10. Somatoform Disorders
Body dysmorphic disorder / Conversion disorder (or Hysterical neurosis, conversion type) / Hypochondriasis (or Hypochondriacal neurosis) / Somatization disorder / Somatoform pain disorder

11. Dissociative Disorders (or Hysterical Neuroses, Dissociative Type)
Multiple personality disorder / Psychogenic fugue / Psychogenic amnesia / Depersonalization disorder / (or Depersonalization neurosis)

12. Sexual Disorders
A. Paraphilias
Exhibitionism / Fetishism / Frotteurism / Pedophilia / Sexual masochism / Sexual sadism / Transvestic fetishism / Voyeurism
B. Sexual Dysfunctions
Sexual desire disorders; Hypoactive sexual desire disorder, Sexual aversion disorder / Sexual arousal disorders; Female sexual arousal disorder, Male erectile disorder / Orgasm disorders; Inhibited female orgasm, Inhibited male orgasm / Premature ejaculation / Sexual pain disorders; Dyspareunia, Vaginismus

13. Sleep Disorders
A. Dyssomnias
B. Parasomnias

14. Factitious Disorders

15. Adjustment Disorder

16. Psychological Factors Affecting Physical Condition

17. V Codes for Conditions Not Attributable To A Mental Disorder That Are A Focus of Attention or Treatment
Academic problem / Adult antisocial behavior / Childhood or adolescent antisocial behavior / Malingering / Marital problem / Noncompliance with medical treatment / Occupational problem / Parent–child problem / Other interpersonal problem / Other specified family circumstances / Phase of life problem or other life circumstance problem / Uncomplicated bereavement

AXIS II

1. Developmental Disorders
A. Mental Retardation
Mild mental retardation / Moderate mental retardation / Severe mental retardation / Profound mental retardation
B. Pervasive Developmental Disorders
Autistic disorder
C. Specific Developmental Disorders
Academic skills disorders / Developmental arithmetic disorder / Developmental expressive writing disorder / Developmental reading disorder / Language and speech disorders / Developmental articulation disorder / Developmental expressive language disorder / Developmental receptive language disorder / Motor skills disorder / Developmental coordination disorder

2. Personality Disorders
Paranoid / Schizoid / Schizotypal / Antisocial / Borderline / Histrionic / Narcissistic / Avoidant / Dependent / Obsessive compulsive / Passive aggressive

ABNORMAL
PSYCHOLOGY

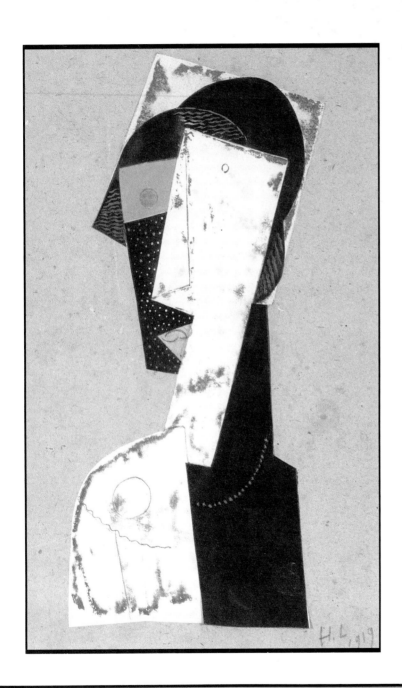

FIFTH EDITION

ABNORMAL
PSYCHOLOGY

GERALD C. DAVISON
University of
Southern California

JOHN M. NEALE
State University of
New York at Stony Brook

WILEY

JOHN WILEY & SONS
New York   Chichester   Brisbane   Toronto   Singapore

Cover and Frontispiece Art / Henri Laurens, *Tête Cubiste*, dated 1919.
Property from the estate of the late James Johnson Sweeney.
Cover Photo / Courtesy of Sotheby's, Inc., New York.
Copyright © Sotheby's, Inc., 1987.

Acquisitions Editor / Deborah Moore
Managing Editor / Joan Kalkut
Production Supervisor / Elizabeth Austin
Copyediting Supervisor / Gilda Stahl
Interior and cover design / Kevin Murphy
Photo Research Manager / Stella Kupferberg
Photo Researchers / Barbara Salz
Joelle Burrows

Library of Congress Cataloging in Publication Data:

Davison, Gerald C.
    Abnormal psychology / Gerald C. Davison, John M. Neale.—5th ed.
        p.   cm.
    Includes bibliographical references.
    ISBN 0-471-63108-6
    1. Psychology, Pathological.   I. Neale, John M., 1943–
II. Title.
RC454.D3   1990
616.89—dc20   89-35932
                                                                    CIP

Printed in the United States of America

10 9 8 7 6 5

To Aaron and Ida

GCD

To Gail and Sean

JMN

GERALD C. DAVISON is Chair and Professor of Psychology at the University of Southern California, where he was also Director of Clinical Training from 1979 to 1984. Previously he was on the psychology faculty at the State University of New York at Stony Brook (1966–1979). In 1969–1970 he was visiting associate professor at Stanford University (where he received his Ph.D. in 1965), and in 1975–76, a National Institute of Mental Health Special Fellow at Harvard (where he obtained his B.A. in 1961). He is a Fellow of the American Psychological Association and has served on the Executive Committee of the Division of Clinical Psychology, on the Board of Scientific Affairs, on the Committee on Scientific Awards, and on the Council of Representatives. He is also a Charter Fellow of the American Psychological Society, on the Advisory Board of the Society for the Exploration of Psychotherapy Integration, and a past president of the Association for the Advancement of Behavior Therapy. He is presently serving on a National Academy of Sciences Committee on Techniques for the Enhancement of Human Performance. In 1988 Davison received an outstanding achievement award from APA's Board of Social and Ethical Responsibility, and in 1989 was the recipient of the Albert S. Raubenheimer Distinguished Faculty Award from USC's College of Letters, Arts and Sciences. His book *Clinical Behavior Therapy*, co-authored in 1976 with Marvin Goldfried, is one of two publications that have been recognized as Citation Classics by the Social Sciences Citation Index. He has been on the editorial board of several professional journals, including the *Journal of Consulting and Clinical Psychology*, *Behavior Therapy*, and *Cognitive Therapy and Research*. His current research program focuses on the relationships between cognition and a variety of behavioral and emotional problems. In addition to his teaching and research, he is a practicing clinical psychologist.

JOHN M. NEALE a Canadian, is Professor of Psychology at the State University of New York at Stony Brook. He received his B.A. from the University of Toronto in 1965 and his Ph.D. from Vanderbilt University in 1969. Thereafter he spent a year as Fellow in Medical Psychology at Langley Porter Neuropsychiatric Institute. His major research interests are schizophrenia and the effects of stress on health and the immune system. In 1974 he won the American Psychological Association's Early Career Award for his research in schizophrenia. He is currently on the editorial boards of several professional journals and was associate editor of the *Journal of Abnormal Psychology*. Recent books include *Readings in Abnormal Psychology* (edited with Jill Hooley and Jerry Davison), *Case Studies in Abnormal Psychology* (with Tom Oltmanns and Jerry Davison), and *Mechanisms of Psychological Influence on Health* (edited with Laura Carstensen).

Preface

Contemporary abnormal psychology is a field in which there are few hard and fast answers. Indeed, the very way the field should be conceptualized and the kinds of questions that should be asked are hotly debated issues. In this book we have tried to present what glimpses there are of answers to two primary questions: what causes psychopathology and which treatments are most effective in preventing or reducing psychological suffering.

It has become commonplace in psychology to recognize the selective nature of perception. Certainly the writing of a textbook is guided by biases on the part of the authors, and our effort is no exception. We share a strong commitment to a scientific approach but at the same time appreciate the often uncontrollable nature of the subject matter and the importance of clinical findings. Rather than pretend that we are unbiased, we have tried to alert readers to our assumptions. Forewarned in this manner, they may consider on their own the merits of our point of view. At the same time, we believe we have succeeded in presenting fairly and comprehensively the major alternative conceptualizations in contemporary psychopathology. A recurrent theme in the book is the importance of points of view or, to use Kuhn's (1962) phrase, paradigms. Our experience in teaching undergraduates has made us very much aware of the importance of making explicit the unspoken assumptions underlying any quest for knowledge. In our handling of the paradigms, we have tried to make their premises clear. Long after specific facts are forgotten, the student should retain a grasp of the basic problems in the field of psychopathology.

A related issue is the use of more than one paradigm in studying abnormal psychology. Rather than force an entire field into, for example, a behavioral paradigm, we argue, from the available information, that different problems in psychopathology are amenable to analyses within different frameworks. For instance, physiological processes must be considered when examining mental retardation and schizophrenia, but for other disorders a cognitive-behavioral theory seems the most helpful. Over the course of our several revisions the importance of a diathesis-stress approach has become more and more evident. Emerging data indicate that many, perhaps most, disorders arise from subtle interactions between organic or psychological predispositions and stressful life events. Our coverage continues to reflect

these hypotheses and findings, strengthening our basic position that a diathesis-stress paradigm is useful in understanding most psychopathologies.

Preparing this fifth edition has given us an opportunity to strengthen many parts of the book and to include significant new material that has appeared since completion of the fourth edition. Those familiar with our earlier efforts will find that our basic orientation has not changed. Our intent is to communicate to students our own excitement about our discipline, particularly the puzzles that challenge researchers in their search for the causes of psychopathology and for ways to prevent and ameliorate it. We try to encourage readers to participate with us in a process of discovery as we sift through the evidence on the origins of psychopathology and the effectiveness of specific interventions. We can mention a small sampling of some of the new material included in this fifth edition: coverage of several neo-Freudian theoreticians (Jung, Adler, Erikson) in Chapter 2; cultural and ethnic biases in psychodiagnosis, behavioral marital assessment, and current research in cognitive assessment and neuropsychological assessment (Chapter 4); epidemiological research (Chapter 5); the neurobiology of anxiety and panic (Chapter 6); critique of the Type A construct and improved methods of assessing stress (Chapter 8); revisions of learned helplessness theory and depression, and neuroendocrine factors in mood disorders (Chapter 9); expanded discussion of personality disorders (Chapter 10); new material on the problems in cocaine use and innovative use of clonidine to ease withdrawal from several addictive drugs (Chapter 11); detailed discussion on AIDS (Chapter 13 and Appendix); neuropsychological research in schizophrenia and the links between somatic and psychological therapies (Chapter 14); the assessment of infant intelligence, treatment of self-injurious behavior, and an extended first-person account of an adult autistic man (Chapter 16); depression in the elderly (Chapter 17); brief psychodynamic psychotherapy and data on its improved effectiveness (Chapter 18); the NIMH Treatment of Depression Collaborative Project, meta-analysis and the effects of psychotherapy, and increasing trends to rapprochement among diverse therapy approaches (Chapter 19); conjoint couples therapy and meta-analyses of its effectiveness (Chapter 20); the aftermath of the John Hinckley case, the case of "Billie Boggs" and the conflicts between civil libertarians and forensic psychiatry and psychology, prediction of dangerousness and commitment (Chapter 21).

Any abnormal psychology textbook published today must attend to the revised third edition of the *Diagnostic and Statistical Manual of Mental Disorders*, and ours is no exception. It has been gratifying to note that many of the changes introduced into DSM-IIIR and its predecessor, DSM-III—recategorizing mood disorders, better operational definitions of each category, omission of homosexuality from the list of mental disorders, a narrower definition of schizophrenia—were anticipated and advocated in our prior editions. To help readers find their way through DSM-IIIR, we provide a summary table on the front endpapers of the book.

We do not, however, accept DSM-IIIR uncritically; those responsible for its compilation are themselves aware of our incomplete and evolving understanding of human suffering. Many times throughout the book we comment critically on this diagnostic scheme. There will be new DSMs, and we hope to make some contribution, along with other colleagues, to the continuing refinement of the manual.

As in the fourth edition, treatments of specific disorders are discussed in the chapters reviewing them. The final section on intervention is also retained, for we continue to believe that only a separate and extended consideration allows us to explore with the reader the many perplexing and intriguing problems encountered by health professionals who try to prevent or treat mental disorders. Chapter 2, the pivotal chapter devoted to paradigms, lays the foundation for Chapters 5 through 17, which describe the various disorders and give what is known about their etiologies and about treating and preventing them.

It is a pleasure to acknowledge the contributions of a number of colleagues who read portions of the manuscript.

Stephen Tiffany
Purdue University

Sarah Burnett
Rice University

Craig Holt
State University of New York at Albany

Joseph Miller
St. Mary's College

John Campbell
Franklin and Marshall College

Thomas A. Martin
Susquehanna University

Seth Kalichman
University of South Carolina

Fred Whitford
Montana State University

Davis J. Lutz
Southwest Missouri State University

Richard Perrotto
Queensborough Community College

Art Skibbe
Appalachian State University

Peter Bankart
Wabash College

Janet Matthews
Loyola University–New Orleans

David M. Wulff
Wheaton College

Robert Deluty
University of Maryland–Baltimore County

Laurence Grimm
University of Illinois–Chicago

J. Powell
California State University–Fresno

Anthony Davids
Brown University

Kenneth Sher
University of Missouri–Columbia

John Belmont
University of Kansas

Leonard Heston
University of Minnesota

Robert Emery
University of Virginia

John McEachin
University of California–Los Angeles

Helpful library research was done at the University of Southern California by Traci Bice, Elizabeth Cameron, Jennifer Dunkin, David A. F. Haaga, Curt Hileman, Steven Holston, Ellie Nezami, and Howard Rowe; and at the State University of New York at Stony Brook by Jack Blanchard, Ann Kring, Antonios Kotsaftis, and Dave Smith. Special thanks go to Marian Williams for drafting and rewriting major portions of Chapters 15 and 16.

We signed on with Wiley in 1971 and continued in this revision to enjoy the skills and dedication of our "Wiley family": Deborah Moore, Beth Austin, Gilda Stahl, Kevin Murphy, Stella Kupferberg, and Serje Seminoff. Special thanks go to Roz Sackoff, who provided many helpful editing and substantive suggestions as we continued our efforts to produce a readable and engaging text without sacrificing scientific accuracy or professional responsibility. We wish to acknowledge the dedicated clerical and administrative assistance of Jill Forthmann, Joan Sterling, and Pat Edson at USC.

For putting up with occasional limited accessibility and mood swings, and for always being there for moral support, our loving thanks go to the most important people in our lives—Eve and Asher Davison, and Kathleen Chambers (GCD) and Gail and Sean Neale (JMN).

Finally, we have maintained the order of authorship as it was for the first edition, decided by the toss of a coin.

Gerald C. Davison
Los Angeles
John M. Neale
July 1989   *Stony Brook*

A Note To The Student

There are several features of this book that we hope will make it easier for you to master and enjoy the material. Some are common to all textbooks, others particular to our book.

1. *Chapter Summaries.* Though a summary appears at the end of each chapter, we recommend that you read it first. Even if you do not understand all of it, you will get some idea of what the chapter is about. Then, when you read it after completing the chapter itself, your enhanced understanding of it will give you an immediate sense of what you have learned in just one reading of the chapter; if something remains unclear in the Summary, you have some indication of what you would do well to reread then and there.

2. *Heads and Subheads.* We have employed four orders of heads. The first and second levels of heads are listed at the beginning of each chapter to provide a general idea of how the chapter is organized. You might also want to flip through the chapter and note the subheads; this will give you a better idea of how the chapter as a whole is organized.

3. *Glossary Terms.* When an important term is introduced, it is italicized and boldfaced. Usually a discussion of that term immediately follows. Of course, the term will probably appear again later in the book, in which case it will not be highlighted in this way. We have provided at the end of the book a detailed dictionary of sorts that includes all these terms. Unlike an ordinary dictionary, a glossary is a very specialized listing of terms and definitions tied to a particular area of study—in the present instance, of course, to abnormal psychology.

4. *Subject and Name Indices.* Also in the back of the book is an index of terms and ideas, the subject index, and a listing of names cited as bibliographic sources, the name index. Sometimes you may wish to know where in the book a certain topic, such as depression, has been discussed. You will find in the subject index that depression is mentioned in more than one context, and the page numbers enable you to look up quickly these several discussions, perhaps to compare how it was dealt with in the different contexts. The name index can help you find a particular reference, though some-times we think that a principal purpose is to enable colleagues to look themselves up quickly to see if they have been cited in someone else's book! (We've certainly been guilty of this "sin.")

5. *DSM-IIIR Table.* On the front endpapers of the book is a summary of the new psychiatric nomenclature, DSM-IIIR. This provides a handy guide to where particular disorders appear in the "official" taxonomy. You will see, as you read our book, that we make considerable use of DSM-IIIR, yet in a selective vein. Sometimes we find it better to discuss theory and research on a particular problem in a way that is different from DSM's conceptualization.

6. *Study Guide.* A *Student Study Guide*, written by Douglas Hindman, is available to help you read and study the textbook. For each chapter there is a summary of the chapter, a list of key concepts, important study questions, and practice tests to encourage active reading and learning. We believe that it is a very helpful study aid.

7. *Supplemental Texts.* Finally, there are two separate books that can enrich your understanding. With Thomas Oltmanns we developed a supplemental paperback text, *Case Studies in Abnormal Psychology*, second edition, based on our own clinical experience with real clients. We hope it gives an appreciation of the range and nature of abnormal behavior. The response from students has been overwhelmingly positive. The other book is a collection of original articles that we edited with Jill Hooley. This volume provides a survey of theoretical and empirical papers that textbook authors and other professionals rely on to find out what researchers are actually doing.

One of the things previous users have liked about our textbook is the way it reads. We hope you, too, will find it engaging and interesting. From time to time students have written us their comments on the book. Should the spirit move you to do so, you can glean our addresses from the brief biographies that appear next to our pictures at the beginning of the book.

GCD AND JMN

Contents In Brief

Part One
Introduction and Basic Issues /1

Chapter One
Introduction: Historical and Scientific Considerations /3
Chapter Two
Current Paradigms in Psychopathology and Therapy /29
Chapter Three
Classification and Diagnosis /61
Chapter Four
Clinical Assessment Procedures /75
Chapter Five
Research Methods in the Study of Abnormal Behavior /109

Part Two
Emotional Disorders and Reactions to Stress /129

Chapter Six
Anxiety Disorders /131
Chapter Seven
Somatoform and Dissociative Disorders /167
Chapter Eight
Psychophysiological Disorders /189
Chapter Nine
Mood Disorders /219

Part Three
Social Problems /251

Chapter Ten
Personality Disorders /253
Chapter Eleven
Psychoactive Substance Use Disorders /277
Chapter Twelve
Sexual Disorders: Gender Identity Disorders and the Paraphilias /321
Chapter Thirteen
Sexual Dysfunctions /351

Part Four
The Schizophrenias /373

Chapter Fourteen
Schizophrenia /375

Part Five
Life-Span Developmental Disorders /409

Chapter Fifteen
Emotional and Behavioral Disorders of Childhood and Adolescence /411
Chapter Sixteen
Learning Disabilities, Mental Retardation, and Autistic Disorder /439
Chapter Seventeen
Aging and Psychological Disorders /475

Part Six
Intervention /511

Chapter Eighteen
Insight Therapy /513
Chapter Nineteen
Cognitive and Behavior Therapies /537
Chapter Twenty
Group, Couples and Family Therapy, and Community Psychology /573
Chapter Twenty-One
Legal and Ethical Issues /601
Appendix /635
Brain Dysfunctions and Abnormal Behavior
Glossary /G-1
References /R-1
Quotation Credits /Q-1
Photo Credits /P-1
Name Index /I-1
Subject Index /I-11

CONTENTS

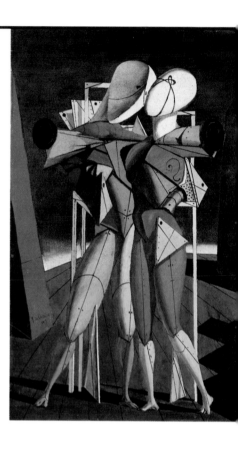

Part One
Introduction and Basic Issues /1

Chapter One
Introduction: Historical and Scientific Considerations /3

The Mental Health Professions /6

History of Psychopathology /7
    Early Demonology /7
    Somatogenesis / 8
    The Dark Ages and Demonology /8
    The Mentally Ill as Witches /10
    Development of Asylums /12
    Moral Treatment /15
    The Beginning of Contemporary Thought /19

Science: A Human Enterprise /22
    Subjectivity in Science: The Role of Paradigms /26
    An Example of Paradigms in Abnormal Psychology /26

Summary /27

Chapter Two
Current Paradigms in Psychopathology and Therapy /29

The Physiological Paradigm /30
    The Choice of Terms /30
    Physiological Approaches to Treatment /32

The Psychoanalytic Paradigm /32
    Classical Psychoanalytic Theory /32
    Post-Freudian Psychodynamic Perspectives /38
    Psychoanalytic Therapy /41

Learning Paradigms /42
    The Rise of Behaviorism /42
    Mediational Learning Paradigms /46
    Applying Learning Points of View to Deviant Behavior /47
    Behavior Therapy /48

The Cognitive Paradigm /49
    Cognitive Behavior Therapy /50
    Learning Paradigms and Cognitive Paradigms /51

The Humanistic Paradigm /52
  Humanistic Therapy /53

Consequences of Adopting a Paradigm /55
  Diathesis-Stress: A Proposed Paradigm /55

Different Perspectives on a Clinical Problem /55
  What is Abnormal? /57

Summary /59

Chapter Three
Classification and Diagnosis /61

DSM-IIIR—The Diagnostic System of the American Psychiatric Association /62
  The Axes /62
  Diagnostic Categories /65

Issues in the Classification of Abnormal Behavior /68
  The Relevance of Classification Per Se /69
  Criticisms of Actual Diagnostic Practice /70
  DSM-III, DSM-IIIR, and Criticisms of Diagnosis /71

Summary /73

Chapter Four
Clinical Assessment Procedures /75

Assessment of Psychopathology /76
  Clinical Interviews /76
  Psychological Tests /78

Assessment of Brain Abnormalities /85
  "Seeing" the Brain /85
  Neuropsychological Assessment /86

Behavioral Assessment /88
  Direct Observation of Behavior /89
  Interviews and Self-Report Measures /92
  Cognitive Assessment /94
  Physiological Measurement /95
  Behavioral Assessment for Behavioral Change /98
  Reliability of Behavioral Assessment /98
  Validity of Behavioral Assessment /99

The Consistency and Variability of Behavior /103
Summary /107

Chapter Five
Research Methods in the Study of Abnormal Behavior /109

Science and Scientific Methods /110
  Testability and Falsifiability /110
  Reliability /110
  The Role of Theory /110

The Research Methods of Abnormal Psychology /112

Epidemiological Research /113
The Case Study /113
The Correlational Method /116
The Experiment /120
Single-Subject Experiment Research /124
Mixed Designs /127
Summary /127

Part Two
Emotional Disorders and
Reactions to Stress /129

Chapter Six
Anxiety Disorders /131
Phobias /133
Subclassification of Phobias /133
The Psychoanalytic Theory of Phobias /136
Behavioral Theories of Phobias /136
Physiological Factors Predisposing to the
Development of Phobias /141
Therapies for Phobias /144
Panic Disorder /146
Generalized Anxiety Disorder /147
Psychoanalytic View /148
Learning View /148
Cognitive-Behavioral View /148
Humanistic View /149
Genetic Studies /149
Neurobiology of Anxiety and Panic /149
Therapies for Generalized Anxiety Disorder /150
Obsessive-Compulsive Disorder /152
Obsessions /154
Compulsions /154
The Psychoanalytic Theory of Obsessive-
Compulsive Disorder /155
Behavioral Theories of Obsessive-Compulsive
Disorder /155
Cognitive Views of Obsessive-Compulsive
Disorder /155
Biological Factors in Obsessive-Compulsive
Disorder /156
Therapies for Obsessive-Compulsive
Disorder /156
Posttraumatic Stress Disorder /157
The Symptoms and Diagnosis /157
Posttraumatic Stress Disorder and the Vietnam
War /158
Treatment of Posttraumatic Stress Disorder /162
Summary /164

Chapter Seven
Somatoform and Dissociative Disorders /167

Somatoform Disorders /168
  Conversion Disorder /168
  Somatization Disorder (Briquet's Syndrome) /170
  Theories of Somatoform Disorders /173
  Therapy for Somatoform Disorders /177

Dissociative Disorders /179
  Psychogenic Amnesia /179
  Psychogenic Fugue /179
  Multiple Personality /179
  Theories of Dissociative Disorders /182
  Therapies for Dissociative Disorders /185

Summary /186

Chapter Eight
Psychophysiological Disorders /189

Stress and Health /191
  The Concept of Stress /191
  Stress and Illness /192
  Moderators and Mediators of Stress /195

Theories of the Stress-Illness Link /197
  Physiological Theories /197
  Psychological Theories /198

Cardiovascular Disorders /199
  Essential Hypertension /199
  Coronary Heart Disease /202

Asthma /207
  A Characterization of the Disease /207
  The Etiology of Asthma /208

Therapies for Psychophysiological Disorders /211
  Hypertension /214
  Type A /214
  Stress Management /215

Summary /217

Chapter Nine
Mood Disorders /219

General Characteristics of Depression and Mania /220
  Depression /220
  Mania /221

Formal Diagnostic Lisings /222

Psychological Theories of Depression /224
  Psychoanalytic Theory /225
  Cognitive Theories /226
  Interpersonal Aspects of Depression /234

Psychological Theories of Bipolar Disorder /235

Physiological Theories of Mood Disorders /235
   The Genetic Data /235
   Biochemistry and Mood Disorders /236
   The Neuroendocrine System /238
Therapy for Mood Disorders /238
   Psychological Therapies /238
   Somatic Therapies /241
Suicide /242
   Facts about Suicide /243
   Perspectives on Suicide /244
   Prediction of Suicide from Psychological
    Tests /246
   Suicide Prevention /247
Summary /249

Part Three
Social Problems /251

Chapter Ten
Personality Disorders /253

Specific Personality Disorders /254

Antisocial Personality Disorder (Sociopathy) /260
   The Case of Dan /260
   The Case of Jim /261
   Cleckley's Concept of Sociopathy /262

*Theory and Research on the Etiology of
 Sociopathy* /263
   The Role of the Family /264
   Genetic Correlates of Sociopathic Behavior /265
   Central Nervous System Activity and
    Sociopathy /265
   Avoidance Learning, Punishment, and
    Sociopathy /267
   Underarousal and Sociopathy /270

Therapies for Personality Disorders /271
   Therapy for the Borderline Personality /272
   Behavior Therapy for Disturbed
    Personalities /272
   Therapy for Sociopathy /273
Summary /274

Chapter Eleven
Psychoactive Substance Use
Disorders /277

Alcoholism /279
   Short-Term Effects of Alcohol /280

Long-Term Effects of Prolonged
    Alcohol Use   /281
Theories of Alcoholism   /284
Therapies for Alcoholism   /289

Sedatives and Stimulants   /293
Sedatives   /293
Stimulants   /295
Theories of the Origins of Drug Addiction   /299
Therapy for the Use of Illicit Drugs   /299

Nicotine and Cigarette Smoking   /302
Prevalence and Consequences of Smoking   /302
Is Smoking an Addiction?   /304
Treatment and Prevention of Cigarette
    Smoking   /304

Marijuana   /309
Frequency of Marijuana Use   /310
Reasons for Use   /310
Effects of Marijuana   /310

LSD and Other Psychedelics   /314
Research on the Effects of Psychedelics   /315
The Problems of Flashbacks   /317

Summary   /318

Chapter Twelve
**Sexual Disorders: Gender Identity
Disorders and the Paraphilias**   /321

Gender Identity Disorders   /323
Transsexualism   /323
Gender Identity Disorder of Childhood   /324
Therapies for Gender Disorders   /325

The Paraphilias   /330
Fetishism   /330
Transvestistic Fetishism   /331
Incest   /332
Pedophilia   /333
Voyeurism ("Peeping")   /334
Exhibitionism   /334
Rape   /336
Sexual Sadism and Sexual Masochism   /339
Paraphilias Not Otherwise Specified   /341
Therapies for the Paraphilias   /341
Therapy for Rape   /343

Homosexuality   /345
Ego-Dystonic Homosexuality in DSM-III   /345
DSM-IIIR and Homosexuality   /347
Future Research   /348

Summary   /348

Chapter Thirteen
Sexual Dysfunctions   /351

*Sexual Disorders and the Human Sexual Response
    Cycle*   /352

*The Sexual Dysfunctions: Descriptions and
Causes* /353
    Sexual Desire Disorders /356
    Sexual Arousal Disorders /356
    Orgasm Disorders /357
    Sexual Pain Disorders /359
Theories of Sexual Dysfunctions /359
    Earlier Sexology /359
    The Ideas of Masters and Johnson /361
    Other Contemporary Views /363
*Behavioral and Cognitive Therapies for Sexual
Dysfunctions* /367
Summary /371

Part Four
The Schizophrenias /373

Chapter Fourteen
Schizophrenia /375

History of the Concept /376
    Kraepelin's and Bleuler's Early Descriptions /376
    The Broadened American Concept /378
    The DSM-IIIR Diagnosis /378
Clinical Symptoms of Schizophrenia /379
    Disorders of Thought /379
    Disorders of Perception and Attention /382
    Motor Symptoms /383
    Affective Symptoms /383
    Impairments in Life Functioning /384
Subcategories of Schizophrenia /384
Research on the Etiology of Schizophrenia /387
    The Genetic Data /387
    Biochemical Factors /392
    Neurological Findings /394
    Social Class and Schizophrenia /395
    Schizophrenia and the Family /396
    High-Risk Studies of Schizophrenia /398
Therapies for Schizophrenia /399
    Somatic Treatments /399
    Psychological Treatments /401
Summary /407

Part Five
Life-Span Developmental Disorders /409

Chapter Fifteen
Emotional and Behavioral Disorders of Childhood and Adolescence /411

Classification /412

Disorders of Undercontrolled Behavior /413
  Attention-Deficit Hyperactivity Disorder /413
  Conduct Disorders /419

Disorders of Overcontrolled Behavior /425
  Childhood Fears /425
  Social Withdrawal /429
  Affective Disorders in Childhood /430

Eating Disorders /431
  Anorexia Nervosa /431
  Bulimia Nervosa /433

Summary /435

Chapter Sixteen
Learning Disabilities, Mental Retardation, and Autistic Disorder /439

Learning Disabilities /440
  Etiology of Learning Disabilities /441
  Intervention with Learning Disabilities /441

Mental Retardation /442
  The Concept of Mental Retardation /442
  Classification of Mental Retardation /445
  Nature of Mental Retardation /446
  Etiology of Mental Retardation /449
  Prevention of Mental Retardation /456
  Treatment for Mental Retardation /457

Autistic Disorder /463
  Descriptive Characteristics /463
  Etiology of Autistic Disorder /468
  Treatment of Autistic Disorder /470

Summary /472

Chapter Seventeen
Aging and Psychological Disorders /475

Concepts and Methods in the Study of Older Adults /476

Some Basic Facts about Older Adults /478

Brain Disorders of Old Age   /485
  Dementia   /485
  Delirium   /489
Psychological Disorders of Old Age   /491
  Depression   /491
  Delusional (Paranoid) Disorders   /494
  Schizophrenia   /496
  Psychoactive Substance Use Disorders   /498
  Hypochondriasis   /499
  Insomnia   /500
  Suicide   /501
  Sexuality and Aging   /501
General Issues in Treatment and Care   /504
  Access to Services   /504
  Provision of Services   /505
  Issues Specific to Therapy with Older
    Adults   /509
Summary   /509

Part Six
Intervention /511

Chapter Eighteen
Insight Therapy /513
The Placebo Effect   /515
Psychoanalytic Therapy   /516
  Basic Techniques and Concepts in
    Psychoanalysis   /516
  Ego Analysis   /519
  Evaluation of Analytic Therapy   /521
Humanistic and Existential Therapies   /524
  Carl Rogers's Client-Centered Therapy   /524
  Existential Therapy   /528
  Gestalt Therapy   /530
Summary   /534

Chapter Nineteen
Cognitive and Behavior
Therapies /537
Counterconditioning   /538
  Systematic Desensitization   /538
  Aversion Therapy   /541
Operant Conditioning   /542
  The Token Economy   /542
  Operant Work with Children   /545

Modeling /546
   Problems Treated by Modeling /546
   The Role of Cognition /547

Cognitive Restructuring /547
   Ellis's Rational-Emotive Therapy /547
   Beck's Cognitive Therapy / 550
   The Therapies of Beck and Ellis—Some
     Comparisons /552
   Social Problem Solving /552
   Some Reflections on Cognitive Behavior
     Therapy /557

Behavioral Medicine /558
   Chronic Pain and Activity /559
   Chronic Diseases and Life-Style /559
   Biofeedback /562

*Generalization and Maintenance of Treatment
  Effects* /563
   Intermittent Reinforcement /563
   Environmental Modification /564
   Self-Reinforcement /564
   Eliminating Secondary Gain /565
   Relapse Prevention /565
   Attribution to Self /566

Some Basic Issues in Behavioral Therapy /566
   Internal Behavior and Cognition /566
   Underlying Causes /567
   Broad-Spectrum Treatment /567
   Relationship Factors /568
   Flesh on the Theoretical Skeleton /568
   Psychoanalysis and Behavior Therapy—A
     Rapprochement? /569

Summary /571

**Chapter Twenty
Group, Couples and Family Therapy,
and Community Psychology** /573

Group Therapy /574
   Insight-Oriented Group Therapy /574
   Behavior Therapy Groups /576
   Evaluation of Group Therapy /578

Couples and Family Therapy /580
   The Normality of Conflict /581
   From Individual to Conjoint Therapy /581
   The Essentials of Conjoint Therapy /583
   Special Considerations /585
   Research in Couples and Family Therapy /585

Community Psychology /586
   Prevention and Seeking /586
   Values and the Question of Where to
     Intervene /587
   Community Mental Health Centers /589

Suicide Prevention Centers and Telephone Crisis
Services /591
The Use of Media to Change Harmful
Life-Styles /593
Halfway Houses and Aftercare /593
Self-Help Movement /594
Competency Enhancement and
Family Problems /594
Overall Evaluation of Community
Psychology Work /595
Summary /597

Chapter Twenty-One
Legal and Ethical Issues /601
Criminal Commitment /602
The Insanity Defense /603
Competency to Stand Trial /609
Civil Commitment /611
Problems in the Prediction of
Dangerousness /611
Recent Trends for Greater Protection /613
Deinstitutionalization, Civil Liberties, and Mental
Health /618
Ethical Dilemmas in Therapy and Research /622
Ethical Restraints on Research /622
Informed Consent /623
Treatment or Research? /624
Confidentiality and Privileged
Communication /625
Who Is the Client? /625
Choice of Goals /629
Choice of Techniques /631
Concluding Comment /632
Summary /632

Appendix
Brain Dysfunctions and Abnormal
Behavior /635
Organic Mental Syndromes /636
Dementia /636
Delirium /637
Amnestic Syndrome /640
Organic Delusional Syndrome /640
Organic Hallucinosis /641
Organic Mood Syndrome /641
Organic Anxiety Syndrome /642
Organic Personality Syndrome /642
Organic Mental Disorders /643
Dementias Arising in the Senium
and Presenium /643

Glossary /G-1
References /R-1
Quotation Credits /Q-1
Photo Credits /P-1
Name Index /I-1
Subject Index /I-11

Highlight Boxes

Chapter One
BOX 1.1
THE SALEM INCIDENT: WITCHCRAFT OR POISONING? /14

BOX 1.2
BENONI BUCK: THE FIRST DOCUMENTED CASE OF MENTAL ILLNESS IN AMERICA /17

BOX 1.3
THE MENTAL HOSPITAL /18

BOX 1.4
HYPNOSIS /22

BOX 1.5
PARADIGM CLASH IN THE STUDY OF HYPNOSIS /24

Chapter Two
BOX 2.1
CRITICISMS OF THE MEDICAL OR DISEASE MODEL OF ABNORMAL BEHAVIOR /31

BOX 2.2
FREUD: THE METHODOLOGICAL AND CONCEPTUAL PROBLEMS /37

BOX 2.3
ECLECTICISM IN PSYCHOTHERAPY: PRACTICE MAKES IMPERFECT /56

Chapter Four
BOX 4.1
WHAT HAPPENS WHEN MINORITY CULTURAL DIFFERENCES ARE CONSIDERED IN PSYCHODIAGNOSIS? /77

BOX 4.2
OPERANT CONDITIONING FINDS ITS HEART /90

BOX 4.3
MEASUREMENT OF AUTONOMIC NERVOUS SYSTEM ACTIVITY /96

BOX 4.4
BEHAVIORAL MARITAL ASSESSMENT /100

BOX 4.5
THE ASSESSMENT OF ANXIETY: IN PURSUIT OF AN ELUSIVE CONSTRUCT /104

Chapter Six
BOX 6.1
LITTLE HANS /134

BOX 6.2
SEX ROLES AND AGORAPHOBIA /135

BOX 6.3
AVOIDANCE CONDITIONING AND PREPAREDNESS /138

BOX 6.4
BEHAVIOR GENETICS /142

BOX 6.5
COMMUNICATION IN THE NERVOUS SYSTEM /150

BOX 6.6
AN HYPOTHESIS ABOUT DELAYED PTSD IN VIETNAM VETERANS /162

Chapter Seven
BOX 7.1
AWARENESS, THE UNCONSCIOUS, AND BEHAVIOR /175

Chapter Eight
BOX 8.1
DESCARTES AND THE MIND-BODY PROBLEM /190

BOX 8.2
IS TYPE A REALLY A USEFUL CONSTRUCT? /206

BOX 8.3
MIGRAINE HEADACHES AND BIOFEEDBACK /212

Chapter Nine
BOX 9.1
DEPRESSION IN WOMEN: A CONSEQUENCE OF LEARNED HELPLESSNESS AND STYLE OF COPING /230

BOX 9.2
LIFE STRESS AND DEPRESSION /233

BOX 9.3
AN EXISTENTIAL THEORY OF DEPRESSION AND
ITS TREATMENT /240

BOX 9.4
SOME MYTHS ABOUT SUICIDE /243

BOX 9.5
CLINICAL AND ETHICAL ISSUES IN DEALING
WITH SUICIDE /249

Chapter Ten

BOX 10.1
KOHUT AND THE NARCISSISTIC
PERSONALITY /258

BOX 10.2
THE ELECTROENCEPHALOGRAM /266

Chapter Eleven

BOX 11.1
ANOTHER LOOK AT AVERSION THERAPY FOR
ALCOHOLICS /291

BOX 11.2
OUR TASTIEST ADDICTION–CAFFEINE /296

BOX 11.3
CLONIDINE AND DRUG WITHDRAWAL /305

BOX 11.4
NICOTINE GUM AND NICOTINE FITS /306

BOX 11.5
THE STEPPING-STONE THEORY—FROM
MARIJUANA TO HARD DRUGS /311

BOX 11.6
NOT AN UPPER OR A DOWNER BUT AN
INSIDE-OUTER /316

Chapter Twelve

BOX 12.1
PSYCHOPHYSIOLOGICAL ASSESSMENT OF
SEXUAL AROUSAL /328

BOX 12.2
ARE RAPISTS SADISTS? /337

BOX 12.3
A PSYCHOPHYSIOLOGICAL ANALYSIS OF
RAPE /339

BOX 12.4
IMPRISONED SEX OFFENDERS: A PROBLEM
FOR SOCIETY /344

BOX 12.5
SOME PROBLEMS IN LOGIC AND THEORY IN
THE STUDY OF HOMOSEXUALITY /346

Chapter Thirteen

BOX 13.1
SOME SEXUAL MYTHS DISPELLED BY MASTERS
AND JOHNSON /354

BOX 13.2
SEXUAL DYSFUNCTION: A BIOENERGETIC
APPROACH /360

BOX 13.3
AIDS: A CHALLENGE FOR THE BEHAVIORAL
SCIENCES /364

BOX 13.4
THERAPY FOR SEXUAL DYSFUNCTIONS BY
MASTERS AND JOHNSON /367

Chapter Fourteen

BOX 14.1
PARANOID DELUSIONS AND REPRESSED
HOMOSEXUALITY /384

BOX 14.2
MAJOR THEORETICAL POSITIONS ON THE
ETIOLOGY OF SCHIZOPHRENIA /388

BOX 14.3
SOME NEGATIVE EFFECTS OF THERAPIES WITH
SCHIZOPHRENIA /402

Chapter Fifteen

BOX 15.1
ENURESIS /414

BOX 15.2
THE ROLE OF MARITAL DISCORD IN CONDUCT
DISORDERS /422

BOX 15.3
PLAY THERAPY AND FAMILY THERAPY: TWO
GENERAL METHODS OF TREATING
CHILDHOOD PROBLEMS /428

BOX 15.4
BEHAVIORAL PEDIATRICS /434

BOX 15.5
DEPRESSION AND EATING DISORDERS /436

Chapter Sixteen

BOX 16.1
MEASURING INFANT INTELLIGENCE /443

BOX 16.2
THE IDIOT SAVANT /458

BOX 16.3
TREATMENT OF SELF-INJURIOUS AND
STEREOTYPED BEHAVIOR /461

BOX 16.4
CLASSIFICATION OF PERVASIVE
DEVELOPMENTAL DISORDERS /464

BOX 16.5
A FIRST-PERSON ACCOUNT OF AN ADULT
AUTISTIC MAN /467

BOX 16.6
THE PERNICIOUS NATURE OF PSYCHOGENIC
THEORIES /469

Chapter Seventeen

BOX 17.1
CEREBROVASCULAR DISEASES—STROKE AND
ITS AFTERMATH /486

BOX 17.2
PREVALENCE OF MENTAL DISORDERS IN
LATE LIFE /492

BOX 17.3
PARTIAL DEAFNESS, GROWING OLD,
AND PARANOIA /496

BOX 17.4
LOSS OF CONTROL AND MINDLESSNESS IN
NURSING HOMES /507

Chapter Eighteen

BOX 18.1
EXCERPT FROM A PSYCHOANALYTIC SESSION,
AN ILLUSTRATION OF TRANSFERENCE /518

BOX 18.2
WHAT DOES THE THERAPIST SEE OF THE
CLIENT IN TRANSFERENCE? /520

BOX 18.3
EXCERPT FROM A CLIENT-CENTERED THERAPY
SESSION /526

BOX 18.4
A GLIMPSE OF FRITZ PERLS /531

Chapter Nineteen

BOX 19.1
TOKEN ECONOMIES, ASYLUMS, AND THE
METRICS OF HUMAN EXISTENCE /544

BOX 19.2
RATIONAL EMOTIVE THERAPY AND EDUCATION
FOR CHILDREN /550

BOX 19.3
NIMH TREATMENT OF DEPRESSION
COLLABORATIVE RESEARCH PROGRAM /553

BOX 19.4
ASSERTION TRAINING /556

BOX 19.5
META-ANALYSIS AND THE EFFECTS OF
PSYCHOTHERAPY /560

BOX 19.6
SELF-CONTROL—OUTSIDE A BEHAVIORAL
PARADIGM? /564

BOX 19.7
RAPPROCHEMENT AND ECLECTICISM—
ANOTHER LOOK /570

Chapter Twenty

BOX 20.1
THERAPY, FOR BETTER OR FOR WORSE /580

BOX 20.2
EMPOWERMENT, SMALL WINS, AND BROAD-
SCALE SOCIAL CHANGE /588

BOX 20.3
COMMUNITY PSYCHOLOGY AND COMMUNITY
MENTAL HEALTH—RELATED BUT
DIFFERENT /590

Chapter Twenty-one

BOX 21.1
THE AFTERMATH OF THE JOHN HINCKLEY
CASE /604

BOX 21.2
THOMAS S. SZASZ AND THE CASE AGAINST
FORENSIC PSYCHIATRY AND
PSYCHOLOGY /608

BOX 21.3
THE STRANGE CASE OF "BILLIE BOGGS" /620

BOX 21.4
THE TARASOFF CASE—THE DUTY TO WARN
AND PROTECT /626

BOX 21.5
NOT CAN BUT OUGHT: AN OPINION ON THE
TREATMENT OF HOMOSEXUALITY /630

Appendix

BOX A.1
STRUCTURE AND FUNCTION OF THE HUMAN
BRAIN /638

Part One

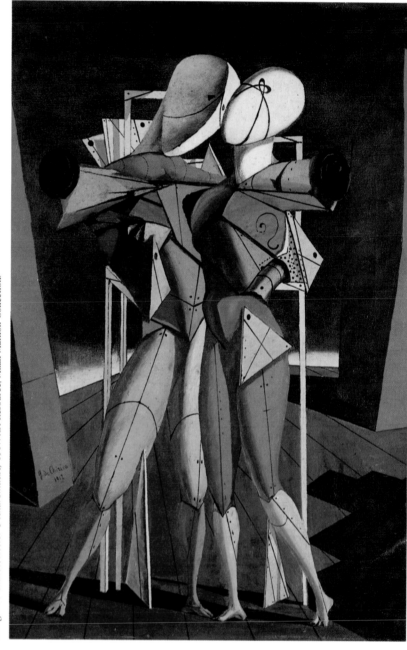

Giorgio de Chirico. *Hector & Andromache*, 1917. Art Resource. Milan Mattioli Collection.

Introduction and Basic Issues

Giorgio de Chirico, *Hector & Andromache*, 1917. Art Resource, Milan Mattioli Collection.

Chapter 1

Introduction: Historical and Scientific Considerations

The Mental Health Professions
History of Psychopathology
　Early Demonology
　Somatogenesis
　The Dark Ages and Demonology
　The Mentally Ill as Witches
　Development of Asylums
　Moral Treatment
　The Beginning of Contemporary Thought
Science: A Human Enterprise
　Subjectivity in Science: The Role of Paradigms
　An Example of Paradigms in Abnormal
　　Psychology
Summary

Slumping in a comfortable leather chair, Ernest H., a thirty-five-year-old city policeman, looked skeptically at his therapist as he struggled to relate a series of problems. His recent inability to maintain an erection when making love to his wife was the immediate reason for his seeking therapy, but after gentle prodding from the therapist, Ernest recounted a host of other difficulties, some of them dating from his childhood but most of them originating during the previous several years.

Ernest's childhood had not been a happy one. His mother, whom he loved dearly, died suddenly when he was only six, and for the next ten years he lived either with his father or with a maternal aunt. His father drank so heavily that he seldom managed to get through any day without some alcohol. Moreover, the man's moods were extremely variable; he had even spent several months in a state hospital with a diagnosis of "manic-depressive psychosis." The father's income was irregular and never enough to pay bills on time or to allow his son and himself to live in any but the most run-down neighborhoods. At times the father was totally incapable of caring for himself, let alone his son. Ernest would then spend weeks, sometimes months, with his aunt in a nearby suburb.

Despite these apparent handicaps, Ernest completed high school and entered the tuition-free city university. He earned his miscellaneous living expenses by waiting table at a small restaurant. During these college years his psychological problems began to concern him. He often became profoundly depressed, for no apparent reason, and these bouts of sadness were sometimes followed by periods of manic elation. His lack of control over these mood swings troubled him greatly, for he had observed this same pattern in his alcoholic father. He also felt an acute self-consciousness with people who he felt had authority over him—his boss, his professors, and even some of his classmates, with whom he compared himself unfavorably. He was especially sensitive about his clothes, which were old and worn compared to those of his peers; their families had more money than his.

It was on the opening day of classes in his junior year that he first saw his future wife. When the tall, slender young woman moved to her seat with grace and self-assurance, his were not the only eyes that followed her. He spent the rest of that semester watching her from afar, taking care to sit where he could glance over at her without being conspicuous. Then one day, as they and the other students were leaving class, they bumped into each other quite by accident, and her warmth and charm emboldened him to ask her to join him for some coffee. When she said yes, he almost wished she had not.

Amazingly enough, as he saw it, they soon fell in love, and before the end of his senior year they were married. Ernest could never quite believe that his wife, as intelligent a woman as she was beautiful, really cared for him. As the years wore on, his doubts about himself, and about her feelings toward him, would continue to grow.

He hoped to enter law school, and both his grades and law school boards made these plans a possibility, but he decided instead to enter the police academy. His reasons, as he related them to his therapist, had to do with doubts about his intellectual abilities, as well as his increasing uneasiness in situations in which he felt himself being evaluated. Seminars had become unbearable for him in his last year in college, and he had hopes that the badge and uniform of a police officer would give him the instant recognition and respect that he seemed incapable of earning on his own.

To help him get through the academy, his wife quit college at the end of her junior year, against Ernest's pleas, and sought a secretarial job. He felt she was far brighter than he and saw no reason why she should sacrifice her potential to help him make his way in life. But at the same time he recognized the fiscal realities and grudgingly accepted her financial support.

The police academy proved to be even more stressful than college. Ernest's mood swings, although less frequent, still troubled him. And like his father, who was now confined to a state mental hospital, he drank to ease his psychological pain. He felt that his instructors considered him a fool when he had difficulty standing up in front of the class to give an answer that he himself knew was correct. But he made it through the physical, intellectual, and social rigors of the academy, and he was assigned to foot patrol in one of the wealthier sections of the city.

Several years later, when it seemed that life should be getting easier, he found himself in even-greater turmoil. Now thirty-two years of age, with a fairly secure job which paid reasonably well, he began to think of starting a family. His wife wanted this as well, and it was at this time that his problems with impotence began. He thought at first it was the alcohol—he was drinking at least six ounces of bourbon every night, except when on the swing shift. Soon, though, he began to wonder whether he was actually avoiding the responsibility of having a child, and later he began to doubt that his wife really found him attractive and desirable. The more understanding and patient she was about his sometimes frantic efforts to consummate sex with her, the less "manly" he felt himself to be. He was unable to accept help from his wife, for he did not believe that this was the "right" way to maintain a sexual relationship. The problems in bed spread to other areas of their lives. The less often they made love, the more suspicious he was of his wife, for she had become even more beautiful and vibrant as she entered her thirties. In addition, she had been promoted to the position of administrative assistant at the law firm where she worked. She would mention—perhaps to taunt him—long, martini-filled lunches with her boss at a posh uptown restaurant.

The impetus for his contacting the therapist was an ugly argument with his wife one evening when she came home from work after ten. Ernest had been elated and agitated for several days. To combat his fear that he was losing control, he had consumed almost a full bottle of bourbon each night. By the time that his wife walked in the door on that final evening, Ernest was already very drunk, and he attacked her both verbally and physically about her alleged infidelity. In her own anger and fear, she questioned his masculinity in striking a woman and taunted him with the disappointments of their lovemaking. Ernest stormed out of the house, spent the night at a local bar, and the next day somehow pulled himself together enough to seek professional help.

Every day of our lives we try to understand other people. Determining why another person does or feels something is a difficult task. Indeed, we do not always understand why we feel and behave as we do. Acquiring insight into what we consider the normal range of expected behavior is arduous enough, but human behavior beyond the normal range, such as that of the policeman just described, is even more perplexing.

When we refer to strange behavior or ideas, we frequently use phrases such as "He's out of his mind," "He's all screwed up," "He's a maniac," "She's a hysteric," or "She's really paranoid." Such terms indicate that as observers we have found a person's behavior inexplicable and can attribute it only to an unbalanced mind. These minds, however, are very often much sounder than such phrases and adjectives imply. Terrifying instances of unusual behavior, although not personally observed by most of us, are very much in the public eye. Hardly a week passes without a violent act, such as an ugly ax murder or multiple slayings, being reported. The assailant is diagnosed by a police officer or mental health authority as a "mental case" and is found to have had a history of mental instability. Sometimes we learn that the person has previously been confined in a mental hospital.

This book is concerned with the whole range of abnormality and with the various explanations for it, both past and present. There are, however, numerous pitfalls in seeking valid explanations. To study abnormal psychology, we must have what might be called "great tolerance for ambiguity," an ability to be comfortable with very tentative, often conflicting pieces of information. Much less is known with certainty about the field than we might hope, presenting problems both for the professional and for the beginning student. Indeed, as already indicated, little is known of why human beings behave in a normal fashion, to say nothing of their abnormal behavior. In approaching the study of psychopathology, we do well to keep in mind that the subject offers few hard and fast answers. Although we shall report such findings as there are, many of the facts that will be introduced will be modified by subsequent research. And yet, as will become evident when we discuss our orientation to scientific inquiry, the study of psychopathology is no less worthwhile because of its ambiguities. The kinds of questions asked rather than the specific answers to those questions constitute the very essence of the field.

Another problem that professionals share with laypeople is the closeness of any human being to the subject matter of behavior. Physicists, for example, would seem better able to detach themselves emotionally from their subject matter than psychologists, particularly those who specialize in the study of abnormal behavior.

The pervasiveness and disturbing effects of abnormal behavior intrude on our lives. Who, for example, has not experienced irrational thoughts and feelings? Or who has not known someone, a friend or perhaps a relative, whose behavior was impossible to fathom? If you have, you realize how frustrating and frightening it is to try to understand and help a person suffering psychological difficulties.

Our closeness to the subject matter, of course, adds to its intrinsic fascination; no wonder that undergraduates courses in abnormal psychology are among the most popular in psychology departments and indeed in the entire college curriculum. Familiarity with the subject matter encourages people to study abnormal psychology, but it has one distinct disadvantage. All of us have already developed certain ways of thinking and talking about behavior, certain words and concepts that somehow seem to *fit*. For example, some may assert that the study of fear should concentrate on the immediate experience of fear; this is technically known as a *phenomenological* approach and is one formal way of setting about the study of human behavior. As behavioral scientists, we ourselves have had to grapple with the difference between what we may *feel* is the appropriate way to talk about human behavior and experience and what we have learned to be more fruitful means of discussing them. Where most people would speak of a "feeling of terror," for example, we might be more inclined to use a phrase such as "fear-response of great magnitude." In doing so we would not be merely playing verbal games. The word "games" does indeed apply in the sense that our procedures have rules, but it does not apply in the sense that we are engaging in activities that do not mean very much or that could just as well be carried out in another fashion. The crucial point is that the concepts and verbal labels we use in the serious study of abnormal behavior must be free of the subjective feelings of appropriateness ordinarily attached to certain human phenomena. We may be asking you, then, to adopt frames of reference different from those you are accustomed to, and indeed different from those we ourselves employ when we are not wearing our professional hats.

The case study with which this chapter began is open to a wide range of interpretations. No doubt you have some ideas about how Ernest's problems developed, what his primary difficulties are, and perhaps even how you might try to help him. We know of no greater intellectual or emotional challenge than deciding both how to conceptualize the life of a person with psychological problems and how best to treat him or her. At the end of the next chapter we refer back to the case of Ernest H. to illustrate how workers from different theoretical orientations might describe him and seek to help.

The Mental Health Professions

The training of clinicians, the various professionals who are regarded as legitimate providers of psychological services, takes different forms. To practice *clinical psychology* (the profession of the authors of this textbook) usually requires a Ph.D. degree, which entails four to five years of graduate study. Training for the Ph.D. in clinical psychology is much like that for the other special fields of psychology—experimental, physiological, social, developmental, aging—with a heavy emphasis on laboratory work, research designs, statistics, and the empirically based study of human and animal behavior. As with these other fields of psychology, the degree is basically a research one, and candidates are required to write a lengthy dissertation on a specialized topic. In addition, however, Ph.D. clinical psychologists learn how to diagnose mental disorders and practice psychotherapy. They take courses in which they master specific techniques under close professional supervision; then, during an intensive internship or postdoctoral training, they gradually assume increasing responsibility for the care of patients.

A *psychiatrist* holds an M.D. degree and has taken postgraduate training, called a residency, wherein he or she has received supervision in psychotherapy. By virtue of the medical degree, the psychiatrist can also continue functioning as a physician—giving physical examinations, diagnosing medical problems, and the like. In actuality, however, the only aspect of medical practice that most psychiatrists engage in is prescribing *psychoactive drugs,* chemical compounds that can change how people feel and think.

The term *psychoanalyst* is reserved for those individuals who have received specialized training at a psychoanalytic institute; the program usually involves serveral years of clinical training as well as an in-depth psychoanalysis of the trainee. Although Sigmund Freud held that psychoanalysts do not need medical training, until recently most psychoanalytic institutes required of their graduates an M.D. and a psychiatric residency. After the B.A., then, it can take up to ten years to become a psychoanalyst.

Other graduate programs prepare people for clinical practice. Some schools have initiated Psy.D. (Doctor of Psychology) programs for training in clinical psychology. The curriculum offered candidates for this new degree is generally the same as that available to Ph.D. students, but there is less emphasis on research and more on clinical training.[1] The assumption is that clinical psychology has advanced to a level of knowledge that justifies—and even requires—intensive training in specific techniques of assessment and therapeutic intervention. A *psychiatric social worker* obtains a Master of Social Work degree. There are also master's and doctoral-level programs in **counseling psychology,** somewhat similar to graduate training in clinical psychology but usually with less emphasis on research.

The actual clinical work conducted by any of these individuals depends for the most part on the orientation of the school attended. By and large, except for the administration of drugs, specific therapies relate very little to the therapist's academic degree.

In addition to professionals who offer therapeutic services to the public, there is a highly diverse group who can be called *psychopathologists.* These people conduct research into the nature and development of the various disorders that their therapist colleagues try to treat. Psychopathologists may come from any number of disciplines; some are clinicians, but the educational backgrounds of others may range from biochemistry to developmental psychology, and their academic degrees are at virtually any level. What unites them is their commitment to the study of how abnormal behavior develops. Since we still have much to learn about psychopathology, the diversity of backgrounds and interests is an advantage, for it is too soon to be certain where major advances will be made. The work of both psychopathologists and clinicians provides the subject matter of this book.

History of Psychopathology

As psychopathologists, our interest is in the causes of deviant behavior. The search for these causes has gone on for a considerable period of time. Before the age of scientific inquiry, all good and bad manifestations of power beyond the control of humankind—eclipses, earthquakes, storms, lightning and thunder, fire, seri-

ous and disabling disease, darkness and light, the passing of the seasons—were regarded as supernatural. Any behavior seemingly beyond the control of the individual was subject to similar interpretation. The earliest writings of the philosophers, theologians, and physicians who studied the troubled mind found its deviancy to reflect the displeasure of the gods or possession by demons.

Early Demonology

The doctrine that a semiautonomous or completely autonomous evil being, such as the devil, may dwell within a person and control his or her mind and body is called **demonology.** The ancient Babylonians had in their religion a specific demon for each disease. Idta was the demon who caused insanity. Similar examples of demonological thinking can be found in the records of early Chinese, Egyptians, and Greeks. Among the Hebrews as well, deviancy was attributed to possession of the person by bad spirits, after God in his wrath had withdrawn protection. Christ is reported to have cured a man with an "unclean spirit" by casting out the devils from within him and hurling them onto a herd of swine. The animals were then said to have become possessed and to have run "violently down a steep place into the sea" (Mark 5:8–13).

Treatment to combat and exorcise demons typically took the form of elaborate prayer rites, noise making, forcing the afflicted to drink terrible-tasting brews, and on occasion more extreme measures such as flogging and starvation to render the body uninhabitable to the devils.

Even in these early times, however, priests learned to temper their incantations with kindness. In Memphis, Egypt, the temple of Imhotep, the deity of healing, became a hospital and medical school. Sleeping in the temple was a principal means of therapy. Patients were also urged to engage in artistic endeavors, to take excursions on the Nile, and to attend concerts and dances. The temples to Asclepius, the Greek god of medicine, were erected near healing springs or on high mountains. The priests of this sect too relied on sleep within the sanctuaries; in their dreams patients were supposedly visited and advised by Asclepius or one of his priests. In the morning they departed cured or began the regimens revealed to them in their dreams. Baths, diet, and walking, riding, and other exercise all played a part in treatment. But those whose erratic behavior lay beyond these healing measures might be chased from the temples by stoning.

---

[1]Only a minority of mental health professionals teach and conduct research in academic and research settings. However, nearly all the empirical work discussed in this book comes from such individuals, who are generally less involved in providing direct mental health services.

Somatogenesis

In the fifth century B.C. Hippocrates (460?–?377 B.C.) received his early medical training at the famous temple of Asclepius at Cos. Often regarded as the father of modern medicine and operating outside the *Zeitgeist* or intellectual and emotional orientation of the times, he separated medicine from religion, magic, and superstition and rejected the prevailing Greek belief that the gods sent serious physical diseases and mental disturbances as punishment. He insisted instead that such illnesses had natural causes and hence should be treated like other more common maladies such as colds and constipation. Hippocrates regarded the brain as the organ of consciousness, of intellectual life and emotion, and it followed that if someone's thinking and behavior were deviant, there was some kind of brain pathology. He is often considered one of the very earliest proponents of a *somatogenic* hypothesis to explain disordered behavior—that something wrong with the *soma* or physical body disturbs thought and action. He also recognized that environmental and emotional stress can damage the body and mind. Hippocrates classified mental disorders into three categories: mania, melancholia, and phrenitis or brain fever. Through his teachings the phenomena of abnormal behavior became more clearly the province of physicians than of priests.

In treating patients, Hippocrates tried to find natural remedies for what he regarded as natural phenomena. For melancholia he prescribed tranquility, sobriety, care in choosing food and drink, and abstinence from sexual activity. Such a regimen was assumed to have a healthful effect on the brain and the body. Because Hippocrates believed in natural causes rather than supernatural, he depended on his own keen observations and made a valuable contribution as a clinician. Remarkably detailed records describing many of the symptoms now recognized in epilepsy, alcoholic delusion, stroke, and paranoia have come down to us from him.

Hippocrates' physiology was rather crude, however, for he conceived of normal brain functioning, and therefore of mental health, as dependent on a delicate balance among four "humors" or fluids of the body, namely, blood, black bile, yellow bile, and phlegm. An imbalance produced disorders. If a person was sluggish and dull, for example, the body supposedly contained a preponderance of phlegm. A preponderance of black bile was the explanation for melancholia, too much yellow bile explained irascibility and anxiousness, and too much blood changeable temperament. Hippocrates' humoral pathology has not withstood later scientific scrutiny. His basic premise, however, that human behavior is directly determined by bodily structures or substances, and that abnormal behavior is produced by some kind of imbalance or even damage, foreshadowed aspects of contemporary thought. In the next seven centuries, before and after the birth of Christ, Hippocrates' naturalistic approach to disorder was generally accepted by other Greeks, such as Plato, Aristotle, and Galen, as well as by the Romans, who adopted the medicine of the Greeks after their city became the seat of power in the ancient world.

The Dark Ages and Demonology

In a massive generalization, historians have often suggested that the death of Galen, the last major physician of the classical era, marked the beginning of the Dark Ages for all medicine and for the treatment and investigation of abnormal behavior in particular.

Indeed, during the third century the imperial power of Rome became invested in the military as it wholly absorbed civilian administration. The one aim of the military was to preserve the frontiers of the overextended empire. The economy collapsed, and intellectual life was greatly diminished. After several centuries of decay, Greek and Roman civilization had finally ceased to be. During these same centuries the churches had gained in influence. The papacy was soon declared independent of the state and became the important element of unity. Christian monasticism, through its missionary and educational work, replaced classical culture.

The Greek physician Hippocrates held a somatogenic view of abnormal behavior, considering insanity a disease of the brain.

Medieval woodcuts of the four temperaments thought by the followers of Galen to result from excesses of the four humors. From left to right: the man with changeable temperament, who has plenty of blood; the melancholy man, full of black bile; the hot-tempered man, who has a surplus of choler or yellow bile; and the sluggish man with too much phlegm.

The monasteries provided care and nursing of the sick, and a few were repositories for the classic Greek medical manuscripts, even though the knowledge within them might not be applied. When monks cared for the mentally disordered, they prayed over them and touched them with relics, or they concocted fantastic potions for them to drink in the waning phase of the moon. The families of the deranged might take them to shrines, or they sometimes disavowed them out of fear and superstition. Many of the mentally ill roamed the countryside, becoming more and more bedraggled and losing more and more of their faculties.

The early church was always both skeptical about witchcraft and disapproving of any effort to practice it. God alone was viewed as all powerful. In 1140 a paragraph of canon law urged the clergy to renounce as fantasies any claims made by wicked women that Satan had empowered them to ride great distances by night on the backs of beasts. But in the next thirty years the dualistic heresy, which ascribed real power to the devil as an equal opponent to God, grew with catastrophic rapidity in western Germany, Flanders, France, and northern Italy. Both the church and the state felt enormously threatened. By 1252 they had put in place all the machinery of the Inquisition. Heretics were tried in an ecclesiastical court and the unrepentant turned over to civil authorities for their punishment, which was usually burning. Papal inquisitors, who were authorized to use torture to obtain confessions and the names of other heretics, were sent to oversee the inquiries into heresy in the threatened bishoprics.

The thirteenth century and the next few saw a populace already suffering from social unrest and recurrent famines and plagues become obsessed with the devil. Witchcraft, now viewed as instigated by the powerful Satan of the heretics, was itself a heresy and denial of God. The reputed practices of witches—attending sabbats, having intercourse with the devil, turning themselves into animals, rendering men impotent, causing a neighbor's wheat to rot, his cattle to sicken, and making people die by melting wax images of them—were no longer regarded as fantasies but believed to take place in fact. Such evil was clearly within the scope of the Inquisition, and so witches began to be hunted and burned throughout Europe, especially in Germany. Faced with inexplicable and frightening occurrences, people tend to seize on whatever explanation is available. The times conspired to heap enormous blame on those regarded as witches.

In 1484 Pope Innocent VIII, in a papal bull, exhorted the clergy of Europe to leave no stone unturned in the search for witches. He sent two Dominicans, Jakob Sprenger and Henricus Institoris, to northern Germany as inquisitors. Two years later they issued a comprehensive and explicit manual, *Malleus Maleficarum* ("the witches' hammer"), to guide the witch hunts. It was a legal and theological document that came to be regarded by Catholics and Protestants alike as a textbook on witchraft. "Carnal lust," insatiable in some women, was the reason they consorted "even with devils" and became witches. Various signs by which witches could be detected, such as red spots or areas of insensitivity on the skin, supposedly made by the claw of the devil when touching the person to seal a pact, were described. And the manual confirmed that the rules the Inquisition followed for heretics applied to the witches. Those accused of witchcraft should be tortured if they did not confess, those convicted and penitent were to be imprisoned for life, and those convicted and unrepentant were to be handed over to the law for execution. The manual specified that a person's sudden loss of reason was a symptom of demonic possession, and that burning was the usual method of driving out the supposed demon. Over the next several centuries hundreds of thousands of women, men, and children are said to have been accused, tortured, and put to death, but records of the period are not reliable.

The first abatement in witch hunting came in Spain, in 1610, when the inquisitor Alonso Salazar y Frías concluded that most of the accusations in Logroño, Navarre, had been false. He ordained that accusations must be accompanied by independent evidence, that torture could not be used, and that the property of the convicted would not be confiscated. Thereafter accusations of witchcraft dropped sharply in Spain. In February 1649 Queen Christina of Sweden wrote a letter to one of her ministers ordering him to free all prisoners accused of witchcraft except those clearly guilty of murder. In France witchcraft trials declined after an edict was issued by Louis XIV in 1682. The last execution of a witch was in Switzerland, in the year 1782.

Tortures by which confessions were extracted from accused witches.

The Mentally Ill as Witches

For some time the prevailing interpretation has been that all the mentally ill of the later Middle Ages were considered witches (Zilboorg and Henry, 1941). In their confessions the accused sometimes reported having had intercourse with the devil and having flown to sabbats, the secret meetings of their cults. These reports have been interpreted by contemporary writers as delusions or hallucinations and thus are taken to indicate that some witches were psychotic. Moreover, to identify people with the "Devil's mark," areas of insensitivity to pain, professional witch prickers went from town to town sticking pins into the bodies of the accused. Because anesthesia is regarded as a symptom of hysteria (see Chapter 7, page 168), the fact that some "witches" did not respond to the prickings is considered evidence of their madness.

More careful analyses of the witch hunts, however, reveal that although some accused witches were mentally disturbed, many more sane than insane people were tried. The delusionlike confessions were typically obtained during brutal torture; words were put on the lips of the tortured by their accusers and by the beliefs of the times. Indeed, in England, where torture was not allowed, the confessions did not usually contain descriptions indicative of delusions or hallucinations. Similarly, insensitivity to pain has many causes, including organic dysfunctions. More important, there are documented cases of deliberate trickery. Often a needle was attached to a hollow shaft so that it did not actually puncture the skin, although to observers it appeared to be penetrating deeply (Schoeneman, 1977; Spanos, 1978).

Witch burning.

The dunking test. If the woman did not drown, she was thought to be in league with the devil.

In this painting St. Catherine is conducting an exorcism, trying to get the evil spirit to leave the woman's body.

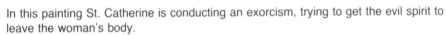

THE COMMONWEALTH OF MASSACHUSETTS

In the Year One Thousand Nine Hundred and Fifty-seven

RESOLVE RELATIVE TO THE INDICTMENT, TRIAL, CONVICTION AND EXE-
CUTION OF ANN PUDEATOR AND CERTAIN OTHER PERSONS FOR "WITCHCRAFT" IN
THE YEAR SIXTEEN HUNDRED AND NINETY-TWO.

Whereas, One Ann Pudeator and certain other persons were indicted, tried, found guilty, sentenced to death and executed in the year sixteen hundred and ninety-two for "Witchcraft"; and

Whereas, Said persons may have been illegally tried, convicted and sentenced by a possibly illegal court of oyer and terminer created by the then governor of the Province without authority under the Province Charter of Massachusetts Bay; and

Whereas, Although there was a public repentance by Judge Sewall, one of the judges of the so-called "Witchcraft Court", and by all the members of the "Witchcraft" jury, and a public Fast Day proclaimed and observed in repentance for the proceedings, but no other action taken in regard to them; and

Whereas, The General Court of Massachusetts is informed that certain descendants of said Ann Pudeator and said other persons are still distressed by the record of said proceedings; therefore be it

Resolved, That in order to alleviate such distress and although the facts of such proceedings cannot be obliterated, the General Court of Massachusetts declares its belief that such proceedings, even if lawful under the Province Charter and the law of Massachusetts as it then was, were and are shocking, and the result of a wave of popular hysterical fear of the Devil in the community, and further declares that, as all the laws under which said proceedings, even if then legally conducted, have been long since abandoned and superseded by our more civilized laws no disgrace or cause for distress attaches to the said descendants or any of them by reason of said proceedings; and be it further

Resolved, That the passage of this resolve shall not bestow on the commonwealth or any of its subdivisions, or on any person any right which did not exist prior to said passage, shall not authorize any suit or other proceeding nor deprive any party to a suit or other proceeding of any defense which he hitherto had, shall not affect in any way whatever the title to or rights in any real or personal property, nor shall it require or permit the remission of any penalty, fine or forfeiture hitherto imposed or incurred.

House of Representatives, August 26, 1957.

Passed, *[signature]* Speaker.

A bill passed in 1957 by the Massachusetts legislature, exonerating a woman who had been executed for witchcraft in 1692.

Evaluations of other sources of information indicate that witchcraft was not the primary interpretation of mental illness. From the thirteenth century onward, as the cities of Europe grew larger, hospitals began to come under secular jurisdiction. Municipal authorities, when they grew powerful, tended to supplement or take over some of the activities of the church, one of these of course being the care of the ill. The foundation deed for the Holy Trinity Hospital in Salisbury, England, dating from the mid-fourteenth century, specified the purposes of the hospital. Among them was that "mad are kept safe until they are restored of reason." British laws during this period allowed both the dangerously insane and the incompetent to be confined in a hospital. Notably, the people to be confined were not described as being possessed (Allderidge, 1979).

Neugebauer (1979) has examined the records from lunacy trials in Britain during the Middle Ages. Beginning in the thirteenth century, these trials were held to determine a person's sanity. The trials were conducted under the Crown's right to protect the mentally impaired, and a judgment of insanity allowed the Crown to become guardian of the lunatic's estate. The defendant's orientation, memory, intellect, daily life, and habits were at issue in the trial. Explanations for strange behavior typically linked it to physical illness or injury or to some emotional shock. Of all the cases that Neugebauer examined, in only *one* was demonological possession referred to. The preponderance of evidence, then, indicates that this explanation of mental disturbance was not as dominant during the Middle Ages as had once been thought (see Box 1.1).

Development of Asylums

Until the end of the Crusades, in the fifteenth century, there were virtually no mental hospitals in Europe. Earlier than this, however, there were thousands of hospitals for lepers. In the twelfth century, for example, England and Scotland had 220 for a population of a million and a half. After the principal Crusades had been waged, leprosy gradually disappeared from Europe, probably because of the break with the eastern sources of the infection. With leprosy no longer of such great social concern, attention seems to have focused on the mad.

Confinement of the mentally ill began in earnest in the fifteenth and sixteenth centuries, sometimes in what had been leprosariums. Some of these **asylums** took in a mixed lot, beggars as well as disturbed people. Beggars were regarded as a great social problem at the time. Indeed, in the sixteenth century, Paris had 30,000 beggars in its population of fewer than 100,000 (Foucault, 1965). These institutions had no specific regimen for their inmates other than to get them to work. But during the same period hospitals geared more specifically for the confinement of the mentally ill also appeared. The Priory of St. Mary of Bethlehem was founded in 1243. By 1403 it housed six insane men, and in 1547 Henry VIII handed it over to the city of London, thereafter to be a hospital devoted solely to the confinement of

A tour of St Mary's of Bethlehem (Bedlam) provides amusement for these two upper-class women. Hogarth captures the poignancy of the scene in this well-known eighteenth-century painting.

The "tranquilizing chair," used by Benjamin Rush as a means of treating mental disorders.

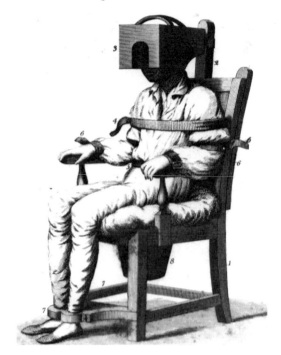

the mentally ill. The conditions in Bethlehem were deplorable. Over the years the word "bedlam", a contraction and popular name for this hospital, became a descriptive term for a place or scene of wild uproar and confusion. Bethlehem eventually became one of London's great tourist attractions, by the eighteenth century rivaling both Westminster Abbey and the Tower of London. Even as late as the nineteenth century, viewing the violent patients and their antics was considered entertainment, and tickets of admission to Bedlam were sold. In the Lunatic's Tower, constructed in Vienna in 1784, patients were confined in the spaces between inner square rooms and the outer walls. There they could be looked at from below by passersby. The first mental hospital in the United States was founded in Williamsburg, Virginia, in 1773 (see Box 1.2).

It should not be assumed, however, that the inclusion of abnormal behavior within the domain of hospitals and medicine necessarily led to more humane and effective treatment. Benjamin Rush (1745–1813), who began practicing medicine in Philadelphia in 1769 and was

BOX 1.1

THE SALEM INCIDENT: WITCHCRAFT OR POISONING?

In December 1691 eight girls who lived in or near Salem Village were afflicted with "distempers," which called for medical attention. Physicians, however, could find no cause for their disorderly speech, strange postures and gestures, and their convulsive fits. One of the girls was the daughter of the minister, Samuel Parris, another his niece. A neighbor soon took it upon herself to have Parris's Barbados slave, Tituba, concoct a "witch cake" of rye meal and the urine of the afflicted, and to feed it to a dog to determine whether witchcraft was indicated. Shortly thereafter, in February 1692, the girls accused Tituba and two elderly women of witchcraft, and the three were taken into custody. In his church records Parris denounced his neighbor's action and stated that until a community member had gone "to the Devil for help against the Devil," there had been no suspicion of witchcraft and no reports of torture by apparitions.

But now the accusations began to spew from the young girls and from other residents of the village. The jails of Salem, of surrounding towns, and even of faraway Boston filled with prisoners awaiting trial. By the end of September, nineteen people had been sent to the gallows, and one man had been pressed to death. The convictions were all obtained on the bases of "spectral evidence"—an apparition of the accused had appeared to the accuser; and the test of touch—an accuser's fit ceased after he or she was touched by the accused. The afflicted girls were present at the trials and often disturbed the proceedings with their violent fits, convulsions, and apparent hallucinations of specters and "familiars." (Familiars are spirits, often in animal form, who are believed to act as servants to a witch.)

Even before the last execution the witchcraft trials were adjourned until November. But the special court appointed earlier by Governor Phips never met again for this purpose. In January 1693 a superior court convened and received the fifty indictments for witchcraft that had already been made by a grand jury. It tried twenty persons, acquitted seventeen, and condemned three, although they were never executed. In May of 1693 Governor Phips or-

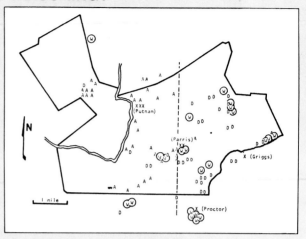

Residence patterns in Salem 1692. The names in parentheses indicate the homes where the "possessed" girls lived. Residents are labeled as follows: X, afflicted girl; W, accused witch; D, defender of an accused witch; and A, accuser. Thirty of the thirty-two adult accusers lived in the western section of the village, and twelve of the fourteen accused witches in the eastern section.

dered a general reprieve; about 150 persons still being held on charges of witchcraft were released, ending the strange episode.

These happenings in Salem are usually discussed as an illustration of how the hapless mentally ill of the era were mistreated through the widespread belief that they were possessed, although the accused witches were for the most part persons of good reputation in the community. The accusers are sometimes proposed to have been schizophrenic, on the basis of their hallucinations. But schizophrenia is not likely to occur simultaneously in a group of young women. Or the episode is sometimes seen as an instance of "mass hysteria"; the witchcraft accusation, once made, mushroomed for some reason. Earlier accusations

also deeply involved in his country's struggle for independence, is considered the father of American psychiatry. He believed that mental disorder was caused by an excess of blood in the brain. Consequently, his favored treatment was to draw from "the insane" great quantities of blood, as much as six quarts over a period of a few months. Little wonder that patients so treated became less agitated (Farina, 1976)! Rush entertained another hypothesis, namely, that many "lunatics" could

be cured by frightening them. In one such recommended procedure the physician was to convince the patient of his impending death. A New England doctor of the nineteenth century implemented this prescription in an ingenious manner. "On his premises stood a tank of water, into which a patient, packed into a coffin-like box pierced with holes, was lowered. . . . He was kept under water until the bubbles of air ceased to rise, after which he was taken out, rubbed, and revived—if he had

of witchcraft in Puritan communities of New England had never had such an outcome, however. Linnda Caporael (1976) has proposed a different theory, that the accusers were suffering from ergot poisoning.

Ergot, a parasitic fungus, grows on cereal grains, principally rye, and its development is fostered by warm, rainy growing seasons. Several of the alkaloids* of ergot contain lysergic acid, from which LSD is synthesized. Ingestion of food made from flour contaminated with ergot can cause crawling sensations on the skin, tingling in the fingers, vertigo, headache, hallucinations, vomiting, diarrhea, and convulsions. The alkaloids of ergot can also induce delirium and mood changes such as mania and depression.

Could ergot poisoning account for the events in question? First, the behavior of the initial accusers is indeed similar to the known effects of ergot poisoning. The girls did report having hallucinations; they also vomited, had convulsions, and said that they felt as though they were being choked and pricked with pins. Second, rye was a well-established crop in Salem, and there had been heavy rains in 1691, which would promote the growth of the fungus. Rye was usually harvested in August and threshed in the late autumn. The onset of the girls' strange behavior occurred at about the time they would be beginning to eat food made from the new grain. The accumulating accusations of witchcraft apparently came to an abrupt halt in the following autumn, when a new supply of grain, grown during a dry 1692, became available. After that time the afflictions of the girls and those of others in Salem were not mentioned in accounts of the period.

Why then did only some people feel that their bodies had been possessed? Caporael argues that the western portion of Salem Village, where the ground is lower and the

meadows are swampy, would be the most likely source of contaminated grain. The pattern of residence of the young girls and of the other accusers fits this hypothesis; they were more likely to reside in or to eat grain grown in the western fields. Most of the accused witches and their defenders lived in the eastern section of the village.

Caporael has presented a compelling set of arguments for her ergot poisoning theory. Of course, it remains a theory, but it is interesting to speculate how many witchcraft persecutions throughout the later Middle Ages may have had ergotism as a root cause.

Painting depicting one of the Salem witch trials.

---

*Alkaloids are organic substances that are found for the most part in seed plants, usually not singly but as mixtures of similar alkaloids. They all contain nitrogen and are the active agents that give a number of natural drugs their medicinal and also their toxic properties.

not already passed beyond reviving!" (Deutsch, 1949, p. 82).

Moral Treatment

A primary figure in the movement for humanitarian treatment of those in asylums was Philippe Pinel (1745–1826). In 1793, while the French Revolution raged, he was put in charge of a large asylum in Paris known as

La Bicêtre. A historian has written of the conditions at this particular hospital.

[The patients were] shackled to the walls of their cells, by iron collars which held them flat against the wall and permitted little movement. . . . They could not lie down at night, as a rule. . . . Oftentimes there was a hoop of iron around the waist of the patient and in addition . . . chains on both the hands and the

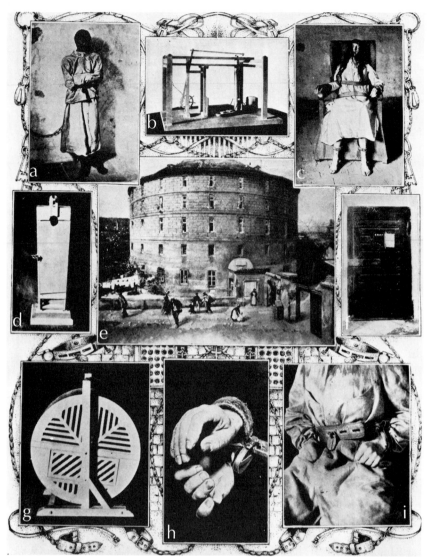

At the Lunatics' Tower (e, center) in Vienna, a remarkable collection of strange instruments and fetters were employed in the treatment of the insane. (a) A lunatic in hood and straitjacket, padlocked to a cell wall. (b) The machine in which lunatics were swung until they were in a state of stupefaction and therefore remained quiet. (c) A maniac strapped in a chair in a position sometimes held for weeks. (d) The "English coffin," in which the lunatic was kept, his face at the hole, for discipline. The face and the box together resembled a standing clock. (f) A cell door with its iron "spy-hole." (g) An enormous wheel, which turned each time the lunatic inside it moved. (h) A maniac's hands in padlocked handcuffs, and (i) Another straitjacketed lunatic.

feet. . . . These chains [were] sufficiently long so that the patient could feed himself out of a bowl, the food usually being a mushy gruel—bread soaked in a weak soup. Since little was known about dietetics, [no attention] was paid to the type of diet given the patients. They were presumed to be animals . . . and not to care whether the food was good or bad. (Selling, 1940, p. 54)

Pinel was reluctantly allowed to remove the chains of the people imprisoned in La Bicêtre and to treat them as sick human beings rather than as beasts. Many who had been excited and completely unmanageable became calm and much easier to handle. Formerly considered dangerous, they strolled through the hospital and grounds with no inclination to create disturbances or to harm anyone. Light and airy rooms replaced their dungeons. Some who had been incarcerated for years were soon restored to health and were eventually discharged from the hospital.

BOX 1.2

BENONI BUCK: THE FIRST DOCUMENTED CASE OF MENTAL ILLNESS IN AMERICA

In seventeenth-century America there were no institutions for the mentally ill; thus there are no records for us to examine so that we might glimpse at early colonial practices. At that time, however, the English Court of Wards and Liveries was responsible for appointing guardians for the mentally ill and their jurisdiction extended to the American colonies. The court could judge an individual to be a "lunatic," in which case a guardian was appointed to watch over the psychotic person and his or her estate until recovery. If the individual was judged an "idiot," the Crown assumed control of the mentally retarded person and his estate.

In 1637 Ambrose Harman of Virginia petitioned King Charles I to have his ward, Benoni Buck, declared an idiot. The petition found its way to the Court of Wards and Liveries, where an official of the King authorized that it be granted. Benoni's parents had died when he was a child, leaving an estate of 750 acres. In the early 1630s Ambrose Harman and his wife had secured custody of Benoni, and

were reimbursed for their expenses by the guardian of the estate. However, the governor of Virginia, Sir John Harvey, wanted to use the proceeds of Benoni's estate to reward public servants and transfer guardianship from year to year. Thus in 1637, Richard Kemp was appointed as a new guardian and payments to the Harmans stopped. Harman then initiated the petition to the Crown.

Legal action followed with Richard Kemp and the governor of Virginia battling Ambrose Harman for custody of Benoni. In March 1638 the Harmans gained custody of Benoni and his estate. Benoni Buck thus became the first documented case of mental illness in America.

Two further points are of interest. First, the case illustrates the common theme of conflict between the social obligation to protect the mentally ill and other social and economic factors. Second, the interchange between the governor of Virginia and the Crown provides an early illustration of Colonial resentment over English interference in American affairs (Neugebauer, 1987).

Freeing the patients of their restraints was not the only humanitarian reform advocated by Pinel.[2] Consis-

tent with the egalitarianism of the new French Republic, he believed that the mental patients in his care were essentially normal people who should be approached with compassion and understanding and treated as individual human beings with dignity. Their reason supposedly having left them because of severe personal and social problems, it might be restored to them through comforting counsel and purposeful activity.

---

[2]Not all scholars agree that Pinel deserves as much adulation as he enjoys. Thomas Szasz (1974), whose influential writings on involuntary hospitalization are reviewed in Chapter 21, points to sections of Pinel's famous *A Treatise on Insanity* (1801). They indicate that he relied on terror and coercion in dealing with patients of the lower classes.

Some early mental hospitals were pleasant retreats. Pictured here is one located in Pennsylvania.

BOX 1.3

THE MENTAL HOSPITAL

Each year about two and a half million Americans are hospitalized for mental disorders. Treatment in public mental institutions is primarily custodial in nature, and the existence of patients is monotonous and sedentary for the most part. After Pinel's revolutionary work in La Bicêtre, the hospitals established in Europe and in this country were for a time relatively small and privately supported. Patients had close contact with attendants, who talked and read to them and encouraged them to purposeful activity. Residents were to lead as normal lives as possible and in general take responsibility for themselves within the constraints of their disorders. This moral treatment, which is estimated to have achieved enviable discharge rates, had to be abandoned in the second half of the nineteenth century, however. The staffs of the large, public mental hospitals being built to take in the many patients for whom the private ones had no room could not provide such individual attention (Bockhoven, 1963). Moreover, these hospitals came to be administered by physicians, who were more interested in the physiological aspects of illness and in the physical well-being of mental patients. The money that once paid the salaries of personal attendants now went into equipment and laboratories.

Mental hospitals in this country today are usually funded either by the federal government or by the state. In fact, the term "state hospital" is taken to mean a *mental* hospital run by the state. They are often old, grim, and somewhat removed from major metropolitan centers. Their costs to society in economic terms are utterly staggering. Some Veterans Administration hospitals and general medical hospitals also contain psychiatric wards.

In addition, there are private mental hospitals. Sheppard and Enoch Pratt near Baltimore, Maryland, and McLean Hospital, in Belmont, Massachusetts, are two of the most famous. The physical facilities of private hospitals tend to be superior to those of state hospitals for one simple reason: the private hospitals have more money. The daily costs to patients in these private institutions can exceed

Depiction of the deplorable conditions existing in some early mental hospitals.

$500 per day and may still not include individual therapy sessions with a member of the professional staff! Although some patients may have medical insurance, usually with a ninety-day limit, such hospitals are clearly beyond the means of most citizens.

A somewhat specialized mental hospital, sometimes called a prison hospital, is reserved for people who have been arrested and judged unable to stand trial and for those who have been acquitted of a crime by reason of insanity (see page 603). They have not been sent to prison, but armed guards and tight security regiment their lives. Treatment of some kind is supposed to take place during their internment.

Many fine books and articles have been written about mental hospitals (Stanton and Schwartz, 1954; Goffman, 1961; Rosenhan, 1973; Moos, 1974). They agree with our own clinical experiences that, even in the best of hospitals, patients usually have precious little contact with psychia-

About the time Pinel began reforming La Bicêtre, a prominent merchant and Quaker, William Tuke (1732–1822), had occasion to be shocked by the conditions at York Asylum in England. He proposed to the Society of Friends that they found their own institution. In 1796 York Retreat was established on a country estate. It provided the mentally ill with a quiet and religious atmosphere in which to live, work, and rest. They discussed their difficulties with attendants, worked in the garden, and took walks through the countryside. In the United States the Friends' Asylum, founded in 1817 in

Pennsylvania, and the Hartford Retreat, established in 1824 in Connecticut, were patterned after the York Retreat. A number of other American hospitals were influenced by the sympathetic and attentive treatment provided by Pinel and Tuke. Of course not all asylums adopted their so-called *moral practices,* but the smaller ones that did achieved remarkable successes. Unfortunately, this personal attention to the patients was no longer possible when the large mental hospitals that are prevalent today began to be built (see Box 1.3) (Bockhoven, 1963).

trists or clinical psychologists. Most of a patient's days and evenings are spent either alone or in the company of other patients and of aides, individuals who often have little more than an elementary school education. As with imprisonment, the overwhelming feeling is of helplessness and depersonalization. Patients sit endless hours in hallways waiting for dining halls to open, for medication to be given out, and for consultations with psychologists, social workers, and vocational counselors to begin.

Except for the most severely disturbed, patients have access to the various facilities of a hospital, ranging from woodworking shops to swimming pools, from gymnasia to proverbial basketweaving shops. Most hospitals require patients to attend group therapy—here a general term indicating only that at least two patients are supposed to relate to each other and to a group leader in a room for a specific period of time. For some patients there are a few sessions alone with a professional therapist.

One nagging problem is that institutionalization is difficult to reverse once people have resided in mental hospitals for more than a year. We recall asking a patient who had improved markedly over the previous several months why he was reluctant to be discharged. "Doc," he said earnestly, "it's a jungle out there." Although we cannot entirely disagree with his view, there nonetheless appear to be at least a few advantages to living on the outside. But this man—a veteran and chronic patient with a clinical folder more than two feet thick—had become so accustomed to the restrictions and care of various Veterans Administration hospitals that the prospect of leaving was as frightening to him as the prospect of entering a mental hospital is to those who have never lived in one. Deinstitutionalization sweeps in the 1970s greatly reduced the number of patients in mental hospitals, but the problems of the chronic patient have yet to be handled adequately (see Chapter 21, page 613).

One treatment now widely applied is ***milieu therapy,*** in which the entire hospital becomes a "therapeutic community" (e.g., Jones, 1953). All its ongoing activities and all its personnel become part of the treatment program. Milieu therapy appears to be a return to the moral practices of the nineteenth century. Social interaction and group activities are encouraged so that through group pressure the patients are directed toward normal functioning. Patients are treated as responsible human beings rather than as custodial cases (Paul, 1969). They are expected to participate in their own readjustment, as well as that of their fellow patients. Open wards allow them considerable freedom. There is some evidence for the efficacy of milieu therapy (e.g., Greenblatt *et al.*, 1965; Fairweather, 1964), the most convincing from a milestone project by Paul and Lentz (1977).

In this ambitious study, Paul and Lentz demonstrated encouraging improvement in chronic "hard-core" patients through both milieu and social-learning therapy. A token economy, which reached into many details of the patients' lives, was combined with other behavior therapy interventions tailored to the particular needs of each resident. Described in more detail on page 542, a token economy rewards patients for behaving in a particular way by reinforcing them with tokens that can be exchanged for privilege or other items patients desire. A host of measures were taken on the behavior of both staff and patients over four and a half years of treatment, with a later eighteen-month follow-up on patients who had since been discharged. The social-learning program was markedly more successful than both milieu therapy, carried out for a matched group at another unit of the mental health center, and routine hospital management of a second matched group in an older Illinois state hospital. Since mental hospitals will be needed for the foreseeable future, especially by people who demonstrate time and again that they have difficulty functioning on the outside, Paul's work is of special importance. It suggests specific ways in which the chronic patient can be helped to cope better not only within the hospital but during periods of discharge as well.

The Beginning of Contemporary Thought

Somatogenesis

After the fall of Greco-Roman civilization, the writings of Galen, a disciple of Hippocrates, were the standard source of information about both physical and mental illness. It was not until the Middle Ages that any change began to take place. One development that fostered progress was the discovery by Vesalius that Galen's presentation of human anatomy was incorrect. Galen had presumed that human physiology mirrored the apes he had studied. It took more than one thousand years for autopsy studies of humans to begin to prove that Galen had been wrong. Empirical medical science received another boost from the efforts of the famous English physician Thomas Sydenham (1624–1689). Sydenham was particularly influential in advocating an empirical approach to classification that subsequently influenced those interested in mental disorders.

One of these was a German physician, Wilhelm Griesinger, who insisted that any diagnosis of mental disorder specify a physiological cause. A textbook of psychiatry, written by his well-known follower, Emil Krae-pelin (1856–1926), and first published in 1883, furnished a classification system to help establish the organic nature of mental illnesses. Kraepelin discerned among mental disorders a tendency for a certain group of *symptoms,* called a *syndrome,* to appear together regularly enough to be regarded as having an underlying physical cause, much as a particular medical disease and its syndrome may be attributed to a physiological dysfunction. He regarded each mental illness as distinct from all others, having its own genesis, symptoms, course, and outcome. Even though cures had not been worked out, at least the course of the disease could be predicted. Kraepelin proposed that there were two major groups of severe mental diseases: dementia praecox, an early term for schizophrenia, and manic-depressive psychosis. He postulated a chemical imbalance as the cause of schizophrenia and an irregularity in metabolism as the explanation of manic-depressive psychosis. Kraepelin's scheme for classifying these and other mental illnesses became the basis for the present diagnostic categories, which will be described more fully in Chapter 3.

Much was being learned about the nervous system in the second half of the nineteenth century but not enough yet to reveal all the expected abnormalities in structure that might underlie mental disorders. Degenerative changes in the brain cells associated with senile and presenile psychoses and some structural pathologies that accompany mental retardation were identified, however. Pellagra and the serious disorientation brought on by it were traced to a vitamin deficiency. Perhaps the most striking medical success was the discovery of the full nature and origin of *syphilis.* The venereal disease syphilis had been recognized for several centuries, and since 1798 it had been known that a number of mental patients manifested a similar and steady deterioration of both physical and mental abilities. These patients were observed to suffer multiple impairments, including delusions of grandeur and progressive paralysis. Soon after these symptoms were recognized, it was realized that these patients never recovered. In 1825 this deterioration in mental and physical health was designated a disease, *general paresis.* Although in 1857 it was established that some patients with paresis had earlier had syphilis, there were many competing theories of the origin of paresis. For example, in attempting to account for the high rate of the disorder among sailors, some supposed that seawater might be the cause. And Griesinger, in trying to explain the higher incidence among men, speculated whether liquor, tobacco, and coffee were implicated. Then in the 1860s and 1870s Louis Pasteur established the *germ*

theory of disease. It thus became possible to demonstrate the relation between syphilis and general paresis. In 1897 Richard von Krafft-Ebing inoculated paretic patients with matter from syphilitic sores. The patients did not develop syphilis, indicating that they had been infected earlier. Finally, in 1905, the specific microorganism causing syphilis was discovered. A causal link had been established between infection, destruction of certain areas of the brain, and a form of psychopathology. If one type of psychopathology had a biological cause, so could others. The search for them was off and running.

Psychogenesis

The search for somatogenic causes dominated psychiatry until well into the twentieth century, no doubt partly because of the stunning discoveries made about general paresis. But in other parts of western Europe, in the late eighteenth century and throughout the nineteenth, mental illnesses were considered to have an entirely different genesis. Various *psychogenic* points of view, attributing mental disorders to psychic malfunctions, were fashionable in France and Austria. For reasons that are not clear to us even today, many people in western Europe were at that time subject to hysterical states (in contemporary terms, conversion disorders): they suffered from physical incapacities that made absolutely no anatomical sense (see page 168).

Franz Anton Mesmer's procedure for transmitting animal magnetism from the *baquet* to his patients.

Franz Anton Mesmer (1734–1815), an Austrian physician practicing in Vienna and Paris in the late eighteenth century, believed that hysterical disorders were caused by a particular distribution of a universal magnetic fluid in the body. Moreover, he felt that one person could influence the fluid of another to bring about a change in the person's behavior. He conducted meetings cloaked in mystery and mysticism, during which afflicted patients sat around a covered *baquet* or tub with iron rods protruding through the cover from the bottles of various chemicals that were beneath. Mesmer would enter a room, clothed in rather outlandish lilac garments, and take various rods from the tub and touch afflicted parts of his patients' bodies. The rods were believed to transmit "animal magnetism" and adjust the distribution of the universal magnetic fluid, thereby removing the hysterical anesthesias and paralyses. Whatever we may think of what seems today to be a questionable theoretical explanation and procedure, Mesmer apparently helped many people overcome their hysterical problems. Our discussion of Mesmer's work under the rubric of psychogenic causes is rather arbitrary, since Mesmer regarded the hysterical disorders as strictly physical. Because of the setting in which Mesmer worked with his patients, however, he is generally considered one of the earlier practitioners of our modern-day **hypnosis** (see Box 1.4). The familiar word mesmerize is the older term for hypnotize. The phenomenon itself, however, was known to the ancients of probably every culture, belonging to the armamentaria of sorcery and magic, of conjurers, fakirs, and faith healers.

Although Mesmer was regarded as a quack by his contemporaries, the study of hypnosis gradually became respectable. A great Parisian neurologist, Jean Martin Charcot (1825–1893), also studied hysterical states, not only anesthesia and paralysis, but blindness, deafness, convulsive attacks, and gaps in memory brought about by hysteria. Charcot initially espoused a somatogenic point of view. One day, however, some of his enterprising students hypnotized a normal woman and suggested to her certain hysterical symptoms. Charcot was deceived into believing that she was an actual hysterical patient. When the students showed him how readily they could remove the symptoms by waking the woman, Charcot changed his mind about hysteria and became interested in nonphysiological interpretations of these very puzzling phenomena. Further psychological theorizing and research were done by Pierre Janet (1859–1947), one of Charcot's pupils. He believed that in hysteria part of the organized system of thoughts, emotions, and sensations broke loose from the rest through a weakness of the nervous system.

Josef Breuer, the Austrian physician and physiologist whose collaboration with Freud was important in the early development of psychoanalysis. He treated only Anna O. by the cathartic method he originated. Becoming alarmed by what would later be called her transference and his own countertransference, he described his procedures to a colleague and turned her treatment over to him.

In Vienna, toward the end of the century, a physician named Josef Breuer (1842–1925) treated a young woman who had become bedridden with a number of hysterical symptoms. Her legs and right arm and side were paralyzed, her sight and hearing were impaired, and she often had difficulty speaking. She also sometimes went into a dreamlike state or "absence," during which she mumbled to herself, seemingly preoccupied with troubling thoughts. During one treatment session Breuer hypnotized Anna O. and repeated some of her mumbled words. He succeeded in getting her to talk more freely and ultimately with considerable emotion about some very disquieting past events. Upon awakening from these hypnotic sessions, she would frequently feel much better. With Anna O. and other hysterical patients Breuer found that the relief and cure of their symptoms seemed to last longer if, under hypnosis, they were able to recall the original precipitating event for the symptom and if, furthermore, their original emotion was expressed. This reliving of an earlier emotional catastrophe and the release of the emotional tension produced by previously forgotten thoughts about the event were called abreaction or catharsis. Breuer's method became known as the ***cathartic method***. In 1895 one of his colleagues joined him in the publication of *Studies in Hysteria*, a book considered to be a milestone

BOX 1.4

HYPNOSIS

A discussion of hypnosis could appear in several chapters of this book; inasmuch as it played a central role in the development of psychogenic theories of psychopathology, we include it here.

An initial question to be asked is what exactly is hypnosis. In view of how often psychologists and psychiatrists employ the term, it is sobering to realize how much heated controversy there is about its very nature. Hilgard (1979) suggests the following characteristics.

1. **Increased Suggestibility.** Hypnotized subjects seem much more open to suggestions from the hypnotist than they would be in a waking state.

2. **Enhanced Imagery and Imagination.** Hypnotized subjects are able to imagine vividly the sensory experiences suggested to them and also report that they are able to retrieve images, sometimes from childhood, with great clarity.

3. **Disinclination to Plan.** The hypnotized subject loses initiative and instead looks to the hypnotist as a source of direction. Indeed, many hypnotized subjects become annoyed when asked to do some planning on their own.

4. **Reduction in Reality Testing.** Many hypnotized subjects readily accept all kinds of perceptual distortions that they would not tolerate when awake. Thus hypnotized subjects may accept suggestions that an animal is talking to them or that someone is present in the room when no one is acutally there. The logic that operates during a hypnotic trance, allowing a person to perceive the world in a way remarkably different from how he or she regards it when awake, has been called "trance logic" (Orne, 1959).

These, then, are what many workers regard as characteristics of hypnotized subjects. As in all aspects of human behavior, not all people manifest all these character-istics in the same way, and it is indeed possible for subjects who otherwise appear to be deeply hypnotized not to give all these noticeable indications at any one time.

Our historical review mentions Mesmer's therapy for hysterical disabilities and subsequent work by Charcot, Janet, and Breuer. During the same period of time, surgeons were "mesmerizing" patients to block pain. For example, in 1842 a British physician, W.S. Ward, amputated the leg of a patient after hypnotizing him. Apparently the patient felt nothing during what would otherwise have been an excruciatingly painful operation. And in 1849 a mesmeric infirmary was opened in London. Hundreds of apparently painless operations were performed while the patients were in hypnotic trances. In the same decade, however, ether was proved to produce insensibility to pain. The term anesthesia had theretofore been applied to the numbness felt in hysterical states and paralysis. Oliver Wendell Holmes is credited with suggesting that it be applied to the effects of this new agent and others like it, and that the agents be called anesthetics. The availability of these chemicals for surgical operations forestalled the continuing use of hypnosis as an alleviator of pain.

The person who is generally credited with coining the modern term hypnotism is James Braid (1795–1860), a British physician who was also hypnotizing people to reduce pain. Unlike Mesmer, however, Braid did not break with his profession, but described what happened in terms that were more consistent with the *Zeitgeist*. He characterized the trance as a "nervous sleep," from which came the name "neurohypnology," later shortened to hypnotism. Braid rejected the mystical orientation of Mesmer and yet continued to experiment with the phenomenon as he saw it. He sought a physiological cause and felt he had found one in his discovery that trances could be readily induced by having people stare at a bright object located somewhat above the line of vision. The object was placed

---

in abnormal psychology. In the next chapter we examine the thinking of Breuer's collaborator, Sigmund Freud.[3]

[3]Anna O., the young woman treated by Breuer with the cathartic method or "*talking cure,*" has become one of the best-known clinical cases in all the psychotherapy literature, and as indicated above, the report of this case and four others in 1895 formed the basis of Freud's important later contributions. But historical investigations by Ellenberger (1972) cast serious doubt on how accurate Breuer's reporting was. Indeed, Anna O.—in reality Bertha Pappenheim, member of a well-to-do Viennese family—was apparently helped only temporarily by Breuer's talking cure! Carl Jung, Freud's renowned colleague, is quoted as saying that, during a conference in 1925, Freud told him that Anna O. had never been cured. Hospital records discovered by Ellenberger confirmed that she continued to rely on morphine to ease the "hysterical" problems that Breuer is reputed to have removed by catharsis. In fact, evidence suggests that some of her problems were organic, not psychological. It is fascinating and ironic to consider that psychoanalysis traces its roots back to an improperly reported clinical case.

Science: A Human Enterprise

In space exploration highly sophisticated satellites are sent aloft to make observations. Astronauts have also been catapulted to the moon, where they use their human senses as well as machines to carry out still more observations. It is possible, however, that certain phenomena are being missed because our instruments do not have sensing devices capable of recording the presence or absence of such phenomena, and because people are not trained to look for them. When the Viking 1 and Viking 2 Mars landers began to forage for life in July and September of 1976, space scientists repeatedly cautioned against concluding that there was no life on Mars just because instruments failed to detect any. Scientists are sophisticated enough by training to know

in front of a person in such a way that the levator muscles of the eyelids had to be strained to keep it in view. Braid suggested that the muscles were markedly affected by having them remain fixed in this position for a given period of time and that somehow this led to nervous sleep or hypnosis. He therefore placed the cause of the sleep inside the subject rather than external to him, as Mesmer had suggested with his concept of animal magnetism. In this way he was able to perform many public demonstrations without incurring the disapproval of his medical colleagues.

As already indicated, the discovery of drugs for anesthesia discouraged the use of hypnosis in medicine, for drugs are clearly more reliable, although more dangerous as well, than hypnotic inductions. In clinical work many practitioners have employed hypnotic procedures for psychotherapeutic purposes, especially during World War II. To relieve the combat exhaustion of frightened and sleepless soldiers, doctors hypnotized them and encouraged them to relive traumatic events in the imagination.

The scientific study of hypnosis had to await the development of relatively objective measures in the 1950s. Perhaps the principal device is that developed at Stanford University by Weitzenhoffer and Hilgard (1959), the Stanford Hypnotic Susceptibility Scale. In the application of this scale, or, more properly, scales, since there are a number of them, the subject is hypnotized and then asked to undertake a series of tasks. For example, the hypnotist may suggest to a subject that his right hand is so heavy that it is doubtful whether he can raise it. Then the hypnotist will ask the subject to try to lift the heavy hand, even though he probably will not be able to do so. The hypnotist observes the degree to which the subject can or cannot raise the hand and gives a plus or minus score. After the subject has been observed at a number of tasks, he is given a score ranging from zero to twelve, and this score is regarded as a measure of how deeply hypnotized he is.

Most of these scales, however, do not measure the more subjective aspects of hypnosis. For example, many hypnotized subjects, even though they have not been specifically told that it may happen, experience sensations such as floating or spinning. Many hypnotists consider such subjective experiences at least as important as the more observable performances tapped by the various scales. As we might expect, this divergence of interests contributes to the controversy within the field, with the more clinically oriented hypnotists rejecting the validity of such scales as the Stanford. They instead content themselves with what subjects report of their subjective reactions.

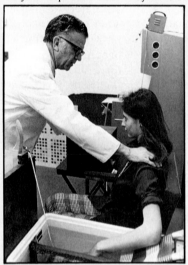

Stanford psychologist Ernest Hilgard, who pioneered the development of a reliable method of assessing hypnotic susceptibility. Here, Hilgard is administering the cold pressor test (See Box 1.3) to a hypnotized subject.

that they are in a bind. Life on another planet can be looked for only with the instruments they themselves have developed, but these devices are limited by their own preconceptions. The tests run on Mars make assumptions about the nature of living matter that may not match what has evolved on this distant planet. Carl Sagan, renowned Cornell space scientist, has cautioned that we may simply be asking the wrong questions. The Viking experiments can determine only whether the Martian soil samples contain earthlike life, but life on Mars could be based on an entirely different chemistry (*Time*, August 2, 1976, p. 23).

This discursion on outer-space exploration is one way of pointing out that scientific observation is a human endeavor, reflecting both the strengths of human ingenuity and scholarship as well as our intrinsic inca-

pacity to be fully knowledgeable about the nature of our universe. Scientists are able to design instruments to make only the kinds of observations about which they have some initial idea. They realize that certain observations are not being made because our knowledge about the general nature of the universe is limited. Thomas Kuhn, a well-known philosopher of science, has put the problem this way: "The decision to employ a particular piece of apparatus and to use it in a particular way carries an assumption that only certain sorts of circumstances will arise" (1962, p. 59). Robert Pirsig, in *Zen and the Art of Motorcycle Maintenance* (1974), expressed the issue somewhat more poetically: "We take a handful of sand from the endless landscape of awareness around us and call that handful of sand the world" (p. 75).

BOX 1.5

PARADIGM CLASH IN THE STUDY OF HYPNOSIS

Box 1.4 reviewed some of the history of hypnosis and its generally accepted characteristics. There is a continuing clash of paradigms in the study of hypnosis, for the very idea that we should talk about hypnosis as a state in which special psychological processes take over has been challenged (e.g., Barber, 1969; Spanos, 1982).

To illustrate the controversy, we shall examine some findings concerning hypnotic analgesia, the reduction of pain by hypnosis. Hilgard, Morgan, and MacDonald (1975) studied subjects who were easily hypnotized and already known to be able to reduce pain substantially when hypnotized. Subjects were required to keep a hand in circulating ice water, called the cold pressor test, and report pain while awake and while hypnotized. As can be seen in Figure 1a, while in the normal waking condition subjects report that pain becomes rapidly more severe during the 45-second period in which the hand is immersed in ice water. Then the subjects were hypnotized, given a suggestion of anesthesia, and asked to report their pain in two ways, verbally as before and also by pressing a key. The two responses were meant to tap two different levels of experience. Subjects were told that through hypnosis it is possible to reach a "hidden part" of the self that is normally inaccessible. The conscious part of the hypnotized subject will verbally report the level of pain experienced. The hidden part, however, will be aware of things going on in the body outside of conscious awareness and will automatically press the key to indicate the pain experienced on this level.

As can be seen in Figure 1a, the two reports in a hypnotized state yielded very different results. As expected, the verbal reports indicated little pain during the 45 seconds. The "hidden observer" key presses, however, signaled substantial pain. Hilgard (1979) interprets these data in a way that clearly ascribes special psychological processes to the hypnotic state. He believes that in hypnotic analgesia the experience of pain is dissociated or separated from conscious awareness. It is experienced unconsciously, behind an "amnesialike barrier." The hidden-observer technique is thought to allow access to this normally unconscious experience.

Hilgard's theory has elicited considerable interest and critical comment, particularly from those who do not believe that hypnosis involves special processes. A study by Spanos, Gwynn, and Stam (1983), for example, attributed the hidden-observer effect to playing a social role. In brief, Spanos and his colleagues believe that the instructions to subjects in Hilgard's studies clearly convey the information that the hypnotized, conscious self will experience little pain and that the hidden part will experience more pain. The experimental situation, then, *demands* a specific pattern of response from subjects, and they provide reports consistent with these demands.

In their experiment Spanos, Gwynn, and Stam examined the responses of easily hypnotized subjects given the cold pressor test in four different situations. The first report was made in a waking state, and the other responses were obtained during hypnotic analgesia but with varying instructions about the hidden observer. In one of these conditions, the uncued, subjects were told that hypnosis would allow a hidden part of them to be reached, but they were given no expectations concerning what their hidden part would experience. In the remaining two conditions, subjects were told that the hidden observer would be either more aware ("The hidden part of you can continue to remain aware of everything going on around it, and everything going on in your body") or less aware (" . . . less aware of everything going on in your body").

Results indicated that ratings of overt pain after each suggestion of analgesia were lower than those given in the waking state, as Hilgard and his co-workers (1975) had found. More important, however, the types of cues subjects were given had an effect on the hidden-observer reports. In the uncued condition, key-pressed reports of pain from the hidden observer did not differ from subjects' ver-

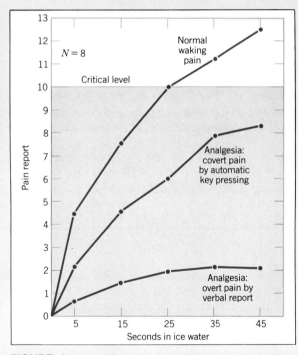

FIGURE 1a
The highest curve indicates the pain that awake subjects felt in one of their hands as they held it in circulating ice water. The small amount of overt pain that they reported verbally when in the same situation but hypnotized and given a suggestion of analgesia is indicated by the lowest curve. The middle curve shows the pain that the hidden parts of their hypnotized selves reported by key pressing. After Hilgard, Morgan, and MacDonald (1975).

bal reports of overt pain. Subjects who expected their hidden observer to be more aware did in fact report more hidden pain than overt. Those who expected their hidden observer to be less aware reported less hidden pain than overt. Clearly, these results suggested that hidden-observer reports can be substantially affected by the information provided by the experimenter. Furthermore, the fact that the level of hidden pain varied with the instructions is contradictory to Hilgard's theory that a high level of unconscious pain is present during hypnotic analgesia.

But the results of the Spanos study have by no means resolved the controversy. For example, Nogrady, McConkey, Laurence, and Perry (1983) performed a study that yielded results more favorable to Hilgard's theory. Subjects were first divided into three groups according to their susceptibility to hypnosis. The subjects of high and medium susceptibility were hypnotized and given several tests. The subjects with little susceptibility were not hypnotized before the tests but rather were instructed to *simulate* the behavior of a hypnotized person. The purpose of the simulation group was to assess the extent to which subjects can determine what is wanted from the cues provided by the experimenter. If the subjects simulating hypnosis behave similarly to those who are actually hypnotized, it can be concluded that the experimenter gave sufficient information to elicit the expected response. Such a result does not prove that hypnotized subjects respond as they do because of the cues given, but it does indicate that either hypnosis or the cues could be operating. On the other hand, if the hypnotized subjects behave differently from the simulators, we can conclude that their behavior is not simply a response to the cues.

In one of the tests administered in the Nogrady study, subjects received electric shocks both to the right hand, which had been suggested to be analgesic, and to the left hand, which had not been the subject of any suggestions.

This pain test was administered twice, the first time after the hypnotic induction or instructions to simulate hypnosis, the second after hidden-observer instructions were given. In the second test subjects were to report the pain level felt by the hidden observer. Subjects were also asked whether they had experienced different levels of awareness, that is, a hidden observer. An important feature of the Nogrady study was to modify somewhat the hidden-observer instructions to give the subjects more leeway. For example, subjects were told that there *may* be another part of them rather than that there *is* another part.

The groups differed significantly in making the hidden-observer response—42 percent of the highly susceptible subjects experienced a hidden observer, but no subject in the other two groups did so! To analyze the pain ratings, the experimenters divided the highly susceptible subjects into two groups according to whether they did or did not have a hidden observer. As can be seen from Table 1a, only the pain ratings reported by the hidden observers of highly susceptible subjects increased for the analgesic hand following the hidden-observer instructions. Thus on both measures the simulating subjects were not able to mimic the behavior of the highly susceptible subjects.

The conflicting findings of the Spanos and Nogrady studies illustrate well the unresolved argument between investigators who believe that hypnosis does involve some special psychological processes and those who believe that it does not. The effects of paradigm can be clearly seen in the publications of each camp. A pro-Hilgard finding will soon elicit a critical commentary or new experiment from the social-role camp, and findings favoring the social-role interpretation usually elicit rebuttals from researchers favoring the view that in hypnosis special psychological processes do take over. The debate is likely to continue to be a lively one for years to come, and it is doubtful whether either camp will ever be convinced that it is wrong.

TABLE 1a
Pain ratings of subjects of varying levels of hypnotic susceptibility (*from Nogrady et al., 1983*)

Group	Analgesic Hand		Control Hand
	Before Hidden-Observer Instructions	After Hidden-Observer Instructions	
High susceptibility			
Hidden observer	3.4	6.2	6.2
No hidden observer	3.6	2.4	8.7
Medium susceptibility	3.9	4.0	8.1
Low susceptibility and simulation	2.8	2.6	6.8

Subjectivity in Science: The Role of Paradigms

We believe that every effort should be made to study abnormal behavior according to scientific principles. It should be clear at this point, however, that science is *not* a completely objective and certain enterprise. Rather, as we can infer from the comment by Kuhn, subjective factors, as well as limitations in our perspective on the universe, enter into the conduct of scientific inquiry. Central to any application of scientific principles, in Kuhn's view, is the concept of **paradigm,** which may be defined as a conceptual framework or model within which a scientist works. A paradigm, according to Kuhn, is a set of basic assumptions that outline the particular universe of scientific inquiry, specifying both the kinds of concepts that will be regarded as legitimate as well as methods that may be used to collect and interpret data. Indeed, every decision about what constitutes a datum, or scientific observation, is made within a paradigm. A paradigm has profound implications for how scientists operate at any given time, for "[People] whose research is based on shared paradigms are committed to the same rules and standards for scientific practice" (Kuhn, 1962, p. 11). Paradigms specify what problems scientists will investigate and how they will go about the investigation.

Although made explicit only when scientists address themselves to philosophy, paradigms are nonetheless an intrinsic part of a science, serving the vital function of indicating how the game is to be played. In perceptual terms a paradigm may be likened to a general **set,** a tendency to see certain factors and not to see others.

In addition to injecting inevitable biases into the definition and collection of data, a paradigm may also affect the interpretation of facts. In other words, the meaning or import attributed to data may depend to a considerable extent on a paradigm (see Box 1.5).

An Example of Paradigms in Abnormal Psychology

A striking demonstration of this "I'll see it when I believe it" feature of science is provided in an experiment by Langer and Abelson (1974). They were interested in how different theoretical orientations might affect the ways in which trained clinicians view the "adjustment" of a person.

Behavior therapy stems from the behaviorism-learning branch of psychology, which sees its purpose to be the objective observation of overt behavior and which has formulated laws that describe learning. Behavior therapists believe that abnormal behavior is acquired according to the same learning principles as normal behavior and that the very designation of a person as mentally ill reflects a social judgment. More traditionally trained clinicians look for the inner conflict supposedly causing disturbed behavior and tend more than behavior therapists to think in terms of mental illness. Langer and Abelson reasoned that behavior therapists might be less swayed by being told that a person was ill than would traditionally trained clinicians. To test this supposition, they conceived the following experiment. A group of behavior therapists and another of therapists trained in **psychoanalysis** were shown a videotape of an interview in progress between two men. Before viewing this videotape, half the subjects in each group were told that the interviewee was a job applicant, the other half that he was a patient. The traditional clinicians who were told that the interviewee was a patient were expected to rate him as more disturbed than those who considered him a job applicant. It was also predicted that the ratings of the two groups of behavior therapists would be less affected by the labels and would thus be rather similar

The videotape shown to all subjects depicted a bearded professor interviewing a young man in his mid-twenties. The interviewee had been recruited through a newspaper advertisement that offered ten dollars to someone who had recently applied for a new job and was willing to be interviewed and videotaped. The fifteen-minute segment chosen from the original interview contained a rambling, autobiographical monologue by the young man in which he described a number of past jobs and dwelt on his conflicts with bureaucrats. His manner was considered by Langer and Abelson to be intense but uncertain; they felt that he could be regarded either as sincere and struggling or as confused and troubled.

A questionnaire measured the clinicians' impressions about the mental health of the interviewee. When the young interviewee was identified as a job applicant, there were no significant differences in the adjustment ratings given by the traditional clinicians and the behavior therapists. But the patient label, as expected, produced sharp differences (Figure 1.1). When the interviewee was identified as a patient, the traditional clinicians rated him relatively disturbed—significantly more so than did the traditional clinicians who viewed the man as a job applicant. In contrast, the behavior therapists rated the "ill" interviewee as relatively well adjusted, in fact, no less adjusted than the other behavior therapists rated the man they considered a job applicant.

Qualitative evaluations obtained from the clinicians supported their ratings. Whereas the behavior therapists described the man as "realistic," "sincere," and

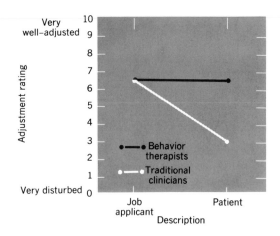

FIGURE 1.1

The mean adjustment ratings given the interviewee, depending on the investigators' description of him and the diagnosticians' training. Adapted from Langer and Abelson (1974).

"responsible," regardless of label, the traditional clinicians who viewed him as a patient used phrases such as "tight, defensive person," "conflict over homosexuality," and "impulsivity shows through his rigidity."

Why, in this particular experiment, did the behavior therapists appear to be unbiased? Langer and Abelson explain it this way. The behavioral approach encourages clinicians to concentrate on overt or manifest behavior and to be skeptical about illness that is not readily apparent. Those with such an orientation had the advantage in this particular study because, however the interviewee rambled, his behavior on balance was not overtly disturbed. The traditional therapists, on the other hand, had presumably been trained to look beyond what is most obvious in a client. Therefore, when the traditional therapists heard the negative ramblings about bureaucrats, they probably paid too much attention to them and inferred that something was basically wrong with the young man.

Langer and Abelson properly alert readers to the limitations of their experiment, reminding them that a different study—perhaps using an interviewee who is obviously disturbed—might put behavior therapists at a disadvantage. The purpose of the experiment, and this discussion of it, is not to pit one orientation against another but rather to illustrate how a paradigm can

affect perception. Indeed, psychopathology can be in the eye of the beholder.

Thus subjective factors in the guise of theoretical persuasions pervade psychology and strongly affect our conception of the nature of abnormal behavior. Scientists, whatever their field, do not resign from the family of human beings when they formulate hypotheses and conduct investigations and controlled research. Perhaps it is especially appropriate for the psychologist-as-scientist to remain aware of this simple, although frequently overlooked, point.

Summary

The study of psychopathology is a search for why people behave, think, and feel in unexpected, sometimes bizarre, and typically self-defeating ways. Much less is known than we would like; this book will focus on the ways in which psychopathologists have been trying to learn the causes of abnormal behavior and what they know about preventing and alleviating it.

A history of the field was provided, indicating its origins in ancient demonology and crude medical theorizing. Since the beginning of scientific inquiry into abnormal behavior, two major points of view have vied for attention: the somatogenic, which assumes that every mental aberration is caused by a physical malfunction; and the psychogenic, which assumes that the sufferer's body is intact and that difficulties are to be explained in psychological terms.

Scientific inquiry was presented as a special way in which human beings acquire knowledge about their world. In a very important sense people see only what they are prepared to see, and certain phenomena may go undetected because scientists can discover only the things about which they already have some general idea. There is subjectivity in science as there is in everyday perception and problem solving.

Hypnosis was reviewed in some detail, both because it occupies an important position in the historical development of the field and because the controversies about hypnosis provide a good example of how the paradigms of science—the sets of basic assumptions that determine the kinds of scientific questions to be asked and the procedures to be used in collecting data—can vary and thus affect the conclusions drawn.

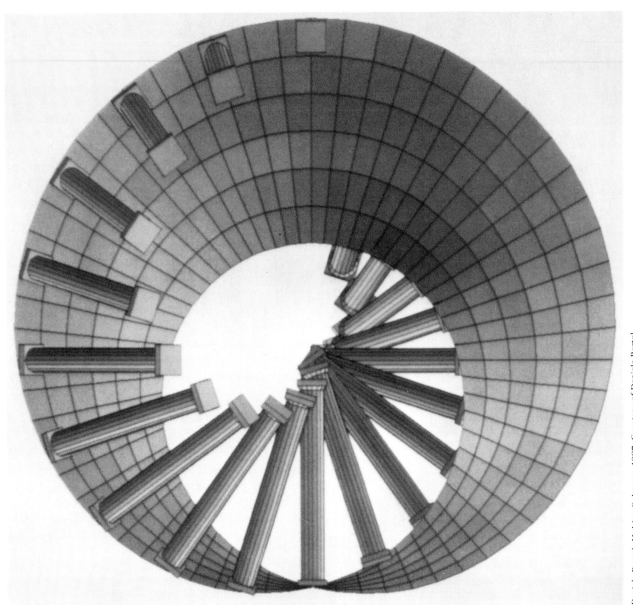

Daniela Bertol. *Mobius Columns*, 1987. Courtesy of Daniela Bertol.

Chapter 2

Current Paradigms in Psychopathology and Therapy

The Physiological Paradigm
The Choice of Terms
Physiological Approaches to Treatment
The Psychoanalytic Paradigm
Classical Psychoanalytic Theory
Post-Freudian Psychodynamic Perspectives
Psychoanalytic Therapy
Learning Paradigms
The Rise of Behaviorism
Mediational Learning Paradigms
Applying Learning Points of View to Deviant Behavior
Behavior Therapy
The Cognitive Paradigm
Cognitive Behavior Therapy
Learning Paradigms and Cognitive Paradigms
The Humanistic Paradigm
Humanistic Therapy
Consequences of Adopting a Paradigm
Diathesis–Stress: A Proposed Paradigm
Different Perspectives on a Clinical Problem
What Is Abnormal?
Summary

Paradigms are self-created, wafer-thin barriers against the pain of uncertainty. (Yalom, 1980, p. 26)

This chapter is concerned with the principal paradigms or models that have been used to conceptualize abnormal behavior, how it develops, and how best to treat it. Different investigators adopt different paradigms, loose sets of general *assumptions* about what should be studied, how to gather data, and how to think about behavior. We shall discuss five major paradigms, or models, of contemporary abnormal psychology: the *physiological paradigm,* the *psychoanalytic,* the *learning,* the *cognitive,* and the *humanistic.* The particular postulates of each paradigm cannot be listed item by item. Instead, we shall try to convey the flavor of the five general points of view.

Many people go about the study of abnormal psychology without explicitly considering the nature of the paradigm that they have adopted. But, as this chapter will indicate, the choice of a paradigm has some very important consequences for the way abnormal behavior is defined, investigated, and treated. In fact, our discussion of paradigms will lay the groundwork for the in-depth examination of the major categories of disorder and of intervention that makes up the rest of the book.

The Physiological Paradigm

What we designate as the physiological paradigm of abnormal behavior is often referred to as the *medical* or *disease model.* We prefer our term for two reasons. First, it has proved difficult to define exactly what is meant by medical model. Second, and more important, arguments about the so-called medical model most often reduce to whether or not behavior is abnormal because of physiological defects.

The Choice of Terms

Let us first examine the prevalent definition of the medical model. As indicated in Chapter 1, the study of abnormal behavior is historically linked to medicine. Many early workers and many contemporaries as well have used the model of physical illness as the basis for defining deviant behavior. Clearly, within the field of abnormal behavior the terminology of medicine is pervasive. As Maher (1966) has noted, "[deviant] behavior is termed *pathological* and is classified on the basis of *symptoms,* classification being called *diagnosis.* Processes designed to change behavior are called *therapies*

and are applied to patients in mental *hospitals.* If the deviant behavior ceases, the patient is described as *cured*" (p. 22).

The critical assumption of the medical paradigm is that abnormal behavior may be likened to a disease. To determine how a disease model can be applied to abnormal behavior, we must first examine the concept of disease as it is employed in medicine. During the Dark Ages a disease was thought to consist simply of observable signs and symptoms, such as a rash and high temperature. As medical science, particularly autopsy studies, increased in sophistication, the observable symptoms were attributed to internal malfunctions. Then, when Louis Pasteur discovered the relation between bacteria and disease, and soon thereafter postulated viruses, the *germ theory* of disease provided a new explanation of pathology. External symptoms were assumed to be produced through infection of the body by minute organisms and viruses. For a time this germ theory was the paradigm of medicine. But it soon became apparent that not all diseases could be explained by the germ theory. Diabetes, for example, a malfunction of the insulin-secreting cells of the pancreas, cannot be attributed to infection. Nor does it even have a single cause. As another example, consider heart disease. A multitude of factors—genetic makeup, stress produced by smoking and obesity, type A behavior (see page 203)—are all related to the frequency of heart disease. Is there a single paradigm, or model, here?

We think not. Because medical diseases themselves vary in their causes and symptoms, asserting that abnormal behavior can be considered a disease clarifies little (see Box 2.1). But all diseases are disturbances of the body's physiological processes. This is why we have chosen the term physiological paradigm. It is meaningful to say that a behavioral abnormality may be attributed, at least in part, to a disruption in one or more physiological processes.

There is now a considerable literature, both research and theory, dealing with physiological factors relevant to psychopathology. For example, heredity probably predisposes a person, through physiological malfunction, to develop schizophrenia (see Chapter 14). Depression may result from a failure of the usual processes of neural transmission (Chapter 9). Anxiety disorders are considered by some to stem from a defect within the autonomic nervous system that causes a person to be too easily aroused (Chapter 6). Other so-called organic brain syndromes can be traced to impairments in structures of the brain (Appendix). In each case a type of psychopathology is viewed as caused by the disturbance of some physiological process. Those working with this paradigm assume that answers to puzzles of psychopathology will be found by concentrating on somatic, that is, bodily, causes.

BOX 2.1

CRITICISMS OF THE MEDICAL OR DISEASE MODEL OF ABNORMAL BEHAVIOR

Although we have argued that the term medical model is not very valuable, it is so widely discussed by psychopathologists and clinicians that an overview of some of its problems may be useful. A common criticism of the medical model is that in examining the abnormal behavior of an individual, the clinician has no independent means of verifying the existence of a disease. In medicine both the symptoms and the factors producing them, that is, the disease process, can often be assessed. It is possible, for example, to determine that an individual has a temperature of 104 degrees. Moreover, the particular germ or microorganism that caused the rise in temperature can also be independently determined, say by taking a throat culture and analyzing the foreign organisms that are present. When a disease model is applied to abnormal behavior, however, it is often not possible to assess independently both the symptoms and the supposed cause of the symptoms. Certain behavior or symptoms are categorized as mental illnesses and given names, but then the name of the illness itself is often cited as an explanation for or cause of these same symptoms. For example, a patient who is withdrawn and hallucinating is diagnosed as schizophrenic; however, when we ask why the patient is withdrawn and hallucinating, we are often told that it is because the patient is schizophrenic. Thus the label schizophrenia is applied to certain behavior and then in addition is specified as a cause of this same behavior. This is a clear example of circular reasoning, something to be avoided in scientific inquiry.

This criticism of the way mental illnesses are assessed is reasonable, but it is not always entirely applicable. Someone holding a medical or disease model point of view could assert that we may make a diagnosis of schizophrenia based on symptoms, without claiming that these symptoms are produced by the presence of schizophrenia. This diagnostician would propose that although we do not now know the cause of the symptoms, future research may uncover the cause(s). For example, some deviant chemical may eventually be located within schizophrenics and be identified as the cause of the disorder. In sum, the more sophisticated disease modeler may acknowledge that we currently have little information about causes of disorders, but that when such information becomes available, it will, in principle, be possible to assess independently both the symptoms and the *etiology* as is the case in medicine.

A second common criticism of applying medical models to abnormal behavior involves an alleged difference between the symptoms of physical illness and the symptoms of mental illness. This argument, most often associated with Thomas Szasz (1960), holds that so-called mental symptoms are a patient's communications about himself and others. When we call such communications symptoms, Szasz asserts, we are making a judgment within a particular social and cultural context. For example, a patient's belief that he is Christ might lead an observer to make a diagnosis of paranoid schizophrenia. Even in this extreme case, however, the diagnosis depends on whether the observer believes the patient's assertion. If the observer gives credence to the patient's statement, the behavior will clearly not be judged a symptom of mental illness.

Szasz and his followers also say that the symptoms of mental illness are *subjective*, whereas those of physical illness are *objective*. This assertion has some merit, but the distinction is not as clear-cut as Szasz would have it (Ausubel, 1961b). For example, a patient who has entered a physician's office may complain that he is suffering pain. But because tolerance of pain differs widely among individuals, how can the physician determine the actual amount of pain the patient is experiencing? Although the importance of subjective factors as they enter into the definition of so-called mental illness should not be minimized, distingushing between mental and physical illnesses on this basis alone is a questionable procedure.

Finally, many people have alleged that so-called mental illnesses have neither a specific etiology nor a specific set of symptoms and thus do not qualify as diseases (e.g., Milton and Wahler, 1969). Our knowledge of the etiologies of psychopathologies is indeed extremely limited. As we have indicated, however, the fact that these etiologies have not been uncovered as yet does not mean that we should stop looking for them.

Our failure to define specific sets of symptoms for many categories of deviant behavior may be a more damning criticism. Specific syndromes have simply not been discerned for all psychopathologies. Again, however, a person wishing to maintain a medical model for mental illness may counter this criticism with the following line of reasoning. Many medical diseases do *not* have a set of specific symptoms. Paresis is a good example. Before it was discovered to be infectious, there was considerable debate whether the symptoms had a physical cause or whether paresis should be considered a psychological disturbance. Proponents of the psychological view argued that the symptoms were not entirely consistent from one person to another, for some patients suffer depression rather than delusions of grandeur. Therefore they did not consider paresis a medical disease. Although paresis was indeed found to have a single causal agent, the manifestations of its *later* stage may *differ markedly from patient to patient.* Thus even an infectious disease may not necessarily have a homogeneous set of symptoms.

Taken together, the information presented here indicates that the decision to view abnormal behavior as a medical disease is determined partly by subjective factors. And, although the medical model is subject to many potential criticisms there is a possible rejoinder for each criticism.

Physiological Approaches to Treatment

An important implication of the physiological paradigm is that surgery or a drug able to alter bodily functioning may well be effective in treating or even preventing certain abnormalities. Certainly if a deficiency in a particular biochemical substance is found to underlie or contribute to some problem, it makes sense to attempt to correct the imbalance by providing appropriate doses of the deficient chemical. Here there is a clear connection between viewing disorder as physiological defect and attempting to correct the fault through a physiological intervention.

As an example, phenylketonuria (PKU) is a form of mental retardation caused by a genetically determined enzyme deficiency that makes the body unable to metabolize phenylalanine into tyrosine. State laws require routine testing of an infant's blood for excess phenylalanine; if the test is positive, a specific diet low in the amino acid is prescribed. Children otherwise doomed to profound mental deficiency can thereby be brought closer to the normal range of intelligence (Chapter 16). The prevention of some of these ravages is a successful example of physiological intervention to correct a physiological anomaly.

Other physiological interventions in widespread use do not necessarily derive from knowledge of what causes a given disorder in the first place. Again, we are notably short on information about etiology, but sedatives, like Valium, can be effective in reducing the tension associated with anxiety disorders. The controversial electroconvulsive shock treatment (ECT) seems to be useful in alleviating severe depression. Neither of these somatic therapies is as yet known to be related meaningfully to possible causes of these disorders, but both are to be regarded as physiological treatments. Further, one can hold a physiological theory about the nature of a mental problem and recommend psychological intervention. Recall from Chapter 1 that Hippocrates proposed *non*somatic therapies—rest for melancholia, for example—to deal with mental disorders that he considered somatic in origin. Contemporary workers also appreciate that nonphysiological interventions can have beneficial effects on the soma (see also Box 8.1, where we discuss Cartesian dualism).

The Psychoanalytic Paradigm

Probably the most widespread paradigm in psychopathology and therapy is the psychoanalytic or psychodynamic, originally developed by Sigmund Freud (1856–1939).

Classical Psychoanalytic Theory

Structure of the Mind

Freud divided the mind or the psyche into three principal parts, the *id, ego,* and *surperego*; each of these are metaphors for specific functions or energies. The id is present at birth and is the part of the personality that accounts for all the energy to run the psyche. It consists of the basic urges for food, water, elimination, warmth, affection, and sex. Freud, trained as a neurologist, regarded the source of all energy of the id as physiological; it is later converted by some means into psychic energy, all of it unconscious, below the level of awareness.

Within the id Freud postulated two basic instincts, Eros and Thanatos. The more important is Eros, which Freud saw as a life-integrating force, principally sexual. The energy of the instinct Eros is called **libido.** Eros, libido, and sexual energy are sometimes indiscriminately equated, but libido and Eros are also occasionally expanded to include all integrative, life-furthering forces, some of which may not be strictly sexual. Thanatos, the death instinct, plays a relatively small role in Freudian thinking, and indeed its energy never received a name.[1]

The id seeks immediate gratification and operates on what Freud called the **pleasure principle.** When the id is not satisfied, tension is produced, and the id strives to eliminate this tension as quickly as possible. For example, the infant feels hunger, an aversive drive, and is impelled to move about, sucking, in order to reduce the tension arising from the unsatisfied drive. This behavior, called reflex activity, is one means by which the id obtains gratification; it represents the organisms's first commerce with the environment. The other means is **primary process,** generating images of what is desired. The infant who wants its mother's milk imagines the mother's breast and thereby obtains some short-term satisfaction of the hunger drive through its wish-fulfilling fantasy. Even in adult life id impulses remain relatively dissociated from the reality-oriented, adaptational processes of the ego. The id, with its need to reduce and eliminate tension, seeks a state of quiescence, which, perhaps ironically, can be achieved only in death.

The second part of the personality, primarily conscious and called the ego, begins to develop out of the id during the second six months of life. The task of the ego is to deal with reality. The ego frowns upon primary

---

[1]One analyst (Wachtel, personal communication, 1983) doubts that Freud ever even used the term. Nowadays people simply refer to an aggressive instinct.

process, for fantasy will not keep the organism alive. Through its planning and decision-making functions, called **secondary process,** the ego realizes that operating on the pleasure principle at all times, as the id would like to do, may not be the most effective way of maintaining life. The ego thus operates on the **reality principle** as it mediates between the demands of reality and the immediate gratification desired by the id.

The ego, however, derives all its energy from the id and may be likened to a horseback rider who receives energy from riding the horse. But a real horseback rider directs the horse with his or her own energy, not depending on that of the horse for thinking, planning, and moving. The ego, on the other hand, derives *all* its energies from the id and yet must direct what it is entirely dependent on for energy.

The superego is the third part of the personality. Essentially, it is the carrier of society's moral standards as interpreted by the child's parents. The superego develops through the resolution of the oedipal conflict, to be discussed shortly, and is generally equivalent to what we call conscience. When the id pressures the ego to satisfy its needs, the ego must cope not only with reality constraints but also with the "right–wrong" moral judgments of the superego. The behavior of the human being, as conceptualized by Freud, is thus a complex interplay of three psychic systems, all vying for the achievement of goals that cannot always be reconciled. This interplay of active forces is referred to as the **psychodynamics** of the personality.

Freud was drawn into studying the mind by his work with Breuer on hypnosis and hysteria (see page 21). The apparently powerful role played by factors of which patients seemed unaware led Freud to postulate that much of our behavior is determined by forces that are inaccesible to awareness. Both the id instincts and many of the superego's activities are not known to the conscious mind. The ego is primarily conscious, for it is the metaphor for the psychic systems that have to do with thinking and planning. But the ego too has important unconscious aspects, the **defense mechanisms,** which protect it from anxiety; these will also be discussed shortly. Basically, Freud considered most of the important determinants of behavior to be **unconscious.**

Freud saw the human personality as a closed energy system; at any one time there is a fixed amount of energy in the id to run the psychic apparatus. The three parts of the personality therefore battle for a share of a specific amount of energy. Moreover, Freud's theorizing was totally deterministic. Natural scientist that he was, Freud saw every bit of behavior, even seemingly trivial slips of the tongue, as having specific causes, some of them unconscious.

Stages of Psychosexual Development

Freud conceived of the personality apparatus as developing through a series of four separate psychosexual stages. At each stage a different part of the body is the most sensitive to sexual excitation and therefore the most capable of providing libidinal satisfaction to the id. The first is the **oral** stage, during which the infant derives maximum gratification of id impulses from excitation of the sensory endings around the mouth. Sucking and feeding are the principal pleasures. In the second year of life the child enters the **anal** stage as enjoyment shifts to the anus and the elimination and retention of feces. In the **phallic** stage, which extends from age three to age five or six, maximum gratifcation comes from stimulation of the genitalia. Between ages six to twelve the child is in a **latency** period, which is not considered a psychosexual stage. During these years the id impulses are less intense and do not play a direct role in motivating behavior. The child behaves asexually, although according to Freud's theoretical scheme all behavior is *basically* driven by id impulses. The final and adult stage is the **genital,** during which heterosexual interests predominate.

The manner in which the growing person at each stage resolves the conflicts between what the id wants and what the environment will provide determines basic personality traits that will last throughout the person's life. For example, a person who in the anal stage experiences either excessive or deficient amounts of gratification, depending on his or her toilet-training regimen, and thus does not progress beyond this stage, is called an **anal personality.** One type, the anal retentive, is considered stingy and sometimes obsessively clean. These traits appear throughout life but receive the greatest attention in adulthood, when people typically seek the help of psychoanalysts. They can, however, be traced back to early events and to the manner in which gratification was provided or denied the child. Freud referred to this "freezing" of development at an earlier psychosexual stage as **fixation.**

Perhaps the most important crisis of development occurs during the phallic stage, around age four, for then, Freud asserted, the child is overcome with sexual desire for the parent of the opposite sex. Threat of dire punishment from the parent of the same sex may cause the child to repress the entire conflict, pushing it into the unconscious. This desire and repression are referred to as the **Oedipus complex** for the male and the **Electra complex** for the female. The dilemma is usually resolved through increased identification with the parent of the same sex and through the adoption of society's mores, which forbid the child to desire its parent. Through this learning of moral values the superego is developed.

(Right) A portrait of Freud at twenty with his fiancé, Martha Bernays. (Below) The room in which Freud saw many of the patients written about in his famous psychoanalytic cases. (Top right page) The ailing Freud sits and works at his desk. (Bottom right page) The Freud family in Vienna 1896. Standing, left to right: Paula (sister), Anna (sister), unidentified girl, Sigmund, Emmauel (half brother), Rosa (sister), Marie (sister), and Simon Nathanson (cousin). Seated, left to right: Adolfine (sister), Amalie (mother), and Jacob (father). Seated in front: Alexander (brother) and an unidentified boy.

Anxiety and Defense

The Two Anxiety Theories Freud proposed two different theories of anxiety. In the first formulation, published in 1895, *neurotic anxiety* was regarded as stemming from the blockage of unconscious impulses. Such impulses are blocked, for example, under conditions of extreme sexual deprivation. When repressed they become susceptible to transformation into neurotic anxiety. In his second theory, proposed in 1926, Freud reversed the relationship between neurotic anxiety and repression. According to the first theory, neurotic anxiety develops through repression of impulses. In the second, anxiety about impulses signals the need for their repression. In a sense, according to the first theory we become anxious because we want things that we do not get; according to the second we are anxious because we fear our wants (Wachtel, 1977). *Neurotic anxiety,* then, is the fear of the disastrous consequences that are expected to follow if a previously punished id impulse is allowed expression.

The second theory viewed birth as the prototypic anxiety situation, for the infant is flooded with excitation over which it can exert no control. After the development of the ego in the first year of life, anxiety becomes a signal of impending overstimulation. The person is warned that he or she is in danger of being reduced to an infantile state of helplessness through overstimulation by id impulses and other forces. Anxiety thus plays a functional role, signaling the ego to take action before being overwhelmed.

Two other kinds of anxiety were described by Freud. *Objective anxiety* refers to the ego's reaction to danger in the external world, for example, the anxiety felt when life is in real jeopardy. This kind of anxiety is the same as realistic fear. *Moral anxiety,* experienced by the ego as guilt or shame, is really fear of the punishment that the superego imposes for failure to adhere to standards of moral conduct.

Perhaps because Freud's earlier views held that repression of id impulses would create neurotic anxiety, we often hear that Freudians preach as much gratification of impulses as possible, lest a person become neurotic. But this is not the case. For Freudians the essence of neurotic anxiety is repression. Being unaware of conflicts lies at the core of neurotic anxiety, rather than simply being reluctant, unwilling, or unable to reduce the demands of the id. A celibate Catholic priest and a nun, for example, are not considered candidates for neurosis provided they consciously acknowledge their sexual or aggressive tendencies. Such individuals do not have to act on these felt needs to avoid neurotic anxiety. They must only remain aware of these needs whenever they vie for expression.

Initially, Freud postulated that traumatic childhood sexual experiences lay behind the neurotic problems of his patients. But by 1897 he came to realize that perverted acts against children would have to be far more prevalent than he was willing or able to assume. He then coupled his patients' reports of such trauma with his own supposition that the unconscious does not distinguish between fact and fantasy. Performing what one commentator has termed a stunning intellectual tour de force (Wachtel, 1977), he proposed that his patients were reporting to him not actual events of their childhood but rather their fantasies. Young children, he assumed, have to deal with intense feelings and longings. Ill-equipped to do so, they are prone to *invent* gratifications. Scientists, wishing to retain certain tenets of their theorizing, can be remarkably creative in adjusting particular aspects of their thinking to accommodate newly emerging evidence. By switching from actual events to fantasies, Freud was able to retain early childhood trauma as the central cause of neurotic anxiety (see Box 2.2).[2]

Defense Mechanisms According to Freud, the discomfort experienced by the anxious ego can be reduced by several maneuvers. Objective anxiety, rooted in reality, can often be handled by removing or avoiding the danger in the external world, or by dealing with it in a rational way. Neurotic anxiety, may be handled through an unconscious distortion of reality by means of a defense mechanism. A defense mechanism is a strategy, unconsciously utilized, that serves to protect the ego from anxiety. Perhaps the most important is *repression,* whereby impulses and thoughts unacceptable to the ego are pushed into the unconscious. Repression not only prevents awareness but also keeps buried desires from growing up (Wachtel, 1977). By remaining repressed, these infantile memories cannot be corrected by adult experience and therefore retain their original intensity. Another defense mechanism, important in paranoid disorders (see Chapter 14), is *projection,* attributing to external agents charcteristics or desires that are possessed by an individual and yet are unacceptable to conscious awareness. For example, a hostile woman may unconsciously find it aversive to regard herself as angry at others and may project her angry feelings onto them; thus she sees others as angry with her. Other defense mechanisms are *displacement,* redirecting emotional responses from a perhaps dangerous object to a substitute, for instance, kicking the cat instead of the

---

[2]In recent years investigators have become aware of a greater prevalence of child molestation within families than we perhaps had wanted to consider. It is possible, then, that Freud seriously underestimated incest and may therefore not have needed to alter his theorizing about traumatic childhood sexual experiences to the extent that he did.

BOX 2.2

FREUD: THE METHODOLOGICAL AND CONCEPTUAL PROBLEMS

Perhaps no investigator of the vagaries of human life has been honored and criticized as much as Freud. During the last years of the nineteenth century and the first years of this century, when he was first espousing his view of infantile sexuality, he was personally vilified. At that time sexuality was little discussed among adults. How scandalous, then, to assert that infants and children were also motivated by sexual drives! In the history of science few have shown greater intellectual integrity and personal bravery than Freud.

Because of his very great importance in the field, some current criticisms of his methodology and concepts will be reviewed. Although we attach considerable importance to case reports compiled by clinicians who are "on the front line," clinical reporting by its very nature presents problems that are extremely difficult to avoid. Freud's theorizing, as well as the thinking of the "**neo-Freudians,**" those who have adapted and changed his basic framework, rests primarily on case studies. Like many clinicians, Freud did not take careful notes during his sessions and had to rely almost completely on recollection. The reliability of his perceptions and recollections is impossible to evaluate. Furthermore, the behavior of a listener affects what a speaker has to say. It is possible that Freud's patients were influenced, at least to some degree, to talk about the childhood events that he was most interested in.

The inferential leaps that are made by Freud and other psychoanalysts may be difficult to accept unless one has a prior commitment to the point of view. The distinction between observation and interpretation is sometimes blurred. Consider an example from the analyst Main (1958). "The little boy who babbles tenderly to himself as he soaps himself in his bath does so because he has taken into himself his tender soaping mother." What, in fact, is readily observed by the average onlooker is the child bathing himself. To see his mother incorporated in the soapy bath play is to operate at a very high level of inference. The paradigm problem is once again evident. What we perceive is strongly colored by the paradigm we adopt.

There is considerable disagreement whether Freud's theorizing should be considered scientific, for it is difficult to disprove or prove. Few of the statements are very explicit. If our view of science requires concepts to be mea-

surable, and theories testable, psychoanalytic thinking cannot be regarded as scientific.

Freud's findings do not have general applicability because his sample of patients was very selective and small. Nearly all his patients were from the upper middle class of early twentieth-century Vienna, hardly a representative sampling of human beings. Nonetheless, Freud was prepared to apply his findings to all humankind. In a related vein, after making limited observations, Freud held that a repressed homosexual inclination was the basis for all paranoid disorders. But he never considered, nor for that matter have others who have accepted his point of view, how many paranoids have not had homosexual desires in the past and, indeed, how many people with repressed homosexuality do not develop into paranoids.

Although Freud insisted that he used concepts like id, ego, superego, and the unconscious as metaphors to describe psychic functions, they seem reified, that is, they are made into independent, behavior-determining agents whose own actions must still be explained. For example, Freud spoke of "immediate and unheeding satisfaction of the instincts, such as the id demands. . . . The id knows no solicitude about ensuring survival." (1937). Thus the id "demands" immediate satisfaction and "knows" certain things. In spite of occasional reminders in psychoanalytic writings that these concepts are meant as metaphors, or as summary statements of functions, they are typically written about as though they had an existence of their own and had a power to push things around, to think, and to act.

It should be obvious by now that the authors of this book view the validity and usefulness of Freud's work with some skepticism. On the other hand, it would be a serious mistake to minimize his importance in psychopathology or, for that matter, in the intellectual history of Western civilization. Freud was an astute observer of human nature. Moreover, his work has elicited the kind of critical reaction that helps to advance knowledge. He was instrumental in getting people to consider nonphysiological explanations for disordered behavior. It is impossible to acquire a good grasp of the field of abnormal psychology without some familiarity with his writings.

---

boss; *reaction formation,* converting one feeling such as hate into its opposite, love; *regression,* retreating to the behavioral patterns of an earlier age; and *rationalization,* inventing a reason for an action or attitude.[3]

---

[3]A psychoanalytic quip defines a rationalization as a *good* reason for an action—but not the *real* reason.

All these defense mechanisms allow the ego to discharge some id energy while at the same time not facing frankly the true nature of the motivation. Because defense mechanisms are more readily observed than other symptoms of a disordered personality, they very often make people aware of their troubled natures and persuade them to consult a therapist.

Post-Freudian Psychodynamic Perspectives

The significance of Freud's theories and clinical work was widely recognized by his contemporaries. A number of them, including Carl Jung and Alfred Adler, met with Freud periodically to discuss psychoanalytic theory and therapy. As may happen when a brilliant leader attracts brilliant followers and colleagues, differences may emerge. From this distinguished group, disagreements arose about a number of important general issues, such as the relative importance of id versus ego; of biological instinctual drives versus sociocultural determinants; of how critical the earliest years of life were in contrast to adult experiences; of whether sexual urges are at the core of motives and actions that are themselves not obviously sexual;[4] of unconscious processes versus conscious ones; and of the reflexlike nature of id impulses versus purposive behavior governed primarily by conscious ego deliberations.

To elaborate on some of these themes, we outline the major ideas of three theorists who adapted Freud's ideas in forging approaches of their own. Others who adapted and modified Freud's theories are discussed in Chapter 18.

Carl Gustav Jung (1887–1961), a Swiss psychiatrist, broke with Freud on many issues in 1914, after a seven-year period during which they had an intense correspondence. Jung proposed ideas radically different from Freud's, ultimately establishing "analytical psychology," a blend of Freudian psychology and, as will be appreciated when we deal with the humanistic paradigm (page 52), humanistic psychology. He de-emphasized the sexual nature of libido and regarded it as general biological life energy; he hypothesized that, in addition to our personal unconscious, which Freud stressed, our "collective unconscious" contains information from the social history of humankind, the repository of all the experiences people have had over the centuries, and, unlike Freud's unconscious, contains positive and creative forces. He also asserted that each of us has masculine and feminine traits that can be blended to forge a creative personality and held that people have spiritual and religious needs that are as basic as their libidinal ones. Jung also catalogued various personality types, perhaps the most important of which is extraversion versus introversion. He also wrote about ***self-actualization,*** a concept central to Carl Rogers, and conceived to be the state of fulfillment when a person balances and gives expression to all aspects of his or her personality. In addition, Jung wrote at length on religious symbolism and the meaning of life, and as a

"I'M A FREUDIAN. IF YOU'RE A JUNGIAN, GO TO A JUNGIAN!"

consequence became quite popular among mystics, novelists, and poets. Finally, whereas Freud regarded current and future behavior as determined primarily from the past, Jung focused on purposiveness, decision making, and goal setting, or what philosophers call *teleogy*. To understand people, then, one has to appreciate their dreams and aspirations, not just the effects of their past experiences, as important as those may be (Jung, 1928).

Alfred Adler's (1870–1937) "individual psychology" (Adler, 1924) was even less dependent on Freud's views of instincts than was Jung's, and Freud remained quite bitter toward the psychiatrist after their relationship ended. Adler, who had been a sickly child in Vienna and had to strive mightily to overcome feelings of inferiority, emphasized striving for superiority, but not in an antisocial sense. Indeed, Adler regarded people as inextricably tied to their society because he believed that fulfillment is found in doing things for the social good. Like Jung, he stressed the importance of working toward goals; and, like Jung, much of his theorizing anticipates later developments in humanistic psychology.[5] One central element in Adler's work was the focus on the individual's *phenomenology* as the key to understanding that person, an emphasis that also anticipates contemporary developments in cognitive behavior

---

[4]An apocryphal (probably false) quip is attributed to Freud, who loved cigars: "Sometimes a cigar is just a good smoke."

[5]Indeed, as one reads about "neo-Freudians" like Jung and Adler, one sometimes wonders why they are considered part of the psychoanalytic tradition rather than the humanistic. No doubt their historical ties to Freud and their close association with him until each broke with "the Master" color our perceptions of their theorizing.

Three important post-Freudians: Alfred Adler, Carl Jung (with his family), and Erik Erikson.

therapy (page 52). Another connection with cognitive behavior therapy is the way Adler worked to help patients change their illogical, mistaken beliefs and expectations; to feel and behave better, one has first to think more rationally. Finally, Adler's interest in growth and prevention of problems, and the betterment of society, influenced the development of child guidance centers and parent education.

Erik Erikson (1902–), who had only the equivalent of a high school diploma, is the final major figure we will discuss here. Erikson is identified as an ego psychologist because he emphasized the formation of ego identity and psychosocial development. Whereas Freud believed that development ended early in life, Erikson's major contribution lies in a field that has come to be called *life-span developmental psychology,* a central thesis of which is that people continue to change and

differentiate through middle age and into their senior years. To get a good sense of the significance of this general viewpoint, consider that "child psychology" used to be synonymous with "developmental psychology," whereas thanks in no small measure to Erikson, people now distinguish between the two, or in a more radical vein, even propose that there be only one developmental psychology and that it refer to the entire life span.

TABLE 2.1
Erikson's eight stages of development

Stage and Approximate Age Range	Psychosocial Crisis	Major Developments
Infancy 0–1	Trust vs. mistrust	In the caregiver–baby relationship, the infant develops a sense of trust or mistrust that basic needs such as nourishment, warmth, cleanliness, and physical contact will be provided.
Early Childhood 1–3	Autonomy vs. shame, doubt	Children learn self-control as a means of being self-sufficient, e.g., toilet-training, feeding, walking, or developing shame and doubt about their abilities to be autonomous.
Play Age 3–6	Initiative vs. guilt	Children are anxious to investigate adult activities, but may also have feelings of guilt about trying to be independent and daring.
School Age 7–11	Industry vs. inferiority	Children learn about imagination and curiosity, develop learning skills, or develop feelings of inferiority if they fail—or if they think they fail to master tasks.
Adolescence 12–20	Identity vs. identity confusion	Adolescents try to figure out who they are, if they are unique, if they want to have a meaningful role in society, how they can establish sexual, ethnic, and career identity. Feelings of confusion can arise over these decisions.
Young Adulthood 20–30	Intimacy vs. isolation	The wish to seek companionship and intimacy with a significant other, or avoid relationships and become isolated.
Adulthood 30–65	Generativity vs. stagnation	The need to be productive—for example, to create products, ideas, or children—or to become stagnant.
Mature Age 65 +	Integrity vs. despair	A review and trying to make sense of one's life, reflecting on completed goals or doubts and despair about unreached goals and desires.

Erikson proposed eight stages through which people progress, each of them characterized by a particular challenge or crisis, the resolution of which affects how the individual deals with each subsequent "psychosocial" stage (Table 2.1). If an earlier crisis is not adequately dealth with, says Erikson, the resolution of subsequent ones is hampered.

To illustrate, let us look at his fifth stage, perhaps the most important one, in which Erikson introduces a term for which he is famous, that of ***identity crisis.*** This

Erikson's fifth stage of development is viewed as very important and includes making vocational choices and developing a sense of personal identity.

crisis, said to occur between the ages of 12 and 20, reflects the transition from childhood to adulthood, a period when each of us creates a sense of ourselves, both the kind of psychological being we are and the kind of life we plan to forge for ourselves. Although the choice of an occupation, role, or profession is important—physician, lawyer, construction worker, mother, father, etc.—one's identity is said to go much deeper. There is concern with the direction of one's life: what things are going to be important and striven after, what kinds of compromises one is prepared to make to achieve one's goals, what kind of person we want to be; in general all the things that go into one's sense of self as a developing adult who is responsible for oneself and who is ready to make commitments to goals and to other human beings. It is a tumultuous time, considering that young people are also trying to come to terms with their sexuality.[6]

[6]Hall, Lindzey, Loehlin, and Manosevitz (1985) suggest that Erikson's own childhood and adolescence may have contributed to the concept of identity crisis. Erikson was born in Germany of Danish parents who were separated before his birth, and he never knew his biological father. He was raised by a German stepfather who he assumed for years was his actual father. Although he looked Nordic because of his biological father, his mother's Jewish ancestry caused him to be taunted by Jewish peers as a "goy" (an uncomplimentary Yiddish term for a non-Jew) and by non-Jewish agemates as a Jew (not an easy thing to be in Germany at that time). He felt out of place after high school and, thinking he might want to become an artist, he wandered around Europe making sketches. He began to teach in Vienna at age 25, where he met Sigmund Freud and his daughter, Anna. Erikson enrolled in the Vienna Psychoanalytic Institute, where he was analyzed by Anna Freud. Erikson would not be the first psychological theorist whose professional interests and ideas were shaped by his own experiences.

Like others who adapted Freud's ideas, Erikson was more optimistic than Freud about people's capacity to change and more positive generally about the nature of existence. The resolution of any psychosocial stage could be reversed, Erikson believed, with appropriate psychotherapy (Erikson, 1959).

Psychoanalytic Therapy

Since Freud's time the body of psychoanalytic thinking has changed in important ways, but all treatments purporting to be psychoanalytic have some basic tenets in common. Classical psychoanalysis is based on Freud's second theory of neurotic anxiety, that it is the reaction of the ego when a previously punished and repressed id impulse presses for expression (Freud, 1949). The unconscious part of the ego, encountering a situation that reminds it of a repressed conflict from childhood—one usually having to do with sexual or aggressive impulses—is overcome by debilitating tension. Psychoanalytic therapy attempts to remove the earlier repression and to help the patient face the childhood conflict and resolve it in the light of adult reality. The repression, occurring so long ago, has prevented the ego from growing in an adult fashion; the lifting of the repression is supposed to enable this relearning to take place.

The essence of psychoanalysis has been captured by Paul Wachtel (1977) in the metaphor of the **woolly mammoth**. Some of these gigantic creatures, frozen alive eons ago, have been recovered so perfectly preserved that their meat can actually be eaten. Neurotic problems were considered by Freud to be the encapsulated residue of conflicts from long ago. Present adult problems are merely reflections or expressions of these "frozen" intrapsychic conflicts.

The patient's neurosis is seen as deriving most essentially from his continuing and unsuccessful efforts to deal with internalized residues of his past [the "woolly mammoth"] which, by virtue of being isolated from his adaptive and integrated ego, continue to make primitive demands wholly unresponsive to reality. It is therefore maintained that a fully successful treatment must create conditions whereby these anachronistic inclinations can be experienced consciously and integrated into the ego, so that they can be controlled and modified. (Wachtel, 1977, p. 36)

A number of techniques are employed by analysts in their efforts to lift repressions. Perhaps the best known is *free association.* The patient, reclining on a couch, is encouraged to give free rein to his or her thoughts, verbalizing whatever comes to mind, without the censoring ordinarily done in everyday life. It is assumed that the analysand can gradually learn this skill, and that defenses built up over many years can eventually be bypassed. **Dream analysis** is another classic analytic technique. Psychoanalytic theory holds that, in sleep, ego defenses are relaxed, allowing normally repressed material to enter the sleeper's consciousness. But since this material is extremely threatening, it usually cannot be allowed into consciousness in its actual form. Rather, the repressed material is disguised, and dreams take on heavily symbolic content. For example, a woman concerned about aggressive sexual advances from men may dream of being attacked by savages who throw spears at her; the spears are considered phallic symbols, substituting for an explicit sexual advance.

Analysis of defenses, long a focus of psychoanalysis, is emphasized even more by contemporary psychoanalysts, who are sometimes referred to as *ego analysts.* They dispute the relatively weak role that Freud assigned the ego. Defense mechanisms, as we have seen, are the ego's unconscious tools for warding off a confrontation with anxiety. For instance, a man who appears to have trouble with intimacy may look out the window and change the subject whenever anything touches on closeness during the course of a session. The analyst will attempt at some point to offer an *interpretation* of the patient's behavior, pointing out its defensive nature, in hopes of stimulating the patient to acknowledge that he is, in fact, avoiding the topic.

Psychoanalytic treatment has in the past extended over several years, with as many as five sessions a week.[7]

Over the past forty or so years, the ideas and work of "neo-Freudians" like Karen Horney and Harry Stack Sullivan (see page 519) and of ego psychologists/analysts like Erik Erikson and Heinz Hartman have blended into "psychoanalytically oriented psychotherapy," sometimes called "psychodynamic therapy." This approach developed in part through the work of Alexander and French (1946), advocates of a briefer, more present- and future-oriented analytic therapy, informed by Freudian concepts like defense mechanisms and unconscious motivation but without relying on the couch and the time-consuming techniques of free association and dream analysis. Such therapy is more active and directive than Freudian therapy, is focused more on present problems and relationships than on childhood conflicts, and is briefer and less intensive.

"The hope of total personality reconstruction is put aside in favor of dealing with more focal and acute problems, but these therapists feel that their work is facilitated by training in and sensitivity to psychoanalytic principles. *A large part of the work of current psychoanalysts is in these briefer forms of therapy; few practice standard psychoanalysis exclusively. (Korchin, 1976, p. 335, emphasis added)*

To our mind, procedural changes do not invariably reflect important theoretical differences. Session frequency and body position matter less than what the patient does with support from the therapist, namely, slowly examining the true sources of tension and unhappiness by a lifting of repression. Psychoanalysis and related therapies are discussed in depth in Chapter 18.

Learning Paradigms

The Rise of Behaviorism

Before we discuss learning paradigms, it will be helpful to trace briefly the rise of behaviorism. Early twentieth-century psychology was dominated by structuralism, which held that the proper subject of study was mental functioning and structure. The goal of psychology, then a very new discipline, was to learn more about what goes on in the mind by analyzing the elementary

---

[7] It is interesting to note that Freud's psychoanalyses seldom lasted longer than six months.

John B. Watson, American psychologist, who was the major figure in making psychology the study of observable behavior rather than an investigation of subjective experience.

constituents making up its contents. To do this, experimental psychologists Wilhelm Wundt (1882–1920), who in Leipzig in 1879 had founded the first formal psychological laboratory and the discipline itself, and Edward Titchener (1867–1927), whose laboratory was at Cornell University, devised elaborate training procedures to teach subjects to report on the most basic aspects of their experiences while being exposed to stimuli. Through painstaking *introspection* subjects would uncover the building blocks of experience and the structure of consciousness. For example, Wundt's subjects listened to a metronome, set to click slowly and sometimes to click fast, sometimes sounding only a few times and then many. The subjects decided that a fast series of clicks made them excited, a slow series relaxed. Just before each click they were conscious of a slight feeling of tension and afterward slight relief.

After some years many in the field began to lose faith in the ability of this kind of introspection to gather useful knowledge about people. The principal problem was that different laboratories gathering data using the introspective method were yielding conflicting data; thus it appeared that introspection was not resolving any problems. This dissatisfaction was brought to a head by John B. Watson (1878–1958), who in 1913 revolutionized psychology with statements such as the following:

Psychology as the behaviorist views it is a purely objective experimental branch of natural science. Its theoretical goal is the prediction and control of behavior.

Introspection forms no essential part of its methods, nor is the scientific value of its data dependent upon the readiness with which they lend themselves to interpretation in terms of consciousness. (p. 158)

To replace introspection, Watson looked to the experimental procedures of the psychologists who were investigating learning in animals. In this way learning rather than thinking became the dominant focus of psychology in the post-Watsonian period. Finding out which stimuli would elicit which directly observable responses was now considered the task of psychology. With such objective S–R information it was hoped that human behavior could be both predicted and controlled.

Classical Conditioning

With the focus of psychology now on learning, a vast amount of research and theorizing was generated. Two types of learning attracted the research efforts of psychologists. The first type, ***classical conditioning,*** had originally been discovered quite by accident by the Russian physiologist Ivan Pavlov (1849–1936) at the turn of the century. In his studies of the digestive system, a dog was given meat powder to make it salivate. Before long Pavlov's laboratory assistants became aware that the dog began salivating when it saw the person who fed it and as the experiment continued, the dog began to salivate even earlier, when it heard the footsteps of its feeder. Pavlov was intrigued and excited by what his laboratory had happened upon and decided to study the dog's reactions systematically. In the first of many experiments, a bell was rung behind the dog, and then the meat powder was placed in its mouth. After this procedure had been repeated a number of times, the dog began salivating as soon as it heard the bell ring and before meat powder was given.

Ivan P. Pavlov, Russian physiologist and Nobel Laureate, responsible for extensive research and theory in classical conditioning. His influence is still very strong in Soviet psychology.

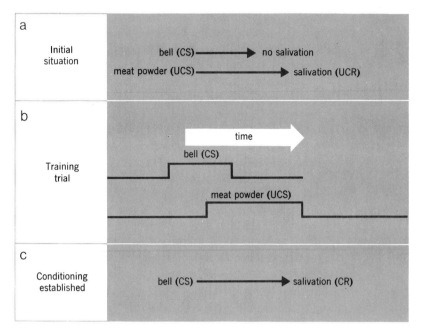

FIGURE 2.1
The process of classical conditioning. (a) Before learning that the meat powder (UCS) elicits salivation (UCR), but the bell (CS) does not. (b) A training or learning trial consists of presentations of the CS, followed closely by the UCS. (c) Classical conditioning has been accomplished when the previously neutral bell elicits salivation (CR).

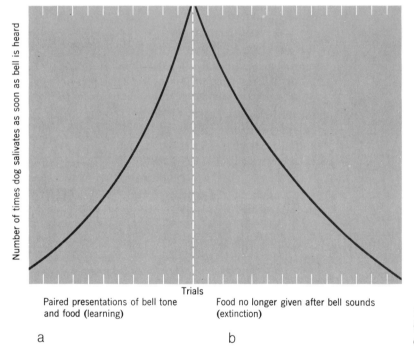

FIGURE 2.2
Classical conditioning: (a) typical learning curve; (b) typical extinction curve.

Since the meat powder automatically elicits salivation, with no prior learning, the powder is termed an *unconditioned stimulus* (UCS) and the response of salivation an *unconditioned response* (UCR). Then when the offering of meat powder is preceded several times by a neutral stimulus, the ringing of a bell (Figure 2.1), the sound of the bell itself (the *conditioned stimulus,* CS) is able to elicit the salivary response (the *conditioned response,* CR). Figure 2.2a is a typical *learning curve.* As the number of paired presentations of the bell and the meat powder increases, the number of salivations elicited by the bell increases. The *extinction curve* in Figure 2.2b indicates what happens to the established CR when the repeated soundings of the bell are later not followed by meat powder: fewer and fewer salivations are elicited, and the CR is extinguished.

Another famous experiment, questionable from an ethical point of view, was conducted by John Watson

B.F. Skinner, perhaps the most influential living psychologist. He is responsible both for the in-depth study of operant behavior and for the extension of experimental findings to American education and society as a whole.

and Rosalie Rayner (1920). They introduced a white rat to an eleven-month-old boy, Little Albert, who indicated no fear of the animal and appeared to want to play with it. But whenever he reached for the rat, the experimenter made a loud noise (the UCS) by striking a steel bar behind Albert's head, causing him great fright (the UCR). After five such experiences Albert became very disturbed (the CR) by the sight of the white rat, even when the steel bar was not struck. The fear initially associated with the loud noise had come to be elicited by the previously neutral stimulus, the white rat (now the CS). This study suggests the possible relation between classical conditioning and the development of certain emotional disorders, in this instance a phobia.

Operant Conditioning

The second principal type of learning drew primarily on the work of Edward Thorndike (1874–1949), begun in the 1890s. Rather than investigating the association between stimuli as Pavlov was to do, Thorndike was interested in the effect that consequences have on behavior. He had observed that alley cats, angered by being caged and making furious efforts to escape, would eventually and accidentally hit the latch that freed them. Recaged again and again, they would soon come to immediately and purposely touch the latch. Thorndike formulated what was to become an extremely important principal, the *law of effect:* behavior that is followed by consequences satisfying to the organism will be repeated, and behavior that is followed by noxious or unpleasant consequences will be discouraged. Thus the

behavior or response that has consequences serves as an instrument, encouraging or discouraging its own repetition. For this reason learning that focuses on consequences was first called instrumental learning.

Over fifty years ago Burrhus Frederick Skinner began applying the law of effect to many different aspects of human behavior. He renamed it the principle of *reinforcement,* the word he prefers to consequences. He argues that freedom of choice is a myth and that all behavior is determined by the positive and negative reinforcers provided by the social environment. The goal of Skinner (1953) and the Skinnerians, like that of Watson, their mentor, is the prediction and control of behavior. These experimenters hope that by analyzing behavior in terms of stimuli, observable responses, and reinforcement, they will be able to determine when certain behavior will occur. The information gathered should then help to indicate how behavior is acquired, maintained, changed, and eliminated. In the Skinnerian approach, often called *operant* because it studies behavior that operates on the environment, abstract terms and concepts are avoided. For example, references to needs, motivation, and wants are conspicuously absent in Skinnerian writings. To provide an entirely satisfactory account of human behavior, Skinner believes that psychology must restrict its attention to directly observable stimuli and responses and to the effects of reinforcement. Psychologists who hold this view do not, as human beings, deny the existence of inner states of mind and emotion. Rather, they urge that investigators not employ such *mediators* in trying to develop a science of behavior.

In a prototypical *operant conditioning* experiment a hungry rat might be placed in a box that has a lever located at one end (the well-known "Skinner box"). Initially the rat will explore its new environment and, by chance, come close to the lever. At this time the experimenter may drop a food pellet into the receptacle located near the lever. After a few such rewards the animal will come to spend more and more time in the area around the lever. But now the experimenter may drop a pellet into the receptacle only when the rat happens to touch the lever. After capitalizing on a few chance touches, the rat begins to touch the lever frequently. With lever touching well established, the experimenter can make the criterion for reward more stringent: the animal must now actually press the lever. Thus the desired operant behavior, lever pressing, is gradually *shaped* by rewarding a series of responses that are *successive approximations.* The number of lever presses increases as soon as they become the criterion for the release of pellets and decreases as soon as the pellet is no longer dropped into the receptacle after a lever press (Figure 2.3).

FIGURE 2.3
(a) Operant conditioning, or instrumental learning, is concerned with the development and maintenance of behavior as a function of its consequences. (b) A typical learning curve, showing increases in responding when the operant behavior is reinforced. (c) A typical extinction curve, showing decreases in responding when the accustomed reward is withheld.

a

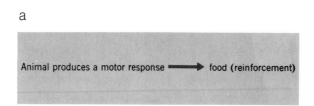

Animal produces a motor response ➡ food (reinforcement)

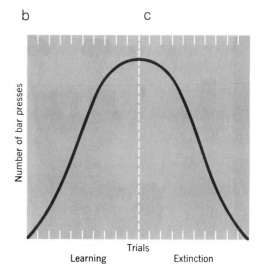

b   c

Number of bar presses

Trials
Learning   Extinction

Modeling

There is a good deal of current interest in yet a third type of learning, ***modeling.*** We all learn by watching and imitating others. Experimental work has proved that witnessing someone perform certain activities can increase or decrease diverse kinds of behavior, such as sharing, aggression, and fear. For example, Bandura and Menlove (1968) used a modeling treatment to reduce fear of dogs in children. After witnessing a fearless model engage in various activities with a dog, initially fearful children showed a decided increase in their willingness to approach and handle a dog.

Modeling has been shown to increase aggressive behavior.

Mediational Learning Paradigms

Among the learning paradigms, modeling illustrates clearly an important issue, namely, the role of mediators in learning and behavior. Consider what happens in the typical modeling experiment. A person watches another do something and immediately shows a change in behavior. No overt responding is necessary for the learning to take place, nor for that matter need the observer be reinforced. Something is learned before the person makes any observable response. Outcomes similar to this one had led learning theorists of the 1930s and 1940s to infer mediators of various kinds in order to explain overt behavior.

In the most general terms, a ***mediational*** theory of learning holds that an environmental stimulus does not initiate an overt response directly; rather it does so through some intervening process. This process is conceptualized as an internal response. Without divorcing themselves from behaviorism, mediational learning theorists adopt the paradigmatic position that, under certain conditions, it is both legitimate and important to go beyond observables. Psychologists, who fondly aspire to the status accorded physicists and chemists, will point out that in these natural sciences ample and effective use is made of supposed entities, like the gluon, which are not directly observed but whose existence is guessed at or inferred to make sense of existing data and to encourage the search for new data.

Consider the mediational learning analysis of anxiety, as developed by O. Hobart Mowrer (1939) and Neal Miller in the late 1930s. In a typical experiment rats were shocked repeatedly in the presence of a neutral stimulus such as the sound of a buzzer. The shock (UCS) produced a UCR of pain, fear, and flight. After

FIGURE 2.4

Schematic representation of Mowrer's account of avoidance learning. The dashed line indicates that the subject is learning to fear the buzzer tone, and the solid line that the subject is learning to avoid the shock.

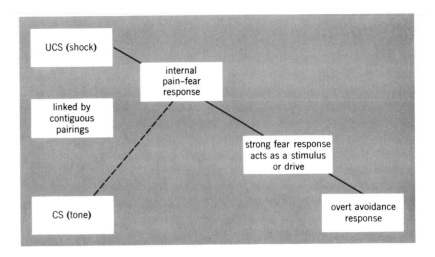

several pairings the fear that was naturally produced by the shock came to be produced by the buzzer, fear being assumed the learnable component of the pain–fear response. It was observed that shock could eventually be omitted, and yet the animal would continue to react fearfully to the previously neutral stimulus (CS). In addition, it was shown (e.g., Miller, 1948) that the rat could learn new responses to avoid the CS. The question became how to conceptualize the finding that animals would learn to *avoid* a harmless event. Mowrer (1947) and others suggested that in this, a typical **avoidance conditioning** experiment, two bits of learning were taking place (Figure 2.4): (1) the animal, by means of classical conditioning, learned to fear the CS, that is, acquired a fear-drive; and (2) the animal, by means of operant conditioning, learned an overt behavior to remove itself from the CS and thus to reduce the fear-drive.

The essential features of this theorizing are that fear or anxiety can be conceived of both as an internal response, which can be learned as observable responses are learned, and as a drive, which can mediate avoidance behavior. Anxiety, then, becomes amenable to the same kind of experimental analysis employed in the investigation of observable behavior. Mowrer and Miller speak of "mediating fear-responses" to point up their assumption that such responses, although inferred, are much the same as overt responses. The knowledge gleaned about overt behavior can therefore, it is hoped, be transferred to the study of mental and emotional life. For instance, if we know that repetition of an overt response without reinforcement leads to the extinction of the response, we can predict that repeated evocation of a fear-response while withholding the expected pain or punishment will reduce the fear. This is no trivial possibility, and indeed, as will be indicated (see page 144), treatments based on such reasoning have helped

people become less fearful of animals and of objects and situations that do not merit such reactions.

Applying Learning Points of View to Deviant Behavior

We are now ready to examine, in general, the application of learning principles to the study of deviant behavior. The crucial assumption of behavioral and learning approaches is that abnormal behavior is learned in the same manner as most other human behavior. This view minimizes the importance of physiological factors. It focuses instead on elucidating the learning processes that supposedly make behavior maladaptive. The gap between normal and abnormal behavior is reduced, since both are viewed within the same general framework; thus a bridge is forged between general experimental psychology and the field of abnormal psychology. Moreover, according to many who have adopted a learning paradigm, abnormality is a *relativistic* concept. Labeling someone or some behavior as abnormal is inextricably linked to a particular social or cultural context.

One very important advantage of applying a learning view in psychopathology is the increased precision of observation. Stimuli must be accurately observed and controlled; the magnitude and rate of responses, and their latency, the rapidity with which they are made, are measured and recorded; and relationships among stimuli, responses, and outcomes are carefully noted. What are taken to indicate unobservable processes such as fear and thought must be stated explicitly; all such unobservables must be described in terms of their measurable outcomes. Although we judge these and other features of learning approaches to deviant behavior to be extremely advantageous, it is difficult to persuade those not already committed to the paradigm that it is adequate. The learning paradigm of abnormal behavior is in much the same position as the physiological paradigm. Just as pertinent physiological malfunctions have not been uncovered, abnormality has not yet been convincingly traced to particular learning experiences. Consider how difficult it would be to show that depression results from a particular reinforcement history. A person would have to be continually observed over a period of years while their behavior is recorded and occurrences of reinforcement noted.

Although adopting a learning explanation of abnormal behavior has clearly led to many treatment innovations (see the following section on behavior therapy), the effectiveness of these treatments does not mean that the particular deviant behavior was learned in the first place. The fact that a treatment based on learning principles is effective in changing behavior does not show that the behavior was itself learned in a similar way. For example, if the mood of depressed persons is elevated by providing them with rewards for increased activity, this fact cannot be considered evidence that the depression and apathy were initially produced by an absence of rewards (Rimland, 1964).

Behavior Therapy

In recent years a number of therapeutic techniques have been developed that are an outgrowth of the learning paradigms. The terms "behavior therapy" and "behavior modification" are applied to them because they were initially asserted to be based on the experimentally tested laws of learning formulated by the behaviorists.

Since in mediation theory anxiety is assumed to be classically conditioned, an effective way to eliminate fear is to associate the conditioned stimulus with a nonfearful response. Referred to as ***counterconditioning,*** this principle of behavior change holds that (see Figure 2.5) a response (R_1) to a given stimulus (S) can be eliminated by eliciting a new response (R_2) in the presence of that stimulus. For example, if a child is afraid of a harmless animal (S), the therapist might attempt to elicit a playful reaction (R_2) in the presence of the animal. Clinical and experimental evidence suggests that this counterconditioning, or substitution of a response, can eliminate R_1.

The counterconditioning principle has played a central role in the innovative thinking of Joseph Wolpe (1958), who devised a set of behavior therapy techniques that he asserts are effective for the reasons just stated. The most widely used technique is ***systematic desensitization.*** A person who suffers from anxiety works with the therapist to compile a list of feared situations, starting with those that arouse minimal anxiety and pro-

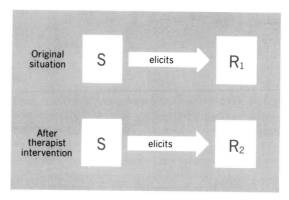

FIGURE 2.5
Schematic diagram of counterconditioning, whereby an original response (R_1) to a given stimulus (S) is eliminated by evoking a new response (R_2) to the same stimulus.

gressing to those that are the most frightening. He or she is also taught to relax deeply. Then step by step, while relaxed, the person imagines the graded series of anxiety-provoking situations. The relaxation tends to inhibit any anxiety that might otherwise be elicited by the imagined scenes. The fearful person becomes able to tolerate increasingly more difficult imagined situations, as he or she climbs the hierarchy over a number of therapy sessions. Clinical and experimental evidence has confirmed that this technique is useful in reducing a wide variety of fears.

The thirty-five-year-old substitute mail carrier who consulted us had dropped out of college sixteen years ago because of crippling fears of being criticized. Earlier, his disability has taken the form of extreme tension when faced with tests and speaking up in class. When we saw him, he was debilitated by fears of criticism in general and of evaluations of his mail sorting in particular. As a consequence, his everyday activities were severely constricted and, though highly intelligent, he had apparently settled for an occupation that did not promise self-fulfillment.

After the client agreed that a reduction in his unrealistic fears would be beneficial, he was taught over several sessions to relax all the muscles of his body while in a reclining chair. We also helped him draw up a list of anxiety-provoking scenes.

You are saying "Good morning" to your boss.

You are standing in front of your sorting bin in the post office, and your supervisor asks why you are so slow.

You are halfway through your route, and it is already 2:00 P.M.

As you are delivering Mrs. Mackenzie's mail, she opens her screen door and complains about how late you are.

Your wife criticizes you for bringing home the wrong kind of bread.

The officer at the bridge toll gate appears impatient as you fumble in your pocket for the correct change.

These and other scenes were arranged in an **anxiety hierarchy,** from least to most fear-evoking. Desensitization proper began with the client being instructed first to relax deeply as he had been taught. Then he was to imagine the easiest item, remaining as relaxed as possible. When he had learned to confront this image without becoming anxious, he went on to the next scene, and so on. After ten sessions the man was able to imagine the most distressing scene in the hierarchy without feeling anxious and gradually his tension in real life became markedly less.[8]

Another behavioral approach is **assertion training,** which encourages people to speak up and react openly when with others, expressing both their positive and negative feelings. In **aversive** ''**conditioning,**'' a stimulus attractive to the patient is paired with an unpleasant event, such as shock to the fingertips, in hopes of endowing it with negative properties. Aversive techniques, somewhat controversial as might be imagined, have been employed to reduce the socially inappropriate attraction that objects have for some people, such as the irresistible appeal a woman's boots may have for a fetishist.

Several behavioral procedures derive from operant conditioning. For example, children who misbehave in

classrooms can be systematically rewarded by the teacher for their socially acceptable behavior whereas their undesirable behavior is ignored and thus eventually extinguished. The **token economy,** a program established in mental hospitals to encourage severely disturbed patients to behave more appropriately, is an operant treatment. Explicit rules are set up for obtaining rewards in the form of tokens or other moneylike scrip. At predetermined intervals patients can trade in their tokens for specific reinforcers, such as a visit to the canteen or a more desirable sleeping arrangement.

Modeling has enjoyed increasing attention as a therapeutic intervention. Bandura, Blanchard, and Ritter (1969) were able to help people reduce their phobias of nonpoisonous snakes by having them view both live and filmed close and successful confrontations between people and snakes. In an analogous fashion, some behavior therapists use **role playing** in the consulting room. They demonstrate to a patient patterns of behaving that might prove more effective than those he or she usually engages in and then have the patient practice them. Lazarus (1971), in his **behavior rehearsal** procedures, demonstrates exemplary ways of handling a situation and then encourages the patient to imitate them during the therapy session. For example, a student who does not know how to ask a professor for an extension on a term paper would watch the therapist portray an effective way of making the request. The clinician would then help the student practice the new skill in a similar contrived role-playing situation.

The Cognitive Paradigm

Cognition is a term that groups together the mental processes of perceiving, recognizing, conceiving, judging, and reasoning. The focus of cognitive psychology is on how people (and animals as well!) *structure* their experiences, how they make sense of them, transforming environmental stimuli into information that is usable. At any given moment we are bombarded by far more stimuli than we can possibly respond to. How do we filter this overwhelming input, put it into words or images, form hypotheses, and arrive at a perception of what is out there? Cognitive psychologists consider the learning process to be much more complex than passively forming new stimulus–response associations. They regard the learner as aware and actively interpreting a situation in the light of what has been acquired in the past, as imposing a perceptual funnel on experience, so to speak. The learner fits new information into an organized network of already accumulated knowledge,

---

[8]Unreferenced case reports such as this one have been drawn from our own clinical files. Identifying features are changed to protect the confidentiality of the individual.

often referred to as a **schema** (Neisser, 1976). New information may fit or, if not, the learner reorganizes the schema to the necessary extent.

Contemporary experimental psychology is very much concerned with cognition. The following situation illustrates how a schema or **cognitive set** may alter the way information is processed and remembered.

The man stood before the mirror and combed his hair. He checked his face carefully for any places he might have missed shaving and then put on the conservative tie he had decided to wear. At breakfast, he studied the newspaper carefully and, over coffee, discussed the possibility of buying a new washing machine with his wife. Then he made several phone calls. As he was leaving the house he thought about the fact that his children would probably want to go to that private camp again this summer. When the car didn't start, he got out, slammed the door and walked down to the bus stop in a very angry mood. Now he would be late. (*Bransford and Johnson, 1973, p. 415*)

Now read the excerpt again, but add the word "unemployed" before the word "man." Now read it a third time, substituting "stockbroker" for "man." Notice how differently you understand the passage. Ask yourself what parts of the newspaper these men read. If this query had been posed on a questionnaire, you might have answered "the want ads" for the unemployed man and "the financial pages" for the stockbroker. Actually, the passage does not specify which part of the paper was read. Your answers would have been erroneous, but in each instance the error would have been a meaningful, predictable one.

Cognitive psychologists study how we acquire, store, and use information. Strict behaviorists, those who follow Skinner in describing behavior in terms of openly observable events, cannot accept cognitive explanations. Cognitive psychologists have until recently paid little systematic attention to how their research findings bear on psychopathology or how they might help generate effective therapies. Now cognitive explanations appear more and more often in the search for the causes of abnormality and for new methods of intervention. A widely held view of depression, for example, places the blame on a cognitive set, the individual's overriding sense of hopelessness (see page 232). Many who are depressed supposedly believe themselves to have no important effect on their surroundings, regardless of what they do. Their destiny seems to them out of their hands and they expect the future to be negative. If depression does develop through a sense of hopelessness, this fact would have implications for how clinicians might treat the disorder.

Some clinicians assert that cognitive theorizing is nothing more than a mediational stimulus–response analysis of behavior (e.g., Wolpe, 1980), similar to the historically important contributions of Mowrer and Miller. We would disagree. A cognitive explanation of behavior is *fundamentally different* from a mediational stimulus–response analysis. The mediational researcher asserts than an environmental stimulus automatically evokes an internal mediational response, which is subject to the same reinforcement principles as are overt responses. The cognitive researcher, in contrast, does not conceptualize perception or thinking as a "little" response. Rather, this worker focuses on how people actively interpret environmental stimuli, and how these transformed stimuli affect behavior. Reinforcement plays a minor role in the theorizing of cognitive psychologists (Davison, 1980).

Although the cognitive paradigm is currently the most active one among psychologists, some criticisms should be noted. The concepts used (e.g., schema) are somewhat slippery and not always well defined. Furthermore, cognitive explanations of psychopathology do not always explain much. To say that depression results from a "negative schema" tells us that depressives think gloomy thoughts. But everyone knows that such a pattern of thinking is actually part of the diagnosis of depression. What is distinctive in the cognitive paradigm is that the thoughts are given causal status, that is, the thoughts are regarded as causing the other features of the disorder, for example, sadness. Left unanswered, however, is the question of where the negative schema came from in the first place. Cognitive explanations of psychopathology tend to focus on current determinants of disorder and not its historical antecedents. As a consequence they have shed little light on the etiology of mental disorders.

Cognitive Behavior Therapy

The cognitive point of view has recently gained widespread attention in behavior therapy. Generally speaking, cognitively oriented behavior therapists attempt to change the thinking processes of their patients in order to influence their emotions and behavior. The following is an early example of **cognitive restructuring** (Davison, 1966).

A man had been diagnosed as paranoid schizophrenic, primarily because of his complaints of "pressure points" on his forehead and other parts of his body. He believed that these pressure points were signals from outside forces helping him to make decisions. These paranoid delusions had been resistant to drug treatment and other psychotherapeutic approaches. The behavior therapist, in examining the man's case history, hypothesized that the patient became very anxious and tense when he had to make a decision, that his anxiety took the form of muscular tension in certain bodily parts, and that the patient misconstrued the tension as "pressure points," signals from helpful spirits. Both patient and therapist agreed to explore the possibility that the pressure points were in fact part of a tension reaction to specific situations. For this purpose the therapist decided to teach the man deep-muscle relaxation, with the hope that relaxation would enable him to control his tensions, including the pressure points.

But it was also important to have the man question his delusional system. So in the first session the therapist asked the patient to extend his right arm, clench his fist, and bend his wrist downward so as to bring the fist toward the inside of the forearm. The intent was to produce a feeling of tension in his forearm; this is precisely what happened, and the man noted that the feeling was quite similar to his pressure points.

Extensive relaxation training enabled the client to begin to control his anxiety in various situations within the hopsital and at the same time to reduce the intensity of the pressure points. As he gained control over his feelings, he gradually came to refer to his pressure points as "sensations," and his conversation in general began to lose its earlier paranoid flavor.

The relaxation training apparently allowed the patient to test a nonparanoid hypothesis about his pressure points, to see it confirmed, and thereby to shake off a belief about these sensations that had contributed to a diagnosis of paranoia.

A prominent cognitive therapist, Albert Ellis (1962), holds that maladaptive feelings and activity are caused by **irrational beliefs.** Through mistaken assumptions people place excessive demands on themselves. A man who believes that he must always be perfect in every-

thing he does feels terrible whenever he makes a mistake. A woman may think "I should be able to win the love and approval of everyone" and then exhaust herself trying to please others. Ellis and his followers, the so-called **rational-emotive** therapists, help their patients to challenge such assumptions and teach them to substitute ideas like "Although it would be terrific never to make a mistake, that doesn't mean I *have* to be without fault."

Another leading cognitive therapist is the psychiatrist Aaron Beck (1967, 1976), whose theorizing and research on depression we examine in detail in Chapters 9 and 19. For now it is sufficient to note that Beck's cognitive focus is on how people distort experience. For example, many depressed individuals **selectively abstract** from a complex event those features that will maintain their gloomy perspective on life, as when a person ignores all the positive occurrences on a given day and fixates exclusively on negative happenings.

Learning Paradigms and Cognitive Paradigms

Are cognitive points of view basically different and separate from the learning paradigms? Much of what we have just said suggests that they are. But the growing field of "cognitive behavior therapy" gives us pause, for here workers study the complex interplay of beliefs, expectations, perceptions, and attitudes on the one hand and overt behavior on the other. For example, Albert Bandura (1977), a leading advocate of changing behavior through cognitive means, argues that a parsimonious way of explaining how different therapies work their improvement is that they increase people's sense of self-efficacy, a belief that they can achieve desired goals (see page 558). *But* at the same time he argues that changing behavior, through behavioral techniques, is the most powerful way to enhance self-efficacy. People like Ellis, by way of contrast, emphasize direct alteration of cognitions through argument, persuasion, Socratic dialogues, and the like to bring about improvements in emotion and behavior. Complicating matters still further, Ellis and his followers also place considerable importance on homework assignments requiring clients to behave in ways that they, presumably blocked by negative thoughts, have been unable to heretofore. Indeed, therapists identified with cognitive behavior therapy work at both the cognitive and behavioral levels, and most of those who employ cognitive concepts and try to change beliefs with verbal means also employ behavioral procedures to alter behavior directly.

Whatever their differences in theory and practice, behavior therapists and cognitive therapist[9] are alike in allying themselves philosophically with their colleagues in experimental psychology. For this reason these approaches are regarded by some (e.g., Davison and Goldfried, 1973; Goldfried and Davison, 1976) not as a set of techniques but rather as a particular epistemological stance, one that demands rigorous standards of proof. Specific techniques, it is assumed, will be revised as new research uncovers better ways of altering and preventing abnormality. The implications of this emphasis on experimental research and methodology will become clearer when behavior therapy and cognitive therapy are discussed in depth in Chapter 19.

The Humanistic Paradigm

Reacting against the dominance of psychology and psychiatry by psychoanalytic and behavioristic views, Abraham Maslow (1908–1970) began exhorting his colleagues of the 1950s to work toward the development of a "third force" in the study of human behavior (Maslow, 1968). Maslow had a much more positive opinion of human nature and potential. He held that the individual is basically sound, whole, healthy, and unique, with an innate drive for growth and self-actualization; that humankind is by nature active, resourceful, purposive, and good; and that human suffering comes from denial of this basic goodness.

The humanistic approach, primarily a development within American mental health circles, has much in common with the existential approach, which derives from European philosophers like Sartre, Kierkegaard, and Heidegger. We will emphasize here the commonalities, but, as detailed in Chapter 18 (page 524), there are some important differences that we will briefly mention. In his influential book on existential psychotherapy, the Stanford University psychiatrist Irvin Yalom portrays these differences as follows:

The existential tradition in Europe has always emphasized human limitations and the tragic dimensions of existence. Perhaps it has done so because Europeans have had a greater familiarity with geographic and ethnic confinement, with war, death, and uncertain existence. The United States (and the humanistic psychology it spawned) bathed in a Zeitgeist of expansiveness, optimism, limitless horizons, and pragmatism. Accordingly, the imported form of existential thought has been systematically altered [as American humanistic psychology has absorbed some of European existentialism]. . . . The European focus is on limits, on facing and taking into oneself the anxiety of uncertainty and non-being. The humanistic psychologists, on the other hand, speak less of limits and contingency than of development of potential, less of acceptance than of awareness, less of anxiety than of peak experiences and oceanic oneness, less of life meaning than of self-realization [and self-actualization], less of apartness and basic aloneness than of 1-thou and encounter. (Yalom, 1980, p. 19)

Consider what this paradigm—known variously as humanistic psychology, existential analysis, the human potential movement, and the personal growth movement—says in contrast to the psychoanalytic and behavioral views already examined. The psychoanalytic paradigm assumes that human nature, the id, is something in need of restraint, that effective socialization requires the ego to mediate between the environment and the basically antisocial, or at best asocial, impulses stemming from physiological urges. (As we have seen with Jung, Adler, and Erikson, neo-Freudian and ego-analytic theorizing de-emphasized these features of classical Freudian thought and introduced concepts that bring contemporary psychoanalytic thinking closer to humanistic and existential approaches.) The behavioral point of view, in considering environmental contingencies of activity—reward and punishment—to be the major determinants of effective and normal behavior, stresses the social consequences of beliefs and actions. In contrast, Carl Rogers (1951), a leading figure in humanistic psychology, asserts that the developing personality goes astray when it concerns itself with the evaluations and expectations of others instead of following its own innate drive for self-fulfillment. Specifically, Rogers postulates an innate tendency to actualize, that is, to realize potentialities. This idea, drawn from Otto Rank (1936), a Viennese psychoanalyst and a member of Freud's inner circle, is basic to Rogers's conception of human beings and therefore crucial to understanding his approach to therapy. In common with Freud and most learning theorists, Rogers holds that people try to reduce the physiological tensions of hun-

---

[9]This issue is reflected in the terminology employed to refer to people like Beck and Ellis. Are they "cognitive therapists" or "cognitive *behavior* therapists"? For the most part we will use the latter term because it denotes both that the therapist regards cognitions as major determinants of emotion and behavior and that he or she maintains the focus on overt behavior that has always characterized behavior therapy. Nonetheless, it is important for the reader to know that Beck, even though he assigns many behavioral tasks as part of his therapy, is usually referred to as the founder of "cognitive therapy" (CT), and that Ellis's rational-emotive therapy (RET) is often spoken of as something separate from behavior therapy.

Developing one's potential or self-actualization is an important aspect of the humanistic paradigm.

ger, thirst, and pain. But Rogers proposes that people by nature seek also to learn new things and otherwise enhance their lives. In other words, people *seek out* pleasurable tension in addition to attempting to reduce unpleasurable tension. All behavior, for Rogers, originates in some way from this innate self-actualizing tendency. Furthermore, people evaluate behavior for its contribution to personal growth and tend to repeat activity that helps them approach this goal.

Rogers assumes that the most effective learning takes place when a person does not have to struggle for or concern herself with approval from others. The most important evaluations come from the person herself, for the self has its innate self-actualizing tendency. When a person receives unconditional positive regard from others, she is not distracted and is better able to evaluate how her own behavior is contributing to enhancement of self.

The phenomenological world of individuals is of utmost importance to all the humanists and existentialists. They regard each of us as having an internal frame of reference that is the product of the totality of earlier experiences. This subjective universe renders each of us unique and gives each of us our own truth. To contact one another, each human being must attempt to view the world through the perspective of the other person. Immediate behavior is guided by the experienced stimulus rather than the external stimulus. A person's actions—in fact entire existence—are decided by the way he or she experiences the world at any given moment. Indeed, one might label this paradigm the phenomenological paradigm instead of the humanistic, so central is the concept of the individual's own unique frame of

reference. We prefer humanistic, however, because there is considerable *content* associated with humanistic psychology whereas phenomenology per se is not associated with any such content.

Finally, the humanistic view reflects an abiding belief in free will. Human beings possess freedom of choice; they initiate action instead of being passively influenced by the environment or driven by internal id impulses. The freedom–determinism issue is an exceedingly complex one that runs through philosophy, literature, psychology, and politics.

Humanistic Therapy

The humanistic paradigm holds that therapists should help people to get in touch with their inner selves, with their true feelings, and to learn to express them without undue concern for what others think. The most prevalent and best-developed form of humanistic therapy is the **client-centered** approach of Carl Rogers. The person seeking therapy is regarded as client rather than patient and becomes responsible for much of his or her own treatment. Consistent with the view that a mature and well-adjusted person chooses what is innately satisfying and actualizing, therapists do not impose goals on their clients. Rather they create conditions during the therapy hour, conditions that enable clients to discover their own basic natures and make their own judgments about what they need, what they want, and how they might maintain and enhance themselves. True to the humanist's positive view of people, the decisions reached by clients are assumed to be good ones.

Carl Rogers (second from right), developer of client-centered therapy, leading a group therapy session.

Pathology supposedly results from undue sensitivity to the judgments of others and a denial of the individual's own nature. People come to adopt negative, limiting attitudes toward themselves and do not remain open to experiences. The basic tool of the client-centered therapist is therefore **unconditional positive regard,** that is, complete and unqualified acceptance and respect for the client's feelings and actions. Through skillful inquiry and attentive listening, the therapist helps clients uncover, clarify, and express their deepest concerns and conflicts. Gradually clients learn to talk in a more honest and emotional way about themselves and thereby gain access to their basically healthy inner natures.

Rogers and other humanistic and existential therapists believe that people must take responsibility for themselves, even when they are troubled. It is often difficult for a therapist to refrain from giving advice, from taking charge of a client's life, especially when the client appears incapable of making his or her own decisions. But workers like Rogers hold steadfastly to the rule that an individual's innate capacity for growth and self-direction will assert itself provided the therapeutic atmosphere is warm, attentive, and receptive. Indeed, it is believed that if the therapist steps in, the process of growth and self-actualization will only be thwarted. Whatever short-term relief might come from the therapist's intervening will sacrifice long-term growth. The therapist must not become yet another person whose wishes the client strives to satisfy.

Humanistic therapists tend to de-emphasize techniques, but most of them utilize **empathy.** In the following excerpt a Rogerian therapist tries to enter the phenomenological universe of the client and view her complaint from her own frame of reference. He then restates what she has expressed to help her clarify her thoughts and feelings—and also to be perceived as someone who understands and cares.

Client: I just can't stand not knowing what Fred's feelings are. Is he really involved with me, or is he just stringing me along?

Therapist: I can see how frustrating it is for you not to know how Fred feels about you, how he views the relationship.

This reflection of feeling is not a simple parroting of the client's words. Rather, the therapist attempts to extract the essence of what she is trying to express—sometimes a feeling only hinted at—and then communicates her concerns back to her, in hopes that she will better understand and acknowledge what is truly at issue. Gradually, encouraged by the empathic acceptance of the therapist, she should gain the self-confidence to listen to feelings from within, which she has shut off as not part of herself.

Empathy is a key component of humanistic therapies.

Consequences of Adopting a Paradigm

The student of abnormal behavior who adopts a particular paradigm necessarily makes a prior decision concerning what kinds of data will be collected and how they will be interpreted. Thus he or she may very well ignore possibilities and overlook other information in advancing what seems to be the most probable explanation. A behaviorist is prone to attribute the prevalence of schizophrenia in lower-class groups to the paucity of social rewards that these people have received, the assumption being that normal development requires a certain amount and patterning of reinforcement. A physiologically oriented theorist will be quick to remind the behaviorist of the many deprived people who do *not* become schizophrenic. The behaviorist will undoubtedly counter with the argument that those who do not become schizophrenic had different reinforcement histories. The physiologically oriented theorist will reply that such *post hoc* or after-the-fact statements can always be made.[10]

Our physiological theorist may suggest that certain biochemical factors that predispose both to schizophrenia and to deficiencies in the intellectual skills necessary to maintain occupational status account for the observed correlation between social class and schizophrenia. The behaviorist will be entirely justified in reminding the physiological theorist that these alleged factors have yet to be found, to which the physiological theorist might rightfully answer, "Yes, but I'm placing my bets that they are there, and if I adopt *your* behavioral paradigm, I may not look for them." To which the learning theorist may with justification reply, "Yes, but *your* assumption regarding biochemical factors makes it less likely that you will look for and uncover the subtle reinforcement factors that in all likelihood account for both the presence and the absence of what you call schizophrenia."

The fact that our two colleagues are in a sense correct and in another sense incorrect is at the same time both exasperating and exciting. They are both correct in asserting that certain data are more likely to be found through work done within a particular paradigm. But they are incorrect to become unduly agitated that each and every social scientist is not assuming that one and the same factor will ultimately be found crucial in the development of all mental disorders. Abnormal behavior is much too diverse to be explained or treated adequately by any of the current paradigms (see Box 2.3). As we subsequently examine various categories of psychopathology, we will find substantial differences in the extent to which physiological and learning paradigms are applicable. As for future discoveries, it is well that psychologists do *not* agree on which paradigm is the *best*. We know far too little to make hard-and-fast decisions on the exclusive superiority of any one paradigm, and there is enough important work to go around. And we will often see that a plausible way of looking at the data is to assume multiple causation. A particular disorder may very well develop through an interaction of physiological defects and environmental factors, a view we turn to next.

Diathesis–Stress: A Proposed Paradigm

A general point of view, one which meaingfully links both physiological and environmental factors, does in fact guide our own search for answers. Termed the **diathesis–stress** approach, it considers the often subtle interaction between a **predisposition** toward disease—the diathesis—and environmental, or life, events disturbing people—the stress. Diathesis refers most precisely to a constitutional predisposition toward illness, but the term may be extended to any characteristic of a person that increases his or her chance of developing a disorder. In the realm of physiology, for example, a number of problems we will consider in later chapters appear to have a genetically transmitted diathesis. That is, having a close relative with the disorder and therefore sharing to some degree his or her genetic endowment increases the person's risk for the disorder. Although the precise nature of these genetic diatheses is currently unknown (i.e., we don't know exactly what is inherited that makes one person more likely than another to develop schizophrenia), it is clear that a biological predisposition is an important component of many psychopathologies. On a psychological level, for example, the cognitive set already mentioned, the chronic feeling of hopelessness sometimes found in the depressed, may be considered a diathesis for depression.

Possessing the diathesis for a disorder increases a person's chance of developing it but does not, by any

---

[10]The behavioral concept of *reinforcement history* poses an interesting dilemma for those sympathetic to any of the learning paradigms. It is invariably invoked whenever a given individual's development is to be explained or when differences between people raised in apparently the same environment are to be accounted for. For example, if identical twins reared by their natural parents become schizophrenic later in life, the clinician holding a learning view will usually assert that they had similar reinforcement histories. When fraternal twins—they do not develop from the same egg and can be so physically unlike that they are of different genders—are raised at home and only one becomes schizophrenic, the learning "explanation" is that their reinforcement histories were different. Such explanations are as circular and as unsatisfactory as the psychoanalyst's inference of unconscious processes, a practice deplored by behaviorists, and with good reason. Neither hypothesis explains anything, nor does either encourage the search for new data.

BOX 2.3

ECLECTICISM IN PSYCHOTHERAPY: PRACTICE MAKES IMPERFECT

A word is needed about paradigms and the activities of therapists. It may appear that the treatments have been presented as though they were practices of separate, non-overlapping schools of therapy. The impression may have been conveyed that a behavior therapist would never listen to a client's report of a dream, nor would a psychoanalyst be caught dead prescribing assertion training to a patient. Such suppositions could not be farther from the truth. Most therapists describe themselves as *eclectics,* workers who employ ideas and techniques from a variety of schools (Garfield and Kurtz, 1974). Therapists often behave in ways that are not entirely consistent with the theories they might hold. For years practicing behavior therapists have listened empathically to clients, trying to make out their perspectives on events, on the assumption that this understanding would help them plan a better program for changing troublesome behavior. Behavioral theories do not prescribe such a procedure, but on the basis of clinical experience, and perhaps through their own humanity, behavior therapists have realized that empathic listening helps them in establishing rapport, in determining what is really bothering the client, and in planning a sensible therapy program. By the same token, Freud himself is said to have been far more directive and done far more to change immediate behavior than would be concluded from his writings alone. A vivid example of this is found in one of Freud's earliest cases as described in Breuer and Freud's *Studies in Hysteria.* Yalom (1980) paraphrased this study and argued that all effective therapists use "throw-ins" and "off the record extras":

In 1892, Sigmund Freud successfully treated Fraulein Elisabeth von R., a young woman who was suffering from psychogenic difficulties in walking. Freud explained his therapeutic success solely by his technique of abreaction, of de-repressing certain noxious wishes and thoughts. However, in studying Freud's notes, one is struck by the vast number of his other therapeutic activities. For example, he sent Elisabeth to visit her sister's grave and to pay a call upon a young man whom she found attractive. He demonstrated a "friendly interest in her present circumstances" by interacting with the family in the patient's behalf: he interviewed the patient's mother and "begged" her to provide open channels of communication with the patient and to permit the patient to unburden her mind periodically. Having learned from the mother that Elisabeth had no possibility of marrying her dead sister's husband, he conveyed that information to his patient. He helped untangle the family financial tangle. At other times Freud urged Elisabeth to face with calmness the fact that the future, for everyone, is inevitably uncertain. He repeatedly consoled her by assuring her that she was not responsible for unwanted feelings, and pointed out that her degree of guilt and remorse for these feelings was powerful evidence of her high moral character. Finally, after the termination of therapy, Freud, hearing that Elisabeth was going to a private dance, procured an invitation so he could watch her "whirl past in a lively dance." One cannot help but wonder what really helped Fraulein von R. Freud's extras, I have no doubt, constituted powerful inverventions; to exclude them from theory is to court error. (p. 4)

Especially today psychoanalysts are paying more attention to overt behavior and the relieving of symptoms than analytic theory would lead them to do. Some contemporary writers, like Paul Wachtel (see page 569), even propose that analysts employ behavior therapy techniques, openly acknowledging that behavior therapy has something to offer in the alleviation of behavior pathology.

These are weighty issues; the final section of this textbook will give them the attention they need and deserve. The reader should be aware of this complexity at the beginning, however, and be spared misconceptions about the intricacies and realities of psychotherapy.

---

means, guarantee that a disorder will develop. The "stress" part of the diathesis–stress paradigm tries to account for how a diathesis may be translated into an actual disorder. Generally speaking, in this context stress refers to some noxious or unpleasant environmental stimulus that could be either physiological or psychological.[11] Examples of the former include oxygen deprivation at birth resulting in brain injury, or poor nutrition during childhood, again leading to some form of brain dysfunction. Psychological stressors include both major traumatic events (e.g., rape, bereavement) and more mundane happenings that many of us experience (e.g., not achieving goals we have set for ourselves).

The key point of the diathesis–stress model is that both the diathesis and the stress are necessary. Certain people have, for example, inherited a physiological predisposition that places them at high risk for schizophrenia (see Chapter 14). Given a certain amount of stress, they are so physiologically constituted that they stand a good chance of becoming schizophrenic. Other

---

[11]"Stress" actually refers to the individual's reaction to a *stressor,* that environmental event that causes stress. For this reason one should probably call this paradigm the diathesis–stress*or* paradigm, but we shall adopt the former term because of its general acceptance among psychopathologists. This distinction is discussed more fully in Chapter 8 (page 191).

people, those at low risk, are not likely to develop schizophrenia, regardless of how difficult their lives are.

Different Perspectives on a Clinical Problem

It will be useful to recall the case of the policeman with which this book began. The information provided is open to a number of interpretations, depending on the paradigm adopted. For instance, if you hold a physiological point of view, you will be attentive to the similarity between the man's alternately manic and depressed states and the cyclical swings of mood suffered by his father. You probably are mindful of the research (to be reviewed in Chapter 9) that suggests a genetic factor in mood disorders. You do not, however, discount environmental contributions to his problems, but you hypothesize that some inherited, probably biochemical, defect predisposes him to break down under stress. After all, not everyone who experiences a difficult childhood and adolescence develops the kinds of problems Ernest H. has. For treatment you may prescribe lithium carbonate, a drug that many consider helpful in reducing the magnitude of mood swings in manic-depression.

Now suppose that you are committed to a cognitive-behavioral perspective, which encourages you to analyze human behavior in terms of reinforcement patterns as well as cognitive variables. You may focus on Ernest's self-consciousness at college, which seems related to the fact that, compared to his fellow students, he had grown up with few advantages. Economic insecurity and hardship may have made him unduly sensitive to criticism and rejection. Moreover, he regards his wife as warm and charming, pointing up his own perceived lack of social skills. Alcohol has been his escape from such tensions. But heavy drinking, coupled with persistent doubt about his own worth as a human being, has interfered with sexual functioning, worsening an already deteriorating marital relationship. As a behavior therapist, you may employ systematic densitization. You teach Ernest to relax deeply as he imagines a hierarchy of situations in which he is being evaluated by others. Or you may decide on rational-emotive therapy to convince Ernest that he need not obtain universal approval for every undertaking. Or, given Ernest's deficiency in social skills, you may choose behavior rehearsal to teach him how to function effectively in social situations in which he has had little experience. His sexual problems might be breached via a Masters and Johnson therapy program of undemanding but increasingly more intimate sexual encounters with his wife.

A psychoanalytic point of view will cast Ernest H. in yet another light. Believing that events in early childhood are of great importance in later patterns of ad-

justment, you may hypothesize that Ernest has blamed his father for his mother's early death. Such strong anger at the father has been repressed, but Ernest has not been able to regard him as a competent, worthwhile adult and to identify with him. Fixation at the oedipal stage of psychosexual development may have made Ernest anxious about authority and kept him from functioning as an adult male. For treatment you may choose dream analysis and free association to help Ernest lift his repressions and deal openly and consciously with his hitherto buried anger toward his father.

If you are a humanist, you will say that Ernest H. has consistently chosen not to follow his inner feelings, his basic nature, and that his pattern of seeking security rather than self-expression has caused his current difficulties and frustrations. He did not follow his inclination to attend law school, but rather became a policeman in order to obtain the instant respect accorded a uniform. He thought about having a child as something he *should* do at the age of thirty-two and thus transformed his sexual relationship into one of duty rather than self-expression. These failures to follow his authentic feelings ended in accusations, frustration, and an explosive outburst. In your sessions with Ernest, you will try to help him trust his innermost feelings and take chances in pursuing his own life goals rather than acting only to counter fear and social pressures. Your emphathic listening will help Ernest to uncover his own needs and to decide for himself what he wants out of life.

What Is Abnormal?

The various paradigms that we have discussed all make some guiding assumption about the nature of abnormal behavior. They do not, however, explicitly define it. The physiological paradigm, for example, asserts that physiological processes make people behave abnormally, and the learning paradigms blame unfortunate experiences. But these paradigms do not tell us exactly what abnormal behavior is. Can we draw a clear-cut distinction between normal and abnormal? Can we offer a satisfactory definition of abnormality?

To address these questions, let us consider some definitions that have been proposed. We will see that no single one is adequate. Each has merit and captures some part of what might be the full definition. But each by itself has too many exceptions to be considered acceptable.

One definition of abnormal behavior is that it is statistically infrequent. Those who adopt the statistical approach measure specific characteristics of people, such as personality traits and ways of behaving, and the dis-

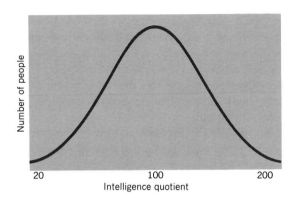

FIGURE 2.6
The distribution of intelligence among adults, illustrating a normal or bell-shaped curve.

tribution of these characteristics in the population. One type of population distribution, the ***normal curve*** (Figure 2.6), depicts the majority of people as being in the middle as far as any particular characteristic is concerned, that is, very few people fall at either extreme. An assertion that a person is normal implies that he or she does not deviate much from the average in a particular trait or behavior pattern.

Statistical infrequency is used explicitly in diagnosing mental retardation. Figure 2.6 gives the normal distribution of intelligence in the population. When an individual's intelligence quotient is below 70,[12] intellectual functioning is considered sufficiently subnormal to be designated as mental retardation.

Although much infrequent behavior indeed strikes us as abnormal, in some instances the relationship breaks down. Having great athletic ability is infrequent but not abnormal in the sense implied here. Only certain infrequent behavior, such as being subject to hallucinations or deep depression, falls into the domain considered in this book. Unfortunately, the statistical definition gives us no guidance in determining what infrequent behavior psychopathologists should study.

Another definition of abnormality invokes the notion of personal suffering: people are to be judged abnormal if their behavior creates great distress and torment in themselves. As with the statistical approach, this definition fits many of the forms of abnormality we consider in this book. People with anxiety disorders and depression truly suffer greatly. But some disorders clearly do not cause acute distress. The sociopath, for example, treats others callously and may continually violate the law without experiencing any guilt, remorse, or anxiety whatsoever. Another difficulty in using personal dis-

comfort as a defining characteristic is that it is inherently subjective. People decide and report on how much they are suffering. The degrees of their distress are difficult to compare, since their standards for defining their own psychological states can vary greatly.

Another concept that has been applied is that of disability. Substance use disorders, for example, are defined principally by how the substance abuse creates social or occupational disability (e.g., poor work performance, serious arguments with spouse). Similarly, a phobia could indicate both distress and disability if, for example, a severe fear of flying prevented someone from taking a job promotion. As with suffering, however, disability applies to some, but not all, disorders. It is not clear, for example, whether transvestism (cross dressing for sexual pleasure) is necessarily a disability. Most transvestites are married, lead conventional lives, and their cross dressing is usually done in private.

Finally, some writers have proposed that abnormal behavior is whatever violates social norms and threatens or makes anxious those observing it. Again, this definition rings true, at least partially. Now the sociopath's callousness fits the definition, as do the sometimes wild behavior of a manic and the strange antics of a schizophrenic. The definition also has the advantage of explicitly making abnormality a relative concept; various forms of unusual behavior can be tolerated, depending on the prevailing cultural norms. But the definition is also at once too broad and too narrow. Criminals and prostitutes, who violate social norms, are usually not studied within the domain of abnormal psychology. The highly anxious person, who is generally regarded as a central character in the field, would not be noticed by many lay observers.

Our position is that no current definition of abnormal behavior is fully satisfactory. Some diagnoses involve infrequency, some involve distress, others disability, and still others norm violations. No single definitional concept is adequate. Over the years a number of the categories of abnormal behavior that appear in official diagnostic manuals have changed, but not because any particular definition of abnormal behavior was adopted. In some cases clinical research has led to the identification of a new syndrome. Infantile autism, for example, first appeared among official psychiatric diagnoses in 1980 even though it was first described in the clinical literature in the 1940s. In others, norms and values have shifted. Over the last century, for example, more and more people have decided that their psychological problems warranted professional help. With this increased flow of patients, therapists and researchers saw problems that were new to them, and new diagnoses emerged. What we present in a text such as this is a list of conditions that are currently thought to be abnormal.

---

[12]Although low intelligence is a principal criterion for defining mental retardation, other diagnostic features must also be considered; see page 443.

The disorders in the list will undoubtedly change with time.

Summary

This chapter has reviewed the major paradigms, or points of view, that are current in the study of psychopathology and therapy. The *physiological* paradigm assumes that psychopathology is caused by an organic defect. Previous discussions of this point of view have taken the form of arguments, pro and con, about a "medical" or "disease" model. But an examination of the meaning of the term medical model reveals that it is actually too vague about etiology to enjoy the status of a formal model of psychopathology. The medical model does have one implication—that psychopathology may be attributed to physiological malfunctions and defects. Therefore we have proposed instead the physiological paradigm. Physiological therapies attempt to rectify the specific organic defects underlying disorders or to alleviate symptoms of disorders that have not been traced to such defects.

Another paradigm derives from the work of Sigmund Freud. The *psychoanalytic* point of view directs our attention to repressions and other unconscious processes that are traced to early childhood conflicts. Whereas present-day ego analysts who are part of this tradition place greater emphasis on conscious ego functions, the psychoanalytic paradigm has generally searched the unconscious and early life of the patient for the causes of abnormality. Therapeutic interventions based on psychoanalytic theory usually attempt to lift repressions so that the analysand can examine the infantile and unfounded nature of his or her fears.

Behavioral, or *learning*, paradigms suggest that aberrant behavior has developed through classical conditioning, operant conditioning, or modeling. More recently, *cognitive* points of view that blame schemata and interpretations for abnormality have been espoused and often blended with the behavioral. Investigators who believe that abnormal behavior may have been learned share a commitment to examine carefully all situations affecting behavior, as well as to define concepts carefully. Behavior therapists try to apply learning and cognitive principles to the direct alteration of overt behavior, thought, and emotion. Less attention is paid to the historical causes of abnormal behavior than to what maintains it, such as the reward and punishment contingencies encouraging problematic response patterns.

The *humanistic* paradigm holds that people can be understood only by appreciating their phenomenology, each person's unique perspective on life, and it assumes further that humankind is by nature good and that psychopathology develops from a blockage or denial of this innate worthiness. Therapists encourage clients to discover and trust their inner true selves and to express their needs and impulses.

The *diathesis–stress* paradigm integrates several points of view. People are assumed to be disposed to react inadequately to particular environment stressors. The diathesis may be constitutional, as appears to be the case in schizophrenia, or it may be extended to the psychological, for example, the chronic sense of hopelessness considered a factor contributing to depression.

A consideration of what is abnormal yielded several criteria, including statistical rarity (e.g., mental retardation), subjective distress (e.g., depression), disability (e.g., a phobia that prevents one from taking a new job that would otherwise be rewarding), and norm violations (e.g., sociopathy). None was found in itself to be satisfactory, and it was concluded that changes will continue to take place over time in what psychopathologists regard as appropriate to their domain of study.

The most important implication of paradigms is that they determine where and how investigators look for answers. Paradigms necessarily limit perceptions of the world, for investigators will interpret data differently according to their points of view. In our opinion it is fortunate that workers are not all operating within the same paradigm, for at this point too little is known about psychopathology and its treatment to settle on any one of them.

Robert Longo. *Tongue to the Heart.* 1984. Courtesy of Metro Pictures.

Chapter 3

Classification and Diagnosis

DSM-IIIR—The Diagnostic System of the American Psychiatric Association

The Axes

Diagnostic Categories

Issues in the Classification of Abnormal Behavior

The Relevance of Classification Per Se

Criticisms of Actual Diagnostic Practice

DSM-III, DSM-IIIR, and Criticisms of Diagnosis

Summary

By the end of the nineteenth century, medicine had progressed far beyond its practice during the Middle Ages, when the common technique of bloodletting was at least part of the treatment of virtually all physical problems. It was gradually recognized that different illnesses required different treatments. Diagnostic procedures were improved, diseases classified, and applicable remedies administered. Impressed by the successes that new diagnostic procedures had achieved in the field of medicine, investigators of abnormal behavior also sought to develop classification schemes that grouped disorders according to symptoms. Moreover, advances in other sciences such as botany and chemistry had followed the development of classification systems, reinforcing hope that similar efforts in the field of abnormal behavior might bring progress.

But during the nineteenth century, and indeed into the twentieth as well, there had been great inconsistency in the way abnormal behavior was classified. By the end of the nineteenth century, the diversity of classifications was recognized as a serious problem that impeded communication among people in the field. In 1889 in Paris, the Congress of Mental Science adopted a single classification system, but it was never widely used. Earlier, in Britain in 1882, the Statistical Committee of the Royal Medico-Psychological Association had produced a classification scheme that, even though revised several times, was never adopted by the members. In the United States, in 1886, the Association of Medical Superintendents of American Institutions for the Insane, a forerunner of the American Psychiatric Association, adopted a somewhat revised version of the British system. Then in 1913 this group accepted a new classification incorporating some of Kraepelin's ideas. But again, consistency did not emerge. The New York State Commission on Lunacy, for example, insisted on retaining its own system (Kendell, 1975).

Nor have more contemporary efforts at achieving uniformity of classification been totally successful. In 1939 the World Health Organization (WHO) added mental disorders to the *International List of Causes of Death*. In 1948 WHO expanded the previous list, and it became the *International Statistical Classification of Diseases, Injuries, and Causes of Death*, a comprehensive listing of all diseases, including a classification of abnormal behavior. Although this nomenclature was unanimously adopted at a WHO conference, the mental disorders section failed to be widely accepted. In the United States, for example, even though American psychiatrists had a prominent role in the WHO effort, the American Psychiatric Association published its own *Diagnostic and Statistical Manual* (DSM-I) in 1952.

In 1969 the WHO published a new classification system, and it was more widely accepted. A second version of the American Psychiatric Association's DSM (DSM-II, 1968) was similar to it, and in Britain a glossary of definitions was produced to accompany it (General Register Office, 1968). But whether a true consensus had been reached was doubtful. The WHO classifications are simply a listing of diagnostic categories; the actual behavior or symptoms that are the basis for the diagnoses are not specified. DSM-II and the British Glossary provided this crucial information, but the symptoms listed by each were not always similar. Therefore actual diagnostic practices still varied widely. In 1980 the American Psychiatric Association published an extensively revised diagnostic manual—DSM-III. A somewhat revised version, DSM-IIIR, appeared in 1987.[1]

In this chapter the major DSM-IIIR categories are given in brief summary. We then examine criticisms of classification in general and of the DSM in particular. In the next chapter we consider the assessment procedures that provide the data on which diagnostic decisions are based.

DSM-III—The Diagnostic System of the American Psychiatric Association

The Axes

A number of major innovations distinguish the third edition and its revised version of the American Psychiatric Association's *Diagnostic and Statistical Manual*. Perhaps the most sweeping is that classification has become **multiaxial**; each individual is to be rated on five separate dimensions or axes (Table 3.1). The multiaxial system, by requiring judgments to be made on each of the five axes, forces the diagnostician to consider a broad range of information. Axis I includes all categories except for the personality and developmental disorders, which make up axis II. Thus axes I and II comprise the classification of abnormal behavior. Axes I and II were separated to ensure that the possible presence of long-term disturbances is considered when attention is directed to the current one. For example, a person who is now a heroin addict would be diagnosed on Axis I as having a psychoactive substance use disorder; he might also have a long-standing antisocial personality disorder, which is found on axis II.

---

[1]Generally when we discuss the DSM our descriptions and comments will apply to DSM-IIIR. When it is necessary to distinguish between DSM-III and DSM-IIIR we will do so. When we discuss the disorders we will sometimes indicate how DSM-IIIR has changed from DSM-III.

TABLE 3.1
DSM-IIIR multiaxial classification system.* Reprinted with permission from the *Diagnostic and Statistical Manual of Mental Disorders, Third Edition, Revised.* Copyright 1987 American Psychiatric Association.

Axis I	Axis II	Axis III
Disorders Usually First Evident in Infancy, Childhood, or Adolescence Organic Mental Disorders Psychoactive Substance Use Disorders Schizophrenia Delusional (Paranoid) Disorder Mood Disorders Anxiety Disorders Somatoform Disorders Dissociative Disorders Sexual Disorders Sleep Disorders Psychological Factors Affecting Physical Condition	Personality Disorders: paranoid, schizoid, schizotypal, histrionic, narcissistic, antisocial, borderline, avoidant, dependent, obsessive-compulsive, passive-aggressive Developmental Disorders: Academic skills disorders, language and speech disorders, mental retardation, pervasive developmental disorder	Physical Disorders and Conditions

Axis IV
Severity of Psychosocial Stressors Scale: Adults

Code	Term	Acute Events	Enduring Circumstances
1	None	No acute events that may be relevant to the disorder	No enduring circumstances that may be relevant to the disorder
2	Mild	Broke up with boyfriend or girlfriend; started or graduated from school; child left home	Family arguments; job dissatisfaction; residence in high-crime neighborhood
3	Moderate	Marriage; marital separation; loss of job; retirement; miscarriage	Marital discord; serious financial problems; trouble with boss; being a single parent
4	Severe	Divorce; birth of first child	Unemployment; poverty
5	Extreme	Death of spouse; serious physical illness diagnosed; victim of rape	Serious chronic illness in self or child; ongoing physical or sexual abuse
6	Catastrophic	Death of child; suicide of spouse; devastating natural disaster	Captivity as hostage; concentration camp experience

Severity of Psychosocial Stressors Scale: Children and Adolescents

Code	Term	Acute Events	Enduring Circumstances
1	None	No acute events that may be relevant to the disorder	No enduring circumstances that may be relevant to the disorder
2	Mild	Broke up with boyfriend or girlfriend; change of school	Overcrowded living quarters; family arguments
3	Moderate	Expelled from school; birth of sibling	Chronic disabling illness in parent; chronic parental discord
4	Severe	Divorce of parents; unwanted pregnancy; arrest	Harsh or rejecting parents; chronic life-threatening illness in parent; multiple foster home placements
5	Extreme	Sexual or physical abuse; death of a parent	Recurrent sexual or physical abuse
6	Catastrophic	Death of both parents	Chronic life-threatening illness

TABLE 3.1 (Continued)

Axis V
Global Assessment of Functioning Scale (GAF Scale)

Consider psychological, social, and occupational functioning on a hypothetical continuum of mental health/illness. Do not include impairment in functioning due to physical (or environmental) limitations.

Code	
90 ⎮ 81	Absent or minimal symptoms (e.g., mild anxiety before an exam), good functioning in all areas, interested and involved in a wide range of activities, socially effective, generally satisfied with life, no more than everyday problems or concerns (e.g., an occasional argument with family members).
80 ⎮ 71	If symptoms are present, they are transient and expectable reactions to psychosocial stressors (e.g., difficulty concentrating after family argument); no more than slight impairment in social, occupational, or school functioning (e.g., temporarily falling behind in school work).
70 ⎮ 61	Some mild symptoms (e.g., depressed mood and mild insomnia) OR some difficulty in social, occupational, or school functioning (e.g., occasional truancy, or theft within the household), but generally functioning pretty well, has some meaningful interpersonal relationships.
60 ⎮ 51	Moderate symptoms (e.g., flat affect and circumstantial speech, occasional panic attacks) OR moderate difficulty in social, occupational, or school functioning (e.g., few friends, conflicts with co-workers).
50 ⎮ 41	Serious symptoms (e.g., suicidal ideation, severe obsessional rituals, frequent shoplifting) OR any serious impairment in social, occupational, or school functioning (e.g., no friends, unable to keep a job).
40 ⎮ 31	Some impairment in reality testing or communication (e.g., speech is at times illogical, obscure, or irrelevant) OR major impairment in several areas, such as work or school, family relations, judgment, thinking, or mood (e.g., depressed man avoids friends neglects family. and is unable to work; child frequently beats up younger children, is defiant at home, and is failing at school).
30 ⎮ 21	Behavior is considerably influenced by delusions or hallucinations OR serious impairment in communication or judgment (e.g., sometimes incoherent, acts grossly inappropriately, suicidal preoccupation) OR inability to function in almost all areas (e.g., stays in bed all day; no job, home, or friends).
20 ⎮ 11	Some danger of hurting self or others (e.g., suicide attempts without clear expectation of death, frequently violent, manic excitement) OR occasionally fails to maintain minimal personal hygiene (e.g., smears feces) OR gross impairment in communication (e.g., largely incoherent or mute).
10 ⎮ 1	Persistent danger of severely hurting self or others (e.g., recurrent violence) OR persistent inability to maintain minimal personal hygiene OR serious suicidal act with clear expectation of death.

*This listing is generally selective rather than complete. A more comprehensive listing of DSM-IIIR categories is given on the front endpapers of this book.

Although the remaining three axes are not needed to make the actual diagnosis, their inclusion in DSM-IIIR indicates recognition that factors other than a person's symptoms should be considered in an assessment. On axis III the clinician indicates any current physical disorders believed to be relevant to the mental disorder in question. In some individuals a physical disorder, a neurological dysfunction, for example, may be the cause of the abnormal behavior, whereas in others it may be an important factor in their overall condition, for example, diabetes in a child with a conduct disorder. Axis IV codes the level of psychosocial stress that the person has been experiencing and that may be contributing to

the disorder. A rating scale of 1 (none) to 6 (catastrophic, e.g., multiple family deaths) is used. Finally, on axis V, the clinician indicates the person's current level of adaptive functioning as well as the highest level during the past year. Life areas to be considered are social relationships, occupational functioning, and use of leisure time. Ratings of current functioning give information about the need for treatment, and the rating of the highest level in the past year is included because the better the person has been functioning, regardless of what problems they have for axes I and II, the better the outlook for the future. Table 3.2 shows how a diagnosis using DSM-IIIR would look.

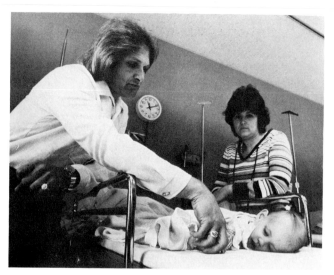

The serious illness of a child and death of a relative or close friend would represent a severe or extreme level of psychosocial stress, Axis IV.

Diagnostic Categories

The following major *diagnostic categories* are to be considered when determining how the patient should be described for axes I and II.

Disorders Usually First Evident in Infancy, Childhood, or Adolescence Within this broad-ranging category are the intellectual, emotional, and physical disorders that usually begin in infancy, childhood, or adolescence. Some of the problems described are anxiety disorders; conduct disorders; eating disorders, such as anorexia nervosa, in which considerable weight is lost through an intense fear of becoming fat; and gender identity disorders, feelings of discomfort and inappropriateness concerning anatomical sex. These disorders are discussed in Chapters 15 and 16.

Organic Mental Disorders In organic mental disorders the functioning of the brain is known to be impaired, either permanently or transiently. The primary symptoms, which vary with the location and extent of the dysfunction, are delirium—clouding of consciousness, wandering attention, incoherent stream of thought, misperceptions; dementia—deterioration of intellectual capabilities, of memory, abstract thinking, judgment, and control over impulses; persistent and recurrent hallucinations; and disturbed emotions. These disorders are studied in Chapter 17 and in the Appendix.

Psychoactive Substance Use Disorders Here the ingestion of various substances—alcohol, opiates, cocaine, amphetamines, and so on—has changed behavior enough to impair social or occupational functioning.

Infantile autism, one of the disorders of childhood, frequently includes a failure to respond socially to others.

TABLE 3.2

Example of a DSM-IIIR multiaxial diagnosis

Axis I: Alcohol Dependence
Axis II: Antisocial Personality
Axis III: Cirrhosis
Axis IV: Psychosocial stressors: death of only child, marital stress. Severity: 6, catastrophic
Axis V: Highest level of adaptive functioning past year: 58; current functioning: 42

Alcohol, one of the most dangerous of drugs, is also one of the most common substances of potential abuse.

The individual may become unable to control ingestion of the substance, or to discontinue it, and may develop withdrawal symptoms if he or she stops using it. These disorders are examined in Chapter 11.

Schizophrenia With schizophrenic disorders the self-care, social relations, and ability of patients to work have deteriorated. Their language and communication are disordered, and they may shift from one subject to another only obliquely related or even completely unrelated. Delusions, such as believing that thoughts not their own have been placed in their heads, are common.

People with schizophrenic or paranoid disorders are often found on urban streets.

Hallucinations, in particular hearing voices that come from outside themselves, plague them. Their emotions are blunted, flattened, or inappropriate, and they have lost contact with the world and with others. These serious mental disorders are discussed in Chapter 14.

Delusional (Paranoid) Disorders The most obvious symptoms of people with these disorders are their delusions of being persecuted. The diagnosis can also be applied to extreme and unjustified jealousy, as when a spouse becomes convinced, without reasonable cause, that his or her partner is unfaithful. DSM-IIIR indicates the difficulty in distinguishing paranoid disorders from *schizophrenia, paranoid type*, noting that in schizophrenia, the more serious disorder, delusions tend to be more bizarre and fragmented and the person also has hallucinations. Paranoid disorders are discussed in Chapter 14.

Mood Disorders In *major depression* the person is deeply sad and discouraged, is also likely to lose weight and energy, and to have suicidal thoughts and feelings of self-reproach. The person suffering *mania* may be described as euphoric, more active than usual, distractable, and possessed of unrealistically great self-esteem. *Bipolar disorder* is diagnosed if the person experiences episodes of mania or of both mania and depression. The disorders of mood are surveyed in Chapter 9.

Depression is one of the most common diagnoses.

Anxiety Disorders Anxiety disorders are those that have some form of anxiety as the central disturbance. Individuals with a *phobia* fear an object or situation so intensely that they must avoid it, even though they know that their fear is unwarranted and unreasonable and disrupts their lives. In *panic disorder with agoraphobia*, the person is fearful of leaving familiar surroundings and is subject to sudden but brief attacks of intense apprehension, so upsetting that he or she is likely to tremble and shake, feel dizzy, and have trouble breathing. The anxiety of *generalized anxiety disorder* is pervasive and persistent. Individuals are jumpy and may have a lump in the throat and a pounding heart. They ruminate and feel generally on edge. The person with *obsessive-compulsive disorder* is subject to persistent obsessions or compulsions. Obsessions are recurrent thoughts, ideas, and images that, uncontrollably, dominate a person's consciousness. A compulsion is an urge to perform a stereotyped act with the seeming but usually impossible purpose of warding off an impending feared situation. Attempts to resist a compulsion create so much tension that the individual usually yields.

The anxiety and numbness suffered in the aftermath of a traumatic event outside the usual range of human experience is called *posttraumatic stress disorder*. Individuals have painful, intrusive recollections by day and bad dreams at night. They find it difficult to concentrate and feel detached from others and ongoing affairs. The anxiety disorders are reviewed in Chapter 6.

Somatoform Disorders The physical symptoms of somatoform disorders have no known physiological cause but seem to serve a psychological purpose. Persons with *somatization disorder*, or Briquet's syndrome, have a long history of multiple physical complaints for which they have taken medicine or consulted doctors. In *conversion disorder* the person reports the loss of motor or sensory function, such as a paralysis, an anesthesia, or blindness. Individuals with *somatoform pain disorder* suffer from severe and prolonged pain. *Hypochondriasis* is the misinterpretation of minor physical sensations as serious illness.

Dissociative Disorders Psychological dissociation is a sudden alteration in consciousness affecting memory and identity. Persons with *psychogenic amnesia* may forget their whole past or more selectively lose memory for a particular time period. With *psychogenic fugue* the individual suddenly and unexpectedly travels to a new locale, starts a new life, and is amnesic for his or her previous identity. The person with *multiple personality* possesses two or more distinct ones, each complex and dominant one at a time. *Depersonalization disorder* is a severe and disruptive feeling of self-estrangement or unreality. Somatoform and dissociative disorders are examined in Chapter 7.

Sexual Disorders The sexual disorders section of DSM-IIIR lists two principal subcategories. In *paraphilias* the sources of sexual gratification—as in exhibitionism, voyeurism, sadism, and masochism— are unconventional. Persons with *sexual dysfunctions* are unable to complete the usual sexual response cycle. Inability to maintain an erection, premature ejaculation, and inhibition of orgasms are examples of their problems. These disorders are studied in Chapter 12 and 13.

Psychological Factors Affecting Physical Condition If an illness appears to be caused, in part, or exacerbated by a psychological condition, the diagnosis for axis I is *psychological factors affecting physical condition*. Referred to previously as psychophysiological or psychosomatic disorders, these conditions are reviewed in detail in Chapter 8.

Sleep Disorders DSM-IIIR distinguishes two major subcategories of sleep disorders. In the *dyssomnias*, sleep is disturbed in amount (e.g., not being able to maintain sleep or sleeping too much), quality (not feeling rested after sleep), or timing (e.g., inability to sleep during conventional sleep times). In the *parasomnias*, an unusual event occurs during sleep (e.g., nightmares, sleepwalking).

Personality Disorders Personality disorders are defined as "inflexible and maladaptive" patterns of behavior. They are listed on axis II. Eleven distinct personality disorders make up the category. In *schizoid personality disorder*, for example, the person is aloof, has few friends, and is indifferent to praise and criticism. The individual with a *narcissistic personality* has an overblown sense of self-importance, fantasizes about great successes, requires constant attention, and is likely to exploit others. The *antisocial personality* has surfaced before the age of fifteen, through truancy, running away from home, delinquency, and general belligerency. Now, in adulthood, he or she is indifferent about holding a job, being a responsible mate or parent, planning ahead for the future and even for tomorrow, and staying on the right side of the law. Previously labeled as psychopaths or sociopaths, antisocial personalities do not feel guilt or shame for transgressing social mores. Chapter 10 covers the personality disorders and examines sociopathy in particular.

"What do you mean, 'Marriage is a two-edged sword'?"

Mankoff a 1989 The New Yorker Magazine

Developmental Disorders There are three subcategories of this axis II category: mental retardation, pervasive developmental disorder (*infantile autism*), and specific developmental disorders, which cover delays in the acquisition of speech, reading, arithmetic, and writing skills. They are studied in Chapters 15 and 16.[2]

Code V

This all-encompassing category is for "conditions not attributable to a mental disorder that are a focus of attention or treatment." Essentially, the category seems to exist so that anyone entering the mental health system can be categorized, even in the absence of mental disorder.[3] Among the individual codes are the following:

academic problem

antisocial behavior

malingering

marital problem

occupational problem

uncomplicated bereavement

Most of these codes will not be covered in this book, although malingering will be discussed in Chapter 7, and assessment of and therapy for marital problems will be presented in Chapters 4 and 20, respectively.

Issues in the Classification of Abnormal Behavior

This review of the major categories of abnormal behavior was brief, for they will be examined in more detail throughout this volume. On the basis of this overview, however, let us scrutinize the usefulness of the system as it exists today. Two major lines of criticism

---

[2]The organization of diagnostic categories in DSM-III and DSM-IIIR differ substantially from the system that appeared in DSM-II. Furthermore, some diagnoses are given for the first time in DSM-III and DSM-IIIR, and some of the categories of DSM-II are no longer listed. The most important of these changes will be discussed in chapters on individual disorders.

[3]In this context it is interesting to recall our discussion of the difficulties of defining mental disorder (page 57). Can these "codes" really be readily distinguished from official diagnoses?

can be distinguished. One group of critics asserts that classification per se is irrelevant to the field of abnormal behavior. The second group of critics finds specific deficiencies in the way diagnoses are made.

The Relevance of Classification Per Se

Those opposed to any attempt to classify argue that whenever we do so we lose information and hence overlook some of the uniqueness of the person being studied.[4] The simple example of casting dice will help to explain this argument. Any of the numbers one through six may come up on a given toss of a single die. Let us suppose, however, that we classify each outcome as odd or even. Whenever a one, three, or five comes up on a roll, we call out "odd," and whenever a two, four, or six appears, we say "even." A person listening to our calls will not know whether the call "odd" refers to a one, three, or five, or whether a two, four, or six has turned up when he or she hears "even." In classification some information must inevitably be lost.

What matters, however, is whether the information lost is *relevant*, which in turn depends on the *purposes* of the classification system. Any classification is designed to group together objects having a common property and to ignore differences in the objects that are not relevant to the purposes at hand. If our intention is merely to count odd and even rolls, it is irrelevant whether a die comes up one, three, or five or two, four, or six. In judging abnormal behavior, however, we cannot so easily decide what is wheat and what is chaff, for the relevant and irrelevant dimensions of abnormal behavior are uncertain. Thus when we do classify, we may be grouping people together on rather trivial bases while ignoring their extremely important differences.

Classification may also stigmatize a person. Consider how you might be affected by being told, for example, that you are a schizophrenic. You might become guarded and suspicious lest someone recognize your disorder. Or you might be chronically on edge, fearing the onset of another "attack." Furthermore, the fact that you are a "former mental patient" could have a great impact on your life. Friends and loved ones now treat you differently, and employment may be difficult to obtain.

There is little doubt that diagnosis can have such negative consequences, but social stigmatization does not appear to be as extensive as once believed. Gove and Fain (1973), for example, followed up a large sample of patients one year after discharge from a hospital. The former patients were interviewed about jobs, social relationships, and outside activities. The patients' descriptions of how they were functioning now and had in the past were not very different. Thus, although we must recognize and be on guard against the possible social stigma of a diagnosis, the problem may not be as serious as generally believed.

Assuming that various types of abnormal behavior do differ one from another, it is essential to classify them, for these differences may constitute keys to the causes and treatments of the various deviant behaviors. For example, the form of mental retardation already mentioned, phenylketonuria, is attributed to a deficiency in the metabolism of the protein phenylalanine, resulting in the release of incomplete metabolites that injure the brain (see page 454). A diet drastically reduced in phenylalanine prevents some of this injury. As Mendels (1970) has noted, however,

had we taken 100, or even 1000, people with mental deficiency and placed them all on the phenylalanine-free diet, the response would have been insignificant and the diet would have been discarded as a treatment. It was first necessary to recognize a subtype of mental deficiency [retardation], phenylketonuria, and then subject the value of a phenylalanine-free diet to investigation in this specific population, for whom it has been shown to have value in preventing the development of mental deficiency. (p. 35)

Forming classes may thus further knowledge, for once a class is formed, additional information may be ascertained about it. Even though the class is only an asserted and not a proven entity, it may still be heuristically[5] useful in that it facilitates the acquisition of new information. Only after a diagnostic class has been formed can people who fit its definition be studied in hopes of uncovering factors that were responsible for the development of their problems and of devising treatments that may help them.

---

[4]The reader is invited to recall our discussions in Chapters 1 and 2 of paradigms and their effect on how we glean information about our world. It appears to be in the nature of humankind that we categorize whenever we perceive and think about anything. Those who argue against classification per se therefore overlook the inevitability of classification and categorization in human thought.

[5]Heuristic is a central word and concept in science. It comes from the Greek *heuriskein*, to discover or find, and is defined in *Webster's* as serving to guide, discover, or reveal, and more specifically as valuable for stimulating or conducting empirical research. The frequent use of this word and its derivatives underlines the importance scientists place on ideas in generating new knowledge.

Criticisms of Actual Diagnostic Practice

More specific criticisms are commonly made of psychiatric classification, the principal ones concerning whether discrete diagnostic categories are justifiable and whether or not the diagnostic classes are reliable and valid. These criticisms were frequently leveled at DSM-II and its predecessor. At the close of this section, we see how DSM-III and DSM-IIIR have come to grips with them.

Discrete Entity versus Continuum

It may be argued that classification, because it postulates discrete entities, does not allow the continuity between normal and abnormal behavior to be taken into consideration. Those who advance this argument, for example, psychopathologists operating within a learning paradigm, hold that abnormal and normal behavior differ only in intensity or degree, not in kind. Therefore discrete diagnostic categories foster a false impression of discontinuity. Rimland (1969) has summarized this position and, in our opinion, effectively criticized it.

The idea is that if it is difficult to make a distinction between two neighboring points on a hypothetical continuum, no valid distinctions can thereafter be made even at the extremes of the continuum. There are thus persons who would argue that the existence of several variations of gray precludes a distinction between black and white. Hokum. While I will agree that some patients in mental hospitals are saner than nonpatients, and that it is sometimes hard to distinguish between deep unhappiness and psychotic depression, I do not agree that the difficulty sometimes encountered in making the distinction between normal and abnormal necessarily invalidates all such distinctions. (pp. 716–717)

In other words, the fact that some distinctions are difficult to make, such as deciding whether sundown is night or day, does not mean it is impossible to distinguish between noon and midnight.

The Issue of Reliability

Whether or not different diagnosticians agree that a given diagnostic label should be applied to a particular person is the test of its **reliability**. Clearly, for a classification system to be useful, those applying it must be able to agree on what is and what is not an instance of a particular class.[6] Thus reliability becomes a primary requisite for judging any classification system.

---

[6]These two components of reliability—agreeing on who is a member of a class and who is not—are referred to as *sensitivity* and *specificity*, respectively. Sensitivity refers to agreement regarding the presence of a specific diagnosis and specificity refers to agreement concerning the absence of a diagnosis.

The reliability of psychiatric diagnosis has been well researched. One exemplary investigation, illustrating the unreliability of older diagnostic systems, was reported by Aaron T. Beck and his colleagues (1962). Beck and three other highly experienced psychiatrists diagnosed 153 patients within one week of their admission to a psychiatric facility. Each patient was interviewed twice in succession by two different psychiatrists. Before beginning their study, the four psychiatrists had met to discuss the current diagnostic manual so that they could agree on its application. No attempt was made to ensure that the four interviewers would employ the same techniques in gathering the information necessary to make their diagnoses, however.

The overall agreement among the psychiatrists, calculated as the number of diagnoses on which they agreed divided by the total number of diagnoses made, was a disappointingly low 54 percent. The data were later reexamined by the same four psychiatrists (Ward *et al.*, 1962) in an attempt to determine why diagnosticians might disagree. Meeting again after they had completed the interviews and made their diagnoses, the psychiatrists found three major reasons why they had not always reached the same determination. First, accounting for 5 percent of the disagreements, were *inconsistencies in the information presented by the patients*. The second major group of diagnostic disagreements, 32.5 percent of them, were attributed to *inconsistencies on the part of the diagnostician*. Differences in interview techniques, in judging the importance of particular symptoms, and in interpreting the same pathology constituted most of these inconsistencies.

The third and largest group of disagreements, comprising 62.5 percent of them, were considered to stem from *inadequacies of the diagnostic system*. The diagnosticians found the criteria unclear. Either too fine distinctions were required, or the classification system seemingly forced the diagnostician to choose a major category that was not specific enough.

The Issue of Validity

Whether or not accurate statements and predictions can be made about a class once it has been formed is the test of its **validity**. We should state at the outset that validity bears a particular relation to reliability; the less reliable a category is, the more difficult it is to make valid statements about the category. If the reliability of diagnosis is not entirely adequate, we can expect that its validity will not be either.

A diagnosis can have three kinds of validity: etiological, concurrent, and predictive. It has **etiological validity** if the same historical antecedents have caused the disorder in the patients diagnosed. In other words, for a diagnosis to be considered etiologically valid, the same factors must be found to have caused the disorder

Diagnostic decisions are made frequently at conferences in which differing professionals share information about a patient.

in the people who comprise the diagnostic group. Consider, for example, the supposition that bipolar disorder is, in part, genetically determined. According to this theory, people with episodes of both depression and mania must have a "family tree" that contains other bipolars. As we shall see in Chapter 9, evidence that supports this theory has been collected, giving this diagnostic category some etiological validity.

A diagnosis has **concurrent validity** if other symptoms or disorderd processes not part of the diagnosis itself are discovered to be characteristic of those diagnosed. Finding that most people with schizophrenia have difficulty in personal relationships is an example. **Predictive validity** refers to similar future behavior on the part of the disorder or patients suffering from it. The disorder may have a specific prognosis; that is, whether recovery is highly likely or whether continuing problems can be expected depends on the diagnostic category being considered. Or members of the diagnostic group may be expected to respond in a similar way to a particular treatment. Bipolar patients, for example, tend to respond well to a drug called lithium carbonate. The fact that this drug does not work well for people in most other diagnostic classes supports the predictive validity of the bipolar diagnosis. We have organized this book around the major diagnostic categories because we believe that they indeed possess some validity. Certain categories have greater validity than others, however;

these differences will become apparent as we discuss each diagnostic classification.

DSM-III, DSM-IIIR, and Criticisms of Diagnosis

DSM-III and DSM-IIIR were devised to be more diagnostically reliable and valid than their predecessors. Each diagnostic category in axes I and II is described much more extensively than was the case in DSM-II. First there is a description of "essential features," then of "associated features." Given next are statements, drawn from the research literature, about age of onset, course, degree of impairment and complications, predisposing factors, prevalence and sex ratio, familial pattern, and differential diagnosis. Finally, specific *diagnostic criteria* for the category are spelled out in a more precise fashion. These are the symptoms and other facts that must be present to justify the diagnosis. Table 3.3 compares the descriptions of a manic episode given in DSM-II to the diagnostic criteria given in DSM-IIIR. Clearly the bases for making diagnoses are decidedly more detailed and concrete in DSM-IIIR.

The explicitness of the DSM-IIIR criteria can be expected to reduce the descriptive inadequacies found by Beck and his colleagues to be the major source of diagnostic unreliability. Results of field testing of DSM-

TABLE 3.3
Description of manic disorder in DSM-II versus DSM-IIIR

> **DSM-II (APA, 1968, p. 36)**
>
> _Manic-depressive illness, manic type._ This disorder consists exclusively of manic episodes. These episodes are characterized by excessive elation, irritability, talkativeness, flight of ideas, and accelerated speech and motor activity. Brief periods of depression sometimes occur, but they are never true depressive episodes.
>
> **Diagnostic Criteria for Manic Syndrome, (APA, 1987, p. 219)***
>
> A. A distinct period of abnormally and persistently elevated, expansive, or irritable mood.
> B. During the period of mood disturbance, at least three of the following symptoms have persisted (four if the mood is only irritable) and have been present to a significant degree:
> (1) inflated self-esteem or grandiosity
> (2) decreased need for sleep, e.g., feels rested after only three hours of sleep.
> (3) more talkative than usual or pressure to keep talking
> (4) flight of ideas or subjective experience that thoughts are racing
> (5) distractibility, i.e., attention too easily drawn to unimportant or irrelevant external stimuli
> (6) increase in goal-directed activity (either socially, at work or school, or sexually) or psychomotor agitation
> (7) excessive involvement in pleasurable activities which have a high potential for painful consequences, e.g., the person engages in unrestrained buying sprees, sexual indiscretions, or foolish business investments
> C. Mood disturbance sufficiently severe to cause marked impairment in occupational functioning or in usual social activities or relationships with others, or to necessitate hospitalization to prevent harm to self or others.

Reprinted with permission from the _Diagnostic and Statistical Manual of Mental Disorders, Third Edition, Revised._ Copyright 1987 American Psychiatric Association.

III were reported in the manual itself and are shown in Table 3.4. As can be seen, the reliabilities vary but are quite acceptable for most of the major categories.[7]

Thus far the description of DSM-III and DSM-IIIR have been in positive terms. The attainment of adequate diagnostic reliability is a considerable achievement, but problems remain. It is unclear, for example, whether

---

[7]Progress has also been made in dealing with the second largest source of diagnostic unreliability, inconsistency on the part of the diagnostician. The use of standardized, reliably scored interviews, discussed in the following chapter, greatly reduces this problem.

TABLE 3.4
Reliabilities for major diagnostic categories achieved in field trials with DSM-III*

Diagnostic Category	Reliability†
Disorders Usually First Evident in Infancy, Childhood, or Adolescence	.65
Organic Mental Disorders	.79
Substance Use Disorders	.86
Schizophrenic Disorders	.81
Paranoid Disorders	.66
Affective Disorders	.69
Anxiety Disorders	.63
Somatoform Disorders	.54
Dissociative Disorders	.80
Psychosexual Disorders	.92
Psychological Factors Affecting Physical Condition	.62
Personality Disorders	.56

*The data shown are from phase I of the field trial. The number of patients was 339.

†These reliabilities use a statistic called kappa, which reflects the percent agreement corrected for chance agreements.

the rules for making diagnostic decisions are ideal. Examining Table 3.3, we see that for patients to be diagnosed as suffering from mania, they must have three symptoms from a list of seven, or four if their mood is irritable. But the reason why three symptoms rather than two or five were selected is unknown (see Finn, 1982). Furthermore, the reliability of axes I and II may not always be as high in everyday usage, for diagnosticians may not adhere as precisely to the criteria as have those whose work was being scrutinized in formal studies. And although the improved reliability of DSM-IIIR _may_ lead to more validity, there is no guarantee that it will. The diagnoses made according to it may not reveal anything useful about the patients. Moreover, subjective factors still play a role in evaluations made according to DSM-IIIR. Consider again the criteria for manic syndrome in Table 3.3. What exactly does it mean to say that the elevated mood must be abnormally and persistently "elevated"? Or what level of involvement in activities with high potential for painful consequences is "excessive?" As another example, on axis V the clinician must judge the patient's highest level of adaptive functioning in the preceding year. The clinician determines what, for the patient, is adaptive and how his or her behavior compares with that of an average person. As Taylor (1983) cautioned for DSM-III, such a judgment sets the stage for cultural biases to creep in, as well as the clinician's own personal ideas of what the average person _should_ be doing at a given stage of life and in particular circumstances. Finally, not all DSM-IIIR classification changes seem positive. The developmental disorders of childhood—of reading, arithmetic, and language—really cover the waterfront! Should a problem like difficulty in learning arithmetic be considered a "psychiatric disorder"? By expanding its coverage, DSM-III and DSM-IIIR seem to have made too many childhood problems into psychiatric disorders, without good justification for doing so.

In sum, although we regard DSM-IIIR as promising, it is far from perfect. Throughout this book, as we present the literature on various disorders, there will be further opportunities to describe both the strengths and weaknesses of this most recent effort of health professionals to categorize mental disorders. What is most heartening about DSM-III and DSM-IIIR, however, is that their attempt to be explicit about the rules for diagnosis will make it easy to detect problems in the diagnostic system. We can expect more changes and refinements over the next several years. In fact, DSM-IV is already in the works.[8]

---

[8]An initial draft of DSM-IV is expected in 1990 and a final one by the end of 1992. Although continuing refinement of diagnostic criteria is certainly desirable, the pace of these revisions may have outpaced real gains in knowledge (Zimmerman, 1988); DSM-IIIR was published in 1987, with the major work toward producing DSM-IV occurring only two or three years later. This short interval barely allows clinicians and researchers to become familiar with one manual and does not permit DSM-IV to really be based on an accumulation of new research.

Summary

The third edition of the *Diagnostic and Statistical Manual of Mental Disorders* (DSM-III), published in 1980 by the American Psychiatric Association, and its revision DSM-IIIR, published in 1987, are the latest in a series of efforts by mental health professionals to categorize the various psychopathologies. A novel feature of these symptoms is their multiaxial organization; every time a diagnosis is made, the clinician must describe the patient's condition according to each of five axes, or dimensions. Axes I and II make up the mental disorders per se; on axis III are listed any physical disorders believed to bear on the mental disorder in question; axis IV is used to indicate the degree of psychological stress the person has been experiencing; and axis V rates the person's highest level of adaptive functioning during the preceding year. A multiaxial diagnosis is believed to provide a more adequate and useful description of the patient's mental disorder.

Both general and specific issues in the classification of abnormality were discussed. Because DSM-III and DSM-IIIR are far more concrete and descriptive than DSM-II, diagnoses based on them are more reliable. Validity, however, remains an open question. It is too soon to know whether more useful knowledge about psychopathology, its prevention, and treatment will be gained through widespread use of DSM-IIIR.

Chapter 4

Clinical Assessment Procedures

Assessment of Psychopathology
> *Clinical Interviews*
> *Psychological Tests*

Assessment of Brain Abnormalities
> *"Seeing" the Brain*
> *Neuropsychological Assessment*

Behavioral Assessment
> *Direct Observation of Behavior*
> *Interviews and Self-Report Measures*
> *Cognitive Assessment*
> *Physiological Measurement*
> *Behavioral Assessment for Behavioral Change*
> *Reliability of Behavioral Assessment*
> *Validity of Behavioral Assessment*

The Consistency and Variability of Behavior

Summary

The account with which this book began, that of the policeman with drinking and marital problems, allowed no opportunity to find out why he was behaving as he was. We did not learn more about him by any of the means commonly available to clinicians—interviews, tests, and a variety of other procedures for assessing behavior. These modes of assessment may occasionally be given different, perhaps more impressive-sounding names. An interview may be called "the psychiatric interview," "the diagnostic interview," or "a depth interview"; tests may be "psychologicals" or "projectives." All clinical *assessment procedures* are more or less formal ways of finding out what is wrong with a person, what may have caused a problem or problems, and what steps may be taken to improve the individual's condition. Some of these procedures are also used to evaluate the effects of therapeutic interventions.

Assessment of Psychopathology

Clinical Interviews

Most of us have probably been interviewed at one time or another, although the conversation may have been so informal that it was not regarded as an interview. To the layperson the word interview connotes a formal, highly structured conversation, but we find it useful to construe the term as any interpersonal encounter, conversational in style, in which one person, the interviewer, uses language as the principal means of finding out about another, the interviewee. Thus a Gallup pollster who asks a college student whom she will vote for in an upcoming presidential election is interviewing with the restricted goal of learning which candidate she prefers. A clinical psychologist who asks a patient about the circumstances of his most recent hospitalization is similarly conducting an interview.

One way in which a *clinical interview* is perhaps different from a casual conversation and from a poll is the attention the interviewer pays to *how* the respondent answers questions—or does not answer them. For example, if a client is recounting her marital conflicts, the clinician will generally be attentive to any emotion accompanying her comments. If the woman does not seem upset about a difficult situation, her answers will probably be interpreted differently than if she were to cry while relating her story.

The paradigm within which an interviewer operates determines the type of information sought and obtained. A psychoanalytically trained clinician can be expected to inquire about the person's childhood history. He or she is also likely to remain skeptical of the verbal reports because the analytic paradigm holds that the most significant aspects of a disturbed or normal person's developmental history are repressed into the unconscious. By the same token, the behaviorally oriented clinician is likely to focus on current environmental conditions that can be related to changes in the person's behavior, for example, trying to determine the circumstances under which the person may become anxious. Thus the clinical interview does not follow a prescribed course but varies with the paradigm adopted by the interviewer. Like scientists, clinical interviewers in some measure find only the information that they look for (Box 4.1).

Great skill is necessary to carry out good clinical interviews, for they are conducted with people who are often under considerable personal stress. Clinicians, regardless of their theoretical orientations, recognize the importance of establishing **rapport** with the client. The interviewer must obtain the trust of the person; it is naive to assume that a client will easily reveal information to another, even to an authority figure with the title "Dr." Furthermore, even a client who sincerely, perhaps desperately, wants to recount intensely personal problems to a professional may not be able to do so without assistance. Indeed, psychodynamic and humanistic clinicians assume that people entering therapy usually are not even aware of what is truly bothering them. Behavioral clinicians, although concentrating more on observables, also appreciate the difficulties people have in sorting out the factors responsible for their distress.

Most clinicians employ the kinds of empathy statements discussed in connection with humanistic therapy (see page 525) to draw clients out, to encourage them to elaborate on their concerns, and to examine different facets of a problem. A simple summary statement of what the client has been saying can help sustain the momentum of talk about painful and possibly embarrassing events and feelings, and an accepting attitude toward personal disclosures dispels the fear that revealing terrible secrets to another human being will have disastrous consequences.

Vast amounts of information can be obtained by means of the interview; its importance in abnormal psychology and psychiatry is unquestioned. Whether the information gleaned can always be depended on is not so clear, however. Clinicians often tend to overlook *situational* factors of the interview that may exert strong influences on what the patient says or does. Consider, for a moment, how a teenager is likely to respond to the question "How often have you used illegal drugs?" when it is asked by a young, informally dressed psychologist and again when it is asked by a sixty-year-old psychologist in a three-piece suit.

BOX 4.1

WHAT HAPPENS WHEN MINORITY CULTURAL DIFFERENCES ARE CONSIDERED IN PSYCHODIAGNOSIS?

If a diagnostician is trying to understand a seemingly abnormal behavior in a member of a minority group—a Black or Hispanic, for example— will he or she best serve the mental health interests of that patient by attending to cultural factors that may distinguish the patient from the majority culture in which he or she lives? If, for instance, the clinician is assessing a Hispanic man who is very emotionally withdrawn, should the clinician consider that lower levels of emotional expressiveness are positively sanctioned among Latins as compared to the Caucasian culture that predominates in this country at this time? In so doing, will the clinician thereby tend to *normalize* this behavior, that is, not believe that it reflects an emotional *disorder*, whereas if the same behavior were found in a Caucasian of the same age, the clinician might find it to be unusual enough to be judged abnormal?

These subtle questions have been addressed in the work of Lopez and his associates at the University of Southern California. The answers are far from clear. In an initial study, Lopez and Hernandez (1986) cast doubt on the idea that including cultural differences in one's diagnostic work necessarily contributes to an accurate and helpful diagnosis. They surveyed a large sample of mental health practitioners in California and found that sometimes clinicians *minimized* the seriousness of a patient's problems by attributing them to a subcultural norm. For example, one clinician reported attaching less psychopathological significance to a Black woman's hallucinations because of his belief that hallucinations are more prevalent among Blacks than among whites. As a result of this, the clinician did not consider a diagnosis of schizophrenia, a decision that may not have been in the woman's best interests. The thrust of this study is that by being respectful and mindful of cultural differences—and believing that what is abnormal in one culture may be normal in another—clinicians can err on the side of minimizing problems and hence reduce the chances of providing appropriate professional intervention.

Lopez extended this study of perceptual bias by examining eleven widely used diagnostic criteria and interview schedules for schizophrenia, affective disorders, and personality disorders (Lopez and Nunez, 1987). Included in these measures and nosologies were several already mentioned or soon to be discussed in this book: the DSM-III (American Psychiatric Association, 1980), the Research Diagnostic Criteria (Spitzer, Endicott, and Robins, 1977), the Diagnostic Interview Schedule (Robins, Helzer, Croughan, and Ratliff, 1981), and the Schedule for Affective Disorders and Schizophrenia (the SADS; Spitzer and Endicott, 1978). If a client's cultural background is considered when making diagnoses, cultural factors will begin to appear in standard diagnostic instruments. If so, this

Cultural differences, although of some potential importance, are not given much attention in DSM-IIIR.

inclusion may be seen as a reflection of the mental health establishment's sensitivity to cultural differences in psychopathology. Furthermore, if cultural factors are found in widely employed instruments, the cognitive activities of clinicians are likely to be shaped or informed by this inclusion; the diagnostic work of clinicians in the field will be marked by a consideration of cultural factors in psychopathology.

The results of the Lopez and Nunez study indicate very minimal mention of cultural variables. The DSM-III, for example, contained only one cultural reference for the three groups of disorders.* Overall, of the eleven instruments, although eight did consider culture, they referred to it very infrequently, revealing an insensitivity to cultural differences in psychopathology.

Taken together the findings of these two studies present a conundrum for the clinician who would include cultural factors in his or her diagnoses of minority patients. If one is sensitive to the role of culture and cultural differences, then one might well interpret a given behavior that is not typical of the general culture as due to a cultural difference and therefore not a sign of psychopathology. If, on the other hand, as Lopez and Hernandez suggest, one recognizes that such an attribution may discourage the clinician from justifiably attributing a behavior to psychopathology, then one should *overlook* or at least downplay the significance of cultural factors when diagnosing and treating a minority client lest one fail to attribute an unusual behavior to a mental disorder and, in so doing, deny necessary care to the client.

---

*It should be mentioned that the DSM-IIIR has more.

The clinical interview is the principal means of collecting information for a diagnosis.

Interviews may vary in the degree to which they are structured. In practice, most clinicians operate from only the vaguest outlines. Exactly *how* such information is collected is left largely up to the particular interviewer. Through years of clinical experience and both teaching and learning from students and colleagues, each clinician has developed ways of asking questions with which he or she is comfortable and which seem to extract the information that will be of maximum benefit to the client. Thus, to the extent that an interview is unstructured, the interviewer must rely on intuition and general experience.

There are times when mental health professionals need to collect standardized information, particularly for making diagnostic judgments on operational criteria. To meet that need, investigators have developed structured interviews such as the Schedule for Affective Disorders and Schizophrenia (Spitzer and Endicott, 1978), which was devised to provide a standard set of questions to elicit the information needed for DSM-III diagnoses. The Structured Clinical Interview for DSM-IIIR (SCID) (Spitzer and Williams, 1985) is now being used by many because its questions allow the best fit to current diagnostic criteria. The SCID is a branching interview (the client's response determines the next question), with detailed instructions to the interviewer concerning when to probe in detail and when to go on to questions about another diagnosis. Most symptoms

are rated on a three-point scale of severity with instructions in the interview schedule for directly translating the symptom ratings into diagnoses. The initial questions pertaining to obsessive-compulsive disorder are presented in Table 4.1. The interviewer begins by asking about obsessions. If the responses elicit a rating of 1 (absent), the interviewer turns to questions about compulsions. If the patient's responses again elicit a rating of 1, the interviewer is instructed to go to the questions for generalized anxiety disorder (GAD). On the other hand, if positive responses are elicited, the interviewer continues with further questions about obsessive-compulsive disorder. Like its predecessor, the Schedule for Affective Disorders and Schizophrenia (Spitzer and Endicott, 1978), the SCID is an important tool for collecting information to make diagnoses. Indeed, the use of structured interviews is clearly a major factor in the improvement of diagnostic reliability that we described in Chapter 3.

Psychological Tests

Psychological tests structure still further the process of assessment. The same test is administered to many people at different times, and the responses collected are analyzed to indicate how certain kinds of people tend to respond. Statistical norms for the test can thereby be established as soon as the data collected are extensive

TABLE 4.1

Section from the Structural Clinical Interview for DSM-IIIR pertaining to Obsessive-compulsive disorder (after Spitzer and Williams, 1985).

Obsessive-Compulsive Disorder Criteria	Interview
Obsessions: (1) Recurrent, persistent ideas, thoughts, impulses, or images that are experienced as intrusive, unwanted, and senseless or repugnant (at least initially). (2) The individual attempts to ignore or suppress them or to neutralize them with some other thought or action. (3) The individual recognizes that they are the product of his or her own mind and not imposed from without (as in thought insertion). **Compulsions:** (1) Repetitive, purposeful and intentional behavior that is performed according to certain rules or in a stereotyped fashion. (2) The behavior is not an end in itself, but is designed to neutralize or prevent extreme discomfort or some dreaded event or situation. However, either the activity is not connected in a realistic way with what it is designed to neutralize or prevent or it is clearly excessive.	**Rating Scale** ? 1 2 3 I would like to ask you if you have ever been bothered by thoughts that kept coming back to you even when you tried not to have them? ? 1 2 3 IF YES: DISTINGUISH FROM BROODING ABOUT PROBLEMS (SUCH AS HAVING A PANIC ATTACK) OR ANXIOUS RUMINATION ABOUT REALISTIC DANGERS: What were they? ? 1 2 3 (What about awful thoughts, or thoughts that didn't make any sense to you—like actually hurting someone even though you didn't want to, or being contaminated by germs or dirt?) [GO TO COMPULSIONS] [DESCRIBE OBSESSIONS] ? 1 2 3 Was there anything that you had to do over and over again and couldn't resist doing, like washing your hands again and again, or checking something several times to make sure you'd done it right? ? 1 2 3 IF YES: What did you have to do? (What were you afraid would happen if you didn't do it?) (How many times did you have to ____? How much time did you spend each day ____?) [GO TO GENERAL ANXIETY DISORDERS SECTION] [DESCRIBE COMPULSIONS] Key to rating scale ? = Inadequate information 1 = Absent or false 2 = Subthreshold 3 = Threshold or true

enough. This process is called **standardization.** The responses of a particular patient can then be compared to the statistical norms. The three basic types are projective personality tests, self-report personality inventories, and tests of intelligence.

Projective Personality Tests

The **Rorschach inkblot test** and the **Thematic Apperception Test** are perhaps the best known **projective techniques.** In both of these tests a set of standard stimuli, vague enough to allow variation in responses, is presented to an individual. In an inkblot test the subject is shown ten blots, one at a time, and asked to tell what figures or objects he or she sees in each of them. Half of the inkblots are in black, white, and shades of gray, two add red splotches, and three are in pastel colors. In the Thematic Apperception Test (TAT), the examinee is shown a series of black and white pictures one by one and asked to tell a story related to each. In both these tests it is assumed that because the stimulus materials are unstructured, the patient's responses will be determined primarily by unconscious processes and will reveal his or her own attitudes, motivations, and modes of behavior. This referred to as the **projective hypothesis.** For example, reporting that one sees eyes on the Rorschach has been said to indicate paranoia. Those of the psychoanalytic bent tend to favor such tests because a preference for ambiguous stimuli is entirely consistent with the psychoanalytic assumption that people defend against unpleasant thoughts and feelings by repressing them into the unconscious. In order to bypass the defense mechanism of repression (see page 36) and get to the basic causes of distress, the real purposes of a test are best left unclear. Indeed, this has to be the case, for psychoanalytic theory asserts that the factors of greatest importance are unconscious.

As might be imagined, the interpretation of the responses to projective tests poses a severe problem, for the examinee is not merely answering yes or no to a series of questions or indicating which of a series of statements are true and which are false. Rather, the person is providing a complex response to a complex stimulus, which is, by design, open to an immense range of interpretations. In many instances the reliability of the scoring of the Rorschach and Thematic Apperception tests is quite low. With extensive training in a particular scoring system, however, examiners can achieve satisfactory levels of agreement (Goldfried, Stricker, and Weiner, 1971). A more serious problem is the often low validities of responses in projective tests. We assume that these responses tell us something important and useful about the person. But as Nunnally (1967) has written,

Picture from the Thematic Apperception Test, introduced in 1935 by Henry Murray and his associates at the Harvard Psychological Clinic. Like the Rorschach, this projective test is designed to reveal unconscious conflicts and concerns.

most projective techniques do a rather poor job of measuring personality traits. . . . In applied settings, the evidence is clear that projective techniques have, at most, only a low level of validity. . . . They do a poor job of differentiating normal people from people who are diagnosed as neurotic and they do a poor job of differentiating various types of mentally ill persons. (p. 497)

The preceding discussion of the Rorschach reflects how these tests were conceptualized and used originally, that is, as a stimulus to fantasy that was assumed to bypass ego defenses. The person's responses were viewed as *symbolic* of internal dynamics, for example, judging a person to have homosexual interests on the basis of his seeing buttocks in the inkblots (Chapman and Chapman, 1969). Current use of the Rorschach concentrates more on the *form* of the person's responses (Exner, 1978), and this approach is of much greater interest nowadays to clinicians. The test is considered more as a perceptual-cognitive task, and the person's responses now are viewed as a sample of how they perceptually and cognitively organize real-life situations. For example, Erdberg and Exner (1984) conclude

Hermann Rorschach (1884–1922), Swiss psychiatrist who during a ride in the country with his two children noticed that what they saw in clouds reflected their personalities. From this observation came his famous inkblot test.

from the literature that respondents who express a great deal of human movement in their Rorschach responses tend to use inner resources when coping with their needs, whereas those whose Rorschach responses can be characterized as involving color are more likely to seek interaction with the environment (p. 335). Rorschach himself suggested this approach in his original manual, *Psychodiagnostics: A Diagnostic Test Based on Perception* (1921), but he died only eight months after publishing his ten inkblots, and his immediate followers devised other methods of interpreting the test.

Personality Inventories

In *personality inventories* examinees are asked to indicate whether a large number of statements do or do not apply to them. The investigators who have been involved in the construction of such *self-report* instruments have usually been well schooled in the general principles of test construction and standardization. It is therefore rare for a personality inventory to lack reliability. Validity, however, still presents a problem, especially if the personality inventory has been designed to reveal unconscious conflicts and the like. Some per-

Inkblots resembling those used by Rorschach.

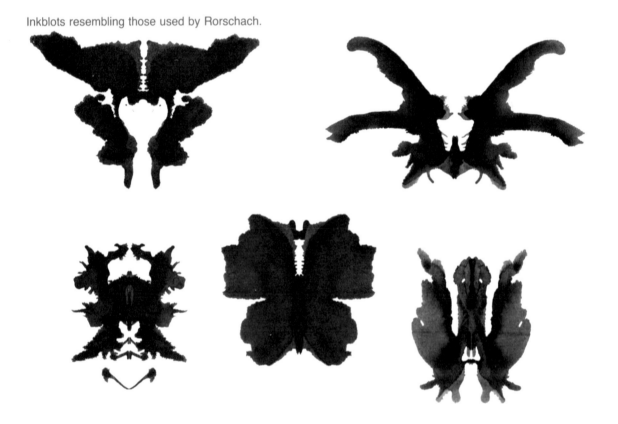

TABLE 4.2
Typical clinical interpretations of items similar to those on the MMPI (*adapted from Kleinmuntz, 1967*)

Scale	Sample Item	Interpretation
Cannot say	This is merely the number of items marked in the "cannot say" category.	A high score indicates evasiveness.
Lie	I have never had a bad night's sleep (false).*	Persons trying to look good (i.e., wholesome, honest) obtain high scores.
Frequency	Everything tastes salty (true).	High scores on this scale suggest lack of interest or a wish to appear abnormal.
Correction	I am more satisfied with my life than most of my friends (true).	High scores on this scale suggest a guarded test-taking attitude.
Hypochondriasis	I wake up tired most mornings (true).	High scorers have been described as cynical and dissatisfied.
Depression	I rarely see the bright side of things (true).	High scorers are usually withdrawn, sad, and troubled.
Hysteria	My fingers sometimes feel numb (true).	High scorers have multiple bodily complaints.
Psychopathic deviate	I did not like school (true).	High scorers tend to be adventurous and antisocial.
Masculinity-femininity	I do not like sports (true).	Men with high scores tend to be artistic and sensitive. High-scoring women have been described as rebellious and assertive.
Paranoia	I am envied by many people (true).	High scorers on this scale tend to be suspicious and jealous.
Psychasthenia	I have a great deal of self-confidence (false).	High scorers are described as anxious, self-doubting, and rigid.
Schizophrenia	I sometimes smell strange odors (true).	Adjectives such as seclusive and bizarre describe high scorers.
Hypomania	I never have any difficulty making decisions (true).	High scorers tend to be outgoing and impulsive.
Social introversion–extroversion	I avoid getting together with people (true).	High scorers are modest and shy; low scorers are sociable and exhibitionistic.

* The true or false responses in parentheses indicate the answer expected if the respondent is to accumulate a high score on this scale.

sonality inventories have been constructed with more specific purposes in mind. Perhaps the best known of these is the Minnesota Multiphasic Personality Inventory (MMPI), which was developed in the early 1940s as an inexpensive device to simplify the differential diagnosis of mental patients. The inventory is called multiphasic because it was designed to detect a number of psychiatric problems.

In developing the test, the investigators relied on factual information. First, many clinicians provided large numbers of statements that they considered indicative of various mental problems. Second, these items were rated as self-descriptive or not by people already diagnosed as having particular disorders. Items that served to discriminate among the patients were retained: that is, items were selected if patients in one clinical group responded to them more often in a certain way than did those in other groups. With additional refinements, sets of these items were established as scales for determining whether or not a respondent should be diagnosed in a particular way. If the individual answered a large number of the items in a scale in the same way as had a certain diagnostic group, his or her behavior was expected to resemble that of the particular diagnostic group. The scales of the instrument do, in fact, relate well to psychiatric diagnoses. Thus the MMPI has been widely used to screen large groups of people for whom clinical interviews are not feasible. Items similar to those on the various scales are presented in Table 4.2.[1] There are several commercial MMPI computerized services that score the test and provide narratives about the respondent. Of course the validity and usefulness of the printout is only as good as the program, which in turn is only as good as the competency and experience of the psychologist who wrote it. Figure 4.1 shows a hypothetical profile. These profiles are used in conjunction with a therapist's evaluation to help diagnose a client.

We may well wonder whether answers that would designate the subject as normal might not be easy to fake. A superficial knowledge of contemporary abnormal psychology would alert even a seriously disturbed person to the fact that, if he wants to be regarded as normal, he must not admit to worrying a great deal about germs on doorknobs. In fact, there is evidence that these tests *can* be "psyched out." In many testing circumstances, however, people do not *want* to falsify their responses, for they want to be helped. Moreover, the test designers have included as part of the MMPI several scales designed to detect deliberately faked responses (see Table 4.2). In one of these, the lie scale,

a series of statements sets a trap for the person who is trying to "look too good." One such item from the lie scale declares "I read the newspaper editorials every night." The assumption is that few people would be able to endorse such a statement honestly. Thus persons who do endorse a large number of the statements in the lie scale might well be attempting to present themselves in a particularly good light. Their scores on other scales are usually viewed with more than the usual skepticism.

Tests such as the MMPI are subject to certain other difficulties. It has been found that many people tend to answer test questions on bases other than the specific content of the question. For example, suppose that a test statement reads, "I attend a party at least once a week." If the individual answers "Yes," or "True," can we conclude without reservation that he or she really attends social gatherings frequently? Research suggests that such answers cannot be accepted as necessarily true, for a certain test-taking or questionnaire "set" may have determined the response. In this instance the subject may have a *social desirability* response set and, believing that attending parties frequently is the "right" thing to do, says "Yes" on this basis. Fortunately, psychologists have developed ways to reduce the influence of such response sets (see Edwards, 1957).

Aptitude tests like the SAT and GRE are taken by large numbers of people.

---

[1]The manner in which the MMPI was constructed is referred to as *empirical*, that is, relying on data or experience rather than speculation. It is also worth noting that the MMPI's diagnostic scheme for the most part incorporated symptoms later listed in the DSM. Not surprisingly, clinicians who disliked the DSM were unenthusiastic about the MMPI. Moreover, because the MMPI was devised using an older diagnostic system, it may not predict DSM-III diagnoses well. Winters, Weintraub, and Neale (1981), for example, found that the MMPI did very poorly in predicting the DSM-III diagnosis of schizophrenia. As this book goes to press, a new version of this widely used test is scheduled for publication. The MMPI-2 has several noteworthy changes designed to improve its validity and acceptability. The original sample fifty years ago lacked representation of racial minorities such as Blacks and native Americans, restricting its standardization sample to men and women who were white, essentially rural Minnesotans; the new version was standardized with a much larger sample that is more similar to 1980 U.S. census figures. A number of items containing allusions to sexual adjustment, bowel and bladder functions, and excessive religiosity have been removed because they were judged in some testing contexts to be needlessly intrusive and objectionable. Sexist wording has been eliminated along with outmoded idioms. Several new items have been added that deal with substance abuse, Type A behavior (see page 203), eating disorders, and interpersonal relationships. The new MMPI is otherwise quite similar to the original, yielding the same scale scores, having the same format, and in general providing continuity with the vast literature already existing on the original MMPI.

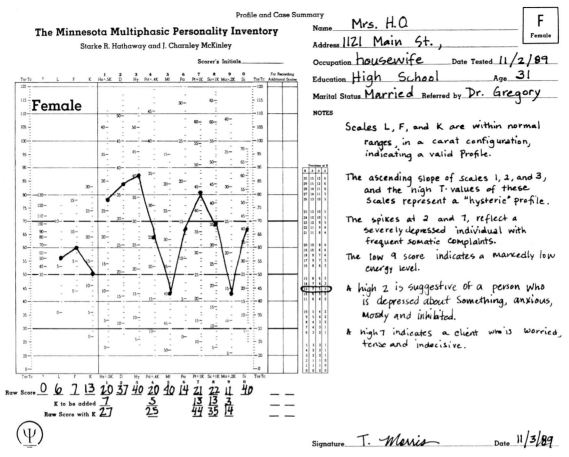

FIGURE 4.1
Hypothetical MMPI profile.

Intelligence Tests

Psychological measures of intelligence play a central role in diagnoses of mental retardation. Alfred Binet, a French psychologist, originally constructed mental tests to help the Parisian school board predict which children were in need of special schooling. *Intelligence testing* has since developed into one of the largest psychological industries. The word aptitude is frequently applied to these widely used standardized procedures. The Scholastic Aptitude Test, the Graduate Record Examination, and the individually administered tests, such as the Wechsler Adult Intelligence Scale and the Stanford-Binet, are all based on the assumption that one sample from an individual's current intellectual functioning can predict how well he or she will perform in school. These tests have other uses as well: in conjunction with achievement tests, to diagnose learning disabilities and to identify areas of strengths and weaknesses for academic planning; to identify children of unusual intellectual potential, the gifted, so that appropriate instruction can be provided them in school; and as part of neuropsychological evaluations, for example, testing periodically a person believed to be suffering from a degenerative dementia so that deterioration of mental ability can be followed over time. Indeed, the Wechsler Adult Intelligence Scale is often used as part of a neuropsychological test battery, an area of assessment we discuss in the next section.

When such tests are evaluated, it is important to keep in mind two points that are only infrequently made explicit by those who have a heavy professional commitment to intelligence testing. First, strictly speaking, the tests measure only what a psychologist considers intelligence to be. The tasks and items on an IQ test are, after all, invented by psychologists—they did not come down to us inscribed on stone tablets. Second,

Psychologist administering the block design subtest of the Wechsler Adult Intelligence Scale. The examinee must manipulate the blocks to duplicate a pattern shown in the small book.

the tests are used widely because they do indeed accomplish what they were designed for, that is, predict who will succeed in our educational system. If and when there are major changes in our school systems, we can expect analogous changes in our definition and assessment of intelligence. Further discussion of IQ tests can be found in Chapter 16.

Assessment of Brain Abnormalities

"Seeing" the Brain

As indicated in Chapter 3, one major section of DSM-IIIR, Organic Mental Disorders, refers to behavioral problems brought on by brain abnormalities. Neurological tests such as checking the patellar reflex, examining the retina for any indication of blood vessel damage, and evaluating motor coordination and perception are useful procedures in diagnosing brain dysfunction. The X-ray can sometimes detect tumors, and the electroencephalograph (EEG) detects abnormalities in the brain's electrical activity (see Chapter 10, p. 266).

Computerized axial tomography, the **CAT scan**, and positron emission tomography, the **PET scan**, are recent advances in assessing brain abnormalities. In the CAT scanner a moving beam of X-rays passes into a horizontal cross section of the patient's brain, scanning it throughout 360 degrees. The moving X-ray detector on the other side measures the amount of radioactivity that gets through; thus it detects subtle differences in tissue density. The computer takes the information and constructs a two-dimensional, detailed image of the cross section, giving it optimal contrasts. Then the patient's head is moved, and the machine scans another cross section of his or her brain. The resulting images can show the locations of tumors and blood clots and the enlargement of ventricles (see page 638), which signals degeneration of tissue.

In PET scanning, a more expensive and invasive procedure, a substance used by the brain is labeled with a short-lived radioactive isotope and injected into the bloodstream of the patient. The radioactive molecules of the substance emit a particle called a positron, which quickly collides with an electron. A pair of high-energy light particles shoot out from the skull in opposite directions and are detected by the scanner. The computer analyzes millions of such recordings and converts them into a motion picture of the functioning brain in horizontal cross section, projected onto a television screen. The images are in color; fuzzy spots of lighter and warmer colors are areas in which metabolic rates for the substance are higher. Moving visual images of the working brain can indicate sites of epileptic seizures, brain cancers, strokes, and trauma from head injuries, as well as the distribution in the brain of psychoactive drugs. The PET scanner is also being used to study possible abnormal physiological processes underlying disorders (see Chapter 14, p. 393).

Newly developed computer-based devices for seeing into the living brain include nuclear magnetic response imaging (NMR), which is superior to CAT scans because it produces pictures of higher quality and does not rely on even the small amount of radiation that CAT (and PET) requires. In NMR the person is placed inside a large circular magnet that causes the hydrogen atoms in the body to move. When the magnetic force is turned off, the atoms return to their original position and thereby produce an electromagnetic signal. These signals are then "read" by the computer and translated into black and white pictures of brain tissue. The implication of this technique's potential is enormous. It may allow us to specify the origin of different abnormalities. All these tools provide startling "pictures" of internal organs and permit the gathering of information about living tissue, including the brain, which neuroscientists, mental health investigators, and medical researchers and practitioners can use both to discover hitherto undetectable tumors and other organic problems and to conduct inquiries into the neural bases of thought, emotion, and behavior.

NMR scanning provides better pictures of the brain than those of the CAT scan.

We might reasonably assume that neurologists[2] and physicians, with the help of such procedures and technological devices, can observe the brain and its functions more or less directly and thus assess brain abnormalities. Many brain abnormalities and injuries, however, involve alterations in structure so subtle or slight in extent that they have thus far eluded direct physical examination.[3]

Neuropsychological Assessment

Since the way the person functions is the problem—what he or she does, says, thinks, or feels—a number of tests assessing behavioral disturbances that are caused by organic brain dysfunctions have been developed by psychologists. The literature on these tests is extensive and, as with most areas of psychology, so too is dis-

agreement about them. The weight of the evidence, however, does seem to indicate that psychological tests have some validity in the assessment of brain damage. They are accordingly called **neuropsychological tests.** One of them is Reitan's modification of a battery or group of tests previously developed by Halstead. The concept of using a battery of tests, each tapping different functions, is critical, for only by studying a person's pattern of performance can an investigator judge accurately whether the person is indeed brain-damaged. But the Halstead–Reitan battery can do even more than this: it can locate the area of the brain that has been affected. Some of the tests in the battery are the following.

1. **Tactual Performance Test.** While blindfolded, the subject tries to fit variously shaped blocks into spaces in a board, using each hand in turn. After finishing this part of the test, the subject tries to draw the board from memory, showing the spaces and the blocks filling them in their proper locations. The purpose of this test is to measure the patient's motor speed response to the unfamiliar and ability to learn to use tactile and kinesthetic cues.

2. **Trail-Making Test.** See Figure 4.2.

3. **Finger Oscillation Task.** In this procedure the subject depresses a key with the index finger as fast as he or she can for five trials of ten seconds each.

4. **Category Test.** The subject, seeing an image on a screen that suggests one of the numbers between one and four, presses a button to show which number he or she thinks it is. A bell indicates that the choice is correct, a buzzer that it is wrong. The subject must keep track of these images and signals in order to figure out the rules for making the correct choices.

---

[2]A neurologist is different from a neuropsychologist, even though both specialists are concerned with the study of the central nervous system. A neurologist is a physician who specializes in medical diseases that affect the nervous system, such as muscular dystrophy or cerebral palsy. A neuropsychologist is a psychologist who studies how dysfunctions of the brain affect the way we think, feel, and behave. As the term implies, a neuropsychologist is trained as a psychologist and, as such, is interested in behavior, but with a focus on the way abnormalities of the brain affect behavior in deleterious ways. Both kinds of specialists contribute much to each other as they work in different ways to learn how the nervous system works and how to ameliorate problems caused by disease or injury to the brain.

[3]Boll (1985), a well-known neuropsychologist, warns us not to be complacent about not finding effects of brain insults or disease using currently available techniques: "Each new diagnostic technique, designed to assess the anatomical, physiological, and behavioral capacity of individuals, has, without exception, been able to document the presence rather than the absence of conditions which have previously not been identifiable but rather considered as basically unreal, or not actually present" (p. 480).

FIGURE 4.2
Sample item from the Trail-Making Test. The subject is instructed to alternate numbers and letters, for example, by drawing a line from 1 to A, A to 2, 2 to B, and so on.

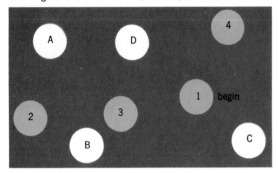

5. Aphasia Screening Test. A number of language abilities are studied by asking the subject to name objects, to identify letters and numbers, to spell, read, write, and pronounce words, to do arithmetic calculations, to identify body parts and pantomime simple actions, and to follow directions.

Performance on the tests is interpreted by drawing on knowledge of the relation between certain brain structures and behavior. Finger tapping, for example, is thought to be controlled by a brain area just in front of the central sulcus (see Box A.1). Control of speech and language tends to be localized in the left cerebral hemisphere. Thus particular deficits suggest that a problem exists in a specific brain area and in one or the other hemisphere.

The Luria–Nebraska battery (Golden, Hammeke, and Purisch, 1978), based on the work of the Russian psychologist Aleksandr Luria (1902–1977), is currently being both widely promoted as an effective neuropsychological test and subjected to much critical scrutiny (Adams, 1980; Kane, Parsons, and Goldstein, 1985; Spiers, 1982). A battery of 269 items makes up 11 sections to determine basic and complex motor skills, rhythm and pitch abilities, tactile and kinesthetic skills, verbal and spatial skills, receptive speech ability, expressive speech ability, writing, reading, arithmetical skills, memory, and intellectual processes. The pattern of scores on these sections, as well as on the pathognomonic scale, the thirty-two items found to be the most discriminating and indicative of overall impairment, reveals damage to the frontal, temporal, sensorimotor, or parietal-occipital area (see Box A.1) of the right or left hemisphere.

For example, patients with lesions in the frontal lobe of the left hemisphere have very high scores—with this battery a zero is given for no errors on the pathognomonic scale. Expressive speech is more extensively disrupted than receptive ability, and motor impairment is greater than tactile. As for motor impairment, patients do better on items testing fine coordination than on those testing complex, sequential movements. High scores on the arithmetic, memory, and intelligence sections indicate severe injuries to the left frontal lobe. Patients with damage in the right parietal-occipital area have generally equal motor and tactile scores. Their motor loss is of spatial analysis and drawing skills. Their worst, or highest, scores will be tactile, motor, arithmetic, and pathognomonic. They make better scores on memory and writing, and the writing score is generally better than the reading (Golden, 1981).

The Luria–Nebraska battery can be administered in two and a half hours, and research demonstrates that this test can be scored in a highly reliable manner (Ma-

Neuropsychological tests assess various performance deficits in the hope of detecting a specific area of neural malfunction. Shown here is the tactual performance test.

Child taking a subtest of the Children's Luria—Nebraska test.

ruish, Sawicki, Franzen, and Golden, 1984; Moses and Schefft, 1984). The Luria–Nebraska is also believed to pick up effects of brain damage that are not (yet) detectable by neurological examination; such deficits are in the cognitive domain rather than in the sensorimotor (which neurological assessments focus on) (Moses, 1983). A particular advantage of the Luria–Nebraska is that one can control for educational level so that a lesser educated person will not receive a lower score solely attributable to limited educational experience (Brickman, McManus, Grapentine, and Alessi, 1984). Finally, a children's version of the Luria–Nebraska (Golden, 1981), for ages 8 to 12, has also been found useful in diagnosing brain damage and in evaluating the educational strengths and weaknesses of children, a very important consideration indeed (Sweet, Carr, Rossini, and Kasper, 1986).

Recent years have brought the development of increasingly sophisticated measurement techniques for detecting negative effects of even minor head injuries. The importance of such advances can be appreciated by the predicament of a school-aged child who receives a minor bump on the head with no obvious sequelae. Instead of being taken out of school and later provided with makeup work and other special considerations, this youngster can sit in school for days, seemingly normal but actually functioning subnormally and not fully understanding the lessons. The child can fall behind, because the injury has gone undetected and therefore unappreciated. Thus, even if the effects of the minor brain insult are themselves temporary, the social and psychological effects can be much longer-lasting (Boll, 1985). Related findings of permanent brain damage have been reported for professional boxers who, despite routine physical examinations that pronounce them entirely fit for bouts, were observed to have neurocognitive impairment as measured by IQ tests (Casson *et al.*, 1984).

A caution to neuropsychological assessors is that they must recognize the simple, yet often unappreciated, fact that "in attempting to appreciate the neurocognitive sequelae of any [brain-injuring] event, one must understand the abilities that the patient has brought to that event" (Boll, 1985, p. 480). This straightforward truth brings to mind the story of the man who, recovering from an accident that has broken all the fingers in both hands, earnestly asks the surgeon whether he will be able to play the piano when his wounds heal. Yes, I'm sure you will, says the doctor reassuringly. That's wonderful, exclaims the man, I don't even know *how* to play the piano *now*!

Behavioral Assessment

As part of the continuing development of behavioral approaches to the study of psychopathology and treatment, interest has been growing in assessment procedures that are different from the Rorschach inkblot test, the TAT, and the MMPI, three of the assessment devices that are intimately related to psychoanalytic theory or to an old diagnostic system. In Chapter 2, learning researchers and behaviorists are described as being interested in *situational determinants* of behavior, that is, in the environmental conditions that precede and follow certain responses. In addition, with the growing interest in cognitive explanations, we can expect the assessments made by behaviorists to include self-reports as well; but, as we shall see, interpretations of self-reports within a behavioral framework differ from those in more traditional assessment.

Traditional assessment concentrates on measuring underlying personality structures and *traits*, such as obsessiveness, paranoia, coldness, aggressiveness, and so on. "A chief aim of the trait approach is to infer the underlying personality structure of individuals and to compare persons and groups on trait dimensions" (Mischel, 1968, pp. 5–6).

Behavioral clinicians, on the other hand, are concerned with four sets of variables, sometimes referred to by the acronym *SORC* (Kanfer and Phillips, 1970). The S stands for stimuli, the environmental situations that precede the problem. For instance, the clinician will try to ascertain which situations tend to elicit an especially high degree of anxiety. The O stands for organismic, referring to both physiological and psychological factors assumed to be operating "under the skin." Perhaps the client's fatigue is caused in part by excessive use of alcohol, or by a cognitive tendency to deprecate the self with such statements as "I never do anything right, so what's the point in trying?" The R refers to overt responses, which probably demand the most attention from behavioral clinicians. They must determine what behavior is problematic, its frequency, intensity, and form. For example, a client might say that she is forgetful and procrastinates. Does she mean that she does not return phone calls, comes late for appointments, or both? Finally, C or consequent variables are events that appear to be reinforcing the behavior in question. When the client avoids a feared situation, does his spouse offer sympathy and excuses, thereby unwittingly keeping the person from facing up to his fears?

SORC factors are those that a behavioral clinician attempts to specify for a particular client. It might be mentioned in passing that O variables are understandably underplayed by Skinnerians; similarly, C variables receive less attention from cognitively oriented behavior therapists than do O variables.

The information necessary for a **behavioral assessment** is gathered by several methods. These include direct observation of the behavior in real life as well as in contrived settings, interviews and self-report measures, cognitive assessment, and physiological measurement.

Direct Observation of Behavior

It is not surprising that behavior therapists have paid considerable attention to careful observation of overt behavior in a variety of settings, but it should not be assumed that they simply go out and *observe*. Like other scientists, they try to fit physical events into a framework consistent with their point of view. This excerpt from a case report by Gerald Patterson and his colleagues (1969), describing an interaction between a boy named Kevin and his mother, father, and sister Freida, serves as the first part of an example.

Kevin goes up to father's chair and stands alongside it. Father puts his arms around Kevin's shoulders. Kevin

"For crying out loud, gentlemen! That's us! Someone's installed the one-way mirror in backward!"

says to mother as Freida looks at Kevin, "Can I go out and play after supper?" Mother does not reply. Kevin raises his voice and repeats the question. Mother says "You don't have to yell; I can hear you." Father says "How many times have I told you not to yell at your mother?" Kevin scratches a bruise on his arm while mother tells Freida to get started on the dishes, which Freida does. Kevin continues to rub and scratch his arm while mother and daughter are working at the kitchen sink. (p. 21)

This informal description could probably be provided by any observer. But a behavioral observer would divide the uninterrupted sequence of behavior into various parts and apply terms that make sense within a learning framework. "Kevin begins the exchange by asking a routine question in a normal tone of voice. This ordinary behavior, however, is not reinforced by the mother's attention; for she does not reply. Because she does not reply, the normal behavior of Kevin ceases and he yells his question. The mother express disapproval—punishing her son—by telling him that he does not have to yell. And this punishment is supported by

BOX 4.2

OPERANT CONDITIONING FINDS ITS HEART

For many years the operant branch of behavior therapy has emphasized—some would say restricted itself to—direct behavioral observation. Their piece of the behavioral or learning paradigm held that the only legitimate datum was behavior that could be reliably observed. In this way, for example, classroom problems were operationalized as the frequency with which children were out of their seats, amount of time children's eyes were not on their books, and other readily observable behaviors. In many ways, this paradigm represented an extreme reaction against decades of assessment that followers of Skinner concluded had not yielded much of value and that was, in any event, too unreliable to include in a scientific account of human behavior.

Over the past fifteen or twenty years, behavioral researchers and therapists have tackled problems of greater and greater complexity and have subjected their own work to the critical scrutiny that once characterized only their examination of "the enemy," namely, the psychoanalysts and humanists. We have already discussed the blurring of the distinctions between schools of thought when we noted the eclecticism of most clinicians (see Box 2.3), and we shall mention other examples of rapprochement throughout the rest of this book. In the present assessment context

we take note of a suggestion made over a decade ago by Montrose Wolf (1978), one of the leading operant behavioral researchers. Wolf proposed that his Skinnerian colleagues expand their paradigmatic focus to include *subjective* measures of people's expressed needs and wants. He arrived at this position, an unlikely one for a radical behaviorist, by a consideration of how one is to judge the *social importance* of a particular change in behavior. This has been a question of far-reaching significance since Skinner himself published *Walden Two*, a Utopian novel that described a small society that espoused the concepts of operant conditioning. Wolf argues that social importance includes the social significance of a treatment goal and the social appropriateness of the behavior change procedures used to achieve the goal. These aspects are, he says, best determined *by asking the people affected*. In other words, people should be asked their views about how their behavior is to be altered and their self-report should be included in any assessment of behavioral change. To be sure, direct observation of overt behavior remains of critical importance, but it is now to be complemented by the subjective evaluations of the people whose behavior is being modified. Operant behavior therapy should "find its heart."

the father's reminding Kevin that he should not yell at his mother." This behavioral rendition acknowledges the consequences of ignoring a child's question. At some point the behavior therapist will undoubtedly advise the parents to attend to Kevin's requests when expressed in an ordinary tone of voice, lest he begin yelling. This example indicates an important aspect of behavioral assessment, namely, its link to *intervention*. The behavioral clinician's way of conceptualizing a situation often implies a way to try to change it.

It is difficult to observe most behavior as it actually takes place, and little control can be exercised over where and when it may occur. For this reason many therapists contrive artificial situations in their consulting rooms or in a laboratory so that they can observe how a client or a family acts under certain conditions. For example, Barkley (1981) has a mother and her hyperactive child spend time together in a laboratory "living room," complete with sofas and television set. The mother is given a list of tasks for the child to complete, such as picking up toys or doing arithmetic problems. Observers behind a one-way mirror watch the proceedings and code the child's reactions to the mother's efforts to control as well as the mother's reactions to

the child's compliant or noncompliant responses. These behavioral assessment procedures yield data that can be used to measure the effects of treatment. For example, Barkley and Cunningham (1979) showed that hyperactive children who were being treated with methylphenidate (Ritalin) were more obedient to their mothers, who, in turn, were more positive in their reactions to their children—as compared to children who had been given placebo medications. Such analogue behavioral observations can facilitate the study of complex interactions between parent and child.

Behavioral observations can also be made by "significant others" in the client's natural environment. For example, the Conners Teacher Rating Scale (Conners, 1969) enables teachers to provide reliable behavioral assessment data on children in classrooms, and the Achenbach Child Behavior Checklist (Achenbach and Edelbrook, 1983) has either parents or teachers rate children's behavior. Box 4.4 illustrates the use of similar scales in the assessment of marital dysfunction.

Most of the research just described is conducted within an operant framework that employs no inferential concepts (see Box 4.2). But behavioral assessment techniques can also be applied within a framework that does

TABLE 4.3
Timed behavioral checklist for performance anxiety (*from Paul, 1966*)

Behavior Observed	Time Period								
	1	2	3	4	5	6	7	8	Σ
1. Paces									
2. Sways									
3. Shuffles feet									
4. Knees tremble									
5. Extraneous arm and hand movement (swings, scratches, toys, etc.)									
6. Arms rigid									
7. Hands restrained (in pockets, behind back, clasped)									
8. Hand tremors									
9. No eye contact									
10. Face muscles tense (drawn, tics, grimaces)									
11. Face "deadpan"									
12. Face pale									
13. Face flushed (blushes)									
14. Moistens lips									
15. Swallows									
16. Clears throat									
17. Breathes heavily									
18. Perspires (face, hands, armpits)									
19. Voice quivers									
20. Speech blocks or stammers									

make use of mediators. For instance, Gordon Paul (1966) was interested in assessing the "anxiety" of public speakers. He decided to count the frequency of behavior that is deemed indicative of this emotional state. One of his principal measures, the Timed Behavioral Checklist for Performance Anxiety, is shown in Table 4.3. Subjects were asked to deliver a speech in front of a group, some members of which were raters trained to consider each subject's behavior every thirty seconds and to record the presence or absence of twenty specific behaviors. By summing the scores, Paul arrived at a

behavioral index of anxiety. This study is one example of how observations of overt behavior have been used to infer the presence of an internal state.

In Paul's study people other than the speaker whose behavior was being described made the observations. For several years behavior therapists and researchers have also asked individuals to observe their *own* behavior, to keep track of various categories of response. The general approach is called ***self-monitoring***. An early application of self-monitoring was used in research to reduce smoking. Subjects were provided with booklets

TABLE 4.4
A behaviorally oriented intake report (*after Goldfried and Davison, 1976*)

<u>Name</u>: BRIAN, James (fictitious name)	<u>Age</u>: 22 <u>Sex</u>: Male
<u>Class</u>: Senior	<u>Date of interview</u>: March 26, 1984
	<u>Therapist</u>: John Doe

1. <u>Behavior during interview and physical description</u>:
   James is a clean-shaven, long-haired young man who appeared for the intake interview in well-coordinated college garb: jeans, wide belt, open shirt, and sandals. He came across as shy and soft-spoken, with occasional minor speech blocks. Although uneasy during most of the session, he nonetheless spoke freely and candidly.

2. <u>Presenting problem</u>:
   (a) <u>Nature of problem</u>: Anxiety in public-speaking situations and in other situations in which he is being evaluated by others.

   (b) <u>Historical setting events</u>: James was born in France and arrived in this country seven years ago, at which time he experienced both social and language problems. His social contacts had been minimal until he entered college; there a socially aggressive friend helped him to break out of his shell. James describes his father as an overly critical perfectionist who would, on occasion, rip up his son's homework if it fell short of the mark. His mother he pictures as a controlling, overly affectionate person who always shows concern about his welfare. His younger brother, who has always been a good student, is continually thrown up to James by his parents as being far better than he.

   (c) <u>Current situational determinants</u>: Interaction with his parents, examinations, family gatherings, participation in classes, initial social contacts.

   (d) <u>Relevant organismic variables</u>: The client appears to be approaching a number of situations with certain irrational expectations, primarily unrealistic strivings for perfection and an overwhelming desire to receive approval from others. He is not taking any medication at this time except as indicated under 10 below.

   (e) <u>Dimensions of problem</u>: The client's anxiety about social relationships and evaluations of himself is long-standing and occurs in a wide variety of day-to-day situations.

   (f) <u>Consequences of problem</u>: His chronic level of anxiety resulted in an ulcer operation at the age of 15. In addition, he has developed a skin rash on his hands and arms, apparently from excessive perspiration. He reports that his nervousness at one time caused him to stutter, but this problem appears to have diminished in recent years. His anxiety when taking examinations has typically interfered with his ability to perform well.

in which they recorded the time each cigarette was lighted at baseline, before treatment had been introduced, during treatment, and after.

Although some research indicates that self-monitoring can provide accurate measurement of such behavior as smoking and the eating of certain foods, many report that the information collected is unreliable (Nelson, 1977). Yet there are ways to improve the accuracy of self-monitoring: by rewarding people for accuracy (Lipinski *et al.*, 1975), by taking care to motivate subjects to be honest and conscientious (Bornstein *et al.*, 1977), by training them in the demands of the particular self-monitoring task (Nelson, Lipinski, and Boykin, 1978), and by informing people that their self-monitoring is in turn being watched by other observers (Nelson, Lipinski, and Black, 1975). At the same time, however, considerable research indicates that behavior may be altered by the very fact that it is being self-monitored (Haynes and Horn, 1982). **Reactivity** of behavior is the phenomenon of its changing because it is being observed. Generally speaking, desirable behavior, such as engaging in social conversation, often increases in frequency when self-monitored (Nelson, Lipinski, and Black, 1976), whereas behavior the subject wishes to reduce, like cigarette smoking, diminishes (McFall and Hammen, 1971). Such findings suggest that the reactivity that is an outcome of self-monitoring can be taken advantage of in therapeutic interventions.

Interviews and Self-Report Measures

For all their interest in direct observation of behavior, behavioral clinicians still rely very heavily on the interview to assess the needs of their clients. Like other clinicians, they make every effort to establish good rapport, creating an atmosphere of trust and caring which

TABLE 4.4 (*Continued*)

3. Other problems:

   (a) <u>Assertiveness</u>: Although obviously a shy and timid individual, James says that lack of assertiveness is no longer a problem with him. At one time in the past, his friends would take advantage of him, but he claims that this is no longer the case. His statements should be followed up, for it is unclear what he means by assertiveness.

   (b) <u>Forgetfulness</u>: The client reports that he frequently misses appointments, misplaces items, locks himself out of his room, and is generally absentminded.

4. <u>Personal assets</u>:

   The client is fairly bright and comes across as a warm, friendly, and sensitive individual.

5. <u>Targets for modification</u>:

   Unrealistic self-statements about how he should fare in social evaluative situations; possible behavioral deficits associated with unassertiveness; and forgetfulness.

6. <u>Recommended treatment</u>:

   It appears that relaxation training would be a good way to begin, especially in light of the client's high level of anxiety. Treatment should then undertake the restructuring of his unrealistic expectations. Behavior rehearsal is a possibility. The best strategy for dealing with forgetfulness is unclear as yet.

7. <u>Motivation for treatment</u>:

   High.

8. <u>Prognosis</u>:

   Good.

9. <u>Priority for treatment</u>:

   High.

10. <u>Expectancies</u>:

    On occasion, especially when going out on a date, James takes a tranquilizer (Valium, 10 mg) to calm himself down. He wants to get away from this and feels that he needs to learn to cope with his anxieties by himself. It would appear that he will be receptive to whatever treatment plan we finally decide on, especially if the emphasis is on self-control of anxiety.

11. <u>Other comments</u>:

    Considering the brief time available between now and the end of the semester, between-session homework assignments should be given.

encourages clients to reveal aspects of their lives that they may not have shown any other person—what London (1964) has poetically called "secrets of the heart." Within this trusting relationship the behavior therapist's job is to determine, by skillful questioning and careful observation of the client's emotional reactions during the interview, the SORC factors already mentioned— the situations in which the problematic behavior occurs, the internal conditions mediating the influence of the environment, the particular patterns of behavior causing distress, and the events that may help to maintain the problem. The authors of this textbook, in their behaviorally oriented clinical work, conduct an initial interview with the goal of writing an intake report like the one shown in Table 4.4.

The self-report inventories that behavior therapists develop are a great deal more specific and detailed than those typically used by nonbehavioral clinicians. For example, McFall and Lillesand (1971) employed a Conflict Resolution Inventory containing thirty-five items that focus on the ability of the respondent to refuse unreasonable requests. Each item describes a specific situation in which a person is asked for something unreasonable. For example, "You are in the thick of studying for exams when a person you know slightly comes into your room and says, 'I'm tired of studying, mind if I come in and take a break for a while?' " Subjects are asked to indicate the likelihood that they would refuse such a request and how comfortable they would be in doing so. Responses to this self-report inventory have been successfully correlated with a variety of direct observational data in research on social skills (Frisch and Higgins, 1986). This and similar inventories are used by the practicing clinician and have helped behavioral researchers measure the outcome of clinical interventions as well.

Cognitive Assessment

The thoughts of patients may be probed both in interviews and by self-report inventories, as we have just seen. Patients reflect backward in time and provide a retrospective and rather general report of their thoughts in certain situations. "When someone criticizes you in class, what thoughts go through your mind?" is a question a client might be asked in an interview or on a paper-and-pencil inventory. The methods by which cognitions of clinical interest are assessed have been reviewed by Kendall and Hollon (1981) and Parks and Hollon (1988). Perhaps the most widely employed are self-report questionnaires. Many of these have been published, and they assess a wide range of cognitions—fear of negative evaluation, tendency to think irrationally, and making negative inferences about life experience.

Replies of subjects to questions asked by interviewers and inventories about their thoughts in certain situations may well be different from what they would report were they able to do so in the immediate circumstance. Moreover, cognitive-behavioral clinicians like Albert Ellis and Aaron Beck make predictions about the kinds of thoughts troubled people will have under very specific conditions. Behavioral researchers have been working on ways to enable subjects to tap into their immediate and ongoing thought processes when confronted with particular circumstances (cf. Parks and Hollon, 1988). Can we show, for example, that a socially anxious person does in fact, as Ellis would predict, view criticism from others as catastrophic, whereas someone who is not socially insecure does not?

The Articulated Thoughts During Simulated Situations (ATSS) method of Davison and his associates (Davison, Robins, and Johnson, 1983) is an example of research allowing the immediate thoughts of individuals to be expressed. In this procedure a subject pretends that he or she is a participant in a situation, such as listening to a teaching assistant criticize a term paper, one which the subject hopes will receive a good grade. Presented on audiotape, the scene pauses every ten or fifteen seconds. During the following thirty seconds of silence, the subject talks aloud about whatever is going through his or her mind in reaction to the words just heard. Then the audiotaped scene continues, stopping after a few moments so that the subject can articulate his or her thoughts another time. One taped scene in which the subject overhears two pretend acquaintances criticizing him or her includes the following segments.

First acquaintance: He certainly did make a fool of himself over what he said about religion. I just find that kind of opinion very closed-minded and unaware. You have to be blind to the facts of the universe to believe that. [Thirty-second pause for subject's response.]

Second acquaintance: What really bugs me is the way he expresses himself. He never seems to stop and think, but just blurts out the first thing that comes into his head. [Thirty-second pause.]

Subjects readily become involved in the pretend situations, regarding them as credible and realistic. The following findings have emerged from several of the studies conducted thus far.

1. The articulated thoughts of subjects hearing the taped criticisms of two pretend acquaintances or the taped disparaging remarks of a pretend teaching assistant about their term paper were more irrational than was their thinking aloud to a neutral tape (Davison, Feldman, and Osborn, 1984; Davison and Zighelboim, 1987).

2. Depressed patients from a psychiatric clinic and fellow outpatients with other psychological disorders listened to a tape describing an outdoor barbecue, one that they had supposedly planned and on which it had rained. The articulated thoughts of the depressed patients were more illogical, as Beck predicts (see page 226), than those of the other outpatients (White, Davison, and White, 1989).

3. Socially anxious therapy patients articulated thoughts of greater irrationality than did nonanxious control subjects (Bates, Campbell, and Burgess, in press; Davison and Zighelboim, 1987).

4. Borderline hypertensive men with the type A behavior pattern (see page 203) articulated more hostile thoughts than did type B's (Weinstein, Davison, DeQuattro, and Allen, 1986) and responded to social criticism with less self-supportive ideation (Williams, Davison, and DeQuattro, 1989).

5. Recent ex-smokers who would subsequently relapse within three months showed a greater tendency to think of smoking without prompting (Haaga, 1987), as well as having fewer negative expectations for smoking than did those who would still be abstinent three months later (Haaga, 1988a).

6. Finally, in an experiment that directly compared ATSS data to overt behavior, Davison, Haaga, Rosenbaum, Dolezal, and Weinstein (1989) found that

articulated thoughts of positive self-efficacy were inversely related to behaviorally indexed speech anxiety, that is, the more anxiously subjects behaved on a timed behavioral checklist measure of public speaking anxiety, the less capable they felt themselves to be while articulating thoughts in a stressful simulated speech-giving situation.

This pattern of results indicates that the method ferrets out people's thinking about both inherently bothersome and "objectively" innocuous situations.

Other cognitive assessment methods have also proven useful. For example, thought-listing has the person write down his or her thoughts prior to or following an event of interest, such as entering a room to talk to a stranger, as a way to determine the cognitive components of social anxiety (Cacioppo, Glass, and Merluzzi, 1979). Different procedures may be more or less useful under different circumstances. For example, open-ended techniques like the ATSS just described may be preferable when investigators know relatively little and want to get general ideas of the "cognitive terrain," whereas more focused techniques like questionnaires may be better—and are certainly more easily scored—when there is more prior knowledge about the cognitions of interest (Haaga, 1988b). So far the various cognitive assessment techniques relate imperfectly to each other (Clark, 1988), but this is perhaps to be expected, given their different formats and the elusive nature of human thought.

The interest in cognitive assessment has recently brought cognitive-behavioral clinicians into contact with literature in experimental cognitive psychology, the branch of empirical psychological research concerned with the ways people transform environmental input into usable information, how they think and plan, remember and anticipate. In addition to self-talk research, workers have developed assessment tools for inferring the existence of a number of cognitive structures, particularly schemata (Bartlett, 1932). A simple example of a schema would be the idea we carry around in our heads of what a face is—a configuration having two eyes, a nose and mouth, and two ears. We are able to identify an object as a face, even when its configuration has much that is unusual about it.

Experimental cognitive psychologists have used the schema concept in understanding memory phenomena (see page 227). An example is from a study by Brewer and Treyens (1981), who brought subjects into a room described as the experimenter's office. After half a minute the subject left the room and their memory was tested for the presence of certain objects. Subjects did very well in recalling such things as a desk and a chair but not at all well in remembering a skull on a shelf. By the same token, subjects reported that there were books in the office; there were none there. The inference can be made that an "office schema" led subjects to recall items that are part of the schema (desk), overlook those that are not (the skull), and even "recall" office-type things that were not there (books).[4]

Clinical researchers have built on this experimental research and infer schemata from distortions in memory. For example, Nelson and Craighead (1977) wanted to test whether depressives encounter their world with a failure schema as posited by Beck. They gave groups of depressed and nondepressed students a task on which they were rewarded or punished 30 percent or 70 percent of the time. In the 70 percent reward condition, the depressed subjects recalled having been reinforced less often than was actually the case. By the same token, in the 30 percent punishment condition, depressed students recalled having received more punishment. These differences in memory are explained in terms of a schema, or cognitive set. For example, the depressed subject believes something like "I am not competent." In this sense a schema is equivalent to a basic, underlying assumption that people have about themselves and their world and that affects the way they perceive, conceptualize, feel, and act.

Physiological Measurement

A number of procedures are used for measuring physiological aspects of behavior. The discipline of **psychophysiology** is concerned with the bodily changes that accompany psychological events (Grings and Dawson, 1978; see Box 4.3). For example, we know that the skin conductance of most people will increase markedly under conditions of psychological, as well as physical, stress.

Experimenters have studied such changes, as well as heart rate, tension in the muscles, blood flow in various parts of the body, and even brain waves (see page 266), while subjects are afraid, depressed, asleep, imagining, solving problems, and so on. Special attention has been paid to the *patterning* of such responses, as when heart rate increases while skin conductivity remains constant.

---

[4]Though usually inferred from such memory data as these, schemata can be assessed from other kinds of data as well. For example, in the articulated thoughts study just noted, Haaga (1988b) inferred a "smoking schema" based on the frequency of smoking themes in think-aloud data collected from ex-smokers imagining themselves in "high risk" situations, like being in the vicinity of cigarettes.

BOX 4.3

MEASUREMENT OF AUTONOMIC NERVOUS SYSTEM ACTIVITY

The mammalian nervous system can be considered to have two relatively separate functional divisions: the **somatic** or voluntary and the **autonomic** or involuntary. Because the autonomic nervous system is especially important in the study of emotional behavior, it will be useful to review its principal characteristics and the ways in which its activity can be monitored.

Skeletal muscles, such as those that move our limbs, are innervated by the voluntary nervous system. Much of our behavior, however, is dependent on a nervous system that operates generally without our awareness and has traditionally been viewed as beyond voluntary control, hence the term autonomic. The autonomic nervous system (ANS) innervates the endocrine glands, the heart, and the smooth muscles that are found in the walls of the blood vessels, stomach, intestines, kidneys, and other organs. This nervous system is itself divided into two parts, the **sympathetic** and **parasympathetic** nervous systems (Figure 4a), which sometimes work in opposition to each other, sometimes in unison. The sympathetic portion of the ANS, when energized, accelerates the heartbeat, dilates the pupils, inhibits intestinal activity, and initiates other smooth muscle and glandular responses that prepare the organism for sudden activity and stress. Indeed, some physiologists view the sympathetic nervous system as primarily excitatory, whereas the other division, the parasympathetic, is viewed as responsible for maintenance functions and more quiescent behavior, such as deceleration of the heartbeat, constriction of the pupils, and speeding up contractions of the intestines. Division of activities is not quite so clearcut, however, for the parasympathetic system may be active during situations of stress. Animals, and human beings to their consternation, may urinate and defecate involuntarily when extremely frightened.

The activities of the ANS are frequently assessed by electrical and chemical measurements and analyses in attempts to understand the nature of emotion. One important measure is heart rate. Each heartbeat generates spreading changes in electrical potential, which can be recorded by an electrocardiograph or on a suitably tuned polygraph. Electrodes are usually placed on both arms and lead to a galvanometer, an instrument for measuring electric currents. The deflections of this instrument may be seen as waves on an oscilloscope, or a pen recorder may register the waves on a continuously moving roll of graph paper. Both types of recordings are called electrocardiograms. More recently available is the cardiotachometer, a device that measures the precise elapsed time between two heartbeats and then instantaneously provides heart rate on a beat-to-beat basis. This technological advance is especially important for experimental psychologists, who are typically interested in bodily changes that occur over short periods of time in response to rapidly shifting circumstances. Generally a fast heart rate is taken to indicate increased arousal.

A second measure is **electrodermal responding**, sometimes referred to as the **galvanic skin response** (GSR). Anxiety, fear, anger, and other emotions increase sweat gland activity. The electrophysiological processes in the cells of these glands change the electric conductance of the skin as well as producing sweat. There are two methods of measuring the electrodermal response. Skin potential may be measured by recording with surface electrodes the very small differences in electrical potential that always exist between any two points on the skin. This voltage shows a pronounced rise after the sweat glands have been stimulated to activity. Or we may determine the current that flows through the skin when a known small voltage derived from an external source is passed betweeen two electrodes pasted to the palm and back of the hand. This current also shows a pronounced increase after activation of the sweat glands. The percentage of change from the normal or baseline reading is for either method the measure of reactivity. High conductance is thought to reflect increased autonomic activity. Since the sweat glands are innervated only by the sympathetic nervous system, increased sweat gland activity indicates sympathetic autonomic excitation and is often taken as a measure of anxiety.

Advances in technology allow researchers to track such things as blood pressure *in vivo* as the person goes about his normal business. The subject wears a portable device that records his blood pressure automatically every few minutes. Combined with self-reports recorded by the subject in a specially designed diary, van Egeren and Madarasmi (1987) have been able to study how people's thoughts and moods co-vary with increases in blood pressure, data of great interest to psychologically oriented researchers in hypertension (see Chapter 8).

A more complete picture of the human being is obtained by assessing physiological functioning along with overt behavior and cognitive activity. If experimenters wonder whether showing schizophrenic patients pictures of their mothers is stressful, they can, in addition to asking the patients how they feel about looking at

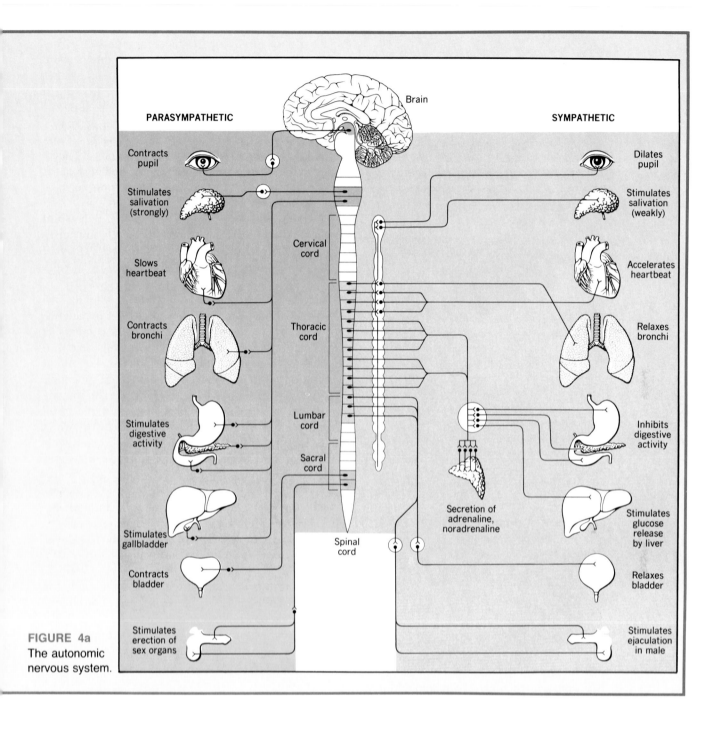

FIGURE 4a
The autonomic nervous system.

the pictures, measure their heart rate and electrical skin activity. Psychophysiological measuring procedures, which are constantly being improved and added to, are relatively unobtrusive. Once the person has adapted to having electrodes pasted on his or her arm, for example, measurement of heart rate does not interfere with many experimental tasks, such as listening to a story or solving a mathematical problem.

Inasmuch as psychophysiology employs highly sophisticated electronic machinery, and inasmuch as many psychologists aspire to be as scientific as possible, they sometimes believe uncritically in these apparently objective assessment devices without appreciating their real limitations and complications. Many of the measurements do not differentiate clearly among emotional states. Blood pressure, for example, increases with a

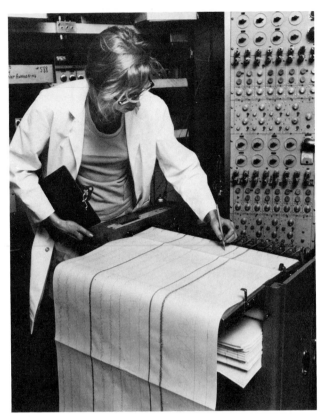

Here a psychologist monitors the output of several channels of a polygraph, a device for measuring a number of physiological responses such as heart rate, blood pressure, respiration, and electrodermal activity.

variety of emotions, not just with anxiety. Special care must be taken to ensure a proper setting for taking measurements so that the data collected are meaningful.

Behavioral Assessment for Behavioral Change

We have already mentioned that a principal aspect of behavioral assessment is its close ties to procedures for changing behavior. Behavior therapists always search thoroughly for the situational determinants of behavior because they believe it can be altered by manipulating the environment. For example, an aggressive youngster might be directly observed to see whether teachers and parents reinforce his abrasive behavior with their attention. If this is the case, the adults can be cautioned to ignore the outbursts as much as possible. This technique contrasts with diagnosing the boy as having a conduct disorder and then seeking the reasons for his general problem. The range of behavior therapies for different disorders, to be described in later chapters, will reveal again and again this direct link between assessment and intervention.

Reliability of Behavioral Assessment

We have now surveyed the major approaches to behavioral assessment. The reader has probably become aware of how much more *direct* this type of assessment is than the traditional techniques, such as the Rorschach described earlier in this chapter. If the behavioral researcher wants to determine how anxious a person is, he or she selects the indicator of anxiety, such as hand tremors or a particular pattern of psychophysiological response recorded on a polygraph, and then measures the person's responses under controlled conditions, as when taking a test.

Are things really so simple? Because a behavioral researcher directly observes a bit of behavior, are better data necessarily being collected? The answer is maybe. Let us examine the problem in terms first of reliability and then of validity.[5]

The reliability of diagnoses depends on whether various diagnosticians agree on how to categorize patients' problems. That of behavioral assessment procedures also depends on whether outcomes are similar. Do two raters using a particular coding system make similar observations of the same event, and does a respondent, when taking two versions of a test judged to be roughly equivalent, make similar scores? For example, Paul (1966), in employing the behavioral checklist shown in Table 4.3, trained his research assistants extensively until two of them, while watching the same subject give a speech, could reach similar judgments of the frequency of the several signs of anxiety.

Over the years the reliability of behavioral assessment has been shown to be affected by several factors. The complexity or difficulty of the assessment task can lower reliability. If an investigator is using a time-sampling procedure as Paul did, whereby raters watch for certain indicators at fixed time intervals, reliability can be enhanced if the interval between observations is long enough to allow raters time to make careful judgments—every minute rather than every ten seconds, for instance—and if the behaviors to be watched for are few rather than many—five, for example, rather than twenty.

Another consideration is the way observers are monitored. At the earliest stages of a research project, the people with overall responsibility, the investigators, usually work very closely with the experimenters, those who actually have contact with the subjects. Before

---

[5]Reliability and validity issues in behavioral assessment are very complex. A sophisticated discussion can be found in Kanfer and Nay (1982). These concepts are important as well in the assessment procedures discussed earlier, like the TAT. For the most part, projectives and personality inventories have good reliability. Their validities are discussed earlier in this chapter.

running a study, the investigators spend many hours with their assistants, ensuring that instructions are being followed and that any behavioral assessments are being done reliably. It has been shown that once the experimenters are left unsupervised—or, more precisely, once they *believe* themselves to be on their own—they tend to become slipshod and hence less reliable as observers (Romanczyk *et al.*, 1973). An effective and ethical way to increase reliability is to inform the experimenters that their work will be checked now and again, without telling them exactly when. This unscheduled observing of the observers seems to keep them on their toes and thus increases reliability (Bernstein and Nietzel, 1980).

The articulated thoughts research described earlier poses a major challenge to establishing reliability because the task is one of content analysis, that is, creating categories (such as hostile thought), defining them clearly (such as a hostile thought is one that indicates a desire to harm), training at least two coders to apply the category to a set of data, and determining that they agree to an acceptable degree (such as concurring 90% of the time on the occurrence of hostile thoughts in a body of think-aloud data). Consider that there is a measure of inference necessary in making such judgments—if a subject articulates "To hell with him!" does this indicate a desire to harm? It is much clearer if the subject says something like "I feel like punching him in the nose." In practice, articulated thoughts research does not favor sweeping inferences and would probably not categorize the first example as a hostile thought. Investigators who use projective instruments like the Thematic Apperception Test, make "deeper" inferences than cognitive-behavioral assessors even though in both approaches efforts are being made to learn what people think about something specific (see Box 4.4).

Validity of Behavioral Assessment

Behavioral researchers have only recently attended to the validity of their measures. As implied in Chapter 3, the validity of any measure is the extent to which it reflects what it is supposed to reflect. For example, if an investigator asserts that frequent lateness is an indicator of hostility, he or she is making a statement about the validity of lateness as a measure of hostility. Is this researcher justified in making such an assertion? Or, put differently, are we prepared to agree that hostility can be assessed by taking note of lateness?

Because behavioral assessment is so much more direct than traditional personality assessment, we can be seduced into assuming validity uncritically and perhaps prematurely. Common sense and the already discussed reactivity of self-monitored behavior, however, suggest that people behave or think differently when they are aware of being watched. For example, Zeigob, Arnold, and Forehand (1975) found that mothers acted more positively toward their children when they knew that they were being observed than when observations were made surreptitiously. Therefore the behavior of the mothers aware of being watched may not provide a valid assessment of their typical level of positive mothering.

Stony Brook psychologist observing and recording the behavior of children in a classroom. He is coding their behavior at regular intervals according to a predetermined set of dimensions.

BOX 4.4

BEHAVIORAL MARITAL ASSESSMENT

Three purposes are served by marital assessment: to advance understanding of relationships; to identify the problems in a relationship to be worked on in therapy; and to measure changes in the relationship brought about by intervention (Margolin, Michelli, and Jacobson, 1988). Behavioral marital assessment in the 1960s and 1970s focused on measuring the rewards and punishments exchanged by spouses (e.g., Stuart, 1976), and this interest in overt behavior and in contingencies continues today. The focus has expanded to include parameters that have been underplayed in the behavioral marital literature but that were traditionally of interest to nonbehavioral therapists; primarily the cognitive components of distress (e.g., unrealistic beliefs and expectations) and the affective components of relationships (e.g., anger and hostility, hurt feelings) (cf. Notarius and Markman, 1989). Of increasing interest as well are so-called systems variables such as dominance and flexibility, global constructs that characterize the nature of a relationship *qua* relationship (e.g., although one person can be angry by himself, he cannot be dominant except in a relationship). Indeed, consonant with the expanding definition of behavior therapy to render it virtually indistinguishable from a general empirical, data-based study of disordered behavior (see page 538), Margolin *et al.* (1988) define behavioral marital assessment as "any instrument or procedure that contributes to an empirically based formulation of the etiology and treatment of marital dysfunction" (p. 443). Rather than quibble about what is or is not "behavioral," let us look at some of the assessment techniques used by behaviorally oriented marital researchers and clinicians. Much of what follows is based on Margolin, *et al.* (1988).

One disarmingly simple measure is Spanier's Dyadic Adjustment Scale (DAS) (Spanier, 1976), a 32-item self-report questionnaire that is filled out by both partners. Cross and Sharpley (1981) found that two DAS items discriminated distressed from satisfied marriages 92 percent of the time: "Rate your marriage, everything considered, from very unhappy to perfectly happy" and "If you had your life to live over, do you think you would marry the same person or a different one?" The latter item probably has some poignancy for anyone who has been in a troubled marriage.

Behavioral marital researchers are interested also in direct observations of overt behavior. A widely used instrument, the Spouse Observation Checklist (SOCL) (Weiss and Perry, 1983), has each partner track the behavior of the other on 408 specific behaviors, such as "Spouse criticized something I made." The checklist is divided into categories on sex, household management, and communication, and includes a daily rating of satisfaction. Though tedious to fill out daily, the SOCL does provide important information on the nature of marital distress and marital satisfaction; for example, distressed couples are more reactive to negative behavior from the partner than are nondistressed couples (Jacobson, Follette, and McDonald, 1982). This finding is not surprising, but another not so obvious one of major importance in understanding marital problems is that distressed couples respond more on the basis of immediate events, both negative *and* positive. If one spouse does something the other dislikes, there is a more marked (negative) reaction than there would be in a good marriage; *and* if one partner does something the other *likes*, there is a strong positive reaction, or as Margolin *et al.* put it, they are "enchanted" by it. The highly focused nature of the SOCL assessment instrument permits the investigator to uncover a relationship between certain classes of behavior and marital satisfaction/dissatisfaction that might escape one's attention with a less structured observational technique.*

Behavioral observation techniques have been extended to marital *interaction* or *communication* between partners, a significant development given the putative importance of communication effectiveness in most theories of marital dysfunction (see Chapter 20, page 580). The Couples Interaction Scoring System (CISS; Gottman, 1979) codes couples' interactions (videotaped in a laboratory setting) for both content and affect. The affect codes, for example, an expression of anger, discriminate best between distressed and nondistressed couples (Notarius, Markman, and Gottman, 1983).

---

*The significance and interest of this finding lie in the inference that distressed partners are overly reactive to and even at the mercy of the immediate or most recent behavior of their spouse. Thus, if one partner frowns at the other, that is a *catastrophe*, but if that partner smiles, then that is *wonderful*. When we later (page 547) examine Ellis's rational-emotive therapy, we shall see how these extreme and opposite reactions can both be considered to arise from the irrational belief that it is crucially important that I not make a mistake, or that it is imperative that I be loved and approved of by everyone all the time. Another way to regard the finding is as a reflection of a lack of faith or trust in the relationship. If one feels loved and accepted by another, then disapproval from them in one situation does not spell doom; by the same token, a specific sign of approval, although always nice to have, is not absolutely necessary to reassure that one is still loved. Hence, the sign of approval does not generate as much immediate (almost frantic) pleasure as it does for a partner in a distressed marriage, who probably is far less certain of spousal regard.

As with any assessment modality, the behavioral observations made by couples during their everyday activities with each other are subject to distortion. Certainly partners do not agree perfectly with each other when they use an instrument even as straightforward as the SOCL (Christensen and Nies, 1980). Interpretive or perceptual factors reduce interrater reliability but are themselves indicative of the important role of cognitive factors in marital dysfunction and assessment.

The recent focus on cognitive assessment in the marital assessment literature has investigators looking at how distressed and satisfied couples differ with respect to such variables as irrational beliefs, attributions for positive or negative behavior from the partner, and expectations about marriage in general. The overall prediction has been borne out that distressed couples distort each other's intentions and behavior in negative, even destructive ways. For example, partners may infer that a compliment is motivated by an external, unstable reason like being persuaded by the therapist to be nice, and/or that a criticism stems from an internal, stable factor such as basic dislike for the other. On a self-report questionnaire called the Relationship Beliefs Inventory, Eidelson and Epstein (1982) found that beliefs such as spouses should know the other's thoughts and feelings without asking and sexual perfection is essential in a good marriage were negatively correlated with marital satisfaction. A clever laboratory-based cognitive assessment was conducted by Jacobson, McDonald, Follette, and Berley (1985). In an analogue discussion, one partner, unbeknownst to the other, was instructed by the experimenter to act positively or negatively during a conflict resolution task. Partners in distressed marriages tended to attribute negative behavior to internal factors (she hates me) whereas those in nondistressed relationships did the same for positive behaviors (she loves me). This study is especially noteworthy in highlighting the ways that direct behavioral observation and experimenter manipulation of variables can be combined with cognitive assessment to yield information that might not be accessible in an interview with the couple and/or by administering standardized questionnaires.

Behavioral marital researchers have already begun to study the emotional or affective dimension of couple conflict. Particularly innovative is John Gottman's work with the above-mentioned CISS, where distressed partners could be distinguished from nondistressed by the nature of their observed inferred affect in laboratory discussion situations (Gottman *et al.*, 1977). In collab-

Lack of communication is one of the domains assessed by the Spouse Observation Checklist.

oration with a psychophysiologist, Robert Levenson, Gottman has more recently been able to use physiologically indexed emotions in a similar way. For example, Gottman and Levenson (1986) found a very high .92 correlation between husband's heart rate during a conflictual discussion and subsequent declines in marital satisfaction. The high heart rate is interpreted as a sign of negative emotion (anger or anxiety); thus, its relationship to subsequent deterioration in the marriage suggests that the presence of physiologically measured negative emotion in the husband predicts (perhaps contributes in a causal way) to later marital dissatisfaction. In addition, they found "physiological linkage" in their distressed couples: during a conflictual discussion, as one partner's heart rate rose, so did the other's. But perhaps of even greater and more general significance is the *methodology* introduced by these investigators—careful observation of behavior in the laboratory under experimenter-controlled conditions with concurrent polygraph assessment of emotion, and correlated with self-report indices of marital satisfaction.

A systems perspective has long characterized the marital literature, and recent efforts have been made by behavioral marital researchers to apply their assessment approach to systems concepts. The basic systems idea is that the unit of analysis should be the relationship, or dyad, and that assessment should be directed at describing its nature. The assumption is that a given behavior is at once a stimulus and a response to both the behaving individual and to the partner, and that its meaning can be understood only within the context of the relationship. For example, Christensen, Sullaway, and King (1982) developed questionnaires that require partners to comment on complex aspects of their relationships, such as whether there is asymmetry marked by one partner's being demanding while the other is in a one-down or subservient posture.

There are still many unexplored issues in marital assessment, and Margolin *et al.* (1988) point to sex roles as an area that has surprisingly attracted little systematic research. None of the instruments outlined here explicitly considers couples and sex roles—How is labor divided in the home? Who controls the finances and what does the other partner think of that? Feminist issues have become a fact of life in many segments of society; it is no longer unusual to see "Ms." as an option for form of address on a demographic questionnaire, for example. But the effects of changing sex roles in intimate relationships are far more complex, especially, say, for a couple married in the 1960s and feeling "sex role strain" in the 1980s. Sociologists would warn us that conflict may well derive in some measure from these issues, and yet marital researchers are only now taking these formally into account in their assessment, and by implication, in their construal of intimate, long-term relationships. What makes this acutely sensitive and important is the inherently moral and political nature of the topic (see Chapter 21, page 629, for an extended discussion of these dimensions of mental health). It is by no means obvious, for example, that a traditional marital arrangement, in which only the husband works outside the home and makes most of the financial decisions for the family, is bad or creates marital stress. By the same token, it is by no means clear that such marriages are certain to promote marital bliss.

The assessment of sex role strain in relationships will not be easy. As with any assessment or data-gathering enterprise, the biases of the observers will inevitably affect how we perceive situations, the kind of measurement instruments we devise, the degree of inference we allow ourselves to make, and the nature of such inferences. This subtle dimension is especially important in marital assessment because we are dealing with what is arguably the most important social and psychological

Different patterns of sex roles have not yet been assessed by marital researchers.

domain of the human animal—his or her intimate, private, and committed relationship to another person. Behavioral workers have perhaps a special challenge because, as Wachtel (1977) has pointed out, they tend to take client complaints at face value and are more reluctant than investigators operating within other paradigms to dig and probe beyond what is fairly obvious. If a woman is annoyed by her husband bringing home business associates at the last minute for dinner, is this a problem to be solved by working out an acceptable exchange—she will make the dinner if he will take care of the cars—or is it the therapist's responsibility to raise the issue of sex roles and encourage a reexamination of how household responsibilities are divided up and whose time is more or less important? This example makes clear that psychological assessment, like other scientific gathering of knowledge, is not a purely objective enterprise. Rather it reflects some bias on the part of the assessor, and the very act of assessing for X rather than for Y constitutes in itself an intervention. The couple's attention is directed to aspects of their relationship that may have escaped their conscious attention and now, by virtue of the therapist's questioning, become a legitimate arena to explore.

Not all behavior, however, is reactive to being measured, and much remains to be learned about this possible source of invalidity (see Haynes and Horn, 1982). We do know that clients and subjects must become accustomed to being observed before the information being collected can be taken seriously. For example, a recorder might run for half an hour before the taped conversation of a group becomes a source of data on group interaction.

Another problem is the **external** or **ecological validity** of an assessment, whether it applies to the actual situations of interest to the researcher or clinician. Imagine that a therapist has a client role-play in the office to determine whether the young woman asserts herself to her mother, the therapist taking the part of the parent. If she proves to be assertive, can the therapist conclude that she has no assertion problems with her mother? It would be hasty to do so. The most obvious consideration is that the therapist is not the client's mother! Moreover, the particular situation selected for role playing, such as asking the mother not to telephone so often, might not touch on other problems requiring more assertion. The client might be able to ask her mother for a loan but not for some baby-sitting help. Any observation made of behavior is necessarily limited. We can *never* observe all conceivable situations; assessment, like any other knowledge-gathering enterprise, always touches on less than exists or could exist. Behavioral assessors must be mindful how restricted their observations are and maintain a modest and cautious attitude about the external validity of their assessments.

Yet another issue are the many distortions that can creep into any observation made by a human being. We have discussed in Chapters 1 and 2 the important roles that paradigms play in science. Any assessor has a point of view and is subject to the effects of this bias. Most importantly, assessors may have expectations and communicate them to subjects. Some years ago Robert Rosenthal (1966) reported on a series of experiments that shocked experimental psychologists and clinicians alike. He demonstrated through review of others' work and by his own ingenious techniques that experimenters can often unwittingly influence the outcome of a study by virtue of having certain expectations about the results. This difficulty of experimenter bias has come to be called the **Rosenthal effect.** But in an interesting demonstration by Kent, O'Leary, and their colleagues (1974), experimenter bias was shown to affect overall conclusions rather than specific behavioral observations. In this study observers used a behavioral coding system as they watched videotapes of children who were being treated for disruptive behavior. One group of observers was told that the treatment would decrease disruptive

behavior, the other that no change was expected. As Rosenthal's studies would suggest, observers afterward made the judgment that disruptive behavior had decreased if they had been told it was expected to. More importantly, however, their *specific behavior recordings* did not show bias. These results indicate the usefulness of relatively objective coding schemes in observing behavior.

Finally, the indicators we choose for measuring what interests us are the most basic issue in the validity of behavioral assessment. Consider the example mentioned earlier, measuring hostility by counting instances of lateness. Is this the best measure of hostility we can select? People might be late frequently for reasons other than hostility. Any person who has had to fight traffic at rush hour can surely come up with at least one example! We would have to take care, then, that a person whose hostility we wish to assess will not be late for nonemotional reasons.

There are many ways to evaluate how meaningful our measures are, and the validity of a wide range of behavioral assessment methods is actively being investigated (see Hersen and Bellack, 1988). Much of the discussion of behavioral marital assessment in Box 4.4 was concerned with establishing the validity of several assessment procedures, for example, finding that fewer "pleases" were reported by distressed couples employing the Spouse Observation Checklist than by couples who were satisfied with their marriages.

These, then, are some of the problems in determining the validity of behavioral assessment and some of the strategies employed to handle them. Behavioral assessment has emerged as one of the liveliest areas of work in clinical psychology and psychiatry (Box 4.5).

The Consistency and Variability of Behavior

Walter Mischel, in *Personality and Assessment* (1968), argued that the environment is a more important determinant of behavior than are personality traits. Trait theorists, as stated earlier, believe that human beings can be described as having a certain "amount" of a characteristic, such as "stinginess" or "obsessiveness," and that their behavior in a variety of situations can be predicted by the degree to which they possess this characteristic. This position implies that people will behave fairly consistently in a variety of situations and will also show stability over time—a highly aggressive person, for example, will be more aggressive than someone low in aggression at home, at work, and at play, and fur-

BOX 4.5

THE ASSESSMENT OF ANXIETY: IN PURSUIT OF AN ELUSIVE CONSTRUCT

Many issues in assessment can be appreciated by considering efforts to measure anxiety, one of the most prevalent emotions and one of great concern to psychopathologists and therapists. They have generally relied on three modes of measurement: self-report questionnaires, observations of overt behavior, and physiological measurements.

Allowing people to describe the phenomena of their emotions in their own terms, as is done in clinical interviews, provides useful information about the one individual interviewed; but this strategy alone makes it difficult to compare the experiences of a number of people and, even more important, to quantify what they say. Researchers have therefore devised various self-report questionnaires that attempt to direct the individual's impressions into standardized terms. The following are some sample items from the Taylor Manifest Anxiety Scale (Taylor, 1953), which consists of fifty items drawn from the MMPI.

I work under a great deal of strain.	True False
I am usually calm and not easily upset.	True False
I sweat very easily even on cool days.	True False
I always have enough energy when faced with difficulty.	True False
My sleep is restless and disturbed.	True False

An anxious person would underline the true and false responses as indicated. The test is scored by simply summing the number of "anxious" responses made by the subject. This score is then assumed to represent the person's general level of anxiety.

The second means of assessing anxiety is to observe overt behavior for reactions and movements that are believed to reflect the internal emotional state—trembling, perspiring, nail biting, fleeing from a situation. Observers trained to administer Paul's (1966) Timed Behavioral Checklist for Performance Anxiety time-sampled the overt behavior of subjects in a stressful situation, recording instances of twenty indices of anxiety whenever they were observed.

Physiological measurements of activities of the autonomic nervous system and the output of certain endocrine glands also indicate levels of anxiety. The availability of these measurements has encouraged researchers to define anxiety in physiological terms. The situation in which physiological measurements are taken is very important, however. What would be revealed, for example, if recording electrodes were attached to a woman who is about to have sexual relations? Both before and during sexual activity the heartbeat is very likely to be faster, blood pressure higher, perspiration greater, and breathing more rapid, all physiological responses that are generally regarded as indicators of sexual excitement as well as of anxiety. But why would we not conclude that our female subject is, indeed, anxious as she contemplates sexual intercourse? As we shall see in Chapter 13, many people are debilitated by fear in sexual situations. How can an investigator distinguish rapid breathing that reflects sexual excitement from rapid breathing that reflects anxiety? Part of the answer necessarily lies in other observations being made concurrently. If at the time physiological measures are being taken the femal subject convincingly reports that she is looking forward to what is to come, and if she ultimately derives great enjoyment from her sexual partner, we would almost certainly choose to interpret her rapid breathing and other physiological responses as indicating sexual arousal. The situation and her self-report of it must be taken into consideration.

Not only are the physiological indicators of anxiety evident in other emotional states, but the many measures of anxiety have been found time and again *not* to correlate well with one another (see Martin, 1961; Lang, 1969). In a stressful situation such as being threatened with painful electric shock, many people report being very nervous, but their heart rates may be lower rather than elevated. An individual taking an important examination for which he

---

thermore will show this trait tomorrow and next week, as well as today. After reviewing the evidence bearing on this question, Mischel concluded that the behavior of people is often not very consistent from situation to situation.

Not surprisingly, Mischel's attack on trait theory elicited a heated debate in the literature. For example, the psychodynamic theorist Paul Wachtel (1977) argues that social-learning theorists like Mischel ignore current psychoanalytic thinking, which does not entirely overlook the way behavior varies in different situations. Moreover, Wachtel argues, the behavior of individuals whom

clinicians tend to encounter may indeed be predictable on the basis of some underlying trait or disposition. Clinical problems may, in fact, be associated with a rigidity or inflexibility to changing conditions.[6]

---

[6]It has been suggested that people at the other extreme, those who "shift with the wind," so to speak, may also be subject to emotional disorder. That is, some forms of disorder may be connected to overdependence on the environment as a guide to behavior. To be totally at the mercy of one's surroundings, like a rudderless ship, would seem to pose as many problems as being insensitive to varying environmental demands (Phares, 1979).

or she is ill-prepared may deny feeling anxious and yet be observed trembling. Moreover, if people are asked to report on their awareness of various signs of anxiety, such as a feeling of tightness in the neck, their avoidance of social gatherings and worrying, their self-reports tend to cluster into one of three fairly independent groups—somatic, behavioral, and cognitive (Lehrer and Woolfolk, 1982). Thus the anxiety reported by people appears to be made up of one of three relatively separate components. One person may have bodily indicators, such as muscle tension and acid stomach, and yet not experience cognitive signs, such as ruminating about an alarming event.

On a more general level many workers regard the concept of anxiety as a useful one for organizing and interrelating data from numerous sources. Maher (1966) and Lang (1969), for example, consider anxiety to be a hypothetical **construct,** a convenient fiction or inferred state that mediates between a threatening situation and the observed behavior of an organism. They also assume that the construct is multifaceted or multidimensional, and that each facet is not necessarily evoked by a given stressful situation or always expressed to the same degree, another explanation of the low intercorrelations for the measures of anxiety.

As a scientific construct, anxiety must be tied to observables, the conditions that produce it and the effects that follow its induction. For this very reason Skinner (1953), as we indicated earlier (see page 45), argues that mediators are not essential in accounting for behavior. Since the construct of anxiety is linked to stimuli and responses, why not dispense with it and talk only of observables? Furthermore, might not the inference of an internal state lead us to believe that an adequate explanation has been found and thereby discourage the continuing search for ways to predict and control behavior?

These are cogent objections, and they have forced workers to exercise great care in their use of the anxiety construct. As will be noted in Chapter 5, investigators who employ mediators such as anxiety do so in hopes of better

organizing their data and of generating hypotheses. We seldom find experimental psychologists speaking about anxiety without being able at any time to explain how and why they infer that the emotional state exists.

Finally, certain experiments would not be undertaken or could not be explained without inferring the mediating state. To illustrate, let us consider an experiment reviewed by Rescorla and Solomon (1967). Dogs were taught to avoid a stimulus (CS) by pairing it repeatedly with a painful shock (UCS). Then they were totally paralyzed with injections of curare, a drug that prevents movement of the skeletal muscles. One group of animals, while paralyzed, were repeatedly presented with the CS, but shock did not accompany it. In Pavlovian, classical conditioning terms, these would be considered attempts to extinguish the conditioned response. Did these animals learn, while paralyzed and unable to move, that the CS was in fact no longer followed by shock? Phrased another way, did the previously learned fear of the CS undergo any extinction? The answer was obtained on a subsequent day when the dogs in this group had completely recovered from the curare and were confronted with the CS. The unshocked presentations of the CS a day or two earlier had indeed reduced avoidance behavior, even though no overt response could have occurred during the curare paralysis. The control animals, who had not been confronted with the CS while paralyzed, did not show a reduction in avoidance behavior.

How do we account for such remarkable findings? Rescorla and Solomon deem it necessary, and legitimate, to infer a mediating fear that was lessened when the dogs were presented with the CS while paralyzed with curare. Clearly something was being unlearned during the time that the dogs could not respond by avoiding the CS. By positing a mediating fear, we can make sense of these findings and relate them to a wealth of other theory and research. The experiment just described does indicate that anxiety, or fear, can be useful as an explanatory device. Nonetheless, the anxiety construct poses continual difficulties for those who employ it.

Wachtel also suggests that people tend to perceive certain kinds of situations in a particular fashion; the perception in effect renders situations that look different to an experimenter equivalent in their own eyes. For example, a person who might be described as paranoid sees threats in seemingly innocuous situations. Insensitivity to circumstances is not his or her problem; rather this person perceives a great many situations as threatening events. In addition, people can *elicit* certain kinds of reactions from their surroundings. The paranoid individual may not only perceive people as threatening but make them so by attacking them first. In effect, he

transforms different situations into similar and dangerous ones. As a result his own behavior varies little.

Wachtel proposes also that a personality disposition can affect the kinds of situations an individual selects or constructs for himself. (This view, it should be mentioned, was espoused by Gordon Allport [1937], the famous Harvard personality psychologist, whose work on traits underlies much of the current debate. Contrary to what some situationalists allege, Allport did not ignore the role of the environment in his theorizing about personality traits; cf. Zuroff [1986].) A generally optimistic person, for example, may seek out situations that confirm his positive outlook, which in turn strengthens his trait-tendency to find and/or to construct similar sanguine situations in the future. There is a constantly reciprocating interaction, then, with personality traits influencing situations one is in, and situations in turn influencing personality. "Consistency over extended periods of time . . . may be the product of extended histories of choosing situations conducive to one's attitudes, traits, and dispositions" (Snyder, 1983, p. 510). Interestingly enough, Wachtel's psychodynamic speculations are consistent with recent social psychological research including that of Bandura (1982), Mischel (1977) himself, Snyder (1983), and Emmons and Diener (1986).

Wachtel goes on to argue that the experiments Mischel attends to are generally done with normals whose behavior is probably more flexible than that of patients. As just mentioned, one of the hallmarks of mental disorder may be rigidity and inflexibility, which is another way of saying that behavior is consistent in a variety of situations. Therefore, by studying basically normal people, social-learning theorists may have concluded that people are more variable than they might had they studied patients.

Mischel, in an important paper published in 1973, replied to some of his critics by suggesting that social-learning theory can indeed incorporate certain personality variables in a more systematic fashion than was made clear in his original pronouncements in 1968. He suggested a set of primarily cognitive "person variables." The expectancy of affecting or not affecting the environment may, for example, be a major factor determining behavior and allowing its prediction.

In the course of the debate touched off by Mischel's important book, a number of psychologists have suggested that his original position was too extreme. Block (1971) challenged Mischel's conclusions regarding the inconsistency of behavior. In examining the studies Mischel used to support his claim, Block finds that most of them have serious flaws. For example, Mischel cites a single study (Burwen and Campbell, 1957) to support his contention that attitudes toward authority figures are not consistent. In this study, Block notes, reliability is not reported for some of the assessments made, and for others the reliability figures were quite low. Low reliability precludes finding strong relationships in measurements and thus of course any degree of consistency in the attitudes assessed. Block also presents information that does show consistency of behavior and was not considered by Mischel. A notable example is Block's own longitudinal study (1971), which indicated considerable consistency of personality as it was assessed in young people when they were attending junior high school, then senior high school, and later when they were adults.

Additional evidence of consistency and stability of behavior comes from Epstein (1979), who also criticized the studies used by Mischel to buttress the situationist position. These studies, noted Epstein, looked only at small bits of behavior, a strategy as inappropriate as it would be to measure IQ by looking at a person's score on a single item. More appropriate is an *averaging* of behavior from a range of situations. In the studies he conducted, Epstein collected data on a number of occasions and was indeed able to demonstrate marked consistency in behavior.

Mischel and Peake (1982), however, have countered these criticisms, pointing out that major assessment studies have all employed multiple measures and observations and yet have still failed to find significant behavioral consistencies. People can indeed be shown to behave consistently if their behavior is sampled more than once in the same kinds of situations, for example, being punctual for a lecture on day 1 as well as for one on day 2. Finding behavior to be similar in similar situations, however, is different from demonstrating that a person is, for example, anxious in situations Y and Z as well as in situation X.

Bandura (1986) has proposed that the heavy reliance of trait theorists on self-report questionnaires colors their conclusions because, he suggests, people may selectively perceive themselves as consistent[7] and respond accordingly on these questionnaires. The questionnaires probe for typical behavior in poorly specified situations, for example, "Do you tend to lose your temper when you get angry?" On the other hand, if people are observed in a variety of different situations, their actual behavior will show itself to be much more diverse and sensitive to environmental differences—a conclusion that can be drawn from a vast literature in social and personality psychology.

Furthermore, Bandura (1986) asserts that Epstein and other trait theorists neglect the *functionality* of performing behavior X in situation Y, that is, whether it pays off to act a certain way in a particular situation. As a social behaviorist, Bandura focuses more than do

---

[7]An intriguing possibility is that the culture fosters a trait orientation to understanding behavior. Most of us grew up with the idea that people can be characterized as "nice," "good-humored," "just," "rotten," and so forth. Pop psychology certainly reflects and fosters this bias, as does astrology, a pseudoscientific field that achieved even greater notoriety than usual when, in May of 1988, it was revealed that a sitting American president and especially his wife consulted an astrologer and apparently regulated some of their daily plans according to her readings. It may also be the case that most of us *value* consistency in our and others' behavior even when, alas, that consistency leads us to conclude that little good is to be expected from a given individual because he is lazy or mean. A belief in traits conveys predictability and perhaps also control: if Joe is "a good guy," then we can rely on him no matter what; and if Jake is "a jerk," then that too can be relied on and planned around, even if we wished he were a different sort of person.

Walter Mischel, the prominent psychologist whose work stimulated the current debate concerning whether traits or situations are the most powerful determinants of behavior.

trait theorists on the situational determinants of behavior, especially the reinforcements anticipated by the individual. "Aggressive acts by delinquents towards parish priests and rival gang members will correlate poorly, however much averaging one does" (p. 10).

What is emerging from this sometimes contentious literature on traits versus behavioral variability is an appreciation for the way personality factors *interact* with different environments, a paradigmatic perspective that overlaps considerably with the diathesis-stress viewpoint that marks our own study of psychopathology.

Summary

Clinicians rely on several modes of assessment in trying to find out how best to describe a patient, in their search for the reasons he or she is troubled, and in designing effective treatments. Described in some detail were clinical interviews, projective tests such as the Rorschach, standardized personality inventories such as the MMPI, intelligence tests, and tomographic and neuropsychological tests for organic brain dysfunction.

In their assessment, behavior therapists gather information on four sets of factors: situational determinants, organismic variables, responses, and the consequences of behavior. Whereas traditional diagnosis, of which DSM-IIIR is an example, seeks to understand people in terms of general traits or personality structure, behavioral and cognitive assessment is concerned more with how people act, feel, and think in particular kinds of situations. Specificity is the hallmark of cognitive and behavioral assessment, the assumption of behavioral clinicians and researchers being that by operating within this framework they will gather more useful information about people. Some of the procedures adopted by behavior therapists, such as direct observation of behavior and behaviorally oriented interviews, were also described. Problems of reliability and validity in behavioral assessment were examined. Current work in behavioral marital assessment was also reviewed.

No concept is at the same time more important and more difficult to define and to measure than anxiety. This elusive concept was discussed separately.

Finally, the lively controversy about how stable human behavior is in varying situations was reviewed. The issue has for years been of both theoretical and practical interest to psychologists. Now, with the development of behavioral models of psychopathology and treatment, it has assumed special importance. The answers are far from in, but it appears prudent to say that behavior is probably more variable than was once thought by traditional personality theorists and also more stable in different situations than those working in the learning paradigm believe.

Fernand Leger, *Follow the Arrow*, 1919. Courtesy of The Art Institute of Chicago. © 1989.

Chapter 5

Research Methods in the Study of Abnormal Behavior

Science and Scientific Methods
  Testability and Falsifiability
  Reliability
  The Role of Theory
The Research Methods of Abnormal Psychology
  Epidemiological Research
  The Case Study
  The Correlational Method
  The Experiment
  Single-Subject Experimental Research
  Mixed Designs
Summary

From our discussion of different ways of conceptualizing and treating abnormal behavior and of problems in its classification and assessment, it should be clear that there is less than total agreement on how abnormal behavior ought to be studied. Our approach to the field is based on the belief that more progress will be made through scientific research than armchair speculation. Abnormal behavior, as we have already noted, has been the subject of theorizing for centuries. We are studying a field that has a high ratio of speculation to data. Because facts are hard to come by, it is important to discuss in some detail the contemporary research methods that are applied in psychopathology.

Science and Scientific Methods

In Chapter 1 we indicated the important role that subjective factors play in the collection and interpretation of data, indeed, in the very definition of what constitutes an observation. Thus there is actually no one science or scientific method, although we often read in college textbooks of "the scientific method." The phrase "as currently practiced" should really be added.

Let us consider science from the point of view of Baruch Spinoza, a famous Dutch philosopher of the seventeenth century. He believed that the scientist's role was to discover God's law. Today we say that Spinoza did not hold a "constructive" view of science. We do not necessarily imply that Spinoza's views were not useful, rather that they can be differentiated from perspectives that emphasize the active role people play in constructing laws and principles. Contemporary scientists tend to regard the laws and theories in existence as constructions or inventions made by scientists. And the rules to be followed in formulating and evaluating these hypotheses and laws are also constructed by people who may very well change them at any time. Science, as currently practiced, is the pursuit of systematized knowledge[1] through observation. Thus the term refers to a method, the systematic acquisition and evaluation of information. It also refers to a goal, the development of principles that explain the information. Contemporary science strives for explanations that are an outgrowth of, and can be modified by, publicly observed evidence. Both observations and explanations must meet the criteria of testability (falsifiability) and reliability.

Testability and Falsifiability

A scientific approach requires first that propositions and ideas be stated in a clear and precise way. Only then can scientific claims be exposed to systematic probes and tests, any one of which could negate the scientist's expectations about what will be found. Statements, theories, and assertions, regardless of how plausible they may seem, must be testable in the public arena and be subject to being disproved. The attitude of science is an extremely doubting one. It is not enough to assert, for example, that particular traumatic experiences during childhood may cause psychological maladjustment in adulthood. This is no more than a possibility or proposition. According to a scientific point of view, such a hypothesis must be amenable to systematic testing that could show it to be wrong.

Reliability

Closely related to testability is the demand that each observation forming a scientific body of knowledge be reliable. Whatever is observed must occur under prescribed circumstances not once but repeatedly. The event cannot be seen or detected only by a single individual or individuals in a given laboratory, community, or country. Instead, it must be reproducible under the circumstances stated, anywhere, anytime. If the event cannot be reproduced, scientists become wary of the legitimacy of the original observation.

The Role of Theory

A *theory* is a set of propositions meant to explain a class of phenomena. A primary goal of science is to advance theories to illuminate the information with which it deals, often by proposing cause–effect relationships. The results of empirical research allow the adequacy of theories to be evaluated. Theories themselves can also play an important role in guiding research by suggesting that certain additional data be collected. The generation of a theory is perhaps the most challenging part of the scientific enterprise—and one of the least understood. It is sometimes asserted, for example, that a scientist formulates a theory simply by considering data that have been previously collected and then deciding, in a rather straightforward fashion, that a given way of talking about them is the most economical and useful.

Although some theory building follows this course, not all does. Aspects too seldom mentioned are the *creativity* of the act and the *excitement* of finding a novel way to conceptualize things. A theory sometimes seems

---

[1]The word science comes from the Latin *scire*, to know.

Sophisticated laboratory equipment represents one method of increasing the reliability of data.

to leap from the scientist's head in a wonderful moment of insight. New ideas suddenly occur to the scientist, and connections hitherto overlooked are suddenly grasped. What seemed obscure or meaningless just a moment before now makes a new kind of sense within the framework that the new theory provides.

In formulating a theory, scientists must often make use of theoretical concepts, unobservable states or processes that are inferred from observable data. Although theoretical concepts are inferred from observable data, they go beyond what can actually be seen or measured. Several advantages may thus be gained. First, theoretical concepts often bridge spatiotemporal relations. For example, in early physics it was noted that a magnet placed close to some iron filings would cause some of the filings to move toward it. How does one piece of metal influence another over the spatial distance? The inferred concept of magnetic fields proved to be very useful in accounting for this phenomenon. Similarly, in abnormal psychology we may often want to bridge temporal gaps with theoretical concepts. If a child has had a particularly frightening experience and his or her behavior is changed for a lengthy period of time, we need to explain how the earlier event is able to exert an influence over subsequent behavior. The unobservable and inferred concept of *acquired fear* has been very helpful in this regard.

Theoretical concepts may also be used to account for already observed relationships. Let us take a classic example proposed by a philosopher of science, Carl Hempel (1958). An early observer of nature has been studying what happens to various objects as they are placed in water. He or she formulates some lawlike generalizations, such as "Wood floats in water, iron sinks." In addition to the fact that a large number of such generalizations would be needed to describe exhaustively the behavior of all objects placed in liquids, exceptions to the generalizations are likely. Iron in a particular shape (boatlike) will float on water, and a water-logged piece of wood will sink. The solution is to propose a theoretical term, in this case specific gravity, that can both simplify descriptions of what will and will not float and allow errorless statements to be made. Specific gravity is the ratio of the weight of an object to its volume. With this theoretical term we can now readily specify what will happen to *any* body placed in *any* liquid. If the specific gravity of the object is less than that of the liquid displaced, the object will float.

Let us now examine a similar and familiar example closer to the field of psychopathology. We may observe that people who are taking an examination, who expect a momentary electric shock, or who are fighting with a companion all have sweaty palms, trembling hands, and a fast heartbeat. If we ask them how they feel, they all report that they are agitated. The relationships can be depicted as shown in Figure 5.1a. Or we could say that all the situations have made these individuals anxious, and that anxiety has in turn caused the reported agitation, the sweaty palms, the faster heartbeat, and the trembling hands. Figure 5.1b shows anxiety as a theoretical concept explaining what has been observed. The first part of the figure is much more complex than the second, where the theoretical term anxiety becomes a mediator of the relationships.

Situations   Behavior

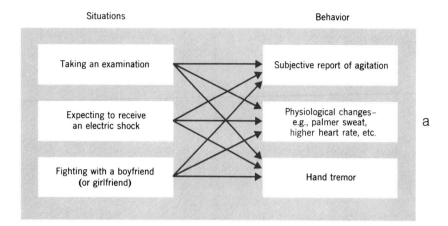

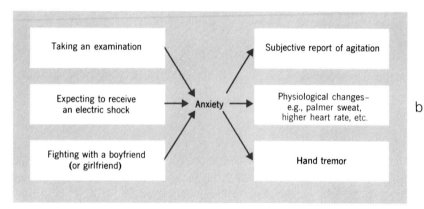

FIGURE 5.1
An illustration of the advantages of using anxiety as a theoretical concept. The arrows in part (b) are fewer and more readily understood. After Miller (1959).

With these advantages in mind, we must consider the criteria to be applied in judging the legitimacy of a theoretical concept. One earlier school of thought, the *operationist,* proposed that each such concept take as its meaning a single observable and measurable operation. In this way each theoretical concept would be nothing more than one particular measurable event. For example, anxiety might be identified as *nothing more* than scoring 50 on an anxiety questionnaire. It was soon realized, however, that this approach would take away from theoretical concepts their greatest advantage. If each theoretical concept is **operationalized** in only one way, its generality is lost. If the theoretical concept of learning, for instance, is identified as a *single* operation or effect that can be measured, such as how often a rat presses a bar, other behavior such as a child performing arithmetic problems or a college student studying this book cannot also be called learning, and attempts to relate the different phenomena to one another might be discouraged. The early operationist point of view quickly gave way to the more flexible position that a theoretical concept can be defined by *sets* of operations or effects. In this way the concept may be linked to several different measurements, each of which taps a different facet of the concept (see Figure 5.1b).

The Research Methods of Abnormal Psychology

All empirical research entails the collection of observable data. Sometimes research will stay at a purely descriptive level, but often researchers will observe several events and try to determine how they are associated or related. In the field of abnormal psychology, for example, there is a large descriptive literature concerning the typical symptoms of people who have been diagnosed as having particular disorders. These symptoms can then be related to other characteristics such as gender or social class; for example, attention deficit disorder is more common in boys than in girls. But science demands more than describing relationships. We often want to understand the *causes* of the relationships we have observed. For example, we want to know *why* attention deficit disorder is found more often in boys than girls.

In this section we describe the most commonly used research methods in the study of abnormal behavior: **epidemiological research;** the **case study;** the **correlation;** the **experiment,** both with **groups** and **single subjects;** and the **mixed design.** Each of the methods varies in the degree to which it permits the collection of adequate descriptive data and the extent to which it allows causal relationships to be inferred.

Epidemiological Research

Epidemiology is the study of the frequency and distribution of illness in a population. In epidemiological research, data are gathered about the rates of illness and possible correlates of illness in a large sample or population. Some key terms in epidemiological research include the following:

prevalence, the proportion of a population that has the disorder being studied at a given point or period of time;

incidence, the number of new cases of a disorder that occur in some period, usually a year;

risk factor, a condition or variable that, if present, increases the likelihood of developing the disorder being studied.

In psychopathology, knowledge of rates of various diagnoses is important for planning health care facilities. Such information has been collected in a recent, large-scale study conducted in three cities—Baltimore, St. Louis, and New Haven (Robins *et al.*, 1984). In each city a careful plan was developed for sampling residents and interviewing them using a specially constructed interview to formulate diagnoses. More than three thousand people were interviewed at each site. Some data from this study are displayed in Table 5.1. The table presents what are called lifetime prevalence rates, the proportion of the sample that had ever experienced a disorder up to the time of the interview. We will make use of the Robins data throughout the book.

Epidemiological research can also contribute to understanding the causes of illness. A classic example comes from a study by an early epidemiologist, John Snow. During an outbreak of cholera in London, Snow was able to determine how the disease had spread and, finally, how to stop the spread. As he examined cases, he learned that most victims drank water from one source, the Broad Street pump. He then hypothesized that cholera was transmitted by contaminated water. He investigated further and showed that rates for the disease were higher in London than in upstream communities, where the water was cleaner. Numerous contemporary examples also attest to the importance of epidemiological research in understanding disease. As we will see in Chapter 7, the various factors that increase risk for heart disease (e.g., smoking, high cholesterol) were discovered in large-scale studies comparing rates of disease in persons with and without the risk factor.

In psychopathology there is no example where epidemiological research has allowed for a convincing etiological theory in any diagnostic category. However, interesting data have been gathered in epidemiological investigations. Depression, for example, is more prevalent in women than in men. Understanding this relationship may provide a clue to the cause of the disorder. Schizophrenia is much more frequent in the lowest social class. Again, if the cause of this relationship were known, it might provide clues to the etiology of the disorder. Epidemiological research may thus provide empirical results that offer avenues to search for causes.

The Case Study

The most familiar and time-honored method of observing others is to study them one at a time and to

TABLE 5.1
Lifetime prevalence of several DSM-III diagnoses from the Robins *et al.* study (after Robins *et al.*, 1984)

Diagnosis	New Haven	Baltimore	St. Louis
Alcohol Abuse/Dependence	11.5%	13.7%	15.7%
Schizophrenia	1.9%	1.6%	1.0%
Manic Episode	1.1%	0.6%	1.1%
Major Depressive Episode	6.7%	3.7%	5.5%
Phobia	7.8%	23.3%	9.4%
Panic Disorder	1.4%	1.4%	1.5%
Obsessive-Compulsive	2.6%	3.0%	1.9%
Somatization	0.1%	0.1%	0.1%
Anorexia	0.0%	0.1%	0.1%
Antisocial Personality	2.1%	2.6%	3.3%

record their behavior. In developing a case study, the clinician collects historical and biographical information from the individual and other sources. A comprehensive case study would cover family history and background, medical history, educational background, jobs held, marital history, and details concerning development, adjustment, personality, the life course, and the current situation. Clinicians may also carefully describe all efforts to treat the individual. Case reports from practicing clinicians may lack the degree of control and objectivity of research done using other methods, but these descriptive histories have played some important roles in the study of abnormal behavior. Specifically, the case history has been used in each of the following ways: (1) to provide a detailed description of a rare or unusual phenomenon and of important, often novel, methods or procedures of interviewing, diagnosis, and treatment; (2) to disconfirm allegedly universal aspects of a particular theoretical proposition; and (3) to generate hypotheses that can be tested through controlled research (Lazarus and Davison, 1971).

Descriptive Uses

In a famous case history of multiple personality reported in 1954, Thigpen and Cleckley described a patient, "Eve White," who assumed at various times three very distinct personalities. Their description of the case required an entire book, *The Three Faces of Eve*. The following brief summary emphasizes the moments in which new personalities emerged and what the separate selves knew of one another.

In this scene from *The Three Faces of Eve*, Eve Black (played by Joanne Woodward) is in a therapy session with her psychiatrist (Lee J. Cobb).

Eve White had been seen in psychotherapy for several months because she was experiencing severe headaches accompanied by blackouts. Her therapist described her as a retiring and gently conventional figure. One day during the course of an interview, however, she changed abruptly and in a surprising way.

As if seized by sudden pain, she put both hands to her head. After a tense moment of silence, both hands dropped. There was a quick, reckless smile, and, in a bright voice that sparkled, she said, "Hi there, Doc!" The demure and constrained posture of Eve White had melted into buoyant repose. . . . This new and apparently carefree girl spoke casually of Eve White and her problems, always using she or her in every reference, always respecting the strict bounds of a separate identity. . . . When asked her name, she immediately replied, "Oh, I'm Eve Black." (p. 137)

After this rather startling revelation, Eve was observed over a period of fourteen months in a series of interviews that ran to almost a hundred hours. A very important part of Eve White's therapy was to help her learn about Eve Black, her other infectiously exuberant self, who added seductive and expensive clothing to her wardrobe and lived unremembered episodes of her life. During this period still a third personality, Jane, emerged while Eve White was recollecting an early incident in which she had been painfully scalded by water from a washpot.

Jane, who from then on knew all that happened to the two Eves, although they did not share in her existence, was "far more mature, more vivid, more boldly capable, and more interesting than Eve White." She also developed a deep and revering affection for the first Eve, who was considered somewhat of a ninny by Eve Black. Jane, however, knew nothing of Eve White's earlier life, except as she learned of it through Eve's memories.

Some eleven months later, in a calamitous session, with all three personalities present at different times, Eve Black emerged and reminisced for a moment about the many good times she had had in the past but then remarked that she did not seem to have real fun anymore. She began to sob, the only time Dr. Thigpen had seen her in tears. She told him that she wanted him to have her red dress to remember her by. All expression left her face and her eyes closed. Eve White opened them. When Jane was summoned a few minutes later, she soon realized that there was no longer any Eve White either and began to experience a terrifying lost event. "No, no . . .!" Oh no, Mother. . . . I can't. . . . Don't make me do it," she cried. Jane, who earlier had known nothing of Eve's childhood, was five years old and at her grandmother's funeral. Her mother was holding her high off the floor and above the coffin and saying that she must touch her grandmother's face. As she felt her hand leave the clammy cheek, the young woman screamed so piercingly that Dr. Cleckley came running from his office across the hall.

The two physicians were not certain who confronted them. In the searing intensity of the remembered moment, a new personality had been welded. Their transformed patient did not at first feel herself as apart, and as sharply distinct a person, as had the two Eves and Jane, although she knew a great deal about all of them. When her initial bewilderment lessened, she tended to identify herself with Jane. But the identification was not sure or complete, and she mourned the absence of the two Eves, as though they were lost sisters. This new person decided to call herself Mrs. Evelyn White.

The case of Eve White, Eve Black, Jane, and eventually Evelyn constitutes a valuable classic in the literature because it is one of only a few detailed accounts of a rare phenomenon, multiple personality. Moreover, in addition to illustrating the phenomenon itself, the original report of Thigpen and Cleckley provides valuable details about the interview procedures that they followed, and it sheds light on the way in which the

"THERE ARE SEVERAL REASONS FOR YOUR PROBLEM: ENVIRONMENTAL STRESS, EARLY CHILDHOOD EXPERIENCE, CHEMICAL IMBALANCE, AND PRIMARILY, THE FACT THAT BOTH OF YOUR PARENTS ARE AS CUCKOO AS A BAVARIAN CLOCK."

woman's behavior may have developed and how the treatment progressed in this one case of multiple personality.

However, the validity of the information gathered in a case study is sometimes questionable. Chris Sizemore's book *I'm Eve* (Sizemore and Pittillo, 1977) indicates the incompleteness of Thigpen and Cleckley's case study just discussed. This woman—the real Eve White—claims that following her period of therapy with them her personality continued to fragment. In all, twenty-one separate and distinct "strangers" have come to inhabit her body at one time or another. Contrary to Thigpen and Cleckley's report, Sizemore maintains that nine of them existed before Eve Black ever appeared. One set of personalities—they usually came in threes—would weaken and fade, to be replaced by others. Eventually her personality changes were so constant and numerous that she might become her three persons in rapid switches resembling the flipping of television channels. The debilitating round robin of transformations and the fierce battle for dominance among her selves filled her entire life. After resolving what she hopes is her last trio, by realizing finally that her alternate personalities were true aspects of herself rather than strangers from without, Chris Sizemore decided to reveal her story as a means of minimizing the past.

The Case History as Evidence

Case histories can provide especially telling instances that negate an assumed universal relationship or law.

Freud, for example, initially believed that his female patients' reports of sexual assaults by their fathers or uncles were accurate descriptions of events and, moreover, that these events had a bearing on the problems being treated. Later, on the basis of a chance finding that the supposed sexual assailant of one of his patients could not have been physically present at the time indicated, he came to believe that some of these sexual assaults were fantasies. This single case provided a negative instance and led Freud to reject his previous idea that his patients' recollections of early sexual assaults were necessarily true.[2]

But the case history fares less well in providing evidence *in favor of* a particular theory or proposition. In the presentation of a case history, the means for confirming one hypothesis and ruling out alternative hypotheses are usually absent. To illustrate this lack of validity, let us consider a clinician who has developed a new treatment for depression, tries it out on a client, and observes that the depression lifts after six weeks of the therapy. Although it would be tempting to conclude that the therapy worked, such a conclusion cannot be drawn because any of several other factors could also have produced the change. A stressful situation in the patient's life may have resolved itself or perhaps (and there is evidence for this) episodes of depression are naturally time–limited. Thus, there are several plausible rival hypotheses that could account for the clinical improvement. The data yielded by the case study do not allow us to determine the true cause of the change.

Generating Hypotheses

Finally, the case study plays a unique and important role because it is very often of great heuristic value. Through exposure to the life histories of a great number of patients, clinicians gain experience in understanding and interpreting them. Eventually they may notice similarities of circumstances and outcomes and formulate important hypotheses that could not have been uncovered in a more controlled investigation.

It is a serious mistake to discount the importance of clinical experience per se. There is nothing mysterious about the fact that repeated exposure to any given set of conditions makes the recipient aware of subtle cues and contingencies which elude the scrutiny of those less familiar with the situation. Clinical experience enables a therapist to recognize problems and identify trends that are usually beyond the perception of novices, regardless of their general expertise. It is at this

level that new ideas will come to the practitioner and often constitute breakthroughs that could not be derived from animal analogues or tightly controlled investigations. Different kinds of data and different levels of information are obtained in the laboratory and the clinic. Each is necessary, useful, and desirable. (Lazarus and Davison, 1971, p. 197)

In summary, the case study is an excellent way of examining the behavior of a single individual in great detail and in generating hypotheses that can later be evaluated by controlled research. Thus it is useful in clinical settings, where the focus is on just one person. In the fields of clinical and personality psychology, some investigators argue that the essence of psychological studies always lies in the unique characteristics of an individual (e.g., Allport, 1961). The case history is an ideal method of study in such an individualistic or **idiographic** context. But in a **nomothetic** context, when only general, universal laws apply, the case study is of limited usefulness. Information collected on a single person may *not* reveal principles that are characteristic of people in general. Furthermore, the case history is unable to provide satisfactory evidence concerning cause–effect relationships.

The Correlational Method

In contrast to the case study, which is a rather informal gathering of information about a single individual, the correlational method requires a more systematic collection of data on particular aspects of a group of research participants. The correlational method is often employed in epidemiological research as well as in other studies where smaller samples are used. Correlational studies address questions of the form "Are variable X and variable Y associated in some way so that they vary together (co-relate)?" In other words, questions are asked concerning relationships; for example, "Is schizophrenia related to social class?" or "Are scores obtained on college examinations related to anxiety?" Thus the **correlational method** establishes whether there is a relationship between or among two or more variables. Numerous examples can be drawn from everyday life. Income correlates positively with the number of luxuries purchased: the higher the income, the more luxuries purchased. Height tends to be positively correlated with weight: taller people are usually heavier. This second relationship, that between height and weight, is by no means perfect, for many individuals are "overweight" or too fat for their height and "underweight" or too thin for their height. The relationship, however, is a strong and positive one.

---

[2]But recall the footnote on page 36. Freud may well have been in error in changing his mind.

TABLE 5.2
Data for determining a correlation*

Individuals	Height	Weight, pounds
John	5'10"	170
Asher	5'4"	120
Eve	5'4"	112
Gail	5'3"	105
Jerry	5'10"	180
Bob	6'1"	175
Gayla	5'2"	100
Steve	5'8"	145
Margy	5'5"	128
Gert	5'6"	143
Sean	5'10"	140
Kathleen	5'4"	116

*For these figures $r = +.93$.

Measuring Correlation

The first step in determining a correlation is to obtain pairs of observations of the variables in question, such as height and weight, on each member in a group of subjects (Table 5.2). Once such pairs of observations are obtained, we can determine how strong the relationship is between the two sets of observations. The most prevalent means of measuring such a relationship was devised by Karl Pearson and is referred to as the Pearson product-moment **correlation coefficient,** denoted by the symbol r. This statistic may take any value between -1.00 and $+1.00$ and measures both the magnitude and the direction of a relationship. The higher the absolute value of r, the larger or stronger the relationship between the two variables. An r of either $+1.00$ or -1.00 indicates a perfect relationship, whereas an r of .00 indicates that the variables are unrelated. If the sign of r is positive, the two variables are said to be **positively related**. In other words, as the values for variable X increase, those for variable Y also tend to increase. Conversely, when the sign of r is negative, variables are said to be **negatively related;** as values for one variable increase, those for the other tend to decrease. The correlation between height and weight, based on the data in Table 5.2, is $+.93$, indi-

cating a very strong positive relationship; as height increases so does weight.

Plotting a relationship graphically will often impart a better feel for it. Figure 5.2 presents diagrams of positive and negative correlations as well as unrelated variables. In the diagrams each point corresponds to two values determined for the given subject, the value of variable X and that for variable Y. In perfect relationships all the points fall on a straight line; if we know the value of only one of the variables for an individual, we can state with certainty the value of the other variable. Similarly, when the correlation is relatively large, there is only a small degree of scatter about the line of perfect correlation. The values tend to scatter increasingly and become dispersed as the correlations become lower. When the correlation reaches .00, knowledge of a person's score on one variable tells us nothing about his or her score on the other.

Statistical Significance

Thus far we have established that the magnitude of a correlation coefficient tells us the strength of a relationship between two variables. But scientists demand a more rigorous evaluation of the importance of correlations and use the concept of **statistical significance** for this purpose. Essentially, statistical significance has to do with the likelihood that the obtained relationship happened by chance and thus would be very unlikely to occur again were the research conducted a second time. A statistically significant correlation is one that is *not* likely to have occurred by chance. Traditionally, in psychological research, a correlation is considered statistically significant if the likelihood is five or less in one hundred that is a chance finding. This level of significance is called the .05 level, commonly written as $p < .05$. In general, as the size of the correlation coefficient increases, the result is more and more likely to be statistically significant.[3]

Statistical significance should not be confused with the social or real-life significance of research results. Research can yield findings that are statistically significant yet devoid of practical importance. Moreover, the level of statistical significance considered acceptable is determined by *social convention*, that is, the rules by which contemporary scientists agree to play the game. Thus if the results of a correlational study have a prob-

---

[1]Whether a correlation attains statistical significance also depends on the number of observations that were made. The greater the number of observations, the smaller r needs to be in order to reach statistical significance. Thus a correlation of $r = .30$ is statistically significant when the number of observations is large, for example, 300, although it would not be significant if only 20 observations have been made.

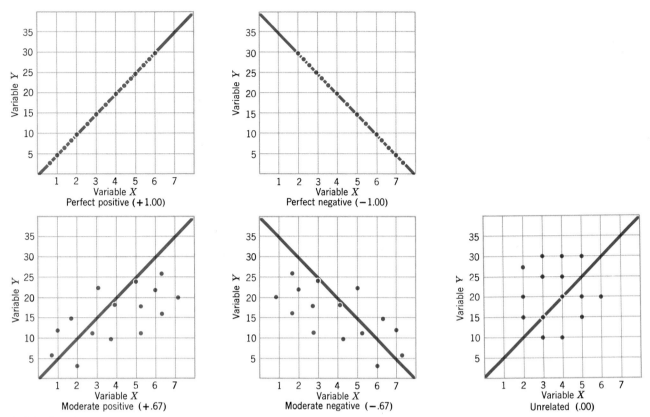

FIGURE 5.2
Scatter diagrams showing various degrees of correlational relationship.

ability of .10 or less that they occurred by chance rather than a probability of .05 or less, it is nowhere mandated that these are chance events and that the study is therefore totally worthless. Investigators may decide that, given the nature of a particular study, these results are quite encouraging and should not be disregarded. Then they must convince their colleagues that these findings are indeed valid. In a sense, science is a game of *persuasion.*

Applications to Psychopathology

The correlational method is widely used in the field of abnormal psychology. Whenever we compare people given one diagnosis with those given another or with normal people, the study is correlational. For example, two diagnostic groups may be compared to see how much stress members of each experienced before the onset of their disorders. Many investigators have also compared the performances of schizophrenics and normal people on laboratory tasks such as proverb interpretation or size estimation and on tests of reaction time (e.g., Kopfstein and Neale, 1972). Often such investigations are not recognized as correlational, perhaps because—as is often so in experiments—subjects come to

a laboratory for testing, or data are analyzed by comparing the average scores of the groups on each test or measure. But the logic of such studies is correlational: the correlation between two variables—being schizophrenic or nonschizophrenic and the average scores of each group on the laboratory test—is what is being examined. Variables such as being schizophrenic or nonschizophrenic are called **classificatory variables.** Schizophrenics have already been so diagnosed before they perform the laboratory task. Other examples of classificatory variables are age, sex, social class, and body build. These variables are naturally occurring patterns and are not manipulated by the researcher, an important requirement for the experimental variables to be discussed shortly. Thus classificatory variables fall into the domain of correlational research.[4]

---

[4]When such classificatory variables are used in correlational research, numbers are assigned as labels to denote values of a variable. For example, schizophrenics could arbitrarily be given the value 0 and normals given the value 1 (or vice versa). The correlation coefficient (technically a point-biserial in this case) can then be computed with values for diagnosis being a column of zeros or ones and the other column the scores on the other variable.

Nor should a classificatory variable such as a psychopathology be manipulated, for both practical and moral reasons. Although inflicting mild pain or discomfort might be (or might not be) ethically acceptable, inducing in an experiment extremely painful but psychologically significant experiences—of the kind people are only too often subjected to in their everyday lives—would be without question highly unethical. Inducing enough distress to cause psychopathology would be indefensible. Thus the correlational technique is the major strategy in studying the vagaries of psychopathology. Using this technique the psychopathologist can determine whether the responses and characteristics of patients correlate with their abnormality.

Directionality and Third-Variable Problems

The correlational method, although often employed in abnormal psychology, has a serious flaw. It does not allow us to determine cause–effect relationships because of two major problems of interpretation, the ***directionality problem*** and the ***third-variable problem.*** With respect to directionality, a sizable correlation between two variables tells us only that they are related or tend to covary with each other, but we do not really know which is cause and which effect. For example, correlations have been found between the diagnosis of schizophrenia and social class; lower-class people are more frequently diagnosed as schizophrenic than are middle- and upper-class people. One possible explanation is that the stresses of living in the lower social classes produce the behavior that is subsequently labeled schizophrenic. But a second and perhaps equally plausible hypothesis has been advanced: it may be that the disorganized behavior patterns of schizophrenic individuals cause them to lose their jobs and thus to become impoverished. The problem of directionality is present in many correlational research designs, hence the often-cited dictum "Correlation does not imply causation."

The directionality problem is best addressed by using a longitudinal design in which variables of interest are studied before a disorder has developed. In this way, the hypothesized "cause" can be measured before the "effect." For example, the most desirable way of collecting information about the development of schizophrenia would be to select a large sample of babies and follow them for the twenty to forty-five years that are the period of risk for the onset of schizophrenia. But such a method would be prohibitively expensive, for only about one individual in a hundred eventually becomes schizophrenic. The yield of data from such a simple longitudinal study would be small indeed. The ***high-risk method*** overcomes this problem; only individuals whose risk of becoming a schizophrenic in adulthood is greater than the average are selected for study. In most of the current research using this methodology, individuals who have a schizophrenic parent are selected for study; a schizophrenic parent increases a person's risk for developing schizophrenia. In addition to studies of schizophrenia, the high-risk method is used with several other disorders, and we will examine these findings in subsequent chapters.

Although correlation does not imply causation, determining whether or not two variables correlate may allow for the *disconfirmation* of certain causal hypotheses. That is, *causation does imply correlation.* For example, if an investigator has asserted that cigarette smoking causes lung cancer, he or she implies that lung cancer and cigarette smoking will be positively correlated. Studies of the two variables must show this positive correlation, or the theory will be disproved.

As for the third-variable problem, it may be that neither of the two variables studied in the correlation produces the other. Rather, some as yet unspecified

People from the lower socioeconomic classes are more likely to develop schizophrenia. This impoverished man may well be suffering from the disorder.

variable or process may be responsible for the correlation. Consider the following example, which points out an obvious third variable.

One regularly finds a high positive correlation between the number of churches in a city and the number of crimes committed in that city. That is, the more churches a city has, the more crimes are committed in it. Does this mean that religion fosters crime or does it mean that crime fosters religion? It means neither. The relationship is due to a particular third variable—population. The higher the population of a particular community, the greater . . . the number of churches and . . . the frequency of criminal activity. (Neale and Liebert, 1980, p. 109)

In psychopathology research there are numerous examples of third variables. For instance, biochemical differences between schizophrenics and normals have frequently been reported. These differences could reflect different diets or the fact that the patients are taking medication for their condition—the differences do not reveal anything telling about the nature of schizophrenia.   Are there any solutions to the third-variable problem? In general, the answer is yes, although the solutions are only partially satisfactory and do not permit unambiguous causal inferences to be made from correlational data. A discussion of these techniques, however, is beyond the scope of this book.[5]

The Experiment

The factors causing the associations and relationships revealed by correlational research cannot, as we have seen, be determined with absolute certainty. The experiment is generally considered to be the most powerful tool for determining causal relationships between events. As an introduction to the basic components of experimental research, let us consider a study of how expressing emotions about past traumatic events is related to health (Pennebaker, Kielcolt-Glaser, and Glaser, 1987). Fifty undergraduates participated in a six-week study, one part of which required them to come to a laboratory for four consecutive days.[6] On each of the four days, half of the subjects were required to write a short essay about a past traumatic event. They were instructed as follows:

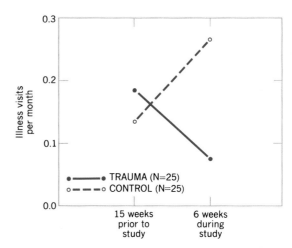

FIGURE 5.3
Health center illness visits for the periods before and during the experiment. After Pennebaker *et al.* (1987).

During each of the four writing days, I want you to write about the most traumatic and upsetting experiences of your entire life. You can write on different topics each day or on the same topic for all four days. The important thing is that you write about your deepest thoughts and feelings. Ideally, whatever you write about should deal with an event or experience that you have not talked with others about in detail.

The remaining subjects also came to the laboratory each day but wrote essays describing their daily activities, a recent social event, the shoes they were wearing, and their plans for the rest of the day . Information about how often the participating undergraduates used the university health center was available for the fifteen-week period before the study began and for the six weeks after it had begun. These data are shown in Figure 5.3. As can be seen, members of the two groups had visited the health center about equally prior to the experiment. After writing the essays, however, the number of visits declined for students who wrote about traumas and increased for the remaining students. (This increase may have been due to seasonal variation in rates of visits to the health center. The second measure of number of visits was taken in February, just before midterm exams.)

Basic Features of Experimental Design
The foregoing example illustrates many of the basic features of an experiment. The researcher typically begins with an ***experimental hypothesis.*** Pennebaker *et al.* hypothesized that expressing emotion about a past event would improve health. Second, the investigator chooses an ***independent variable*** that can be manipu-

---

[5]A readable presentation of the techniques to handle directionality and third variables can be found in Neale and Liebert's *Science and Behavior* (1986).

[6]There were more components to the research than will be described here. We present the major aspects of the design and results.

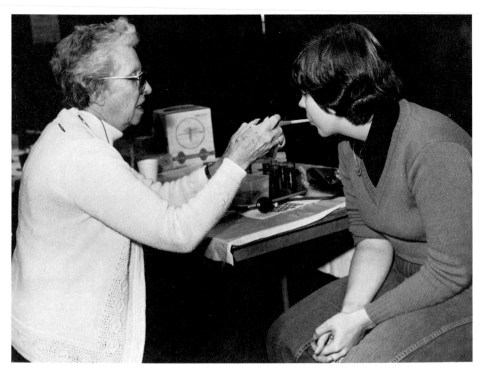

Visits to the student health center was the dependent variable in the Pennebaker et al. study.

lated, that is, some factor that will be under the control of the experimenter. Pennebaker *et al.* had some students write about past traumatic events and others about mundane happenings. Finally, the researcher arranges for the measurement of a ***dependent variable,*** which is expected to depend on or vary with manipulations of the independent variable. The dependent variable in this study was visits to the health center. When in such an investigation differences between groups are indeed found to be a function of variations in the independent variable, the researcher is said to have produced an ***experimental effect.***

Internal Validity

An additional feature of any experimental design is the inclusion of at least one ***control group.*** A control group is necessary if the effects in any experiment are to be attributed to the manipulation of the independent variable. In the Pennebaker *et al.* study the control group wrote about mundane happenings. The data from the control group provide a standard against which the effects of expressing emotion can be compared.

To illustrate this point with another example, consider a study of the effectiveness of a particular therapy in modifying some form of abnormal behavior. Let us assume that persons with poor self-concepts have asked for treatment and that they undergo therapy designed to remedy their condition. At the end of six months the patients are reassessed, and it is found that their self-concepts have improved compared to what they were at the beginning of the study. Unfortunately, such an investigation would not produce internally valid data. The improvement in self-concept from the beginning of the treatment to the end could have been brought about by several factors in addition to or instead of the particular treatment employed. For example, it may be that certain environmental events occurred within the six months and produced the improvement. Or it may be that people with a poor self-concept acquire better feelings about themselves with the mere passage of time. Variables such as these are often called ***confounds;*** they, like the third variables in correlational studies, confound the results, making them impossible to interpret.[7] Studies in which the effect obtained cannot be attributed with confidence to the independent variable are called ***internally invalid*** studies. The design of ***internally valid*** research, that is, research in which the effect obtained can be confidently attributed to the manipulation of the independent variable, is a primary goal in social sciences.

In the example just outlined, ***internal validity*** could have been secured by the inclusion of a control group.

---

[7]These confounds, and others described in this chapter, are unfortunately widespread in research on the effects of psychotherapy, as will be documented often throughout this book, especially in Part 6.

Such a group might have consisted of individuals with poor self-concepts who did *not* receive the therapeutic treatment. Changes in the self-concepts of these control subjects would constitute a **baseline** or standard against which the effects of the independent variable can be assessed. If a change in self-concept is brought about by particular environmental events, quite beyond any therapeutic intervention, the experimental group receiving the treatment and the control group receiving no treatment are equally likely to be affected. On the other hand, if after six months the self-concepts of the treated group have improved more than those of the untreated control group, we can be relatively confident that this difference is, in fact, attributable to the treatment.

The mere inclusion of a control group, however, does not ensure internal validity. To illustrate, let us consider another study of therapy, this time the treatment of two hospital wards of psychiatric patients. An investigator may decide to select one ward to receive an experimental treatment and then select another ward as a control. When the researcher later compares the frequencies of deviant behavior in these two groups, he or she will want to attribute any differences between them to the fact that patients in one ward received treatment and those in the other did not. But the researcher cannot legitimately draw this inference, for there is a competing hypothesis that cannot be disproved—that even before treatment the patients who happened to receive therapy might have had a lower level of deviant behavior than the patients who became the control group. The principle of experimental design disregarded in this defective study is that of **random assignment**.

Random assignment is achieved by ensuring that every subject in the research has an equal chance of being assigned to any of the groups. For example, in a two-group experiment a coin can be tossed for each subject. If the coin turns up heads, the subject is assigned to one group; if tails, he or she is assigned to another. This procedure minimizes the likelihood that differences between or among the groups after treatment will reflect pretreatment differences in the samples rather than true experimental effects. Random assignment was employed in the Pennebaker experiment.

Even with both a control group and random assignment, the results of the research may still be invalid. An additional source of error is the potential biasing influence of the experimenter or observers. This is the "Rosenthal effect" already mentioned in Chapter 4. As Rosenthal (1966) has suggested, the expectancies of an experimenter about the outcome of a study may conspire to produce results favorable to the initial hypothesis. He or she may subtly manipulate the subject to

give expected and desired responses. Although the pervasiveness of these effects has been questioned (Barber and Silver, 1968; Kent *et al.*, 1974), experimenters must remain on guard lest their results be influenced by their own expectations. To avoid biases of this type, many studies apply the so-called **double-blind** procedure. For example, in an investigation comparing the psychological effects of two drugs, the person dispensing the pills is kept ignorant (i.e., blind) about their actual content, and the subject is also not informed about the treatment he or she is receiving. With such controls the behavior observed during the course of the treatment is probably not influenced by biasing.[8]

Earlier, we briefly defined the term experimental effect, but we have yet to learn how it can be decided that an effect is important. To evaluate the importance of experimental results, as with correlations, researchers determine their statistical significance. A *significant* difference between groups is one that has little probability of occurring by chance alone. Thus this difference can be expected to occur whenever the same experiment is repeated. A difference between groups in an experiment, like a correlation, is typically considered statistically significant if the likelihood is five or less in one hundred that it is a chance finding.

External Validity

The extent to which the results of any particular piece of research can be generalized beyond the immediate experiment is the measure of their **external validity**. For example, if investigators have demonstrated that a particular treatment helps a group of patients, they will undoubtedly want to determine whether this treatment will be effective in ministering to other patients, at other times, and in other places. Pennebaker *et al.* would hope that their findings generalize to other instances of emotional expression (e.g., confiding to a close friend), to other situations, and to people other than those who participated in the experiment.

The external validity of the results of a psychological experiment is extremely difficult to determine. For example, there is the reactivity of observed behavior: merely knowing that one is a subject in a psychological experiment often alters behavior, and thus results are produced in the laboratory that may not automatically be produced in the natural environment. In many instances results obtained from investigations with laboratory animals such as rats have been generalized to human beings. Such generalizations are hazardous,

---

[8] Even with the double-blind procedure however, results may not be interpretable. Some drugs exert such strong effects that both patients and observers are keenly aware of who is taking the drug and who the placebo.

since there are enormous differences between *Homo sapiens* and *Rattus norvegicus*. Researchers must be continually alert to the extent to which they claim generalization for findings, for there are, in fact, no entirely adequate ways of dealing with the questions of external validity. The best that can be done is to perform similar studies in new settings with new participants so that the limitations, or the generality, of a finding can be determined.

Analogue Experiments

The experimental method is judged to be the most telling way to determine cause–effect relationships. The effectiveness of treatments for psychopathology is usually evaluated by the experimental method, for it has proved a powerful tool for determining whether a therapy reduces suffering. As you may well have surmised, however, the method has in fact been little used by those seeking the causes of abnormal behavior. Suppose that a researcher has hypothesized that a child's emotionally charged, overdependent relationship with his or her mother causes schizophrenia. An experimental test of this hypothesis would require assigning infants randomly to either of two groups of mothers! The mothers in one group will have undergone an extensive training program to ensure that they are able to create a highly emotional atmosphere and foster overdependence in children. The mothers in the second group will have been trained not to create such a relationship with the children they care for. The researcher then waits until the subjects in each group reach adulthood and determines how many of them become schizophrenic. Obviously, such an experimental design already contains insurmountable practical problems. But practical issues are hardly the principal ones that must concern us. Consider the ethics of such an experiment. Would the potential scientific gain of proving that an overdependent relationship with a person's mother brings on schizophrenia outweigh the suffering that would surely be imposed on some of the participants? In almost any person's view it would not. (Ethical issues are considered in greater detail in Chapter 21.)

In an effort to take advantage of the power of the experimental method, research on the causes of abnormal behavior has taken the **analogue** approach. Investigators have attempted to bring a *related* phenomenon, that is, an analogue, into the laboratory for more intensive study. In this way, internally valid results may be obtained, although the problem of external validity may be accentuated. In one type of analogue study, behavior is rendered temporarily "abnormal" through experimental manipulations. For example, lactate infusion can elicit a panic attack, hypnotic suggestion can produce "blindness," and threats to self-esteem

Early in their development monkeys need a mother, even if only a cloth surrogate like this one. Monkeys reared in isolation later show signs of both emotional distress and depression. When we generalize these findings about monkeys to human beings, we have used the monkey studies as analogues.

can increase anxiety and depression. If "pathology" can be experimentally induced by any one of these manipulations, the same process, existing in the natural environment, might well be a cause of the disorder. The key to interpreting such studies lies in the validity of the dependent variable as an analogue of a true clinical state. Are transient increases in anxiety or depression, for example, reasonable analogues of their clinical counterparts? Results of such experiments must be interpreted with great caution, and care must be taken about generalizing the results, but they do provide valuable hypotheses about the origins of psychopathology.

In another type of analogue study, subjects are selected because they are considered similar to patients given certain diagnoses. A large amount of research, for example, has been conducted with college students who were selected for study because they scored high on a paper-and-pencil measure of anxiety or depression. The question here is whether these anxious or depressed students are adequate analogues for those with an anxiety disorder or major depression. Some research bearing on this issue will be discussed in Chapter 9.

Whether experiments are regarded as analogues depends not on the experiment itself but rather on the use to which it is put. We can very readily study avoidance behavior in a white rat by running experiments with rats. The data collected from such studies are not analogue data if we limit our discussion to the behavior of rats. They become analogue data only when we draw implications from them and apply them to other domains, such as anxiety in human beings.

Some of the animal experiments we examine in later chapters are analogue in nature, with their results being generalized to human beings (e.g., see Chapter 9, page 228). It will be important to keep in mind that we are arguing by analogy when, for example, we attempt to relate reactions to stress of white rats to anxiety in people. At the same time, however, we do not agree with those who regard such analogue research as totally and intrinsically worthless for the study of human behavior. Although human beings and other mammals differ on many important dimensions, it does not follow that principles of behavior derived from animal research are necessarily irrelevant to human behavior.

Single-Subject Experimental Research

Experiments do not always have to be conducted on *groups* of people. In this section we shall consider experimental designs for studying a single subject.

The strategy of relying on a single subject appears to violate many of the principles of research design that we have discussed. As with the case study, there is no control group to act as a check on a single subject. Moreover, generalization will be difficult because the findings may relate to a unique aspect of the one individual whose behavior we have explored. Hence the study of a single individual would appear unlikely to yield any findings that could possess the slightest degree of internal or external validity. But, as we shall see, the experimental study of a single subject *can* be an effective research technique for certain purposes.

A method developed by Tate and Baroff (1966) for reducing the self-injurious behavior of a nine-year-old boy, Sam, serves as an example. The child, who had been diagnosed as psychotic, engaged in a wide range of self-injurious behavior, such as banging his head against the floors and walls, slapping his face with his hands, punching his face and head with his fists, hitting his shoulder with his chin, and kicking himself. Despite his self-injurious behavior, Sam was not entirely antisocial. In fact, he obviously enjoyed contact with other people and would cling to them, wrap his arms around them, and sit in their laps. This affectionate behavior gave the investigators the idea for an experimental treatment.[9]

---

[9]The use of the adjective experimental in this context prompts us to distinguish between two different meanings of the word. As applied to the research methods that have been discussed, the adjective refers to the manipulation of a variable that allows conclusions of a cause–effect relationship to be drawn. But here the word refers to a treatment whose effects are unknown or only poorly understood. Thus an "experimental drug" is one about which we know relatively little; however, such a drug might well be used in a correlational design or reported in a case study.

The study ran for twenty days. For a period of time on each of the first five days, the frequency of Sam's self-injurious actions was observed and recorded. Then on each of the next five days the two adult experimenters accompanied Sam on a short walk around the campus, during which they talked to him and held his hands continuously. The adults responded to each of Sam's self-injurious actions by immediately jerking their hands away from him and not touching him again until three seconds after such activity had ceased. The frequency of the self-injurious acts was again recorded. As part of the experiment, the schedule was then systematically reversed. For the next five days there were no walks, and Sam's self-afflicting behavior was again merely observed. Then for the last five days the experimenters reinstated their experimental procedure. The dramatic reduction in undesirable behavior induced by the treatment is shown in Figure 5.4. The design of such experiments, usually referred to as a **reversal,** or ABAB, **design** requires that some aspect of the subject's behavior be carefully measured during a given time period, the baseline (A), during a period when a treatment in introduced (B), during a reinstatement of the conditions that prevailed in the baseline period (A), and finally during a reintroduction of the experimental manipulation (B). If behavior in the experimental period is different from that in the baseline period, reverses when the experimentally manipulated conditions are reversed, and "re-reverses" when the treatment is again introduced, there is little doubt that the manipulation, rather than chance or uncontrolled factors, has produced the change.

The reversal technique cannot always be employed, however, for the initial state of a subject may not be recoverable, as when treatment produces an irreversible change. Moreover, in studies of therapeutic procedures, reinstating the original condition of the subject or patient would generally be considered an unethical practice. Most therapists would be extremely unwilling to act in any way that might bring back the very behavior for which a client has sought help, merely to prove that a particular treatment was indeed the effective agent in changing the behavior.

In situations where the reversal technique does not apply, the method of choice is the **multiple-baseline** procedure. Here two or more behaviors are selected for study. For example, if a child has "learning problems," both mathematical and reading performances might be picked as the two areas for treatment. When observing the child, the experimenter may notice that he or she is inattentive during lessions and proceed to collect baseline data on the degree of attentiveness during *both* mathematics *and* reading sessions. Rewards are then given the child for attention paid to the math-

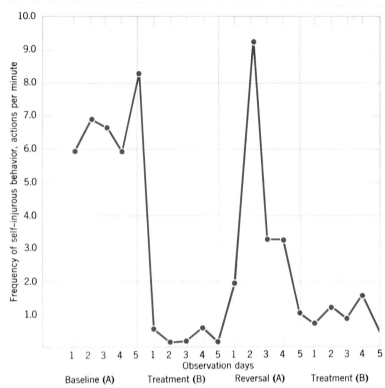

FIGURE 5.4
Effects of a treatment for self-injurious behavior in an experiment with an ABAB single-subject design. Note the rapid shifts in frequency of problem behavior as treatment is introduced (B), withdrawn (A), and finally reinstated (B). Adapted from Tate and Baroff (1966).

ematics lessons but not for attention paid during reading sessions. Again, the attentiveness of the child during both kinds of lessons is measured. Finally, in a third phase of the experiment, the child is rewarded for attention paid during reading as well as mathematics lessons.

A hypothetical pattern of the attentiveness of the child during the course of the experiment is shown in Figure 5.5. If such a pattern were indeed obtained, it would provide convincing evidence that the introduction of reward, and not other factors, was responsible for modifying the child's behavior. Had some uncontrolled environmental influence improved the child's attention, it presumably would have worked equally well during both mathematics and reading classes. Moreover, if reward were not the agent responsible for change, attentiveness during mathematics lessons would not have markedly improved as compared to attentiveness during reading sessions. Thus, by choosing two baselines of behavior to be modified (hence the term multiple baselines), the investigator was able to eliminate certain possible sources of invalidity.

As indicated earlier, even though an experiment with a single subject demonstrates an experimental effect, no generalization may be possible. The fact that a particular treatment works for a single subject does not necessarily imply that the treatment will be universally

effective. If the search for more widely applicable treatment is the major focus of an investigation, the single-subject design has a serious drawback. It may well help investigators to decide whether large-scale research with groups is warranted, however.

FIGURE 5.5
Outcome of a multiple-baseline, single-subject experiment that rewarded attention, initially during lessons in mathematics but not during reading lessons, and ultimately during both mathematics and reading instruction.

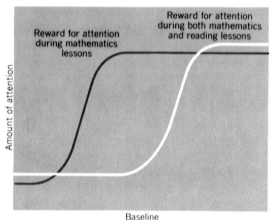

Mixed Designs

The experimental and correlational research techniques that we have just discussed can be combined in what is called a mixed design. In a mixed design, subjects who can be divided into two or more discrete and typically nonoverlapping populations are assigned as groups to each experimental condition. The two different types of populations, for example, schizophrenics and phobics, constitute a classificatory variable. That is, the variables schizophrenia and phobia were not manipulated, nor were they created by the investigator, and they can only be correlated with the manipulated conditions, which are true experimental variables.

To illustrate how a mixed design is applied, we shall consider an investigation of the effectiveness of three types of therapy (the experimental variable) on psychiatric patients who were able to be divided into two groups on the basis of the severity of their illnesses (the classificatory variable). The question was whether the effectiveness of the treatments varied with the severity of illness. The hypothetical outcome of such a study is presented in Figure 5.6. The (b) part of the figure shows the results obtained when the patients were divided into two groups, on the basis of the severity of their problems. The (a) part of the figure illustrates the unfortunate conclusions that would be drawn were the patients not able to be divided into those with severe and those with less severe illnesses. When all patients were grouped together, treatment 3 produced the greatest amount of improvement. Therefore, when no information about differential characteristics of the patients is available, treatment 3 would be preferred. When the severity of the patients' difficulties is considered, however, treatment 3 would no longer be the therapy of choice for *any* of the patients. Rather, as seen in Figure 5.6b, for those with less severe illness treatment 1 would be selected and for patients with more severe illness treatment 2 would be preferred. Thus a mixed design can identify which particular treatment applies best to which group of subjects.

In interpreting the results of mixed designs, we must be continually aware of the fact that one of the variables (severity of illness in our example) is not manipulated. Therefore the problems we have previously noted in interpreting correlations are to be found in interpreting the results of mixed designs as well.

Yet the inclusion of a manipulated variable, particularly one with multiple levels, does offer some advantages. Consider a study (Neale, 1971) in which schizophrenic and control subjects were administered an information-processing task of four different levels of complexity. The subjects were briefly presented with visual displays containing one, four, eight, or twelve alphabetic characters. Their task was to search the display and tell the experimenter whether it contained a

FIGURE 5.6
Effects of three treatments on patients whose symptoms vary in degree of severity. In (a), when the severity of the illness is not known and the patients are treated together, treatment number 3 appears to be best. In (b), the same data as in (a) are reanalyzed, dividing patients by severity. Now, treatment 3 is no longer best for any patients.

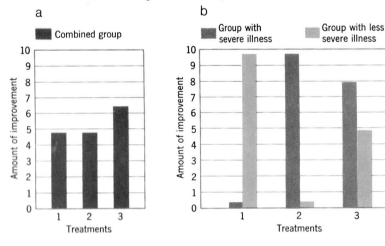

T or an *F*. The results of this investigation showed that schizophrenics differed from control subjects whenever the two groups saw more than one letter. This pattern is referred to as a ***differential deficit.*** The schizophrenics' performance was poorer than the control subjects' in one but not all the conditions. A differential deficit is more informative than a simple deficit on a single task. Maher (1974) explains why:

With the hypothesis that bulls are characterized by a desire to break Royal Worcester China, we stock a shop exclusively with that item, turn the bulls loose, and watch the ensuing destruction. Our hypothesis is duly confirmed—especially if our control group is composed of mice. (p. 2)

Maher goes on to point out that "just as bulls tend to break any kind of china, patient populations tend to do poorly at many tasks." In other words, the demonstration of a simple deficit provides little specific information, because the poor performance could be caused by any number of factors. A differential deficit, however, allows certain plausible rival hypotheses to be ruled out. The equality of performances of schizophrenics and control subjects when only a single letter was presented makes it unlikely that the schizophrenics' difficulties with larger displays could be attributed to a general failure to comprehend the task. If the schizophrenic subjects had been unable to understand the task or comply with the experimenter's instructions, they would not have done as well as control subjects in determining whether a single letter was a *T* or an *F*.

Our survey of the major research methods of abnormal psychology is now complete. It should be apparent that there is no perfect method that will easily reveal the secrets of psychopathology and therapy. Our task in subsequent chapters will be to attempt to synthesize the information yielded by investigations, conducted with varying methodologies, and to apply these results to advance knowledge of the field.

Summary

Science represents an agreed-upon problem-solving enterprise, with specific procedures for gathering and interpreting data in order to build a systematic body of knowledge. The position taken in this book is that scientific statements must have the following characteristics: they must be testable in the public arena, they must be subject to falsification, they must derive from reliable observations, and although they may contain references to unobservable processes, the concepts inferred must be linked to observable and measurable events or outcomes.

It is important to consider the various methods that scientists employ to collect data and arrive at conclusions. Clinical case studies serve unique and important functions in psychopathology, such as allowing rare phenomena to be studied intensively in all their complexity. Case studies also encourage the formulation of hypotheses that can be tested later through controlled research. Epidemiological research gathers information about the prevalence of disorder and about risk factors that increase the probability of disorder.

Correlational methods are the important means of conducting research in abnormal psychology, for diagnoses are classificatory and not experimentally manipulated variables. In correlational studies, statistical procedures allow us to determine the extent to which two or more variables correlate or co-vary. Conclusions drawn from nearly all correlational studies cannot legitimately be interpreted in cause–effect terms, however, although there is great temptation to do so.

The experimental method entails the manipulation of independent variables and the careful measurement of their effects on dependent variables. An experiment usually begins with a hypothesis to be tested, that manipulation of one variable will cause another to change in a specific way. Subjects are generally assigned to one of at least two groups: an experimental group, which experiences the manipulation of the independent variable, and a control group, which does not. If differences between the experimental and control groups are observed on the dependent variable, we can conclude that the independent variable did have an effect. Since it is important to ensure that experimental and control subjects do not differ from one another before the introduction of the independent variable, they are assigned randomly to groups. Experimenters must guard against bias by keeping themselves unaware of what group a given subject is in, experimental or control. If these conditions are met, the experiment has internal validity. The external validity of the findings, whether they can be generalized to situations and people not studied within the experiment, can be assessed only by performing similar experiments in the actual domain of interest with new subjects.

Single-subject experimental designs that expose one subject to different treatments over a period of time can provide internally valid results, although the generality of conclusions may be limited. Mixed designs are combinations of experimental and correlational methods. For example, two different kinds of patients (the classificatory variable) may be exposed to various treatments (the experimental variable).

A science is only as good as its methodology. Thus students of abnormal psychology must appreciate the rules that social scientists currently abide by if they are to be able to evaluate the research and theories that form the subject matter of the remainder of this book.

Part Two

Juan Genovés. *La Ruta*. 1980. Private collection. Courtesy of Marlborough Gallery, Inc.

Emotional Disorders
and Reactions to Stress

Richard Bosman. *Drowning Man I.* 1981. Courtesy of Brooke Alexander Collections.

Chapter 6

Anxiety Disorders

Phobias
   Subclassification of Phobias
   The Psychoanalytic Theory of Phobias
   Behavioral Theories of Phobias
   Physiological Factors Predisposing to the
      Development of Phobias
   Therapies for Phobias
Panic Disorder
Generalized Anxiety Disorder
   Psychoanalytic View
   Learning View
   Cognitive-Behavioral View
   Humanistic View
   Genetic Studies
   Neurobiology of Anxiety and Panic
   Therapies for Generalized Anxiety Disorder

Obsessive-Compulsive Disorder
   Obsessions
   Compulsions
   The Psychoanalytic Theory of Obsessive-
      Compulsive Disorder
   Behavioral Theories of Obsessive-Compulsive
      Disorder
   Cognitive Views of Obsessive-Compulsive Disorder
   Biological Factors in Obsessive-Compulsive
      Disorder
   Therapies for Obsessive-Compulsive Disorder
Posttraumatic Stress Disorder
   The Symptoms and Diagnosis
   Posttraumatic Stress Disorder and the Vietnam
      War
   Treatment of Posttraumatic Stress Disorder
Summary

How would you like to be a tame, somewhat shy and unagressive little boy of nine, somewhat shorter and thinner than average, and find yourself put three times a week, every Monday, Wednesday, and Friday, as regularly and inexorably as the sun sets and the sky darkens and the globe turns black and dead and spooky with no warm promise that anyone anywhere ever will waken again, into the somber, iron custody of someone named Forgione, older, broader, and much larger than yourself, a dreadful, powerful, broad-shouldered man who is hairy, hard-muscled, and barrel-chested and wears immaculate tight white or navy-blue T-shirts that seem as firm and unpitying as the figure of flesh and bone they encase like a mold, whose ferocious, dark eyes you never had courage enough to meet and whose assistant's name you did not ask or were not able to remember, and who did not seem to like you or approve of you? He could do whatever he wanted to you. He could do whatever he wanted to me. (Heller, 1966, p. 236)

This excerpt from Joseph Heller's second novel, *Something Happened,* portrays the terrified helplessness of a nine-year-old boy who has to interact every other school day with a burly gym teacher. As described by his equally fearful father, the youngster has an overwhelming anxiety about his gym class, a situation into which he is forced and from which he cannot escape, a situation that makes demands on him that he feels utterly unable to meet. Once again a gifted novelist captures the phenomenology—the direct experience—of an important human emotion in a way that speaks vividly to each of us.

There is, perhaps, no other single topic in abnormal psychology that is as important and controversial as anxiety. This emotional state can occur in many psychopathologies and is a principal aspect of the disorders to be considered in this chapter. Furthermore, anxiety plays an important role in the study of the psychology of normal people, for very few of us go through even a week of our lives without experiencing some measure of what we would all agree is the emotion called anxiety, or fear. But the briefer periods of anxiety that beset the normal individual are hardly comparable in intensity or duration, nor are they as debilitating, as those suffered by someone with an anxiety disorder.

The specific disorders considered in this chapter and the next were for a considerable period all regarded as forms of *neuroses.* They were conceptualized through Freud's clinical work with his patients, and thus the diagnostic category of neuroses was inextricably bound up with psychoanalytic theory. DSM-II offered the following definition:

Anxiety is the chief characteristic of the neuroses. It may be felt and expressed directly, or it may be controlled unconsciously and automatically by conversion, displacement and various other psychological mechanisms. Generally, these mechanisms produce symptoms experienced as subjective distress from which the patient desires relief. (APA, 1968, p. 39)

The behavior encompassed by the forms of neuroses varied greatly—the fear and avoidance of the phobic, the irresistible urge to perform certain acts over and over again found in compulsives, the paralyses and other "neurological" symptoms of conversion hysterics. How could such diverse problems be grouped into a single category? Although the observed symptoms differ, all neurotic conditions were *assumed,* according to the psychoanalytic theory of neuroses, to reflect an underlying problem with repressed anxiety.

Over the years many psychopathologists questioned this assumption and their doubts are reflected in the manner in which DSM-III progressed through several drafts on the way to its final form. At one point the category of neuroses was dropped entirely. But in the introduction to the final version it was noted that "the omission of the DSM-II diagnostic class of Neuroses has been a matter of great concern to many clinicians," and the category has been restored, at least partially.[1] In DSM-IIIR the old categories of neuroses are distributed in several new diagnostic classes that form new sections: anxiety disorders, the topic of this chapter, and somatoform disorders and dissociative disorders, both of which are covered in Chapter 7. In our view neurosis is an undesirable diagnostic category because no data support the assumption that all such patients share some common problem or set of symptoms. In all likelihood many people will continue to use the term—indeed it is part of our everyday vocabulary and appears throughout the book—but in this chapter and the next the presentation is organized according to the newer diagnostic categories.

Anxiety disorders are diagnosed when subjectively experienced feelings of anxiety are clearly present. DSM-IIIR proposes five principal categories: ***phobic disor-***

---

[1]*Psychosis* is another term that is part of our everyday vocabulary and that was prominent in DSM-II. Certain diagnoses in DSM-IIIR—pervasive developmental disorders, some organic mental disorders, schizophrenic and paranoid disorders, and some mood disorders—are recognized as psychoses, although they are not generally grouped as such. Individuals with a psychosis generally suffer extreme mental unrest and have lost contact with reality. Their hallucinations and delusions—false perceptions and misguided beliefs, which are a jumble of distortions and impossibilities but are firmly accepted by them—so take them over that they are often unable to meet even the most ordinary demands of life. Psychotic persons are more likely to need confinement.

Fear and avoidance of heights is classified by DSM-IIIR as a simple phobia.

ders, panic disorder, generalized anxiety disorder, obsessive-compulsive disorder, and *posttraumatic stress disorder.*

Phobias

Psychopathologists define a phobia as a disrupting, fear-mediated avoidance, out of proportion to the danger posed by a particular object or situation and, indeed, recognized by the sufferer as groundless. For example, when people are extremely fearful of heights, closed spaces, snakes, or spiders, provided there is no objective danger and their distress is sufficient to disrupt their lives, the label phobia is likely to be applied to their avoidance and fear.[2]

Over the years complex terms have been formulated as names for such unwarranted avoidance patterns. In each instance the suffix "phobia" is preceded by a Greek word for the feared object or situation. The suffix is derived from the name of the Greek god Phobos, who frightened his enemies. Some of the more familiar terms are claustrophobia, fear of closed spaces; agoraphobia, fear of public places; and acrophobia, fear of heights. More exotic fears have also been given Greek-derived names, for example, ergasiophobia, fear of writing; pni-

gophobia, fear of choking; and taphephobia, fear of being buried alive. All too often the impression is conveyed that we understand how a particular problem originated or even how to treat it merely because we have an authoritative-sounding name for it. Nothing could be farther from the truth, however. As with so much else in the field of abnormal psychology, there are more theories and jargon pertaining to phobias than there are firm findings.

In comparison to other diagnostic categories, phobias are relatively common in the general population. For example, Agras, Sylvester, and Oliveau (1969) found a rate of 7.7 per 100 in a population study done in New England. A more recent and more extensive survey found a rate of 5.9 per 100, with women having a substantially higher rate, 8.0, than men, 3.4 (Myers *et al.,* 1984). The Agras study, however, revealed that most of the phobias recorded were relatively mild, with only 2.2 per 1000 rated as severely disabling. Indeed, many specific fears do not cause enough hardship to compel an individual to seek treatment. For example, if a person with an intense fear or phobia of snakes lives in a metropolitan area, he or she will probably have little direct contact with the feared object and may therefore not believe that anything is seriously wrong.

Subclassification of Phobias

Up to now we have been discussing phobias as though they are alike in every respect except for the object or

---

[2]Phobias of childhood will be discussed in Chapter 15.

BOX 6.1

LITTLE HANS

A classic case of phobia, reported by Freud in 1909, was that of a five-year-old boy, Little Hans, who was afraid of horses and thus would not venture out of his home. The importance of this case is attested to by many psychoanalytic scholars. Ernest Jones, Freud's famous biographer, calls it "the brilliant success of child analysis" (1955, p. 289); and Glover, a respected scholar, terms it "a remarkable achievement . . . [constituting] one of the most valued records in psychoanalytic archives" (1956, p. 76).

Freud's analysis of Little Hans was based on information reported in letters written to Freud by the boy's father; Freud actually saw the child only once. Two years before the development of his phobia, when he was three, Hans was reported to have "a quite peculiarly lively interest in the part of his body which he used to describe as his widdler." When he was three and a half his mother caught him with his hand on his penis and threatened to arrange for his penis to be cut off if he continued "doing that." At age four and a half, while on summer vacation, Hans is described as having tried to "seduce" his mother. As his mother was powdering around his penis one day, taking care not to touch it, Hans said, "Why don't you put your finger there?" His mother answered "Because that would be piggish." Hans replied "What's that? Piggish? Why?" Mother: "Because it's not proper." Hans, laughing: "But it's great fun." These events were taken by Freud as proof that Hans had strong sexual urges, that they were directed toward his mother, and that they were repressed for fear of castration. According to Freud's first theory of anxiety (see page 36), this sexual privation would ultimately be transformed into neurotic anxiety.

The first signs of the phobia appeared about six months later while Hans was out for a walk with his nursemaid. After a horse-drawn van had tipped over, he began crying, saying that he wanted to return home to "coax" (caress) with his mother. Later he indicated that he was afraid to go out because a horse might bite him, and he soon elab-

orated on his fears by referring to "black things around horses' mouths and the things in front of their eyes."

Freud considered this series of events to reflect Hans's oedipal desire to have his father out of the way so that he could possess his mother. His sexual excitement for his mother was converted into anxiety because he feared that he would be punished. Hans's father was considered the initial source of his son's fear, but the fear was then transposed to a symbol for his father—horses. The black muzzles and blinders on horses were viewed as symbolic representations of the father's moustache and eyeglasses. Thus, by fearing horses, Hans was said to have succeeded unconsciously in avoiding the fear of castration by his father—even though it was the *mother* who had threatened this punishment—while at the same time arranging to spend more time at home with his principal love-object, his mother.

There are many other details in the case study, which occupies 140 pages in Freud's *Collected Papers*. In our brief account we have attempted to convey the flavor of the theorizing. We agree with Wolpe and Rachman (1960) that Freud made large inferential leaps from the data of the case. First, the evidence for Hans's wanting sexual contact with his mother is minimal, making it debatable that Hans wanted to possess his mother sexually and replace his father. Second, there is little evidence that Hans hated or feared his father, and in the original case report it is stated that Hans directly denied any symbolic connection between horses and his father. This denial was interpreted as evidence for the connection, however. Third, there is no evidence, or any reason to believe, that intense sexual excitement was somehow translated into anxiety. Indeed, the fact that Hans became afraid of horses after being frightened by an accident involving a horse may be more parsimoniously explained by the classical conditioning model, although this interpretation has its own problems (see page 136).

situation that is fearfully avoided. Behaviorists have been remiss in not considering whether there are important differences between fearing a small animal and fearing the prospect of leaving the house. This neglect of the content of the phobia is consistent with the fact that the behaviorists take a functional stance rather than a topographical one (Wilson and Davison, 1969). *Topography* here means specification of the actual physical behavior. Thus avoidance of a snake is topographically different from avoidance of heights, for the simple reason that a snake is not a height. Within a *functional*

framework, adopted by most behaviorists, fear of snakes and fear of heights are viewed as equivalent in the means by which they are acquired, in how they might be changed, and so on.

If behaviorists underplay the content of phobias, analysts go to the other extreme, seeing great significance in the phobic object as a symbol of an important unconscious fear. In a celebrated case reported by Freud, Little Hans was afraid of encountering horses if he went outside (see Box 6.1). Freud paid particular attention to Hans's reference to the "black things around horses'

BOX 6.2

SEX ROLES AND AGORAPHOBIA

In numerous surveys more women than men are found to be agoraphobic (Brehony and Geller, 1981). Even allowing for the possibility that women may admit to such problems more readily than men, the numbers still indicate that most agoraphobics are women. Why?

In recent years, as part of women's liberation and appreciation of how women have been and are still being stereotyped, agoraphobia has been explained in terms of traditional sex roles. Consider the following. Clinical descriptions of agoraphobics employ such words as passive, shy, and dependent, descriptors traditionally applied to women (Bem, 1974; Broverman *et al.,* 1970). It may be, as Fodor (1978) suggests, that being agoraphobic is in part a logical, although exaggerated, extension of the stereotyped female role. Until recently, and still in many seg-

ments of American and other societies, it has been more acceptable for a woman than for a man to be housebound. Any indications that men might be housebound would be more readily criticized, hence encouraging their continuing forays into the outside world and giving them opportunities to extinguish fears of leaving their homes.

Sex-role models in some media still support the female stereotype. A task force of the National Organization for Women determined from a study of children's readers that female characters in them are usually portrayed as helpless, home-oriented, passive, dependent, fearful, and incompetent compared to males (Brehony and Geller, 1981). As these stereotypes change, there should be corresponding shifts in the male–female sex ratio of agoraphobics.

---

mouths and the things in front of their eyes." The horse was regarded as representing the father, who had a moustache and wore eyeglasses. Freud theorized that fear of the father had become transformed into fear of horses, which were then avoided by Hans. Countless other such examples might be cited; the principal point

is that psychoanalysts believe that the content of phobias has important symbolic value.

Simple Phobias

Although easy to define, simple phobias are the rarest seen in clinical practice. The most common sources of these phobias are animals (e.g., dogs, snakes, insects), heights, closed spaces, air travel, and blood. Only 3 percent of all phobics have them. The majority of these simple phobias occur in women, and they begin very often in early childhood (Marks and Gelder, 1966).

Agoraphobia

A complicated syndrome, **agoraphobia**[3] (from the Greek *agora,* place of assembly, marketplace), is a cluster of fears centering around public places and being unable to escape or find help should the individual suddenly become incapacitated. Fears of shopping, encountering crowds, and traveling are often a part of agoraphobia. From a patient's point of view, agoraphobia is surely very distressing. Consider how limiting it must be to be afraid of leaving the house. Perhaps for this reason agoraphobia is the most common phobia seen in the clinic, constituting roughly 60 percent of all phobias examined. Most agoraphobics are women (see Box 6.2), and the majority develop their problems in adolescence

THE FAR SIDE   By GARY LARSON

© 1988 Universal Press Syndicate

Anatidaephobia: The fear that somewhere, somehow, a duck is watching you.

---

[3] DSM-IIIR now considers agoraphobia as a subtype of panic disorder. As will be seen below, one view of agoraphobia is that in some people it develops from panic attacks, so prevalent have repeated panic attacks been seen in the histories of agoraphobics. However, we have elected to discuss agoraphobia in this section on phobias because so much of the clinical and research literature addresses it in these terms.

and early adulthood. The disorder often begins with recurrent panic attacks. Numerous other symptoms are also evident, including tension, dizziness, minor checking compulsions—seeing that the screen door is latched, no intruder is under the bed, the iron is off—rumination, depression, and fear of going mad. One study found that 93 percent of a sample of agoraphobics also reported fears of heights and enclosed spaces such as subways and elevators (Buglass *et al.*, 1977). But many agoraphobics have ''good days,'' when they can move about with relative ease. Being with a trusted companion can also help them leave the house. Psychophysiological responses confirm the clinical impression that agoraphobics are subject to a rather diffuse, nonspecific anxiety. Recordings taken of their autonomic activity usually show high levels of arousal, even when they are supposedly relaxing (Marks, 1969).

Social Phobias

A *social phobia,* sometimes referred to in its milder forms as social anxiety, is a persistent, irrational fear generally linked to the presence of other people. The individual tries to avoid a particular situation in which he or she might be scrutinized and reveal signs of anxiousness or behave in an embarrassing way. Speaking or performing in public, eating in public, using public lavatories, or virtually any other activity that might be carried out in the presence of others, can elicit extreme anxiety. Although this phobia is not uncommon, social phobics seek help much less frequently than do agoraphobics. As might be expected, onset is generally during adolescence, when social awareness and interaction with others are assuming much more importance in the person's life.

Severe fear of public speaking is one form of social phobia.

The Psychoanalytic Theory of Phobias

As is true of many of the anxiety disorders, Freud was the first to attempt to account sytematically for the development of phobic behavior. According to Freud, phobias are a defense against the anxiety that is produced by repressed id impulses. This anxiety is displaced from the id impulse that is feared to an object or situation that has some symbolic connection to it. These objects or situations—for example, elevators or closed spaces—then become the phobic stimuli. By avoiding them, the person is able to avoid dealing with repressed conflicts. As discussed in Chapter 2 (page 36), the phobia is the ego's way of warding off a confrontation with the real problem, a repressed childhood conflict.

More recently, another psychoanalytic theory of phobias has been proposed by Arieti (1979). According to him, repression is of a particular interpersonal problem of childhood rather than of an id impulse. Arieti theorizes that, as children, phobics first lived through a period of innocence during which they trusted the people around them to protect them from danger. But then these children came to fear that adults, usually the parents, were not reliable. This mistrust, or generalized fear of others, was something they could not live with; in order to be able to trust people again, they unconsciously transformed this fear of others into a fear of impersonal objects or situations. The phobia supposedly surfaces when, in adulthood, the person undergoes some sort of stress. As is true of most psychoanalytic theorizing, evidence in support of these views is restricted to conclusions drawn from uncontrolled clinical case reports.

Behavioral Theories of Phobias

As in psychoanalytic theory, the primary assumption of all behavioral accounts of phobias is that such reactions are learned. But the exact learning mechanisms and what is actually learned in the development of a phobia are specified differently in the various behavioral theories.

The Avoidance Conditioning Model

Historically, Watson and Rayner's (1920) demonstration of the apparent conditioning of a fear or phobia in Little Albert (see page 44) is considered the model of how a phobia may be acquired. Learning theorists have elaborated on the case by asserting that the classically conditioned fear of an objectively harmless stimulus forms the basis of an operant avoidance response. This formulation, based on the two-factor theory originally proposed by Mowrer (1947), holds that phobias develop from two related sets of learning (see page 72). (1) Via classical conditioning a person can learn to fear a neutral stimulus (the CS) if it is paired with an intrinsically painful or frightening event (the UCS). (2) Then the person can learn to reduce this conditioned fear by escaping from or avoiding the CS. This second kind of learning is assumed to be operant conditioning; the response is maintained by its reinforcing consequences.

Certain clinically reported phobias seem to fit such a model rather well. For example, a phobia of a specific object has sometimes been reported to have developed after a particularly painful experience with that object. Some people become intensely afraid of driving an automobile after a serious accident, or of descending stairs after a bad fall. Other phobias apparently originate in similar fashion.

A young boy would often pass a grocery store on errands and when passing would steal a handful of peanuts from the stand in front. One day the owner saw him coming and hid behind a barrel. Just as the boy put his hand in the pile of peanuts the owner jumped out and grabbed him from behind. The boy screamed and fell fainting on the sidewalk.

The boy developed a phobia of being grasped from behind. In social gatherings he arranged to have his chair against the wall. It was impossible for him to enter crowded places or to attend the theater. When walking on the street he would have to look back over his shoulder at intervals to see if he was closely followed. (Bagby, 1922)

A major problem exists in the application of this model, however. The fact that Little Albert's fear and certain clinically reported phobias were acquired through conditioning can *not* be taken as evidence that *all* fears and phobias are acquired by this means. Rather, the evidence demonstrates only the *possibility* that some fears *may* be acquired in this particular way. Indeed, other clinical reports suggest that phobias may develop *without* prior frightening experience. Many individuals with severe fears of snakes, germs, airplanes, and heights tell clinicians that they have had no particularly unpleasant experiences with any of these objects or situ-

ations.[4] In a systematic study Keuthen (1980) found that half of a sample of phobics could recall no upsetting experience in the feared situation. Similarly, many people who have had a harrowing automobile accident or a bad fall down stairs do *not* become phobic to automobiles or stairs. Thus the avoidance conditioning model cannot account for the acquisition of all phobias.

Furthermore, attempts to replicate Watson and Rayner's experiment and demonstrate again the acquisition of fear via classical conditioning have for the most part *not* been successful. For example, English (1929) attempted to condition fear in a fourteen-month-old girl by pairing the presentation of a duck with a loud noise. Despite fifty trials, no conditioned response to the duck was established. In a more extensive investigation Bregman (see Thorndike, 1935) tried to condition fear in fifteen infants of about the same age as Little Albert, using various CSs and a loud bell as the UCS. Again, relatively few fears were acquired by the subjects. (From an ethical point of view, it is fortunate that these workers failed to produce phobias in their young subjects.)

There is actually very little experimental evidence to support the contention that human beings can be classically conditioned to fear neutral stimuli even when such stimuli are paired repeatedly with primary aversive stimuli, such as electric shock (e.g., Davison, 1968b; Dawson, Schell, and Banis, 1986). Ethical considerations have of course restrained most researchers from employing highly aversive stimuli with human beings, but considerable evidence indicates that fear is extinguished rather quickly when the CS is presented a few times without the reinforcement of moderate levels of shock (Bridger and Mandel, 1965; Wickens, Allen, and Hill, 1963). Finally, it is also unclear whether the model itself is an accurate portrayal of a phobia. The essence of phobic behavior is the fear and avoidance elicited by the CS. However, in the avoidance learning literature, an animal's fear of the CS quickly declines and it has proved difficult (perhaps impossible) to train an animal to avoid a CS (Mineka, 1985).

In sum, the data we have reviewed suggest that not all phobias are learned through avoidance conditioning. Such a process *may* be involved in the etiology of some phobias, but other processes must also be implicated in their development (see Box 6.3).

---

[4]Such accounts are called *retrospective* reports, that is, reports made by people looking back into their past, sometimes for many, many years. Since memory of long-ago events is often distorted, such reports must be viewed with some skepticism. The fact that many phobics cannot recall traumatic experiences with their now-feared objects may indeed be distortions of memory. Accounts of traumatic episodes may be questioned on the same grounds. Retrospective reports are discussed again on page 263.

BOX 6.3

AVOIDANCE CONDITIONING AND PREPAREDNESS

Perhaps the avoidance conditioning view of phobias would be more valid if modified enough to take into account the fact that certain neutral stimuli may be more likely to become classically conditioned stimuli than others. Pavlov (1928) did not address this question, stating that "every imaginable phenomenon of the outer world affecting a specific receptive surface of the body may be converted into a CS" (p. 88).

Seligman (1971) has suggested that phobias may well reflect classical conditioning to stimuli that an organism is physiologically predisposed to be sensitive to. Accordingly, classical conditioning experiments that show quick extinction of fear may have employed CSs that the organism was really not "prepared" to learn to associate with UCSs.

An example from the research that has given rise to this ***preparedness*** notion may make this hypothesis clearer. Garcia and his associates (Garcia, McGowan, and Green, 1972) found that rats could learn to avoid the taste of a given food if nauseated following its ingestion—even if the nausea did not begin for many hours. In contrast, they could not be aversively conditioned to the *sight* of food if they were nauseated in its presence but had not actually tasted it. Similarly, rats could readily learn to avoid a light paired with shock (a common experimental finding), but they could not learn to avoid taste paired with shock. Thus, as seen in Figure 6a, gustatory sensations and illness (taste–nausea) are readily associated, as are visual and tactile modalities (light–shock). But visual stimuli and illness (sight of food–nausea) and gustatory and tactile sensations (taste–shock) are not.

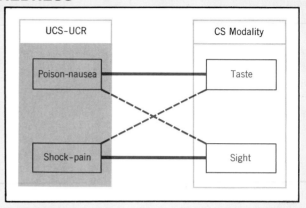

FIGURE 6a
The organism may be prepared through innate sensitivity to learn certain associations but not be prepared to learn others. Solid lines indicate easily made associations; dashed lines connect classes of stimuli that are difficult to associate.

Seligman has provided a personal illustration of the operation of this process.

Sauce Béarnaise is an egg-thickened, tarragon-flavored concoction, and it used to be my favorite sauce. It now tastes awful to me. This happened several years ago. . . . After eating filet mignon with Sauce Béarnaise, I became violently ill and spent most of the night vomiting. The next time I had Sauce Béarnaise, I couldn't bear the taste of it. At the time I had no ready way to account for the change, although it seemed to fit a classical conditioning

Modeling

Phobic responses may also be learned through imitating the reactions of others. As we have previously noted (see page 46), a wide range of behavior, including emotional responses, may be learned by witnessing a model. The learning of phobic reactions by observing others is generally referred to as ***vicarious conditioning***. In one study Bandura and Rosenthal (1966) arranged for subjects to watch another person, the model (a confederate of the experimenter), in an aversive conditioning situation. The model was hooked up to an impressive-looking array of electrical apparatus. Upon hearing a buzzer, the model withdrew his hand rapidly from the arm of the chair and feigned pain. The physiological responses of the subjects witnessing this behavior were recorded. After the subjects had watched the model "suffer" a number of times, they showed an increased frequency of emotional responses when the buzzer sounded. The subjects began to react emotionally to a harmless stimulus even though they had had no direct contact with a noxious event.

Vicarious learning may also be accomplished through verbal instructions. That is, phobic reactions can be learned through another's description of what might happen as well as by observing another's fear. As an example from everyday life, a mother may repeatedly warn her child not to engage in some activity lest dire

paradigm: CS (sauce) paired with US (illness) and UR (vomiting) yields CR (nauseating taste). [Although I learned that flu had caused the nausea and others with me did not get sick . . .], I could not later inhibit my aversion. (Seligman and Hager, 1972, p. 8)

This and related research prompted Seligman to hypothesize that some associations, and thereby phobias, are easily learned by human beings and are not readily extinguished. Marks (1969), in a related observation, points to the fact that human beings tend to be afraid of certain types of objects and events. People may have phobias of dogs, cats, and snakes–but few lamb phobics have been encountered. It is even more remarkable how few people phobically avoid electric outlets, which do present certain dangers under specified circumstances.

Some more direct evidence that certain fears are easily learned comes from a conditioning study in which different types of stimuli were used as the CS (Öhman, Erixon, and Löfberg, 1975). All subjects viewed three sets of pictures varying in content–snakes, houses, and faces. Half the participants received a shock (UCS) immediately after viewing each slide of snakes. The remainder received shocks after viewing slides either of houses or of faces. The GSR served as the CR and was analyzed for both the conditioning trials and for a subsequent extinction series. During the conditioning part of the study, the GSRs of the groups of participants receiving shocks after viewing slides of any of the three classes of stimuli were about the same. During extinction, however, the CR to the slides of houses or faces quickly diminished, whereas the CR to slides of snakes

remained strong. Thus the CR was more durably associated with the sight of snakes, which are a fairly common elicitor of clinical phobias.

In a later study, (Hugdahl, Fredrikson, and Öhman, 1977), the subjects' level of physiological arousal (see page 96) was also found to be related to the extent to which fears can be conditioned. People with high levels of arousal were more readily made fearful of stimuli easily associated with the emotion than were those with lower levels. These findings suggest that people, particularly those with high levels of arousal, are "prepared" to fear certain stimuli.

Seligman has also linked his preparedness theory to psychoanalytic concepts. He proposed that the kind of symbolism mentioned in psychoanalytic theory may one day be found to have a basis in the sensitivities of people and what they are prepared to associate and to learn. Hans, after all, came to fear horses after he saw one of them fall down in the street in a rather memorable incident. But he did not become afraid of the van that tipped over, and he must have observed other dramatic incidents and been struck by particularly vivid aspects of them during his walks with the nursemaid. Although the symbolic connection with the father is still unclear unless Freud's hypothesis is accepted, it does seem significant that the particular incident mentioned in the case report loomed larger than others, and that in its aftermath Hans came to be afraid of horses. Even through not all investigators are convinced that people are prepared to acquire conditioned responses to certain stimuli (see Bitterman, 1975; Evans, 1976; McNally and Reiss, 1982), the preparedness hypothesis nevertheless appears worth exploring.

consequences ensue. Vicarious examples can apparently be provided through words. (We should not assume, however, that such learning is necessarily a product of conditioning).

The clearest demonstration of the potential importance of observational learning comes from a study by Mineka and her colleagues (1984). Adolescent rhesus monkeys were reared with parents who all had an intense fear of snakes. During the observational learning sessions, the offspring saw their parents interact fearfully with real and toy snakes as well as nonfearfully with neutral objects. After six sessions, the fear of the adolescent monkeys was indistinguishable from that of

the parents. A three-month follow-up showed that the fear was durable.

As with classical conditioning, however, vicarious learning experiments fail to provide a complete model for all phobias. First, phobics who seek treatment do not often report that they became frightened after witnessing someone else's distress. Second, many people have been exposed to the bad experiences of others but have not themselves developed phobias.

Operant Conditioning

Phobic reactions may also be learned by virtue of the positive consequences that follow. Avoidance responses

Monkeys in Mineka's study of modeling and fear of snakes. (Top) Fear is elicited by the approach of a snake. (Bottom) The snake now elicits an even stronger fear response.

may be directly rewarded and thereby learned. For example, a daughter who wants to stay close to a parent may invent excuses so that she does not have to attend school. If the mother or father gives in to these excuses, the child is directly rewarded by being allowed to stay

home with the adult. In this instance fear is not mentioned as a mediator. The child avoids school simply because it produces favorable results.

Although some phobias may develop because of the payoff provided by the environment, the fact that the lives of many phobics become severely limited through their compelling need to avoid harmless situations strains the general applicability of the theory.

Research on Social Anxiety

Phobias of small animals, elevators, and heights can disrupt people's lives, to be sure, but not to the extent that social phobias can. To be excessively sensitive to the opinions of others, to be constantly embarrassed about how one acts—these concerns interfere markedly in meaningful activities, for the simple reason that human beings are social creatures, spending much of their time with others or, when alone, reflecting about how others might regard their actions. Accordingly, a great deal of research has been conducted on social phobias.

There are three major models of social anxiety. The first conceives of social anxiety as stemming from an unfortunate episode that classically conditioned the individual in the manner already described. Presumably a socially sensitive person lived through very unpleasant events in the presence of other people, thereby learning to associate fear with others. The second model considers a lack of social skills or inappropriate behavior as the cause of social anxiety. According to this view, the individual has not learned how to behave so that he or she feels comfortable with others, or the person repeatedly commits faux pas, is awkward, and socially inept, and is often criticized by social companions. Support for this model comes from findings that socially anxious people are indeed rated as being low in social skills (Twentyman and McFall, 1975) and that the timing and placement of their responses in a social interaction are impaired (Fischetti, Curran, and Wessberg, 1977). Socially anxious people also tend to rate themselves negatively. For example, Clark and Arkowitz (1975) had male, high and low anxious, subjects participate in social interactions with female confederates. Thereafter the males rated their own performance, and undergraduate raters who viewed the interactions completed the same ratings. The highly anxious subjects rated their performance considerably lower than did the raters.

More recently, the ways people think in social situations have been stressed (Glass and Merluzzi, 1981). For example, Beck and Emery (1985) have proposed that socially anxious people operate within a ***vulnerability schema.*** They are continually concerned with danger and harm and with what unpleasant events might befall them in the future. Results from research as-

Socially anxious people are uncomfortable when around others.

sessing these cognitions support their theory (Beck *et al.*, 1987). Direct evidence comes from the study by Davison and Zighelboim (1987) mentioned in Chapter 4. The thoughts of two groups of subjects were compared—by the Articulated Thoughts During Simulated Situations method—as they role-played participation in a neutral situation and one in which they were being sharply criticized. One group of subjects were volunteers from an introductory psychology course, and the others were undergraduates referred from the student counseling center and identified as shy, withdrawn, and socially anxious. The thoughts articulated by the socially anxious subjects in both the stressful and neutral situations were more negative than those of the control subjects.

Here are examples of some of the thoughts expressed by socially anxious subjects as they imagined themselves being criticized:

I've been rejected by these people. I have this very depressed feeling, a feeling of rejection. There is no place to turn to now. There is no way to eliminate that feeling I have inside.

I think I am boring when I talk to people. I often think I should not talk at all.

I should maybe not be so argumentative and maybe let things drop even if I don't like the way they are . . . like if I am not happy with the situation. Just for the sake of everybody else, to keep everybody else happy, I should let things go at times. [These thoughts reflect the belief that one must be loved and approved of by everyone.]

Physiological Factors Predisposing to the Development of Phobias

Both psychoanalytic and learning theories look to the environment for the cause and maintenance of phobias. Indeed, as already indicated, the primary assumption of both theories in that phobias are learned. But why do some people acquire unrealistic fears whereas others do not, given similar opportunities for learning? Perhaps those who are adversely affected by stress have a physiological malfunction (a diathesis) that somehow predisposes them to develop a phobia following a particular stressful event.

Autonomic Nervous System

What characteristic may be important in determining the susceptibility of individuals to particular environment experiences? One way people may react differently to certain environmental situations is the ease with which their autonomic nervous sytems become aroused. Lacey (1967) has referred to a dimension of autonomic activity that he calls stability-lability. Labile or "jumpy" individuals are those whose autonomic systems are readily aroused by a wide range of stimuli. Clearly, because of the extent to which the autonomic nervous system is involved in fear and hence in phobic behavior, a dimension such as ***autonomic liability*** would assume considerable importance. Since there is reason to believe that autonomic lability is to some degree genetically determined (Eysenck, 1957; Lacey, 1967), the heredity (see Box 6.4) of individuals may very well have a significant role in the development of phobias.

BOX 6.4

BEHAVIOR GENETICS

When the ovum, the female reproductive cell, is joined by the male's spermatozoan, a zygote or fertilized egg is produced. It has forty-six chromosomes, the number characteristic of the human being. Each chromosome is made up of thousands of *genes*. The genes are the carriers of the genetic information (DNA) that is passed from parents to child. Each cell of the human body will contain a full complement of chromosomes and genes in its nucleus.

Behavior genetics is the study of individual differences in behavior that are attributable in part to differences in genetic makeup. The total genetic makeup of an individual, consisting of inherited genes, is referred to as the *genotype*. An individual's genotype is the unobservable, physiological genetic constitution, in contrast to the totality of observable characteristics, which is referred to as the *phenotype*. The genotype is fixed at birth, whereas the phenotype changes and is generally viewed as the product of an interaction between the genotype and experience. For example, an individual may be born with the capacity for high intellectual achievement. Whether he or she develops this genetically given potential depends on such environmental factors as rearing and education. Any measure of intelligence (IQ) is therefore best viewed as an index of the phenotype.

On the basis of the distinction made between phenotype and genotype, we realize that various clinical syndromes are disorders of the phenotype. Thus it is not proper to speak of the direct inheritance of schizophrenia or anxiety disorders. At most, only the genotypes for these disorders can be inherited. Whether these genotypes will eventually engender the phenotypic behavior disorder will depend on environment and experience; a predisposition (diathesis) may be inherited but not the disorder itself.

The two major methods of study in behavior genetics are to compare members of a family and pairs of twins. Members of a family are compared because we can determine, on the average, how many genes are shared by two blood relatives. For example, children receive half their genes from one parent and half from the other. Siblings will, on the average, be identical in 50 percent of their genetic background. In contrast, relatives not as closely related share fewer genes. For example, nephews and nieces share 25 percent of the genetic makeup of an uncle. If a predisposition for a mental disorder can be inherited, a study of the family should reveal a correlation between the number of shared genes and the incidence of the disorder in relatives. The starting point in such investigations is to collect a sample of individuals who bear the diagnosis in question; these are referred to as *index cases* or *probands*. Then relatives are studied to determine the frequency with which the same diagnosis might be applied to them.

In family studies the investigator capitalizes on the degree of genetic similarity in family members. Shown here is a marked similarity in physical appearance.

In the twin method *monozygotic* (MZ) and *dizygotic* (DZ) pairs of twins are compared. MZ twins develop from a single fertilized egg and are genetically identical. DZ pairs develop from separate eggs and on the average are only 50 percent alike genetically, actually no more alike than two siblings. MZ twins are always the same sex, but DZs or fraternal twins can be either the same sex or opposite in sex. Again, such studies begin with diagnosed cases and then search for the presence of the disorder in the other twin. When the twins are similar diagnostically, they are said to be *concordant*. To the extent that a predisposition for a mental disorder can be inherited, concordance for the disorder should be greater in MZ pairs than in DZ pairs.

Although the methodology of the *family* and *twin studies* is clear, the data they yield are not always easy to interpret. Let us assume that neurotic parents have been found to produce more than the average number of neurotic offspring. Does this mean that anxiety disorders are genetically transmitted? Not necessarily. The greater number of anxiety disorders could as well reflect child-rearing practices and exposure of the children to neurotic adult models. Consider also a finding of greater concordance for schizophrenia among MZ than among DZ twins. Again, such data do not necessarily inplicate heredity, since MZ twins, perhaps because they look so much alike, may be raised in a more similar fashion than are DZs, thus accounting for the greater concordance for schizophrenia among them. There are, however, special but infrequent circumstances that are not subject to the aforementioned problems: a child reared completely apart from its abnormal parents and MZ twins reared separately from very early infancy. A high freqeuncy of anxiety disorders in children reared apart from their anxious parents would offer convincing support for the theory that genetic factors figure in these disorders. Similarly, greater concordance of separately reared MZ twins than of DZ twins would offer compelling evidence that a predisposition for a disorder can be inherited.

Identical or monozygotic twins are genetically identical. Fraternal or dizygotic twins are no more alike genetically than siblings and can be either the same or opposite in sex. The identical twins in the two photos were separated when very young and reared apart from one another. Even so, they are amazingly alike as adults. In their homes both have workshops in which they build furniture.

Genetic Studies

Several studies have questioned whether a genetic or innate factor is involved in anxiety disorders, although most have not been directly concerned with whether such a factor is implicated in the formation of phobias per se. In a family study of anxiety disorders, Harris and her fellow workers (1983) found that the first-degree relatives of individuals with agoraphobia were at greater risk for it or one of the other anxiety disorders than were the first-degree relatives of nonanxious control subjects. Noyes *et al.* (1986) have also found that relatives of agoraphobics are at higher than usual risk for both agoraphobia and panic disorder. Similarly, Torgersen (1983) found more concordance for agoraphobia in identical twins than in fraternal twins.

These data do not unequivocally implicate innate factors, however. Although close relatives share genes, they also have considerable opportunity to observe and influence one another. The fact that a son and his father are both afraid of heights may indicate not a genetic component but rather direct modeling of the son's behavior after that of his father (or, both factors could be involved). In sum, although there is some reason to believe that genetic factors are involved in the etiology of phobias, there has as yet been no clear-cut demonstration of the extent to which they may be important.

Therapies for Phobias

Throughout the book, after reviewing theories about the causes of the various disorders, we will briefly describe the principal therapies for them. The treatment sections of Chapter 2 were meant to furnish the reader with a context for understanding these discussions of therapy. An in-depth study and evaluation of therapy is reserved for the final section of the book.

Psychoanalytic Approaches

Psychoanalytic treatments of phobias generally attempt to uncover the repressed conflicts that are assumed to underlie the extreme fear and avoidance characteristic of these disorders. Because the phobia itself is regarded as *symptomatic* of underlying conflicts, it is not dealt with directly. Indeed, direct attempts to reduce phobic avoidance are contraindicated because the phobia is assumed to protect the person from repressed conflicts that are too painful to confront. The various techniques that have been developed within the psychoanalytic tradition are used in various combinations to help lift the repression. During free association (see page 42) the analyst listens carefully to what the patient mentions in connection with any references to the phobia. The analyst also attempts to discover clues to the repressed origins of the phobia in the manifest content of dreams. Exactly what the therapist believes these repressed origins to be depends, of course, on the particular psychoanalytic theory held. An orthodox analyst will look for sexual conflicts, whereas an analyst holding to Arieti's interpersonal theory will encourage patients to examine their generalized fear of other people.

The contemporary ego analysts focus less on historical insights, rather they encourage the patient to confront the phobia, even though they continue to view it as an outgrowth of an earlier problem. Alexander and French in their classic book, *Psychoanalytic Therapy* (1946), spoke of the "corrective emotional experience" in therapy, by which they meant the patient's confrontation with what is so desperately feared. They observed that "Freud himself came to the conclusion that in the treatment of some cases, phobias for example, a time arrives when the analyst must encourage the patient to engage in those activities he avoided in the past" (p. 39). Wachtel (1977) has even more boldly recommended that analysts employ the fear reduction techniques of behavior therapists, such as systematic desensitization.

Behavioral Approaches

The principal behavioral treatment for phobias is systematic desensitization (Wolpe, 1958). The phobic individual imagines a series of increasingly frightening scenes while in a state of deep relaxation. Both clinical and experimental evidence indicates that this technique is effective in eliminating or at least reducing phobias (Wilson and O'Leary, 1980). Some behavior therapists have, over the years, come to recognize the importance of exposure to real-life phobic situations, sometimes during the period in which a patient is being desensitized in imagination, sometimes instead of the imagery-based procedure. Indeed, evidence is beginning to accumulate on the long-term effectiveness of treating agoraphobics by graded exposures to real-life crowds and public places (Emmelkamp, 1986; Munby and Johnston, 1980).

One of the most impressive clinical research programs on the treatment of agoraphobia comes from David Barlow's Center for Stress and Anxiety Disorders at the State University of New York at Albany. In this program phobic women—nearly all their patients are women—participate with their spouses or with significant others in group meetings during which encouragement and exhortation are given for exposure *between* therapy sessions. Gradual forays away from the home are nurtured by the nonphobic participants and then discussed at the weekly group meetings. With twelve group meetings plus a few follow-up sessions, outcomes of this approach are very positive (Barlow and Waddell, 1985).

David Barlow, noted anxiety researcher at SUNY, Albany.

Fearful clients who are treated through modeling are exposed to either filmed or live demonstrations of other people interacting fearlessly with the phobic object. ***Flooding*** therapy forces exposure to the source of the phobia at full intensity. The extreme discomfort that is an inevitable part of this procedure has tended to discourage therapists from employing it, except perhaps as a last resort.

Behavior therapists who favor operant techniques ignore the fear assumed to underlie phobias and attend instead to the overt avoidance of phobic objects and to the approach behavior that must replace it. They treat approach like any other operant and shape it according to the principle of successive approximation. The real-life exposures to the phobic object are graded, and the client is rewarded for even minimal successes in moving closer to it.

Many behavior therapists attend both to fear and to avoidance, using techniques like desensitization to reduce fear and operant shaping to encourage approach. Lazarus, Davison, and Polefka (1965) first proposed this two-pronged strategy. At the initial stages of treatment, when fear and avoidance are both very great, the therapist concentrates on reducing the fear through relaxation training and graded exposures to the phobic situation. As therapy progresses, however, fear becomes less of an issue and avoidance more. A phobic individual has often over time settled into an existence in which other people cater to his or her incapacities and thus in a way reinforce the person for having a phobia. As the person's anxieties diminish, he or she is able to approach what used to be terrifying; this overt behavior should be positively reinforced—and avoidance discouraged—by relatives and friends as well as by the therapist.

Especially for agoraphobics, the spouse, who will usually be the husband, should be involved in treatment. Clinical reports suggest that, by being overly so-licitous and supportive—perhaps out of his own understandable concern of his wife's plight, perhaps to satisfy some inner need of his own to be dominant—he may have unwittingly "conspired" to perpetuate his wife's agoraphobia (Brehony and Geller, 1981). Indeed, Milton and Hafner (1979) found that as the wife improves, an already distressed marital relationship can worsen.[5]

Agoraphobics, indeed, may present a unique set of problems for therapists in planning effective treatment strategies. The clinical literature notes in particular the "fear of fear" that most agoraphobics complain about. Theirs seems to be a "portable phobia" (Brehony and Geller, 1981). They are greatly concerned about becoming the slightest bit nervous, for fear that their nervousness will escalate into a panic attack, in which they may lose control and suffer possible harm and social embarrassment (see the discussion of panic disorder later in this chapter).

Cognitive treatments for phobias have been viewed with skepticism because of a central defining characteristic. As stated in DSM-IIIR, the phobic fear "is recognized by the individual as excessive or unreasonable" (p. 243). Thus if an otherwise well-functioning person is intensely afraid of something that, intellectually, he or she acknowledges to be relatively harmless, of what use can it be to alter the person's thoughts about it? One proposal comes from Ellis; he suggests that a phobia is maintained by irrational beliefs such as "If something seems dangerous or fearsome, you must be terribly occupied with and upset about it" or "It is easier to avoid than to face certain life difficulties." The client is taught to dispute the irrational belief whenever encountering the phobic object or situation. But even Ellis, with his strong cognitive bias, encourages clients to approach and confront what they fear. His intellectual debates with clients may very well help goad them into real-life exposures, which will extinguish the fear. Indeed, there is no evidence that eliminating irrational beliefs alone, without exposures to the fearsome situations, reduces phobic avoidance (Williams and Rappoport, 1983).

---

[5] This phenomenon is one of several lying at the core of the ***family therapy*** movement, described in detail in Chapter 20 (page 580). It should be mentioned, however, that this family systems view of agoraphobia has not gone unchallenged. Bland and Hallam (1981) argue that data do *not* support the contention that improvement in the wife's agoraphobia worsens the marital relationship. Rather, they suggest, "dissatisfied spouses remained dissatisfied; satisfied spouses tended to become more satisfied as the patient's phobia improved" (p. 338). Indeed, Barlow's clinical research program has found that successful *in vivo* exposure treatment in which husbands are involved leads to *improved* marital satisfaction (Himadi, Cerny, Barlow, Cohen, and O'Brien, 1986). Perhaps the very process of involving the husband in his wife's therapy contributes to an improvement of marital problems per se, unrelated to the agoraphobia.

All these various therapies for phobias have a recurrent theme, namely, the need for the phobic to desist from customary avoidance of the phobic object or situation and to begin facing what has been deemed too fearsome, too terrifying. To be sure, analysts consider the fear to reside in the buried past and therefore delay direct confrontation, but eventually they too encourage it (e.g., Zane, 1984). Indeed, Freud stated: "One can hardly ever master a phobia if one waits until the patient lets the analysis influence him to give it up. One succeeds only when one can induce them to go about alone and to struggle with their anxiety while they make the attempt" (Freud, 1919, p. 400).[6] Thus all these therapies reflect a time-honored bit of folk wisdom, one that tells us that we must face up to what we fear. As an ancient Chinese proverb puts it, "Go straight to the heart of danger, for there you will find safety."

Somatic Approaches

Drugs that reduce anxiety are referred to as sedatives or **anxiolytics.** Barbiturates were the first major category of drugs used to treat anxiety disorders, but because of undesirable side effects and their addictive properties, they were supplanted in the 1950s by two other classes of drugs—propanediols (e.g., Miltown) and benzodiazepines (e.g., Valium). The latter are widely used today and are of demonstrated benefit (Greenblatt and Shader, 1972). Some studies also suggest that antidepressants like imipramine are useful in treating agoraphobia (Johnston et al., 1988; Zitrin, Klein, and Woerner, 1980), especially when dysphoria (depressed mood) is part of the clinical picture (Marks, 1983).

The problem in treating phobias and other anxiety disorders with drugs, however, is that they may be difficult to discontinue. All too often people calmed down by anxiolytics (sometimes referred to as tranquilizers) find themselves still fearful when weaned from the drugs (Marks, 1981a); consequently, they tend to become dependent on them for long periods of time.[7] In fact, in their efforts to reduce their anxiety, many phobics and other anxious people use anxiolytics or alcohol on their own. The use and abuse of drugs and alcohol are not uncommon among anxiety-ridden people.

---

[6]Freud's apparent appreciation of *in vivo* exposure to what is actually feared should not overshadow the greater emphasis he and most analytically oriented workers place on ferreting out the repressed childhood antecedents of the phobia.

[7]Evidence indicates that dependence on frequently prescribed sedatives such as Miltown (meprobamate) and Valium (diazepam) is a serious problem after a month or so of steady ingestion. Withdrawal from these drugs resembles that found with barbiturates, though it is not as dangerous. Further, the risks of lethal overdose are not as great as with barbiturates. As with opiates, however, babies born of tranquilizer-dependent mothers are themselves dependent and suffer withdrawal.

Panic Disorder

In panic disorder there is a sudden and inexplicable attack of a host of jarring symptoms—labored breathing, heart palpitations, chest pain, feelings of choking and smothering; dizziness, sweating, and trembling; and intense apprehension, terror, and feelings of impending doom. **Depersonalization** and **derealization,** feelings of being outside one's body and of the world's not being real, and fears of losing control, of going crazy, or even of dying may beset and overwhelm the patient. Panic attacks occur frequently, perhaps once weekly or more often; usually last minutes, rarely hours; and are sometimes linked to specific situations, such as driving a car. The rate of panic disorder is about 0.7 percent for men and slightly over 1 percent for women (Myers et al., 1984). For the diagnosis to be applied, the person must experience at least four attacks in a four-week period or an attack must be followed by at least one month of intense fear concerning the possibility of recurrence. In DSM-IIIR, panic attacks are diagnosed as either with or without agoraphobia, the former being much more common. Over 80 percent of patients diagnosed as having one of the other anxiety disorders also experience panic attacks, although not with the frequency that justifies a diagnosis of panic disorder (Barlow et al., 1985). Coexistence of panic disorder and major depression is also common (Breier et al., 1986).

Panic disorder does run in families (Crowe et al., 1987) and has greater concordance in identical twin pairs than in fraternal twins (Torgersen, 1983). Further, evidence suggests a physiological cause for a proportion of diagnosed cases. Specifically, a cardiac malfunction, mitral valve prolapse (MVP) syndrome, can produce symptoms very similar to those of a panic attack. It has been hypothesized that some individuals with MVP syndrome become alarmed at their sensations of heart palpitations and thereby contribute to their escalation. They consider the palpitations a panic attack (Kantor, Zitrin, and Zeldis, 1980). Indeed, this physical problem is very frequent in patients diagnosed as having panic disorder (Crowe et al., 1980). The therapy implied by their reactions would be to explain to such MVP sufferers exactly what is happening to them, that the palpitations are rarely harmful, and that they are not in themselves signals of anxiety. Perhaps this reattribution could forestall the rapid buildup of anxiety in people with MVP syndrome.

Another line of physiological inquiry has linked panic disorder to overactivity in the β-adrenergic nervous system. The β-adrenergic system controls the activity of many of the organ systems affected in a panic attack, and therefore heart palpitations, sweating, and choking become evidence of β-adrenergic overactivity. Drugs that block the activity of this division of the nervous system, β-blockers, do reduce anxiety. More recently, however, the benzodiazepines have been found more effective than β-blockers in treating panic disorder (Noyes *et al.*, 1984). Similarly, when persons with the disorder are infused with lactate in an attempt to induce a panic attack, β-blockers are ineffective in preventing the lactate-induced panic (Gorman *et al.*, 1983), whereas antidepressants have been able to do so (Liebowitz *et al.*, 1984). Therefore the β-adrenergic theory appears questionable at this time.

More recently, theorizing about the mechanism of lactate's effect has taken a different direction. One approach proposes that panic attacks are linked to hyperventilation or overbreathing (Ley, 1987). Hyperventilation may activate the autonomic nervous system, thus leading to the familiar somatic aspects of a panic episode. Lactate sensitivity, in turn, is thought to result from chronic hyperventilation. Based on the finding that breathing air containing higher than usual amounts of CO_2 can generate a panic attack, oversensitive CO_2 receptors have also been proposed as a mechanism that could stimulate hyperventilation (Gorman *et al.*, 1988).

A strong psychological component may also be present here, namely, how the physiological sensations of panic are perceived (Clark, 1986). Attributing these sensations to a "medical condition," for example, may lessen the likelihood of developing panic disorder and its associated agoraphobia (Breier *et al.*, 1986). Panic disorder patients also ruminate about serious illnesses, both physical and mental (Hibbert, 1984). In this overconcern they may amplify slight physical sensations into signs of impending disaster, which could then spiral into full-blown panic.

Both antidepressants and anxiolytics such as the benzodiazepines have shown some success as biological treatments. The evidence for the effectiveness of aprazolam, a benzodiazepine derivative, is particularly compelling as it has been obtained in a large-scale, multinational study (Ballenger *et al.*, 1988). Based on the assumption that hyperventilation is central to panic disorder, Clark, Salkovskis, and Chalkley (1985) showed patients how a mild panic attack could be created by *voluntarily* hyperventilating. They then taught them techniques of slow breathing. Within two weeks most patients had benefited from this "respiratory control" treatment.

Generalized Anxiety Disorder

"WHAT A RELIEF. NOW I CAN FOCUS MY FREE-FLOATING ANXIETY ON TO SOMETHING SPECIFIC."

The patient, a twenty-four-year-old mechanic, had been referred for psychotherapy by his physician, whom he had consulted because of dizziness and difficulties in falling asleep. He was quite visibly distressed during the entire initial interview, gulping before he spoke, sweating, and continually fidgeting in his chair. His repeated requests for water to slake a seemingly unquenchable thirst were another indication of this extreme nervousness. Although he first related his physical concerns, a more general picture of pervasive anxiety soon emerged. He reported that he nearly always felt tense. He was apprehensive of possible disasters that could befall him as he worked and interacted with other people. He reported a long history of difficulties in interpersonal relationships, which had led to his being fired from several jobs. As he put it, "I really like people and try to get along with them, but it seems like I fly off the handle too easily. Little things they do upset me too much. I just can't cope unless everything is going exactly right."

The individual with generalized anxiety disorder is chronically and persistently anxious. The anxiety and worry are typically linked to all-encompassing life situations, for example, chronic terror concerning a possible accident befalling a child or persistent worries about financial difficulties. So pervasive is this distress that it is sometimes referred to as "free-floating" anxiety. Somatic complaints—sweating, flushing, pounding heart, upset stomach, diarrhea, frequent urination, cold, clammy hands, dry mouth, a lump in the throat, shortness of breath—are frequent and reflect hyperactivity of the autonomic nervous system. Pulse and respiration rates too may be high. The person may also report disturbances of the skeletal musculature: muscle tension and aches, especially of the neck and shoulders; eyelid and other twitches; trembling, becoming tired easily, and an inability to relax. He or she is easily startled, fidgety, restless, and sighs often. As for the state of mind, the person is generally apprehensive, often imagining and worrying about impending disasters, such as losing control, having a heart attack, or dying. Impatience, irritability, insomnia, and distractibility are also common, for the person is all "on edge."

Psychoanalytic View

Psychoanalytic theory regards the source of generalized anxiety as an unconscious conflict between the ego and id impulses. The impulses, usually sexual or aggressive in nature, are struggling for expression, but the ego cannot allow this because it unconsciously fears that punishment will follow. Since the source of the anxiety is unconscious, the person experiences apprehension and distress without knowing why. The true source of anxiety, namely, previously punished id impulses that are striving for expression, is ever present. In a sense there is no way to evade anxiety; if the person escapes the id, he is no longer alive. Anxiety is felt nearly all the time. The phobic may be regarded as more fortunate since, according to psychoanalytic theory, his or her anxiety is displaced onto a specific object or situation, which can then be avoided. The person with generalized anxiety disorder has not developed this type of defense and thus is constantly anxious.

Learning View

Learning theorists (e.g., Wolpe, 1958) attempting to account for generalized anxiety carefully examine the environmental elicitors of the anxiety. For example, a person anxious most of his or her waking hours might well be fearful of social contacts. If that individual spends a good deal of time with other people, it may be more useful to regard the anxiety as tied to these circumstances rather than to any internal factors. This behavioral model of generalized anxiety, then, is identical to one of the learning views of phobias. The anxiety is regarded as having been classically conditioned to external stimuli, although the range of conditioned stimuli is considerably broader.

Cognitive-Behavioral View

A cognitive-behavioral model of generalized anxiety focuses on control and helplessness. Mandler (1966) suggests that the feeling of not being in control is a central characteristic of all views of anxiety. According to psychoanalytic theory, the ego is anxious because it is threatened with overstimulation that it cannot control. Learning theory sees people as confronted with painful stimuli over which they have no control until they learn to avoid them. This concept of ***helplessness*** had earlier been examined by workers in several disciplines.

Richter (1957), in an article entitled "On the Phenomenon of Sudden Death in Animals and Man," quoted the following anthropological observation from an earlier source.

A Brazilian Indian condemned and sentenced by a so-called medicine man is helpless against his own emotional response to this pronouncement—and dies within hours. In Africa a young Negro knowingly eats the inviolably banned wild hen. On discovery of his "crime" he trembles, is overcome by fear and dies in twenty-four hours. In New Zealand a Maori woman eats fruit that she only later learns has come from a taboo place. Her chief has been profaned. By noon the next day she is dead. (Basedow, 1925, cited in Richter, 1957, p. 191)

That such seemingly supernatural events actually occur in primitive societies may be difficult for us to believe. Walter Cannon (1942), a well-known American physiologist of the earlier part of this century, studied reports of such "voodoo" deaths and concluded that they do take place and are worthy of serious scientific study.

Experimental psychologists have also been interested in related phenomena. In a classic experiment Mowrer and Viek (1948) trained rats to obtain food. Then they were all shocked at the feeding place. One group was able to terminate the shock by performing a certain behavior. Each member of the second group was yoked to, that is paired with, a member of the first so that the amount and duration of shock received by the pair were identical. But the members of the second group were unable to terminate the shock. The group of rats who had control over shock exhibited less fear than did those animals who were yoked helplessly to a partner.

Similar findings have emerged in studies of humans. Early on, Haggard (1943) showed that human subjects who administered electric shocks to themselves were less anxious about the situation than those who received the same amount and intensity of shock but who had no control over its administration. Furthermore, Pervin (1963) found that electric shocks that could be controlled were preferred to those that could not be controlled. Another study indicated that intellectual performance is superior when the subjects believed that they had control over the order in which they took a series of tests (Neale and Katahn, 1968). And in yet another study, in which human beings received aversive stimulation, Staub, Tursky, and Schwartz (1971) indicated that "the ability to predict and control events in the environment is important for the comfort and safety of organisms. Consequently . . . lack of control . . . may become intrinsically aversive" (p. 157). In all this experimental work with human beings, stressful events that the subjects could exert some control over were less anxiety-provoking than those over which no control could be exercised. Some research (e.g., Geer, Davison, and Gatchel, 1970) also suggests that in certain circumstances the control need only be perceived by the subject and not actually be real.

In addition to feeling that they cannot control stressors they encounter, a number of other cognitive processes may be linked to GAD. The content of cognitions of patients with GAD involves themes of danger. Benign events are misperceived as involving threats and cognitions focus on anticipated future disasters (Beck *et al.*, 1987). The attention of patients with GAD is easily drawn to stimuli suggesting possible physical harm or the possibility of social misfortune (e.g., criticism, embarrassment, or rejection) (MacLeod *et al.*, 1986).

Humanistic View

A statement on how humanistic workers explain phobias and generalized and other anxiety disorders has not been offered until now because their thinking about all of them is generally the same and not specific. As indicated in Chapter 2, humanists hold human nature to be basically good and beautiful, with psychological problems resulting from a denial of this innate worth. Thus the individual becomes anxious in various ways when his or her basic nature is not expressed. Humanistic psychologists believe that neurotic individuals are particularly preoccupied with two conflicting self-concepts. They have accepted the unfavorable opinion of

themselves held by others, which interferes with their own more natural, self-enhancing image. Their energy is expended on this conflict rather than on self-actualization.

Genetic Studies

Genetic researchers have also examined anxiety disorder. In one study (Slater and Shields, 1969) comparisons were made of seventeen identical pairs of twins and twenty-eight fraternal pairs; one twin of each pair had been diagnosed as having anxiety neurosis. Of the identical co-twins, 49 percent were also diagnosed as having anxiety neurosis. In contrast, only 4 percent of the fraternal co-twins were so diagnosed. Torgersen (1983), however, found the same concordance for generalized anxiety disorder in identical and fraternal twin pairs. Thus, at this time, the data are equivocal.

Neurobiology of Anxiety and Panic

In considering neurobiological factors relevant to generalized anxiety disorder, we will consider panic disorder again. The reason is that theorists in this area make an important distinction between the physiology of panic anxiety and what they often term anticipatory anxiety, which is viewed as similar to the anxiety of GAD (e.g., Gray, 1982).

Panic anxiety is viewed by many as being linked to the noradrenergic system and particularly the locus ceruleus, a nucleus in the pons. The locus ceruleus is the major noradrenergic nucleus and has projections to many other brain areas—cortex, limbic system, and brain stem. Redmond (1977) discovered that electrical stimulation of the locus ceruleus caused monkeys to respond with what appeared to be a panic attack, thus suggesting that naturally occurring panic might be based on noradrenergic overactivation. Subsequent research has indeed shown that drugs that stimulate the locus ceruleus (e.g., yohimbine) can elicit panic attacks whereas drugs that reduce activity in the locus ceruleus (e.g., clonidine) have anxiolytic properties (e.g., Charney *et al.*, 1984; Siever and Uhde, 1984). Although all evidence does not support the theory (e.g., other measures of noradrenergic activation have failed to discriminate patients with panic disorder from controls; Woods *et al.*, 1987), interest in it remains active.

The most prevalent neurobiological model for generalized anxiety comes from knowledge concerning the operation of the benzodiazepines, which are an effective treatment. A receptor in the brain has been discovered that is linked to an inhibitory neurotransmitter called γ-aminobutyric acid (GABA) (see Box 6.5). It is be-

BOX 6.5

COMMUNICATION IN THE NERVOUS SYSTEM

The nervous system is composed of billions of neurons. Although differing in some respects, each neuron has four major parts (Figure 6b): (1) the cell body; (2) several dendrites, its short and thick extensions; (3) one or more axons, but usually only one, long and thin, extending a considerable distance from the cell body; and (4) terminal buttons on the many end branches of the axon. When a neuron is appropriately stimulated at its cell body (primarily inhibitory messages) or through its dendrites (primarily excitatory messages), a nerve impulse, which is a change in the electric potential of the cell, travels down the axon to the terminal endings. Between the terminal endings of the sending axon and the receiving neurons there is a small gap, the synapse (Figure 6c).

For a nerve impulse to pass from one neuron to another, it must have a way of bridging the synaptic space. The terminal buttons of each axon contain synaptic vesicles, small structures that are filled with chemicals called neurotransmitters. A neuron synthesizes and stores only one principal neurotransmitter. Neuropeptides (chains of amino acids), which serve as auxiliary neurotransmitters, may be stored by themselves in a neuron, with another neuropeptide, or with a principal neurotransmitter, whose action it supports or modifies. Nerve impulses cause the synaptic vesicles to release their transmitter substances, which flood the synapse and can then stimulate an adjacent neuron. The molecules of a transmitter fit into receptor sites in the postsynaptic neuron and thereby transmit the impulse.

Several principal transmitters have been identified; those belonging to two major compound groups, the catecholamines and the indoleamines, have been implicated in mood and emotion and therefore in psychopathology. Substances in both groups are monoamines, which means that their molecules contain a single amino group (NH_2). The catecholamines, each with a catechol portion ($C_6H_6O_2$), are norepinephrine, epinephrine, and dopamine. The two indoleamines, each with an indole portion (C_8H_7N), are serotonin and tryptamine. Serotonin and tryptamine are found in greater quantities in other bodily tissues than in the central nervous system. Serotonin, for example, occurs in large amounts in cells of the mucous membranes of the intestines. Norepinephrine is a neurotransmitter of the peripheral sympathetic nervous system. Of these monoamines, norepinephrine, epinephrine, dopamine, and ser-

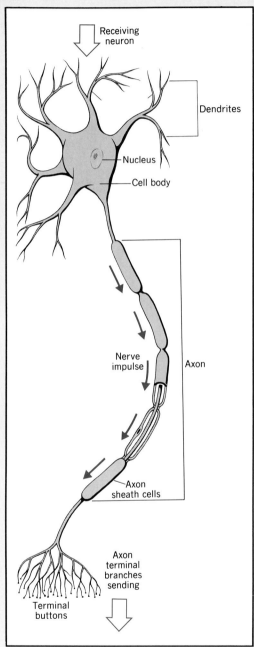

FIGURE 6b
The neuron, the basic unit of the nervous system.

lieved that when there is neural excitation stimulated by anxiety, the benzodiazepines reduce anxiety by enhancing release of GABA. Similarly, drugs that block or inhibit the GABA system lead to increases in anxiety (Insell, 1986). As with most new theories, much remains to be learned but the approach seems destined to enhance our understanding of anxiety.

Therapies for Generalized Anxiety Disorder

As might be expected from their view of generalized anxiety disorder, that it stems from repressed conflicts, most psychoanalysts work to help patients confront the true sources of their conflicts. Treatment is much the same as that for phobias.

Behavioral clinicians approach generalized anxiety

otonin appear for certain to be neurotransmitters of the central nervous system. At least some of the particular pathways in the brain served by these transmitters have been identified.

To understand the theory and research relating neurotransmitters to psychopathology, we need to know how these substances are synthesized within the neuron from the amino acids tryosine and tryptophan. Table 6a presents this information. Finally, we need to consider the mechanisms by which the neurotransmitters are *inactivated* following their release. The catecholamines norepinephrine and dopamine are for the most part pumped back (reuptake) into the presynaptic neuron. The remainder of these substances is deactivated in the synapse by the enzyme catechol-*O*-methyltransferase (COMT). Catecholamines within the presynaptic neuron can be deactivated by the enzyme monoamine oxidase (MAO), which is present in the mitochondria, the powerhouses supplying the energy for the activities of all cells. Serotonin is also taken up again into the presynaptic neuron. It is deactivated within the presynaptic neuron and in the synapse by MAO.

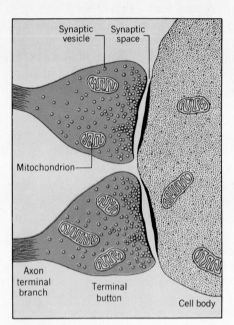

FIGURE 6c
A synapse showing the terminal buttons of two axon branches in close contact with a very small portion of the cell body of another neuron.

TABLE 6a
Biosynthesis of the catecholamines and indoleamines

Catecholamines	Indoleamines	
Tyrosine ↓ tyrosine hydroxylase*	Tryptophan ↓ tryptophan hydroxylase	tryptophan decarboxylase
Dopa ↓ dopa decarboxylase	5-Hydroxytryptophan ↓ dopa decarboxylase	→ Tryptamine
Dopamine ↓ dopamine-β-hydroxylase	Serotonin	
Norepinephrine ↓ norepinephrine-*N*-methyltransferase		
Epinephrine		

*The substances on the arrows are the enzymes that catalyze the reactions.

in various ways. If they can *construe* the anxiety as a set of responses to identifiable situations, the free-floating anxiety can be reformulated into one or more phobias. For example, through situational assessment (see page 88) a behavior therapist may determine that the generally anxious client seems more specifically afraid of criticizing others and of being criticized by them. The anxiety appears free-floating only because the client spends so many hours with other human beings. Systematic desensitization becomes a possible treatment. However, difficulties in assessing specific causes of the anxiety suffered by such patients as well as by those with panic disorder have led behavioral clinicians to prescribe more generalized treatment, such as intensive relaxation training, in the hopes that its anxiety-inhibiting potential will help reduce the patient's overall tension level (Barlow *et al.*, 1984).

If a feeling of helplessness seems to underlie the pervasive anxiety, the therapist will help the client acquire whatever skills might engender a sense of competence, the vital "self-efficacy" that Bandura (1977) speaks of. The skills may be taught by verbal instructions, modeling, or operant shaping—and very likely some judicious combination of the three (Goldfried and Davison, 1976).

Humanistic treatment of generalized anxiety encourages the person to sense what he or she truly needs and wants at any given time and to develop the trust to express those needs and satisfy those wants. For example, an aim of **Gestalt therapy,** one of the humanistic therapies, is to help the client become aware of moment-to-moment feelings and perceptions. Ingenious exercises are often used to achieve this goal. In the **empty-chair technique** the client is instructed to talk to a person who is significant in their life, or to a feeling, as though that individual or emotion were sitting in an empty chair nearby. Gestalt therapists believe that by this unusual procedure clients will confront their most basic wants and fears. The increased awareness and insight that follow are assumed to be both necessary and sufficient for the alleviation of a host of psychological problems, including anxiety.[8] Client-centered therapists, following the work of Carl Rogers, provide a warm, nonjudgmental atmosphere in which the client will be better able to come upon his or her innermost feelings.

Anxiolytics, such as those mentioned earlier for the treatment of phobias, are probably the most widespread treatment for generalized anxiety disorder. A psychoactive drug is viewed by medical practitioners as especially appropriate for a disorder defined by its pervasiveness, for the simple reason that once it takes effect, a drug will continue to work for several hours in whatever situation clients find themselves. Unfortunately, many tranquilizing drugs have undesirable side effects, ranging from drowsiness and depression to physical addiction and damage to certain bodily organs.

Community psychologists or psychiatrists have yet another approach to generalized anxiety, and to most other psychological disorders. They view human suffering as a normal reaction to abnormal or untenable living conditions. Rather than help the individual cope with or adjust to an environment considered brutalizing, community workers strive for social change. Their work is very different indeed from any discussed so far;

much of Chapter 20 is devoted to a close examination of **community psychology**.

Obsessive-Compulsive Disorder

Obsessive-compulsive disorder affects between 1 and 3 percent of the population (Myers *et al.*, 1984). The disorder itself usually begins in early adulthood, often following some stressful event such as pregnancy, childbirth, family conflict, and difficulties at work (Kringlen, 1970). During an episode of depression, patients occasionally develop obsessive-compulsive disorder, and significant depression is often found in obsessive-compulsive patients (Rachman and Hodgson, 1980).

Obsessions are intrusive and recurring thoughts and images that come unbidden to the mind and appear irrational and uncontrollable to the individual experiencing them. Whereas many of us may have similar fleeting experiences, the obsessive has them with such force and frequency that they interfere with normal functioning. Cameron (1963) gives an example illustrating the onset of an obsessive thought in a forty-two-year-old mother.

"RONALD IS EXTREMELY COMPULSIVE."

---

[8]See page 530 for an in-depth examination of Gestalt therapy.

> She was serving the family dinner one evening when she dropped a dish on the table and smashed it. The accident appalled her. While clearing up the fragments she was seized with an unreasonable fear that bits of glass might get into her husband's food and kill him. She would not allow the meal to proceed until she had removed everything and reset the table with fresh linen and clean dishes. After this, her fears, instead of subsiding, reached out to include intense anxiety over the possibility that she herself and the children might be killed by bits of glass. (p. 384)

Obsessions may also take the form of extreme doubting, procrastination, and indecision. The patient may be unable to come to a conclusion and cease reconsidering an issue (Salzman and Thaler, 1981).

A *compulsion* is an irresistible impulse to repeat some ritualistic act over and over again. The activity, however, is not realistically connected with its apparent purpose or is clearly excessive. Lady Macbeth washed her hands continually after the murder of King Duncan. Often an individual who continually repeats some action fears dire consequences if the act is not performed. The sheer frequency with which an act is repeated may often be staggering. One woman treated by one of the authors of this book washed her hands over 500 times per day, despite the painful sores that resulted. She reported that she had a very strong fear of contamination by germs and could temporarily alleviate this concern only by washing her hands. Frequently reported compulsions have to do with cleanliness and orderliness, sometimes achieved only by elaborate ceremonies that take hours and even most of the day; with avoiding particular objects, such as staying away from anything brown; with repetitive "magical" protective practices, such as counting, saying particular numbers, touching a talisman or a particular part of the body; and with checking, going back seven or eight times to make certain that already performed acts were actually carried out—lights, gas jets, faucets turned off, windows fastened, doors locked, the silver chest hidden away beneath the guest tablecloths.

Bernice was forty-six when she entered treatment. This was the fourth time she had been in outpatient therapy, and she had previously been hospitalized twice. Her obsessive-compulsive disorder had begun twelve years ago, shortly after the death of her father. Since then it had waxed and waned and currently was as severe as it had ever been.

Bernice was obsessed with a fear of contamination, a fear she vaguely linked to her father's death from pneumonia. Although she reported that she was afraid of nearly everything, because germs could be anywhere, she was particularly upset by touching wood, "scratchy objects," mail, canned goods, and "silver flecks." By silver flecks Bernice meant silver embossing on a greeting card, eyeglass frames, shiny appliances, and silverware. She was unable to state why these particular objects were special sources of possible contamination.

To try to reduce her discomfort, Bernice engaged in a variety of compulsive rituals which took up almost all her waking hours. In the morning she spent three to four hours in the bathroom, washing and rewashing herself. Between each bath she would have to scrape away the outside layer of her bar of soap so that it would be totally free of germs. Mealtimes also lasted for hours, as Bernice performed her rituals—eating three bites of food at a time, chewing each mouthful three hundred times. These were meant "magically" to decontaminate her food. Even Bernice's husband was sometimes involved in these mealtime ceremonies, and he would shake a teakettle and frozen vegetables over her head to remove the germs. Bernice's rituals and fear of contamination had reduced her life to doing almost nothing else. She would not leave the house, do housework, or even talk on the telephone.

We hear people described as compulsive gamblers, compulsive eaters, and compulsive drinkers. But even though such individuals may report an irresistible urge to gamble, eat, and drink, such behavior is not clinically regarded as a compulsion because it is often engaged in with pleasure and is not "ego-alien." A true compulsion is viewed by the person as somehow foreign to his or her personality. Stern and Cobb (1978), for example, found that 78 percent of a sample of compulsives viewed their rituals as either "rather silly or absurd."

Howard Hughes, the famous industrialist, suffered from an obsessive fear of contamination. Here, on a trip to London, Hughes has lined the windows of his Rolls-Royce with newspaper to protect himself from unclean air.

A frequent consequence of obsessive-compulsive disorder is the negative effect it can have on the individual's relations with other people, especially with members of the family. A person saddled with the irresistible need to wash his hands every ten minutes, or touch every doorknob he passes, or count every tile in a bathroom floor is likely to cause concern and even resentment in a spouse, children, friends, or co-workers. And the antagonistic feelings experienced by these significant others are likely to be tinged with guilt, for at some level they understand that the person cannot really help doing these senseless things. Finally, the undesirable effects on others can, in turn, be expected to have additional consequences, engendering feelings of depression and generalized anxiety in the obsessive-compulsive person and setting the stage for even further deterioration of personal relationships. For such reasons family therapists (Hafner, 1982; Hafner *et al.*, 1981) have suggested that obsessive-compulsive disorder is sometimes embedded in marital distress and actually substitutes for overt marital conflict. This speculative hypothesis cautions therapists to consider marital treatment as well as therapies that focus on the individual.

The content of obsessions and compulsions has been investigated by Akhter and his colleagues (1975). After interviews with eighty-two obsessive-compulsive patients, five distinguishable forms of obsession and two of compulsion were identified.

Obsessions

1. **Obsessive Doubts.** Persistent thoughts that a completed task had not been adequately accomplished were found in 75 percent of the patients. "Each time he left his room a twenty-eight-year-old student began asking himself 'Did I lock the door? Am I sure?' in spite of a clear and accurate remembrance of having done so" (p. 343).

2. **Obsessive Thinking.** Seemingly endless chains of thoughts, usually focusing on future events, were reported by 34 percent of those interviewed. A pregnant woman tormented herself with these thoughts: "If my baby is a boy he might aspire to a career that would necessitate his going away from me, but he might want to return to me and what would I do then, because if I . . ." (p. 343).

3. **Obsessive Impulses.** Seventeen percent had powerful urges to perform certain actions, ranging from rather trivial whims to grave and assaultive acts. "A forty-one-year-old lawyer was obsessed by what he understood to be the 'nonsensical notion' of drinking from his inkpot but also the serious urge to strangle an apparently beloved only son" (p. 343).

4. **Obsessive Fears.** Twenty-six percent were anxious about losing control and doing something that would be socially embarrassing. "A thirty-two-year-old teacher was afraid that in the classroom he would refer to his unsatisfactory sexual relations with his wife, although he had no wish to do so" (p. 344).

5. **Obsessive Images.** Persisting images of some recently seen or imagined event plagued 7 percent of the sample. A patient " 'saw' her baby being flushed away in the toilet whenever she entered the bathroom" (p. 344).

Compulsions

1. **Yielding Compulsions.** Compulsive urges seemingly forced actions on 61 percent of the patients. "A twenty-nine-year-old clerk had [a notion] that he had an important document in one of his pockets. He knew that this was not true, but found himself impelled to check his pocket, again and again" (p. 344).

2. **Controlling Compulsions.** Diverting actions apparently allowed 6 percent of the patients to control a compulsive urge without giving in to it. "A sixteen-year-old boy with incestuous impulses controlled the anxiety these aroused by repeatedly and loudly counting to ten" (p. 344).

Additional information on the content of compulsions is provided by Rachman and Hodgson's (1980) analysis of the responses of obsessive-compulsive patients to a questionnaire. The two major compulsions centered around cleaning and checking. In addition, many patients complained of what Rachman and Hodgson call primary obsessional slowness. Dressing, personal hygiene, folding clothes, and the like can take up so much of the patients' days that they are unable to meet other obligations.

The Psychoanalytic Theory of Obsessive-Compulsive Disorder

In psychoanalytic theory obsessions and compulsions are viewed as similar, resulting from instinctual forces, sexual or aggressive, which are not under control because of overly harsh toilet training. The person is thus fixated at the anal stage. The symptoms observed represent the outcome of the struggle between the id and the defense mechanisms; sometimes the id predominates, sometimes the defense mechanisms. For example, when obsessive thoughts of killing intrude, the forces of the id are dominant. More often, however, the observed symptoms reflect the partially successful operation of one of the defense mechanisms. For example, an individual fixated at the anal stage may by reaction formation resist his urge to soil and become compulsively neat, clean, and orderly.

Alfred Adler (1931), an early colleague of Freud who broke with the master because he did not agree with Freud's libido theory, viewed obsessive-compulsive disorders within the framework of his theory that pathology results when children are kept from developing a sense of competence by their doting or excessively dominating parents. Saddled with an inferiority complex, people may unconsciously adopt compulsive rituals in order to carve out a domain in which they exert control and can feel proficient. Adler proposed that the compulsive act allows a person mastery of *something,* even if only the positioning of writing implements on a desk.

Behavioral Theories of Obsessive-Compulsive Disorder

Behavioral accounts of obsessions and compulsions (Meyer and Chesser, 1970) consider them learned behavior reinforced by their consequences. One set of consequences is the reduction of fear. For example, compulsive hand washing is viewed as an operant escape-response that reduces an obsessional preoccupation with contamination by dirt or germs. Similarly,

compulsive checking may reduce anxiety about whatever disaster the patient anticipates were the checking ritual not completed. Anxiety as measured by self-report (Hodgson and Rachman, 1972) and psychophysiological responses (Carr, 1971) can indeed be reduced by such compulsive behavior. Research has also shown, however, that not all compulsive acts reduce anxiety to the same degree. Rachman and Hodgson (1980) report that patients with a cleaning compulsion are more often able to lessen their anxiety than patients with a checking compulsion. Furthermore, the reduction of anxiety cannot account for obsessions. Indeed, the obsessions of obsessive-compulsive patients make them anxious (Rabavilas and Boulougouris, 1974), much as do the somewhat similar intrusive thoughts of normal subjects about stressful stimuli, such as a scary movie (Horowitz, 1975).

How, then, might we account for obsessive thoughts? First, Rachman and deSilva (1978) have shown that most people occasionally experience unwanted ideas that are similar in content to obsessions. Among normals, however, these cognitions are tolerated or dismissed. But for the obsessive, the thoughts may be particularly salient and elicit great concern. The obsessive may then begin to try to actively suppress these troubling thoughts, with unfortunate consequences.

Wegner *et al.* (1987) studied what happens when people are asked to suppress a thought. Two groups of college students were asked to either think about a white bear or not to think about one. One group expressed and then inhibited; the other group did the reverse. Thoughts were measured by having subjects verbalize their thoughts aloud and also by having them ring a bell every time they thought about a white bear. Two findings are of particular note. First, attempts to inhibit were not fully successful. Second, the students who first inhibited thoughts of a white bear had more subsequent thoughts about it once the inhibition condition was over. Trying to inhibit a thought may therefore have the paradoxical effect of inducing preoccupation with it.

Cognitive Views of Obsessive-Compulsive Disorder

In a related but more cognitive view, Carr (1974) proposes that obsessive-compulsives, when in a situation that has a potentially undesirable or harmful outcome, overestimate the likelihood that the harmful outcome will occur. In other words, the obsessive-compulsive has an "If anything can go wrong, it will" view of life. This cognitive set, according to Carr, necessitates avoiding the sources of threat and thus increases the likelihood of obsessive-compulsive behavior.

A study by Sher, Frost, and Otto (1983) employed cognitive tasks to test the idea that compulsive checkers suffer from a memory deficit for actions performed—Did I turn off the stove?—and for distinguishing between reality and imagination—Maybe I just *imagined* I turned off the stove. In both instances the person would be inclined to reduce uncertainty by checking whether in fact the stove is turned off. The results supported the first hypothesis in that compulsive checkers had poorer recall of prior actions; the second hypothesis was not unequivocally supported. The experiment is significant in that it construes at least one kind of compulsivity as a problem in a certain kind of memory, and tests this hypothesis via procedures that come from basic experimental research in cognition. This kind of experimentation has been employed for some years in schizophrenia research but is only recently being followed in empirical work with other psychological disorders.

Biological Factors in Obsessive-Compulsive Disorder

Encephalitis, head injuries, and brain tumors have all been associated with the development of obsessive-compulsive disorder (OCD) (Jenike, 1986). Neurochemically, interest has focused on serotonin. Clomipramine, a tricyclic antidepressant that blocks the reuptake of serotonin, has proved to be a useful therapy in OCD. Furthermore, research with drugs that can stimulate the serotonin receptor indicates that they can exacerbate the symptoms of OCD (Zohar *et al.*, 1988). Carey and Gottesman (1981) have also reported evidence consistent with a genetic contribution to OCD. Although it is premature to conclude that biological factors are known to predispose to OCD, we can expect the search for a physiological diathesis to increase in the coming years.

Therapies for Obsessive-Compulsive Disorder

Psychoanalytic treatment for obsessions and compulsions resembles that for phobias and generalized anxiety, namely lifting repression and allowing the patient to confront what he or she is truly afraid of—that a particular impulse will be gratified. The intrusive thoughts and irresistible behavior are not appropriate targets for therapeutic change, serving as they do to protect the ego from the repressed conflict.

The failure of psychoanalytic procedures has prompted some analytic workers to advocate taking a more action-oriented approach to these disorders. Salzman (1980), for example, warns that free association merely feeds into the patient's obsessionalism; hence he suggests that the analyst be more directive in guiding the discussion. He hypothesizes that the indecision one sees in most obsessive-compulsives derives from a need for guaranteed correctness before any action can be taken (Salzman, 1985). Patients therefore need to learn to tolerate the uncertainty and anxiety that all people feel as they confront the reality that nothing is certain or absolutely controllable in life.[9] He suggests as well that the analyst encourage the patient to abandon the ego defense of acting compulsively. The ultimate focus of the treatment, however, remains on insight into unconscious determinants.

Active interruption of the "symptoms," a trend in psychoanalytic treatment, is the core of behavioral approaches to obsessive-compulsive disorders. Generally speaking, behavioral treatment of obsessive thoughts has concentrated either on reducing the anxiety assumed to underlie them, in procedures such as desensitization, or on a technique called thought stopping. This straight-forward procedure has the client signal to the therapist when an obsessive thought creeps into consciousness, at which time the therapist shouts "Stop!" Not surprisingly, the client is startled and realizes immediately that this interruption has driven out the unwanted cognition. The client is then trained to utter "Stop" subvocally whenever intrusive thoughts or images invade consciousness. Data on the efficacy of this technique are meager indeed, however (Marks, 1981b), as are other available treatments for obsessive ruminations that are not associated with compulsive rituals (Marks, 1983).

The most widely used and generally accepted behavioral approach to compulsive rituals entails exposure with response prevention (Rachman and Hodgson, 1978).[10] This entails having the person expose herself to situations that elicit the compulsive act—such as touching a dirty dish—and then refraining from performing the accustomed ritual—handwashing.

Although in the short term such curtailment is very arduous and unpleasant for clients, the extreme discomfort is believed worth enduring to alleviate these

---

[9]The hypothesized need of the obsessive-compulsive not to err suggests that a rational-emotive approach might also be useful: the person may harbor an irrational belief that he or she must never make a mistake.

[10]This modern treatment of compulsive rituals was anticipated by Pierre Janet, who discovered a number of unplanned cures of obsessive-compulsive disorder brought about through the institutional practices of the military and of religious orders. Their rules and strictures, which did not tolerate obsessive-compulsives' performing their "uncontrollable" actions, remedied their condition (Marks, 1981a).

disabling problems. Clearly, however, conditions must be such that the client can be persuaded to go along with the treatment. Sometimes control over rituals is possible only in a hospital. Victor Meyer (1966), a renowned behavioral expert in the treatment of compulsions, pioneered the development of a controlled environment at Middlesex Hospital in London, England. There staff members are specially trained to restrict the patient's opportunities for engaging in ritualistic acts. Generalization of the treatment to the home requires that family members become involved. Suffice it to say that preparing them for this work is no mean task, requiring as it does skills and care that go beyond whatever specific behavioral technique is being employed. The general response prevention approach is widely accepted as the most promising available treatment for compulsions, though its efficacy is far from 100 percent.

The monoamine oxidase inhibitors and the tricyclics, drugs that are more commonly used in treating depression (see Chapter 9), are sometimes given to obsessive-compulsives. Both classes of drugs have yielded beneficial results (Jenike, 1986). The desperation of mental health workers, surpassed only by that of the sufferers, explains the occasional use of psychosurgery in treating obsessions and compulsions. The procedure in current use is called a **modified leucotomy;** it involves severing 2–3 centimeters of white matter in the cingulum, an area near the corpus callosum. Side effects from this procedure are rare and it appears to be effective in patients for whom other treatments have failed (Tippin and Henn, 1982).

Obsessive-compulsive disorder is overall one of the most difficult psychological problems to treat.

Traumatic life experiences, like a devastating earthquake, can cause posttraumatic stress disorder.

Posttraumatic Stress Disorder

The Symptoms and Diagnosis

In posttraumatic stress disorder (PTSD) a traumatic event or catastrophe of the worst order, such as rape,[11] combat, a natural disaster, serious threat to the safety of loved ones, or seeing another person maimed or killed, brings in its aftermath difficulties with concentration and memory, an inability to relax, impulsiveness, a tendency to be easily startled, disturbed sleep, anxiety, depression, and above all a psychic numbing. Previously enjoyed activities lose their interest. There

is a feeling of estrangement from others and from "the passing parade" and, if the trauma was shared and took the lives of companions, a deadening sense of guilt for having survived. As for the experience itself, the person has great difficulty keeping it out of mind although trying in many ways to do so. "Flashbacks"—vivid and intrusive recollections of the painful event—and recurring nightmares and dreams of it are common. Posttraumatic stress disorder may be acute, chronic, or delayed. It is believed to be more severe and longer lasting after a trauma caused by human beings, as in war, physical assaults, or torture, than after a catastrophe of nature, such as a flood or an earthquake. Symptoms often worsen when the individual is exposed to situations that resemble the original trauma: a thunderstorm may remind a soldier of the firings and rumbles of the past unendurable bloody battle.

DSM-IIIR alerts us to the fact that children can suffer from PTSD, but they may show it differently from adults. Sleep disorders with nightmares about monsters are

---

[11]The aftermath of sexual assault is discussed in a separate section on rape in Chapter 12 (page 336).

common as are general behavioral changes, as when a previously garrulous and sociable youngster becomes very quiet and withdrawn and loses interest in normal play activities or school. Conversely, a previously quiet child may begin to act aggressively. Some children develop the idea that they will not become adults. In addition, the child may lose already acquired developmental skills such as toilet habits or even language skills. Most importantly, young children have much more difficulty talking about their upset and concern than do adults; this feature is especially important to remember in cases of possible physical or sexual abuse by adults.

The anxiety disorders discussed so far in this chapter seem to share an important characteristic: they cannot be adequately explained on environmental grounds alone. In contrast, people diagnosed as having posttraumatic stress disorder, although surely different from one another in countless ways before trauma, do have in their lives a major, salient, and powerful happening—in the words of DSM-IIIR "a psychologically distressing event that is outside the range of usual human experience" (p. 247). DSM-IIIR goes on to state, as the literature on trauma had for years, that "the stressor producing this syndrome would be markedly distressing to almost anyone" (p. 247).

Although clinicians had written about a disorder that they called traumatic neurosis, DSM-II itself lacked a specific category for stress disorders of some duration. The posttraumatic stress disorder listed in DSM-III and DSM-IIIR represents no small change in overall point of view, for it constitutes a formal recognition that, regardless of premorbid history, many people may be adversely affected by overwhelming catastrophic stress, and that their reaction should be distinguished from other disorders. The newly listed disorder can be seen, then, as shifting the "blame" for the problem from the survivor to the event. Instead of implicitly concluding that the person would be all right were he or she made of sterner stuff, DSM-IIIR acknowledges the onerousness of the traumatizing circumstances (Haley, 1978).

We must not overlook entirely the role of premorbid factors, however, for the simple reason that not all people subjected to the same kind of trauma develop PTSD. It is more a question of emphasis. The externally imposed trauma is a clear, powerful, and completely obvious circumstance in the lives of those who do suffer emotional wounds.

Recent research has begun to examine "person variables" that distinguish between those who do and do not develop PTSD following combat. For example, in a study of Israeli veterans of the 1982 war with Lebanon, development of PTSD was associated with a "depres-

sive attributional style" (see page 230) and a tendency to cope by focusing on their emotions (e.g., "I wish I could change how I feel.") rather than on the problems themselves (Mikhliner and Solomon, 1988; Solomon *et al.*, 1988).

On the other hand, a recent detailed review of premorbid factors in PTSD among Vietnam veterans failed to show consistent contributions from such variables as age, race, socioeconomic status, level of education, or depression. The strongest and most consistently found predictor was severity of combat-related exposure (Foy, Carroll, and Donahoe, in press). Foy *et al.* (1987) suggest that premorbid factors like family history of psychopathology may play a contributory role only when the severity of the stressor is relatively low.

The reader is invited to reflect on whether these reactions to trauma should even be considered abnormal. If most people are indeed significantly distressed by severe trauma, why should PTSD be of concern to psychopathologists any more than the tendency of most people to become dehydrated when deprived of liquids and exposed for hours to temperatures in excess of a hundred degrees? To be sure, PTSD can and should be studied and treated, but perhaps both activities can be conducted without considering the phenomenon as abnormal.

Posttraumatic Stress Disorder and the Vietnam War

Combat Stress in Earlier Wars

During war, military personnel must contend with devastating stress, and some of them break down. The American Civil War was the first one in which the psychological disintegration suffered under the rigors of battle was acknowledged as a clinical entity. William Hammond, Surgeon General of the Union Army, considered it to be "nostalgia," meaning a severe melancholia brought on by protracted absence from home. The incidence of nostalgia was reported to be 2.34 cases per 1000 troops in the first year of the Civil War, and 3.3 in the second. In addition, 20.8 per 1000 troops were discharged for "paralysis" and 6 per 1000 for insanity (Bourne, 1970).

In World War I, the first global conflict, the term used was "shell shock," reflecting the somatogenic belief that the soldier's brain suffered chronic concussions through the sudden and severe atmospheric pressure changes from nearby explosions. Eventually, the soldier's dazed loss of self-command, his tremulousness and terror were recognized as the cumulative emotional and psychological reaction to the strain of war. But those who succumbed were also regarded as vulnerable

Prior to the Vietnam War, returning soldiers were greeted with enthusiastic demonstrations.

to stress, as having a "breaking point." Some maladjustment extending back before their service in the war had presumably predisposed them to their breakdown. In World War II and the Korean War the great weariness of a soldier, his sleeplessness, startle at the slightest sounds, inability to speak, terror, and either stupor or agitated excitement were called "exhaustion" and then "combat fatigue" (Figley, 1978a), putting the blame clearly on the stressful circumstances of battle.

Combat Stress in the Vietnam War

What was unusual about the psychological breakdowns during and in the aftermath of the Vietnam War? As Figley (1978b) has noted, this war was believed at first to have caused far fewer psychological casualties than did World War I or II—1.5 percent in Vietnam[12] versus 10 percent in World War II—perhaps because battle duty was more intermittent and limited in time. A tour of duty was one year long. Each soldier had his DEROS, his date expected to return from overseas, and thus a day on which he would no longer have to go into combat (Bourne, 1970). His DEROS must have helped

him to gird himself for this one year of duty and to concentrate his energies on staying alive.

After men had been home for a few months or years, however, signs of great distress began to appear. The public was made aware of this disorder through veterans who availed themselves of the free medical and psychological services offered by the Veterans Administration. Many of these veterans had also returned with drug problems. Were these men malingering? Were they to be considered somehow weak or lazy, unable and unwilling to reenter civilian life?

The listing of posttraumatic stress disorder in DSM-III eventually made it easier for Vietnam veterans to obtain help within the Veterans Administration system. They were acknowledged to have a recognized mental disorder. Their treatment centered on the combat stress itself and not on any emotional "weakness" presumed to have existed prior to the war, or on the veteran's own efforts to deal with their stress, such as abusing drugs.

Efforts have been made to document the extent of PTSD among Vietnam veterans. Penk and his colleagues (1981) studied 87 combat veterans and 120 who had not seen combat. All had sought treatment for substance abuse at a Veterans Administration medical center. The veterans were compared on their answers to questions designed specifically by Figley to tap into their life problems since leaving military service. Overall, the combat veterans showed significantly more stress, which statistical techniques indicated was not likely to be explained by adjustment differences before the war

---

[12]Figley also notes, however, that stress-related difficulties may have been underreported, for the military resorted to administrative discharges to rid itself of those with "discipline problems." Rather than recognizing problems as produced by stress and taking responsibility for treating them, the military, asserts Figley, often shipped the troubled soldiers home with a dishonorable discharge, the cruel irony then being that these men would be denied necessary mental health services by the Veterans Administration (Figley and Leventman, 1980).

Visiting the Vietnam War Memorial is an emotional experience for veterans.

experience. Moreover, those who saw heavy combat were more distressed than those who saw light. In particular, combat veterans reported significantly more problems identified as part of the PTSD syndrome than did controls, such as getting along poorly with others, finding it difficult to become emotionally close to someone, to trust others, to express feelings; having family or marriage problems; being unable to sleep and to control temper; being nervous much of the time. These findings have been confirmed by a clinical research team at the West Los Angeles Veterans Administration Hospital, where upwards of 70 percent of high-combat patients and about 30 percent of low-combat patients were diagnosed with PTSD (Foy, Resnick, Sipprelle, and Carroll, 1987).[13] These findings confirm the claims made by veterans' groups since the end of the Vietnam War that those who saw combat, especially heavy combat, have many stress-initiated psychological problems, even though in some cases their reactions have been delayed until well after their return to civilian life.

An Unpopular War

Several factors other than the abbreviated and time-limited periods of combat differentiated the Vietnam War from others in recent history. It was extremely unpopular and controversial, and it was a war that this country did not win in spite of the infusion of billions of dollars, fatalities exceeding 58,000, and many more seriously wounded and permanently maimed. The military men, after their one-year tour of duty, returned home alone and quickly by jet. There were no battalions of soldiers arriving stateside together at war's end, no parades, no homecomings, indeed, none of the grateful hoopla that all of us have seen in newsreels taken of the end of World War II. To make matters worse, the soldiers were subjected to criticism and sometimes abuse from those who regarded them as murderers for their participation in what many in the United States had come gradually to regard as an immoral war. Here is one example from many cited by Figley and Leventman (1980).

Walking across the Boston Commons his first day home, his service uniform and gear fully apparent, he was greeted by peace demonstrators with shouts of "Killer! How many babies did you burn over there?" Returning home, his brother offered, "You asshole! Why did you go to Vietnam anyway?" Seeking solace and companionship that night in the American Legion Hall, he was confronted with "Hey buddy! How come you guys lost the war over there?" (p. xxv)

The alienation and meaninglessness of the war that the soldiers had just left are summed up well in this excerpt.

Winning the hearts and minds of the Vietnamese was

[13]Note: these estimates are likely to be high because a hospitalized sample of Vietnam veterans was used.

the goal. But hamlets were destroyed only to increase the number of Vietcong recruits. Containment policies and confusing restrictions often resulted in GIs taking and retaking the same hill or hamlet five or six times a year. . . . Faulty intelligence reports, fabricated body counts, an invisible enemy, high civilian involvement, an inability to measure positive military results, and awareness of divided political support at home all contributed to a sense of deep despair and anomie among combatants in Vietnam. (Figley and Leventman, 1980, p. xxiii)

Existential philosophy teaches us that people must find meaning and purpose in their lives. Sheer survival is important, but men and women suffer distress and depression if they cannot develop some sense of self-worth in what they do. It is terrible enough for soldiers to see a friend torn up by shrapnel, or to plunge a bayonet into the throat of a man designated as the enemy. How much worse are these experiences if soldiers know that back home people are protesting the morality of their being in the war in the first place? Many American soldiers in Vietnam began to harbor their own doubts about the value and legitimacy of their being there.

The Returned Soldier's Lot

The military have always suffered dearly after as well as during war. Their economic lot when peace is re-

stored often lags behind that of the men who remained at home. Highly decorated soldiers have sometimes found themselves in miserable poverty upon return to civilian life. Yet for the most part the veterans of wars have been welcomed back as patriots and incorporated into the fabric of society, even if they were on the losing side, as the South was in the Civil War. This was not the case for those who served in Vietnam. Their continuing dislocation may have contributed to the long-term effects of the trauma of combat (Box 6.6).

Moreover, men from the working class and minority groups were overrepresented in the military forces in Vietnam. Their cohorts in civilian society were those who do not fare well, which undoubtedly added to the estrangement that the veterans felt and to their job difficulties when they returned home (Figley and Leventman, 1980). As pointed out by the French sociologist Émile Durkheim (1897), group support can help people endure considerable stress. Many Vietnam veterans lacked this.

In addition, the most intimate aspects of the home-lives of veterans were sometimes disturbed by their battle experiences. Haley (1978), a social worker with extensive experience treating Vietnam veterans, provides a chilling and poignant account of how the particular nature of the war affected one soldier years afterward.

Because of the guerrilla nature of the Vietnam war, the "enemy" could be anyone, including women and chil-

There was a great contrast between the ways America welcomed home its soldiers from World War II and from the Vietnam War.

BOX 6.6

AN HYPOTHESIS ABOUT DELAYED PTSD IN VIETNAM VETERANS

Why were there delays, sometimes years, before some of the combat-related PTSD symptoms began to show up in many returning Vietnam veterans? We would suggest that perhaps the stressors eliciting the symptoms did not occur until *after* the return home. The combat stressors themselves may have sensitized soldiers to react with great stress to the often hostile reception that awaited them after discharge. This lack of welcome (at best) may have robbed them of the healing effects that a warm and appreciative populace and family provided veterans who returned from our more popular or at least more widely accepted wars. Veterans of World War II, for example, may have also been predisposed to develop PTSD upon returning home but may have been protected from it by the strong social support that awaited them.

This hypothesis is consistent with the developing literature on "secondary trauma," said to occur "when the survivor of a traumatic event subsequently is held responsible for the event or is seen in some vague, ill-defined, collusive relationship with agents of the primary traumatic event. . . . Examples could include the rape victim who 'brought it on herself . . . dressing, behaving seductively . . .' or the Vietnam veteran who 'deserved his misfortune . . . should feel guilty . . . shouldn't have been

there in the first place.' " (Foy *et al.*, 1987). Indirect but intriguing support for this idea can be found in research that shows the healing effects of social support in reducing the negative sequelae of stress (e.g., Cohen and Wills, 1985); PTSD sufferers may find themselves rejected by others because of the very nature of their symptoms—suspiciousness, depression, apathy, low tolerance for intimacy.

This perspective implies that PTSD is virtually *inevitable*, with some people being spared its worst effects because of social support and acceptance once the actual crisis is past. Rather than focusing on why some people develop PTSD after a stressor, one might consider why some do *not*.*

---

*When we discuss the aftermath of rape (page 336), we shall see that rape crisis intervention is actually based on this posttrauma perspective: professional opinion holds that it is normal for a sexually abused individual to be traumatized and that therefore it is important to have in place readily available support systems to prevent the stressor from causing the development of PTSD. We see this also when crisis intervention professionals go to scenes of horror or destruction, for example, an unprovoked shooting spree at a school or other public place, immediately after the event and before any one individual seeks out mental health assistance.

---

dren. Thus, some stress responses are activated by closeness to women and the responsibility of marriage, a wife's pregnancy and the birth of a child. Veterans who have fought and killed women and children during combat often find it impossible to make a smooth transition to the roles of husband, protector and father. One veteran had warned his close friend, the squad medic, not to go near a crying baby lying in a village road until they had checked the area. In his haste to help the child, the medic raced forward and "was blown to bits" along with the child, who had been booby-trapped. The veteran came into treatment three years later, after a period of good adjustment, because he was made fearful and anxious by his eight-month-old daughter's crying. He had been unable to pick her up or hold her since her birth despite his conscious wish to "be a good father." (p. 263)

Treatment of Posttraumatic Stress Disorder

The treatment of combat-related stress has for some time been guided by the three principles of immediacy, proximity, and expectancy (Lifton, 1976). When signs of stress, such as sleeplessness, are detected, the soldier

is removed immediately to a quiet area as near as possible to his fighting unit and his comrades. There he is encouraged to talk things out and to rest. The soldier is also made aware that he is expected to return soon to his unit, for anxiety is regarded as an inevitable aspect of war, not sufficient cause to be excused from military responsibilities. Those severely affected are given more intensive therapy.

As stated earlier, during World War II combat-exhausted soldiers were hypnotized. They were also treated by narcosynthesis (Grinker and Spiegel, 1945), a procedure that might be considered a drug-assisted abreaction à la Breuer. The soldier was sedated with an intravenous injection of sodium Pentothal, enough to make him very drowsy. The therapist then told him in a matter-of-fact voice that he was on the battlefield, in the front lines, and if necessary and possible, mentioned circumstances of the particular battle. The patient would usually begin recalling sometimes frightening events that he had perhaps forgotten, often with intense emotion. Many times the actual trauma was relived and even acted out by the patient. As the patient gradually returned to the waking state, the therapist would continue encouraging him to discuss the terri-

Rap sessions, a form of group therapy for Vietnam veterans, played an important role in treating their posttraumatic stress disorder.

fying events, the hope being that he would realize that they were in the past, no longer a threat. In this fashion a synthesis, or coming together, of the past horror with the patient's present life was worked for (Cameron and Magaret, 1951).

The Veterans Administration, which had served veterans of World War II as well as those of the Korean War, was not prepared at first to address the psychological plight of the Vietnam vet. First of all, many had left the service with "bad paper," that is, with less than honorable discharges. Some of the offenses for which a soldier could receive undesirable discharges included "character and behavior disorders," "alcoholism," and "drug addiction" (Kidder, 1978). It seems likely that some of these men were suffering from the trauma of combat. Not until 1979—six years after the truce was signed with North Vietnam—was upgrading of dishonorable discharges effected through the assistance of the American Civil Liberties Union (Beck, 1979).

But in 1971, earlier than these governmental efforts that have helped bring more Vietnam veterans within the purview of the Veterans Administration hospital system, the psychiatrist Robert Jay Lifton was approached by antiwar veterans from the New York–New Haven area to work with them in forming "rap groups." Initiated by the men themselves, these veterans' groups had a twofold purpose: a therapeutic one of healing themselves and a political one of forcing the American

public to begin to understand the human costs of the war (Lifton, 1976). The rap groups spread outward from New York City until, in 1979, Congress approved a $25 million package establishing Operation Outreach, a network of ninety-one storefront counseling centers for psychologically distressed Vietnam veterans. In 1981 funding was extended for three additional years.

The rap groups have focused on the residual guilt and rage felt by the veterans: guilt over what their status as soldiers had called on them to do, in fighting a guerrilla war in which enemy and ally were often impossible to distinguish one from the other; and rage at being placed in the predicament of risking their lives in a cause to which their country was not fully committed. Discussion extends as well to present life concerns, such as relationships with women and feelings about masculinity, in particular, the "macho" view of physical violence. Antidepressant medication has also been used, but with equivocal results (Lerer *et al.*, 1987).

The treatment of PTSD should also, argue Stanton and Figley (1978), encompass the complexities of the veteran's family life. Does he feel guilt over infidelities or rage at his wife's extramarital involvements while he was away? Is he having trouble with the increased independence of his wife, which she developed out of necessity in his absence and may be reluctant to give up on his return, especially in this era of raised feminist consciousness?

Group therapy is discussed in some detail in Chapter 20 (page 574). For now it suffices to say that in the rap groups—and in the more conventional group therapy sessions in the 172 Veterans Administration hospitals across the country—at least two factors have probably helped the veterans. For perhaps the first time they could partake of the company of returned comrades-in-arms and feel the mutual support of others who had shared their war experiences. They were also able finally to begin confronting, in often emotional discussions, the combat events whose traumatic effects had been suppressed and thereby not looked at. As people have known for many, many years, in order for individuals to come to terms with fearsome happenings, to loose themselves from the hold that events can have over them, they must, in effect, return to the events and expose themselves fully.

Summary

People with anxiety disorders feel an overwhelming apprehension that seems unwarranted. DSM-IIIR lists five principal diagnoses: phobic disorders; panic disorder, generalized anxiety disorder, obsessive-compulsive disorder, and posttraumatic stress disorder.

Phobias are intense, unreasonable fears that disrupt the life of an otherwise normal person. They are relatively common. Agoraphobia is fear of being outside one's home; social phobia is fear of social situations in which one may be scrutinized by other people. Other simple phobias are fears of animals, of closed-in spaces, and of heights. The psychoanalytic view of phobias is that they are a defense against repressed conflicts. Behavioral theorists have several ideas of how phobias are acquired—through classical conditioning, the pairing of an innocuous object or situation with an innately painful event; through operant conditioning, whereby a person is rewarded for continuing avoidance; through modeling, imitating the fear and avoidance of others; and through cognition, by making a catastrophe of a social mishap that could be construed in a less threatening fashion. But not all people who have such experiences develop a phobia. Perhaps a genetically transmitted physiological diathesis, lability of the autonomic nervous system, predisposes certain people to acquire phobias.

A patient suffering from panic disorder has sudden inexplicable and periodic attacks of intense anxiety. Panic attacks frequently precede the onset of agoraphobia. Some people who have panic attacks also suffer from mitral valve prolapse syndrome. They may regard their heart palpitations as evidence of anxiety and escalate them into full-blown panics. A number of laboratory manipulations (e.g., lactate, hyperventilation) can induce panic attacks in those with the disorder. Panic disorder patients, in general, ruminate about serious illnesses, both physical and mental; they may magnify slight physical sensations until they are overwhelmed.

In generalized anxiety disorder, sometimes called "free-floating anxiety," the individual's life is beset with virtually constant tension and apprehension. Psychoanalytic theory regards the source as an unconscious conflict between the ego and id impulses. Behavioral theorists assume that, with adequate assessment, this pervasive anxiety can be pinned down to a finite set of anxiety-provoking circumstances, thereby likening it to a group of phobias. A sense of helplessness can also cause people to be anxious in a wide range of situations. Humanistic theorists find that people go into anxiety states when they accept the unfavorable opinions others hold of them and do not express their basic self-worth. Biological approaches focus on the therapeutic effects of the benzodiazepines and their relevance to the neurotransmitter GABA.

People with obsessive-compulsive problems have intrusive, ego-alien thoughts and feel pressured to engage in stereotyped rituals lest they be overcome by frightening levels of anxiety. This disorder can become quite disabling, interfering not only with the life of the unfortunate who experiences the difficulties but also with the lives of those close to the person. Psychoanalytic theory posits strong id impulses that are under faulty and inadequate ego control. In behavioral accounts, compulsions are considered learned avoidance responses.

There are many therapies for anxiety disorders. Psychoanalytic treatment tries to lift repression so that childhood conflicts can be resolved; direct alleviation of the manifest problems is discouraged. In contrast, behavior therapists employ a range of procedures, such as systematic desensitization and modeling, designed to reduce the fear and avoidance. Dissuading compulsives from their rituals is an apparently effective although initially arduous technique. Rational-emotive therapy attempts to substitute more realistic self-statements for irrational beliefs. Humanistic therapies help the person discover his or her denied needs and wants and assume responsibility for satisfying them.

Perhaps the most widely employed treatments are anxiolytic drugs, dispensed by medical practitioners. Drugs, however, are subject to abuse, and their long-term use may have untoward and still inadequately understood side effects. Weaning a person from reliance on a chemical that reduces anxiety is also a problem.

Finally, posttraumatic stress disorder was examined, with particular attention given to the delayed reactions of many veterans of the Vietnam War. These anxiety reactions are often the fate of those who have suffered life-threatening trauma that would evoke extreme distress in most individuals. Treatment is by intense remembrances of the traumatic events. If we are to understand the veterans of Vietnam who suffer from this disorder and how best to render complete their return to and reintegration into society, we must grapple with the moral and political aspects of this conflict. The particular horrors and unpopularity of the war seem to lie at the core of the veteran's problems in adjusting to civilian life.

George Grosz. *Untitled*, 1920. Kunstsammlung Nordheim-Westfalen, Düsseldorf.

Chapter 7

Somatoform and Dissociative Disorders

Somatoform Disorders

    Conversion Disorder

    Somatization Disorder (Briquet's Syndrome)

    Theories of Somatoform Disorders

    Therapy for Somatoform Disorders

Dissociative Disorders

    Psychogenic Amnesia

    Psychogenic Fugue

    Multiple Personality

    Theories of Dissociative Disorders

    Therapies for Dissociative Disorders

Summary

A twenty-seven-year-old male was brought to a hospital emergency room after being picked up by the police for lying down in the middle of a busy intersection. He said that he wanted to die and was very depressed. He had no memory for any events prior to being picked up by the police. He didn't know his name nor anything about his life history

Several neurological tests were administered and revealed no abnormality. After six days in hospital, hypnosis was begun. Over the first three hypnotic sessions, details of the patient's past life emerged but not his name nor the events that led up to his hospitalization. During the fourth and fifth sessions, the remaining details came forth. The man had just come to town, looking for work. Two men noticed his toolbox, approached him, and asked if he wanted a job. All three then left in a pickup truck and after smoking some marijuana the patient was forced, at gunpoint, to have sex with the other men (Kasniak *et al.,* 1988)

Complaints of bodily symptoms that suggest a physical defect or dysfunction, some rather dramatic in nature, but for which no physiological basis can be found are diagnosed as *somatoform disorders.* As illustrated by the opening case, *dissociative disorders* are rarer, even more dramatic disruptions of consciousness, memory, and identity. The somatoform and dissociative disorders seem to serve some purpose or need of those who suffer them (Table 7.1). Both categories of disorder are very rare, and carefully collected prevalence data are not readily available.

TABLE 7.1
Somatoform and dissociative disorders

Somatoform Disorders
Conversion disorder
Somatization disorder (Briquet's syndrome)
Somatoform pain disorder
Hypochondriasis
Body dysmorphic disorder
Dissociative Disorders
Psychogenic amnesia
Psychogenic fugue
Multiple personality
Depersonalization disorder

Somatoform Disorders

The physical symptoms of somatoform disorders, which have no known physiological explanation and are not under voluntary control, are assumed to be linked to sometimes rather discernible psychological factors. In this chapter, we shall focus our discussion on two major forms of somatoform disorders: *conversion disorder* and *somatization disorder,* sometimes called *Briquet's syndrome.* DSM-IIIR also proposes three other somatoform disorders, about which little information is available. In *somatoform pain disorder* the person is preoccupied with pain that cannot be accounted for by organic pathology, even after extensive investigation. The pain may have a temporal relation to some conflict or stress, or it may allow the individual to avoid some hated activity and to secure attention and sympathy not otherwise available. This diagnosis is problematic because the subjective experience of pain is always a psychologically influenced phenomenon; that is, pain is not just a sensory experience in the same way that vision or hearing are. Therefore, deciding when a pain becomes a somatoform pain is likely to be difficult. In *body dysmorphic disorder* the person is preoccupied with an imagined or exaggerated defect in appearance, for example, facial wrinkles, excess facial hair, or the shape or size of the nose. These concerns are distressing and lead to frequent consultations with plastic surgeons. Here again, though, subjective factors and matters of taste play a role. When, for example, does one's vanity become a body dysmorphic disorder?

In *hypochondriasis* the person is preoccupied with fears of having a serious disease. He or she overreacts to ordinary physical sensations and minor abnormalities—such as irregular heartbeat, sweating, occasional coughing, a sore spot, stomachache—as evidence for this belief and cannot be medically persuaded otherwise. Hypochondriasis is not very well differentiated from somatization disorder.

Conversion Disorder

Symptoms

In conversion disorders the operations of the musculature or sensory functions are impaired, although the bodily organs themselves and the neuromuscular apparatus are sound. The classic conversion symptoms suggest neurological disease. We find reports of partial or complete paralyses of arms or legs; seizures and coordination disturbances; paresthesia, a sensation of pricking, tingling, or creeping on the skin; anesthesias (Figure 7.1), the loss or impairment of sensations; analgesias, insensitivity to pain—all occurring in physiologically normal people. Vision may be seriously disturbed: the person may become partially or completely blind or have "tunnel vision," wherein the visual field is constricted as it would be were the observer peering through a tunnel. Aphonia, loss of the voice and all but whispered speech; anosmia, loss or impairment of the sense of smell; and false pregnancy are other conversion disorders.

Conversion symptoms by their very nature suggest that they, like psychogenic (somatoform) pain, are linked to psychological factors. They usually appear suddenly in stressful situations, allow patients to avoid some activity or responsibility, or secure them badly wanted attention. The term "conversion" originally derived from Freud, who thought that the energy of a repressed instinct is diverted into sensory-motor channels and blocks functioning. Thus anxiety and psychological conflict were believed to be *converted* into physical symptoms. Some of the people suffering conversion disorders may in fact seem complacent, even serene, and not particularly eager to part with their symptoms. Nor do they connect them with whatever straits they may be in.

Hysteria, the earlier term for conversion disorders, has a long history dating back to the earliest writings on abnormal behavior. Hippocrates considered it an affliction limited solely to women and brought on by the wandering of the uterus through the body. The Greek word *hystera* means womb. Presumably the wandering uterus symbolized the longing of the body for the production of a child. Freud considered the specific nature of the hysterical symptom to relate either to the repressed instinctual urge or to its repressing counterforce, representing them in disguised form. A hysterical convulsion might be the symbolic expression of a forbidden sexual wish, and a hysterical paralysis the manifestation of self-punishment for a hidden aggressive urge. Conversion symptoms usually develop in adolescence or early adulthood. An episode may end abruptly, but sooner or later the disorder is likely to return, either in its original form or with a symptom of a different nature and site. Conversion disorders are found primarily in females. For example, of fifty conversion disorders appearing at a clinic, Folks, Ford, and Regan (1984) identified forty-four women. During both world wars, however, a large number of males developed conversionlike difficulties in combat (Ziegler, Imboden, and Meyer, 1960).

Diagnostic Problems

Diagnostically, it is important to distinguish a conversion paralysis or sensory dysfunction from similar problems that have a true neurological basis. Sometimes this is an easy task, as when the paralysis does not make anatomical sense. A classic example is the glove anes-

FIGURE 7.1
Hysterical anesthesias can be distinguished from neurological dysfunctions. On the left are shown the patterns of neural innervation of the skin. On the right are superimposed typical areas of anesthesias in hysterical patients. The hysterical anesthesias do not make anatomical sense. (Adapted from an original painting by Frank H. Netter, M.D. From *The CIBA Collection of Medical Illustrations,* copyright © by CIBA Pharmaceutical Company, Division of CIBA-GEIGY Corporation.)

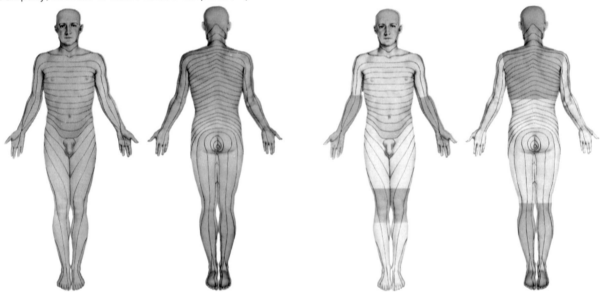

"Well you can go back to Dr. Kendrick and tell him that I said your broken arm has an organic cause."

thesia, an area of insensitivity in the part of the hand that would be covered by a glove (see Figure 7.1). For years this was the textbook illustration of anatomical nonsense because the nerves here run continuously from the hand up the arm. But a newly recognized disease, carpal tunnel syndrome, can produce symptoms like those of glove anesthesia. Nerves in the wrist run through a tunnel formed by the wrist bones and membranes; the tunnel can become swollen and may pinch the nerves, leading to tingling, numbness, and pain in the hand.

Since the majority of paralyses, analgesias, and sensory failures do have organic causes, true neurological problems may sometimes be misdiagnosed as conversion disorders. Slater and Glithero (1965) investigated this disturbing possibility in a follow-up of patients who nine years earlier had been diagnosed as suffering from conversion symptoms. An alarming number, in fact 60 percent, of these individuals had either died in the meantime or developed symptoms of physical disease! A high proportion had diseases of the central nervous system. Similarly, Whitlock (1967) compared the incidence of organic disorders in patients earlier diagnosed as having depressive reactions, anxiety reactions, or both. Organic disorders were found in 62.5 percent of the patients earlier diagnosed as having conversion disorders and in only 5.3 percent of the other groups. The most common organic problem was head injury, generally found to have occurred about six months before the onset of the conversion symptoms. Other common organic problems were stroke, encephalitis, and brain tumor. Finally, Watson and Buranen (1979) found that

25 percent of patients whose symptoms had been considered conversion reactions actually had physical disorders.

From these data we can see that some symptoms labeled as conversion reactions and thought to have psychological causes may, in fact, be physical disorders. We have already learned that the assessment of organic problems is still far from perfect. Therefore it is not always possible to distinguish between psychologically and organically produced symptoms. The diagnosis of conversion disorder may be applied too frequently; some individuals diagnosed in this way may have an organic problem that has gone undetected. The damage that such inappropriate diagnoses can do is sobering to contemplate.

A second diagnostic problem with conversion disorders is differentiating them from **malingering,** which is faking an incapacity in order to avoid a responsibility. In trying to discriminate conversion reactions from malingering, clinicians may attempt to decide whether the symptoms have been consciously or unconsciously adopted.[1] This means of resolving the issue is at best a dubious one, for it is difficult if not impossible to know with any degree of certainty whether behavior is consciously or unconsciously motivated. One aspect of behavior is sometimes revealing, however, *la belle indifférence*—a relative lack of concern, the adoption of a blasé attitude toward the symptoms out of keeping with their severity and supposedly long-term consequences. But these patients also appear willing and eager to talk endlessly and dramatically about them. In contrast, the malingerer is likely to be more guarded and cautious, perhaps because he or she considers interviews a challenge or threat to the success of the lie. But this distinction is not foolproof, for only about one-third of people with conversion disorders show *la belle indifférence* (Stephens and Kamp, 1962). Further, a stoic attitude sometimes is found among patients with verified medical diseases.

Somatization Disorder (Briquet's Syndrome)

In 1859 the French physician Pierre Briquet described a syndrome that has since borne his name and now in

---

[1] Two DSM-IIIR diagnoses, *malingering* and *factitious disorders*, should also be mentioned. Both are applied to people whose conversionlike symptoms or psychological symptoms are under voluntary control. In malingering the symptoms are obviously linked to a recognizable goal, the altering of the individual's circumstances. An example would be a claim of physical illness to avoid standing trial. In a factitious disorder the motivation for adopting the physical or psychological symptoms is much less clear. Apparently the individual for some unknown reason wants to assume the role of "patient."

TABLE 7.2
Various symptoms and their frequency as reported by a sample of patients with Briquet's syndrome (*after Perley and Guze, 1962*)

Symptom	Percent Reporting	Symptom	Percent Reporting	Symptom	Percent Reporting
Dyspnea (labored breathing)	72	Weight loss	28	Back pain	88
Palpitation	60	Sudden fluctuations in weight	16	Joint pain	84
Chest pain	72	Anorexia	60	Extremity pain	84
Dizziness	84	Nausea	80	Burning pains in rectum, vagina, mouth	28
Headache	80	Vomiting	32	Other bodily pain	36
Anxiety attacks	64	Abdominal pain	80	Depressed feelings	64
Fatigue	84	Abdominal bloating	68	Phobias	48
Blindness	20	Food intolerances	48	Vomiting all nine months of pregnancy	20
Paralysis	12	Diarrhea	20	Nervous	92
Anesthesia	32	Constipation	64	Had to quit working because felt bad	44
Aphonia (loss of voice above a whisper)	44	Dysuria (painful urination)	44	Trouble doing anything because felt bad	72
Lump in throat	28	Urinary retention	8	Cried a lot	70
Fits or convulsions	20	Dysmenorrhea (painful menstruation, premarital only)	4	Felt life was hopeless	28
Faints	56			Always sickly (most of life)	40
Unconsciousness	16	Dysmenorrhea (prepregnancy only)	8	Thought of dying	48
Amnesia	8	Dysmenorrhea (other)	48	Wanted to die	36
Visual blurring	64	Menstrual irregularity	48	Thought of suicide	28
Visual hallucination	12	Excessive menstrual bleeding	48	Attempted suicide	12
Deafness	4	Sexual indifference	44		
Olfactory hallucination	16	Frigidity (absence of orgasm)	24		
Weakness	84	Dyspareunia (painful sexual intercourse)	52		

DSM-IIIR is referred to as somatization disorder. Recurrent, multiple somatic complaints for which medical attention is sought but which have no apparent physical cause are the basis of this diagnosis. Common complaints include headaches, fatigue, allergies, abdominal, back, and chest pains, genitourinary symptoms, and palpitations. Conversion symptoms may also be present.[2] Visits to physicians, sometimes to a number of them simultaneously, are frequent, as is the use of medication. Hospitalization and even surgery are common (Guze, 1967). Menstrual difficulties and sexual indifference are frequent (Swartz *et al.*, 1986). Patients are given to histrionics, presenting their complaints in a dramatic, exaggerated fashion or as part of a long and complicated medical history. Many believe that they have been ailing all their lives. The lifetime prevalence of somatization is estimated at .1 percent (Robins *et al.*, 1984).

The colloquial term for these problems is hypochondria, but DSM-IIIR draws a distinction between hypochondriasis and somatization disorder. In the first the patient is preoccupied with the fear of having a specific and serious physical disease, whereas in the second the patient's concern is with the many symptoms themselves. As noted at the beginning of this chapter, such a distinction appears to be of dubious value. Table 7.2 gives a picture of the pervasiveness of health problems reported by people with Briquet's syndrome.

Somatization disorder typically begins in late adolescence and is more common in women than in men (Kroll, Chamberlain, and Halpern, 1979; Cloninger *et al.*, 1986). Anxiety and depression are frequently reported, as are a host of behavioral and interpersonal problems, such as truancy, poor work records, and mar-

---

[2] In fact, somatization disorder and conversion disorder share many of the same symptoms. It is not uncommon for both diagnoses to be applicable to the same patient (e.g., Ford, Folks, and Regan, 1984).

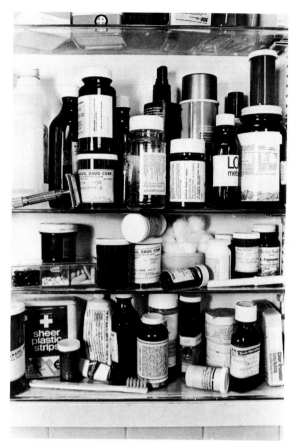

The medicine chest of a patient with somatization disorder.

ital difficulties. Somatization disorders also seem to run in families; they are found in about 20 percent of the first-degree relatives of index cases (Arkonac and Guze, 1963). The following case illustrates one woman's complaints.

Alice was referred to the psychological clinic by her physician, Joyce Williams. Dr. Williams had been Alice's physician for about six months and in that time period had seen her twenty-three times. Alice had dwelt on a number of rather vague complaints—general aches and pains, bouts of nausea, tiredness, irregular menstruation, and dizziness. But various tests—complete blood workups, X-rays, spinal tap, and so on—

had not revealed any pathology.

Upon meeting her therapist, Alice immediately let him know that she was a somewhat reluctant client: "I'm here only because I trust Dr. Williams and she urged me to come. I'm physically sick and don't see how a psychologist is going to help." But when Alice was asked to describe the history of her physical problems, she quickly warmed to the task. According to Alice, she had always been sick. As a child she had had episodes of high fever, frequent respiratory infections, convulsions, and her first two operations, appendectomy and tonsillectomy. As she continued her somewhat loosely organized chronological account of her medical history, Alice's descriptions of her problems became more and more colorful (and probably exaggerated as well): "Yes, when I was in my early twenties I had some problems with vomiting. For weeks at a time I'd vomit up everything I ate. I'd even vomit up liquids, even water. Just the sight of food would make me vomit. The smell of food cooking was absolutely unbearable. I must have been vomiting every ten minutes." During her twenties Alice had gone from one physician to another. She saw several gynecologists for her menstrual irregularity and dyspareunia (pain during intercourse) and had dilatation and curettage (scraping the lining of the uterus). She had been referred to neurologists for her headaches, dizziness, and fainting spells, and they had performed EEGs, spinal taps, and even a CAT scan. Other physicians had ordered X-rays to look for the possible causes of her abdominal pain and EKGs for her chest pains. Both rectal and gallbladder surgery had also been performed.

When the interview finally shifted away from Alice's medical history, it became apparent that she was a highly anxious person in many situations, particularly those in which she thought she might be evaluated by other people. Indeed, some of her physical complaints could be regarded as consequences of anxiety. Furthermore, her marriage was quite shaky, and she and her husband were considering divorce. Their marital problems seemed to be linked to sexual difficulties stemming from Alice's dyspareunia and her general indifference toward sex.

Theories of Somatoform Disorders[3]

Psychoanalytic Theory

Conversion disorder occupies a central place in psychoanalytic theory, for in the course of treating such cases Freud was led to many of the major concepts of psychoanalysis. Conversion disorders offered him a clear opportunity to invoke the concept of the unconscious. Consider for a moment how you might try to make sense of a patient's report that she awakened one morning with a paralyzed left arm. Your first reaction might be to give her a series of neurological tests to assess possible physiological causes of the paralysis. Let us assume that these tests are negative: no evidence of neurological disorder is present. You are now faced with choosing whether to believe or to doubt the patient's communication. One the one hand, she might be lying; she may know that her arm is not paralyzed but has decided to "fake" paralysis to achieve some end. This would be an example of malingering. But what if you believe the patient? Now you are almost forced to consider that unconscious processes are operating. On a conscious level the patient is telling the truth; she believes and reports that her arm is paralyzed. Only on a level that is not conscious does she know that her arm is actually normal.

In their *Studies in Hysteria* (1895) Breuer and Freud proposed that a conversion disorder is caused by an experience that had created great emotional arousal. The affect, however, was not expressed, and the memory of the event was cut off from conscious experience. Two reasons were suggested to explain why the affect associated with the experience was not expressed. The experience may have been so distressing that the person could not allow it to enter consciousness and therefore repressed it. Or the experience may have occurred while the person was in an abnormal psychological state, such as semihypnosis. In both situations, Breuer and Freud proposed, the specific conversion symptoms are related to the traumatic event that caused them.

Anna O. (see p. 21), for example, while watching at the bedside of her seriously ill father, had dropped off into a waking dream with her right arm over the back of her chair. She saw a black snake emerge from the wall and come toward her sick father to bite him. She tried to ward it away, but her right arm had gone to sleep. When she looked at her hand, her fingers turned

into little snakes with death's heads. The next day a bent branch recalled her hallucination of the snake, and at once her right arm became rigidly extended. Thenceforward it acted the same way whenever some object revived her hallucination. Later, when Anna O. fell into her absences and took to her own bed, the contracture of her right arm became chronic and extended to paralysis and anesthesia of her right side.

In his later writings Freud formulated a theory of conversion disorder in which sexual impulses became primary. Specifically, he hypothesized that conversion disorders are rooted in an early, unresolved Electra complex. The young female child becomes incestuously attached to her father, but these early impulses are repressed, producing both a preoccupation with sex and, at the same time, an avoidance of it. At a later period of her life, sexual excitement or some happenstance reawakens these repressed impulses, at which time they are transformed or converted into physical symptoms that represent in distorted form the repressed libidinal urges or the repressing forces. Thus the primary gain from conversion disorder is the avoidance of previously repressed id impulses. Freud allowed, however, that there could also be a *secondary gain* from the symptoms. That is, they might allow the patient to avoid or escape from some currently unpleasant life situation. Modern psychoanalytic theorists, however, do not all agree that conversion disorders stem from the Electra complex. Some (e.g., Sperling, 1973) see the problem originating much earlier, during the oral period, when the basic security system of the infant is taking form.

A contemporary psychodynamic interpretation of one form of conversion disorder, hysterical blindness, has been offered by Sackeim, Nordlie, and Gur (1979). The starting point of their analysis is experimental studies of hysterically blind people whose behavior on visual tests shows that they are being influenced by the stimuli, even though they explicitly deny seeing them.

A case in point was described by Theodor and Mandelcorn (1973). The patient, a sixteen-year-old, had experienced a sudden loss of peripheral vision, reporting that her visual field had become tubular and constricted. Although a number of neurological tests had proved negative, the authors wanted to be even more certain that they were not dealing with a neurological problem. So they arranged a special visual test in which a bright, oval target was presented either in the center or in the periphery of the patient's visual field. On each trial there were two time intervals, which were bounded by the sounding of a buzzer. The target was illuminated during one of the intervals, and the young woman's task was to report which one.

---

[3]Much of the theorizing in this area has been directed toward hysteria and thus assumes that conversion disorder and somatization disorder are similar etiologically. Although this assumption is unsupported, we have little choice but to present the theories as they exist.

When the target was presented in the center of the visual field, the patient always correctly identified the time interval during which it was illuminated. This had been expected since she had not reported any loss of central vision. What happened when the oval was presented peripherally? The patient could be expected to be correct 50 percent of the time by chance alone; the authors reasoned that this would be the outcome if she were truly "blind" in peripheral vision. For the peripheral showings of the target, however, the young woman was correct only 30 percent of the time. She had performed significantly more poorly than would a person who was indeed blind! The clinicians reasoned that she must have been in some sense aware of the illuminated stimulus, and that she wanted, either consciously or unconsciously, to preserve her "blindness" by performing poorly on the test.

Grosz and Zimmerman (1970), on the other hand, observed almost perfect visual performance by a hysterically blind adolescent girl. Fifteen-year-old Celia's initial symptom was a sudden loss of sight in both eyes, followed thereafter by severe blurring of vision. Celia claimed not to be able to read small or large print. Celia had set high standards for herself and did very well at school. Her busy parents, continually rushing off on their own many activities, professed concern about their four children's education but often left Celia responsible for the three younger children. When Celia's vision blurred so severely, her parents became obliged to read her studies to her. Even so, testing revealed that Celia could with no difficulty identify objects of various sizes and shapes and count fingers at a distance of fifteen feet. When three triangles were projected on three display windows of a console, two of the triangles inverted, one of them upright, in 599 trials out of 600 she pressed the switch under the upright triangle, the correct response, which then turned off a buzzer for five seconds.

Sackeim and his colleagues argue that a two-stage defensive reaction can account for these conflicting findings. First, perceptual representations of visual stimuli are blocked from awareness, and on this basis people report themselves blind. Second, information is still extracted from the perceptual representations. If subjects feel that they must deny being privy to this information, they do more poorly than they would do by chance on perceptual tasks. If subjects do not need to deny to themselves having such information, they perform the task well but still maintain that they are blind. Whether hysterically blind people unconsciously need to deny receiving perceptual information is viewed as being dependent on personality factors and motivation.

Are the people who claim that they are blind and yet on another level respond to visual stimuli being truthful? Sackeim and his colleagues report that some patients with lesions in the visual cortex, rather than damage to the eye, say that they are blind and yet perform well on visual tasks. They have vision, but they do not *know* that they can see. So it is possible for people to claim truthfully that they cannot see and at the same time give evidence that they can. On a more general level, a dissociation between awareness and behavior has been reported in many perceptual and cognitive studies (see Box 7.1). In a laboratory setting, Sackeim and his colleagues tested their assumption that motivation has a bearing on this dissociation. They hypnotized two susceptible subjects, gave each a suggestion of total blindness, and then tested them on a visual discrimination task. One was given instructions designed to motivate her to maintain her blindness. She was expected to deny her perceptions and perform more poorly than chance on the visual task. The other subject was not so explicitly urged to maintain her blindness and was expected to do better than chance on the task. A third subject was asked to simulate the behavior of someone who had been hypnotized and given a suggestion of total blindness.

The results agreed with the predictions. The subject highly motivated to maintain blindness indeed performed more poorly than chance, and the less motivated subject performed perfectly, even though still reporting that she was blind. The simulator performed, for the most part, at a chance level. In a postexperimental interview she stated that she had deliberately tried to simulate chance performance. As Sackeim and his colleagues have proposed, verbal reports and behavior can apparently be unconsciously separated from one another. Hysterically blind persons are able to say that they cannot see and yet at the same time be influenced by visual stimuli. The way in which they show signs of being able to see may depend on how much they need to be considered blind.

Sociocultural Theory

Sociocultural theories are based on the supposed decrease in conversion disorders over the last century. Although Charcot and Freud seemed to have had an abundance of female patients with this sort of difficulty, contemporary clinicians rarely see anyone with such problems. A number of hypotheses have been proposed to explain this apparent decrease. For example, those of a psychoanalytic bent point out that in the second half of the nineteenth century, when the incidence of conversion reactions was apparently high in France and Austria, sexual attitudes were quite repressive and may have contributed to the increased incidence of the disorder. The decline of the conversion reaction, then, is attributed to a general relaxing of sexual mores and also to the greater psychological and medical sophistication of twentieth-century culture, which is more tolerant of

BOX 7.1

AWARENESS, THE UNCONSCIOUS, AND BEHAVIOR

The first experimental psychologists working in the last two decades of the nineteenth century realized very soon that we are unaware of much that goes on in our minds as we perceive and encode stimuli from our environment. Much of the workings of the mind proceeds out of our awareness. Consider a recent example. In studying selective attention, researchers often use a dichotic-listening task in which separate tapes are played to each ear; subjects are asked to attend to only one of them. Subjects usually report later on that they know little about the sounds that came into the unattended ear. *But these unattended stimuli can affect behavior.* For example, Wilson (1975) had people listen to a human voice played into one ear while tone sequences were played in the unattended ear. Subjects reported having heard no tones. Furthermore, in a memory task in which they listened to tone sequences played earlier and others that had not been played, the subjects were unable to distinguish between the two types. Despite this demonstration that the subjects did not recognize tone stimuli played previously, another measure had a startling result. When subjects in Wilson's study were asked to rate how much they liked a series of tone sequences, the ones that had been presented earlier to the unattended ear were preferred to novel sequences. Some aspects of the tone sequences played during the dichotic-listening task must have been absorbed, even though subjects said that they had not heard them and demonstrated that they did not recognize them. It is known that familiarity affects judgments of tone stimuli similar to those Wilson used. Familiar sequences are liked better than novel ones. A similar phenomenon has been observed with vision (Kunst-Wilson and Zajonc, 1980). Subjects were presented with different shapes for one millisecond (one-thousandth of a second). Their ability to recognize later the shapes that they had seen was essentially nil. But when they rated how much they liked the shapes, they preferred the ones that they had "seen" to new ones that were presented.

A series of studies reported by Nisbett and Wilson (1977) also indicates that awareness, as measured by verbal report, is not always a very accurate indication of the effect stimuli have on behavior. In one of their studies, Nisbett and Wilson first had subjects memorize a list of word pairs. For some subjects the pairs of words were specially constructed so that they would be likely to have an effect of subjects' performances in a second part of the study. For example, one of the word pairs these subjects first memorized was "ocean–moon." This pair was expected to make them more likely to respond "Tide" when they were later asked to name a detergent. The results agreed with expectation: subjects who had memorized the special word pairs gave double the number of expected associations as subjects who had not memorized them. Right after the second part of the test, subjects were asked why they had

given their particular responses. Even though they could still recall the word pairs, subjects almost never mentioned them as bringing their responses to mind. Instead they gave reasons such as "My mother uses Tide" or "Tide is the most popular detergent."

The studies just described provide laboratory evidence for the operation of unconscious processes. But do they generalize to more naturalistic dependent variables? A recent study indicates that the answer is yes. Bornstein, Leone, and Galley (1987) investigated whether subliminal exposure to a person's face would influence subsequent interactions with that person. Subjects participated with two confederates of the experimenter in a task in which they had to read ten poems and as a group decide on the gender of the author of each poem. By prior arrangement the two confederates disagreed on seven of the ten, putting the subject in the role of tie breaker. Prior to judging the poems, half of the subjects viewed, for 4 milliseconds, five presentations of a slide of one of the confederates. The other half saw a slide of the second confederate. (Pilot data had already shown that exposures like these could not be discriminated from blank flashes of light.) This manipulation, based on the earlier work of Wilson and Kunst-Wilson and Zajonc, was expected to increase liking for the confederate whose photograph had been viewed and hence change behavior toward that confederate. The major dependent measure was which confederate subjects chose to agree with concerning their judgments of the gender of the authors of the poems. Consistent with the hypothesis of the study, subjects agreed with the confederate whose slide they had "seen" 68 percent of the time, a statistically significant effect.

These experiments, which are but a small sampling of current research making a similar point, are closely related to the psychoanalytic concept of the unconscious. Contemporary investigators have begun to corroborate Freud's view that some human behavior is determined by unconscious processes. But the unconscious processes are understood in a different way. Freud postulated the existence of "the" unconscious, a repository of instinctual energy and repressed conflicts and impulses. Contemporary researchers reject the energy reservoir and repression, holding more simply that we are not aware of everything going on around us and of some of our cognitive processes.* At the same time, these stimuli and processes of which we are unaware can affect behavior powerfully. This recent research suggests that understanding the causes of human behavior will be a difficult task. It will not be sufficient merely to ask someone "Why did you do that?"

---

*In a sense, the distinction resides in whether "unconscious" is a noun, as Freud used it, or an adjective, as contemporary researchers employ the term. As an adjective, "unconscious" can encourage further exploration into the factors that render something unavailable to awareness.

Charcot demonstrates hypnosis with a conversion disorder case to a class of medical students.

anxiety than it is of dysfunctions that do not make physiological sense.

A study by Proctor (1958) provides evidence for the theory. The incidence of conversion reaction was found to be particularly high among children who were patients at the University of North Carolina Medical School Psychiatric Clinic. In interpreting this very high incidence, 13 percent, the author noted that most of the children came from rural areas where the socioeconomic status of the inhabitants was low and little education was provided for them. Moreover, the religious background of these people was generally strong and fundamentalist. The mid-twentieth-century conditions in this area of North Carolina may have approximated in some respects those prevailing in nineteenth-century France and Austria. Similarly, in the Folks *et al.* study of fifty cases, diagnoses of conversion disorder were more common among rural residents and those of lower socioeconomic status, Further evidence supporting this sociocultural view comes from studies showing that the diagnosis of hysteria has declined in industrialized societies (e.g., England; Hare, 1969) but has remained more common in undeveloped countries (e.g., Libya; Pu *et al.*, 1986).

Behavioral Theory

A behavioral account of the development of conversion disorders has been proposed by Ullmann and Krasner (1975). In their opinion the person with a conversion reaction attempts to behave according to his or her own conception of how a person with a disease affecting the motor or sensory abilities would act. This theory raises two questions. Are people capable of such behavior? Under what conditions might such behavior be most likely to occur?

Considerable evidence supports an affirmative answer to the first question, that people can adopt patterns of behavior that match many of the classic conversion symptoms. For example, paralyses and analgesias, and blindness as we have seen, can be induced in people under hypnosis. Similarly, chemically inert drugs called placebos have reduced the pain of patients who had been considered truly ill. As a partial answer to the second question, Ullmann and Krasner specify two conditions that increase the likelihood that motor and sensory disabilities will be imitated. First, the individual must have some experience with the role to be adopted. He or she may have had similar physical problems or may have observed them in others. Second, Ullmann and Krasner note that the enactment of a role must be rewarded. An individual will assume a disability only if it can be expected either to reduce stress or to reap other positive consequences. For Ullmann and Krasner, conversion disorders are the same as malingering in that the person adopts the symptom to gain some end.

Grosz and Zimmerman's patient, Celia, who was mentioned earlier, did not act in accord with Ullmann and Krasner's theory, however. The very intelligent

Celia performed perfectly in the visual discrimination task while still claiming severely blurred vision. Such a pattern of behavior seems a rather clumsy enactment of a role. If you wanted to convince someone that you could not see, would you always correctly identify the upright triangle? Again, Celia's actions seem more consistent with the theorizing offered by Sackeim and his co-workers. On the level of conscious awareness, Celia probably saw only blurred images, as she claimed. But during the test the triangles were distinguished on an unconscious level, and she could pick out the upright one, whichever console window it appeared in.[4]

Another behavioral view of somatoform disorders, at least of Briquet's syndrome, holds that the various aches and pains, discomforts, and dysfunctions are unrealistic anxiety manifesting itself in particular bodily systems. Perhaps the extreme tension of an individual localizes in his stomach muscles, and he feels nauseous and even vomits. Once normal functioning is disrupted, the maladaptive pattern may strengthen because of the attention it receives or the excuses it provides. In a related vein, reports of physical symptoms have been seen as a strategy used to "explain" poor performance in evaluative situations. Attributing poor performance to illness is psychologically less threatening than attributing it to some personal failing (Smith, Snyder, and Perkins, 1983).

Biological Factors

Genetic and physiological factors have been suggested as playing some role in the development of conversion disorders. Slater (1961) investigated concordance rates in twelve identical and twelve fraternal pairs of twins. Probands of each pair had been diagnosed as having the disorder, but none of the co-twins in either of the two groups manifested a conversion reaction. Similarly, Gottesman (1962) found the reactions of identical twins (MZ) to statements on the hysteria scale of the MMPI to be no more similar than those of fraternal twins (DZ). More recently, Torgerson (1986) has reported the results of a twin study of the somatoform disorders. Among the probands were ten cases of conversion disorder, twelve of somatization disorder, and seven of pain disorder. No co-twin had the same diagnosis as his/her proband! Even the overall concordance for somatoform disorder was no higher in the MZ than in the

DZ pairs. Genetic factors, then, from the studies done so far, seem to be of no importance.

Several studies have examined physiological reactions in patients with conversion symptoms. The question asked is whether patients' verbal reports have physiological correlates. For example, are the areas of the body in which analgesia or anesthesia is reported less physiologically responsive? Unfortunately, results are contradictory (Hernández-Peón, Chávez-Ibarra, and Aguilar-Figueroa, 1963; Levy and Muskin, 1973).

A hint of a nuerophysiological explanation of why emotions connected with conversion disorders remain unavailable to conscious awareness comes from studies showing that conversion symptoms are more likely to occur on the left side of the body than on the right (Galin, Diamond, and Braff, 1977; Ford and Folks, 1985; Stern, 1977). In most instances these left-side body functions are controlled by the right hemisphere of the brain. Thus the majority of conversion symptoms may be related to the functioning of the right hemisphere. Research on patients who have had the hemispheres of their brains surgically disconnected to prevent the spread of epileptic seizures has shown that the right hemisphere can separately generate emotions, and indeed it is suspected of generating more of them than does the left hemisphere. Conversion symptoms would in this way be neurophysiologically linked to emotional arousal. Furthermore, this same research indicates that the right hemisphere depends on the neural passageways of the corpus callosum (see Box A.1, page 638) for connection with the left hemisphere's verbal capacity to describe and explain emotions and by these means to gain awareness of them. In conversion disorders it may be that the left hemisphere somehow blocks impulses carrying painful emotional content from the right hemisphere. Thus individuals with a conversion disorder make no connection between it and their troubling circumstances or their emotional needs. This is an intriguing bit of speculation.

Therapy for Somatoform Disorders

Not surprisingly, people with hypochondriacal complaints, and also those with conversion disorders and pain disorder, go far more often to physicians than to psychiatrists and nonmedical clinicians like psychologists, for they define their problems in somatic terms. They are not open to psychological explanations of their predicaments and therefore resent referrals to "shrinks." Many such patients try the patience of their physicians, who often find themselves prescribing one drug or medical treatment after another in hopes of remedying the somatic complaint.

---

[4]Celia's visual problems had gained her crucial attention and help from her parents, which is in the nature of conversion disorders as well as of malingering. Three years after the onset of her visual difficulties Celia suddenly and dramatically recovered clear sight while on a summer trip with her parents across the country to the West Coast. In June she had graduated from high school with grades well above average.

Psychoanalysis of course has a special connection to conversion disorders, inasmuch as many of Freud's patients were women who suffered from these phenomena. The "talking cure" that psychoanalysis developed into was based on the assumption that a massive repression had forced psychic energy to be transformed or converted into puzzling anesthesias or paralyses. The catharsis of the patient as she faced up to the infantile origins of the repression was assumed to help, and even today free association and other efforts to lift repression are a common approach. Psychoanalysis and psychoanalytically oriented psychotherapy have not been demonstrated to be particularly useful with conversion disorders, however, except perhaps to reduce the patient's concern about her disabling problems (Ochitil, 1982).

Behavioral clinicians consider the high levels of anxiety associated with somatization disorder, or Briquet's syndrome, to be linked to certain situations. Alice, the woman described earlier, revealed herself to be extremely anxious about her shaky marriage and about situations in which other people might judge her. Techniques like systematic desensitization or any of the cognitive therapies could be addressed to her fears, the reduction of which would help to lessen somatic complaints. But it is likely that more treatment would be needed, for a person who has been "sick" for a period of time has grown accustomed to weakness and dependency, to avoiding everyday challenges rather than facing them as an adult. Chances are that people who live with Alice have adjusted to her "infirmity" and are even unwittingly reinforcing her for her avoidance of normal adult responsibilities. Family therapy, then, would be called for to help Alice and the members of her family change the web of relationships in order to support her movements toward greater autonomy. Assertion training and *social-skills training*—coaching Alice in effective ways to approach and talk to people, to keep eye contact, give compliments, accept criticism, make requests—could be useful in helping her acquire, or reacquire, means of relating to others and meeting her needs that do not begin with the premise "I am a poor, weak, sick person."

In vivo exposure was used in the treatment of two patients with psychogenic nausea. The individuals were encouraged to expose themselves to the situations that were making them nauseous, much as one would have a phobic person confront a particular fear. The authors concluded that the favorable outcomes were due to extinction of the anxiety underlying the nausea (Lesage and Lamoontagne, 1985).

Behavior therapists have applied to somatoform disorders a wide range of techniques intended to make it worthwhile for the patient to give up the symptoms. A case reported by Liebson (1967) is an example of this tack. A man had relinquished his job because of pain and weakness in his legs and attacks of giddiness. Liebson helped the patient return to full-time work by persuading his family to refrain from reinforcing him for his idleness and by arranging for the man to receive a pay increase if he succeeded in getting himself to work. A reinforcement approach, then, attempts to provide the patient with greater incentives to get better than to remain incapacitated. Another important consideration with any such operant tactic, as noted by Walen, Hauserman, and Lavin (1977), is to make it possible for the patient not to lose face when parting with the disorder. This is, the therapist should appreciate the possibility that the patient will feel humiliated at becoming better through treatment that does not deal with the "medical" problem.

An excellent illustration is provided by Macleod and Hemsley (1985). They treated a forty-nine-year-old man who had developed aphonia, the inability to speak above a whisper, following an injection to his neck. Although physical examinations were all negative, the patient maintained that his speech difficulty was caused by the injection. Macleod and Hemsley decided not to challenge the patient's attribution and instead accept it, telling the man that a series of exercises would be necessary to strengthen the damaged muscles. Treatment consisted of having the patient repeat nursery rhymes into a microphone that was attached to a polygraph that provided constant monitoring and feedback concerning volume. During each treatment session the patient was required to increase his speech level. Initially, volume increased steadily but soon a plateau was reached. One day, however, the patient stopped off for a beer before his therapy session and on this day his speech returned to normal.[5]

Because somatoform disorders are rarer than other problems people take to mental health professionals, no true research has been done on the relative efficacy of different treatments. Case reports and clinical speculation are, for now, the only sources of information on how to help people with these puzzling disruptions in bodily functions.

---

[5]Through a series of unfortunate incidents, however, the treatment gains were not maintained. The patient attributed his cure, in part, to the beer, and his wife decided that this was a newsworthy event and informed the local newspaper. The story was then picked up by the national press and television, and the manufacturer of the beer he had drunk even began an advertising campaign with him as the focus. The resulting humiliation was too much, and the aphonia returned as well as depressive symptoms that required hospitalization.

Dissociative Disorders

DSM-IIIR distinguishes among three major dissociative disorders—*psychogenic amnesia, psychogenic fugue,* and *multiple personality*—in all of which there is an "alteration in the normally integrative functions of consciousness, identity, or motor behavior" (p. 269). Important personal events cannot be recalled, or customary identity is temporarily lost. The individual may even wander far from his or her usual surroundings. *Depersonalization disorder,* in which the person's perception or experience of the self is disconcertingly and disruptively altered,[6] is also described as a dissociative disorder. But its inclusion is recognized as controversial because there is no disturbance of memory.

Psychogenic Amnesia

In psychogenic amnesia the person suddenly becomes unable to recall important personal information, usually after some stressful episode. (See the case at the opening of this chapter.) The holes in memory are too extensive to be explained by ordinary forgetfulness. There are four types of psychogenic amnesia: localized, selective, continuous, and generalized. Most often the memory loss is for all events during a limited period of time following some traumatic experience (localized), such as witnessing the death of a loved one. More rarely the amnesia is for only selected events during a circumscribed period of distress (selective), is continuous from a traumatic event to the present (continuous), or is total (generalized), covering the person's entire life. During the period of amnesia, the person's behavior is otherwise unremarkable, except that the memory loss may bring some disorientation and purposeless wandering. With total amnesia the patient will not recognize relatives and friends, but he or she will retain the ability to talk, read, and reason and perhaps his or her talents and whatever knowledge of the world and how to function in it had previously been acquired. The amnesic episode may last several hours or as long as several years. Then it usually disappears as suddenly as it came on, with complete recovery and only a small chance of recurrence.

Memory loss is common in many organic brain disorders as well. But psychogenic amnesia and memory loss caused by a brain disease can be fairly easily distinguished. In organic disorders memory fails slowly over time and is not linked to life stress. Furthermore, recovery is rare or incomplete, and other symptoms, such as inattention and emotional upset, are also present.

Psychogenic Fugue

If a person not only becomes totally amnesic but suddenly moves away from home and work and assumes a new identity, the diagnosis of psychogenic fugue is made. Sometimes the assumption of the new identity can be quite elaborate, with the person taking on a new name, new home, new job, and even a new set of personality characteristics. He or she may succeed in establishing a fairly complex social life, all without questioning the inability to remember the past. More often, however, the new life does not crystallize to this extent and the fugue is of briefer duration. It consists for the most part of limited, but apparently purposeful, travel, during which social contacts are minimal or even avoided. Fugues typically occur after the person has experienced some severe stress, such as marital quarrels, personal rejections, war service, or a natural disaster. Recovery, although varying in the time it takes, is usually complete; the individual does not recollect what took place during the flight from his or her usual haunts.

Multiple Personality

Consider what it would be like to have a multiple personality, as did Chris Sizemore, the woman with the famous "three faces of Eve" (see page 114). People tell you about things you have done that seem out of character, events that you have no memory of. You yourself have been waking up each morning with the remains of a cup of tea by your bedside—and you do not like to drink tea. How can you explain these happenings? If you were to seek treatment, might you not worry whether the psychiatrist or psychologist will believe you? Perhaps the clinician will think you psychotic.

Each of us has days when we are not "quite ourselves." This is assumed to be quite normal and is not what is meant by multiple personality. According to DSM-IIIR, a proper diagnosis of multiple personality

---

[6]In a depersonalization episode individuals rather suddenly lose the sense of self. Their limbs may seem drastically changed in size, or they may have the impression that they are outside their bodies, viewing themselves from a distance. Sometimes they feel mechanical, that they and others too are robots, or they move as though in a dream, in a world that has lost its reality. Similar, but much more intense, episodes sometimes occur in schizophrenia. The schizophrenic's experience, however, does not have the "as if" quality that the person in depersonalization reports. The schizophrenic's estrangement from the self is real and complete.

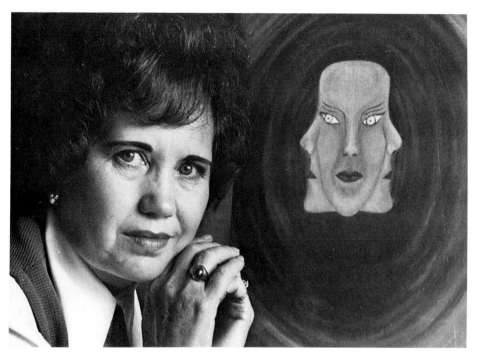

Chris Sizemore, the woman who was the subject of the famous "three faces of Eve" case.

requires that a person have at least two separate "ego states," two different modes of being and feeling and acting that exist independently of each other, coming forth and being in control at different times.[7] At least one ego state usually has no contact with the other, that is, the person in ego state A has no memory for what state B is like, or even any knowledge of having an alternate state of being. The existence of different states must furthermore be chronic and severe, not attributable to the ingestion of some drug, for example.

Each personality is fully integrated and complex, with its own behavior patterns, memories, and relationships; they determine the nature and acts of the individual when the particular personality is in command. Usually the personalities are quite different, even

opposites of one another. The original and subordinate personalities are all aware of lost periods of time, and the voices of the others may sometimes echo into their consciousness, even though they do not know to whom these voices belong. When an individual has more than two subpersonalities, each of these is to some extent aware of the others. In fact, they may talk to each other and be constant companions. The disorder may begin in early childhood or later, but it is rarely diagnosed until adolescence. Multiple personality is more chronic and serious than other dissociative disorders, and recovery may be less complete.

The case of Eve White was at one time the most carefully documented report of multiple personality in the clinical literature. But now a number of other cases have been described. One such account appeared in 1976 in the *Journal of Abnormal Psychology*. "The Three Faces of Evelyn" is a detailed history by Robert F. Jeans, the psychiatrist who treated the woman.

[7]Cases of multiple personality are frequently mislabeled in the popular press as schizophrenic reactions. This diagnostic category, discussed in greater detail in Chapter 14, derives part of its name from the Greek root *schizo*, which means "splitting away from," hence the confusion. A split in the personality, wherein two or more fairly separate and coherent systems of being exist alternatively in the same person, is different from the split between cognition and affect that is said to produce the schizophrenic's bizarre behavior. Bliss (1980) and Rosenbaum (1980) both believe that multiple personality has indeed often been misdiagnosed as schizophrenia by clinicians. The number of cases of multiple personality fell off shortly after the term schizophrenia was introduced. A diagnostician may also inadvertently suggest to a patient a particular way of interpreting his or her symptoms. A schizophrenic patient who hears voices may, for example, be led to *interpret* them as evidence that he or she has multiple personality.

Jeans provides the following background on his patient. He was consulted in December 1965 by a Gina Rinaldi, referred to him by her friends. Gina, single and thirty-one years old, lived with another single woman and was at the time working successfully as a writer at a large educational publishing firm. She was considered an efficient, businesslike, and productive person, but her friends had observed that she was becoming forgetful and sometimes acted out of character. The youngest of nine siblings, Gina reported that she had been sleepwalking since her early teens; her present roommate had told her that she would sometimes scream in her sleep.

Gina described her mother, then age seventy-four, as the most domineering woman she had ever known. She reported that as a child she had been quite a fearful and obedient daughter. At age twenty-six Gina got braces for her teeth, and at age twenty-eight she had had an "affair," her first, with a former Jesuit priest, although it was apparently not sexual in nature. Then she became involved with "T.C.," a married man who assured her he would get a divorce and marry her. She indicated that she had been faithful to him since the start of their relationship. Partly on the basis of Jeans's analysis of one of Gina's dreams, the psychiatrist concluded that she was quite uncomfortable about being a woman, particularly when a close, sexual relationship with a man might be expected of her. But T.C. did not come through with his promised divorce, stopped seeing Gina regularly, and generally fell out of her favor.

After several sessions with Gina, Jeans began to notice a second personality emerging. "Mary Sunshine," as she came to be referred to by Jeans and Gina, was quite different from Gina. She seemed to be more childlike, more traditionally feminine, ebullient, and seductive. Gina felt that she herself walked like a coal miner, but Mary certainly did not. Some quite concrete incidents indicated Mary's existence. Sometimes Gina found in the sink cups that had had hot chocolate in them—neither Gina nor her roommate liked this beverage. There were large withdrawals from Gina's bank account that she could not remember making. One evening while watching television, Gina realized that she was crying and remarked to herself that it was stupid to feel sad about the particular program she was viewing. She even discovered herself ordering a sewing machine on the telephone, although she disliked sewing; some weeks later she showed up for her therapy session wearing a new dress that Mary had sewn. At work, Gina reported, people were finding her more pleasant to be with, and her colleagues took to con-

sulting her on how to encourage people to work better with one another. All these phenomena were entirely alien to Gina. Jeans and Gina came to realize that sometimes Gina was transformed into Mary.

Then one day T.C. showed up again. Gina was filled with scorn and derision for him, yet she heard herself greeting him warmly with the words "Gee, I missed you so much! It's good to see you!" (Apparently the psychoanalytically oriented therapy was softening the hitherto impermeable boundaries between the separate ego states of Gina and Mary.) Gina was also surprised to hear T.C. reply on this occasion, "All you ever wanted was to please me. You've done nothing but cater to my every whim, nothing but make me happy." Mary must have been active in the earlier relationship that Gina had had with this man.

Now more and more often Jeans witnessed Gina turning into Mary right before his eyes in the consulting room. T.C. accompanied Gina to a session during which her posture and demeanor became more relaxed, her tone of voice warmer. When T.C. explained that he really cared for her, Gina, or rather Mary, said warmly, "Of course, T., I know you do."

At another session Mary was upset and, as Jeans put it, chewed off Gina's fingernails. Then the two of them started having conversations with each other in front of Jeans.

A year after the start of therapy, an apparent synthesis of Gina and Mary began to emerge. At first it seemed that Gina had taken over entirely, but then Jeans noticed that Gina was not as serious as before, particularly about "getting the job done," that is, working extremely hard on the therapy. Jeans, probably believing that Mary wanted to converse with him, encouraged Gina to have a conversation with Mary. The following is what was said by the patient: "I was lying in bed trying to go to sleep. Someone started to cry about T.C. I was sure that it was Mary. I started to talk to her. The person told me that she didn't have a name. Later she said that Mary called her Evelyn. . . .I was suspicious at first that it was Mary pretending to be Evelyn. I changed my mind, however, because the person I talked to had too much sense to be Mary. She said that she realized that T.C. was unreliable but she still loved him and was very lonely. She agreed that it would be best to find a reliable man. She told me that she comes out once a day for a very short time to get used to the world. She promised that she will come out to see you [Jeans] sometime when she is stronger." (Jeans, 1976, pp. 254–255).

Throughout January Evelyn appeared more and more often, and Jeans felt that the patient was improving rapidly. Within a few months the patient seemed to be Evelyn all the time, and this woman soon married a physician. Now, years later, she still has had no recurrences of the other personalities.

Interviews concerning the possibility of child sexual abuse make use of anatomically correct dolls.

Theories of Dissociative Disorders

According to the psychoanalytic view of dissociative disorders, one part of the mind or consciousness splits off or becomes dissociated from another part. The types of dissociative disorder are tied together etiologically in psychoanalytic theory, being viewed as instances of a massive repression, usually relating back to the unacceptable infantile sexual wishes of the oedipal stage. In adulthood these oedipal yearnings increase in strength until they are finally expressed, often as an impulsive sexual act. The ordinary form of repression is obviously no longer sufficient; the whole event must be obliterated from consciousness. The person succeeds in this by splitting off an entire part of the personality from awareness (Buss, 1966) or by acquiring a new identity for the dissociated portion of the self. In similar reasoning, Bliss (1980) believes that multiple personality is established in childhood by self-hypnosis. The new personalities are thought to be a way of coping with extremely disturbing events. Two pieces of evidence support Bliss's theory. First, many cases of multiple personality report severe childhood traumas. For example, the results from a survey of therapists who work with multiple personalities indicated that 80 percent of their clients had suffered physical abuse in childhood and almost 70 percent had been subjected to incest (Putnam *et al.*, 1983). Other estimates of physical and sexual abuse in childhood are even higher—97 percent (Kluft, 1984). Second, available data indicate that multiple personalities are high in hypnotizability. Bliss (1983), for example, found that multiples scored much higher than controls on the Stanford Scales of Hypnotic Susceptibility (see page 23).

Learning theorists have generally construed these rare phenomena as avoidance responses that serve to protect the individual from highly stressful events. Although not employing the concept of repression and not emphasizing the overriding importance of infantile sexual conflicts, the behavioral view of dissociative disorders is not dissimilar to psychoanalytic speculations about them. One clinician has gone so far as to suggest that all cases of fugue are nothing more than malingering. When Symonds (reported in Merskey, 1979) sees a case of fugue, he says, "I know from experience that your pretended loss of memory is the result of some intolerable emotional situation. If you tell me the whole story I promise absolutely to respect your confidence, will give you all the help I can, and will say to your doctor and relatives that I have cured you by hypnotism." According to Symonds, such words have never failed to elicit an admission from the patient that the fugue was contrived. This is an extreme view, however.

A study by Spanos, Weekes, and Bertrand (1985) supports the possibility that a person may adopt another personality to avoid punishment. The experimental manipulations were derived from an actual interview that had been conducted with Kenneth Bianchi, the Hillside strangler, while he was supposedly under hypnosis during a pretrial meeting with a mental health professional to determine his legal responsibility for his crimes. The interviewer (I) asked for a second personality to come forward.

I: . . .I've talked a bit to Ken but I think that perhaps there might be another part of Ken that I haven't talked to. And I would like to communicate with that other part. And I would like that other part to come to talk with me. . . . And when you're here, lift the left hand off the chair to signal to me that you are here. Would you please come, Part, so I can talk to you? . . ., Part, would you come and lift Ken's hand to indicate to me that you are here? . . . Would you talk to me, Part, by saying "I'm here"? (Schwarz, 1981, pp. 142–143)

Bianchi (B) answered "Yes" to the last question, and then he and the interviewer had the following conversation.

I: Part, are you the same as Ken or are you different in any way. . . .

B: I'm not him.

I: You're not him. Who are you? Do you have a name?

B: I'm not Ken.

I: You're not him? Okay. Who are you? Tell me about yourself. Do you have a name I can call you by?

B: Steve. You can call me Steve. (pp. 139–140)

While speaking as Steve, Bianchi stated that he hated Ken because Ken was nice, and that he, Steve, with the help of his cousin, had murdered a number of women. Bianchi's plea in the case became not guilty by reason of insanity; he claimed that he suffered from multiple personality.[8]

Undergraduate subjects in the Spanos study were all told that they would play the role of an accused murderer and that, despite much evidence of guilt, a plea of not guilty had been entered. They were also told that they were to participate in a simulated psychiatric interview that might involve hypnosis. Then the subjects were taken to another room and introduced to the "psychiatrist," actually an experimental assistant. After a number of standard questions, the interview diverged for subjects assigned to one of three experimental conditions. Subjects in the *Bianchi condition* were given a rudimentary hypnotic induction and were then instructed to let a second personality come forward, just as Bianchi's interviewer had done. Subjects in the *Hidden Part condition* were also hypnotized and given information suggesting that they may have "walled off" parts of themselves. These instructions, however, were less explicit than those for the first condition. Subjects in a final condition were not hypnotized and were given even less explicit information about the possible existence of a hidden part.

After the experimental manipulations, the possible existence of a second personality was probed directly by the "psychiatrist." In addition, subjects were asked questions about the facts of the murders. Finally, in a second session, subjects who had acknowledged the presence of another personality were asked to take two personality tests twice—once each for their two personalities.

Eighty-one percent of subjects in the Bianchi condition adopted a new name, and many of these admitted guilt for the murders. Even the personality test scores of the two "personalities" differed considerably. Clearly, when the situation demands, people can adopt a second personality. Spanos *et al.* suggest that people who present as multiple personalities may have a rich fantasy life and considerable practice imagining that they are other people, especially when they find themselves in a situation in which, like Bianchi, there are inducements and cues to behave as though a previous act had been committed by another personality. We should remember, however, that this demonstration illustrates only that such role playing is possible and in no way demonstrates that all cases of multiple personality have such origins.

---

[8]Bianchi was found guilty. His insanity plea did not hold up because evidence indicated that his role enactment differed in important ways from how true multiple personalities and deeply hypnotized subjects act (Orne, Dinges, and Orne, 1984).

High susceptibility to becoming hypnotized is a characteristic of multiple personalities.

If dissociative disorders are regarded as problems in memory, experimental research on memory might be brought to bear in trying to understand them. A recent area of investigation, *state-dependent memory*, offers some promise. In this phenomenon people are better able to recall an event if they are in the same psychic state as when it happened. If they are in a greatly different state when they try to remember, for example, sad now and happy then, memory of the earlier event is poor. Experimental research on state-dependent memory has manipulated mood by hypnosis and confirmed that recall is much better if mood at the time of learning matches mood at the time of recall. One of Bower's (1981) studies demonstrating this finding is outlined in Table 7.3. Two groups of subjects were first hypnotized and asked to get themselves into a happy or a sad mood. All subjects then learned a list of sixteen words. Next, subjects learned a second list of words to create interference with their initial learning. Subjects learned this second list in the affective state opposite that in which they had learned the original list. Finally, subjects were tested for their recall of the first list. During this recall test, mood for some subjects was the same as during initial learning, and for some subjects it was not. As can be seen from the results given in Figure 7.2, mood had a strong effect on memory. Recall was much better if mood during recall matched mood during learning. Bower has recently likened this dissociation between memories learned in contrasting states to the different directories in a computer data base—these directories are compartmentalized according to the mood prevailing during learning (inputting, in computerese)—and to enter them easily for recall or retrieval one needs to be in the same emotional state that one was in during learning (Bower, 1986).

In applying the concept of state-dependent memory to dissociative disorders, Bower notes that there are

TABLE 7.3

Moods created by hypnosis in the three parts of a study to demonstrate state-dependent learning (*from Bower, 1981*)

Learn First Word List	Learn Second (Interference) Word List	Recall Test
Happy	Sad	Happy Sad
Sad	Happy	Sad Happy

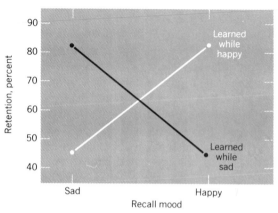

FIGURE 7.2

Results of the study of state-dependent learning outlined in Table 7.3, showing the effects of mood on memory. After Bower (1981).

often major mood differences in the several ego states of a person with multiple personality. Similarly, in fugue a person escapes from an emotionally charged situation into a calmer existence. The different emotional states may, in part, account for the selective memory loss. Indeed, (usually partial) amnesia is more likely to be observed between two personalities that show radically different emotional styles. But what determines when a shift occurs in ego state, and furthermore, if there are more than two such states, as there usually are, what factors influence the shift to a particular state over another? Bower speculates that when ego state A, say, a happy personality, gets into an anger-provoking situation, she may then switch to a hostile personality, ego state B, as a way to cope with the challenge. This may explain the shifts from one personality to another.

We are unfortunately able to go little beyond these rather vague theories and analogue data. Information is scant, principally because of the rarity of these disorders. Dissociative disorders remain among the most poorly understood clinical syndromes.

Therapies for Dissociative Disorders

Dissociative disorders suggest, perhaps better than any other, the plausibility of Freud's concept of repression. For in all three—amnesia, fugue, and multiple personality—people behave in ways that very assuredly indicate they have forgotten earlier parts of their lives. And since these people may at the same time be unaware even of having forgotten something, the hypothesis that

they have repressed massive portions of their lives is a compelling one.

Consequently, for dissociative disorders, psychoanalytic treatment is perhaps administered with more élan than for other psychological problems. The goal of lifting repressions is the order of the day, pursued in ways with which we are already familiar.

We have already encountered examples of the treatment of multiple personality disorder. The common element in these therapies is an attempt by the therapist to "fuse" the different personalities, to encourage and help the patient accept them as but different facets of his or her "one self." This characteristic is found not only in traditional analytically oriented approaches (e.g., Kluft, 1984, 1985), but in cognitive behavioral ones as well (cf. Caddy, 1985).

Combs and Ludwig (1982) suggest that some patients with acute amnesia can regain lost memories if the therapist patiently encourages them to tell their life stories as completely as possible, without skipping over difficult-to-remember parts. This recounting of their lives can be combined with a modified free-association technique focusing on remembered events that took place just before the hole in memory. Thus, if the patient seems to be jumping forward in time, the therapist encourages him or her to free-associate to the event just preceding the memory gap (Parfitt and Gall, 1944). The therapist should all along suggest strongly that memory will be regained and should not imply that the patient is deliberately lying or malingering. In some cases, Combs and Ludwig propose, all that is necessary is the "tincture of time", a period during which the patient is separated from his or her stressful surroundings and given quietness, general support, and encouragement.

As discussed in Chapter 1, psychological theorizing about mental disorders began with Mesmer's work on hypnosis in Vienna and Paris in the late eighteenth century and Charcot's work in Paris in the second part of the nineteenth century. They apparently succeeded in removing various hysterical symptoms[9] by rather di-

---

[9]Hysteria is of course the familiar vernacular diagnosis of several millenniums' standing. Hysterical neurosis was one of the neurotic diagnoses in both DSM-II and DSM-I, covering both conversion disorder and the dissociative disorders. In DSM-IIIR conversion disorder is one of the somatoform disorders, and dissociative disorders make up a separate major section. Thus contemporary psychiatric thinking regards as fundamentally different two sets of problems formerly considered closely related. But hypnotism was and still is employed in treatment for hysteria, meaning both conversion disorder and the several dissociative disorders.

rect suggestion. Then Breuer and Freud encouraged patients to talk, while hypnotized, about their problems and especially about the earlier origins of them. Therefore psychoanalysis had its beginnings in hypnosis. But Freud eventually abandoned the practice in favor of techniques like free association, for he came to believe, mistakenly though it may be, that enduring cures are not possible by means of hypnosis.

Through the years practitioners have continued to hypnotize patients suffering from dissociative disorders, supposing that something special about the hypnotic state would permit the person access to hidden portions of the personality—to his or her lost identity or to a set of events precipitating or flowing from a trauma.

Some physicians have used sodium Amytal, the "truth serum," to induce a hypnoticlike state, again assuming that painful repressed memories will be brought forth and remove the "need" for the dissociative disorder. A number of dramatic case studies in the clinical literature attest to the efficacy of both hypnosis and barbiturates like sodium Amytal, but little of certainty can be said about their actual effectiveness because almost nothing approximating controlled research has been done.[10] When Dysken (1979) did compare the effects on amnesic patients of sodium amobarbital and normal saline acting as a placebo, he failed to find significant differences in the amount of new information remembered.

Perhaps because of the rarity of dissociative disorders, the behavioral treatment of them has been little discussed in the published literature. Walton (1961) reported on the successful therapy he devised for a sleepwalker who tried to harm his wife nearly every night for six months during somnambulistic episodes. (Somnambulism was listed as a hysterical dissociative dis-

order in DSM-II.) Analyzing the case much as a psychoanalyst would, Walton determined that the thirty-five-year-old man, an architectural assistant, was very shy and inhibited, especially in relation to his authoritarian and rigid mother. His wife was at the time trying to force him to do things he objected to and reminded him of his domineering mother. Assertion training helped the man to treat his mother with firmness and to express his negative feelings directly. The sleepwalking incidents were soon eliminated. In general, behavioral clinicians might encourage the person to imagine and discuss aspects of the trauma being avoided in memory and might even desensitize him or her to situations related to the onset of the disorder. Recovering memory of the stressful event of course signals that it is no longer avoided.

Summary

In somatoform disorders physical symptoms for which no physiological basis can be found are the problem. The sensory and motor dysfunctions of conversion disorders, one of the two principal types of somatoform disorders, suggest neurological impairments, but ones that do not always make anatomical sense; the symptoms do, however, seem to serve some psychological purpose. In somatization disorder, or Briquet's syndrome, multiple physical complaints, which are not adequately explained by physical disorder or injury, eventuate in frequent visits to physicians, hospitalization, and even unnecessary surgery.

Theory concerning the etiology of these disorders is very speculative and focuses primarily on conversion disorders. Psychoanalytic theory proposed that in conversion disorders repressed impulses are converted into physical symptoms. Behavioral theories focus on the more or less conscious and deliberate adoption of the symptoms as a means of obtaining a desired goal. In therapies for somatoform disorder, analysts try to help the client face up to the repressed impulses, and behavioral treatments attempt to reduce anxiety and to reinforce behavior that will allow relinquishment of the symptoms.

Dissociative disorders are disruptions of consciousness, memory, and identity. An inability to recall important personal information, usually after some traumatic experience, is diagnosed as psychogenic amnesia. In psychogenic fugue the person moves away,

---

[10]To illustrate the problem inherent to case studies, we offer this personal observation. While working in a mental hospital some years ago, one of the authors encountered on the ward a man suffering from partial amnesia. He did not recognize members of his family when they came to visit him but could still recall most other events in his life. Many efforts were made to restore his memory, ranging from hypnotic suggestions to drug therapy. Both sodium Amytal and Methedrine, a powerful stimulant, were administered. Methedrine intravenously. It was hoped that Methedrine would energize his nervous system and "dislodge" the blocks to memory, much as Drano is used to open a clogged drain. In all these attempts the patient was cooperative and even eager for a positive outcome, but none of them worked. The unsuccessful treatment was never written up for publication. There is a strong editorial bias against publishing reports of failed clinical treatments, as indeed there is against publishing inconclusive results of experiments. This, a general problem for psychology and psychiatry, is a special detriment when, as for dissociative disorders, there is little in the way of controlled research.

assumes a new identity, and is amnesic for his or her previous life. The person with multiple personality has two or more distinct and fully developed ones, each with unique memories, behavior patterns, and relationships that determine the individual's nature and acts when it comes forth. Psychoanalytic theory regards dissociative disorders as instances of massive repression of some undesirable event or aspect of the self. Behavioral theories similarly consider dissociative reactions to be avoidance responses motivated by high levels of anxiety. Both analytic and behavioral clinicians focus their treatment efforts on the anxiety associated with the forgotten memories, since it is viewed as etiologically significant.

Roy Lichtenstein, *Girl with Tear III*, 1977. © Roy Lichtenstein, private collection.

Chapter 8

Psychophysiological Disorders

Stress and Health
>   The Concept of Stress
>   Stress and Illness
>   Moderators and Mediators of Stress

Theories of the Stress–Illness Link
>   Physiological Theories
>   Psychological Theories

Cardiovascular Disorders
>   Essential Hypertension
>   Coronary Heart Disease

Asthma
>   A Characterization of the Disease
>   The Etiology of Asthma

Therapies for Psychophysiological Disorders
>   Hypertension
>   Type A
>   Stress Managment

Summary

In Chapter 6 we discussed voodoo death, a seemingly supernatural phenomenon whereby a curse from a witch doctor dooms his victim to extreme physical suffering and death. To explain such events, Cannon (1942) proposed that vital bodily organs are irreparably harmed if the autonomic nervous system is maintained in a highly aroused state through prolonged psychological stress, and there is no opportunity to take effective action to relieve the stress. Inasmuch as the arousal of the autonomic nervous system is also regarded as one of the bodily indications of emotion, it is not surprising that psychopathologists have concerned themselves with physical diseases involving this system, in the belief that psychological factors may be implicated. In the expression of emotion, the bodily changes of autonomic arousal are viewed as transient; in psychophysiological disorders the usually reversible autonomic and hormonal responses to stress can cause irreversible tissue damage.

Psychophysiological disorders, such as asthma, ulcers, hypertension, headache, and gastritis, are characterized by genuine physical symptoms that are caused or can be worsened by emotional factors. The present term, psychophysiological disorders, is now preferred to one that is perhaps better known, psychosomatic disorders. *Psychosomatic* connotes quite well the principal feature of these disorders, that the psyche or mind is having an untoward effect on the soma or body. The structure of both these terms, in fact, implies that mind and body are separate and independent, although they may, at times, influence each other (see Box 8.1). Dualism is a deeply ingrained paradigm of human thought. Yet the hope was that these terms would foster a monistic rather than dualistic view of the human being, since "all functioning and all diseases are both mental and physical, because both mental and physiological processes are going on continuously" (Sternbach, 1966, p. 139). Instead of speaking of the emotions as causing body dysfunctions, we could instead, as Graham (1967) has noted, regard the psyche and soma as one and the same. Psychological and physical explanations of disease are then simply two alternative ways of describing the same events.

At the outset, two important points must be firmly established. First, a psychophysiological disorder is a real disease involving damage to the body. The fact that such disorders are viewed as being caused by emotional factors does not make the affliction imaginary. People can just as readily die from "psychologically produced"

BOX 8.1

DESCARTES AND THE MIND–BODY PROBLEM

One of the most influential statements about the "mind–body" problem is found in the writings of the brilliant French philosopher of the seventeenth century René Descartes (1596–1650). Being a deeply religious Catholic, he assumed that human beings differed from other animals by virtue of having a soul and thus being partly divine. But like the other animals, human beings had a body as well. Although the body was said to work on mechanical principles—Descartes was fascinated by the mechanical models of the body's workings that were prevalent at the time—these mechanics were seen to be under the control of the soul, or mind. But how could the body, operating like a machine, be affected by the soul, which is spiritual and nonphysical? How could two such basically different substances, in fact, "touch" each other? If the mind was to affect the body, there must be some point of *contact.* The pineal gland, located in the midbrain, was postulated by Descartes as the locus of this critical interaction, the point at which the mind could direct the mechanics of the body. By dualizing human beings in this way, with this vital connection between the mind and the body, Descartes felt that he could retain his religious view of people as being partly divine and yet an integral part of the rest of the animal world.

René Descartes, the French philosopher who proposed a dualistic view of mind and body.

high blood pressure or ulcers as from similar diseases produced by infection or physical injury. Second, psychophysiological disorders should be distinguished from conversion disorders, which were discussed in Chapter 7. Conversion disorders do not involve actual organic damage to the body, and they are generally considered to affect function of the voluntary musculature. In contrast, in psychophysiological disorders, bodily tissues *are* damaged.

Psychophysiological symptoms and disorders are quite common in industrialized societies, although they are apparently rare among nonindustrialized groups, such as the Australian aborigines and the American Indians. Schwab, Fennell, and Warheit (1974), for example, interviewed a randomly selected sample of close to 1700 Americans (Table 8.1). Over 40 percent of the respondents reported having had headaches during the previous year, and 50 percent reported a range of gastrointestinal symptoms. Actual disorders such as hypertension, however, were not as common as the less serious symptoms they were questioned about.

Psychophysiological disorders as such do not appear in DSM-IIIR as they did in earlier versions of the DSM. Because virtually all physical diseases are now viewed as potentially related to psychological stress, a psychophysiological disorders category would become a complete listing of all diseases. Instead of such a cumbersome, overlapping system, DSM-IIIR requires that a diagnostic judgment be made on axis I, to indicate the presence of a *psychological factor influencing a physical condition,* and also on axis III, to specify that physical condition.

TABLE 8.1
Percentages of people* reporting psychophysiological symptoms and conditions for the previous year (*from Schwab, Fennell, and Warheit, 1974*)

Symptoms and Conditions	Yes— Regularly, percent	Yes— Occasionally, percent	No, percent
Symptoms			
Headaches	8.7	38.0	53.4
Indigestion	6.4	27.5	66.1
Constipation	6.9	19.6	73.5
Nervous stomach	5.2	17.5	77.3
Stomachaches	3.7	18.8	77.5
Diarrhea	0.9	14.4	84.8
Conditions			
Hypertension	6.2	8.0	85.8
Asthma	1.9	2.9	95.2
Ulcers	0.9	1.4	97.6
Colitis	0.4	0.9	98.7

*N = 1647.

Stress and Health

The Concept of Stress

In 1936, Hans Selye introduced the ***general adaptation syndrome (GAS),*** a model used to describe the biological reaction to sustained and unrelenting physical stress. There are three phases of the model. During the first phase, the alarm reaction, the autonomic nervous system is activated to resist the stress. If the stress is too powerful, gastrointestinal ulcers form, the adrenal glands become enlarged, and there is atrophy of the thymus. During the second phase, resistance, the organism adapts to the stress through available coping mechanisms. If the stressor persists or the organism is unable to respond effectively, the third phase, a stage of exhaustion, follows and the organism dies or suffers irreversible damage (Selye, 1950).

Eventually, Selye's concept of stress found its way into the psychological literature but with substantial changes in the way it was defined. Some researchers followed Selye's lead and continued to consider stress as a response to environmental conditions, defined on the basis of such diverse criteria as emotional upset, deterioration of performance, or physiological changes like increased skin conductance or increases in the levels of certain hormones. For other researchers, however, stress became a stimulus and was identified with a long list of environmental conditions—electric shock, boredom, uncontrollable stimuli, catastrophic life events, daily hassles, and sleep deprivation (Appley and Trumball, 1967). For the most part, the term stress is used today to denote a stimulus that can produce changes in behavior, cognition, emotion, and physiology. As such, stress is a construct in the same way we discussed for anxiety (page 111).

Richard Lazarus (1968) has been an important figure in the study of psychological stress and has elaborated it in several ways. For Lazarus, stress cannot be objectively defined. Rather, he suggests that the way we perceive or appraise the environment determines when stress is present. More specifically, stress occurs when a situation is appraised as exceeding the person's adaptive resources. This is an important notion for it allows us to account for individual differences in how people respond to the same event. Taking a final examination may be a stress for some people and merely a challenge for others.

Also relevant to individual differences in response to stressful situations is the concept of coping. Even among those who appraise a situation as stressful, the effects of the stress may vary depending on how an individual copes with the event. Lazarus and his colleagues have identified two broad dimensions of coping (Lazarus and Folkman, 1984). Problem-focused coping includes taking direct action to solve the problem or seeking information that will be relevant to the solution. An example would be developing a study schedule to reduce end-of-semester pressure by not being faced with insurmountable amounts of reading. Emotion-focused coping subsumes efforts to reduce the negative emotional reactions to stress, for example, by distracting oneself from the problem, relaxing, or seeking comfort from others. It is important to mention that effective coping varies with the situation; distraction may be an effective way of dealing with the emotional upset produced by impending surgery but would be a poor way to handle the upset that could be produced by the discovery of a lump on the breast (Lazarus and Folkman 1984).

Stress and Illness

What is the evidence for the view that all illness is, in part, stress-related? For years it had been known that various physical diseases could be produced in laboratory animals who were exposed to severe stress. Usually the diseases studied in this fashion were the classic psychophysiological disorders, such as ulcer and hypertension. More recent evidence has broadened the range of diseases that appear to be stress-related. Sklar and Anisman (1979), for example, first induced tumors in mice with a transplant of cancerous tissue and then studied the impact of stress on growth of the tumors. In animals exposed to electric shock, the tumors grew more rapidly and the animals died earlier.

Out of research like this, and many other demonstrations of the pervasive role of psychological factors in health, came the fields of **behavioral medicine** and **health psychology.** Since the 1970s, these new areas have dealt with the role of psychological factors in all facets of health and illness. Beyond studying the etiological role that stress can play in illness, workers in these fields study psychological treatments (e.g., biofeedback for migraine headache), the maintenance and promotion of healthful behaviors, (e.g., dietary change to reduce cholesterol intake and thus lessen the risk of heart attack), and the health care system itself (e.g., how to better deliver services to underserved populations) (Schwartz and Weiss, 1977; G. Stone, 1982).

The Social Readjustment Rating Scale

Human research on the effects of stress on health has sought to measure the amount of life stress a person has experienced and then correlate this with illness. A number of instruments have been developed to measure

Major life changes can precipitate both medical and psychological problems.

life stress. One such test, whose items appear in Table 8.2, is the Social Readjustment Rating Scale (SRRS). In using the SRRS, the respondent simply checks off the life events that have been experienced during the time period in question. But merely summing the *number* of events would not work, for different *amounts* of stressfulness are inherent in different events. To solve this problem, Holmes and Rahe (1967) gave a list of life events to a large group of subjects and asked them to rate each item according to its "intensity and [the] length of time necessary to accommodate . . . *regardless of the desirability of the event*." Marriage was arbitrarily assigned a stress value of 500; all other items were then evaluated using this reference point. For example, an event twice as stressful as marriage would be assigned a value of 1000, and an event one-fifth as stressful as marriage would be assigned a value of 100. The average ratings assigned to the events by the respondents in Holmes and Rahe's study are also shown in Table 8.2.

The ratings that indicate differential stressfulness of events are totaled for all the events actually experienced to produce a Life Change Unit (LCU) score, a weighted sum of events. The LCU score is then related to illness. Rahe and Holmes (unpublished), for example, studied a sample of 200 physicians. Health problems (infectious diseases, allergies, musculoskeletal problems, and psychophysiological disorders) were strongly related to LCU scores. When an LCU score of less than 200 was recorded, 37 percent of the life crises were associated with deterioration of health. But when an LCU score greater than 300 was recorded, 79 percent of the life crises were accompanied by health problems. Other studies have shown that LCU scores are related to heart attacks (Rahe and Lind, 1971), fractures (Tollefson, 1972), leukemia onset (Wold, 1968), and colds and fevers (Holmes and Holmes, 1970).

We have, then, some promising information on the relationship between psychological stress and physical illness. But caution is in order before we assert that the relationship is a causal one. Illness, for example, could cause a high life change score as when chronic absenteeism brings dismissal from a job. And the reports of stressful events in such studies could also be contaminated by knowledge of subsequently occurring illnesses. That is, someone who has experienced many illnesses may search hard for recent stressors to "explain" them. Furthermore, many of the studies have used a retrospective method; participants were asked to recall both the illnesses and the stressful life events that they had experienced over the previous two years. As mentioned previously (see page 137), retrospective reports are subject to considerable distortion and forgetting. Furthermore, self-reports of illness may not yield a true reflection of disease. For example, someone under stress

TABLE 8.2

Social readjustment rating scale (*from Holmes and Rahe, 1967*)

Rank	Life event	Mean value
1	Death of spouse	100
2	Divorce	73
3	Marital separation	65
4	Jail term	63
5	Death of close family member	63
6	Personal injury or illness	53
7	Marriage	50*
8	Fired at work	47
9	Marital reconciliation	45
10	Retirement	45
11	Change in health of family member	44
12	Pregnancy	40
13	Sex difficulties	39
14	Gain of new family member	39
15	Business readjustment	39
16	Change in financial state	38
17	Death of close friend	37
18	Change to different line of work	36
19	Change in number of arguments with spouse	35
20	Mortgage over $10,000	31
21	Foreclosure of mortgage or loan	30
22	Change in responsibilities at work	29
23	Son or daughter leaving home	29
24	Trouble with in-laws	29
25	Outstanding personal achievement	28
26	Wife begins or stops work	26
27	Begin or end school	26
28	Change in living conditions	25
29	Revision of personal habits	24
30	Trouble with boss	23
31	Change in work hours or conditions	20
32	Change in residence	20
33	Change in schools	20
34	Change in recreation	19
35	Change in church activities	19
36	Change in social activities	18
37	Mortgage or loan less than $10,000	17
38	Change in sleeping habits	16
39	Change in number of family get-togethers	15
40	Change in eating habits	15
41	Vacation	13
42	Christmas	12
43	Minor violations of the law	11

*Marriage was arbitrarily assigned a stress value of 500; no event was found to be any more than twice as stressful. Here the values are reduced proportionally and range up to 100.

may focus on minor physiological sensations and thereby increase symptom reporting.[1]

The SRRS can also be criticized for *assuming* a particular definition of stress, namely, that any change is stressful, whether it is a change usually regarded as negative, such as being fired from a job, or as positive, such as marrying. The available evidence is, in fact, contradictory, but it would seem to indicate that the undesirable aspects of events are as important as the fact that they change lives (Redfield and Stone, 1979). Another problem is that items on the SRRS were not selected to sample systematically all major stresses. As you peruse Table 8.2, you can probably identify stressful events that you have experienced but that are not on the list.

The Assessment of Daily Experience

Consideration of these problems led Stone and Neale (1982) to develop a new assessment instrument, the Assessment of Daily Experience (ADE), designed to allow individuals to record and rate their daily experiences in prospective investigations. They chose a twenty-four-hour day as the unit of analysis because they felt that a thorough characterization of this period was possible without major retrospective-recall bias. With this period as the unit of analysis, the specific life events to be rated must include more mundane happenings than are found in previous life-event inventories. Yet the inventory would not exclude major events that have been retrospectively reported in other inventories; they can still be recorded, probably with greater reliability. Furthermore, there is theoretical and clinical support for the idea that minor daily events are related to illness. These events may be subjectively important to individuals for reasons not addressed by the researcher. How events are appraised may be linked to past experience with similar events (e.g., many failures with it), to more general personality characteristics (an anxious individual faced with a public speaking engagement), or to the cultural–religious background of the individual (divorce for a strict Catholic). Furthermore, there is now direct evidence that these minor events are related to illness (Jandorf *et al.*, 1986).

The objective was to construct a checklist of daily events that would characterize an individual's experience. These events would then be rated on several dimensions to assess respondents' psychological reactions to them. Because the instrument was to be used on a daily basis over substantial time periods, it was important that the recording task itself not be excessively

onerous. Devising a relatively small but representative set of event *categories,* rather than a lengthy checklist of specific events, was the solution to this problem. The first step in developing the scale was to obtain a sample of daily activities. Twenty-six couples recorded their experiences in a diary for fourteen days. These events were then independently reviewed and a list of categories was created and arranged in outline form. A sample page from the booklet is presented in Table 8.3.

TABLE 8.3

Sample page from Stone and Neale's (1982) Assessment of Daily Experience scale. Respondents indicate whether an event occurred by checking the circles to the left of the list of events. If an event does occur, it is then rated on the dimensions of desirability, change, meaningfulness, and control using the enclosed spaces to the right.

WORK RELATED ACTIVITIES

Concerning Boss, Supervisor, Upper Management, etc.

○ Praised for a job well done □ ○ ○ $\triangle_{01}$

○ Criticism for job performance, lateness, etc.
□ ○ ○ $\triangle_{02}$

Concerning Co-workers, Employees, Supervisees, and/or Clients

○ Positive emotional interactions and/or happenings with co-workers, employees, supervisees, and/or clients (work related events which were fulfilling, etc.)
□ ○ ○ $\triangle_{03}$

○ Negative emotional interactions and/or happenings with co-workers, employees, supervisees, and/or clients (work related events which were frustrating, irritating, etc.)
□ ○ ○ $\triangle_{04}$

○ Firing or disciplining (by Target) □ ○ ○ $\triangle_{05}$

○ Socializing with staff, co-workers, employees, supervisees, and/or clients □ ○ ○ $\triangle_{06}$

General Happenings Concerning Target at Work

○ Promotion, raise □ ○ ○ $\triangle_{07}$

○ Fired, quit, resigned □ ○ ○ $\triangle_{08}$

○ Some change in job (different from the above, i.e., new assignment, new boss, etc.) □ ○ ○ $\triangle_{09}$

○ Under a lot of pressure at work (impending deadlines, heavy workload, etc.) □ ○ ○ $\triangle_{10}$

---

[1]The concept of overreaction to symptoms and overreporting them is similar to the diagnosis of somatization disorder, described in Chapter 7, page 170.

The procedure is as follows: Husbands (Targets) and wives (Observers) first work through the ADE independently, recording the husband's experiences of the day. They then reconvene and go through the event categories together to produce a master list of the husband's experiences that day. With this procedure the husband must confirm events he recorded but were not observed by his wife, she can remind him of some experiences, and the couple can discuss and agree upon how experiences are to be classified on the ADE.

With an assessment of daily experiences in hand, Stone, Reed, and Neale (1987) began a study of the relationship between life experience and health. Daily symptoms and health-related behaviors were collected using a modified version of the Daily Health Record from the Health in Detroit Study (Verbrugge, 1979). The section on symptoms asks if a subject had any symptoms or discomforts during the day: if so, they are recorded in an open-ended format along with any health-related behavior changes and treatments sought or administered.

Seventy-nine subjects provided at least twelve weeks of continuous, daily data. The goal was to examine the relationship between undesirable and desirable events and the onset of episodes of infectious illness. Infectious illness was selected as the criterion variable for two reasons. First, in a community sample, respiratory illness occurs with sufficient frequency to allow it to be analyzed as a distinct category. Second, respiratory infection maximizes the opportunity to detect "lagged effects" of events on symptom onset. Lagged effects offer the clearest evidence that events are having an effect on symptoms. With rhinovirus infection (a principal cause of the common cold), for example, there is a two- to five-day lag between encountering the virus and peak symptom onset. Therefore, it would be possible for stress to increase risk of illness but with symptoms not being apparent for two to five days. In contrast, with other illnesses such as headache, same-day effects are more probable, and render causal interpretation of effects more difficult.

After examining each subject's data, thirty were identified as having episodes of infectious illness. Next, the daily frequency of undesirable and desirable events that occurred from one to ten days before the start of an episode was examined. For each subject a set of control days, without an episode, was also selected with the restriction that the control days matched the others for day of the week. This was done to control for the higher frequency of desirable and lower frequency of undesirable events that are typically reported on weekends; since subjects serve as their own controls, any weekend effects would be the same for days preceding episodes and for control days. The means of undesirable

events for the days preceding episode starts is shown in Figure 8.1; parallel data for desirable events are shown in Figure 8.2. It was expected that several days before the onset of the illness episode there would be an increase in undesirable events and a decrease in desirable events relative to control days. The results showed that for desirable events there were significant decreases three and four days prior to episode onset. For undesirable events, there were significant increases at four and five days before the episode onset.

These results are the first to show a relationship between life events and health, with both variables measured in a daily, prospective design. Most sources of confounding in prior life-events studies have therefore been avoided in this study, and we can now come much closer to asserting that life events play a causal role in increasing vulnerability to episodes of infectious illness. One of the strongest and most interesting aspects of the pattern of events preceding symptom episodes is that there is a peak in undesirable events and a trough in desirable ones several days prior to onset, yet the two days just before onset have average rates of desirable and undesirable events. Speculation that the results are caused by some bias, such as individuals feeling poorly prior to flagrant symptom onset, thus influencing perception of events, is unlikely as most potential biases would produce a change in the frequency of events on days just prior to the onset of symptoms.

Moderators and Mediators of Stress

Even with a demonstration that life events are related to the onset of illness, important questions remain. We have already noted that the same life experience can apparently have different effects in different people. Conceptually, this raises the possibility that there are other variables that moderate the stress–illness relationship. We will describe research on one of the most important of these moderators—social support. A second important question concerns the mechanism, usually physiological, by which stress exerts its effects. Through what process are the effects of psychological stress mediated? We will discuss one example of such a physiological mediator—changes in the immune system.

Social Support

Cohen and Wills (1985) have distinguished two major aspects of social support—structural and functional. Structural support refers to a person's network of social relationships, for example, marital status and number of friends. Functional support is concerned more with the *quality* of a person's relationships. For example,

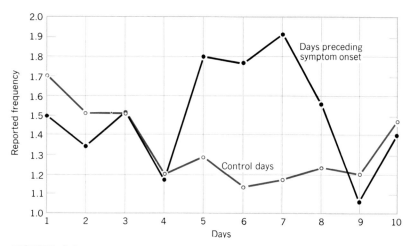

FIGURE 8.1
Number of undesirable events for the ten days preceding an episode of respiratory infection. After Stone, Reed, and Neale (1987).

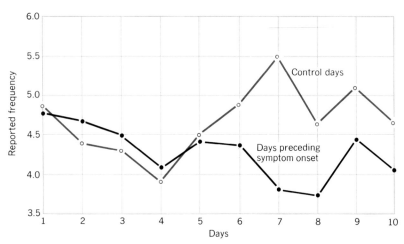

FIGURE 8.2
Number of desirable events in the ten days preceding an episode of respiratory infection. After Stone, Reed, & Neale (1987).

does a person believe they have close friends they can call on in a time of need?

Structural support is a well-established predictor of mortality. For example, Schoenbach *et al.* (1986) found that total mortality in an elderly population was related to lower levels of structural support. Similarly, Ruberman *et al.* (1984) found that among men who had experienced a myocardial infarction (heart attack), lower levels of structural support were related to subsequent death. The role of functional support in predicting death, however, is currently unclear (Cohen, 1988).

Both forms of social support have been related to disease onset. For example, Seeman and Syme (1987) found that higher levels of functional support were related to lower rates of atherosclerosis (clogging of the arteries). Structural support has also been related to various aspects of cardiovascular disease (Reed *et al.*, 1983).

How does social support exert its beneficial effects? One possibility is that higher levels of social support increase the occurrence of positive *health behaviors,* for example, eating a healthy diet, not smoking, and moderating alcohol intake. Such relationships were found in a study of the elderly (Blazer, 1982). Alternatively, social support (or lack of it) could have a direct effect on biological processes. For example, low levels of social support are related to an increase in negative emotions (Kessler and McLeod, 1985; see also our earlier discussion of PTSD on p. 162), which in turn could have effects on levels of some hormones and on the immune system (Kielcolt-Glaser *et al.*, 1984).

Physiological Mediation

A host of physiological changes occur during stress that could mediate the role of stress on illness, for example, increases in heart rate and blood pressure, or increases in secretions of hormones. Recent research also suggests that stress affects the immune system, which is an important consideration in infectious diseases, cancer, and allergies. To illustrate this we will discuss one aspect of the immune system—secretory immunity—in some detail and return to Stone and Neale's research that we described earlier.

The secretory component of the immune system exists in the fluids that bathe the mucosal surfaces of the body (i.e., tears, saliva, gastrointestinal, vaginal, nasal, and bronchial secretions) and at those surfaces at the ports of entry for invading bacteria and viruses. A glycoprotein found in these secretions, called Immunoglobulin A or IgA, contains antibodies that are viewed as the body's first line of defense against invading viruses and bacteria. They prevent the virus or bacterium from binding to mucosal tissues.

A recent study by Stone *et al.* (1987) showed that changes in antibody in IgA were linked to changes in mood. Throughout an eight-week study period a group of dental students came to the laboratory three times a week where their saliva was collected and a brief psychological assessment conducted. When the students experienced relatively high levels of negative mood, there was less antibody present than on days with low levels of negative mood. Similarly, antibody level was higher on days with higher levels of positive mood.

Prior research (e.g., Stone and Neale, 1984) had shown that daily events affect mood. It is therefore quite possible that daily events affect the fluctuations in mood, which in turn suppress synthesis of the secretory IgA antibody. The process could operate as follows. An increase in undesirable life events coupled with a decrease in desirable life events produces increased negative mood, which in turn depresses antibody levels in secretory IgA. If, during this period a person is exposed to a virus, he or she will be at increased risk for the virus to infect the body. Following infection, the overt symptoms of respiratory illness begin several days later. These findings illustrate well the complex interplay among psychological and physiological variables in the etiology of psychophysiological disorders.

Theories of the Stress–Illness Link

In considering the etiology of psychophysiological disorders, we are confronted with three questions. (1) Why does stress produce illness in only some people who are exposed to it? (2) Why does stress sometimes cause an illness and not a psychological disorder? (3) Given that stress produces a psychophysiological disorder, what determines which one of the many disorders it will be?

Answers to these questions have been sought by both physiologically and psychologically oriented theorists. Physiological approaches attribute particular psychophysiological disorders to specific weaknesses or overactivity of an individual's organ systems in responding to stress. Psychological theories account for specificity by positing particular emotional states for particular disorders.

Physiological Theories

Somatic-Weakness Theory
Genetic factors, earlier illnesses, diet, and the like may disrupt a particular organ system, which may then become weak and vulnerable to stress. According to the **somatic-weakness theory,** the connection between stress and a particular psychophysiological disorder is the weakness in a specific bodily organ. Like a tire that blows out at its weakest or thinnest portion, in the human body a congenitally weak respiratory system might predispose the individual to asthma.

Specific-Reaction Theory
Some investigators argue that there are differences, probably genetically determined, in the ways individuals respond to stress. People have been found to have their own particular patterns of autonomic response to stress. The heart rate of one individual may increase, whereas another person any react with increased respiration rate but no change in frequency of heartbeats (Lacey, 1967). According to **specific-reaction theory,** individuals respond to stress in their own idiosyncratic way, and the body system that is the most responsive may be a likely candidate for the locus of a subsequent psychophysiological disorder. Someone reacting to stress with considerable secretion of stomach acid may be more vulnerable to ulcers, and someone reacting to stress with blood pressure elevation may be more susceptible to essential hypertension. Later in this chapter, when we consider particular psychophysiological disorders, substantial evidence in support of both somatic-weakness and specific-reaction theories will be presented.

Evolution Theory and Autonomic Balance
A psychophysiological disorder usually affects a single organ system that is controlled by the autonomic nervous system. In a healthy body the actions of the two branches of this system, the sympathetic and the parasympathetic—which work sometimes in unison, sometimes against each other to manage the body's internal affairs—must always be kept in a complex and delicate

balance. The two systems act in concert. A burst of sympathetic activity must soon be redressed by increased activity of the parasympathetic. The healthy body can sustain prolonged overactivity of one or the other system on occasion, but for the viscera, blood vessels, and glands to act effectively and to remain unharmed, neither system can overexpend energy for protracted periods of time.

External, physical danger stimulates the sympathetic system to prepare the body for fight or flight. It increases heart rate, blood pressure, and rate of breathing. The liver releases a large supply of sugar into the bloodstream. The blood vessels of the limb muscles and other skeletal muscles dilate to ready them for strenuous activity. At the same time blood vessels of the stomach, intestines, skin, and brain constrict. But actual physical danger is usually transient. After the body has either fled or fought, its muscles relax, heart rate slows down again to normal, blood flow to the brain increases, and digestion resumes, all under the direction of the parasympathetic system.

Our brains have evolved to the point that they perceive other than physical threats (Simeons, 1961), and imagined or social dangers such as anger provoked by an annoying present situation, regrets about the past, and worries about the future all stimulate sympathetic system activity. But resentment and regret and worry cannot as readily be fought or escaped from as external threats, nor do they easily pass. They may keep the sympathetic system aroused and the body in a continual state of emergency, sometimes for far longer than it can bear. Under these circumstances, moreover, the necessary balancing of sympathetic and parasympathetic actions is made that much more difficult and can go awry. Thus the distressed thoughts that evolution has made possible bring about bodily changes that both persist longer than they were meant to and that contribute to an imbalance between sympathetic and parasympathetic activity. Our higher mental capacities, it is theorized, subject our bodies to physical "storms" that they are not built to withstand.

Psychological Theories

Psychoanalytic Theory

Franz Alexander (1950) has perhaps been the most prominent of the psychoanalytic theorists who have concerned themselves with psychophysiological reactions. In his view the various psychophysiological disorders are products of unconscious emotional states specific to each disorder. For example,

It would appear that the crucial factor in the pathogenesis of ulcer is the frustration of the dependent, help-

seeking and love-demanding desires. When these desires cannot find gratification in human relationships, a chronic emotional stimulus is created which has a specific effect on the functions of the stomach. (p. 103)

Alexander assumed that ulcer patients have repressed their longing for parental love in childhood, and that this repressed impulse causes the overactivity of the autonomic nervous system and of the stomach, leading to ulcers. Physiologically, the stomach is continuously preparing to receive food, which the person has symbolically equated with parental love.

Undischarged hostile impulses are viewed as creating the chronic emotional state responsible for essential hypertension.

The damming up of his hostile impulses will continue and will consequently increase in intensity. This will induce the development of stronger defensive measures in order to keep pent-up aggressions in check. . . . Because of the marked degree of their inhibitions, these patients are less effective in their occupational activities and for that reason tend to fail in competition with others, . . . envy is stimulated and . . . hostile feelings toward more successful, less inhibited competitors are further intensified. (p. 150)

Alexander formulated this unexpressed-anger or "anger-in" theory on the basis of his observations of patients undergoing psychoanalysis. His hypothesis continues to be pursued in present-day studies of the psychological factors in essential hypertension (see page 201).

Conditioning Theories

Both classical and operant conditioning have been suggested as having a role in psychophysiological disorders, although conditioning is probably best viewed as a factor that can exacerbate an already existing illness rather than cause it. Consider a person who is allergic to pollen and thus vulnerable to asthma attacks. It has been theorized that through classical conditioning neutral stimuli paired with pollen could also come to elicit asthma, thus broadening the range of stimuli that can bring on an attack (Bandura, 1969). The asthmatic attacks might also be viewed as operant responses producing rewards. For example, a child could "use" asthma as an excuse for not participating in unpleasant activities. Dworkin and his colleagues (1979) have proposed that hypertension too may be reinforcing. Their hypothesis begins with the assumption that many people live in surroundings that stimulate their aggressive tendencies but also discourage overt aggression. Animal research has shown that rage reactions can be inhibited by stimulation of the baroreceptors, which are pressure-sensitive neural cells located, among other places in the cardiovascular system, within the walls of the arch of the aorta and of the nearby carotid sinuses.[2] Perhaps, then, a simiilar mechanism operates in human beings. High blood pressure may stimulate the baroreceptors and thus help inhibit maladaptive aggressive responses.

None of these accounts excludes the importance of physiological factors in psychophysiological disorders. Classical and operant conditioning hypotheses typically assume that the physical symptoms already exist. Thus any learning model of a psychophysiological disorder requires a physiological predispositon, a diathesis of some kind.

Our general overview of theories concerning the etiology of psychophysiological disorders is complete. We turn now to a detailed review of the disorders that have attracted the most attention from researchers—*cardiovascular disorders, (hypertension, coronary heart disease), asthma,* and *migraine headache.*

Cardiovascular Disorders

Although the rate of death from cardiovascular disease has been decreasing since 1964, it still remains a problem of great magnitude. Over 100 billion dollars a year is spent on its treatment and research, and it is still the leading cause of death in the United States, claiming almost one million people per year (Weiss, 1986). The two forms to be discussed in this section are hypertension and coronary heart disease (CHD). Coronary heart disease is of major significance because, of the cardiovascular diseases, it is the single greatest cause of death. Hypertension is a factor not only in CHD but in stroke. It is generally agreed that many of the deaths from cardiovascular diseases are premature and can be prevented by dealing with one or more of the known risk factors (Price, 1982).

Essential Hypertension

Without question, one of the most serious psychophysiological disorders is hypertension, commonly called high blood pressure. This disease disposes people to atherosclerosis (clogging of the arteries), heart attacks, and

strokes (see Chapter 17) and it can also cause death through kidney failure. In fact, no more than 10 percent of all cases in the United States are attributable to an identifiable physical cause. Hypertension without an evident organic cause is called ***essential hypertension.*** Recent estimates are that varying degrees of hypertension are found in 15 to 33 percent of the adult population of the United States; as many as 10 percent of American college students have hypertension, most of them remaining unaware of their illness. Unless people have their blood pressure checked, they may go for years without knowing that they are hypertensive. The disease, then, is known as "the silent killer."

Lyght (1966) has offered the following description of the course of hypertension and the symptoms associated with the disorder.

Hypertension frequently is present for many years without symptoms or signs other than an elevated blood pressure. In the majority of cases, increased blood pressure first appears during early adult life (mean age of onset, the early thirties.) These patients may complain of fatigue, nervousness, dizziness, palpitation, insomnia, weakness and headaches at some time in the course of the disorder. . . . The mean age of death for untreated patients is in the fifties, and their average life expectancy probably is close to twenty years from the onset, with extremes of from several years to many decades. (pp. 218 ff)

Blood pressure is measured by two numbers; one represents systolic pressure and the other represents diastolic pressure. The systolic measure is the amount of arterial pressure when the ventricles contract and the heart is pumping; the diastolic measure is the degree of arterial pressure when the ventricles relax and the heart is resting. A normal blood pressure in a young adult would be 120 (systolic) over 80 (diastolic).

Essential hypertension is currently viewed as a heterogeneous condition brought on by many possible disturbances in the various systems of the body that are responsible for regulating blood pressure. Blood pressure may be elevated by increased cardiac output, the amount of blood leaving the left ventricle of the heart per minute; by increased resistance to the passage of blood through the arteries, that is, by vasoconstriction; and by an increase in the body's volume of fluids. The combination of physiological mechanisms that contribute to regulation of blood pressure is extremely complex. The sympathetic nervous system, hormones, and salt and water metabolism, as well as central nervous system mechanisms, are all involved (Weiner, 1977). Many of these controlling physiological mechanisms can be affected by psychological stress.

---

[2]The carotid sinus is a slight enlargement of the carotid artery at the point where it bifurcates into an external branch supplying the face, scalp, tongue, teeth, and other external parts of the head and an internal branch supplying the brain, eye, and other internal structures. The rich supply of sensory nerve endings in its walls constitutes a major mechanism regulating heart rate and blood pressure.

Because hypertension produces no obvious effects in someone with the disease, blood pressure levels should be routinely tested.

Stress, "Anger-In", and Blood Pressure Increase

Various stressful conditions have been examined to determine their role in the etiology of essential hypertension. Stressful interviews, natural disasters, anger, and anxiety have been found to produce short-term elevations in blood pressure (Innes, Millar, and Valentine, 1959; Ruskin, Board, and Schaffer, 1948; Ax, 1953). Kasl and Cobb (1970) have examined the effects of the loss of employment. They studied a group of workers beginning two months before their jobs were to be terminated and for two years subsequent to loss of employment. A control group, consisting of men in similar occupations who did not lose their jobs, was examined for the same twenty-six month period. Each participant in the study was visited at home several times by a nurse during six separate periods so the blood pressure could be measured. For the control subjects there were no overall changes in blood pressure. In the men who lost their jobs, however, elevated blood pressure was found with anticipation of job loss, after termination of employment, and during the initial probationary period of a new job. Those who had great difficulty finding stable employment suffered the longest periods of high blood pressure.

In another group of studies (Hokanson and Burgess, 1962; Hokanson, Burgess, and Cohen, 1963; Hokanson, Willers, and Koropsak, 1968; Stone and Hokanson, 1969), based in part on psychoanalytic theory, Jack Hokanson and his colleagues attempted to determine whether blood pressure elevation is associated with the inhibition of aggression. Subjects were given a task but were angered almost immediately by the interruptions of a supposed fellow subject, actually a confederate of the experimenter. Later on, half of the subjects were given the opportunity to retaliate against their harasser.

The results of this classic series of investigations indicate that harassment of course causes blood pressure to rise but that, for males, aggressing against a source of frustration then helps blood pressure to decrease. With no opportunity to aggress against the frustrater, blood pressure is significantly slower to decrease after frustration. Only aggression directed at a low-status frustrater (college student) proved helpful in decreasing blood pressure, however, not that directed toward a high-status frustrater (visiting professor). These findings did not hold for female subjects.

Hokanson favors the following interpretation of his data: "*Any* social response can be viewed as having arousal-reducing concomitants, if that response has been previously instrumental in terminating or avoiding aggression in others" (Stone and Hokanson, 1969, p. 72).

Hokanson's interpretation explains why aggression directed toward a high-status frustrater was not effective. Presumably, subjects have learned that it does not pay to retaliate against a high-status aggressor. Thus an aggressive response will *not* help to reduce arousal since such responses have not previously been rewarding. Similarly, Hokanson's position accounts for the fact that aggressive responses do not seem to reduce arousal for females. Social and cultural conditions prevailing for them when these studies were conducted dictated that the response to frustration not be aggression.

A study by Harburg and others (1973) extends Hokanson's ideas to the natural environment and to the high incidence of hypertension among black Americans. Harburg and his colleagues chose two areas of Detroit in which to conduct their investigation. In one area, the high-stress location, the crime rate was substantial, population density, mortality rates, and frequency of marital breakups were all high, and the socioeconomic status of residents was generally low. Conditions in the low-stress area were more favorable.

In each area groups of married black and white men were selected for study. During a visit to the participants' homes, a nurse took blood pressure readings, the respondents were interviewed, and a specially designed test was administered. The test presented hypothetical situations and asked the participants how they would respond. An example follows.

Now imagine that you were searching to find another place to live in, and finally found one for sale or rent which you liked, but the owner told you he would not sell or rent to you because of your religion, national

Harburg and his coworkers found that blacks living in high-stress areas were likely to have high blood pressure, particularly if they felt guilty about expressing anger.

origin or race. How would you feel about that? The response categories . . . were as follows: (1) "I'd get angry or mad and show it, (2) I'd get annoyed and show it, (3) I'd get annoyed, but would keep it in, (4) I'd get angry or mad but would keep in it, (5) I wouldn't feel angry or annoyed." (p. 280)

Participants were also asked how they would feel if they had become angry and showed it. The dimension assessed here was guilt, and the possible responses ranged from very guilty to no feelings of guilt at all.

Blood pressure was higher among the black males than among the whites; and blacks living in the high-stress area had higher blood pressure than blacks living in the middle-class neighborhoods. Thus previous statistics revealing racial differences in blood pressure were substantiated, but with the important reservation that environmental stress is also a major factor. When responses on the test were related to blood pressure, the following pattern emerged: for all subjects except blacks in the middle-class neighborhood, holding anger in and feeling guilt were related to higher blood pressure levels.

Harburg's findings, a reanalysis of them (Gentry *et al.*, 1981, 1982), and a replication by Dimsdale, *et al.* (1986) have pointed out the role of "anger-in" in the development and maintenance of high blood pressure. Ongoing research (e.g., Spielberger *et al.*, 1984) is correlating blood pressure in normal subjects with their scores on the Anger Expression Scale, a twenty-four-item self-report inventory asking subjects the various ways in which they react when they are angry or furious (Spielberger, 1988). Do they control their temper? Do they keep things in? Do they slam doors or argue with others? A study of adolescents (Johnson, 1984, re-

ported in Spielberger *et al.*, 1984) found strong and positive correlations between elevated blood pressure and the tendency to suppress anger. Similar findings have emerged for adults (Goldstein *et al.*, 1988). Suppressed anger, through its continual activation of the autonomic nervous system, may in time cause elevations in blood pressure to become fixed, that is, it may cause essential hypertension.[3]

The mechanism inducing long-term essential hypertension would necessarily involve some structural changes in the organism. For ethical reasons no experimental work has been done with human beings to determine whether short-term increases in blood pressure will develop into prolonged hypertension, but some research has been done on animals.

In general, true hypertension has proved elusive in the laboratory. In many studies using electric shock as a stressor, blood pressure increased during the period when the animal was stressed but returned to normal when the stress was removed. Somewhat more successful in producing long-term blood pressure elevations are studies that have used more naturalistic stress, such as competing with other animals for food (Peters, 1977). But the overall picture indicates that some predisposing factor or factors are required if stress, such as the activation of the autonomic nervous system by suppressed anger, is to bring on essential hypertension.

---

[3]We should not conclude, however, that inhibiting anger is the only way to increase blood pressure. As an illustration we can consider a series of studies involving what is termed active, effortful coping. In their research, Obrist and his colleagues (e.g., 1978) used a reaction time (RT) task in which subjects were told they would receive an electric shock if they did not respond quickly enough. Good performance led to a monetary bonus. The RT task yielded significant increases in both heart rate and systolic blood pressure.

Patient undergoing angioplasty to detect atherosclerosis.

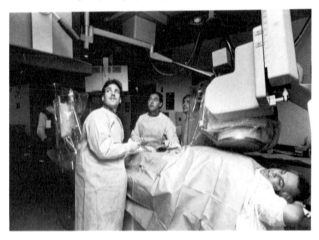

Predisposing Factors

In research with animals, several powerful diatheses have been identified—rearing in social isolation (Henry, Ely, and Stephens, 1972), a high level of emotionality (Farris, Yeakel, and Medoff, 1945), and sensitivity to salt (Friedman and Dahl, 1975). In the salt study, the researchers worked with two strains of rats who had been bred to be either sensitive or insensitive to the impact of their diet. The sensitive rats reliably developed hypertension and died on a high-salt diet. These salt-sensitive rats were also likely to show sustained blood pressure elevations when placed in an experimentally created conflict situation.

Unfortunately, the information on physiological predispositions for hypertension in human beings is not very clear. Several studies have, however, demonstrated that hypertensives show greater blood pressure reactivity, reacting to stress and other novel situations with blood pressure increases that are larger than those of normal people (Engel and Bickford, 1961; Shapiro, 1961). In the Engel and Bickford study twenty female hypertensive patients and twenty control subjects were exposed to various stressors. Fifteen of the twenty hypertensives showed an increase in blood pressure, but only five of the controls did. In a similar vein Hodapp, Weyer, and Becker (1975) studied the blood pressure of hypertensive patients and normal controls while they rested, while they attended to colored slides of landscapes, and while they performed a demanding cognitive task (the stressor). The blood pressure of all subjects increased during the stress task. But in the hypertensives blood pressure was elevated, in relation to that recorded during the rest period, even when they were simply viewing the slides.

The research on blood pressure reactivity as a possible physiological predisposition cannot be regarded as conclusive, however, for the individuals being studied were *already* hypertensive. Their reactivity might have been a *result* rather than a *cause* of their hypertension. To be conclusive, studies must begin with individuals who have the predisposition but have not yet developed essential hypertension. In one such longitudinal study, Wood *et al.* (1984) followed up subjects who many years earlier had their blood pressure monitored during a stress task. Those who had reacted strongly were five times more likely to be hypertensive. Further support for the importance of reactivity comes from high-risk research comparing individuals with and without a positive history for hypertension (e.g., Hastrup *et al.*, 1982). As anticipated, people with a positive family history showed greater blood pressure reactivity to stress. Coupled with other research showing the heritability of blood pressure reactivity (Matthews and Rakaczky, 1987) and the heritability of hypertension, blood pressure reactivity becomes a good candidate for a genetically transmitted diathesis. There is little doubt that essential hypertension is caused by an interplay between a diathesis and a stress.

Coronary Heart Disease

A Characterization of the Disease

Coronary heart disease (CHD) takes two principal forms, angina pectoris and myocardial infarction or heart attack. The symptoms of **angina pectoris** are periodic chest pains, usually located behind the sternum and frequently radiating into the left shoulder and arm. The principal cause of these severe attacks of pain is an insufficient supply of oxygen to the heart, which, in turn, is traced to coronary atherosclerosis, a narrowing or plugging of the coronary arteries by deposits of fatty material. Angina is generally precipitated by physical or emotional exertion and is commonly relieved by rest or medication. Serious physical damage to heart muscle rarely results from an angina attack, for blood flow is reduced but not cut off. **Myocardial infarction** (MI) is a much more serious disorder and is the leading cause of death in the United States today. Like angina pectoris, myocardial infarction is caused by an insufficient oxygen supply to the heart. The oxygen insufficiency, more extreme than in angina pectoris, results from coronary artery disease, either a general curtailment of the heart's blood supply through atherosclerosis or from coronary occlusion, a sudden obstruction of a large coronary artery by deposits or by a blood clot. In both instances parts of the heart muscle die. In addition to this greater severity and possibility of death, myocardial infarction differs from angina in that it is not necessarily precipitated by exertion, and the pain is longer and more severe (Friedberg, 1966).

The American Heart Association lists seven factors related to increased risk for CHD; age, sex (males are at a greater risk), cigarette smoking, elevated blood pressure, elevated serum cholesterol, an increase in the size of the left ventricle of the heart, as revealed by electrocardiogram, and diabetes (Insull, 1973). The risk for heart disease generally increases with the number and severity of these factors. Still, Jenkins (1976) has concluded that these traditional risk factors leave at least half of the etiology of CHD unexplained. Indeed, less attention was paid to contributing causes such as overweight, poor exercise habits, consumption of fatty foods, and smoking in the 1930s than is now, and yet in earlier decades the incidence of CHD and related cardiovascular diseases was much less. It has also been pointed out that in the Midwest, where people's diets are highest in saturated fats—from eating considerable amounts of red meat, for example—and where smoking rates are especially high, the incidence of CHD is low compared to that in more industrialized parts of the United States. And anyone who has visited Paris is aware of the intemperate smoking and the fat-rich diets of the French population—and yet CHD is relatively low there. *Why?*

Type A Behavior Pattern

Clinical Description The search for other causes of CHD has begun to focus on psychological factors such as stress and personality. Such considerations actually go back many years. In 1910 the Canadian physician Sir William Osler (1849–1919) described the typical angina patient as "vigorous in mind and body, and the keen and ambitious man, the indicator of whose engines is always set at full speed ahead" (Chesney, Eagleston, and Rosenman, 1980, p. 256). More recent evidence indicates a relationship between CHD and such stressors as an overload of work, chronic conflict, and the life stressors tapped by the SRRS (Jenkins, 1971, 1976; Rahe and Lind, 1971). The most promising evidence linking CHD to psychological variables, however, comes from investigations pioneered by two cardiologists, Meyer Friedman and Ray Rosenman (Friedman, 1969; Rosenman *et al.*, 1975). In 1958 they identified a coronary-prone behavior pattern, called *type A.* The type A individual has an intense and competitive drive for achievement and advancement; an exaggerated sense of the urgency of passing time, of the need to hurry; and considerable aggressiveness and hostility toward others. Type A persons are overcommitted to their work, often attempt to carry on two activities at once, and believe that to get something done well, they must do it themselves. They cannot abide waiting in lines and they play every game to win, even when their opponents are children they are impatient and hostile. Fast-thinking, fast-talking, and abrupt in gesture, they often jiggle their knees, tap their fingers, and blink rapidly. Too busy to notice their surroundings or to be interested in things of beauty, they tabulate success in life in numbers of articles written, projects under way, and material goods acquired. The type B individual, on the other hand, is less driven and relatively free of such pressures.

Assessment of Type A Type A and B individuals have been reliably identified by means of the Structured Interview (Rosenman *et al.*, 1964), in which questions are asked about the intensity of ambitions, competitiveness, the urgency of deadlines, and hostility.

Interviewer: When you are in your automobile, and there is a car in your lane going *far too slowly* for

"*I don't care if they are moving better over there. This is the fast lane. This is where I live.*"

Drawing by Handelsman; © 1983, *The New Yorker Magazine*, Inc.

you, what do you do about it? Would you *mutter* and *complain* to yourself? Honk your horn? Flash your lights? Would anyone riding with you know that you were *annoyed*?

Interviewer: If you make a date with someone for, oh, two o'clock in the afternoon, would you *be there* on *time*? Always? Never? If you are kept waiting, do you *resent* it? Would you *say* anything about it? Why or why not?

Anger and hostility are now regarded as core components of the Type A construct.

Seldom taking more than fifteen minutes, the interviewer asks the questions in a manner that is abrupt and fast-paced, rather than warm and empathic. Although the interview is highly structured, its protocol requires the interviewer to push the respondent with challenging, probing follow-up questions delivered in a pressured fashion. For example, if the respondent says that he played games with his children to win when they were six, the interviewer might well ponder aloud, almost in disbelief, "Even with a six-year-old?" The interviewer also interrupts the subject now and then in the middle of an answer in order to keep things moving and to try to elicit hostility. The originators of this novel assessment device believe that only by nudging and goading the interviewees can reliable discriminations be made between type A and type B individuals.

At the end of the interview, the interviewer makes his or her own judgment whether the person is type A or B, but the more critical assessment is made later on when highly skilled raters listen to and view tapes of the interview and watch very closely for two sets of information: the content of what the person says and how he or she said it. Indeed, the tenor of the responses is deemed more important. For example, question 13 is delivered in a hesitant, halting manner, almost as though the interviewer has lost his or her place or wandered off in thought to something else.

Interviewer: Most people who work have to get up fairly early in the morning. In your particular case, uh-what-time-uh-do-you-uh, ordinarily uh-uh-uh-get up?

By the time the interviewer begins to uh-uh, it is obvious what the rest of the question is going to be. Note is taken whether the subject provides the answer before the question is completed, and whether he or she does so in an impatient, even hostile way, as if to say, "Hell, let's get on with this damned interview!" Answers to other questions also allow the raters to determine the subject's hostility, impatience, and sense of time urgency. Rosenman, in fact, believes that the interviewer should be a type A person.

There are several other techniques for detecting type A personality (see Chesney, Eagleston, and Rosenman, 1980; Matthews, 1982). A self-report inventory of type A behavior, the Jenkins Activity Survey (Jenkins, Rosenman, and Zyzanski, 1961), has been used extensively in the literature. It is now clear, however, that it does not relate well to the Structured Interview. Some of the inconsistencies in the type A literature are likely the result of using different assessment devices (Matthews, 1982).

Predictive Validity Furthermore, the Structured Interview appears to be better than the Jenkins Activity Survey (JAS) at picking up hostility, which is increasingly being viewed as "the bad actor" (Weinstein, Davison, DeQuattro, and Allen, 1985) in contributing to coronary heart disease. In contrast, the JAS is better at detecting the person's job involvement, competitive striving, and fast pace of living (Matthews, 1982). Evidence supporting the predictive validity of the type A pattern comes from the Western Collaborative Group Study (WCGS) (Rosenman *et al.*, 1975). In a double-blind prospective investigation, 3524 men aged thirty-nine to fifty-nine were to be followed over a period of eight and a half years. Some 3154 men completed their participation in the study. Individuals who had been identified as type A by the Structured Interview were more than twice as likely to develop CHD than were type B men. In addition, type A men with CHD were more than five times as likely to have a second myocardial infarction than were other individuals with CHD. Traditional risk factors—parental history of heart attacks; high blood levels of cholesterol, triglycerides, and lipids; diabetes; elevated blood pressure; cigarette smoking; lack of education; and lack of exercise—were also found to be related to CHD, but even when these factors were controlled for, type A individuals were still twice as likely to develop CHD.[4] These findings from the WCGS have provided strong evidence that type A behavior contributes to the development of CHD. Equally impressive, one study has shown that patients who have undergone angiography and been found to have extensive atherosclerosis also tend to be type A personalities (e.g., Blumenthal *et al.*, 1978). (In this procedure a catheter is inserted into the heart so that a photosensitive dye can be introduced to permit filming of the coronary arteries.)

Further research has been spurred by the success of the WCGS, such as the identification and study of type A women (Waldron, 1978) and attempts to identify subsets of type A behavior that may be related to specific manifestations of coronary disease (Jenkins,

---

[4]These findings are sometimes misinterpreted as meaning that type A's are highly likely to develop CHD. The WCGS did not show this, nor did its report intend such an implication. What the findings do reveal is *relative* risk: 7 percent of the initially well subjects had developed coronary disease at the eight-and-a-half-year point; of this small percentage two-thirds were type A and one-third type B. Since half the subjects were rated as type A and the other half as type B, the risk was twice as high for the type A's as the the the B's (Chesney, Eagleston, and Rosenman, 1980). The overwhelming majority of type A's do *not* develop CHD; rather, type A personality is *one* of the significant risk factors in CHD. By the same token, many type B's *do* develop CHD.

Zyzanski, and Rosenman, 1978). Evidence collected by this second line of investigation suggests that "future angina" individuals may be more in a hurry, irritable, and competitive than "future MI" individuals.

More recent studies have not, however, unequivocally supported the predictive utility of type A behavior. For example, in the Multiple Risk Factor Intervention Trial (Shekelle *et al.*, 1983), type A failed to predict either mortality or myocardial infarction in subjects with multiple risk factors. Similarly, other studies have not found a relationship between type A and angiographically determined coronary artery disease (Williams, 1987).

There are several reasons for these conflicting results. First, some of the negative findings have come from studies that did not use the Structured Interview (SI) to assess type A. As we have already noted, non-SI assessments probably do not adequately measure type A. Second, the predictive power of type A may be limited. For example, Williams *et al.* (1986) found that type A predicted coronary artery disease only among people under the age of fifty. In fact, type B's over fifty had more severe disease! Thus, when studying

a population with a broad age range, unless the data are analyzed separately according to age, it is unlikely that a type A–CHD relationship would be established. Finally, it is possible that an overall type A score is not the best measure of coronary-prone behavior (see Box 8.2).

Mechanisms of Type A How does a set of *psychological* characteristics mediate a *physiological* disease of the heart? Type A's are generally higher in heart rate reactivity to stressful laboratory situations than type B's (see Manuck and Krantz, 1986, for a review). Excessive changes in heart rate and the consequent alterations in the force with which blood is pumped through the arteries could injure arteries. Heart rate reactivity has been related to CHD in several different research contexts. Manuck, Kaplan, and Clarkson (1983) studied monkeys who were being fed a special diet designed to promote atherosclerosis. On the basis of a laboratory stress test the animals were divided into high versus low heart rate reactors. Subsequently, the high heart rate reactors developed twice as much atherosclerosis as the low reactors. In a study of humans, heart rate reactivity

"*Well, my biological clock is ticking, too, and it's saying that if I don't make partner by forty I'm history.*"

BOX 8.2

IS TYPE A REALLY A USEFUL CONSTRUCT?

As already mentioned serious doubts have arisen about the predictive validity of the type A construct. In January 1988, *The New England Journal of Medicine* published an article by Ragland and Brand (1988) that reported on an analysis of men from the original WCGS study who had one coronary event. The question they posed to the data was whether subjects who died from a subsequent coronary attack were more likely to be type A than B. They found the opposite to be true! Although type A's were at higher risk for CHD within the eight and a half years of the study, *after* an initial coronary event they died less often from CHD than did type B's. Perhaps type A's reacted to their first coronary event in a more adaptive fashion, for example, by altering some of their health habits in a more conscientious and effective manner. Among other things, this startling and unexpected findings casts serious doubt on the advisability of secondary prevention of CHD via reduction of type A characteristics.

So controversial did the editors of the *Journal* consider the report that they invited a leading cardiovascular researcher, Dimsdale (1988), to write an introduction to place these negative findings into perspective. He did so by reviewing the literature we have just covered but with attention to some *un*successful attempts to replicate the original WCGS findings. His conclusions were several: (1) he lamented the fact that ideological fervor in opposing camps has apparently discouraged attempts to replicate or reconcile conflicting data; (2) he pointed to the heterogeneous nature of type A and to the fact that different indices of it correlate imperfectly (a conclusion Matthews [1982] had

come to earlier); and (3) he suggested that one of the components of type A, hostility, may be worthy of special attention, a conclusion we ourselves came to in the previous edition of this textbook.

Does this mean that type A is dead as an organizing framework for research into coronary artery and heart disease? We have addressed this question in the following fashion. We ask our Ph.D. students in Psychology whether they would propose the type A construct *today* in light of what we are learning about the role of psychological factors in CAD/CHD. Students' answers invariably discuss the findings on hostility and usually end up with the position that they would *not* put forward the type A construct given what has been learned in recent years. This is not a bad answer—but it overlooks one important factor in the nature of science and in the nature of type A research as it has evolved over the past forty years, namely, the *heuristic* function of theory. It is through the attention to personality factors via type A that behavioral scientists and physicians have examined closely the psychological factors in medical illnesses such as CAD/CHD, and it may seem ironic that it took two *physicians*, Rosenman and Friedman, to argue the case for psychological variables.

For these reasons it is important to understand the course of theory and research on type A, even if future findings encourage workers to drop the construct in favor of something less heterogeneous, like hostility. Indeed, twenty years from now it is likely that workers will criticize hostility as too global a construct and will focus on a narrower aspect of it.

to the cold pressor test predicted the development of CHD in a twenty-three-year follow-up study (Keys *et al.*, 1971). Alternatively, the release of catecholamines or corticosteroids in stressful situations could damage the arteries or increase the extent to which platelets aggregate, thus increasing the likelihood of blockage in the arteries (Herd, 1986).

On a more psychological level, we can ask what there is about type A's that puts them at risk. One way of addressing this question is to examine individual items from the Structured Interview to see which ones are the best predictors of CHD. In the analysis of the interview data from the WCGS done by Matthews and her colleagues (1977), only seven of the whole set of items discriminated between type A individuals who developed CHD and those who did not. Three of these items were related to self-reports of impatience and hostility, one was self-reported competitiveness, and the remain-

der were aspects of voice style, such as explosiveness. In further analysis of these data, hostility has emerged as the major predictor of CHD (Hecker *et al.*, 1988). Consistent with these findings are results reported earlier (Chapter 4, page 94) that type A is associated with high levels of hostile cognition (Weinstein, Davison, DeQuattro, and Allen, 1986). Recent findings (e.g., Williams *et al.*, 1986) also suggest that cynicism is a major factor within the type A complex. The rate of occlusion of coronary arteries was especially high in type A's who had earlier endorsed MMPI items reflecting a cynical or hostile attitude. Similar findings were reported earlier by Barefoot, Dahlstrom, and Williams (1983). Following up medical students who were healthy when they took the MMPI twenty-five years earlier, they found a higher rate of CHD and death in those whose answers had indicated cynicism toward others. What is not yet clear is the best way to conceptualize these results. Is hostility the critical component? Or is it the cynical attitude that is assessed with the MMPI items? Further research will be needed to explore this issue.

Asthma

A Characterization of the Disease

Purcell and Weiss (1970) have described **asthma** in the following way.

Asthma is a symptom complex characterized by an increased responsiveness of the trachea, major bronchi, and peripheral bronchioles to various stimuli, and is manifested by extensive narrowing of the airways which causes impairment of air exchange, primarily in expiration, [thus inducing] wheezing. [The airways may be narrowed] because of edema [an accumulation of excess watery fluid in the tissues] of the walls, increased mucus secretion, spasm of the bronchial muscles, or the collapse of the posterior walls of the trachea and bronchi during certain types of forced expiration. (p. 597)

Asthma attacks occur intermittently and with variable severity; the frequency of some patients' attacks may increase seasonally when certain pollens are present. The airways are not continually blocked; rather the respiratory system returns to normal or near normal either spontaneously or after treatment, thus allowing asthma to be differentiated from chronic respiratory problems like emphysema (Creer, 1982). The major structures of the respiratory system are shown in Figure 8.3.

Most often, asthmatic attacks being suddenly. The patient has a sense of tightness in the chest, wheezes, coughs, and expectorates sputum. Subjective reactions include panic-fear, irritability, and fatigue (Kinsman *et al.*, 1974). A severe attack is a very frightening experience indeed. The immense difficulty of getting air into and out of the lungs feels like suffocation, and the raspy, harsh noise of the gasping, wheezing, and coughing compounds the individual's terror. He or she may become exhausted by the exertion and fall asleep as soon as breathing is more normal.

The asthma sufferer takes a longer time than normal to expire air, and whistling sounds can be detected throughout the chest. These sounds are referred to as rales. Symptoms may last an hour or less or may continue for several hours or sometimes even days. Between attacks no abnormal signs may be detected when the individual is breathing normally, but forced, heavy expiration will often allow the rales to be heard through a stethoscope.

One patient, to be described in the following case history, had his first attack at age nine. His condition worsened until he was thirteen, after which he was symptom-free for ten years. From that time on, however, his condition deteriorated to an unusual degree, and the patient eventually died of respiratory complications—an outcome which fortunately is rare.

Abundant data from this patient's life suggest the importance of emotional factors in precipitating exacerbations of his asthma. He gives a graphic description of developing wheezing and shortness of breath upon separation from his mother. Once, while away on a trip with either her or his grandmother (it is not clear which), in a strange hotel, separated from his companion by a wall, he suffered through the night, having the feeling that his wheezes might be loud enough to be heard and bring her in to rescue him.

He described clearly the relationship of his symptoms to odors. His response to the scent of flowers may have had an allergic basis. That seems less likely in the case of the scent of "lovely ladies," which he stated also gave him asthma. So did certain "bad" smells, of asparagus and cigar smoke. . . . He had many conflicts around weeping, frequently described being dissolved in tears, but always with the implication that he never really was exhausting the reservoir of "sobbing." . . .

At the time of his brother's marriage, the patient was jealous; he managed to forget to mail the 150 invitations to the ceremony that had been entrusted to him. In the church he was almost more prominent than the bride, walking down the aisle just before the ceremony, gasping for breath, and wearing a fur coat, although the month was July. (Knapp, 1969, p. 135)

Somewhere between 2 and 5 percent of the population is estimated to have asthma. A third of asthma sufferers are children, and about two-thirds of these youngsters are boys (Graham *et al.*, 1967; Purcell and

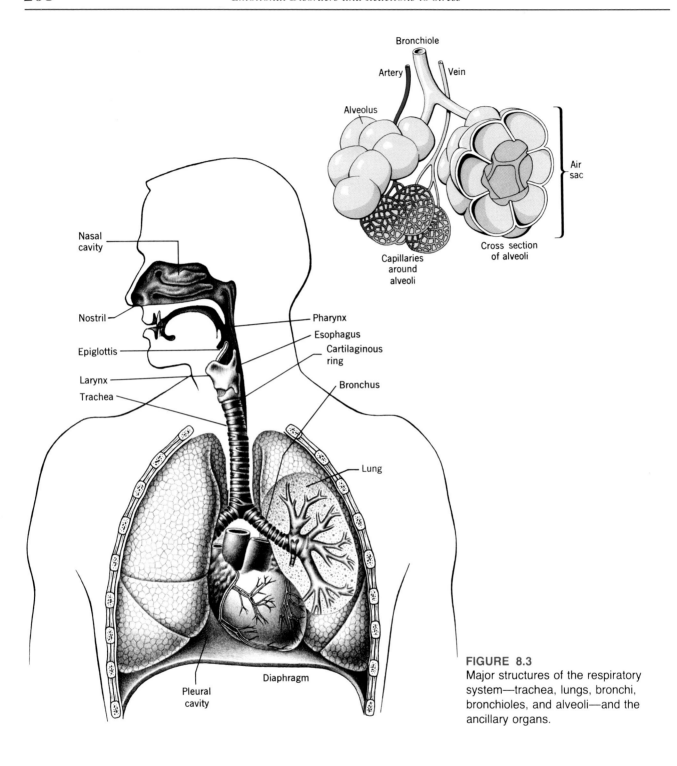

FIGURE 8.3
Major structures of the respiratory system—trachea, lungs, bronchi, bronchioles, and alveoli—and the ancillary organs.

Weiss, 1970). Williams and McNicol (1969) studied 30,000 seven-year-old Australian schoolchildren. They found a high correlation between the age of onset of the symptoms and the length of time the disorder lasted. If onset occurred prior to age one, 80 percent were found to be still wheezing five years later. With ages of onset from three to four, 40 percent were still wheezing five years later, and with an onset age of five or six, only 20 percent

were still wheezing five years later. Thus the earlier the disorder begins, the longer it is likely to last.

The Etiology of Asthma

Much of the debate concerning the importance of psychological factors in the development of asthma relates to whether or not emotionality is always implicated. To investigate the etiology of asthma, Rees (1964) divided the various possible causes into three categories, allergic, infective, and psychological. The cells in the respiratory tract may be especially sensitive to one or more substances or allergens such as pollen, molds, fur, and dust, bringing on asthma. Respiratory infections, most often acute bronchitis, can also make the respiratory system vulnerable to asthma. Anxiety, tension produced by frustration, anger, depression, and anticipated pleasurable excitement are all examples of psychological factors thay may, through induced emotionality, disturb the functioning of the respiratory system and thus cause asthma.

Rees studied 388 asthmatic children admitted consecutively to the asthmatic outpatient clinic of St. David's Hospital in Cardiff, Wales. The part played by allergic factors was assessed through the case histories that were taken and by making cutaneous and inhalation reaction tests with suspected allergens. Patients were also exposed to suspected allergens and inert substances without their knowing which was which. The importance of infective factors was determined through the case histories and X-rays, by examining sputum, and by searching for pus or other evidence of infection in the nose, sinuses, and chest. The potential importance of psychological factors was assessed through the case histories and by direct behavioral observations. The principal results of Rees's study demonstrate the importance of conceptualizing asthma as a disease with multiple causes. As can be seen from Table 8.4, psychological factors were considered a dominant cause in only 37 percent of the cases, and in 30 percent of the cases psychological variables were regarded as totally unimportant—a conclusion at odds with the popular notion that asthma is always psychosomatic.

Rees's data showed also that the different causes of asthma varied in importance depending on the age of the individual. For those asthmatic individuals less than five years of age, the infective factors predominated.

TABLE 8.4
Relative importance of allergic, infective, and psychological factors in the etiology of asthma (*from Rees, 1964*)

Factors	Relative Importance, percent		
	Dominant	Subsidiary	Unimportant
Allergic	23	13	64
Infective	38	30	32
Psychological	37	33	30

From ages six to sixteen the infective factors still predominated, but psychological variables increased in importance. In the range from ages sixteen to sixty-five, psychological factors decreased in importance until about the thirty-fifth year, thereafter becoming more consequential again.

Psychological Factors Producing Asthma
Rees's studies have demonstrated that some, but by no means all, cases of asthma have psychological factors as a primary cause. Yet even when asthma is originally induced by an infection or allergy, psychological stress can precipitate attacks. Kleeman (1967) interviewed twenty-six patients over an eighteen-month period. According to the reports of these patients, 69 percent of their attacks began with an emotional disturbance.

A study by Luparello *et al.*, (1971) indicates the "power of suggestion" in inducing asthma attacks, even in individuals whose allergic reactions are regarded as the primary cause of their disorder. Forty asthmatics and a control group of another forty persons were told that they were participating in a study of air pollution. The experimenter explained to each subject that he wanted to determine what concentrations of various substances would induce wheezing. The asthmatics were told that they would inhale five different concentrations of an irritant or allergen that had previously been established as a contributing cause of their asthma attacks. They were led to believe that each successive sample would have a higher concentration of the allergen, but in fact they were given only five nonallergenic saline solutions to inhale. The control subjects were told that they were inhaling pollutants that could irritate the bronchial tubes and make it difficult for them to breathe. Fourteen out of the forty asthmatic patients reacted with significant airway obstruction, and twelve went on to develop full-fledged attacks. None of the controls had any pathological respiratory reactions. Later the twelve subjects who had developed asthma attacks were given the same saline solution to inhale but were told that the solution was a bronchodilator. The condition of all twelve improved, confirming the role of suggestion in some asthmatics.

The Role of the Family
Several researchers have considered parent–child interactions to be important in the etiology of asthma. In one investigation Purcell and his colleagues (1969) chose a group of twenty-two children. For thirteen children psychological factors were considered the principal precipitants of their asthma. For the other nine allergic or infective factors were considered more significant. These twenty-two children were studied over a considerable length of time that was subdivided into four periods.

The first was an initial baseline period during which the children lived as usual with their families. In the second period the children still lived with their families, but all were informed that all family members except for the asthmatic child would soon be moved out for a two-week period. In the third period the children lived in their own homes but with a substitute mother, and in the fourth they were reunited with their parents. If the psychological factor disturbing one subgroup was the parent–child relationship, these children should improve when their parents lived apart from them. The children whose asthma was considered induced principally by allergic or infective factors would show no such improvement. The data supported the predictions remarkably well. Seventy percent of the thirteen children who were predicted to do well without their parents improved during the separation phase. Of the nine children whose condition was primarily caused by infective factors and was not predicted to improve with their parents away, only one benefited from the separation.

Not all research, however, finds that parent–child relationships figure in asthma. Gauthier and his co-workers (1977, 1978) studied young asthmatic children and their mothers through a battery of questionnaires and interview and by making observations in the home. Most of the children and their mothers were well adjusted. The children's level of development was normal for their age, and they were independent and successful at coping with their surroundings.

The research we have reviewed is thus not completely consistent regarding the role that the home life of asthmatics plays in their illness. Furthermore, even if we allow that family relations are consequential in asthma, we cannot always tell whether the various familial variables are causal agents or maintaining agents. Although certain emotional factors in the home may be important in eliciting early asthmatic attacks in some children, in others the illness may originally develop for nonfamilial reasons, and then the children's parents may unwittingly reward various symptoms of the syndrome. For example, the parents may cater to the child and treat him specially because of his asthma. Current recommendations for the treatment of asthmatic children supply indirect support for this thesis. Doctors prescribe no special treatment and no overprotection. Instead, asthmatic children are urged to lead as normal a life as possible, even to the extent of participating in athletic events. An attempt is made, then, to keep the children from considering their sickness as the dominating factor in their lives. This attitude is well illustrated in the following interaction presented by Kluger (1969, p. 361).

Patient: I can't go to school today because my asthma is worse.

Doctor: I know, but since it's not contagious why can't you be in school?

Patient (Irritated): Because I'm having trouble breathing!

Doctor: I can see that, but you'll have trouble breathing whether you go to school or not. Remaining in bed won't help your breathing.

Patient: (disgustedly): Boy, they don't even let you be sick in this hospital!

Personality and Asthma

It has often been suggested that particular constellations of personality traits are linked to asthma. Several investigators have found that asthmatic individuals have a great many so-called neurotic symptoms: dependency and maladjustment (Herbert, 1965), meekness, sensitivity, anxiety, meticulousness, perfectionism, and obsessions (Rees, 1964). But most of this work consisted of comparing asthmatics to a normal control population. Neuhaus (1958) compared the personality test scores of asthmatic children to those of both a normal group of children and a group of children with cardiac conditions. As in other studies, the asthmatics were found to be more neurotic than those who were normal. But, and this is the important point, *the cardiac children were like the asthmatics more neurotic than normal children.* Thus the increased neuroticism of asthmatic children may reflect only reactions to a chronic illness; neuroticism scores on personality tests are higher the longer the patient has been sick (Kelly and Zeller, 1969).

Physiological Predisposition

Now that the importance of various stresses in eliciting asthmatic attacks has been documented, we must attempt to account for the fact that not all individuals exposed to such stressors develop asthma. Rees (1964) found that 86 percent of the asthmatics examined had had a respiratory infection before asthma developed. Only 30 percent of his control subjects had been so afflicted. This study can be regarded as evidence that inheriting a weak organ, establishing a reaction pattern, or both may figure in the etiology of asthma. Individuals whose asthma is primarily allergic may have an inherited hypersensitivity of the respiratory mucosa, which then overresponds to usually harmless substances such as dust or pollen. There is evidence that the incidence of asthma has a familial pattern consistent with genetic transmission of a diathesis (Konig and Godfrey, 1973). Finally, there is some indication that asthmatics have a less than normally responsive sympathetic nervous system (Miklich *et al.*, 1973; Mathe and Knapp, 1971). Activation of the sympathetic nervous system is already known to reduce the intensity of an asthmatic attack.

In conclusion, a diathesis–stress explanation once again seems to fit the data on a psychophysiological disorder. Once the respiratory system is predisposed to asthma, any number of psychological stressors can interact with the diathesis to produce the disease.

Therapies for Psychophysiological Disorders

Since psychophysiological disorders are true physical dysfunctions, sound psychotherapeutic practice calls for close consultation with a physician. Whether high blood pressure is organically caused or, as in essential hypertension, linked to psychological stress, the diuretic chlorthalidone will increase excretion by the kidneys of sodium chloride, and thus reduce its presence in arterial walls and in turn their constriction. Asthma attacks can be alleviated by oral inhalation or injection of agents that dilate the bronchial tubes, one of the most effective being epinephrine. The help that drugs provide in ameliorating the damage and the discomfort in the particular body systems cannot be underestimated. Mental health and medical professionals recognize, however, that most drug interventions treat only the symptoms; they do not deal with the fact that the person is reacting emotionally to psychological stress. Although the evidence suggests that the predisposition for a particular organ breakdown is inherited or at least somatically based, nonetheless, the manner in which a person responds psychologically indicates that psychotherapeutic interventions are appropriate.

Therapists of various persuasions agree in the most general terms that reducing anxiety is the best way to alleviate the suffering from psychophysiological disorders. The particular disorder, whether it be essential hypertension, coronary heart disease, or an asthma attack, is considered a consequence of anxiety or to be linked with it in some way. Psychoanalytically oriented workers employ techniques such as free association and dream analysis, as they do with other anxiety sufferers, in their efforts to help the egos of their patients confront the supposed infantile origins of their fears. Ego analysts, however, like Franz Alexander, consider specific emotional states to underlie the several disorders and try to strengthen present functioning. Thus they would encourage someone with essential hypertension, viewed as laboring under a burden of undischarged anger, to assert himself and thereby siphon it off.

Client-centered therapists similarly regard people beset with psychophysiological disorders as needing to reduce anxiety, but they place special blame on the individual's conflict with society. Hypertension and coronary heart disease are considered the physiological evidence of the stress felt by those who comply with an establishment whose values go against their own best interests. The goal of the attentive listening and empathic reflection of client-centered therapists is to help clients see the physiological price paid for social conformity and make responsible decisions about changing their mode of living.

Behavior therapists employ their usual range of procedures for reducing anxiety—systematic desensitization, rational-emotive therapy, and assertion training—depending on the source of tension. If the person does not know how to act in a particular situation, behavior rehearsal and shaping may help him or her acquire necessary skills.

Obviously psychophysiological disorders are of special interest to those in the field of behavioral medicine. Treatments are devised to lessen habits known to contribute to illness.[5] For example, one important area of research is to help people stop smoking cigarettes, which has been linked to a host of medical problems. These therapists also work on methods to help people lose weight (Marston and Marston, 1980). Carrying around extra pounds, especially as people grow older, can contribute to coronary heart disease and to hypertension. One way to help asthma patients is to teach them how to discriminate better when they are having an attack. Many patients do not recognize their own symptoms and do not respond appropriately. But they can become more attuned to them and thereby better able to follow a treatment regimen (Creer, Renna, and Chai, 1982).

In recent years behavioral researchers have been exploring the clinical uses of **biofeedback** as a means of improving somatic functioning. Biofeedback provides people with prompt and exact information, otherwise unavailable, on heart rate, blood pressure, brain waves, skin temperature, and other autonomic bodily functions. The particular internal physiological process is detected and amplified by a sensitive electronic recording device. The person knows instantaneously, through an auditory or visual signal, the rate of the process, whether it is too high or too low or just right. Numerous studies have shown that most people, if given the task, for example, of raising their heart rates or lowering their blood pressure, can do so with the help of biofeedback (Elmore and Tursky, 1978; Shapiro, Tursky, and Schwartz, 1970). What is not yet clear is whether through biofeedback they can achieve results that are of clinical significance. Biofeedback will be evaluated in greater depth in Chapter 19. Box 8.3 presents an example of promising clinical research.

---

[5]A community-based approach is described in Chapter 20 (page 593).

BOX 8.3

MIGRAINE HEADACHE AND BIOFEEDBACK

When I am in a migraine aura (for some people the aura lasts fifteen minutes, for others several hours), I will drive through red lights, lose the house keys, spill whatever I am holding, lose the ability to focus my eyes or frame coherent sentences, and generally give the appearance of being on drugs, or drunk. The actual headache, when it comes, brings with it chills, sweating, nausea, a debility that seems to stretch the very limits of endurance. That no one dies of migraine seems to someone deep into an attack, an ambiguous blessing. (From Joan Didion, *The White Album*, pp. 170–171. Reprinted by permission of Wallace Literary Agency, Inc. Copyright © 1968, 79 by Joan Didion.)

Migraine headaches are estimated to afflict up to 10 percent of the general population. Some people have these attacks as often as every few days, others only a few times in their lives. The headache pain itself is usually on one side, almost as though the head were divided in two by an impermeable wall. It has been said that only those actually afflicted with this most common of psychophysiological disorders can know how extreme is the suffering associated with migraine.

A distinction is usually made between classic migraine and common migraine. In classic migraine (as described in the passage above) the person has prodromal symptoms, symptoms experienced before the onset of the headache itself. They take the form of tension, wakefulness, declining energy and drive, and sometimes visual disturbances that are seen first as a shimmering haze, then as zigzag lines. In both types of migraine it is known that the headache itself is caused by sustained dilation, or increase in size, of the extracranial vasculature, principally of the temporal artery, which trifurcates to supply the side of the head. Almost universally, the headache is initially a pulsing pain on one side of the head, coinciding with each heartbeat as the blood is pumped through the expanded extracranial arteries. The pain is caused by these dilated arteries triggering pain-sensitive nerve fibers in the scalp. As the headache progresses, the pain becomes steadier. The arteries thicken and rigidify, making stimulation of the extracranial nerve fibers constant rather than pulsing (Elmore, 1979). Recent evidence indicates that the scalp arteries of migraine victims are more sensitive to autonomic nervous stimulation than those of normal people. Other evidence points to a general instability in vasomotor control, which appears to be the inherited diathesis that

predisposes these unfortunates to reacting to stress with this debilitating disorder.

For many years there has been a controversy about the causes of the extracranial vascular dilation. As we have already noted, in classic migraine, visual disturbances are among the prodromal symptoms. These precursors to the headache itself, according to some researchers, are caused by intense constriction, or narrowing, of the internal carotid artery and its branches, the cranial arteries supplying blood to the brain and to the visual system. Somehow, the theorizing goes, this initial constriction of the internal cranial arteries produces the subsequent rebound dilation of the external carotid artery and its branches, in particular of the temporal arteries, that is the immediate cause of the migraine headache itself.

Consequently, there are two competing schools of thought regarding the best way to treat migraine: one concentrates on the intracranial vasoconstriction during the prodromal stage, and the other on the extracranial vasodilation of the headache phase. The first tries to dilate internal arteries by reducing sympathetic activity, the second to constrict external arteries by increasing sympathetic activity. Sympathetic activity can be reduced through such psychological techniques as deep-muscle relaxation training (Jacobson, 1929); autogenic training, a method promoting relaxation through suggestions of heaviness and warmth* (Luthe and Schultz, 1969); and a Westernized version of transcendental mediation (Benson, 1975). Of particular importance for our present discussion are studies that employ biofeedback to increase hand temperature as a means of shifting blood supply to the periphery and away from the brain. Clinical reports of research conducted originally at the famous Menninger Clinic in Topeka, Kansas (Sargent, Green, and Walters, 1972, 1973), claimed marked improvement in a number of migraine patients who were taught to warm their hands through biofeedback training and then to initiate hand warming on their own at the slightest warning that a headache was coming on. Unfortunately, these studies were flawed by serious methodological problems. Nothing indicated that patients actually learned to warm their hands, and the judgments of improvement were unsystematic and impressionistic (El-

---

*A series of six exercises trains patients to regulate their breathing and heart rates and to make their extremities feel heavy and warm, the stomach warm, and the forehead cool. Autogenic training is considered a combination of relaxation training and self-hypnosis.

more, 1979). The Menninger reports, however, did stimulate a series of more rigorous clinical studies some of which showed that *cooling* of the hands produced equally significant reductions in migraine (e.g., Gauthier, Bois, Allaire, and Drollet, 1981). Some researchers have concluded that it is the reduction in general sympathetic autonomic arousal that is the operative factor, and that this can be brought about by a variety of techniques including hypnosis and muscle relaxation (Blanchard *et al.*, 1978).

The second treatment for migraine focuses on increasing sympathetic activity in order to halt extracranial artery dilation. Through biofeedback the individual is trained to reduce the amplitude of pulsations in the superficial temporal arteries, in other words to constrict the arteries at the site of the actual migraine headache.

Graham and Wolff (1938) had earlier given migraine sufferers ergotamine tartrate, a powerful vasoconstrictive drug, and found significant lowering of pulse in the superficial temporal arteries and in the occipital, the extracranial arteries at the side and rear of the head; patients also reported less headache pain. As with many drugs, however, the very vasoconstriction that appeared to alleviate the migraine had some serious side effects, such as nausea and numbness and even gangrene in the extremities. Indeed, if too strong a dose is given when the internal arteries are constricting, the person could die (Reed, Katkin, and Goldband, 1985). These side effects encouraged work on psychological methods of constricting just the extracranial arteries. A number of researchers have demonstrated that patients find relief from migraine by learning to lower extracranial artery pulse via biofeedback (e.g., Friar and Beatty, 1976).

From an examination of the migraine treatment literature, Elmore and Tursky (1981) concluded that a study was needed to compare the two competing approaches to treatment. They also wanted to demonstrate by careful physiological measurement that whatever response was asserted to have been acquired via biofeedback was in fact acquired, and to determine whether therapy gains were maintained by following up patients for a period of time after their training.

Elmore and Tursky divided a sample of twenty-three adults suffering from migraine into two groups: one received eight sessions of biofeedback training to raise hand temperature, and the other eight sessions of biofeedback training to lower temporal pulse. Both groups had a ninth session without feedback to test whether members could perform the learned response on their own. To achieve the respective goals of their groups, raising hand temperature or lowering temporal pulse, subjects were to generate images of warmth or coolness, or to adopt any technique, other than tensing the muscles, that seemed to work for them. They were also encouraged to practice these strategies every day for about fifteen minutes and at the slightest warning that a headache was about to begin. For a month before and following treatment all subjects recorded the occurrence and intensity of headache in a specially designed pain and discomfort diary. If the people lowering temporal pulse did better than the hand-warming people, it could be concluded that migraine should be treated by *increasing sympathetic* nervous system activity. To relieve migraine headaches people need merely constrict the extracranial arteries. Superiority of hand warming, in contrast, would indicate that earlier on vasodilation is necessary *in order* to prevent the intracranial vasoconstriction believed by the Menninger group to trigger the later extracranial vasodilation.

Physiological measurements taken during the biofeedback training showed that members of each group did in fact learn the skill they were being taught. Moreover, the subjects lowering temporal pulse showed a pattern of general sympathetic nervous system activation and the hand-warming group showed deactivation of this system, demonstrating that the respective training procedures had the intended effects on the autonomic nervous system. Finally, the all-important treatment results: the people lowering temporal pulse achieved significantly more improvement during the one-month posttreatment evaluation than did the hand-warming subjects. Specifically, they reported fewer than half the headaches suffered before treatment, ingested significantly less headache medication, and tended to rate as less painful whatever headaches they had. In contrast, members of the hand-warming group rated their posttreatment headaches as significantly more painful and somewhat longer lasting than those suffered before treatment. The results, then, pose a serious challenge to the view that migraine is caused by sympathetic overarousal and that, generally speaking, people with this disorder should try to reduce their sympathetic nervous activity through relaxation training or tension-reducing drugs. Rather, treatment should be aimed more directly at constriction of the extracranial arteries, although other findings continue to lend support to the original Menninger idea about the benefits of biofeedback-induced hand warming to reduce vasoconstriction (Blanchard, *et al.*, 1982). The picture is far from clear.

Biofeedback procedures are being applied in the treatment of a number of psychophysiological disorders. Demonstrated here is a technique sometimes used to relieve headaches.

Hypertension

Because some antihypertensive drugs have undesirable side effects, such as drowsiness, lightheadedness, and erectile difficulties for men, and because some medical research suggests that long-term use of certain drugs for mild hypertension may have harmful effects (Medical Research Council, 1981), many investigations have been undertaken on nonpharmacological treatments for borderline essential hypertension. The general approach has been to teach people relaxation techniques, sometimes using biofeedback for muscle tension (Blanchard and Miller, 1977). Indeed, as will be described in Chapter 19, the first applications of biofeedback to human problems were for hypertension (e.g., Shapiro, Tursky, and Schwartz, 1970). The available evidence suggests that it is relaxation that has a favorable effect on hypertension, presumably by lowering sympathetic nervous system arousal; biofeedback may help certain people learn to relax, but there is little evidence for any specific effects from biofeedback (Johnston, 1985). It

is, though, unclear how enduring relaxation treatment effects are (Patel, *et al.*, 1985). It will probably depend ultimately on whether the person maintains the acquired skill to relax and that in turn will depend on whether the person remains motivated to practice that skill.

In a recently completed clinical trial, DeQuattro and Davison (Lee, DeQuattro, Cox, Pyter, Foti, Allen, Barndt, Azen, and Davison, 1987) found that intensive relaxation, conducted in weekly sessions over two months and using at-home practice with audiotaped instructions, significantly reduced blood pressure in borderline hypertensives (7 mm Hg systolic and 10 mm Hg diastolic), more so than did a control condition that included state-of-the-art medical advice and instructions concerning diet, weight loss, and other known risk factors. (It should be noted that the relaxation group also received the same medical information that the control subjects were given.) Furthermore, these effects were stronger among those hypertensives previously assessed to have high sympathetic arousal than among those with lower levels, confirming the hypothesis of Esler *et al.* (1977) that there is a subset of hypertensives with relatively high resting levels of sympathetic arousal who may be especially well suited for sympathetic dampening therapies like relaxation. This finding is one of the few in the psychotherapy or behavioral medicine literature that suggests a "fit" between a type of problem and a type of intervention. For example, hypertensives with low levels of sympathetic nervous system arousal may benefit more from a cognitive therapy approach—their hypertension may be sustained by the thoughts they carry in their heads more than by what their sympathetic nervous system is doing. (Of course the logical alternative exists that sympathetic arousal itself might be in part sustained by negative cognitive patterns and that cognitive interventions are one way to reduce this arousal and hence the consequent hypertension.)

Research (e.g., Wadden, 1984) is just beginning on designing cognitive therapy treatment packages suitable for essential hypertensives—presumably these packages should help patients control their anger and anxiety by learning to think less catastrophically and more realistically about negative life events (Jacob and Chesney, 1986).

Type A

Researchers in behavioral medicine also address the challenge of altering the driven, overcompetitive patterns of the type A individual, who has been shown to be at higher risk for heart disease. Within the past ten years or so, about a dozen studies have been conducted on how to lessen or change type A behavior. Because most of them have provided a narrow treatment of short duration, for example, a few sessions of relaxation training, not surprisingly their results have been modest (Price, 1982). A significant exception is the Recurrent Coronary Prevention Project (Friedman *et al.*, 1982), funded by the National Heart, Lung, and Blood Institute.

The overall purpose of this project was to see whether the type A behavior of men who had suffered a heart attack could be changed in the direction of type B, and whether fewer of these patients than those given only cardiological counseling would then have a second heart attack. The treatment expected to improve subjects the most attempted to alter their type A behavior as well as the environmental, cognitive, and physiological factors believed to contribute to their personality. Thus subjects practiced talking more slowly and listening to others more closely instead of interrupting them, and were also encouraged to reduce excessive activities and demands and to relax more. They watched fewer television programs featuring violence and competitiveness (an environmental switch), and they attempted to alter their silent, internal self-talk by believing that events are not necessarily direct challenges to them, and by considering that type A behavior may not be essential to success, which is a cognitive (actually philosophical) change. They also complied with their physicians' drug and diet prescriptions to improve their physiological state. Results were encouraging: type A behavior can be measurably changed. Moreover, after three years of treatment, for men who had received type A counseling the risk of a second heart attack was 7.2 percent annually, compared to 13.2 percent for type A men who received only cardiological counseling (Friedman and Ulmer, 1984; Friedman *et al.*, 1984; Powell *et al.*, 1984; Thoresen *et al.*, 1985). Interestingly, there are indications that reductions in hostility may have been particularly important, consistent with its increasing importance in type A research and in psychophysiological disorders generally (Haaga, 1987; see Box 8.2 for conflicting findings).

But there are many obstacles to reducing type A patterns in our culture. Price (1982) enumerates two. First, in an industrialized and competitive society such as ours, type A behavior pays off, at least in the short run, in increased productivity and achievement, even though personal happiness may be sacrificed. Second, being a type A person is in many ways a cultural norm in the United States and in other countries as well. Often it takes a heart attack to force a type A person even to consider giving up the aggressive, individualistic struggle to gain as many material rewards as possible

in the shortest amount of time, and instead to treasure leisure time and to value people, including the self, for their intrinsic worth rather than for their achievements and status.

Some work by Matthews (e.g., 1978) has assessed type A behavior in children and the ways in which young people learn the values and behavior of the type A personality. She has found, for example, that mothers of type A boys continually "up the ante" for reinforcement. The child is set ever-higher goals for the same degree of reward from the mother. The mass media and most of our schools exhort children to "Be number one," "Don't make mistakes," "Don't waste time," "Increase your production," "Upward and onward." It seems likely that developmental psychologists will find more and more evidence that type A behavior is taught to youngsters from early childhood on and may therefore be extremely difficult to change.

Thus shifting from type A behavior in an effort to prevent or at least reduce the incidence of coronary heart disease challenges the very essence of our advanced and advancing society. A perhaps unintended consequence of the burgeoning literature and research on the type A personality may well be a searing examination of some of the most basic values upon which modern Western civilization is built. Surely, however, psychology can advocate that different values be presented in schools and in the mass media. And the Recurrent Coronary Prevention Project, in which patients were encouraged to place less emphasis on achievement and on rushing and more on pausing to smell the flowers, to enjoy the moment, on living life in the slow rather than the fast lane, indicates that through their own efforts individuals can alter their type A personalities and in the process make themselves happier as well as healthier.[6]

Stress Management

In recent years the field of "stress management" has developed as part of the increased emphasis on stress and health that we discussed earlier. In industry, in government, in universities, in the military, and among people generally, we read of individuals participating in workshops on stress management, even when they do not have diagnosable problems. It has, in other words, become socially acceptable to be stressed and to learn ways (other than therapy) for reducing or managing that stress. There are several approaches under the rubric of stress management, and more than one is

---

[6]Of course these philosophical speculations will have to be revised if hostility rather than "excessive" achievement and time-urgency turns out to be "the culprit" in type A's contribution to risk for cardiac disease.

Stress management training, often involving relaxation, has become a more and more frequently utilized service.

Redesigning the work space, easily accomplished with movable panels, can reduce job stress.

typically followed in any given instance (Davison and Thompson, 1988).

Individual Approaches

Arousal Reduction In arousal reduction we find training in muscle relaxation, sometimes assisted by biofeedback. Although the evidence is uncertain for the need to use the complex instrumentation required for proper biofeedback of minute levels of muscle tension

or certain patterns of electroencephalographic activity, there is confirmation that teaching people to relax deeply and to apply these skills to real-life stressors can be helpful in lowering their stress levels.

Cognitive Restructuring Included under cognitive restructuring is the work of Ellis (1962) and Beck (1976), already briefly described in Chapters 2 (page 51) and 6 (page 141) and to be described more fully in Chapters 9 (page 239) and 19 (page 547). The focus here is on altering people's belief systems and improving the clarity of their logical interpretations of experience on the assumption that our intellectual capacities can affect how we feel and behave. This includes what can simply be called the provision of information to reduce uncertainty and enhance people's sense of control, a theme from Chapter 6.

Behavioral Skills Training Because it is natural to feel overwhelmed if one lacks the skills to execute a challenging task, stress management often includes instruction and practice in necessary skills as well as general issues like time management and effective setting of priorities.

Environmental Change Approaches

The work of *community psychologists* is relevant in this approach (see Chapter 20, page 586). Whereas the individual strategies just described aim at helping the individual deal with a particular environment, one can also take the position that sometimes the environment is the problem and that change is best directed to altering it. (As we shall see in Chapter 20, this approach highlights the political and ethical dimensions of any behavior change enterprise.) For example, a work environment could be redesigned with partitions to provide some privacy, rather than require secretarial workers to sit together in a large open area. Of course stressed individuals themselves can sometimes make environmental changes if they can employ some of the individual techniques discussed earlier. There need be no sharp separation between these two general stress management approaches.

Summary

Psychophysiological disorders are physical diseases produced, in part, by psychological factors, primarily stress. Such disorders usually affect organs innervated by the autonomic nervous system, such as those of the respiratory, cardiovascular, gastrointestinal, and endocrine systems. Research has questioned how psychological stress produces a particular psychophysiological

disorder. Some workers have proposed that the answer lies in the specifics of the stressor or psychological characteristics of the person. Theories and some evidence link inhibition of aggression to hypertension, and the type A personality to heart attacks. Other theories propose that stress must interact with a physiological diathesis: for hypertension a tendency to respond to stress with increases in blood pressure, for heart attacks a sympathetic nervous system that releases too much norepinephrine, and for asthma a respiratory system that overresponds to an allergen or one that has been weakened by prior infection. Although we have spoken of psychological stress affecting the body, it must be remembered that the *mind* and the *body* are best viewed as two different ways of talking about the same organism.

Psychophysiological disorders no longer appear in DSM-IIIR. Instead, the diagnostician can make a diagnosis of psychological factor affecting physical condition and then note the condition on axis III. This change reflects the growing realization that life stress is relevant to all disease, not just those that previously were considered as psychophysiological disorders. To illustrate this we described research showing that life stress was related to episodes of respiratory infection. Important issues in current work on life stress and health include moderators of the relationship (e.g., social support) and specifying the physiological mechanisms (e.g., the immune system) through which stress can exert its effects.

Because psychophysiological disorders represent true physical dysfunctions, medications are usually called for. The general aim of psychotherapies for these disorders is to reduce anxiety. Behavioral medicine, a new field of specialization in behavior therapy, tries to find psychological interventions that can improve the patient's physiological state. It has developed ways of helping people to relax, smoke less, eat fewer fatty foods, and, using biofeedback, gain control over various autonomic functions, such as heart rate and blood pressure. One study has developed methods by which type A victims of heart attacks can abandon their angry, driving ways.

Finally, the emergent field of stress management was described; people without diagnosable problems avail themselves of techniques that can help them cope with the inevitable stress of everyday life.

Pablo Picasso, *Portrait of Jaqueline with Crossed Hands.* 1954. © 1989 ARS, New York/SPADEM/Art Resource.

Chapter 9

Mood Disorders

**General Characteristics of Depression
and Mania**

Depression

Mania

Formal Diagnostic Listings

Psychological Theories of Depression

Psychoanalytic Theory

Cognitive Theories

Interpersonal Aspects of Depression

**Psychological Theories of
Bipolar Disorder**

**Physiological Theories of
Mood Disorders**

The Genetic Data

Biochemistry and Mood Disorders

The Neuroendocrine System

Therapy for Mood Disorders

Psychological Therapies

Somatic Therapies

Suicide

Facts about Suicide

Perspectives on Suicide

Prediction of Suicide from Psychological Tests

Suicide Prevention

Summary

Melancholia, a term derived from the Greek words *melan* meaning black and *choler* meaning bile, and mania, derived from the Greek word *mainesthai*, to be mad, were two of the three types of mental disorder recognized by Hippocrates in the fourth century B.C. By the second century A.D. the physician Aretaeus of Cappadocia had suggested a relationship between melancholia and the apparently opposite emotional state of mania. In the late nineteenth century, as we have seen, the famous German psychiatrist Emil Kraepelin listed two major types of psychoses. One, schizophrenia, will be discussed in Chapter 14. The other, **manic-depressive illness,** which was considered to be the disturbance of all patients showing "affective excess," is one of the principal mood (formerly called affective) disorders discussed in this chapter.

General Characteristics of Depression and Mania

Depression

"Depression is the common cold of psychopathology, at once familiar and mysterious" (Seligman, 1973). Just as most people experience at least moments of anxiety every week of their existence, so will each of us probably have more than an ample amount of sadness during the course of our lives, although perhaps not to the degree or with the frequency that the diagnosis depression is warranted. Often depression is associated with other psychological problems and with medical conditions. The man who has trouble maintaining his erection during intercourse can become depressed about his sex life. The woman who has had a hysterectomy may suffer depression over what she incorrectly believes to be a loss of her femininity. Agoraphobics may become despondent because of their inability to venture out of their homes. Alcoholics may be depressed by their inability to control their drinking and by the social and employment problems that their drinking has provoked. In these and many other instances depression is best viewed as secondary to another condition. Our discussion of depression in this chapter will focus on people for whom this affective disorder is the *primary* problem.

The following eloquent account is from a person who would be regarded as suffering from profound depression. Clearly, anxiety also plays a part in deepening the despair.

I was seized with an unspeakable physical weariness. There was a tired feeling in the muscles unlike any-

thing I had ever experienced. A peculiar sensation appeared to travel up my spine to my brain. I had an indescribable nervous feeling. My nerves seemed like live wires charged with electricity. My nights were sleepless. I lay with dry, staring eyes gazing into space. I had a fear that some terrible calamity was about to happen. I grew afraid to be left alone. The most trivial duty became a formidable task. Finally mental and physical exercises became impossible; the tired muscles refused to respond, my "thinking apparatus" refused to work, ambition was gone. My general feeling might be summed up in the familiar saying "What's the use?" I had tried so hard to make something of myself, but the struggle seemed useless. Life seemed utterly futile. (Reid, 1910, pp. 612–613)

There is general agreement on the most common signs and symptoms of depression (Robins and Guze, 1970; American Psychiatric Association, 1987).

1. Sad, depressed mood.
2. Poor appetite and weight loss or increased appetite and weight gain.
3. Difficulties in sleeping (insomnia); not falling asleep initially, not returning to sleep after awakening in the middle of the night, and early morning awakenings; or in some depressed patients a desire to sleep a great deal of the time.
4. Shift in activity level, becoming either lethargic (psychomotor retardation) or agitated.
5. Loss of interest and pleasure in usual activities.
6. Loss of energy, great fatigue.
7. Negative self-concept; self-reproach and self-blame, feelings of worthlessness and guilt.
8. Complaints or evidence of difficulty in concentrating, such as slowed thinking and indecisiveness.
9. Recurrent thoughts of death or suicide.

Paying attention is an exhausting effort for the depressed. They cannot take in what they read and what other people say to them. Conversation is also a chore, for many prefer to sit alone and to remain silent. They speak slowly, after long pauses, using few words and a low, monotonous voice. Others are too agitated and cannot sit still. They pace, wring their hands, sighing and moaning all the while or complaining. When depressed individuals are confronted with a problem, no ideas for its solution occur to them. Every moment has a great heaviness, and their heads fill and reverberate with self-recriminations. Depressed people may also neglect personal hygiene and appearance and make numerous hypochondriacal complaints of aches and pains that apparently have no physical basis. Utterly dejected and completely without hope and initiative, they may be apprehensive, anxious, and despondent much of the time.

A single individual seldom shows all the aspects of depression; the diagnosis is typically made if at least a few signs are evident, particularly a *mood* of profound sadness that is out of proportion to the person's life situation. Fortunately, most depression, although recurrent, tends to dissipate with time. But an average untreated episode may stretch on for six to eight months or even longer. When depression becomes chronic, the patient does not always snap back to an earlier level of functioning between bouts.

Mr. J. was a fifty-one-year-old industrial engineer who, since the death of his wife five years earlier, had been suffering from continuing episodes of depression marked by extreme social withdrawal and occasional thoughts of suicide. His wife had died in an automobile accident during a shopping trip which he himself was to have made but had canceled because of professional responsibilities. His self-blame for her death, which became evident immediately after the funeral and was regarded by his friends and relatives as transitory, deepened as the months, and then years, passed by. He began to drink, sometimes heavily, and when thoroughly intoxicated would plead to his deceased wife for forgiveness. He lost all capacity for joy—his friends could not recall when they had last seen him smile. Once a gourmet, he now had no interest in food and good wine, and on those increasingly rare occasions when friends invited him for dinner, this previously witty, urbane man could barely manage to engage in small talk. As might be expected, his work record deteriorated markedly. Appointments were missed and projects haphazardly started and then left unfinished.

Mania

Some people who suffer from episodic periods of depression also at times suddenly abound with joyful elation and become hyperactive, overconfident, and full of impractical, grandiose plans. Although there are clinical reports of individuals who experience **mania** but not depression, such a condition is apparently quite

Depression was Marilyn Monroe's frequent adversary and disrupter of her personal life and professional life. She fought many bouts of it throughout her career and earlier and then lost a final one.

rare. Mania has the following signs and symptoms.

1. Elevated, expansive, or irritable mood.

2. Extraordinary increase in activity level—at work, socially, or sexually.

3. Unusual talkativeness, rapid speech, and the subjective impression that thoughts are racing.

4. Less than the usual amount of sleep needed.

5. Inflated self-esteem; belief that one has special talents, powers, and abilities.

6. Distractibility; attention easily diverted.

7. Involvement in activities that are likely to have undesirable consequences, such as reckless spending.

The manic stream of remarks is loud and incessant, full of puns, jokes, plays on words, rhyming, and interjections about nearby objects and happenings that have attracted the speaker's attention. This speech is very difficult to interrupt. It also reveals the manic's so-called *flight of ideas.* Although small bits of talk are coherent, the individual shifts rapidly from topic to topic. The manic need for activity may cause the individual to be annoyingly sociable and intrusive, constantly and sometimes purposelessly busy, and unfortunately oblivious to the obvious pitfalls of his or her endeavors. Any attempt to curb all this momentum can bring quick anger and even rage. Mania usually comes on suddenly, over the period of a day or two. Untreated episodes may last from a few days to several months.

The following description of a case of mania comes from our files. The irritability that is often part of this state was not found in this patient.

Mr. M., a thirty-two-year-old postal worker, had been married for eight years. He and his wife lived comfortably and happily in a middle-class neighborhood with their two children. In retrospect there appeared to be no warning for what was to happen. On February the twelfth Mr. M. let his wife know that he was bursting with energy and ideas, that his job as a mail carrier was unfulfilling, and that he was just wasting his talent. That night he slept little, spending most of the time at a desk, writing furiously. The next morning he left for work at the usual time but returned home at eleven a.m., his car filled to overflowing with aquaria and other equipment for tropical fish. He had quit his job and then withdrawn all the money from the family's savings account. The money had been spent on tropical fish equipment. Mr. M. re-

ported that the previous night he had worked out a way to modify existing equipment so that fish "won't die anymore. We'll be millionaires." After unloading the paraphernalia, Mr. M. set off to canvass the neighborhood for possible buyers, going door to door and talking to anyone who would listen.

The following bit of conversation from the period after Mr. M. entered treatment indicates his incorrigible optimism and provocativeness.

Therapist: Well, you seem pretty happy today.

Client: Happy! Happy! You certainly are a master of understatement, you rogue! (Shouting, literally jumping out of his seat.) Why I'm ecstatic. I'm leaving for the West Coast today, on my daughter's bicycle. Only 3100 miles. That's nothing, you know. I could probably walk, but I want to get there by next week. And along the way I plan to contact a lot of people about investing in my fish equipment. I'll get to know more people that way—you know, Doc, "know" in the biblical sense (leering at the therapist seductively). Oh, God, how good it feels. It's almost like a nonstop orgasm.

Formal Diagnostic Listings

Two major *mood disorders* are listed in DSM-IIIR, *major depression* and *bipolar disorder.* The symptoms of major depression, sometimes also referred to as *unipolar depression,* are the profoundly sad mood and disturbances of appetite, weight, sleep, and activity level (becoming either lethargic or agitated). Major depression is one of the most widespread of the disorders considered in this book. Approximately 8 to 11 percent of men and 18 to 23 percent of women will be clinically depressed at least once in their lives (Weissman and Myers, 1978; Woodruff, Goodwin, and Guze, 1974). The disorder is more frequent among members of the lower socioeconomic classes (Hirschfeld and Cross, 1982). The critical symptoms of bipolar disorder are the elated or irritable mood, talkativeness, and hyperactivity of mania, as well as episodes of depression. These symptoms must be severe enough to cause serious impairment in social or occupational functioning or to require hospitalization. Interestingly, people who suffer only manic episodes are diagnosed as having bipolar disorder. The reason is that these patients are similar to those with episodes of both mania and depression on many other variables (e.g., family history, response to treatment). The prevalence of bipolar disorder is much lower than that of major depression—about 1 percent of the population (e.g., Weissman and Myers, 1978).

The validity of the Major (Unipolar) Depression vs. Bipolar Disorder Distinction

There is abundant evidence that the bipolar–unipolar distinction is an important one. Those suffering the two disorders differ in ways other than whether they have manic episodes. For example, when bipolars are depressed, they typically sleep more than usual and are lethargic, whereas unipolars have insomnia and are agitated. Unipolar depression usually has a later age of onset than does bipolar disorder, the average ages being thirty-six and twenty-eight, respectively. Moreover, more relatives of individuals with bipolar disorder have affective disorders than do the relatives of those with unipolar depression. Lithium carbonate (see page 242) is more therapeutic for bipolars who are currently depressed than it is for unipolars. All these differences add to the validity of the bipolar–unipolar distinction (Depue and Monroe, 1978).

Heterogeneity within the Categories

A problem remaining in the classification of mood disorders, however, is their great heterogeneity. Some bipolar patients, for example, suffer the full range of symptoms of both mania and depression almost simultaneously or, alternating rapidly, every few days. Other patients have only the symptoms of either mania or depression during a clinical episode. So-called bipolar II patients have episodes of major depression but only a less severe form of mania, called hypomania; they also have family members with bipolar disorder. Some researchers advocate diagnosing these individuals as having bipolar disorder itself, but the evidence that they should be is still insufficient (Depue and Monroe, 1978).

Unipolar depression too has great heterogeneity. In DSM-II, attempts were made to deal with this diversity. The factors distinguishing among various types of unipolar depression were age of onset, the presence or absence of stress, and whether or not the patient was psychotic. Involutional melancholia, one of the DSM-II categories, was thought to occur at the "change of life," when both men and women go through physiological changes that make it less likely that they will be able to reproduce. Stress was not viewed as an important etiological factor; rather physiological (hormonal) changes were believed to cause this kind of depression. But no evidence substantiates this belief.

In two other DSM-II diagnoses, neurotic and psychotic depression, a life event was assumed to have brought on the reactions, but deciding whether depression was indeed caused by environmental stress proved troublesome.

DSM-IIIR retains the option of diagnosing a depressed patient as psychotic but drops the notion of neurotic depression. Depressed patients are diagnosed as psychotic if they are subject to delusions and hallucinations. The presence of delusions appears to be a useful distinction among unipolar depressives (Nelson and Bowers, 1978; Glassman and Roose, 1981): depressed patients with delusions do not generally respond well to the usual drug therapies for depression, but they do respond favorably to these drugs when they are combined with the drugs commonly used to treat other psychotic disorders such as schizophrenia.

According to DSM-IIIR, some unipolar depressives may fit the melancholic subtype. They find no pleasure in any activity and are unable to feel better even temporarily when something good happens. Their depressed mood is worse in the morning. They awaken about two hours too early, lose appetite and weight, and are either lethargic or extremely agitated. Furthermore, they had no personality disturbance prior to their first episode of depression and respond well to biological therapies. The validity of the distinction between depressions with or without melancholia has not been established (Zimmerman *et al.*, 1986).

Finally, DSM-IIIR states that both bipolar and unipolar disorders can be subdiagnosed as *seasonal*. The criterion is at least three prior episodes of a mood disturbance (at least two of which must have been con-

Light fixture used in the treatment of seasonal mood disorder.

secutive), in which the disorder began and ended within a consecutive sixty-day period. For example, someone might experience three episodes of depression that began between October 1 and November 30 and that ended between February 1 and March 30. Most research on the concept of seasonal mood disorder has been done on patients who had winter depression and mania in the spring or summer (e.g., Rosenthal *et al.*, 1986); the most prevalent explanation was that the mood disorders were linked to changes in the length of daylight hours. Indeed, therapy for these winter depressions involves exposing the patients to bright, white light (Rosenthal *et al.*, 1985). In DSM-IIIR, however, the diagnostic criteria allow for a summer depression and winter episode of mania. If this change proves to be valid, some reconceptualization of the concept of seasonal mood disorders will be necessary.

Chronic Mood Disorders

DSM-IIIR lists two long-lasting disorders in which mood disturbances are predominant. Although the symptoms of individuals with either of these disorders have been evident for at least two years, they are not severe enough to warrant a diagnosis of major depression or bipolar disorder. In *cyclothymic disorder,* the person has frequent periods of depression and hypomania. These periods may be mixed, alternate, or separated by periods of normal mood lasting as long as two months. Cyclothymics have paired sets of symptoms in their periods of depression and hypomania. During their depression they feel inadequate; during their hypomania their self-esteem is inflated. They withdraw from people, then seek them out in an uninhibited fashion. They sleep too much and then too little. Depressed cyclothymics have trouble concentrating and their productivity decreases; but during hypomania their thinking becomes sharp and creative and their productivity increases.

The person with *dysthymic disorder* is chronically depressed, either persistently or with periods of normal mood lasting a few days or weeks, never more than a month or two at a time. Besides feeling blue and losing pleasure in usual activities and pastimes, the person has at least several other signs of depression, such as insomnia or sleeping too much; feeling inadequate, ineffective, and drained of energy; pessimism; being unable to concentrate and to think clearly; avoiding the company of others. Data collected by D. Klein and his associates (1988) have validated dysthymia as a form of depression and shown that it appears to be a particularly severe form of this disorder.

Both of the chronic mood disorders may occur in people who also, from time to time, have full-blown episodes of major depression or bipolar disorder. The prognosis for patients with major depression who also have dysthymic disorder has been found to be especially poor (Keller *et al.*, 1982).

Psychological Theories of Depression

Depression has been studied from several perspectives. We shall discuss psychoanalytic views, which emphasize

Several well-known figures who suffered from depression—Abraham Lincoln, Edgar Allan Poe, Fyodor Dostoyevsky, Sylvia Plath.

the unconscious conflicts associated with grief and loss; cognitive theories, which focus on the depressed person's self-defeating thought processes; interpersonal factors, which relate to how depressed people interact with others; and physiological theories, which concentrate on what the central nervous system is doing at the neurochemical level. It will be seen that each theoretical position emphasizes one or another aspect of depression at the expense of others.

Psychoanalytic Theory

It is not always easy to distinguish between sadness, which is normal, and depression, which is not. The contrast between normal grief and abnormal depression is the focal point of Abraham's (1911) original attempt to interpret depression through psychoanalytic theorizing. It is also the focus of Freud's (1917) celebrated paper, "Mourning and Melancholia." Abraham was Freud's student and Freud's work was an elaboration of Abraham's theorizing.

Freud saw the potential for depression being created early in childhood. He theorized that during the oral period the child's needs may be insufficiently or oversufficiently gratified. The person therefore remains "stuck" in this stage and dependent on the instinctual gratifications particular to it. With this arrest in psychosexual maturation, this fixation at the oral stage, he or she may develop a tendency to be excessively dependent on other people for the maintenance of self-esteem.

From this happenstance of childhood, how can the adult come to suffer from depression? The reasoning is complex, assuming as it does that several unconscious processes are a part of mourning. Freud hypothesized that after the loss of a loved one the mourner first **introjects** or incorporates the lost person; he or she identifies with the lost one, perhaps in a fruitless attempt to undo the loss. Because, as Freud asserted, we unconsciously harbor negative feelings against those we love, the mourner now becomes the object of his or her own hate and anger. In addition, the mourner also resents being deserted and feels guilt for real or imagined sins against the lost person. The period of introjection is followed by the period of **mourning work**, during which the mourner recalls memories of the lost one and thereby separates himself from the person who has died and loosens the bonds that introjection has imposed.

The grief work can go astray in overly dependent individuals and develop into an ongoing process of self-abuse, self-blame, and depression. Such individuals do not loosen their emotional bonds with the person who has died, rather they continue to castigate themselves for the faults and shortcomings perceived in the loved

The psychoanalyst theory of depression likened it to mourning.

one who has been introjected. The mourner's anger toward the lost one continues to be directed inward. This theorizing is the basis for the widespread psychodynamic view of depression as anger turned against oneself.

One further point must be made. Since many people can become depressed and remain so without having recently suffered the loss of a loved one, it became necessary to invoke the concept of "**symbolic loss**" in order to keep the theoretical formulation intact. For example, a person may unconsciously interpret a rejection as a total withdrawal of love.

Little research has been generated by psychoanalytic points of view, neither Freud's nor those of others that are not discussed here. The little information available does not support the theory. Dreams and projective tests should theoretically be means of expressing unconscious needs and fears. Beck and Ward (1961) analyzed the dreams of depressed people and found themes of loss and failure, not of anger and hostility. An examination of responses to projective tests established that depressives identify with the victim, not the aggressor. Other data also contradict the views of Abraham and Freud. If depression comes from anger turned inward, we would expect depressed people to express little hostility toward others. This was not found to be the case; depressed individuals often express intense anger and hostility toward people close to them (Weissman, Klerman, and Paykel, 1971).

At the same time, however, psychonalytic ideas have found their way into more recent theorizing. For instance, irrational self-statements such as "It is a dire necessity that I be universally loved and approved of," to which Ellis attributes much human suffering, might be devastating for Freud's "oral personality" in the deepening depression following the loss of a loved one. Although Freud cloaked his clinical impressions in theoretical terms that have been rejected by many contemporary writers, we must appreciate that some of his basic suppositions have a continuing influence.

Cognitive Theories

Discussions of the feeling of helplessness in Chapter 6 and of Ellis's concept of irrational beliefs in Chapter 2 and elsewhere indicate that cognitive processes play a decisive role in emotional behavior. In some theories of depression as in some concerning anxiety, thoughts and beliefs are regarded as causing the emotional state. In a way Freud is a cognitive theorist too, for he viewed depression as resulting from a person's belief that loss is a withdrawal of affection.

Beck's Theory

An important contemporary theory of depression that regards thought processes as causative factors is Aaron Beck's (1967; 1985). His central thesis is that depressed individuals feel as they do because they commit characteristic errors in thinking. From an examination of his therapy notes, he found that his depressed patients tended to distort whatever happened to them in the direction of self-blame, catastrophes, and the like. Thus an event interpreted by a normal person as irritating and inconvenient, for example, the malfunctioning of an automobile, would be interpreted by the depressed patient as yet another example of the utter hopelessness of life. Beck's position is not that depressives think poorly or illogically in general, rather, depressives draw illogical conclusions and come to evaluate negatively themselves, their immediate world, and their future. They see only personal failings, present misfortunes, and overwhelming difficulties ahead.

According to Beck, in childhood and adolescence, depressed individuals have acquired, through loss of a parent or an unrelenting succession of tragedies, or the social rejection of peers, or the criticisms of teachers, or the depressive attitude of a parent, a negative schema. All of us have schemata of many kinds; by these perceptual sets, these "mini-paradigms," we order our lives.

The negative schemata that depressed persons have acquired are activated whenever new situations they encounter resemble in some way, perhaps only remotely, the conditions in which the schemata were learned. Moreover, the negative schemata of depressives fuel, and are fueled by, certain cognitive distortions which lead these sufferers to misperceive reality. Thus an ineptness schema can make depressives expect to fail most of the time; a self-blame schema burdens them with responsibility for all misfortunes; and their negative self-evaluation schema constantly reminds them of their worthlessness. The following is a list of the principal cognitive distortions of the depressive.

1. **Arbitrary Inference.** A conclusion drawn in the absence of sufficient evidence or of any evidence at all. For example, a man concludes that he is worthless because it is raining the day that he is hosting an outdoor cocktail party.

2. **Selective Abstraction.** A conclusion drawn on the basis of but one of many elements in a situation. A worker feels worthless when a product fails to function, even though she is only one of many people who have produced it.

3. **Overgeneralization.** An overall sweeping conclusion drawn on the basis of a single, perhaps trivial, event. A student regards his poor performance in a single class on one particular day as final proof of his worthlessness and stupidity.

4. **Magnification and Minimization.** Gross errors in evaluating performance. A woman, believing that she has completely ruined her car (magnification) when she sees that there is a slight scratch on the rear fender, regards herself as good for nothing; or a man still believes himself worthless (minimization) in spite of a succession of praiseworthy achievements.

These distortions could of course be used within a schema of positive self-evaluation, by a person who distorts what he sees so as to *enhance* his view of himself. For example, he can selectively abstract from the success of a project on which he worked with many others, the conclusion that he himself has great ability and was primarily responsible for the good outcome. The depressed person, however, by these errors in thinking, confirms his self-deprecatory schema and finds himself unworthy and responsible for calamities.

It is important to appreciate the thrust of Beck's position. Whereas many theorists have seen people as victims of their passions, creatures whose intellectual capacities can exert little if any control over feelings—this is Freud's basic position—in the theory just outlined, the cause–effect relationship operates in the opposite direction. Our emotional reactions are considered to be a function of how we construe our world, and indeed the interpretations of depressives are found not to mesh very well with the way most people view the world. Beck sees depressives as the victims of their own illogical self-judgments.

At least two points need to be demonstrated when evaluating Beck's theory. First, depressed patients, in contrast to nondepressed individuals, must actually judge themselves in the illogical ways that Beck has enumerated. This first point was initially confirmed by Beck's clinical observations, which suggest that depressed patients do, in fact, manifest at least some of the distortions listed by him (Beck, 1967).

Further support for this general proposition comes from a number of sources. Questionnaires have been developed to assess depressive-distorted cognitive biases in reacting to stories about college students in problematic situations (Krantz and Hammen, 1979) and to allow subjects to report negative automatic thoughts (Hollon and Kendall, 1980). In general, depressives' responses to these questionnaires agree with expectations based on Beck's theory. As indicated in Chapter 4, an experiment employing the Articulated Thoughts During Simulated Situations procedure found the thinking of depressive patients illogical (White, Davison, and White, 1989). In perceiving and recalling information, depressives would seem to have negative schemata, for they perceive information in more negative terms (Roth and Rehm, 1980) and recall their incorrect answers better than their correct ones (Nelson and Craighead, 1977).

However, another body of research does not support the assertion that cognition is invariably distorted among depressives. For example, expectancy of success is actually quite accurate in depressives whereas normals overestimate the likelihood of success (Lobitz and Post, 1979). Similarly, in another study depressives were more accurate than normals in monitoring their level of social skill (Lewinsohn et al., 1980). Thus, although depressives are consistently pessimistic, they are not always cognitively distorted (Layne, 1986). An important task for future research will be to understand the conditions under which depressives distort reality and when they seem to perceive it more clearly than normals. Another challenge is to understand why a depressed person is saddened by his sometimes accurate judgments whereas a nondepressed individual is not.

Second, it should be demonstrated that the cognitive distortion of depressives does not follow upon an emotional disturbance, that it does in fact *cause* the depressed mood. Many studies in experimental psychology have in a general way shown that a person's mood can be influenced by how he or she construes events. But manipulating affect has also been shown to change thinking (e.g., Isen et al., 1978). No study that we know of directly demonstrates that the various emotional and physical aspects of depression are truly secondary to, or a function of, the negative schemata that Beck believes operate in this disorder. Beck has found that depression and cognitive distortions are *correlated*, but a specific causal relationship cannot be determined from such data; depression could cause negative and illogical thoughts, or negative and illogical thoughts could cause depression.

Indeed, one longitudinal study of the relationship between cognition and depression found that negative and illogical thinking did not precede depression (Lewinsohn et al., 1981). A large sample of community residents completed a battery of tests measuring cognition and depression and were then followed up eight months later. Of particular interest were the results of the earlier tests assessing the thinking of people who later became depressed.

Prior to becoming depressed, [future depressives] did not subscribe to irrational beliefs, they did not have lower expectancies for positive outcomes or higher expectancies for negative outcomes . . . nor did they perceive themselves as having less control over the events in their lives (p. 218).

In our view the relationship in all likelihood works both ways; depression can probably make thinking negative and illogical, and negative, illogical thinking can probably cause depression.

In spite of these irresolutions, an important advantage of Beck's theory is that it is testable and has encouraged considerable research on depression. One of the areas now being pursued, for example, is how different schemata might interact with particular life stressors and lead to the onset of depression. For example, one person may regard the adequacy of their social relationships as the most important aspect of their well-being, whereas for another occupational achievement might be central. For the socially oriented person, life stress related to interpersonal themes (e.g., divorce or breaking up a relationship) would have great impact, whereas for the achievement oriented individual a failure to meet some goal would do so. Evidence collected by Hammen and her colleagues (1985) supports the general usefulness of such a conceptualization. Even more important, as discussed later in this chapter (see page 239), Beck's work has encouraged therapists to focus directly on depressed patients' thinking in order to change and alleviate their feelings (Beck, 1976).

Learned Helplessness: A Cognitive-Learning Theory

Martin Seligman's (1974) *learned-helplessness* theory of depression suggests that although anxiety is the initial response to a stressful situation, it is replaced by depression if the person comes to believe that control is unattainable. In some ways this model is similar to the ego-analytical view of Bibring (1953), who proposed that depression follows "the ego's shocking awareness of its helplessness in regard to its aspirations" (p. 39).

Initially Seligman's view was a noncognitive mediational learning theory, formulated to explain the behavior of animals who received inescapable electric shock. In the first part of the experiment several dogs are put in a box with electric grids in the flooring and subjected to numerous painful electric shocks from which they cannot escape. In the second part these animals, as well as dogs who did not have the prior experience with inescapable shock, are placed in a similar apparatus. The difference is that now painful shock can be avoided if the dogs learn to leap over a partition to another compartment of the so-called shuttle box as soon as they hear a warning buzzer or see a light come on. The behavior of the dogs is markedly affected by whether they were earlier exposed to inescapable shock. Animals who have not had the earlier experience become quite upset when they receive the first few electric shocks but fairly soon thereafter learn to leap over the partition when they hear or see the conditioned stimulus, and thereby avoid further painful shock. The animals who have had the earlier experience with inescapable shock behave quite differently. Soon after receiving the first shocks, they stop running around in a distressed manner; instead they seem to give up and passively accept the painful stimulation. Not surprisingly, they do not acquire the avoidance response as efficiently and effectively as the control animals do. Most of them in fact lie down in a corner and whine. On the basis of these observations Seligman proposed that animals can acquire what might be called a "sense of helplessness" when confronted with uncontrollable aversive stimulation. This helplessness later tends seriously and deleteriously to affect their performance in stressful situations that *can* be controlled. They appear to lose the ability and motivation to learn to respond in an effective way to painful stimulation.

On the basis of this and other work on the effects of uncontrollable stress, Seligman felt that learned helplessness in animals can provide a model for at least certain forms of human depression. He noted similarities between the manifestations of helplessness observed in animal laboratory studies and at least some of the symptoms of depression. Like many depressed people, the animals appear passive in the face of stress, failing to initiate action that might allow them to cope.

TABLE 9.1

Sample items from the Beck Depression Inventory
(*after Beck, 1967*)

Attitudes		Depression Inventory
Sadness*	0	I do not feel sad.
	1	I feel sad.
	2	I am sad all the time and I can't snap out of it.
	3	I am so sad or unhappy that I can't stand it.
Pessimism	0	I am not particularly discouraged about the future.
	1	I feel discouraged about the future.
	2	I feel I have nothing to look forward to.
	3	I feel that the future is hopeless and that things cannot improve.
Guilt	0	I don't feel particularly guilty.
	1	I feel guilty a good part of the time.
	2	I feel quite guilty most of the time.
	3	I feel guilty all of the time.
Self-dislike	0	I don't feel disappointed in myself.
	1	I am disappointed with myself.
	2	I am disgusted with myself.
	3	I hate myself.
Self-accusations	0	I don't feel I am any worse than anybody else.
	1	I am critical of myself for my weaknesses or mistakes.
	2	I blame myself all the time for my faults.
	3	I blame myself for everything bad that happens.
Suicidal ideas	0	I don't have any thoughts of killing myself.
	1	I have thoughts of killing myself, but I would not carry them out.
	2	I would like to kill myself.
	3	I would kill myself if I had the chance.

*The words to the left do not appear in the actual inventory but are given here to indicate what attitudes each group of items is meant to measure. A total score is obtained by summing the numbers (0, 1, 2, or 3) associated with a subject's response to each item.

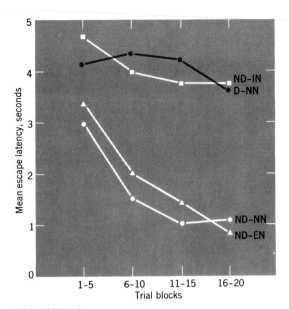

FIGURE 9.1

Subjects who were depressed and those who were not depressed but had experienced inescapable noise acted more slowly to escape noise than did those in the other two groups. After Klein and Seligman (1976).

ND-IN: subjects rated as nondepressed; were previously subjected to inescapable noise (the "helpless" group).

D-NN: subjects rated as depressed on Beck Depression inventory; were not previously subjected to noise.

ND-NN: subjects rated as nondepressed; were not previously subjected to noise.

ND-EN: subjects rated as nondepressed; were previously subjected to escapable noise.

They develop anorexia, having difficulty in eating or retaining what is eaten, and lose weight. Further, one of the neurotransmitter chemicals, norepinephrine, was found to be depleted in Seligman's animals (see Box 6.5, page 150). Drugs that increase levels of norepinephrine have been shown to alleviate depression in human beings. Although effectiveness of treatment does not, as we have often indicated, prove etiology, the fact that depression is reduced by a drug that increases the level of norepinephrine is consistent with the finding that learned helplessness in animals is associated with lower levels of the chemical.

Experiments with human beings have yielded results similar to those of experiments done with animals. People who are subjected to inescapable noise, or inescapable shock, or who are confronted with unsolvable problems, fail later to escape noise and shock and solve simple problems (e.g., Hiroto and Seligman, 1975; Roth and Kubal, 1975). Moreover, the performance of tasks by college students who rate as depressed on the Beck Depression Inventory (BDI; Table 9.1) is similar to that of nondepressed students who have earlier been subjected to these same helplessness-inducing experiences (Miller, Seligman, and Kurlander, 1975; Klein and Seligman, 1976) (Figure 9.1).

In 1978 a revised version of the learned-helplessness model was proposed by Abramson, Seligman, and Teasdale,[1] for several inadequacies of the theory and unexplained aspects of depression had become apparent. Some studies with humans, for example, had indicated that "helplessness inductions" actually led to subsequent facilitation of performance (e.g., see Wortman and Brehm, 1975). In addition, many depressed people hold themselves responsible for their failures. If they regard themselves as helpless, how can they blame themselves? The essence of the revised theory lies in the concept of **attribution** (Weiner *et al.*, 1971), and in this way it blends cognitive and learning elements. Given a situation in which the individual has experienced failure, he or she will try to attribute the failure to some cause. In Table 9.2 the Abramson, Seligman, and Teasdale formulation is applied to indicate the ways in which a college student might attribute his failure on the mathematics portion of the Graduate Record Examination. Three questions are asked. Are the reasons for failure believed to be internal (personal) or environmentally caused (universal)? Is the problem believed to be stable or unstable? How global or specific is the inability to succeed perceived to be?

---

[1]Miller and Norman (1979) independently published a theory very similar to this reformulation.

TABLE 9.2

Attributional schema of depression: Why I failed my GRE math exam

Degree	Internal (Personal)		External (Universal)	
	Stable	Unstable	Stable	Unstable
Global	I lack intelligence.	I am exhausted.	These tests are all unfair.	It's an unlucky day, Friday the thirteenth.
Specific	I lack mathematical ability.	I am fed up with math.	The math tests are unfair.	My math test was numbered "13."

BOX 9.1

DEPRESSION IN WOMEN: A CONSEQUENCE OF LEARNED HELPLESSNESS AND STYLE OF COPING?

Depression occurs more often in women than in men. Research involving both patients in treatment and surveys of community residents consistently yields a 2:1 female:male ratio (Nolen-Hoeksema, 1987). Understanding the cause of this gender difference may yield some further clues to the etiology of depression.

Radloff (1975) speculates that the higher levels of depression among women are best explained as a consequence of learned helplessness. The feminist literature would agree (e.g., Bernard, 1973; Chesler, 1972), for it blames the greater incidence of mental problems among women on their lack of personal and political power. Feminists take the position that more women than men become depressed because their social roles do not encourage them to feel competent. What women do does not seem to count compared to the greater power that men have in society. In fact, it may be that little girls are *trained* to be helpless (Broverman, Broverman, and Clarkson, 1970). Consistent with these speculations are data showing that girls' behavior is less likely than boys' to elicit consequences from both parents (Maccoby and Jacklin, 1974) and teachers (Dweck *et al.*, 1978). Furthermore, girls are more likely to attribute success to luck or the favors of others (unstable) and failures to global and stable factors (Dweck, 1975).

Nolen-Hoeksema (1987) has proposed an equally plausible account of these gender differences, referring to characteristic differences in the way men and women cope with stress. When responding to depression, men typically en-gage in activities that will distract them from their mood, for example, engaging in some physical activity or watching television. Women, on the other hand, are less active, tend to ruminate about their situation, and blame themselves for being depressed (e.g., Kleinke *et al.*, 1982). This ruminative reaction is then seen as amplifying the state of depression and negative mood, perhaps by interfering with attempts to problem-solve.

Assume for the moment that Nolen-Hoeksema is correct. How does it come about that women have more of a ruminative response style to stress and sadness than do men? She seeks answers in sex-role learning that begins during childhood. It is part of the masculine stereotype to be active and coping rather than reflecting on one's feelings and the reasons for them. Men learn to be less emotionally "tuned in" than women. By the same token this sex-linked learning may teach women that they are by nature more emotional and that therefore depressive episodes are natural and unavoidable.

The implications for treatment are clear according to this view. Depressed women—and men, to be sure—should be encouraged to increase their coping and pleasure-producing activity rather than dwell on their moods and search for causes of depression. Problem solving should also be nurtured. In a preventive vein, Nolen-Hoeksema suggests that parents and other caretakers encourage girls to adopt active behavior in response to negative moods.

The attributional revision of helplessness theory postulates that the way the person explains failure will determine its subsequent effects. Global attributions should increase the generality of the effects of failure. Attributions to stable factors will make them long term. Finally, attributing the failure to internal characteristics is more likely to diminish self-esteem, particularly if the personal fault is also global and persistent.

People become depressed, the theory suggests, when they attribute negative life events to stable and global causes. Whether self-esteem collapses too depends on whether they blame the bad outcome on their own inadequacies. The depression-prone individual is also thought to show a "depressive attributional style," a tendency to attribute bad outcomes to personal, global, stable faults of character. When persons with this style (a diathesis) have unhappy, adverse experiences (stressors), they become depressed and self-esteem shatters (Peterson and Seligman, 1984; see Box 9.1).

Some research gives direct support to the reformulated theory. Seligman and his colleagues (1979) have devised the Attributional-Style Questionnaire (ASQ; Table 9.3) and, as predicted by the theory, found that depressed college students did indeed more often attribute failure to personal, global, persistent inadequacies than did nondepressed students.

Metalsky, Halberstadt, and Abramson (1987) have linked attributional style to depressed mood. A study was conducted with college students taking a course in introductory psychology. Early in the semester the students completed the ASQ and a questionnaire concerning their grade aspirations. An adjective checklist was used to collect mood information on two occasions before the midterm exam. Mood was then assessed right after receipt of grades from the exam and again two days later.

According to the reformulated helplessness theory, a tendency to attribute negative events to global and

TABLE 9.3
Instructions and sample item from the Attributional-Style Questionnaire
(*from Seligman et al., 1979*)

Please try to vividly imagine yourself in the situations that follow. If such a situation happened to you, what would you feel would have caused it? While events may have many causes, we want you to pick only one—the *major* cause if this event happened to *you*. Please write this cause in the blank provided after each event. Next we want you to answer some questions about the *cause* and a final question about the *situation*. To summarize, we want you to:

1. Read each situation and vividly imagine it happening to you.
2. Decide what you feel would be the *major* cause of the situation if it happened to you.
3. Write one cause in the blank provided.
4. Answer three questions about the *cause*.
5. Answer one question about the *situation*.
6. Go on to the next situation.

SAMPLE:

YOU HAVE BEEN LOOKING FOR A JOB UNSUCCESSFULLY FOR SOME TIME.

1. Write down *one* major cause _____

2. Is the cause of your unsuccessful job search due to something about you or something about other people or circumstances? (Circle one number)

Totally due to other people or circumstances						Totally due to me
1	2	3	4	5	6	7

3. In the future when looking for a job, will this cause again be present? (Circle one number)

Will never again be present						Will always be present
1	2	3	4	5	6	7

4. Is the cause something that just influences looking for a job, or does it also influence other areas of your life? (Circle one number)

Influences just this particular situation						Influences all situations in my life
1	2	3	4	5	6	7

5. How important would this situation be if it happened to you? (Circle one number)

Not at all important						Extremely important
1	2	3	4	5	6	7

persistent inadequacies, as determined by the ASQ, should predict a more depressed mood in those students who received a poor grade. A poor grade was defined as a failure to match aspirations; this score was weighted by the importance attached to this negative event by the subjects.

The results differed depending on which of the post-exam mood assessments was examined. The outcome of the exam was the major determinant of students' initial mood changes. Those who did poorly became more depressed. Two days later, however, the unstable, specific students had recovered but the stable, global students were still mildly depressed. Following a suggestion by Weiner (1986), Metalsky *et al.* propose that a negative event elicits an immediate emotional response that occurs before any attributions are even made. Subsequently, causal interpretations are sought and a pattern of global, stable attributions makes the initial depressive response last longer.

The latest version of the theory (Abramson, Metalsky, and Alloy, in press) has moved even further away from the original formulation. Some forms of depression (hopelessness depressions) are now regarded as caused by a state of hopelessness, an expectation that desirable outcomes will not occur and that the person has no responses available to change this situation. (The latter part of the definition of hopelessness, of course, refers to helplessness, the central concept of earlier versions of the theory.) As in the attributional reformulation, negative life events (stressors) are seen as interacting with diatheses to yield a hopelessness state. One diathesis is the attributional style pattern that has already been described. However, the theory now considers the possibility that there are other negative diatheses—a tendency to infer that negative life events will have severe negative consequences and a tendency to draw negative inferences about the self.

One advantage of the hopelessness theory is that it can deal directly with co-morbidity of depression and anxiety disorders. In Chapter 6, we noted that panic disorder, agoraphobia, obsessive-compulsive disorder, and PTSD all occurred frequently with depression. Accounting for this pattern poses a major challenge for many theories, for they deal only with a single diagnosis. Alloy, Kelly, Mineka, and Clements (in press) point out several important features of co-morbidity. First, cases of anxiety without depression are relatively common but pure depression is rare. Second, longitudinal studies reveal that anxiety diagnoses typically precede depression. On the basis of a good deal of prior evidence (e.g., Mandler, 1972; Bowlby, 1980), Alloy and her colleagues propose that an expectation of helplessness creates anxiety. When the expectation of helplessness becomes certain, a syndrome with elements of

both depression and anxiety will ensue. Finally, if the perceived probability of the occurrence of negative events becomes certain, hopelessness develops. Although the theory is promising, some problems do need to be addressed in future work.

1. Which type of depression is being modeled? In his original paper Seligman attempted to document the similarity between learned helplessness and "reactive depression," depression indicated in DSM-II to be brought on by stressful life events. But Depue and Monroe (1978) have demonstrated that learned helplessness resembles the symptoms of a bipolar patient in a depressive episode more than it does those of any form of unipolar depression. Clearly, neither Seligman's dogs nor human beings in helplessness studies have exhibited both mania and depression. Seligman's (1978) solution to this problem was to bypass the traditional classification schemes and regard learned helplessness as a model for "helplessness depression." Similarly, Abramson *et al.* (in press) now talk about a hopelessness depression. Only future research will tell whether these solutions are more than circular statements.

2. Can college student populations provide good analogues? Although some research on learned helplessness has been done with clinical populations (e.g., Abramson *et al.*, 1978), many studies have examined college students who are selected on the basis of scores on the Beck Depression Inventory. This inventory was not, however, designed to *diagnose* depression, only to allow an assessment of severity in a clinically diagnosed group. Indeed, accumulating evidence indicates that selecting subjects solely on the basis of elevated BDI scores does not yield a group of people who can serve as a good analogue for those with clinical depression. Hammen (1980), for example, found that high scorers, with a mean of 18.37, were down to an average of only 10.87 when retested two to three weeks later. This transient nature of a high BDI score is particularly important because it is common research practice to test potential subjects with the BDI and then have them participate in a research study several weeks or even months later. Hammen's results, then, caution us that some subjects designated as depressed on the BDI might not in fact be depressed by the time the actual study takes place.

3. Are the findings specific to depression? This issue is raised by the results of a learned-helplessness study that Lavelle, Metalsky, and Coyne (1979) conducted with subjects classified as having high or low test anxiety. The subjects with high test anxiety performed a task poorly after going through a laboratory situation

BOX 9.2

LIFE STRESS AND DEPRESSION

In Chapter 8 we described research on the relationship between life stress and the occurrence of various physical illnesses. A great deal of similar research has been done to show that life stress is also linked to the onset of depression. Many of these studies have used the same general methodologies that we described earlier: a group of depressed people and a control group are given a life events checklist and asked to indicate which items had been experienced in the past six months or year. The data consistently show that depressives report more stressful events (Paykel, 1979), although it remains possible that their recall is biased by their current psychological state. More recently, investigators studying life events and depression, like their counterparts studying life events and illness, have turned their attention to possible moderators of the stress–depression relation. Billings, Cronkite, and Moos (1983), for example, found that depressives have fewer social resources available to them and are less likely to try to solve the problems they face.

In an attempt to study similar issues and at the same time to improve the quality of data, Brown and Harris (1978) began a large-scale study of depressed women in London. Instead of using a life events checklist, they constructed a detailed interview and carefully trained interviewers to question subjects about any recent adversities that had distressed them. The truthfulness of the women's reports was checked by interviewing relatives. Moreover, trained members of the research staff rated the stressfulness of the events, rather than letting the respondents do the evaluation. Using these methods, Brown and Harris found that 61 percent of depressive women but only 25 percent of the control subjects had experienced a severely disturbing life event in the nine months prior to the interview. The majority of these misfortunes were long term and wrenching, such as separation from a key person, for example, her husband, a life-threatening illness of someone close, a major disappointment, or loss of her job. Social supports were also found to be crucial. When the women were divided into those who had an intimate friend in whom they confided and those who did not, the effects of stress were quite different. Only 10 percent of the women with an intimate relationship who experienced a misfortune became depressed; the corresponding figure for the women without a confidant was 37 percent! Thus, stress has a much greater impact on women with few social supports.

---

inducing helplessness. Thus the learned-helplessness phenomenon may not be specific to depression. Similarly, highly anxious persons blame their failures on themselves, just as depressives do (Doris and Sarason, 1955). The newer hopelessness theory may fare better in distinguishing between anxiety and depression.

4. Are attributions relevant? At issue here is the underlying assumption that people actively attempt to explain their own behavior to themselves and that the attributions they make have subsequent effects on behavior. Some research indicates that making attributions is not a universal process. For example, Hanusa and Schulz (1977) allowed subjects in a helplessness experiment to make open-ended attributions about their successes or failures. Subjects did not spontaneously report either, and even after probing, the reported attributions did not fall into specific categories. Furthermore, relating attributions to behavior has been difficult. Indeed, in a series of experiments, Nisbett and Wilson (1977) showed that people are frequently unaware of the causes of their behavior.[2]

Even if we allow that attributions are relevant and powerful determinants of behavior, we should note that many findings suppporting the learned-helplessness theory have been gathered by giving individuals the ASQ or by determining how they explain laboratory-induced successes or failures. When depressives were asked about the five most stressful events of their lives, however, their attributions did not differ from those given by normal subjects (Hammen and Cochran, 1981; see Box 9.2).

---

[2]The attribution literature makes the basic assumption that people *care* what the causes of their behavior are. This central idea is the brainchild of psychologists whose business it is to explain behavior. It may be that psychologists have projected their own need to explain behavior onto other people! Laypeople may simply not reflect on why they act and feel as they do to the same extent that psychologists do.

5. Some research has refuted some aspects of the theory. In a series of studies, Alloy and Abramson (1979) examined one of its central points, that depressed people perceive themselves as having little control over their lives. Subjects were placed in various experimental situations manipulated by the experimenter to give predetermined percentages of contingency between their responses and an outcome. After subjects had experienced some actual percentage or level of control, they were asked how much control they *believed* that they had had. Contrary to the theory, depressed students did not underestimate their degree of control. Using a classic experimental situation to induce helplessness in subjects, Ford and Neale (1985) similarly found that the students did not underestimate their control on the subsequent task.

One key assumption of all versions of learned-helplessness theory is that the depressive attributional style is a persistent part of the makeup of depressed people. Using a battery of measures, including the ASQ, Hamilton and Abramson (1983) carefully tested diagnosed depressives on two occasions, first while they were in the midst of an episode of depression, and again just before they were discharged from the hospital. Results from the first assessment revealed the expected depressive pattern on the ASQ. But the information gathered just before the patients were discharged indicated that the pattern was no longer present.

Learned helplessness theory has clearly stimulated a great deal of research and further theorizing about depression. It seems destined to continue to do so for many years to come.

Interpersonal Aspects of Depression

In this section, we discuss aspects of depression that generally involve relationships between the depressed person and others. Some of the data we present may be relevant to the etiology of depression and some to its course.

In Chapter 8 we discussed the role of social support in health. The concept has also been applied to research on depression. Depressives have spare social networks and regard them as less supportive. As shown clearly in Box 9.2, reduced social support lessens the individual's ability to handle negative life events.

Is it simply fate that confronts the depressive with an inadequate level of social support? Perhaps, but it is also possible that the depressed person plays a role. One possibility is that depressed people are low in social skills (Lewinsohn, 1974). A number of studies have

Having a close friend to confide in makes it less likely that a person will become depressed after experiencing some major life stress.

indeed demonstrated such deficits across a variety of measures—interpersonal problem solving (Gottlib and Asarnow, 1979), speech patterns, and maintenance of eye contact (Gottlib and Robinson, 1982; Gottlib, 1982).

As suggested by Coyne (1976), depressed people may elicit negative reactions from others. This possibility has been studied in a variety of ways, ranging from telephone interactions with depressed patients, listening to audiotapes of depressed patients, and even in face-to-face interactions. These data show that depressives have an aversive interpersonal style that elicits rejection from others (for a review see Gottlib and Whiffin, in press). Not surprisingly, given these findings, depression and marital discord frequently co-occur and the interactions of depressed people and their spouses are characterized by hostility (Kowalik and Gottlib, 1987). Indeed, Hooley (1986) has shown that the critical comments of spouses of depressed people are a significant predictor of recurrence of depression.

Do any of these interpersonal characteristics of depressed people precede the onset of depression? Some research using the high-risk method (see page 119) suggests that the answer is yes. For example, the behavior of elementary-school-aged children of depressed parents is rated negatively by both teachers and peers (Weintraub, Liebert, and Neale, 1975; Weintraub, Prinz, and Neale, 1978). In sum, interpersonal behavior appears to play a major role in depression.

Psychological Theories of Bipolar Disorder

Bipolar disorder has been neglected by both psychological theorists and researchers, probably because only between 5 to 10 percent of depressions are found in people who also have bouts of mania. In general, theories of the depressive phase of bipolar disorder are similar to theories of unipolar depression. The manic phase of the disorder is seen as a defense against a debilitating psychological state. The specific negative state that is being avoided varies from theory to theory. One of our own cases illustrates why many theorists have concluded that the manic state serves a defensive function.

A forty-two-year-old male was currently in his third manic episode. During each he had had the classic pattern of manic symptoms, and much of his manic behavior centered around a grandiose delusion that he was the world's greatest businessman. "Did you know that I've already bought twenty companies today?" he stated at the beginning of a therapy session. "Not even Getty or Rockefeller have anything on me." From sessions between episodes, it was apparent that success in business was indeed a central concern to the patient. But he was far from successful. His parents had loaned him money to start several companies, but each had gone bankrupt. He was obsessed with matching the business successes of his wealthy father, but as the years passed his opportunities to do so were slipping away. It seemed, therefore, that his manic grandiosity was protecting him from a confrontation with his lack of business success—a realization that would likely have plunged him into a deep depression.

Clinical experience with manics as well as studies of their personalities when they are in remission indicate that they appear well adjusted between episodes. But if mania is a defense, it must be a defense against something, although probably not a characteristic that would be readily self-reported. Using means other than a conventional paper-and-pencil test Winters and Neale (1985) have recently tested the notion that manics, even when between episodes, have little self-esteem.

Manics, unipolar depressives, and normal subjects were given two tests, a self-esteem inventory and a pragmatic inference test. The second was meant to be a subtle measure of the manics' expected low self-esteem. In the pragmatic inference test subjects first read a paragraph describing a series of events, some of which had a positive outcome, the others a negative one. Subjects were then given a test that appeared to measure their recall of each story. Some items actually assessed recall of facts, but others forced the subject to go beyond the information and draw an inference. For example, one story concerned a man who was currently out of work. The reason for his unemployment was not stated directly, but the story was constructed to allow either of two inferences to be drawn. The subject could infer that the man was unemployed through no fault of his own but because the economy was poor. Or the subject could infer that the man's poor work record kept him unemployed. People with low self-esteem were expected to make the second inference.

The results agreed exactly with expectation. On the paper-and-pencil measure of self-esteem, both the manics and normal subjects scored higher than the depressives. But on the pragmatic inference test the manics performed like the depressives; both groups drew the second inferences and revealed their low self-esteem. Thus the self-esteem of manics may be very low. Generally, however, their feelings of inadequacy are successfully defended against.

Physiological Theories of Mood Disorders

Since physiological processes are known to have considerable effects on moods, it is not surprising that investigators have sought physiological causes for depression and mania. Moreover, disturbed physiological processes must of course be part of the causal chain if a predisposition for a mood disorder can be genetically transmitted. Evidence indicating that a mood disorder is, in part, inherited would, then, provide some support for the view that the disorder has a physiological basis.

The Genetic Data

Research on genetic factors in unipolar depression and bipolar disorder has used the family, twin, and adoptee methods. Estimates of the frequency of mood disorders in first-degree relatives of bipolars range from about 10 to 20 percent (Slater, 1938; Perris, 1969; Brodie and

Leff, 1971; Hays, 1976). Approximately 6 percent of the relatives of bipolar probands are at risk for bipolar disorder (Rice *et al.*, 1987). Risk among the relatives increases with early onset of the disorder among the probands. These figures are higher than those for the general population. Notably, among the first-degree relatives of bipolar index cases, there are more cases of unipolar depression than bipolar disorder. For example, James and Chapman (1975), in a thorough study conducted in New Zealand, found the morbidity risk estimates for the first-degree relatives of bipolars to be 6.4 percent for bipolar disorder and 13.2 percent for unipolar depression. Allen (1976) has reviewed concordance data for bipolar disorder in twins. Overall, the concordance rate for bipolar disorder in identical twins was 72 percent and in fraternal twins only 14 percent. The evidence supports the notion that bipolar disorder may have a heritable component.

The information available on unipolar depression indicates that genetic factors, although important, do not figure to the same extent that they do in bipolar disorder. In fact, although the relatives of unipolar probands are at increased risk for unipolar depression, their risk is less than that among relatives of bipolar probands (Andreasen *et al.*, 1987). Relatives of unipolar probands are also not at especially high risk for bipolar disorder. Early onset of depression and co-morbidity with an anxiety disorder or alcoholism confer greater risk on the relatives (Weissman *et al.*, 1986). Studies of unipolar depression in twins usually report MZ concordances of about 40 percent and DZ concordances of about 11 percent (Allen, 1976).

Earlier we mentioned the great heterogeneity of unipolar depressions. Some of the genetic data collected over the past decade bear on this issue. Winokur (1979) has noted differences in the disorders found in the first-degree relatives of unipolars. Both male and female first-degree relatives of men whose depression occurs for the first time rather late in life, after age forty, are at about equal risk for depression. But for male and female first-degree relatives of women whose first episode of depression begins earlier, the pattern is different. The female relatives are at greater risk for depression than male relatives, who are at greater risk for alcoholism and sociopathy. Although these data are not yet fully understood, they do suggest that the diagnosis unipolar depression may actually cover several disorders with different etiologies.

Taken together, the family and twin studies suggest that both *bipolar disorder* and *unipolar depression have heritable components*. This conclusion is further supported by studies that have used the adoption method. Mendlewicz and Rainer (1977) found more mood disorders in the biological parents than in the adoptive

parents of bipolar adoptees. Also, Cadoret (1978a) found more mood disorders in adopted children whose biological parents had an affective disorder. Finally, Wender *et al.* (1986) found that the biological relatives of adopted index cases were eight times more likely to have a mood disorder.

An exciting development in genetic research on mood disorders is the use of what is called *linkage analysis.* The technique involves studying the occurrence of mood disorder across a family pedigree and simultaneously assessing some other characteristic—a genetic marker—for which the genetics are fully understood (e.g., red-green color blindness is known to result from mutations on the X chromosome). When the genes are linked, that is, when they are sufficiently close together on a chromosome, the family pedigree will tend to show that the two traits being examined are inherited together. There are two reports of successful linkage analysis, with different results. Egeland and her colleagues (1987) have reported an analysis of linkage in a large composite family of the Old Order Amish. Large family size, prohibition of alcohol and drug use, and the closed nature of Amish society made it ideal for study. Based on earlier research, Egeland and her colleagues examined two markers on chromosome 11, insulin and a cancer gene. In the pedigree examined, a predisposition to affective disorder was governed by a dominant gene at the tip of the short arm of chromosome 11. In other research, Biron and his colleagues (1987) found linkage between bipolar disorder and the X chromosome in three pedigrees studied in Israel. These results indicate that we might expect the mood disorders to have genetic heterogeneity (i.e., to result from different genes in different people with the disorders). It may be that mutations at different loci are related to a predisposition to mood disorders in different people.

Biochemistry and Mood Disorders

Two major theories have been proposed relating depression to *neurotransmitters* (see Box 6.5). One theory suggests that depression results from low levels of *norepinephrine;* the other points to low levels of *serotonin*. The norepinephrine theory also postulates that an excess of this neurotransmitter causes mania (Schildkraut, 1965).

The actions of drugs provided the clues on which both theories are based. In the 1950s two particular groups of drugs, the *tricyclics* and the *monoamine oxidase inhibitors,* were found to be effective in relieving depression. Studies revealed that they also increase the levels of both serotonin and norepinephrine in the brains of animals. This information only suggested that depression is caused by low levels of these substances, but it encouraged further explorations. Another piece of evidence favoring both theories was provided by reserpine, a drug sometimes used in the treatment of hypertension. Also in the 1950s reserpine had been isolated by a research team working in Switzerland. It is an alkaloid of the root of *Rauwolfia serpentina*, a shrub that grows in India. Hindu physicians have for centuries administered powdered rauwolfia as a treatment for mental illness. Reserpine became one of the compounds to initiate the modern era of psychopharmacology and to revolutionize the care and treatment of mental patients. This drug and chlorpromazine were given to schizophrenics to calm their agitation. Reserpine did indeed relax and sedate them but was soon contraindicated since depression was a serious side effect in about 15 percent of the patients taking it (e.g., Lemieux, Davignon, and Genest, 1965). Reserpine was discovered to reduce levels of both serotonin and norepinephrine by impairing the process by which these substances are stored within the synaptic vesicles, allowing them instead to become degraded by monoamine oxidase.

So far we have examined *indirect* evidence for each theory. It would be ideal if the levels of norepinephrine, serotonin, or both could be measured within the brains of depressed people. This has not yet been done, so we must take another tack. Two approaches have been used. The first measures metabolites of these neurotransmitters, the by-products of the breakdown of serotonin and norepinephrine, as they are found in urine, blood serum, and the cerebrospinal fluid. The problem with such measurements is that they are not direct reflections of *brain* levels of either serotonin or norepinephrine, since serotonin is involved in other bodily processes and norepinephrine also acts in the peripheral nervous system.

A second strategy would be to choose drugs other than the antidepressants and reserpine that are known either to increase or to decrease the brain levels of serotonin and norepinephrine. A drug raising the level of a neurotransmitter should alleviate depression; one reducing it should deepen depression or induce it in normal subjects. This strategy also has its problems, however. Most drugs have multiple effects, making it difficult to choose one that accomplishes a specific purpose without complicating side effects.

These problems notwithstanding, what can be said of the validity of these theories that blame low levels of norepinephrine or serotonin for depression and high levels of norepinephrine for mania? First, a series of studies conducted by Bunney and Murphy and their colleagues at the National Institute of Mental Health monitored closely the urinary levels of norepinephrine itself in a group of bipolar patients as they cycled through

stages of depression, mania, and normalcy. Urinary levels of norepinephrine decreased as patients became depressed (Bunney *et al.*, 1970) and increased during mania (Bunney, Goodwin, and Murphy, 1972). Despite such evidence, however, it has become clear that the theory that a lack of norepinephrine causes depression is untenable. Several lines of evidence support this conclusion. 3-Methoxy-4-hydroxyphenyl glycol (MHPG) is considered to be norepinephrine's principal metabolite. According to the theory, low levels of norepinephrine should be reflected by low levels of urinary MHPG. Although depressed bipolars have generally been shown to have low levels of urinary MHPG, the amount of MHPG in the urine of unipolars does not differ from that of controls (e.g., Muscettola *et al.*, 1984).

Studies of serotonin rely on 5-hydroxyindoleacetic acid (5-HIAA), a major metabolite of serotonin that is present in cerebrospinal fluid. It can be measured to determine the level of the transmitter in the brain and spinal cord. A fairly consistent body of data indicates that 5-HIAA levels are low in the cerebrospinal fluid of depressives (see McNeal and Cimbolic, 1986, for a review). Studies also show that ingestion of L-tryptophan, which acts as a serotonin precursor, relieves depression, especially when used in combination with other drugs (Coppen *et al.*, 1972; Mendels *et al.*, 1975). Furthermore, p-cholorophenylalanine (PCPA), which suppresses serotonin synthesis by blocking tryptophan hydroxylase, reduces the therapeutic effect of drugs that usually lessen depression (Shopsin, Friedman, and Gershon, 1976).

We have already indicated that effective antidepressants increase levels of norepinephrine and serotonin and that knowledge of this formed a keystone of the norepinephrine and serotonin theories of depression. It now appears, however, that the therapeutic effects of tricyclics and MAO inhibitors do *not* depend on an increase in the levels of neurotransmitters. The earlier findings were not incorrect; tricyclics and MAO inhibitors do indeed increase levels of norepinephrine and serotonin *when they are first taken*. But after several days the levels of neurotransmitters return to what they had been earlier. This information is crucial because it does *not* fit with our knowledge of the time that must pass before antidepressants become effective. Both tricyclics and MAO inhibitors take from seven to fourteen days to relieve depression! Thus a simple increase in norepinephrine or serotonin is not a plausible mechanism (Heninger, Charney, and Menkes, 1983). Another key finding that has prompted a move away from the original theories comes from studies of new antidepressants. Although they are not yet commercially available, several drugs—for example, mianserin and zimeldine—seem to be effective antidepressants (Cole,

1986), and neither of these drugs simply increases the amount of norepinephrine or serotonin!

What is the impact of these new findings on the old theories? Researchers are now examining whether tricyclics and MAO inhibitors may act against depression by altering postsynaptic receptors. At this time, results are contradictory and difficult to interpret. Antidepressants seem to decrease the sensitivity of β-adrenergic receptors yet increase the sensitivity of serotonin receptors (McNeal and Cimbolic, 1986). This attention to receptors means that new methodologies must be developed to study receptor sensitivity in human beings. Most of our current knowledge of the functioning of receptors comes from animal studies. As yet, the methods used in human studies are indirect. The next few years of research will undoubtedly see further refinements so that receptor functions can be more thoroughly explored.

The Neuroendocrine System

Many studies also suggest a role for the neuroendocrine system in depression. The limbic area of the brain (see Box A.1) is closely linked to emotion and also has effects on the hypothalamus. The hypothalamus, in turn, controls various endocrine glands and thus the levels of hormones they secrete. Hormones secreted by the hypothalamus also affect the pituitary and the hormones it produces. Of particular relevance to depression is the hypothalamic–pituitary–adrenal cortical axis. It is thought that this system is overactive in depression.

Various findings support this proposition. Levels of cortisol (an adrenocortical hormone) are high in depressives and this finding even led to the development of a biological test for depression—the dexamethasone suppression test (DST). Dexamethasone is a glucocorticoid that suppresses cortisol secretion. When given dexamethasone during an overnight test, some depressives, especially those with melancholia, were found to "escape" from the usual suppressing effects (Carroll, 1982; Poland *et al.*, 1987). The interpretation is that the failure of dexamethasone to suppress cortisol reflects overactivity in the hypothalamic–pituitary–adrenal cortical axis. This failure to show suppression normalizes when the depressive episode ends, indicating that it might be a nonspecific response to stress. Another finding linking high levels of cortisol to depression is found in a disease called Cushing's syndrome. Abnormal growths on the adrenal cortex lead to oversecretion of cortisol and an ensuing depression. Hypercortisolemia in depression may also be linked to the neurotransmitter theories we just discussed. High levels of cortisol may lower the density of serotonin receptors (Roy *et al.*,

1987) and impair the function of noradrenergic receptors (Price *et al.*, 1986).

These biological data lend some support to theories that affective disorders have physiological causes. Does this mean that psychological theories are irrelevant or useless? Not in the least. To assert that behavioral disorders have a basis in somatic processes is to state the obvious. No psychogenic theorist would deny that behavior is mediated by some kinds of bodily changes. The question rather is how psychological and physiological factors interact. We have already grappled with this philosophical issue in Chapter 8. It may well be, for example, that alteration of norepinephrine receptors does cause certain kinds of depression, but that an earlier link in the causal chain is "the sense of helplessness" or "paralysis of will" that psychological theorists have proposed as the disabler.

Therapy for Mood Disorders

Most episodes of depression lift after a few months, although the time may seem immeasurably longer to the depressed individual and to those close to him. That most depressions are self-limiting is fortunate. However, mental health workers have not forsaken the depressed person. Depression is too widespread and too incapacitating, both to the person[3] and to those around him or her, not to treat the disorder. Current therapies are both psychological and somatic. Singly or in combination, they turn out to be quite effective.

Psychological Therapies

Because depression is considered to be derived from anger unconsciously turned inward, psychoanalytic treatment tries to help the patient achieve insight into the repressed conflict and often encourages outward release of the hostility supposedly working inward. In the most general terms, the goal of analytic therapy is to uncover latent motivations for the patient's depression. A man may, for example, blame himself for the the death of a loved one, as did the engineer described earlier, but repress this belief because of the pain it causes. The patient must first be guided to confront the fact that he holds this belief, after which the therapist

---

[3]Depression can be more than a serious inconvenience. It can be life-threatening, for the risk of suicide is especially great in depressed individuals. The last section of this chapter is devoted to suicide.

can help him realize that his guilt is unfounded. The recovery of memories of stressful circumstances of the patient's childhood, at which time feelings of inadequacy and loss may have developed, should also bring relief.

Research on the effectiveness of dynamic psychotherapy in alleviating depression is sparse (Klerman, 1988). The few investigations carried out have not found such treatment making a significant impact on the problem (Hollon and Beck, 1979). For example, psychoanalytic therapy combined with tricyclic drugs, which have proved useful, does not lift mood any more than do the drugs by themselves (Daneman, 1961; Covi *et al.*, 1974). **However, recent findings from a large scale study (p. 553) suggest that some forms of psychodynamic therapy are effective for unipolar depression.**

In keeping with their cognitive theory of depression, that the profound sadness and shattered self-esteem of depressed individuals are caused by errors in their thinking, Aaron Beck and his associates have worked for several years to devise a cognitive therapy aimed at altering aberrant thought patterns. The therapist tries to persuade the depressed person to change his or her opinions of events and of the self. When a client states that she is worthless because "Nothing goes right. Everything I try to do ends in a disaster," the therapist offers examples contrary to this overgeneralization, such as competences that the client is either overlooking or discounting. The therapist also instructs the patient to monitor her "private monologues" with herself and to identify all patterns of thought that contribute to depression. She is then taught to think through her negative prevailing beliefs, to understand how they prevent her from making more realistic and positive assumptions and from more accurately interpreting adversity.

Although developed independently of Ellis's rational-emotive method, Beck's analyses are similar to it in some ways. For example, he suggests that depressed people are likely to consider themselves totally inept and incompetent if they make a mistake. This can be considered an extension of one of Ellis's irrational beliefs, that the individual must be competent in all things in order to be a worthwhile person.

Beck also includes more strictly behavioral components in his treatment of depression. Especially when patients are severely depressed, Beck encourages them to *do* things, such as getting out of bed in the morning, and discourages them from doing other things, such as attempting suicide. Beck gives his patients activity assignments that will provide them with successful experiences and allow them to think well of themselves. But the overall emphasis is on cognitive restructuring, on persuading the person to think differently. If a change

in overt behavior will help in achieving that goal, fine. Behavioral change by itself, however, without altering the errors in logic that Beck asserts depressed people commit, cannot be expected to alleviate depression in any significant way.

A widely cited comparative therapy by Rush and his colleagues (1977), discussed in Chapter 19 (page 551), has indicated that Beck's cognitive therapy is more successful in alleviating unipolar depression than the common regimen of administering an antidepressant drug, the tricyclic imipramine (Tofranil). This superiority, maintained at a six-month follow-up and also at twelve months (Kovacs *et al.*, 1981), has encouraged many other researchers to adopt the therapy and to develop it further. Previous research had shown imipramine to be superior to insight-oriented psychotherapy in treating depression, which renders all the more impressive the finding that Beck's cognitive therapy was better than a standard course of pharmacotherapy. These original findings have since been replicated and extended by other investigators (e.g., Hollon, DeRubeis, Tuason, Weimer, Evans, and Garvey, 1989; Seligman *et al.*, 1988; Simons, Murphy, Levine, and Wetzel, 1985; Teasdale, Fennell, Hibbert, and Amies, 1984), including data showing that Beck's therapy has a prophylactic effect in preventing subsequent bouts of depression (Blackburn, Eunson, and Bishop, 1986). This growing body of research has prompted Beck to conclude in a clinical vein that "it would seem desirable that if a patient is placed on drugs, to offer him cognitive therapy in addition. However, if he is receiving cognitive therapy [already], it is not clear that adding drugs would be indicated except for the more severely depressed patients in a hospital outpatient clinic" (Beck, 1986, p. 3).

Sometimes a person has reason to be depressed. A woman who is disheartened because of the way that she is treated by men might be better advised by a feminist therapist, who will encourage her to resist continued subjugation by an overbearing spouse or boss, than by an equally well-intentioned cognitive therapist, who might try to teach her that the treatment she receives from husband or supervisor is not all that bad. As with forms of therapy for a wide range of human problems, the therapist must confront the moral and political implications of his or her work. Should I help the client alter her life situation, or should I help her adjust? Indeed, the very fact that the woman is depressed may indicate that she is ready for a change in her social and personal relations with others. The depression, then, may be a healthy sign, one that should be heeded as a signal that all is not well in her life.

Although Seligman's learned-helplessness theory is a widely held conception of depression, as yet no spe-

BOX 9.3

AN EXISTENTIAL THEORY OF DEPRESSION AND ITS TREATMENT

In 1959 a remarkable book, *From Death Camp to Existentialism,* was published by Viktor Frankl, an Austrian psychiatrist who during World War II had spent three horrible years in Nazi concentration camps. His wife, brother, and parents, imprisoned with him, all lost their lives. Revised since its initial appearance and retitled *Man's Search for Meaning* (1963), Frankl's book vividly describes the humiliation, suffering, and terror experienced by camp prisoners. Frankl goes on to tell how he and others managed to survive psychologically in the brutalizing conditions of the death camps.

Frankl concluded that he was sustained emotionally by having succeeded somehow in finding meaning in his suffering and relating it to his spiritual life. The spirit gives the individual freedom to transcend circumstances, and freedom makes him responsible for his life. Frankl believes that psychopathology, particularly depression, ensues when a person has no purpose in living. Out of his concentration camp experiences he developed a psychotherapeutic approach called **logotherapy,** after the Greek word *logos,* translatable as meaning.

The task of logotherapy is to restore meaning to the client's life. This is accomplished first by accepting in an empathic way the subjective experience of the client's suffering, rather than conveying the message that suffering is sick and wrong and should therefore not be regarded as normal. The logotherapist then helps the client make some sense out of his or her suffering by placing it within a larger context, a philosophy of life in which the individual assumes responsibility for his or her existence and for pursuing the values inherent in life. Nietzche has said, "He who has a why to live for can bear with almost any how."

It may be useful to relate Frankl's views on depression and its treatment to learned helplessness. Certainly the concentration camp induced helplessness and hopelessness, an utter disbelief that an individual could exert any

control over his or her life. Profound depression was commonplace. Logotherapy might be an effective way to reverse the helplessness depressed people experience in contemporary society, under less horrific and brutal conditions. By accepting responsibility for their lives and by seeking some meaning even in trying circumstances, they may achieve a sense of control and competence indispensable to forging an acceptable existence.

Viktor Frankl's best known technique is called paradoxical intention. Patients are told to indulge their symptoms intentionally. If a depressed man has been unable to leave his bed until noon, he should stay there until evening. Exaggeration can bring this symptom under conscious control.

---

cific program of therapy based on this view has been developed. One recent study by Seligman *et al.* (1988) did find that unipolar depressives successfully treated at Beck's Center for Cognitive Therapy at the University of Pennsylvania showed changes in their attributional style in the direction of less global, internal, and stable attributions for negative events. Similar findings have been reported by Firth-Cozens and Brewin (1988) employing both cognitive therapy and a less behavioral, "exploratory" treatment. Although these findings are consistent with the attributional reformulation of the learned-helplessness theory of depression, they do not provide data relevant to a specific therapy based on that

theory since it was Beck's therapy and a nonbehavioral method that were reported on. Overall, the growing research literature on learned helplessness has sensitized therapists in a general way to the need that many depressed people have to achieve a sense of competence and of control over events in their lives, and indeed to the need that all human beings have to believe that they command their own destinies (see Box 9.3).

One of the few studies attempting to match type of patient to type of treatment was done by McKnight, Nelson, Hayes, and Jarrett (1984). Adult women diagnosed as having a mood disorder were assigned either to rational-emotive therapy or social skills training and then switched to the other treatment in an alternating treatments design. Significant and enduring (one-year follow-up) treatment effects, which did not differ from each other, were found on a variety of measures for both therapies. What is particularly interesting in this study is that, prior to treatment, a subset of three subjects had been identified as having special difficulties with irrational thinking and the other three with social skills deficits. A close analysis of session-by-session progress showed that the irrational group benefited more from RET than from social skills training, with the reverse holding true for the socially deficient patients. The implication is clear: depression can be caused by a variety of factors, and optimal treatment should be chosen on the basis of efforts to match those factors with the nature of a given therapy (Haaga and Davison, 1989).

Somatic Therapies

There are a variety of somatic therapies for depression and mania. Perhaps the most dramatic, and controversial, treatment for depresson is **electroconvulsive therapy** (ECT). ECT was originated by two Italian physicians, Ugo Cerletti and Lucio Bini, in the early twentieth century. Cerletti had been interested in epilepsy and was seeking a means by which its seizures could be

experimentally induced. The "solution" became apparent to him during a visit to a slaughterhouse, where he saw animals rendered unconscious by electric shocks administered to the head. Shortly thereafter he found that by applying electric shocks to the sides of the human head, he could produce full epileptic seizures. Not long thereafter, in 1938 in Rome, he used the technique on a schizophrenic patient.

In the decades that followed, ECT was used with both schizophrenic and psychotically depressed patients, usually in hospital settings. For the most part its use nowadays is restricted to profoundly depressed individuals. ECT entails the deliberate induction of a seizure and momentary unconsciousness by passing a current of between 70 and 130 volts through the patient's brain. Electrodes were formerly placed on each side of the forehead, but now the standard procedure is to put one on the temple of the nondominant cerebral hemisphere. In the past the patient was usually awake until the current triggered the seizure, and the electric shock often created frightening contortions of the body, sometimes even causing bone fractures. Now the patient is given a short-acting anesthetic, then an injection of a strong muscle relaxant before the current is applied. The convulsive spasms of the body muscles are barely perceptible to onlookers, and the patient awakens a few minutes later, remembering nothing about the treatment.

This woman has just undergone shock treatment. Oxygen is being administered because the muscle relaxant given earlier interferes with breathing.

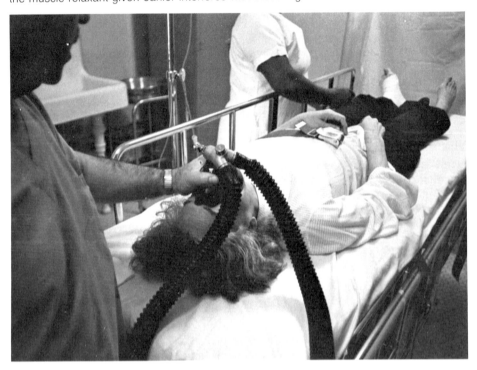

Inducing a seizure still remains a drastic procedure, however. Why should anyone in his right but depressed mind agree to undergo such radical therapy, or how could a parent or a spouse consent to such treatment if the patient is judged legally incapable of giving consent? The answer is simple. Although we don't know why, ECT may be the optimal treatment for severe depression (Klerman, 1972, 1988). Most professionals, though, acknowledge the risks involved—memory loss that can be prolonged, although unilateral ECT to the nondominant hemisphere now erases fewer memories than did bilateral ECT; confusion; perhaps even some brain damage when shocks are administered repeatedly. Clinicians typically resort to ECT only after less drastic treatments have been tried and found wanting. In considering *any* treatment that has negative side effects, the person making the decision must be aware of the consequences of not providing any treatment at all. Given that suicide is a real possibility among depressed people, and given a moral stance that values the preservation of life, the use of ECT, at least after other treatments have failed, is regarded by many as defensible and responsible.

The two major categories of antidepressant drugs are the tricyclics, such as imipramine (Tofranil) and amitriptyline (Elavil), and the monoamine oxidase (MAO) inhibitors, such as Parnate. Since the MAO inhibitors have by far the more serious side effects, the tricyclics are more widely used. These medications have been established as effective in a number of double-blind studies (Davidson *et al.*, 1988; Morris and Beck, 1974).Both types of drugs are believed to ameliorate depression by facilitating neural transmission. Practitioners do not rely exclusively on drugs like Tofranil because once the patient has withdrawn from the drug, relapse is more often the rule than the exception (Klerman, 1975). "Symptomatic relief" is, as already stated, of no small importance in problems like depression, but the patient should be able to stop taking the drug during periods when symptoms have lessened. The simple truth is that, at least so far, no chemical has been found that can "cure" depression.

Even if a chemical agent manages to alleviate a bout of depression only temporarily, that benefit in itself should not be underestimated, given the potential for suicide in depression and given the extreme anguish and suffering borne by the individual, and usually by the family as well. Moreover, the judicious use of a drug may make unnecessary an avenue of intervention and control that many regard as very much a last resort, namely, being placed in a psychiatric hospital. Many clinicians recommend combining antidepressant medications with some form of psychological intervention (Klerman, 1988).

People with the mood swings of bipolar disorder are often helped by carefully monitored dosages of **lithium,** an element, taken in a salt form, lithium carbonate. The fact that lithium carbonate cannot be patented like other drugs discouraged pharmaceutical companies for years from marketing it; only minimal profits are to be made. Lithium is now taken regularly and prophylactically, that is, every day in the absence of problems in order to prevent radical shifts in mood (Davis, 1976; Prien *et al.*, 1984). One of the consequences of the medication, however, is that it prevents bipolars from feeling extremely good on occasion (Honigfeld and Howard, 1978), and it is not always easy for them to forgo occasional euphoria. Indeed, two or three hospitalizations are often necessary before the patient's cooperation is enlisted; unfortunately by the time this is achieved, major damage has been wreaked on career, marriages, finances, and reputation. Because of possibly serious, even fatal side effects, lithium has to be prescribed and used very carefully.

Suicide

In classical Rome, in the period just preceding the Christian era, the quality of life was viewed as far more important than how long one lived. "Living is not good, but living well. The wise man, therefore, lives as well as he should, not as long as he can. . . . He will always think of life in terms of quality not quantity" wrote the first-century Roman Stoic philosopher Seneca (as cited in Shneidman, 1973, p. 384). Then in its first centuries, Christianity was a persecuted religion; many early Christians committed suicide in acts of martyrdom (Heyd and Block, 1981). Western thought changed radically in the fourth century, when St. Augustine proclaimed suicide a crime because it violated the Sixth Commandment, Thou shalt not kill. St. Thomas Aquinas elaborated on this view in the thirteenth century, declaring suicide to be a mortal sin because it usurped God's power over life and death. So, although neither the Old Testament nor the New explicitly forbids suicide, the Western world came to regard it as a crime and a sin (Shneidman, 1973). The irony is that the Christian injunctions against suicide, deriving from a profound respect for life, contributed to persecution of those who attempted to take their own lives. Indeed, as late as 1823 anyone in London who took his own life was buried with a stake pounded through his heart, and not until 1961 did suicide cease to be a criminal offense in England. In this country only Oklahoma and Alabama consider suicide a crime, but what penalty can be

BOX 9.4

SOME MYTHS ABOUT SUICIDE

There are many prevalent misconceptions about suicide (Pokorny, 1968; Shneidman, 1973).

1. *People who discuss suicide will not commit the act.* The fact is that up to three-quarters of those who take their lives have communicated beforehand, perhaps as a cry for help, perhaps to taunt.

2. *Suicide is committed without warning.* The falseness of of this belief is readily indicated by the preceding statement. The person usually gives many warnings, such as saying that the world would be better off without him, or making unexpected and inexplicable gifts to others, often of his most valued possessions.

3. *Only people of a certain class commit suicide.* Suicide is actually neither the curse of the poor nor the disease of the rich. People in all classes commit suicide.

4. *Membership in a particular religious group is a good predictor that a person will not consider suicide.* It is mistakenly thought that the strong Catholic prohibition against suicide makes the risk that Catholics will take their lives much lower. This is not supported by the evidence, perhaps because an individual's formal religious identification is not always an accurate index of true beliefs.

5. *The motives for suicide are easily established.* The truth is that we do not fully understand why people commit suicide. For example, the fact that a severe reverse in finances precedes a suicide does not mean that the reversal adequately explains the suicide.

6. *All who commit suicide are depressed.* This fallacy may account for the tragic fact that signs of impending suicide are overlooked because the person does not act despondently. Many of the people who take their lives are *not* depressed. In fact, some people appear calm and at peace with themselves.

7. *A person with a terminal physical illness is unlikely to commit suicide.* A person's awareness of impending death does not preclude suicide. Perhaps the wish to end their own suffering or that of their loved ones impels many to choose the time of their death.

8. *To commit suicide is insane.* Although most suicidal persons are very unhappy, most do appear to be completely rational and in touch with reality.

9. *A tendency to commit suicide is inherited.* Since suicides often run in families, the assumption is made that the tendency to think in terms of self-annihilation is inherited. There is no evidence for this.

10. *Suicide is influenced by seasons, latitude, weather fronts, barometric pressure, humidity, precipitation, cloudiness, wind speed, temperature, and days of the week.* There are no good data to substantiate any of these myths.

11. *Suicide is influenced by cosmic factors such as sunspots and phases of the moon.* No evidence confirms this.

12. *Improvement in emotional state means lessened risk of suicide.* The fact is that people often commit the act after their spirits begin to rise and their energy level improves; this appears to be especially true of depressed patients.

13. *Suicide is a lonely event.* Although the debate whether to commit suicide is waged within the individual's head, deep immersion in a frustrating, hurtful relationship with another person—a spouse, a child, a lover, a colleague—may be a principal cause.

14. *Suicidal people clearly want to die.* Most people who commit suicide appear to be ambivalent about their own deaths.

---

imposed on someone who has committed suicide! Some states do categorize suicide attempts as misdemeanors, but, these offenses are seldom prosecuted. On the other hand, there are laws in every state that make it a crime to encourage or advise suicide (Shneidman, 1987).

Suicide is discussed in this chapter because many depressives have suicidal thoughts and sometimes make genuine attempts to take their own lives; moreover, it is generally believed that more than half of those who try to kill themselves are depressed and despondent at the time of the act. A significant number of people who are not depressed, however, make suicidal attempts, some with success.[4]

Facts about Suicide

No single theory is likely to take into account all the available information about suicide. The diversity of

---

[4]For that matter, other disorders are associated with suicide (Linehan and Shearin, 1988). The rate for male alcoholics is 75 times greater than for the general population of men (Kessel and Grossman, 1961), and up to 13 percent of schizophrenics commit suicide (Roy, 1982). Still, our focus here is on issues and factors in suicide that transcend specific diagnoses.

known facts may help us appreciate how complex and multifaceted self-intentioned death is (Resnik, 1968; Gibbs, 1968; Douglas, 1967; Holinger, 1979; Shneidman, 1973; Seiden, 1974; National Center for Health Statistics, 1988). (See Box 9.4 for myths about suicide.)

1. Every twenty minutes someone in the United States kills himself, and this rate—close to 31,000 a year—is probably a gross underestimate. The suicide rate in the United States is about 12.8 per 100,000. It rises in old age, and between the ages of seventy-five and eighty-four, the rate reaches 25.2 per 100,000.

2. Although no official attempt data are available it is estimated that between 240,000 and 600,000 people attempt suicide each year. This means that for every actual suicide in the United States, between eight and twenty people have made an attempt![5]

3. About half of those who commit suicide have made at least one previous attempt.

4. Three times as many men kill themselves as women, although the ratio may be approaching twice as many men as women, for women are becoming a higher-risk group.

5. Three times as many women as men attempt to kill themselves but do not die.

6. Divorced men are three times more likely to kill themselves than married men.

7. Suicide is found in both the very old and the very young—even in those older than ninety years and younger than ten years.

8. Suicide is found at all social and economic levels but is especially frequent among psychiatrists, physicians, lawyers, and psychologists.

9. No other kind of death leaves in friends and relatives such long-lasting feelings of distress, shame, guilt, puzzlement, and general disturbance. Indeed, these survivors are themselves victims, having an especially high mortality rate in the year following the suicide of their loved one.

10. Guns are the most common means of suicide in the United States. Men usually choose to shoot or hang themselves. Women are more likely to use sleeping pills.

11. Suicide ranks eighth as a cause of death among adults in general; it ranks third after accidents and homicides among those aged fifteen to twenty-four.

It is estimated that each year upward of 10,000 American college men and women attempt to kill themselves.

12. The rates for suicide among whites and native American youths are more than twice those for blacks. The highest rates of suicide in the United States are for white males between the ages of twenty and seventy-nine.

13. The rates of suicide for adolescents and children in the United States are increasing. As many as 1900 young people between the ages of fifteen and nineteen are believed to kill themselves each year, and attempts are made by children as young as six. But the rates are far below those of adults.

14. Hungary is the country with the highest rate of suicide in the world. Czechoslovakia, Finland, Sweden, and Austria also have high incidences.

15. Suicide rates go up during depression years, remain stable during years of prosperity, and decrease during war years.

Perspectives on Suicide

In imagining a suicide, we usually think of a person deliberately performing a dramatic act explicitly chosen to end life almost immediately—the woman on the ledge of the tall building, the man with the gun next to his temple, the child with the bottle of mother's sleeping pills. But suicidologists also regard people as being suicidal when they act in self-destructive ways that can cause serious injury or death after a prolonged period of time, such as the diabetic who neglects his insulin and dietary regimen; or the alcoholic who will not seek help, despite his awareness of the damage being done to his body. Sometimes termed subintentioned death, these apparent suicides complicate still further the task of understanding suicide and gathering statistics on it (Shneidman, 1973).

Perspectives on suicide can be found in many domains (Shneidman, 1987). Novelists like Herman Melville and Leo Tolstoy have provided insights on suicide, as have writers who themselves have killed themselves, like Virginia Woolf and Sylvia Plath. Ordinary people as well have left behind letters and diaries that can be studied for insights into the phenomenology of people who commit suicide.

Many philosophers have also written searchingly on the topic, like Descartes, Voltaire, and Kant, and especially existentialists like Heidegger and Camus, who grapple with the inherent meaninglessness of life and with Man's need and responsibility to forge for himself whatever meaning he can construct out of what appears to be a dark existence.

---

[5]Another way to look at these estimates is that at least five million living Americans have attempted to kill themselves.

While acknowledging that perhaps 90 percent of suicides could be given a DSM-IIIR diagnosis, Shneidman (1987) reminds us that the overwhelming majority of schizophrenics and those with mood disorders do *not* commit suicide and that the *perturbation* of mind that he posits as a key feature of a suicide is not a mental illness (see Box 9.4).

It appears that media reports of suicide may spark an increase in suicides. This disturbing possibility was discussed by Bandura (1985), who reviewed research by Phillips (1974, 1977, 1985) that shows that (1) suicides rose by 12 percent in the month following Marilyn Monroe's death; (2) publicized accounts of self-inflicted deaths of people other than the famous also are followed by significant increases in suicide (suggesting that it is publicity rather than the fame of the suicide that is important); and (3) publicized accounts of murder-suicides are followed by increases in fatal auto and plane crashes where the driver and others are killed. Finally, (4) media reports of natural deaths of famous people are not followed by increases in suicide, suggesting that it is not grief per se that is the influential factor.

Mintz (1968) has summarized the numerous motivations for suicide mentioned in the literature: aggression turned inward; retaliation by inducing guilt in others; efforts to force love from others; efforts to make amends for "perceived" past wrongs; efforts to rid oneself of unacceptable feelings, such as sexual attraction to members of one's own sex; the desire for reincarnation; the desire to rejoin a dead loved one; and the desire or need to escape from stress, deformity, pain, or emotional vacuum. Many contemporary mental health workers regard suicide in general as an individual's attempt at problem solving, conducted under considerable stress and marked by a consideration of a very narrow range of alternatives, of which self-annihilation appears the most viable (Linehan and Shearin, 1988).

Psychoanalytic Theories of Suicide

Freud proposed two major hypotheses to account for suicide. One is an extension of his theory of depression and basically views suicide as murder. When a person loses someone whom he or she has ambivalently loved and hated, and introjects that person, aggression is directed inward. If these feelings are strong enough, the person will commit suicide. The second theory postulates that the death instinct, Thanatos, can turn inward and make the person take his or her life.

Freud's views on suicide are subject to many of the problems raised earlier in this text about psychoanalytic theorizing. Moreover, a careful analysis of suicide notes by Tuckman, Kleiner, and Lavell (1959) provides information that is in marked disagreement with the psychoanalytic position. They found that only a minority

of the notes expressed hostility. In fact, about half expressed gratitude and affection for others. A possible rebuttal—which would be difficult or impossible to test—might be that a suicide note, written at the conscious level, could not be expected to reflect repressed hostility.

Durkheim's Sociological Theory of Suicide

Durkheim (1897), after analyzing the records of suicide for various countries and during different historical periods, viewed self-annihilation as a sociological phenomenon and distinguished three different kinds. ***Egoistic suicide*** is committed when a person has too few ties to the society and community. These people feel alienated from others, cut off from the social supports that are important to keep them functioning adaptively as social beings. ***Altruistic suicides,*** in contrast, are viewed by Durkheim as responses to societal demands. Some people who commit suicide feel very much a part of a group and sacrifice themselves for what they take to be the good of society. The self-immolations of Buddhist monks and nuns to protest the fighting during the Vietnam War would fit into this category. Some altruistic suicides, such as the hara-kiri of the Japanese, are literally required as the only honorable recourse in the circumstances. Finally, ***anomic suicide*** may be triggered by a sudden change in a person's relations to society. A successful businesswoman who suffers severe financial reverses may experience ***anomie,*** a sense of disorientation, because what she believed to be her normal way of living is no longer possible for her. Anomie can pervade a society in disequilibrium, making suicide more likely.

As with all sociological theorizing, Durkheim's hypotheses have trouble accounting for the differences among individuals in a given society in their reactions to the same demands and conditions. Not all those who unexpectedly lose their money commit suicide. It appears that Durkheim was aware of this problem, for he suggested that individual temperament would interact with any of the social pressures that he found causative.

A Psychological Approach to Suicide

Shneidman's psychological approach to suicide (1987) is summarized in Table 9.4, which contains the ten most frequent characteristics, not all of them to be found in each and every suicide.

This view regards suicide as (almost always) a conscious effort to seek a solution to a problem that is causing intense suffering. To the sufferer, this solution ends consciousness and unendurable pain—what Melville in *Moby Dick* termed an "insufferable anguish". All hope and sense of constructive action are gone. Still—and this is of central importance in prevention—

The Buddhist flag covers the body of a young girl who set herself on fire. Self-immolation is a form of altruistic suicide.

most suiciders are ambivalent. "The prototypical suicidal state is one in which an individual cuts his or her throat, cries for help at the same time, and is genuine in both of these acts. . . . Individuals would be happy not to do it, if they didn't have to" (Shneidman, 1987, p. 170). Cognitively there is a narrowing of the perceived range of options; when not in a highly perturbed suicidal state, the person is capable of seeing more choices in dealing with stress. People planning suicide usually communicate their intention, sometimes as a cry for help, sometimes as a withdrawal from others, a search for inviolacy. Common behaviors include giving away treasured possessions and putting one's financial affairs in order.

TABLE 9.4

The ten commandments of suicide
(*from Shneidman, 1987, p. 167*)

I. The common purpose of suicide is to seek a solution	VI. The common cognitive state in suicide is ambivalence
II. The common goal of suicide is the cessation of consciousness	VII. The common perceptual state in suicide is constriction
III. The common stimulus in suicide is intolerable psychological pain	VIII. The common action in suicide is egression
IV. The common stressor in suicide is frustrated psychological needs	IX. The common interpersonal act in suicide is communication of intention
V. The common emotion in suicide is hopelessness–helplessness	X. The common consistency in suicide is with lifelong coping patterns

Prediction of Suicide from Psychological Tests

Psychologists have attempted to predict suicide on the basis of scores on psychological tests. It would of course be of immense theoretical and practical advantage to be able to predict from test results who might consider the act. Many investigators have studied the personality characteristics of those who have attempted suicide. An unavoidable difficulty with this kind of research stems from the fact that the personality tests can seldom be given to numbers of people who may *later* kill themselves. Furthermore, in addition to the problem of obtaining data before a suicide attempt has been made, it is impossible to collect information, other than biographical accounts from relatives and a few other sources, after the deed has been done. Much of the literature, then, consists of reports of psychological tests given to people *after* they have made an aborted attempt at suicide. Clearly, the information obtained from such tests

Jo Roman, in her early sixties and suffering from breast cancer that was not yet critical, methodically planned her death for fifteen months. She was determined to spare herself and her dear ones the pain and great emotional strain of a terminal illness. While she could still "function to my satisfaction," she bid her husband, daughter, and a close friend goodnight and farewell, swallowed thirty-five sleeping pills and a glass of champagne, and went quietly to bed.

will reflect the fact that those tested have recently tried and failed to kill themselves. Their state of mind is likely to be quite different from what it had been before the attempt. For example, many who have tried unsuccessfully to take their lives feel extremely guilty and embarrassed. It is impossible to know with any exactness how test scores and interview behavior are affected by such postattempt factors.

Although these problems might have affected test results, several studies have found significant correlations between suicide intent and hopelessness. Especially noteworthy are Aaron Beck's findings, based on prospective data, that hopelessness is a strong predictor of suicide (Beck *et al.*, 1985; Beck, 1986), more so than is depression (Beck, Kovacs, and Weissman, 1975). The expectation that, at some point in the future, things may look no better than they do right now seems to be more instrumental than depression per se in propelling a person to take his or her life. Beck and his group have also developed the Suicidal Intent Scale (Beck, Schuyler, and Herman, 1974) and the Scale for Suicide

Ideation (Beck, Kovacs, and Weissman, 1979), both of which show promise in helping us to understand and predict those at high risk for serious suicide attempts.

Another avenue of research has focused on the cognitive characteristics of people who attempt suicide. It has been suggested that suicidal individuals are more rigid in their approach to problems (e.g., Neuringer, 1964) and less flexible in their thinking (Levenson, 1972). Constricted thinking could account for their apparent inability to seek solutions to life problems other than taking their own lives (Linehan *et al.*, 1987). Others have suggested that such people may also be impulsive, the assumption being that they would not attempt to kill themselves were they to reflect carefully on their behavior. A study by Patsiokas, Clum, and Luscomb (1979) addressed some of these questions. They administered several tests to a group of psychiatric patients who had been admitted to a hospital for having attempted suicide, as well as to a control group made up of psychiatric patients with no history of having tried to take their own lives. Flexibility of thinking was measured by the Alternative Uses Test (Wilson *et al.*, 1975), in which the person has to list as many different uses for a series of common objects as possible. Also given was the Matching Familiar Figures Test (Kagan, 1965). Each item of this test has at the top a picture of a familiar object. The person chooses the correct matching figure from six below, one of them identical and the other five varying in a minute detail difficult to detect. The impulsive person supposedly responds too quickly and makes many errors, rather than taking the time to reflect and examine the figures closely.

In general, the results confirmed the hypothesis that people who attempt suicide are more rigid than control subjects, lending support to the clinical observation that they seem almost myopically incapable of thinking of alternative solutions to problems and might therefore tend to settle on suicide as the only way out. Little evidence linked impulsiveness to attempted suicide, however. The researchers speculate that the measure used may not be a valid index of impulsiveness as it relates to suicide. Another interpretation, more plausible to us, is that taking one's own life is not an impulsive act at all but is generally done after considerable reflection and doubt.

Suicide Prevention

Shneidman's (1985, 1987) general approach to suicide prevention is threefold: try to reduce the intense psychological pain and suffering, lift the blinders (expand the constricted view the person has, help them see options other than continued suffering or nothingness),

Suicide prevention centers typically have hotlines that are staffed 24 hours a day.

and encourage the person to pull back even a little from the self-destructive act. He gives the example of a wealthy, elegant college student who was single, pregnant—and suicidal with a clearly formed plan. The only solution she could think of besides suicide was never to have become pregnant, even to be virginal again.

I took out a sheet of paper and began to widen her blinders. I said something like, "Now, let's see: You could have an abortion here locally." She responded, "I couldn't do that." I continued, "You could go away and have an abortion." "I couldn't do that." "You could bring the baby to term and keep the baby." "I couldn't do that." "You could have the baby and adopt it out." Further options were similarly dismissed. When I said, "You can always commit suicide, but there is obviously no need to do that today," there was no response. "Now," I said, "let's look at this list and rank them in order of your preference, keeping in mind that none of them is optimal." (Shneidman, 1987, p. 171)

Shneidman reports that just drawing up the list had a calming effect. Her lethality—her drive to kill herself very soon—receded and she was able to rank-order the list, even though she found something wrong with each item. *But* an important goal had been achieved: she had been pulled back from the brink and was in a frame of mind to consider courses of action other than dying or being a virgin again. "We were then simply 'haggling' about life, a perfectly viable solution" (P. 171).

Suicide prevention centers rely heavily on demographic factors (Shneidman, Farberow, and Litman, 1970). Workers receiving phone calls from people in suicidal crises have before them a checklist to guide their questioning of each caller, for they must immediately assess how great the risk of suicide may be. For example, a caller would be regarded as a lethal risk if he is male, middle-aged, divorced, and living alone and has a history of previous suicide attempts. And usually the more detailed and concrete the suicide plan, the higher the risk. More information on suicide prevention centers is provided in Chapter 20 (page 591). Box 9.5 discusses some general clinical issues and gives guidelines for handling suicidal patients.

An investigative procedure is the *psychological autopsy,* pioneered at the Los Angeles Suicide Prevention Center (Shneidman, Faberow, and Litman, 1970). In effect, these workers analyze information obtained from crisis phone calls, from interviews with relatives and friends of those who are thinking about suicide or who are believed to have committed the act, and sometimes from notes left behind by those who have died. The purpose is to determine the actual mode of death and, if judged intentional, the reasons for it.

Of particular interest is a study (Shneidman and Farberow, 1970) of notes left by people who subsequently committed suicide. In the Los Angeles area, at the time this work was done, about 15 percent of suicides left notes, and the contents of these notes were analyzed by judges trained to rate them on the presence or absence of instructions and specific themes, such as self-blame, discomfort, death as relief, and the like. Having determined that such ratings could indeed be made reliably by independent judges, Shneidman and Farberow compared these actual suicide notes with simulated notes prepared for them by individuals who were *not* oriented toward killing themselves but who were matched to those who had on such demographic variables as age, sex, and social class. These control subjects had been instructed to write as *if* they were about to commit suicide. The genuine notes contained a greater number of instructions, such as suggestions about raising the children and explicit orders about how to dispose of the body; there was also evidence of significantly more anguish and hostility in the genuine notes.

BOX 9.5

CLINICAL AND ETHICAL ISSUES IN DEALING WITH SUICIDE

Although it is not true, as stated at the beginning of this section, that people are invariably depressed when they commit suicide or attempt to do so (also see Box 9.4), suicide must always be considered a danger when working with those who are profoundly depressed. The despair and utter hopelessness of their existence may make them see suicide as the only solution, the only exit. In fact, sometimes the sole reason a depressed individual does *not* attempt suicide is that he or she cannot summon the energy to formulate and implement a suicide plan. In working with a seriously depressed individual, the clinician must be especially careful as the patient *emerges from* the low point of depression, for the sadness and hopelessness may still be strong enough to make self-annihilation appear the only option *and* now the person begins to have enough energy to do something about it. Because so many who commit suicide are depressed, treatment of this condition is at the same time an intervention that clinicians hope will reduce the risk of suicide.

Clinicians have to work out for themselves an ethic regarding a person's right to end his or her life. What steps is the professional willing to take to prevent a suicide? Confinement in a straitjacket on the back ward of a hospital? Or, as is more common in these modern times, sedation administered against the patient's wishes and strong enough that the person is virtually incapable of taking any action at all? And for how long will extraordinary measures be taken? The clinician realizes, of course, that many,

perhaps even most, suicidal crises pass; the suicidal person is likely to be grateful afterward that he or she was prevented from destroying the self when it seemed the only course. But to what extremes is the professional prepared to go in the interim to prevent a suicide attempt?

The therapist should not hesitate to inquire directly whether the client has thought of suicide. Experienced clinicians and suicidologists do not believe that the idea can be put into another person's head, that the risk of suicide can be increased merely by asking about it. On the contrary, opening up the topic for discussion can be the first step of a therapeutic intervention (Beck *et al.*, 1979). It is important to adopt a phenomenological stance, to view the suicidal person's situation as he sees it, rather than convey in any way that he is a fool or is crazy to have settled on suicide as a solution to his woes. This Rogerian empathy for suicidal people is sometimes referred to as "tuning in" by those who work in suicide prevention centers. In addition, the clinician treating a suicidal person must be prepared to devote more energy and time than he or she usually does, even to psychotic patients. Late-night phone calls and visits to the patient's home may be frequent. Finally, the therapist should realize that he or she is likely to become a singularly important figure in the suicidal person's life—and be prepared both for the extreme dependency of the patient and for the hostility and resentment that sometimes greet efforts to help.

As is the case in nearly all areas of abnormal psychology, not as much is known about suicide as we would like. In this instance the lack of information is all the more worrisome, since the very existence of many people is at stake. Fortunately those who have devoted their professional lives to preventing suicide are not waiting for all the data to come in before attempting to intervene. The absence of a good theory does not preclude action. Working principles can be derived from available statistical studies, which already identify at least some of the individuals who are likely to make lethal attempts. Shneidman has summed up his own involvement with suicide prevention as follows:

If we have not unequivocally demonstrated that we singlehandedly effected a drastic reduction in the suicide rate of Los Angeles, we have at least served thousands of people who are perturbed, undoubtedly saved

some lives, indisputably increased the communication among mental health and other agencies in the community, and directly and indirectly raised the consciousness and lowered the taboo about the topic of suicide throughout the country. (1987, p. 164)

Summary

DSM-IIIR lists two principal mood disorders. In major or unipolar depression the person experiences profound sadness as well as a number of related problems, such as sleep and appetite disturbances, loss of energy and self-esteem. In bipolar disorder the person has episodes either of mania alone or of both mania and depression. With mania the person's mood is elevated or irritable and he or she becomes extremely active, talkative, and distractible.

Psychological theories of depression have been couched in psychoanalytic, cognitive, and interpersonal terms. Psychoanalytic formulations stress unconscious identification with a loved one whose desertion of the individual has made him or her turn anger inward. Beck's cognitive theory ascribes causal significance to negative and illogical self-judgment. According to learned-helplessness theory, early experiences in inescapable, hurtful situations instill a sense of helplessness that can evolve into depression. These individuals are likely to attribute failures to their own general and persistent inadequacies and faults. A revised version of this theory links depression to a state of hopelessness. Interpersonal theory focuses on deficits in depressed people and the negative responses they elicit from others. These same theories are applied to the depressive phase of bipolar disorder. The manic phase is considered to be a defense against a debilitating psychological state.

Physiological theories suggest an inherited predisposition for mood disorders, bipolar disorder in particular, and linkage analyses may provide information concerning the chromosome on which the gene is located. Early neurochemical theories related the phenomena of depression and mania to abnormally depleted and copious amounts of the neurotransmitters that pass on neural impulses in particular nerve tracts of the brain. Recent research focuses on the postsynaptic receptor rather than simply the amount of various transmitters. Overreaction of the hypothalamic–pituitary–adrenal axis is also found among depressives.

There are several psychological and somatic therapies for affective disorders and especially for depression. Psychoanalytic treatment tries to give the patient insight into childhood loss and inadequacy and into later self-blame. The aim of the cognitive therapy of Beck is to uncover negative and illogical patterns of thinking and teach more realistic ways of viewing events, the self, and adversity. The learned-helplessness theory of depression, although not generating as yet a particular set of therapy procedures, does make therapists aware of the apparent need of people to believe that they exercise control over their lives. The existential logotherapy encourages depressed people to make spiritual sense of their suffering, to feel free and responsible for their lives, and to find meaning and purpose in existence.

A range of somatic treatments is also available; often used in conjunction with a psychological treatment, they can be very effective. Electroconvulsive shock and several antidepressant drugs have proved their worth in lifting depression. It has become possible for patients to avoid the excesses of manic and depressive periods through careful administration of lithium carbonate.

Finally, the topic of suicide was explored, although self-annihilative tendencies are not restricted to those who are depressed. A review of the facts and myths about suicide indicates that any single theory is unlikely to account for its great diversity, but that the information already gathered can be applied to prevent it.

Most large communities have suicide prevention centers, and most therapists at one time or another have to deal with patients in suicidal crisis. Clinical evidence suggests that suicidal persons need to have their fears and concerns understood but not judged, and that workers must gradually and patiently point out to them that alternatives to self-destruction are there to be explored.

Part Three

Social Problems

Ed. Paschke, *Violencia*, 1980. Collection of the Whitney Museum of American Art, gift of Sherry and Ann Koppel in memory of Miriam and Herbert Koppel.

Chapter 10

Personality Disorders

Specific Personality Disorders

Antisocial Personality Disorder (Sociopathy)

The Case of Dan

The Case of Jim

Cleckley's Concept of Sociopathy

Theory and Research on the Etiology of Sociopathy

The Role of the Family

Genetic Correlates of Sociopathic Behavior

Central Nervous System Activity and Sociopathy

Avoidance Learning, Punishment, and Sociopathy

Underarousal and Sociopathy

Therapies for Personality Disorders

Therapy for the Borderline Personality

Behavior Therapy for Disturbed Personalities

Therapy for Sociopathy

Summary

Personality disorders, previously called "character disorders," are a group of diagnoses based on a trait approach to personality (see page 103). DSM-IIIR proposes that personality disorders occur when personality traits are inflexible and maladaptive, producing either behavioral impairment or emotional distress.

According to DSM-IIIR, *personality disorders* are to be indicated on axis II, which means that their presence or absence is to be considered whenever a diagnosis is made. They were placed on a separate axis to ensure that diagnosticians would pay greater attention to their possible presence. Sometimes, a diagnostic interview will point directly to the presence of a personality disorder but it is often the case that someone who has come to a clinic has an axis I disorder (such as panic disorder) that, quite naturally, is a primary focus of attention. Placing the personality disorders on axis II is meant to guide the clinician to consider whether personality disorder is also present.

Personality disorders had little diagnostic reliability as they were defined in previous editions of the DSM (e.g., Beck *et al.*, 1962). Although DSM-III changed a number of the names given to specific personality disorders and attempted to improve the clarity of the definitions, in the field trials of DSM-III the reliability of diagnoses of personality disorders was lower than that of most other categories. And this rather low reliability figure was for personality disorders *as a class* rather than for the specific disorders. Even though personality disorders were diagnosed in over 50 percent of the patients in field trials of DSM-III, the reliabilities of some of the individual personality disorders were totally inadequate. These low reliabilities, however, may have been caused by the lack of a good assessment device in the DSM-III field trials. More recent work with structured interviews specially designed for assessing personality disorders indicates that good reliabilities can be achieved (Loranger *et al.*, 1984; Widiger *et al.*, 1988).

Problems still remain with this diagnostic category, however. In DSM-IIIR it is noted that it is often difficult to diagnose someone with a single, specific personality disorder. The reason is that many disordered people exhibit a wide range of traits that make several diagnoses applicable. For example, Widiger, Frances and Trull (1987) found that 55 percent of patients with borderline personality disorder also met the diagnostic criteria for schizotypal personality disorder, 47 percent for antisocial personality disorder, and 57 percent for histrionic personality disorder. Data such as these are particularly discouraging when we try to interpret the results of research comparing patients with a specific personality disorder to some control group. If, for example, we find that borderlines differ from normals, have we learned anything specific to borderline personality disorder or do the findings relate to personality disorders in general or perhaps even to another diagnosis?

These data suggest that the categorical diagnostic system of DSM-IIIR may not be ideal for classifying personality disorders. The personality traits that comprise the data for classification form a continuum; that is, most of the relevant characteristics are present in varying degrees in most people.[1] The diagnostic categories are in fact defined by the extremes. This suggests that a dimensional approach to classification (see Chapter 3, page 70) may be more appropriate. Indeed, a dimensional system was considered for inclusion in DSM-IIIR but consensus could not be reached on which dimensions to include (Widiger *et al.*, 1988). A promising effort in the direction of dimensional classification has been reported by Widiger *et al.* (1987). A large sample of patients was assessed on all the symptoms relevant to a diagnosis of personality disorder. The correlations among the symptoms were then analyzed to see if a smaller number of dimensions could explain the relationships. Three dimensions were found to do so:

1. Social involvement; positive and friendly vs. not involved with other people.
2. Assertion/Dominance vs. Passive Submission.
3. Anxious rumination vs. Behavioral acting out.

Using a dimensional approach to classification, each patient would be assessed, described, and scored on each dimension. For example, a person diagnosed by DSM-IIIR as an avoidant personality would score below average on the first and second dimensions, and above average on the third.

Specific Personality Disorders

Personality disorders are grouped into three clusters in DSM-IIIR. Individuals in the first cluster of three in the following list seem odd or eccentric, those with the next three disorders seem dramatic, emotional, or erratic, and those with any of the last cluster of four disorders appear anxious or fearful.[2]

Paranoid Personality Disorder The *paranoid personality* is suspicious of people. He or she expects to be mistreated by others and thus becomes secretive and is

---

[1]This is a good place to remind readers about medical student syndrome. With the personality disorders we come closest to describing characteristics that we all possess. Therefore, it is especially important to be aware that an actual disorder is defined by the extremes of several personality traits.

BOX 10.1

PERSONALITY DISORDERS IN NEED OF FURTHER STUDY

DSM-IIIR has proposed diagnostic criteria for new personality disorders that are not formal diagnoses but "categories in need of further study." By far the most controversial is Self-Defeating Personality Disorder, originally put forward as Masochistic Personality Disorder but changed lest it be assumed that the sufferer obtains any sort of (disguised) sexual satisfaction from it. Feminists were particularly angered by the term masochism. The central criteria are that the person is drawn to situations in which he or she is going to suffer and the person undermines pleasurable experiences (e.g., by rejecting opportunities for pleasure, by responding with guilt to a positive event, by being uninterested in people who treat him or her well, and by preventing others from helping him or her). These behaviors should not occur only when the person is feeling depressed (otherwise a mood disorder would be the more appropriate diagnosis). No assumption is made that the person actually gets pleasure from feeling bad.

One of the objections to labeling such behavior patterns as psychopathological is that it threatens to "blame the victim," to shift the responsibility for interpersonal pain from those who punish to those who are punished. Those working with battered women are especially concerned, fearing that women who are regularly beaten up by their mates will be viewed as having "asked for it," albeit in subtle ways. The response of DSM-IIIR has been to list as an exclusion criterion that "the behaviors...do not occur only in response to, or in anticipation of, being physically, sexually, or psychologically abused." But critics appear unappeased by this.

Another proposed personality disorder is Sadistic Personality Disorder, the principal criteria of which are demeaning and aggressive behaviors like beating up others in the service of no goals other than inflicting harm, being an overly harsh disciplinarian, being amused by the suffering of others including animals, intimidating others to get his or her own way, and being fascinated by violence, weapons, or the martial arts. Exclusion criteria are that these behaviors not be directed at only one person and that they not be solely for the purpose of sexual arousal (as in Sexual Sadism). It is, of course, too early to discuss these diagnoses in more detail because the necessary data are not available. Whether they will become part of DSM-IV remains to be seen.

continually on the lookout for possible signs of trickery and abuse. Such individuals are extremely jealous and tend to blame others even when they themselves are at fault. Paranoid personalities are also overly sensitive, quick to take offense, argumentative, and tense. They may also read hidden messages into events, for example, believing that their neighbor's dog deliberately barks in the early morning to disturb them.

Schizoid Personality Disorder The **schizoid personality** has difficulties in forming social relationships and usually has few close friends. He or she appears dull and aloof and without warm, tender feelings for other people. Indifferent to praise, criticism, and the sentiments of others, individuals with this disorder are "loners" and pursue solitary interests.

Schizotypal Personality Disorder The **schizotypal personality** usually has the interpersonal difficulties of the schizoid personality. But along with these are a number of other symptoms that are more eccentric, although they are not severe enough to warrant a diagnosis of schizophrenia (see Chapter 14). Schizotypal personalities may have "*magical thinking*"—superstitiousness, beliefs that they are clairvoyant and telepathic—and recurrent *illusions*—they may sense the presence of a force or a person not actually there. Speech may also contain words used in unusual and unclear fashion. Behavior and appearance may also be eccentric (e.g., talking to oneself or wearing dirty and disheveled clothing); ideas of reference and delusional beliefs are common. In a study of the relative importance of these symptoms for diagnosis, Widiger, Frances, and Trull (1987) found that paranoid ideation, ideas of reference, and illusions were most telling. Schizotypal personality disorder and schizophrenia are probably related to each other through genetic transmission of a predisposition. More first-degree relatives of schizophrenics are given the diagnosis than are relatives of individuals in control groups; the disorder may thus be a mild form of schizophrenia (Spitzer, Endicott, and Gibbon, 1979).

Drawing by Sempé; © 1982 The New Yorker Magazine, Inc.

"I demand to know what hidden forces are impeding my progress and strewing my path with obstacles!"

Borderline Personality Disorder The ***borderline personality*** reveals instability in relationships, mood, and self-image. For example, attitudes and feelings toward other people may vary considerably and inexplicably over short periods of time. Emotions are also erratic and can shift abruptly, particularly to anger. Borderline personalities are argumentative, irritable, and sarcastic. Their unpredictable and impulsive behavior, such as gambling, spending, sex, and eating sprees, is potentially self-damaging. These individuals have not developed a clear and coherent sense of self and remain uncertain about their values, loyalties, and choice of career. They cannot bear to be alone. So they tend to

have a series of intense one-to-one relationships that are usually stormy, transient, and brief, for they also have little capacity to evaluate others and no real concern for them. Subject to chronic feelings of depression and emptiness, they may make manipulative attempts at suicide. Of all these varied symptoms, unstable and intense interpersonal relationships appear as a critical feature (Modestin, 1987).[2]

---

[2]Patients with both borderline and schizotypal personality disorders would probably have been diagnosed as schizophrenic using DSM-II criteria. Designating the behavior of these people as the criteria for these two personality disorders is one way that DSM-IIIR has narrowed the schizophrenia diagnosis (see Chapter 14).

The character portrayed by Glenn Close in the film *Fatal Attraction* had many characteristics of the borderline personality.

Clinicians and researchers have used the term borderline personality for some time, but they have given it many meanings. Originally, the term implied that the patient was on the borderline between neurosis and schizophrenia; recent research, however, has not supported this view.

The current conceptualization of borderline personality derives from several sources. After reviewing the available literature and interview studies of borderline personalities, Gunderson, Kolb, and Austin (1981) devised an interview for collecting information necessary for the diagnosis. They also proposed a set of specific diagnostic criteria similar to those that ultimately appeared in DSM-III. The DSM-III criteria for borderline personality were established through a study done by Spitzer, Endicott, and Gibbon (1979). They began by examining research done in Denmark on whether heredity figures in schizophrenia. This genetic research had found more schizophrenia in the relatives of schizophrenics than in the general population and had also shown that these relatives had high rates of other disorders. These disorders were termed the schizophrenia spectrum or borderline schizophrenia. By carefully analyzing these cases, Spitzer and his colleagues determined that one particular clinical syndrome *did* appear to be related to schizophrenia through an inherited predisposition. This syndrome became DSM-III's schizotypal personality disorder. They also identified another syndrome not related to schizophrenia through a predisposition, and this became DSM-III's borderline personality disorder. DSM-IIIR maintains these distinctions.

Much controversy still surrounds the diagnosis of borderline personality disorder. It has become apparent that borderline personalities make up a very heterogeneous group. For example, Pope and his co-workers (1983) found that about half of their sample of borderline personalities also had either major depression or bipolar disorder. These people responded well to the usual somatic treatments for these mood disorders. In addition, their first-degree relatives had a higher incidence of mood disorders than that of the general population. Pope and his colleagues found too that most of their borderline personalities could also be diagnosed as having another personality disorder—histrionic, narcissistic, or antisocial. A great deal of overlapping symptomatology has even been reported between borderline and schizotypal personality disorders (Serban, Conte, and Plutchik, 1987). The data therefore suggest a large overlap among the various personality disorders, an undesirable state of affairs given that these are viewed as distinct diagnoses.

This heterogeneity notwithstanding, what further can we say about borderline personality? It is an intriguing disorder that is both common and serious, hence the attention given it; it begins in adolescence, and it is more frequent in women than in men (McGlashan, 1983). Furthermore, the disorder runs in families, with high rates in first-degree relatives of index cases (Baron *et al.*, 1985; Loranger, Oldham, and Tulis, 1983).

Histrionic Personality Disorder The diagnosis *histrionic personality,* formerly called hysterical personality, is applied to people who are overly dramatic and

BOX 10.2

KOHUT AND THE NARCISSISTIC PERSONALITY

In recent years many psychoanalytically oriented clinicians have regarded as the prevalent disorder of our time the narcissistic personality, a person whose remarkable sense of self-importance, complete self-absorption, and fantasies of limitless success mask a very fragile self esteem. Constantly seeking attention and adulation, narcissistic personalities are underneath extremely sensitive to criticism and deeply fearful of failure. Sometimes they seek out others whom they can idealize, because they are disappointed in themselves, but they generally do not allow anyone to be genuinely close to them. Their personal relationships are few and shallow; when people inevitably fall short of their unrealistic expectations, they become angry and rejecting. The inner lives of narcissists are similarly impoverished because, despite their self-aggrandizement, they actually think very little of themselves and are without resources.

At the center of this contemporary interst in narcissism is Heinz Kohut, whose two books *The Analysis of the Self* (1971) and *The Restoration of the Self* (1977) have established a variant of psychoanalysis known as self psychology. His basic idea is that parents must respond to their children with respect, warmth, and empathy if the children are to acquire a normal sense of self-worth. But a mother may further her own needs rather than being empathic with her child.

A little girl comes home from school, eager to tell her mother about some great successes. But this mother, instead of listening with pride, deflects the conversation

Heinz Kohut, the psychoanalytically oriented psychiatrist who founded self psychology and has written extensively about narcissism.

from the child to herself [and] begins to talk about her own successes which overshadow those of her little daughter. (Kohut and Wolf, 1978, p. 418)

A youngster neglected in this way has trouble accepting her own shortcomings. She may develop into a narcissistic personality, neurotically striving to bolster her sense of self through unending quests for love and approval from others.

always drawing attention to themselves. These individuals, while displaying emotion extravagantly, are noted as actually being shallow of emotion. They are also given to angry overreactions to minor annoyances and to quick boredom with normal routines. Interpersonal problems are frequent and include manipulativeness, seductiveness, dependence, and constant demands on others. Speech is often vague and impressionistic. Although DSM-IIIR states that the diagnosis is more common among women, Reich (1987) did not find support for this. The histrionic personality is sometimes regarded as superficially charming by other people, but also as vain, ungenuine, and inconsiderate.

Narcissistic Personality Disorder **Narcissistic personalities** have a grandiose view of their own uniqueness and abilities. They are preoccupied with fantasies of great successes and crave the admiration and attention

of others. To say that they are self-centered is almost an understatement. Their interpersonal relationships are disturbed by their lack of empathy; by feelings of envy; by exploitiveness, taking advantage of others; and by feelings of entitlement, expecting others to do special, not-to-be-reciprocated favors for them.

The diagnosis of narcissistic personality disorder has its roots in modern psychoanalytic writings. Kernberg (1970) described the grandiosity and egocentric behavior of narcissists as a defense against the rage that they feel toward their parents, whom they perceive as cold and indifferent. Kohut (1966) has proposed that the narcissistic personality develops as a way of coping with perceived shortcomings in the self that rankle, because parents do not provide support and empathy. The child who receives such help learns to deal with his or her shortcomings more adaptively. Although these etiological speculations have not been empirically tested, the descriptions of narcissism by these psychoanalytic writers had a major impact on the DSM-IIIR diagnosis (see Box 10.2).

Advoidant Personality Disorder **Avoidant personalities** are keenly sensitive to the possibility of social rejection and humiliation and are therefore reluctant to enter into relationships, even though they yearn for closeness and for the affection and acceptance of others. They suffer from low self-esteem, being dismayed by their own personal shortcomings and devaluing all their achievements. There is considerable overlap between the features of avoidant personality disorder and dependent personality disorder (Trull, Widiger, and Frances, 1987).

Dependent Personality Disorder **Dependent personalities** lack self-confidence and self-reliance, passively allowing their spouses to assume responsibility for deciding where they should live, what jobs they should hold, with whom they should be friendly. They are unable to make demands on others, and they subordinate their own needs to ensure that they do not break up the protective relationships they have established. They are very sensitive to criticism and disapproval and are devastated when close relationships end. Submission is part of the traditional stereotype for feminine behavior; more women than men are diagnosed as having dependent personalities. Their belittlement of themselves brings to mind the colloquialism "inferiority complex."

Obsessive-Compulsive Personality Disorder **Obsessive-compulsive personalities** are perfectionists, preoccupied with details, rules, schedules, and the like. They are work- rather than pleasure-oriented and have inordinate difficulty making decisions and allocating time. Their interpersonal relationships are often poor because they demand that everything be done their way. They are generally serious and formal and are unlikely to express warmth and friendliness.[3] This dysfunctional attention to work and productivity is found more often in men than women.

Passive-Agressive Personality Disorder **Passive-agressive personalities** indirectly resist the demands of others, both in social situations and at work. The resistance, which is thought to be aggression in disguise, takes the form of thoroughgoing stubbornness and ineffectuality. They are habitually late for appointments, do not return phone calls, procrastinate, and "forget." This persistent behavior pattern usually provokes further problems, such as marital discord and not being offered promotions. The dawdling of passive-aggressive personalities can be considered a hostile way of controlling others without assuming responsibility for their own anger. Of all the personality disorders, this one is probably most often hurled as an epithet by people who in their everyday lives are frustrated by the passive-aggressive behaviors of some of their colleagues.

The personality disorders make up what many researchers regard as an unreliable, cluttered grab bag of a category. Ironically, the descriptions of them may seem to fit some of the members of our own families and some of our acquaintances, not to mention ourselves! Each of us develops over the years some apparently persistent means of dealing with life's challenges, a certain "style" of relating to other people. One person is overly dependent, another challenging and aggressive; yet another is very shy and avoids social contact, and another is more concerned with appearances and bolstering his or her precious ego than with relating honestly and on a deep level with others. To be sure, DSM-IIIR would not have these personalities diagnosed unless the patterns of behavior are longstanding, pervasive, and dysfunctional, but the essential disturbances listed for the various personality disorders no doubt bring to mind the shortcomings of friends, colleagues—and oneself.

The reader may also have noticed that descriptions of some of the personality disorders are similar to those of diagnostic categories discussed elsewhere. Generally speaking, a person judged to have, for example, a paranoid personality disorder is less disturbed than a person with paranoid schizophrenia or a paranoid disorder (see page 386). People given one of these three diagnoses, however, all have in common a tendency to be overly suspicious, guarded, and thin-skinned. But it can be very difficult to distinguish personality disorders from others that bear a resemblance (Nathan *et al.*, 1968), underlining once again their problematic status as a separate group of psychological disturbances.

Although data are few on the disorders just described, one personality disorder omitted from the foregoing list is more reliably diagnosed and has attracted the attention of researchers for many years. **Antisocial personality disorder** is unfortunately a prevalent diagnosis. The rest of this chapter will be devoted to what is known about the disruptive individuals whose deep-

---

[3] It may occur to the reader that these traits can be very adaptive in certain situations. It is a standing joke, for example, that success in graduate school goes to those who are obsessive-compulsive. The issues are more serious, however, for they go to the heart not only of the appropriateness of considering such people to have a mental disorder, but also of the demands placed on people working for advanced degrees. Consider as well the kinds of people selected for graduate study, and the kinds of professionals these students are likely to become.

seated ethical and moral maladjustments frequently bring them into serious conflict with their associates and with society.

Antisocial Personality Disorder (*Sociopathy*)

In current usage the terms **sociopath** and **psychopath** appear interchangeably with antisocial personality. The concept has an interesting history. At the very beginning of the nineteenth century, Philippe Pinel conceived of *manie sans délire*. Pinel chose this term to indicate that the patient he described was violently insane (*manie*) but did not show other symptoms (*sans délire*) common among the insane. In 1835 James Prichard, an English psychiatrist, described the disorder "moral insanity" in an attempt to account for behavior so far outside the usual ethical and legal codes that it seemed a form of lunacy. The man whose nature prompted Pinel's term was an easily angered aristocrat who had whipped a horse, kicked a dog to death, and thrown a peasant woman into a well. Since the early concept was used to explain a wide range of strange behavior, it is not surprising that it came to function somewhat as a wastebasket diagnosis, encompassing those inclined not only to violence but to unconventional practices as well.

About four percent of adult American men and one percent of women are estimated to have antisocial personalities (Robins *et al.*, 1984). Business executives, politicians, and physicians, plumbers, salespeople, carpenters, and bartenders—they are to be found in all walks of life. Prostitutes, pimps, confidence men, murderers, and drug dealers are by no means the only sociopaths.

Before considering current views of antisocial personality, we shall examine excerpts from two case histories that illustrate the scope of sociopathic reactions. The first case illustrates many of the classic characteristics of the sociopath but is unusual in that the person described was neither a criminal nor in psychiatric treatment at the time that the data for the case study were collected. This is an important point, for the majority of sociopaths who are the subjects of research studies have broken the law and been caught for doing so. Only rarely do we have the opportunity to examine in detail the behavior of an individual who fits the diagnostic definition but yet has managed not to break the law. The second case history presents the more usual picture of the criminal sociopath.

The Case of Dan

This case history was compiled by a psychologist, Elton McNeil (1967), who happened to be a personal friend of Dan's.

Dan was a wealthy actor and disc jockey who lived in an expensive house in an exclusive suburb and generally played his role as a "personality" to the hilt. One evening, when he and McNeil were out for dinner, Dan made a great fuss over the condition of the *Shrimp de Johnge* that he had ordered. McNeil thought that the whole scene had been deliberately contrived by Dan for the effect it might produce, and he said to his companion,
"I have a sneaking suspicion this whole scene came about just because you weren't really hungry." Dan laughed loudly in agreement and said, *"What the hell, they'll be on their toes next time."* *"Was that the only reason for this display?"* . . . *"No,"* he replied, *"I wanted to show you how gutless the rest of the world is. If you shove a little they all jump. Next time I come in, they'll be all over me to make sure everything is exactly as I want it. That's the only way they can tell the difference between class and plain ordinary. When I travel I go first class."*
"Yes, . . . but how do you feel about you as a person—as a fellow human being?"
"Who cares?" he laughed. *"If they were on top they would do the same to me. The more you walk on them, the more they like it. It's like royalty in the old days. It makes them nervous if everyone is equal to everyone else. Watch. When we leave I'll put my arm around that waitress, ask her if she still loves me, pat her on the fanny, and she'll be ready to roll over any time I wiggle my little finger."* (p. 85)

Another incident occurred when a friend of Dan's committed suicide. Most of the other friends whom Dan and McNeil had in common were concerned and called the psychologist to see whether he could provide any information about why the man had taken his life. Dan did not. Later, when McNeil mentioned the suicide to Dan, all he could say was "That's the way the ball bounces." In his public behavior, however, Dan's attitude toward the incident appeared quite different. He was the one who collected money and presented it personally to the new widow. In keeping with his character, however, Dan remarked that the widow had a sexy body that really interested him.

These two incidents convey the flavor of Dan's behavior. McNeil had witnessed a long succession of similar events, which led him to conclude that

[The incidents] painted a grisly picture of life-long abuse of people for Dan's amusement and profit. He was adept at office politics and told me casually of an unbelievable set of deceptive ways to deal with the opposition. Character assassination, rumor mongering, modest blackmail, seduction, and barefaced lying were the least of his talents. He was a jackal in the entertainment jungle, a jackal who feasted on the bodies of those he had slaughtered professionally. (p. 91)

In his conversations with Dan, McNeil was also able to inquire into Dan's life history. One early and potentially important event was related by Dan.

I can remember the first time in my life when I began to suspect I was a little different from most people. When I was in high school my best friend got leukemia and died and I went to his funeral. Everybody else was crying and feeling sorry for themselves and as they were praying to get him into heaven I suddenly realized that I wasn't feeling anything at all. He was a nice guy but what the hell. That night I thought about it some more and found that I wouldn't miss my mother and father if they died and that I wasn't too nuts about my brothers and sisters for that matter. I figured there wasn't anybody I really cared for but, then, I didn't need any of them anyway so I rolled over and went to sleep. (p. 87)

The moral depravity described long ago by Pinel and Prichard clearly marks Dan's behavior. A person may be otherwise quite rational and show no loss of contact with reality and yet behave in a habitually and exceed-

ingly unethical manner. This final excerpt illustrated Dan's complete lack of feeling for others, a characteristic that will later be seen to have considerable relevance in explaining the behavior of the sociopath.

The Case of Jim

A case of a more typical sociopath was reported by Bintz and Wilson as reprinted in Milton and Wahler, 1969.

Jim, the fourth child in a family of five, grew up in the lower social class of a small Midwestern town. During his childhood the member of his family who made the greatest impression on him was his older brother, whom he described as follows.

He was always a bully, promiscuous, and adventurous. He was always involved with some local girl, before I was even old enough to realize what was going on. He started drinking early, and had several scrapes with the law. He had rough companions, whom I later inherited, who helped me on my way.

He married a tramp, ended up in a stolen car, and was given the choice of jail or the army, as this was the Korean war time. I cannot directly link him to my life of crime, although he introduced me to those who later helped me along. Also, he condoned some of my early petty thievery. (Bintz and Wilson, as reprinted in Milton and Wahler, 1969, p. 92)

During early adolescence Jim engaged in many petty antisocial acts. For example, on one occasion he stole some change from his mother's pocketbook. His father reacted by whipping both brothers until Jim confessed. Once Jim admitted that he had taken the money, however, the punishment ended. This became standard practice for the family, with Jim being able to avoid punishment by confessing as soon as he was accused of misbehavior, regardless of whether or not he was guilty. Moreover, the petty thievery that Jim committed in the community was generally successful, and even when he was caught consequences were minimal.

Jim's first serious trouble with the law occurred when he was charged with raping a young woman whom he had picked up at the local skating rink. He was sentenced to five years at a reform school but received an immediate parole with the condition that he would be sent to reform school if he violated parole. After several parole violations such as petty theft and speeding, he was sentenced to one year at the reform school. By the time he was released a year later, he had become a young hoodlum. Jim himself stated that the principal consequence of the year in reform school had been the opportunity afforded him to fraternize with more experienced thieves. Shortly thereafter Jim and a friend committed their first major theft, stealing $1700 from a tavern safe. Then the same pair attempted to burglarize a lumberyard but were unable to open the safe. The next day they were arrested, and the burglary tools were found in Jim's car. He served a ninety-day sentence for attempted burglary. Three months after being released, Jim was incarcerated again, this time for statutory rape. As soon as he was free again, he and a friend planned another robbery. They reasoned that a bootlegger would be a good target for a holdup for, being outside the law himself, he would be reluctant to report the incident to the police. They bungled the job badly, however, and both were sentenced to five-year terms. Jim served three of the five years and upon his release met the woman he was soon to marry. He described her as follows.

Diane was a tramp, I could tell from the start. She forced the introduction and the first date. I had sexual relations with her on the first date, she was my third sexual partner on that particular day. She was neat, but not really attractive. The next four and a half months we were intimate almost every night. She wanted to marry, I did not. I could not see myself married to this plain-looking tramp. In fact, toward the last, I was trying to think of a scheme to get rid of her. (p. 100)

During this period Jim held a job, but he soon began to sink deeper and deeper into debt. Eventually, an opportunity for another theft presented itself. Again the job was spectacularly unsuccessful and Jim was sentenced to ten years in the state penitentiary. While in the county jail, before the trial, he was visited often by Diane and finally married her just before going to prison. As a substitute for a wedding ring, Jim had the words "Love me, Diane" tattooed on his penis.

Cleckley's Concept of Sociopathy

Both of these case histories illustrate many of the symptoms of the sociopathic syndrome as it has been defined by Hervey Cleckley in his classic book, *The Mask of Sanity* (1976). On the basis of his vast clinical experience, he formulated a set of criteria by which to recognize the disorder. Cleckley's work continues to be accepted as providing the classic description of sociopathy.

1. Considerable superficial charm and average or above average intelligence.
2. Absence of delusions or other signs of irrational thinking.
3. Absence of anxiety or other "neurotic" symptoms; considerable poise, calmness, and verbal facility.
4. Unreliability, disregard for obligations; no sense of responsibility, in matters of little and great import.
5. Untruthfulness and insincerity.
6. Lack of remorse, no sense of shame.
7. Antisocial behavior which is inadequately motivated and poorly planned, seeming to stem from an inexplicable impulsiveness.
8. Poor judgment and failure to learn from experience.
9. Pathological egocentricity, total self-centeredness; incapacity for real love and attachment.
10. General poverty of deep and lasting emotions.
11. Lack of any true insight, inability to see oneself as others do.
12. Ingratitude for any special considerations, kindness, and trust.
13. Fantastic and objectionable behavior, after drinking and sometimes even when not drinking—vulgarity, rudeness, quick mood shifts, pranks.
14. No history of genuine suicide attempts.
15. An impersonal, trivial, and poorly integrated sex life.
16. Failure to have a life plan and to live in any ordered way, unless it be one promoting self-defeat.

Cleckley's indicators of sociopathy are somewhat different from the DSM-III criteria for the diagnosis of antisocial personality disorder. The DSM-III criteria referred to more specific aspects of behavior, such as inability to hold a job and be a responsible parent and failure to honor financial obligations. But DSM-III omitted some of the characteristics that Cleckley would regard as being of central importance, such as inability to learn from experience and poverty of emotional reactions. DSM-IIIR restores what DSM-III omitted, namely, lack of remorse, although it is not a *necessary* or *defining* characteristic (i.e., it need not be present but is one of many features that can lead to the diagnosis).

For the concept of sociopathy to be useful, it must be easily differentiated from criminal behavior. Criminality refers to law breaking as defined by a given society at a given point in time. The sociopath is viewed as not responding emotionally after committing an act that generally elicits shame and guilt in most people. Thus Cleckley's criteria *no sense of responsibility* and *no sense of shame* are particularly important. Hare's (1980) research has also verified these two faults as indicative of sociopathy.

Lack of shame and guilt is presumably linked to the sociopath's inability to learn from experience, in particular to avoid punishment. The sociopath continues to engage in the same antisocial activities, even though they prove unsuccessful, and even though his or her intelligence is perhaps above average. Learning to avoid actions that continually fail may be mediated by emotional arousal; because sociopaths do not become emotionally aroused, they may be less likely to suffer from and to change their unproductive and antisocial ways.

Before examining the existing research on the sociopathic syndrome, we should emphasize again that most of it has been conducted on sociopaths who have already been convicted as criminals. Individuals such as Dan have rarely been studied in research settings. We must therefore keep in mind that the available literature may not allow us to generalize about the behavior of sociopaths who elude arrest and the subsequent label of criminal.

Sociopathy begins in childhood, with a diverse range of antisocial behavior including theft.

Theory and Research on the Etiology of Sociopathy

The Role of the Family

Since much sociopathic behavior violates social norms, it is not surprising that many investigators have focused on the primary agent of socialization, the family, in their search for the explanation of such behavior. McCord

and McCord (1964) concluded, on the basis of a classic review of the literature, that lack of affection and severe parental rejection were the primary causes of sociopathic behavior. Several other studies have related sociopathic behavior to the parents' inconsistencies in disciplining their children and in teaching them their responsibilities to others (Bennet, 1960). Furthermore, the fathers of sociopaths are likely to be antisocial in their behavior.

But such data on early rearing must be interpreted with extreme caution. They were gathered by means of *retrospective reports;* we have already seen (see page 137) that the information obtained in this way may be of little value. When people are asked to recollect the early events in the life of someone who is now known to be a sociopath, their knowledge of adult status may affect what they remember or report about childhood events. Deviant incidents are more likely to be recalled, whereas more typical or normal incidents that do not match with the person's current behavior may be overlooked.

One way of avoiding the problems of retrospective data is to follow up in adulthood a large group of individuals who as children were seen at a child guidance clinic. In one such study very detailed records had been kept on the children, including the type of problem that had brought them to the clinic and considerable information relating to the family (Robins, 1966). Ninety percent of an initial sample of 584 cases were located

Antisocial behavior in childhood predicts adult sociopathy.

pathic personality. Such boys had a history of truancy, theft, staying out late, and refusing to obey parents. They lied gratuitously, and showed little guilt over their behavior. They were generally irresponsible about being where they were supposed to be or taking care of money. (p. 157)

In addition to these characteristics, aspects of family life mentioned earlier were again found to be consequential. Both inconsistent discipline and no discipline at all predicted sociopathic behavior in adulthood, as did antisocial behavior of the father.

In sum, the research we have reviewed emphasizes the importance of child-rearing practices. The fathers of sociopaths appear to provide a model for antisocial behavior. We must caution, however, that poor training in socialization has been implicated in the etiology of a *number* of clinical syndromes, including delinquent, neurotic, and even psychotic behavior (Wiggins, 1968), and that many individuals who come from what appear to be similarly disturbed social backgrounds do *not* become sociopaths or develop any other behavior disorders. This point is important: adults may have no problems whatsoever in spite of the inconsistent and otherwise undesirable manner of their rearing. Thus, although family experience is probably significant in the development of sociopathic behavior, it can not be the whole story.

Genetic Correlates of Sociopathic Behavior

Twin and Adoptee Studies

Most of the studies concerned with the possible genetic basis for sociopathic behavior have focused on criminality or antisocial behavior rather than on sociopathy per se. The data collected are therefore difficult to interpret since, as already emphasized, not all sociopaths are criminals nor all criminals sociopaths. Lange's research (1929) comparing concordance rates for criminality in identical and fraternal twins showed them to be a great deal higher for identical twins, supporting the theory that genetic factors may be involved. Kranz (1936), in a study that used better sampling procedures, found the following patterns of concordance: identical twins, 66 percent; fraternal twins of the same sex, 54 percent, fraternal twins of the opposite sex, 14 percent. Although at first glance these data also seem to support the notion that genetic factors are important, they in fact give only slight support to this hypothesis. The critical piece of information is the marked *difference* in concordance rates of fraternal twins of the same sex and those of fraternal twins of the opposite sex. Both of these pairs of twins are equally alike genetically, but

thirty years after their referral to the clinic.[4] In addition to the clinic cases, 100 control subjects who had lived in the same geographic area served by the clinic but who had not been referred to it were also followed up in adulthood.

By interviewing the now-adult people chosen for both the experimental and control samples, the investigators were able to diagnose and describe any maladjustments of these individuals. Then adult problems were related back to the characteristics that these people had had as children to find out which of them predicted sociopathic behavior in adulthood. Robin's summary brings to mind the category Conduct Disorder, which will be discussed in Chapter 15, where we take up antisocial behavior in juveniles:

If one wishes to choose the most likely candidate for a later diagnosis of sociopathic personality from among children appearing in a child guidance clinic, the best choice appears to be a boy referred for theft or aggression who has shown a diversity of antisocial behavior in many episodes, at least one of which could be grounds for Juvenile Court appearance, and whose antisocial behavior involves him with strangers and organizations as well as with teachers and parents . . . more than half of the boys appearing at the clinic [with these characteristics were later] diagnosed socio-

---

[4]It should be appreciated that being able to track down this large a percentage of individuals thirty years after their contact with the clinic is an incredible feat.

"Which are you—a victim of society or a crook?"

we can expect the parental rearing practices to which they are exposed to be markedly different. Fraternal twins of the same sex are probably treated more alike than are fraternal twins of the opposite sex. This evidence, in point of fact, implicates environmental factors.

But more recent adoptee studies suggest that heredity may indeed play a role in both criminality and sociopathy. With the help of the extensive social records kept in Denmark, Hutchings and Mednick (1974) and Mednick, Gabrielli, and Hutchings (1984) examined rates of criminality in the adoptive and biological relatives of adoptees who had acquired criminal records. Schulsinger (1972) performed a similar study with sociopathy as the misconduct of interest. Both studies of criminality found it at a higher rate in the biological relatives of criminals than in the adoptive relatives. Schulsinger found more sociopathy in the biological relatives of sociopaths. Studies done in the United States of adopted children whose biological parents were antisocial personalities also point to a genetic predisposition (e.g., Cadoret *et al.*, 1985).

More complicated studies have examined both the criminality and the alcoholism of adoptees (Bohman *et al.*, 1982; Cloninger *et al.*, 1982). A large sample of adopted individuals were classified according to whether they had criminal records, a history of alcoholism, both, or neither. Criminals who were also alcoholic repeatedly committed violent offenses; risk for criminality in these individuals was linked to their own alcoholism but not to any criminal behavior of their biological parents. Nonalcoholic criminals tended to commit petty crimes, such as property offenses; their risk for criminality was associated with their biological parents' history of committing similar crimes as well as with instability in their placements before they were finally adopted. Thus these data again suggest that some forms of criminal behavior may have a genetic component.

Central Nervous System Activity and Sociopathy

Many early studies examined brain wave activity (see Box 10.3) in sociopaths and various groups of control subjects. Ellingson (1954) reviewed these studies and reported that in thirteen out of fourteen of them, investigating a total of about 1500 sociopaths, between 31 and 58 percent of the sociopaths showed some form of electroencephalogram (EEG) abnormality. The most frequent form of abnormality was slow-wave activity, which is typical of the infant and young child but not of the normal adult. The slow waves were widespread throughout the brain.

BOX 10.3

THE ELECTROENCEPHALOGRAM

The ***electroencephalogram*** or EEG is a graphic recording of the electrical activity of the brain. The brain is known to be continuously active, chemically and electrically, throughout life, even in sleep. Individual neurons of the central nervous system fire spontaneously at regular or irregular intervals, creating differences in electric potentials, that is, fluctuations in voltage. The fluctuations in voltage in the cortex, the portion of the brain immediately below the skull, can be picked up by two or more sensitive electrodes pasted to the scalp. The recording machine, the ***electroencephalograph,*** amplifies the pulsations one to two million times and connects them to a pen recorder (or recorders) that registers them on a continuously moving roll of graph paper as a pattern of oscillations. The spontaneous activity of the brain, known as its waves, varies in different cortical areas and in the other, less accessible portions of the brain. Perhaps most importantly, the dominant brain waves reflect the degree to which the brain has been aroused.

In a normal adult subject, awake but resting quietly with eyes closed, the dominant rhythm has a frequency of between 8 and 13 pulsations or cycles per second (cps) and an amplitude of from 40 to 50 microvolts. This low-frequency, high-voltage wave is called the ***alpha*** rhythm. When a stimulus is presented, the alpha rhythm is replaced by a high-frequency (14 to 25 cps), low-voltage rhythm, the ***beta*** rhythm. If very low frequency waves are found dominant in the awake adult, they are considered abnormal. These ***slow waves***, which are sometimes found in sociopaths while they are awake, are referred to as the ***theta*** (4 to 7 cps) and the ***delta*** (less than 4 cps) rhythms. Delta rhythms in normals occur during deep sleep; theta waves are commonly recorded from subcortical parts of the brain.

The electroencephalogram records electrical activity from several sources on the subject's scalp as well as muscles in the face.

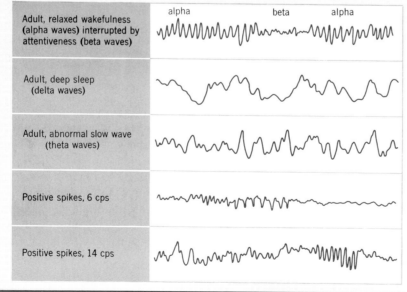

Adult, relaxed wakefulness (alpha waves) interrupted by attentiveness (beta waves)	alpha beta alpha
Adult, deep sleep (delta waves)	
Adult, abnormal slow wave (theta waves)	
Positive spikes, 6 cps	
Positive spikes, 14 cps	

FIGURE 10a
Patterns of electrical activity in the brain recorded by electroencephalograph. After Hare (1970).

Later findings reviewed by Syndulko (1978) generally agree with the earlier ones. Most studies report rather high frequencies of EEG abnormalities in sociopaths and the presence of slow waves and positive spikes in particular. **Positive spikes** occur in the temporal area of the brain and consist of bursts of activity with frequencies of 6 to 8 cycles per second (cps) and 14 to 16 cps. Not all sociopaths show EEG abnormalities, however, and it is unclear whether those who do differ in any other way from those who do not. Furthermore, the brain waves of sociopaths are not abnormally slow in all experimental contexts. Hare and Jutai (1985), for example, found the usual high levels of slow-wave activity when sociopaths were resting, but later, when they played an exciting videogame, their brain waves were the same as those of normal subjects.

Specific interpretations of the sociopath's EEG abnormalities remain highly speculative at this time. Hare (1970), for example, interprets the high frequency of slow-wave activity to indicate a dysfunction in inhibitory mechanisms, which, in turn, lessens the sociopath's ability to learn to forestall actions that are likely to get him or her into trouble. Although this interpretation is consistent with studies of the negligible effects of past punishment on sociopaths, it certainly is not the only one possible. But the *inability* of sociopaths *to learn to avoid or escape from punishment* has been an important subject of research.

Avoidance Learning, Punishment, and Sociopathy

As we have previously noted, in defining the sociopathic syndrome, Cleckley pointed out the inability of these persons to profit from experience; thus they do not try to avoid the negative consequences of social misbehavior. Cleckley also remarked that they were not neurotic and seldom anxious. From these clinical observations, Lykken (1957) deduced that sociopaths may have few inhibitions about committing antisocial acts because they experience so little anxiety. He performed several tests to determine whether sociopaths do indeed have low levels of anxiety. One of these tests involved avoidance learning.

A group of male sociopaths, judged to be so on the basis of Cleckley's criteria, were selected from a penitentiary population. Their performance on an avoidance learning task was compared to that of non-sociopathic penitentiary inmates[1] and of college students. It was of course critical that only avoidance and

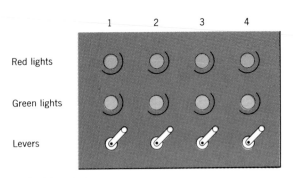

FIGURE 10.1

The apparatus devised by Lykken (1957) for his study of avoidance learning in sociopaths.

For the first lever press assume that lever 3 is correct, that is, that pressing it lights the green bulb; that levers 1 and 4 are incorrect, lighting red bulbs; and that pressing lever 2 lights a red bulb and gives the subject a shock. For the second lever press the meaning of the levers may change entirely; for example, lever 2 may be correct, levers 3 and 4 incorrect, and lever 1 may give the shock. The subjects had to learn a sequence of twenty correct lever presses.

not learning mediated by other possible rewards be tested. If a subject perceives that his task is to learn to avoid pain, he may be motivated not only by the desire to avoid the pain but also by a desire to demonstrate his cleverness to the investigator. To ensure that no other motives would become manifest, Lykken made the avoidance learning task *incidental*. He used the following apparatus. On a panel in front of the subject there were four red lights in a horizontal array, four green lights below each of the red ones, and a lever below each column, as illustrated in Figure 10.1. The subject's task was to learn a sequence of twenty correct lever presses, but for each he first had to determine by trial and error which of the four alternatives was correct. The correct lever turned on a green light. Two of the remaining three incorrect levers turned on red lights, indicating an error. The third incorrect lever delivered an electric shock to the subject. The location of the correct lever was of course not always the same. The subject was told simply to figure out and to learn the series of twenty correct lever presses. He was not informed that avoiding shock was desirable or possible, only that shock was randomly administered as a stimulant to make him do well. Thus the task yielded two measures of learning: the total number of errors made before the subject learned the correct sequence of twenty presses and the number of errors made that produced shock. Avoidance is measured by this second index.

In terms of the overall number of errors made, there were no significant differences among any of the groups in Lykken's study. The college students, however, were

---

[1] In the literature such people are sometimes referred to as neurotic sociopaths. We have avoided using this confusing term since, by definition, a sociopath is not neurotic.

apparently best able to remember the sequence of presses that produced shock and thus sharply decreased their proportion of shocked errors. The sociopaths made the most shocked errors, but the differences between their shocked errors and those of the other penitentiary inmates only approached statistical significance. The results of Lykken's investigation therefore tentatively support the hypothesis that sociopaths operate under lower levels of anxiety than do normal individuals.

Lykken also tried to verify his reduced-anxiety hypothesis by giving his subjects standard psychological tests for measuring anxiety, such as the Taylor Manifest Anxiety Scale. On these tests the sociopaths showed lower levels of anxiety, providing further confirmation for the low anxiety theory.

Lykken's pioneering work was subsequently followed up by Schachter and Latané (1964). These investigators reasoned that if sociopaths fail to learn to avoid unpleasant stimuli because they have little anxiety, a procedure that increases their anxiety should help them learn to shun punishment. Inasmuch as anxiety is viewed as being related to activity of the sympathetic nervous system, they injected Adrenalin, an agent whose effects mimic sympathetic activity, in order to increase anxiety.

Sociopathic and nonsociopathic prisoners from a penitentiary were studied with the same task and apparatus that had been devised by Lykken. The subjects were led to believe that the effects of a hormone on learning were being investigated. Testing took place on two consecutive days. Half received a placebo injection on the first day of testing and half an injection of Adrenalin. On the second day of testing, the injections received by the subjects were reversed.

The results of Schachter and Latané's experiment were important in several ways. First, the overall number of errors provided confirmation for Lykken's results: no difference was found between the sociopathic and nonsociopathic prisoners in the total number of errors committed in learning the sequence, whether they had been injected with Adrenalin or the placebo. Second, the nonsociopathic prisoners injected with the placebo markedly reduced their proportion of shocked errors after a number of runs, but the sociopaths injected with the placebo showed no such improvement. In this part of the study, the difference between the performances of the two groups of prisoners was greater than that revealed in Lykken's experiment and considerably larger than the amount necessary for statistical significance. Third, and most important, when injected with Adrenalin, the sociopaths showed a great reduction in the number of shocked errors, but the nonsociopathic prisoners *were* adversely affected by the

Stanley Schachter, social psychologist at Columbia University, known for his theory that emotion has both cognitive and physiological aspects. He has investigated the relation between arousal in the autonomic nervous system, emotion, and sociopathy.

Adrenalin and did not learn to avoid the shock in their state of high arousal (Figure 10.2). Thus the hypothesis of the anxiety-free and *underaroused* sociopath received considerable support from the work of Schachter and Latané.[6]

In a guessing game situation, Newman, Kosson, and Patterson (1987) also studied how sociopaths fail to learn from negative experiences. In each trial the subjects were shown playing cards on a computer-generated video display. If a face card appeared the subject won five cents; if a non-face card appeared the subject lost five cents. After the presentation of each card the subject had the option to continue or to end the game. The probability of losing was controlled by the experimenter and started at 10 percent for the first 10 cards played. Thereafter, the probability of losing increased in 10 percent steps with each succeeding block of ten cards until it reached 100%. Sociopathic prison inmates continued to play the game longer than nonsociopathic inmates. Indeed, in the condition just described, nine of twelve sociopaths never quit even though they lost money on nineteen of the last twenty trials.

The same game was played with groups of socio-

---

[6]The finding that the Adrenalin injection apparently worsened the avoidance learning performance of the nonsociopathic prisoners is difficult to interpret. A follow-up test by Schachter and Latané did not reproduce this effect.

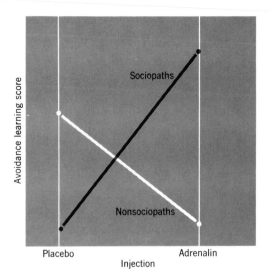

FIGURE 10.2

Results of Schrachter and Latané's study (1964) of the effects of Adrenalin on avoidance learning in sociopathic and nonsociopathic prisoners. Higher scores reflect better avoidance learning; increasing arousal through Adrenalin helped the sociopaths to learn to avoid shock by activating their otherwise underaroused autonomic nervous systems.

pathic and nonsociopathic prisoners with one procedural variation—a five-second waiting period was imposed after feedback thus delaying the decision about whether to play again or quit. This manipulation dramatically reduced the number of trials for which sociopaths played the game. In this condition they did not differ from the nonsociopathic prisoners. Imposing a delay may therefore force sociopaths to use feedback and thus behave less impulsively.

An avoidance learning study by Schmauk (1970) qualifies the findings of Lykken as well as those of the other studies we have discussed. He showed that a particular kind of punishment, losing money, can have an effect on sociopaths. He tested three groups: sociopathic prisoners, nonsociopathic prisoners, and a control group consisting of farmworkers and hospital attendants. As in the previous studies, an avoidance learning task was devised, but this time three different aversive stimuli could be avoided: a physical punishment—electric shock; a tangible punishment—losing a quarter from an initial pile of forty; and a social punishment—the experimenter's saying "wrong" to the subject. There were again no differences among the groups in the total number of errors made before the task was mastered. The major finding of this study (Figure 10.3) indicated that the sociopath's avoidance performance varies with the nature of punishment. When the punishments confronting them were physical and

social, the members of the control group were vastly superior to the sociopaths in learning to avoid punishment. But the sociopaths outdid the controls in learning to avoid the tangible punishment of losing a quarter. The nonsociopathic prisoners did better than the sociopaths in learning to avoid physical punishment but less well in avoiding social punishment.

It appears then that sociopaths *can* learn to avoid punishment. The differences found between sociopaths and nonsociopaths in previous investigations may reflect not a general deficit in avoidance learning ability but rather the fact that some punishments have no meaning for the sociopath. Evidently, sociopaths will learn to avoid punishment that is relevant to their system of values, and money may very well be particularly motivating to them.

An alternative explanation of these results has been suggested by Newman and Kosson (1986). They pointed out that Schmauk's tangible punishment condition differed from shock avoidance in several respects. Most important to Newman and Kosson was the fact that in the tangible punishment condition the punishment was very salient. Subjects saw the stack of quarters in front of them and could keep their winnings. In contrast, in the shock avoidance condition subjects were not even told that the shock could be avoided.

On the basis of this reasoning, Newman and Kosson hypothesized that salience of the punishment was the

FIGURE 10.3

Mean avoidance learning scores plotted for three subject groups confronted by three different punishments, physical, tangible, and social. The sociopaths readily learned to avoid punishment when it cost them money. After Schmauk (1970).

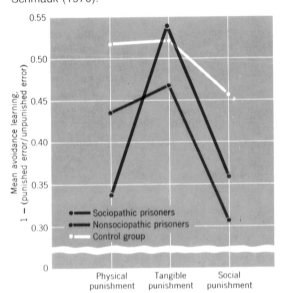

critical variable and tested it by studying sociopaths and controls on two versions of a discrimination learning task. In one condition subjects were rewarded when they responded correctly and punished when they made an error. In the second condition subjects were not rewarded for a correct response; they were only punished for errors. The punishment should be more salient in the second condition because it is the only consequence to which a subject must attend.

Comparison of the number of punished errors in each condition supported the hypothesis. Sociopaths did not differ from controls in the punishment-only condition but in the reward and punishment condition they showed their usual performance deficit, making more punished errors than did controls. Getting the sociopath's attention may be what's needed for a punishment to be effective.

Underarousal and Sociopathy

Sociopaths have often been described as not responding emotionally when confronted by both familiar and new situations that most people would find either stressful or unpleasant. Cleckley (1976) has written about this aspect of their behavior.

Regularly, we find in [the sociopath] extraordinary poise rather than jitteriness or worry, a smooth sense of physical well-being instead of uneasy preoccupations with bodily functions. Even under concrete circumstances that would for the ordinary person cause embarrassment, confusion, acute insecurity, or visible agitation, his relative serenity is likely to be noteworthy. (p. 340)

This description is remarkably consistent with the Schachter and Latané finding that sociopaths do not ordinarily avoid electric shock but that they do so when their autonomic arousal is increased by injections of Adrenalin. Because of the assumed central role of the autonomic nervous system in states of emotion, several investigators have examined sociopaths both for their resting levels of autonomic activity and for their patterns of autonomic reactivity to various classes of stimuli.

Most studies indicate that in resting situations sociopaths have lower than normal levels of skin conductance. Furthermore, their skin conductance is less reactive when they are confronted with intense or aversive stimuli. A different picture emerges, however, when heart rate is examined. The heart rate of sociopaths is like that of normal people under resting con-

ditions, and their heart rate reactivity to neutral stimuli is also unremarkable. But in situations in which sociopaths anticipate a stressful stimulus, their hearts beat faster than those of normal people anticipating stress.

These physiological reactions indicate that the sociopath cannot be regarded as simply underaroused, for measurements of skin conductance and heart rate are inconsistent. Basing his theorizing in part on Lacey's work (1967), Hare (1978) focuses on the *pattern* of psychophysiological responses of sociopaths. Faster heartbeats are viewed as a concomitant of gating out or reducing sensory input and thus lowering cortical arousal. Thus the increased heart rate of sociopaths who are anticipating an aversive stimulus would indicate that they are "tuning it out." Their skin conductance is then less reactive to an aversive stimulus because they have been able effectively to ignore it. That is, with skin conductance considered an index of anxiety, that of sociopaths does not increase to any extent after expected aversive stimulation because they have already dealt with it by screening it out. This interpretation of the physiological reactions of sociopaths is plausible and consistent with the studies reviewed earlier on avoidance learning. Further research by Hare and his associates has confirmed that both in their behavior and in their physiological responses (Jutai and Hare, 1983) psychopaths are particularly adept at ignoring stimuli.

The fact that sociopaths are underaroused or are better able to control their arousal has additional implications. Quay (1965) suggested that the sociopath's impulsiveness, thirst for excitement, and inability to tolerate routine and boredom are fostered by their lesser emotional reactivity and by their ability to block out arousing sensory input and thus stem cortical arousal. Quay's reasoning is based on the hypothesis that there is an optimal level of arousal for human beings. When arousal is too high an individual will take steps to reduce it, and when it is too low the individual will take steps to increase it. Much of the sociopath's "thrill seeking" behavior could then be viewed as an attempt to increase his or her arousal enough to approach this optimal state.

If it is true that sociopaths seek excitement to raise their arousal levels, we might expect their performance on a tedious and monotonous task to be especially poor. Orris (1967) tested prisoners on such a task. The findings bore out the prediction. Sociopathic prisoners performed less well than did the others. We might also predict that given a choice, sociopaths will prefer novel and complex stimuli. Such stimuli are generally viewed as having high-arousal properties, and thus the sociopath might be expected to show a preference for them. Skrzypek (1969) tested this hypothesis on a sample of sociopathic and other prisoners and found that socio-

Some research suggests that the thrill seeking of sociopaths is an attempt on their part to make up for a level of arousal that is chronically too low.

paths indeed showed a somewhat greater preference for novelty and complexity than did the other prisoners.

The case histories, studies, and theories that we have reviewed show the sociopath to be an individual who does not react as most of us do. In particular, he has almost no anxiety, so it can have little deterrent effect. Moreover, because the sociopath is in greater control of his negative emotional reactions, arousal is actually sought. And because the sociopath is deficient in planning and in inhibition, he behaves impulsively. These are possible reasons for the sociopath's misconduct without regret and for his thrill seeking without regard for society's rules.

Therapies for Personality Disorders

There is as little research-based information on treating personality disorders as there is information on how they develop. There is, though, a lively and burgeoning clinical case literature on therapies for many of the personality disorders. Though the ideas outlined in the following are for the most part based on the clinical experiences of a small number of mental health profes-

sionals, and not on studies that contain suitable controls, these therapeutic guidelines are all that is available on treating personality disorders.

A sense of what the literature contains can be appreciated from some ideas put forth by Millon (1981) in his widely known book on personality disorders (Millon was part of the DSM-III team that worked on the personality disorders). He suggests that:

1. Therapy with dependent personalities is facilitated by the fact that these people seek out stronger others on whom they rely. They therefore make willing and receptive patients. However, this trait can make them *too* dependent on the therapist and less likely to make their own decisions and to take responsibility for themselves. Millon suggests that nondirective approaches work better than behavioral ones because they foster independence.

2. Histrionic personalities do not remain in therapy for long, especially when sources of anxiety are probed (as most therapists, regardless of theoretical orientation, will do). Millon proposes cognitive therapy to help the histrionic personality learn to think rather than to act impulsively.

3. Passive-aggressive personalities make treatment difficult because of their very problem—they forget appointments, come late, and fail to do between-

session appointments. Psychoanalytic techniques of interpreting such resistance may be helpful.

4. The schizoid personality might be helped to reduce isolation through behavioral techniques such as social skills training.

However, it is noteworthy that, like others who write about and work with personality disorders, Millon is very cautious about expecting too much from therapy when the range of problems is so broad and all-encompassing.

Therapy for the Borderline Personality

A number of drugs have been tried in the pharmacotherapy of borderline personality disorder, most notably antidepressants and neuroleptics. However, most of the available data come from uncontrolled clinical trials (Gunderson, 1986). The exception to this is a double-blind, placebo-controlled study showing the effectiveness of neuroleptics (Soloff *et al.*, 1986).

The borderline personality disorder has attracted a great deal of attention in recent years. The leading theoretician is Otto Kernberg (1985), whose "object relations theory" operates from the basic assumption that borderline personalities have weak egos and therefore inordinate difficulty tolerating the regression (probing of childhood conflicts) that occurs in psychoanalytic treatment. The weak ego fears being flooded by primitive primary process thinking. Kernberg's modified analytic treatment has the overall goal of strengthening the patient's weak ego. Therapy involves analysis of a principal defense of the borderline person, namely, "splitting," or dichotomizing into all good or all bad and not integrating positive and negative aspects of a person into a whole. Somehow this defense protects the borderline's weak ego from intolerable anxiety. The borderline must also be helped to reality-test (though it is not clear in what way this is different from the overall psychoanalytic goal of helping patients discriminate between irrational childhood-based fears and adult reality). Kernberg's approach is more directive than that of most analysts: he gives the patient concrete suggestions for behaving more adaptively and will hospitalize if the patient's behavior becomes dangerous to either the self or others. His opinion that such patients are inappropriate for classical psychoanalysis is consistent with a long-term study conducted at the world-famous analytically oriented Menninger Clinic (Stone, 1987).

An approach that combines client-centered empathy with behavioral problem solving is suggested by Linehan (1987). What she calls "dialectical behavior ther-apy" centers on the therapist fully accepting borderlines with all their contradictions and acting out, empathically validating their (distorted) beliefs with a matter-of-fact attitude toward their suicidal and other dysfunctional behavior. The behavioral aspect of the treatment involves helping the patient learn to problem-solve, that is, to acquire more effective and socially acceptable ways of handling their daily living problems. Work is also done on improving their interpersonal skills and in controlling their anxieties. After many months of intensive treatment, limits are set on their behavior, consistent with what Kernberg recommends.

Behavior Therapy for Disturbed Personalities

Behavior therapists, in keeping with their attention to situations rather than to traits, have no specific treatments as such for histrionic personality, borderline personality, or any of the other personality disorders designated by DSM-IIIR. Rather they analyze the problems that, taken together, might be considered by an enthusiast of DSM-IIIR to reflect a personality disorder. For example, the man diagnosed as having a paranoid personality will be very sensitive to criticism. This sensitivity may be treated by systematic desensitization or rational-emotive therapy (see Chapter 2, page 51). His argumentativeness and hostility when he disagrees with other people will push them away from him and provoke counterattacks from them. The behavior therapist may help the man learn more adaptive ways of disagreeing with other people. A passive-aggressive individual might be given assertion training on the assumption that learning more forthright ways to express displeasure will reduce his reliance on indirect methods. Social skills training in a support group might be considered a way to encourage avoidant personalities to be more bold in initiating contacts with other people. This technique, perhaps combined with rational-emotive therapy, may help them not catastrophize when their efforts to reach out do not succeed, as is bound to happen (Turkat and Maisto, 1985).

One aspect of a personality disorder commands the attention of any skilled behavior therapist, as well as that of any other professional helper, namely, the alleged deeply ingrained, long-standing, and pervasive nature of the problem. A man will bear the diagnosis of paranoid personality only if his tendency to be suspicious and guarded is chronic and permeates his overall psychological functioning. Any therapist working with him must therefore consider the broad implications of his problem. Before a highly suspicious person can express emotion openly and appropriately, he must make

Prisons have failed as vehicles of rehabilitation.

major and difficult changes in his assumptions about people and in his general mode of functioning. In other words, therapy must take into consideration the pervasive, wide-ranging nature of a person's particular personality disorder and, in addition, the person's general intractableness.

Therapy for Sociopathy

As for the treatment of antisocial personality disorder, there is unusual—and unfortunate—agreement among therapists of varying theoretical persuasions: sociopathy is virtually impossible to treat (Cleckley, 1976; McCord and McCord, 1964).

It may be that people with the classic symptoms listed by Cleckley are, by their very natures, incapable of

benefiting from any form of psychotherapy. The most likely reason is that they are unable to form any sort of trusting, honest relationship with a therapist. A person who lies almost without knowing it, who cares little for the feelings of others and understands his own even less, who appears not to realize that what he is doing is morally wrong, who lacks any motivation to obey society's laws and mores, and who, living only for the present, has no concern for the future is all in all an extremely poor candidate for therapy. In fact, one clinician, experienced in working with sociopaths, has suggested three general principles.

First, the therapist must be continually vigilant with regard to manipulation on the part of the patient. Second, he must assume, until proven otherwise, that information given him by the patient contains distortions and fabrications. Third, he must recognize that a working alliance develops, if ever, exceedingly late in any therapeutic relationship with a psychopath. (Lion, 1978, p. 286)

To be sure, many valiant attempts have been made to establish tenable connections with sociopaths, but both the published literature and informal communications among mental health professionals support the conclusion that true sociopathy cannot be reached through clinical efforts. Similar negative conclusions are to be drawn as well about somatic methods—electroconvulsive shock, drugs such as Dilantin, stimulants, and sedatives, and psychosurgery.[7] There is, however, some evidence that antianxiety agents can, in large doses, reduce hostility in sociopaths (Kellner, 1982) and there is some very tentative evidence that sociopaths who had attention deficit disorder (see Chapter 15, page 413) as children might benefit from the drug Ritalin, which has had some positive effects with hyperactive youngsters (Stringer and Josef, 1983).

Since many sociopaths spend time in prison for crimes that they have been convicted of, the discouraging results of imprisonment as rehabilitation are traced at least in part to the inability to modify sociopathic behavior. As criminologists have stated repeatedly (e.g., Wilkins, 1969), our prison system seems to operate more as a school for crime than it does as a place where criminals, and sociopaths, can be rehabilitated. Ramsey Clark, a former United States attorney general, put it this way: "Prisons in the United States today are more often than not manufacturers of crime . . . [They] are usually little more than places to keep people—warehouses of human degradation" (1970, p. 213). For a time in the 1970s, there was interest in developing new therapy programs for prisoners. Operant conditioning regimens, usually token economies, were established for especially violent prisoners, and different kinds of group therapy tried to encourage the more tractable prisoners to assume some responsibility for their behavior. For a variety of reasons, including the claims of civil liberties groups that therapy in a prison setting is unconstitutional, fewer therapeutic efforts are now made on behalf of prisoners. Indeed, the trend seems to be to regard imprisonment as simply

punishment for transgression against society. Little attention is paid to trying to help those convicted so that they will "go straight" upon release.

An interesting argument in favor of incarceration is that psychopaths often "settle down" in middle age and thereafter (Craft, 1969). Whether through physiological changes, eventual insight into their self-defeating natures, or simply becoming worn out and unable to continue in their finagling ways, many sociopaths grow less disruptive as they approach forty. Prison, therefore, protects society from the antisocial behavior of "active" sociopaths, with release considered more plausible when the prisoner enters a stage of life in which the excesses of his sociopathy are less in evidence.

Summary

The category of personality disorders is an extremely broad and heterogeneous one. Personality disorders are grouped into three clusters in DSM-IIIR. Individuals in the first cluster are odd and eccentric; those in the next dramatic and emotional; and those in last anxious and fearful. There is little information on most of the personality disorders. The notable exception is sociopathy, the dominant pattern of which is repeated antisocial behavior without regret or shame. In addition, sociopaths are thought to be unable to learn from experience, to have no sense of responsibility, and to establish no genuine emotional relationships with other people. Research on their families indicates that sociopaths had fathers who themselves were antisocial and that discipline was either absent or inconsistent. Genetic studies, particularly those using the adoptee method, suggest that a predisposition to sociopathy is inherited. The core problem of the sociopath may be that impending punishment creates no inhibitions about committing antisocial acts. A good deal of overlapping evidence supports this view: (1) sociopaths have abnormal amounts of slow-wave EEG activity, which may reflect a failure of the usual inhibitory processes; (2) sociopaths are slow at learning to avoid shock, a deficit that can be reduced by heightening the sociopath's level of physiological arousal; and (3) sociopaths, according to their electrodermal responses, show little anxiety but, as indicated by their faster heat rates, seem better able than normal people to tune out aversive stimuli.

Little is know about effective therapy for the various personality disorders, for several reasons. The poor reliability of the diagnoses and the tendency to use the

---

[7]An ethical problem can arise from this notion that sociopaths have a poor prognosis. If a prisoner is considered a sociopath, those in charge of decisions about parole and release are naturally concerned whether he has really changed his ways. His good behavior in prison may merely reflect his manipulativeness and ability to "con" people. The person designated a sociopath may thus be at a serious disadvantage in obtaining just treatment from the judicial system.

category as a grab bag make it difficult to evaluate reports of therapy. Therapy for the sociopath in particular holds little promise for a successful outcome. In addition to the pervasiveness and apparent intractability of the uncaring and manipulative life style, the antisocial personality is by nature a poor candidate for therapy. People who habitually lie and lack insight into their own or others' feelings—and have no inclination to examine emotions—will not readily establish a trusting and open working relationship with a therapist.

Roy Carruthers, *Three Smokers*, 1977. Courtesy of ACA Galleries, New York.

Chapter 11

Psychoactive Substance Use Disorders

Alcoholism
   Short-Term Effects of Alcohol
   Long-Term Effects of Prolonged Alcohol Use
   Theories of Alcoholism
   Therapy for Alcoholism
Sedatives and Stimulants
   Sedatives
   Stimulants
   Theories of the Origins of Drug Addiction
   Therapy for the Use of Illicit Drugs
Nicotine and Cigarette Smoking
   Prevalence and Consequences of Smoking
   Is Smoking an Addiction?
   Treatment and Prevention of Cigarette Smoking
Marijuana
   Frequency of Marijuana Use
   Reasons for Use
   Effects of Marijuana
LSD and Other Psychedelics
   Research on the Effects of Psychedelics
   The Problem of Flashbacks
Summary

Alice was 54 when her family finally persuaded her to check into an alcohol rehabilitation clinic. She had taken a bad fall down her bedroom steps while drunk and it may have been this event that finally got her to admit that something was wrong. Her drinking had been out of control for several years. She began each day with a drink, resulting in total intoxication by the afternoon. She seldom had any memory for events after noon of any day.

Since early adulthood she had drunk regularly but rarely during the day, and never to the point of drunkenness. The sudden death of her husband in an automobile accident two years earlier had triggered a quick increase in her drinking, and within six months she had slipped into a pattern of severe alcohol abuse. She had little desire to go out of her house and had cut back on social activities with family and friends. Repeated efforts by her family to get her to curtail her intake of alcohol had only led to angry confrontations.

From prehistoric times humankind has used various substances in the hope of reducing physical pain or altering states of consciousness. Almost all peoples have discovered some intoxicant that affects the central nervous system, relieving physical and mental anguish or producing euphoria. Whatever the aftermath of taking such substances into the body, their effects are usually pleasing, at least initially.

Alcoholic beverages from the fermentation of many fruits and grains, of milk, honey, and molasses, and even of tree sap; opium, the dried milky juice obtained from the immature fruit of the opium poppy; hashish and marijuana from *Cannabis*, the hemp plant; and cocaine, an alkaloid extracted from coca leaves—these are the major natural drugs that have a long history of both use and abuse, and that continue to present problems for society. In the United States and other Western countries, morphine, an alkaloid extracted from opium, and heroin, derived from morphine, are more prevalent than the raw opium, and dried marijuana is used more often than hashish. The use of inhalants and solvents also has a history in humankind's efforts to alter their feelings and consciousness—William James, the famed American psychologist of the late nineteenth and early twentieth century, praised the effects of nitrous oxide; and people have used and still do use agents like paint thinner, glue, chloroform, and nutmeg, especially when socially sanctioned drugs like alcohol are not at hand. A number of newer synthetic and synthesized drugs are also available, most importantly the barbiturates, the amphetamines, LSD, and PCP. Of all the potentially dangerous drugs, the one craved by the greatest number of people is nicotine, the principal alkaloid of tobacco.

Many of those who abuse drugs use more than one drug at any given time. ***Polydrug abuse*** poses a serious health problem because the effects of some drugs when taken together are synergistic, that is, the effects of each interact to produce an especially strong reaction. For example, mixing barbiturates with alcohol is a common means of suicide, be it intentional or accidental. Alcohol is believed to have contributed to deaths from heroin as well, for evidence indicates that alcohol can dramatically reduce the amount of narcotic that need be taken for it to be a lethal dose. The pathological use of substances that affect the central nervous system falls into two categories: psychoactive substance abuse and psychoactive substance dependence. Together, these constitute the major category, Psychoactive Substance Use Disorders.

Alcoholic beverages provide one of the major substances of abuse.

DSM-IIIR defines *psychoactive substance dependence* as the presence of three of the following symptoms for at least one month.

1. The person uses more of the substance or uses it for a longer time than intended.

2. The person recognizes excessive use of the substance; may have tried to reduce it but has been unable to do so.

3. Much of the person's time is spent in efforts to obtain the substance or recover from its effects.

4. The person is intoxicated or suffering from withdrawal symptoms at times when responsibilities need to be fulfilled (e.g., work).

5. Many activities (work, recreation, socializing) are given up or reduced in frequency because of the use of the substance.

6. Problems in health, social relationships, and psychological functioning occur (e.g., excessive use of alcohol is often linked to depression).

7. *Tolerance* develops, requiring larger doses (at least a 50 percent increase) of the substance to produce the desired effect.

8. *Withdrawal symptoms* develop when the person stops taking the substance or reduces the amount.[1]

9. The person uses the substance to relieve the withdrawal symptoms (e.g., drinking alcohol early in the morning because the first unpleasant feelings of withdrawal are beginning).

Psychoactive substance abuse is a less severe version of dependence. It is diagnosed when the person's use of a substance is maladaptive but not severe enough to meet the diagnostic criteria for dependence.

The DSM-IIIR section Psychoactive Substance Use Disorders considers only the *behavior* associated with the regular use of substances that interfere with everyday life. If a person who is addicted to a drug is denied it and therefore thrown into withdrawal, that person would be diagnosed as having a substance dependence

and, in addition, would receive a diagnosis of psychoactive substance-induced organic mental disorder. An example is alcohol withdrawal delirium, commonly known as the DTs (see page 283). In this chapter, then, which covers all psychological and physical problems created by drugs, we necessarily deal with facets of drug abuse that DSM-IIIR puts into more than one major section.

Alcoholism

Written reports of the use of wines, beers, and other alcoholic beverages date back to 3000 B.C., but not until about 800 B.C. was the distillation process applied to fermented beverages, making possible the preparation of the highly potent liquors that are available today. Alcohol consumption has risen, both in America and in most other countries. In 1940, for example, 30 percent of the American population were drinkers and 2 percent problem drinkers. By 1970, 68 percent of the population drank, 9 percent problematically (Caddy, 1983). As of 1985, 86 percent of the population reported having consumed alcohol, and about 12 percent reported using it twenty or more days each month (NIDA, 1988). In the large American epidemiological study described on page 113, lifetime prevalence rates for alcoholism defined by DSM-III criteria were over 20 percent for men and just under 5 percent for women (Robins *et al.*, 1984).

Although most of the people who have a drinking problem do not seek professional help, alcoholics do constitute a large proportion of new admissions to mental and general hospitals. The suicide rate of alcoholics, especially of women alcoholics, is much higher than that of the general population. A third of all suicides have alcohol as a contributing cause. Moreover, some estimate that alcohol is implicated in at least 25,000 highway deaths each year, about half the total number. Alcohol may be a factor as well in airplane crashes, industrial accidents, and mishaps in the home. Alcohol also presents law enforcement problems, for about one-third of all arrests in the United States are for public drunkenness. Homicide is an alcohol-related crime—over half of all murders are believed committed under its influence—and so too are parental child abuse, spouse abuse, and sexual offenses (Brecher, 1972; National Institute on Alcohol Abuse and Alcoholism, 1983). The overall cost of problem drinking in the United States—from absenteeism to damaged health—was estimated in 1983 to be more than 116 billion dollars (National Council on Alcoholism, 1986). It is judged that up to

---

[1]Tolerance and withdrawal were at one time used to define the term addiction, implying that addiction was a physiological process rather than a psychological dependency. This distinction is not viewed by DSM-IIIR as a useful one; one reason is the difficulty in distinguishing between people believed to be physically dependent on a drug and those thought to be psychologically dependent. Furthermore, even classic addiction with obvious tolerance and withdrawal is not always disabling, as when a patient becomes addicted to prescribed pain medication. Nonetheless, the drug abuse literature reviewed in this chapter does speak of addiction as a physiological dependency, so we will discuss theories and data in a way that distinguishes physical dependency from psychological abuse.

Many highway fatalities are due to drunk driving. Here a breathalyzer test is being administered.

40 percent of patients in general hospitals are being treated for alcohol-related disorders. Alcoholics use health services four times more than do nonalcoholics, and their medical expenses are twice as high as those of nondrinkers (*The Harvard Medical School Mental Health Letter*, 1987). The human costs, in terms of broken lives and losses to society, are incalculable (Jaffe, 1985).

As in the more general diagnoses of substance abuse and dependence, DSM-IIIR distinguishes between *alcohol dependence* and *alcohol abuse*. Important components of alcohol dependence include tolerance or withdrawal reactions, such as morning "shakes" and malaise, which can be relieved only by taking a drink. Persons who begin drinking early in life develop their first withdrawal symptoms in their thirties or forties. The pattern of drinking indicates that it is out of control. Individuals will need to drink daily, being unable to stop or cut down despite repeated efforts to abstain completely or to restrict drinking to certain periods of the day. They may go on occasional binges, remaining intoxicated for two, three, or more days. Sometimes they consume a fifth of alcohol at a time. They may suffer "blackouts" for the events that took place during a bout of intoxication; their craving may be so overpowering that they are forced to ingest alcohol in a nonbeverage form, such as hair tonic. Such drinking of course causes social and occupational difficulties, quarrels with family or friends, sometimes violence when intoxicated, frequent absences from work or loss of job, and arrest for intoxication or for traffic accidents. Polydrug abuse often involves alcohol, and DSM-IIIR indicates that nicotine dependence is especially com-

mon in association with heavy drinking, as any visit to a cocktail lounge will confirm (though we do not mean to imply that all those in cocktail lounges are alcoholics).

Short-Term Effects of Alcohol

Physiological Effects

After being swallowed, alcohol does not undergo any of the processes of digestion. A small part of the alcohol ingested passes immediately into the bloodstream through the stomach walls, but most of it goes into the small intestines and from there is absorbed into the blood. It is then broken down, primarily in the liver, which can metabolize about one ounce of 100 proof (that is, 50 percent alcohol) whiskey per hour. Quantities in excess of this amount remain in the bloodstream. Whereas absorption of alcohol can be very rapid, removal is always slow. Many of the effects of alcohol vary directly with the level of concentration of the drug in the bloodstream, which in turn depends on the amount ingested in a particular period of time, the presence or absence in the stomach of food to retain the alcohol and reduce its absorption rate, the size of the individual's body, and the efficiency of the liver.

Because the drinking of alcoholic beverages is accepted in most societies, alcohol is rarely regarded as a drug, especially by those who drink. But it is indeed a drug and acts as a depressant on the central nervous system. The initial effect of alcohol is stimulating. Tensions and inhibitions are reduced, and the individual may experience an expansive feeling of sociability and well-being. Some people, though, become suspicious and even violent. Larger amounts interfere with complex thought processes; then motor coordination, balance, speech, and vision are impaired. At this stage of intoxication, some individuals become depressed and withdrawn. Alcohol is capable of blunting pain and in larger doses of inducing sedation and sleep. Before modern techniques of anesthesia were discovered, liquor was often administered to a patient about to undergo surgery.

Behavioral Effects

Studies have determined that the short-term effects of alcohol on social drinkers are complex. Jones and Parsons (1975) reviewed a number of experiments that suggest, among other things, that effects vary depending on whether the person is becoming drunk or sobering up. In one such experiment Jones and Parsons (1971) assessed the abstract problem-solving ability of drinkers. Those on the downward part of the curve, that is, drinkers becoming sober, performed significantly better with a particular level of alcohol in their blood than did those who were getting high and had the same level. A person apparently thinks better, at a given stage of intoxication, if he or she is becoming less drunk than if becoming more so. The short-term memories of those becoming sober appear to be similarly good and those becoming intoxicated to be similarly poor (Jones, 1973).

It now appears that some of the short-term effects of ingesting small amounts of alcohol are more strongly related to beliefs about the effects of the drug than to its chemical action on the body. For example, alcohol is commonly thought to stimulate aggression and increase sexual responsiveness. Research has shown, however, that these reactions may not be caused by alcohol itself but by beliefs about alcohol's effects. Subjects in experiments demonstrating these points are told that they will be consuming a quantity of alcohol but, in fact, are given an alcohol-free beverage with its taste disguised so that they will not see through the ruse. They subsequently become more aggressive (Lang *et al.*, 1975) and more sexually aroused (Wilson and Lawson, 1976). Indeed, subjects who merely believe that they have drunk alcohol, but have not, sometimes act the same way as subjects who have actually consumed the drug. Once again, cognitions have a demonstrably powerful effect on behavior.

Studies of alcohol's effects on sexual responding confirm Shakespeare's observation that "Lechery, sir, it provokes, and it unprovokes: it provokes the desire but it takes away the performance" (*Macbeth*, Act II, Scene 3). In the first experiment published on the effects of alcohol on the physiology of sexual responding, a plethysmograph was used to determine genital blood flow (see Box 12.2, page 328). Farkas and Rosen (1976) showed male subjects an erotic film after they had drunk one of four concentrations of alcohol ranging from 0 percent (pure orange juice) to 0.075 percent, which corresponds to about five drinks of straight whiskey. In each case the amount of alcohol could not be detected by the taste of the drink. The men who ingested more alcohol had less penile erection. Thus, in a laboratory setting, the more alcohol consumed, the more it took away from "performance."

Do women respond in the same way? Wilson and Lawson (1976) confirmed that female physiological sexual arousal was also reduced by drinking a large amount of alcohol. But when the women *believed* that they had drunk alcohol, they reported feeling sexually aroused even though, if the amount was large, their vaginal blood flow indicated little arousal. As psychologists have learned more than once, the Bard of Avon had great insight into the workings of humankind.

Long-Term Effects of Prolonged Alcohol Use

The possible long-term effects of prolonged drinking are vividly illustrated in the following case history.

At the time of his first admission to a state hospital at the age of twenty-four, the patient, an unmarried and unemployed laborer, already had a long history of antisocial behavior, promiscuity and addiction to alcohol and other drugs. . . . There had been eight brief admissions to private sanatoria for alcoholics, a number of arrests for public intoxication and drunken driving, and two jail terms for assault.

The patient had been born into a wealthy and respected family in a small town. The patient's father, a successful and popular businessman, drank excessively and his death at the age of fifty-seven was partly due to alcoholism. The mother also drank to excess. The parents exercised little control over the patient as a child, and he was cared for by nursemaids. His father taught him to pour drinks for guests of the family when he was very young and he reported that he began to drain the glasses at parties in his home before he was six; by the time he was twelve he drank almost a pint of liquor every weekend and by seventeen was drinking up to three bottles every day. His father provided him with money to buy liquor and shielded him from punishment for drunken driving and other consequences of his drinking.

The patient was expelled from high school his freshman year for striking a teacher. He then attended a private school until the eleventh grade, when he changed the date on his birth certificate and joined the Army paratroops. After discharge, he was unemployed for six months; he drank heavily and needed repeated care at a sanatorium. When a job was obtained for him he quit within a month. On his third arrest for drunken driving he was jailed. His father bailed him out with the warning that no more money would be forthcoming. The patient left town and worked as an unskilled laborer—he had never acquired any useful skills—but returned home when his father died. During the next few years he was jailed for intoxication, for blackening his mother's eyes when he found a male friend visiting her, and for violating probation by getting

Some alcoholics end up on skid row.

drunk. He assaulted and badly hurt a prison guard in an escape attempt and was sentenced to two additional years in prison. When released, he began to use a variety of stimulant, sedative and narcotic drugs as well as alcohol. (Rosen, Fox, and Gregory, 1972, p. 312)

Course of the Disorder

The life histories of male alcoholics were once considered to share a common progression. On the basis of an extensive survey of 2000 such men, Jellinek (1952) described the male alcoholic as passing through four stages on the way to his addiction. In the *prealcoholic* phase the individual drinks socially and also on occasion rather heavily to relieve tension and to forget about his problems. In the second *prodromal stage* drinking may become furtive and may also be marked by blackouts. The drinker remains conscious, talks coherently, and carries on other activities, without even appearing to be greatly intoxicated, but later has no recall of the occasion. Alcohol begins to be used more as a drug and less as a beverage.

Jellinek terms the third phase *crucial*, choosing this adjective because he sees the alcoholic in this stage as being in severe danger of losing everything that he values. He has already lost control of his drinking. Once he takes a single drink, he continues to consume alcohol until he is too sick or in too much of a stupor to drink anymore. The individual's social adjustment also begins to deteriorate. He starts to drink during the day, and this becomes evident to his employer, family, and friends. The alcoholic neglects his diet, has his first bender, a

several-day period of excessive drinking, and may experience hallucinations and delirium when he stops drinking. At this stage the individual still has the ability to abstain. He can give up alcohol for several weeks or even months at a time, but if he has just one drink the whole pattern will begin again.

In the final *chronic stage* drinking is continual, and benders are frequent. The individual lives only to drink. His bodily systems have become so accustomed to alcohol that they must be supplied with it or he suffers withdrawal reactions. If liquor is not available to him, he will consume any liquid he can find that contains alcohol—shaving lotion, hair tonic, various medicinal preparations, whatever. He suffers from malnutrition and other physiological changes. He neglects his personal appearance and, having lost his self-esteem, feels little remorse about any aspect of his behavior. Finally, he ceases to care at all about family and home, about friends, occupation, and social status.

Jellinek's description has been widely cited, but the available evidence is not always corroborative. One study found that blackouts do *not* occur in conjunction with modest drinking and that many alcoholics have never experienced a blackout (Goodwin, Crane, and Guze, 1969). Other data question the commonly accepted notion that a single drink stimulates an irresistible impulse to continue drinking (Marlatt, Demming, and Reid, 1973). Alcoholics "primed" with an initial drink, one they believed to be nonalcoholic, later consumed no more alcohol than did social drinkers. Finally, there is much less consistency in the progression from problem drinking to alcoholism than Jellinek implied. In a four-year follow-up of problem drinkers, Clark and Cahalan (1976) found much variability in outcome. Furthermore, patterns of maladaptive use of alcohol are more variable than Jellinek implied. For example, heavy use of the drug may be restricted to weekends or long periods of abstinence may be interspersed with binges of continual drinking for several weeks.

A growing body of evidence also indicates that Jellinek's account does not apply to alcoholic women. Alcoholism usually begins at a later age in women than in men and very often after an inordinately stressful experience, such as the death of a husband or a serious family crisis. For women the time interval between the onset of problem drinking and alcoholism is briefer. Alcoholic women tend more than men to be steady drinkers and to drink alone; they are also less likely to engage in binge drinking (Hill, 1980; Wolin, 1980).

Physiological Effects

In addition to the psychological deterioration brought on by alcoholism, severe physiological damage is a serious consequence of chronic drinking. Almost every tissue and organ of the body is affected by the prolonged consumption of alcohol. The malnutrition suffered may be severe. Because alcohol provides calories—a pint of 80 proof spirits supplies about half a day's caloric requirements—alcoholics often reduce their intake of food. But the calories provided by alcohol are "empty"; they do not supply the nutrients essential for health. Alcohol also contributes directly to malnutrition by impairing the digestion of food. In the older chronic alcoholic a deficiency of B-complex vitamins is believed to cause severe memory loss (Korsakoff's psychosis, page 640). A drastic reduction in the intake of protein contributes to the development of cirrhosis of the liver, a disease in which some liver cells become engorged with fat and protein, impeding their function, and some cells die, triggering an inflammatory process. When scar tissue develops, blood flow is obstructed. Cirrhosis ranks eighth among causes of death in the United States, and for many years deaths from alcohol-related cirrhosis have remained constant at approximately 5 per 100,000 of the population (Malin *et al.*, 1982). The disease is more common in women alcoholics than in male. Alcohol per se also disturbs liver functions and damages liver cells. Other common physiological changes include damage to the endocrine glands and pancreas, heart failure, hypertension, and capillary hemorrhages, which are responsible for the swelling and redness in the face, and especially of the nose, of chronic alcoholics. Prolonged use of alcohol also appears to damage brain cells, especially those in the frontal lobes, causing cortical atrophy and other changes in structure (Parsons, 1975).

Heavy alcohol consumption during pregnancy can retard the growth of the fetus and infant and can cause cranial, facial, and limb anomalies as well as mental retardation. The condition is known as ***fetal alcohol syndrome.*** Even moderate drinking can produce less severe but undesirable effects on the fetus, leading the National Institute on Alcohol Abuse and Alcoholism to counsel total abstention during pregnancy as the safest course (*Alcohol, Drug Abuse and Mental Health Administration News*, May 2, 1980). Indeed, in 1988 it became law in several states to require explicit warnings where alcohol is served or sold that drinking can cause birth defects.

The effects of the abrupt withdrawal of alcohol from an alcoholic may be rather dramatic, for the body has become profoundly accustomed to the drug. Subjectively, the patient is often anxious, depressed, weak, restless, and unable to sleep. Tremors of the muscles, especially of the small musculatures of the fingers, face, eyelids, lips, and tongue, may be marked, and there is an elevation of pulse, blood pressure, and temperature. In relatively rare cases an alcoholic who has been drinking for a number of years may also suffer from ***delirium tremens*** (DTs) when the level of alcohol in the blood drops suddenly. He becomes delirious as well as trem-

Customers in bars must now be warned of the dangers of drinking during pregnancy.

ulous. His hallucinations are primarily visual, but they may be tactile as well. Unpleasant and very active creatures—snakes, cockroaches, spiders, and the like—may appear to be crawling up the wall or all over the alcoholic's body, or they may fill the room. Feverish, disoriented, and terrified, the alcoholic may claw frantically at his skin to rid himself of the vermin, or he may cower in the corner to escape an advancing army of fantastic animals.

The delirium and physiological paroxysms caused by withdrawal of alcohol indicate that the drug is addictive. Increased tolerance is also evident. Mello and Mendelson (1970) found that some alcoholics could drink a quart of bourbon a day without showing signs of drunkenness. Moreover, levels of alcohol in the blood of these people were unexpectedly low after what would usually be viewed as excessive drinking.

Although changes in the liver enzymes that metabolize alcohol can account to some extent for tolerance, most researchers now believe that the central nervous system is implicated. Alcohol can, for example, increase the fluidity of nerve cell membranes and by this process alter electrical conduction in the brain (National Institute on Alcohol Abuse and Alcoholism, 1983).

In short, *the psychological, physiological, and social consequences of prolonged consumption of alcohol are extremely serious.* Because the alcoholic's own functioning is so severely disrupted, the people he interacts with are also deeply affected and hurt by his conduct. Society too suffers, for the alcoholic is unlikely to be able to hold a job. As mentioned earlier, the accumulated costs—the money spent on liquor, the time lost in work efficiency, the damage of traffic accidents,

A vivid portrayal of the delirium tremens scene of a play.

the expense of physicians and psychologists—run to well over 100 billion dollars each year. The human tragedy, much more devastating, is virtually incalculable.

Theories of Alcoholism

In trying to understand alcoholism, we must draw a distinction between conditions that induce a person to *start* drinking and those that play the central role in *maintaining* the behavior. After years of continual, heavy drinking the alcoholic consumes alcohol both for its primary reinforcing effects and because it reduces the unpleasant feelings of withdrawal. Furthermore, episodes of withdrawal distress may become conditioned to a variety of environmental stimuli so that craving becomes virtually constant (Wikler, 1980). But these effects do not explain why an individual initially develops a drinking habit. Those who attempt to explain the origins of heavy drinking refer to either psychological or physiological factors. Within each of these two broad categories there are several theories.

Psychological Theories

Psychoanalytic Views Most analytic accounts of alcoholism point to fixation at the oral stage of development as the precipitating cause. Early mother–child interactions supposedly either frustrate dependency needs

during this stage of maturation or satisfy them to too great an extent. The various psychoanalytic theories therefore differ in the function attributed to excessive drinking. For example, Adams (1978) proposed that the male alcoholic's experience with an overprotective mother has created a strong need to remain dependent. When this need is frustrated, he becomes angry and aggressive and feels guilty about his impulses. He drinks heavily to reduce these impulses and also to punish those who withhold affection from him. Fenichel (1945), in contrast, stated that being neglected by the mother turns the young male child toward his father, which in turn produces unconscious homosexual impulses. These repressed impulses compel him to drink in bars with other men, an activity that supposedly allows the alcoholic to obtain some of the emotional satisfaction he has not received from women. (It is not clear what the psychodynamic significance of solitary drinking would be.) Bergler (1946), emphasizing the self-destructive nature of alcoholism, hypothesized that alcohol dependence is a means of attempting to destroy a bad mother with whom the individual has identified. Little evidence is available to support these hypotheses.

Other analytic accounts of alcoholism describe excessive drinking as a defense mechanism adopted to reduce emotional conflicts or eliminate guilt (Wurmser, 1981). A common analytic quip defines the superego as the part of the personality that is soluble in alcohol.

Personality and Alcoholism Many investigations have attempted to measure the personalities of alcoholics. Two points must be made about this research. First, no profile of a single "alcoholic personality" has been obtained. More typically a number of personality patterns are found among alcoholics (e.g., Skinner, Jackson, and Hoffman, 1974). Second, the research design of such studies suffers from the problems of interpretation that are inherent in correlational work. For example, if a given personality pattern is highly correlated with alcoholism, did the former cause the latter, or vice versa?

Some studies however, have employed a longitudinal design, which is more appropriate for studying the relationship between personality and alcoholism. Two important personality characteristics have emerged from this work. The first is hyperactivity in childhood. For example, in a prospective study spanning over ten years, Hechtman, Weiss, and Perlman (1984) found that hyperactivity was an important predictor of later alcohol abuse. The second is antisocial behavior (Jones, 1968). Notably, hyperactivity and antisocial behavior are themselves highly correlated and there are some indications that it is antisocial behavior that has the greater ability to predict adult outcomes (see Chapter 15, page 416). Indeed, antisocial personality, itself linked to similar patterns in biological parental background, is predictive of drug abuse problems generally, including alcoholism (Cadoret *et al.*, 1986).

Epidemiological Studies There is great cross-national variation in alcohol consumption (see Table 11.1). Norway's average of 5.4 liters of 100 proof alcohol per person is only about one-fifth of France's average of 24.1 liters. These statistics are based on government records of the tax revenues from the sale of alcoholic beverages. The taxes are then converted to an estimate of absolute alcohol so that the alcoholic content of different beverages can be averaged for the number of people over the age of fifteen.

It has been proposed that the greater the consumption in a culture, the greater will be the rate of alcoholism (Ledermann, 1956). The consumption statistics in Table 11.1 would thus be a direct reflection of cross-national differences in the rates of alcoholism. Cultural attitudes and patterns of drinking therefore influence the likelihood of drinking heavily and therefore of abusing alcohol.

A study carried out by McCord, McCord, and Gudeman (1959, 1960) also reveals the importance of ethnic and cultural backgrounds in the etiology of alcoholism of males in the United States. Young men who had been intensively studied several years earlier as adolescents were followed up. In examining the earlier histories of those who had become alcoholics, the inves-

TABLE 11.1

Alcohol consumption in litres of absolute alcohol per capita for those aged 15 years and older

Country	1960	1973	Change*
France	27.3	24.1	−12
Italy	19.1	21.1	10
Spain	11.9	18.5	55
Luxembourg	13.8	18.5	34
West Germany	10.2	16.8	65
Portugal	15.3	17.9	17
Russia	10.4	14.7	41
Switzerland	12.5	19.3	54
Austria	10.9	16.0	47
Belgium	11.7	14.5	24
Hungary	9.2	13.2	43
Australia	9.5	12.2	28
New Zealand	9.3	11.7	26
East Germany	7.8	12.3	58
Yugoslavia	8.0	10.5	31
United States	7.8	10.6	36
Denmark	6.1	11.0	80
Canada	7.8	11.1	42
Great Britain	6.8	10.0	47
Sweden	5.9	8.0	36
Netherlands	3.8	10.1	166
Poland	6.2	9.2	48
Republic of Ireland	4.9	9.0	84
Finland	3.9	7.8	100
Norway	3.6	5.4	50

Note: From "Alcohol Consumption and Alcohol Problems from an Epidemiological Perspective" by J. deLint, 1978, *British Journal of Alcohol and Alcoholism,* **13,** 75–85. Copyright © 1978 by Pergamon Press. Adapted by permission.
*1960 = 100.

tigators found the relation of alcoholism and ethnic background to be significant. More young men with American Indian, western and eastern European, and Irish backgrounds were alcoholic than were those of Italian and other Latin extractions. The investigators also found a relation between alcoholism and social class: more of the alcoholics were from the middle class than from the lower class.

Epidemiologists studying alcoholism also examine the broad social contexts in which people live. Fillmore and Caetano (1980) found unusually high levels of alcoholism among sailors, railroad workers, and people in the "drink trade"—restaurant owners, bartenders, waiters, and liquor dealers. In all these occupations heavy drinking is normative, that is, almost expected as part of the job, and alcohol is readily available to these men. A survey of occupational drinking by Mannello and Seaman (1979) showed that 14 percent of railroad workers

Vinicultural societies, like France and Italy, have high rates of alcohol abuse.

drank on the job, 5 percent came to work drunk or got drunk on duty, and 20 percent reported to work with hangovers. These are alarming statistics, considering the fact that railroad personnel are responsible for the physical safety of hundreds of thousands of people each day. In sum, social and cultural factors play an important role in the etiology of alcoholism.

Learning Views The notion that the consumption of alcohol can *reduce distress* is advanced in learning-based accounts of alcoholism. An early experiment by Conger (1951) demonstrated that alcohol can relieve fear. First, animals were trained in a classic approach–avoidance situation: after having been trained to feed in a particular place, the animals were subjected to shock when they approached their food. Half of the animals were then injected with alcohol. These animals were found to approach the food more readily than did the controls. The fear that had become associated with the goal was apparently decreased by the alcohol in the bloodstream of the animals. Other investigations have replicated this work and also shown that conflict increases alcohol consumption (Freed, 1971; Von Wright, Pekanmaki, and Malin, 1971).

Generalizing from these studies, we might argue that drinking alcohol is a learned response that is acquired and maintained because it reduces distress. However, should not the extremely serious long-term negative effects of alcohol outweigh the transient relief from stress felt when alcohol is first consumed? Dollard and Miller (1950) offered as a solution to this seeming paradox the concept of a ***delay of reward gradient.*** According to

this formulation, the effectiveness of both rewards and punishments, in terms of their impact on any particular behavior, tends to decrease as they become farther and farther removed in time from the response. Thus a small but immediate reward exerts a more powerful effect than a larger one that does not immediately follow the response. Similarly, an immediate punishment is a much more effective agent of change than a punishment imposed several days, weeks, or even months later. In this sense the short-term reduction of distress offered by alcohol is seen as a rather large and immediately reinforcing benefit. Conversely, the longer-term negative effects of alcohol are of no avail in discouraging its consumption because they are suffered so long after the actual drinking.

The theory that the alcoholic drinks because alcohol reduces tension does not, however, appear to account for the maintenance of heavy drinking over long periods of time. For example, Nathan and his colleagues (1970) reported a study in which alcoholics residing in a specially designed hospital ward were carefully observed. The patients were allowed to work to obtain points that could later be exchanged for alcohol. Although the patients themselves reported that they drank to relieve anxiety and depression, an assessment of their moods by means of a self-report adjective checklist indicated that they were actually *more* anxious and depressed after drinking. Similar results were reported by Mendelson (1964).

Although several studies do indicate that alcohol can reduce tension (e.g., Sher and Levenson, 1982) in people who are not yet alcoholic, there are also conflicting findings (e.g., Thyer and Curtis, 1984). Perhaps alcohol reduces tension in only some people, making them more likely to drink heavily. Researchers looking for a link between the tension-reducing effects of alcohol and various personality characteristics have, however, had disappointing results.

Other investigators who examined the inconsistent results focus on the situation in which alcohol is consumed. Steele and Josephs (1988) have proposed that alcohol produces its tension-reducing effect by altering cognition and perception. Specifically, they theorize that alcohol impairs cognitive processing and narrows attention to the most immediately available cues, resulting in what the authors term "alcohol myopia." Tension can then be reduced in two ways. First, the intoxicated person has less cognitive capacity to distribute between ongoing activity and worry. Second, if a distracting activity is available, attention will be diverted to it rather than focusing on worrisome thoughts. However, in some situations alcohol could increase tension, for example, when an intoxicated person has no distractors present and therefore focuses all his limited processing capacity

TABLE 11.2

Results of the Steele and Josephs (1988) experiment showing differential effects of alcohol on anxiety*

Group	Amount of anxiety at beginning of wait period	Amount of anxiety halfway through wait period
No alcohol/slides	54.6	56.4
Alcohol/no slides	57.4	66.8
No alcohol/no slides	56.5	55.5
Alcohol/slides	63.5	53.0

*The larger the percentage the higher the anxiety.

on unpleasant thoughts. In this case, the discouraged person can become even more depressed as he drinks alone.

In an experiment designed to test this theory, subjects were led to believe that they would have to give a speech on the topic "What I dislike most about my body and personal appearance." Half the subjects were given alcohol (gin and tonic; 1 ml ethanol/kg of body weight); the other half were led to believe they were getting alcohol but just got tonic (disguised so the deception would not be obvious). After the beverages were consumed, there was a fifteen-minute waiting period before the speech was to be delivered. During this waiting period, half the subjects in each group were given a distracting task of making esthetic judgments of art slides while the other half of each group sat quietly.

The dependent variable was anxiety, which had been assessed several times by a self-report measure. Some of the data are shown in Table 11.2. As can be seen, anxiety ratings remained virtually unchanged among the no alcohol subjects from the beginning of the waiting period to the halfway point, and, as predicted by the theory, anxiety decreased in subjects who were given alcohol and were distracted by the slides. The cognitive and perceptual effects of the alcohol altered the subjects so that their focus was on the art slides and not on the upcoming self-deprecating speech. Also as predicted, anxiety increased in subjects who received alcohol and were not distracted. Apparently, these people focused excessively on the upcoming stress and became even more anxious as time passed.

Physiological Theories

Among animals a preference for alcohol or indifference to it varies with the species. By using selective mating within a species showing a preference, animals that greatly prefer alcohol to other beverages can be bred (Segovia-Riquelme, Varela, and Mardones, 1971). There is also evidence that alcoholism in human beings runs in families. A number of studies indicate that relatives and children of alcoholics have higher than expected rates of alcoholism. Studies indicating greater concordance for alcoholism in identical twins than in fraternal twins also point toward a possible role of heredity. Although these findings are consistent with the genetic transmission of a predisposition, these individuals might also have become alcoholics through exposure to drinking.

One study, however, examined alcoholism in the adopted male offspring of alcoholics, thus allowing the role of heredity to be more precisely specified (Goodwin et al., 1973). One hundred seventy-four subjects were chosen from an initial pool of 5483 male babies who were adopted in Copenhagen between 1924 and 1947. Subjects were divided into three groups.

1. *N* = 67: One and sometimes both biological parents of each subject (proband) in the experimental group had been hospitalized for alcoholism. The probands had been adopted within six weeks of birth by nonrelatives and had had no subsequent contact with biological relatives.

2. *N* = 70: Each subject in this control group was matched for age and time of adoption with a subject in group 1. None of the biological parents of these control subjects had a record of psychiatric hospitalization.

3. *N* = 37: The subjects in this control group were matched for age and time of adoption with subjects in group 1. At least one biological parent of each of these control subjects had been hospitalized for a psychiatric condition other than alcoholism or schizophrenia.

When this original sample was followed up, 133 subjects were located and interviewed. (Those who could

TABLE 11.3

The alcohol-related problems of offspring of alcoholics, adopted and raised by others, compared with those of controls

(*from Goodwin et al., 1973*)

Problems	Probands, percent (N = 55)	Controls, percent (N = 78)
Ever divorced	27	9
Any psychiatric treatment	40	24
Psychiatric hospitalization	15	3
Drinking problems Hallucinations (as withdrawal symptoms)	6	0
Loss of control	35	17
Repeated morning drinking	29	11
Treated for drinking	9	1
Alcoholic diagnosis	18	5

not be located or who refused to be questioned were proportionately distributed across groups.) The subjects, who had a mean age of thirty at the time of the follow-up, were interviewed by a psychiatrist blind to their group assignment. Questions covered their drinking practices, psychopathology, and demographic variables. Since the subjects in the two control groups did not differ on any of the classificatory variables except having or not having a parent with a record of psychiatric hospitalization, they were combined into one comparison group for purposes of analysis. Problems that significantly discriminated between the two groups are given in Table 11.3.

As can be seen, the two groups are easily distinguished from each other on the basis of alcohol-related measures. Thus the results suggest that in men a predisposition toward alcoholism can be inherited.

Subsequent research has generally confirmed Goodwin's findings for adopted males (e.g., Cadoret, Cain, and Grove, 1980). The results of studies with adopted daughters, however, are less clear. Goodwin and his colleagues (1977) found little evidence for any genetic contribution, but Bohman, Sigvardsson, and Cloninger (1981) found adopted daughters to be susceptible to alcoholism if their biological mother was alcoholic.

Large-scale adoptee research conducted in Sweden has raised the possibility that there are subtypes of alcoholism with different genetic bases (Cloninger *et al.*,

1981). The investigators divided their sample of biological parents into two groups according to their pattern of alcohol abuse. One group of biological parents had an adult onset of alcoholism, no history of criminal behavior, and were believed to be episodic alcoholics. The second group of parents had both an early onset of drinking problems and a history of antisocial behavior. They were viewed as the continual alcoholics.

For the first adoptee subtype (bingers), both genes and environment seemed necessary to produce disorder. An alcoholic parent and exposure to a pattern of heavy drinking in the adoptive home predicted alcoholism in these subjects. In contrast, the children whose biological parents continually used alcohol had only a genetic effect, but their risk of alcoholism was increased markedly. This effect held only for male adoptees.

In speculating on what might be inherited as a diathesis for alcoholism, Goodwin (1979) proposes the ability to tolerate alcohol. To become an alcoholic, a person first has to be able to drink a lot, in other words, be able to tolerate large quantities of alcohol. Some ethnic groups, notably Asians, may have a low rate of alcoholism because of their physiological intolerance. Indeed, about three-quarters of Asians experience unpleasant effects from small quantities of alcohol. Noxious effects of the drug may then protect a person from alcoholism.

Goodwin's hypothesis focuses on short-term effects, possibly on how alcohol is metabolized or on how the central nervous system responds to alcohol. Animal research indicates that genetic components are at work in both these processes (Schuckit, 1983). Corroborating this notion are recent findings from research using the high-risk method. Typically, studies have compared young, nonalcoholic adults with a first degree alcoholic relative to similar individuals without a positive family history for the disorder. Although there have been inconsistencies in published results, two findings have recently been replicated by Schuckit and Gold (1988), in one of the best studies yet reported. Of a number of variables examined, two were the strongest discriminators between groups:

1. Sons of alcoholics self-reported less intoxication than controls after a dose of alcohol.

2. Sons of alcoholics showed a smaller hormonal response (cortisol and prolactin) to the alcohol.

The smaller response of the sons of alcoholics may at first seem puzzling but it may well fit with the notion that you have to drink a lot to become an alcoholic. A small response to alcohol may provide a context for heavier than normal drinking.

Therapy for Alcoholism

The havoc created by alcoholism, both for the drinkers themselves and for their families, friends, employers, and communities, makes this problem the most serious public health issue in this country. As already mentioned, no dollar figure can be put on the human tragedy that is a direct result of this most prevalent form of drug abuse. For these reasons industry spends large sums of money in support of various alcohol rehabilitation programs for employees, in the knowledge that for every dollar spent in this way, many more dollars will be returned in improved functioning of workers. Television and radio carry public service messages about the dangers of alcoholism, in attempts to discourage people from beginning to drink to excess and to encourage those already affected to own up to their problem and seek help. Calling excessive drinking a disease is believed preferable to holding persons responsible for their drinking; presumably this lessens guilt and allows them to mobilize their resources to seek help and combat their alcoholism.

Traditional Hospital Treatment

Both public and private hospitals around the world have for many years provided retreats for alcoholics, sanctums where individuals can "dry out" and avail themselves of a variety of individual and group therapies, which they will need. The withdrawal from alcohol—*detoxification*—can be very painful, both physically and psychologically, and usually takes about one month. Tranquilizers are sometimes given to ease the anxiety and general discomfort of withdrawal. Because many alcoholics misuse tranquilizers, some clinics try gradual tapering off without tranquilizers rather than a sudden cutoff of alcohol. The alcoholic will also need carbohydrate solutions and B vitamins and perhaps an anticonvulsant.

Among the treatments available for the alcoholic to choose from is disulfiram, or Antabuse, which discourages drinking by causing violent vomiting if alcohol is ingested. Many alcoholics are naturally reluctant to take the drug, but if they can be motivated to do so, Antabuse can be an effective therapy (Bourne, Alford, and Bowcock, 1966). The effects of Antabuse last about four days. If the alcoholic patient agrees to take the drug every four days, he is fairly certain not to drink. This buys time, a precious commodity. For the first time in a long while, the person has the chance to live without booze, to experience a football game without beer, a business luncheon without a martini, an evening at home without cocktails. Problems underlying the reliance on alcohol can become more evident. The therapist will be better able to evaluate what needs to be worked on

in treatment, and with any luck the patient may begin to see the possibility of dealing with his problems without alcohol (Goodwin, 1982).

Alcoholics Anonymous

The largest and most widely known self-help group in the world is Alcoholics Anonymous (AA), founded in 1935 by two recovered drinkers. It currently has 30,000 chapters and a membership numbering more than a million people in the United States and ninety-one other countries throughout the world. An AA chapter runs regular and frequent meetings at which newcomers rise to announce that they are alcoholics, and older sober members give testimonials, relating the stories of their alcoholism and indicating how their lives are better now. The group provides emotional support, understanding, and close counseling for the alcoholic and a social life to relieve isolation. Members are urged to call upon one another around the clock when they need companionship and encouragement not to relapse into drink.

The belief is instilled in each AA member that alcoholism is a disease one is never cured of, that continuing vigilance is necessary to resist taking even a single drink lest uncontrollable drinking begin all over again. The important religious and spiritual aspect of AA is evident in the twelve steps of AA shown in Table 11.4. Two related self-help groups are of more recent origin. The relatives of alcoholics meet in Al-Anon Family Groups for mutual support in dealing with their alcoholic family members. Alateen is for the children of alcoholics, who also require support and understanding.

Alcoholics Anonymous meeting. AA is the largest self-help group for those with drinking problems.

TABLE 11.4
Twelve suggested steps of Alcoholics Anonymous

1. We admitted we were powerless over alcohol—that our lives had become unmanageable.
2. Came to believe that a power greater than ourselves could restore us to sanity.
3. Made a decision to turn our will and our lives over to the care of God *as we understood Him.*
4. Made a searching and fearless oral inventory of ourselves.
5. Admitted to God, to ourselves, and to another human being the exact nature of our wrongs.
6. Were entirely ready to have God remove all these defects of character.
7. Humbly asked Him to remove our shortcomings.
8. Made a list of all persons we had harmed, and became willing to make amends to them all.
9. Made direct amends to such people wherever possible, except when to do so would injure them or others.
10. Continued to take personal inventory and, when we were wrong, promptly admitted it.
11. Sought through prayer and meditation to improve our conscious contact with God *as we understand Him,* praying only for knowledge of His will for us and the power to carry that out.
12. Having had a spiritual awakening as the result of these steps, we tried to carry this message to alcoholics and to practice these principles in all our affairs.

Source: The Twelve Steps and Twelve Traditions. Copyright © 1952, by Alcoholics Anonymous World Services, Inc. Reprinted with permission of Alcoholics Anonymous World Services, Inc.

Unfortunately, the claims made by AA about the effectiveness of its treatment have rarely been subjected to scientific scrutiny. Available findings indicate that they should be viewed with some caution. For example, as many as 80 percent of people who join AA drop out (Edwards *et al.,* 1967). Furthermore, without follow-up it is impossible to know how enduring are the short-term changes that AA may effect. Since return to excessive drinking is the norm rather than the exception for alcoholics, the absence of such information prevents an adequate evaluation of what many regard as the best treatment for alcoholism.

Aversion Therapy

Behavioral researchers have been studying the treatment of alcoholism for many years. In fact, one of the earliest articles on behavior therapy concerned aversive "conditioning" of alcoholism (Kantorovich, 1930). With these procedures a problem drinker is shocked or made nauseous while looking at, reaching for, or beginning to drink alcohol. The aversive stimulus may also be vividly imagined in a procedure called **covert sensitization** (Cautela, 1966). Using a hierarchy of scenes designed to extinguish the desire to drink, the alcoholic is instructed to imagine being made violently and disgustingly sick by his or her drinking. The scientific and ethical complexities of aversion therapy are explored in Box 11.1.

Behavioral Contracting

Making a contract with the alcoholic is promising. An alcoholic in an institution agrees to refrain from excessive drinking in exchange for particular rewards, such as weekend passes or better living conditions on the ward. Provided that a patient can be persuaded to enter into the necessary contract, there is some evidence that control over drinking can be achieved (Nathan and Goldman, 1979).

Controlled Drinking

Until recently it was generally agreed that alcoholics had to abstain completely if they were to be cured,[2] for they were said to have no control over their imbibing once they had taken that first drink. Although this continues to be the abiding belief of Alcoholics Anonymous, the research mentioned earlier calls this assumption into question: drinkers' *beliefs* about themselves and alcohol may be as important as the physiological addiction to the drug itself. Indeed, considering the difficulty in our society of avoiding alcohol altogether, it may even be *preferable* to teach the problem drinker to imbibe with moderation. A drinker's self-esteem will certainly benefit from being able to control a problem and from feeling in charge of his or her life.

In the earliest training for controlled drinking, an outpatient was allowed to drink to a moderate level of intoxication and blood alcohol. He or she was then informed if the level of blood alcohol rose above a certain percent (Lovibond and Caddy, 1970). Thereafter when the person drank, he or she was supposedly able to keep the blood level of alcohol low.

Findings of one treatment program suggested that at least some alcoholics can learn to control their drinking and improve other aspects of their lives as well (Sobell and Sobell, 1976, 1978). Alcoholics attempting to control their drinking were given shocks when they chose straight liquor rather than mixed drinks, gulped their

---

It is widely believed that alcoholics are in fact never really cured, rather, that they can be in remission and must constantly fight the temptation to drink to excess.

BOX 11.1

ANOTHER LOOK AT AVERSION THERAPY FOR ALCOHOLICS

Based on the preparedness research reviewed earlier (page 138) and on recent animal research on conditioned taste aversion employing illness as the UCR (cf. Chambers, 1985), there is renewed interest in and evidence supporting the use of emetics (nausea-inducing drugs) in aversion therapy for alcoholics.

In an earlier study and consistent with the preparedness literature, Cannon and Baker (1981) showed that emetic-based aversion therapy produced a stronger aversion than that generated by using painful electric shock as the UCS. The conditioned response measures included heart rate increases, alcohol consumption, and subjective ratings of alcohol. Following up their subjects six months and a year later, Cannon, Baker, and Wehl (1981) found that the emetic therapy subjects were abstinent for more days than the shock subjects. (It is puzzling that at one-year follow-up, the emetine subjects were still more abstinent than the electric shock ones but *not* more so than control subjects, who had received no aversion therapy at all.) Significantly, abstinence was positively correlated with conditioned heart rate increases, a physiological measure considered to reflect classical conditioning.

A small sample and some ambiguity in the results prompted Cannon, Baker, Gino, and Nathan (in press) to conduct a more ambitious study with sixty alcoholics residing voluntarily in a private hospital specializing in emetic aversion therapy for substance abusers. There were two variations of emetic aversion: Regular (REG), in which subjects swallowed alcoholic drinks, were given a maximum dose of the nausea-producing drug emetine, and became ill and vomited, and Smell, Swish and Spit (SSS), in which patients did not swallow alcohol and were given a lower dose of emetine that made them feel awful, but did not make them vomit. There were five treatment sessions for both variations every other day. It is relevant to note that, like the other patients at the hospital, these subjects were highly motivated to stop drinking and participated in the various individual and group therapy sessions designed to teach alcoholics how to cope with life and find satisfaction without alcohol. Fifty-seven of the sixty subjects were interviewed one year after discharge, and efforts were also made to confirm their reports of abstinence or relapse with family members.

The abstinence rates for the REG and SSS treatments were similar—almost half the subjects in each group had not relapsed by the end of one year—even though subjects generally found the REG regimen more unpleasant than the SSS. Comparable conditioned aversions were established for all subjects as indexed by greater heart rate increases to alcohol post-treatment than to control beverages (those not paired with emetine-produced nausea). Electromyographic recordings of tension in facial muscles showed the same pattern as did self-report ratings and judgments made by those who saw videotapes of subjects tasting either alcohol or control beverages.

The key question in this study was whether degree of conditioned taste aversion predicted abstinence, that is, whether a person was more likely to remain dry after a year if he had shown significant aversive conditioning during the actual treatment. The results here were largely negative, albeit with a tendency for conditioned heart rate increase to be correlated with relapse at six-month (but not one-year) follow-up. Tendency to relapse after aversion therapy was positively associated with less social stability, having drunk more with neighbors prior to treatment, and having lower income.

Though not without its critics (Wilson, 1987), these admittedly mixed findings provide the strongest support to date for the efficacy of emetic aversion therapy in producing conditioned taste aversions *and* contributing to abstention from alcohol when the treatment is part of a multicomponent therapy program (not unlike the conclusions to be drawn later with cigarette smoking). That a low level of emetine, enough to produce illness but not vomiting, achieved effects similar to the maximal levels given in the REG treatment indicates that more patients (like those with hernias, for example) might be suitable for less risky and less arduous aversion therapy. Whether drastic treatment is worth the extreme discomfort and threat to health as compared to less distasteful and less grueling interventions is a subject for both future research and ethical discussion.*

---

*The controversial nature of aversion therapy is reflected in the Cannon *et al* report that, since completion of their research, the corporation that owned the hospital discontinued use of aversion therapy in all twenty-one of its institutions to improve their ability to recruit patients.

drinks down too fast, or took large swallows rather than sips. They were also given problem-solving and assertiveness training, watched videotapes of their inebriated selves, and identified the situations precipitating their drinking so that they could settle on a less self-destructive course of action. Their improvement was greater than that of alcoholics who tried for total abstinence and who were given shocks for any drinking at all. Several years later, however, these findings came under sharp attack. Many controlled-drinking patients did in fact continue to drink heavily and were not open with follow-up interviewers about their drinking practices (Pendery, Maltzman, and West, 1982). This issue is quite controversial (Marlatt, 1983). Many workers in the field continue to question the wisdom of **controlled drinking** for alcoholics, being concerned that for many the belief that they can imbibe with moderation will prove to be an illusion.

There may be a way to resolve this apparent inconsistency in findings and philosophy. Investigators at the Rand Corporation, a research institute in Santa Monica, California, determined that for some patients—alcoholics under forty with relatively little dependency on alcohol—controlled drinking seemed a better goal in rehabilitation than total abstinence. The opposite was true for older, more addicted drinkers, however (Armor, Polich, and Stambul, 1976, 1978). Of particular interest is the finding that moderate drinking rather than abstinence seems to work for some alcoholics who have gone through a total-abstinence program (Marlatt, 1983). In other words, although their treatment goal had been to cease all drinking, some of the patients adopted a pattern of moderate, off-and-on drinking while maintaining employment and other common indicators of any successful therapy.[3]

Contemporary controlled-drinking treatment programs do much more than the earliest ventures, which concentrated on teaching patients to monitor their blood alcohol levels. Patients are taught other ways of responding to situations that might lead to excessive drinking. Learning to resist social pressures to drink; assertiveness, relaxation, and stress management training, sometimes including biofeedback and meditation; and exercise and better diets will all help to bolster them. They are also taught that a lapse will not inevitably precipitate a total relapse and should be regarded as a learning experience. Sources of stress in their work, family, and relationships are examined. To be able to control their drinking, they must become active and responsible in anticipating and resisting situations that might tempt excesses (Marlatt, 1983).

Clinical Considerations

A general problem with attempts to treat alcoholism has been the therapist's often unstated assumption that all people who drink to excess do so for the same rea-

sons. Thus an analyst may assume that problem drinkers are trying to escape from intolerable feelings of dependency. A humanistic theorist may hold that the excessive drinker escapes into the haze of alcohol because he or she lacks courage to face problems and deal with them in an open, direct fashion. A behavior therapist favoring aversive treatment believes that reducing the attraction alcohol or its taste has for drinkers will help them abstain. As we might expect, excessive drinking is a complex human problem and it may be too simple to assume that all people drink for the same reason (Lazarus, 1965). A more sophisticated and comprehensive clinical assessment considers the place that drinking occupies in the person's life.[4] A woman in a desperately unhappy marriage, with meaningless time on her hands at home, now that her children are in school and no longer need her constant attention, may seek the numbing effects of alcohol just to help the time pass and to avoid facing her life dilemmas. Making the taste of alcohol unpleasant for this woman by pairing it with shock or an emetic seems neither sensible nor adequate. The therapist should concentrate on the marital and family problems and try to reduce the psychological pain that permeates her existence. She will also need help in tolerating the withdrawal symptoms that come with reduced consumption. Without alcohol as a reliable anesthetic, she will need to mobilize other resources to confront her hitherto avoided problems. Social-skills training may help her to do so.

In addition, alcoholism is sometimes associated with other mental disorders, in particular affective disorders and sociopathy (Goodwin, 1982). The clinician must conduct a broad-spectrum assessment of the patient's problem, for if heavy drinking stems from the desperation of deep depression, a regimen of Antabuse or any other treatment focused only on alcohol is unlikely to be of lasting value.

Even with the many treatment programs to help alcoholics live without their drug, it has been estimated that no more than 10 percent of alcoholics are ever in

---

[3]There is a definitional issue here. Are these younger drinkers really alcoholics? Some show no signs yet of tolerance and withdrawal. They might be called "problem drinkers" (Lang and Marlatt, 1982), people whose lives are seriously disrupted by periods of drunkenness but who have no clear signs of physical addiction. But to those who regard alcoholism as a progressive disease with an inexorable course of ever stronger addiction, such drinkers are incipient alcoholics, for whom total abstinence is the only sensible goal.

[4]Sound clinical practice can benefit also from empathy for what is involved in breaking an entrenched, overlearned pattern of behavior, whether there is a physical dependence or not. "It is helpful for any therapist who is going to work with alcoholics to personally give up some longstanding habit, such as smoking . . . [or] overeating. The therapist should keep a careful log of the behavior and a subjective account of the difficulties associated with the behavior change, especially noting relapse days. After several months of personal attempts at habit change, it is easier for a therapist to be empathic with alcoholics. . . . [Also] attending AA meetings is an excellent way of learning more about the subjective experience of being an alcoholic and helps the therapist to develop an appreciation of the pain involved in alcoholism and abstinence" (McCrady, 1985, pp. 262–263). It is interesting to note that this advice comes from a psychologist operating within a learning paradigm; cf. our earlier discussion of eclecticism in the practice of psychotherapy (page 56).

professional treatment and upwards of 40 percent cure themselves. How does such "spontaneous recovery" take place? Among the apparent factors are a new marriage, a new job, a religious or spiritual experience or conversion, a near-fatal auto accident while driving drunk, or being shaken by a serious illness. What is not clear is why some people can stop compulsive drinking after a serious crisis while others react by seeking the solace of the bottle (Vaillant, 1983). Whatever combination of factors that help alcoholics become abstinent or controlled drinkers, what seems important is *social support* for their efforts, whether it be from family, friends, work setting, or from self-help groups such as AA (McCrady, 1985).

Opium den in New York City's Chinatown.

Sedatives and Stimulants

Until 1914 addiction to drugs was disapproved in the United States, but it was tolerated. The 1914 Harrison Narcotics Act changed this, making the unauthorized use of various drugs illegal and those addicted to them criminals. The drugs to be discussed, not all of which are illegal, may be divided into two general categories. The major **sedatives,** called "downers," slow the activities of the body and reduce its responsiveness. In this group of drugs are the organic narcotics—opium and its derivatives morphine, heroin, and codeine—and the synthetic barbiturates such as seconal. The second group, the **stimulants** or "uppers," such as cocaine, act on the brain and the sympathetic nervous system to increase alertness and motor activity. The amphetamines, such as benzedrine, are synthetic stimulants; cocaine is a natural stimulant extracted from the coca leaf.

Sedatives

Narcotics

Opium, originally the principal drug of illegal international traffic, was known to the people of the Sumerian civilization dating as far back as 7000 B.C. They gave the poppy that supplied this narcotic the name by which it is still known and that means "the plant of joy." Opium is a mixture of about eighteen alkaloids, but until 1806 people had no knowledge of these substances to which so many natural drugs owe their potency. In that year the alkaloid **morphine,** named after Morpheus, the Greek god of dreams, was separated out from raw opium. This bitter-tasting powder proved to be a powerful sedative and pain reliever. Before its addictive properties were noted, it was commonly used

in patent medicines. In the middle of the century, when the hypodermic needle was introduced in the United States, morphine began to be injected directly into the veins to relieve pain. Many soldiers wounded in battle and those suffering from dysentery during the Civil War were treated with morphine and returned home addicted to the drug. Concerned about administering a drug that could disturb the later lives of patients, scientists began studying morphine. In 1874 they found that morphine could be converted into another powerful pain-relieving drug, which they named **heroin.** It was used initially as a cure for morphine addiction and was substituted for morphine in cough syrups and other patent medicines. So many maladies were treated with heroin that it came to be known as G.O.M. or "God's own medicine" (Brecher, 1972). Heroin, however, proved to be even more addictive and more potent than morphine, acting more quickly and with greater intensity. By 1909 President Theodore Roosevelt was calling for an international investigation of opium and the opiates.

Opium and its derivatives morphine and heroin produce euphoria, drowsiness, reverie, and sometimes a lack of coordination. Heroin has an additional initial effect, the "rush," a feeling of warm, suffusing ecstasy immediately following an intravenous injection. The addict sheds worries and fears and has great self-confidence for four to six hours, but then experiences letdown, bordering on stupor. Because these drugs are central nervous system depressants, they relieve pain. All three are clearly addicting in the physiological sense, for users show both increased tolerance of the drugs and withdrawal symptoms when they are unable to obtain another dose.

Our understanding of the process of addiction to opiates has increased greatly over the past decade. In the early 1970s several laboratories reported the presence in vertebrate brains of what appeared to be specific opiate receptors, that is, cell components to which opiates bind to produce euphoria and analgesia. Because it seemed unlikely that such receptors had developed to interact with opiate alkaloids in the environment, a search began for internally produced (endogenous) opiates. By 1975 such compounds, called **endorphins,** had been discovered in several species, including human beings (Goldstein, 1976). Apparently our bodies can produce natural opiates. Endorphins are thought to be the body's own pain relievers and may play a crucial role in addiction. Ingesting an exogenous opiate, such as heroin, may halt the normal production of endorphins. When the exogenous substance is no longer supplied, an individual could be left with no opiates in the body, either exogenous or endogenous, precipitating withdrawal reactions.

Reactions to not having a dose of heroin may begin within eight hours of the last injection, at least after high tolerance has built up. During the next few hours the individual will typically have muscle pain, will sneeze, sweat, become tearful, and yawn a great deal; the symptoms resemble influenza. Within thirty-six hours the withdrawal symptoms have become more severe. There may be uncontrollable muscle twitching, cramps, chills alternating with excessive flushing and sweating, and a rise in heart rate and blood pressure. The addict is unable to sleep, vomits, and has diarrhea. These symptoms typically persist for about seventy-two hours and then diminish gradually over a five- to ten-day period.

In spite of enormous difficulties in data gathering, the considered opinion is that there are more than half a million heroin addicts in the United States. Although this number appears to have remained stable over the past decade, there have been changes in the demographics of heroin abusers. In 1979, 36 percent of the heroin abusers admitted for emergency room treatment were over thirty years of age; by 1983, 58 percent of these admissions were over thirty. Similarly, the percentage of those over thirty years of age admitted to heroin treatment programs increased from 41 percent in 1979 to 50 percent in 1983. When combined with declining number of new cases, the conclusion is that current heroin abusers were initiated into its use in the 1960s and therefore represent an aging of this population of drug addicts (Kozel and Adams, 1986).

Even more serious than the physical effects are the social consequences of narcotic addiction. The drug and obtaining it become the center of the abuser's existence,

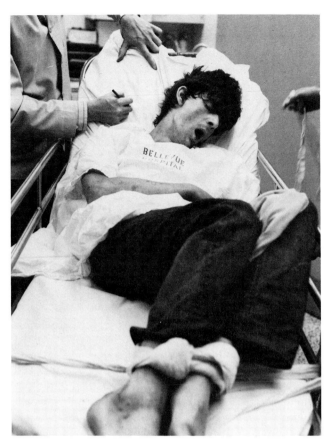

Overdosing is a constant danger to heroin addicts.

structuring all activities and social relationships. Since narcotics are illegal, addicts must deal with the underworld to maintain their habits. The high cost of the drugs—addicts must often spend $100 and more per day for their narcotics—means that they must either have great wealth or acquire money through illegal activities, such as prostitution or selling drugs themselves.[5] Thus the correlation between addiction and criminal activities is rather high, undoubtedly contributing to the popular notion that drug addiction per se causes crime.

Barbiturates and Other Sedatives

Barbiturates were synthesized as aids for sleeping and relaxation. The first was produced in 1903, and since then hundreds of derivatives of barbituric acid have been made. When properly prescribed and used, barbiturates can be safe and effective. Two types are usually distinguished—long-acting barbiturates for prolonged

---

[5] Recent indications are that heroin use is increasing in the upper socio-economic classes. For many years dependence has been many times higher among physicians and nurses than in any other group of comparable educational background. This problem is believed to arise from a combination of the relative availability of opiates in medical settings and the stresses under which people often work in such environments (Jaffe, 1985).

sedation and short-acting barbiturates for prompt sedation and sleep. The short-acting drugs are usually viewed as addicting. Initially, the drugs were considered highly desirable and were prescribed very frequently. In the 1940s, however, a campaign was mounted against them because they were discovered to be addicting, and physicians prescribed barbiturates less frequently. Today in the United States they are manufactured in vast quantities, enough, it is estimated, to supply each man, woman, and child with fifty pills per year. Many are shipped legally to Mexico and then brought back into the country and trafficked illegally. The majority of polydrug abusers choose a barbiturate or other sedative as one of their drugs.

Barbiturates (pentobarbital, secobarbital, and amobarbital) relax the muscles and in small doses produce a mildly euphoric state.[6] With excessive doses, however, speech becomes slurred and gait unsteady. Impairment of judgment, concentration, and ability to work may be extreme. The user loses emotional control and may become irritable and combative before falling into a deep sleep. Very large doses can be fatal because the diaphragm muscles relax to such an extent that the individual suffocates. As we have indicated in Chapter 9, barbiturates are frequently chosen as a means of suicide. But many users accidently kill themselves by drinking alcohol, which potentiates, or magnifies, the depressant effects of barbiturates. With prolonged excessive use the brain can become damaged and personality deteriorates.

Increased tolerance follows prolonged use of the barbiturates, and the withdrawal reactions after abrupt termination are particularly severe and long lasting and can even cause sudden death. The delirium, convulsions, and other symptoms resemble those following abrupt withdrawal of alcohol.

Three types of abusers can be distinguished. The first group fits the stereotype of the illicit drug abuser: adolescents and young adults, usually male and often antisocial, who use the drugs to alter their moods and consciousness, sometimes mixing them with other drugs. The second group consists of middle-aged, middle-class, "respectable" individuals who begin their use of sedatives under a physician's orders, to alleviate sleeplessness and anxiety, and then come to use larger and larger doses until they are addicted. These people rely less on street purchases because they are generally able to obtain refills of their drug prescriptions whenever they wish, sometimes switching doctors so as not to raise

suspicion. The third group are health professionals, physicians and nurses, who have easy access to these drugs and often use them to self-medicate for anxiety-related problems (Shader, Caine, and Meyer, 1975; Liskow, 1982).

Stimulants

Amphetamines

In seeking a treatment for asthma, the Chinese-American pharmacologist Chen studied ancient Chinese descriptions of drugs. He found a desert shrub called ma-huang commended again and again as an effective remedy. After systematic effort Chen was able to isolate an alkaloid from this plant that belongs to the genus *Ephedra;* ephedrine did indeed prove highly successful in treating asthma. But relying on the shrub for the drug was not viewed as efficient, and so a search began for a synthetic substitute. The ***amphetamines*** were the result of this search (Snyder, 1974).

The first amphetamine, Benzedrine, was synthesized in 1927. Almost as soon as it became commercially available in the early 1930s as an inhalant to relieve stuffy noses, the public discovered its stimulating effects. Physicians thereafter prescribed it and the other amphetamines soon synthesized to control mild depression and appetite. During World War II soldiers on both sides were supplied with the drugs to ward off fatigue; today amphetamines are sometimes used to treat hyperactive children (see page 418).

Amphetamines such as Benzedrine, Dexedrine, and Methedrine produce effects similar to those of norepinephrine in the sympathetic nervous system. They are taken orally or intravenously and can be addicting. Wakefulness is heightened, intestinal functions are inhibited, and appetite is reduced—hence their use in dieting. The heart rate is increased and blood vessels in the skin and mucous membranes constrict. The individual becomes alert, euphoric, and more outgoing and is possessed with seemingly boundless energy and self-confidence. Larger doses can make the person nervous, agitated, and confused, subjecting him or her to palpitations, headaches, dizziness, and sleeplessness. Sometimes the high-level user becomes so suspicious and hostile that he or she can be dangerous to others. There are some reports that large doses taken over a period of time induce a state quite similar to paranoid schizophrenia, including its delusions. This state can persist beyond the time that the drug is present in the body. Frequent ingestion of large amounts of amphetamines is also believed to cause brain damage.

Tolerance develops rapidly so that mouthfuls of pills are required to produce the stimulating effect. As tol-

---

[6]Methaqualone, a sedative sold under the trade names Quaalude and Sopor, is similar in effect to barbiturates and has become a popular street drug. Besides being addictive, it has other dangers—internal bleeding, coma, and even death from overdose.

BOX 11.2

OUR TASTIEST ADDICTION—CAFFEINE

What may be the world's most popular drug is seldom viewed as a drug at all, and yet it has strong effects, produces tolerance in people, and even subjects habitual users to withdrawal. Users and nonusers alike joke about it, and most readers of this book have probably had some this very day. We are of course referring to caffeine, a substance found in coffee, tea, cocoa, cola and other soft drinks, in some cold remedies, and in some diet pills.

Coffee, introduced from Arabia and Turkey in the fifteenth and sixteenth centuries, was, like tobacco, initially considered abhorrent to Europeans and Americans. "Proper" people regarded it as hazardous and drinking it unseemly because of its stimulating effects, which sometimes included "blasphemous" speech. Yet its popularity spread. People found that it "quickens the spirits," and they liked its taste, which improved with the addition of sugar, making the beverage even more popular. In 1652 the first London coffeehouse was established. In 1854 the first coffeehouses appeared in Constantinople. It is impossible to picture present-day Western culture and much of Eastern without the ceremony and sociability of moments shared over cups of coffee (Brecher, 1972).*

Two cups of coffee, containing between 150 and 300 milligrams of caffeine, affect most people within half an hour. Metabolism, body temperature, and blood pressure all increase; urine production goes up, as most of us will attest; there may be hand tremors, appetite can diminish, and, most familiar of all, sleepiness is warded off. Extremely large doses of caffeine can cause headache, diarrhea, nervousness, severe agitation, even convulsions and death. Such deaths, though, are virtually impossible unless

"Jump-start?"

Drawing by Stevenson; © 1989 The New Yorker Magazine, Inc.

the individual grossly overuses tablets containing caffeine, for the drug is rapidly excreted by the kidneys without any appreciable accumulation.

Habitual users find it difficult to begin their day without their usual mug or two of the brew and, when they cannot, sometimes suffer such withdrawal symptoms as headaches, irritability, and mood changes. Although parents usually deny their children access to coffee and tea, often they do allow them to imbibe caffeine-laden cola drinks, hot chocolate, and cocoa, and to eat chocolate candy and coffee- and chocolate-flavored ice cream (Berger and Dunn, 1982). Thus our addiction to caffeine can begin to develop as early as six months of age, the form of it changing as we move from childhood to adulthood.

*Some of these cups of coffee are these days decaffeinated, as health-conscious consumers try to avoid or escape from the craving for caffeine. But it is not unusual to hear regular, caffeinated coffee referred to as "real" coffee. In turn, decaffeinated versions endeavor valiantly to establish themselves as legitimate coffee beverages.

---

erance increases, the user may stop taking pills and inject Methedrine, the strongest of the amphetamines, directly into the veins. The so-called speed freaks give themselves repeated injections of the drug and maintain intense and euphoric activity for a few days, without eating or sleeping (a "run"), after which they are exhausted and depressed and sleep or "crash" for several days. Then the cycle starts again. After several repetitions of this pattern, the physical and social functioning of the individual will have deteriorated considerably. Behavior will be quite erratic and hostile, and the speed freak may become a danger to himself and to

others. Of particular concern is the fact that as many as 20 percent of high school students have taken amphetamines at least once, and its use among younger adolescents is on the increase (Goodwin and Guze, 1984).

Cocaine

The Spanish conquistadors introduced coca leaves to Europe. The Indians of the Andean uplands, to which the coca shrubs are native, chew the leaves, but the Europeans chose to brew them instead in beverages. The alkaloid *cocaine* was extracted from the leaves of the coca plant in 1844 and has been used since then as a local anesthetic. In 1884, while still a young neurologist in Vienna, Sigmund Freud began using cocaine to combat his depression. Convinced of its woundrous effects, he prescribed it to a friend with a painful disease and published one of the first papers on the drug, "Song of Praise," which was an enthusiastic endorsement of the exhilarating effects he had experienced.[7] One of the early products using coca leaves in its manufacture was Coca-Cola, the recipe for which was concocted by an Atlanta druggist in 1886. For the next twenty years Coke was the real thing, but in 1906 the Pure Food and Drugs Act was passed and the manufacturer switched to coca leaves from which the cocaine had been removed.

In addition to its pain-reducing effects, cocaine acts rapidly on the cortex of the brain, heightening sensory awareness and inducing a thirty-minute state of euphoria. Sexual desire is accentuated, and feelings of self-confidence, well-being, and indefatigability suffuse the user's consciousness. An overdose may bring on chills, nausea, and insomnia, as well as a paranoid breakdown and terrifying hallucinations of insects crawling beneath the skin. Chronic use often leads to changes in personality that include heightened irritability, impaired social relationships, paranoid thinking, and disturbances in eating and sleeping (*Scientific Perspectives on Cocaine Abuse*, 1987). As users take larger and larger doses of the purer forms of cocaine now available, they are more often rushed to emergency rooms and may die of an overdose, often from a myocardial infarction (heart attack) (Kozel, Crider, and Adams, 1982). Because of its strong vasoconstricting properties, cocaine may pose special dangers in pregnancy, for the blood supply to the developing fetus may be compromised.

Cocaine can be sniffed ("snorted"), smoked in pipes or cigarettes, swallowed, or even injected into the veins like heroin; some heroin addicts in fact mix the two drugs in a combination known as "speedball," which is taken orally. In the 1970s cocaine devotees in this country adopted a practice similar to that used in parts of South America for enhancing the effects of the drug. To separate, or free, the most potent component of cocaine, they heat cocaine with ether. When purified by this chemical process, the cocaine base—or "freebase"—is extremely powerful. Called white tornado, baseball, or snow toke, it is usually smoked in a water pipe or sprinkled on a normal or marijuana cigarette. It is rapidly absorbed into the lungs and carried to the brain in a few seconds, and induces an intense, two-

Early ad proclaiming the beneficial effects of drinking Coca-Cola.

minute high, followed by restlessness and discomfort. Some freebase smokers go on marathon binges lasting up to four days (Goodwin and Guze, 1984). The freebasing process is hazardous, however, because ether is flammable. Comedian Richard Pryor nearly died from the burns he suffered when the ether he was using ignited.

In the mid-1980s there appeared on the streets a new form of freebase called "crack," a marketing ploy that has brought about an increase in freebasing and in casualties. Because it is available in small, relatively inexpensive doses ($10 for about 100 milligrams versus the $100 per gram that users formally had to shell out to obtain cocaine), younger and less affluent buyers have begun to experiment with the drug and to get addicted (Kozel and Adams, 1986). Many public health and police officials regard crack as the most dangerous and perhaps most addicting illicit drug that society has to cope with.

Cocaine use soared in the 1970s and 1980s. The dramatic increase in use is evident in these statistics. In

---

[7] Freud subsequently lost his enthusiasm for cocaine after nursing a physician friend, to whom he had recommended the drug, through a night-long psychotic state brought on by it.

Crack use has increased greatly in the 1980s. Shown here is a seller in the Times Square area of New York City.

1974 it was estimated that 5.4 million Americans had tried cocaine at least once; in 1982 this figure had risen to 21.6 million. Current users of the drug numbered 1.6 million in 1974; in 1982 they numbered 4.2 million (National Institute on Drug Abuse, 1983); and in 1985 this had grown to 5.8 million (Kozel and Adams, 1986). This is an increase of over 260 percent in 11 years! In 1984 cocaine use among high school seniors increased slightly, all regions considered, but it jumped by over 40 percent among seniors in the Northeastern states. More than 10 percent of high school seniors in this region reported being current users (*The New York Times*, January 8, 1985), though it is believed that, unlike the case for marijuana and LSD, the chances of initiating cocaine use persist well into adulthood.

The economics of cocaine provides staggering figures for money spent by heavy users. In 1985 people snorting cocaine once a day spent more than $1500 a week for the drug. Others using it more often reported spending much more, being able to support their expensive habit because they themselves sold the drug or were independently wealthy (Siegel, 1982). In the early 1980s

cocaine cost $2000 an ounce, making it approximately five times more expensive than gold. It was a status symbol in the 1920s among Hollywood performers, and in the 1980s it reemerged with similar meaning for actors, athletes, and others in the better-paid strata of our society. Now the cost of cocaine has begun to decrease, and people from all segments of society are using it (Adams and Durell, 1984).

Is cocaine addicting? Until very recently it was believed not to be, but data gathered over the past decade indicate otherwise (*Scientific Perspectives on Cocaine Abuse*, 1987): ceasing cocaine use appears to cause a severe withdrawal syndrome. Gawin and Kleber (1986) suggest a triphasic scheme:

Crash can last from nine hours to four days, depending on the length and intensity of the preceding binge. Within a few hours of abstaining, craving increases so strongly that cocaine is used if at all available. The person becomes quite miserable and depressed, cannot sleep, and is confused. The craving diminishes gradually. Paranoia is common as is suicidal thinking. Then fatigue and a desire to sleep take over. "Crash" refers both to the initial dysphoria followed by a crash in mood and to the later sleepiness and crash of activity.

Withdrawal can last from one to ten weeks. At first there is a return to near normality, with little craving and with a recognition of the negative consequences of cocaine use. But within a few days craving increases, and memories of the euphoria from binging become more vivid. Environmental reminders ("conditioned stimuli") of previous highs exacerbate the desire and lead to designing plans to obtain the drug. Relapse occurs if there is availability.

Extinction is indefinite. If there is no relapse, the person experiences a period of near-normal affect but with periodic, albeit controllable, cravings that can last quite a long time. The person remains vulnerable to environmental "triggers" for months afterward. (One former intravenous user experienced a need for cocaine when blood was drawn months later for a laboratory test.)

Current laboratory as well as field-based research indicates more and more that this drug can take hold of people with as much tenacity as has been demonstrated for years with the established addictive drugs. Indeed, cocaine may have the most powerful positive reinforcing properties of all the drugs we discuss in this chapter. Animals will select cocaine over access to food and water, even to the extent that they die (Aigner and Balster, 1978). Nor do the mass media lack reports of the social, psychological, economic, and legal damage that some will subject themselves to in order to continue taking the drug (Grabowski, 1984).

Theories of the Origins of Drug Addiction

Physiological Theories

Many have regarded the physiologial changes in the body effected by drugs as the most important factor in drug addiction. Because the physiology of the body has been changed by the drug, it reacts when the substance to which it has become accustomed is no longer administered. To avoid withdrawal reactions, the addict continues taking the drug. With enough repetition— how much is not known—the person is ensnared by changes in bodily chemistry and the concomitant severity of withdrawal reactions. The addict is regarded as an unwitting victim of physiological reactions, continuing to use the drug to ward off the distress of withdrawal.

Ausubel (1961a) challenged this interpretation, alleging that the effects of withdrawal from heroin, for example, are in reality no more severe than a bad case of influenza. Anecdotal evidence exists to support Ausubel's claim that the effects of withdrawal from heroin are not as severe as is often imagined. However, the apparent increase in availability of purer forms of heroin and of stimulants like cocaine is likely to exacerbate the withdrawal problems of addicts.

Psychological Theories

Psychological theories of the origin of drug addiction usually emphasize reduction of distress and the pleasant feeling and euphoric state that the drugs produce. These theories also attempt to explain why particular kinds of people seem to "need" these effects. An association has often been noted between criminality, drug abuse, and antisocial personality disorder. In this context drug abuse may be considered as part of the thrill-seeking behavior of the sociopath discussed in Chapter 10. We might also expect narcotics to be used by anxious individuals in order to reduce their distress. Drug addicts have also been found to be deviant on various personality questionnaire measures. But we must question whether these personality characteristics antedated the addiction and caused it. For example, we might find that drug addicts tend to be more suspicious than nonusers. To conclude that suspiciousness contributes to the use of drugs would not be justified, for it might well be the addict's *reaction* to his illegal status as a drug user.

Some similarities in family background have been identified in the life histories of drug addicts (Chein *et al.*, 1964). In many cases the father is absent from the home of the future addict. If the father is present, he tends to be a shadowy figure or to be overtly hostile and distant. If present he may also serve as a model for criminal behavior, and the relations between the mother and father are likely to be stormy. Chein and his colleagues therefore proposed that the personality defects of the drug addict, whatever they are, were developed through family background. Initial experiences with addicting drugs were also shown to be nonaccidental. Most addicts were found to have been introduced knowingly to the drugs, not by an adult but rather by a member of their peer group, suggesting the importance of peer pressure and curiosity. Boredom and aggravation are probably contributing factors. In ghettoes where narcotics are readily available, and the culture of the streets prevails, the incidence of drug use is especially high.

Therapy for the Use of Illicit Drugs

Central to the treatment of those who use illicit drugs is detoxification, withdrawing the person from the drug itself. Heroin withdrawal reactions range from relatively mild bouts of anxiety, nausea, and restlessness for several days, to more severe and frightening bouts of delirium and apparent madness, depending primarily on the purity of the heroin that the individual has been using. Someone high on amphetamines can be brought down by appropriate dosages of one of the phenothiazines, a class of drugs more commonly used to treat schizophrenics (see page 399), although it must be kept in mind that the speed freak may also have been using other drugs in conjunction with amphetamines. As for barbiturates, withdrawal reactions from these drugs, as already noted, are especially severe, even life-threatening; they begin about twenty-four hours after the last dose and reach their maximum two or three days later. They have usually abated by the end of the first week, but they may last a month if doses have been large. Withdrawal from these drugs is best done gradually, not "cold turkey,"[8] and should take place under close medical supervision (Honigfeld and Howard, 1978).

Detoxification is but the first way in which therapists try to help the addict or drug abuser, and perhaps ironically it is the easiest part of the rehabilitation process. Finding a way to enable the drug user to function on his or her own, without drugs, is an arduous task that promises more disappointment and sadness than success for both helper and client. Nonetheless, a great number of efforts are made, many of them financed heavily by federal and state governments.

Drug Treatment

Two widely used drug therapy programs for heroin addiction are the administration of **heroin substitutes** and

---

[8]This expression comes from the goosebumps that commonly appear during abrupt withdrawal from opiates. The skin of the person resembles that of a plucked turkey (Jaffe, 1985).

of *heroin antagonists.* In the first category are *methadone* and methadyl acetate, both synthetic narcotics. Originally developed by Dole and Nyswander (1966), these agents are designed to take the place of heroin. Since they are themselves narcotics, successful treatment merely converts the heroin addict into a methadone addict. This occurs because methadone is *cross-dependent* with heroin; that is, by acting on the same central nervous system receptors, it becomes a substitute for the original dependency. Abrupt discontinuation of methadone results in its own pattern of withdrawal reactions, which are not as severe as those from heroin, hence its potential therapeutic properties for weaning the addict altogether from drug dependence (Jaffe, 1985). The addict must come to a clinic once a day and swallow methadone in the presence of a staff member, three times a week for methadyl acetate. Indeed, many methadone users manage to hold jobs, commit no crimes, and stay away from other illicit drugs (Cooper *et al.,* 1983), but many others do not. Some abuse alcohol. Clearly premorbid behavioral patterns and life circumstances play a role in how a given individual will react to methadone treatment. Moreover, since methadone does not give the addict a euphoric high, many will return to heroin if it becomes available to them. In addition, when methadone is injected, rather than taken orally as it is supposed to be, its effects on some addicts are similar to those of heroin (Honigfeld and Howard, 1978). Not surprisingly, an illegal market in methadone has developed, which would seem to be defeating the purpose of its use. Finally, a great number

Methadone is a heroin substitute that is designed to take the place of a heroin addiction.

of people drop out from methadone programs, in part because of side effects, such as insomnia, constipation, excessive sweating, and diminished sexual function.

Cyclazocine and naloxone are heroin antagonists. After being gradually withdrawn from heroin, addicts receive increasing dosages of either of these drugs, which prevents them from experiencing any high should they later take heroin. The drugs have great affinity for the cells that heroin usually binds to. Their molecules occupy the cells, without stimulating them, and heroin molecules have no place to go. The antagonist, then, changes the whole nature of heroin; it simply will not produce the euphoric effect that the addict seeks. As with methadone, however, addicts must make frequent and regular visits to the clinic, which requires motivation and responsibility on their part. In addition, addicts do not lose the actual craving for heroin for some time.

The societal need to address opiate dependence has been accentuated in recent years by the AIDS epidemic, for it has been known for some time that the sharing of needles—a practice common among many addicts—is a principal means of transmitting this fatal disease. So serious is the problem that proposals have been made to provide addicts with free sterile needles without attempting to influence them to stay off the drug.

As mentioned earlier, cocaine is now viewed as a physically addicting drug. One consequence of this is a search for drugs that will ease the symptoms of withdrawal and perhaps also attack the physical basis of the addiction. Tricyclic antidepressants like imipramine are being explored with some success, and Box 11.3 (page 305) discusses the utility of clonidine, an antihypertensive medication, in easing withdrawal in a variety of addicting drugs including cocaine. Psychological approaches are also being employed, such as contingency contracting (operant conditioning) and Cocaine Anonymous, both in widespread use with alcoholics, as we have seen. In the most general terms, as with any abused drug, patients are encouraged to examine the role of cocaine in their lives and to attempt to meet in more healthful ways whatever needs are being met by this quite dangerous drug.

Psychological Treatment

Indeed drug abuse cannot be dealt with solely by some form of chemotherapy. People turn to drugs for many reasons, and even though in most instances their current drug taking is controlled primarily by a physical addiction, the entire pattern of their existence is bound to be influenced by the drug and must therefore command the attention of whoever would hope to remove the drug from their lives. The difficulty of maintaining abstinence is attributable in a major way to environmental stimuli that can influence the recovering addict. Needles, neighborhoods, and others with whom one used to take drugs can readily become secondary reinforcers, thereby eliciting a craving for the substance (Wikler, 1980). Alcoholics and cigarette smokers have similar experiences.

Drug abuse is treated in the consulting rooms of psychiatrists, psychologists, and other mental health workers. The several kinds of psychotherapy are applied to drug use disorders as they are to the other human maladjustments. Little can be said, however, about the relative efficacy of psychoanalytic, behavioral, and humanistic therapies in helping people to break their dependence on drugs (Liskow, 1982).

Self-help residential homes or communes, with which most readers are familiar, are the most widespread psychological approach to dealing with heroin addiction and other drug abuse. Modeled after Synanon,[9] a therapeutic community of former drug addicts founded by Charles Dederich in Santa Monica, California, in 1958, these residences are designed to restructure radically the addict's outlook on life so that illicit drugs no longer have a place. Daytop Village, Phoenix House, Odyssey House, and other drug rehabilitation homes share the following features.

1. A total environment in which drugs are not available and continuing support is offered to ease the transition from regular drug use to a drug-free existence.

2. The presence of often charismatic role models, former addicts who appear to be meeting life's challenges without drugs.

3. Direct, often brutal confrontation in group therapy, in which the addict is goaded into accepting responsibility for his problems, and for his drug habit, and urged to take charge of his life.

4. A setting in which the addict is respected as a human being rather than stigmatized as a failure or a criminal.

5. Separation of the addict from previous social contacts, on the assumption that these relationships have been instrumental in fostering the addictive life-style.

There are several obstacles to evaluating the efficacy of residential drug treatment programs. First, since entrance is voluntary only a small minority of dependent users enter such settings. (Jaffe, 1985). Furthermore, because the dropout rate is high, those who remain cannot be regarded as representative of the population of people addicted to hard drugs. Their motivation to go straight is probably much higher than average; therefore any improvement they might make will in part reflect their uncommon desire to rid themselves of their habit, rather than the specific qualities of the treatment program. Second, the role of mental health professionals is either nonexistent or very marginal because of an explicit antagonism toward "shrinks" and social workers. Further, adequately designed research on the outcomes of these programs has not been undertaken. Such self-regulating residential communities, however, may help a large number of those who stay in them for a year or so (Jaffe, 1985).

Prevention

It is generally acknowledged that by far the best way to deal with drug abuse is to *prevent* it in the first place. In recent years we have seen well-known sports and entertainment figures urge audiences not to experiment with illicit drugs, especially cocaine. Whereas the message in the 1960s and the 1970s was often that certain drugs—especially the psychedelics (to be discussed later)—would help people realize their potential or at least provide an escape from the humdrum and the stressful, the message as we begin the 1990s is that mind-altering drugs interfere with psychological functioning and with the achievement of our personal best and that, above all, these drugs are harmful to the body and can even cause unexpected death. "Just say 'no'" has replaced "Turn on, tune in, drop out." Also better appreciated are the *relationships* among drug usage patterns. It now appears, for example, that marijuana may be one factor in subsequent more serious drug abuse (see p. 311), a hypothesis that in the 1960s was ridiculed by young people for whom marijuana was as much a form of political and social protest as a mind-altering excursion. (The case for the dangers of marijuana per se was not readily made twenty-five years ago, and it was the absence of good scientific data—available now—that buttressed the argument that harsh legal penalties against "grass" were politically motivated.)

Adequate prevention requires more knowledge of the developmental paths to drug use. For example, are youngsters from particular family and socioeconomic backgrounds at risk for initiation into the use of a drug that, once taken, quickly fosters dependency? Does the early use of tobacco predispose to the snorting of cocaine or the smoking of marijuana? Are young people who have low self-esteem or who show conduct disorder problems at risk for drug abuse? Such information will not only help clinical researchers target subgroups to-

---

[9]Like its founder, Charles Dederich, who in 1980 pleaded no contest to a charge of attempting to murder a lawyer for Synanon members by placing a poisonous snake in his mailbox, Synanon has fallen on hard times. It has been emulated by others, but Synanon itself eventually lost its mission. It grew large and wealthy through its business enterprises, and it has been brought to court for acts of violence and for holding residents against their will.

Attitudes toward drug abuse have changed. (left) Photo of a 1960s rally to legalize marijuana. (right) Rally to foster "saying no" to drugs.

ward whom preventive efforts can be most fruitfully directed but can also shed light on the whys and hows of people's initiation into and continuation of substance abuse and dependence.

Nicotine and Cigarette Smoking

The history of tobacco smoking bears much similarity to the use of other addictive drugs (Brecher, 1972). Its popularity spread through the world from Columbus's commerce with the native American Indians. It did not take long for sailors and merchants to imitate the Indians' smoking of rolled leaves of tobacco—and to experience, as the Indians did, the increasing craving for the stuff. When not smoked, tobacco was chewed or else ground into small pieces and inhaled as snuff.

Some idea of the addictive qualities of tobacco can be appreciated by considering how much people would sacrifice to maintain their supplies. In sixteenth-century England, for example, tobacco was exchanged for silver ounce for ounce. Poor people squandered their meager resources for their several daily pipefuls. Even the public tortures and executions engineered as punishment by the Sultan Murad IV of Turkey during the seventeenth century could not dissuade those of his subjects who were addicted to the weed.

Prevalence and Consequences of Smoking

The threat to health that smoking poses has been documented convincingly by the United States Surgeon General in a series of reports since 1964. Among the

medical problems associated with, and almost certainly caused or exacerbated by, long-term cigarette smoking are lung cancer, emphysema, cancer of the larynx and of the esophagus, and a number of cardiovascular diseases. The most probable harmful components in the smoke from burning tobacco are nicotine, carbon monoxide, and tar; the latter consists primarily of certain hydrocarbons, many of which are known carcinogens (Jaffe, 1985). Among the many statistics on the health hazards of smoking is the estimate that thirty- to thirty-five-year-old, two-pack-a-day cigarette smokers have a mortality rate twice that of nonsmokers. Mortality risk increases less sharply for cigar smokers and even less for pipe smokers, an apparent function of the fact that cigar and pipe smokers seldom inhale and therefore take less of the harmful ingredients in tobacco smoke into their body. The good news is that health risks decline dramatically over a period of five to ten years following cessation, to levels only slightly above those of nonsmokers, although the destruction of lung tissue is not reversible (Jaffe, 1985). And as with alcohol, the socioeconomic cost to society is considerable: smokers compile each year over 80 million extra days of lost work and 145 million extra days of disability. Health costs associated with cigarettes in the United States run about $30 billion annually, and about 350,000 people—almost 1,000 Americans a day—die prematurely each year as a result of smoking.

These findings appear, after many years, to be having some limited influence on smokers and their consumption of tobacco. Since the first Surgeon General's report there has been a welcome decrease in smoking among adults (Warner, 1977). Yet as of 1982, 33 percent of adult Americans were still smokers, puffing more than 600 billion cigarettes a year. What is even more alarming, smoking among teenage boys did not at once change

and that among teenage girls actually *increased*. An encouraging note is that only 20 percent of high school seniors were smokers in 1982, suggesting that future prevalence figures for adults will continue to decline (Jaffe, 1985).

The attraction of smoking for young people has caused concern, for smoking is very difficult to give up once the habit and the addiction have been established. Researchers surmise that the widely publicized health dangers of smoking may be making an impact. Through peer pressure and social support not to smoke, the "macho" image of the male smoker and the supersophisticated image of the female smoker seem to be losing their appeal.[10]

Most people who smoke acknowledge that it is hazardous to their health, and yet they continue to engage in what might be viewed as suicidal behavior. Perhaps one of the most tortured addicts was Sigmund Freud,

who continued smoking up to twenty cigars a day in the full knowledge that they were seriously taxing his heart and causing cancerous growths in his mouth. When his jaw was later almost entirely removed and replaced by an awkward artificial one, Freud suffered great difficulty swallowing and endured excruciating pain. But he was still unable to bear the anguish of abstaining. Although many heavy smokers do succeed in stopping, Freud's tragic case was certainly not the exception.

The health hazards are not restricted to those who smoke. The smoke coming from the burning end of a cigarette, the so-called sidestream smoke, contains higher concentrations of ammonia, carbon monoxide, nicotine, and tar than does the smoke actually inhaled by the smoker. Nonsmokers can suffer lung damage, possibly permanent, from extended exposure to cigarette smoke (Bennett, 1980). At the very least, many non-smokers greatly dislike the smell of smoke from burning tobacco, and some have allergic reactions to it. Moreover, when mothers-to-be smoke, their infants are more likely to be born prematurely and to have lower birth weights and birth defects.

---

[10]But young people emulate their familial elders as well as their peers. If both parents and an older sibling smoke, a youngster is four times as likely to do so than if none of the other family members smokes.

In recent years various local governments have passed, or tried to pass, ordinances regulating where cigarettes may or may not be smoked in public places and work settings. Smoking is banned in many supermarkets and on buses and other public conveyances, including some airline flights. Restaurants must often post signs indicating whether they have an area for nonsmokers. Workplaces with more than fifty employees must either ban smoking on the premises or restrict it to designated areas. Many nonsmokers express enthusiastic approval of such measures, but pressure from smokers and from the tobacco industry sometimes defeats efforts to enact laws. Some smokers object virulently to what they view as undue infringement on their rights.

Is Smoking an Addiction?

For some people smoking is a pleasurable accompaniment to their relaxing activities, and for others a necessary aid to their coping with challenging situations in our achievement-oriented society (Mausner, 1973). A smoker receives satisfaction from handling the pack, removing the cigarette, perhaps tapping one end against a firm surface to pack the tobacco more firmly, an act that probably has no real effect, especially on a filter cigarette; lighting the cigarette and perhaps sharing the match with a friend; and taking puffs at intervals during a relaxing conversation or an exhilarating task requiring concentration, such as reading a psychology textbook. Such social and psychological factors are not to be overlooked in attempts to understand why people begin and continue to smoke. Nonetheless, there is growing evidence that the **nicotine** in tobacco is a powerful addictive drug, with experienced smokers showing both tolerance and withdrawal symptoms. It is important, though, to distinguish among different kinds of smokers. Those smoking more than two packs a day are almost surely addicted to nicotine, whereas those who limit smoking, for example, to social situations and consume less than a pack a day do indeed smoke from habit, but they may not be addicted. In any event, like cocaine and the opiates, nicotine is known to produce pleasurable effects in both animals (Goldberg *et al.*, 1981) and humans who have smoked regularly (Henningfield *et al.*, 1983).

Although upward of four million American smokers are estimated to quit on their own each year, over three-quarters of them return to smoking within twelve months. Regular smokers trying to escape from the weed report problems such as disruption of sleep, nausea, headaches, constipation, excessive eating, increased anxiety, difficulty in concentrating, irritability—in short, all the signs and symptoms we are accustomed to seeing por-

trayed humorously by screen characters or displayed by friends and loved ones in the throes of "nicotine fits." And these withdrawal symptoms can persist for many weeks, even months. As with other addictions, the most readily available relief is a bit more of the same—another cigarette and the nicotine "hit" it provides to a body grown dependent on it. Nonsmokers tend to berate the nicotine addict with allegations of no will power and lack of concern for self and others. From all we know, however, these people are waging an extremely difficult battle with a true addiction (Jarvik, 1979). It has been estimated that one out of five people who have refrained from smoking for as long as nine years continues at least occasionally to crave a cigarette (Fletcher and Doll, 1969). In fact, in July 1988 the Surgeon General asserted that available scientific evidence has proven that nicotine dependency is at least as powerful as dependency on heroin, the clear implication being that many smokers are basically drug addicts.

The rather general agreement that nicotine is addictive, and that at least heavy smokers are addicted, has raised concern about the proliferation of low-nicotine cigarettes. Smokers who switch to such cigarettes in the numbers they are accustomed to smoke each day will experience acute withdrawal symptoms, as happens to smokers who stop "cold turkey" in an effort to abstain from cigarettes altogether (Schachter, 1977). Regular smokers will therefore smoke more of these "improved" cigarettes or take greater numbers of puffs and inhale more deeply than they did when smoking those containing higher levels of nicotine. They do this to maintain their nicotine levels (Benowitz and Jacob, 1984). Thus Schachter (1978) questions current social policy that encourages the development and marketing of low-nicotine cigarettes. Since the products of incomplete combustion of tar during the smoking process itself, rather than nicotine, are the principal agents causing cancer and other harm, it might be preferable to develop low-tar–high-nicotine cigarettes; these would provide the nicotine addict with the drug he or she craves but at the same time reduce the risks associated with tar. Nicotine may, however, through stimulation, contribute to or exacerbate cardiovascular disease. All things considered, it is better not to begin smoking at all, or, if the habit is established, to concentrate personal and professional efforts on reducing or eliminating it.

Treatment and Prevention of Cigarette Smoking

Of the more than thirty million smokers who have quit since 1964, it is believed that 95 percent did so without

BOX 11.3

CLONIDINE AND DRUG WITHDRAWAL

Perhaps the most exciting new development in the treatment of substance dependence is the use of clonidine, an antihypertensive drug that appears to ease the withdrawal symptoms from alcohol, opiates, cocaine, and nicotine. An early report by Bjorkqvist (1975) with alcoholics was followed by a brief account on opiates by Gold, Redmond, and Kleber in 1978, who gave clonidine to five former morphine addicts who had become addicted to methadone. The clonidine alleviated the withdrawal symptoms from methadone abstention and also helped actually wean them from the methadone. These results were subsequently replicated (e.g., Gold, Pottash, Sweeney, and Kleber, 1980; Washton and Resnick, 1980), though some have found that clonidine's effects are not quite so good as morphine itself (Jasinski, Johnson, and Kocher, 1985).

Why did workers try this drug at all? Previous research by Gold *et al.* (1978) had shown that when they stimulated in monkeys the locus coeruleus, a nucleus in the brain that produces most of the norepinephrine, the result mimicked withdrawal from morphine. It is also known that both morphine and clonidine reduce such noradrenergic activity. Since morphine reduces withdrawal from itself (obviously), the investigators reasoned that perhaps clonidine could too, without the negative addicting effects of morphine.

More recently there have been reports that clonidine can also be useful in weaning people from nicotine dependence. The effects of clonidine for smoking withdrawal in fifteen heavy smokers were reported by Glassman, Jackson, Walsh, Roose, and Rosenfeld (1984) in a double-blind comparison of a placebo, a benzodiazepinelike tranquilizer, and clonidine. Every subject was given each of the drugs but on separate days, each time after having abstained from cigarettes for twenty-four hours. In this way comparisons among the two drugs and the placebo could be made with each subject contributing data in each condition, an unusually powerful research strategy called a crossover design. Of the thirteen (of fifteen) subjects who preferred a drug to the placebo, ten preferred clonidine. Both active drugs reduced tension, irritability, and restlessness, but only clonidine ameliorated craving, the most aggravating part of drug withdrawal. The results clearly showed superiority of clonidine over the other two conditions in reducing the craving component of withdrawal from nicotine.

But what of the actual clinical effects of clonidine in helping people stop smoking? The challenge of long-term abstention from cigarettes extends far beyond the acute withdrawal period for which clonidine seems to be beneficial. For one thing, most smokers probably *like* to smoke, over and above whatever relief they obtain from nicotine withdrawal by lighting up and replenishing their bodies with the craved drug. In the context of a "behavioral counseling" program developed by the American Lung Asso-

ciation, Glassman *et al.* (1988) compared clonidine to a placebo in heavy smokers who had been unsuccessful in previous attempts to quit. Because of the focus on the withdrawal effects of clonidine, only those subjects who had cut down their smoking by at least 50 percent during the first few days of clonidine or placebo treatment were included. Four weeks of clonidine or placebo treatment followed, with smoking diaries checked during weekly visits, as well as blood assays done to determine the presence of nicotine. After four weeks the drugs were withdrawn gradually and then the effects on smoking evaluated. There was also a six-month follow-up. The results showed the expected superiority of clonidine, similar to the earlier reports with alcohol and morphine. Interestingly, this was due entirely to the benefit derived by the women in the study—for men there was no clonidine–placebo difference, something that the authors believe might have been due to insufficient dosage.*

According to Glassman *et al.*, the fact that clonidine has been found to reduce withdrawal discomfort among opiate, alcohol, and now nicotine addicts and the fact that clonidine is known to reduce noradrenergic activity in the brain lend support to the physiological hypothesis that high levels of noradrenergic activity in the locus coeruleus underlie withdrawal from addicting drugs. Future research will have to examine these effects more closely, especially their interactions with psychosocial interventions that have to be included once the acute withdrawal period is past. The hope is that by combining the interventions, the former addict will be less likely to resume his or her reliance on harmful drugs to escape from life stress.

Indeed, emergent data and theorizing about the biological substrates of positive and negative reinforcement suggest that treatment for addicting drugs must attend not only to easing the pain of withdrawal, as clonidine does, but also to the positive reinforcing effects of the drug (Wise, 1987). These two effects seem to be subserved by different parts of the brain, consistent with the well-known clinical observation that a detoxified addict—one who has gotten past withdrawal—can still have a positive craving for the particular drug based on memories of its initially positive reinforcing effects. Arguing from animal and biological research, Wise proposes that treatment programs must attend to the pleasures that can be achieved with use of a drug, and not only to detoxification. Nondrug substitutes for the positive rewards of drugs like cocaine and heroin have to be found.

---

*It should be mentioned that the *absolute* success rates were typically modest. To wit, only about half of the clonidine subjects were abstinent immediately after treatment, and of these almost half resumed smoking by the six-month follow-up, consistent with the rest of the smoking cessation literature.

BOX 11.4

NICOTINE GUM AND NICOTINE FITS

Each of the thousands of "hits" that the smoker administers to himself or herself each day during the consumption of a pack or two of cigarettes delivers nicotine to the brain in seven seconds. Available since 1984 by doctor's prescription, gum containing nicotine, sold under the trade name Nicorette, may help smokers endure the nicotine withdrawal that accompanies any effort to stop smoking. The nicotine in gum is absorbed much more slowly and steadily. The rationale is that providing the addicting drug by gum will help unlink the act of smoking from the nicotine "hit." At the same time cessation of smoking is disconnected from the nicotine "fit" or withdrawal. The long-term goal, of course, is for the former smoker to be able to cut back on the use of gum as well, eventually eliminating reliance on nicotine altogether. There is evidence, however, that ex-smokers can become dependent on this gum. Moreover, in doses that deliver an amount of nicotine equivalent to smoking one cigarette an hour, the occurrence of cardiovascular changes like blood pressure increase can be dangerous to people with cardiovascular diseases. Even so, some experts believe that even were the smoker to stay with the gum indefinitely, his or her situation would be healthier than obtaining nicotine by smoking because at least the poisons in the smoke will be avoided.

Some well-controlled, double-blind studies suggest that nicotine gum is useful in a limited way. Jarvis and his co-workers (1982) in Great Britain found better abstinence at one-year follow-up by people chewing nicotine gum than by those chewing a placebo gum. A series of studies at the University of California at Los Angeles by Schneider, Jarvik, and their associates (1983) had less positive but still encouraging outcomes. The greatest difference between nicotine and placebo gum groups was found early in treatment, between weeks 3 and 6, and at six months. After one year the nicotine gum groups had relapsed noticeably—only 30 percent of them were still abstinent—and yet they were still better than the control group, only 20 percent of whom were still abstinent.

A closer analysis of the UCLA data revealed an interesting finding. The logic of chewing nicotine gum is that it will help a person stop smoking by supplying the nicotine otherwise obtained from cigarettes. This implies that a person who is highly dependent on cigarettes will benefit more than a person less so, for there will be a better fit between the state of the smoker, who has a great need for nicotine, and the drug treatment, in which the gum supplies nicotine. Jarvik and Schneider (1984) divided the smokers in the just-described study into those with great and little dependence, based on their answers to a questionnaire by Fagerstrom (1978). People were asked how much they inhale, whether they smoke when sick or in forbidden places, and whether their cigarettes contain large or small amounts of nicotine. Table 11a shows the number of smokers abstinent at one-year follow-up as a function of whether they were rated as having great or little dependence on nicotine. The 41 percent abstinence rate for people highly dependent on nicotine (7 out of 17) is considerably higher than the zero percent success rate for subjects who were considered to be less nicotine dependent.

However, nicotine gum does not duplicate the effects of an inhaled cigarette. It does not produce the "peak" in plasma nicotine that an average cigarette does, nor does it raise nicotine blood levels as high (Russell, Feyerabend,

---

professional help (National Cancer Institute, 1977; U.S. Department of Health and Human Services, 1982).[11] Some smokers attend smoking clinics or consult with professionals for specialized smoking reduction programs. The American Cancer Society and the Church of the Seventh Day Adventists have been especially active in offering programs to help people stop smoking. And, as mentioned earlier, more and more nonsmokers object to people smoking in restaurants, trains, airplanes, and public buildings. The social context, then, provides many more incentives and support to stop smoking than existed twenty-five years ago, when the Surgeon General first warned of the serious health hazards associated with cigarette smoking. Even so, it is estimated that not more than half of those who go through smoking cessation programs succeed in abstaining by the time the program is over; and only about one-third of those who have succeeded in the short term actually remain away from cigarettes after a year (Hunt and Bespalec, 1974; Schwartz, 1987).

Smoking Cessation Treatments

The most encouraging results come from behavioral programs, especially those employing the so-called **rapid-smoking treatment** (Lando, 1977; Lichtenstein *et al.*, 1973; Harris, Birchler, Wahl, and Schmal, 1973). The procedure calls for a smoker to sit in a poorly ventilated room and puff much faster than normal, per-

---

[11]Investigations have begun on these large numbers of people who quit without being in a formal program. What enables a particular individual to stop? How does this person survive the withdrawal from nicotine, a hellish period of time that can last for months, some say even years? What homegrown techniques do these people use? What commonalities exist among these do-it-yourselfers (Ockene, 1984)?

and Cole, 1976). These differences probably account for the limited (though significant) benefits of the gum in reducing withdrawal once a smoker abstains. Smokers would prefer to get their nicotine from a cigarette! On the other hand, these differences are an integral part of the process of weaning the nicotine addict from his or her drug.

Not everyone is advised to use the gum. Contraindications include active ulcers and pregnancy. Smokers with certain forms of heart disease are also poor candidates (Schneider, 1987). The person must also be warned about and encouraged to put up with some of the side effects, which can include flatulence, hiccups, nausea, and throat irritation.

Research indicates that "clinic support" is important. This entails monitoring the use of the gum for the first week, daily encouragement, and discussion of coping skills. The gum must be chewed slowly as well as intermittently and then discarded after about twenty minutes; enough pieces must be chewed to provide relief from withdrawal, as many as fifteen pieces a day, and this regimen may last for several months, with a gradual tapering; and it should

TABLE 11a

Numbers of abstainers and smokers as a function of nicotine dependence (*after Jarvik and Schneider, 1984*)

	Great Dependence	Little Dependence
Abstinent	7	0
Smoking	10	8

be kept on hand "for emergencies" (Schneider, 1987). Data do point clearly to its usefulness in reducing withdrawal symptoms in the first few crucial days of abstinence (Schneider and Jarvik, 1984), but something other than replacement of cigarette nicotine is clearly necessary to keep people from later smoking.

The best results are found when the gum is combined with a behaviorally oriented treatment (Hall, Tunstall, Rugg, Jones, and Benowitz, 1985; Killen, Maccoby, and Taylor, 1984). When nicotine gum was prescribed as part of a physician's *unsolicited* advice to stop smoking, it had no measurable effect (Crofton *et al.*, 1983).

Compliance in chewing the gum has turned out to be a problem. In one setting not more than half of the smokers given prescriptions for the gum actually purchased it, and those who did failed to stay with the gum for the recommended period of time. Moreover, most of those who do chew the gum do not participate in psychological treatment programs at the same time, something recommended by the Food and Drug Administration. Some of these problems might be due in part to the failure of physicians to motivate the smoker properly; it has been reported that most did not counsel the patient to try to stop smoking nor did they stay in touch with the patient to provide the necessary support and follow-up (Hughes, 1985). Experimentation is under way with transdermal nicotine delivery through a polyethylene patch taped to the arm, from which nicotine is slowly and steadily released into the body without the patient having to do anything (but not remove the patch). It is too early to say how effective this mode of administration is, but it does avoid most of the compliance and side effect problems inherent in nicotine gum.

haps as often as every six seconds. After a number of such daily sessions, many smokers report less desire to smoke; in fact, as might be expected, the rapid-smoking sessions make most of the participants ill. In aversive-conditioning terms, rapid smoking uses the natural consequences of the act, smoke, as an aversive UCS to discourage puffing on a cigarette. Though results are not entirely consistent across studies, there is some evidence that the technique is effective, especially when it is part of a multicomponent program. Furthermore, data suggest that its efficacy is due to a true conditioned taste aversion (Baker and Brandon, 1988). However, other controlled smoking techniques achieve outcomes comparable to rapid smoking and without the risk that the latter might hold for people with cardiopulmonary disease (Horan, Linberg, and Hacket, 1977). For example, there is *focused smoking*, in which the person

smokes for a sustained period of time but at a slow or normal rate, and *rapid puffing*, similar to rapid smoking but without inhaling (Baker and Brandon, 1988; Danaher, Jeffery, Zimmerman, and Nelson, 1980).

Behavioral treatments have thus far focused on the overt act of smoking. Given the addictive nature of the smoking habit, the disappointing results are not surprising. Until more is known of how to eliminate the addiction or at least of how ex-smokers might learn to tolerate withdrawal symptoms for long periods of time, it is unrealistic to expect great advances in treatment. Box 11.4 describes research on a promising new method of withdrawing from the nicotine of cigarettes, by chewing nicotine gum.

And yet, as important as addiction is in heavy smoking, smoker A may also have trouble quitting for psychological reasons, and they may be quite different from the reasons that keep smoker B puffing away. When two such smokers are exposed to the same treatment package, it is unlikely to help both. Unfortunately, in their zeal to make an impact on the smoking problem, workers have for many years put smokers in standardized programs. Since there are probably many different reasons people have trouble quitting, there will have to be diverse methods to help them stop. Indeed, the most promising treatments overall are multicomponent programs that contain group discussions, training in how to cope with situations that ordinarily trigger smoking, and either directed smoking (rapid smoking, focused smoking, or rapid puffing, see above) or nicotine replacement (see Box 11.4) (Baker and Brandon, 1988).

Probably the most widespread "intervention" is advice or direction from a physician to stop smoking. Each year millions of smokers are told by their doctors to stop smoking—because of hypertension, heart disease, lung disease, diabetes, or on general grounds of preserving or improving health. Indeed, it is difficult to imagine a medical professional condoning the use of tobacco (smoked or chewed) given the weight of the scientific evidence about its numerous health dangers. At the same time it is doubtful that this medical advice does much good! Although there is some evidence that a physician's advice can get some people to stop smoking, at least for a while, especially when this advice is combined with nicotine gum (Russell, Merriman, Stapleton, and Taylor, 1983), much more needs to be learned about the nature of the advice, the manner in which it is given, its timing, and other factors that must surely play a role in whether an addicted individual is prepared and able to alter his or her behavior primarily because a doctor has said it is unhealthy.

Media campaigns are one component of the war against smoking.

Smoking Prevention Programs

In light of the difficulties in desisting from smoking once the habit and addiction are established, *prevention* of smoking, developing ways of discouraging young people even from experimenting with tobacco, has become a top priority among health researchers, with encouragement from the Surgeon General. What measures hold promise for persuading young people to resist smoking? Although many young people now apparently do fear disastrous consequences later in life and resist cigarettes, smokers, young and old alike, seem able to discount the possibility that they are at higher risk of coronary heart disease or lung cancer—the "It won't happen to me" syndrome. Indeed, although heavy smokers are eleven times as likely as nonsmokers to develop lung cancer, large numbers of heavy smokers live longer and healthier lives than do nonsmokers. In addition, it is the nature of young people to have a limited time perspective. Teenagers would seem to be more concerned with next Saturday evening's festivities or next Friday's math exam than with their life situation at age sixty.

Recent years have seen scores of school-based programs aimed at preventing the onset of tobacco use by young people. A review of 143 such programs indicates marked success in delaying the onset of smoking (Tobler, 1986). Several components are to be found in such efforts (Hansen, Johnson, Flay, Graham, and Sobel, 1988):

1. **Peer Pressure Resistance Training.** Instruction is given about the nature of peer pressure and ways to say no. Evans and his co-workers (1981), for example, developed films that portray teenagers resisting appeals from friends to try smoking. The idea is to teach assertive ways to refuse invitations to smoke, not an easy matter for young people, for whom peer approval and acceptance are acutely important. Schinke and Gilchrist (1985) taught resistance strategies to sixth-graders and found less smoking two years later than among a control group who received only attention and information about the harmful effects of smoking.

2. **Correction of Normative Expectations.** Since many young people believe that cigarette smoking is more prevalent (and by implication, "more OK") than it actually is, some programs have provided factual information about true prevalence rates. One survey, for example, found that close to 70 percent of teenagers believed that their teachers probably smoked (Jarvik *et al.*, 1977); in fact, a survey of actual smoking by teachers showed the rate to be about 20 percent (American Cancer Society, 1976).

3. **Inoculation against Mass Media Messages.** Some

programs try to counter the positive images of smokers that we are all subjected to in the media. But at least for several years there have been no cigarette ads on television or radio, and print ads have to contain explicit warnings about the dangers of smoking.[12]

4. **Information about Parental and Other Adult Influences.** Since it is known that parental smoking is strongly correlated with (and most probably contributes to) smoking by the children, some programs point out this fact and argue that this aspect of one's parents' behavior does not have to be imitated.

5. **Peer Leadership.** Most programs involve peers of recognized status to enhance the impact of the nonsmoking messages being conveyed.

6. **Affective Education, Self-Image Enhancement.** A number of programs have focused on the idea that intrapsychic factors like poor self-image and lack of stress-coping ability underlie smoking onset in young people. A careful comparison of this approach with a program that emphasized social pressure resistance training combined with most of points 1–5 found that it was far less effective in preventing use of tobacco as well as alcohol and marijuana (Hansen *et al.*, 1988). In fact, there were indications that the affective education program actually *increased* drug use over a period of three years, perhaps by unintentionally suggesting drug experimentation to deal with life stress.

7. **Other Components.** Additional features of preventive programs include information about the harmful effects of smoking (a common element in adult smoking cessation programs) and efforts to produce a public commitment not to smoke, like making a commitment on videotape.

It has been said often that cigarette smoking is difficult to discourage because the short-term gratification outweighs the long-term negative effects. One way to lessen the former is to introduce immediate negative consequences, and this strategy underlies aversion therapies for smoking. Another strategy would be to increase the cost of cigarettes, perhaps by raising the federal excise taxes on them. It has been estimated, for example, that a fourfold increase in the 1982 excise tax of 8 cents a pack might decrease teenage consumption by more than 50 percent and adult use by 15 percent

(Gesten and Jason, 1987). Such changes would have profound positive health effects. However, such an effort would be extremely difficult to bring to fruition in light of the politics of tobacco farming in the United States and the fact that cigarette usage is more widely accepted in other countries than it is in the United States. Behavioral and medical scientists have the important and formidable challenge of trying to understand better why people begin smoking, why they continue, and why it is so very difficult for most of them to give up the habit.

Marijuana

Marijuana consists of the dried and crushed leaves and flowering tops of the hemp plant, *Cannabis sativa.* It is most often smoked, but it may be chewed, prepared as a tea, or eaten in baked goods. **Hashish,** much stronger than marijuana, is produced by removing and drying the resin exude of the tops of high-quality cannabis plants. Both marijuana and hashish have been known for thousands of years, and their poor reputation among the general public dates back many centuries. For example, the English word assassin comes from the Arabic word *hashishāshin,* which means those addicted to hashish, and which was the name given an order of

Early recreational use of hashish in a fashionable apartment in New York City. An 1876 issue of the *Illustrated Police News* carried this picture with the title "Secret Dissipation of New York Belles: Interior of a Hasheesh Hell on Fifth Avenue."

---

[12]There is a massive incongruity in such ads. Billboards portray young, attractive people frolicking in sylvan settings, lighted cigarettes dangling from between their fingers, with a foot-high message at the bottom boldly proclaiming that the Surgeon General has determined that smoking is proven to be a major determinant of premature death from a host of incurable diseases.

Muslims who took hashish and murdered Christians at the time of the Crusades. In early American history the plant was extensively cultivated not for smoking but for its fibers, which were used in the manufacture of cloth and rope. By the nineteenth century the medicinal properties of *Cannabis* resin were noted, and it was a recommended treatment for rheumatism, gout, depression, cholera, and neuralgia, as well as being smoked for pleasure. Until 1920 marijuana was little seen in the United States, but with the passage of the Eighteenth Amendment, which prohibited the sale of alcohol, marijuana began to be brought across the border from Mexico and smoked for intoxication by members of the lower classes. Unfavorable reports in the press attributing crimes to marijuana use led to the enactment of a federal law against the sale of the drug in 1937. It is today illegal in most countries, many of which are bound by a United Nations treaty prohibiting its sale (Goodwin and Guze, 1984).[13]

Frequency of Marijuana Use

Periodically the National Institute of Drug Abuse (NIDA), a federal agency charged to investigate drug use in this country by encouraging investigators through awards of grants, publishes the results of surveys taken of youths, ages twelve to seventeen; young adults, eighteen to twenty-five; and those over twenty-six. They are questioned about current drug use, past use, frequency of use, range of drugs used, and so forth. In general, trends over the past twenty years suggest that the use of marijuana peaked in 1979 and is now showing a slight decline. For example, the following percentages of those between the ages of twelve and seventeen reported having used marijuana at least once: 14 percent in 1972, 31 percent in 1979, 27 percent in 1982, and 24 percent in 1985 (*Marijuana Research Findings: 1980; National Survey on Drug Abuse, 1979; National Survey on Drug Abuse, 1982;* Kozel and Adams, 1986). Among adults aged eighteen to twenty-five, the figures were 48 percent in 1972, 53 percent in 1974, 68 percent in 1979, 64 percent in 1982, and 61 percent in 1985. It is estimated that around 10 percent of Americans of all ages are current users of marijuana.

A very interesting relationship is found between use among high school seniors and their perceptions of the harmfulness of marijuana. Use peaked in 1978, when almost 11 percent of seniors reported use *daily;* at that time only 12 percent of seniors believed there was risk associated with occasional use and 35 percent believed

there was risk with regular use. Compare this to 1985, when daily use had plummeted to 5 percent; 25 percent now believe it is harmful to use it occasionally and 70 percent believe it is harmful if used on a regular basis (Kozel and Adams, 1986).

Reasons for Use

In the middle and late 1960s, social activism was prevalent among young people, and use of marijuana appeared to have political and generational significance. Along with hallucinogens, marijuana was declared to be a drug of the young, and its illegality may have enhanced its appeal among those who were in their then magical years below the age of thirty.

Marijuana remains popular because of its pleasurable effects. People report enjoying good feelings of being "high" and relaxed, usually without the hangover common with alcohol. They generally find that space seems larger, time is drawn out, and perceptions are enhanced; a feeling of serene detachment and composure is created. Many consider marijuana an easy escape from their everyday lives, and many value the sociality of sharing joints, and the accompanying camaraderie— sitting quietly with friends and acquaintances, touching, conversing, and listening to music. When penalities for use of marijuana were reduced and people in all walks of life numbered themselves among its champions, the sweet scent of marijuana in parks and even some theaters became almost commonplace in some parts of the country.

Effects of Marijuana

A great deal of research has been conducted on marijuana. Like most other drugs it is apparently not without its risks. Science has generally found that the more we learn about a drug, the less benign it turns out to be. Marijuana is no exception (Box 11.5).

Psychological Effects of Marijuana

The intoxicating effects of marijuana, as of most drugs, depend in part on potency and size of the dose. We have already stated that smokers of marijuana find it makes them feel relaxed and sociable. Large doses have been reported to bring rapid shifts in emotion, to dull attention, fragment thoughts, and impair memory. Extremely heavy doses have sometimes been found to induce hallucinations and other effects similar to those of LSD, including extreme panic, sometimes arising from the belief that the frightening experience will never end. Dosage can be difficult to regulate because the behavioral effects can lag inhalation by more than half

---

[13]As will be seen in this section, the marijuana story is full of ironies. One is that marijuana is the biggest cash crop in agriculture-rich California.

BOX 11.5

THE STEPPING-STONE THEORY—FROM MARIJUANA TO HARD DRUGS

A concern that has been prevalent for some time is expressed in the so-called "stepping-stone theory" of marijuana use. According to this view, marijuana is dangerous not only in itself but as a first step that can lead young people to become addicted to hard drugs like heroin. In the late 1960s, when information on the harmfulness of marijuana was scant, the issue was basically a political and generational one. People in their teens and college years believed that the older generation, lacking scientific data to discourage marijuana use, had concocted the stepping-stone theory, which itself lacked empirical support, to justify harsh legal penalties for marijuana use and sale. Since there was little disagreement that the hard drugs were very harmful, marijuana was said to be so too because it was a first step to a career of abusing these drugs.

Studies done in the late 1970s and early 1980s established several specific dangers from using marijuana, as we have seen (Jones, 1983). The scientific question remains whether marijuana is, in fact, a stepping-stone to more serious substance abuse. The question may not be a difficult one to answer. It is clear that most people who have used marijuana *do not* go on to drugs like heroin and cocaine. So, if by "stepping-stone" we mean that there is an *inevitability* of escalating to a more serious drug, the case is definitely not made for marijuana. However, we do know

that many—but far from all—who abuse heroin and cocaine began their drug experimentation with marijuana. Indeed, cigarette smokers are more likely to use marijuana than nonsmokers and, at least in the United States, users of marijuana are more likely than nonusers to experiment later with heroin and cocaine (Kandel, 1984). Furthermore, the single best predictor of cocaine use in adulthood is heavy use of marijuana during adolescence (Kozel and Adams, 1986; Kandel, Murphy, and Karus, 1985). Perhaps there is a third variable that can link all such drugs including the legal drug, alcohol. There is growing evidence that users of even legal drugs are at higher risk for using illegal drugs. It is likely that the use of an illegal (or even legal) substance puts one in the company of like-minded others. Social supports develop that even encourage the use of drugs to escape from stressors and from the tedium of many people's lives.

Thus, better than a stepping-stone theory might be a "network" theory, for network implies a complex set of relationships where cause and effect are virtually impossible to isolate but where it is acknowledged that there is some degree of association among many variables. Marijuana is part of the picture, but only one of many contributing factors to involvement in harmful substance use.

---

an hour; many users have in this way gotten themselves much higher than they had intended. People who have had psychological problems before using any psychoactive drug are generally believed to be at highest risk for having negative reactions to it.

The major active chemical in marijuana has been isolated and named delta-9-tetrahydrocannabinol (THC). Since 1974 the marijuana available in this country has been very potent, as much as ten times stronger than that sold earlier.[14] Thus in the early 1970s the most widely available domestic *Cannabis* contained about 0.4 percent THC; samples studied in 1979, in contrast, averaged more than 4 percent and in the early 1980s as much as 6 percent. Hash oil, a concentrated liquid marijuana extract, has been found to be as much as 28 percent THC. The picture is complicated, however, by the fact that *Cannabis* contains more than 400 compounds in addition to THC. Many of these compounds are believed to exert psychological effects either by

themselves or in conjunction with one another and with THC.

Let us examine the psychological effects of marijuana more closely. An abundance of scientific evidence indicates that marijuana interferes with a wide range of cognitive functions. And since *Cannabis* available in recent years is stronger, actual short-term effects on people's minds are probably greater than they were found to be in the laboratory studies, which were conducted for the most part in the late 1960s. A number of tests—digit-symbol substitution (substituting symbols for numbers), reaction time tests, repeating series of digits forward and backward, arithmetic calculations, reading comprehension and speech tests—all revealed intellectual impairment (*Marijuana Research Findings: 1980*). Of special significance are loss of short-term memory and state-dependent learning—the inability, when sober or "straight," to recall material learned when high. Given both the numbers of high school students who use marijuana regularly and the strength of *Cannabis* today, it would seem that significant numbers of students may be seriously hindering their learning.

Several studies have demonstrated that being high

---

[14]The potency of the leaves is thought to vary with the region in which the hemp plant is cultivated. The leaves of plants grown in hot, relatively dry climates contain larger amounts of THC.

on marijuana diminishes complex psychomotor skills necessary for driving. Highway fatality and driver arrest figures indicate that marijuana plays a role in a significant proportion of accidents and arrests; a study in California, for example, found that of 1800 blood samples taken from people arrested for driving while intoxicated, 24 percent had detectable levels of marijuana (Reeve, 1979, cited in *Marijuana Research Findings: 1980*). Marijuana has similarly been found to impair manipulation of flight simulators. Some performance decrements measurable after smoking one or two joints containing 2 percent THC can persist for up to eight hours after a person believes he or she is no longer high, creating the very real danger that people will attempt to drive or to fly when they are not functioning adequately.

Does long-term use of marijuana affect intellectual functioning in any consistent way? Studies requiring memory and problem solving that were conducted in Egypt and in India in the late 1970s indicated some deterioration in users compared to nonusers (Soueif, 1976; Wig and Varma, 1977). It is impossible to know, however, whether these differences existed before heavy drug use and whether they might have been associated with poor diet. American college students do not show these deficits, so it would be premature to conclude that chronic use of the drug brings intellectual deterioration.

Recent survey findings suggest, however, that heavy use of marijuana during teenage years may well contribute to psychological problems in adulthood. Kandel *et al.* (1986) interviewed 1004 adults in their mid-twenties who had been part of a 1971 New York public high school survey of drug use. They found indications of deleterious effects of heavy marijuana use, including more separation or divorce, more delinquency, increased tendencies to consult mental health professionals, and less stable employment patterns among women. The authors do caution, however, that the specific effects of a single drug, like marijuana, are very difficult to disentangle from the effects of other drugs that marijuana users sometimes use, especially alcohol and cocaine.

Somatic Effects of Marijuana

Some preliminary, tentative evidence indicates that marijuana may be harmful to reproduction. Two studies of male chronic users found lower sperm counts and less motility of the spermatozoa, suggesting that fertility might be decreased, especially in men who are already marginally fertile (Hembree, Nahas, and Huang, 1979; Issidorides, 1979). It is conceivable, notes the 1980 Public Health Service Marijuana Report, that negative effects on sperm may be greatest in young smokers. The

junior high and high school male students of today may be tampering with their present and future fertility.

As for female reproduction, a study with female "street users" yielded consistent findings, namely, frequent failure to ovulate normally and shortened fertility periods. Moreover, researchers have discovered that marijuana constituents can cross the placental barrier[15] in rats and thus may affect the development of a fetus (Vardaris *et al.*, 1976). Experiments with female rhesus monkeys, using THC levels comparable to fairly heavy use by human beings, found abnormally frequent loss of the fetus in those who became pregnant (Sassenrath, Chapman, and Goo, 1979). All these studies have their share of methodological problems, but the outcomes for animals and human beings do raise the possibility that moderate and heavy use of marijuana interferes with reproduction. People interested in bearing children need to exercise caution and prudence with *any* drug and should avoid the use of all but strictly necessary and medically supervised drugs if they believe that they might be pregnant.

In the short term, marijuana makes the eyes bloodshot and itchy, dries the mouth and throat, increases appetite, and may raise blood pressure somewhat. There is no evidence that smoking marijuana has untoward effects on the normal heart. The drug apparently poses a danger to people with already abnormal heart function, however, for it does elevate heart rate, sometimes dramatically. As a NIDA report suggests, this fact may become of particular concern as present smokers grow older. The relatively healthy thirty-year-old marijuana users of today are the fifty-year-olds of tomorrow, with a statistically greater chance of having a cardiovascular system impaired for other reasons, such as atherosclerosis. If they are still using the drug then, their hearts will be more vulnerable to its effects. In addition, it is possible that long-term use of marijuana, like the chronic use of tobacco, may be harmful in ways that cannot be predicted from the short-term effects studied so far (Jones, 1980).

Indications are that long-term use of marijuana may seriously impair lung structure and function. Even though marijuana users smoke far fewer cigarettes than do persons using tobacco, most inhale marijuana smoke more deeply and retain it in their lungs for much longer periods of time. Since marijuana has some of the same

---

[15]The placenta is the porous membrane forming the sac in which a fetus develops. In studying whether a chemical in the pregnant woman's body might affect the fetus, scientists try to determine whether it can penetrate the placenta or whether this membrane filters it out. If the agent can get through this barrier, there is presumptive— suggestive but not definite—evidence that the fetus is affected.

carcinogens as regular cigarettes, harmful effects may be greater than would be expected were only the absolute number of cigarettes or pipefuls considered. What are these unfavorable pulmonary effects? First, a research team at the University of California at Los Angeles found that the amount of air a person can expel following a deep breath, called vital capacity, is reduced as much from smoking one marijuana cigarette a day as from smoking sixteen conventional cigarettes a day (Tashkin, Clavarese, and Simmons, 1978). Second, since marijuana cigarettes are generally "homemade," they are not filtered as are most tobacco cigarettes nowadays; the smoke contains significantly higher levels of tar, which, like the tar from conventional cigarettes, has been found to cause cancer when applied to the skin of laboratory animals. Moreover, marijuana smoke contains 70 percent more benzopyrene, another known cancer-causing agent, and 50 percent more carcinogenic polyaromatic hydrocarbons than does the smoke from regular cigarettes (Cohen, 1981). The risk of lung cancer from regular, prolonged use of marijuana cannot be overlooked.

Is marijuana addictive? Recent information suggests that indeed it may be, contrary to widespread earlier belief that it is not. It began to be suspected that tolerance could develop when American servicemen returned from Vietnam accustomed to concentrations of THC that would be toxic to domestic users. Controlled observations have confirmed that habitual use of marijuana does produce tolerance (Nowlan and Cohen, 1977).[16] Whether long-term users suffer physical withdrawal when accustomed amounts of marijuana are not available is less clear. When subjects abstain after a period of heavier-than-normal smoking in the laboratory, appetite is lost and other withdrawal symptoms such as irritability, nausea, and diarrhea do develop (Jones, 1977; Jones and Benowitz, 1976; Jones, 1983). Withdrawal was also found in a study in which users selected their own number of joints, smoked in their usual manner, and then stopped (Mendelson, Rossi, and Meyer, 1974). If people do develop a physical dependency on marijuana, it is far less serious than what we know to be the case with nicotine, cocaine, and alcohol.

Ours is known to be a drug-taking culture. At any one time many individuals have circulating in their bloodstreams one or more chemicals that have been swallowed, injected, sniffed, or smoked. How drugs *interact* with one another, the combination of marijuana and alcohol in particular, is of no little concern.

Evidence from studies of both animals and human beings indicates that simultaneous use of alcohol and marijuana more seriously impairs perception, cognition, and motor activity than does either drug alone. The synergistic effect also extends to physiological processes; for example, heart rate is faster and eyes become more bloodshot. Marijuana can enhance the effects of other drugs such as barbiturates and amphetamines. Although this interactive force of THC is complex and inadequately understood, people should be aware of it and govern themselves accordingly (Siemens, 1980).

Therapeutic Effects of Marijuana

In a seeming irony, therapeutic uses of marijuana came to light during the same period that negative effects of regular and heavy usage of the drug were indicated. In the 1970s a number of double-blind studies (e.g., Salan, Zinberg, and Frei, 1975) showed that THC and related drugs can reduce for some cancer patients the nausea and loss of appetite that accompany chemotherapy. Marijuana often appears to reduce nausea when other antinausea agents fail, and THC is available for oral administration in hundreds of hospitals today under special arrangement with the U.S. Government (Jaffe, 1985; Poster, Penta, Bruno, and Macdonald, 1981).[17] It is also a treatment for glaucoma, a disease in which outflow of fluid from the eyeball is obstructed. A 1971 study by Hepler and Frank had shown that smoking marijuana reduced intraocular pressure in normal subjects. Later studies showed that oral ingestion of delta-9-THC, especially when combined with conventional treatment of the eye disease, reduces intraocular pressure in glaucoma sufferers (Hepler, Frank, and Petrus, 1976).

Research continues on these and other therapeutic uses of marijuana, but as yet none is regarded as standard medical practice (Cohen, 1980). Moreover, since such medical treatments tend to be attempted with older people, the potential benefits have to be measured against physical risks. It will be unfortunate if the illegality of marijuana in many states hinders scientific study of its

---

[16]The question whether marijuana is physically addicting is complicated by "reverse tolerance." Experienced smokers need only a few "hits" or puffs to become high from a marijuana cigarette that a less experienced user puffs many times in order to reach a similar state of intoxication. Reverse tolerance is directly opposite to tolerance for an addicting drug like heroin. The substance THC, after being rapidly metabolized, is stored in the body's fatty tissue and then released very slowly, over as long a period as a month, which may explain people's reverse tolerance for it.

[17]Phenothiazines, used in the treatment of schizophrenia, have been used with some success to reduce the subjective effects of marijuana that can be troubling to patients undergoing chemotherapy. Also used is *Nabilone*, a synthetic compound that produces fewer of marijuana's psychological effects (Weintraub and Standish, 1983).

LSD and other psychedelic drugs were part of the hippie culture of the 1960s.

positive uses, especially for serious medical conditions inadequately dealt with by conventional treatments.[18]

LSD and Other Psychedelics

In 1943, a Swiss chemist, Albert Hofmann, recorded a description of an illness he had seemingly contracted.

Last Friday . . . I had to interrupt my laboratory work . . . I was seized with a feeling of great restlessness and mild dizziness. At home, I lay down and sank into a not unpleasant delirium, which was characterized by extremely exciting fantasies. In a semiconscious state with my eyes closed . . . fantastic visions of extraordinary realness and with an intense kaleidoscopic play of colors assaulted me. (Cited by Cashman, 1966, p. 31)

Earlier in the day Dr. Hofmann had manufactured a

few milligrams of *d*-lysergic acid diethylamide, a drug that he had first synthesized in 1938. Reasoning that he might have unknowingly ingested some and that this was the cause of his unusual experience, he deliberately took a dose and confirmed his hypothesis.

After Hofmann's experiences with **LSD** in 1943, the drug was referred to as psychotomimetic because it was thought to produce effects similar to the symptoms of a psychosis. Then the term **psychedelic**, from the Greek words for soul and to make manifest, was applied to emphasize the subjectively experienced expansion of consciousness reported by users of LSD and two other drugs, **mescaline** and **psilocybin**.[19] In 1896 mescaline, an alkaloid and the active ingredient of peyote, was

---

[18]Yet additional risks may have to be considered even for very ill cancer patients. Dr. Steve Kagen (as reported by *The New York Times*, February 19, 1981) found that marijuana contains a fungus particularly dangerous to people whose immune systems are impaired, and those of cancer patients undergoing chemotherapy are. In the lungs of a healthy person the immune system fights off the fungus, and the individual suffers mild cough or fever. Patients with immune systems weakened by the drugs fighting their cancer may develop a more serious version of the infection, which can cause death.

---

[19]A new psychedelic joined the ranks of illegal drugs on an emergency basis on July 1, 1985. Ecstasy, which refers to two closely similar synthetic compounds, MDA (methelenedioxyamphetamine) and MDMA (methelendioxymethamphetamine), is chemically similar to mescaline and to the amphetamines and is the psychoactive agent in nutmeg. MDA was first synthesized in 1910, but it was not until the 1960s that its psychedelic properties came to the attention of the drug-using, consciousness-expanding generation of the sixties. Today it is popular on some college campuses. Users report that the drug enhances intimacy and insight, improves interpersonal relationships, elevates mood, and promotes aesthetic awareness. It can also cause muscle tension, rapid eye movements, nausea, faintness, chills or sweating, and anxiety, depression, and confusion. The Drug Enforcement Administration considers the use of Ecstasy to be unsafe and a serious threat to health. Indeed, a number of deaths have been reported from accidental overdose (Climko, Roehrich, Sweeney, and Al-Razi, 1987). There have been a few isolated reports on its successful use as an adjunct in psychotherapy because of its presumed ability to facilitate access to feelings (e.g., Naranjo, Shulgin, and Sargent, 1967).

isolated from small, disklike growths of the top of the peyote cactus. The drug has been used for centuries in the religious rites of Indian peoples living in the Southwest and northern Mexico. Psilocybin is a crystalline powder that Hofmann isolated from the mushroom *Psilocybe mexicana* in 1958. The early Aztec and Mexican cultures called the sacred mushrooms "god's flesh," and the Indians of Mexico still use them in their worship today.

During the 1950s these drugs were given in research settings to study what were thought to be psychotic experiences. In 1960 Timothy Leary and Richard Alpert of Harvard University began an investigation of the effects of psilocybin on institutionalized prisoners. The early results, although subject to several confounds, were encouraging: released prisoners who had a psilocybin trip proved less likely to be rearrested. At the same time the investigators started taking trips themselves and soon had gathered around them a group of people interested in experimenting with psychedelic drugs. By 1962 their activities had attracted the attention of law enforcement agencies. As the investigation continued, it became a scandal, culminating in Leary and Alpert's departure from Harvard. The affair seemed to give tremendous impetus to the use of the ***hallucinogens,*** particularly since the manufacture of LSD and the extraction of mescaline and psilocybin were found to be relatively easy and inexpensive.

After leaving Harvard, Leary and Alpert founded the International Foundation for Internal Freedom, an organization that emphatically espoused the desirability of psychedelic trips. It can probably be said that the proselytizing efforts of Leary and Alpert shifted attention from the supposedly psychotic experiences induced by the drugs to their mind-expanding effects.[20]

The use of LSD and other psychedelics peaked in the 1960s; by the 1980s only 1 or 2 percent of people could be classified as regular users, and even these "acid heads" do not indulge more than once or twice every two weeks (*National Survey on Drug Abuse: Main Findings 1982* (1983)). However, marijuana is used fairly frequently between trips. There is no evidence of withdrawal symptoms during abstinence and only equivocal evidence of tolerance (Jaffe, 1985).

Research on the Effects of Psychedelics

The typical dose of LSD is extremely small, from about 100 to 350 micrograms, administered as a liquid absorbed in sugar cubes or as capsules or tablets; for psilocybin the usual dose is about 30,000 micrograms; and for mescaline the usual dose is between 350,000 and 500,000 micrograms. The effects of LSD and mescaline usually last about twelve hours and those of psilocybin about six hours. Although the chemical structure of LSD is well known, the way it produces its psychological effects is not.

The following description is of the general effects of LSD, but it is also appropriate for the other psychedelics:

Synesthesias, the overflow from one sensory modality to another, may occur. Colors are heard and sounds may be seen. Subjective time is also seriously altered, so that clock time seems to pass extremely slowly. The loss of boundaries [between one's sense of self and one's environment] and the fear of fragmentation create a need for a structuring or supporting environment; and in the sense that they create a need for experienced companions and an explanatory system, these drugs are "cultogenic." During the "trip," thoughts and memories can vividly emerge under self-guidance or unexpectedly, to the user's distress. Mood may be labile, shifting from depression to gaiety, from elation to fear. Tension and anxiety may mount and reach panic proportions. After about 4 to 5 hours, if a major panic episode does not occur, there may be a sense of detachment and the conviction that one is magically in control . . . . While the user may be greatly impressed with the drug experience and feel a greater sensitivity for art, music, human feelings, and the harmony of the universe, there is little evidence for long-term changes in personality, beliefs, values, or behavior. (Jaffe, 1985, p. 564)

The effects of the psychedelics, like those of other kinds of drugs, depend on a number of psychological variables in addition to the dose itself. A subject's set, that is, attitudes, expectancies, and motivations about taking drugs, are widely held to be important determinants of reactions to psychedelics. Among the most prominent dangers of taking LSD is the "bad trip." Some aspect of experience after taking the drug creates anxiety, which escalates and can sometimes develop into a full-blown panic attack. Often the specific fear is of going crazy. These panics are usually short-lived and subside as the drug is metabolized. A minority of people, however, go into a psychotic state that can require hospitalization and extended treatment (Box 11.6). It

[20]Like many of the "old timers" in the psychedelic drug revolution, Alpert now espouses an Eastern meditation philosophy that urges people to forsake drugs and work instead on creating their own meaningful "trips" without the aid of chemical agents. Known as Baba Ram Dass, he has lectured and written eloquently about the possibility of cultivating expanded states of consciousness; those who would devote the necessary time and energy to meditation techniques will be open to such experiences, according to Ram Dass.

BOX 11.6

NOT AN UPPER OR A DOWNER BUT AN INSIDE-OUTER

In 1956 Parke Davis and Company, a large pharmaceutical firm, synthesized a new anesthetic. Although effective in large doses, it was found to cause agitation and disorientation as a patient regained consciousness. When administered in smaller doses, it induced a psychoticlike state. In 1965 this new drug, *phencyclidine,* was taken off the market, and by 1978 its legal manufacture was discontinued in the United States.

Phencyclidine (PCP) was first seen in illegal use in Los Angeles in 1965. It soon turned up in the Haight-Ashbury district of San Francisco under the name "PeaCe Pill" and was sold as a psychedelic, but it quickly gained a bad reputation because many users had negative reactions. In the late 1960s and early 1970s the drug spread to other parts of the country until, by 1979, it had turned up in most states. Its prevalence has declined sharply in the 1980s.

As sold on the street, PCP is known by dozens of names—among which are angel dust, elephant tranquilizer, cadillac, cozmos, Detroit Pink, embalming fluid, Killerweed, horse crystal, PeaCe Pill, wac, and zombie—and has been marketed falsely as LSD, psilocybin, cocaine, and other drugs. It is available in many forms and degrees of purity and in most colors. In granular form it contains between 50 and 100 percent phencyclidine. This angel dust is usually available as mint or parsley that has been sprinkled with PCP powder or liquid and sealed in zip-lock plastic bags. The most popular ways to take PCP are in mint or parsley joints and in commercial cigarettes that have been dipped in liquid PCP or had a string dipped in liquid PCP passed through them. But the drug can also be injected intravenously, swallowed, put in the eyes as drops, "snorted" like cocaine, and smoked in a pipe.

The effects of PCP depend largely on the dosage. The user generally has jerky eye movements (nystagmus) alternating with a blank stare, is unable to walk heel-to-toe in a straight line (gait ataxia), and has great rigidity of the muscles. Hallucinations and delusions are also experienced by some. All the sensory systems become overly sensitive so that users are extremely susceptible to any stimulation and are best left alone. When touched, they are likely to flail and become so agitated and combative that it takes several people to restrain them. Their incoherence and lack of communicativeness do not allow them to be "talked down" from their high. With very high dosages—actually, as little as a single gram—there are usually a deep and prolonged coma, seizures, apnea or periods of no breathing, sustained high blood pressure, and sometimes even death from heart and lung failure or from ruptured blood vessels in the brain. No medication to reverse the effects of PCP has yet been found. People seldom remember afterward what happened while they were on the drug.

Phencyclidine is not an upper or a downer, nor is it a psychedelic. Some workers refer to it as an "inside-outer," a term that to some extent conveys the bizarre and extreme nature of its effects.

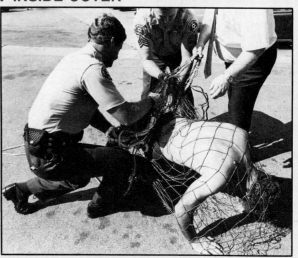

A net had to be used to capture this PCP user.

How long do the effects of PCP last? The way it is ingested and the dosage seem to play a role. Onset is usually between one and five minutes after smoking a treated cigarette; effects peak after about half an hour and then do not dissipate for up to two days. Since PCP remains in the body for several days, it can accumulate if ingested repeatedly. Chronic users who have taken the drug several times a week for six months experience cognitive distortions and disorientation for several months afterward, even for as long as two years after use has ceased. In addition, personality often changes, there can be memory loss, and the user may experience severe anxiety, depression, and aggressive urges (Aniline and Pitts, 1982).

More than 100 deaths from ingesting PCP were reported in Los Angeles County in 1978 alone. These fatalities were caused in a number of ways. One man who was swimming drowned because he lost his spatial orientation; others have expired because of severe respiratory depression or uncontrollable increase in body temperature. Information about the drug is too limited at this time to know more about its long-term effects. Its addictiveness and other consequences are likely to be difficult to determine because most PCP users take other drugs as well.

Those who use PCP frequently are apparently very young, averaging fifteen years of age. The drug is often used with alcohol. Abusers tend to be arrested more often for substance-related offenses than those taking the other drugs discussed in this chapter, and they tend as well to have overdosed on more occasions. The PCP user, then, seems to be more socially deviant, perhaps more often sociopathic, than abusers of other illicit substances.

In light of how terrifying and dangerous the drug is, it is not surprising that its popularity has declined in the 1980s. More surprising perhaps is that it was ever popular at all!

should be noted that there is no indication that LSD or the other psychedelics are addicting.

Some of the individual studies on psychological sets of people taking psychedelics have been relatively simple, others complex. Expectancies were examined by Metzner, Litwin, and Weil (1965). Before receiving 25,000 to 30,000 micrograms of psilocybin, subjects were asked, "How apprehensive are you about taking the drug?" and "How good do you feel about taking the drug today?" Reports of greater apprehension about taking the drug correlated significantly with increased anxiety, headache, and nausea during the drug experience itself. Other studies confirm the great importance of the person's psychological set to the nature of the drug effects (Linton and Langs, 1964; Klee and Weintraub, 1959; Von Felsinger, Lasagna, and Beecher, 1956).

Pahnke (1963) performed a considerably more remarkable and original piece of research. He attempted to maximize all the situational variables that might contribute to a religious or mystical experience. Subjects in his investigations were theological students who first attended a meeting at which they were told of the possibilities of having religious experiences after taking psilocybin. Twenty students were given psilocybin and twenty an active placebo by a double-blind procedure. Nicotinic acid was given as the placebo because it does produce some similar effects, such as a tingling sensation in the skin. After receiving the drug or the placebo, each subject participated in a two-and-a-half-hour-long religious service that included meditation, prayers, and the like. To heighten the significance of the occasion, Pahnke had chosen to conduct the experiment on Good Friday. After the service, each subject wrote a description of his experience and answered an extensive questionnaire. The mystical and transcendental experiences of those who took psilocybin were found to be significantly greater than those who took the placebo.

The Problem of Flashbacks

One of the principal concerns about ingesting LSD is the possibility of *flashbacks*—"the transient recurrence of psychedelic drug symptoms after the pharmacologic effects of such drugs have worn off and [there has been] a period of relative normalcy" (Heaton and Victor, 1976, p. 83). Little is known about these flashback "trips" except that they cannot be predicted or controlled. The available evidence does not support the hypothesis that they are caused by drug-produced physical changes in the nervous system. For one thing, only 15 to 30 percent of users of psychedelic drugs are estimated ever to have

flashbacks (e.g., Stanton and Bardoni, 1972). Moreover, there is no independent evidence of measurable neurological changes in these drug users. The flashback, which seems to have a force of its own and may come to haunt people weeks and months after they have taken the drug, is a very upsetting phenomenon for those it besets.

Heaton and Victor (1976) determined to explore a possible psychological explanation of flashbacks. Heaton had been mindful of previous evidence indicating that extreme relaxation and sensory deprivation can produce in some people sensations and experiences very similar to those reported during flashbacks. In an earlier study (1975) he had demonstrated that *expectancy* of a flashback increased the chances that former LSD users, after swallowing a placebo capsule and then undergoing mild sensory deprivation, would report such experiences, whether or not they had *previously* had flashbacks. The belief that they had taken a drug that would produce a flashback proved more important than a past history of such phenomena.

Heaton and Victor therefore speculated that some drug users, believing that flashbacks are likely, may *attend selectively* to naturally occurring altered states of consciousness and then *label* them flashbacks of a previous drug trip. But why would they allow their thinking to take such a course? Employing various scales from the MMPI, the two researchers developed measures of thinking in a logical, reality-oriented fashion and in a looser, inner-fantasizing mode. They then recruited thirty male volunteer drug users in a Western metropolitan area from clinics and counseling agencies serving young people, including "street people." Half claimed no previous history of flashbacks; the others reported such experiences. The two groups, satisfactorily matched on classificatory variables such as age and the number of times that they had previously taken psychedelics, were tested on the selected MMPI scales. Then all subjects swallowed a capsule, which they were told would probably produce a flashback in experienced drug users like themselves, and underwent brief sensory deprivation. On a second occasion all subjects were given a different capsule, this time with the expectation that it would *not* produce a flashback. Both capsules were placebos.

The group of LSD users who reported earlier flashbacks did show significantly more loose fantasizing, as measured by the MMPI scales. They were also found to have poorer social and sexual adjustment, an uneven school and work history, and often a history of bizarre thinking. And the subjects who scored especially high in loose thinking did indeed report many flashback experiences during the sensory deprivation, even when they had been told that the capsule ingested would *not* produce such effects.

Although it is impossible to know whether the personality described predated the tendency to have flashbacks, the results are useful. They suggest that

under environmental conditions which pull for altered states of consciousness anyway, [loose-thinking] subjects have less ability (and possibly less desire) to maintain reality-oriented mental activity. . . . [Furthermore,] if the subject labels his initial sensations as the beginning of a flashback, expectations . . . are self-fulfilling to the extent that they selectively direct attention to psychedelic sensations. (Heaton and Victor, 1976, p. 89)

Summary

Using substances to alter mood and consciousness is virtually a human characteristic, and so also is the tendency to abuse them. DSM-IIIR distinguishes between psychoactive substance dependence and psychoactive substance abuse. Dependence refers to excessive use of the substance and serious impairments due to its use. Some workers equate it with physical addiction, especially when tolerance and withdrawal are present. Substance abuse is a less severe version of dependence.

Alcohol has a variety of short-term and long-term effects on human beings, and many are tragic in nature, ranging from poor judgment and motor coordination, and their dire consequences for the alcoholic and society, to addiction, which makes an ordinary productive life impossible and is extremely difficult to overcome. As with other addicting drugs, people come to rely on alcohol less for how good it makes them feel than for an escape from feeling bad.

Less prevalent but more notorious, perhaps because of their illegality, are the so-called hard drugs, the narcotic heroin and the barbiturates such as Seconal, which are sedatives, and the amphetamines and cocaine, which are stimulants; all are addicting, most of all cocaine. Heroin has been of special concern in recent years because stronger varieties have become available. Barbiturates have for some time been implicated in both intentional and accidental suicides; they are especially lethal when alcohol is taken at the same time. Cocaine use has risen dramatically in the past few years. Its extremely high cost and elaborate paraphernalia made it a rather ''trendy'' drug in some circles, but now it costs somewhat less and is used by all segments of society.

Nicotine, especially when taken into the body via the inhaled smoke from a cigarette, has worked its addictive power on humankind for centuries and, in spite of somberly phrased warnings from public health officials, continues in widespread use. Of special concern is the smoking of school-aged youngsters and teenagers. Each year the government and private individuals spend millions of dollars to dissuade people from beginning the habit or to help those already addicted to desist from smoking; and each year millions of dollars are spent by the government and private individuals promoting the cultivation and sale of tobacco products. Neither the psychological-medical nor economic-political issues have easy solutions.

Marijuana is smoked by a large number of young Americans although its use has declined in the 1980s. Arguments for deregulation of marijuana have stressed its supposed safety, in comparison to the known harm caused by the habitual use of alcohol, which is a legal and integral part of our culture. But currently available evidence indicates that marijuana when used with regularity is not benign. Significantly stronger varieties of marijuana are now available than were in the early 1970s. Furthermore, there is evidence that marijuana constituents may adversely affect fertility, fetal development, heart function in people who already have coronary problems, and pulmonary function. It also appears to be addicting. Ironically, at the same time that the possible dangers of this drug began to be uncovered, marijuana was found to ease the nausea of cancer patients undergoing chemotherapy and to reduce the excessive intraocular pressure of glaucoma sufferers.

Phencyclidine, known as PCP or angel dust, is a relative newcomer on the drug abuse scene. Though it is used by very few, there is a legal and public health concern about it, for people on PCP are unpredictable and often violent and have such seriously impaired judgment that they can inadvertently kill themselves.

The so-called psychedelics, LSD, mescaline, and psilocybin, are taken by many to alter or expand consciousness. Their use reflects humankind's desires not only to escape from unpleasant realities but probably to explore inner space as well.

Therapies to discourage use of many of these drugs are often confrontational in nature. Residential and outpatient programs confront alcoholics and other drug addicts with the immorality or stupidity of their behavior and encourage in them a resolve to alter the mode of their lives, leaving no room for chemical crutches. Behavioral clinicians, until fairly recently, employed primarily aversive techniques with abusers of alcohol and tobacco, but they now include in their repertoire procedures designed to reduce anxiety and enhance social skills. Anxiety and the lack of such skills may be underlying reasons why people turn to drugs as a means of coping with life.

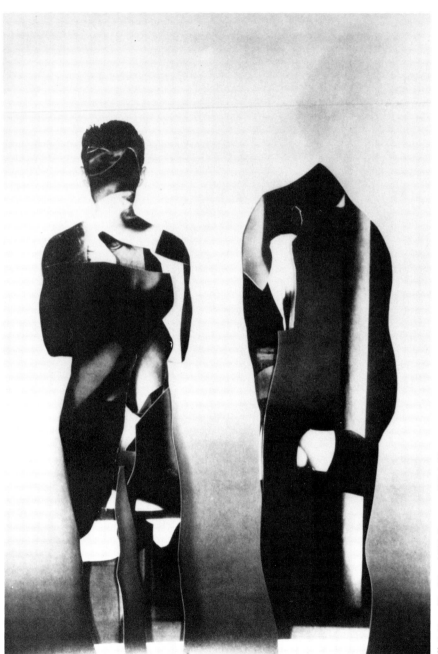

Chris Fiore, *The Other*, 1987. Courtesy of Chris Fiore.

Chapter 12

Sexual Disorders: Gender Identity Disorders and the Paraphilias

Gender Identity Disorders
    Transsexualism
    Gender Identity Disorder of Childhood
    Therapies for Gender Identity Disorders
The Paraphilias
    Fetishism
    Transvestistic Fetishism
    Incest
    Pedophilia
    Voyeurism ("Peeping")
    Exhibitionism
    Rape
    Sexual Sadism and Sexual Masochism
    Paraphilias Not Otherwise Specified
    Therapies for the Paraphilias
    Therapy for Rape
Homosexuality
    Ego-Dystonic Homosexuality in DSM-III
    DSM-IIIR and Homosexuality
    Future Research
Summary

William V. is a twenty-eight-year-old computer programmer who currently lives alone. He grew up in a rural area within a conservative family with strong religious values. He has two younger brothers and an older sister. William began to masturbate at age fifteen; his first masturbatory experience took place while he watched his sister urinate in an outdoor toilet. Despite considerable feelings of guilt, he continued to masturbate two or three times a week while having voyeuristic fantasies. At the age of twenty he left home to spend two years in the navy.

On a summer evening at about 11:30 P.M., William was arrested for climbing a ladder and peeping into the bedroom of a suburban home. Just before this incident he had been drinking heavily at a cocktail lounge featuring a topless dancer. When he had left the lounge at 11:15 P.M. he had intended to return to his home. Feeling lonely and depressed, however, he had begun to drive slowly through a nearby suburban neighborhood, where he noticed a lighted upstairs window. With little premeditation, he had parked his car, erected a ladder he found lying near the house, and climbed up to peep. The householders, who were alerted by the sounds, called the police, and William was arrested. Although this was his first arrest, William had committed similar acts on two previous occasions.

The police referred William's case for immediate and mandatory psychological counseling. William described a lonely and insecure life . . . to his therapist—six months before the arrest, he had been rejected in a long-term relationship, and he had not recovered from this emotional rejection. As an unassertive and timid individual, he had responded by withdrawing from social relationships, and increasing his use of alcohol. His voyeuristic fantasies, which were present to begin with, became progressively more urgent as William's self-esteem deteriorated. His arrest had come as a great personal shock, although he recognized that his behavior was both irrational and self-destructive. (Rosen and Rosen, 1981, pp. 452–453)

Of all the aspects of human suffering that command the attention of psychopathologists and clinicians, few touch the lives of more people than problems involving sex. Oftentimes the problem is exacerbated by bad counsel and misinformation—such as the belief held not so long ago that masturbation should be avoided at all costs because it was immoral and might even weaken the mind. This chapter and the next consider the full range of human sexual thoughts, feelings, and actions that are generally regarded as abnormal and dysfunctional and, with one exception, are listed in DSM-IIIR as *Sexual Disorders* (Table 12.1). The single exception is the Gender Identity Disorders, which have been moved from the sexual disorders to the axis I category *Disorders Usually First Evident in Infancy, Childhood, or Adolescence*. The reason for this shift is that it is now believed that problems in **gender identity** almost always begin in childhood. We have decided to discuss them

TABLE 12.1
Sexual disorders (*from DSM-IIIR*)

A. Gender Identity Disorders (now listed on Axis I)
  1. Transsexualism
  2. Gender identity disorder of childhood
  3. Atypical gender identity disorder
B. Paraphilias
  1. Fetishism
  2. Transvestistic fetishism
  3. Pedophilia
  4. Exhibitionism
  5. Voyeurism
  6. Sexual masochism
  7. Sexual sadism
  8. Frotteurism
  9. Paraphilias not otherwise specified (e.g., coprophilia, necrophilia)
C. Sexual Dysfunctions
  1. Sexual desire disorders
    a. Hypoactive sexual desire disorder
    b. Sexual aversion disorder
  2. Sexual arousal disorders
    a. Female sexual arousal disorder
    b. Male erectile disorder
  3. Orgasm disorders
    a. Inhibited female orgasm
    b. Inhibited male orgasm
    c. Premature ejaculation
  4. Sexual pain disorders
    a. Dyspareunia
    b. Vaginismus
D. Other Sexual Disorders
  1. Sexual disorder not otherwise specified, e.g., distress over one's sexual orientation

here, however, because their *sexual* component seems more important than the likely fact of their early origin.

Our study of the Sexual Disorders is divided into two chapters: the present chapter examines theory and research in the gender identity disorders and the paraphilias, with some critical discussion of *ego-dystonic homosexuality,* a controversial category that was new in DSM-III and that appears in the current nomenclature in only an indirect way. Included also in the present chapter are incest and rape, which do not appear as separate listings in DSM-IIIR but which merit examination in an abnormal psychology textbook. The next chapter addresses *sexual dysfunctions,* disruptions in normal sexual functioning to be found among many people who are in otherwise reasonably sound psychological health.

Gender Identity Disorders

"Are you a boy or a girl?" "Are you a man or a woman?" For virtually all people—even those with serious mental disorders such as schizophrenia—the answer to such questions is immediate and obvious. Also unequivocal is the fact that others will agree with the answer given. Our sense of ourselves as male or female, or what is called gender identity, is so deeply ingrained from earliest childhood that, no matter the stress suffered at one time or another, the vast majority of people are certain beyond a doubt of their gender.

Some people, however, and more often they are men, feel deep within themselves from early childhood that they are of the opposite sex. The evidence of their anatomy—normal genitals and the usual secondary sex characteristics, such as beard growth for men and developed breasts for women—does not persuade them that they are what others see them to be. A male transsexual, then, can look at himself in a mirror, see an ordinary man, and yet announce to himself that he is a woman. Furthermore, he will often try to convince the medical profession to bring his body in line with his gender identity; many transsexuals undergo genital surgery and hormone treatment to make their bodies assume as much as possible the anatomy of the opposite sex.

Transsexualism

DSM-IIIR defines a *transsexual* as an adult who has "a persistent discomfort and sense of inappropriateness

about [his or her] assigned sex[1] . . . . In addition, there is persistent preoccupation, for at least two years, with getting rid of one's primary and secondary sex characteristics and acquiring the sex characteristics of the other sex" (p. 74). Excluded are schizophrenics who on very rare occasions claim to be of the other sex, as well as people who are biologically intersexed, that is, possess both male and female organs, as in *hermaphroditism.*

Transsexuals, sometimes called "gender dysphorics," generally suffer from anxiety and depression, not surprising in light of their psychological predicament. A male transsexual's interest in men will be interpreted by him as a conventional heterosexual preference, given that he is "really" a woman. Predictably, transsexuals often arouse the disapproval of others when they choose to cross-dress in clothing of the other sex. Indeed, for a man to dress as a woman is illegal in many states. Many male-to-female transsexuals who are getting ready to undergo sex-reassignment surgery carry letters from their physicians or therapists informing police authorities that their cross-dressing is an important early aspect of treatment. Cross-dressing is less of a problem for female-to-male transsexuals because contemporary dress fashions allow women to don clothing very similar to that worn by men. DSM-IIIR estimates the prevalence of transsexualism to be very slight, one in 30,000 for males and one in 100,000 in females.

The question is often raised whether it is not delusional for a person with a penis to believe he is a woman. DSM-IIIR asserts that "the insistence by a person with Transsexualism that he or she is of the other sex is, strictly speaking, not a delusion since what is invariably meant is that the person *feels like* a member of the other sex rather than truly believing he or she *is* a member of the other sex" (p. 75). Case studies of many transsexuals reveal, however, that such people express the conviction that they are, in fact, members of the opposite sex. Their statements imply more than the "as if" feelings that DSM-IIIR claims are prevalent. Research has provided conflicting findings (e.g., Langevin, Paitich, and Steiner, 1977; Hunt, Carr, and Hampson, 1981). But perhaps it matters little whether transsexuals are delusional or not; their condition remains what it is.

---

[1]There is a subtle and interesting difference here from DSM-III, which referred to *anatomic* sex rather than assigned sex, "i.e., the sex that is recorded on the birth certificate" (p. 71). The implication is that, admittedly very rarely, the assigned sex could be other than the anatomic sex and that a sense of alienation from the former is to be regarded as transsexual *even if* the assignment at birth had been erroneous. The DSM-IIIR language points up the importance placed on the sex to which an infant is *assigned* as separable from that child's actual anatomical situation.

Etiology

The long-standing and apparently unchangeable nature of the transsexual's incongruous gender identity has led researchers to speculate that transsexuals are hormonally different from those with normal gender identity. Perhaps a woman who believes that she is a man has an excess of androgens such as testosterone and androsterone, hormones known to promote the development and maintenance of male secondary sex characteristics. In a review of several such investigations, Meyer-Bahlburg (1979) found the results to be equivocal: some female transsexuals have elevated levels of male hormones, but most of them do not. Differences, when they are found, are difficult to interpret. Many transsexuals use sex hormones in an effort to alter their bodies in the direction of the sex to which they believe they belong. Even though a researcher may study only transsexuals who have not taken such exogenous hormones for a few months, relatively little is known at present about the long-term effects of earlier hormonal treatment. In any event, the available data do not clearly support an explanation of transsexualism in terms of hormones. Even less conclusive is the research on possible chromosomal abnormalities.

Gender Identity Disorder of Childhood

We know that most transsexuals who have been studied by sex researchers report a history of profound opposite-sexed styles in childhood—femininity in boys and masculinity in girls. An examination of **gender identity disorder of childhood** might therefore provide clues to the etiology of transsexualism. The children given this diagnosis are profoundly feminine boys and profoundly masculine girls, youngsters whose behavior, likes, and dislikes do not fit our culture's rules for what is appropriate for the two sexes. Thus a boy may not like rough-and-tumble play, may prefer the company of little girls, don women's clothing, and insist that he will grow up to be a girl. He may even claim that his penis and testes are disgusting. Many gender disordered children harbor the belief that as they grow, their genitalia will somehow change into those of the opposite sex, a belief that can be construed as a child's version of the adult transsexual's wish for sex-change surgery. The onset of the disorder is before the age of six.

The very categorization of boys and girls as having their own masculine and feminine ways is so heavily laden with value judgments and stereotyping that considering opposite behavioral patterns abnormal may seem unjustified. But some evidence suggests that these patterns can come from a physical disturbance. Human and other primate offspring of mothers who have taken sex hormones during pregnancy may frequently behave like the opposite sex *and* have anatomical abnormalities. For example, girls whose mothers took synthetic progestins during pregnancy, to prevent uterine bleeding, were found to be "tomboyish" during their preschool years (Ehrhardt and Money, 1967). Progestins are considered precursors of androgens, the male sex hormones. Other young tomboys also had genitalia with male characteristics, which suggests a link between the progestins taken by their mothers and male physical features (Green, 1976). Young boys whose mothers ingested female hormones when they were pregnant were found to be less athletic as young children and to engage less in rough-and-tumble play than their male peers (Yalom, Green, and Fisk, 1973). Although such children were not necessarily abnormal in their gender identity, the mother's ingestion of prenatal sex hormones did give them higher than usual levels of cross-gender interests and behavior.

The cross-gender behavior that many, perhaps most, little children engage in now and then may, in some homes, receive too much attention and reinforcement from parents and other relatives. Interviews with the parents of children who have become atypical frequently reveal that they did not discourage, and in many instances clearly encouraged, cross-dressing behavior. This is especially true for feminine boys. Many mothers, aunts, and grandmothers found it "cute" that the little fellow enjoyed putting on mommy's old dresses and high-heeled shoes, and very often they instructed the youngster on how to apply lipstick, eyeshadow, and rouge. Family albums often contain photographs of the young boys fetchingly attired in women's clothing. Such reactions on the part of the family to an atypical child have probably contributed in a major way to the conflict between his or her anatomical sex and the acquired gender identity (Green, 1974). Indeed, Richard Green's noteworthy prospective, longitudinal study of feminine boys and tomboy girls[2] reveals that, as compared to a control group of nontomboys, tomboy girls were more likely to choose their fathers as a favored parent (and presumably to regard their fathers rather than their mothers as a role model) and were more likely to have mothers who themselves were tomboys as children and

---

[2]What's a tomboy? The definition in this study was for the girl to be regarded as one by her parents and to have the following characteristics: "(1) a peer group which was at least half male; (2) a preference for traditionally masculine attire such as a baseball jacket and cap; (3) a low interest in dress-up dolls (e.g., Barbie); (4) a preference for male roles when engaging in make-believe games; (5) a stronger interest in sports than most same-age girls; and (6) a more than rarely expressed desire to be a boy" (Williams *et al.*, 1985, p. 722). The data described here were collected on Long Island, New York, during the mid 1970s.

who were more accepting of their daughters' masculine behavior (Williams, Goodman, and Green, 1985). The possible modeling and operant shaping of more masculine behavior within the family may, as Williams *et al.* speculate, be supplemented by the positive reinforcement these girls might experience from their male peer groups as a result of their tomboyish behavior.

Research with infants and very young children whose genitals have both male and female characteristics indicates that surgery to correct this problem needs to be performed by the age of three, the time by which a child has achieved a sense of gender identity that is very difficult to change later on (Money, Hampson, and Hampson, 1955). Indeed, the gender assigned several of these children was later found to conflict with at least one anatomic sex criterion, such as the indication of sex by their chromosomes. Such children already over the age of three kept the gender to which they had been assigned. The web of evidence, then, points to the criticalness of how a very young child, under three years of age, is treated by the adults around him. Dressing a child as a boy, giving him (or her!) a male name, and encouraging him to engage in traditional masculine activities are major influences on the development of gender identity. In contradiction to widespread belief, anatomy is not always destiny.

These findings, however, should *not* be interpreted to mean that encouraging gentleness in a little boy or assertiveness, even aggressiveness, in a little girl will probably lead to a gender identity disorder. Indeed, *most GID children do not become transsexual in adulthood, even without professional intervention* (Zucker *et al.*, 1984), although many develop a homosexual orientation (Coates and Person, 1985; Green, 1985). Investigators working in this field are very much aware of the culture-relative aspects of masculinity and femininity, and of the difference between enjoying activities more typical of the opposite sex and actually believing that one *is* of the opposite sex. We do know that the vast majority of little boys engage in varying amounts of "feminine" play and little girls in varying amounts of "masculine" play with no identity conflicts whatsoever (Green, 1976).[3] Gender identity disorder of childhood and the adult disorder of transsexualism are rare, far less prevalent than could be expected from the numbers of little boys who play with dolls and of little girls who engage in vigorous, physical-contact sports.

Indeed, Sandra Bem (1984) takes the view that we need not consider any behavior or interest as gender-related except those that concern anatomy or reproduction. She argues that children should enjoy the freedom to behave in both conventional and nontraditional ways without risking punishment from parents or peers. A little boy who shows tenderness to a doll and a little girl who does not should not be made to worry and doubt themselves. Taking the argument a step further, would transsexuality itself disappear if sex-role stereotyping ceased to exist? Then a man would regard his traditionally feminine traits and interests as a normal *masculine* variation, rather than as a pathognomonic sign of being a woman trapped in a man's body (see Raymond, 1979). He would need to be more accepting of any sexual attraction to members of his own sex, however, an attraction that transsexuals regard as heterosexual.

Therapies for Gender Identity Disorders

Sex-Change Surgery

Innovations in surgical procedures, coupled with advances in hormonal treatments and a sociocultural atmosphere that would permit their implementation, have allowed many transsexuals to pursue their wish to become in some respects a member of the opposite sex. The treatments to be described, however, do *not* biologically transform a man or woman into the opposite sex.

In **sex-change surgery** where a man takes on the physical characteristics of a woman, his genitalia are almost entirely removed, with some of the tissue retained to form an artificial vagina. At least a year before the operation, appropriate female hormones are given to develop the breasts, soften the skin, and change the body in other ways; they have to be taken indefinitely after the surgery (Green and Money, 1969). Most male-to-female transsexuals have to undergo extensive and costly electrolysis to remove beard and body hair, and they receive training to raise the pitch of their voice; the female hormones prescribed do not make hair distribution and the voice less masculine. Some male-to-female transsexuals also have plastic surgery on their chin, nose, and Adam's apple to rid them of masculine largeness. At the same time the transsexual begins to live as a female member of society in order to experience as fully as possible what it is like. The genital surgery itself is not done until a one- or two-year trial period has been completed. Conventional heterosexual intercourse is possible for male-to-female transsexuals, although pregnancy is out of the question since only the external genitalia are altered.

---

[3]This is not to say that feminine boys are not subject to considerable stress. Our society has a low tolerance for boys who act like girls. In contrast, girls can be tomboys and still conform to acceptable standards of behavior for girls (Williams, Goodman, and Green, 1985).

A 1960 picture of James Morris, who after sex-change surgery became Jan Morris, shown in a 1974 photograph.

For female-to-male transsexuals the process is more arduous. The penis that can be constructed is small and not capable of normal erection; artificial supports are therefore needed for conventional sexual intercourse. An operation now available extends the urethra into the newly constructed penis to allow the person the social comfort of being able to use public urinals. Less cosmetic follow-up is needed than for male-to-female transsexuals because the male hormones prescribed drastically alter fat distribution and stimulate the growth of beard and body hair. The relatively greater ease of the female-to-male change may come in part from our society's lesser focus on the physical attributes of men. A small, soft-spoken man is more acceptable to society than a large, hulking woman.

DSM-IIIR indicates that the ratio of male transsexuals to female transsexuals seeking help ranges from a high of eight to one to a low of one to one. In the first comprehensive book on female-to-male transsexuals, Lothstein (1983) reports that each year more and more women are applying for sex-reassignment surgery.

The first sex-change operation took place in Europe in 1930, but the surgery that attracted worldwide attention was performed on an ex-soldier, Christine (originally George) Jorgensen, in Copenhagen in 1952. Some years later Jan (originally James) Morris, a well-known journalist, published *Conundrum* (1974), a sensitive and highly personal account of her life as a man and her subsequent alteration to a woman.

For many years the Gender Identity Clinic at Johns Hopkins University School of Medicine was a leading American facility for these operations, but in the 1980s their sex-change program was terminated. This termination was justified on the basis of a now widely cited and controversial report from Johns Hopkins by Meyer and Reter (1979), the first outcome study that included a group of control transsexuals who did not undergo sex-change surgery. It was concluded that "sex reassignment confers no advantage in terms of social rehabilitation" (p. 1015). These negative findings were embraced so readily by the Johns Hopkins Clinic and several hospitals that they seemed, so to speak, "exactly what the folks wanted to hear" in order to justify, on scientific grounds, terminating their sex-change surgery programs. The Meyer–Reter study, however, was strongly criticized by Fleming, Steinman, and Bocknek (1980) on a number of methodological grounds. Indeed the outcome for sex-reassignment may not be as bleak as portrayed by the Meyer–Reter study. Abramovitz's (1986) careful review of twenty years of research indicates that there is an overall improvement in social adaptation rate of two-thirds resulting from sex-change surgery, with female-to-males showing somewhat greater success than males-to-females. However, caution is warranted in drawing conclusions because of glaring inadequacies in research design in most of the studies—these include such missteps as subjects appearing in more than one report; subjects who committed suicide not being counted as no-improvement because they were not available at follow-up; and inadequate information provided on the exact nature of hormonal and surgical modification. As for the Meyer–Reter (1979) study, Abramovitz (1986) points out that the markedly shorter follow-up period for the unoperated controls worked against finding better results for the surgical group of transsexuals (the longer follow-up period for the surgery patients may well have allowed more problems to come to light over time). He concludes that "an observer [of reactions to the Meyer–Reter Hopkins report] may well suspect that this incident warrants a chapter in the social psychology of medicine" (p. 187).

In the face of these controversies, sex-change programs continue in many medical-psychological settings; it is estimated that each year in the United States upward of 1000 transsexuals are surgically altered to the opposite sex. And yet, the long-term effectiveness, or even wisdom, of sex transformation surgery is difficult to evaluate (Lothstein, 1980). Given that people who go to great lengths to have this surgery performed claim that their future happiness depends on the change, should this surgery be evaluated in terms of how happy such people are afterward? If so, it can be safely said that some transsexuals who have crossed over anatomically are better off, others are not. But as people make their way through life, many events bring them a greater or lesser amount of fulfillment or even just ease. If a surgically altered transsexual becomes dismally unhappy, is the venture to be indicted as antitherapeutic? Transsexuals who undergo these procedures often cut their ties to former friends and family members and to aspects of their previous lives—"Was it *I* who played tailback on the football team?" Considerable stress is the lot of those who choose to divorce themselves from the past, for the past contributes to our sense of ourselves as people, as much as do the present and the future. A transsexual who has surgery, then, confronts challenges few others have occasion to face; adjustment to the new life should perhaps be evaluated more leniently.

All experienced therapists, whatever their theoretical persuasion, are wary of a client who says "If only . . . ." The variations are legion: "If only I were not so fat. . . ." "If only I were not so nervous. . . ." "If only I had not left school before graduation. . . ." Following each "if only" clause is some statement indicating that life would be far better, even wonderful . . . if only. Most of the time the hopes expressed are an illusion; things are seldom so simple. The transsexual, understandably focusing on the discrepancy be-

tween gender identity and biological makeup, blames his or her present dissatisfactions on the horrible trick nature has played. But he or she usually finds that sex change falls short of solving life's problems. It may handle this one set of them, but it usually leaves untouched other difficulties that all human beings are subject to, such as conflicts at work, with intimates, and even within one's self.

Even proponents of sex-change surgery have for some time advocated psychotherapy to help transsexuals adjust to their new lives. Instructional materials for transsexuals, their friends, and relatives are available from the Harry Benjamin Gender Dysphoria Association, named after the New York endocrinologist who in the 1950s was a pioneer in his clinical work with transsexuals. Whether transsexuals choose sex-change surgery or not, they need a good deal of supportive psychotherapy and counseling to help them through their conflicts, anxiety, and depression (Roberto, 1983).

The dilemmas faced by professionals and by society-at-large are summed up vividly by Abramovitz (1986):

From the perspective of many psychiatrists and psychologists, the surgeon who performs a sex-change operation is at best naively colluding [with the patient] on a psychotic odyssey and at worse [sic] surrendering to mercenary instincts. To physicians skeptical of psychosocial models of mental illness and face-to-face with with the agony of a pleading transsexual, however, surgical treatment holds out the promise of a lasting cure. Although not generally regarded as curative in and of itself, the sex change is thought to offer reassurance for a weak gender identity under constant emotional siege. (p. 183)

Alterations of Gender Identity

Are sex-change operations indeed the only option? They used to be considered the only viable treatment, for psychological attempts to shift gender identity had consistently failed. Gender identity was assumed too deep-seated to alter. Apparently successful procedures for altering gender identity through behavior therapy have been reported, however. One treatment (Rekers and Lovaas, 1974) was of a five-year-old boy who, since age two, had been cross-dressing and showing the other familiar signs of gender identity disorder. Concurring with the therapist's judgment that conforming to societal standards of masculinity would benefit the boy in both the short and long run, the child's parents began, as instructed, to compliment and otherwise support him whenever he played with traditionally male toys, rather than those commonly preferred by girls, and whenever he engaged in other little-boy activities. Feminine mannerisms were discouraged. After only six months of

BOX 12.1

PSYCHOPHYSIOLOGICAL ASSESSMENT OF SEXUAL AROUSAL

Let us examine closely some important innovations in physiological measurement. In 1966 Masters and Johnson startled researchers and lay people alike by their direct physiological assessments of men and women during states of great sexual arousal. The measures they used primarily were muscle tension and blood volume in various parts of the cardiovascular system. In addition, they employed ingenious photographic devices to record changes in the color of various tissues of the vagina during the sexual arousal of women. More recently behavioral researchers have been using two genital devices for measuring sexual arousal in men and in women, and each of them enjoys validation in giving rather specific measurements of sexual excitement. Both are sensitive indicators of vasocongestion of the genitalia, that is, the flooding of their veins with blood, a key physiological process in sexual arousal.

The penile plethysmograph (Freund, 1963; Bancroft, Jones, and Pullan, 1966) has been used successfully to measure the sexual arousal of men in a variety of experiments. A plethysmograph is a device that measures blood flow. The most widely used penile plethysmograph is a strain gauge, consisting of a very thin rubber tube filled with mercury or a circular piece of light surgical steel, either of which can be placed around the penis (Barlow *et al.*, 1970) with ease and in privacy. As the penis fills with blood during sexual excitement, the tube or steel stretches, changing the electrical resistance of the mercury or steel; through appropriate wiring the increase in resistance is transformed into tracings on a polygraph. Increase in the length of the penis correlates fairly well with increase in circumference, and both of them are a function of engorgement of the penis with blood during sexual excitement. The strain gauge, then, provides a useful measure

of sexual responding in men. More recent research uses other modes of assessment that focus on temperature changes (Webster and Hammer, 1983) and blood flow (Bancroft and Bell, 1985) in the penis; early findings suggest that erection in the male may be more complicated than hitherto believed.

Similarly direct and specific measurement of female sexual arousal was not at first possible. Only indirect measures such as those used by Masters and Johnson were available, and these are unsatisfactory for both aesthetic and practical reasons. Fortunately, a vaginal plethysmograph was eventually invented by Sintchak and Geer (1975). This device is shaped like a small menstrual tampon and has a light at the tip. The light reflected from the vaginal walls is recorded and provides a measure of the amount of blood they contain, an indicator of sexual arousal in women. Like the penile strain gauge, the vaginal probe is easily put in place by subjects in total privacy. An important validational study of this device was reported by Geer, Morokoff, and Greenwood (1974). They showed female undergraduates erotic and nonerotic films. Any differences between the measurements of the two groups of subjects during the viewings could be taken as evidence that the vaginal probes provide a valid measure of sexual excitement. The women watching the sexual film showed much greater blood flow than did the subjects watching the control film. It is of interest that heart rate measurements taken concurrently did not differentiate the two groups of subjects, confirming the desirability of specific genital measures. Other measures are under study as well, including temperature sensors (thermistors) for detecting changes in the labia (Henson, Rubin, Henson, and Williams, 1977) and in the vagina (Fisher *et al.*, 1983).

intensive treatment, the boy was typically masculine, and he was still so at a two-year follow-up. Although it might be objected that encouraging play with guns while discouraging play with dolls only reinforces cultural stereotypes (Winkler, 1977), this child may have been spared considerable psychological hardship by bringing his gender identity into conformity with his biological makeup.[4]

An even more dramatic reversal of gender identity was reported by Barlow, Reynolds, and Agras (1973). In their behavioral treatment of a seventeen-year-old male transsexual, gender role was broken down into

concrete components, such as mannerisms, interpersonal behavior, and fantasies, and the client was given training to change each component. He was initially made aware of the effeminate manner in which he stood, sat, walked, and talked. Then through modeling, rehearsal, and video feedback, and through voice retraining, he was taught the ways of doing them judged masculine by the culture. Almost immediately the staring and ridicule of his peers lessened, and he returned to high school part time. The young man's social skills improved as he was taught to make eye contact and conversation and to express his positive feelings through appropriate smiles and other means.

He still felt himself to be a female, however, and had fantasies and urges to have intercourse with men. Therapy then focused on his fantasy life. During train-

[4]We have stated that most GID children do not become transsexuals, even without special treatment. Not knowing whether this particular child would "grow out of it," the parents and the therapists decided to intervene.

Subjects soon become relatively unaware of the presence of genital plethysmographs on their bodies and of the wiring to the polygraph. This degree of unobtrusiveness, desirable in any assessment procedure, is particularly important in studying sexual behavior, about which many people are self-conscious. The technical innovations and availability of these devices have spurred a remarkable volume of research on human sexual behavior. Of course, it would be naive to assert that these genital devices have no effect on how subjects respond in a laboratory. Furthermore, volunteers for such studies have had more sexual experiences than those who do not volunteer (Wolchik, Spencer, and Lisi, 1983); hence findings based on their reactions cannot be reliably generalized. Still, these measures are proving useful in research, and their possible clinical utility can be appreciated from a report by Abel, Cunningham-Rathner, Becker, and McHugh (1983), who confronted a mixed group of paraphiliac sex offenders with the results of the physiological assessment of their penile tumescence to a range of stimuli. Many who had earlier denied unconventional sexuality admitted to it after seeing the laboratory results and being assured of confidentiality. This interesting finding suggests that psychophysiological measures can enhance the reliability of self-reports (Rosen and Beck, 1988).

The physiology of the human body, however, presents problems for the assessment of sexual arousal by genital plethysmographs. In the earliest stages of arousal, the penis lengthens faster than it grows in circumference (Davidson *et al.*, 1981); the circumference, which is what the strain gauge measures, can initially *decrease* as the penis lengthens. Many studies of male sexual arousal focus on these early stages, what may be termed sexual *interest*. More-

over, it has been found that circumference measures often reach their maximum before full erection is achieved, thereby providing unreliable assessment at the upper range of sexual arousal as well. The vaginal plethysmograph is extremely sensitive to temperature; the body temperature of women is known to fluctuate, depending on the phase of the menstrual cycle (Beck, Sakheim, and Barlow, 1983).

Genital arousal measures are also subject to faking and distortion by subjects who wish to hide their preferences for certain classes of stimuli, for example, imagining negative events while being exposed to unconventional stimuli in order to suppress their arousal (Laws and Holmen, 1978). It is clear that not all sexuality can be measured in terms of genital responding. Although many studies find high correlations between subjective reports of arousal and physiological measures of the kind just described, these relationships are not one to one (Rosen and Beck, 1988). Indeed, in the Geer *et al.* validational study described earlier, there was no relationship between the vaginal probe measures and subjects' estimates of their own sexual arousal. It may be that under the relatively low levels of arousal produced in this, and related, studies, subjects' own estimates of their sexual arousal are based on affective cues that are not highly correlated with physiological state. It may also be that some subjects are guilty about feeling sexual and may underreport to an experimenter whatever physical sexual feelings they are aware of and/or that are being detected by the photoplethysmograph (Morokoff, 1985). Overall, however, the data being reported by laboratory sex researchers hold considerable promise for shedding light on an area of human conduct previously shrouded in mystery, embarrassment, and an often harmful mythology.

ing sessions a female therapist encouraged him to imagine himself in sexual situations with attractive women; she also embellished his fantasies by describing foreplay in explicit detail. He was instructed to generate such fantasies when encountering women as he went about his daily activities. After thirty-four training sessions over a period of two months, the client's desire to change sex dropped dramatically, and fantasies about men decreased in number as those about women increased. He was now beginning to think of himself as a man, and the attraction he still occasionally felt toward men took place without gender role reversal, that is, the attraction was that felt by one man toward another.

Measures of sexual arousal with the penile plethysmograph (see Box 12.1) more definitely revealed that he was still attracted to men and not women, so ther-

apeutic effort was now devoted to increasing the arousal felt toward women and decreasing that felt toward men. Slides of women were paired with slides of men, the idea being to classically condition sexual arousal to women by associating them with the arousal felt toward slides of males. This procedure, followed by aversion therapy sessions to reduce the attractiveness of slides of males, promoted the desired change to a heterosexual pattern of arousal. Interestingly, during this period the young man's manner of standing, sitting, and walking became even more traditionally masculine. He also felt much better about himself and had returned to high school on a full-time basis. Five months after the end of treatment, the young man reported for the first time masturbating to orgasm while imagining himself with a woman. A one-year follow-up found him going steady with a woman and engaging in "light petting." He no longer thought of himself as a woman. Five years later the man's gender identity continued to be masculine and his sexual orientation heterosexual (Barlow, Abel, and Blanchard, 1979).

The work of Barlow and his colleagues represents the first successful change of gender identity in an adult transsexual and as such raises the possibility that cross-sex identity is amenable to change. The clinicians themselves acknowledge that this particular client might have been different from other transsexuals because he did consent at the outset to participate in a therapy program aimed at changing his gender identity. Most transsexuals refuse such treatment as inappropriate; for them sex-reassignment surgery is the only legitimate goal.[5]

The Paraphilias

The term *paraphilia* denotes that there is a deviation (*para-*) in what the person is attracted to (*-philia*). In those suffering the disorders,

The essential feature . . . is recurrent intense sexual urges and sexually arousing fantasies generally involving either (1) nonhuman objects, (2) the suffering or humiliation of oneself or one's partner (not merely simulated), or (3) children or nonconsenting persons. The diagnosis is made only if the person has acted on these urges, or is markedly distressed by them. . . . The imagery in a paraphilic fantasy is frequently the stimulus for sexual excitement in people without a Paraphilia. For example, female undergarments are sexually exciting for many men; such fantasies and urges are paraphilic only when the person acts on them or is markedly distressed by them. (Reprinted with permission from the *Diagnostic and Statistical Manual of Mental Disorders, Third Edition, Revised.* Copyright 1987 American Psychiatric Association, p. 279)

The DSM-IIIR definition of paraphilias differs from that in DSM-III in an important way. As part of the increasing "liberalization" of the DSM, DSM-IIIR allows for people to have the same fantasies and urges that a paraphiliac has (like exhibiting the genitals to an unsuspecting stranger) but not to be diagnosed if the fantasies are not recurrent and intense, and if he or she has never acted on the urges *or is not markedly dis-*

tressed by them. Thus, unlike DSM-III, DSM-IIIR declines to construe unconventional fantasies and urges as abnormal unless a person has acted them out or is distressed by having such recurrent and strong urges.

Paraphilias are, according to DSM-IIIR, often multiple rather than single and can also be an aspect of other mental disorders, such as schizophrenia or one of the personality disorders. Prevalence statistics indicate that paraphiliacs are almost always men; only in masochism does one find appreciable numbers of women, but even here they are outnumbered by a ratio of twenty to one. Finally, the fact that some paraphiliacs seek nonconsenting partners indicates that there will be legal consequences.

Fetishism

A fetishist, almost always a male, is sexually enthralled by some inanimate object. His disorder of *fetishism* takes the form of

recurrent, intense, sexual urges and sexually arousing fantasies, of at least six months' duration, involving the use of nonliving objects (fetishes). . . . Usually the fetish is required or strongly preferred for sexual excitement, and in its absence there may be erectile failure in males. The diagnosis is not made when the fetishes are limited to articles of female clothing used in cross-dressing, as in Transvestic Fetishism [see below], or when the object is genitally stimulating because it has been designed for that purpose, e.g., a vibrator. (Reprinted with permission from the *Diagnostic and Statistical Manual of Mental Disorders, Third Edition, Revised.* Copyright 1987 American Psychiatric Association, p. 282)

Beautiful shoes, sheer stockings, gloves, toilet articles, fur garments, and especially underpants are common sources of arousal for fetishists. Some can carry on their fetishism by themselves in secret by fondling, kissing, smelling, or merely gazing at the adored object as they masturbate. Others need their partner to don the fetish as a stimulant for intercourse. Fetishists sometimes become primarily interested in making a collection of the desired objects, and they may commit burglary week after week to add to their hoard.

Subjectively, the attraction felt by the fetishist toward the object is involuntary and irresistible. The degree of the erotic focalization distinguishes fetishisms from the ordinary attraction that high heels and net stockings may hold for heterosexual men. The disorder usually begins by adolescence, although the fetish may have acquired special significance even earlier, during childhood.

----

[5]In their follow-up report on the seventeen-year-old transsexual, Barlow, Abel, and Blanchard (1979) described two additional cases treated in the same way. These two men, in their mid-twenties, were on the route to sex-change surgery but then had second thoughts. The behavioral retraining succeeded again in altering gender identity but not their attraction to men.

Psychoanalytic theorists generally consider fetishisms and other paraphilias to serve some sort of defensive function, warding off castration anxiety about normal sexual contacts. Learning theorists usually invoke some kind of classical conditioning in the person's social-sexual history. For example, a young man may, early in his sexual experiences, masturbate to pictures of women dressed in black leather. Indeed, one experiment (Rachman, 1966) lends some mild support to learning propositions. Male subjects were repeatedly shown slides of nude and alluring females interspersed with slides of women's boots. The subjects were eventually aroused by the boots alone. The "fetishistic attraction" induced, however, was weak and transient.

Box 6.3 (page 138) discussed the possibility that people are "prepared" to learn to become phobic to certain objects. It is also possible that human beings are prepared to learn to be sexually stimulated by certain classes of stimuli. If mere association with sexual stimulation were all there is to acquiring a fetishism through classical conditioning, would not objects such as ceilings and pillows be found high on the list of fetishes (Baron and Byrne, 1977)? At this point it would be premature to conclude that fetishisms are established through classical conditioning.

Transvestistic Fetishism

When a man is sexually aroused by dressing in the clothing of the opposite sex while still regarding himself as a member of his own sex, the term ***transvestistic fetishism*** or transvestism is applied to his behavior. A transvestite may also enjoy appearing socially as a woman; some female impersonators become performers in nightclubs, catering to the delight that many sexually conventional people take in skilled cross-dressing. Unless the cross-dressing is associated with sexual arousal, however, DSM-IIIR does not consider impersonators as transvestic. Transvestism should not be confused with homosexuality; transvestites are heterosexual, and only a few homosexuals ever on occasion "go in drag." As mentioned earlier, it is illegal in many jurisdictions to appear cross-dressed in public.

Transvestites, who are always males according to DSM-IIIR, by and large cross-dress episodically rather than on a regular basis. They tend to be otherwise masculine in appearance, demeanor, and sexual preference. Most are married. The cross-dressing usually takes place in private and in secret and is known to few members of the family. The compulsion to cross-dress may become more frequent over time but only rarely develops to a change in gender identity, that is, to the man's believing that he is actually a member of the female

Transvestites at a social outing.

sex. On the other hand, some transvestites do report *feeling* like a woman when they are cross-dressing.

Case histories of transvestites often refer to childhood incidents in which the little boy was praised and fussed over for looking "cute" when wearing female attire. Paradoxically, some male transvestites recall "petticoat punishment" from their childhood—being punished through the humiliation of being forced to don girls' clothing (American Psychiatric Association, 1987, p. 289). Learning accounts assume the disorder results from the conditioning effects of repeatedly masturbating when cross-dressing, similar to the supposed classical conditioning connection between arousal and the object adopted as a fetish. Some clinicians believe transvestism represents for a beleaguered male a refuge from the responsibilities he sees himself bearing solely by virtue of being male in our society. Female clothing, then, is believed to have *meaning* for transvestites that is more complex and encompassing than sheer sexual arousal; trying to explain transvestism solely in sexual terms may therefore be an oversimplification.

Incest

The taboo against **incest** seems virtually universal in human societies (Ford and Beach, 1951). A notable exception was the marriages of Egyptian pharaohs to their sisters or other females of their immediate families. In Egypt it was believed that the royal blood should not be contaminated by that of outsiders. Some anthropologists consider the prohibition against incest to have served the important function of forcing more widely spread social ties and consequently greater social harmony than would have been likely had family members chosen their mates only from among their own. The incest taboo makes sense according to present-day scientific knowledge. The offspring from a father—daughter or a brother—sister union has a greater probability of inheriting a pair of recessive genes, one from each parent. For the most part, recessive genes have negative physiological effects, such as serious birth defects. The incest taboo, then, has adaptive evolutionary significance (Geer, Heiman, and Leitenberg, 1984).

Incest,[6] which includes all forms of sexual contact, seems most common between brother and sister. The next most common form, which is considered more pathological, is between father and daughter. In a well-known study on sex offenders, Gebhard and his associates (1965) found that most fathers who had relations with physically mature daughters tended to be very devout, moralistic, and fundamentalistic in their religious beliefs.[7] There is also evidence that the structure of families in which incest occurs is unusually patriarchal and traditional, especially with respect to the subservient position of women relative to men (Alexander and Lupfer, 1987). Furthermore, it is believed that incest is more prevalent when the mother is absent or disabled (Finkelhor, 1979); this may happen because mothers otherwise usually protect their daughters from intrafamilial sexual abuse. Fathers who commit incest may be sexually frustrated in their marriage yet feel constrained, for religious reasons, from seeking gratification through masturbation, prostitutes, or extramarital affairs. For them it is preferable to keep sexual contacts within the family (Frude, 1982). Other evi-

dence, however, indicates that incestuous relationships can be found in families of all religious and socioeconomic backgrounds (Rosen and Rosen, 1981). Very few instances of mother–son incest are reported.

Statistics on the incidence of incest are notoriously difficult to collect; family members are very reluctant to report the offenders to the authorities, sometimes from fear of violence from the offending father, particularly when he drinks heavily (Mey and Neff, 1982). Family members may also realistically fear that the child or father can be legally removed from the home, which would have a major negative impact on the very existence of the family. So seriously does the public view this sexual offense, that in recent years many state laws *require* professionals such as physicians, psychologists, and teachers to report occurrences of incest to legal authorities even when the discovery is made in the context of an otherwise confidential relationship.

Incest is now acknowledged to happen much more often than had earlier been assumed. A study of 796 college students found that an astounding 19 percent of the women and 8.6 percent of the men had been sexually victimized as children. Of the victimized women, 28 percent had had incestuous relations, of the men, 23 percent (Finkelhor, 1979). More recent survey data confirm these findings (Siegel *et al.*, 1987). When states pass more effective legislation on reporting incidents of incest, confirmed cases increase 50 to 500 percent.

Explanations of incest run the gamut from sexual deprivation to the Freudian notion that human beings have basic human desires for such relationships. Some older explanations tended to "blame the victim" (Ryan, 1971): Bender and Blau (1937) described a number of children who had been involved in incestuous relationships as having "unusually attractive and charming personalities" (p. 511) and, because of their seductiveness, as not being totally innocent parties. In addition to being morally repugnant, this hypothesis is refuted by the information available (Meiselman, 1978).

There is a growing body of evidence bearing on the long-term effects of incest (as well as of the disorder discussed below, pedophilia). A number of studies reviewed by Geer, Heiman, and Leitenberg (1984) and by Burnam *et al.* (1988) suggest that the adverse psychological impact on the child can be serious, evidenced by later prostitution, promiscuity, drug abuse, depression, anxiety disorders, and psychosexual dysfunction. One recent study found that a long-term effect of sexual abuse *in general*, that is, including abuse by others from outside the home, was an increased vulnerability to subsequent sexual assault: "the actual occurrence of abuse, regardless of perpetrator, appeared to [play a role] . . . in instilling an expectation of victimization"

---

[6]For some reason incest does not appear in DSM-IIIR.

[7]The association that some have reported between strong religious beliefs and the disorders of incest and pedophilia should not be taken to mean that being religious, even "rigidly" so, predisposes one to these sexual disorders. It may be that some people, overcome by the intensity of their attraction to their own or others' children, seek solace and forgiveness in religion. In any event, the data are only correlational, and hence are open to different interpretations.

(Alexander and Lupfer, 1987, p. 244). Although it is important to note that this interpretation is not equivalent to a degrading "she asked for it," it does point to the possibility that victims of childhood sexual abuse are adversely affected in how they learn to deal assertively with unwanted sexual advances in their adult lives.

Pedophilia

Pedophiles are adults, usually men at least as far as police records indicate, who derive sexual gratification through physical and often sexual contact with prepubertal children.[8] Older adolescents may also be pedophiles, although the disorder most frequently begins in middle age. Violence is seldom a part of the molestation, although some pedophiles frighten the child by, for example, killing her pet and threatening further harm if the youngster tells her parents. Sometimes the pedophile, or child molester, is content to stroke the child's hair, but he may also manipulate the child's genitalia, encourage the child to manipulate his, and, less often, attempt intromission. The molestations may be repeated over a period of weeks, months, or years if they are not discovered by other adults or protested by the child. A minority of pedophiles, who might also be classified as sexual sadists or antisocial personalities (sociopaths), do inflict serious bodily harm on the object of their passion. Groth *et al.* (1982) regard such individuals, whether sociopathic or not, as child rapists and fundamentally different from pedophiles by virtue of their wish to hurt the child physically at least as much as to obtain sexual gratification.

Two major distinctions are drawn between incest and pedophilia. First, by definition, incest is between members of the same family. Second, and more importantly, incest victims tend to be older than the object of a pedophile's desires. It is more often the case that a father becomes interested in his daughter when she begins to mature physically, whereas the pedophile is interested in the youngster precisely because she is sexually immature. In defining pedophilia, state laws vary on a prescribed upper age limit for those who are to be considered children.

Pedophiles are often rigidly religious and moralistic.

As with most of the aberrant sexual behavior that has been described there is a strong subjective feeling of compulsion in the attraction that draws the pedophile to the child. According to Gebhard and his colleagues (1965), pedophiles generally know the children they molest, being a next-door neighbor or friend of the family. Most older heterosexual pedophiles are or have been married at some time in their lives.

As with incest, it is not known with any degree of precision how widespread child molestation is; since most instances occur between the child and someone known to him or her and to the family, many more cases are assumed to go unreported to authorities than come to their attention. Indeed, in 1984 several day-care centers across the country were alleged to be the sites of ongoing child molestation by the owners and staff, heightening public awareness of, and outrage at, the extent of the problem. The general estimate is that from 10 to 15 percent of children and young adolescents are subjected to at least one incident of molestation by an adult (Mrazek, 1984).

Of all the paraphilias, more is known about pedophilia, specifically that many pedophiles were themselves the victims of sexual abuse in childhood (American Psychiatric Association, 1987, p. 285); it may be that modeling is the best way to conceptualize the role of these early experiences. Common among psychoanalytic hypotheses are nonsexual bases for child molestation, such as an idealization of childhood, the need for mastery, debilitating anxiety about adult sexual relationships, and a sense of having failed socially and professionally in the adult world (Lanyon, 1986).

One of the biggest problems faced by mental health and law enforcement officials is obtaining testimony from a child that is credible in a court of law. The accused criminal has the right to face and question his accuser, and parents are often unwilling to expose their victimized children to the probing questions of a defense attorney. There may also be skepticism about some of the stories children tell of sexual abuse, perhaps because of our own acute discomfort with the very idea that an adult would take this sort of advantage of a trusting and helpless child. In fact, expert opinion is that children very rarely invent molestation incidents (Summit, 1983). A new breed of forensic expert has arisen in recent years, who employs dolls to help the child communicate what was done to him or her, with questions like "Can you show me with these two dolls what Mr. X did to you?" Efforts to find and prosecute child molesters have become increasingly vigorous, no doubt spurred on by moral outrage and by greater appreciation of the harmful effects they can have on their victims (Browne and Finkelhor, 1986).

---

[8] It is a matter of some debate whether to classify as pedophiles people (usually men) who "resort to" sexual contacts with children only under extreme stress and for whom child molestation is not a primary organizing factor in their lives. The DSM seems not to consider such "situational" molesters, concentrating instead on what can be termed "preference" molesters (Lanyon, 1986).

Voyeurism ("Peeping")

Now and then a man may by chance happen to observe a nude woman without her knowing he is watching her. If his sex life is primarily conventional, his act is voyeuristic, but he would not generally be considered a voyeur.

The essential feature of [voyeurism] is recurrent, intense, sexual urges and sexually arousing fantasies . . . involving the act of observing unsuspecting people, usually strangers, who are either naked, in the process of disrobing, or engaging in sexual activity. . . . The act of looking ("peeping") is for the purpose of achieving sexual excitement, and no sexual activity with the person is sought. Orgasm, usually produced by masturbation, may occur during the voyeuristic activity, or later in response to the memory of what the person has witnessed. Often these people enjoy the fantasy of having a sexual experience with the observed person, but in reality this does not occur. In its severe form, peeping constitutes the exclusive form of sexual activity. (Reprinted with permission from the *Diagnostic and Statistical Manual of Mental Disorders, Third Edition, Revised.* Copyright 1987 American Psychiatric Association, pp. 289–290)

A true voyeur, who is almost always a man, will not find it particularly exciting to watch a woman who is undressing for his special benefit. The element of risk seems important, for he is excited by his anticipation of how the woman would react if she knew he was watching.[9] Some voyeurs derive special pleasure from secretly observing couples having sexual relations. As with all categories of behavior that are against the law, frequencies of occurrence are difficult to assess, since the majority of *all* illegal activities go unnoticed by the police.

From what we know, voyeurs tend to be young, single, submissive, and fearful of more direct sexual encounters with others (Katchadourian and Lunde, 1972; McCary, 1973). Their peeping serves as a substitute gratification and possibly gives them a sense of power over those watched. They do not seem to be otherwise disturbed, however. After all restrictions against the

The surreptitious voyeur, unable to manage closer sexual encounters, invades from a distance the privacy of a disrobing stranger.

sale of pornographic materials to adults had been lifted in Denmark, one of the few observed effects of this liberalization was a significant reduction in peeping, at least as reported to the police (Kutchinsky, 1970). It may be that the increased availability of completely frank pictorial and written material, which is typically used in masturbation, satisfies the needs that had earlier made voyeurs of some men without other outlets.

Exhibitionism

Voyeurism and exhibitionism together account for close to a majority of all sexual offenses that come to the attention of police. It should come as no surprise that exhibitionists are frequently arrested for what is legally termed "indecent exposure"; the very nature of their disorder compels them to expose themselves to people who are shocked or at least offended by the act. Again, the frequency of **exhibitionism** is much greater among men. A quip holds that a man surreptitiously looking at a nude woman is a voyeur, but that a woman looking at a naked man is watching an exhibitionist. Like many statements about human sexuality, this one implies that women are less sexual than men. The exhibitionist has

recurrent, intense, sexual urges and sexually arousing fantasies, of at least six months' duration, involving the exposure of [his] genitals to a stranger [in most instances an adult woman or girl]. The person has acted on these urges, or is markedly distressed by them. Sometimes the person masturbates while exposing him-

---

[9]That voyeurs have an impoverished social life and engage in surreptitious peeping instead of making conventional sexual and social contacts with women suggests another way to understand their preference for spying on unaware women. If the woman were to be aware of the man's actions and continue nonetheless to allow herself to be watched, the man might well conclude that she has some personal interest in him. This possibility would be very threatening to the voyeur and, because of his fear, less sexually arousing. Perhaps then it is not the risk of being discovered that arouses the voyeur. Rather, undiscovered peeping, because it protects the heterosexual voyeur from a possible relationship with a woman, is the least frightening way for him to have contact with her.

self (or fantasizing exposing himself). If the person acts on these urges, there is no attempt at further sexual activity with the stranger. . . . In some cases the desire to surprise or shock the observer is consciously perceived or close to conscious awareness. In other cases, the person has the sexually arousing fantasy that the person observing him will become sexually aroused. (Reprinted with permission from the *Diagnostic and Statistical Manual of Mental Disorders, Third Edition, Revised.* Copyright 1987 American Psychiatric Association, p. 282)

The urge to expose seems overwhelming and virtually uncontrollable to the exhibitionist or "flasher" and is apparently triggered by anxiety and restlessness as well as by sexual arousal. Because of the compulsive nature of the urge, the exposures may be repeated rather frequently and even in the same place and at the same time of day. Apparently exhibitionists are so strongly driven that, at the time of the act, they are oblivious to the social and legal consequences of what they are doing (Stevenson and Jones, 1972). In the desperation

and tension of the moment, they may suffer headache and palpitations and have a sense of unreality. Afterward they flee in trembling and remorse (Bond and Hutchison, 1960). Only rarely does the exhibitionist seek physical contact with his unwilling observer; even less often is a more violent sexual offense, such as rape, a danger (Rooth, 1973). Generally, the exhibitionist is immature in his approaches to the opposite sex and has difficulty in interpersonal relationships. Over half of all exhibitionists are married, but their sexual relationships with their wives are not satisfactory (Mohr, Turner, and Jerry, 1964).

The penile plethysmograph described in Box 12.1 was used in a study of male exhibitionists in an effort to determine whether they are sexually aroused by stimuli that do not arouse nonexhibitionists (Fedora, Reddon, and Yeudall, 1986). Compared with normals and with sex offenders who had committed violent assaults, the exhibitionists showed significantly greater arousal to slides of fully clothed women in nonsexual situations, such as riding on an escalator or sitting in a park, while showing *similar* levels of sexual interest in erotic and sexually explicit slides.[10] These results are consistent with the hypothesis that exhibitionists misread cues in "the courtship" phase of sexual contact, in the sense that they construe certain situations to be sexual that are judged to be nonerotic by nonexhibitionists.

The search to determine how exhibitionism develops has turned up very little. One of many psychodynamic theories views the problem as stemming from a repressed fear of castration and the exhibitionist's need to reassure himself that he is still a man. Such speculations are unsupported by any data, nor have they contributed to the development of effective therapies. An intriguing learning hypothesis emphasizes the reinforcing aspects of masturbation. McGuire, Carlisle, and Young (1965) reported on the development of exhibitionism in two young men who were surprised during urination by an attractive woman. When the embarrassment had passed and they were in private, the thought of being discovered in this way aroused them and they masturbated while fantasizing the earlier experience. After repeated masturbating to such fantasies, they began to exhibit. The report suggests that repeated association of sexual arousal with images of being seen by a woman classically conditioned the men to become aroused through exhibiting. No controlled evidence, however, clearly supports this learning explanation of exhibitionism.

---

[10]In light of the widespread concern that exhibitionists might be physically threatening, it is interesting to note that there was a marginally significant tendency for them to be *less* aroused than either control group by slides that depicted violence.

Rape

The Crime

Few other antisocial acts are viewed with more disgust and anger than the obtaining of sexual gratification from an unwilling partner through **forcible rape.** A second category, **statutory rape,** refers to sexual intercourse between a male and any female who is a minor. The typical age of consent, as decided by state statutes, is eighteen years. It is assumed that a younger person should not be held responsible for her sexual activity, but it has been suggested in recent years that the age be lowered. A charge of statutory rape can be made even if it is proved that the girl entered into the situation knowingly and willingly. Thus statutory rape need not involve force, being simply a consummated intercourse with a female minor that was reported to the police. The focus here is on forcible rape.

In the past rape was considered an offense not against the victim but against the property rights of the woman's husband, father, or brothers. Even now in most states a forcible sexual assault by a husband on his wife is not legally recognized as rape. Moreover, certain women have "bad" reputations with the police of their communities. Under these circumstances a truly forceful and even violent rape may not be categorized as such in the station house, especially when the man's status in the community is higher than that of the victim. Thus a biased incidence of rape, as well as of other unconventional sexual behavior, may be obtained if attention is restricted to police records. Moreover, there is the unfortunate fact that the woman may feel great shame attached to her involuntary role in rape. Perhaps as many as twenty rapes occur for every one reported to the police; but even though underreported, the incidence of rape is increasing faster than incidences of murder, assault, and robbery. Rape is the fastest-growing violent crime in the United States.[11]

Noteworthy too is the frequency with which men subject women to coerced sexual activity that stops short of rape. In a survey of undergraduate men, Rapaport and Burkhart (1985) found that many had sexually manhandled women against their will. For example, 37 percent had placed their hand on a woman's breast, 31 percent had removed or disarranged underclothing, and 30 percent had touched the genital area of a protesting woman.

The Victim and the Attack

A prevalent belief is that the victims of rape are always young and attractive. This is a myth. Although many victims do indeed fit this description, many others do not. Age and physical appearance are no barriers to some rapists; they might choose children as young as one year old and women in their eighties. In almost all instances of forced rape, there is sexual intercourse, but other activities as well—fellatio and cunnilingus—are sometimes demanded of or performed on the victim. In what is sometimes termed sadistic rape, the rapist inflicts serious physical harm on the victim's body, such as inserting foreign objects into the vagina or pulling and burning her breasts. Some rapists murder and mutilate (Holmstrom and Burgess, 1980). Little wonder then that rape is considered as much an act of violence and aggression as a sexual act.

Rape victims are often traumatized by the experience, both physically and mentally (Calhoun, Atkeson, and Resick, 1982; Resick, Veronen, Calhoun, Kilpatrick, and Atkeson, 1986). In the minutes or seconds preceding rape, the woman begins to recognize her dangerous situation but can scarcely believe what is about to happen to her. During the moments of the attack, she is first and foremost in great fear for her life. The physical violation of her body and the ripping away of her freedom of choice are enraging. But the victim also feels her vulnerability in not being able to fight off her stronger attacker and usually finds her capacity for resistance seriously compromised by her terror. For weeks following the rape, many victims are extremely tense and deeply humiliated; they feel guilt that they were unable to fight harder and have angry thoughts of revenge. Many have nightmares about rape. In a study of women admitted to a large city hospital for emergency treatment immediately following rape, Burgess and Holmstrom (1974) found that half ultimately changed their place of residence or at least their telephone number. A large number had trouble in the sexual relationships with husbands or lovers. Masters and Johnson (1970) too found among their dysfunctional couples a number of women who had developed negative attitudes toward sex with their husbands following rape. Some victims of rape develop phobias about being outdoors or indoors, or in the dark, depending on where the rape took place. They may also for a time fear being alone or in crowds or having anyone behind them. For good reason DSM-IIIR mentions rape as one of the traumata that can give rise to posttraumatic stress disorder.

The Rapist

The vast majority of rapes are almost surely planned— it is inaccurate to say that rape is the spontaneous act of a man whose sexual impulses have gone out of control (Harrington and Sutton-Simon, 1977). The rapist may have a sadistic streak, but unlike the sadist he often does not know the victim beforehand and attacks some-

---

[11]In many jurisdictions the definition of rape includes not only vaginal penetration but oral and anal entry as well.

BOX 12.2

ARE RAPISTS SADISTS?

As we have observed in previous editions of this textbook, rape per se does not appear as a separate disorder in the DSM and is not even to be found in the subject index of DSM-IIIR. It is, though, mentioned in several places in DSM-IIIR, for example, as part of Antisocial Personality Disorder, as a cause of Posttraumatic Stress Disorder, and in Sexual Sadism and Sexual Masochism. Of particular interest to us is the following discussion in the listing for Sexual Sadism, where distinctions are drawn between sadism and rape:

Differential diagnosis. Rape or other sexual assault may be committed by people with this disorder [Sexual Sadism]. In such instances the suffering inflicted on the victim is far in excess of that necessary to gain compliance, and the visible pain of the victim is sexually arousing. In most cases of rape, however, the rapist is not motivated by the prospect of inflicting suffering, and he may even lose sexual desire while observing the victim's suffering. Studies *of rapists indicate that fewer than 10% have Sexual Sadism. Some rapists are apparently aroused by coercing or forcing a nonconsenting person to engage in intercourse and are able to maintain sexual arousal even while observing the victim's suffering.* However, unlike the person with Sexual Sadism, such people do not find the victim's suffering sexually arousing. (Reprinted with permission from the *Diagnostic and Statistical Manual of Mental Disorders, Third Edition, Revised.* Copyright 1987 American Psychiatric Association, pp. 287–288, emphasis added)

The emphasized sections raise this question: Given that most people being raped are terrified, feeling pain, or at the very least objecting strenuously and pleading for release, and given the fact that most rapists do obtain sexual gratification from their assault, how can the DSM speak of only 10 percent of rapists as being sadists?

one who is unwilling. Moreover, the sadist usually has an established, ongoing relationship with a masochist (see below). In many cases a pattern of repeated rape is part of a sociopathic life-style.

Recent research by Knight and Prentky (in press) has attempted to classify rapists on the basis of factors such as the motivation for the rape as well as on personal characteristics. Four main motivations for rape were identified in a large sample of rapists at the Massachusetts Treatment Center for convicted sex offenders. *Opportunistic rape* involved an unplanned, impulsive assault. In *pervasively angry rape,* the act was motivated by anger, the rapist often inflicting physical injury on the victim. In *sexual rape,* the primary motivation appeared to be an enduring sexual preoccupation that could encompass sadistic elements. Finally, in *vindictive rape,* sexual assaults included violence and behaviors designed to degrade and humiliate the victim (Box 12.2).

The incidence of sexual dysfunction during rape may be high. Interviews with 170 men convicted of sexual assault revealed that erectile failure as well as premature and retarded ejaculation during their criminal act had occurred for a third of these men, although almost none reported having these problems in his consenting sexual relations. Only one-fourth of the men gave no evidence of sexual dysfunction during rape (Groth and Burgess, 1977).

Sexism and the subjugation of women through rape were explored in depth by Susan Brownmiller (1975) in her best-selling book *Against Our Will.* Her thesis is that rape is "nothing more or less than a conscious process of intimidation by which all men keep all women in a state of fear" (p. 5). She garners evidence from history, both ancient and modern. In the Babylonian civilization (3000 B.C.), for example, a married woman was the property of her husband. If she was raped, both she and the rapist were bound and tossed into a river. The husband could choose to save her, or he could let her drown, just punishment for "her adultery." The views of the ancient Hebrews were no more enlightened; a married woman who had been raped was com-

Demonstration against rape and its link to pornography.

monly stoned to death along with her attacker. When an unbetrothed virgin was raped within the walls of the city, she was similarly stoned, for it was assumed that she could have prevented the attack simply by crying out.

These penalties that different societies have imposed on raped women, together with the fact that men with their generally superior strength can usually overpower women, buttress Brownmiller's argument that rape has served in the past and still serves to intimidate women. The Crusaders raped their way across Europe in the eleventh through thirteenth centuries on their holy pilgrimages to free Jerusalem from the Muslims, the Germans in World War I raped as they rampaged through Belgium, and American forces raped in Vietnam as they "searched and destroyed." Brownmiller contends that rape is actually *expected* in war. In her view, membership in the most exclusive males-only clubs in the world—the fighting forces of most nations—encourages a perverse sense of masculine superiority and creates a climate in which rape is acceptable.

Who is the rapist? Is he primarily the psychopath who seeks the thrill of dominating and humiliating a woman through intimidation and often brutal assault? Is he an ordinarily unassertive man with a fragile ego who, feeling inadequate after disappointment and rejection in work or love, takes out his frustrations on an unwilling stranger? Or is he the teenager, provoked by a seductive and apparently available young woman who, it turns out, was not as interested as he in sexual intimacy? Is he a man whose inhibitions against expressing anger have been dissolved by alcohol? The best answer is that the rapist is all these men, probably in a combination of several of these circumstances.

If we rely on crime reports for information, men arrested for rape tend to be young—usually between fifteen and twenty-five years of age—poor, unskilled, and not well educated. They come from the lower classes, in which, sociologists assert, violence is more the norm than in the middle class. About half of them are married and living with their wives at the time of the crime. A fourth to a third of all rapes are carried out by two or more men. Given the knowledge that rape is seriously underreported, however, it would be a mistake to generalize about rapists from information gleaned from police files. Indeed, in some instances the rapist is the victim's husband (Russell, 1982).

Some theoreticians believe that rape is part and parcel of the cultural stereotypes of masculinity and femininity, whereby the male's role in sexual relationships is to be aggressive and the female's passive yet seductive. The woman is expected to resist the man's advances; the man is expected to overcome her resistance. It may be that some acts of rape are committed through faulty communication between the man and the woman.

The woman's "Maybe" is interpreted as "Yes" by the man, who proceeds on the assumption that the woman "really" wants to be intimate, only to be sorely disappointed and unable to accept her ultimate refusal (Gagnon, 1977). This view of rape would of course apply only to instances in which the two people know each other—in more than a third of reported rapes they do—not to the large number of assaults that occur on streets and through forced entry into the woman's home. Nor does this view account for the extreme brutality that is often part of the assault.

Bandura (1986) suggests that exposure to certain forms of pornography may dispose some men to act aggressively toward women in sexual situations. In a review of research on the topic, he concludes that whereas pleasant erotica does not increase sexual aggressiveness, erotica that demeans women or entails violence toward and domination of them does (Malamuth, Feshbach, and Jaffe, 1977). Indeed, there is evidence that hardcore pornography—which typically derogates women—leads male viewers to become more lenient in their thinking about rape offenders (Linz, Donnerstein, and Penrod, 1988; Zillman and Bryant, 1984). Violent pornography that portrays women as initially resisting but then enjoying rape fosters the idea that women like to be sexually assaulted (Malamuth and Check, 1981). Moreover, one-third of a sample of college men admitted that they might rape if they could avoid arrest, and they tended to subscribe to the myth that women who are raped ask for it by the way they dress and act (Malamuth, 1981). Even male students who regard rape as unacceptable are aroused by portrayals of rape if the woman is depicted as having an orgasm during the assault (Malamuth and Check, 1983).

Emerging from the study of rape, and of other patterns of unconventional sexual behavior, is the fact that sexuality can serve many purposes. Indeed, an act we label as sexual because it involves the genitalia may sometimes be better understood in nonsexual terms. The classic study of sex offenders (Gebhard *et al.*, 1965) concluded that up to 33 percent of rapists carried out the act to express aggression rather than for sexual satisfaction. Rapists, in the opinion of many (e.g., Brownmiller, 1975; Gagnon, 1977), aggress against others for reasons only remotely related to sex per se (see Box 12.3). Many feminist groups object to the classification of rape as a *sexual* crime at all, for it can mask the basically assaultive and typically brutal nature of the act, and it creates an atmosphere in which the sexual motives of the *victim* are questioned. Although a person who is beaten and robbed (without being sexually abused) is hardly suspected of secretly wanting to be attacked, by cruel irony the victims of rape must often prove their moral "purity" to husbands, friends, police—even to themselves. What, after all, did *they* do that might have

BOX 12.3

A PSYCHOPHYSIOLOGICAL ANALYSIS OF RAPE

Discussions of rape are based almost entirely on the work of historians, sociologists, political analysts, and journalists. Experimental psychologists also have been trying to bring something of the phenomenon into the laboratory. The work of Abel and his colleagues (1977) is a good example of this kind of research.

In their initial study these workers developed a methodology that relied on the penile plethysmograph to help them distinguish between rapists and nonrapists. Most of the rapists had long histories of forcible sexual assaults on women, and some on men as well. Control subjects had histories of other types of unconventional sexual behavior, such as exhibitionism, pedophilia, and homosexuality.

The independent variable in the experiment consisted of two kinds of erotic audiotapes. The story recorded on one tape was of mutually enjoyable intercourse with a suitable partner; the other audiotape was of a rape of that same partner. The enjoyable scene of intercourse portrayed the partner as willing, loving, and utterly involved with the subject. In the rape scene the victim resisted and was in physical as well as emotional pain. According to the plethysmograph, rapists were significantly more aroused by the rape tape than were the nonrapist subjects, the expected pattern. But interestingly, the rapists were highly aroused by the mutually enjoyable intercourse tape as well! In fact, this tape aroused them no less than the rape scene. And the nonrapists, although much more aroused by the lovemaking than by the rape, nonetheless showed some mild arousal when listening to the rape story.

Abel then went on to use the same method to investigate the rapist's response to aggression. Are rapists aroused by aggression if the incident does not conclude with sexual assault? How does arousal from aggression relate to arousal from rape? Some of the rapists already studied listened to three additional tapes. One of them depicted a man slapping, hitting, and holding a woman down against her will, but without ensuing intercourse. On the second the man had forcible intercourse with the same victim. The rapists also listened to a tape of nonviolent sexual intercourse with a willing partner. Results revealed that the aggression scene generated some sexual arousal, but only 40 percent of that generated by the rape scene and an even smaller percent than was generated by the tape of mutually satisfying nonaggressive intercourse.

Abel and his colleagues then compared the plethysmograph records of individual rapists with their case histories. Some case histories indicated a preference for conventional intercourse, with rape resorted to if the victim was unwilling. These men had relatively small erections to the aggression story, greater response to the rape, and the greatest response to the conventional intercourse. For other rapists, whose histories showed repeated, often sadistic assaults on women, erections to mutually enjoyable intercourse were minimal, but arousal was markedly increased when aggression was added, enough to equal rape. Moreover, high levels of arousal were elicited by the aggression tape. Hence the picture is not a simple one. Some men apparently resort to rape only when loving intercourse is unavailable, whereas others seem to *require* violence-with-sex forced on an unwilling and frightened victim. These findings have been fairly well replicated with other samples of rapists and nonrapist controls (Barabee, Marshall, and Lanthier, 1979; Quinsey and Chaplin, 1984), and similar research has been done with child molesters (Abel, Becker, Murphy, and Flanagan, 1981) and other paraphiliacs (Abel, Blanchard, and Barlow, 1981).

How does this sort of research relate to the discussions in the text? Consider, for example, Brownmiller's thesis that rape is man's way of intimidating, even denigrating, women. Her historical-political analysis might at first appear a world apart from the laboratory research of Abel. But this is not really the case. The question that Abel's kind of laboratory research does not address—and can probably *never* address—is *why*. Why are certain men sexually stimulated when pain is inflicted on an unwilling victim? What is there about the one-down relationship between a rapist and his victim that excites him? Brownmiller and others find the causes in the broad sweep of history and more particularly in the power relationship between men and women. Their independent variables, if you will, are male machismo, the deliberate degradation of women, and the desire to intimidate by aggression. Abel and other laboratory researchers examine men at the end of a long shaping process. The rapists they have studied are products of their social-learning history. To figure out *why* they aggress is the larger, more important question. The search should take investigators into the domain of sociologists, political scientists, and historians.

contributed to the incident, especially if the rapist is not a complete stranger? But there are indications that the stigma of rape is being lessened by more enlightened views, coming in large measure from women's liberation groups and from books such as Brownmiller's.

Sexual Sadism and Sexual Masochism

The majority of **sadists** establish relationships with **masochists** to derive mutual sexual gratification. Sadism and masochism are found in both heterosexual and homosexual relationships, though it is estimated that

Harnesses used in some sado-masochistic activities.

upward of 85 percent are exclusively or predominantly heterosexual (Moser and Levitt, 1987). Unlike the other paraphilias, a substantial proportion of sadists and masochists are women. Sadism and masochism seem to begin by early adulthood, and most such individuals are relatively comfortable with their unconventional sexual practices (Spengler, 1977). Moser and Levitt (1987) estimate that millions of Americans engage in sexual practices that involve the infliction of pain or humiliation (though far fewer engage in such practices often or intensively enough to be diagnosed as sadists or masochists). The majority of sadists and masochists lead otherwise conventional lives, and there is some evidence that they are above average in income and educational status (Moser and Levitt, 1987; Spengler, 1977). The sadist may derive full orgastic pleasure by inflicting pain on his or her partner, and the masochist may be completely gratified by being subjected to pain. For other partners the sadistic and masochistic practices are a prelude to sexual intercourse. A married couple seen for behavior therapy had practiced the following ritual.

*As a prelude to sexual intercourse, the young man would draw blood by cutting a small incision on the palm of his wife's right hand. She would then stimu-*late his penis, using the blood of her right palm as a lubricant. Normal intercourse will then ensue, and the moment the wife felt her husband ejaculating, she was required to dig her nails deep into the small of his back or buttocks. (Lazarus and Davison, 1971, pp. 202–203)

Although a great many are "switchable," that is, able to take both dominant and submissive roles, masochists seem to outnumber sadists. For this reason "bondage and discipline" services may constitute a considerable portion of the business of a house of prostitution. The manifestations of sexual masochism are also varied. (Some are self-inflicted.) DSM-IIIR provides some vivid examples of masochism:

restraint (physical bondage), blindfolding (sensory bondage), paddling, spanking, whipping (flagellation), beating, electrical shocks, cutting, "pinning and piercing" (infibulation), and humiliation (such as being urinated or defecated upon, being forced to crawl and bark like a dog, or being subjected to verbal abuse). Forced cross-dressing may be sought for its humiliating associations. The term infantilism is sometimes used to describe a desire to be treated as a helpless infant and clothed in diapers. One particularly dangerous form of Sexual Masochism, called "hypoxyphilia," involves sexual arousal by oxygen deprivation. In this form, the person produces oxygen deprivation by means of a noose, ligature, plastic bag, mask, chemical (often a volatile nitrite that produces a temporary decrease in brain oxygenation by peripheral vasodilation), or chest compression. . . . (Reprinted with permission from the *Diagnostic and Statistical Manual of Mental Disorders, Third Edition, Revised.* Copyright 1987 American Psychiatric Association, p. 286)

Some sadists murder and mutilate. Fortunately, however, most of the time sadism and masochism are restricted to fantasies and are not then regarded as disorders, according to DSM-IIIR, unless the person is "markedly distressed by them."[12] The increasing number of "sex shops" in large cities do a lucrative business in providing pictorial and written materials to those who need at least the vicarious experience of pain in order to satisfy themselves sexually.

---

[12]This a constant theme in DSM-IIIR, that is, that it is okay to have very unconventional fantasies provided that one does not act on them or that one is not bothered by them. If, then, the social milieu supports "creativity" in at least fantasies, we can expect more people not to be bothered by the stories they tell themselves and the pictures they generate in their minds while having sex. We may have, then, more sadistic and/or masochistic fantasies but less diagnosable sadism and masochism.

The shared activities of a sadist and a masochist are heavily "scripted." Pain, humiliation and domination, or both take place as part of a story that the two agree to act out together. Themes of submission–domination appear to be as important as inflicting physical pain. The activities of the masochist and sadist assume for both parties a certain fictional *meaning* that heightens sexual arousal. The masochist, for example, may be a mischievous child, who must be punished by a discipline-minded teacher; or a slave from ancient times, recently sold to a powerful sultan. Cognitive theorists like Gagnon and Simon (1973) hold that any explanation of sadomasochistic sexual patterns must take into account the fabrications that the partners weave into their actions.

How can it happen that a person, often quite normal in other respects, must inflict or experience suffering, directly or vicariously, in order to become sexually aroused? If it is assumed, as some psychoanalysts do, that pain provides sexual pleasure, the answer is readily available; unfortunately, this "explanation" really explains nothing. Another psychoanalytic theory, restricted to men, holds that the sadist has a castration complex and inflicts pain to assure himself of his power and masculinity. It may also be that in childhood or adolescence sadomasochistic elements were present while orgasms were experienced. Although it is plausible to suggest that classical conditioning may have occurred, there are as yet no data to support this theory. A related hypothesis suggests that the physiological arousal from inflicting and experiencing pain is not, in fact, dissimilar to sexual excitement. In the early stages of being sexualized, discriminations may be difficult to make, especially if the pain-inducing act also includes sexual elements. In this way the individual may learn to label pain-produced arousal as sexual. Interesting as it may be, this hypothesis is also purely speculative at this time.

Paraphilias Not Otherwise Specified

The paraphilias here are a miscellaneous group of unconventional activities, all of them having impressive and mysterious names, none of them being well understood. Among them are the following.

Coprophilia. Obtaining sexual gratification from handling feces.

Frotteurism. Obtaining sexual gratification by rubbing against or fondling an unsuspecting, nonconsenting person. Intercourse is not involved. Note: In DSM-IIIR this diagnosis has its own separate listing, whereas the other paraphilias discussed in this section continue to be relegated to a catchall miscellaneous category.

Klismaphilia. Achieving sexual excitement by means of an enema administered by another person.

Necrophilia. Being sexually intimate with a corpse.

Telephone scatologia. Making obscene phone calls for sexual gratification.

Zoophilia. Being sexually intimate with animals.

Therapies for the Paraphilias

A prevalent psychoanalytic view of the paraphilias is that they arise from a "character disorder," an older term for personality disorder, and that they are therefore exceedingly difficult to treat with any reasonable expectation of success. This perspective is probably the one also held by the courts and by the lay public (Lanyon, 1986). In fact, psychoanalytic and humanistic-existential approaches have made few notable contributions to therapy of these disorders.

Behavior therapists have made relatively *few* assumptions about deep-seated personality defects among paraphiliacs and have instead concentrated on the particular pattern of unconventional sexuality and tried to develop therapeutic procedures for changing only this aspect of the individual's makeup.

In the earliest stages of behavior therapy, paraphilias were narrowly viewed as attractions to inappropriate objects and activities. Looking to experimental psy-

"When I said you were allowed one phone call, I did not mean another obscene one."

(Drawing by Charles Addams; © 1974, The New Yorker Magazine, Inc.)

chology for ways to reduce these attractions, workers fixed on aversion therapy. Thus a boot fetishist would be given shock or an emetic when looking at a boot, a transvestite when cross-dressing, a pedophile when gazing at a photograph of a nude child, and so on. Sometimes these negative treatments were supplemented by training in social skills and assertion, for many of these individuals relate poorly to others in ordinary social situations and even more poorly if at all through conventional sexual activity. There is some reason to believe that aversion therapy can have some beneficial effects on pedophilia, transvestism, exhibitionism, and fetishism (Marks and Gelder, 1967; Marks, Gelder, and Bancroft, 1970).

The aversive stimulus has also been presented in imagination, via **covert sensitization** (Cautela, 1966). Instead of being shocked or made nauseous with a drug while confronting the objects or situations to which he is inappropriately attracted, the paraphiliac, with assistance and encouragement from the therapist, pairs in imagination the unwanted (but pleasurable) arousal and an aversive stimulus. In a variation called covert punishment, the fantasized aversive stimulus may concern the aftermath of his act. The pedophile may imagine that his wife and daughter catch him fondling a little girl, that the police arrest him in the street, that his crime is reported in the newspapers, that he loses his job and goes to jail. There is some evidence for the effectiveness of covert sensitization in reducing unconventional arousal, although increases in conventional arousal seem to depend on more positive approaches, such as **orgasmic reorientation** (Brownell, Hayes, and Barlow, 1977).

This latter procedure aims to help paraphiliacs respond sexually to stimuli or situations that for them do not have the accustomed appeal. Individuals are confronted with a conventionally arousing stimulus while they are responding sexually for other, undesirable reasons. In the first clinical demonstration of this technique, Davison (1968a) instructed a young man troubled by sadistic fantasies to masturbate at home in the following manner.

When assured of privacy in his dormitory room . . . he was first to obtain an erection by whatever means possible—undoubtedly with a sadistic fantasy, as he indicated. He was then to begin to masturbate while looking at a picture of a sexy, nude woman (the "target" sexual stimulus). . . . If he began losing his erection, he was to switch back to his sadistic fantasy until he could begin masturbating effectively again. Concentrating again on the . . . picture, he was to continue masturbating, using the fantasy only to regain the erec-

tion. As orgasm was approaching, he was at all costs to focus on the . . . picture. . . . (p. 84)

The client was able to follow these instructions and over a period of weeks began to find conventional pictures, ideas, and images sexually arousing. The therapist, however, had to complement the orgasmic procedure with some covert sensitization for the sadistic imaginings. The follow-up after a year and a half found the client capable of conventional arousal, although he apparently reverted to his sadistic fantasies every now and again. This dubious outcome has been reported for other instances of orgasmic reorientation, but behavior therapists continue to explore its possibilities, and some workers believe it to be the treatment of choice for increasing conventional sexual arousal in paraphiliacs (Abel, Mittelman, and Becker, 1985).

A sensible program of treatment must always consider the multifaceted nature of a particular disorder. An exhibitionist, for example, may experience a great deal of tension in connection with his urge to expose himself; it would therefore make sense to desensitize him to women who "turn him on." After imagining them in a succession of street and other public scenes, until they no longer make him anxious, he may be more relaxed when he encounters these types of women in public places and so may not feel the urge to expose (Bond and Hutchison, 1960). Other paraphiliacs might be questioned about social situations and aspects of relating to women that cause them undue discomfort. They could be desensitized to these women in hopes of becoming generally less anxious. Social skills training and sex education are often called for as well, to address deficits that are commonly found among paraphiliacs. The availability of an adult sexual partner also strengthens the potential for long-term improvement. A noteworthy clinical observation is that relapse from sexual reorientation therapy is sometimes observed when patients abuse drugs or alcohol, indicative of the need to deal with such concurrent problems as well (Rosen and Beck, 1988).

There is a call for a multifaceted approach in the treatment of incest, a problem that is increasingly viewed as involving an entire family—the victim, the spouse, and siblings as well. A **family systems** approach is advocated here, whereby the entire family is involved in therapy sessions that are primarily insight-oriented, aimed at helping all members understand why the father (in most instances) turns to a daughter for emotional support and sexual gratification. The best known program of this kind is the Child Abuse Treatment Program in Santa Clara County, California, which reports that over 90 percent of fathers can be returned to their families and that there is only a 1 percent recidivism rate (Giarretto, 1982). Considerable research is needed, however, to replicate these findings and to uncover why this complex (and expensive) treatment approach effects beneficial change (Lanyon, 1986).

Efforts to control illegal and socially disapproved paraphiliac behavior among sex offenders recently have included drugs like Medroxyprogesterone acetate (MPA) that are believed to reduce testosterone levels in men, reduce the frequency of erections and ejaculations, and thereby, presumably, inhibit unconventional sexual arousal and consequent disapproved behavior. The results so far are quite inconclusive. Berlin and Meinecke (1981) found that after periods of MPA administration ranging from five to twenty years, seventeen of twenty sex offenders did not engage in paraphiliac behaviors; however, when the drug was discontinued, most reverted to their forbidden ways. It would appear that this "sexual appetite suppressant" may have to be taken indefinitely, a possibility that raises many ethical issues, including the sometimes serious side effects of long-term use, such as infertility and diabetes. Even more serious are questions of its efficacy; in some cases even when testosterone levels are reduced, paraphiliac arousal and behavior are still present (Wincze, Bansal, and Malamud, 1986). This seemingly anomalous outcome is actually consistent with recent animal research on the complex role of testosterone and other hormones in the regulation of sexual behavior (Chambers, Resko, and Phoenix, 1982); even in infrahumans, there is not a one-to-one relationship between levels of sex hormones and sexual behavior.

The paraphilias have been the focus of considerable behavior therapy research. The evidence that aversion therapy, assertion training, social skills training, covert sensitization, desensitization, and other behavior therapy procedures can effect enduring and significant changes in the paraphilias is meager when the usual standards of scientific evidence are applied (see Chapter 5). In our zeal to be rigorous, however, we should not dismiss these early results.

Therapy for Rape

Unlike most of the disorders dealt with in this book, rape has the dubious distinction of presenting two different challenges to the mental health professional: treating the man who has committed the act and treating the woman who has been the victim.

A number of therapy programs have been developed to reduce the tendency of men to rape. In some prisons group therapy of a confrontational nature has been em-

ployed in efforts to encourage convicted rapists to take responsibility for their violence toward women and to explore more decent ways of handling their anger and relating to the opposite sex. But the effectiveness of these programs has for the most part not been studied. Most rapists perpetrate their assaults many times in their lives, and prison terms have little demonstrable effect on reducing the future incidence of rape. Therapists who try to help men who rape have to consider a wide range of causes that might underlie the problem—loneliness, deficient social skills, fear of dealing with women in conventional ways, actual hatred for women, inability or unwillingness to delay gratification, perhaps especially after excessive drinking, and exaggerated conceptions of masculinity that relegate women to an inferior status.

Surgical castration and the just-mentioned chemical lowering of testosterone levels as therapies rest on the assumption that rape is primarily a sexual act. It should be borne in mind, however, that erectile capacity is not necessary for rape; the violent behavior itself is not directly addressed by these drastic medical measures (Geer, Heiman, and Leitenberg, 1984). Further, there is the question of the effectiveness of castration as a therapy (see also Box 12.4).

Considerable effort is expended in helping the victims of sexual assaults (e.g., Peters, 1977; Sutherland and Scheri, 1977). A number of rape crisis centers and telephone hot lines have been established across the country, some of them associated with existing hospitals and clinics, others operating on their own. Staffed both by professionals and by female volunteers, who may themselves have been rape victims in the past, these

Staff member at a rape crisis center.

BOX 12.4

IMPRISONED SEX OFFENDERS: A PROBLEM FOR SOCIETY

Sex offenders, those who are convicted of rape, child molesting, voyeurism, and exhibitionism, are usually imprisoned. Sometimes, but not always, specially designed treatment programs are available to help the prisoner with his problem, but the success rates are not encouraging (Furby, Weinrott, and Blackshaw, 1989). Indeed, recidivism among those who have served long prison terms is very high, and a large percentage of sex crimes are committed by repeat offenders (Rosen and Beck, 1988).

To begin with, virtually all therapies require the active cooperation of the patient (except for castration, removal of the testicles, a procedure considered by many as barbaric and, furthermore, ineffective). They generally have little chance of succeeding when forced on a person. Moreover, when therapy takes place in a prison, conditions may be too restrictive for the prisoner to become truly involved in his treatment. Finally, above and beyond the inherently coercive surroundings, professional knowledge of how to treat unconventional patterns of sexuality is quite limited. Until recently, therapeutic efforts were very punitive in nature, consisting for the most part of aversion therapy. Many critics believe that such radical treatments reflected society's wish to punish the offender for his heinous acts rather than any desire to help him.

The 1970s saw a curtailment of treatment. Lawsuits were brought on behalf of prisoners who objected to certain therapeutic interventions on the grounds that their civil rights were being violated. And indeed, some sex offenders were being subjected to extremely painful and unethical practices in the name of behavior modification. Actions by the courts have brought much-needed protection to many prisoners, but at the same time it may have a price: clinicians have been discouraged from developing treatments that could conceivably have controlled behavior threatening to society as well as to the offender himself. An additional problem is that many sex offenders are minors; one estimate is that males between the ages of thirteen and seventeen commit 20 percent of the reported forcible rapes in this country (Sourcebook of Criminal Justice Statistics, 1983) as well as a significant proportion of other sexual offenses such as exhibitionism, frotteurism, and child molesting (Becker, 1988). How shall society hold such youngsters—many of them diagnosable as conduct disordered (see Chapter 15 for what is believed to be a precursor to adult antisocial personality disorder)—responsible for their harmful behavior?

Finally, the descriptions of sex offenders indicate the complexity of their behavior. A man who feels compelled to exhibit himself to unwilling observers would seem to suffer from a host of underlying psychological problems. If he is a lonely person, unable to initiate even casual, let alone intimate, relationships with women, chances are that many areas of his life require careful attention. Such work requires much skill, patience, and time—which our society does not have in abundance when it comes to treating the sex offender.

centers offer support and advice. Women from the center accompany the rape victim to the hospital and to the police station, where they help her with the legal procedures and with recounting the events of the attack. They may later arrange for examinations for pregnancy and venereal disease and for psychological counseling. These empathic companions help the victim get started in expressing her feelings about her ordeal, and they urge her to continue her venting with her own relatives and friends. If the attacker or attackers have been apprehended, the women from the center urge the victim to go through with the prosecution. They attend both her meetings with the district attorney and the trial itself.

As already indicated, rape victims, far more than the victims of other violent crimes, tend to examine their own role in provoking or allowing the attack; counsel-

ing, therefore, has to concentrate on alleviating the woman's feelings of responsibility and guilt. When long-term counseling is available, attention is often paid to the woman's ongoing relationships, which may be disrupted or otherwise negatively affected by the rape. Husbands and lovers often acquire the culture's suspicion of the victim and must be kept from viewing their loved one as guilty or tainted by the experience.

Attitudes and support systems now encourage the victim to report rape and pursue the prosecution of the alleged rapist, but the legal situation is still problematic. Estimates are that only a very small percentage of rapists are convicted of their crimes. Any familiarity of the victim with her assailant argues strongly against his ultimate conviction. The victim's role in her own assault continues to be examined. And even though many rapists rape hundreds of times, they are only occasionally

Gay rights demonstration.

imprisoned for an offense. Society must be attentive and active to ensure that the victim's rights are defended by the legal system.

Homosexuality

Although homosexuality does not appear in DSM-IIIR as a clearly definable category, we believe that sufficient controversy remains about these patterns of emotion and behavior—among both lay people and health professionals—to warrant consideration of the topic. A historical overview will provide a perspective on some of the many issues surrounding the ways we view those whose sexual preferences include or are restricted to members of their own sex. (See Box 12.5 for several other problems and issues on the topic.)

From the time that DSM-II was published in 1968 until 1973, it listed *homosexuality* as one of the "sexual deviations." During 1973 the Nomenclature Committee of the American Psychiatric Association, under pressure from many professionals, and particularly from gay activist groups, recommended to the general membership the elimination of the category homosexuality and the substitution of *sexual orientation disturbance*. This

new diagnosis was to be applied to gay men and women who are "disturbed by, in conflict with, or wish to change their sexual orientation." The members of the psychiatric association voted on the issue, in itself a comment on the conduct of science in the twentieth century. The change was approved, but not without vehement protests from a number of renowned psychiatrists who had for some time been identified with the traditional view that homosexuality reflects a fixation at an early stage of psychosexual development and is inherently abnormal.

The controversy continued among mental health professionals, but as DSM-III was being developed during the late 1970s, it became increasingly clear that the new nomenclature would maintain the tolerant stance toward homosexuality that had become evident in 1973. The DSM-III category, *ego-dystonic homosexuality,* referred to a person who is homosexually aroused, finds this arousal to be a persistent source of distress, and wishes to become heterosexual.

Ego-Dystonic Homosexuality in DSM-III

As for all categories of disorder, DSM-III contained for ego-dystonic homosexuality a discussion of predisposing factors.

BOX 12.5

SOME PROBLEMS IN LOGIC AND THEORY IN THE STUDY OF HOMOSEXUALITY

HOMOPHOBIA AND EXCLUSIVE HOMOSEXUALITY

Those who argue that heterosexuality is normal and homosexuality abnormal often make the statement that exclusive homosexuality is unknown in the animal kingdom when members of the opposite sex are available. It is also proposed that heterosexual contacts are maximized in all species so that adequate reproduction can take place. Moreover, it is apparently the case that in no human culture has exclusive homosexuality been encouraged for sizable numers of people.

These arguments are cogent, but they overlook one essential characteristic of human sexuality, namely, that *bisexuality is more prevalent than exclusive homosexuality* (Kinsey, Pomeroy, and Martin, 1948). Churchill (1967) made the provocative suggestion that exclusive homosexuality may well be encouraged by antihomosexual societies such as our own. Because sexual contacts betwen members of the same sex are so severely condemned, some bisexuals may be forced into making a choice and *thereby* become committed to contacts with members of their own sex rather than continuing to find sexual relationships with members of both sexes meaningful. What some call *homophobia* (Weinberg, 1972) may actually help create exclusive homosexuality.

GENDER IDENTITY AND HOMOSEXUAL PREFERENCE

Psychoanalytic theory and to a degree behavioral theories as well hold male homosexuality to be a problem in gender identity: a man can become homosexual because he has not adopted his society's definition of manhood. Making love to a man rather than to a woman is assumed to be possible only for men who do not share a given society's conception of masculinity.

Other theorists and writers dispute whether homosexuals have an inappropriate gender identity. Churchill (1967), for example, refers to the comradeship and homosexual love that existed among many Greek warriors; Plato commented on the military advantages of homosexual relationships, for they seemed to foster great ferocity in battle on the part of men driven to protect their lovers. Is it reasonable to regard a brave soldier as lacking a masculine gender identity?

Moreover, only 2 percent of the homosexuals were rated by their analysts as "effeminate" (Bieber *et al.*, 1962); this finding of masculinity among male homosexuals was borne out in a study by Evans (1969), in which 95 percent of the homosexuals rated themselves as "moderately or strongly masculine." Indeed, in his renowned "Three Contributions to the Theory of Sex" (1905), Freud asserted, "In men, the most perfect psychic manliness may be united with . . . homosexuality."

Many male homosexuals have a firm identification of themselves as men (Silverstein, 1972); the same holds true for lesbians, who usually identify themselves as women (Martin and Lyon, 1972). To be sure the stereotype of the limp-wristed, lisping "fag" probably contributes to the misconception, or at least overgeneralization, of male homosexuality as feminine behavior. And the stereotype of the "butch" or "dyke" who wears her hair clipped and dresses in tailored clothing similarly fosters the misconception that the lesbian is somehow less of a woman and more of a man. But we must bear in mind that homosexuals grow up in the same cultures as everyone else! They learn that preferring a same-sexed partner implies being less of a man or less of a woman, and they may come to adopt traits of

---

Since homosexuality itself is not considered a mental disorder, the factors that predispose to homosexuality are not included in this section [or anywhere in DSM-III]. The factors that predispose to Ego-Dystonic Homosexuality are those negative societal attitudes toward homosexuality that have been internalized. In addition, features associated with heterosexuality, such as having children and [a] socially sanctioned family life, may be viewed as desirable and incompatible with a homosexual arousal pattern (American Psychiatric Association, 1980, p. 282).

What do these statements mean? Consider the plight of the homosexual growing up in contemporary society.

To suggest that a person comes voluntarily to change his sexual orientation is to ignore the powerful environmental stress, oppression if you will, that has been telling him for years that he should change. To grow up in a family where the word "homosexual" was whispered, to play in a playground and hear the words "faggot" and "queer," to go to church and hear of "sin" and then to college and hear of "illness," and

the opposite gender. To explain homosexuality itself as simply an error in gender identity is probably wrong. "Gender roles are not a mold in which we pour our sexuality" (Gagnon, 1977, p. 242).

DIFFERENCES AND PATHOGENICS

For many years theories have been proposed, and data collected, on the origins of homosexuality. Psychoanalysts, learning theorists, and physiologically oriented workers have compared homosexuals with heterosexuals for differences in their psychological or physical makeup. Perhaps the most widely cited study is that carried out by Bieber and several of his colleagues (1962). Case records of 106 homosexual patients were compared with those of 100 heterosexual patients. These two groups were being seen by 77 New York psychoanalysts. Among the differences found was that the homosexual male analysands more often had "close-binding intimate mothers" and emotionally detached, hostile fathers. Overlooking for present purposes a number of methodological flaws in the study—the most important being that all the 106 homosexuals were being analyzed and were not representative of homosexuals en masse, most of whom are not in therapy—we ask whether these differences demonstrate that homosexuality per se is pathological and that having such parents is pathogenic, that is, causes illness.

Bieber and his colleagues clearly believe so.

[*The close-binding intimate mother*] *exerted an unhealthy influence on her son through preferential treatment and seductiveness on the one hand and inhibiting, over-controlling attitudes on the other. In many instances, the son was the most significant individual in her life and the husband was usually replaced by the son as her love ob-*

ject. . . . We are led to believe that . . . maternal close-binding intimacy and paternal detachment-hostility is the "classic" pattern and most conducive to promoting homosexuality . . . in the son. (pp. 47, 144)

The implication of this study and of many others is that any differences found between homosexuals and heterosexuals constitute evidence that homosexuality is abnormal and that the difference itself is pathogenic. Is there anything wrong with this line of reasoning?

Let us take an analogous situation. Suppose we found that women who are now good golfers had as children attended public schools more often than did women who are poor golfers. Suppose also that their golfing ability is the only consistent difference between the two groups. Under what circumstances would we conclude that childhood experiences in private schools are pathogenic, causing pathology or illness? The answer is simple: going to a private school is pathogenic if its outcome, being a poor golfer, has already been judged pathological. If we do not make this a priori judgment, we cannot talk of a difference between two groups as indicative of pathology in one of the groups, and we cannot regard the presumed cause a pathogenic one. The most we can say is that the two groups are *different* from each other.

This logic can be applied to Bieber's study.

One cannot attach a pathogenic label to a pattern of child rearing unless one a priori labels the adult behavior pattern as pathological. . . . What is wrong with [a "close-binding intimate mother"] unless you happen to find her in the background of people whose current behavior you judge beforehand to be pathological? (Davison, 1976, p. 159)

finally to the counseling center that promises to "cure," is hardly [to live in] an environment of freedom and voluntary choice. The homosexual is expected to want to be changed and his application for treatment is implicitly praised as the first step toward "normal" behavior. (Silverstein, 1972, p. 4)

DSM-III took the position then that a homosexual was abnormal if he or she had been persuaded by this prejudiced society-at-large that his or her sexual orientation is inherently deviant. Yet DSM-III also asserted that

this was not the case! Ego-dystonic homosexuality could also develop when a homosexual was frustrated or hurt by societal prejudices against his or her desire to establish a home with another person of the same sex.

DSM-IIIR and Homosexuality

When we commented on DSM-III's ego-dystonic homosexuality category in the previous edition of this textbook, we suggested that *if DSM-III's explicit support of homosexuality is able to help win for the life-style greater acceptance than it has today, eventually there will be fewer social and legal sanctions against homosexual partners' setting up households and raising children, whether they be adopted or the offspring of earlier heterosexual liaisons of one or both of them. The homosexual will then be able to enjoy more of what is now the heterosexual "package." The DSM will have influenced itself out of this new category, ego-dystonic homosexuality.* (Davison and Neale, 1986, p. 309)

This may well have happened, for DSM-IIIR contains no specific mention of homosexuality as a disorder in its own right. In the years following publication of DSM-III in 1980, very little use was made by mental health professionals of the ego-dystonic homosexuality diagnosis. Was it because homosexuals in therapy were no longer asking for sexual reorientation? Perhaps the greater tolerance of homosexuality—despite the AIDS crisis (page 364) and the erroneous allegation that it was a homosexual problem and maybe even God's punishment for their sins—helped gay people seek therapy for problems unrelated to their sexual orientation. Perhaps also some gay people, as gay activists had been urging for the previous twenty years, were no longer willing to tolerate the prejudice against their sexual orientation and were seeking assistance in resisting societal biases against them. It may also have been that clinicians had begun to focus more on problems like anxiety and depression in gay clients without seeing these problems as necessarily connected with a wish to become heterosexual. It is impossible to establish the exact reasons, but it is clear that by the time the American Psychiatric Association was ready in 1987 to publish the DSM-IIIR, it had decided that even the watered-down diagnosis of ego-dystonic homosexuality should not be included. Instead, in its catchall category of Sexual Disorder Not Otherwise Specified, there is given the example of "persistent and marked distress about one's sexual orientation" (p. 296).

It is noteworthy that this definition does not specify a particular sexual orientation. Thus, while the door is still open for a diagnosis of ego-dystonic homosexuality, the psychiatric nosology now appears to allow as well for ego-dystonic *hetero*sexuality. Our own expectation is that *neither* of these diagnoses is going to be made very often.

Future Research

The position that has evolved over the past fifteen to twenty years, that homosexuality per se is not a mental disorder, along with the position that a person is not disordered unless he or she is markedly distressed by their sexual orientation, has important implications for how social scientists might be spending their time studying homosexuality. Rather than searching for why some people prefer members of their own gender as sexual mates, and rather than investigating and applying methods for changing homosexuals' orientation in the direction of heterosexuality, clinicians and researchers might better focus on how people in general deal with their sexuality and on how to help those homosexually inclined to resist the pressures that still are applied by those directing them toward heterosexuality. Furthermore, as discussed in Box 21.5 (page 630), mental health workers might direct their energies to the institutional, community psychology level and try to eliminate societal prejudices against homosexuality; homophobia continues to be prevalent among both lay and professional people (Forstein, 1988), and mental health professionals could be attempting more vigorously to reduce this widespread fear and abhorrence of homoeroticism. Fewer and fewer state laws any longer legislate against homosexuality; as these legal proscriptions are eliminated, social biases may also slowly mollify. As a consequence of all these changes, the very societal conditions that underlie ego-dystonic homosexuality may disappear and with them, as indicated above, the last vestige of homosexuality from the list of recognized mental disorders.

Summary

In this chapter we examined three categories of sexual disorders. The gender identity disorders—transsexualism and gender identity disorder of childhood—are deep and persistent convictions of individuals that their anatomic sexual makeup and the psychological sense of self as a man or a woman and as a boy or a girl are discrepant. Thus a man who is a transsexual is masculine in his physical endowment but considers himself a woman and would like to live as such. Early child-rearing practices may have encouraged the young child to believe that he or she was of the opposite sex. These problems are of significant theoretical interest, for they illustrate the early plasticity of our beliefs about ourselves as males and females. For a time the only kind of help available to such individuals was sex-change surgery, to bring their bodies into line in some degree with gender identity. Now, however, there is preliminary evidence that behavior therapy can alter specific aspects of the transsexual's behavior—mannerisms, tone of voice, sexual fantasies—and bring gender identity into line with anatomy.

In the paraphilias, unusual imagery and acts are persistent in sexual excitement or gratification; fetishism, transvestistic fetishism, pedophilia, incest, and sexual sadism are examples of such problems. Rape, although it is not described in DSM-IIIR, is a pattern of behavior of considerable social and psychological trauma for the victim. The very inclusion of rape in a discussion of human sexuality is a matter of some controversy, for many workers regard rape as an act of aggression and violence rather than of sex. The most promising treatments for the paraphilias are behavior therapies, such as training in social skills to help the person have ordinary relations with members of the opposite sex.

DSM-IIIR does not contain any specific mention of homosexuality, thus continuing a process of "liberalization" that began in 1973, when DSM-II introduced a variation of the diagnosis that was to be applied only to those homosexuals disturbed by their sexual orientation. The current nomenclature alludes to those distressed by their sexual orientation without specifying whether that orientation is hetero- or homosexual.

Shinkichi Tajiri. *Granny's Knot*, 1967–1968. The National Trust for Historic Preservation. Nelson A. Rockefeller Collection.

Chapter 13

Sexual Dysfunctions

Sexual Disorders and the Human Sexual Response Cycle

The Sexual Dysfunctions: Descriptions and Causes

Sexual Desire Disorders

Sexual Arousal Disorders

Orgasm Disorders

Sexual Pain Disorders

Theories of Sexual Dysfunctions

Earlier Sexology

The Ideas of Masters and Johnson

Other Contemporary Views

Behavioral and Cognitive Therapies for Sexual Dysfunctions

Summary

The preceding chapter described the unconventional patterns of sexual behavior of a small minority of the population. But many "ordinary" people are likely to have problems that interfere with conventional sexual enjoyment during the course of their lives. Our concern in this chapter is with a range of sexual problems that are considered to represent inhibitions in the normal sexual response cycle.

A psychological problem has consequences not only for the individual but also for those with whom he or she is involved. Individuals unable to interact socially with others are inevitably cut off from many opportunities in life and, furthermore, often have low opinions of themselves. They can be a source of frustration and guilt for a spouse, a child, or a friend. This aspect of human emotional problems is especially important in our consideration of *sexual dysfunctions,* for they are usually evident in intimate personal relationships. A marriage is bound to suffer if one or both of the partners fear the sexual relationship. And most of us, for better or for worse, base part of our self-concept on our sexuality. Do we please the people we love, do we gratify ourselves, or, more simply, are we able to enjoy the fulfillment and relaxation that can come from a pleasurable sexual experience? Sexual dysfunctions can be of such severity that tenderness itself is lost, let alone the more intense satisfaction of sexual activity. It will be helpful to keep these points in mind in this review of the various sexual dysfunctions and, at the end of the chapter, of some of the therapies for them.

Sexual Disorders and the Human Sexual Response Cycle

As indicated in Table 12.1 (page 322), DSM-IIIR divides sexual dysfunctions into four principal categories: sexual desire disorders, sexual arousal disorders, orgasm disorders, and pain disorders. It is important to note that these disorders were called *psycho*sexual dysfunctions in DSM-III; the "psycho" part of the term was dropped in the current edition in formal recognition of the accumulating evidence that biological factors play a role in many of these problems.

In the most general terms, Sexual Dysfunctions are defined as an "inhibition in the appetitive or psychophysiologic changes that characterize the complete sexual response cycle" (American Psychiatric Association, 1987, p. 290). The difficulty should be persistent and recurrent, a clinical judgment that the DSM acknowledges entails a degree of subjectivity. The diagnosis is

Havelock Ellis (1859–1939), a British writer on the psychology of sex and a humane and discerning man, understood at the turn of the century the sexual capacities of women, children, and old people.

not to be made, however, if the disorder is believed to be due *entirely* to a medical illness (such as advanced diabetes, which can cause erectile problems in men) or if it is believed to be due to another Axis I disorder (such as major depression).

How does DSM-IIIR conceptualize "the sexual response cycle"? The current position is a distillation of previous proposals by Havelock Ellis (1906), Masters and Johnson (1966), and Kaplan (1974). The work of Masters and Johnson twenty-five years ago signaled a

Helen Singer Kaplan, noted sex therapist who introduced the appetitive phase to the sexual response cycle.

The noted sex researchers and therapists, William H. Masters and Virginia Johnson. Their pioneering work helped launch a more candid and scientific appraisal of human sexuality.

revolution in the nature and intensity of research in and clinical attention to human sexuality. They extended the earlier interview-based breakthroughs of the Kinsey group (Kinsey *et al.*, 1948, 1953) to make direct observations and physiological measurements of people masturbating and having sexual intercourse.[1] DSM-IIIR distinguishes four phases in the human sexual response cycle, which itself is quite similar in men and in women:

1. **Appetitive.** Introduced by Kaplan (1974), this stage refers to sexual interest or desire, often associated with sexually arousing fantasies.[2]

2. **Excitement.** Masters and Johnson's original first stage, this refers to "a subjective sense of sexual pleasure and accompanying physiologic changes . . . [which in men includes] penile tumescence, leading to erection . . . [and in women are] vasocongestion in the pelvis, vaginal lubrication, . . . swelling of the external genitalia . . . and breast tumescence" (American Psychiatric Association, 1987, p. 291). (Tumescence refers to the flow of blood into tissues. It takes different forms in men and women, as noted.) If stimulation is adequate, tension builds to a peak into the next stage.

3. **Orgasm.** In this phase sexual pleasure peaks in ways that have fascinated poets and the rest of us ordinary people for thousands of years. In men ejaculation feels inevitable and indeed almost always occurs (except for rare instances where some men can occasionally have an orgasm without ejaculating and vice versa). In women there are contractions of the walls of the outer third of the vagina. In both sexes there is general muscle tension and involuntary pelvic thrusting.

4. **Resolution.** This last of Masters and Johnson's stages refers to the relaxation and sense of well-being that usually follow an orgasm. In men there is an associated refractory period, during which further erection and arousal are not possible (but for varying periods of time across individuals and even within the same person across occasions). Women, however, are usually able to respond again with sexual excitement almost immediately, an ability that permits multiple orgasms.

It is important to note the "constructive" nature of this rendition of the human sexual response cycle. As we said, there have been different proposals over time; Havelock Ellis, for example, spoke only of **tumescence** and **detumescence**. The DSM-IIIR view is one of many conceivable *inventions* or conceptual schemes created by scientists as a way to organize and discuss a body of information (Gagnon, 1977; Kuhn, 1962). We are about to see how the current DSM uses this scheme to describe sexual dysfunctions. Finally, it is worth mentioning that sex researchers speak in terms of *averages,* which after all are by definition a mathematical way to summarize a *range* of scores or observations. So, a given individual's responses can differ noticeably from a group average and yet not be considered abnormal (Box 13.1).

[1]Although it is generally assumed that the data collected by Alfred Kinsey in the 1940s and 1950s were based entirely on interviews, John Gagnon, formerly associated with Kinsey's Institute for Sex Research in Bloomington, Indiana, has called attention to the extent to which Masters and Johnson built on work done earlier at the Institute. Many findings of the Kinsey group, published later in the Kinsey reports, were obtained through the direct observation and filming of sexual activity. The social climate of the day, however, discouraged Kinsey from acknowledging that this group had, in fact, gathered information on human sexuality through direct observation (Gagnon, 1977).

[2]Masters and Johnson omitted this stage because, we believe, they used well-functioning volunteers in their landmark laboratory work. The issue of desire or readiness to be sexual did not arise. This is a good example of how the nature of one's knowledge-gathering techniques—in this case the kinds of subjects studied—constrains the kinds of information one obtains.

The Sexual Dysfunctions: Descriptions and Causes

A particular disorder may be lifelong, or it may have been acquired after a period of normal functioning; it may be generalized, or it may occur only in particular situations or with certain partners; and it may be total or partial. Each of the disorders may show up either during sexual activity with another person or during

BOX 13.1

SOME SEXUAL MYTHS DISPELLED BY MASTERS AND JOHNSON

The impact of Masters and Johnson's work was considerable in contributing to our knowledge of the physiology of human sexuality. Perhaps more important, it helped make the scientific study of sex legitimate and acceptable. By knowing how the body functions to achieve maximum sexual response, Masters and Johnson were able to elaborate methods of treating sexual dysfunction. Even before their 1966 book was published, the information obtained through research was being put to use in the treatment phase of their work (Masters and Johnson, 1970).

The artificial circumstances in which Masters and Johnson gathered their findings limit their generality somewhat, however. And we should be mindful that physiological research can tell us little about the *psychological* components of human sexuality. Masters and Johnson were nonetheless able to provide firm data on certain controversial points and to dispel a few myths.

1. Although the ***clitoris*** (Figure 13a) is very important in transmitting sexual stimulation in the female, it has been a mistake to advise men to try to stimulate it continually during intercourse. During the excitement phase the clitoris retracts, making access to it extremely difficult and even painful for some women. In point of fact, it is very difficult to have intercourse without stimulating the clitoris *indirectly,* which is the type of stimulation that some women seem to prefer.

2. Masters and Johnson were able to document that orgasms in women obtained from stimulation of the clitoris, without entrance into the vagina, are as intense as and indeed physiologically indistinguishable from orgasms obtained by having an erect penis in the vagina.

   Probably few pieces of misinformation have caused more consternation than Freud's insistence that the vaginal orgasm is superior to the clitoral orgasm. He asserted, and practitioners have parroted to hundreds of thousands of people for years since, that a woman who can have an orgasm only by stimulation of her clitoris is settling for second best; further, that failure to have an orgasm via stimulation of the vagina by the man's penis is a sign of psychosexual fixation and immaturity. The Freudian theory is explained nicely by John Gagnon.

Everyone goes through certain psychosexual stages, one of which involves masturbation as the important overt sexual activity. This stage occurs early in life as part of the parade of changes toward heterosexual genital maturity, that is, intercourse with a person of the opposite sex. Masturbation is infantile; intercourse is mature; being mature is better than being infantile. When women masturbate, they touch the clitoris; when women have intercourse, they have a penis in the vagina. Since masturbation is infantile, pleasures achieved by touching the clitoris are infantile. Sexual maturity [therefore] requires that women move from having orgasms produced by touching the clitoris to having orgasms produced by the penis in the vagina. The site of sensation [is] supposed to move from clitoris to vagina. (From *Human Sexualities*, p. 138. Copyright © 1977, by Scott, Foresman and Company. Reprinted by permission.)

Even before the work of Masters and Johnson, some sexologists had been trying to disabuse people of this notion (e.g., A. Ellis, 1961), pointing out that the walls of the *vaginal barrel* are poorly supplied with sensory nerve endings, whereas the clitoris, like the glans of the penis, is amply supplied. The fact that orgasms achieved by masturbation and manual manipulation by the partner, both of which typically concentrate on the clitoris and surrounding areas, were found to create at least as much excitation as intercourse pretty much puts to rest the bugaboo about clitoral orgasms.

Many authorities now believe that all female orgasms are evoked by stimulation of the clitoris, whether the friction is applied directly or through coitus. The orgasm itself, however, is expressed by rhythmic contractions of vaginal muscles. This dichotomy may be the source of the myth of clitoral versus vaginal orgasms (Kaplan, 1974). Of course these findings in no way imply that the insertion of the penis and the movements of coitus are not extremely enjoyable to women.*

3. Having simultaneous orgasms, a goal held up in numerous marriage manuals as indicating true love and compatibility, was not shown to be a mark of superior sexual achievement. In fact, it can often distract each of the partners from his or her own sexual pleasure.

---

*Creative speculation continues on female orgasm. Perry and Whipple (1981) described a spot the size of a nickel located within the vagina, the stimulation of which was asserted to cause orgasm in some women without clitoral stimulation and to be accompanied by an ejaculation. Named the G-spot for the German physician, Grafenberg, who first described it, this location was touted as further evidence against the hegemony of Freudian viewpoints on female sexuality. Subsequent research has, however, not confirmed the initial and highly publicized findings (Rosen and Beck, 1988).

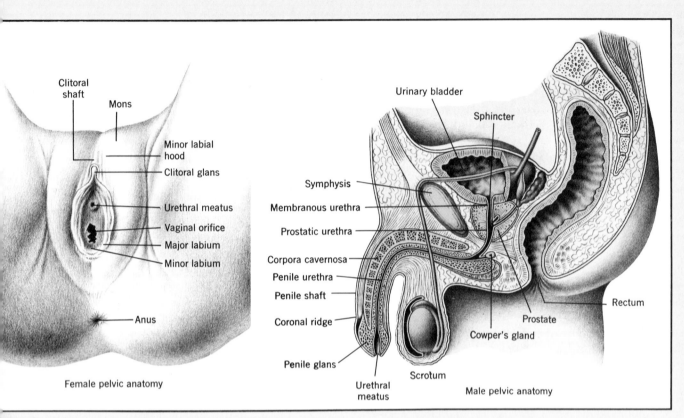

RE 13a

or view of female genitalia and cross section of male. (From Alvin Nason and Rob-
eHaan, *The Biological World.* New York: Wiley, 1973.)

4. It was also found that not only do most women *not* object to intercourse during menstruation, but they even tend to enjoy it more, particularly during the second half of the period.

5. During the second trimester of pregnancy, women seem to desire intercourse at least as much as when not pregnant. Although there is some danger of spontaneous abortion in the early stages, particularly for women who have a history of spontaneous miscarriage, most women continue to desire sexual stimulation, sometimes until they go into labor. At any rate, little harm seems to come to the woman or to the fetus through intercourse, at least during the first six months of pregnancy.

6. Various myths about the male's penis were also dispelled. The size of a man's erect penis was not found to be a factor in the enjoyment he can derive himself

and impart to his sexual partner. The vagina is a potential not an actual space; that is, it distends just enough to accommodate the penis. Hence a very large penis will not create more friction for the man or the woman than a smaller one. Furthermore, penises that are small when flaccid may double in size when erect, whereas penises that are large in the limp state increase less proportionately. In other words, there does not seem to be as much variation in the size of the *erect* penis as had been assumed. The idea that the size of a man's penis is an index of his virility was completely dispelled.†

—————

†Some women have voiced disagreement with Masters and Johnson's conclusion about the merit of a large penis. No doubt psychological variables, as well as the purely physiological ones that Masters and Johnson have dealt with, play a part in determining how an individual woman reacts.

masturbation. The prevalence of disturbances is believed to be so great that people should not assume that they need treatment only because they sometimes experience one or more of these problems. In the diagnostic criteria for each sexual dysfunction, DSM-IIIR uses the phrase "recurrent and persistent" to underscore the fact that a problem must be serious indeed before a diagnosis is made.[3] Further, DSM-IIIR does not state whether the sexual partner is of the opposite sex or same sex, another sign of the growing liberalization of the attitude of the mental health professions toward homosexuality.

In our discussions of DSM-IIIR categories of sexual dysfunctions, we describe what is believed to cause these human problems. It is important to bear in mind, however, that most of these generalizations about etiology are based on clinical reports of investigators like Masters and Johnson (1970), Kaplan (1974), and other sex therapists. As with all clinical reports, information provided by clients and interpreted by therapists is subject to distortion and selective attention. Moreover, no studies compare groups of dysfunctional patients with appropriate control groups for the presence or absence of causative factors. For example, an unpleasant experience with a prostitute at age seventeen may seem to be a major cause of a thirty-year-old man's erectile problem, but countless other men have had a similar negative experience *without* developing a sexual problem.

Any points made about etiology are therefore necessarily tentative. Although this caveat can be issued for any section of this book, it is particularly appropriate to bear in mind here, considering the likelihood that the lives of many readers will be touched in some way by what is being discussed.

Sexual Desire Disorders

DSM-IIIR distinguishes two kinds of sexual desire disorders: **hypoactive sexual desire disorder** refers to deficient or absent sexual fantasies and urges; **sexual aversion disorder** represents a more extreme form of the first in which the person actively avoids nearly all genital contact with another. In making either diagnosis the clinician should take into consideration the patient's age, health, and life circumstances. DSM-IIIR estimates that about 20 percent of the adult population has hypoactive sexual desire disorder.

Of all the DSM-IIIR diagnoses, what is colloquially referred to as "low sex drive" seems the most problematic, for how frequently *should* a person want sex? In practice, the reason a person even goes to a clinician in the first place and ends up with this diagnosis is probably that *someone else* is dissatisfied with his or her interest in sex *with them*. The hypoactive desire category appeared for the first time in DSM-III in 1980 under the title of inhibited sexual desire[4] and may owe its existence to the higher expectations people have about being sexual. It is striking that entire books, for example, Leiblum and Rosen (1988), are being written about a disorder that fifteen years ago was hardly talked about in professional sexology circles.

We know little about the causes of either hypoactive sexual desire or sexual aversion disorder. Probably the most definite evidence is that certain drugs, especially sedatives and narcotics, can dull a person's sexual desires. A partner's sexual dysfunction may also be implicated: a woman who is constantly frustrated by her partner's erectile problems or inept lovemaking may decide that sex is just not worth the aggravation and disappointment. Interpersonal problems of the partners can also be expected to affect their interest in sex with each other; Stuart, Hammond, and Pett (1987) found that relationships in which the hypoactive desire disorder was present are marked by distrust, anger, power struggles, and poor communication. In general, the importance that sex has in someone's life can vary tremendously. Unlike hunger and thirst, an "appetite" for sex need not be satisfied or even exist in order for the individual to survive and, it seems, to live happily.

Sexual Arousal Disorders

The two subcategories of arousal disorders are **female sexual arousal disorder** and **male erectile disorder**. The former used to be called "frigidity" and the latter "impotence." These and the orgasm disorders to follow assume that the person has sexual stimulation that is adequate in "focus, intensity, or duration" (American Psychiatric Association, 1987, p. 293). In other words, if the situation is simply that the person's partner repeatedly does not do what he or she *likes*, the diagnosis would not be made.

---

[3]What is defined as normal and desirable in human sexual behavior varies with time and place. Contemporary views, as reflected in DSM-IIIR, point to *inhibitions* of sexual expression as causes of abnormality. In contrast, during the nineteenth and early twentieth centuries the Western world regarded *excess* as the culprit. It is well to keep these varying temporal and cultural norms in mind as we continue our study of human sexual dysfunction.

---

[4]It is interesting to note that the DSM-III term "inhibited" was deemed by those who produced DSM-IIIR as suggesting psychodynamic causality. For DSM-IIIR, preference was given to the more descriptive "hypoactive" (Lief, 1988).

In the woman, there is either inadequate vaginal lubrication for comfortable completion of intercourse *or* an absence of a subjective sense of sexual excitement and pleasure during sex. In the man there is either failure to attain or maintain an erection through completion of the sexual activity *or,* as with the woman, lack of subjective pleasure. Note that for both sexes there is equal consideration given to how one *feels* about the sexual activity; presumably a man with erectile disorder, for example, could maintain his erection but (somehow) not be "turned on" by his partner.

Besides the fears of performance and spectator role to be discussed below as general causes of sexual dysfunctions, some specific reasons are believed to underlie female arousal problems. A woman may not have learned adequately what she finds sexually arousing and may even lack knowledge about her own anatomy. Coupled with a shyness about communicating her needs, she may find the behavior of her partner to be unstimulating and even aversive.

Helen Singer Kaplan (1974) has outlined a wide range of erectile problems for men. Some get an erection easily but lose it as they enter the woman's vagina. Others are flaccid when intercourse is imminent but maintain an erection easily during fellatio. Some men are erect when the partner dominates the situation, others when they themselves are in control. Some suffer complete erectile failure, being unable to maintain an erection under any circumstances. Others have problems only with people they care for deeply. Moreover, an obvious aspect of the problem is that it is, in fact, obvious. A woman can go through the motions of lovemaking, but sexual intercourse is usually stalemated if the man is not erect. A great deal is at stake if the penis becomes flaccid when it "should" be erect.[5] For

this reason, perhaps, an "impotent" male is sometimes and unfortuntely regarded as less than a man.

Organic factors may cause erectile problems, and include certain medications, such as Mellaril, one of the phenothiazines used in treating psychoses; some drugs for hypertension, angina, and heart disease; alcohol in large amounts; obesity; and generally any disease or hormonal imbalance that can affect the nerve pathways or blood supply to the penis (Geer, Heiman, and Leitenberg, 1984). The majority of erectile difficulties, however, are believed to be psychological in nature (Rosen and Rosen, 1981), brought on by performance fears and other preoccupations that distract men from "egoless" involvement in and enjoyment of sexual relations.

Orgasm Disorders

Three kinds of orgasm disorders are described in DSM-IIIR, one for women and two for men. ***Inhibited female orgasm*** refers to absence of orgasm after a period of normal sexual excitement. The stimulation can come from masturbation or from having sex with a partner, although the DSM indicates that "in some of these females [who do not have orgasms during intercourse unless there is concomitant manual clitoral stimulation], this does represent a psychological inhibition that justifies the diagnosis" (p. 294).

---

[5]Male erectile problems are complicated. Although an extended discussion is beyond the scope of this book, a few additional observations would seem in order. The fact that the state of a man's penis is obvious both to him and to his partner is generally regarded as placing a unique set of pressures on him that are not the fate of a woman who suffers from inhibited sexual excitement. But the woman's situation is not easy either. The very fact that she can have sexual relations without being aroused has no doubt contributed to neglect of the woman's needs and desires. Moreover, the man's self-esteem is not the only one threatened if he becomes flaccid; the partner too, whether it be a woman or another man, often has doubts about sexual adequacy—is she not sexy enough, not lovable enough, not creative or "liberal" enough? Finally, replacement of impotence and frigidity by the phrase sexual arousal disorder can be considered an advance. Impotence implies that the man is not potent, or in control, or truly masculine, and negatively backs up the macho conception of masculinity that many people are challenging. Frigidity implies that the woman is emotionally cold, distant, unsympathetic, unfeeling. Both terms are derogatory and encourage as well a search for causes *within* the person, rather than focusing attention on the relationship, the domain contemporary investigators explore for answers and solutions.

Until recently a distinction was not generally made between problems a woman may have in becoming sexually aroused and those she may have in reaching an orgasm. Although as many as 20 percent of all adult women rarely if ever experience an orgasm (Kinsey *et al.*, 1953), far fewer are believed to remain unaroused during lovemaking. Kaplan (1974) argues that this distinction, made too in DSM-IIIR, is an important one, for "as a general rule, women who suffer from orgasmic dysfunction are responsive sexually. They may fall in love, experience erotic feelings, lubricate copiously, and also show genital swelling" (p. 343). In fact, she argues that failure to have orgasms should not be regarded as a disorder at all, rather as a normal variation of female sexuality.

Numerous reasons have been put forward to explain anorgasmia. Perhaps many women, unlike men, have to *learn* to become orgasmic. That is, the capacity to have an orgasm may not be innate in females as it is in males. In men ejaculation, which almost always is accompanied by orgasm, is necessary for reproduction. A woman may to some extent learn to have coital orgasms through earlier masturbation; survey findings indicate that women who masturbated little or not at all before they began to have intercourse were much more likely to be nonorgasmic than women who had (Kinsey *et al.*, 1953; Hite, 1976; Hoon and Hoon, 1978). These are, of course, correlational data; some third factor may be responsible both for infrequent masturbation and for diminished ability to have orgasms. Lack of sexual knowledge also appears to play a role according to clinical data; many nonorgasmic women, as well as those who experience little excitement during sexual stimulation, are unaware of their own genital anatomy and therefore have trouble knowing what their needs are and communicating them to a partner.

Women have different "thresholds" for orgasm. Although some have orgasms quickly and without much clitoral stimulation, others seem to need intense and prolonged stimulation, whether during foreplay or intercourse. The reaction of a woman's partner can contribute to the problem; a man may conclude that he and his penis are inadequate if the female asks for manual stimulation of her clitoris during intercourse.

Another factor may be fear of losing control. The French have an expression for orgasm, *le petit mord,* the little death. Some women fear that they will begin screaming uncontrollably, make fools of themselves, or faint. A related source of inhibition is a belief, perhaps poorly articulated, that to let go and allow the body to take over from the conscious, controlling mind is somehow unseemly. The state of a relationship is also not to be overlooked: although some women can enjoy

making love to a person they are angry with, or even despise, most hold back under such circumstances.

Inhibited male orgasm and ***premature ejaculation*** are the two male orgasm disorders described in DSM-IIIR. Masters and Johnson (1970) used the somewhat pejorative term ejaculatory incompetence for the inability of the man to ejaculate within the vagina. The DSM-IIIR diagnosis inhibited male orgasm would be applied to problems of ejaculating during intercourse, masturbation, manual or oral manipulation by a partner, and anal intercourse.

Difficulty in ejaculating is relatively rare, although some have suggested it is becoming more prevalent as men deem it desirable to delay their orgasms for long periods of time (Rosen and Rosen, 1981); indeed, sex without orgasm has even been proposed in recent years as an ultrasophisticated form of male sexuality. It may be that some men are learning the skill too well! More prosaic causes have also been put forth: fear of impregnating a female partner, withholding love, expressing hostility, and, as with female anorgasmia, fear of letting go. In rare instances the problem may be traced to a physical source, such as taking certain tranquilizers (Munjack and Kanno, 1979).

Masters and Johnson (1970) spoke of premature ejaculation when a man is unable to inhibit his orgasm long enough for his partner to climax in 50 percent of their sexual encounters. Many people were concerned about stipulating the problem in terms of a *partner's* responsiveness. In DSM-IIIR this difficulty is handled as follows: "Persistent or recurrent ejaculation with minimal sexual stimulation before, upon, or shortly after penetration and before the person wishes it. The clinician must take into account factors that affect the duration of the excitement phase, such as age, novelty of the sexual partner or situation, and frequency of sexual activity" (American Psychiatric Association, 1987, p. 295). Note that consideration is given to the preference of the man himself. In our view, however, it would be naive to overlook the extent to which a partner may influence the patient's judgment that ejaculation is occurring before he wishes it.

Premature ejaculation is probably the most prevalent sexual dysfunction among males, a problem for 30 percent of men at any given time (American Psychiatric Association, 1987). In general, it is associated with considerable anxiety. Sometimes the man ejaculates even before he penetrates the vagina but more usually within a few seconds of intromission. Although the human being is more than a relatively hairless ape, evolutionary theory informs us that rapid ejaculation has survival value, for any animal is particularly vulnerable to surprise attack when copulating. Hence the more quickly copulation can occur, the better. Kinsey, himself a biologist, suggested that ejaculating quickly should not be regarded as a problem in human beings. Such a view, however, considers only the reproductive function of intercourse, ignoring its recreational and interpersonal functions (Rosen and Rosen, 1981). Indeed, concern about ejaculating "too soon" may be regarded as part and parcel of the undue emphasis placed on coitus as the ultimate in sexual behavior. The problem for couples who prize conventional sexual intercourse above all other sexual activities is that erection is slowly lost after an ejaculation, with many men finding continued stimulation unpleasant and sometimes painful. If lovemaking stops when the penis is no longer hard, ejaculation may indeed sometimes be premature. But if, as sex therapists advise, couples expand their repertoire of activities to include techniques not requiring an engorged penis, gratification of the partner is eminently possible *after* the man has climaxed. Indeed, when the focus is removed from penile–vaginal intercourse, a couple's anxieties about sex usually diminish sufficiently to permit greater ejaculatory control in the male and sexual intercourse of longer duration. It will be interesting to observe whether shifts in sexual norms and practices alter the concept of premature ejaculation.

Sexual Pain Disorders

DSM-IIIR lists two pain disorders associated with sex, *dyspareunia* and *vaginismus.* Dyspareunia is diagnosed when there is persistent or recurrent pain before, during, or after sexual intercourse. In women the diagnosis should not be made when the pain is believed to be due to lack of vaginal lubrication (when presumably female sexual arousal disorder would be diagnosed) or when it is judged to be a function of the second pain disorder, vaginismus. This latter problem is marked by involuntary spasms of the outer third of the vagina to such a degree that intercourse is not possible.

Dyspareunia is almost always caused by a medical problem such as infections of the vagina or uterus, or in the male, infections of the glans of the penis. Vaginismus, though defined in sexual terms by DSM-IIIR, can be observed also during pelvic examinations.

Since the spastic contractions of the muscles prevent intercourse, it is not surprising that one theory supposes that the woman wishes, perhaps unconsciously, to deny herself, her partner, or both the pleasures of sexual intimacy. As plausible as this idea may seem, no evidence supports it. Indeed, women with vaginismus can often have sexually satisfying lives through clitoral stim-

ulation, if the partner agrees. Clinical reports also suggest fear of pregnancy and negative attitudes about sex in general, the latter often traceable to rape or to having been molested in childhood (LoPiccolo and Stock, in press). Masters and Johnson found that for a number of couples the man's inability to maintain an erection preceded the development of vaginismus in his wife; for some women, then, the sexual problems of their partners are so anxiety-provoking that a condition like vaginismus may develop.

Theories of Sexual Dysfunctions

Earlier Sexology

Psychoanalytic views have assumed that sexual dysfunctions are symptoms of underlying repressed conflicts. The analyst considers the symbolic meaning of the "symptom" both to understand its etiology and to guide treatment. Since sexual dysfunctions bring discomfort and psychological pain to both the individual and to his or her partner, and since unimpaired sexuality is inherently pleasurable, the theme of repressed anger and aggression competing with the gratification of sexual needs pervades psychoanalytic writings. Thus a man who ejaculates so quickly that he frustrates his female partner may be expressing repressed hostility to women who remind him unconsciously of his mother. A woman with vaginismus may be expressing her repressed penis envy by threatening to castrate a man who would hope to enter her vagina. There is little evidence for the validity or even the usefulness of psychoanalytic theories of sexual dysfunctions. In fact, many contemporary psychoanalysts now recognize the inability of their therapy to help people with sexual dysfunction and supplement it with the more direct techniques of behavior therapy (LoPiccolo, 1977).

Humanists view psychosexual dysfunctions in the same way that they view other disorders. A sexual dysfunction is considered to reflect the crippling anxiety and inhibition of a person who is failing to fulfill his or her own potential (see Box 13.2).

The most comprehensive account of the etiology of human sexual dysfunction was offered by Masters and Johnson in their widely acclaimed book *Human Sexual Inadequacy* (1970). Let us first examine their suggestions and then consider modifications and extensions of their ideas that have been proposed more recently.

BOX 13.2

SEXUAL DYSFUNCTION: A BIOENERGETIC APPROACH

Wilhelm Reich (1942), Austrian psychoanalyst, agreed with Freud in placing human sexuality at the center of psychology but, unlike Freud, he studied sexual functioning directly. He concluded that the basis for all anxiety was the inability to achieve full and repeated sexual satisfaction. Thus the goal of therapy was to teach people to achieve sexual satisfaction by releasing muscular tension and allowing the free flow of sexual energy. Although one of Reich's extreme notions—that a vital energy "orgone" pervades nature and can be accumulated for bodily use by sitting in a specially designed box—discredited his other theories in the early fifties, they reemerged in the work of Alexander Lowen (1958). The *bioenergetic approach* is followed by some American psychologists and psychiatrists, especially on the West Coast.

According to the bioenergetic view, sexual dysfunctions such as premature ejaculation and inhibited orgasm are caused by chronic tensions as they affect the muscles of the body. These chronic tensions are said to develop when powerful emotions like fear, anger, and sexual excitation are "blocked." The "blocking" is described as being not only cognitive but physical. Bioenergetic analysts speak of such phenomena as "the dead pelvis" in describing the body posture of those individuals who do not experience orgasm as the full and rhythmic involuntary pelvic movements indicative of sexual satisfaction. The task of bioenergetic therapy is to teach people to relax the body's musculature and establish freedom of movement during sex.

Bioenergetic therapy generally proceeds at both the cognitive and physical levels. At the cognitive level the therapist employs traditional psychodynamic procedures to help the patient achieve insight into the thoughts and feelings that sustain a rigid and sexually dysfunctional body posture. At the physical level the patient is instructed in a series of exercises designed to remove body tensions and breathing irregularities and to promote freedom of pelvic movement. Some bioenergetic therapists loosen tense areas of the body through deep-muscle massage. While the patient is being massaged, he or she is encouraged to recall and express any emotions that are experienced in order to ensure that emotional blocks and muscle tensions are not reinstated.

Bioenergetics, following Reich, places sexual dysfunction at the heart of all emotional and behavioral problems and has the same therapy goal for all clients, the restoration of sexual functioning. This goal may be appealing to some, but others have criticized it as contributing to a cultural obsession with sexual gratification and kindling unrealistic expectations of sexual fulfillment (Keen, 1979).

Because bioenergetic therapy has not been properly evaluated in controlled studies, its effectiveness is difficult to judge. Bioenergetics does, however, offer a unique view of human sexual inadequacy.

Bioenergetic therapy considers sexual dysfunctions to be caused by chronic anxiety and tension. Here Alexander Lowen performs deep-muscle massage to remove tension.

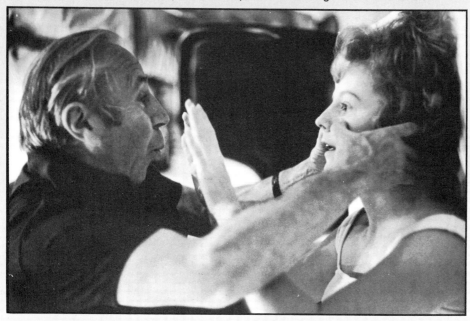

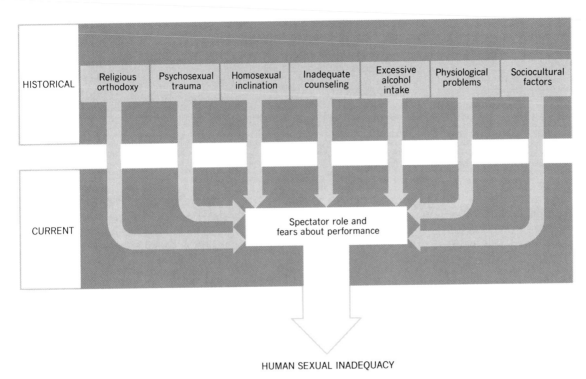

HISTORICAL	Religious orthodoxy	Psychosexual trauma	Homosexual inclination	Inadequate counseling	Excessive alcohol intake	Physiological problems	Sociocultural factors

CURRENT

Spectator role and fears about performance

HUMAN SEXUAL INADEQUACY

FIGURE 13.1
Historical and current causes of human sexual inadequacies, according to Masters and Johnson.

The Ideas of Masters and Johnson

In the most general sense, DSM-IIIR has incorporated the theorizing of Masters and Johnson (see Figure 13.1) in proposing reasons for the sexual dysfunctions. The key variables are said to be *fears of performance* and the adoption of a **spectator role,** both of which have the person focusing undue attention on performance rather than allowing the kind of accepting and "ego-less" participation that, they assert, will allow sexual arousal to build to orgasm. Or, as they put it: "fear of inadequacy is the greatest known deterrent to effective sexual functioning, simply because it so completely distracts the fearful individual from his or her natural responsivity by blocking reception of sexual stimuli . . ." (Masters and Johnson, 1970, pp. 12–13).

Viewed as the *current* or proximal reasons for sexual dysfunctions, performance fears and the spectator role are believed to have any one of several *historical* antecedents, such as religious orthodoxy and psychological trauma.

Religious Orthodoxy One or both partners may have negative attitudes toward sex because they have been brought up with strict religious beliefs that denigrate sexual enjoyment. For example, a woman with vagin-ismus who was interviewed by Masters and Johnson had been

taught that almost any form of physical expression might be suspect of objectionable sexual connotations. . . . She was prohibited when bathing from looking at her own breasts either directly or from reflection in the mirror for fear that unhealthy sexual thoughts might be stimulated by visual examination of her own body. Discussion with a sibling of such subjects as menstruation, conception, contraception, or sexual functioning were taboo. . . . Mrs. A. entered marriage without a single word of advice, warning, or even good cheer from her family relative to marital sexual expression. The only direction offered by her religious advisor relative to sexual behavior was that coital connection was only to be endured if conception was desired. (p. 254)

Psychosexual Trauma Some patients trace their fears of sexual contact to particularly frightening or degrading experiences during early sexual encounters. One young man had been assured by a prostitute that "He would never be able to get the job done for any woman—

if he couldn't get it done here and now with a pro.'' One woman could date her vaginismus to a gang rape from which she suffered severe physical and psychological damage.

Homosexual Inclinations Men with erectile problems and nonorgasmic women may be unable to enjoy heterosexual relations because they have homosexual inclinations.[6]

Inadequate Counseling Bad advice from professional workers may create or exacerbate sexual inadequacies. Some men were told by physicians that erectile problems are incurable, others that they are a natural part of the aging process. A few had been warned by clergymen that their problem was God's punishment for sins.

Excessive Intake of Alcohol An erectile problem sometimes begins with undue concern about a normal reduction in sexual responsiveness brought on by excessive drinking (see page 281). In the typical pattern suggested by Masters and Johnson, a man who works very hard may develop a habit of drinking a good deal. Large amounts of alcohol are known to interfere with erections, while at the same time, ironically, lowering inhibitions. Having drunk too much, the man may find later in bed that no erection develops. Instead of attributing his lack of sexual arousal to drinking, however, he begins to ruminate. Fear accumulates, and after a number of failures he may become unable to have an erection. The wife often attempts to be understanding and supportive of the husband. He, for any number of reasons, interprets this solicitude as further questioning of his masculinity. Or the wife, concerned that she may no longer be sexually attractive to her husband, pushes for sexual encounters and aggravates the situation. Soon she may refrain from any physical contact whatsoever, even affectionate hugs and kisses, for fear that the husband will interpret this as a demand for intercourse. The communication of the couple worsens, intensifying the man's anxiety and setting a pattern difficult to reverse without professional assistance.

Vaginismus As yet another example of the intimate relation between the sexual reactions of the two partners, Masters and Johnson found that some men develop erectile problems because of the partner's vaginismus.

Physiological Causes Some of the disorders are attributable to physical damage. As indicated earlier, clitoral or vaginal infections, torn ligaments in the pelvic region, scar tissue at the vaginal opening from incisions made during childbirth (episiotomies), and—especially in older, postmenopausal women—insufficient lubrication of the vagina may make intercourse painful for women. Infection of the glans of the penis, which can develop when it is not kept clean, may cause dyspareunia in men. A minority of men with erectile problems are found to suffer from metabolic disturbances through diabetes, and in others sexual arousal is dulled by the use of certain tranquilizers.[7]

Sociocultural Factors Especially in female dysfunctions, cultural biases play a role. "Sociocultural influence more often than not places the woman in a position in which she must adapt, sublimate, inhibit, or even distort her natural capacity to function sexually in order to fulfill her genetically assigned role. Herein lies a major source of woman's sexual dysfunction" (Masters and Johnson, 1970, p. 218). The man has the blessing of society to develop sexual expressiveness, but the woman, at least until recently, has not had this freedom, and her needs have often been ignored. And of course compounding her difficulties is the fact that she does not require sexual arousal to function adequately as a partner during sexual intercourse.

According to laboratory studies reported in *Human Sexual Response,* women seem capable both of multiple orgasms and of more sustained, more frequent, and more physiologically intense sexual arousal than men,

---

[6]When Masters and Johnson published their clinical report on the nature and treatment of "human sexual inadequacy" in 1970, the sociopolitical climate was not as accepting of homosexuality as it is today. Their treatment program was exclusively heterosexual in its focus; hence the presence in one of the partners of a homosexual preference was seen as an etiological factor. The alternative view that the problem lay with a decision of the homosexual partner to try to maintain a heterosexual marriage was not explicitly considered.

[7]Spinal cord lesions, depending on how complete they are and where they are located, may cause paralysis and loss of sensation either in the legs (paraplegia) or in both arms and legs (quadraplegia). A person who cannot move his or her arms and legs is sometimes considered incapable of sexual excitement. This is not so. A review by Higgins (1978) documents erections and ejaculation in a number of paralyzed men.

which makes the neglect of their sexuality particularly ironic.

Other Contemporary Views

One question suggested by the distinction drawn by Masters and Johnson between the historically relevant factors and the spectator role and fear of performance is whether causes alleged to be of only historical importance might not be of more immediate concern to some people. Might not a woman's *current* religious beliefs inhibit her involvement in and enjoyment of sexual relations? Or consider the woman who was traumatized as a teenager by a gang rape. Might not the memory of that incident intrude itself upon her consciousness whenever she finds herself in an intimate situation? Masters and Johnson would reply that a religious belief or memory acts on the present by putting the person in a spectator role rather than as an uncritical participant, thus preserving the integrity of their theoretical model. Be that as it may, religious beliefs and sexual traumas might conceivably hinder a person's sexual behavior in a very direct and immediate way.

Masters and Johnson considered sexual dysfunctions as problems in and of themselves and not inevitably caused by deeper-seated intrapsychic or interpersonal difficulties. The couples whose treatment formed the basis of their second book, *Human Sexual Inadequacy* (1970), had marriages that in spite of the sexual problems, were marked by caring and closeness. But as the Masters and Johnson therapy techniques became widespread and were applied by others, sex therapists were seeing people whose relationships were seriously impaired. It is not difficult to imagine why a marriage or other relationship might deteriorate when the couple has not had intercourse for years. By the time a therapist is consulted, he or she is faced with the chicken-and-egg conundrum. It is impossible to know whether the hostility between the two people caused the sexual problem or vice versa. The working assumption of most therapists is that couples have both sexual and interpersonal problems. Clearly, it is unrealistic to expect a satisfying sexual encounter when, for example, the man is angry with the woman for spending more and more time outside the home, or when the woman resents the man's insensitive dealings with their children. Such negative thoughts and emotions can intrude themselves into the sexual situation and thereby inhibit whatever arousal and pleasure might otherwise be found.

BANG. YOU'RE DEAD!

That's how serious AIDS is.

Anyone can get the AIDS virus by having sex with an infected person. And you just can't be sure who's infected. The carrier often doesn't know, and can have the virus years before the symptoms start showing up.

And once you get AIDS, you'll likely die. No ifs, ands or cures.

Not having sex is one sure way to avoid AIDS. But if you have sex, use a condom.

AIDS Because the one thing you don't want to hear is "You've got AIDS."

If you think you can't get it, you're dead wrong.

Fear of contracting AIDS may well become another contributor to sexual dysfunction.

As with other disorders, Albert Ellis (1971) emphasizes the role of irrational thinking in the development and maintenance of sexual dysfunctions. Thus a woman who cannot have orgasms during intercourse is assumed to be *demanding* of herself that she have one. Indeed, the often-used phrase "achieve an orgasm" may reflect our society's maladaptive view of sexual satisfaction as something to be pursued and won, much as people chase after approval and recognition. Ellis's term for this kind of self-defeating, demanding thinking—"musturbation"—seems appropriate here. Many sexologists, in-

BOX 13.3

AIDS: A CHALLENGE FOR THE BEHAVIORAL SCIENCES*

There is no greater public health threat today than Acquired Immune Deficiency Syndrome. This invariably fatal illness has two unique, interrelated characteristics that make it appropriate for discussion in an abnormal psychology textbook: (1) it is not presently curable or preventable by medical means; and (2) it *is* preventable by psychological means. Indeed, for the present and foreseeable future, the only realm in which we *know* progress can be made is in changing people's attitudes and behavior, and in particular their sexual activities.

DESCRIPTION OF THE DISEASE

First identified in 1981, AIDS has emerged as the most serious infectious epidemic of modern times. Indeed, it has been compared to the Black Plague of the Middle Ages. It is estimated that between 300,000 and 480,000 Americans will be diagnosed with AIDS by 1991, but as many as two million are believed infected now with the precursor to AIDS, the human immunodeficiency virus (HIV) (Curran, 1985). As many as 100 million people worldwide are likely to become infected with HIV in the next few years.

Although the medical intricacies of AIDS are beyond the scope of this book, it is important to understand a few fundamentals. AIDS is a disease in which the body's immune system is severely compromised, putting the individual at high risk for opportunistic diseases such as Kaposi's sarcoma, rare forms of lymph cancer, and a wide range of dangerous fungal, viral, and bacterial infections. Medical authorities suspect AIDS when an otherwise healthy person presents with an illness that he or she would not likely have unless the immune system is malfunctioning. (People who have had an organ transplant, for example, are at risk for such opportunistic diseases because they are given drugs that suppress the immune system so that the body will not reject the new organ. In a sense, the AIDS patient is someone who presents similarly, without having taken the antirejection, immunosuppressant medication. The big difference, of course, is that the transplant patient is kept in an antiseptic intensive care hospital environment while his or her immune system is being *artificially*—and *temporarily*—compromised.) Strictly speaking, people do not die of AIDS as much as they die of fatal infectious diseases that AIDS makes them vulnerable to.

AIDS also attacks the central nervous system (Nurnberg, Prudic, Fiori, and Freedman, 1984), sometimes leading to problems in memory and concentration many months before an AIDS-related illness appears. One recent study (Navia, Cho, Petito, and Price, 1986) found that of seventy AIDS patients autopsied at death, fewer than 10 percent had normal brains, and that most of them had exhibited what has come to be called AIDS Dementia Complex, a deterioration in memory, thought, judgment, and motor coordination that is now believed to be caused directly by the HIV virus (see Appendix page 644). Another study found that AIDS-diagnosed children between the ages of thirty months and six years showed retardation in language and motor skills development attributable to AIDS Dementia Complex (Ultmann *et al.*, 1985). Most AIDS patients die within a few years of their first opportunistic illness. In our present state of knowledge, *all die eventually*.

If a person tests positive for HIV, it means that the HIV virus has destroyed a large number of T-4 or "helper T" lymphocytes, cells that are at the core of the body's immune system, the system that fights off the many infections that humans are exposed to daily but resist rather routinely most of the time. All people who test HIV-positive develop AIDS, usually within eight years, but some first develop AIDS-related complex, ARC, which is less severe than AIDS and which develops into AIDS.

SPREAD OF THE DISEASE

The AIDS crisis is exacerbated by the fact that many untested HIV-positive people feel healthy and are unaware of their illness. They can infect others, in the ways described below, and contribute to what some have called a ticking time bomb in the health of the human race. Once diagnosed with AIDS, drug therapy such as AZT can bring about some improvement and perhaps even prolong life, but available data offer little encouragement that lives can be saved over the long haul (and "long" is seldom more than a few years). While millions are being spent on developing a vaccine against the HIV virus, the focus is now squarely on behavioral science research and practice for prevention and control.

The core of the problem is risky sexual practices, not sexual orientation. Although in this country almost two-thirds of AIDS patients are homosexual or bisexual males and about one-fifth are intravenous drug users, in central and west Africa AIDS is contracted primarily through heterosexual relations. HIV is present only in blood, semen, and vaginal secretions and can be transmitted only when infected liquids get into the bloodstream. AIDS cannot be "caught" through casual social contact or even by living with an AIDS or HIV-positive person, provided reasonable care is taken to avoid blood contact. Risky sexual behavior includes anal or vaginal intercourse without a condom, and probably also "unprotected" oral–genital contact and finger or hand insertion into the anus or vagina. The other category of risky behavior is found among *intravenous drug users who share unsterilized needles* and

---

*This discussion on AIDS relies heavily on the work of Kelly and St. Lawrence (1988a, 1988b).

thus can introduce HIV-carrying blood into the bloodstream of another. Perhaps the most tragic victims are infants born to HIV-positive mothers, for the virus can cross the placental barrier and infect the developing fetus.

PREVENTION OF THE DISEASE

The primary focus in prevention is on changing sexual *practices*, not the least reason being that many people in monogamous relationships do not, in fact, restrict their sexual activity to the relationship, and certainly young people are sexually active with several partners before settling into a presumably monogamous union. Exposure can of course be eliminated by being in a monogamous relationship with a partner who tests negative for HIV.

Prevention, therefore, is best directed at encouraging sexually active people to use condoms. They are about 90 percent effective in preventing HIV infection. People are also urged to explore the pleasures of low-risk sex such as mutual masturbation and frottage (body rubbing without insertion of the penis into the vagina, mouth, or anus of the partner). Note that for the most part this advice holds for same- or opposite-sexed partners. Prevention for IV drug users includes the above-mentioned measures, but precautions for them should also include the use of new or sterilized needles and, best of course, getting off drugs altogether.

But how can changes be brought about, especially (at least for heterosexuals) in a generation of sexually active people for whom "the pill" marked a welcome liberation from the need to use condoms? Also daunting is the challenge of changing the attitudes and practices of adults for whom the 1960s ushered in a period of "sexual liberation," restrained to be sure by the danger of herpes and other venereal diseases but not by the certainty of dying. Kelly and St. Lawrence (1988a, 1988b) draw on social psychological and behavior therapy theory and research to suggest principles that can form the basis of effective interventions. Educational messages should (1) emphasize the risk of certain behaviors; (2) make clear the vulnerability of people who engage in such behaviors; (3) demonstrate how changes in behavior can reduce risk; and (4) persuade the person that the benefits of making behavioral changes outweigh the inconvenience and loss of satisfaction from continuing with the high-risk behavior. The information itself needs to be presented so that people know exactly what they should be doing and why; and the communication has to be frequent and conveyed in a supportive, optimistic (yet realistic) way by respected persons with whom the audience can identify. Also important are social support and encouragement, such as what we saw in Chapter 11 with cigarette smokers trying to kick the habit.

Kelly and St. Lawrence review a number of such efforts and document beneficial changes like reduced patronage of gay bathhouses and increases in monogamous relationships. However, in cities where AIDS is less a problem than in centers like New York and San Francisco, high-risk behavior seems to be common, perhaps because of a (mistaken) sense of personal invulnerability when there is not an epidemic in one's immediate vicinity. This certainly seems to be the case, especially among young heterosexuals who continue to see the problem as mostly limited to gays and drug users and who perhaps wish to distance themselves from a disease that bears the social stigma of those whom it affects the most at the present time. There is, then, little evidence that high-risk behavior among heterosexuals has markedly changed.

Media efforts and the greater visibility of condoms in stores need to be supplemented by programs such as that described by Kelly, St. Lawrence, Hood, and Brasfield (1988), who provided apparently healthy gay men over several months with assertion practice (saying no to high-risk overtures and asking for low-risk practices), encouragement to reduce "cruising" and other high-risk ways of meeting people, and up-to-date information on AIDS. Results indicated reductions in high-risk sex.

Such cognitive-behavioral approaches to prevention might, we believe, benefit from some social psychological research inspired by Milton Rokeach's work on values (1973; Ball-Rokeach and Rokeach, 1984). Rokeach holds that human behavior is controlled in important ways by values, for example, involvement in civil rights is associated with a person valuing equality more than freedom of choice. In a technique he calls value self-confrontation, Rokeach and others have shown that if one confronts an individual with a discrepancy between the values held by those whom the person wishes to emulate and the values the person currently holds, one can influence the individual to change his or her behavior in an enduring fashion.

What might be the implications for AIDS prevention? It is possible—and remains to be researched—that people who are successful in changing from high- to low-risk sexual practices differ in their *values* from those who do not. For example, they may value wisdom more than happiness. If this be the case, then informing HIV-negative people of this fact may encourage them to change their own values (or maintain them if they match those of successful behavior-changers) and thereby regard their sexuality in a way that promotes more healthful, less risky behavior in the interests of a long-term benefit. Research inspired by Rokeach (e.g., Schwartz and Inbar-Saban, 1988) would seem to be of particular importance to social scientists concerned with behavioral risk reduction in AIDS because to be meaningful, any behavioral changes brought about need to be enduring ones. Cognitive change aimed at a "deep" level like values may be superior to changes that are more superficial.

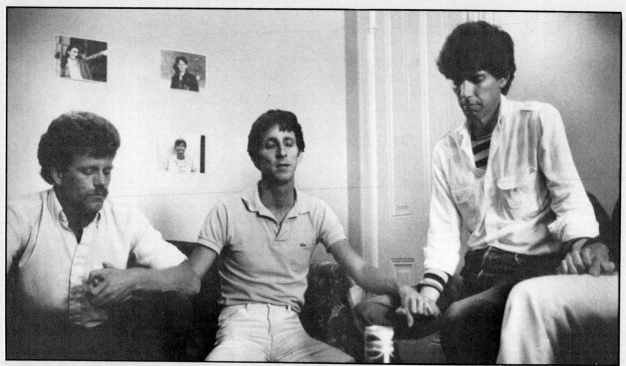

Group support is one of the components of current therapy with AIDS patients.

THERAPY FOR AIDS PATIENTS

What can mental health professionals offer those already afflicted with AIDS? Anxiety and depression are common, as is a sense of outrage that Nature has perpetrated such a sick joke on humankind. The self-hate that gays sometimes have is bound to be exacerbated if the homosexual patient accepts the still-prevalent (but diminishing) harangue that AIDS is God's punishment for sexual perversion. Therapy entails supporting the person in seeking whatever experimental medical treatments are available and acceptable, and helping the person make contact with whatever AIDS support groups are in the area. Stress management approaches (page 215) can also be beneficial, though one cannot and should not deny the objective gravity of the situation. What also seems in our view to be emerging in the clinical literature is the appropriateness of an existential approach that encourages examination of the meaning of one's life and of one's impending death as well, and of the importance of achieving some manner of resolution, including the making out of one's will, saying goodbye, in short, doing what has long been believed to be useful and meaningful as one confronts his or her mortality and obligations to those about to be left behind. No doubt a religious belief in an afterlife can bring comfort both to the patient and to his or her loved ones. Social support

from family and friends, and from other AIDS sufferers, is also of benefit (Kelly, St. Lawrence, Hood, Smith, and Cook, 1988).

The fact that most of those dying of AIDS are young and in what would have been their most productive years underscores the personal and social tragedy. Those who test HIV-positive but do not yet have AIDS or ARC are also stressed by the developing knowledge that they will almost certainly contract AIDS. With such individuals Kelly and St. Lawrence advise encouragement of healthful practices such as exercise, less alcohol consumption, and good nutrition, all of which *may* have positive effects on the immune system. Indeed, since little is known about the biological and psychological factors that may determine when an HIV-positive individual will develop AIDS, there is much research to be done in hopes of buying time.

Finally, AIDS is as much a political, legal, and moral issue as it is a medical and psychological one. Issues of mandatory testing and even of quarantine will be raised as the numbers of AIDS cases and deaths increase. We shall all ultimately have to confront our values and our prejudices, our deepest fears and most urgent desires, as we negotiate a period of uncertainty and threat that few of us have ever had to face.

cluding Masters and Johnson, appreciate that such thoughts can preclude sexual enjoyment.

"Why doesn't he touch me more there, rather than here?" "Why does she stop stroking just as I'm getting excited?" As mentioned earlier, people may lack knowledge of sexual anatomy and functioning and more specifically be unaware of the likes and dislikes of a partner. Unfortunately, just caring for the partner may not be enough in establishing a mutually satisfying sexual relationship. In fact, Kaplan (1974) suggests that inhibiting anxiety can arise when one partner wants *too much* to please his or her partner; this may, though, be a special case of performance anxiety. People who have sexual problems are also often found to lack knowledge and skill (LoPiccolo and Hogan, 1979). A woman may be left "hanging" short of orgasm by a lover who does not appreciate the importance of clitoral stimulation; the husbands of nonorgasmic women are often reported to be awkward lovers (Kaplan, 1974; LoPiccolo, 1977).

The assumption that sexual anxiety inhibits sexual arousal and performance has been challenged by data from psychophysiology laboratories that show that anxiety experimentally induced by certain films or by the threat of electric shock actually *increases* genital arousal as compared to no-anxiety conditions (Barlow, Sakheim, and Beck, 1983; Hoon, Wincze, and Hoon, 1977). This finding, however, holds only for fully functional subjects; those who have been identified as sexually dysfunctional become *less* aroused under shock-threat conditions (Beck, Barlow, Sakheim, and Abrahamson, 1984). Perhaps there is something arousing for functional people when there is danger involved during sex, a theme many people can relate to from their earliest sexual experiences in parked cars and other similar situations. If so, anxiety may play less of a role in the etiology of some sexual dysfunctions than it does in the maintenance of them.

Another problem is poor communication between partners. For any number of reasons—embarrassment, distrust, dislike, resentment, depression, to name but a few—one lover may not inform the other of his or her preferences, likes, and dislikes. Then he or she often misinterprets the failure of the partner to anticipate or mind-read as not really caring. Although sexual communication is frequently inadequate in distressed marriages and is therefore tended to in marital therapy (see page 582), it can also be poor in people who are otherwise compatible. Open discussions of sex by partners, among friends, in the media, and even in professional training programs are after all relatively recent phenomena.

Although concerns about contracting a venereal disease have probably long been a distractor and hence an inhibitor of sexual pleasure between people, the spread of Acquired Immune Deficiency Syndrome among sexually active individuals has no doubt become yet another reason for many of the sexual dysfunctions; Box 13.3 discusses AIDS in detail.

Finally, as with many of the other psychological problems dealt with in this book, it is not known why some people have in their backgrounds or in their present lives one or more of the factors believed to be of etiological significance and yet do not have a sexual dysfunction. Why a person develops one sexual dysfunction rather than another is also a puzzle.

Behavioral and Cognitive Therapies for Sexual Dysfunctions

Perhaps in no area of psychotherapy have behavioral and cognitive therapies been more notably successful than in treating sexual dysfunctions. Several adequately controlled outcome studies (e.g., Obler, 1973; Heiman and LoPiccolo, 1983; Mathews, *et al.*, 1976), plus the

"STAY TUNED FOR THE LATEST ON BONDAGE, QUICKIES, DELAYED ORGASMS, VIBRATORS AND PREMATURE EJACULATION ON 1320 A.M., YOUR ALL-SEX STATION."

BOX 13.4

THERAPY FOR SEXUAL DYSFUNCTIONS BY MASTERS AND JOHNSON

In 1970 the publication of Masters and Johnson's *Human Sexual Inadequacy* generated an excitement in the mental health community that is seldom encountered. This book reported on a therapy program carried out with close to 800 sexually dysfunctional people. Each couple had traveled to St. Louis and spent two weeks attending the Reproductive Biology Research Foundation for intensive therapy by day and doing sexual homework in a motel at night. Away from home, they were free of domestic distractions and able to make their stay a sort of second honeymoon. Many of the Masters and Johnson techniques had been used by therapists for some time; and, although some methodological problems have been uncovered by workers who have examined their report closely (Zilbergeld and Evans, 1980), other therapists using their techniques have had the same high rates of success (Andersen, 1983). Masters and Johnson virtually created the sex therapy movement, and their work therefore deserves a detailed description.

The therapy attempts to reduce or eliminate fears of performance and to take the participants out of their maladaptive spectator role. Then, it is hoped, the couple will be able to enjoy sex freely and spontaneously.

Each day the couple meets with a dual-sex therapy team, the assumption being that men best understand men and women best understand women. For the first several days the experiences of all couples are the same, regardless of their specific problem. An important stipulation in these early days is that sexual activity between the two partners is expressly forbidden. A complete social and sexual history is obtained during the first two days, and physical examinations are conducted to determine whether there are organic factors to be dealt with.

During the assessment interviews considerable attention is paid to the so-called *sexual value system,* the ideas of each partner about what is acceptable and needed in a sexual relationship. Sometimes this sexual value system must be changed for one or both partners before sexual functioning can improve. For example, if one partner regards sexuality as ugly and unacceptable, it is doubtful whether even the most powerful therapy can help that person and the partner enjoy sex.

On the third day the therapists begin to offer interpretations about why problems have arisen and why they are continuing. In all cases the emphasis is on the problems in the relationship, not on particular difficulties of either partner. A basic premise of the Masters and Johnson therapy is that "there is no such thing as an uninvolved partner in any marriage in which there is some form of sexual inadequacy" (1970, p. 2). Whatever the problem, the couple is encouraged to see it as their mutual responsibility. At this time the clients are introduced to the idea of the spectator role. They are told, for example, that a male with erectile problems usually worries about how well or poorly he is doing rather than participating freely. It is pointed out to the couple that this pattern of observing himself, although totally understandable in context, is blocking his natural responses and greatly interfering with sexual enjoyment.

At the end of the third day an all-important assignment is given to the couple, namely to engage in *sensate focus.* The couple is instructed to choose a time when they feel "a natural sense of warmth, unit compatibility . . . or even a shared sense of gamesmanship" (Masters and Johnson, 1970, p. 71). They are to undress and give each other pleasure by touching each other's bodies. The co-therapists appoint one marital partner to do the first "pleasuring" or "giving"; the partner who is "getting" is simply to enjoy being touched. The one being touched, however, is *not* required to feel a sexual response and, moreover, is responsible for immediately telling the partner if something becomes distracting or uncomfortable. Then the roles are switched. Attempts at intercourse are still forbidden. To Masters and Johnson this approach is a way of breaking up the frantic groping common among these couples. The sensate-focus assignment may promote contact where none has existed for years; if it does, it is a first step toward gradually reestablishing sexual intimacy.*

Sensate focusing may uncover deep animosities that have hitherto remained hidden. Most of the time, however,

---

*Details of other direct therapies, some of them going beyond what Masters and Johnson describe, are available in LoPiccolo and LoPiccolo, 1978; Rosen and Rosen, 1981; Gagnon, 1977; Kaplan, 1974.

overwhelming weight of clinical evidence, indicate the greater effectiveness of learning and cognitive approaches in treating sexual dysfunctions. The overall success rates for the kind of direct cognitive-behavioral approaches described below, however, are far from perfect, and erectile problems in men seem especially difficult to treat, with improvement being effected in as few as 30 percent of cases (Crown and D'Ardenne, 1982).

The pioneering work of Masters and Johnson (1970)

partners begin to realize that encounters in bed can be intimate without necessarily being a prelude to sexual intercourse. On the second evening the partner being pleasured is instructed to give specific encouragement and direction by placing his or her hand on the hand of the giving partner in order to regulate pressure and rate of stroking. The touching of genitals and breasts is also now allowed. Still, however, there is no mention of an orgasm, and the prohibition on intercourse remains in effect. Diagrams are presented if the partners are ignorant of basic female and male anatomy, as they often are. After this second day of sensate focusing, treatment branches out according to the specific problem or problems of the couple. As an illustration, we will outline the therapy for inhibited female orgasm.

After the sensate-focus exercises have made the couple more comfortable with each other in bed, the woman is encouraged to focus on maximizing her own sexual stimulation without trying to have an orgasm. As a result her own sexual excitement usually builds. The therapists give her partner explicit instructions about generally effective means of manually manipulating the female genital area, although ultimate decisions are made by the female partner, who is encouraged to make her wishes clear to the man, moment by moment. In the treatment of the dysfunction, as in the treatment for others, it is emphasized that at this stage having orgasms is not the focus of interaction between partners.

After the woman has begun to enjoy being pleasured by manual stimulation, the next step is to move the source of sensate pleasure from the man's hand on her body to his penis inside her vagina. She is told to place herself on top of the man and gently insert the penis; she is encouraged simply to tune in to her feelings. When she feels inclined, she can begin slowly to move her pelvis. She is encouraged to regard the penis as something for her to play with, something that will provide her with pleasure. The male can also begin to thrust slowly. At all times, however, the woman must be able to decide when and what should happen next.

When the couple is able to maintain this containment for minutes at a time, without the man thrusting forcefully toward orgasm, a major change has usually taken place in

their sexual interactions: for perhaps the first time the woman has been allowed to feel and think sexually, and indeed selfishly, about her own pleasure. In their subsequent encounters most couples begin to have mutually satisfying intercourse.

Clinicians must be extremely sensitive in presenting these various treatment procedures to a couple whose problems may stretch back many years. Sometimes the couple discuss sex for the very first time at the Masters and Johnson clinic. The calm and open manner of the therapists puts the couple at ease, encouraging in them both a commitment to follow certain instructions and a more open attitude toward sex and the activities that people may engage in together when making love. Although behavioral prescriptions are specific, the therapists can never lose sight of the atmosphere that must be maintained in the consulting room and, it is hoped, transferred over to the privacy of the bedroom, where much of the *actual* therapy takes place. As in other forms of behavior therapy, there is a strong emphasis on technique, but interpersonal factors set the stage for behavior to change.

Sex clinics have sprung up everywhere, based in general on the Masters and Johnson model, and many mental health professionals have incorporated direct sex therapy techniques into their practices. Researchers have investigated various aspects of the treatment package. One question is whether a dual-sex therapy team is really necessary for all couples; this does not seem to be the case (Fordney-Settlage, 1975; Husted, 1975). Another question concerns the effectiveness of daily intensive therapy as compared to the more usual outpatient practice of once-weekly sessions; data indicate no advantage to the intensive Masters–Johnson regimen (Heiman and LoPiccolo, 1983). Some clinicians now rely on electrically powered vibrators when treating inhibited female orgasm; with proper instructions many nonorgasmic women first learn to enjoy orgasms through self-stimulation with these little machines (Barbach, 1975; Dodson, 1974). The pursuit and enhancement of sexual pleasure for its own sake is being legitimized. Although some are concerned about this trend and dub it "sexual athletics," on the whole relaxation of strictures regarding sexuality promises greater satisfaction for most people (Gagnon and Davison, 1974).

in the treatment of sexual dysfunctions is described in Box 13.4. Over the past twenty years therapists and researchers have elaborated upon this early report and added to the armamentarium of clinicians who seek to improve the sexual lives of dysfunctional patients. In

the following we shall describe several approaches and procedures (LoPiccolo and Hogan, 1979; LoPiccolo and Stock, 1986). A therapist may choose only one technique for a given case, but the complex and multifaceted nature of sexual dysfunctions usually demands several.

Sex Education Because many dysfunctional people are ignorant of basic facts about human sexuality, most therapists devote time and effort to educating their clients in sexual anatomy and the physiological processes of intercourse. An unintentional but important effect of such instruction is to make legitimate the explicit discussion of sex, taking it out of the realm of unspoken taboo and mystery and reducing some of the anxiety and embarrassment surrounding this previously avoided topic.

Anxiety Reduction Techniques Well before the publication of the Masters–Johnson therapy program, behavior therapists appreciated that their frightened clients needed gradual and systematic exposure to anxiety-provoking aspects of the sexual situation. Wolpe's systematic desensitization and *in vivo desensitization,* that is, by real-life encounters, have been employed with apparently high degrees of success (Hogan, 1978; Andersen, 1983), especially when they are combined with skills training; people highly anxious about sex have often failed to learn to do a number of necessary and preliminary things. In vivo desensitization would appear to be the principal technique of the Masters–Johnson program, although additional components probably contribute to its overall effectiveness.

Directed Masturbation Employed primarily for women who have seldom if ever had an orgasm, this technique involves persuading the patient of the propriety and normality of masturbation (for often such women have never masturbated), instructing her in female anatomy, encouraging stroking oneself in pleasurable ways, and finally exploring those masturbation methods that are most effective in bringing her to high levels of sexual arousal and to orgasm (LoPiccolo and Lobitz, 1972). Those women who have partners are invited to include them in the various stages of the program. Sessions with the therapist are supplemented by assigned reading, such as *Becoming Orgasmic,* a self-help book by Heiman, LoPiccolo, and LoPiccolo (1976), and occasionally by specially designed videotapes that illustrate masturbation. In most instances nonorgasmic women learn to have orgasms while masturbating and while their partners manually or orally bring them to orgasm. However, in fewer than half of the cases does this ability transfer to conventional penile–vaginal intercourse (LoPiccolo and Stock, 1986).

Skills and Communication Training To improve sexual skills and communication, therapists assign written materials, show clients videotapes and films that demonstrate explicit sexual techniques, discuss techniques with them, and encourage them to express their likes and dislikes to their partners (e.g., McMullen and Rosen, 1979). All these training procedures also expose the client to anxiety-laden material; this desensitizing aspect appears to be an additional benefit.

Procedures to Change Attitudes and Thoughts In what are called *sensory-awareness procedures,* the client is encouraged to tune in to the pleasant sensations that accompany even incipient sexual arousal. The sensate-focus exercises described in Box 13.4, for example, are a way of opening the individual to truly sensual and sexual feelings. Rational-emotive therapy tries to substitute less self-demanding thoughts for "musturbation," the "I must" thoughts often causing problems for sexually dysfunctional people.

Shifts in Routines Therapists may encourage a couple to make "dates" with each other, to take the phone off the hook, hang a "Do Not Disturb" sign on the bedroom door, or agree not to have intercourse for a given period of time. The assumption is that any such specific shifts from habitual behavior can have positive reinforcing consequences and be beneficial to the sexual relationship.

Marital Therapy As noted earlier, sexual dysfunctions are often embedded in a distressed marital or other close relationship. Troubled couples usually need special training in communications skills. Marital therapy is discussed in more detail in Chapter 20.

Psychodynamic Techniques A man may not at first admit that he cannot have an erection, in which case the therapist must listen between the lines of what he says. A woman may be reluctant to initiate sexual encounters because, although she may not verbalize it to the therapist, she considers such assertiveness unseemly and inappropriate to her traditional female role. In such instances the general analytic view that clients are often unable to express clearly to their therapists what truly bothers them can help in proper assessment and planning for behavioral treatment. Kaplan (1974) articulates well the blend of psychodynamic therapy with direct behavioral treatment. No doubt elements of nonbehavioral therapy are to be found in the actual practices of sex therapists, even if they are not made explicit by these workers when they discuss their techniques in journals or with colleagues. Readers may wish to recall the earlier discussion of eclecticism in therapy (Box 2.3, page 56) to remind themselves of the complexity of the therapeutic enterprise.

Medical and Physical Procedures Although our study of sexual dysfunctions has referred to relatively few underlying somatic problems, therapists must not ignore their possibility, especially if dyspareunia and complete erectile dysfunction are the disorders. When depression is part of the clinical picture and has severely diminished sex drive, antidepressant drugs can be helpful (Winokur, 1963). Tranquilizers are also used as an adjunct to anxiety reduction techniques, although the depressant effects of these drugs may be detrimental to sexual functioning. Most therapists use drugs only when psychological procedures are found wanting.

The self-help trend is quite evident among sexually dysfunctional people as well as among those who strive to enhance already satisfying sex lives. For greater arousal and ecstatic enjoyment of sex, some people rely on chemicals. Amyl nitrite is a peripheral vasodilator, but unfortunately it sometimes has the potentially fatal side effect of heart failure. It is inhaled from a small glass vial, usually by homosexual men, just before orgasm to intensify and prolong it. Alcohol disinhibits in small amounts; marijuana, hashish, cocaine, LSD, and other psychedelics have effects that are variable and often dramatic. Other chemicals are touted for their presumed aphrodisiac, or sexually stimulating, properties. For example, cantharides or Spanish fly, a preparation of powdered blister beetles that is taken internally, creates inflammation and itching in the genitals, sensations experienced by some people as sexually arousing. The most that can be said about any of these drugs is that their efficacy is yet to be established, although their benefits to some people under some circumstances, as well as their dangers to others, are attested to by enthusiastic testimonials and by dire warnings.

Implanting a rigid plastic rod or a system of hydraulic tubes in a chronically flaccid penis and removal of the clitoral hood, in hopes of enhancing clitoral stimulation, are surgical procedures. These are radical steps to take, but implantations in the penis will usually allow the physically disabled man to have an erection. Major medical complications, however, have been reported for a significant number of such operations (Malloy, Wein, and Carpiniello, 1980). Alterations of the female genitalia are seemingly unnecessary, since the clitoris can be gently rubbed either during or separately from intercourse, Finally, simple physical exercise may have some favorable impact on sexual difficulties, although the effects may be general and placebo in nature; people who jog or otherwise maintain their bodies in good physical condition probably feel generally better about themselves and may thereby improve their sex lives. One set of exercises does appear to have some specific benefit for nonorgasmic women, namely, the Kegel (1952) exercises for regularly contracting and thereby strengthening the pubococcygeal musculature surrounding the vagina.

Summary

Few emotional problems are of greater interest to people nowadays than the sexual dysfunctions, disruptions in the normal sexual response cycle that seem to be caused by inhibitions and that rob many people of sexual enjoyment. DSM-IIIR categorizes these disturbances into four groups: sexual desire disorders, sexual arousal disorders, orgasm disorders, and pain disorders. Disorders can very in severity, in chronicity, and in their pervasiveness, occurring generally or only with certain partners and in particular situations. In no instance should a person believe himself or herself to have a sexual dysfunction unless the difficulty is persistent and recurrent; all of us quite normally experience sexual problems on an intermittent basis throughout our lives.

The particular sexual dysfunctions were described and their presumed causes discussed. Although organic factors must be considered, especially for instances of dyspareunia and complete erectile failure, the etiology of the disorders usually lies in a combination of unfavorable attitudes, difficult earlier experiences, fears of performance, assumption of a spectator role, and lack of specific knowledge and skills. Sex-role stereotypes may play a part in some dysfunctions: a man who has trouble maintaining his erection is often called impotent, the implication being that he is not much of a man; and a woman who does not have orgasms with regularity is often termed frigid, the implication being that she is generally cold and unresponsive. The problems of females in particular appear to be linked to cultural prejudices against their sexuality, ironic in light of laboratory data indicating that women are capable of more frequent sexual enjoyment than men.

Information on the causes of sexual dysfunction derives almost entirely from uncontrolled case studies and most therefore be viewed with caution. The absence of solid data on etiology has not deterred therapists from devising seemingly effective behavioral and cognitive interventions. Direct sex therapy, behavioral in nature and aimed at reversing old habits and teaching new skills, was propelled into public consciousness by the appearance of the Masters and Johnson book *Human Sexual Inadequacy* in 1970. Their method hinges on gradual, unthreatening exposure to increasingly intimate sexual encounters and the sanctioning of sexuality by credible and sensitive therapists. Education in sexual anatomy and physiology; anxiety reduction techniques; skills and communications training; procedures to change attitudes and thoughts; shifts in routines; marital therapy, when the sexual problem is embedded, as it often is, in a snarled relationship; psychodynamic techniques; and a variety of medical and other physical procedures are other means applied by sex therapists. Controlled data are just beginning to appear, but there is good reason to be optimistic about the ultimate ability of the mental health professions to help most people achieve at least some relief from crippling sexual inhibitions. Consideration was also given to the health crisis of Acquired Immune Deficiency Syndrome; the nature of the illness was described as were some of the efforts by behavioral scientists to help people reduce their chances of contracting AIDS by changing from risky to safer sexual practices.

Part Four

Paul Klee. *Physionomic Lightning.* 1927. © 1989 ARS, New York/Cosmopress.

The Schizophrenias

Paul Klee, *Physionomic Lightning*, 1927. © 1989 ARS, New York/Cosmopress.

Chapter 14

Schizophrenia

History of the Concept
  Kraepelin's and Bleuler's Early Descriptions
  The Broadened American Concept
  The DSM-IIIR Diagnosis
Clinical Symptoms of Schizophrenia
  Disorders of Thought
  Disorders of Perception and Attention
  Motor Symptoms
  Affective Symptoms
  Impairments in Life Functioning
Subcategories of Schizophrenia
**Research on the Etiology
  of Schizophrenia**
  The Genetic Data
  Biochemical Factors
  Neurological Findings
  Social Class and Schizophrenia
  Schizophrenia and the Family
  High-Risk Studies of Schizophrenia
Therapies for Schizophrenia
  Somatic Treatments
  Psychological Treatments
Summary

All of a sudden things weren't going so well. I began to lose control of my life and, most of all, myself. I couldn't concentrate on my schoolwork, I couldn't sleep, and when I did sleep, I had dreams about dying. I was afraid to go to class, imagined that people were talking about me, and on top of that I heard voices. I called my mother in Pittsburgh and asked for her advice. She told me to move off campus into an apartment with my sister.

After I moved in with my sister, things got worse. I was afraid to go outside and when I looked out of the window, it seemed that everyone outside was yelling, "kill her, kill her." My sister forced me to go to school. I would go out of the house until I knew she had gone to work; then I would return home. Things continued to get worse. I imagined that I had a foul body odor and I sometimes took up to six showers a day. I recall going to the grocery store one day, and I imagined that the people in the store were saying "Get saved, Jesus is the answer." Things worsened—I couldn't remember a thing. I had a notebook full of reminders telling me what to do on that particular day. I couldn't remember my schoolwork, and I would study from 6:00 P.M. until 4:00 A.M. but never had the courage to go to class on the following day. I tried to tell my sister about it, but she didn't understand. She suggested that I see a psychiatrist, but I was afraid to go out of the house to see him.

One day I decided that I couldn't take this trauma anymore, so I took an overdose of 35 Darvon pills. At the same moment, a voice inside me said, "What did you do that for? Now you won't go to heaven." At that instant I realized that I really didn't want to die. I wanted to live, and I was afraid. I got on the phone and called the psychiatrist whom my sister had recommended. I told him that I had taken an overdose of Darvon and that I was afraid. He told me to take a taxi to the hospital. When I arrived at the hospital, I began vomiting, but I didn't pass out. Somehow I just couldn't accept the fact that I was really going to see a psychiatrist. I thought that psychiatrists were only for crazy people, and I definitely didn't think I was crazy yet. As a result, I did not admit myself right away. As a matter of fact I left the hospital and ended up meeting my sister on the way

home. She told me to turn right back around because I was definitely going to be admitted. We then called my mother, and she said she would fly down on the following day. (O'Neal, 1984, pp. 109–110)

Although the diagnosis of schizophrenia has existed now for about a century and the disorder has spawned more research than any other, we are far from understanding this serious mental disorder. The massive and extreme disruptions of thoughts, perceptions, emotions, and behavior that are schizophrenia are what people generally refer to as madness. In this chapter we consider first how schizophrenia is and has been diagnosed and in so doing find that through the decades there has been widespread disagreement. Then we examine research on the etiology of schizophrenia and therapies for the disorder.

History of the Concept

Kraepelin's and Bleuler's Early Descriptions

The concept of **schizophrenia** was initially formulated by two European psychiatrists, Emil Kraepelin and Eugen Bleuler. Kraepelin first presented his concept of **dementia praecox,** the early term for schizophrenia, in 1898. Two major groups of endogenous, or internally caused, psychoses were differentiated, manic-depressive illness and dementia praecox. Dementia praecox included several diagnostic concepts—dementia paranoides, catatonia, and hebephrenia—already singled out and regarded as distinct entities by clinicians in the previous few decades. Although *symptomatically* these disorders are very diverse, Kraepelin believed that they shared a common core. His term, dementia praecox, reflected what he believed the common core to be—an early onset (praecox) and a progressive intellectual deterioration (dementia). Among the major symptoms that Kraepelin saw in such patients were hallucinations, delusions, negativism, attentional difficulties, stereotyped behavior, and emotional dysfunction. Thus Kraepelin focused on both the course and the symptoms in defining the disorder, although he often emphasized the former over the latter.

Kraepelin did not move much beyond a narrow definition of schizophrenia and an emphasis on description. In the eighth edition of his textbook, for example, he

Emil Kraepelin (1856–1926), the German psychiatrist whose descriptions of dementia praecox have proved remarkably durable in the light of contemporary research.

Eugen Bleuler (1857–1939), the Swiss psychiatrist who contributed importantly to our conceptions of schizophrenia and coined the term.

grouped the symptoms of dementia praecox into thirty-six major categories, assigning hundreds of them to each. He made little effort to interrelate these separate symptoms and stated only that they all reflected dementia and a loss of the usual unity in thinking, feeling, and acting. The view of the next major figure, Eugen Bleuler, however, represented both a specific attempt

to define the core of the disorder and a move away from Kraepelin's emphasis on prognosis in defining the disorder.

In describing schizophrenia, Bleuler broke with Kraepelin on two major points: he believed that the disorder in question did not necessarily have an early onset and that it did not inevitably progress toward dementia. Thus Bleuler was much less attentive to the *course* of the disorder than was Kraepelin, and the label dementia praecox was no longer considered appropriate. In 1908 Bleuler proposed his own term, schizophrenia, from the Greek words *schizien* meaning "to split" and *phren* meaning "mind," to capture what he viewed as the essential nature of the condition.

Psychoanalytic theory had a major influence on Bleuler's view of schizophrenia. Most importantly, Bleuler was led to attempt for schizophrenia what Freud had tried to accomplish for the neuroses—to specify underlying psychological processes that might be at the root of the various disturbances of schizophrenic patients.

Bleuler, like Kraepelin, had noted the great range of distress and dysfunction evident in schizophrenic patients. But Bleuler went much further than Kraepelin in trying to specify a common denominator or essential property that would link the various disturbances together. The metaphorical concept that he adopted for this purpose was the "breaking of associative threads." For Bleuler associative threads joined not only words but thoughts. Thus goal-directed, efficient thinking and communication were possible only when these hypothetical structures were intact. The notion that associative threads are disrupted in schizophrenics was then used to "account" for other problems. The attentional difficulties of schizophrenics, for example, were viewed by Bleuler as resulting from a loss of purposeful direction in thought, which in turn caused passive responding to objects and people in the immediate surroundings. In a similar vein, blocking, a seeming total loss of a train of thought, was considered a complete disruption of the associative threads for the subject under discussion.

Although Kraepelin recognized that a small percentage of patients who originally manifested symptoms of dementia praecox did not deteriorate, he preferred to limit this diagnostic category to patients who had a poor prognosis. Bleuler's work, in contrast, led to a broader concept of schizophrenia and a more pronounced theoretical emphasis. He placed patients with a good prognosis in his group of schizophrenias and in addition included as schizophrenic "many atypical melancholias and manias of other schools, especially hysterical melancholias and manias, most hallucinatory confusions, some 'nervous' people and compulsive and impulsive patients and many prison psychoes" (1923, p. 436).

The Broadened American Concept

Bleuler had a great influence on the American concept of schizophrenia. Over the first part of the twentieth century, its breadth was extended considerably. At the New York State Psychiatric Institute, for example, about 20 percent of patients were diagnosed schizophrenic in the 1930s. The numbers increased through the 1940s and in 1952 peaked at a remarkable 80 percent. In contrast, the European concept of schizophrenia remained narrower. The percentage of patients diagnosed schizophrenic at Maudsley Hospital in London stayed relatively constant, at 20 percent, for a forty-year period (Kuriansky, Deming, and Gurland, 1974).

The reasons for the increase in the frequency of American diagnoses of schizophrenia are not difficult to find. Several prominent figures in the history of American psychiatry, following Bleuler's lead, expanded the concept of schizophrenia to an even greater extent.

Adolf Meyer (1866–1950), considered by many to have been the dean of American psychiatry (e.g., Zilboorg and Henry, 1941), argued that diagnostic categories were often arbitrary and artificial (e.g., Meyer, 1917, 1926). His approach to schizophrenia was flexible and did not rely on either specific symptoms or progressive deterioration for a definition of the disorder.

The American conception of schizophrenia was also broadened by investigators who suggested additional schizophrenic subtypes.[1] For example, in 1933 Kasanin described nine patients who had all been assigned diagnoses of dementia praecox. The onset of the disorder had been sudden for all of them and their recovery relatively rapid. Noting that theirs could be said to be a combination of both schizophrenic and affective symptoms, Kasanin suggested the term "schizoaffective psychosis" to describe the disturbances of these patients. This diagnosis subsequently became part of the American concept of schizophrenia, and was listed in DSM-I (1952) and DSM-II (1968).

The schizophrenia category was further expanded by Hoch and his colleagues, who argued that schizophrenia often "masquerades" as other disorders. They suggested the terms "pseudoneurotic schizophrenia" (Hoch and Polatin, 1949) and "pseudopsychopathic schizophrenia" (Hoch and Dunaif, 1955) to describe anxious, withdrawn persons with serious interpersonal problems

who also have neurotic or psychopathic symptoms. Hoch argued that even though these patients often lack the more classic symptoms of schizophrenia, they reveal, on closer examination, the cognitive and emotional disorganization he considered to be the hallmark of the disorder. As a result of such opinions, many patients who would otherwise have been diagnosed as suffering from neuroses, affective disorders, and personality disturbances were in this country considered to be schizophrenic.

In the 1960s and 1970s the ***process-reactive*** dimension was another key means of maintaining the broad concept of schizophrenia in the United States. As soon as Bleuler had observed that the onset of schizophrenia was not always at a young age and that deterioration was not a certain course, clinicians began to observe other differences between those whose onset was later and who sometimes recovered and those whose onset was earlier and who usually deteriorated further. Some schizophrenics had been relatively deviant, apathetic individuals for many of their young years, suffering gradual but insidious depletion of thought, emotion, interests, and activity. Others, usually later in life, had a rather rapid onset of more severe symptoms. The term *process,* indicating some sort of basic physiological malfunction in the brain, was chosen for insidiously developing schizophrenia and *reactive* for what appeared suddenly after stress. For the last thirty years in the United States the process-reactive dimension has been extensively studied. Earlier social and sexual adjustment, as measured, for example, by the Phillips Scale (1953), became a means of distinguishing schizophrenics and determining their chances for recovery. Those with a *good premorbid* adjustment were more likely to have only an episodic problem and to have a good prognosis. Process schizophrenia, then, which has followed an earlier poor adjustment of patients at school, work, and in their sexual and social lives, may be equated with Kraepelin's original description of dementia praecox. The inclusion of reactive patients in the definition helped extend the American concept.

A prevailing interest in treatment also played a role in broadening the American concept of schizophrenia. Both Bleuler and Meyer had rejected the notion that deterioration was inevitable, thus allowing the possibility of intervention and the restitution of reason. Harry Stack Sullivan (1892–1949) shared this optimistic view and became the first major theorist to develop a systematic psychological treatment for schizophrenia. He emphasized the underlying emotional and cognitive factors motivating what he considered to be the schizophrenic's withdrawal from interpersonal relationships. Other behavior did not play an important role in Sullivan's definition of the disorder. Because he believed

---

[1]Both Kraepelin and Bleuler had suggested that schizophrenia could be divided into specific types, but the subtypes discussed here went considerably beyond their proposals.

that personality could be observed only in interpersonal relations, he, in fact, maintained that there were *no* fundamental criteria for the disorder (Sullivan, 1929).

The DSM-IIIR Diagnosis

With the publication of DSM-III and DSM-IIIR, the American conception of schizophrenia has moved considerably from the broad definition we have been discussing to a new definition that narrows the range of patients diagnosed schizophrenic in four ways. First, the diagnostic criteria are presented in explicit and considerable detail. Second, patients with symptoms of an affective disorder are specifically excluded. Many patients with a DSM-II diagnosis of schizophrenia actually had an affective disorder (Cooper *et al.,* 1972). Schizophrenia, schizoaffective type, is now listed as *schizoaffective disorder*[2] in a separate section, Psychotic Disorders Not Elsewhere Classified. Third, DSM-IIIR requires six months of disturbance for the diagnosis. The six-month period must include at least one week of the active phase, defined by the presence of at least two of the following—delusions, hallucinations, incoherence or loose associations, catatonic behavior, and flat or inappropriate affect. The remaining time required can be either a prodromal (before the active phase) or residual (after the active phase) period. Problems during either the prodromal or residual phases include social withdrawal, impaired role functioning, blunted or inappropriate affect, lack of initiative, vague and circumstantial speech, impairment in hygiene and grooming, odd beliefs or magical thinking, and unusual perceptual experiences. Thus are eliminated patients who have a brief psychotic episode, often stress-related, and then recover quickly. DSM-II's acute schizophrenic episode is now diagnosed as either *schizophreniform disorder* or *brief reactive psychosis,* which are also listed in the new section. In schizophreniform disorder the psychotic symptoms—emotional turmoil, fear, confusion, vivid hallucinations—must not persist for more than six months. A brief reactive psychosis must not last longer than one month and is brought on by extreme stress, such as bereavement. Fourth, what DSM-II may have regarded as mild forms of schizophrenia are now diagnosed as personality disorders—schizotypal and borderline—as we saw in Chapter 10 (page 255).

It cannot be concluded, however, that with the appearance of DSM-IIIR we have reached a final answer to the problem of diagnosing schizophrenia. The DSM-IIIR criteria are not accepted universally and, in fact, a number of different sets of diagnostic criteria are still frequently used. Endicott and her colleagues (1982) compared diagnoses made by the sets of criteria of ten different diagnostic systems. The number of patients identified by these systems as schizophrenic ranged from a low of six to a high of forty-four! Thus the breadth of the schizophrenia concept remains an issue even in contemporary research.

The foregoing serves as background for a more detailed description of the behavior of schizophrenics. The diagnostic symptoms to be presented rely heavily on the DSM-IIIR criteria as well as on information collected in a large-scale investigation of schizophrenia, the International Pilot Study of Schizophrenia (IPSS), conducted by the World Health Organization (Sartorius, Shapiro, and Jablonsky, 1974).

Clinical Symptoms of Schizophrenia

The symptoms of schizophrenic patients can be organized into disturbances in several major areas—thought, perception and attention, motor behavior, affect or emotion, and life functioning. The range of problems of people diagnosed as schizophrenic is very extensive, although patients who are so diagnosed will typically have only *some* of them. DSM-IIIR determines for the diagnostician how many problems must be present, and in what degree, to justify the diagnosis. Unlike most diagnostic categories that we have considered, there is *no essential* symptom that must be present. Thus schizophrenic patients differ from one another more than do patients with other disorders. The heterogeneity of schizophrenia suggests that it would be appropriate to try to subdivide schizophrenics into types who manifest particular constellations of problems. After reviewing the major symptoms, we shall examine the types of schizophrenia.[3]

Disorders of Thought

The term **thought disorder** refers to problems both in the *form* of thought—the organization of ideas, speak-

---

[2]Schizoaffective disorder is to be diagnosed only when the clinician cannot decide between an affective disorder and schizophrenia or schizophreniform disorder. Onset and usually recovery are rapid, as indicated earlier.

[3]Although we describe the symptoms of schizophrenia in detail, it must be kept in mind that diagnostically the duration of the disorder is regarded as at least as important, if not more so, in allowing schizophrenia to be distinguished from the symptomatically similar schizophreniform disorder and brief reactive psychosis.

ing so that a listener can understand; and in its *content*—the actual ideas that are expressed. We examine first the form of thought in schizophrenia.

Disorders of Thought Form

In response to an initial, seemingly simple question to a schizophrenic patient, this conversation ensued:

> *"How old are you?"*
> *"Why I am centuries old, sir."*
> *"How long have you been here?"*
> *"I've been now on this property on and off for a long time. I cannot say the exact time because we are absorbed by the air at night, and they bring back people. They kill up everything; they can make you lie; they can talk through your throat."*
> *"Who is this?"*
> *"Why, the air."*
> *"What is the name of this place?"*
> *"This place is called a star."*
> *"Who is the doctor in charge of your ward?"*
> *"A body just like yours, sir. They can make you black and white. I say good morning, but he just comes through there. At first it was a colony. They said it was heaven. These buildings were not solid at the time, and I am positive that this is the same place. They have others just like it. People die, and all the microbes talk over there, and prestigitis you know is sending you from here to another world. . . . I was sent by the government to the United States to Washington to some star, and they had a pretty nice country there. Now you have a body like a young man who says he is of the prestigitis."*
> *"Who was this prestigitis?"*
> *"Why, you are yourself. You can be prestigitis. They make you say bad things; they can read you; they bring back Negroes from the dead."* (White, 1932, p. 228)

This excerpt illustrates the ***incoherence*** sometimes found in the conversation of schizophrenics. Although the patient may make repeated references to central ideas or a theme, the images and fragments of thought are not connected. It is difficult to understand exactly what the patient is trying to tell the interviewer. In addition, the patient used the work "prestigitis" several times, a ***neologism*** or new word that he had made up himself and that is probably meaningless to the listener.

Thought may also be disordered by ***loose associations,*** in which case the patient may be more successful in communicating with a listener but has difficulty sticking to one topic. He or she seems to drift off on a train of associations evoked by an idea from the past. Schizophrenic patients have themselves provided descriptions of this state.

> *My thoughts get all jumbled up. I start thinking or talking about something but I never get there. Instead, I wander off in the wrong direction and get caught up with all sorts of different things that may be connected with things I want to say but in a way I can't explain. People listening to me get more lost that I do. . . . .*
>
> *My trouble is that I've got too many thoughts. You might think about something, let's say that ashtray and just think, oh! yes, that's for putting my cigarette in, but I would think of it and then I would think of a dozen different things connected with it at the same time.* (McGhie and Chapman, 1961, p. 108)

Other disturbances in thought form are ***poverty of speech***—the amount of discourse is reduced; ***poverty of content***—the amount of speech is adequate but it conveys little information; ***perseveration***—words and ideas are persistently repeated; and ***blocking***—a train of speech is interrupted by silence before an idea is completed and then the thought being conveyed cannot be recalled.

Disturbances in the form of thought were regarded by Bleuler as the principal clinical symptom of schizophrenia and remain one of the DSM-IIIR criteria for the diagnosis. But evidence indicates that the thinking of many schizophrenics is not faulty in form. Furthermore, the presence of thought disorder does not discriminate well between schizophrenics and other psychotic patients, such as some of those with affective disorders (Andreasen, 1979). For example, manic patients show as much loosening of associations as do schizophrenics, and depressives are equivalent to schizophrenics in poverty of speech.

Disorders of Thought Content

Deviance in *content* of thought seems more central to schizophrenia than confusion in form of thought. The thoughts of 97 percent of schizophrenics in the IPSS were found disordered in a very fundamental way, through *lack of insight.* When asked what they thought was wrong or why they had been hospitalized, schizophrenics seemed to have no appreciation of their condition and little realization that their behavior was unusual.

No doubt each of us is, at one time or another, rather concerned because we believe that others think badly of us. Perhaps much of the time this belief is well justified. Who, after all, can be universally loved? Fortunately, we either learn to live with this belief, or, if it is false, are readily able to dispel it. Many schizophrenics, however, are subject to ***delusions,*** holding beliefs that the rest of society would generally disagree with or view as misinterpretations of reality. As with formal thought disorder, however, delusional beliefs are found also among patients in other diagnostic categories, notably mania and psychotic depression.

Consider for a moment what life would be like if you were firmly convinced that numbers of people did not like you, indeed that they disliked you so much that they were plotting against you. Some of these persecutors have sophisticated listening devices that allow them to tune in on your most private conversations and gather evidence in a plot to discredit you. None of those around you, including your loved ones, is able to reassure you that these people are not spying on you. In fact, even your closest friends and confidants are gradually joining your tormentors and becoming members of the persecuting community. You are naturally quite anxious or angry about your situation, and you begin your own counteractions against the imagined persecutors. Any new room you enter must be carefully checked for listening devices. When you meet a person for the first time, you question him or her at great length to determine whether he or she is part of the plot against you.

Simple **persecutory** delusions were found in 65 percent of the IPSS sample. Schizophrenics' delusions may also take several other forms. Some of the most important of these have been described by the German psychiatrist Kurt Schneider (1959). The following catalogue of delusions is drawn from Mellor (1970).

1. **Delusional Percept.** A normal perception, for some reason, takes on a special significance for the patient and an often elaborate delusional system quickly develops. The following is an example of such a transformed percept.

A young Irishman was at breakfast with two fellow lodgers. He felt a sense of unease, that something frightening was going to happen. One of the lodgers pushed the salt cellar towards him (he appreciated at the time that this was an ordinary salt cellar and his friend's intention was innocent). Almost before the salt cellar reached him he knew that he must return home, "to greet the Pope, who is visiting Ireland to see his family and to reward them . . . because Our Lord is going to be born again to one of the women. . . . And because of this they [all the women] are all born different with their private parts back to front." (p. 18)

2. **Somatic Passivity.** The patient is a passive, unwilling recipient of bodily sensations imposed by an external agency.

Kurt Schneider, a German psychiatrist, proposed that particular forms of hallucinations and delusions, which he calls first-rank symptoms, are central to defining schizophrenia.

A twenty-nine-year-old teacher described "X-rays entering the back of my neck, where the skin tingles and feels warm, they pass down the back in a hot tingling strip about six inches wide to the waist. There they disappear into the pelvis which feels numb and cold and solid like a block of ice. They stop me from getting an erection." (p. 16)

3. **Thought Insertion.** Thoughts, which are not the patient's own, have been placed in his or her mind by an external source.

A twenty-nine-year-old housewife said "I look out of the window and I think the garden looks nice and the grass looks cool, but the thoughts of Eamonn Andrews come into my mind. There are no other thoughts there, only his. . . . He treats my mind like a screen and flashes his thoughts on it like you flash a picture." (p. 17)

4. **Thought Broadcast.** The patient's thoughts are transmitted, so that others know them.

A twenty-one-year-old student [found that] "As I think, my thoughts leave my head on a type of mental ticker-tape. Everyone around has only to pass the tape through their mind and they know my thoughts." (p. 17)

5. Thought Withdrawal. The patient's thoughts are "stolen" from his or her mind by an external force, suddenly and unexpectedly.

A twenty-two-year-old woman [described such an experience]. "I am thinking about my mother, and suddenly my thoughts are sucked out of my mind by a phrenological vacuum extractor, and there is nothing in my mind, it is empty. . . . " (pp. 16–17)

The next three delusions pertain to the experiencing of feelings and the carrying out of actions and impulses that have been imposed on the patient by some external agent.

6. "Made" Feelings. *A twenty-three-year-old female patient reported, "I cry, tears roll down my cheeks and I look unhappy, but inside I have a cold anger because they are using me in this way, and it is not me who is unhappy, but they are projecting unhappiness onto my brain. They project upon me laughter, for no reason, and you have no idea how terrible it is to laugh and look happy and know it is not you, but their emotions."* (p. 17)

7. "Made" Volitional Acts. *A twenty-nine-year-old shorthand typist described her [simplest] actions as follows: "When I reach my hand for the comb it is my hand and arm which move, and my fingers pick up the pen, but I don't control them. . . . I sit there watching them move, and they are quite independent, what they do is nothing to do with me. . . . I am just a puppet who is manipulated by cosmic strings. When the strings are pulled my body moves and I cannot prevent it."* (p. 17)

8. "Made" Impulses. *A twenty-nine-year-old engineer [who had] emptied the contents of a urine bottle over the ward dinner trolley [tried to explain the incident]. "The sudden impulse came over me that I must do it. It was not my feeling, it came into me from the X-ray department, that was why I was sent there for implants yesterday. It was nothing to do with me, they wanted it done. So I picked up the bottle and poured it in. It seemed all I could do."* (p. 18)

Disorders of Perception and Attention

Schizophrenic patients frequently report that the world seems somehow different or even unreal (derealization) to them. Some mention changes in the way their bodies feel. Parts of their bodies may seem too large or too small, objects around them too close or too far away. Or there may be numbness or tingling and electrical or burning sensations. Patients may feel as though snakes are crawling inside the abdomen. Or the body may become so depersonalized that it feels as though it is a machine. Some patients become hypersensitive to sights, sounds, and smells. They may find it torment to be touched. Light may seem blinding and noise becomes an agony. Others remark that their surroundings are not as they used to be, that everything appears flat and colorless. Some schizophrenics report difficulties in attending to what is happening around them.

I can't concentrate on television because I can't watch the screen and listen to what is being said at the same time. I can't seem to take in two things like this at the same time especially when one of them means watching and the other means listening. On the other hand I seem to be always taking in too much at the one time, and then I can't handle it and can't make sense of it. . . . [Or, as another patient stated] When people are talking, I just get scraps of it. If it is just one person who is speaking, that's not so bad, but if others join in then I can't pick it up at all. I just can't get in tune with the conversation. It makes me feel all open—as if things are closing in on me and I have lost control. (McGhie and Chapman, 1961, p. 106)

The most dramatic distortions of perception are called **hallucinations,** sensory experiences in the absence of any stimulation from the environment. They occur most often in the auditory modality and less often in the visual. Seventy-four percent of the IPSS sample reported having auditory hallucinations.

Some hallucinations are thought to be particularly important diagnostically because they occur more often in schizophrenics than in other psychotic patients. Schneider (1959) has described these, and we again rely on Mellor (1970) for examples.

1. Audible Thoughts. *A thirty-two-year-old housewife complained of a man's voice speaking in an intense whisper from a point about two feet above her head. The voice would repeat almost all the patient's goal-directing thinking—even the most banal thoughts. The patient would think, "I must put the kettle on" and after a pause of not more than one second the voice would say "I must put the kettle on." It would often say the opposite "Don't put the kettle on."* (p. 16)

2. Voices Arguing. *A twenty-four-year-old male patient reported hearing voices coming from the nurse's office. One voice, deep in pitch and roughly spoken, repeatedly said "G.T. is a bloody paradox," and another higher in pitch said "He is that,* *he should be locked up." A female voice occasionally interrupted, saying "He is not, he is a lovely man."* (p. 16)

3. **Voices Commenting.** *A forty-one-year-old housewife heard a voice coming from a house across the road. The voice went on incessantly in a flat monotone describing everything she was doing with an admixture of critical comments. "She is peeling potatoes, got hold of the peeler, she does not want that potato, she is putting it back, because she thinks it has a knobble like a penis, she has a dirty mind, she is peeling potatoes, now she is washing them. . . ."* (p. 16)

Motor Symptoms

Disturbances in motor activity are obvious and bizarre. The schizophrenic may grimace or adopt strange facial expressions. He or she may gesture repeatedly, using peculiar and sometimes complex sequences of finger, hand, and arm movements—which often seem to be purposeful, odd as they may be. Some schizophrenics manifest an unusual increase in the overall level of activity. There may be much excitement, wild flailing of

Catatonic posturing, although rare today, was apparently more common before modern drug therapies were introduced.

Inappropriate affect was the key feature in diagnosing hebephrenic schizophrenia.

the limbs, and great expenditure of energy similar to that seen in mania. At the other end of the spectrum is ***catatonic immobility:*** unusual postures are adopted and maintained for very long periods of time. A patient may stand on one leg, with the other tucked up toward the buttocks, and remain in this position virtually all day. Catatonic patients may also have what is referred to as ***waxy flexibility.*** Another person can move their limbs into strange positions that will then be maintained for long periods of time.

Affective Symptoms

Two affective abnormalities are found in a number of schizophrenic patients. In patients with ***flat affect*** virtually no stimulus can elicit an emotional response. The shallowness or complete blunting of emotion renders the schizophrenic apathetic. The patient may stare vacantly, the muscles of his face flaccid, his eyes lifeless. When spoken to he answers in a flat and toneless voice. Flat affect was found in 66 percent of the IPSS schizophrenics. Other patients have ***inappropriate affect.*** The emotional responses of these individuals are out of context—the patient may laugh on hearing that her mother has just died or become enraged when asked a simple question about how a new garment fits. These schizophrenics are likely to shift rapidly from one emotional state to another for no discernible reason. Although this symptom is quite rare, when it does appear it is of considerable diagnostic importance.

BOX 14.1

PARANOID DELUSIONS AND REPRESSED HOMOSEXUALITY

According to DSM-IIIR, paranoid delusions are the most obvious symptoms of both paranoid schizophrenia and the **delusional (paranoid) disorders.** A person with a delusional disorder is troubled by persistent persecutory delusions or by delusional jealousy, the unfounded conviction that the spouse or lover is unfaithful. But unlike the paranoid schizophrenic, he or she has no thought disorder, no hallucinations, and no bizarre delusions. The person speaks and reasons coherently and carries out daily responsibilities. A circumscribed delusional system is the one and fundamental loss of contact with reality. People with paranoid disorder rarely seek treatment through their own volition, but when they become contentious and initiate litigation, others may bring them for care.

Freud's theory, commonly accepted even today by most analytic workers, is that paranoid delusions result from repressed homosexual impulses that are striving for expression. The anxiety stemming from their threatened expression is handled primarily by the defense mechanism of projection, attributing to others feelings that are unacceptable to one's own ego (Freud, 1915). The basic unconscious thought is "I, a man, love him" or "I, a woman, love her." Freud considered the common paranoid delusions of persecution and grandiosity to derive from distortions, and then projection, of this basic homosexual urge.

In **delusions of persecution** the homosexual thought "I, a man, love him," being unacceptable to the ego, is converted into the less threatening statement "I, a man, hate him." Since the emotion expressed by this premise is also less than satisfactory, it is further transformed by projection into "He hates me, so I am justified in hating him." The final formulation may be "I hate him because he persecutes me." Freud asserted that the persecutor is always a person of the same sex who is unconsciously a love object for the individual.

Delusions of grandiosity (megalomania) begin with a contradiction of the homosexual impulse. The sentence "I, a man, love him" is changed into "I do not love anyone." But since libido must be invested in or attached to some-

thing or someone, the psychic reality becomes "I love only myself."

One of Freud's lesser-known cases of a patient with paranoid delusions is of special interest, for it seems initially to challenge Freud's basic tenet that the persecutor must be a person of the same sex. The kinds of inferences that constitute the argument of this case study are typical of those made by Freud in his attempts to understand his clinical data and to test his hypotheses.

Freud was consulted by a lawyer in Vienna who had been hired by a woman to sue a male business associate for making indecent allegations about her. She stated that the man had had photographs taken of them while they were making love and was now threatening to bring disgrace upon her. Because of the unusual nature of her allegation, the lawyer had persuaded her to see Freud so that he could offer an opinion.

The woman, about thirty years of age, was an attractive single person who lived quietly with her mother, whom she supported. A handsome man in her firm had recently begun to court her. After much coaxing he had persuaded her to come to his apartment for an afternoon together. They became intimate, at which point she was frightened by a clicking noise coming from the direction of a desk in front of the window. The lover told her that it was probably from a small clock on the desk. As she left the house that afternoon, she encountered two men, one of them carrying a small package. They appeared to whisper something to each other secretively as she passed. By the time she reached home that evening, she had put together the following story. The box was a camera, the men were photographers, and her lover was an untrustworthy person who had arranged for photographs to be taken of them while they were undressed. The following day she began to berate the lover for his untrustworthiness, and he tried equally hard to rid her mind of her unfounded suspicions. Freud read one of the letters that the man had written to the woman. It struck him that the lover was indeed sincere and honest in denying involvement in such a plot.

Impairments in Life Functioning

Besides the specific symptoms that have been described, schizophrenics have many impairments of what should be the daily routines of their lives. In adolescence the preschizophrenic usually has few social skills, few friends, and no intimates. Dating is infrequent and academic difficulties are common. After leaving high school most schizophrenics are relatively unsuccessful in obtaining and holding a job, and they become ever more seclusive and actively avoid the company of other people. They even keep a definite physical distance from

others and may have difficulty looking people in the eye. Personal hygiene and grooming may become quite cursory. After they have experienced full-blown episodes of schizophrenia, they continue to have many similar problems even between episodes.

Subcategories of Schizophrenia

Three of the types of schizophrenic disorders that are now included in DSM-IIIR—**hebephrenic, catatonic,** and

At this point Freud faced a dilemma common in scientific inquiry. What should the investigator do when confronted with an instance that negates his hypothesis? The persecutor of the young woman appeared to be a member of the opposite sex. Freud could, of course, have completely abandoned his theory that paranoid delusions originate in homosexual impulses. Instead, he looked more closely into the case to see whether there were subtle factors that would allow him, in the end, to preserve the integrity of his theory.

During the second meeting with Freud, the woman changed the story somewhat. She admitted that she had visited the man twice in his apartment, not once, and that only on the second occasion had she heard the suspicious noise. After the first and uneventful visit—as far as her paranoia was concerned—she had been disturbed by an incident that she had witnessed at the office. The next day she had seen her new lover speaking in low tones to an older woman who was in charge of the firm. The older person liked the younger woman a great deal, and the younger woman in turn found that her employer reminded her of her own mother. She was therefore very concerned about their conversation and became convinced that her suitor was telling the woman about their lovemaking the previous afternoon.

Then it occurred to her that her lover and her employer had been having a love affair for some time. At the first opportunity she berated her lover for telling their employer of their lovemaking. He naturally protested and after a while succeeded in undoing her suspicions. Then she made her second visit to his apartment and heard the reputed clicking.

Let us examine Freud's comments on this portion of the case history.

These new details remove first of all any doubts as to the pathological nature of her suspicion. It is easy to see that the white haired elderly manageress is a mother-substitute, that in spite of his youth the lover had been put in the place of the father, and that the strength of the mother-complex has driven the patient to suspect a love-relationship between these ill-matched partners, however unlikely such a relation might be. Moreover, this fresh information resolves the apparent contradiction with the view maintained by psychoanalysis, that the development of a delusion of persecution is conditioned by an overpowerful homosexual bond. The original persecutor—the agency whose influence the patient wishes to escape—is here again not a man but a woman. The manageress knows about the girl's love-affairs, disapproves of them, and shows her disapproval by mysterious allusions. The woman's attachment to her own sex hinders her attempts to adopt a person of the other sex as a love object. (1915, p. 155)

To protect herself unconsciously from her own homosexual impulses, the young woman is presumed to have developed a paranoid delusion about the man and her employer. A crucial aspect of the case, according to Freud, was the click that the woman had heard and interpreted as the sound of a camera shutter. Freud assumed that this click was actually a sensation or beat in her clitoris. Her sexual arousal, then, provided the basis for her paranoid delusion of being photographed.

Freud allowed himself a great deal of unverified inference in this particular case. Because he wanted to hold to a homosexuality-based theory of paranoia, he inferred that the woman regarded her female superior as a substitute for her mother, that she had an undue homosexual attachment to her own mother and by generalization to this older woman, and that the click that she heard and construed in paranoid fashion to be the sound of a camera shutter was really sexual excitement.*

---

*A more general problem with the psychoanalytic theory of paranoia is that many paranoids are *aware* of their homosexual interests. If so, they should have no need unconsciously to form defensive projections.

paranoid—were initially proposed by Kraepelin many years ago. The present descriptions of Kraepelin's original types provide further information on what schizophrenia is like and on the great diversity of behavior that relates to the diagnosis.

Disorganized Schizophrenia

Kraepelin's hebephrenic form of schizophrenia is called *disorganized* schizophrenia by DSM-IIIR and is characterized by a number of rather diffuse and regressive symptoms. Hallucinations and delusions—sexual, hypochondriacal, religious, and persecutory—are profuse and less organized than those of the paranoid schizophrenic. The patient may be subject to bizarre ideas, often involving deterioration of the body. Much of the patient's behavior is marked by a pattern of silliness and absurdity. He may grimace or have a meaningless smile on his face. He giggles childishly and speaks incoherently, stringing together similar-sounding words and inventing neologisms. He is constantly changeable, breaking into inexplicable fits of laughter and crying. All in all, his life seems a tangled skein of delusions, mannerisms, and busy, inconsequential rituals. He may tie a ribbon around his big toe or move incessantly, pointing at objects for no apparent reason. He frequently deteriorates to the point that he becomes incontinent, voiding anywhere and at any time. And he completely neglects his appearance, never bathing, brushing his teeth, or combing his hair.

Catatonic Schizophrenia

The most obvious symptoms of the **catatonic** type of schizophrenia are the motor disturbances discussed earlier. Such individuals typically alternate between catatonic immobility and wild excitement, but one or the other type of motor symptoms may predominate. The onset of catatonic reactions may be more sudden than other forms of schizophrenia, although the person has probably already shown some apathy and withdrawal from reality. The limbs of the immobile catatonic may become stiff and swollen; in spite of apparent obliviousness, he or she may later relate all that occurred during the stupor. In the excited state the catatonic may shout and talk continuously and incoherently, all the while pacing with great agitation. This form of schizophrenia is seldom seen today, perhaps because drug therapy works effectively on these bizarre motor processes.

Paranoid Schizophrenia

A diagnosis of paranoid schizophrenia is assigned to a substantial number of incoming patients to mental hospitals. The key to this diagnosis is the presence of prominent delusions. Usually they are of persecution, but sometimes they may be **grandiose** delusions: individuals may have an exaggerated sense of their own importance, power, knowledge, or identity. Or they may be plagued by **delusional jealousy,** believing their sexual partner to be unfaithful. Vivid auditory and visual hallucinations may also accompany the delusions. These patients often develop what are referred to as **ideas of reference:** they incorporate unimportant events within a delusional framework, reading personal significance into the trivial activities of others. They think that phrases of overhead conversations apply to them, and the continual appearance of a person on a street where they customarily walk means that they are being watched. What they see on television or read in magazines also somehow refers to them. Paranoid schizophrenics are agitated, argumentative, angry, and sometimes violent. But they remain emotionally responsive, although they may be somewhat stilted, formal, and intense with others. And they are more alert and verbal than other schizophrenics; their thought processes, although deluded, have not fragmented (see Box 14.1).

Positive and Negative Symptoms

The Kraepelinian types still form the basis of current diagnostic systems, yet many have questioned their usefulness. Diagnosing types of schizophrenia is extremely difficult, which often means that diagnostic reliability is dramatically reduced. Furthermore, the types have little predictive validity: knowing that a patient has been diagnosed as having one or another form of schizophrenia does not give us information that will be helpful in treatment or in predicting the course of the problems. Finally, there is considerable overlap among types. For example, patients with all forms of schizophrenia may have delusions. Thus the Kraepelinian system of subtyping has not proved to be an optimal way of trying to deal with the variability in schizophrenic behavior.

Supplemental types that have been added by the DSM are also flawed, as definitions of the **undifferentiated** and **residual** types will indicate. The undifferentiated type is for patients who either have psychotic symptoms that do not fit into any other types or have symptoms of more than one type. The diagnosis of residual schizophrenia "should be used when there has been at least one episode of Schizophrenia but the [current] clinical picture . . . is without prominent psychotic symptoms, though signs of the illness persist" (American Psychiatric Association, 1987, p. 198). Clearly, schizophrenia is a disorder with a wide range of possible symptoms. Indeed, Bleuler wrote of the "group of schizophrenias," implying that it is not one but a set of disorders, each perhaps with a different etiology.

Because of this symptomatic variability among schizophrenics there is continuing interest in establishing subtypes. The system currently attracting much interest distinguishes between positive and negative symptoms. **Positive symptoms** consist of excesses, such as hallucinations, delusions, and bizarre behavior. **Negative symptoms** consist of behavioral deficits. In contrast to positive symptoms, negative symptoms are not thoroughly assessed in standard interviews. Andreasen (1982) has therefore developed a new instrument, the Scale for the Assessment of Negative Symptoms, so that they can be reliably rated. This scale assesses four negative symptoms.

1. **Affective Flattening.** A blunting of emotions.
2. **Alogia.** A group of language deficits, including poverty of speech, poverty of content of speech, blocking, and long delays before responding.
3. **Avolition-Apathy.** A lack of interest, drive, and energy manifested as inattention to grooming and hygiene, difficulty in seeking and keeping a job, and a low level of general activity.
4. **Anhedonia-Asociality.** An inability to experience pleasure and feel intimacy, together with little in-

terest in recreational activities, sex, and social re-lationships.[4]

With reliable ratings of both positive and negative symptoms, it becomes possible to divide schizophrenic patients into those with positive symptoms, negative symptoms, and "mixed" symptoms. Andreasen and Olsen (1982), for example, evaluated fifty-two patients diagnosed as schizophrenics according to DSM-III and found that sixteen could be regarded as having negative symptoms, eighteen positive symptoms, and eighteen mixed. Evidence relevant to the validity of this distinction will be given when we discuss the possible roles of dopamine and brain pathology in the etiology of schizophrenia.

TABLE 14.1

Summary of major European family and twin studies of the genetics of schizophrenia (*after Gottesman, McGuffin, and Farmer, 1987*)

Relation to Proband	Percentage Schizophrenic
Spouse	1.00
Grandchildren	2.84
Nieces/nephews	2.65
Children	9.35
Siblings	7.30
DZ twins	12.08
MZ twins	44.30

Research on the Etiology of Schizophrenia

We have now considered *how* schizophrenics differ from normal people in the ways they think, speak, perceive, and imagine. We are now ready to ask *what* can explain the scattering and disconnections of their thoughts, their inappropriate emotions or lack of them, their misguided delusions and bewildering hallucinations. In contrast to other disorders considered in this book, broad theoretical perspectives like psychoanalysis and learning theory have not had much of an impact on research in schizophrenia. Therefore we provide only a brief overview of major theoretical positions in Box 14.2. The specific areas of etiological research are examined in detail, however.

The Genetic Data

Suppose that you wish to find an individual who you know will one day be diagnosed as a schizophrenic and where no behavior patterns or other symptoms can be considered. This problem, suggested by Paul Meehl (1962), has one solution with close to an even chance of picking a potential schizophrenic. *Find an individual who has a schizophrenic identical twin.* There now exists a convincing body of literature indicating that a predisposition for schizophrenia is transmitted genetically. The major methods employed in this research, as in other behavior genetics research projects, are family and twin studies. The findings obtained from these studies will be discussed first and thereafter we will discuss studies of adopted children.[5]

Family Studies

Table 14.1 presents a summary, compiled by Gottesman, McGuffin, and Farmer (1987), of the risk for schizophrenia in various relatives of schizophrenic index cases. In evaluating the figures of this table, bear in mind that the risk for schizophrenia in the general population is a little less than one percent. Quite clearly, relatives of schizophrenics are at increased risk, and the risk increases as the genetic relationship between proband and relative becomes closer. Therefore the data gathered by the family method support the notion that a predisposition for schizophrenia can be transmitted genetically. And yet relatives of a schizophrenic proband share not only genes but also common experiences. A schizophrenic parent's behavior could be very disturbing to a developing child. The influence of the environment cannot be discounted as a rival explanation for the higher morbidity risks.

Twin Studies

Concordance rates for MZ and DZ twins also appear in Table 14.1. Concordance for the identical twins (44.3) is clearly greater than that for the fraternal twins (12.08), but it is less than 100 percent. This is important, for if genetic transmission were the whole story of schizophrenia and one twin was schizophrenic, the other twin would be guaranteed a similar fate because MZ twins are genetically identical.

---

[4]Andreasen (1982) originally included attentional impairment as a negative symptom but subsequent research (e.g., Harvey, 1987) indicates that it is more strongly related to positive symptoms.

[5]Most of the major genetic studies of schizophrenia were conducted before the publication of DSM-III. Fortunately, genetic investigators collected extensive descriptive data on their samples, allowing them to be rediagnosed using newer diagnostic criteria. Reanalyses using DSM-III criteria have substantiated the conclusions reached earlier (e.g., Kendler and Gruenberg, 1984).

BOX 14.2

MAJOR THEORETICAL POSITIONS ON THE ETIOLOGY OF SCHIZOPHRENIA

PSYCHOANALYTIC THEORY

Because Freud himself dealt primarily with neuroses, he had relatively little to say about schizophrenia. He did occasionally speculate on its origins, though, using some of the psychoanalytic concepts that he applied to all disordered personalities. His basic notion was that schizophrenics have regressed to a state of "primary narcissism," a phase early in the oral stage before the ego has differentiated from the id. There is thus no separate ego to engage in reality testing—a crucial function whereby the ego takes actions that test the nature of its social and physical environment. By regressing to narcissism, schizophrenics have effectively lost contact with the world; they have withdrawn the libido from attachment to any objects external to themselves. Freud thought that the cause of the regression was an increase, during adulthood, in the intensity of id impulses, especially sexual ones. Contemporary psychoanalytic theorists give primacy to aggressive impulses. Whether the threats of the intense id impulses provoke schizophrenia or a neurosis depends on the strength of the ego. Neurotics, having developed a more stable ego, will not regress to the first psychosexual stage, as schizophrenics do, and consequently will not lose contact with reality.

Few data bear on the psychoanalytic position. The theory has generated intriguing and speculative analysis of case history material but little research. Studies showing that schizophrenics have cognitive deficits could be said to demonstrate that the egos of schizophrenics have been impaired. But even so, ego impairment need not be precipitated by an increase in id impulses, nor need it end in a regression to a childhood state. Finally, no one has presented evidence that ego impairments cause schizophrenia.

LABELING THEORY

In a radical departure from the traditional conceptualization of schizophrenia, Scheff (1966) suggested that the disorder is a learned social role. This position, also known as *labeling theory,* is essentially unconcerned with etiology. Rather, Scheff argues that the crucial factor in schizophrenia is the act of assigning a diagnostic label to the individual. Presumably this label then influences the manner in which the person will continue to behave, based on the stereotypic notions of mental illness, and at the same time determines the reactions of other people to the individual's behavior. The social role, therefore, *is* the disorder, and it is determined by the labeling process. Without the diagnosis, Scheff argues, deviant behavior—or to use his term, residual rule breaking—would not become stabilized. It would presumably be both transient and relatively inconsequential.

By residual rules Scheff means the rules that are left over after all the formal and obvious ones, about stealing

and violence and fairness, have been laid down. The examples are endless. "Do not stand still staring vacantly in the middle of a busy sidewalk." "Do not talk to the neon beer sign in the delicatessen window." "Do not spit on the piano." Scheff believes that one-time violations of residual rules are fairly common. However, normal people, through poor judgment or bad luck, may be caught violating a rule and be diagnosed as being mentally ill. Once judged so, they are very likely to accept this social role and will find it very difficult to rejoin the sane. Employment will be denied them and other people will know about their pasts. In the hospital they will receive attention and sympathy and be free of all responsibilities. So once there they actually perceive themselves as mentally ill and settle into acting crazy as is expected of them.

Scheff's theory has some intuitive appeal. Most people who have worked for any amount of time at a psychiatric facility have witnessed abuses of the diagnostic process. Patients are sometimes assigned labels that are poorly justified.

Scheff's theory has a number of serious problems, however, indicating that it is, at most, of secondary importance to our understanding of schizophrenia. First of all, Scheff refers to deviance as residual rule breaking, and as described it is indeed merely that. However, calling schizophrenia residual rule breaking trivializes a very serious disorder. Second, very little evidence indicates that unlabeled norm violations are indeed transient, as Scheff implies. Third, information regarding the detrimental effects of the social stigma associated with mental illness is inconclusive (Gove, 1970).

An important correlate of the labeling position is the notion of cultural relativism, according to which definitions of abnormality should be very different in cultures different from our own because of the wide variation in social norms and rules. As an example, proponents of labeling theory might argue that the visions of a shaman are the same as the hallucinations of a schizophrenic but cultural differences allow a favorable response to shamans.

This and several other questions were addressed by Murphy (1976) in a report of her investigations of the Eskimos and Yoruba. Contrary to the labeling view, both cultures had a concept of "being crazy" that is quite similar to our definition of schizophrenia. The Eskimos call it "nuthkavihak," and it includes talking to oneself, refusing to talk, delusional beliefs, and bizarre behavior. The Yoruba call the phenomenon "were" and include similar symptoms under this rubric. Notably, both cultures also have shamans but draw a clear distinction between their behavior and that of "crazy" people.

A final perspective on labeling theory is found in an

Murphy's anthropological research established a clear distinction between the behavior of shamans and that of the mentally ill.

anecdote related by colleagues of Paul Meehl, the famous schizophrenia theorist. Meehl was giving a lecture on genetics and schizophrenia when someone in the audience interrupted him to point out that he thought that schizophrenics behaved in a crazy way because others had labeled them schizophrenic. Meehl had the following reaction:

I just stood there and didn't know what to say. I was thinking of a patient I had seen on a ward who kept his finger up his ass "to keep his thoughts from running out," while with his other hand he tried to tear out his hair because it really "belonged to his father." And here was this man telling me that he was doing these things because someone had called him a schizophrenic. What could I say to him? (Kimble, Garmezy, and Zigler, 1980, p. 453)

AN EXPERIENTIAL THEORY

Ronald Laing, a Scottish existential psychiatrist, has offered a view of schizophrenia that is similar in some respects to labeling theory. For him schizophrenia is not an illness but a label for another kind of problematic experience and behavior.

The experience and behavior that gets labelled schizophrenic is a special sort of strategy that a person invents in order to live in an unlivable situation . . . the person has come to be placed in an untenable position. He cannot make a move or make no move without being beset by contradictory pressures, both internally, from himself, and externally, from those around him. He is, as it were, in a position of checkmate. (1964, p. 186)

Under such stress he will no longer masquerade as the false outer self society expects of him. Rather he retreats from reality backward into his inner world. There he passes through regressive changes, but it is a voyage of discovery on which he may meet and make peace with his true inner self. Then he may emerge again into reality with a whole and authentic identity. Laing considers the family to be the primary culprit producing behavior that is labeled schizophrenia. In what Laing calls *mystification,* the parent has systematically stripped the child's feelings and perceptions about himself and the world of all validity, so that he has come to doubt his hold on reality.

Rather than trying to remove the patient's symptoms, Laing argues that we should accept his or her experience as valid, understandable, and potentially meaningful and beneficial. The schizophrenic is on a psychedelic trip, necessitated by untenable environmental demands, and is in need of guidance—not control—if the destination of that trip is to be a state of enlightenment.

Laing's ideas are popular among those who object to what they consider to be hypocrisies of society and of the mental health establishment. Those who experience the suffering associated with schizophrenia may also take comfort in the belief that they are going through a positive growth process. At this point, however, there is little evidence that experiencing schizophrenia can make a "better person" of the patient. When released from the hospital, most schizophrenics who had a poor premorbid adjustment live a marginal existence and are isolated from social relationships.

In sum, none of the major theoretical positions discussed has much support. Freud's views of regression to the oral stage; labeling theory, which postulates that schizophrenia is role taking reinforced by the attitudes of diagnosticians and mental hospital staff; and Laing's hypothesis that schizophrenia is a trip to improved functioning—all are without substantiating evidence.

TABLE 14.2

Concordance in MZ and DZ twins as defined in three ways (*from Gottesman and Shields, 1972*)

Definition of Concordance	Concordance, percent	
	MZ	DZ
1. Hospitalized and diagnosed schizophrenic	42	9
2. Hospitalized but not schizophrenic, plus those with first-grade concordance	54	18
3. Not hospitalized but abnormal, plus those with first-grade and second-grade concordance	79	45

Gottesman and Shields (1972) studied all twins treated at the Maudsley and Bethlem hospitals in London, England, between the years 1948 and 1964. One of the problems of any twin study of schizophrenia is how to judge concordance. Recognizing the potential problems and biases involved in making psychiatric diagnoses, often of people who were not hospitalized, Gottesman and Shields devised a three-grade system of concordance. All probands were, of course, hospitalized schizophrenics. The co-twins with the first grade of concordance were also hospitalized and diagnosed schizophrenic. Co-twins with the second grade of concordance were hospitalized but not diagnosed as schizophrenic; those with the third grade were abnormal but not hospitalized. Concordance rates for the MZ and DZ twins in the sample, figured cumulatively for the three grades, are shown in Table 14.2. As the definition of concordance is broadened, its rate increases in both MZ and DZ pairs, but concordance of the MZs is always significantly higher than that of the DZs.

Gottesman and Shields have also examined the relationship between severity of schizophrenia in the proband and the rate of concordance. Severity was defined in terms of the total length of hospitalization and the outcome, that is, whether the patient recovered enough to leave the hospital and then engage in gainful employment. When one of a MZ pair was judged severely ill, concordance rates went up dramatically. For example, pairs of MZ twins were divided into two groups; in one group the probands had had less than two years of hospitalization and in the other more than two years of hospitalization. The concordance rate for the first group was 27 percent and for the second 77 percent.

Questions have been raised about the interpretation

of data collected on twins. Some have argued that the experience of being an identical twin may itself predispose toward schizophrenia. If schizophrenia is considered an "identity problem," it might be argued that being a member of an identical pair of twins could be particularly stressful. But schizophrenia occurs about as frequently in single births as in twin births. If the hypothesis were correct, simply being a twin would have to increase the likelihood of becoming schizophrenic—which it does not (Rosenthal, 1970).

But the most critical problem of interpretation remains. Since the twins have been reared together, a common deviant environment rather than common genetic factors could account for the concordance rates. A clever analysis, supporting a genetic interpretation of the high concordance rates found for identical twins, was performed by Fischer (1971). She reasoned that if these rates indeed reflected a genetic effect, the children of even the discordant, or nonschizophrenic, identical co-twins of schizophrenics should be at high risk for schizophrenia. These nonschizophrenic twins would presumably have the genotype for schizophrenia, even though it was not expressed behaviorally, and thus might pass along an increased risk for the disorder to their children. In agreement with this line of reasoning, the rate of schizophrenia and schizophreniclike psychoses in the children of nonschizophrenic co-twins of schizophrenic probands was 9.4 percent. The rate among the children of the schizophrenic probands themselves was only slightly and nonsignificantly higher, 12.3 percent. Both rates are substantially higher than those found in an unselected population.

Dworkin and his colleagues have reevaluated the major twin studies according to the positive–negative symptom distinction discussed earlier (Dworkin and Lenzenweger, 1984; Dworkin *et al.*, 1987). Ratings of positive and negative symptoms were compiled from published case histories of the twins and compared for probands of concordant and discordant pairs. No differences emerged for positive symptoms but probands from concordant pairs were higher in negative symptoms than probands from discordant pairs. These data suggest that negative symptoms have a stronger genetic component than positive ones.

Adoptee Studies

A study of children of schizophrenic mothers reared from early infancy by adoptive parents has provided more conclusive information on the role of genes in schizophrenia. This study eliminated the possible effects of a deviant environment. Heston (1966) was able to follow up forty-seven people who had been born to schizophrenic mothers while they were in a state mental hospital. The infants were separated from the mothers at birth and raised by either foster or adoptive parents.

TABLE 14.3
Subjects separated from their schizophrenic mothers in early infancy (*from Heston, 1966*)

Assessment	Offspring of Schizophrenic Mother	Control Offspring, Mothers Not Schizophrenic
Number of subjects	47	50
Mean age at follow-up	35.8	36.3
Overall ratings of disability (low score indicates more pathology)	65.2	80.1
Number diagnosed schizophrenic	5	0
Number diagnosed mentally defective	4	0
Number diagnosed sociopathic	9	2
Number diagnosed neurotic	13	7

In addition, fifty control subjects were selected from the same foundling homes that had placed the children of schizophrenic mothers. The control group was matched to the schizophrenics by sex, where they were eventually placed, and for the length of time in a child care institution. As one might expect, exact matching in each case was not always possible. All forty-seven subjects were born between 1915 and 1945.

The follow-up assessment, conducted in 1964, consisted of an interview, MMPI, IQ test, social class ratings, and the like. A dossier on each of these subjects was then rated independently by two psychiatrists, and a third evaluation was made by Heston. Ratings were made on a 0 to 100 scale of overall disability and, whenever possible, psychiatric diagnoses were offered. Ratings of disability proved to be quite reliable, and when the number of diagnostic categories was reduced to four—schizophrenia, mental deficiency, sociopathy, and neurosis—diagnostic agreement was also acceptable.

The control subjects were rated as less disabled than were the children of schizophrenic mothers. Similarly, thirty-one of the forty-seven children of schizophrenic mothers (66 percent) were given a psychiatric diagnosis, but only nine out of fifty control subjects (18 percent) were. None of the control subjects was diagnosed schizophrenic, but 16.6 percent of the offspring of schizophrenic mothers were so diagnosed.[6] In addition to this

greater likelihood of being diagnosed schizophrenic, the children of schizophrenic mothers were more likely to be diagnosed mentally defective, sociopathic, and neurotic (Table 14.3). They had been involved more frequently in criminal activity, had spent more time in penal institutions, and had more often been discharged from the armed services for psychiatric reasons. Heston's study clearly supports the importance of genetic factors in the development of schizophrenia. Children reared without contact with their so-called "pathogenic mothers" were still more likely to become schizophrenic than were the controls.

A study similar to Heston's was carried out in Denmark under Kety's direction (Kety *et al.*, 1968, 1976). In Denmark a lifelong and up-to-date listing of the address of every resident is kept, and a National Psychiatric Register maintains records on every psychiatric hospitalization in the country. The starting point for the investigation was a culling of the records of all children who had been adopted at an early age between the years 1924 and 1947. All adoptees who had later been admitted to a psychiatric facility and diagnosed schizophrenic were selected as the index cases. From the remaining cases the investigators chose a control group who had no psychiatric history and who were matched to the index group on variables such as sex and age. Both the adoptive and the biological parents and the siblings and half-siblings of the two groups were then identified, and a search was made to determine who of them had a psychiatric history. As might be expected if genetic factors figure in schizophrenia, the biological relatives of the index cases were diagnosed schizophrenic more often than were members of the general population. The adoptive relatives were not.

---

[6]The 16.6 percent figure was *age-corrected*. By this process raw data are corrected to take into account the age of the subjects involved. If a subject in Heston's sample was only twenty-four at the time of the assessment, he might still have become schizophrenic at some later point in his life. The age correction procedure attempts to account for this possibility.

Evaluation of the Genetic Data

All the data collected so far indicate that genetic factors play an important role in the development of schizophrenia. Earlier twin and family studies deserved the criticism of environmentalists, who found that investigators had not acknowledged upbringing as a possible contributing factor. But later studies of children of schizophrenic mothers and fathers, who were reared in foster and adoptive homes, plus the follow-up of relatives of adopted schizophrenics, indicate the importance of genetic transmission, for the potential biasing influence of the environment had been virtually removed. As Seymour Kety, the highly regarded schizophrenia researcher, has quipped, "If schizophrenia is a myth, it is a myth with a heavy genetic component" (9174).

We cannot conclude, however, that schizophrenia is a disorder completely determined by genetic transmission. The less than 100 percent concordance rate of identical twins would argue against this, and we must always keep in mind the distinction made between phenotype and genotype (see page 142). The diathesis–stress model, introduced in Chapter 2, seems appropriate for guiding theory and research into the etiology of schizophrenia. Genetic factors can only be predisposers for a behavioral disorder. Stress is required to render this predisposition an observable pathology. And yet the exact sources of stress are rather vague at this point. Low social class and certain patterns of family interaction are two areas we will discuss. There is also some evidence that, in the weeks preceding hospitalization, schizophrenics experience an increased number of stressful life events (Brown and Birley, 1968). But, on the whole, additional research is needed on how particular environmental stressors trigger schizophrenia in an already predisposed person.

Biochemical Factors

Speculation concerning possible biochemical[7] causes of schizophrenia began almost as soon as the syndrome was identified. Kraepelin thought in terms of a chemical imbalance, as already indicated, for he believed that poisons secreted from the sex glands affected the brain to produce the symptoms. Carl Jung suggested the presence of "toxin X," a mystery chemical that he thought would eventually be identified. The demonstrated role of genetic factors in schizophrenia also suggests that biochemicals should be investigated, for it is through

the body chemistry and physiological processes that heredity may have an effect.

The extensive and continuing search for possible biochemical cuases has a principal difficulty to overcome. If an aberrant biochemical is found in schizophrenics and not in control subjects, the difference in biochemical functioning may have been produced by a third variable rather than by the disorder. Most schizophrenic patients, for example, take psychoactive medication. Although the effects of such drugs on behavior diminish quite rapidly once they are discontinued, traces of them may remain in the bloodstream for very long periods of time, making if difficult to attribute a biochemical difference between schizophrenic and control subjects to schizophrenia per se. Prolonged drug therapy may also lead to changes in the very process of neural transmission. Institutionalized patients may also smoke more, drink more coffee, have a less nutritionally adequate diet than various control groups, and they may be relatively inactive. All these variables can conspire to produce biochemical differences between schizophrenic and control patients that confound attempts to seek deviant biochemicals in schizophrenics. Nonetheless, the search for biochemical causes of schizophrenia proceeds at a rapid rate. Tremendous advances now allow a much greater understanding of the relation between biochemistry and behavior. At present no biochemical theory has unequivocal support but because of the great amount of effort that continues to be spent in the search for biochemical causes of schizophrenia, we shall review one of the best-researched factors.

Excess Dopamine Activity

The theory that schizophrenia is brought on by excess activity of the neurotransmitter dopamine is based principally on information concerning the mode of action of drugs that are effective in treating schizophrenia. If the biochemical activity of a therapeutically effective drug is understood, or at least hypothesized, the process responsible for the disorder may be guessed at too.[8] The *phenothiazines* (see page 399), in addition to alleviating some symptoms of schizophrenia, produce side effects resembling Parkinson's disease. Parkinsonism is known to be caused, in part, by low levels of dopamine in a particular nerve tract of the brain (see page 646). It is therefore supposed that phenothiazines interfere with dopamine activity. Phenothiazine molecules are assumed, because of the structural similarities to the dopamine molecule (Figure 14.1), to fit into and thereby

---

[7]This section is necessarily technical, and for readers who have not studied biochemistry, it may be unusually difficult to follow. We want to provide the details, however, for those who have this background. For those who lack it, we hope at least to convey the logic and general trends in the research on biochemical factors.

---

[8]Although the therapeutic effects of a drug may provide a *clue* to the causes of the disorder it helps to alleviate, we must be mindful once again that treatment effects cannot logically prove the case for etiology or even for the current causes of the problem in question.

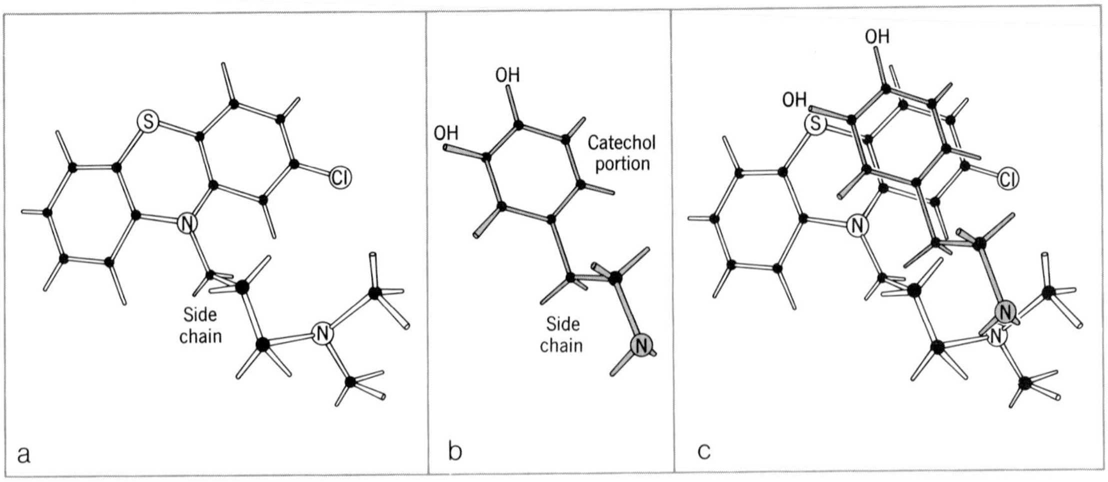

FIGURE 14.1
Conformations of (a) chlorpromazine, a phenothiazine, and (b) dopamine and (c) their superimposition, determined by X-ray crystallographic analysis. Chlorpromazine blocks impulse transmission by dopamine by fitting into its receptor sites. Adapted from Horn and Snyder, 1971.

block postsynaptic receptors in dopamine tracts. From this speculation about the action of the drugs that help schizophrenics, it is but a short inductive leap to view schizophrenia as resulting from excess activity in dopamine nerve tracts.

Further indirect support for the theory of **excess dopamine activity** comes from the literature on amphetamine psychosis. Amphetamines can produce a state that closely resembles paranoid schizophrenia, and they can exacerbate the symptomatology of a schizophrenic (Angrist, Lee, and Gershon, 1974). The amphetamines are thought to act either by directly releasing catecholamines into the synaptic cleft or by preventing their inactivation (Snyder *et al.*, 1974). We can be relatively confident that the psychosis-inducing effects of amphetamines come from their impact on dopamine, rather than norepinephrine, for phenothiazines are antidotes to amphetamine psychosis.

The major metabolite of dopamine, homovanillic acid, has been examined, with the expectation that it would be present in greater amounts in schizophrenics. Homovanillic acid can be measured in cerebrospinal fluid by treating patients with probenecid, a drug that prevents the transfer of homovanillic acid from cerebrospinal fluid to blood. But Bowers (1974) found that before drug treatment schizophrenics had lower levels of homovanillic acid than patients with affective illness, and that levels of homovanillic acid in schizophrenics increased when they were reassessed during treatment. Post and his colleagues (1975) found no differences in levels of homovanillic acid in schizophrenics and several control groups.

The theory of excess dopamine transmission is not strongly refuted by the evidence collected in the studies of homovanillic acid. Dopaminergic overactivity has not, perhaps, been specified precisely enough. The predictions of increased levels of homovanillic acid assume that the dopamine-releasing neurons are overactive. But it may be that in schizophrenia dopamine *receptors* are overactive or oversensitive. In fact, the work on the phenothiazines' mode of action would suggest that the dopaminergic receptors are a more likely locus of disorder. Indeed, some postmortem studies of schizophrenics' brains have revealed that dopamine receptors may have either increased in number or been hyperactive (Lee and Seeman, 1977; Mackay *et al.*, 1982). If increased activity of the dopaminergic receptors is the key to schizophrenia, the data concerning levels of homovanillic acid are not crucially relevant.

In an impressive study, Wong *et al.*, (1986) used positron emission tomography (PET) (cf. page 85 in Chapter 4) to study dopamine receptors in schizophrenic patients who had never been treated with drugs. It has now been discovered that there are two main classes of dopamine receptors called D1 and D2. They differ in the biochemical process by which they interact with neurotransmitter and stimulate the postsynaptic cell. Wong and his colleagues focused their efforts on the D2 receptor, the one on which phenothiazines work. In this application of PET technology a chemical that is known to bind to dopamine receptors is radioactively labeled and injected into the patient. When the substance reaches the brain and binds to dopamine receptors, the positrons that are emitted interact with electrons; an annihilation results and two photons are emitted. A series of crystalline detectors, mounted in rings around the patient's head, detect the photons and computers use this information to develop an image of the brain, in this case of the density of dopamine receptors. Corroborating the dopamine theory, the density of D2 receptors was found to be significantly greater in the drug-naive schizophrenics than in either a group of drug-treated schizophrenics or normals.

Other research on the excess-dopamine-activity theory has revealed that it may not be applicable to all schizophrenics. Some studies have now shown, for example, that amphetamines do not worsen the symptoms of all patients (e.g., Kornetsky, 1976), and one study has even reported that symptoms lessen after an amphetamine has been administered (Kammen et al., 1977). Furthermore, phenothiazines have been shown to benefit only a subgroup of patients. In both instances the divergent results are related to the positive–negative symptom distinction noted earlier (see page 386). Amphetamines worsen positive symptoms and lessen negative ones. Phenothiazines lessen positive symptoms but have little or no effect on negative symptoms (Haracz, 1982). The dopamine theory appears to apply only to schizophrenics with positive symptoms.

Even in this more limited context, the hypothesis cannot be regarded as having been proved, for it has difficulty handling some other effects. For example, phenothiazines gradually lessen positive schizophrenic symptoms over a period of several weeks, but the drugs rapidly block dopamine receptors, and after several weeks tolerance should have developed (Davis, 1978). This disjunction between the clinical and pharmacological effects of phenothiazines is difficult to understand within the context of the theory. It is also puzzling that phenothiazines have to reduce dopamine levels or receptor activity to *below normal*, producing Parkinsonian side effects, if they are to be therapeutically effective. According to the theory, reducing dopamine levels or receptor activity to normal should be sufficient for a therapeutic effect, but apparently it is not. Thus, although the dopamine explanation remains the most actively researched biochemical position, it is not likely to be a complete theory of the biochemistry of schizophrenia.

Evaluation of Biochemical Data

The history of research on whether biochemicals figure in schizophrenia has been one of discovery followed by failures to replicate. Many methodological problems plague this research, and many confounds, unrelated to whether or not a subject is schizophrenic, can produce biochemical differences. Thus we must maintain a cautious attitude toward the excess-dopamine-activity theory. Furthermore, studies on biochemicals can indicate only that a particular substance and its physiological processes are associated with schizophrenia. Dopamine activity might become excessive *after* rather than *before* the onset of the disorder.

Neurological Findings

The search for a brain lesion that causes schizophrenia, like that for a biochemical, began as early as the syndrome was identified. But the research did not prove promising, for studies when replicated did not yield the same findings. Interest gradually waned over the years. In the last two decades, however, spurred by a number of methodological advances, the field has reawakened and yielded some promising evidence (Seidman, 1983; Weinberger, Wagner, and Wyatt, 1983). A percentage of schizophrenics—the exact number cannot be specified—have been found to have observable brain pathology.

Postmortem analysis of the brains of schizophrenic patients is one source of this evidence. These studies consistently reveal abnormalities in schizophrenics' brains, although the specific problems reported vary from study to study (Weinberger, Wagner, and Wyatt, 1983). Even more impressive are the images obtained in CAT scan studies. Researchers were quick to apply this new tool to the living brains of schizophrenics. Thus far these images of living brain tissue, with a resolution of less than one millimeter, have most consistently revealed that a proportion of schizophrenics have enlarged ventricles, suggesting deterioration or atrophy of brain tissue. Large ventricles are in turn correlated with impaired performance on neuropsychological tests, poor premorbid adjustment, poor response to drug treatment, and the presence of negative symptoms (Weinberger et al., 1980; Andreasen et al., 1982).[9] A variety of data suggest that the frontal lobes are also of particular importance. In studies of the sulci (the shallow furrows in the cerebral cortex), frontal rather than general atrophy is found (Doran et al., 1985). In applications of PET scanning in which glucose metabolism is studied in various brain regions while subjects perform psychological tests, schizophrenics show low metabolic rates in the frontal lobes (Buchsbaum et al., 1984). Schizophrenics also perform poorly on the Wisconsin Card Sorting Test, a neuropsychological test that assesses frontal cortical functioning (Goldberg et al., 1987).

---

[9]Enlarged ventricles are also found in the CAT scans of other psychotic patients and are not specific to schizophrenia (Rieder et al., 1983).

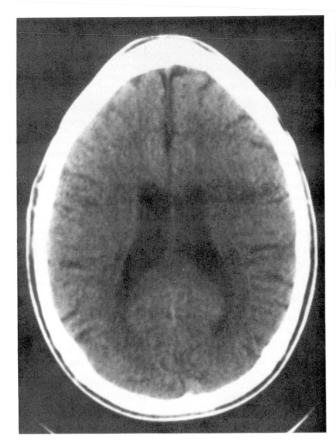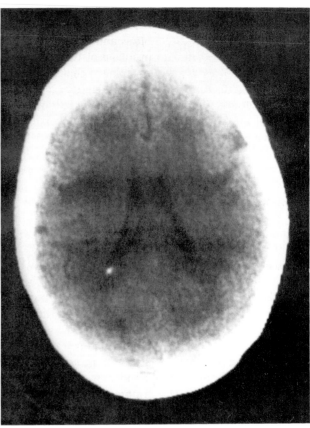

CAT scan images of the brain in horizontal section. The ventricles show up as dark areas toward the center. The ventricles of the brain of the schizophrenic (left) are clearly enlarged as compared to those of a normal brain (right).

A possible interpretation of these neurological abnormalities is that they result from infection by a virus that invades the brain and damages it. Some data suggest that the infection could occur during fetal development. Mednick and his colleagues (1988) addressed this possibility in a study performed in Helsinki, Finland. During a five-week period in 1957 Helsinki had experienced an epidemic of influenza virus. Rates of schizophrenia were examined in adults who had been exposed during their mothers' pregnancies. Those exposed during the second trimester of pregnancy had much higher rates than those exposed in either of the other trimesters or in nonexposed controls. This is an intriguing finding, especially since cortical development is in a critical stage of growth during the second trimester.

All the evidence suggests that these malfunctionings are likely to appear in patients with chronic, negative symptoms. Thus investigators may be on the verge of isolating a subgroup of schizophrenic patients who have signs of brain pathology and suffer negative symptoms.

Social Class and Schizophrenia

Numerous studies have shown a relation between social class and the diagnosis of schizophrenia. The highest rates of schizophrenia are found in central city areas inhabited by the lowest socioeconomic classes (e.g., Hollingshead and Redlich, 1958; Srole *et al.*, 1962). The relationship between social class and schizophrenia does not show a continuous progression of higher rates of schizophrenia as the social class becomes lower. Rather, there is a decidedly sharp difference between the number of schizophrenics in the lowest social class and those in others. In the ten-year Hollingshead and Redlich study of social class and mental illness in New Haven, Connecticut, the rate of schizophrenia was found to be twice as high in the lowest social class as in the next to the lowest. The findings of Hollingshead and Redlich have been confirmed cross-culturally by similar community studies carried out in countries such as Denmark, Norway, and England (Kohn, 1968).[10]

---

[10]There is perhaps one exception to this finding: the relationship may disappear in nonurban areas (Clausen and Kohn, 1959).

The correlations between social class and schizophrenia are consistent, but they are still difficult to interpret in causal terms. Some people believe that being in a low social class may in itself cause schizophrenia. This is called the *sociogenic hypothesis.* The degrading treatment a person receives from others, the low level of education, and the unavailability of rewards and opportunity, taken together, may make membership in the lowest social class such a stressful experience that the individual develops schizophrenia.

But another explanation of the correlation between schizophrenia and low social class has also been suggested, the *social-drift theory.* During the course of their developing psychosis, schizophrenics may "drift" into the poverty-ridden areas of the city. The growing cognitive and motivational problems besetting these individuals may so impair their earning abilities that they cannot afford to live elsewhere. Or they may by choice move to areas where little social pressure will be brought to bear on them and where they can escape intense social relationships.

One way of resolving the conflict between these two differing theories is to study the social mobility of schizophrenics. Three studies (Schwartz, 1946; Lystad, 1957; Turner and Wagonfeld, 1967) have found that schizophrenics are downwardly mobile in occupational status. But an equal number of studies have shown schizophrenics *not* to be downwardly mobile (Hollingshead and Redlich, 1958; Clausen and Kohn, 1959; Dunham, 1965). Kohn (1968) suggested another way of examining this question. Are the fathers of schizophrenics also from the lowest social class? If they are, this could be considered evidence in favor of the hypothesis that lower-class status is conducive to schizophrenia, for class would be shown to *precede* schizophrenia. If the fathers are from a higher social class, the drift hypothesis would be the better explanation.

Goldberg and Morrison (1963) conducted such a study in England and Wales. They reported that the occupations of male schizophrenic patients were less remunerative and prestigious than those of their fathers. Turner and Wagonfeld (1967) conducted a similar study in the United States and found evidence for both the sociogenic and drift hypothesis. Fathers of schizophrenics were more frequently from the lowest social class, supporting the sociogenic hypothesis. But at the same time many of these schizophrenics were lower in occupational prestige than their fathers, supporting the drift hypothesis. Thus it appears that both theories are partially correct. Some, but not all, of the relationship between social class and schizophrenia can be accounted for by the drift hypothesis. Social class appears to play a causal role, but the exact way in which the stresses associated with it exert their effect remains unknown.

Schizophrenia and the Family

Many theorists have regarded family relationships, especially those between a mother and her son, as crucial in the development of schizophrenia. The view has been so prevalent that the term *schizophrenogenic mother* has been coined for the supposedly cold and dominant, conflict-inducing parent who is said to produce schizophrenia in her offspring (Fromm-Reichmann, 1948). These mothers have also been characterized as rejecting, overprotective, self-sacrificing, impervious to the feelings of others, rigid and moralistic about sex, and fearful of intimacy.[11]

Another prominent early theory is the *double bind* proposed by Bateson and his colleagues (1956). These writers believed that an important factor in the development of schizophrenic thought disorder is the constant subjection of an individual to a so-called double-bind situation. A double-bind has the following aspects.

1. The individual has an intense relationship to another, so intense that it is especially important to be able to understand communications from the other person accurately so that the individual can respond appropriately.

2. The other person expresses two messages when making a statement, one of which denies the other.

3. The individual cannot comment on the mutually contradictory messages and cannot withdraw from the situation or ignore the messages.

In their original paper Bateson and his colleagues gave the following example.

A young man who had fairly well recovered from an acute schizophrenic episode was visited in the hospital by his mother. He was glad to see her and impulsively put his arm around her shoulders whereupon she stiffened. He withdrew his arm and she asked, "Don't you love me anymore?" He then blushed and she said, "Dear, you must not be so easily embarrassed and afraid of your feelings." The patient was able to stay with her only a few minutes more and following her departure he assaulted an aide. . . .

Obviously, this result could have been avoided if the young man had been able to say, "Mother, it is obvious that you become uncomfortable when I put my arm around you, and you have difficulty accepting a gesture of affection from me." However, the schizophrenic patient doesn't have this possibility open to him. An intense dependency in training prevents him

---

[11]It is noteworthy that most theories implicating family processes in the etiology of abnormal behavior focus almost exclusively on the mother. Sexism?

from commenting upon his mother's communicative behavior, though she comments on his and forces him to accept and to attempt to deal with the complicated sequence. . . .

The impossible dilemma thus becomes: "If I am to keep my tie to my mother, I must not show her that I love her, but if I do not show her that I love her then I will lose her." (pp. 258–259)

Controlled studies evaluating these two theories have not yielded supporting data. Studies of families of schizophrenics have, however, revealed that they differ in some ways from normal families, for example, showing vague patterns of communication and high levels of conflict. But whether these family processes should be viewed as playing a causal role in the development of schizophrenia is questionable. It is equally plausible that the conflict and unclear communication are a response to having a young schizophrenic in the family. Indeed, some evidence favors this interpretation. For example, Liem (1974) had a number of families with a schizophrenic son and control families with a normal son participate in an object identification task. The "communicator" was given the task of describing common objects, such as lamp or match, and concepts, such as teacher or child, so that a listener could identify them. Each schizophrenic son and each normal son had a turn in the role of communicator. Each set of parents took a role together as a communicator. Later parents and sons responded to different tapes, giving an answer after each description. The parents responded to tapes made by their own son, by an unknown nonschizophrenic son, and by an unknown schizophrenic son. The sons responded to tapes made by their own parents, unknown parents of a normal son, and unknown parents of a schizophrenic son.

How does this study relate to the possible role of the family in the etiology of schizophrenia? If unclear communication by the parents of a schizophrenic is assigned a *causal* role, we might expect their descriptions to be indeed inadequate and confusing to anyone who listens to them. In contrast, if the parents of a schizophrenic are *reacting* to their child's disorder, we would not expect their descriptions to be inadequate, but we would expect *all* parents to have difficulty interpreting the tape-recorded communications of a schizophrenic son. This second pattern is the one borne out by Liem's study. In the author's own words:

The communication disorder of schizophrenic sons had an immediate, observable, negative effect not only on the parents of schizophrenic sons but on all parents who heard and attempted to respond to them. Disorder was not observed in the communications of par-

TABLE 14.4
Adjustment of adopted-away children of schizophrenic parents related to maladjustment of adoptive families (from Tienari et al., 1987)

Clinical Ratings of Children	Degree of Family Maladjustment		
	None/mild	Moderate	Severe
Healthy/mild disturbance	39	9	3
Moderate	10	9	24
Severe	0	11	16

ents of schizophrenic sons nor were their communications found to adversely affect sons who heard and responded to them. (p. 445)

Studies like Liem's, however, may not accurately reflect actual everyday interactions between a schizophrenic and his or her parents. Therefore we cannot conclude that the faulty communications of parents play no role in the etiology of schizophrenia. Indeed, some recent findings suggest that they do. One of these studies is the University of California at Los Angeles Family Project (Goldstein and Rodnick, 1975). In this project adolescents with behavior problems were studied intensively along with their families. A five-year follow-up revealed that a number of the young people had developed schizophrenia or schizophrenia-related disorders. The investigators were then able to relate these disorders discovered at follow-up to any deviance in the communications of parents that had been evident five years earlier. Communication deviances of parents were indeed found to be a predictor of the later onset of schizophrenia in their offspring, supporting its significance (Norton, 1982). It does not appear, however, that communication deviance is a *specific* etiological factor for schizophrenia since parents of manics are equally high on this variable (Miklowitz, 1985).

Further evidence favoring some role for the family comes from a very substantial adoption study being conducted in Finland by Tienari and his colleagues (1987). A large sample of adopted-away offspring of schizophrenic mothers has been studied along with a control group. As of 1987, 112 children of schizophrenics and 135 controls had been assessed. Unlike Heston's adoption study, extensive data were collected on various aspects of family life in the adoptive families. Data on the adjustment of the children were related to data collected on their adoptive familes. The families were categorized into levels of maladjustment based on material from clinical interviews as well as psychological tests. The major data are shown in Table 14.4. As can be seen, more severe problems in adopted children of schizophrenics are clearly associated with more "pathological" environments. Also notable in this study was the fact that family environment was *not* related to psychopathology in the control adoptees. Both a genetic predisposition (diathesis) and a noxious environment (stress) are therefore necessary to increase risk for psychopathology.

A series of studies conducted in London indicate that the family can also have an important impact on the adjustment of patients *after* they leave the hospital. Brown and his colleagues (1966) conducted a nine-month follow-up study of a sample of schizophrenics who returned to live with their families after being discharged from the hospital. Interviews were conducted with parents or spouses before discharge and rated for the number of critical comments made about the patient and for expressions of hostility toward or emotional overinvolvement with him or her. On the basis of this variable, called ***expressed emotion*** (EE), families were divided into those revealing a great deal, high-EE families, and those revealing little, low-EE families. At the end of the follow-up period, 10 percent of the patients returning to low-EE homes had relapsed. In marked contrast, 58 percent of the patients returning to a high-EE home had gone back to the hospital in the same period! This research, which has since been replicated (Vaughn and Leff, 1976; Leff, 1976; MacMillan *et al.*, 1981; Koenigsberg and Hadley, 1986); indicates that the environment to which patients are discharged has great bearing on whether or not they are rehospitalized. What is not yet clear, however, is exactly how to interpret the effects of EE. Is EE causal or do these attitudes reflect a reaction to the patients' behavior? For example, if the condition of a schizophrenic begins to deteriorate, family concern and involvement may be increased. The other side of this coin is that family criticism and efforts to control the schizophrenic may also increase. Indeed, bizarre or dangerous behavior by the schizophrenic can be seen to call for limit-setting and other familial efforts that come under the rubric of expressed emotion (Kanter, Lamb, and Loeper, 1987). Finally, a focus on expressed emotion runs the risk of needlessly blaming the family for the patient's illness, provoking the kind of guilt and hurt that will be dealt with in our discussion of infantile autism (Box 16.5).

High-Risk Studies of Schizophrenia

How does schizophrenia develop? An earlier method of answering this question was to construct developmental histories by examining the childhood records of those who had later become schizophrenics. This research did indeed show that those who were to become schizophrenics were different from their contemporaries even before any serious problems were noted in their behavior. Albee and Lane and their colleagues repeatedly found preschizophrenics to have a lower IQ than members of various control groups, which usually consisted of siblings and neighborhood peers (Albee, Lane, and Reuter, 1964; Lane and Albee, 1965). Investigations of the social behavior of preschizophrenics yielded some interesting findings; for example, teachers have described male schizophrenics as having been disagreeable in childhood and female schizophrenics as passive (Watt *et al.*, 1970; Watt, 1974). Both have been described as delinquent and withdrawn (Berry, 1967).

But these findings are gross and nonspecific; certainly the traits mentioned would also be found in children and adolescents who are not destined to become schizophrenic. The major limitation of this type of developmental research is that the data on which it relies were not originally collected with the intention of describing preschizophrenics or of predicting the development of schizophrenia from childhood behavior. More specific information is required if developmental histories are to be a source of new hypotheses.

The high-risk method, described in Chapter 5, can yield such information. The first such study of schizophrenia was begun in the 1960s by Sarnoff Mednick and Fini Schulsinger. Denmark was chosen because the registries of all people make it possible to keep track of them for long periods of time. Mednick and Schulsinger selected as their high-risk subjects 207 young people whose mothers were chronic schizophrenics and had had poor premorbid adjustment. It was decided that the mother should be the parent suffering the disorder because paternity is not always easy to determine and because schizophrenic women have more children than do schizophrenic men. Then 104 low-risk subjects, individuals whose mothers were not schizophrenics, were matched to the high-risk subjects on variables such as sex, age, father's occupation, rural–urban residence, years of education, and institutional upbringing versus rearing by the family.

In 1972 the now-grown men and women of the high-risk sample and of the low-risk group were followed up through a number of measures, including a diagnostic battery. Seventeen of the high-risk subjects, nine men and eight women, were diagnosed schizophrenic. None of the control men and women was so diagnosed. The follow-up also revealed that six high-risk subjects had committed suicide, as compared to none of the low-risk subjects. Looking back to the information collected on the subjects when they were children, the investigators

Sarnoff Mednick, of the University of Southern California, and Fini Schulsinger, of the University of Copenhagen, pioneers in applying the high-risk longitudinal method of studying schizophrenia.

found that several circumstances predicted the later onset of schizophrenia. For boys, separation from parents early in life and being brought up in an institution predicted later schizophrenia (Walker *et al.*, 1982). The separation from their parents was also related to an early onset of schizophrenia in their mothers and to lower-class status. The mothers of the schizophrenic boys had more pregnancy and birth complications while carrying and delivering them. For girls, the only circumstance predicting schizophrenia was an early onset of the disorder in their mothers, which in turn related to lower-class status (Mednick, Schulsinger, and Griffith, 1981). These early returns, granted that they come from a small study, seem to suggest that the etiology of schizophrenia may differ for men and women.

In the wake of Mednick and Schulsinger's pioneering study a number of other high-risk investigations began. Some of them have yielded information concerning the prediction of adult psychopathology. The New York High-Risk Study found that a composite measure of attentional dysfunction predicted behavioral disturbance at follow-up (Cornblatt and Erlenmeyer-Kimling, 1985). Furthermore, low IQ has been a characteristic of the first high-risk children to be hospitalized (Erlenmeyer-Kimling and Cornblatt, 1987). In an Israeli study, poor neurobehavioral functioning (poor concentration, poor verbal ability, lack of motor control and coordination) predicted schizophrenialike outcomes as did earlier interpersonal problems (Marcus *et al.*, 1987). As subjects in other studies mature we will gain further glimpses of the development of this debilitating disorder.

Therapies for Schizophrenia

The puzzling, often frightening array of phenomena that plague schizophrenics makes one wonder how they can possibly he helped. The history of psychopathology, reviewed in Chapter 1, is in many respects a history of humankind's efforts, often brutal and unenlightened, to deal with schizophrenia. Although some of the insane people condemned centuries ago as witches or confined in foul asylums may have suffered from problems as prosaic as food poisoning or syphilis (see pages 14 and 20), there seems little doubt that many, were they to be examined now, would carry a diagnosis of schizophrenia. Until the advent of deinstitutionalization, somatic and psychological therapies for schizophrenia were for the most part administered within a hospital.

Somatic Treatments

Shock and Psychosurgery

The general warehousing of severely disturbed patients in mental hospitals earlier in this century, coupled with the shortage of professional staff, created a climate that allowed, perhaps even subtly encouraged, experimentation with radical somatic interventions. In the early 1930s, inducing a coma with large dosages of insulin was introduced by Sakel (1938), who claimed that up to three-quarters of the schizophrenics he treated showed significant improvement. But later findings by others were less encouraging, and ***insulin coma therapy***, which presented serious risks to health, including irreversible coma and even death, was gradually abandoned.

In 1935 Moniz, a Portuguese psychiatrist, introduced the ***prefrontal lobotomy***, a surgical procedure that destroys the tracts connecting the frontal lobes to lower centers of the patient's brain. His initial reports, like those of Sakel for insulin coma therapy, claimed high rates of success (Moniz, 1936), and for twenty years thereafter hundreds of mental patients underwent variations of psychosurgery, especially if their behavior was violent. Many of them did indeed quiet down and could even be discharged from hospitals. But during the 1950s this intervention too fell into disrepute, for several reasons. Many patients suffered serious losses in their cognitive capacities—which is not surprising, given the destruction of parts of their brain believed responsible for thought and became dull and listless, or even died. The principal reason for its abandonment, however, was the introduction of drugs that seemed to reduce the behavioral and emotional excesses of many patients.

One Flew Over the Cuckoo's Nest provides a compelling illustration of the horrors of older mental hospitals and the treatments then in use.

Electroconvulsive therapy (ECT) has been in use since its development in 1938 by Cerletti and Bini. Electrodes are placed on both temples, more recently on only one temple, and a current of between 70 and 130 volts is applied for a fraction of a second. A seizure is thereby induced, followed by a period of unconsciousness. In the treatment of schizophrenia, ECT has, like psychosurgery, proved to be basically ineffective and has given way to the several psychotropic medications, although it remains an apparently effective treatment for profoundly depressed patients.

Drug Therapies

Without question the most important development in the treatment of the schizophrenia disorders was the advent in the 1950s of several drugs collectively referred to as antipsychotic medications. They are also called **neuroleptics** because, in addition to their beneficial effects, they have side effects similar to the behavioral manifestations of neurological diseases. One of the more frequently prescribed neuroleptic drugs, **phenothiazines,** was first produced by a German chemist in the late nineteenth century and used to treat parasitic worm infections of the digestive system of animals. However, it was not until the discovery of the antihistamines by Bovet in the 1940s that phenothiazines were given any attention; antihistamines have a phenothiazine nucleus! Reaching beyond their use to treat the common cold and asthma, the French surgeon Laborit pioneered the use of antihistamines to reduce surgical shock. He no-

ticed that they made his patients somewhat sleepy and less fearful about the impending operation. Laborit's work encouraged the drug companies to reexamine antihistamines in light of their tranquilizing effects. Shortly thereafter a French chemist, Charpentier, prepared a new phenothiazine derivative and called it chlorpromazine. It proved very effective in calming schizophrenics. Phenothiazines are now believed to block impulse transmission in the dopaminergic pathways of the brain, which gives them their therapeutic properties.

Chlorpromazine (trade name: Thorazine) was first used therapeutically in the United States in 1954 and rapidly became the preferred treatment for schizophrenics. By 1970 over 85 percent of all patients in state mental hospitals were receiving chlorpromazine or one of the other phenothiazines. In recent years two other neuroleptics have also been given to schizophrenics, the butyrophenones (trade name: Haldol) and the thioxanthenes (trade name: Taractan). Both seem generally as effective as the phenothiazines. Each class of drug seems able to reduce positive schizophrenic symptoms but has less effect on the negative ones.

Although the phenothiazine regimen reduces the positive symptoms of schizophrenia, so that patients can be released from the hospital, it should not be viewed as a cure. Typically, patients are kept on so-called *maintenance doses* of the drug; they continue to take their medication and return to the hospital or clinic on occasion for adjustment of the dose level. But released patients who are maintained on phenothiazine medication may make only marginal adjustment to the community. As mentioned earlier, the phenothiazines keep

Mental hospitals no longer retain patients for long periods of time. The result is that many ex-patients can be found on the streets of urban centers.

the positive symptoms from returning but have little effect on negative symptoms, such as social incompetence. In addition, reinstitutionalization is frequent. Although the phenothiazines reduced long-term institutionalization significantly, they also made possible the revolving-door pattern of admission, discharge, and readmission.

Some progress has been made in at least slowing down the revolutions per minute of the door. We know that applying social-learning principles in aftercare homes is one way of helping deinstitutionalized patients remain in the community (Paul and Lentz, 1977). There is also some evidence that a maintenance program of drugs plus a form of psychotherapy is effective at preventing relapse (Hogarty *et al*, 1974). One group of released patients received drugs plus a treatment program called major role therapy. In this therapy ex-patients are helped to assume productive social roles in the community and to reestablish personal relationships through the active help of a counselor. Then gradually they make more and more daily decisions on their own. Members of this group were rated as better adjusted after eighteen months of treatment than three other groups of released patients who received only the drug, only a placebo, and a placebo plus major role therapy.

Finally, the potentially serious side effects of phenothiazines must be noted. Patients generally report that taking the drug is disagreeable, causing dryness of the mouth, blurred vision, grogginess, and constipation. Among the other common side effects are low blood pressure and jaundice. Perhaps this unpleasantness is one of the reasons maintenance programs have proved so difficult. It is a problem to get patients to take these drugs initially and to keep them on medication once they have left the hospital (Van Putten *et al.*, 1981).[12] For this reason, patients are now frequently treated with long-lasting neuroleptics (e.g., fluphenazine decanoate) that require an injection every few weeks.

Even more disturbing are the extrapyramidal side effects; they stem from dysfunctions of the nerve tracts that descend from the brain to spinal motor neurons. Extrapyramidal side effects resemble symptoms of neurological diseases, as just mentioned. These side effects most closely resemble the symptoms of Parkinson's disease. People taking phenothiazines have "pill-rolling" tremors of the fingers, a shuffling gait, muscular rigidity, and drooling. Other side effects include dystonia, a disordered tonicity of tissues, and dyskinesia, an abnormal motion of voluntary and involuntary muscles. They cause arching of the back and a twisted posture of the neck

TABLE 14.5

Nine-month relapse rates of schizophrenics discharged, with and without maintenance medication, to low-EE homes and to high-EE homes with little and much family contact (*from Vaughn and Leff, 1976*)

Drug Status	Family Atmosphere and Contact		
	Low EE	High EE, Little Contact	High EE, Much Contact
Maintenance medication	12%	15%	53%
No drugs	15%	42%	92%

and body. Akasthesia is an inability to remain still; people pace constantly, fidget, and make chewing movements and other movements of the lips, fingers, and legs. These perturbing symptoms can be treated by drugs used with patients who have Parkinson's disease. In a muscular disturbance of older patients, called tardive dyskinesia, the mouth muscles involuntarily make sucking, lip-smacking, and chin-wagging motions. This syndrome affects from 10 to 20 percent of patients treated with phenothiazines for a long period of time (Kane *et al.*, 1986).

Because of these serious side effects, current clinical practice calls for treating patients with the smallest possible doses of drugs. The routine use of maintenance doses is also regarded as risky and many patients now take drug holidays—scheduled periods when they do not take any medication. Some relief from the symptoms of tardive dyskinesia is obtained from the administration of GABA agonists (Thaker *et al.*, 1987).

In spite of the many difficulties, phenothiazines are the best available treatment for schizophrenics and will undoubtedly continue to be the primary treatment until something better is discovered.[13] They are surely preferable to the straitjackets formerly used to restrain patients.

Psychological Treatments

Psychodynamic Therapy

Efforts to treat schizophrenia have by no means all been somatic. Freud did little, either in his clinical practice

---

[12]Some hold the opinion that patients are *smart* not to take phenothiazines for extended periods of time.

[13]Recent research indicates that a new drug, clozapine, can produce therapeutic gains in schizophrenics who did not respond positively to phenothiazines (Kane *et al.*, 1988). Interestingly, clozapine does not appear to produce its therapeutic effect by blocking dopamine receptors. Unfortunately, it can also impair the functioning of the immune system, making patients vulnerable to infection.

BOX 14.3

SOME NEGATIVE EFFECTS OF THERAPIES WITH SCHIZOPHRENICS

A discussion of therapy with schizophrenics must include mention of iatrogenic (caused by the method of treatment) negative effects. In a review of such negative effects, Drake and Sederer (1986) note the following cautions:

1. Intensive, intrusive, especially psychoanalytic treatments can be more than some schizophrenics can handle, especially when close therapeutic relationships are encouraged. Many patients subjected to such treatments need longer hospitalizations, become symptomatically worse, and are more likely to leave treatment. It is believed that the problem is emotional overstimulation (see page 397 for the data on harmful effects of expressed emotion in families), especially when regression is encouraged (as is frequently the case in analytically oriented therapies). Therapies that appear to be more effective are those that focus on practical issues like finding a job or behaving in nondisruptive ways and that permit the therapist to give straightforward advice and be a sounding board for reality testing.*

2. Milieu therapy can be harmful if, as above, the environment is overly stimulating, for example, when there are lively group discussions that encourage affective exploration of self and others, or otherwise emotionally provocative discussions. Furthermore, milieu therapies

that encourage democratic decision making and antihierarchical power can be confusing and negative for many schizophrenic patients. Although this latter generalization is inconsistent with data such as those reported by Paul and Lentz (1977), as well as other proponents of milieu therapy, the cautionary note is useful as a check on unbridled professional enthusiasm for assuming that seriously mentally ill patients (at least when they are actively psychotic) have the same needs and capacity for power-sharing as do normal individuals. There are probably also differences among milieu therapies, and those that are only moderately stimulating may be best suited for schizophrenics.

3. As in milieu therapy, excessive uncovering and self-disclosure during group therapy is not as helpful as groups that foster reality-testing and teach social skills. A review of forty-three studies of group therapy with hospitalized schizophrenics suggests that although there may be some benefit from both psychodynamic insight-oriented and behaviorally oriented approaches, there is some indication that the former carries a risk of negative effects (Kanas, 1986).

4. The noted negative side effects of neuroleptics (see page 400) and other pharmacotherapies that are used with schizophrenics present serious iatrogenic problems. In addition to physical sequelae like tardive dyskinesia, patients can develop psychotic explanations for drug-produced effects, such as concluding that the FBI is interfering with their thinking via malevolent radio waves.

---

*It is sometimes said that this kind of intervention is not *therapy* at all, rather "just" advice-giving and such. The issue depends of course on one's definition of therapy, a question considered in Chapter 18.

---

or through his writings, to adapt psychoanalysis to the treatment of schizophrenics; he believed them to be incapable of establishing the close interpersonal relationship that is essential for analysis. It was Harry Stack Sullivan, the American psychiatrist, who pioneered the use of psychotherapy with schizophrenic hospital patients. Sullivan established a ward at the Sheppard and Enoch Pratt Hospital in Towson, Maryland, in 1923 and developed a psychoanalytic treatment reported to be markedly successful. He held that schizophrenia reflected a return to early childhood forms of communication. The fragile ego of the schizophrenic, unable to handle the extreme stress of interpersonal challenges, regresses. Therapy therefore requires the patient to learn adult forms of communication and achieve insight into the role that the past has played in current problems. Sullivan advised the very gradual, nonthreatening development of a trusting relationship. For example, he

recommended that the therapist sit somewhat to the side of the patient in order not to force eye contact, which is deemed too frightening in the early stages of treatment. After many sessions, and with the establishment of greater trust and support, the analyst begins to encourage the patient to examine his or her interpersonal relationships.

A similar ego-analytic approach was proposed by Frieda Fromm-Reichmann (1889–1957), a German psychiatrist who emigrated to the United States and worked for a period of time with Sullivan at Chestnut Lodge, a private mental hospital in Rockville, Maryland. Fromm-Reichmann was sensitive to the symbolic and unconscious meaning of behavior, attributing the aloofness of schizophrenics to a wish to avoid the rebuffs suffered in childhood and thereafter judged inevitable. She treated them with great patience and optimism, making it clear that they need not take her into their world or give up their "sickness" until they were completely ready to do so. Along with Sullivan, Fromm-Reichmann (1952) helped establish psychoanalysis as a major treatment for schizophrenia.

Paradoxes are inherent to psychoanalytic thought. Whereas Sullivan and Fromm-Reichmann trod gingerly and gently into the defensive structure of their patients, John Rosen (1946) in his ***direct analysis*** drives a Mack truck. He agrees with his analytic colleagues that therapy must establish communication and foster insight, but he parts company with them about the fragility of the schizophrenic's ego. Rosen believes it strong enough to handle direct, often brutal confrontation, although always in a supportive relationship.[14] The following excerpt describes part of a therapy session with a young male catatonic schizophrenic.

For the first hour, his productions were repetitious and revealed that he was actively hallucinating. He made reference to numerous sexual adventures. He spoke as follows: "This is a wonderful airplane. It's over the Atlantic Ocean. I can see her down there. My mother. She's floating. Here I go. A dive bomb. I have her centered. Here I go. Here I go."

Following this symbolic incestuous experience, the patient screamed in terror and appeared to plead for mercy with his father. "Don't cut off my balls. Please don't cut them off. Please, papa, please." Since the plea was directed toward "papa," the physician said he was "papa," that he had seen what happened and that everything would be all right. The patient received permission to have these thoughts about his mother and was promised that there would be no punishment. (1946, p. 193)

Rosen becomes the omnipotent, nurturant protector of his patients. In some instances he actually feeds and caresses them to lend reality to their regression and enable them to reexperience problems from early childhood that are assumed to underlie their psychosis. Patients spend virtually all their waking hours in the company of the therapist and his assistants, being harangued through threats and coaxed through promises to interpret and relinquish their psychotic behavior. Rosen is, understandably, a controversial figure, and his claims for a 100 percent cure rate do little to reduce the controversy. Indeed, there is evidence that such intrusive interaction can be harmful (see Box 14.3).

---

[14]Those who have worked with Rosen attest to his unusual ability to establish a supportive relationship with many patients so that they are not frightened or otherwise disturbed by his unorthodox techniques.

Existential and Humanistic Therapies

Existential and humanistic therapies have made little if any impact on schizophrenic disorders. As writers in this tradition have themselves suggested (e.g., Corey, 1977), to make responsible choices and thus become truly human and to face the existential realization that the individual is ultimately alone in the world are high-level demands and very probably beyond the capacities of the patients described in this chapter. A schizophrenic's response to the expounding of existential-humanistic goals might well be "They should be my worst problems." When people must struggle even to reason logically, to avoid violating social norms, and to attend to the world as most people see it, rather than to their own of frightening demons and persecutors, they do not have the luxury of contemplating ultimate aloneness and the awesome responsibility of making choices, of creating existence anew every day. But empathic listening and efforts to reassure patients that they will not be hurt are certainly beneficial. Clinical lore, for example, tells us not to challenge the paranoid's delusions, lest we become part of them. The person who believes that the C.I.A. is broadcasting messages into his or her mind and keeping tabs on daily thoughts and activities needs an empathic ear.

Evaluation of Insight Therapies

The overall evaluation of insight-oriented psychotherapy with schizophrenics thus far justifies little enthusiasm for applying it with these severely disturbed people (Feinsilver and Gunderson, 1972). More recent results from a long-term follow-up of patients bearing a diagnosis of schizophrenia and discharged after treatment between 1963 and 1976 at the New York State Psychiatric Institute confirm the lack of success of insight-oriented psychotherapy (Stone, 1986). These patients had received drugs in addition to what was described as analytically oriented therapy. An analysis of data from half the sample of more than 500 indicates that the patients were doing poorly. It may be, as Stone hypothesizes, that gaining psychoanalytic insight into one's problems and illness may worsen a schizophrenic patient's psychological condition. Earlier, great claims of success were made for the analyses done by Sullivan and Fromm-Reichmann, but a close consideration of the patients they saw indicates that many tended to be only mildly disturbed and might not even have been diagnosed schizophrenic by the strict DSM-IIIR criteria for the disorder.

What little research has been done on Rosen's direct analysis is methodologically flawed; in any event, good evidence is lacking of the value in this approach. A widely cited study by Carl Rogers and his associates (1967) examining client-centered therapy with schizophrenics indicated that empathic listening by an exceptionally genuine therapist can help establish a good therapeutic relationship, but no inroads on the actual clinical problems of schizophrenics were made (May, 1974). This failure to ease their condition is consistent with research indicating that client-centered therapy is most successful with people who can involve themselves deeply in therapy from the outset. Expecting such involvement from schizophrenics is unrealistic (Shilling, 1984). Finally, a study by May (1968; May *et al.*, 1976) failed to show that psychoanalysis added anything to a phenothiazine regimen. Although experienced clinicians often believe that they themselves, or other highly gifted therapists, can make a positive impact on certain schizophrenics, and this may indeed happen when some therapists work with some patients, evidence obtained through controlled scientific research does not indicate that insight into themselves and the past is of much help to schizophrenics.

Family Therapy and Expressed Emotion

Family therapy was conceived in the 1950s in response to theories of schizophrenia that proposed abnormal family relationships as causes. Subsequent research has attempted to help schizophrenics discharged from a mental hospital to remain at home. Since high levels of expressed emotion have been linked with relapse and reinstitutionalization, a family therapy team at the University of Southern California decided to try to lower, through cognitive and behavioral means, the emotional intensity of the households that schizophrenics returned to (Falloon *et al.*, 1982, 1985).

Family therapy sessions took place in the patients' homes, with family and patient participating together. The importance of the patient's taking his or her medication regularly was stressed. The family was also instructed in ways to express both positive and negative feelings in a constructive, empathic manner and to defuse tense, personal conflicts through collaborative problem solving. The patient's symptoms were explained to the family, and ways of coping with them and of reducing emotional turmoil in the home were suggested. It was made clear to patient and family alike that schizophrenia is primarily a biochemical illness, but that proper medication and the kind of psychosocial treatment they were receiving can reduce stress on the patient and prevent relapses and deterioration. Treatment extended over the first nine months after the patient returned home, when the danger of relapse is especially great.

This family treatment, aimed at calming the home life of the family, was compared to an individual therapy in which the patient was seen alone at a clinic, with supportive discussions centering on problems in daily living and on developing a social network. Family members of patients in this control group were seldom seen, and when they were, it was not in conjoint home sessions with the patients. These control patients received the typical individual, supportive management in widespread use in aftercare programs for schizophrenics.

Ongoing assessments were made of the patient's symptomatology, with special attention given to signs of relapse, such as delusions of control and hallucinations. Family members were also evaluated for their problem-solving skills and for the emotions they expressed toward the patient. All patients, including the controls, were maintained on antipsychotic medication, primarily Thorazine, which was monitored and adjusted throughout the project by a psychiatrist unaware of which patients were receiving family therapy and which individual therapy.

In all, thirty-six patients were treated, eighteen in the family therapy group and eighteen in the individual therapy control group. Those receiving family therapy fared much better. Only one person in this group had a major clinical relapse, as compared to eight in the control group. Further, of the schizophrenic episodes occurring in the control group, two-thirds were considered major whereas only one-third in the family therapy group were so categorized. Finally, hospital readmission rates were consistently different: half (nine) of the eighteen control patients were returned to the hospital whereas only 12 percent of the eighteen family therapy patients had to return.

In interpreting their results, the investigators were properly mindful of the possibility that the patients in family therapy may have improved more than the controls because they took their neuroleptic medications more faithfully; indeed, family therapy subjects did comply better with their medication regimens. However, other studies have shown that drugs alone do not adequately prevent deterioration in patients such as these: the family therapy seems also to have been important.

A larger scale and more complex study by Hogarty *et al.* (1986) confirms these findings while at the same time raising some curious complications. Like the Falloon study, Hogarty *et al.* emphasized to high-EE families and to the 103 recently discharged patients the importance of remaining on prescribed neuroleptic medication after hospital discharge. Three treatment conditions were created:

1. Family education to reduce EE, that is, engendering realistic expectations of their schizophrenic family member, trying to decrease their guilt and anxiety, and in general encouraging a "cooling out" of the

emotionally charged home atmosphere (this is equivalent to the Falloon *et al.* family treatment).

2. Social skills training, which focused on changing the patient's behavior so as to reduce family EE, namely, by teaching the patient to avoid and handle conflict, to abstain from behaving in ways that might elicit high-EE behavior in the family, and to express positive feelings in hopes of reducing family dissatisfaction. This patient-focused treatment was based on the social skills training approaches of behavior therapists such as Liberman, King, DeRisi, and McCann (1975), Wallace *et al.* (1980), and Hersen and Bellack (1976).

3. Both treatments 1 and 2.

There was also a control group, which received only maintenance drug therapy in a supportive relationship with a nurse practitioner. The drug maintenance treatment was given to patients in the other three groups as well; as with Falloon *et al.*, medication was regarded as

After hospitalization, many patients are discharged to group homes or halfway houses where they can receive support from others.

a necessary mainstay of any conceivably successful aftercare program.

Compared to the control group's 41 percent relapse rate, only 19 percent of the patients in the family therapy group relapsed, confirming the usefulness of family therapy in alleviating the relapse problem over a period of one year. In the social skills condition, which concentrated on changing patient behavior to reduce family EE, the relapse rate was only 20 percent (Bellack, Turner, Hersen, and Luber, 1984; Wallace and Liberman, 1985). Notably the combined family plus social skills group experienced *no* relapse. Of the ninety families who completed the study, sixty-one agreed to be interviewed a second time at one-year follow-up (when patient relapse was assessed). *No* patient relapsed if he or she had returned to a home in which EE had become lower over the course of the year. This was independent of treatment; indeed in five of the control families, EE was reduced significantly. Consistent with the importance of lowering EE is the finding that among households that remained high on EE, relapse in both family treatment (33 percent) and social skills training (29 percent) was no different from that in controls (42 percent). *But,* the combination of family treatment plus social skills training produced significantly lower relapse (0 percent) even when EE remained high. There thus seemed to be something special about the combination of family and social skills training that helped the patient avoid relapse even when expressed emotion remained high in the home.[15]

The authors caution against inferring that high EE *causes* relapse, for it is possible that EE initially diminished early in the year following hospital discharge but increased at the time of the patient's relapse—the relapse being caused by entirely different problems—and perhaps an increase in EE is caused by the relapse rather than the other way around. This is very plausible since one can expect an increase in turmoil and family concern if and when the patient begins to deteriorate, as may happen if readmission to hospital is imminent. Other cautions include the fact that EE seems to work differently for female patients—high relapse rates have been found for *low*-EE families where the patient is a woman. Also, at a two-year follow-up, relapse rates rise for all treatments, suggesting that EE reduction (primarily for male patients) only delays rather than prevents relapse. There is much yet to be learned about the usefulness of lowering EE.

---

[15]Hogarty *et al.* report that a future publication will indicate that such nonrelapsed patients from families that did *not* lower their EE do not turn out to be as well adjusted. This finding underscores the importance of lowering familial expressed emotion.

Behavior Therapy

Social skills training as a means of reducing expressed emotion is generally viewed as a form of behavior therapy. In addition, operant conditioning techniques, another means of behavior therapy, have been employed in mental hospitals; this work is discussed in greater detail in Chapter 19. For our present purposes we should note that hundreds of hospitalized patients, most of them carrying a diagnosis of schizophrenia, have lived in a token economy instituted to eliminate specific behavior, such as hoarding towels; to teach more socially appropriate responses, such as combing hair and arriving on time at dining halls; and to encourage activity, such as doing chores on the ward (Ayllon and Azrin, 1968). The study by Paul and Lentz (1977) demonstrated the potential of a carefully designed and meticulously implemented therapy program based on social-learning principles (see Chapter 19). Seriously ill schizophrenics were released to shelter care and three even to independent living.[16] At the present time it is generally acknowledged among mental health professionals that therapy programs with a learning framework are the most effective psychological procedures for helping schizophrenics function better. But behavior therapy is seldom claimed to make such thoroughgoing changes that we can speak of curing people with this group of mental illnesses. Behavioral interventions do, however, reverse somewhat the effects of institutionalization, fostering social skills such as assertiveness in people whom attendants have reinforced for passiveness and compliance.

General Trends in Treatment

A general trend seems to be emerging in attitudes toward and treatment of schizophrenia. Only a generation ago many if not most mental health professionals and laypeople believed the primary "culprit" to be the psychological environment, and most especially the family—because the seeds for schizophrenia were seen as having been sown in early childhood. The thinking now is that a biological, and probably a genetic, factor predisposes a person to become schizophrenic. The twin and high-risk studies reviewed earlier in this chapter provide strong supporting evidence for this view. More careful research is needed about the *kind of stressor* that can trigger a schizophrenic break in a predisposed individual. In our view, the most promising contemporary approaches to treatment as discussed below make good use of this increased understanding.

1. Information about current scientific knowledge is conveyed to both family and patient. They are given realistic information about schizophrenia as a disability that can be controlled but that is probably lifelong. Like many other chronic disabilities, medication is necessary to maintain control and allow the patient to perform daily activities. But what is *not* necessary and what is even counterproductive is the guilt of family members, especially parents, believing that something in the patient's upbringing has caused the problem. (This issue is also dealt with in Chapter 16, Box 16.6, where we discuss psychogenesis as a pernicious hypothesis in infantile autism.) Considerable effort is devoted in many treatment programs to dispel this sense of culpability while at the same time encouraging a focus on the physiological diathesis and the associated need for medication.[17]

2. Efforts are made to reduce the stress experienced by the patient on discharge. This is done both by reducing hostility, overinvolvement or intrusiveness, and criticality of the family—what has been termed expressed emotion—and by providing medication that is believed to have a quieting effect, perhaps by helping the patient think more clearly about his or her world and by directly reducing anxiety. The means employed to reduce stress include teaching family members to reduce their EE, teaching the patient how to interact with his or her family so as to reduce EE in the home, and in general trying to improve the patient's social skills so that he can function more normally outside the hospital and probably reduce the EE he might encounter both inside and outside the home.

3. Networking among affected families is also being encouraged (Greenberg *et al.*, 1988) to reduce the isolation and stigma that is associated with having a member who is schizophrenic. Support groups and even formal organizations are increasingly available to help families cope with the stress associated with having a member who is schizophrenic.

Concluding Remarks on the Integration of Somatic and Psychological Interventions

The justified enthusiasm for drugs that reduce hallu-

---

[16]The criterion of being discharged from a mental hospital is more complicated than may appear on the surface. A treatment may help a person leave a hospital, yet that person may still be able to live only a marginal existence. Keith and his colleagues (1976) concluded that only half of schizophrenics who are released from mental hospitals are able to assume full occupational and social responsibilities.

[17]The use of medication in this context is interesting and complex. Our mention of it here implies that the drugs are aimed at the biological predisposition. But in fact, the drugs could also be regarded as a way to reduce environmental stress, the second facet of the current approach to schizophrenia.

cinations and delusions and even sometimes improve the clarity of thought runs a risk of ignoring psychological components that are likely to be necessary for effective and humane intervention. There are many reasons why somatic and psychological approaches need to be integrated.

1. We know that long-term use of phenothiazines and other neuroleptics can have seriously negative side effects such as tardive dyskinesia. Some patients complain of affective blunting and interference with thinking, reminding one of the "fog machine" that Ken Kesey talked about being turned on in the hospital ward in his classic novel *One Flew Over the Cuckoo's Nest.* Although there are hopes that newly developed drugs will avoid some of these nontrivial drawbacks, the general history of medication cautions us to remain mindful of the iatrogenic problems of many pharmaceuticals.

2. As already noted, neuroleptics have little if any effect on negative symptoms such as social withdrawal and behavioral deficits. Many schizophrenics need to learn or relearn ways of interacting with their world, of dealing with the emotional challenges that all people face as they negotiate life. A "wonder" drug that alleviates symptoms still leaves untouched the basic tendency of the predisposed individual to react abnormally in later stressful situations.

3. Another consideration, sometimes lost when only group averages are examined, is that many patients do not improve from the available antipsychotic drugs. Much more needs to be learned about *individual differences,* and although some of these variations will no doubt be found to exist in the somatic realm, it is held by some experts that psychological factors, including the phenomenological realm of the patient, will prove to be important (Carpenter, 1986).

4. The family therapy work with high EE has alerted us to the interplay between the somatic and the psychological. At the very least, even a highly effective drug cannot have its effects on a patient who does not take it. Although medication can be forced upon a person in a hospital setting, and new technologies may make it possible to administer a drug to an uncooperative patient—as with a slow release device implanted under the skin—issues of civil rights and respect for human dignity are not to be overlooked. An empathic, supportive, and trusting relationship with the patient is always necessary and important.

Regrettably, professional turf battles threaten to interfere with the integration of somatic and psychological therapies. The late 1980s have seen some medical practitioners blocking psychologists from obtaining hospital privileges. Some psychological practitioners have taken antagonistic stances against drug therapies and neuropsychological discoveries on grounds that seem to be less than purely scientific. These interdisciplinary squabbles are not new, but they seldom contribute to advances in knowledge or improvements in patient care. We would do well to recall some of the past extreme positions taken by in-groups believing themselves to be the recipients of "Truth," only to find years later that these positions taken with utmost certainty and not a little bigotry to the out-group were discredited and seen to be ridiculous at best and harmful at worst. Well before all the answers are in, logic and experience dictate that comprehensive treatment be both somatic and psychological.

Summary

The pioneering efforts of Kraepelin and Bleuler led to two views of schizophrenia. Kraepelin's work fostered a descriptive approach and a narrow definition, whereas Bleuler's theoretical emphasis led to a very broad diagnostic category. Bleuler had a great influence on the American conception of schizophrenia. His influence, together with the American interest in treatment and the addition of several poorly defined types of schizophrenia, served to make the American concept excessively inclusive. By the middle of the twentieth century the differences in the way schizophrenia was diagnosed in America and Europe were vast. With the advent of DSM-III and DSM-IIIR, the American concept of schizophrenia has become narrower and more similar to a European view. The basic symptoms are disturbances in thought—incoherence, loose associations, lack of insight, and delusions; in perception and attention—distractibility and hallucinations; in motor behavior—grimacing, gesturing, and flailing of limbs or catatonia and waxy flexibility; and in affect—flat or inappropriate. Schizophrenics also have little social competence and considerable difficulty holding jobs. A review of the schizophrenic types proposed by Kraepelin and in DSM-IIIR indicates the great variability in the behavior of schizophrenic patients. Schizophrenics have recently been typed by their positive symptoms—their excesses such as hallucinations, delusions, and outlandish behavior; and by their negative symptoms—their flattened emotions, poverty of speech, apathy, and anhedonia.

Research has tried to determine the etiological role of specific variables such as social class, the family, genetic and biochemical factors, and brain pathology.

The data on genetic transmission are impressive. The adoptee studies, which are relatively free from most criticisms that can be leveled at family or twin studies, show a strong relation between having a schizophrenic parent and the likelihood of developing the disorder. Perhaps the genetic predisposition has biochemical correlates, although research in this area permits only tentative conclusions. At this time the excess-dopamine-activity theory appears the most promising in helping to explain the schizophrenia of those with positive symptoms. The brains of schizophrenics with negative symptoms, however, have enlarged ventricles, cortical and cerebellar atrophies, and a reduced metabolism in the frontal areas.

The diagnosis of schizophrenia is more frequently applied to members of the lowest social class. Available information indicates this is so in part because the stresses of lower-class existence are great and in part because the disorder keeps schizophrenics from achieving higher social status. Vague communications and conflicts are evident in the family life of schizophrenics and probably contribute to their disorder. Level of expressed emotion (EE) in families has been shown to be an important determinant of relapse.

Much of the information we have reviewed is consistent with a diathesis–stress view of schizophrenia. Investigators have turned to the high-risk method, studying children who are particularly vulnerable to schizophrenia by virtue of having a schizophrenic parent. Mednick and Schulsinger have found that circumstances predicting maladjustment in adulthood differ for boys and girls. Having mothers who suffered an early onset of schizophrenia and were poor predicted the development of schizophrenia in girls. As for boys, these circumstances plus their mothers' difficulties in carrying and delivering them predicted who would become schizophrenic.

There are both somatic and psychological therapies for schizophrenia. Insulin and electroshock treatments and even surgery were in vogue earlier in the century, but none is employed to any extent nowadays, primarily because antipsychotic drugs, in particular the phenothiazines, are now available. In numerous studies these medications have been found to have a major and beneficial impact on the disordered lives of schizophrenic patients. They have also been very much a factor in the deinstitutionalization of hospital patients. But drugs alone are unlikely to be the answer, for schizophrenics need to be taught or retaught ways of dealing with the challenges of everyday life, and perhaps as well to resolve the intrapsychic problems believed by some therapists to underlie their symptoms. Ego-analytic theory assumes that schizophrenia represents a retreat from the pain of childhood rejection and mistreatment; the relationship gradually and patiently established by the analyst offers the patient a safe haven in which to explore repressed traumas. Direct analysis agrees that childhood conflicts lie at the core of schizophrenia but regards the patient's ego as not too fragile for an assaultive analysis of defenses. Good evidence for the efficacy of these treatments is not plentiful, although case studies of dramatic cures are many in both the professional and popular literature. Family therapy, aimed at reducing high levels of EE, has been shown to be valuable in preventing relapse. More recently behavioral treatments have helped patients discharged from mental hospitals to meet the inevitable stresses of family and community living, and, when discharge is not possible, to lead more ordered and constructive lives within an institution.

Part Five

Joan Miró, *Jack-in-the-Box*, 1953. © 1989 ARS, New York/ADAGP/Art Resource.

Lifespan
Developmental Disorders

Lee N. Smith, *The Last Stand*, 1984. Private collection. Courtesy of Texas Gallery, Houston. Photo: Rick Gardner.

Chapter 15

Emotional and Behavioral Disorders of Childhood and Adolescence

Classification
Disorders of Undercontrolled Behavior
   Attention-Deficit Disorder with Hyperactivity
   Conduct Disorders
Disorders of Overcontrolled Behavior
   Childhood Fears
   Social Withdrawal
   Affective Disorders in Childhood
Eating Disorders
   Anorexia Nervosa
   Bulimia Nervosa
Summary

"Nothing is more precious than a young child" (O'Leary and Wilson, 1975, p. 39). And few events in an adult's life are more emotionally draining than being close to a child who is hurt, physically or psychologically. Until now we have discussed psychological problems that affect a significant proportion of the adult population. As upsetting as it may be to have a friend or relative who suffers from depression, or from unpredictable bouts of anxiety, or from the myriad of thought and emotional disruptions of schizophrenia, it is much more disturbing to see such problems in a child. Children are judged to have few emotional resources with which to cope with problems. The extreme dependency of troubled children on their parents and guardians adds to the sense of responsibility that these people feel, and to their guilt, whether it be justified or not.

Most psychodynamic, behavioral, and even biological theories find childhood experience and development to be critically important to adult mental health. In addition, most theories regard children as more malleable than adults and thus more amenable to treatment. We would therefore expect the disorders of children to have been the focus of voluminous research into etiology, prevention, and treatment. Until recently, however, they have been given considerably less attention than adult problems.

Disorders associated with the course of adult development and aging have received even less attention than those of childhood. The disorders of these two periods, childhood and aging, can be treated together as a new research and clinical endeavor, the study of the problems of lifespan development. In this chapter we discuss emotional and behavioral disorders of childhood and adolescence. Chapter 16 covers developmental disorders in which the acquisition of cognitive, language, motor, or social skills is disturbed. These disorders include learning disabilities and the most severe of developmental disorders, mental retardation and pervasive developmental disorders (especially autism), which are usually chronic and often persist into adulthood. Chapter 17 discusses the psychological disorders of older adults.

Classification

The classification of childhood disorders has changed radically over the last thirty years. Consistent with the scant research efforts then being expended on the problems of childhood, DSM-I and DSM-II treated them primarily as downward extensions of adult disorders.

Children were often given diagnoses that had originally been created for adults. The major adult categories of psychoses, neuroses, and personality disorders of DSM-II, for example, were all applied to children as well. The only unique section for disorders of children was Behavior Disorders of Childhood and Adolescence. The ineffectiveness of this system is indicated by the fact that most children seen by mental health professionals received a diagnosis of adjustment reaction, a very broad one indeed, or no diagnosis at all (Achenbach, 1982).

Recognizing a need for change in the classification system, the Group for Advancement of Psychiatry (GAP), an organization of psychiatrists devoted to a careful scrutiny of their field, proposed a very different diagnostic scheme for children (GAP, 1966). Although the work was still linked to psychodynamic theory, the GAP committee began creating a developmentally oriented diagnostic system tailored specifically to childhood disorders. These efforts were incorporated and extended in DSM-III. Whereas DSM-II contained one section with seven specific diagnoses to be applied uniquely to children, DSM-III contained a section with forty specific diagnoses gathered in nine general groups. DSM-IIIR has continued this expansion of diagnostic categories.

DSM-IIIR reflects the burgeoning interest in childhood disorders; the number of advisory committee members consulting on disorders of childhood and adolescence increased from seventeen for DSM-III to seventy-four for DSM-IIIR. Revisions of the diagnostic manual reflect the growing influence of the field of developmental psychopathology, which studies disorders of childhood within the context of knowledge about normal life-span development. Understanding normal developmental changes allows us to identify behaviors that are appropriate at one stage but are considered disturbed at another. For example, although defiant behavior is quite common at age two or three, the persistence of such behavior at ages five or six is considered much more problematic. Maturational differences in children also affect the manner in which symptoms are expressed, and make many childhood disorders both distinct from adult psychopathology and more difficult to classify. Although we agree that child problems should not be viewed as downward extensions of adult problems, it is also possible to diagnose children as having disorders such as Major Depression or Post-Traumatic Stress Disorder, if they meet the adult criteria.

Before proceeding further, it is important to note that childhood disorders differ from adult disorders in a very central way. Whereas most adults identify *themselves* as having a problem, most children are so identified *by others*. The difference between "I have a problem" and "You have a problem" is great. When people refer themselves for treatment, we can be reasonably sure that they have problems for which they desire help. When a child is referred for treatment, on the other hand, all we really know is that someone perceives this child as disordered. Why does the person see this child as needing treatment? Is this boy really unmanageable or does he just remind his mother of her divorced husband? Is this girl really distractible or is she merely bored by school? The evidence indicates that although the child's actual behavior plays a major role in how adults perceive him or her, many other factors also enter into the perception (Ross, 1981).

In our survey of childhood and adolescent disorders, we make only partial use of DSM-IIIR for section organization. More useful in our view is a consideration based on a review of the studies of disordered children that found consistent evidence for two broad clusters of childhood symptoms. Children with symptoms from one cluster are called either *undercontrolled* or externalizers and are said to show behavior excesses. Children who have symptoms from the other cluster are said to be *overcontrolled*, to be internalizers, or to have behavior deficits (Achenbach and Edelbrock, 1978). The key to the distinction between these clusters lies in whether the child's way of reacting creates a problem for others or affects the self primarily. These two clusters are discussed first, followed by a discussion of the eating disorders of anorexia nervosa and bulimia nervosa (Box 15.1).

Disorders of Undercontrolled Behavior

The undercontrolled child lacks or has insufficient control over behavior that is expected in a given setting and is appropriate to the child's age. Because of such failings, the undercontrolled child is frequently an annoyance to both adults and peers. Two general categories of undercontrolled behavior are frequently differentiated, attention-deficit hyperactivity disorder and conduct problems (called "disruptive behavior disorders" in DSM-IIIR).

Problems of undercontrol are defined by the type, form, and frequency of the behavior. The high frequency of much "problem" behavior in the general population of children, such as fidgeting in class, makes it questionable, however, whether isolated incidents should be considered abnormal. Other behavior, such as assaulting a teacher, is by topography alone considered abnormal by most people.

Attention-Deficit Hyperactivity Disorder

Everybody probably knows at least one child considered to be hyperactive, and this child is most likely to be a school-age boy. These youngsters often behave impulsively or act before thinking, a pattern that may lead both to social friction and to academic failure. They have difficulty focusing on a single activity and often shift erratically from one task to another without finishing those projects they begin. Many of these children tend not to maintain the behaviors expected of them for more than a few minutes—whether this involves sustained attention to a task or a game, patient waiting for a desired event, or modulation of spontaneous verbal and motor behaviors. They seem to have remarkably high energy levels, approaching activities with striking and sometimes formidable intensity.

A hyperactive child's mother might report that he has difficulty remembering not to trail his dirty hand along the clean wall as he runs from the front door to the kitchen. His peers may find that he spontaneously changes the rules while playing Monopoly or soccer. His teacher notes that he asks what he is supposed to do immediately after detailed instructions were presented to the entire class. He may make warbling noises or other strange sounds that inadvertently disturb anyone nearby. He may seem to have more than his share of accidents—knocking over the tower his classmates are erecting, spilling his cranberry juice on the linen tablecloth, or tripping over the television cord while retrieving the family cat—and thereby disconnecting the set in the middle of the Superbowl game.

A hyperactive child is all too frequently "in trouble"—with his peers, his teachers, his family, his community. His social faux pas do not seem to stem from negativism or maliciousness. In fact, he is often quite surprised when his behaviors elicit anger and rejection from others. Nor does he seem to have any basic deficits or disabilities—either in intellectual or in interpersonal spheres. He seems almost normal in every way, but yet he has inordinate and pervasive difficulties getting along in the everyday world. This is the puzzle of hyperactivity—a puzzle that continues to perplex and intrigue child health and education specialists.
(Whalen, 1983, pp. 151–152)

As the foregoing description suggests, the term "hyperactive" is familiar to most people, especially to parents and teachers. Other diagnoses that have in the past been used to describe inattentive and impulsive youngsters include minimal brain dysfunction, which clearly suggested that subtle brain damage caused the behavioral problems, and hyperkinesis, which is from the Greek words *hyper* meaning over and *kinesis* meaning

BOX 15.1

ENURESIS

Infants have no bladder or bowel control and must continually be diapered. As the child becomes older, toilet training begins. Some children learn toileting at eighteen months, others at thirty months, and so on. When is it no longer "normal" to be unable to control the bladder? The answer, as determined by cultural norms and statistics, is fairly arbitrary.

DSM-IIIR and other classification systems distinguish between those who wet during sleep, which is nocturnal enuresis, and those who wet themselves while awake, which is called diurnal enuresis. Daytime continence is established earlier. When a child falls behind in bladder control, it is usually for the nighttime hours. It is estimated that at age five, between 16 and 25 percent of children wet at night (this figure includes those who used to stay dry but have regressed). By age seven and one-half, 7 percent are still wetting, and by age ten, 5 percent remain nocturnal bed wetters (Pierce, 1980, 1985).

In the United States, the most commonly accepted cutoff for regarding nocturnal wetting as an actual problem is between three and four years of age (age five in DSM-IIIR), at which time the estimated incidence of bed-wetting is 10 to 15 percent of the age group (Baller, 1975). In contrast, Bettelheim (1969) reported that on an Israeli kibbutz 40 percent of the nine-year-olds wet their beds, but the caretakers do not consider this a problem. Apparently there is more bed-wetting but less enuresis in Israel!

Clearly, age is not the only factor that enters into a diagnosis of enuresis. Baller (1975) offers a four-part definition of nocturnal enuretics as

persons who (1) involuntarily wet the bed; (2) show no evidence of urinary, organic pathology; (3) are three and one half years of age or more; and (4) have simply con-

tinued the nighttime wetting habits of infancy ("primary enuresis") or have . . . fallen into a pattern of bed-wetting ("secondary enuresis") that averages more than twice a week. (p. 15)

This fourth criterion is a commonly made distinction, one found also in DSM-IIIR. Primary enuretics, who represent two-thirds of all enuretics (Starfield, 1972), have wet the bed from infancy, whereas secondary enuretics were once able to remain dry at night but have apparently lost the capacity.

One consistent finding about enuresis is that the likelihood of an enuretic having a first-degree relative who also wets is very high, approximately 75 percent (Bakwin, 1973), evidence for either physiological or psychological theories of etiology. Bed-wetting usually occurs about four hours after the onset of sleep, or after the last enuretic incident (Sorotzin, 1984). Hospitalization between the ages of two and four, the birth of a sibling, and entering school are precipitating stressors.

THEORIES OF ENURESIS

As many as 10 percent of all cases of enuresis are caused by purely medical conditions. The most common of the known physical causes is urinary tract infection. Approximately one in twenty female and one in fifty male enuretics have such an infection. Treatment of the infection oftentimes does not stop the enuresis, however. Other infrequent but known physical causes are chronic renal or kidney disease, tumors, diabetes, and seizures (Kolvin, MacKeith, and Meadow, 1973). Because of the substantial incidence of physical causes of enuresis, most professionals refer enuretics to physicians before beginning psychological treatment.

Learning theorists believe that enuresis results from a failure of toilet training.

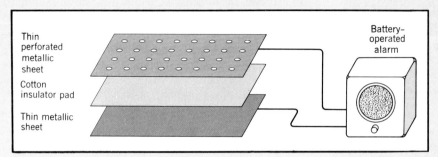

FIGURE 15a

The bell and pad apparatus for halting bed-wetting, devised by Orval Hobart and Willie Mae Mowrer.

Some psychoanalytic theorists have suggested that enuresis serves as a symbol for other conflicts. Enuresis has been hypothesized to be both symbolic masturbation and a disguised means of demonstrating spite toward parents (Mowrer, 1950). A related notion considers enuresis a symptom of a more general psychological disorder. Many investigators disagree, however, finding other personal problems to be a reaction to the embarrassment and guilt of wetting, rather than being causes of enuresis. Children will of course lose self-esteem if their peers ostracize them and their parents become angry and rejecting. When bladder control is gained, most of the correlated problems are also likely to disappear (Starfield, 1972; Baller, 1975).

Learning theorists propose that children wet when toilet training begins at too early an age, when training is lax and insufficient reinforcement is given for proper toileting, and more specifically when children do not learn to awaken as a conditioned response to a full bladder or to inhibit sufficiently relaxation of the sphincter muscle controlling urination (Mowrer and Mowrer, 1938; Young, 1965; Baller, 1975). Bladder control, the inhibition of a natural reflex until voluntary voiding can take place, is after all a skill of considerable complexity. Although no single learning theory has received much empirical support, treatments based on learning models have proved quite successful (Doleys, 1977).

TREATMENT OF ENURESIS

In the late 1930s Mowrer and Mowrer (1938) introduced the *bell and pad,* a treatment for nocturnal enuresis based on learning principles. Over the years the procedure has proved markedly successful in reducing or eliminating bedwetting. Although relapses can be common, it is estimated that 75 percent of enuretic children will learn to stay dry through the night with the help of this remarkably simple device (Doleys, 1977).

The bell and a battery are wired to the pad, which is composed of two metallic foil sheets, the top one perforated, separated by a layer of absorbent cloth (Figure 15a).

The pad is inserted into a pillowcase and placed beneath the child at bedtime. When the first drops of urine, which acts as an electrolyte, reach the cloth, the electric circuit is completed between the two foil sheets. The completed circuit sets off the bell, which awakens the child immediately or soon after he begins to wet. He is then able to stop urination, turn off the device, and go to the bathroom.

Mowrer and Mowrer (1938) viewed the bell and pad as a classical conditioning procedure wherein an unconditioned stimulus, the bell, wakes the child, the unconditioned response. The bell is paired with the sensations of a full bladder so that they eventually become a conditioned stimulus that produces the conditioned response of awakening, before the bell sounds. Others have questioned the classical conditioning theory, suggesting instead that the bell, by waking the child, serves as a punisher and thus reduces the undesirable behavior of wetting.* Other methods that use an operant conditioning rationale instead of or in addition to the bell and pad procedure have also proved quite successful (Doleys, 1977).

A rather different learning treatment for enuresis is based on the theory that enuretics have an abnormally small functional bladder capacity. Children perform exercises to increase gradually the volume of urine that they can retain before voiding (Starfield, 1972). For instance, a child may be asked to drink a large glass of water and not to urinate for thirty minutes. The next day the time might be stretched to thirty-five minutes, and so on; rewards are provided for the steps along the way. In this manner the child's capacity to hold urine without voiding is gradually increased, the hope being that the enlarged capacity will reduce wetting. Although often useful, retention control training has not proved as effective as the bell and pad (Doleys, 1977)

---

*In actual practice the bell usually wakes the child's parents too; their reactions may serve as an additional incentive for the child to remain dry.

A hyperactive child looking at her star chart for the week. At the end of the week, stars are exchanged for tangible rewards.

motion. DSM-IIIR has renamed these terms **attention-deficit hyperactivity disorder** (ADHD). The focus now is on the difficulty the child has in concentrating on the task at hand for an appropriate period of time and involvement in non-goal-directed overactivity. These inattentive children seem to have particular difficulty controlling their activity in situations that call for sitting still, such as at school or at mealtimes. When required to be quiet, they appear unable to stop moving or talking. They are often described as being "on the go," as "running like a motor." They are also disorganized, erratic, and tactless, obstinate, and bossy. Their activities and movements seem haphazard. They quickly wear out their shoes and clothing, smash their toys, and soon exhaust their family, teachers, and friends.

As Whalen (1983) cautions, it is important not to apply the ADHD diagnosis to youngsters who are rambunctious, "overactive," or a bit distractible, for in the early school years children are often so. ADHD is best reserved for truly extreme and persistent cases. Those who worry that DSM-IIIR diagnoses may stigmatize children unnecessarily (e.g., Garmezy, 1977) remind us that words like "rambunctious" may really mean no more than that the child is more lively and more difficult to control than a parent or teacher would like.

Not surprisingly, the inattention and impulsiveness of ADHD children are often associated with academic difficulties. In fact, some workers believe that learning disabilities (see page 440) and ADHD are so closely related that they are sometimes indistinguishable from each other. To be sure, more than three-quarters of a sample of ADHD children were found to have serious learning problems, and more than one-third of learning-disabled children to be hyperactive (Safer and Allen, 1976). But these same statistics indicate also that the overlap is not complete; some ADHD children, for example, do very well in school. For the time being, efforts are being made to keep the two categories separate while acknowledging their relatedness (Whalen, 1983).

An even more difficult distinction to make is that between ADHD and conduct disorder. Since an overlap of 30 to 90 percent between the two categories has been found (Hinshaw, 1987), some researchers have asserted that the two types of undercontrolled behavior are actually the same disorder (Quay, 1979). On the other hand, validational studies have revealed differences between the two; hyperactivity is associated more with off-task behavior in school, cognitive and achievement deficits, and a better long-term prognosis, whereas children with conduct problems and aggression are more likely to have antisocial parents, family hostility, low socioeconomic status, and a much higher risk for delinquency and substance abuse in adolescence (Hinshaw, 1987; Loney, Langhorne, and Paternite, 1978). The comorbidity of both disorders, which is frequent in clinic-referred children, apparently combines the worst features of both, as these children are the most likely to be rejected by their peers and have the poorest long-term prognosis. In concluding a careful review of the literature comparing the two disorders, Hinshaw (1987) recommends continuing to view hyperactivity and conduct disorder as separate but related disorders. Unfortunately, much of the research on hyperactive children confounds ADHD with conduct problems and aggressiveness, making the findings about hyperactivity less clear.

The problems of hyperactive children begin in early infancy; they are slower to establish eating and sleeping patterns (Campbell, 1985), and they fail to reach developmental milestones, such as walking, at the expected ages (Hartsough and Lamber, 1985). Furthermore, even during infancy there are deviations in activity level; some are overactive but others, interestingly enough, are too passive (Werry, Weiss, and Douglas, 1964). By the preschool years their inattentiveness and overactivity are evident. They do not follow through when given small chores by their parents, and they knock over their baby sister's pile of blocks when asked to play with her. At this stage in their lives, they are often considered temperamental and emotional children (Schain and Reynard, 1975). Their problems attract real notice when they enter school, probably because of the greater degree of structure evident in most elementary school settings. One study (Stewart *et al.,* 1966) com-

TABLE 15.1
Classroom behavior of ADHD and control children (*from Stewart et al., 1966*)

Behavior	Control, percent (N = 33)	Hyperactive, percent (N = 37)
Overactive	33	100
Can't sit still	8	81
Fidgets	30	84
Leaves class without permission	0	35
Can't accept correction	0	35
Temper tantrums	0	51
Fights	3	59
Defiant	0	49
Doesn't complete project	0	84
Doesn't stay with games	3	78
Doesn't listen to whole story	0	49
Moves from one activity to another in class	6	46
Doesn't follow directions	3	62
Hard to get to bed	3	49
Unpopular with peers	0	46
Talks too much	20	68
Wears out toys, furniture, etc.	8	68
Gets into things	11	54
Unpredictable	3	59
Destructive	0	41
Unresponsive to discipline	0	57
Lies	3	43

pared teacher ratings of the behavior of hyperactive and control children (Table 15.1). The actions and attitudes rated make a good catalogue of hyperactivity.

Many hyperactive children have inordinate difficulties getting along with peers and establishing friendships (Whalen and Henker, 1985), probably because their behavior is annoying to others. Although these children are usually friendly and talkative, they often miss subtle social cues, misinterpret peers' intentions, and make unintentional social mistakes. ADHD children are often knowledgeable about correct social actions in hypothetical situations but do not translate this knowledge into appropriate behavior in real-life social interactions. This ineptitude, often combined with impulsive aggressiveness, leads hyperactive children to be rejected by their peers, even in new social groups (Whalen and Henker, 1985).

It is estimated that 8 to 9 percent of elementary school boys and 2 to 3 percent of girls have ADHD (Miller, Palkes, and Stewart, 1973). At one time it was thought that hyperactivity simply went away by adolescence. From a review of the literature, however, Wallander and Hubert (1985) offer the tentative conclusion that ADHD-diagnosed young people continue to have adjustment problems throughout adolescence and some into young adulthood. Their overactivity tends to diminish in adolescence and adulthood, but these young people have more problems finishing school than normal adolescents. Their employment histories are comparable to those of normal individuals, perhaps because they are no longer in the highly structured and cognitively demanding school setting where ADHD tends to show up prominently. And yet in adulthood some of these ADHD people, mostly men, are more likely to abuse alcohol and to have greater numbers of car accidents than do individuals in the general population. Unfavorable outcomes are found both among those who were treated as youngsters and among those who were not.

Physiological Theories of ADHD

The search for causes of ADHD is complicated by the heterogeneity of children given this diagnosis; any factor found to be associated with the syndrome is perhaps linked with only some of those carrying the diagnosis.

A predisposition toward ADHD may be inherited. Morrison and Stewart (1971), for example, found that 20 percent of hyperactive children had a parent who had been hyperactive. The corresponding figure for control children was 5 percent. Similar results have been reported by Gross and Wilson (1974), and the findings have held up in more methodologically sophisticated adoption studies (Morrison and Stewart, 1973; Cantwell, 1975). However, all the available studies on genetic causes of ADHD have been hampered by methodological problems: hyperactive subjects were chosen by unreliable methods; there were no other psychiatric control groups used (such as conduct disordered children); and the experimenters who interviewed the parents were not blind to the children's diagnoses (McMahon, 1980). More rigorous studies are needed before the hypothesis that ADHD is inherited can be confirmed.

A biochemical theory of hyperactivity, proposed by Feingold (1973), has enjoyed much attention in the popular press. He had been treating a woman for allergies while she was concurrently being seen by a psychiatrist for uncontrollable, frenetic behavior. Feingold thought that the patient might be allergic to aspirin and other salicylate compounds, so he prescribed a diet free of them. Both her allergic symptoms and her overactivity rapidly and dramatically diminished. Feingold soon noted the prevalence of salicylates and other similar chemicals in food additives and embarked on a study in which hyperactive children were kept on a diet free of food additives. Many responded favorably, and his work was subsequently replicated (Hawley and Buckley, 1974). Thus it seemed possible that the central nervous systems of some hyperactive children, perhaps through a genetically transmitted predisposition, are upset in some way by food additives. It is unlikely, though, that more than a small percentage of cases of hyperactivity are caused by sensitivity to food additives. Well-controlled studies of the Feingold diet have found that very few such children respond positively (Goyette and Conners, 1977).

There is some evidence that ADHD children suffer from abnormally low levels of arousal in the central nervous system. For example, their cerebral spinal fluid has low levels of homovanillic acid, the major metabolite of dopamine (Shaywitz, Cohen, and Shaywitz, 1978). But, as Whalen (1983) cautions, the cause–effect relations are not straightforward. For example, we know that stress can alter neurotransmitter metabolism; since many ADHD children are probably under abnormally high levels of stress because of the troubles their behavior gets them into, their biochemical differences may be a consequence of, rather than a cause of, their hyperactive behavior. The underarousal theory, however, remains an important one for researchers to pursue.

Some ADHD children show signs of possible brain damage. Their mothers have often had difficult pregnancies (Hartsough and Lamber, 1985), and in infancy hyperactive children are more likely to have had seizures, encephalitis, cerebral palsy, and head injury (Conners *et al.,* 1972). Furthermore, hyperactive behavior can be brought on by lead poisoning (Wiener, 1970). And many hyperactive children show abnormal EEGs (Gross and Wilson, 1974) in addition to "soft" neurological signs, such as clumsiness, confusion of right and left, and poor balance and coordination. However, the neurological signs linked to hyperactivity are also common in other groups of clinic-referred children (Campbell and Werry, 1986), and no data currently available allow greater and more meaningful specification of the vague term brain damage (Sroufe, 1975).

The success of psychostimulant medication in treating hyperactive children was once considered to be additional evidence in support of a physiological theory of hyperactivity. Amphetamines, as discussed in Chapter 11, heighten the adult's sense of energy. Yet they have the effect of increasing attention and decreasing activity level in hyperactive children. This apparently paradoxical effect was taken as evidence for abnormal physiological processes in hyperactive children. Such an interpretation is no longer viable, for some evidence demonstrates that normal children also respond to amphetamines with increased attention and decreased activity (Rapoport *et al.,* 1978). The once presumed "paradoxical effect" has proved to be the normal response of children to psychostimulants.[1]

Psychological Theories of ADHD

Bettelheim (1973) proposed a diathesis–stress theory, suggesting that hyperactivity develops when a predisposition to the disorder is coupled with unfortunate rearing by parents. A child with a disposition toward overactivity and moodiness is stressed further by a mother who easily becomes impatient and resentful. The child is unable to cope with the mother's demands for obedience, the mother becomes more and more negative and disapproving, and the mother–child relationship ends up a battleground. With a disruptive and disobedient pattern already established, the demands of school cannot be handled, and the behavior of the child is often in conflict with the rules of the classroom.

The Fels Research Institute's longitudinal study of child development supplies some evidence that is consistent with Bettelheim's position (Battle and Lacey, 1972). Mothers of hyperactive children were found to be critical of them and relatively unaffectionate, even during the children's infancy. These mothers continued to be disapproving of their children and dispensed severe penalties for disobedience. The parent–child relationship, however, is bidirectional, the behavior of each being determined by the reactions of the other. The influence of hyperactive children's behavior on the actions of their mothers has also been demonstrated (Barkley and Cunningham, 1979). It is plausible, though, that a critical and unaffectionate mother might exacerbate the problems of a hyperactive child (Cunningham and Barkley, 1979).

Finally, although no comprehensive theory has been proposed, two ways in which learning might figure in hyperactivity should be mentioned. First, hyperactivity could be reinforced by the attention it elicits. Second, as Ross and Ross (1982) suggest, hyperactivity may be modeled on the behavior of parents and siblings.

Treatment of ADHD

As already indicated, two somatic treatments for hyperactivity are in use. Stimulant drugs, especially methylphenidate or Ritalin, have been prescribed for this disorder since the early 1960s (Sprague and Gadow, 1976). One estimate is that during the school year 1 to 2 percent of American children are given Ritalin or one of the amphetamines in efforts to control their hyperactivity (Henker and Whalen, 1980). The other somatic

---

[1]In addition to this empirical disconfirmation, the reader is reminded of the logical fallacy of concluding etiology from the effectiveness of treatment.

intervention is the so-called Feingold diet, promulgated by Feingold's 1975 book, *Why Your Child Is Hyperactive,* and by numerous parent associations throughout the country. These associations publish complete diets made up of foods that do not contain such things as artificial flavors and colorings, preservatives, and natural salicylates.

We have already said that few hyperactive children are helped by the Feingold diet. A number of controlled studies comparing stimulants with placebos in double-blind designs indicate dramatic short-term improvements in concentration, goal-directed activity, classroom behavior, fine motor activity, and reduced aggressive behavior and impulsivity in many ADHD children (Weiss, 1983). However, research indicates that such drugs do not improve academic achievement over the long haul (Weiss, 1983) and have little effect on long-term social outcome (Satterfield, Hoppe, and Schell, 1982); in fact, they may sometimes *interfere with* academic performance when administered in doses strong enough to reduce hyperactivity (Sprague and Sleator, 1977).

Despite the absence of a comprehensive theory, treatments of ADHD children based on learning principles have demonstrated at least short-term success in improving both social and academic behavior. In these treatments the behavior of the children is monitored both at home and in school, and they are reinforced for doing the appropriate thing, such as remaining in their seats and working on assignments. Point systems and star charts are frequently a part of these programs; the youngsters earn points and the younger children earn stars for behaving in certain ways. They can then of course "spend" their earnings for backup rewards. It is of special interest that the focus of these operant programs is on improving academic work, completing household tasks, or learning specific social skills, rather than on reducing signs of hyperactivity, such as running around and jiggling (O'Leary *et al.*, 1976). The therapists devising these interventions conceptualize hyperactivity as a deficit in certain skills rather than as an excess of disruptive behavior. Although hyperactive children have proved very responsive to these programs, the optimal treatment for the disorder may require the use of both stimulants and behavior therapy.

Conduct Disorders

The term **conduct disorders** encompasses a wide variety of undercontrolled behavior. There is no single definition. Aggression, lying, destructiveness, vandalism, theft, and truancy are actions usually covered by the general, and rather vague, category of conduct disorders. The connecting thread in this array of behaviors is violation of societal norms and the basic rights of others. The patterns and severity of the acts go beyond the mischief and pranks common among children and adolescents.

Two types of conduct disorders are commonly identified (American Psychiatric Association, 1987; Quay, 1986). The diagnosis **conduct disorder-group type** applies to children who perpetrate frequent antisocial or delinquent acts—truancy, serious lying, stealing, vandalism—as part of a group of peers. **Conduct disorder-solitary aggressive type** is the diagnosis when the essential feature is aggressive physical behavior, initiated by the individual not as part of a group. The latter type of conduct problem is associated with poor social skills, failure to respond to treatment, and a poorer prognosis for adult living than any other disorder except autism (Quay, 1986).

Perhaps more than any other childhood disorder, conduct problems are defined by the impact of the child's behavior on people and surroundings. Schools, parents, and peers usually decide what undercontrolled behavior is unacceptable conduct. Preadolescents and adolescents are often identified as conduct problems by legal authorities. Moral judgments are inherent in our conception of the disorder, for the very term "conduct" carries with it the connotation of "good" and "bad." Moreover, since much of the behavior considered a conduct problem has a high base rate in the general population, a certain level of aggression or disobedience must be "normal." Even juvenile delinquency is difficult to define. As indicated in Table 15.2, a wide variety of illegal acts are committed by a significant proportion of "nondelinquent" populations.[2]

An excerpt from the case history of Tom serves to illustrate the difficulty of defining conduct disorders in terms of behavior alone.

> He entered the church, now, with a swarm of clean and noisy boys and girls, proceeded to his seat and started a quarrel with the first boy who came handy. The teacher, a grave, elderly man, interfered; then turned his back a moment and Tom pulled a boy's hair in the next bench,

---

[2] "Juvenile delinquency" is a legal, not a psychological, term, referring to acts committed by a young person, usually less than eighteen years of age, that are either generally illegal, such as assault or robbery, or illegal only for people of a certain age, such as truancy. It is not surprising, then, that many youngsters who are diagnosed as conduct-disordered run afoul of the law and are judged to be juvenile delinquents by our system of juvenile justice. A young person with a conduct disorder, however, might well evade legal detection.

TABLE 15.2

Frequency of illegal activities in nondelinquent male populations (*from Short and Nye, 1958*)

Delinquent Act	Admit Committing Act, percent			Admit Committing Act More Than Once or Twice, percent		
	Midwestern Students	Western Students	Training School Boys	Midwestern Students	Western Students	Training School Boys
Driving a car without a license	81.1	75.3	91.1	61.2	49.0	73.4
Skipping School	54.4	53.0	95.3	24.4	23.8	85.9
Fist fighting	86.7	80.7	95.3	32.6	31.9	75.0
Running away	12.9	13.0	68.1	2.8	2.4	37.7
School probation or expulsion	15.3	11.3	67.8	2.1	2.9	31.3
Defying parents' authority	22.2	33.1	52.4	1.4	6.3	23.6
Stealing items worth less than $2	62.7	60.6	91.8	18.5	12.9	65.1
Stealing items worth from $2 to $50	17.1	15.8	91.0	3.8	3.8	61.4
Stealing items worth more than $50	3.5	5.0	90.8	1.1	2.1	47.7
Gang fighting	24.3	22.5	67.4	6.7	5.2	47.4
Drinking beer, wine, or liquor	67.7	57.2	89.7	35.8	29.5	79.4
Using narcotics	1.4	2.2	23.1	0.7	1.6	12.6
Having sexual relations	38.8	40.4	87.5	20.3	19.9	73.4

Source: From Adams and Unikel, *Issues and Trends in Behavior Therapy,* © 1973. Courtesy of Charles C. Thomas, Publisher, Springfield, Illinois.

> and was absorbed in his book when the boy turned around; stuck a pin in another boy, presently, in order to hear him say "Ouch!" and got a new reprimand from his teacher. (p. 494)

"But as I was saying," said Aunt Polly, "he warn't bad, so to say—only mischievous. Only, just giddy, and harum-scarum, you know. He warn't any more responsible than a colt. He never meant any harm, and he was the best-hearted boy that ever was." (p. 503)

Based on this sample of Tom's behavior, are we to conclude that he has a conduct disorder? Certainly he is aggressive and disobedient, two of the more frequent indications. And the impact of Tom's behavior on his companions and the Sunday school session is a disruptive one, as we can be sure both Tom's Sunday school teacher and his classmates would report. The excerpt, however, was taken from *The Adventures of Tom Sawyer,* by Mark Twain (1876). Tom Sawyer a conduct problem? No! For over one hundred years Tom has been considered the prototypical All-American boy. Something about Tom, perhaps his cleverness and his affection for Becky, keeps us from thinking of him as a boy with conduct problems. Although he was devilish, even Aunt Polly acknowledged that Tom was not *really* a ruffian.

The factors that make the actions of one child be considered a conduct problem and the same actions of another be accepted as "normal" are intriguing. Unfortunately, they are largely unspecified in the psychological literature. Fertile ground for speculation is provided by the contrast between Tom Sawyer and Huck Finn, who would likely be diagnosed as having a conduct disorder. "Huckleberry was cordially hated and dreaded by all the mothers of the town, because he was idle, and lawless, and vulgar and bad" (p. 464). The fact that Huck had no "proper" family may have been one factor swaying the opinions of the townspeople.

We do not wish to overstate the labeling bias of society, however. Many qualities of the child's behavior itself must be considered in the diagnosis of conduct disorders. Perhaps the two most important criteria for deciding whether a given act is aggressive or problematic are the frequency with which it occurs and the intensity of the behavior (Herbert, 1978). Thus one fight in a year is not a problem, but one fight per week is. (The percentage of young people committing a delinquent act the second time is sometimes dramatically less than the percentage who do it once, as indicated in Table 15.2.) Similarly, whereas stealing a candy bar is a minor incident, stealing a car is a felony. These criteria of frequency and intensity do not fully solve the problem of defining conduct disorders, but they are important considerations.

Because of the definitional difficulties, the prevalence of conduct disorders is impossible to estimate accurately. With little doubt, however, they are quite common. Approximately one-third of all referrals made to child guidance clinics are for conduct problems (Wiltz and Patterson, 1974). Furthermore, since it is estimated that most children with conduct problems do not receive treatment (Bahm, Chandler, and Eisenberg, 1961), clinic referrals would not reflect the true prevalence of these problems. If both of these suppositions are accurate, conduct disorders must be the most frequent psychological problem of childhood.

Conduct problems are from three to ten times more frequent in males than in females, although their incidence in females may be increasing (Herbert, 1978). Generally, the more serious the delinquent act, the greater the ratio of males to females committing it. Juvenile crime is a major problem, particularly in the more violent categories of robbery and aggravated assault. The rate of juvenile crime increased greatly in the 1960s and 1970s and has now leveled off at this high frequency.

The prognosis for children diagnosed as having conduct disorders is poor. Robins (1966, 1972), in her thirty-year follow-up study of adults who as children had been seen in a child guidance clinic (see page 263), found that fully 50 percent of them had in their younger years been incarcerated in correctional institutions, and that the majority of the people in this clinic sample continued to be antisocial in their behavior during adulthood. Aggressive behavior, in particular, has been found to be as stable as IQ, persisting from preschool and childhood into adulthood (Quay, 1986). As is the case with hyperactivity, it is clear that conduct problems are not simply outgrown.

Etiology of Conduct Disorders

Numerous theories have been offered for the etiology of conduct disorders. Physiological explanations are suggested by the fact that a higher incidence of antisocial behavior is found in the relatives of delinquent children than in the general population (Cloninger, Reich, and Guze, 1975). Furthermore, twin studies show con-

"DON'T YOU REALIZE, PETER, THAT WHEN YOU THROW FURNITURE OUT THE WINDOW AND TIE YOUR SISTER TO A TREE, YOU MAKE MOMMY AND DADDY VERY SAD?"

sistently higher concordance rates for antisocial behavior in identical pairs than in fraternal pairs (Eysenck, 1975). The effects of rearing are indicated by findings that families of these children frequently lack cohesiveness (Craig and Glick, 1963), and that they have experienced the stresses of marital discord and divorce (Rutter, 1971; Emery and O'Leary, 1979; see Box 15.2).

An important part of normal child development is the growth of moral awareness, acquiring a sense of what is right and wrong and the ability, even desire, to abide by rules and norms. Most people refrain from hurting others, not only because it is illegal but because it would make them feel guilty to do otherwise. Research into the backgrounds of conduct-disordered youngsters has shown a pattern of family life lacking in factors believed to be central to the development of a strong moral sense. Strong affection between child and parents; making firm moral demands on the child; using sanctions in a consistent manner; punishing psychologically rather than physically, to induce anxiety and guilt rather than anger; and reasoning and explaining things to the child all help in this development (Herbert, 1982; Hoffman, 1970; Wright, 1971).

BOX 15.2

THE ROLE OF MARITAL DISCORD IN CONDUCT DISORDERS

The role that separation and divorce play in fostering conduct problems and delinquency has been an issue of debate. The incidence of delinquency is greater in one-parent families than in two-parent families (e.g., Glueck and Glueck, 1959). Some have argued that separation from a parent by itself causes delinquency (Bowlby, 1973). If this assumption is correct, parents would be wise to stay together "for the child's sake."

But research evidence contradicts this conclusion. McCord, McCord, and Thurber (1962) compared the rates of gang delinquency in the sons from three groups of homes. The three types consisted of happy single-parent homes, happy homes inhabited by both parents, and unhappy single-parent homes. The researchers found that rates of delinquency of sons from the two types of happy homes were very similar, but the unhappy single-parent homes produced a greater percentage of delinquents. On the basis of this finding, they concluded that discord, not separation, was the more likely cause of delinquency. The confounding of two factors, separation and marital conflict, would explain the misinterpretations of the results of other studies. Comparisons of homes broken by death with homes broken by divorce support the conclusion that discord is the important factor. A parent's death, unlike a parent's absence through separation or divorce, is not associated with a higher incidence of conduct disorder in the children (Felner, Stolberg, and Cowen, 1975; Rutter, 1979). Although the separation per se does have disruptive effects, family conflict is apparently the key contributor to delinquency and conduct problems.

Emery (1982) discusses several theories proposed to explain how marital discord adversely affects children. The modeling hypothesis suggests that interparental conflict sets an example of using hostility and aggression as a way of handling problems; the parents' behaviors are imitated by the children (particularly boys), who are then seen as conduct disordered. Another theory suggests that parents who

Marital discord and divorce are sometimes associated with conduct disorders.

have marital problems are less consistent in their discipline techniques, leading to undercontrolled behavior in the children. A third possibility, proposed by Minuchin (1974), is that children develop problems as a way of distracting parents from their own conflict.

Each of these theories (and others) may prove useful in describing the mechanism that links marital turmoil with children's problems. They all seem to suggest that parents should minimize their children's involvement in marital conflict, for example, by not arguing about marital or discipline issues in front of the children.

Conduct-disordered children, like the sociopaths discussed in Chapter 10, seem to be deficient in this moral awareness, viewing antisocial acts as exciting and rewarding, indeed as central to their very self-concept (Ryall, 1974). Some psychodynamic theorists have explained conduct problems and delinquency as "disorder(s) in the functioning of the superego" (Kessler, 1966, p. 303). In psychoanalytic theory the superego is the part of the psyche that governs behavior according to societal and parental rules; thus conduct problems are traced to a failure of conscience and moral development.

Several other psychological theories have merit. Learning theories that look to both modeling and op-

erant conditioning have received considerable attention as explanations of the development and maintenance of conduct problems. Bandura and Walters (1963) were among the first to point out the obvious, that children can learn aggressiveness from parents who behave in this way. Children may also imitate aggressive acts that are seen elsewhere, such as on television (Liebert, Neale, and Davidson, 1973). Since aggression is an effective, albeit unpleasant, means of achieving a goal, it is likely to be reinforced. Thus, once imitated, aggressive acts will probably be maintained.

Bandura and Walters (1959) found that the families of antisocial adolescents use physical punishment more often than control families and are more likely to reward aggressive acts. A later study by Hetherington and Martin (1979) confirmed and extended these findings. Youngsters in treatment for aggressive or antisocial behavior were likely to have siblings and fathers who themselves had records of aggressive and criminal behavior. These studies, although limited by a cross-sectional design,[3] indicate that modeling and reinforcement are part of the etiology of at least some conduct problems.

Patterson (1986) has offered a more specific explanation of how conduct problems are rewarded in families. His *coercion hypothesis* is best demonstrated by an example from our clinical files.

> Chris was an eight-year-old boy brought to the clinic by his mother, who described him as unmanageable. Whenever his mother refused to comply with Chris's requests, he became upset. At these times Chris would be stubborn, uncooperative, and verbally abusive. Occasionally he would throw a temper tantrum and lie down on the floor, kicking his feet and screaming. His mother usually ignored Chris's behavior for a few minutes, but she gave in to his demands when his tantrums became too difficult for her to bear. This sequence of agitation and giving in had become habitual, particularly when the mother was busy. When she felt rushed and perturbed, she gave in to Chris almost immediately.

The coercion hypothesis postulates that both Chris and his mother are rewarded in this sequence of events. Chris is rewarded by getting his own way, his mother by the cessation of Chris's obnoxious behavior. Through this mutual rewarding both Chris's conduct problems and his mother's acquiescence are likely to be maintained. Therapy based on the coercion hypothesis would direct the mother never to give in to Chris while he is misbehaving and thereby extinguish his conduct problem. The coercion hypothesis seems a likely model, but it explains only how obstreperous behavior is *maintained*, not how it first *develops*.

In any discussion of conduct disorders and delinquency, the work of sociologists must be recognized. Social class and urban living in particular are related to the incidence of delinquency. High unemployment, poor educational facilities, disrupted family life, and a subculture that deems delinquency acceptable have all been found to be contributing factors (Gibbons, 1975). Any comprehensive theory of delinquency and conduct disorders would need to include these consistent sociological findings.

Treatment of Conduct Disorders

The management of conduct disorders poses a formidable challenge to contemporary society. Sociologists and politicians, as well as community psychologists, working on the assumption that poor economic conditions create most of the problem, argue for a fairer distribution of income and for job programs and other large-scale efforts to alleviate the material deprivation of the lower classes, among whom, as previously noted, delinquency is often found.

As meritorious as such proposals might be on moral and political grounds, the broad sociological view gives too little consideration to two simple facts: only a minority of lower-class youngsters are "hoods," and conduct problems are to be found in sizable numbers among children and adolescents of middle- and upper-class families.[4] Mischief and crime of well-to-do young people are underrepresented in police statistics because the status and social influence of their families often keep these children from being booked and incarcerated, as poorer youngsters are. Although sociological considerations may play some role in planning treatments, we emphasize here psychological methods aimed more at the particular individuals and their families.

Some of the young people with undersocialized conduct disorder are the sociopaths of tomorrow. Just as precious little in the way of effective psychological treatment has been found for sociopathy, so are there few ways to reach young people who commit violent and antisocial acts with little remorse or emotional involvement. These callous young individuals, most of them male, "graduate from" training schools and youth farms to lives of crime and dissoluteness, interrupted by extended periods of incarceration in prisons. Recidivism

---

[3]The findings are only correlational. In such cross-sectional studies it is possible that the aggressiveness of the children elicits physical punishment from their parents. A longitudinal study would show if a cause–effect relationship exists. Say, for example, a child is not aggressive at age five but lives in a home in which he is punished physically. By age ten he may have become an aggressive youngster. Because punishment preceded the child's aggression, we are better able to draw a causal inference.

[4]One view of the juvenile delinquency of young people from affluent backgrounds holds that, with time on their hands, they sometimes make the conscious choice to engage in antisocial acts, not out of any felt economic need but as a way to fill their leisure hours. They supposedly engage in a bit of deliberation, weighing the positive consequences against the negative.

TABLE 15.3
Parents' data for targeted behaviors of aggressive child (*from Patterson, Cobb, and Ray, 1973*)

Child	Targeted Behaviors for Which Parent Data Available	Mean for Baseline Data	Mean for Intervention Data
Fred	Noncompliance, hitting	.150	.000
Carl	Noncompliance, temper tantrums	.068	.009
Zeke	Noncompliance, tease	.150	.005
Will	Noncompliance, lies	.005	.003
Ted	Noncompliance, demands	.043	.002
Hal	Noncompliance, swear	.021	.000
Mark	Noncompliance, hitting, yelling	.040	.005
Sam	Noncompliance, steal, hitting	.115	.005
Roy	Noncompliance	.124	.040
Steve	Noncompliance, hitting, yelling, surliness	.063	.000
Jack	Tease	.025	.003
Oren	Noncompliance	.082	.017
Craig	Noncompliance, bickering	.026	.003
Mean		.070	.007

Source: From Adams and Unikel, *Issues and Trends in Behavior Therapy,* © 1973. Courtesy of Charles C. Thomas, Publisher, Springfield, Illinois.

is the rule. One of society's most enduring problems is how to deal with people whose social consciences appear grossly underdeveloped.

Some of the most promising approaches to treating conduct disorder involve intervening with the parents or families of the antisocial child. Gerald Patterson and his colleagues have worked for over two decades developing and testing a behavioral program of parent-management training, in which parents are taught to modify their responses to their children so that prosocial rather than antisocial behavior is consistently rewarded. Parents are taught social-learning principles through readings and presentations, and are taught to use techniques such as positive reinforcement when the child exhibits positive behaviors and time-out and loss of privileges for aggressive or antisocial behavior. Sessions include practicing the techniques and a discussion of difficulties the parents may encounter when applying the methods to an antisocial child. Patterson's group has demonstrated the effectiveness of this program as evidenced both by parents' and teachers' reports of children's behavior and by direct observation of behavior at home and at school (see Table 15.3) (Patterson, 1982). Parent-management training has even been shown to improve the behavior of siblings and reduce depression in mothers involved in the program (Kazdin, 1985).

Although parent-focused intervention is often the treatment of choice for children with conduct disorder, these are situations when direct intervention with the disturbed individual is more appropriate. Parent-man-

agement training requires a great deal of time and effort from at least one parent and can be difficult to carry out in families with multiple social problems. In fact, research has demonstrated that parent-focused training is much less effective in families with low socioeconomic status or marital discord, and when there is psychopathology in one or both parents (Kazdin, 1985).

Research by Dodge and Frame (1982) suggests a direction for cognitive therapy. They examined the cognitive processes associated with aggressive behavior and found a cognitive bias that might underlie such antisociality. Their finding was that aggressive boys interpret ambiguous acts (such as being bumped in line) as hostile. This biased view may lead such boys to retaliate aggressively to actions that may not have been intended to be provocative. Their peers, remembering these aggressive acts, may tend to aggress more often against them, further angering the aggressive children. This cycle can lead to peer rejection and further aggression.

Anger-control training is one promising method of teaching aggressive children self-control in anger-provoking situations. Hinshaw, Henker, and Whalen (1984) helped children learn to withstand verbal attacks without responding aggressively using distracting techniques such as humming a tune, saying calming things to themselves, or turning away. The children than practiced these self-control methods while a peer provoked and insulted them.

These methods are preventive, focusing mainly on younger children who have not yet exhibited serious

Direct training in controlling anger is now being used with aggressive children.

criminal or delinquent behavior. Once conduct-disordered children or adolescents have come into contact with the juvenile justice system, it becomes much more difficult to redirect them to a prosocial way of life. In fact, studies of "diversion" suggest that avoiding contact with the court system is essential to success in treating delinquents. Davidson *et al.* (1987) compared several types of treatments, all having the common element of pairing a college student with a juvenile delinquent for 6–8 hours per week in the community. They found that the specific content of those meetings (behavioral contracting versus focusing on empathy, unconditional positive regard, and communication skills) was less important than the factor of removal from the justice system. Even a watered-down treatment involving minimal supervision by the college volunteers was superior to a more rigorous treatment where supervision was administered within the court building by a court caseworker (even though the juveniles had no contact with the court during treatment).

Disorders of Overcontrolled Behavior

Overcontrolled behavior, as indicated earlier, usually creates more problems for the individual child than for others.[5] Unlike undercontrolled children whose behavior is judged by others, children with problems of overcontrol frequently complain of bothersome fears and tenseness; of feelings of shyness, of being unhappy and unloved; and of being inferior to other children. Symptoms of overcontrolled behavior are similar to those of the adult problems of anxiety and depression. The three specific problems of overcontrol we shall discuss are frequently found in the same child: childhood fears, social withdrawal, and depression (Quay, 1979). The first two problems are roughly equivalent to the DSM-IIIR listings ***separation anxiety disorder*** and ***avoidant disorder.*** Childhood depression is not a specific diagnostic category in DSM-IIIR; as will be seen, the evidence for depression in children is controversial.

Childhood Fears

Most children have many fears that are apparently "outgrown" in the normal course of development. For example, Jersild, Markey, and Jersild (1933) interviewed 398 children of ages five to twelve. Fear of the following were expressed by substantial numbers: supernatural events, for example, ghosts and witches, 19.2 percent; being alone, in the dark, or in a strange place, being lost, 14.6 percent; attack or danger of attack by animals, 13.7 percent; bodily injury, falling, illness, operations, hurt and pains, 12.8 percent. The results of a similar study of generally younger children appear in Figure 15.1. Certain types of fears diminish as children become older. Experience with various everyday objects apparently takes away their fearsomeness. But imaginary fears magnify and are acquired by more and more children as they gain in months and years. Later on, by the time children are in the sixth grade, fears of imaginary creatures have been abandoned, but fears of bodily injury and physical danger have increased (Bauer, 1976).

The suffering experienced by a fearful child should not be underestimated. In contrast to adults, who are usually able to acknowledge that many of their fears are baseless, children do not have enough years behind them to adopt this realistic perspective (Wicks-Nelson and Israel, 1984). As recounted in DSM-IIIR, children's fears often affect them physically: they have headaches, stomachaches, and nausea, and they vomit. Children may have a near-obsessive concern that parents will be hurt during an absence, or that they will never see them again. They may be subject to nightmares and insomnia, indeed, to an overwhelming sense

---

[5]We must not, however, underestimate the toll taken on parents, family members in general, and teachers by the problems described in this section.

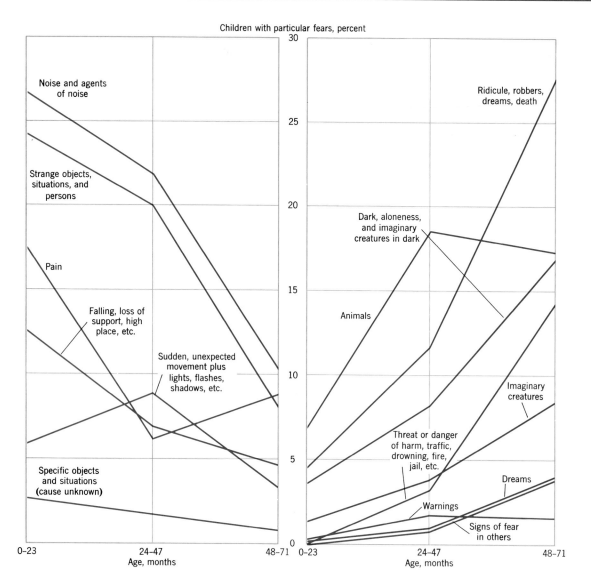

FIGURE 15.1
Relative frequency of fears of various kinds shown by children of different ages who were observed by parents and teachers in the Jersild and Holmes study (1935). After Gray (1971).

of dread and apprehension that permeates their young lives and robs them of the simple pleasures that childhood can bring. Perhaps the sense of helplessness spoken of earlier aggravates a situation that is already grim in the eyes of the child.[6]

School Phobia
One childhood fear, **school phobia,** has attracted the

most attention, for not only is it disabling to the child and disruptive to the household, but it also appears to be a true phobia, an extreme avoidance that does not usually just go away with the passage of time. Furthermore, it has serious academic and social consequences for the youngster. Waldfogel (1959) offers the following definition.

School phobia refers to a reluctance to go to school because of acute fear associated with it. Usually this dread is accompanied by somatic symptoms with the gastrointestinal tract the most commonly affected. . . . The somatic complaints come to be used as an auxil-

---

[6]Some children have an entirely new fear, the fear that the world will be annihilated in a thermonuclear holocaust. Parents and professionals alike have difficulty providing the same kind of ironclad reassurance that they can offer when, for example, a youngster is afraid of the dark.

The first day of school for an obviously frightened child.

*iary device to justify staying at home and often disap-
pear when the child is reassured that he will not have
to attend school. The characteristic picture is of a child
nauseated or complaining of abdominal pain at breakfast and desperately resisting all attempts at reassurance, reasoning, or coercion to get him to school. In
its milder forms, school phobia may be only a transient symptom; but when it becomes established, it can
be one of the most disabling disorders of childhood,
lasting even for years.* (pp. 35–36)

The frequency of school phobias has been estimated
at 17 per 1000 children per year (Kennedy, 1965), and
is more common in boys than in girls. School phobia is
thought to be rooted both in actual fear of being in
school and in separation anxiety, but primarily in separation anxiety. Since the beginning of school is often
the first circumstance that requires lengthy and frequent
separations of children from their parents, separation
anxiety is frequently a principal cause of school phobia.

In fact, school phobia is listed in DSM-IIIR as one of
several manifestations of separation anxiety disorder.

If separation anxiety largely accounts for school phobias that commence with enrollment in school, how are
the serious school phobias that develop later to be explained? Johnson and his colleagues (1941) have offered
one interpretation. First some environmental event,
which may be related to the school setting itself, elicits
increased anxiety in the child. At the same time the
mother becomes increasingly anxious about some problem of her own. A dependent relationship between
mother and child may then conspire to increase further
the anxiety that occurs naturally when mother and child
are separated by the child's going to school. Thus the
child starts to avoid school, and the mother does not
protest too strongly. She may even unwittingly reward
the child's nonattendance for her own purposes. Given
that the dependent relationship works both ways, the
child being dependent on the mother and the mother
being dependent on the child, the mother may not wish
to lose her child to the school each day. Several factors
may therefore conspire to keep the child from school.
Initial, perhaps realistic, fears may make the young
child withdraw from school to seek the comforting figure of her mother. This dependency on her mother is
consoling and reinforces both mother and child for
avoiding the feared situation. Finally, since the object
of fear is not confronted, actual fears are not reduced
and may, in fact, be worsened.[7]

Treatment of Childhood Fears

How are childhood fears overcome? As Figure 15.1
indicates, many simply dissipate with time and maturation. Perhaps the most widespread means of helping
children overcome fears, employed by millions of parents, is to expose them gradually to the feared object,
often while acting simultaneously to inhibit their anxiety. If a little girl fears strangers, a parent takes her
by the hand and walks her slowly toward the new person. Mary Cover Jones (see page 538) was the first
psychologist to explain this bit of folk wisdom as a counterconditioning procedure.

Indeed, contemporary therapists have by and large
built on folk wisdom in helping children overcome fears.
Exposure is generally agreed to be the most effective
way of eliminating baseless fear and avoidance. Modeling has also proved effective, both in laboratory studies
(e.g., Bandura, Grusec, and Menlove, 1967) and in
countless clinical treatments; for example, another child,
one the fearful child is likely to imitate, demonstrates

---

[7]For a general discussion of the etiology of phobias, the reader is
referred back to Chapter 6, page 136.

BOX 15.3

PLAY THERAPY AND FAMILY THERAPY: TWO GENERAL METHODS OF TREATING CHILDHOOD PROBLEMS

Many of the childhood disorders discussed in the present chapter, and even the more serious problems to be reviewed in the next, are treated by two general methods, *play therapy* and *family therapy*.

Children are usually less verbal than adults, at least in the sense that is needed for psychoanalytic and client-centered therapy. Moreover, children are often more reluctant than older clients to voice their concerns and complaints directly and openly. Through the pioneering work of Melanie Klein (1932) and Anna Freud (1946b), play became an analytic vehicle for delving into a child's unconscious, taking the place of the free association and recounting of dreams that mean so much in analytic treatment of adults. It is assumed that in play therapy a child will express his or her feelings about problems, parents, teachers, and peers. A play therapy room is equipped with puppets, blocks, games, puzzles, drawing materials, paints, water, sand, clay, toy guns and soldiers, and a large inflated rubber clown, Bobo, to punch. These toys will, it is hoped, help draw out inner tensions and concerns. A dollhouse inhabited by parental and child dolls is a common fixture. The therapist may encourage a young male client to place the figures in "any room you wish," to position the dolls in a way "that makes you feel good." The child may assemble members of the little family in the living room, except for the father, who is placed in his study. "What is Daddy doing?" the therapist will ask. "He's working. If he weren't such a meanie, he'd come out and play with the kids." The therapist will then, as he or she would for an adult, interpret for the boy the wish he seems reluctant to express openly.

In nondirective play therapy, such as that practiced by Virginia Axline (1964), the relationship between the therapist and child developed through play is used to provide a corrective emotional experience for the child. Rather than interpreting the child's symbolic expressions, the client-centered therapist responds to the child's words and actions in an empathic manner, demonstrating unconditional acceptance.

There has been little controlled research to evaluate the claims made for play therapy by its adherents. What evidence is available, however, does not find it to be notably effective (Barrett, Hampe, and Miller, 1978; Phillips, 1985). One area of promise is play therapy with cognitive-behavioral components. For example, short-term puppet play containing rehearsal and modeling has been demonstrated to help reduce anxiety in children about to undergo surgery (Cassell, 1965).

Whatever ultimate purposes may be served by play therapy, at the very least it is likely to help the adult therapist

Play therapy is often used to test children with limited verbal skills.

establish rapport with a youngster. An adult client might respond favorably to a therapist who is empathic, kindly, and replete with professional degrees, but a little girl is likely to be suspicious and regard "Dr. X" as an ally of her parents or teacher, with no real interest in her. Therapists of varying persuasions, including behavior therapists who would eschew the symbolic significance an analytic worker might see in the child's play, commonly use a playroom to establish a relationship with a young client and perhaps also to determine from what the child says and does with toys the youngster's perspective of the problem.

Because children usually live with their parents and siblings, and because their lives are so inextricably bound up with them, many therapists examine and attempt to alter patterns of interactions in families rather than see the troubled child or young adolescent alone. Family therapy (page 580) too is practiced by therapists of all persuasions. Practitioners hold that the child's problem has been caused or is maintained by disturbed relationships within the family. For example, the father may have defaulted on his own responsibilities, forcing a male child to take a more adult role than he feels ready to assume. As we have pointed out many times, however, treatments that help alleviate a problem may in no way indicate its etiology. The fact that clarifying and altering disturbed family relationships relieve the disorders of children does not mean that the disturbed relationships themselves caused their problems in the first place. Many clinical reports and the intrinsic plausibility of family therapy suggest that future studies will back up claims of success made by enthusiasts.

fearless behavior. Offering rewards for moving closer to a feared object or situation can also be encouragement to a fearful child.[8] When the fear and avoidance of a school phobic child are very great and of long duration, they may require desensitization through direct, graduated exposure plus operant shaping. In one of our cases, the therapist started with walks to school with nine-year-old Paul. Next the boy, one step at a time on successive days, entered the schoolyard, then an empty classroom after school, attended the opening morning exercises and then left, sat at the desk, spent time in school, all with the therapist beside him, then with the therapist out of sight but still nearby. In the last steps, when anxiety seemed to have lessened, promises to play the guitar for Paul at night, comic books, and tokens that would eventually earn the boy a baseball glove were the enticements for attending school (Lazarus, Davison, and Polefka, 1965).

Finally, some new situations may be threatening not only for children but for adults as well, because the person lacks the knowledge and skills to deal with them. Thus a child's fear of the water may very well be based on a reasonable judgment that danger lurks there because he or she cannot swim. Parents and therapists must see to it that children have the opportunity to acquire knowledge and relevant skills.

Treatment outcome studies suggest that time-limited treatment of children's phobias can be very effective. For example, Hampe, Noble, Miller, and Barrett (1973) treated 67 phobic children for eight weeks, using either a behavioral or insight-oriented therapy. Sixty percent of the treated children were free of their phobia at the end of the eight-week period and did not experience a relapse or additional emotional problems during the two-year follow-up period. Eighty percent of the sample (those just mentioned plus others who sought further treatment elsewhere) were free of symptoms after two years, with only 7 percent continuing to experience a severe phobia. The authors conclude that, although many childhood phobias go away on their own, treatment greatly hastens recovery (Box 15.3).

Social Withdrawal

Most classrooms have in attendance at least one or two children who are extremely quiet and shy. Oftentimes these same children will play only with family members or familiar peers, avoiding strangers both young and old. Their shyness may prevent them from acquiring

Shy children keep to themselves in playgrounds, all the while wanting to join in.

skills and participating in a variety of activities that most of their agemates enjoy, for they avoid playgrounds and games played by neighborhood children. Although some youngsters who are shy may simply be "slow to warm up," withdrawn children never do, even after prolonged exposure to new people. Extremely shy children may refuse to speak at all in unfamiliar social circumstances; this is called ***elective mutism.*** In crowded rooms they cling and whisper to their parents, hide behind the furniture, and cower in corners. At home they ask their parents endless questions about situations that worry them. Withdrawn children usually have warm and satisfying relationships with family members and family friends, and they do show an eagerness for affection and acceptance. Because the point at which shyness or withdrawal becomes a problem varies, no statistics of the frequency of ***social-withdrawal disorder*** have been compiled.

Theories of the etiology of social withdrawal are not well worked out. It is often suggested that anxiety interferes with social interaction and thus causes the child to avoid social situations. Or withdrawn children may simply not have the social know-how that facilitates interaction with their agemates. The finding that isolated children make fewer attempts to make friends and are less imaginative in their play may indicate a deficiency in certain social skills. Finally, isolated children may have become so because they have in the past spent most of their time with adults; they do interact more freely with adults than with other children (Scarlett, 1980).

---

[8]Of course both modelling and operant treatments involve exposure to what is feared.

Treatment for withdrawal or social avoidance disorders is similar to the treatment of childhood fears. In one innovative study, youngsters were helped by viewing films in which other isolated children gradually engage in and come to enjoy play with their peers (O'Connor, 1969). Another group of researchers paired undergraduate volunteers with socially isolated children on the playground during recess (Allen *et al.*, 1976). The goal was to help start group games that would include the target child and give *in vivo* feedback to the child about which behavior promoted or inhibited positive interactions with other children. By the end of the six-month program, the volunteers were standing on the sidelines, observing the children playing with their peers.

Some shy children lack specific social skills needed for peer interaction. Skills such as asking questions (Ladd, 1981), giving compliments, and starting conversations with agemates (Michelson, Sugai, Wood, and Kazdin, 1983) may be taught in small groups or pairs, with interactions videotaped so the child and "coach" can observe and modify the new behaviors.

Affective Disorders in Childhood

Clinical reports in the literature describe what appear to be instances of both major depression and bipolar disorder in children. The DSM-IIIR leaves the door open to controversy about the diagnosis of childhood depression by including the criteria for it as part of the criteria for adult depression. The manual goes on to describe "age-specific features" that are likely to accompany depression in children and adolescents. For example, prepubertal depressed children are described as likely to have somatic complaints and psychomotor agitation, and adolescents with depression are likely to demonstrate antisocial behavior, alcohol and drug use, and sensitivity to rejection in love relationshps.

On the other hand, Lefkowitz and Burton (1978) point out that some symptoms included in the diagnosis of (adult) depression are very common in childhood. For example 37 percent of girls and 29 percent of boys have poor appetite at age six (MacFarlane, Allen, and Honzik, 1954). Whereas Lefkowitz and Burton (1978) argue that such statistically prevalent behavior should be considered a transient phenomenon of normal child development, Costello (1980) points out that common behaviors may still have clinical significance. In addition, although individual *symptoms* of depression are quite common in children, the whole *syndrome* of depressive disorder (e.g., as defined by DSM-IIIR) appears to have more meaning as a guide for targeting children who need intervention.

Researchers have reported widely varying findings on the prevalence of childhood depression. Rutter, Tizard, and Whitmore (1970), using conservative criteria, conducted an extensive survey of children on the Isle of Wight; they found that fewer than 1 percent were depressed. In marked constrast, other studies (e.g., Weinberg *et al.*, 1973) have reported much higher figures. Reasons for the contradictory findings lie in part in using a wide age range of subjects as well as different sex ratios, varying patient samples (such as inpatient versus outpatient), and different diagnostic criteria (Cantwell, 1983). Another problem in diagnosing childhood depression has been the practice by some researchers of choosing a very broad range of behavior to indicate its presence. To this range they couple the notion of "masked depression," which is behavior not considered indicative of depression in adults—such as hyperactivity, psychophysiological reactions, school problems, aggression—yet nonetheless thought to reflect an "underlying" depression in children. Clearly, such an expansive definition, which is unsupported by data, means that a large number of diagnoses will probably be invalid.

How shall we then conceptualize depression in children? Developmental psychologists remind us that children are *not* miniature versions of adults. It may therefore be unwise to assume that depression will take the same form in youngsters that it does in adults. In part, of course, the problem is to arrive at a consensual definition of childhood depression that will be useful in investigation and treatment. Achenbach and Edelbrock (1981) had parents bringing their children for mental health services and parents of control children rate their respective youngsters on a number of items. The item "unhappy, sad, or depressed" was applied to no more than 13 percent of the control children between the ages of four and sixteen. But referred children had this item applied to them by their parents with much greater frequency. Rates ranged from 43 percent for four- and five-year-old boys to 80 percent for twelve- and thirteen-year-old girls. Other items applied by parents that correlated strongly with sad affect for children between the ages of six and eleven were complaints of loneliness, feels too guilty, feels worthless or inferior, nervous, sulks a lot, worrying, too fearful or anxious, feels he or she has to be perfect, self-conscious or easily embarrassed, and fears he or she might think or do something bad. As Achenbach (1982) comments, although these complaints and disconsolating feelings are rather different from the DSM-IIIR criteria for depression in adults (see page 220), they do seem to reflect depression.

If we accept that some children present the depression syndrome, we must ask what causes a child to become depressed? Several theories of etiology have been suggested. As discussed in Chapter 9, evidence supports the role of a genetic factor in adult depression. Perhaps genetics are implicated in childhood depression as well. Studies of children have also focused on family relationships, hypothesizing that such factors play an important role in child psychopathology. Puig-Antich and colleagues (Puig-Antich *et al.*, 1985) interviewed mothers of three groups of children: depressed, normal, and a group with psychiatric diagnoses other than affective disorders. Several aspects of interpersonal functioning distinguished depressed children from the other groups: the mother–child relationship of depressed children was characterized by less communication, less warmth, more hostility, and less time spent in activities together; relationships between the father and the depressed child revealed more tension and hostility and less warmth; depressed children were less able to maintain a "best friend" and were more likely to be teased by their peers; and the sibling relationships of depressed children were especially difficult. Although these interpersonal problems were less pronounced after successful treatment with antidepressant medication (peer relationships, in particular, showed improvement), the previously depressed children still experienced interpersonal relationships that were significantly worse than those of normal children. The authors point out that it is not yet clear whether poor social bonds cause depression in children, whether depression produces persistent impairments in social relationships, or whether some third variable causes both depression and interpersonal difficulties.

Suicide is the third most common cause of death among young people in the United States, exceeded only by accidents and homicide. It is conceivable that some of their deaths deemed accidental are actually suicides, a number of them subintentioned.[9] Depression in young people heightens suicide risk, especially for those between the ages of fifteen to nineteen. But even at much younger ages children, lacking the time perspective that comes with maturity, can become so despondent, so completely without hope of things becoming better, that they attempt to end their lives. However, as we have discussed previously (see page 243), suicide is not always linked to depression. Adolescents appear to commit suicide far less from depression than from personal conflicts and developmental crises, such as the breakup of a love affair (Achenbach, 1982; Cytryn and

McKnew, 1979). Moreover, one study found that adolescents treated for a suicide attempt were three to six times more likely than controls to have had previous contact with the Department of Social Services because of child abuse or neglect charges (Deykin, Alpert, and McNamarra, 1985).

Eating Disorders

Anorexia Nervosa

Anorexia nervosa is a life-threatening disorder unaccounted for by any known physical disease. The term anorexia means severe loss of appetite, and nervosa indicates for emotional reasons. Interestingly, the word anorexia is a misnomer because many anorexics do not initially so much lose their appetites as fear eating (Achenbach, 1982). Serious weight loss, an intense fear of becoming obese, and a refusal to eat sufficiently to gain or maintain body weight are three principal symptoms of this mysterious disorder. The self-starvation imposed by anorexics brings about physiological changes that are sometimes difficult to reverse; estimates vary, but approximately 5 percent die. Another 25 percent of anorexics continue in the unremitting course of their disorder at two-year follow-up, and the remainder gain weight back as a result of treatment (Hsu, 1980).

Anorexia is far more common in young women than in men. Ratios as high as twenty female anorexics for one male have been reported; approximately one of every 200 school-aged women is anorexic (Crisp, Palmer, and Klucy, 1976). Onset of the weight loss most commonly begins during adolescence, shortly after the beginning of menstruation. Amenorrhea, failure to menstruate regularly, is a characteristic feature of anorexia nervosa, often starting before weight loss has become noticeable. These young women begin losing weight because, being a little plump or sometimes obese, they decide to diet; but the dieting continues far beyond reasonable bounds. Anorexics may take laxatives and exercise extensively and frantically to lose weight. The manic energy expended in excessive physical activity is amazing, considering their emaciation.

Anorexics are preoccupied with food, even when they are struggling not to ingest it. They become interested in its preparation, collecting cookbooks, trying new recipes, and planning and cooking elaborate meals of many courses and special dishes for others. Many anorexics do not admit to feeling any hunger, but others say they do feel hungry but force themselves not to eat. Admission to feeling hungry is associated with binge eat-

---

[9]This loss of life is clearly tragic, but the fact that suicide is the third-ranking cause of death in young people should be placed in perspective. Young people and children are far less likely than adults to die from disease. Therefore their deaths are more likely to be from accidents and suicide. The *rates* of suicide in children and adolescents are actually quite low, nowhere near those of adults.

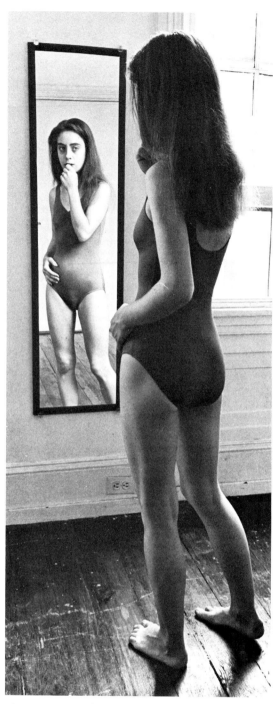

A young anorexic woman studying her body in an attempt to overcome her belief that she is too fat.

A commonly reported phenomenon of anorexia is a distorted body image. Despite their protruding ribs and hipbones, their skull-like faces, their broomstick limbs, anorexics do not view themselves as being too thin. Rather, in frequent scrutinizings of their figures in mirrors, they either continue to see themselves as too fat or feel that they have finally arrived at an attractive weight. Anorexics are often described as "good girls." They are well-behaved, conscientious, quiet, and often perfectionistic.

The Etiology of Anorexia Nervosa

Theories of anorexia are varied and largely unsubstantiated. Some psychological explanations of the disorder have been based on Freud's notion that eating can be a substitute for sexual expression. Thus the anorexic's refusal to eat is thought to indicate fear of increasing sexual desires or perhaps of oral impregnation (Ross, 1977).

Learning theorists have suggested that anorexia may be a weight phobia (Crisp, 1967) or a striving to effect the image of the beautifully slim woman so extensively modeled and emulated by our society (Bemis, 1978). A review of centerfolds from *Playboy Magazine* revealed that the height and weight of models decreased significantly over a twenty-year period. Similarly, Miss America Pageant contestants have become thinner, and the winners of these contests are thinner still, weighing far less than the average American woman (Garner, Garfinkel, Schwartz, and Thompson, 1980). Others view anorexia as a reflection of conflict, between wanting to attain independence and selfhood within the family and a fear of growing up. Finally, a variety of organic explanations have been offered. Abnormal functioning of the part of the hypothalamus known to control eating, sexual activity, and menstruation is perhaps the leading physiological theory; however, it is not yet known whether disturbance in hypothalamic functioning is a cause of anorexia, a result of the weight loss and caloric restriction, or caused by the emotional distress of the patient (Garfinkel and Garner, 1982).

Therapy for Anorexia Nervosa

The treatment of anorexia is a two-tiered process. The immediate goal is to help the young woman gain weight in order to avoid medical complications and the possibility of death. An anorexic may have to be hospitalized if any food is to be gotten into her at all. She has often become so weak and her physiological functioning so disturbed that she badly needs hospital treatment. Intravenous feeding will provide necessary nourishment in life-threatening situations. Some success in producing immediate increases in body weight has been achieved by behavior therapy programs in which the

ing or bulimia, followed by self-induced vomiting, an eating pattern found in almost half of all anorexics. Anorexics who are also bulimic are more impulsive, depressed, and anxious than others and may be particularly difficult to treat (Casper *et al.*, 1980; Garfinkel, Moldofsky, and Garner, 1980). Anorexics in general deny having a problem that needs treatment.

hospitalized anorexic is isolated as much as possible and given mealtime company, then periods of access to a television set, radio, or phonograph, walks with a student nurse, mail, and visitors as rewards for eating and gaining weight. The second goal of treatment, long-term maintenance of gains in body weight, is not reliably achieved by medical, behavioral, or traditional psychodynamic interventions (Box 15.4) (Bemis, 1978).

One mode of treatment that may be able to produce long-term gains for anorexics is family therapy. Like most other treatments, family therapy has been insufficiently studied for its long-term effects. One report, however, suggests that as many as 86 percent of fifty anorexic daughters treated with their families were still functioning well when assessed at times ranging from three months to four years after treatment (Rosman, Minuchin, and Liebman, 1976). Salvador Minuchin and his colleagues, who represent but one of several "schools" of family therapy, have done considerable work on anorexia nervosa. The treatment they have developed is called the family lunch session.

Before the specific treatment is described, a basic assumption in Minuchin's family treatment has to be made clear. He believes that "sick" family members, especially children, serve to deflect attention away from underlying conflict in family relationships. The illness is the family psychopathology become manifest, so to speak. In these families, members are both rigid and deeply enmeshed in one another's lives, overprotect the children, and do not acknowledge conflicts. Thus the sickness acts to reduce friction surrounding these basic family disturbances. By providing an alternative focus of attention, the illness lessens the tension between family members. Minuchin believes that troubled families therefore act in a way that keeps the "sick" family member in the patient role (Minuchin *et al.*, 1975).

A recent review of studies on the family interactions of anorexia nervosa patients provides some support for Minuchin's theory. For example, families of anorexics were found to be more enmeshed, as evidenced by stronger coalitions between each parent and the anorexic child than between the parents as marital partners. Videotaped role-plays among anorexic families reveal a lack of conflict resolution, focus on the daughter, and parents rarely talking directly to one another (Kog and Vandereycken, 1985).

To treat the disorder, Minuchin attempts to redefine it as interpersonal rather than individual and to bring the family conflicts to the fore. Thus, it is theorized, the symptomatic family member is freed from having to maintain his or her problem, for it no longer deflects attention from the dysfunctional family.

Families of anorexics are seen by the therapist during mealtime, since the conflicts related to anorexia are believed to be most evident then. There are three major goals for these lunch sessions: (1) changing the patient role of the anorexic; (2) redefining the eating problem as an interpersonal one; and (3) preventing the parents from using their child's anorexia as a means of avoiding conflict. One strategy is to instruct each parent to try individually to force the child to eat. The other parent may leave the room. The individual efforts are expected to fail. But through this failure and the frustration of each, the mother and father may now work *together* to persuade the child to eat. Thus, rather than being a focus of conflict, the child's eating will produce cooperation and increase parental effectiveness in dealing with the child (Rosman, Minuchin, and Liebman, 1975). Given the only moderate successes of other treatments devised for anorexics, family therapy appears promising.

Bulimia Nervosa

For some time **bulimia nervosa** was regarded as an occasional accompaniment to anorexia, but it is now recognized by DSM-IIIR as an eating disorder separate from anorexia nervosa. Bulimia is from the Greek words *bous* meaning head of cattle and *limos* meaning hunger. Often referred to as the binge–purge syndrome, it consists of episodes of gross overeating followed by induced vomiting or overdoses of laxatives to rid the body of the enormous amount of food just ingested. Unlike the anorexic, the bulimic does not necessarily have abnormally low weight, but patients with both disorders do share an abnormal concern with body size, having a morbid fear of becoming fat. The anorexic and the bulimic both make persistent attempts to lose weight, but only the anorexic actually reduces food intake (Schlesier-Stropp, 1984).[10]

The foods bulimics choose have a texture that allows them to be eaten rapidly. They gobble them down, with little chewing, in a short span of time, and then may go in search of more food. A typical binge might consist of two packages of cookies and a loaf of bread, a gallon of milk and a half gallon of ice cream, a basket of fried chicken, and fistfuls of candy and pastries (*The New York Times,* October 20, 1981). Bulimics are painfully aware that their uncontrollable eating pattern is abnormal. They often feel disgust, helplessness, and panic while the binge is upon them. The purge is a source of relief for most victims. In fact, Rosen and Leitenberg (1985) assert that bulimics purge to reduce the anxiety caused by binging. Their vomiting serves as an escape response that frees them from normal inhibitions against

---

[10]As noted earlier, aspects of both disorders are indeed found in some people; these individuals are sometimes referred to as bulimarexics.

BOX 15.4

BEHAVIORAL PEDIATRICS

An earlier discussion of behavioral medicine (see page 211) enumerated several applications of psychological knowledge to the prevention and treatment of physical disease, for example, altering the type A behavior pattern as a way of reducing the incidence of later coronary heart disease. Psychological attention has been paid to childhood and adolescent diseases as well.

Russo and Varni (1982) propose a normal person–abnormal situation (NPAS) model as a way of conceptualizing a field called **behavioral pediatrics.** An acutely or chronically ill child is a young person who may have psychological problems because he or she has been placed, by illness, in a complex and stressful predicament. Many sick children suffer considerable pain and sometimes defacement and have to spend long periods of time in a hospital, away from parents, siblings, and the comforting surroundings of their homes and neighborhoods.

In general, behavioral pediatrics combines behavior therapy and pediatrics to manage disease in children. It concerns itself with parent–child, school–child, and medical team–child relations (Varni and Dietrich, 1981). Some specific examples of recent work in behavioral pediatrics will convey the scope and aims of this burgeoning and promising field (Kellerman and Varni, 1982).

In recent years, many forms of childhood cancer, such as acute lymphoblastic leukemia, have become treatable; some types can even be treated so effectively that they go into remission and the children are alive five years after the onset of cancer. With such improvement, however, come new problems of a psychological nature for both patients and families—learning to live with the disease and its treatment.

Concealing from a youngster the true nature of his or her illness, and how life-threatening it is, increases rather than decreases anxiety (e.g., Spinetta, 1980). Open communication with the child is advocated. Research advises maintaining the child in his or her regular school as much as possible (Katz, 1980). Because cancer and its treatment can bring physical disfigurement, such as hair loss, the child should be taught to handle the teasing that often awaits any youngster who looks different; assertion training and learning to ignore the hurtful remarks can be helpful.

Pain accompanies both the diagnosis and treatment of childhood cancer. A child with leukemia must undergo frequent and regular bone marrow aspiration. The doctor inserts a long needle into the middle of the thigh bone and extracts some marrow. It hurts. And it is not the kind of pain to which the individual readily habituates (Katz, Kellerman, and Siegel, 1980). The experience takes a toll on the young patient, and on the parents as well. Specialists in behavioral pediatrics have developed hypnotic imagery techniques that teach the child to relax, thereby reducing the trauma of this inevitable medical event. Children who develop anticipatory anxiety before undergoing other painful medical procedures have been helped by viewing films of a coping model (Jay *et al.,* 1982). Systematic desensitization to situations associated with the pain, such as entering the hospital and sitting in the waiting room, can reduce the level of anxiety with which a patient comes to the medical procedure and in turn to some extent the pain.

---

overeating. Thus, binging often becomes more extreme after the individual has "discovered" the use of purging to control their previous anxiety about overeating.

The prevalence of bulimia is difficult to estimate because the eating and purging are done in great secrecy, and body weight is generally within normal limits. The guilt-ridden victims are so careful to hide their disorder that those who live with them may not know of it. One estimate is that in the United States more than five million people, mostly women, are bulimic, binging–purging at least once a week, and sometimes spending upward of a hundred dollars a day on food, usually high-calorie carbohydrates (Ely, 1983).

In her review of the bulimia literature, Schleiser-Stropp (1984) provides the following portrait of the typical binge eater. She is likely to be a Caucasian woman in her mid-twenties who began overeating at about age eighteen and began purging, usually by vomiting, about a year later. She is usually within the normal weight range for her age and height, and her family history has an unusually high incidence of obesity and alcoholism. Several other points should be noted from Schlesier-Stropp's review: (1) very few men have been diagnosed as bulimic; (2) bulimia is a problem of adolescence and early adulthood, with very, very few cases beginning after age thirty; (3) overeating tends to precede purging by as much as three years; (4) the frequency of binging–purging cycles varies considerably, with some people doing so once a day, others once or so a week, still others as often as thirty times a week.

Bulimics also frequently suffer periods of depression (see Box 15.5) and anxiety as well as guilt over their inability to control binging. Their costly binge–purges can take up so many of their hours that social activities are restricted and financial resources squandered. In a study of 275 bulimics, Mitchell, Hatsukami, Eckert, and

Reducing anxiety can be of more general importance. An extremely anxious child, for example, may avoid the medical procedure or may begin to lose weight. Weight loss will decrease his or her chances of surviving cancer (Dewys *et al.*, 1980).

Children and adolescents with other medical problems have also been helped by behavioral pediatrics. Chronic arthritic pain in the joints is a serious problem for hemophiliacs, people whose blood lacks a critical clotting factor. Varni (1981) has successfully treated such pain by hypnotic imagery techniques, teaching his patients both to relax and to increase blood flow to the affected joint. A higher surface temperature about the joint diminishes the need for pain medications, many of which have the undesirable side effect of inhibiting platelet aggregation, thus worsening an already bad blood-clotting condition. When children with asthma are in no physical danger, paying little attention to their attacks can lessen their severity and duration (Creer, Weinberg, and Molk, 1974), although the asthma itself is by no means cured by this operant procedure.

Obesity in children is highly predictive of obesity in adulthood, which is, as we know, a major risk factor for such diseases as hypertension, heart disease, and diabetes. Childhood obesity has also been associated with low social competence, behavior problems, and poor self-concept (Banis *et al.*, 1988). Behavioral investigators have been working to help overweight youngsters alter their eating habits, their exercise practices, and other aspects of their life-styles that appear to contribute to the caloric intake

and how it is or is not burned off (Epstein, Masek, and Marshall, 1978). For example, obese children, like obese adults, eat faster, take bigger bites, and chew their food less than do age peers of normal weight (Drabman *et al.*, 1979). When their parents are also involved in treatment, weight can be lost permanently (Aragone, Cassady, and Drabman, 1975).

Another topic in behavioral pediatrics is known as *therapeutic compliance.* How can we get people to do the things that are necessary to prevent or manage an illness (Varni and Wallander, 1984)? Juvenile diabetes serves as a good example of the challenge facing the youngsters and families affected. Urine must be tested several times a day to determine glucose (sugar) levels so that food intake and the amount of insulin can be adjusted. Indeed, diet itself poses a major challenge to youngsters. They must learn to resist candy and other sweets. Their meals need to be timed to coincide with the peak action of an insulin injection so that the insulin does not lower glucose levels abnormally. Activity and exercise must also become part of the regimen, for they exert their own natural, insulin-like effect of utilizing glucose in the cells (Hobbs, Beck, and Wansley, 1984). With no cure of diabetes in sight, diabetics need to accept both their condition and the required regulation of some of the most basic of human drives. The complex set of self-care skills that a young person needs in order to cope with this serious but treatable disease is now benefiting from clinical research in behavioral pediatrics (Epstein *et al.*, 1981).

Pyle (1985) found that 70 percent experienced difficulties with intimate or interpersonal relationships, 53 percent reported family problems, and 50 percent had work impairment. Many bulimics are suicidal as well.

There are also physiological consequences, especially if the purging is done by vomiting. Sore throats, swollen salivary glands, and destruction of tooth enamel by the acidic vomitus have been reported in a significant number of bulimics; intestinal damage, nutritional deficiencies, and dehydration can also result. Menstrual irregularities, found frequently among female anorexics, are less severe among female bulimics (Ely, 1983; Schlesier-Stropp, 1984).

When untreated, bulimia is unlikely to go away. Few systematic studies of different interventions have been made. Attempts to change women's beliefs that thinness is equated with success (Garver and Rosen, in press; Boskind-Lodahl and White, 1978), assertion

training (White and Boskind-White, 1981), elaborate self-monitoring of food intake (Fairburn, 1980), and preventing the bulimic from vomiting after her binge (Agras *et al.*, 1989; Rosen and Leitenberg, 1982; Rossiter and Wilson, 1985) have all been tried. They have all had some successes, as have antidepressant drugs (Hughes, Wells, Cunningham, and Ilstrup, 1986; Pope and Hudson, 1984). It must be concluded, however, that little is known about the effective treatment of bulimia, reflecting our inadequate understanding of the disorder.

Summary

DSM-III greatly expanded the range of diagnoses applicable to children, and its revised version, DSM-IIIR,

BOX 15.5

DEPRESSION AND THE EATING DISORDERS

It has long been noticed that both anorexics and bulimics are often depressed. In a sample of 105 hospitalized anorexics, Eckert and his colleagues (1982) found high levels of depression, especially in the anorexics with the most severe eating difficulties.

Recent evidence suggests that, for some women, the onset of depression precedes symptoms of an eating disorder (Piran, Kennedy, Garfunkel, and Owens, 1985), and that depressed and nondepressed anorexics may show biochemical differences (Biederman *et al.*, 1984). Rather than trying to prove either that the depression is always the *result* of the eating disorder or that anorexia and bulimia are caused by affective disturbance, Swift and colleagues suggest a multidimensional model, where biological, psychological, familial, and sociocultural factors interact reciprocally (Swift, Andrews, and Barklage, 1986).

Let us assume that depression is indeed connected to anorexia and bulimia. But which is the cause and which the effect? If an anorexic loses 25 percent of her body weight, the drop in her body temperature and the starvation may cause biochemical changes that bring on depression. Similar harmful somatic changes can take place in bulimia. From a psychological point of view, the loss of control, guilt, and shame that accompany these eating disorders could easily eventuate in a clinical depression. On the other hand, depression could conceivably cause anorexia. Bruch (1980), a psychoanalytic theorist, suggests that a young woman may compensate for her depressed feelings by seeking to be thin and desirable; finding that as she loses weight her depression does not lift, she seeks to lose still more. Bruch (1981) also suggests that anorexia might be regarded as an adolescent female manifestation of depression. Looking to her appearance as both the cause and potential cure of her depression, the young woman loses more and more weight.

Although not all anorexics, and not all bulimics, are depressed, nor all depressed young women anorexic or bulimic, the relation between depression and both anorexia and bulimia is strong. What is needed are longitudinal studies that carefully observe young women over time for changes in their affective states as well as for the emergence of eating disorders (Hilterbrand, 1983).

Winokur, March, and Mendels (1980) looked at the incidence of affective disorder in the families of anorexics and control subjects, the assumption being that they would be higher in the relatives of those with eating disorders if in fact depression and anorexia are linked. The hypothesis was confirmed. The fact that the affective problems of family members often predated the onset of the patient's anorexia argues against the explanation that relatives became depressed as a reaction to the eating problem. In addition, Pope and Hudson (1984) have reported marked success in treating bulimia with antidepressant drugs. These lines of evidence point to a connection between depression and both anorexia and bulimia.

---

reflects the continuing burgeoning of interest in childhood disorders. Attention-deficit disorders and conduct problems are disorders of undercontrolled behavior. The attentional problems of hyperactive children, who are "running motors" in situations that call for sitting still, are now viewed as primary; the DSM-IIIR diagnosis is attention-deficit hyperactivity disorder. Genetic studies, evidence of neurological problems and underarousal of the central nervous system, and the fact that hyperactive behavior can be induced by head injuries, brain diseases, and lead poisoning point to a physiological cause. The role of parents in influencing the course of the disorder is also supported by some data. Stimulant drugs and rewards for staying focused on a task help to calm ADHD children. Conduct disorders cover aggression, lying, theft, vandalism, and other acts that violate social norms. A genetic predisposition, marital discord of parents, poor rearing in moral awareness, modeling and direct reinforcement of deviant behavior, and living in city slums are considered etiological fac-

tors. Teaching parents to reinforce prosocial behavior and diverting delinquents from the court system have proved promising interventions.

School phobia, social withdrawal, and depression are disorders of overcontrolled behavior. School phobia, a fear and refusal to go to school, is usually treated by gradual exposure to the feared situation, sometimes coupled with rewards for attending school. Children who withdraw socially are assumed to do so because of anxiety and poor social skills. The frequency of depression in children is not known for certain. Nor do we know for sure whether depressed children have symptoms different from those of depressed adults. Play therapy and family therapy are often applied to disorders of overcontrolled behavior. Behavioral pediatrics helps children adjust to serious illness.

The final disorders discussed are two enormously irregular eating patterns of adolescents. In anorexia nervosa the individual does not eat enough to maintain a healthy weight and, if not stopped, starves herself to death. It is much more common in adolescent women than in men. None of the several theories of anorexia—fear of becoming sexually mature, weight phobia, striving for the slim image so esteemed by our society, conflict between wanting selfhood within the family and a fear of growing up, and physiological dysfunctions—has clear support. Treatment of the disorder is difficult, although family therapy appears promising. In bulimia, sometimes found in anorexics but also considered to be a separate disorder, the individual indulges herself in binges of eating and then induces vomiting or takes a laxative to rid her body of the food. Although not as life-threatening as anorexia, bulimics suffer serious health consequences from their vomiting and forced bowel movements, such as tooth decay and damage to the intestines. In both eating disorders, depression may play a role, not just as an understandable consequence but as a cause as well.

Rhonda Wall, *Human Nature*, 1988. Courtesy of Rhonda Wall.

Chapter 16

Learning Disabilities, Mental Retardation, and Autistic Disorder

Learning Disabilities
  Etiology of Learning Disabilities
  Intervention with Learning Disabilities
Mental Retardation
  The Concept of Mental Retardation
  Classification of Mental Retardation
  Nature of Mental Retardation
  Etiology of Mental Retardation
  Prevention of Mental Retardation
  Treatment for Mental Retardation
Autistic Disorder
  Descriptive Characteristics
  Etiology of Autistic Disorder
  Treatment of Autistic Disorder
Summary

In the previous chapter we examined several emotional and behavioral disorders of childhood. In this chapter the focus is on developmental disorders: learning disabilities, mental retardation, and autism, which are characterized predominantly by a disturbance in the acquisition of cognitive, language, motor, or social skills. The course of these disorders tends to be chronic, usually persisting into adulthood. Learning disabilities signify inadequate development in a specific area of academic, language, speech, or motor skills, which is not due to mental retardation, autism, a demonstrable physical or neurological disorder, or deficient educational opportunities. Such children are usually of average or above average intelligence, but have difficulty learning some specific skill (e.g., arithmetic or reading), thus impeding their progress in school.

In contrast, mental retardation and autism interfere markedly with the entire developmental process, and many of the children affected are unlikely to become well-functioning adults. Not only are these disorders lifelong but, if severe, they disrupt all of a life. Mentally retarded and autistic children are similar in a number of respects. The majority of autistic children score significantly below average on intelligence tests, and many children with mental retardation make ritualistic hand movements, body-rock, and are injurious to themselves, actions that are even more frequent in those with autism. Educational interventions can also be similar for children with the two disorders. Both autism and the moderate, severe, and profound forms of mental retardation become evident in infancy or in very early childhood. Retardation and autism are, however, different problems of development.

mental health clinics. The disorders are from two to four times more common in males than in females.

The following specific developmental disorders are identified in DSM-IIIR.

Academic Skills Disorders Children with ***developmental reading disorder,*** better known as ***dyslexia,*** have significant difficulty with word recognition and reading comprehension. When reading orally, they omit, add, and distort words. This disorder, present in 2 to 8 percent of school-age children, does not preclude great achievements. It is widely known that Nelson Rockefeller, former governor of New York and former vice president of the United States, suffered from dyslexia.

In ***developmental arithmetic disorder,*** the child may have difficulty with "linguistic skills" (such as coding written problems into mathematical symbols), "perceptual skills" (such as recognizing numerical symbols), "attention skills" (such as remembering to add in "carried" numbers), and "mathematical skills" (such as counting objects or following sequences of mathematical steps). This disorder is apparently not common.

Developmental expressive writing disorder, a new category in DSM-IIIR, describes an impairment in the ability to compose the written word (including spelling errors, grammatical or punctuation errors, or poor paragraph organization) that is serious enough to interfere significantly with academic achievement or daily activities requiring such writing skills. No systematic data have yet been collected on the prevalence of this disorder.

Language and Speech Disorders ***Developmental language disorders*** can be both ***receptive,*** wherein the child

Learning Disabilities

DSM-IIIR lists several classes of ***specific developmental disorders,*** better known as ***learning disabilities,*** in which a child fails to develop to the degree expected by his intellectual level in a specific academic, language, or motor skill area. As the diagnostic manual states, "the inclusion of these categories in a classification of 'mental disorders' is controversial, since many of the children with these disorders have no other signs of psychopathology" (American Psychiatric Association, 1987, p. 40). These disabilities, however, do fall into the category of mental disorder according to the definition offered by DSM-IIIR (p. 401): "clinically significant behavioral or psychological pattern . . . associated with . . . disability." Learning disabilities are usually identified and treated within the school system rather than through

Children with developmental articulation disorder are given special training to help them speak more clearly.

has trouble understanding spoken language, or ***expressive,*** wherein the child has difficulty expressing himself or herself in speech. A child with the receptive form may seem to be deaf, so deficient is he or she in comprehending what is being said. A youngster with the expressive form of the disorder may seem eager to communicate but have inordinate difficulty finding the right words. By age four, the child speaks only in short phrases. Old words are forgotten when new ones are learned, and the use of grammatical structures is considerably below age level.

Unlike children who have trouble understanding or finding words, youngsters with ***developmental articulation disorder*** both comprehend and are able to use a substantial vocabulary, but their words sound like baby talk. "Blue" comes out "bu," and "rabbit" sounds like "wabbit." They have not learned articulation of the later-acquired speech sounds, such as r, sh, th, f, z, l, and ch. With speech therapy, complete recovery occurs in almost all cases, and milder cases may recover spontaneously by age eight.

Developmental Coordination Disorder In this motor skills disorder, also new to DSM-IIIR, children show marked impairment in the development of motor coordination that is not explainable by mental retardation or a known physical disorder. The young child may have difficulty tying shoelaces and buttoning shirts, and when older with model-building, playing ball, and printing or handwriting. The diagnosis is made only if the impairment interferes significantly with academic achievement or with activities of daily living.

Etiology of Learning Disabilities

Both physiological and psychological factors are possible causes of the several learning disabilities. Answers are far from in. Earlier the learning disabilities were linked to "minimal brain damage"; however, although reduced oxygen supply at birth is more common in dyslexics than in normal children (Kawi and Pasamanick, 1958), neurological tests show no differences between normal and learning-disabled children (McGuiness, 1985). Twin studies several years ago confirmed the heritability of learning disabilities (Mathaney, Dolan, and Wilson, 1976), and more recent research has begun to pinpoint which specific learning problems are inherited and which may have psychological or other physiological bases. Evidence recently reviewed by Pennington and Smith (1988) suggests that whereas simple word reading and spelling skills are genetically influenced, reading comprehension seems not to be.

Psychological theories have in the past focused on visual perceptual deficits as underlying dyslexia. One popular hypothesis suggested that children with reading problems *perceive* letters in reverse order or mirror image, mistaking, for example, a "d" for a "b". However, no relationship has been found between letter confusions at age five to six and subsequent reading ability (Calfee, Fisk, and Piontkowski, 1985), and one does not need to be able to *see* to have reading problems—blind people may have difficulty learning to read Braille (McGuiness, 1981). Recent research points to language-processing problems (including perception of speech as well as written material) and deficiencies in verbal memory as the core deficits underlying dyslexia (Mann and Brady, 1988).

McGuiness (1985) notes that any theory of learning disabilities must explain the clear sex difference in the disorders, as boys are two to four times more likely to have a learning disability than girls. It may be that structural or hormonal differences between male and female brains account for some of the variation in learning between the sexes. For example, damage to the left hemisphere causes more deficits in language in males than in females; females have a greater representation of language in the right hemisphere (Kimura, 1983; Mateer, Polen, and Ojemann, 1982). This finding suggests that boys are more vulnerable to language and reading disabilities.

Another promising hypothesis concerns the differences in sensorimotor integration between boys and girls (McGuiness, 1985). Boys are said to be involved in more gross motor activities as young children. Gross motor control skills become integrated primarily with sensory input to the *visual* system and the position of limbs in space, leading to efficiency in visuomotor integration (which males are better at than females). In contrast, it is hypothesized that girls are geared more toward fine motor control, which includes speech structures, that becomes integrated primarily with the *auditory* system, leading to girls' superior language skills.

Intervention with Learning Disabilities

One cannot underestimate the anxiety of parents whose otherwise normal child lags behind in reading or cannot speak effectively and normally for his or her age. Professional attempts to remedy learning disabilities have been subject to somatic, educational, and psychological fads—from the use of stimulants and tranquilizers to training the child in motor activities believed to have been inadequately mastered at a younger age in hopes of reorganizing neuronal connections in the brain.

Currently, several methods are being used to treat learning disabilities. Linguistic approaches focus on instruction in listening, speaking, reading, and writing skills in a logical, sequential, and multisensory manner (Lyon and Moats, 1988). Solan (1982) points out the importance of "readiness" to learn. Most children do not have the auditory and visual discrimination skills necessary for reading until age six and one-half. If they are taught to read before those readiness skills are developed, they often cannot retain, integrate, and generalize the reading skills they learn. Reading-disabled children at age six or so may simply not be ready to begin instruction in reading. Readiness skills may need to be specifically taught before reading instruction is attempted.

Cognitive approaches identify and remedy deficits in metacognitive skills (Lyon and Moats, 1988). For example, a student might be taught first to analyze the nature of the problem ("Check if I'm supposed to add or subtract on this arithmetic problem"), then devise a plan for approaching the problem ("I have to remember to carry the numbers"), and monitor and adjust his performance ("I went too quickly that time; I need to slow down").

For all children, but especially those with learning disabilities, a success-oriented approach is essential. Most learning-disabled children have probably experienced a great deal of frustration and failure that erode their motivation and confidence. Behavioral programs that reward small steps can be helpful in increasing the child's motivation, focusing attention on the learning

task, and reducing behavioral problems caused by frustration.

Mental Retardation

Kevin is a twenty-three-year-old man who was diagnosed in childhood as having moderate to severe mental retardation. He has been in educational programs since he was six years of age. At present he feeds and dresses himself but needs help in selecting clothing to wear and must be "checked" to ensure that everything is appropriate before going out. He finds his way around his community without getting lost, but he cannot take buses alone. He can go on errands to the grocery store about two blocks from his home, but he takes a note for the storekeeper and does not know whether he has been given the correct change. He is reliable in helping with simple household chores, such as making beds, setting the table, running the vacuum cleaner, and helping with simple tasks in the kitchen. His scores on the Wechsler Adult Intelligence Scale are very much below normal. The psychologist reported that Kevin did not respond on some verbal tasks, which had to be marked "Fail"; she did not know, however, whether he could have responded correctly were his speech better. Kevin's speech is indeed barely understandable, with many articulation problems, but he does respond to directions and requests. He functions adequately in a sheltered workshop on simple tasks, such as stuffing bags, simple assembly, and attaching stickers in correct places. He understands that he is paid for work and talks about using the money he makes, but he must be supervised in selecting purchases. He functions socially at the level of a six-year-old. (Adapted from Grossman, 1983)

The Concept of Mental Retardation

DSM-IIIR bases its definition of mental retardation and the criteria for its diagnosis on standards set in 1973 by the American Association of Mental Deficiency, whose

Cognitive interventions for learning disabilities typically focus on strategies for dealing with academic problems.

BOX 16.1

MEASURING INFANT INTELLIGENCE

For the past fifty years, psychologists have been searching for a way to predict later intelligence from the performance of infants. Most such attempts have involved measuring sensory and motor functioning, such as hand–eye coordination, response to sound, and social responsiveness during the first year of life (Brooks and Weinraub, 1976). Although these measures are useful for learning about normal development and cross-cultural differences in infancy, they have proven to be poor predictors of later intellectual functioning as well as ineffective measures of the efficacy of intervention or enrichment programs.

Fagan and Singer (1983) have made strides in the development of a new type of measure that holds promise for tapping the "intelligence" of infants. Their work explores the *visual recognition memory* of infants, that is, the child's ability to recognize a familiar stimulus. Capitalizing on the infant's predilection to attend more to novel stimuli

than to familiar objects, Fagan and Singer can determine whether an infant recognizes a previously presented object. They have discovered that infants' ability to remember and recognize visual stimuli is far better at predicting intelligence measured at age seven than are the sensorimotor measures. In addition, groups of infants expected to differ in later intelligence (such as Down's syndrome and premature babies versus normal infants) were found to differ in visual recognition memory.

In addition to contributing to our understanding of the nature of intelligence at different ages, Fagan and Singer's work may result in a test that can be used to screen infants suspected to be at risk for a slower rate of development, for determining the effects of early intervention programs, and for measuring cognitive functioning in individuals for whom verbal tests are inappropriate, such as those who have a severe mental handicap.

definition states mental retardation to be "significantly subaverage general intellectual functioning existing concurrently with deficits in adaptive behavior and manifested during the developmental period." Let us examine these several criteria.[1]

Intelligence Test Scores as a Criterion

The first component of the definition requires a judgment of intelligence. Since there is no universal agreement on what constitutes general intellectual functioning, some might have difficulty accepting even this component. Most psychologists, however, rely on performance on standardized intelligence tests to determine intellectual functioning.

Performance on such tests may be used to determine a person's mental age, for items making up these tests are ordered by difficulty. National norms have been established to indicate the age levels at which most children are successful with the particular items. A person's mental age is the age level that is the norm for the items they are able to pass. For example, if a twelve-year-old girl is able to answer correctly items most nine-year-olds are able to pass, but not the items passed by the majority of older children, her mental age is nine.

Scores on IQ tests are standardized in such a way that 100 is the mean and 15 is the standard deviation

(a measure of how scores are dispersed both above and below the average). This means that approximately two-thirds of the population receive scores between 85 and 115. Those with a score of 70 are two standard deviations below the mean of the population, and are considered to have "significant subaverage general intellectual functioning." Approximately 2.5 percent of the population fall into this category.

The use of standardized IQ tests to assess children suspected of having mental retardation presents several problems. First, the age norms were derived from samples of white, middle-class children. Generalizing to chidren from different racial or cultural backgrounds may not be valid. Second, few of the intelligence tests have been validated for IQ scores of less than 70. Individuals of low intellectual functioning were not adequately represented in the groups taking the tests when the scales were being compiled and standardized. Third, physical handicaps are not taken into account by several of the most reliable and frequently used IQ tests. Fourth, because a child with mental retardation may not be as familiar with the testing situation or be motivated to do well like other children, he or she may obtain a spuriously low IQ score (Box 16.1)

Adaptive Behavior as a Criterion

Adaptive behavior refers to the individual's "effectiveness in areas such as social skills, communication, and daily living skills, and how well the person meets the standards of personal independence and social respon-

---

[1] The reader should note that there are similarities between mental retardation and autistic disorder, making these disorders difficult to differentiate. Throughout this chapter we discuss the similarities and differences where they are useful for the reader.

TABLE 16.1

Sample items from the Vineland Adaptive Behavior Scales (*from Sparrow, Balla, and Cicchetti, 1984*)

Age Level	Adaptive Ability
2 years	Says at least fifty recognizable words.
	Removes front-opening coat, sweater, or shirt without assistance.
5 years	Tells popular story, fairy tale, lengthy joke, or plot of television program.
	Ties shoelaces into a bow without assistance.
8 years	Keeps secrets or confidences for more than one day.
	Orders own meal in a restaurant.
11 years	Uses the telephone for all kinds of calls, without assistance.
	Watches television or listens to radio for information about a particular area of interest.
16 years	Looks after own health.
	Responds to hints or indirect cues in conversation.

sibility expected of his or her age by his or her cultural group" (American Psychiatric Association, 1987, p. 29). The adaptive skills a child is expected to learn are caring for the self; acquiring concepts of time and money; being able to use tools, to shop, and to travel by public transportation; and becoming socially responsive and self-directive. The adolescent is expected to be able to apply academic skills, reasoning, and judgment to daily living and to participate in group activities. The adult, of course, is expected to be self-supporting and to assume social responsibilities.

Several tests have been constructed to assess adaptive behavior, the best known being the American Association of Mental Deficiency Adaptive Behavior Scale (ABS) (Nihira *et al.*, 1974) and the Vineland Adaptive Behavior Scales, formerly the Vineland Scale of Social Maturity (Sparrow, Balla, and Cicchetti, 1984; Table 16.1).

Although impairments in adaptive behavior have long been included in the definition of mental retardation, only recently have the tests been adequately standardized with firmly established norms. One problem with many assessments of adaptive behavior, however, is that they fail to consider the environment that the person must adapt to. A person who lives in a small rural community where everyone is acquainted may not need as complex skills as someone who lives in New York City. Youngsters who are quite competent working at

farm chores, walking to school, and shopping at the local general store may, when transported to a city, be considered deficient in adaptive behavior if they are not able to ride the subway to school or buy groceries at a store where a foreign language is spoken. Since the requirements of one setting may be more complex than those of another, a criterion based on what the average, middle-class white and urban child does may not be valid.[2] An effective and valid assessment of adaptive behavior should therefore consider the interaction between the child and the surroundings he or she must function in.

Another problem with assessing adaptive behavior is that the distinction between it and intelligence is sometimes blurred. Charlesworth (1976), an ethological psychologist who studies intelligence from an evolutionary perspective, believes that the ability to adapt to the environment is the hallmark of intelligence. According to this view, adaptive behavior scores are a more valid measure of intelligence than scores on IQ tests, which require more abstract thinking. Critics of the ethological perspective, however, point out that the cockroach has been best able to adapt to the environment, as evidenced by its length of time on earth, longer than that of any other creature. Not many people would be willing to claim that the cockroach is more intelligent than human beings.

Time of Onset as a Criterion

A final definitional criterion mandates that mental retardation be manifest before adulthood, that is, before age eighteen. This rules out classifying as mental retardation any deficits in intelligence and adaptive behavior from traumatic accidents or illnesses occurring later in life. For the majority of children with more severe impairments, diagnosis can usually be made during infancy, or sometimes, through *amniocentesis* (see page 451), even before the child is born. The majority of children considered mentally retarded, however, are not identified as such until they enter school. These children have no obvious physiological, neurological, or physical manifestations, and thus their problems become apparent only when they are not able to keep up with their peers in school. Once these mildly retarded children leave school and become absorbed into the community and work world, their mental retardation may become less evident once again. The increased prevalence of mental retardation in school-age children has led some researchers to consider it a school phenomenon.

---

[2]By the same token, city children may find themselves at a loss with some of the activities expected of youngsters living on a farm!

Adaptive behaviors, like opening buttons or tying shoelaces, are important in the definition of mental retardation.

Classification of Mental Retardation

Four levels of mental deficiency are now recognized by DSM-IIIR, each of them a specific subaverage range on the far left of the normal distribution curve of measured intelligence. The IQ ranges given are not of course the sole basis of diagnosis, for deficiencies in adaptive behavior are also a criterion of mental retardation. Some persons falling in the mildly retarded range based on IQ may have no deficits in adaptive behavior and thus would not be considered mentally retarded. The American Association on Mental Deficiency suggests that the IQ criterion be applied only after deficits in adaptive behavior have been identified. The following is a summary of how individuals at each level of mental retardation are described by Robinson and Robinson (1976).

Mild Mental Retardation (50–55 to 70 IQ) The mildly retarded comprise about 85 percent of all those who have IQs less than 70. They are not always distinguishable from normal youngsters until they enter school. By their late teens they can usually learn academic skills at about a sixth-grade level. As adults they are likely to be able to maintain themselves in unskilled jobs or in sheltered workshops, although they may need help with social and financial problems. Further, they may marry and have children of their own. Only about one percent are ever institutionalized, usually in adolescence for behavior problems. Most of the mildly retarded show no signs of brain pathology and are members of families whose intelligence and socioeconomic levels are low.

Moderate Mental Retardation (35–40 to 50–55 IQ) About 10 percent of those with IQs less than 70 are moderately retarded. Brain damage and other pathologies are frequent. The moderately retarded may have physical defects and neurological dysfunctions that hinder fine motor skills, such as grasping and coloring within lines, and gross motor skills, such as running and climbing. During childhood these individuals are eligible for special classes in which the development of self-care skills rather than academic achievement is emphasized. The moderately retarded are unlikely to progress beyond the second-grade level in academic subjects and can manage this learning only in later childhood or as adults. They may, however, learn to travel alone in a familiar locality. Many are institutionalized. Although most can do useful work, few hold jobs except in sheltered workshops or in family businesses. Most live dependently within the family or in supervised group homes. Few have friends of their own, but they may be left alone without supervision for several hours at a time. Their retardation is likely to be identified in infancy or early childhood, for their sensorimotor coordination remains poor, and they are slow to develop verbal and social skills. In contrast to mildly retarded children, moderate retardates and those more seriously retarded are found in all socioeconomic groups.

Severe Mental Retardation (20–25 to 35–40 IQ) About 3–4 percent of those with IQs of less than 70 are severely retarded. They commonly have congenital physical abnormalities and limited sensorimotor control. Genetic disorders and environmental insults, such as severe oxygen deprivation at birth, account for most of this degree of retardation. Most are institutionalized and require constant aid and supervision. For children in this group to be able to speak and take care of their own basic needs requires prolonged training; the self-care training that is provided in the special classes within the school system is usually inadequate except for the upper portion of this group. As adults the severely retarded may be friendly but can usually communicate only briefly on a very concrete level. They engage in very little independent activity and are often lethargic, for their severe brain damage leaves them relatively passive and the circumstances of their lives allow them little stimulation. They may be able to perform very simple work under close supervision.

Profound Mental Retardation (below 20–25 IQ) One to two percent of the retarded are profoundly so, requiring total supervision and often nursing care all their lives. Intensive training may improve motor development, self-care, and communication skills. Many have severe physical deformities as well as neurological damage and cannot get around on their own. There is a very high mortality rate during childhood.

Classification and Educability

Educational psychologists have developed an "education" classification system that parallels DSM-IIIR and aids in the instructional programming of those with mental retardation.

Labels such as "educable" and "trainable" are sometimes substituted for "mild" and "moderate" mental retardation, respectively. The present trend, however, is away from educational placement based on the student's degree of mental retardation and toward an individualized placement based on the person's strengths, weaknesses, and the amount of instruction needed. For example, in New York State a student who needs considerable one-on-one instruction because of deficient intellectual functioning may be placed in the same classroom with a child who needs intensive instruction because of emotional problems or physical handicaps. Thus students are identified by the classroom environment that they are judged to need. This approach can lessen the stigmatizing effects of being considered retarded.

Nature of Mental Retardation

Figure 16.1 presents a visual scheme to illustrate the nature and etiology of mental retardation. We shall refer to this figure several times in the chapter.

Deficiencies in Adaptive Skills

As pictured in the outer ring of Figure 16.1, a retarded person is generally limited at least to some extent in six skills needed for daily living—communication, social skills, academic skills, sensorimotor skills, self-help skills, and vocational skills. A discussion of these adaptive skills provides a means of comparing degrees of mental retardation and the help that these children need.

Communication Although most children develop spontaneously the ability to speak and communicate, children with mental retardation may need help. Those

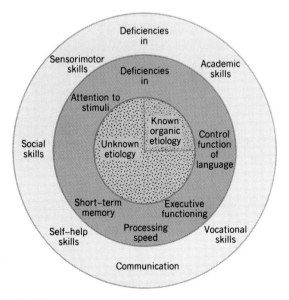

FIGURE 16.1

The causes of mental retardation and the adaptive skills and the general cognitive abilities that are wanting in retarded people.

with mild handicaps may require only minimal support to achieve effective communication, such as being assigned to a speech class. Children with more severe disabilities, however, may need years of intensive language training in order to express effectively their basic needs and feelings.

Some children are taught alternate means of communication, either to replace or to facilitate speech. Many children considered too disabled to use language can communicate effectively by sign language, communication boards and gestures, and photographs or drawings of common objects and actions (Fristoe and Lloyd, 1979).

Social Skills It is not uncommon for children who are mildly retarded to have difficulties making and keeping friends. The more seriously retarded children show little awareness of social conventions. For example, many moderately and severely retarded youngsters seem overly friendly, wanting to be held and hugged by people whom they have just met. Children who are profoundly retarded may appear to be unaware of those who approach them.

Even children who are profoundly retarded, however, are capable of some social behavior. A child with multiple physical handicaps may be unable to talk or to reach out to someone but will smile at a favorite person. Because social behavior is not expressive does not mean that the person is not responding to social events. The individual may be experiencing more emotion than he or she is able to express.

Academic Skills Academic skills, such as reading, writing, and mathematics, pose difficult problems for children with even mild mental handicaps. Still, many can learn enough arithmetic to shop effectively, to balance checkbooks, and to budget their money. They may also competently read recipes, how-to-manuals, or just-for-fun books. Few teachers attempt to teach these skills, in their usual sense, to children with more severe handicaps. But many of these children have learned, with adequate instruction, "functional academics," for example, reading signs and labels frequently found on their daily route or using a calculator at a store.

Sensorimotor Skills The degree of sensorimotor impairment is not consistently related to the degree of mental retardation. To be sure, many severely and profoundly retarded children have serious motor and sensory impairments. Children may also have physical disabilities but little or no mental impairment. Unfortunately, many children with physical disabilities, such

as cerebral palsy[3] or hearing loss, may appear to be mentally retarded and subsequently be given an inappropriate educational curriculum. As clinicians become more aware of these problems and as assessment procedures become more sophisticated, fewer diagnostic errors are being made.

Self-Help Skills Self-help skills are exercised in the routine activities of daily living—bathing, dressing, eating, using a telephone. Many children with mild and moderate retardation have all these skills. Children with profound retardation often require extensive, arduous training and supervision in order to perform these basic tasks. But many of these children also have physical disabilities; a movement that is simple for a nonhandicapped person may pose a real challenge for someone with a limited range of motion.

Vocational Skills One goal of education is to prepare children for a vocation. By the time most youngsters with mild mental retardation have finished school, they have acquired most of the skills needed to support themselves with a job in a competitive marketplace. In fact, although children's mild handicaps may be quite apparent in an academic setting, these handicaps may not be apparent in the world of work. Children with moderate mental retardation may also have acquired some work skills, and many do get jobs. They are usually simple jobs, structured and supervised, in sheltered workshops or family businesses.

Retarded people do clerical, maintenance, and laundry work; packaging; electronic and other light assembly; cutting metals, drilling, and other machine work; farming, gardening, and carpentry. They are also in the domestic and food services and in other service fields. Some are taught to participate in the care and training of those more retarded than themselves and benefit greatly from the experience. Many retarded workers are very persistent, accurate, and punctual employees.

Deficiencies by Age Level

Often, rather than describing a person's performance by the degree of retardation, it is given by age level. An eighteen-year-old woman with severe mental retardation may be described as having communicating abilities comparable to those of the average six-year-old. Another person, scoring within the range of moderate

---

[3]Some people with cerebral palsy are very likely to be underestimated. Difficulties in walking and speaking, problems in using hands in a smooth, coordinated fashion, uncontrollable facial grimaces—these are frequently interpreted by others as signs that intelligence is defective. Although the majority of those with cerebral palsy do have IQs below the average, many individuals achieve uncommonly high levels of distinction that require superior intellectual functioning.

retardation, may be expected to achieve social skills comparable to those of a seven- or eight-year-old and no better.

This type of description is based on certain assumptions. First, skills are assumed to develop in the same course for all people, regardless of their degree of mental ability. Second, the ultimate level of performance reached by a person with mental retardation is assumed to be less than that of a nonretarded person. Finally, the age level reached in one skill, such as communication, will be approximately the same as the age level reached in another, such as social skills.

These assumptions, although logically consistent, have not been substantiated. The way skills develop may depend in part on the primary cause of the mental retardation. For example, a fourteen-year-old boy diagnosed as moderately retarded and having specific brain damage may be unable to add one plus one yet have little problem reading and writing. Thus, although his academic performance may average out to that of a six-year-old, his and that of a normal six-year-old are really not comparable. In addition, by describing him as "at a six-year-old level," we are tempted to treat him as though he were six years old instead of fourteen. A boy of fourteen certainly has different experiences and emotions than a younger child, whether mentally retarded or not.[4]

Deficiencies in General Cognitive Abilities

The middle ring of Figure 16.1 consists of general cognitive abilities that people with mental retardation lack, at least to some extent. Researchers who specialize in mental retardation have studied two aspects of cognitive abilities that are hypothesized as responsible for the observed deficits in adaptive behavior. *Structural features,* for example, the frontal lobe, refer to fixed, unmodifiable components of the brain that affect cognitive and adaptive functioning. *Control processes,* in contrast, are those aspects of cognitive abilities that can presumably be improved through training (Atkinson and Shiffrin, 1969; Baumeister, 1984). Although researchers differ in their emphases on fixed versus modifiable aspects of cognitive functioning, most agree that both components are important to an understanding of mental retardation.

Attention to Stimuli Zeaman and Hanley (1983) review evidence indicating that persons with mental retardation attend to different dimensions of a stimulus than people of normal intelligence. Discrimination learning tasks require subjects to select correctly between two objects on the basis of one or more specific dimensions, such as color, size, or shape. Researchers have found that younger children and retarded individuals attend more to color than to form, whereas older children and normal adults pay more attention to form. In addition, mentally retarded individuals attend more readily to the position of the object than to its other dimensions. For example, a retarded person may use a "response set," such as always selecting the choice on the left, or alternating left and right positions, and ignore dimensions of the problem such as color or shape that could guide him to a correct solution.

Does the preference of retarded individuals for the position of a stimulus indicate the presence of a control process or a structural feature? Evidence that retarded persons can be taught to attend to the relevant dimensions rather than to position suggests that control processes are functioning. On the other hand, several findings indicate that structural features are predominant: (1) prior to training, most retarded individuals show the preference for position; (2) despite countertraining in attention to the relevant dimensions of the problem, retarded individuals sometimes continue to attend to an irrelevant dimension, such as position; and (3) when training ends, subjects usually regress to their earlier preferences (Zeaman and Hanley, 1983).

Short-Term Memory Deficits The well-documented presence of short-term memory deficits in mentally retarded persons again raises the question of fixed versus modifiable deficiencies in cognitive functioning. Although the long-term memories of normal children and those with mental retardation have been found to be the same, retarded individuals have much poorer short-term memory.

A control process hypothesis to explain this deficit centers on a correctable failure to use rehearsal strategies in solving problems. Given a list of ten items to remember, normal children will rehearse the items or find cues to help them remember them. Some researchers (Butterfield and Belmont, 1975; Detterman, 1979) suggest that, although retarded children do not use such rehearsal strategies on their own, they can be taught to do so, with a resulting improvement in their short-term memory abilities.

More recent evidence, however, points to a structural deficit in the memory capacity of mentally retarded children. To study short-term memory capacity separately from voluntary cognitive processes such as rehearsal, Ellis, Deacon, and Wooldridge (1985) presented stimuli (letters or pictures) briefly, and prevented rehearsal by requiring both the normal and the mentally retarded to attend immediately to a distracting stimulus. In this procedure, the superior rehearsal strategies of

---

[4]A normal six-year-old is also different in many ways from a retarded fourteen-year-old who is functioning at a six-year-old level.

the normal subjects are inhibited, enabling the experimenter to examine short-term memory ability apart from the effects of rehearsal. The Ellis *et al.* (1985) studies demonstrated deficiencies in short-term memory in mentally retarded individuals, suggesting a structural deficit in their memory capacity.

Processing Speed Further evidence for structural deficits in the functioning of mentally retarded individuals is found in research on the speed of processing information. An example of this type of experiment is the "inspection time" study, which attempts to measure processing speed while keeping cognitive strategies (control processes) to a minimum. Nettelbeck (1985) gave subjects a simple discrimination task, such as identifying the longer of two lines. The task (stimulus) is flashed briefly on a screen, followed by a "mask" (a different pattern) to halt processing. Inspection time is defined as the length of exposure to the initial stimulus that the subject requires to reach 100 percent accuracy. Mildly retarded subjects require about twice as much exposure time as nonretarded control subjects, suggesting a deficit in their processing speed, a presumed structural problem.

Executive Functioning Other researchers suggest that retarded children have general deficits in "executive functioning" (Butterfield and Belmont, 1977). The children fail to generalize strategies to other times and to other settings. Although the appropriate use of memory strategies is one aspect of executive functioning, it includes as well "metacognitive" activities such as knowing how to plan, to monitor progress, to solve problems, and to check outcomes for completeness and corrections. People with and without retardation may have strategic ability but not be able to apply it.

Control Function of Language Russian developmental psychologists have long been interested in discovering general cognitive deficits in individuals with mental retardation. Their work is being translated into English and is being incorporated into experimental studies of mental retardation done in the United States. Lev Semenovich Vygotsky (1896–1934) had an extensive theory of thought and speech that regarded them as stemming from separate roots but later coinciding. He also theorized that private speech branches off from social speech and assumes a control function. The control function of language is crucial to intelligent behavior and develops in three stages (Vygotsky, 1978). A child's behavior is first controlled or regulated by instructions from other people. Then the child imitates these instructions aloud, and they serve as a cue or guide to behavior. The process is completed when the child's

formerly spoken words become internalized, when they become inner speech. This natural internalizing process may break down in retarded children.

Etiology of Mental Retardation

The innermost circle of Figure 16.1 (page 446), which we focus on in this section, represents the responsible causal agent of mental retardation. In only 25 percent of the mentally retarded population can this primary cause be specifically identified.

No Identifiable Etiology

Although moderate and severe mental retardation are found equally in boys and girls, mild mental retardation is slightly more common in boys. It is likely that much of this discrepancy is due to differences in the development of adaptive behavior in males and females: male psychosocial development in childhood lags behind that of females, possibly leading boys to be judged more readily as mildly retarded. When strict objective measures are used, such as an IQ of 70 or less, the prevalence of mild mental retardation in males and females is almost equal (Richardson, Katz, and Koller, 1986).

In general, persons with severe or profound mental retardation have an identifiable organic brain defect, whereas persons with less severe mental retardation do not. Persons whose mental retardation is associated with identifiable organic impairments are found in much the same percentages throughout all socioeconomic, ethnic, and racial groups. In contrast, persons with mild or moderate mental retardation are overrepresented in the lower socioeconomic classes.

Two theories have been proposed to explain why some people with no identifiable brain defect do not function within the normal range of intelligence. One, proposed by Edmund Zigler (1967), is called the developmental theory. Zigler argued that a person with mild retardation for which no organic cause is indicated should not be viewed as having a structural deficit, but rather as "a perfectly normal expression of the population gene pool, of slower and more limited intellectual development than the individual of average intellect" (Zigler, 1967, p. 298). According to this model, the differences found between retarded persons and normal children with matched mental age are not due to a cognitive defect, but to motivational factors. Specifically, the social deprivation common in institutions for the retarded, the history of task failures, and the lesser importance of reinforcers such as being told one is correct lead retarded individuals to have lower motivation for performing cognitive tasks than normal children of the same mental age. Presumably, strengthening those motivational variables should improve the performance of mildly retarded children, although they still would not be expected to perform at normal levels because of their slower growth and lower peak of intellectual development.

Research reviewed by Weisz and colleagues has lent support, albeit inconsistent, to this developmental theory of mental retardation. Weisz and Yeates (1981) found that mentally retarded subjects with no organic cause for their retardation performed comparably to mental-age-matched controls on certain intellectual tasks, suggesting that retarded persons develop cognitively in the same way as normal persons, just more slowly. This finding supports Zigler's view. However, Weiss, Weisz, and Bromfield (1986) found that on information-processing tasks, retarded individuals performed significantly below their mental-age-matched controls. This latter finding suggests that there are indeed structural differences between mentally retarded and normal individuals, challenging the developmental theory.

The alternative view to Zigler's is that brain damage, too slight to be detected by currently available methods, causes mild retardation. Baumeister and MacLean (1979), for example, propose that a trauma during the birth of infants, as well as other prenatal and perinatal conditions, damages the brain enough to cause mild retardation. But other factors, including the environment, may make the same degree of impairment manifest itself differently. The effects of the environment could explain the relatively few persons in the upper socioeconomic classes with mild retardation. Consider two persons with equal structural impairment, one from an upper socioeconomic level and one from a lower level. The first individual's slight deficit could be compensated for by the enriched background. The second individual's deficit might be exaggerated by impoverished circumstances. To show signs of retardation, a socially advantaged person must have more extensive damage, which is impervious to help from an enriched upbringing.

Although researchers have attempted to determine the nature of the proposed physical brain impairment, results have thus far been inconclusive (Baumeister and MacLean, 1979; Karrer, Nelson, and Galbraith, 1979). Some evidence suggests, however, that the synaptic connections in the brains of children with mental retardation are less complex and less differentiated than those of normal children (Huttenlocher, 1974; Purpura, 1976). Unfortunately, the minor physical defects responsible for mild to moderate retardation are readily observable only in postmortem studies. Their presence is also somewhat of a chicken-and-egg question. Does the environmental deprivation or the structural deficit

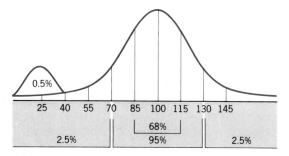

FIGURE 16.2
Normal curve showing the theoretical distribution of IQ scores. The bump on the left represents the actual frequency of severe and profound retardation with organic causes.

occur first? For example, studies of animals raised in a deprived environment found their brains to be smaller in size (Krech, Rosenzweig, and Bennett, 1966).

Known Organic Etiology

The approximately 25 percent of people with mental retardation that has a known single organic cause inflate the incidence of retardation in the population over what would be statistically expected were no abnormal conditions present. These individuals create what is referred to as a "bump" at the bottom end of the normal curve (Figure 16.2). Genetic conditions, infectious diseases, accidents, prematurity, chemicals, and environmental hazards are six categories of organic impairment.

Genetic or Chromosomal Anomalies Four percent of all recognized pregnancies have chromosomal abnormalities. The majority of these pregnancies, however, end in spontaneous abortions or miscarriages. Only about one-half of one percent of the babies who are born have a chromosomal abnormality (Smith, Bierman, and Robinson, 1978). A significant proportion of these infants die soon after birth. Of the babies that survive, the largest percent have ***Down's syndrome*** or ***trisomy 21.***

Down's syndrome is named after the British physician Langdon Down, who first described the clinical signs in 1866. In 1959 the French geneticist Jerome Lejeune and his colleagues identified its genetic basis. Human beings usually possess forty-six chromosomes, inheriting twenty-three from each parent by means of the germ cells. Individuals with Down's syndrome almost always have forty-seven chromosomes instead of forty-six. During maturation of the egg, something goes wrong so that the two chromosomes of pair 21, the smallest ones, fail to separate. If this egg is fertilized, uniting with a sperm, there will be three of chromosome 21; thus the technical term trisomy 21. Down's syndrome is found in approximately one out of 800 to 1200 live births.

All of a woman's eggs remain in prophase 1 of meiosis, basically in a suspended state of division, from the time that they were formed, when the woman was merely a fetus, until they begin to mature after puberty, usually one at a time. The longer this period, the greater the chance for damage to pairs of chromosomes that would prevent their eventual separation. For this reason the incidence of Down's syndrome increases dramatically for mothers over the age of thirty-five; in 1973 women over thirty-five had little more than 13 percent of all pregnancies but bore more than one-half of the infants with trisomy 21.

Unlike women, after puberty men form new germ cells daily. Recent research, however, indicates that in as many as 25 percent of Down's syndrome cases the father's sperm carries the extra chromosome (Magenis *et al.*, 1977). Again, age at conception is implicated, in this instance advanced paternal age.

Fortunately, the amniotic fluid in which the fetus is immersed within the uterus contains cells and other substances from the fetus. A small amount of the fluid can be withdrawn by needle in the sixteenth week, a process called amniocentesis. The cells are cultured and later reveal whether there are three chromosomes 21. A new method, chorionic villi biopsy, can be performed even earlier, in the tenth week, which is an important advantage. The villi, tiny protrusions on the chorion, the outermost membrane surrounding the fetus, are tissue from the conceptus. They are taken by suction or clipping and removed directly through the mother's cervix. Cells of this tissue are cultured and then analyzed.

The IQs of people with Down's syndrome are in the mild to moderate range of mental retardation. In addition, they have many rather distinctive physical signs of their syndrome: short and stocky stature; oval, upward-slanting eyes; the epicanthic fold, a prolongation of the fold of the upper eyelid over the inner corner of the eye; sparse, fine, straight hair; a wide and flat nasal bridge; square-shaped ears; a large, furrowed tongue, protruding because the mouth is small and its roof low; short, broad hands with stubby fingers; a general loose-jointedness, particularly in the ankles; and a broad-based walk. Perhaps 40 percent of children with Down's syndrome have heart problems; a small minority may have blockages of the upper intestinal tract; and about one in six dies during the first year. Mortality after age forty is high; at autopsy, brain tissue generally shows deterioration similar to that in Alzheimer's disease. Plastic surgeons have recently attenuated some of the more obvious facial distinctions of young people with Down's syndrome. Despite their mental retardation,

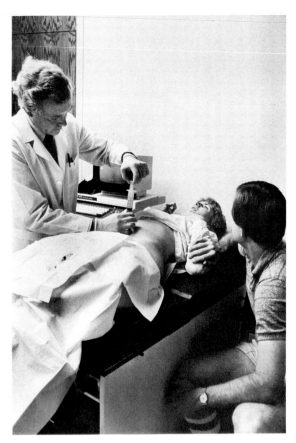

Amniocentesis can be used to diagnose Down's syndrome in a developing fetus.

most of these children can learn to read, to write, and even to do math.

Researchers have identified certain individuals with malformations of the X chromosome (Harvey, Judge, and Wiener, 1977). Specifically, the X chromosome may actually break in two—hence the name *fragile X syndrome.* Physical symptoms associated with fragile X include facial features such as large, underdeveloped ears, a long, thin face and a broad nasal root, and enlarged testicles in males. More importantly, the majority of males and about one-third of females with fragile X are moderately mentally retarded, and many also show attention deficits and hyperactivity. Females who do not manifest outward symptoms can still be carriers and may pass the syndrome on to their children. Among those who are not retarded, many have learning disabilities and speech and language difficulties (Bergman, Dykens, Watson, Ort, and Leckman, 1987). Fragile X is the second leading cause of mental retardation with a chromosomal basis, after Down's syndrome (Dykens, Leckman, Paul, and Watson, 1988), and has recently been implicated as a cause of some cases of autism as well (Fisch, Cohen, Wolf, Brown, Jenkins, and Gross, 1986).

The development of a child with Down's syndrome, sensitively photographed by his father.

Recessive-Gene Diseases When a pair of defective recessive genes misdirect the formation of an enzyme, metabolic processes are disturbed. The problem may affect development of the embryo in the uterus or become important only much later in life.

In *phenylketonuria* (PKU) the infant, born normal, soon suffers from a deficiency of liver enzyme, phenylalanine hydroxylase, which is needed to convert phenylalanine, an amino acid of protein food, to tyrosine. Phenylalanine and its derivative phenylpyruvic acid build up in the body fluids, eventually giving the urine a musty odor and ultimately wreaking irreversible brain damage. The unmetabolized amino acid interferes with the process of myelination, the sheathing of neuron axons. This sheathing is essential for the rapid transmittal of impulses and thus of information; the neurons of the frontal lobes are particularly affected. Little wonder that mental retardation is profound.

Although PKU is a rare disease with an incidence of about one in 14,000 live births, it is estimated that one person in seventy is a carrier of the recessive gene. There is a blood test for prospective parents who have reason to suspect that they might be carriers. Fortunately too, after the PKU newborn has consumed milk for several days, an excess amount of unconverted phenylalanine can be detected in its blood. State laws require that the necessary test be given. If the test is positive, the parents are urged to provide the infant a diet low in phenylalanine. When the diet is restricted as early as the third month and until the age of six, when brain differentiation is relatively complete, cognitive development improves, sometimes to within the normal range (*Collaborative Study of Children Treated for Phenylketonuria*, 1975).

Several hundred other recessive-gene diseases have been identified, many of them causing mental retardation. Only a very small percentage of the cases of mental retardation is accounted for by any *single* disease. Genetic counseling can help future parents find out whether their backgrounds suggest that they are at risk for carrying certain of these recessive genes, and amniocentesis and chorionic villi biopsy can reveal the presence of some of these problems in the fetus.

If the fetus is found to have genetic abnormalities, the parents usually have the option of abortion. Supporters of selective abortion refer to the poor quality of life of a retarded individual as well as to the emotional costs to the parents and the costs to society to provide care. Opponents of selective abortion claim that all life is sacred and that such fetuses have the right to life. It is not an easy issue.

Infectious Diseases While in utero, the fetus is at increased risk of mental retardation from maternal infectious diseases. The consequences of these diseases are more serious during the first trimester of pregnancy, when the fetus has no detectable immunological response. In addition, the first trimester is a critical period in the development of the brain. Cytomegalovirus, toxoplasmosis, rubella, herpes simplex, and syphilis are all maternal infections that may cause both physical deformities and mental retardation of the fetus. The mother may experience slight or even no symptoms from the infection, but the effects on the developing fetus can be devastating. Pregnant women who go to prenatal clinics are given a blood test for syphilis. Today women who contemplate having a child can take a blood test to determine whether they are immune to rubella (German measles); nearly 85 percent of American women are. A woman who is not should be vaccinated at least six months before becoming pregnant. If a fetus contracts rubella from its mother, it is likely to be born with brain lesions that cause mental retardation.

After birth, infectious diseases can also affect a child's developing brain. Encephalitis and meningococcal meningitis may cause irreversible brain damage and even death if contracted in infancy or early childhood. These infections in adulthood are usually far less serious, probably because the brain is largely developed by about the age of six. There are several forms of childhood meningitis, a disease in which the protective membranes of the brain are acutely inflamed and fever is very high. Even if the child survives and is not severely retarded, it is likely that onset of moderate or mild retardation will occur. Other disabling aftereffects are deafness, paralysis, and epilepsy.

Accidents In the United States accidents are the leading cause of severe disability and death in children over one year of age. Falls and automobile accidents are among the most common mishaps in early childhood and may cause varying degrees of head injury and mental retardation. The institution of laws mandating that children riding in automobiles wear seat belts may play a major role in reducing the incidence of mental retardation in young children.

Prematurity A baby is considered premature if delivered two or more weeks before term. Premature infants who survive have an increased risk of developing mental retardation. Although the relation between prematurity and mental retardation is quite high, it is difficult to substantiate prematurity per se as a causal factor. Many factors—poverty, teenage motherhood, inadequate nutrition, and poor prenatal care—all figure in prematurity. Additionally, premature infants may develop other medical problems that place them at increased risk for mental retardation.

Prematurity is associated with mental retardation.

There is some evidence that preterm infants may not get off to a good start in social development. Field and her colleagues (1979, 1980) have compared the patterns of mothers' interactions with their preterm infants to those of mothers with full-term infants. Those between mothers and preterm infants have less synchrony, sensitivity, give and take, and turn taking. Field suggests that parents of preterm infants may be disappointed in their infants because they expect them to act their birth age, rather than their age since conception in the womb.

Noxious Chemical Substances   In the early 1960s a presumably harmless drug called thalidomide was prescribed in England, Canada, West Germany, and Scandinavia for pregnant women experiencing morning sickness. Thus they took the drug during the critical embryonic period. Many of the babies born to these mothers had arms and legs resembling the buds that precede limb development in the human embryo, a condition called phocomelia. Although thalidomide was quickly taken off the market, for thousands of infants the damage was already done.

The havoc wreaked by thalidomide was extreme, but it can serve to underscore the point that the ingestion of any chemical substance by a pregnant woman may cause the development of the fetus to diverge in a serious way from its normal track. One such chemical in widespread use is alcohol.

Consumption of even one or two glasses of wine each day during the first trimester of pregnancy increases by 10 percent the probability that the infant will be born with *fetal alcohol syndrome.* FAS consists of both physical symptoms—small head, widely spaced eyes, a flat nose, a deep upper lip, and a small stature that never catches up—and mental retardation. The risk of FAS increases with the amount of alcohol consumed, but even if the mother has only one or two alcohol binges during pregnancy, the infant may still develop FAS. As with many hazards, the risk to the fetus is greatest during the first trimester. Many women do not realize that they are pregnant until the later part of the first trimester. Thus, even if the mother quits drinking as soon as the pregnancy becomes known, some damage to the fetus may already have been done. Many states now require restaurants, bars, and liquor stores to post warnings that drinking alcohol during pregnancy can cause birth defects.

Environmental Hazards   Several environmental pollutants can cause poisoning and mental retardation. These include mercury, which may be transmitted through affected fish, and lead, which is found in lead-based paints, smog, and the exhaust from automobiles burning leaded gasoline. Lead poisoning can cause kidney and brain damage as well as anemia, mental retardation, seizures, and death. Lead-based paint is now pro-

Eating chips of lead-based paint, found on old buildings, can cause mental retardation.

hibited, but it is still on the walls of lower-income housing and by this time is old and flaking.

The increasing technology of our society creates environmental hazards. The intent of a medical treatment is to do good, but an unforeseen consequence may be mental retardation. One such medical procedure—the diphtheria-pertussis-tetanus (DPT) vaccine—carries such iatrogenic dangers, that is, problems induced inadvertently by the doctor. The DPT vaccine protects thousands of children from pertusis, a dangerous childhood disease more commonly known as whooping cough. The pertussis part of the vaccine, however, causes a high rate of adverse reactions in the children inoculated. These range from redness and swelling around the vaccinated area, to persistent crying or high-pitched screaming, to brain damage and sometimes even death. The DPT vaccine is estimated to be responsible for approximately fifty cases of severe mental retardation each year.

Although the potential side effects of the DPT vaccine were known in the early 1940s, the majority of the population remains unaware of the risks. A group of parents, Dissatisfied Parents Together, whose children have been adversely affected by the DPT vaccine, advocate federal legislation that would allow compensation for the families of DPT victims. The proposed legislation would also require doctors to give parents all the information available on the vaccine before it is administered and to report all adverse reactions.

Programs like Project Head Start try to prevent mild mental retardation.

Prevention of Mental Retardation

In the early 1960s a national effort was begun to prevent retardation. The President's Panel on Mental Retardation stated that if we would apply all the knowledge available, one-half of all new cases of mental retardation could be prevented (Begab, 1974). Prevention depends, of course, on understanding the factors causing retardation. The known organic causes present a fairly straightforward challenge and opportunity, and many of them can now be counteracted, as already indicated. For the majority of cases in which etiology is not as obvious, prevention becomes considerably more problematic.

Eugenics Movement

Historically, eugenics[5] has been practiced in an effort to decrease the numbers of mentally retarded people. Eugenics advocates that breeding be selective to increase, from one generation to another, the proportion of persons with better than average hereditary endowments. Social Darwinism had contributed the belief that mental retardation was caused largely by heredity. In 1903 the American Breeders Association was formed to devise guidelines and set up policies by which people should be allowed to conceive and bear children. Two remedies for mental retardation were advocated, segregation and sterilization.

Many large institutions were constructed in which retarded individuals could live apart from the rest of the population. Most were no more than warehouses for anyone unfortunate enough to do poorly on newly constructed intelligence tests (Blatt, 1966). The majority of residents were newly arrived immigrants, members of racial minorities, children with physical handicaps, and indigents.

Although forced segregation reduced the number of children born to couples with one partner of questionable intelligence, it did not stop couples within institutions from bearing children. In Indiana, in 1907, the first mandatory sterilization law for women with mental retardation was passed. By 1930 twenty-eight states had these laws. Although their unconstitutionality was ques-

---

[5]Eugenics should be distinguished from genetic counseling. Parents who learn through a counselor that they are at risk for giving birth to a handicapped infant are advised about the odds and the care that would be necessary for the child, and given other information that might help them reach a decision in a difficult predicament. In contrast, eugenics tries to create babies who, it is believed, will have certain qualities that may make them *superior*. During the Third Reich the Nazis wanted to increase the numbers of blond, blue-eyed Aryan children. Nowadays there are "sperm banks" in which are stored the frozen sperm of men of uncommon professional distinction, such as brilliant scientists and writers, the hope being that, at some later time, a woman will apply to be impregnated by sperm judged to be genetically superior.

tioned, forced sterilization continued to be practiced in many institutions through the 1950s. In the 1960s safeguards were passed to protect the rights of individuals with mental retardation to marry and bear children.

Early Intervention

As the importance of environmental factors in the incidence of mental retardation became more widely recognized, prevention efforts turned to early intervention for children at risk through the impoverished circumstances of their rearing. Prevention of mild mental retardation depends on early identification and training of susceptible people. Researchers are working both to improve the procedures for identifying children at risk and to design the most effective preventive programs.

Certainly the best-known, large-scale effort to raise the achievement and intellectual level of disadvantaged children is Project Head Start. Its purpose is to prepare children socially and culturally to succeed in the regular school setting by giving them experiences that they are missing at home. The impetus for Head Start came during the 1960s, when national attention was directed to problems of hunger and civil rights. If the thousands of children from culturally disadvantaged families were to have the same educational opportunities as other children, the poverty cycle would have to be broken and the standard of living raised considerably.

The core of the Head Start program is community-based preschool education, focusing on the development of early cognitive and social skills. In addition, Head Start contracts with professionals in the community to provide children with health and dental services, including vaccinations, hearing and vision testing, medical treatment, and nutrition information (North, 1979). Mental health services are an important component of Head Start programs. Psychologists may help to identify children with psychological problems and consult with teachers and staff to help make the preschool environment sensitive to psychological issues, for example, by sharing knowledge of child development, consulting on an individual case, or helping staff address parents' concerns (Cohen, Solnit, and Wohlford, 1979). Social workers can serve as advocates for the child's family, linking families with needed social services and encouraging parents to get involved with their children's education (Lazar, 1979).

A comparison of Head Start children with other disadvantaged children who attended either a different preschool or no preschool was conducted by Lee, Brooks-Gunn, and Schnur (1988). The Head Start children improved significantly more than both control groups on social-cognitive ability and motor impulsivity; the relative improvement was especially strong for black children, and particularly those with below-average initial ability. Although the Head Start program succeeded in enhancing the functioning of the neediest children, the authors note that these children were still behind their peers in terms of absolute cognitive levels after one year in the program.

Treatment for Mental Retardation

Over the past two hundred years attitudes have swung like a pendulum from optimism and interest in educating the "feeble-minded" to bleak pessimism (Crissey, 1975). Édouard Seguin, a French physician and educator of the nineteenth century, was convinced that education was a universal right and that "idiots" were among the neediest. Considering mental retardation to be a weakness in the nervous system, he devised teaching methods to correct specific disabilities. After leaving Paris in 1848, he settled in Ohio and was instrumental in setting up special schools throughout the northeastern United States, one of them the Pennsylvania Training School for Idiots. (The reader will note how the connotative meanings of terms change. Nowadays health professionals would never use the word idiot, let alone include it in the name of an institution.) But disillusionment set in later in the century when the goals that had been confidently worked toward earlier were not attained. The children did not become normal, and the institutions grew and grew. Perhaps retarded individuals were just "born that way" and little could be done for them, except to maintain them and protect them from the intellectual demands of society. But in the past few decades of this century, there have again been serious and systematic attempts to educate retarded children to as full an extent as possible. Most retarded people can acquire the competencies needed to function effectively in the community (Box 16.2).

Deinstitutionalization

Since the 1960s the trend has been to provide retarded individuals with educational and community services rather than institutional care. Like the emptying of mental hospitals, this is called "deinstitutionalization." According to the Developmentally Disabled Assistance and Bill of Rights Act, passed by Congress in 1975, retarded individuals have a right to appropriate treatment in the least restrictive residential setting. Ideally, moderately retarded people live in small- to medium-sized homelike residences that are integrated into the community. A transition period gradually prepares the individual for the move from the institution to the community home. Medical care is provided the residents, and trained, live-in supervisors and concerned aides see to their special needs around the clock. Residents are

BOX 16.2

THE IDIOT SAVANT

One particularly interesting phenomenon, usually regarded as a special form of mental retardation, is the ***idiot savant,*** a retarded person with superior functioning in one narrow area of intellectual activity. A classic case history was reported by Scheerer, Rothman, and Goldstein (1945), who studied their subject intensively from his eleventh year through his sixteenth. During this period they gave the boy numerous problem-solving tasks and intelligence tests. L. was described as follows.

1. He had been failing at school, showing little interest in classroom activities and interacting minimally with classmates.

2. L. had developed the unusual talent of being able to provide, with little apparent thought, the day of the week for any date between 1880 and 1950. A favorite pastime was to ask people their birth dates and then immediately tell them on which day of the week they had been born and when their birthday would fall in any other given year, past or future. L. had been performing this feat since the age of seven. Scheerer and his collegues point out, however, that he had no grasp of which of two people was the older, designating always the person whose birthday fell in an earlier part of the year. For example, he would regard anyone born on June 10 as being older than someone born on September 13, quite overlooking the year of birth or the physical appearance of the two people.

3. L. could quickly spell forward or backward practically any word pronounced to him, *but* without knowing its meaning or caring to.

4. The boy had a very well developed but unusual musical ability. He could play many melodies on the piano by ear, that of Beethoven's "Moonlight Sonata," for example, but he seemed to have no grasp of what he was doing and took no enjoyment in it. He ignored any

instructions or comments on his playing. Moreover, "he sings the accompaniment or the Italian words [to several operas] as they sound to him. Without knowing the language he reproduces it phonetically" (p. 2).

5. L.'s arithmetic ability was also unusual. He could, for example, add ten to twelve two-digit numbers as fast as they were recited to him, but he was unable to learn to add larger numbers. He could also count by 16 very rapidly—1, 17, 33, 49, and so on—but without any understanding of what the numbers meant; for instance, he could not state that 20 is larger than 8.

6. He easily learned the Gettysburg Address at age fourteen by rote memory, but without understanding its meaning.

Scheerer and his colleagues found L. to test at an IQ of 50 on the Binet scale. In their attempt to explain L.'s behavior, they rejected the idea that an idiot savant has a supernormal *ability* in one area. Rather they suggested that this kind of individual lacks the crucial ability to reason abstractly and that, given this serious handicap, he copes with the world by channeling his energy into rote memory feats. He develops rote skills to an unusually high degree because he can in essence do little else with his cortex. L.'s IQ rating was low because he could not perform tasks that children must handle in order to score in the normal range when they are eleven or older—namely, tasks requiring abstract reasoning. For instance, shown an absurd picture of a man in the rain holding an umbrella upside down, the boy at age fifteen said "Yes, the man is holding an umbrella upside down. I don't know why, there is a lot of rain there" (p. 10). The overall problem was summarized by these workers as "a general impairment of abstract capacity . . . , L. [even] succeeded in his own performance-specialties without having a genuine understanding of their meaning . . ." (p. 59).

In *Rain Man*, Dustin Hoffman portrayed an autistic savant.

encouraged to participate in the household routines to the best of their ability. Severely retarded children may live at home or in foster-care homes provided with educational and psychological services. Many mildly retarded persons who have jobs and are able to live independently have their own apartments. Others live together in semi-independent apartments of three to four retarded adults. The aid of a counselor is generally provided only in the evening.

Unfortunately, some large institutions have been closed down and the residents discharged without having a supervised community placement to go to. Other institutions have been renovated to provide a more homelike atmosphere. Residents, typically severely retarded, are often clustered in cottages on the institution grounds. They are no longer living in barracks, but because institutions are often located outside the city limits, they have few opportunities to shop in stores, take public transportation, and come in contact with normal people. At present, the majority who remain in institutions are severely and profoundly retarded people who have physical handicaps as well (Scheerenberger, 1984).

Early Intervention

Whereas programs like Head Start can help prevent mild mental retardation in disadvantaged children, other early intervention programs have been developed to improve the eventual level of functioning of more seriously retarded individuals (without actually preventing the retardation). A number of pilot projects with Down's syndrome children have intervened during infancy and young childhood to attempt to improve the functioning of these children. These programs typically include systematic home- and treatment-center-based instruction in language skills, fine and gross motor skills, self-care, and social development. Specific behavioral objectives are defined, and, in an operant fashion, children are taught skills in small sequential steps, structured according to their progress in previous steps (e.g., Clunies-Ross, 1979).

Studies of these programs indicate consistent improvements in fine motor skills, social acceptance, and self-help skills. Unfortunately, the programs appear to have little effect on gross motor skills and linguistic abilities, and long-term improvements in IQ and school performance have not been demonstrated. It is not yet clear whether the benefits of the programs are greater than what parents can provide in the home without special training (Gibson and Harris, 1988).

Public Law 94-142

In 1975 the United States Congress passed Public Law 94-142, the Education for All Handicapped Children Act. Passage of this law represented substantial gains for the educational rights of children with handicaps and, in addition, secured their integration into the community. Both mentally retarded and autistic children have benefited from this federal law. Specifically, it includes five provisions.

1. **All handicapped children between the ages of three and twenty-one have the right to a free, appropriate public education.** Before the passage of this law, school districts could refuse to accept into their schools children with mental, emotional, or physical handicaps. Parents of children with disabilities were often left with three choices: to pay for a private school, to attempt to care for their child at home, or to institutionalize the child. Because few parents could afford private schools or had the resources needed to care for their child at home, many children ended up in institutions. When P.L. 94-142 was enacted, handicapped children could receive an appropriate education in a public school, giving their parents a break from caretaking responsibilities during the day.

2. **Individual educational programs (IEPs) are mandated for each handicapped child, with annual reevaluations.** The right of access to the public schools, in and of itself, does not guarantee that handicapped children will develop to their fullest potential. In fact, special education classrooms have often been little more than day-care centers providing virtually no functional learning. Or, if instruction was provided, it was often not appropriate to the students' ages and levels of functioning and did not teach them the skills that they needed. P.L. 94-142 guarantees that training will be carefully tailored to the individual child. The goals for the children are determined at an IEP conference that must include, at the least, an administrator of the educational agency, the teacher, the children's parents, and, if possible, the students themselves. Further, P.L. 94-142 mandates that the goals for each IEP be reevaluated at least once a year to ensure that they continue to be relevant to what the child needs to learn and is capable of learning.

3. **Students are entitled to education in the least restrictive environment.** The "least restrictive environment" provision of P.L. 94-142 has been subject to differences in interpretation. In the abstract, such an environment is one that allows the handicapped student to develop mentally, physically, and socially with the fewest barriers while at the same time providing necessary support. To some, the least restrictive environment means that the children are edu-

Many retarded children are now "mainstreamed" into regular classrooms.

cated at the same schools as normally achieving youngsters and are "mainstreamed" into some of their classrooms. Others would say that a segregated school provides the resources and intensive training required by handicapped children.

Programs that are sensitive to the problems inherent in mainstreaming appear likely to yield positive results for students both with and without handicaps. Normal children can learn early in life that there is tremendous diversity among human beings and that a child may be different in some very important ways and yet be worthy of respect and friendship. With support from parents and teachers, normal children may reach adulthood without the burden of prejudice of earlier generations. Such an eventuality would benefit both the normal child and the emotionally or cognitively handicapped agemate.

4. **The right to procedural due process is guaranteed.** If the parents with a handicapped student or the students themselves believe that the education is not appropriate, or that the student's due process is being violated, they may protest to the proper school administrators. Often parents will believe that their child should be eligible for special services, but because of the testing cutoff points the child may not receive the necessary classification and thus miss out on the extra resources. Other parents may believe that the school is not teaching the students what they need to know after they graduate. P.L. 94-142 mandates that interested parties have the right to protest, to participate in hearings and appeals, and to have an attorney present.

The defendants in a legal case in Pennsylvania argued that some children who are severely and profoundly impaired tend to learn much more slowly than other children and tend much more quickly to forget what they have learned. The court concluded that a state rule limiting the school year to 180 days kept such children from obtaining an appropriate public education and, accordingly, violated P.L. 94-142. Year-round education was provided.

5. **States that comply with these statutes receive federal assistance.** Each state is required to report to the federal government whether or not its school districts are complying with the provisions of P.L. 94-142. When they do not comply, moneys are withheld from educational programming.

Teaching Strategies

Therapies based on the writings of Freud and Rogers, which rely heavily on verbal ability, indeed verbal facility, have had limited applicability in treating retarded people. But verbal exchanges with retarded individuals are of course possible and necessary. Moderately and mildly retarded children can use advice from a counselor or other adult; they all need to be reassured about the competencies that they have, and they can obtain encouragement and support from what kind and trustworthy people tell them (Robinson and Robinson, 1976). Play therapy has been adapted for treatment of retarded children; for example, water and finger paints in unstructured sessions for the severely retarded, and coloring books and puzzles in more structured meetings with those less so (Leland and Smith, 1965).

Therapists treat retarded children with behavioral methods, in particular ***applied behavior analysis***[6] and cognitive behavior therapy. The former is most often used to teach severely and profoundly retarded children and those with autism the adaptive skills mentioned earlier: communication, self-help, and social and vocational skills. Children with mild and moderate mental retardation are given cognitive therapy to improve their general cognitive functioning. Other teaching approaches focus on nonvocal communication and computer-assisted instruction.

Applied Behavior Analysis Children with severe and profound retardation usually need intensive instruction to be able merely to feed, toilet, and groom themselves. To teach a severely retarded child a particular routine, the therapist usually begins by analyzing and dividing the targeted behavior, such as eating, into smaller com-

---

[6]In the behavioral literature on mental retardation, this term is used more frequently than operant conditioning, but the two terms refer to the same kinds of assessments and interventions.

BOX 16.3

TREATMENT OF SELF-INJURIOUS AND STEREOTYPED BEHAVIOR

Many mentally retarded and autistic individuals, particularly those with severe disabilities, engage in persistent, repetitive, stereotyped behavior. Some of these behaviors are self-injurious, such as head-banging, face-slapping, biting, pinching, and scratching, whereas others (such as rocking, twirling, mouthing, or wall-patting) do not present a physical danger. Nevertheless, these maladaptive behaviors compete with more socially acceptable adaptive behaviors and interfere with attempts to educate them.

A fourteen-member task force organized by the Association for the Advancement of Behavior Therapy (AABT) explored the effectiveness of behavior therapy for treating self-injurious behavior (Favell *et al.*, 1982). They pointed out that reassuring the child resulted in a dramatic *increase* in self-injury, presumably because the comforting served as a positive reinforcement for the behavior (Lovaas, Freitag, Gold, and Kossorla, 1965). Behavior therapists have worked at applying operant principles to the problem of stereotyped behavior. One effective combination involves giving positive reinforcement when the child is *not* engaging in the target behavior, and using "overcorrection" (having the child practice alternative behaviors over and over) after each instance of self-injurious or stereotyped behavior. These procedures have been found to be effective for many children, but not for all.

A controversial alternative is punishment. Behavior therapists have used such aversive consequences as squirting lemon juice in the mouth or applying a mild shock (enough to be noxious, but not physically harmful) to the arm or leg immediately following each incident of self-injurious behavior. Of course some therapists and laypeople have understandably been concerned about the use of aversive procedures, particularly in institutional settings with patients who may be unable to give informed consent. But research has demonstrated that punishment may be the most effective, indeed the only effective, method of reducing self-injurious behavior in intractable cases (Gorman-Smith and Matson, 1985). Proponents of the procedure assert that dangerous behaviors, for example, those that may cause serious head injury, justify the use of aversive procedures. The AABT task force concludes their report by advocating that punishment be reserved for those situations where more benign procedures have failed, where the client is in imminent and extreme physical danger, or when the self-injurious behavior is so intrusive as to prevent participation in habilitative and humanizing activities. In addition, they propose guidelines for ensuring that the procedures are used with caution, including required training and supervision by qualified experts, review of treatment by a Human Rights Committee and a Peer Review Committee, informed guardian consent, and rigorous evaluation of the effects of the treatment in each individual case.

---

ponents: pick up spoon, scoop food from plate onto spoon, bring spoon to mouth, remove food with lips, chew and swallow food. Operant conditioning principles are then applied to teach the child these components of eating. For example, the child may be reinforced for successive approximations to picking up the spoon until he or she is able to do so. The chain may start at the first step of the sequence, picking up the spoon, and add further components till the last one is mastered; this is referred to as "forward chaining." Or the child may be taught the last step first, chewing and swallowing the food. Each time a step is mastered, the next-earlier step is taught. With this "backward chaining" procedure the student accomplishes the goal, actually eating the food, during each training period. The learning is slow and requires great patience from the teacher. Nevertheless, both forward and backward chaining have been effective in teaching needed skills to children with severe and profound handicaps.

Applied behavior analysis is used also to reduce inappropriate and self-injurious behavior. Children with severe and profound mental handicaps who live in institutions are especially prone to stereotyped behaviors performed in isolation—repetitive, rhythmic, self-stimulatory motions, such as rocking back and forth, swaying, rolling the head—and to aggression against the self or toward other children and staff. These maladaptive movements and injurious actions can often be reduced by reinforcing substitute responses (see Box 16.3).

The significance of learning self-care and of reducing stereotypes and injurious actions must not be underestimated. Toilet-trained children, for example, are more comfortable, are liked better by the staff, and can leave the ward for other rooms and leave the building to play on the grounds. Mastering toilet training and learning to feed and dress themselves may even mean that severely retarded children can live at home. Most retarded people face discrimination from others, whose negative attitudes are based in part on the sometimes gross violations of norms committed by them. Being able to act more normally will increase their chances of interacting meaningfully with others. Moreover, the self-esteem that comes from learning to take better care of oneself is extremely bolstering.

Cognitive Behavior Therapy As we indicated earlier, retarded children fail to use strategies in solving problems, and when they do have strategies, they often do not apply them effectively. Self-instructional training, for example, teaches retarded children to guide their actions through speech. Meichenbaum and Goodman (1971) outline a five-step procedure based on a Russian theory for self-instructional training. First the instructor performs the task, speaking instructions aloud to herself while the child watches and listens. Then the child listens and performs the task while the instructor speaks instructions to him. The child repeats the task twice again, first giving himself instructions aloud, then whispering them. Finally, he is ready to perform the task while uttering self-talk instructions to himself.

Self-instructions have been employed to teach children self-control and to pay attention, as well as to master more academic tasks. Johnston and her colleagues (1980) have found self-instruction effective for teaching metacognitive skills in helping mildly retarded children learn to add and subtract. The children ask themselves, "How do I begin?" and "What kind of math problem is this?" They are also given answers to these questions. For example, "It's an add problem. I can tell by the sign." To self-instruct themselves in specific arithmetic techniques for carrying and borrowing, the children may learn to say, "I start with the top number in the one's column. Since it has two numbers, I have to carry." A question designed to foster monitoring or checking skills might be, "Is the answer right? I need to check it." Finally, the children learn to reinforce themselves for correct answers, "I got it right. I'm doing very well."

Ross and Ross (1973) implemented an exemplary modeling program based on a finding by Milgram (1973) that retarded children do not use mediators to make associations as effectively as normal children do. They gave one group of children whose IQs ranged from 40 to 80 special game sessions in which they watched nonretarded children using sentences to link words together. Control retarded children continued in the usual curriculum of the school at which the study was being carried out. During the school year the special group of retarded children showed marked increases in their measured IQ, and eleven of the thirty were actually transferred from the special classes to regular ones; the control children did not show such improvement.

Cognitive behavior therapy has also been applied to improving the social skills of retarded individuals. Although focus on concrete behavioral skills is important, it is also clear that many mentally retarded individuals experience ridicule during adolescence and may develop negative attitudes about social interaction that prevent them from forming satisfying social relationships, even with adequate social skills. Lindsay (1986) used cognitive therapy methods to reduce anxiety and negative self-statements in mildly mentally retarded adults, and found that negative attitudes toward socializing could be reduced.

Nonvocal Communications It is estimated that over 70 percent of mentally retarded individuals have some type of speech difficulty (Fristoe and Lloyd, 1979); though some of these people can be taught to communicate through speech, behavior modification techniques for teaching speech have not been successful with many retarded and autistic individuals. These failures have led to a shift in emphasis from trying to teach articulation and language to emphasis on other means of communication. Most promising have been efforts to teach severely retarded and autistic individuals to communicate through sign language and other nonvocal methods. Communication systems taught include the American Sign Language used by the deaf and "communication boards" with pictures or symbols that mute persons use to indicate wants or needs. Individuals who are unable to point can direct a beam of light mounted on the head to communicate. Some encouraging findings of studies on nonvocal communication suggest that not only can handicapped individuals often learn to communicate more easily through nonvocal means than through speech, but people who have learned to sign often begin using speech spontaneously (Lloyd and Karlan, 1984).

Computer-Assigned Instruction Evidence suggests that computer-assisted instruction may be especially well

The use of computers is an important aspect of current educational training of the mentally retarded.

suited for education of mentally retarded individuals; the visual and auditory components of computers maintain the attention of often distractible students; the level of material presented can be individualized, ensuring success experiences; and the computer can meet the needs of mentally retarded individuals for numerous repetitions of material without becoming bored or impatient (as a human teacher might!). Computer-assisted instruction programs are shown to be superior to traditional methods for teaching the mentally retarded spelling, money handling, number conservation, text reading, word recognition, handwriting, and visual discrimination (Conners, Caruso, and Detterman, 1986).

Autistic Disorder

Imagine that you are walking into a community group home for children with developmental disabilities. You are taking a class on mental retardation, and one of the requirements is to volunteer some time in this home. As several of the children rise to greet you, you become aware of some minor or major physical signs. One child has slanted eyes and a flat nose, characteristic of Downs syndrome. Another makes spastic movements, which you recognize as signs of cerebral palsy. A third child may call to you from a wheelchair with grunting noises and communicate with a combination of hand gestures and pictures. So far the children are as you expected from your readings.

Finally, you notice a fourth child in the room. He is standing in front of the fish tank. As you approach him, you notice his graceful, deft movements, the dreamy, far-away look in his eye, and you find him hauntingly attractive. You naturally assume that he is a visitor to the group home or a sibling of one of the residents. You start talking to him about the fish. Instead of acknowledging your comment, or even your presence, he begins rocking back and forth while continuing to smile, as if enjoying a private joke. When the group home director enters the room, your first question is about the boy at the fish tank. The director tells you that he is autistic.

Descriptive Characteristics

From the time when it was first distinguished, **autistic disorder** has seemed to have a mystical aura about it. The syndrome was first identified in 1943 by a psychiatrist at Harvard, Leo Kanner, who noticed that eleven disturbed children behaved in ways that were not com-

mon in children with mental retardation or with schizophrenia. He named the syndrome early infantile autism because he observed that "there is from the start an *extreme autistic aloneness* that, whenever possible, disregards, ignores, shuts out anything that comes to the child from the outside" (Kanner, 1943). Kanner considered autistic aloneness the most fundamental symptom, but he also found that these eleven had been unable from the beginning of life to relate to people in the ordinary way, were severely limited in language, and had a great obsessive desire that everything about them remain exactly the same. Despite its early description by Kanner and others (e.g., Rimland, 1964), the disorder was not accepted into official diagnostic nomenclature until the publication of DSM-III in 1980 (Box 16.4).

Rutter (1976) identified, in addition to a failure to develop social relations and to learn language, the ritualistic and compulsive activities of autistic children. Autism begins in early childhood, and indeed can be evident in the first weeks of life. Infants do not seem to care whether they are held and do not smile or look at their caretakers. They could be characterized as seeming not to need affection. Autism occurs relatively infrequently in the general population, in approximately three or four infants out of 10,000. Studies indicate that about four times more boys have autism than girls. Autistic children are found in all socioeconomic classes and in all ethnic and racial groups.

Parents may attribute their autistic infant's behavior to several factors. They may believe that the baby will "grow out of it" and become more responsive as it matures. They may adapt to the infant, believing that the behavior is normal, just different from what they expected. Other parents may realize that something is very wrong but be unable to admit it to themselves. Sometimes they fear that the baby is deaf. Parents may first realize that something is seriously awry when the infant misses an important developmental marker. For example, the absence or peculiarity of speech development by age two often compels parents to determinedly pursue an accurate diagnosis.

Autism and Mental Retardation

Kanner believed that autistic children were probably of average intelligence. He based this conclusion on their good physical condition and on their skill at some tasks requiring rote memory or spatial ability. Empirical investigations indicate, however, that approximately 80 percent of autistic children score below 70 on standardized intelligence tests. Because of the significant number of autistic children who are also mentally retarded, it is sometimes difficult to differentiate the two disabilities.

BOX 16.4

CLASSIFICATION OF PERVASIVE DEVELOPMENTAL DISORDERS

There has been a good deal of confusion in the classification of serious disorders that begin in childhood. DSM-II used the diagnosis *childhood schizophrenia* for these conditions, implying that they were simply an early onset form of adult schizophrenia. But the available evidence did not support this supposition and instead demonstrated many differences between childhood and adult schizophrenia. For example, delusions and hallucinations did not seem to be prevalent among the children formerly considered schizophrenic. Although the sex ratio is about equal among adult schizophrenics, the so-designated schizophrenia of childhood was more common among males. Lotter (1966) indicated the ratio as 2.5 to 1, but Rutter (1967) placed it at 4.3 to 1. Moreover, unlike adult schizophrenia, the supposed childhood schizophrenia was not preponderant in the lower classes. Finally, in a well-executed, ten-year follow-up study of psychotic children, many of whom could be regarded as childhood schizophrenics, Lockyer and Rutter (1969) did not find that they had become adult schizophrenics. We must therefore conclude that the evidence does not favor viewing adult schizophrenia and the so-called childhood schizophrenia as two closely related disorders.

As a partial replacement for the earlier childhood schizophrenia diagnosis, DSM-III proposed *childhood onset pervasive developmental disorder.* The diagnosis was given to children with profound disturbances in social relations and "oddities of behavior" that began after thirty months but before twelve years of age. The term infantile autism was reserved for those cases where symptoms began before thirty months of age.

The major change in DSM-IIIR is elimination of age of onset as a criterion for autism; this change recognizes the difficulty in establishing age of onset retrospectively through parents' reports. Autistic disorder is now considered to be a severe kind of *Pervasive Developmental Disorder,* the primary distinction being that autistic children do not attain a significant level of development prior to the onset of the problem. Later onset cases, more likely to be diagnosed as the more general pervasive developmental disorder, are also more likely to show delusions and hallucinations, have a course of remission and exacerbation, to not suffer as much cognitive impairment, and to have a more favorable prognosis, owing to the competencies that have been established during the early years of development. The majority of the research underlying the discussion of autism in this chapter applies to those cases in which onset is before age two.

But there *are* important differences. Although retarded children usually score consistently poorly on all parts of an intelligence test, the scores of autistic children may have a more differentiated pattern. In general, autistic children do worse on tasks requiring abstract thought, symbolism, or sequential logic, all of which may be associated with language. They usually obtain better scores on items requiring visual-spatial skills, such as matching designs in block design tests and in putting together disassembled objects (DeMyer, 1975; Rutter and Lockyer, 1967). In addition, like the idiot savant described earlier, they may have isolated skills reflecting great talent, such as multiplying two four-digit numbers rapidly in their heads. They may also have exceptional long-term memory, being able to recall the exact words of a song heard years earlier. In addition, sensorimotor development is the area of greatest relative strength among autistic children. Retarded children are much more delayed in areas of gross motor development such as learning to walk. In contrast, autistic children, who may show severe and profound deficits in cognitive abilities, can be quite graceful and adept at swinging, climbing, or balancing.

Because of the social nature of autistic children's disability, standard scores on intelligence tests have been questioned. In fact, autistic children used to be referred to as "untestable." Although testing an autistic child is difficult because such children generally will not sit still, follow directions, or attend to the task at hand, modifications of testing procedures have made it possible to evaluate autistic youngsters meaningfully. For example, concrete reinforcements, such as giving candy for paying attention to a task and not hand-flapping, usually succeeds in focusing the child's attention long enough to administer a test. In addition, care must be taken to choose tests that are appropriate for the child's developmental level and skills; administering a test requiring expressive verbal responses is clearly inadequate for determining the cognitive abilities of a nonverbal autistic child (Freeman and Ritvo, 1976).

Extreme Autistic Aloneness

The social deficits of autistic children also differentiate them from the mentally retarded. In a sense autistic children do not withdraw from society—they never joined it to begin with. Normal infants may show signs of at-

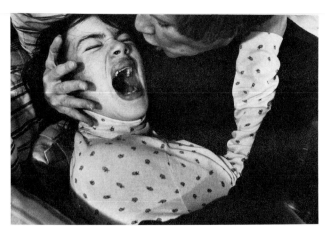

Autistic children may actively resist close interactions with other people.

tachment, usually to mother, as early as three months. In autistic children this early attachment is virtually absent. They do not smile or reach out or look at their mothers when being fed. Infants may reject parents' affection by refusing to be held or cuddled, arching their back when picked up to minimize the contact normal infants—and parents—love. Although normal infants often coo or cry or fret to attract parental attention, autistic children seldom initiate contact with the caregiver, except when hungry or wet. Indeed, such children are often described as "good babies" because they make few demands. Autistic infants are content to sit quietly in their playpens, completely self-absorbed, never noticing the comings, goings, and doings of other people. However, by age two or three many autistic children do form some emotional attachment to their parents or to other caregivers.

Impaired attachment to parents is not the only way in which the autistic child's social development is poor. The child never approaches others and may look through or past people or turn his back on them. When play is initiated by someone else, however, the autistic child may be compliant and engage in the selected activity for a period of time. Physical play such as tickling and wrestling may actually appear to be enjoyable to the child.

Few autistic children may be said to have friends. Not only do they seldom initiate play with other children, but potential friends, like parents, usually receive little responsiveness from the autistic child. Autistic infants may avert their gaze if parents try to communicate with them, and they are described as engaging in less eye contact than their peers. The sheer amount of eye gaze may sometimes be relatively normal, but not the way in which it is used. Normal children eye-gaze to gain someone's attention or to direct the other person's attention to an object. The autistic child generally does not do this (Mirenda, Donnellan, and Yoder, 1983).

Some autistic children appear not to recognize or distinguish one person from another. They do become preoccupied with and form strong attachments to keys, rocks, a wire mesh basket, light switches, a large blanket; to mechanical objects such as refrigerators and vacuum cleaners. If the object is something that they can carry, they walk around with it occupying their hands and keeping them from learning to do more useful things.

There are conflicting views of whether social withdrawal is a primary or secondary characteristic of autism. Kanner (1943) believed it was primary, and that other features were a result of the child's emotional withdrawal and failure to interact with the world around him. Fein and colleagues (Fein, Pennington, Markowitz, Braverman, and Waterhouse, 1986) present evidence in favor of viewing social withdrawal as the primary feature of autism, noting that even children with Down's syndrome, severe retardation, brain damage, or environmental deprivation do not show the kinds of social aloofness present even in high-functioning autistic children. However, it is also possible that the core deficit is an inability to process certain kinds of sensory input, which leaves the child helpless to understand and respond to the world around him (Rimland, 1964).

Communication Problems

Even before the period when language is usually acquired, autistic children have deficits in communication. Babbling, a descriptive term for the utterances of infants before they actually begin to use words, is less frequent in autistics and conveys less information than does that of other infants. Ricks (1972), for example, played tape recordings of the babbling of both autistic and mentally retarded infants to their own mothers and to other mothers. Although all mothers understood best the babbling of their own infants, the babbling of the autistic children was less meaningful to other mothers than was the babbling of the mentally retarded children.

By two years of age, most normally developing children use words to represent objects in their surroundings and construct one- and two-word sentences to express more complex thoughts. About 50 percent of all autistic children never learn to speak at all (Rutter, 1966). Even when they do, many peculiarities are found, among them *echolalia.* The child echoes, usually with remarkable fidelity and in a high-pitched monotone, what he or she has heard another person say. The teacher may ask an autistic boy, "Do you want a cookie?" The child's response will be "Do you want a cookie?" This is immediate echolalia. In delayed echolalia the child may be in a room with the television on and with others conversing and appear to be completely uninterested. Several hours later or even the next day, the child may echo a word or phrase from the conversation or television program. Mute autistic children who later do acquire some functional speech through training usually first pass through a stage of echolalia.

In the past most educators and researchers believed that echolalia served no functional purpose. But Prizant (1983) and others have suggested that echolalia may actually be an attempt to communicate. The boy who was offered a cookie decides at a later time that he does want one. He will approach the teacher and ask, "Do you want a cookie?" Although the child may not know what each of the individual words means, he has certainly learned that the phrase is connected with getting a cookie.

Another abnormality common in the speech of autistic children is **pronoun reversal.** The children refer to themselves as "he," or "you," or by their own proper names. Pronoun reversal is closely linked to echolalia. Since autistic children often use echolalic speech, they will refer to themselves as they have heard others speak of them; pronouns are of course misapplied. For example,

Parent: "What are you doing, Johnny?"

Child: "He's here."

Parent: "Are you having a good time?"

Child: "He knows it."

If normal speech is built up, this pronoun reversal might be expected to disappear. It has been reported, however, to be highly resistant to change (Tramontana and Stimbert, 1970); some children have required very extensive training even after they have stopped parroting the phrases of other people.

Neologisms, made-up words or words used with other than their usual meaning, are another characteristic of autistic children's speech. Neologisms may also be a consequence of echolalia. If a word or phrase heard earlier is repeated later by the autistic child, it may be inappropriate to the present situation. Autistic children may also change slightly the original words or phrase. These alterations may develop into made-up words.[7]

Children with autism are very literal in their use of words. If a father rewarded a child by putting him on his shoulders when he learned to say the word "yes," then the child might say the word "yes" to mean that he wanted to be lifted onto his father's shoulders. In

the reverse, called metaphorical languge, the child may say, "Do not drop the cat" to mean the more general "no," because his mother had used these emphatic words when he was about to drop the family kitten.

Communication deficiencies may leave a lasting mark of social retardation on the child. The link between social skills and language is made evident by the often spontaneous appearance of affectionate and dependent behavior in these children after they have been trained to speak (Churchill, 1969; Hewett, 1965).

Compulsive and Ritualistic Acts

Autistic children become extremely upset over changes in daily routine and their surroundings. An offer of milk in a different drinking cup or a rearrangement of furniture may make them cry or bring on a temper tantrum. Even common greetings must not vary.

Each morning she had to be greeted with the set phrase "Good morning, Lily, I am very, very glad to see you." If even one of the very's was omitted, or another added she would start to scream wildly. (Diamond, Baldwin, and Diamond, 1963, p. 304)

An "obsessional" quality, similar to the preservation of sameness, pervades the behavior of autistic children in other ways. In their play they may continually line up toys or construct intricate patterns out of household objects. They may become preoccupied with train schedules, subway routes, and number sequences. By adolescence, full-blown obsessions sometimes appear.

Autistic children are also given to stereotypical behavior, peculiar ritualistic hand movements, and other rhythmic movements, such as endless body rocking, hand flapping, and walking on tiptoe. They spin and twirl string, crayons, sticks, and plates, twiddle their fingers in front of their eyes, and stare at fans and spinning things. They may also become preoccupied with manipulating a mechanical object and be very upset when interrupted. Often toys are used in a compulsive and ritualistic manner rather than for their intended purpose.

Stereotyped behavior is especially counterproductive and interferes with attempts to teach autistic children. While engaged in self-stimulatory behavior, they are totally preoccupied and unresponsive to the environment (Lovaas, Litrownik, and Mann, 1971). This behavior may serve as a powerful form of reinforcement that autistic children can administer to themselves, seriously restricting their responsiveness to other reinforcers (Lovaas, Newsom, and Hickman, 1987).

---

[7]All children make up words in this fashion. Normal children, however, alter their idiosyncratic words as they listen to the speech of others and are corrected by those who care for them.

BOX 16.5

A FIRST-PERSON ACCOUNT OF AN ADULT AUTISTIC MAN

Excerpted below, with some punctuation and spelling corrections made by the professionals who published the account (Volkmar and Cohen, 1985), is a first-person report by a twenty-two-year-old man who had been treated for autism as a very young child at the Yale Child Study Center and who had returned to gain access to his records. In the course of many meetings with the staff, he decided to write an account of his experiences as an autistic child and now as a young adult. This depiction is unusual because autistic children seldom acquire enough cognitive and linguistic abilities to communicate in this way.

"Tony" had been described by his parents as having, from the first weeks of life, avoided human contact, never smiled responsively to others, and been preoccupied with his hands and with spinning objects. When examined at twenty-six months of age at the Yale Center, he did not speak, exhibited bizarre and highly stereotyped behavior, and showed no interest in others. After treatment at the center, he was able to enter a special-education program in a public school and was even able to attend a private high school until the tenth grade. His WAIS IQ at the time he wrote his autobiographical account was 94 Verbal, 92 Performance, and 93 Full Scale, which placed him just a little below the average, and was described as "a testament to his intellectual abilities" (Volkmar and Cohen, 1985, p. 48). When he contacted the center, he was employed as an assembler in a local industry.

Tony's account of his life contains features that are often found in autistic disorder, such as his sense of social isolation, his inability to empathize with others, unusual sensory experiences, and pervasive anxiety (and occasional abuse of alcohol in attempts to diminish it). Less typical of such individuals are the anger and aggressive tendencies he reports, and perhaps also his desire to be considered normal and interest in the opposite sex. The reader should note (perhaps with dismay) that Tony succeeded in obtaining a driver's license and enlisting in the Army.

AUTISM: "THE DISEASE OF ABOMINATION"

Tony W.

I was living in a world of daydreaming and Fear revolving aboud my self I had no care about Human feelings or other people. I was afraid of everything! I was terrified to go in the water swimming, (and of) loud noises; in the dark I had severe, repetitive Nightmares and occasionally hearing electronic noises with nightmares. I would wake up so terrified and disoriented I wasnt able to Find my way out of the room for a few miniuts. It felt like I was being draged to Hell. I was afraid of simple things such as going into the shower, getting my nails cliped, soap in my eyes. . . . I rember Yale Child Study Ctr. I ignored the doctors and did my own thing such as make something and played or idolize it not caring that anybody was in the room. I was also very hat(e)full and sneakey. I struggled and breathed hard because I wanted to kill the

gunia pig; as soon as the examiner turned her back I killed it. I hated my mother becaus she try to stop me from being in my world and doing what I liked; so I stoped and as soon as she turn her back I went at it agen. I was very Rebellious and sneaky and distructive. I would plot to kill my mother and destroy the world. . . . I also (had) a very warp sence of humor and learn(ed) perveted thing(s) verry quickly. I used to lash out of controll and repeat sick, perverted Phrases as well as telling people violent, wild, untrue things to impress them. . . . I like machanical Battery Power toys or electronic toys. Regular toys such as toy trucks, cars that wernt battery powered didnt turn me on at all. I was terrified to learn to ride the bybycle. One thing I loved that not even the Fear could stop was Airplanes. I saw an air show the planes—f4s— were loud. I was allway(s) Impressed by Airplanes. I drew picutres and had severeal Airplane models. The Test came when we went to D.C. I was so Anxious and Hyper to go on the plane I drove my Parrents nut. The only peace they had is when I heard the turbines reving at the end of the runway. Then I knew we were taking off. Soon as the plane took off I was amazed. I started to yell y(a)h HO! I loved every minuit of it. I allways loved Hi tech thing(s)—Planes, Rockets. . . . I dont or didnt trust anybody but my self—that still (is) a problem today. And (I) was and still (am) verry insucure! I was very cold Harted too. I(t) was impossible for me to Give or Receive love from anybody. I often Repulse it by turning people off. Thats is still a problem today and relating to other people. . . . I woudl hear electronic Noises and have quick siezious (seizures) in bed and many other ph(y)sical problems. Often I have to be Force to get things done and (was) verry uncordinated. And was verry Nervious about everything. And Feared People and Social Activity Greatly. . . . I lived with my father and the(n) saw the so call(ed) normal, sick teenage world. I was 14. I set my will (to) be normal like everybody else. (I) look(ed) up to people in school and did what they did to be accepted and put (up) more of a show to hide the problems and be Normal. I forced(d) my self to Know all the top rock groups, smoke pot, and drink and (tried to) have a girl friend. This was the 9th grade and 10th. I constantly got in trouble in school and did som(e) real crazy things to be cool. Like everybody else I thought I was all normal. Most of it was a failure. More people hated me then ever. . . . I went into the army and got in lots of Fights with people. So I got dicarged (discharged). . . . I worked a few more Jobs and hung around w/some Crazy people I knew from school and got drunk a lot and did distructive things, Magnified Fears and Peronia on pot. I never got Fired from a job. My problems havn't changed at ALL from early childhood. I was Just able to Function. And it still (is) the same today—1983. (Volkmar and Cohen, 1985, pp. 49– 52)

467

Prognosis in Autistic Disorder

What happens to such severely disturbed children when they reach adulthood? Kanner (1973) reported on the adult status of nine of the eleven children whom he had described in his original paper on autism. Two developed epileptic seizures; one of them died, and the other was in a state mental hospital. Four others had spent most of their lives in institutions. Of the remaining three, one had remained mute but was working on a farm and as an orderly in a nursing home. The last two made at least somewhat satisfactory recoveries. Although both still live with their parents and have little social life, they are gainfully employed and have some recreational interests.

Other follow-up studies corroborate the generally gloomy picture of adult autistics (e.g., Rutter, 1967; Treffert, McAndrew, and Dreifuerst, 1973; Lotter, 1974). From his review of all published studies, Lotter (1978) concluded that only 5 to 17 percent of autistic children had made a relatively good adjustment in adulthood, leading independent lives but with some residual problems, such as social awkwardness. Most of the others had limited lives, and about half were institutionalized (see Box 16.5).

Etiology of Autistic Disorder

Psychological Bases of Autism

Since Kanner first described autism, researchers have been seeking its cause. Some of the same reasons that led Kanner to consider autistic children to be average in intelligence, their normal appearance and apparently normal physiological functioning, led others to regard autism as environmentally caused.

One of the best-known of the psychological theories was formulated by Bruno Bettelheim (1967). The basic supposition of his theory is that autism closely resembles the apathy and hopelessness found among inmates of German concentration camps during World War II. Bettelheim hypothesizes that the young infant has rejecting parents and is able to perceive their negative feelings. He finds that his own actions have little impact on their unresponsiveness. The child comes to believe "that [his] own efforts have no power to influence the world, because of the earlier conviction that the world is insensitive to [his] reactions" (p. 46).

This experience of helplessness, which appears to be similar to the learned helplessness discussed earlier (see page 228), is viewed as extremely frustrating and frightening for the child. But he is unwilling to communicate his fears because he feels that nothing good can come from it. He never really enters the world but builds the "empty fortress" of autism against pain and disappointment. His only activities—his ritualistic hand movements and echolalic speech—are a means of shutting out the world. An elaborate fantasy life is created, and insistence on sameness is the rule that brings permanence and order. Autistic children remain safe only if everything about them stays put. Since the essential purpose of most activity is to bring about change, autistic children avoid any sort of action; their universe centers on a static environment, beyond which they will not move.

Some behavioral theorists, like those who are psychoanalytically oriented, have postulated that certain childhood learning experiences cause autism. Ferster (1961), in an extremely influential article, suggested that the inattention of the parents, especially of the mother, prevents establishment of the associations that make human beings reinforcers. And because the parents have not become reinforcers, they cannot control the child's behavior, the end result being autistic disorder.

Both Bettelheim and Ferster, as well as others, have stated that parents play the crucial role in the etiology of autism. Many investigators have therefore studied the characteristics of these parents; for a psychogenic theory of a childhood disorder to have any plausibility at all, something very unusual and damaging about the parents' treatment of their children would have to be demonstrated.

In his early papers, Kanner described the parents of autistic children as cold, insensitive, meticulous, introverted, distant, and highly intellectual (Kanner and Eisenberg, 1955). Others (e.g., Singer and Wynne, 1963; Rimland, 1964) have also noted the detachment of parents of autistic children, although Rimland has used less pejorative adjectives. Singer and Wynne have described several means by which these parents "disaffiliate" themselves from their children. Some are cynical about all interpersonal relations and are emotionally cold; others are passive and apathetic; and still others maintain an obsessive, intellectual distance from people.

Systematic investigations, however, have failed to confirm these clinical impressions. For example, Cox and his colleagues (1975) compared the parents of autistic children to those of children with receptive aphasia (a disorder in understanding speech); the two groups did *not* differ in warmth, emotional demonstrativeness, responsiveness, and sociability. Similarly, DeMyer and her co-workers (1972) did not find the parents of autistic children to be rejecting, nor did Cantwell, Baker, and Rutter (1978) or McAdoo and DeMyer (1978) find psychiatric disorders in parents, using standard measures like the MMPI. The weight of the evidence is over-

BOX 16.6

THE PERNICIOUS NATURE OF PSYCHOGENIC THEORIES

Readers of this book have no doubt noticed that the authors are often critical of some psychogenic theories, both psychoanalytic and learning. In addition to our aspirations to provide as scientifically accurate a textbook as possible, we are concerned about the impact that theories may have on people. Consider, for a moment, what your feelings might be if a psychiatrist or psychologist were to tell you that your unconscious hostility has caused your child to be mute at the age of six. Or how would you feel if you were told that your commitment to professional activities has brought about the autistic behavior patterns of your child? The fact is, of course, that the truth of these allegations has yet to be demonstrated, and considerable information even contradicts these views. But in the meantime a tremendous emotional burden is placed on parents who have, over the years, been told that they are at fault.

As Rimland (1964) has suggested, considering autism psychogenic in origin is not only an inadequate hypothesis but also a pernicious one.

---

whelming: there is nothing remarkable about the parents of autistic children. In fact, such parents raise other perfectly normal and healthy siblings.

Even if we were to ignore these findings, the direction of a possible correlation between parental characteristics and autism is not easily determined. Any deviant behavior could be a reaction to the child's abnormality rather than the other way around. Moreover, there is no evidence that any kind of emotional maltreatment, deprivation, or neglect can produce behavior that resembles the syndrome of autism (Ornitz, 1973; Wing, 1976) (see Box 16.6). Indeed, the very early onset of autism and an accumulation of neurological and genetic evidence imply a physiological basis for this puzzling disorder.

Physiological Bases of Infantile Autism

Genetic Factors Genetic studies of autism are difficult to conduct because the disorder is so rare. Indeed, the family method presents special problems because autistic persons almost never marry. In cases where autistics have siblings, the rate of autism in their brothers and sisters is about 2 percent (Rutter, 1967). Although this is a small percentage, it represents a fiftyfold increase in risk as compared to the morbidity risk in the general population.

Evidence of the importance of genetic factors in autism is provided by a methodologically sound study conducted by Folstein and Rutter (1978). In ten pairs of fraternal twins, one of whom had autism, there was no concordance of the co-twins. But in the eleven pairs of identical twins, one of whom had autism, the concordance rate was 36 percent: four of the co-twins had autism. In addition to examining concordance for autism, Folstein and Rutter also looked for cognitive disabilities, such as delayed speech, problems in saying words properly, and low IQ, in the co-twins. Concordance for cognitive impairment was 82 percent for the MZ pairs and 10 percent for the DZ. Thus the identical twin of an autistic is very likely to have difficulties of speech and intellect, but the fraternal twin of an autistic is not. Autism is apparently linked genetically to a broader deficit in cognitive ability. Further support for this position comes from finding a higher incidence of a spectrum of learning disabilities in the families of autistic children (August, Stewart, and Tsai, 1981). Taken together, the evidence from family and twin studies supports a genetic basis for autistic disorder.

Neurological Factors Early EEG studies of autistic children indicated that many had abnormal brain wave patterns (e.g., Hutt *et al.*, 1964). Other types of neurological examination have also revealed signs of damage in a large percentage of autistic children (Bosch, 1970; DeMyer *et al.*, 1973; Gubbay, Lobascher, and Kingerlee, 1970). Further evidence supporting the possibility of neurological dysfunction includes a recent study using magnetic resonance scans of the brain, which found that portions of the cerebellum were underdeveloped in autistic children (Courchesne *et al.*, 1988). This abnormality was present in fourteen out of eighteen autistic subjects. The degree of neurological abnormality or central nervous system dysfunction seems to be related to the severity of the autistic symptoms. In adolescence 30 percent of those who had severe autistic symptoms as children begin having epileptic seizures. Furthermore, the prevalence of autism in children whose mothers had rubella during the prenatal period is approximately ten times higher than that in the general population of children. A syndrome similar to autism may follow in the aftermath of meningitis, encephalitis, and tuberous sclerosis and develop through PKU, all of which may affect central nervous system functioning. These findings, plus the degree of mental retardation, would seem to link autism and brain damage.

Autism cannot, however, be attributed solely to general brain damage for two reasons. First, not all autistic children show signs of brain damage. Second, children may have brain damage but no symptoms of autism. In fact, most children who are brain-damaged are not autistic. With increasing sophistication in our knowledge of brain function and the instruments used to assess it, clearer evidence of the links between autism and brain dysfunction is likely to emerge in the future.

Treatment of Autistic Disorder

Special Problems in Treating Autistic Children

Educational programs for autistic children usually try to relieve their symptoms and improve their communication, social skills, and adaptive behavior so that they can become more independent. Autistic children have several problems that make teaching them difficult, however. First, they do not adjust normally to changes in routines, including special events and substitute teachers. Second, their behavior problems and self-stimulatory movements may interfere with effective teaching. Although the similar behavior of children with other disabilities may intrude on the teacher's efforts, it does not do so with the same frequency and severity.

Third, it is particularly difficult to find reinforcers that motivate autistic children. Normal children like to explore and control their surroundings, but not children with autism. For reinforcers to be effective with autistic children, they must be explicit, concrete, or highly salient. A widely used method of increasing the range of reinforcers that autistic children respond to is to pair social reinforcement with primary reinforcers such as food.

A further problem that often interferes with the learning of autistic children is their overselectivity of attention. When the child's attention becomes focused on one particular aspect of a task or situation, other properties, including relevant ones, may not even be noticed. For example, in sign language training, the instructor often says a word while making its sign in the presence of the referent object or its image. Students, it is assumed, will learn to associate the sign with the spoken word and the object. Children with autism are more likely to attend to only one of the cues, however (Lovaas *et al.*, 1971). An autistic child may appear to

have learned to associate the sign with several spoken words and the object but has attended instead to the instructor's mouth movements. The child then will not select the correct object when he hears the word or sees the sign but only when he watches the instructor's lips move.

An additional concern, one which educators and therapists of autistic children share with educators of retarded children, is the youngsters' inability to generalize the learning. The overselective nature of autistic children's attention makes generalization especially difficult for them. For example, the child who learned several words by watching the instructor's lip movements may not comprehend the same words spoken by another person with less pronounced movements of the lips. In other words, the child's response may be contingent on a nonessential aspect of the situation, which is usually not present if the context is changed. In spite of all these problems, educational programs for students with autism have achieved some positive results.

Behavioral Treatments

Mental health professionals agree that autistic children have been helped through modeling and operant conditioning. Behavior therapists have helped autistic children talk (Hewett, 1965), modified their echolalic speech (Carr, Schreibman, Lovaas, 1975), encouraged them to play with other children (Romanczyk *et al.*, 1975), and helped them become more generally responsive to adults (Davison, 1964).

In an early case report, which has served as an exemplar for over twenty-five years of conditioning treatments for autism, Wolf, Risley, and Mees (1964) reduced the incidence of tantrums by regarding them as operant behavior maintained by adult attention. They isolated the boy in a room for short periods of time whenever he threw a temper tantrum. The acting out was soon eliminated. This *time–out* procedure, whereby a person is temporarily excluded from situations in which positive reinforcement might be obtained, has proved effective with a number of behavioral problems and with children other than those diagnosed as autistic. For extreme and dangerous behavior, such as self-mutilation, brief but strong punishment may be necessary (see Box 16.3).

Work by Donnellan and her colleagues (1984) extends applied behavior analysis to the communicative aspects of some autistic children's aggressive behavior. According to these researchers, many of their tantrums and outbursts may be caused by their inability to communicate in a more positive, socially appropriate manner. They describe a twelve-year-old boy with autism and moderate mental retardation. The boy's parents wanted to be able to take him on shopping trips and other community outings. When in public he would vocalize loudly and repetitively, however, causing considerable disturbance.

The first step in treating the boy's outbursts was to search for consistencies in the conditions that brought them on. The researchers observed that the boy went into his vocal tantrums when confronted by noise and crowds. The next question the researchers asked was what the boy might be communicating with his inappropriate behavior. They thought that he might be trying to say, "I'm anxious and overwhelmed by the noise and crowds." With other autistic children in other situations, possible answers might be, "This task is too difficult." "I'm frustrated." "I'm bored." "I don't feel good." "I want some attention."

Donnellan and her co-workers decided to teach the autistic boy an alternate method of decreasing his overstimulation while in the community. They taught him to use a stereo headset with a cassette tape. Whenever he felt the need to reduce stimulation, he could put on the headset rather than have a verbal tantrum. Gradually, he needed the headset less and less as he learned to adapt to public places.

Ivar Lovaas, a behavior therapist, noted for his operant conditioning treatment of autistic and schizophrenic children.

Ivar Lovaas, a leading clinical researcher at the University of California at Los Angeles, describes an intensive operant program with very young (under four years) autistic children (Lovaas, 1987). Therapy encompassed all aspects of the children's lives for more than forty hours a week over more than two years. Parents were trained extensively so that treatment could continue during almost all waking hours of the children's lives. Nineteen youngsters receiving this intensive treatment were compared to forty controls who received a similar treatment for less than ten hours per week. All children were rewarded for being less aggressive, more compliant, and more socially appropriate, including talking and playing with other children. The goal of the program was to mainstream the children, the assumption being that autistic children, as they improve, benefit more from being with normal peers rather than remaining by themselves or with other seriously disturbed children.

The results were quite dramatic and encouraging for the intensive therapy group. Their measured IQs averaged 83 in first grade (after about two years in the intensive therapy) compared to about 55 for the controls; twelve of the nineteen reached the normal range as compared to only two (of forty) in the control group. Furthermore, nine out of the nineteen intensives were promoted to second grade in a normal public school, whereas only one of the much larger control group achieved this level of normal functioning. This ambitious study confirms the need for heavy involvement of both professionals and parents in dealing with the extreme challenge of autistic disorder. Although such intensive treatment is expensive and time-consuming, the long-term dependence and loss of productive work in less intensively treated autistic children represent a far greater cost to society than a treatment that enables many of these children to achieve a normal level of functioning.

Autism, like mental retardation, places considerable stress on a family. Because autistic children have few or no physical handicaps and some isolated normal and even superior abilities, their parents may even hope that the diagnosis is erroneous. One way to ease the parents' burden is to instruct them about the nature of autistic disorder, especially the virtual certainty that it does not have a psychogenic cause. Relieved of the guilt associated with this pernicious belief, some parents will want to become involved in the education of their child. There is reason to expect that the education provided by parents is more beneficial to the child than clinic- or hospital-based treatment. In work similar to that of Lovaas, Koegel and his colleagues (1982) have demonstrated that after only 25 to 30 hours of parent training, autistic children's improvements on standardized tests and behavioral measures were similar to those after over 200 hours of direct clinic treatment. Koegel concluded that parent training is superior in generalizing learning because parents are present in many different situations, and, when training their children, they may actually spend more time with them in recreational and leisure activities.[8]

Psychodynamic Treatment

A very different treatment of autism was developed over many years by Bruno Bettelheim (1967, 1974) at the Orthogenic School of the University of Chicago. Bettelheim argued that a warm, loving atmosphere must be created to encourage the child to enter the world. Patience and what Rogerians would call unconditional positive regard were believed to be necessary for the child to begin to trust others and to take chances in establishing relationships. Bettelheim and his colleagues reported many instances of success, but the uncontrolled nature of their observations makes it difficult to know what the active ingredients might have been. Bettelheim's treatment may contain more direct instruction, systematic reinforcement, and extinction than comes through in the published reports. By the same token, of course, reports of behavior therapists usually underplay the rapport building that undoubtedly provides the context for their programs.

Drug Treatment

There is evidence that some autistic children have elevated blood levels of serotonin (Ritvo *et al.*, 1970). Researchers from eighteen to twenty medical centers under the leadership of Ritvo at UCLA have studied the effectiveness of a drug known to lower serotonin levels in rats and monkeys. In hopes of reducing their serotonin levels and thereby improve behavior and cognitive functioning, investigators administered fenfluramine to autistic children. This drug, an amphetamine derivative, is an appetite suppressant for adults sold under the trade name Pondimine.

Results of early studies administering fenfluramine to autistic children were quite positive; not only were serotonin levels lowered, but IQs and behavior were significantly improved (Geller *et al.*, 1982, 1984; Ritvo *et al.*, 1983). However, although several reports replicated the initial findings (Ritvo *et al.*, 1986), concerns have been raised about negative side effects (particularly excessive sedation, increased irritability, and transient weight loss). Furthermore, several investigators have failed to demonstrate improvements in cognitive or behavioral functioning (Campbell, 1987, 1988). In fact, in one recent study, children on placebo performed better at a laboratory learning task than children taking fenfluramine, suggesting that the drug actually *inhibited* learning (Campbell *et al.*, submitted for publication). Future research is needed to identify reasons for the discrepant findings in different laboratories, and to clarify which autistic children, if any, are likely to benefit from the drug.

Summary

Specific developmental disorders, better known as learning disabilities, are diagnosed when a child fails to develop to the degree expected by his or her intellecutal level in a specific academic, language, or motor skill area. These disorders, which are two to four times more prevalent in males than in females, are usually identified and treated within the school system rather than through mental health clinics.

The diagnostic criteria for mental retardation are subaverage intellectual functioning and deficits in adaptive behavior, with onset before the age of eighteen. Four levels of retardation are designated, ranging from the profound when IQ is less than 20 to mild when IQ is 50 to 70. Researchers have identified adaptive skills and general cognitive abilities that are wanting in retarded children. The more severe forms of mental retardation usually have a physiological basis, such as the chromosomal trisomy that causes Down's syndrome. Certain infectious diseases suffered by the pregnant mother, such as rubella and syphilis, or affecting the child directly, for example, encephalitis, can stunt cognitive and social development. So can malnutrition, severe falls, and automobile accidents that injure the brain. For the mild range of retardation, which is by far the most prevalent, no identifiable brain damage is evident. Environmental factors are considered the principal causes. Among the specific findings are that these people come from lower-class homes in which deprivation is great.

Researchers try to prevent mild retardation by giving children at risk through impoverished circumstances special preschool training and social opportunities. Many retarded children who would have been institutionalized are now being educated in the public schools

---

[8]At the same time, it must be clearly stated that some autistic and other severely disturbed children can be adequately looked after only in a hospital or in a group home staffed by mental health professionals. Moreover, the circumstances of some families preclude the home care of their seriously disturbed child. The fact that effective treatments can be implemented by parents should not be transformed into a must-do for those who are already living their lives and taking care of other normal children under trying circumstances.

under the mainstreaming provisions of P.L. 94–142. In addition, using applied behavioral analysis, self-instructional training, and modeling, behavior therapists have been able to treat successfully many of the behavioral problems of retarded individuals as well as improve their intellectual functioning.

Autistic disorder, one of the pervasive developmental disorders, usually begins before the age of thirty months. The major symptoms are extreme autistic aloneness, a complete failure to relate to other people; communication problems, either a failure to learn any language or speech irregularities such as echolalia and pronoun reversal; and preservation of sameness, an obsessive desire that daily routines and surroundings be kept exactly the same. On the basis of early clinical reports, some psychologically biased theorists had concluded that the coldness and aloofness of parents and their rejection of their children bring on autism, but recent research gives no credence to such notions. Although no certain physiological basis of autism has been found, a number of facts make such a cause plausible: its onset is very early; both family and twin studies give evidence of a genetic predisposition; the EEGs of some autistic children are abnormal, and other neurological tests also reveal abnormalities; a syndrome similar to autism can develop after meningitis and encephalitis and through PKU; and many autistic children have the low intelligence associated with brain dysfunctions.

The most promising treatments of autism have often used procedures that rely on modeling and operant conditioning. Although the prognosis for autistic children remains poor in general, Lovaas' recent work suggests that with intensive behavioral treatment, up to half of these children may be able to lead normal lives.

Edvard Munch, *Self Portrait by the Window*, circa 1940. Oslo Kommunes Kunstsamlinger, Munch-Museet.

Chapter 17

Aging and Psychological Disorders

Concepts and Methods in the Study of Older Adults

Some Basic Facts about Older Adults

Brain Disorders of Old Age

    Dementia

    Delirium

Psychological Disorders of Old Age

    Depression

    Delusional (Paranoid) Disorders

    Schizophrenia

    Psychoactive Substance Use Disorders

    Hypochondriasis

    Insomnia

    Suicide

    Sexuality and Aging

General Issues in Treatment and Care

    Access to Services

    Provision of Services

    Issues Specific to Therapy with Older Adults

Summary

The more fortunate readers of this book will grow old one day. When and as you do, physiological changes are inevitable, and there may be many emotional and mental changes as well. We are concerned here less with physical changes than with the psychological aspects of growing old. Does society treat the elderly in ways that may set them on a downward slide to senescence and even death? Are the aged at higher risk for mental disorders than the young? Are earlier emotional problems of anxiety and depression likely to become worse in old age? Do these emotional problems develop in people who did not have them when younger? Is it reasonable to expect a satisfying sex life in old age? Is the ability to remember and to think rationally subject to unavoidable deterioration? Finally, are some therapies especially appropriate to our elders, and does society devote suitable monetary and intellectual resources to the development of effective ways of helping our older citizens? As life expectancy extends into the seventies and beyond, what is the professional community doing *now* to acquire knowledge and techniques that can make old age more meaningful than it has been for past generations, in the United States and in many other countries?

The elderly in this country are not treated very well. The process of growing old, although inevitable for us all, is abhorred, even resented. Perhaps the lack of regard for senior citizens stems from our own deep-seated fear of and misconceptions about growing old. The old person with serious infirmities is an unwelcome reminder that some of us may one day walk with a less steady gait, see less clearly, taste food less sharply, enjoy sex less frequently and with apparently less intensity, and fall victim to some of the many diseases and maladies that are the lot of most old people before they depart this world.

Growing old may be especially disagreeable for women. Even with all the consciousness raising carried out by the feminist movement in the past two decades, women still have trouble accepting the wrinkles and sagging that become more and more prominent with advancing years. The cosmetics industry and plastic surgery make billions of dollars a year by exploiting the fear women have been taught to have about looking their age. Although gray hair at the temples and even a bald head are often considered distinguished in a man, a great many women who have the financial means to buy a few more years of youthful appearance do so. And so the psychological problems of aging may be especially severe for women.

Older adults suffer discrimination because of "ageism . . . a form of prejudice . . . that individuals experience at various points in their lives. Individuals may be too young to vote, drive, or drink alcohol, too young to receive a pension and Medicare, or too old to teach in a university" (Kimmel, 1988, p. 175). Ageism can also be seen when a person older than seventy-five is ignored in a social gathering on the assumption that she has nothing to contribute to the conversation. Like any prejudice (Allport, 1954), ageism ignores the *diversity* among people in favor of employing stereotypes (Gatz and Pearson, 1988).

Mental health professionals have until recently almost phobically ignored the behavioral and emotional problems of the elderly. There is misinformation, such as the belief that intellectual deterioration is widespread and inevitable, that depression among old people is untreatable, that sex is a lost cause. Although those who provide mental health services are probably not extremely ageist (Gatz and Pearson, 1988), their attitudes and practices merit special attention because of the influence they have over policies that affect the lives of older adults.

The relative inattention to mental health problems of the aging is both a cause and an effect of the inattention to professional training. For this reason, in June 1981, the American Psychological Association sponsored a conference on geriatric clinical training. Its purpose was to bring together experts from around the country to formulate guidelines for proper training of clinicians for the aging, as well as to encourage the development of such programs. In just the past few years research and training in gerontology have begun to be introduced into curricula of schools and universities preparing people for health professions.

Concepts and Methods in the Study of Older Adults

Diversity in Older Adults

Before we consider psychological disorders in late life, some basic concepts critical to the study of aging should be introduced. In any discussion of the differences between the elderly and those not yet old, the elderly are usually defined as those over the age of sixty-five. The decision to use this age was set largely by social policies, not because age sixty-five is some critical point at which the physiological and psychological processes of aging suddenly begin. To have some rough demarcation points for better describing the diversity of the elderly, gerontologists have divided those over sixty-five into three groups: the young-old, those sixty-five to seventy-four; the old-old, those seventy-five to eighty-four; and the oldest-old, those over eighty-five. The health of

Cohort effects refer to the fact that people of the same chronological age may differ considerably depending on when they were born.

these groups differs in important ways. The word diversity is well applied to the older population. Not only are older people different from one another, but they are more different from one another than are individuals in any other age group! In essence, people tend to become less alike as they grow older.[1]

Age, Cohort, and Time-of-Measurement Effects

Chronological age is not as simple a variable in psychological research as we might expect, for being any age is associated with a host of other factors. For example, diet, medical care, and social habits all change with time; we must be cautious when we attribute differences in age groups solely to the effects of aging, for other factors associated with age may be at work. Being seventy in 1990 is different from having been seventy in 1960. In the field of aging, therefore, as in studies of earlier development, including childhood, a distinction is made between the contributions of what are called **age effects, cohort effects,** and **time-of-measurement effects** (Schaie and Hertzog, 1982). The two major research designs used to assess developmental change, the **cross-sectional** and the **longitudinal,** clarify these terms.

In cross-sectional studies the investigator compares different age groups at the same moment in time on the variable of interest. Suppose that in 1985 I take a poll and find that many of my interviewees who are over seventy speak with a European accent, whereas those in their thirties and forties do not. Can I conclude that as people grow older they develop European accents? Hardly! Cross-sectional studies do not examine the *same* people over time; they allow us to make statements only about *age differences* in a particular study or experiment, not about *age changes* over time.

A *cohort* is a group of people who have a vital statistic in common, here being born within a certain time period. In the hypothetical study just mentioned, many in the older sample or cohort came to this country from abroad. A longitudinal study selects one cohort and then periodically retests it, using the same measure over a number of years. Thus it allows us to trace individual patterns of consistency or change over time and to analyze how behavior in early life relates to behavior in old age.

Conclusions drawn from longitudinal studies are restricted to the particular cohort chosen, however, for each cohort is unique. This limitation is a problem of longitudinal studies. For example, if a cohort is studied from 1940 to 1980 and its members are found to suffer a decline in sexual activity as they enter their sixties, we cannot conclude that the sexuality of those in a cohort studied from 1980 to 2020 will decline when they reach the same age. Improvements over time in health care and other variables might benefit the sexual activity of the younger cohort. Longitudinal studies have an-

---

[1]That all old people are alike is a prejudice held by many younger people. To know that a man is sixty-seven years old is, in itself, to know very little about him. And yet a moment's honest reflection may indicate to the reader that certain traits come to mind when we hear that a man is sixty-seven. The many *differences* in people who are sixty-five and older will become increasingly evident in the course of reading this chapter.

other problem. Unfortunately, people often drop out of them as they proceed, creating a source of bias commonly called "selective mortality." The least able subjects are the most likely to drop from a study; the non-representative people who remain are usually healthier than the general population. Thus, findings based on longitudinal studies may be too optimistic concerning the amount of decline in sexual activity over the life span.

Contrary to popular belief, longitudinal studies do not allow us to measure pure age changes. Time-of-measurement effects also have to be considered. For example, because of a coronary risk scare in 1980, many people in a cohort may give up drinking coffee between the time of their first measurement in 1970 and their next measurement in 1985. At the next evaluation their physical health—which usually declines—may actually have *improved* because fewer have drunk coffee since the 1980 scare, a time-of-measurement effect.

Diagnosing Psychopathology in Later Life

The revision of the DSM has not changed psychiatric diagnoses drastically as they affect older adults; what few changes have been made will be discussed in later sections. The nature and manifestation of mental disorders are apparently assumed to be the same in adulthood and old age, even though little research supports this assumption (LaRue, Dessonville, and Jarvik, 1985). We often do not know what certain symptoms of older adults mean because we have few specifics about psychopathology in the elderly (Zarit, Eiler, and Hassinger, 1985). For example, somatic symptoms are generally more prevalent in late life, but these symptoms are also evident in depression in older adults. Are the somatic symptoms of a depressed older adult necessarily a part of depression? Or might they (also) reflect physical decline?

Range of Problems

We already know that mental health may be tied to the physical and social problems in a person's life. Although this can be true at any age, no other group of people have more of these problems than the aged. They have them all—physical decline and disabilities, sensory and neurological deficits, the cumulative effects of a lifetime of many unfortunate experiences and social stresses. However, it is important also to remember that in addition to a lifetime of exposure to losses and other stressors, older adults may have a large amount of positive life experiences, coping mechanisms, and wisdom on which to draw. To understand the psychopathology of older adults, we must take into account many typical physical, psychological, and social forces of later life. It is to these that we now turn.

Some Basic Facts about Older Adults

Numbers of Older People

The proportion of older people in the population has increased greatly during the past century. This increase is attributable to many factors, in particular decreased infant, childhood, and maternal mortality, as well as improved sanitation and the effective control of infectious diseases. In 1900 only 4 percent of the United States population was over age sixty-five. As of 1987, these figures had risen to 12.2 percent or 29 million people over the age of sixty-five. From 1980 to 1987, the second fastest growing age segment—second only to people aged thirty-five to forty-four years—was those eighty-five years and older, increasing from 2,240,000 persons to 2,867,000 persons, a rate of 28 percent. Another perspective on these trends is the steady increase in median age of the United States population, from 29.4 years in 1960 to 32.1 years in 1987 (U.S. Bureau of the Census, 1988). This steady growth in the older population is expected to continue: while the total United States population grows by one-third between 1982 and 2050, the fifty-five-plus age group is expected to increase at the rate of 115 percent! Thus, by the year 2000, older persons are predicted to represent 13.1 percent of the population. By the year 2030, the percentage may climb to 21.1 percent, a result of the baby boomers of the 1950s reaching sixty-five and older (U.S. Bureau of the Census, 1986). No wonder the graying of the population

The "oldest-old," now 1% of the population, are projected to be 5% of the population by 2050.

has been considered one of the most significant trends of the century.

Although in the years to come all segments of the elderly population are expected to grow rapidly, the fastest-growing subgroup will be the "old-old," those seventy-five and over. The U.S. census estimate is that those older than eighty-five—the "oldest-old"—constituting about 1 percent of the population today (2.8 million), could represent 5 percent in 2050 (over 16 million).[2]

Characteristics of the Aged Population

This is the era of increasing numbers of older persons but of more older women in particular. Men today can expect to live to be about seventy-nine years old; women will live to about eighty-three. Because of this discrepancy in life expectancy, the health, social, and economic problems of the elderly, particularly of the old-old, are often the problems of women. As we might expect, given these figures, most older men are married and most older women are widowed: approximately 80 percent of men in the sixty-five to seventy-four age group are married compared to 49 percent of the women; of people over seventy-five, seven out of ten women are widowed, and seven out of ten men are married. Not only do women live longer than men, thus losing their spouses, but men tend to marry women younger than themselves, keeping theirs. In addition, elderly widowed men have a remarriage rate seven times that of widows (U.S. Bureau of the Census, 1986).

A largely invisible group of older adults are homosexuals. It has been suggested that between 5 and 10 percent of older adults are gay, consonant with estimates for the general population (Lipman, 1984). Although, as we have seen recently, there is a measure of greater acceptance of homosexuality as an alternative life-style rather than as a mental illness, it seems likely that the current cohort of older gays is less open about

their sexual orientation than are younger people and thus suffer from isolation and self-stigmatization (Kimmel, 1979). (The extent of continuing stigmatization in society at large should not be underestimated, despite the changes in DSM-IIIR and among many mental health professionals.) Still, many older homosexuals are in "close couple" committed relationships and otherwise have social support networks that help them deal both with ageism and with continuing biases against homosexuality in American society (Bell and Weinberg, 1978).

Physical Decline

Many physical functions unquestionably decline with age. Aging affects the entire body, including all the major systems—musculoskeletal, cardiovascular, respiratory, nervous, gastrointestinal, urinary, integumentary, reproductive, endocrine, and immune (Kenney, 1982). The capacity for homeostatic regulation is reduced. All five senses as well suffer a loss, thereby affecting perception. The lens of the eye yellows and becomes less accommodative, visual acuity decreases, and sensitivity to glare increases. Hearing is diminished, particularly the ability to perceive high-frequency sounds. Older people respond less quickly, and take longer to do many tasks and to recover from stress (Blazer and Siegler, 1984). The conservative driving habits of older adults are a wise adaptation to the slowdown in their reaction time and to diminished visual acuity.

The physical losses of aging are reflected in the health problems of older adults. The incidence of chronic illnesses increases with age. Over 80 percent of older persons have at least one chronic condition, and 50 percent have two or more (Jarvik and Perl, 1981). Arthritis, hypertension, heart problems, hearing and visual impairments, and diabetes are the most frequent debilities. In addition, although the incidence of acute illnesses and accidental injuries decreases with age, their impact is often more severe and protracted in the old (Hickey, 1980); for example, bones broken in a fall heal more slowly.

Yet in the face of these apparent losses in bodily performance, it has been estimated that at least 80 percent of people sixty-five and over are able to carry out major daily activities and otherwise function with a considerable degree of independence. Although the average older person may be afflicted with one or more chronic ailments, they are not necessarily limited severely by them. In fact, a survey of older adults reveals substantial gains in relative health from 1961 to 1981 (Palmore, 1986), for several likely reasons. First, later cohorts are healthier; those reaching sixty-five in 1980, for example, have benefitted from better medical care throughout their lives than those who achieved that age

---

[2]These U.S. census figures and projections have recently been challenged by Guralnik, Yanagashita, and Schneider (1988), researchers from the National Institute on Aging (NIA) and the University of Southern California. They estimate that those over eighty-five will grow to nearly 24 million by the year 2040. Furthermore, they estimate that by 2040, those over sixty-five will number 87 million, 25 percent of the U.S. population, again above census projections. The principal reason for these differences is that Guralnik *et al.* are factoring in predicted improvements in health care with consequent declines in the death rate of 2 percent a year; the U.S. census did not assume such changes in making their projections. Consider, for example, the recent dramatic drop in deaths from the number one cause of death, heart disease, as a result of changes in life-styles (e.g., better eating and exercise habits). Major breakthroughs in the prevention and treatment of most forms of cancer are also predicted by the USC and NIA researchers. (On the other hand, a disease that was *not* considered is AIDS, which is certain to reduce by many hundreds of thousands the numbers of those below age sixty-five who will reach old age.)

The stereotype is that aging brings a steady decline and inactivity. The fact of aging, however, is diversity.

Meals on Wheels is one of the programs that supports older adults in their efforts to be independent.

in 1960. Second, Medicare and Medicaid have made major contributions to the health care of the later cohorts. And third, many helpful nutritional, social, and psychological programs have been instituted in recent years, such as Meals on Wheels, senior citizens centers in many communities, and other programs designed to support the efforts of older adults to remain healthy, active, and relatively independent.

IQ Changes

Does measured IQ decline with age? Methodological problems abound in research attempting to answer this question, but some patterns have been observed (Botwinick, 1977). Contrary to popular belief, there is no simple relation between age and intelligence. Findings suggest that some intellectual abilities do not decline with age, whereas others do. Horn distinguishes between *fluid intelligence* and *crystallized intelligence.* The former refers to cognitive abilities such as short-term memory and performance based on psychomotor speed, and it tends to decline as people age; the latter is composed of such things as vocabulary, and this kind of intelligence is believed not to decline and even sometimes to improve with age (Horn and Donaldson, 1976; Horn, 1985). The achievement of better scores on verbal tests than on performance tests has been observed so universally that it is called the classic aging pattern (Botwinick, 1977). One recent analysis of longitudinal data found increases in overall IQ through early adulthood (age thirty-two), a plateau until the fifties, and then some decline after age sixty (Hertzog and Schaie, 1988). After age eighty a decline in IQ is the rule for most people (Schaie, 1980).

There are some general problems in evaluating studies of intelligence, however, and they are relevant as well to studies of learning and memory difficulties. The age declines in IQ are neither as considerable as cross-sectional studies imply nor as minimal as longitudinal studies indicate, but rather are somewhere in the middle. Cross-sectional studies confuse age-related performance with the poorer health of the older cohort, whereas, as mentioned earlier, people studied longitudinally are usually healthier than the general population. When age and health are contrasted in the same study, health rather than age appears to account for declines in intellectual functioning (Siegler and Costa, 1985). Thus we do not know exactly what causes the declines in IQ that have been noted. Were we able to improve the health of the older population, perhaps the age differences in IQ that have been reported would be reduced.

It is important to note that whatever IQ declines have been found are so small that their practical significance is questionable (Schaie, 1980).[3] Moreover, intelligence tests, which after all were designed for much younger people, do not measure important cognitive phenomena such as wisdom and creativity (Clayton and Birren, 1980), or the complex capacity to make good use of the experiences and knowledge of a lifetime.

Learning and Memory

The individual's ability to learn and remember is obviously important in IQ testing. Although older adults tend to perform more poorly than their younger counterparts in experiments, the differences can be reduced by altering certain aspects of the situation. For example, providing the aged more time to learn new material reduces age differences, often completely. And older people will abandon some of their cautiousness when given rewards for responding (Botwinick, 1984).

There is evidence that older people do less well than younger people on memory tasks that demand considerable organization of the material to be memorized (Poon, 1985). They also perform less effectively tasks that require divided attention; older people apparently have a more limited cognitive capacity available to them at any one moment (Craik, 1977). Older adults seem to be less proficient at encoding material, transferring it into long-term memory, and eventually getting it back out again. Recognition declines less with age than does recall (Perlmutter and Hall, 1985). "Who was the thirty-fifth president of the United States?" is an example of a free-recall question. A recognition question on the same topic gives cues and asks "Was the president assassinated in Dallas in November 1963 Kennedy or Johnson?" Older people answer this question about as well as younger people.

---

[3]Recall our earlier discussion of statistical versus clinical significance (page 117).

Although age brings some decline in cognitive abilities, losses are not severe enough to prevent high-level intellectual pursuits.

On a practical level, we might ask whether the decrements in the learning and memory abilities of older people, as measured in careful laboratory settings, reflect true functional deficits in their everyday lives. As people age, they adapt to all kinds of changes in their environment, and all this involves learning. The kinds of memory tasks used in experiments may uncover deficits that have no impact on day-to-day functioning.

Indeed, one recent large national survey ($N = 14,783!$) found that only 15 percent of persons over the age of fifty-five complained of frequent memory problems and that 25 percent said that they never had problems; significantly, only 23 percent of those over age eighty-five reported having frequent problems (Cutler and Grams, 1988). Similar findings were reported by Sunderland, Watts, Baddeley, and Harris (1986), who found very few reports, by noninstitutionalized older adults and by those who knew them, of problems like forgetting where one has put something, forgetting what one has just said to another, and having to go back and check whether one had done something. Interpretation of these data, however, is complicated by the fact that they correlate imperfectly with laboratory and real-life measures of memory; that is, a person may not complain about a memory problem and yet have one, and a person, especially a depressed one, may complain about and yet not have an actual problem remembering things (Gilewski and Zelinski, 1986; Herrmann, 1982; Poon, 1985; Sunderland *et al.*, 1986). Furthermore, although older adults do tend to believe that their memory has declined over the years, very few feel that they are handicapped by forgetfulness in everyday life (Sunderland *et al.*, 1986).

Memory problems point up a general issue of attribution in thinking about aging. Older adults are "known" to be forgetful, and when they are, their failing memory is attributed to the inevitable process of aging. Medications taken by the older individual and health problems, however, may account for the impairments. In fact, when health was held constant for a group of patients, performance on learning and memory tasks was not related to age (Hulicka, 1967). In another study half of a sample of people over sixty complained of memory problems, but their complaints were not reflected on objective tests of memory (Lowenthal *et al.*, 1967). It may be that elderly people accept the cultural stereotype of forgetful old folks and then attach special significance to occasions when they have forgotten something (Kahn *et al.*, 1975). This can create worry and anxiety, which, in turn, can interfere with memory and other intellectual performance. Readers of this book under the age of sixty-five can confirm for themselves how often they forget another's name or how often they cannot remember why they have gotten up from studying and gone into another room. Younger people seemingly forget more easily that they have been forgetful, an interesting irony indeed!

Personality

Do people undergo predictable personality changes in old age or over the life span? In more general terms, do people's personalities change appreciably as they move from adulthood to old age? From a number of cross-sectional and longitudinal studies, it appears that stability rather than change is the rule (Costa and McCrae, 1978; Costa, McCrae, Zonderman, Barbano, Lebowitz, and Larson, 1986; Costa, Zonderman, McCrae, Cornoni-Huntley, Locke, and Barbano, 1987; McCrae and Costa, 1984; Siegler, George, and Okun, 1979), indicating that at least some aspects of personality (e.g., neuroticism) "are largely unaffected by aging and all of its accompanying events (e.g., death of parents, menopause, retirement) [and suggesting] that powerful mechanisms must maintain characteristic functioning, or return individuals to their usual levels after brief periods of readjustment" (Costa *et al.*, 1986, p. 148).

Medical Care

Medical expenses constitute a potential financial headache, and therefore a cause of stress, for the elderly. The Medicare program passed in 1965 as part of the Social Security law was intended to provide adequate medical care within the means of even the poor, but this has not happened. It has been estimated that in 1967 Medicare covered about 46 percent of medical expenses for the elderly; by the late 1970s this had dropped to 38 percent (Butler and Lewis, 1982). For outpatient services, patients have had to make contributions to the plan themselves, and like most private health insurance plans there are deductibles and co-payments by the patient (colloquially referred to as the "medigap"). In some states health care for older adults can be supplemented by Medicaid, a joint federal and state program designed as a companion to Medicare.

In June 1988, Medicare coverage was extended for catastrophic health care. This new expansion offers un-limited hospital stays after the beneficiary pays $564 for only the first day (previously patients had to pay $135 a day after the sixtieth day—hence the term "cata-strophic care" to describe the new law) and some cov-erage of drugs (in 1991 it will cover half of the drug costs after the patient has paid $600 in a given year—previously there was no coverage at all by Medicare). How well the new plan, which is being phased in be-tween 1989 and 1991, will meet the still unmet health care needs of older adults remains to be seen (Rosen-blatt, 1988).

Assuming the elderly can obtain and pay for medical care, how good is it? The answer seems to be, not very. The chronic health problems of old people are not ap-pealing to physicians because they seldom diminish. In fact, many maladies of old people—such as hearing loss, visual impairments, loss of mobility, aches and pains, especially in the feet (Pearson and Gatz, 1982), and a steadily declining cardiovascular system—are unlikely to get better and must somehow be adjusted to. The elderly come to rely heavily on their relationships with health care providers, but these providers may become impatient with them because they complain continually about not getting well or they become depressed.[4] Older people do not always take medication as instructed. Their relations with family members who must look after them are likely to suffer. The ailing elderly are sometimes torn both by feelings of guilt for needing so much from others and by anger against these younger people whom they have spent so many of their "good years" looking after and sacrificing for. The sons and daughters also have feelings of guilt and anger (Zarit, 1980).

Income
According to a 1988 report from the U.S. Census Bu-reau, in 1986, 32.4 million Americans, or 13.6 percent, were living in poverty (U.S. Department of Commerce, U.S. Bureau of the Census, 1988). Before Medicare was instituted for the elderly in 1965, the economic situation for older adults was far worse in this country—35 percent were living below the poverty line in 1959,

Many older adults are in the "near poor" category, and live under marginal circumstances.

the figure for all Americans being 22 percent. It is clear, then, that the government assistance programs of Pres-ident Lyndon Johnson's "Great Society" have had a beneficial impact on all people, especially seniors. But older adults continue to face more difficult economic challenges than younger citizens. And if we look at what are called "the near poor," or those living at 125% of the official poverty level, an additional 10 percent—22.4%—or a total of 6 million older adults are living under very marginal circumstances. This is considerably worse than for those under the age of sixty-five.

The situation is even more dismal for nonwhites and women, essentially the consequence of years of dis-crimination in pay and in access to jobs. The 13.6 per-cent poverty rate for all Americans breaks down into 11 percent for whites, 31 percent for blacks, and 22 percent for Hispanics. And the poverty rate for women is about two times that for men. Especially hard hit are older women living alone, many of whom are widowed after having seen their family life savings drained by the terminal illness of their husbands. At triple jeopardy are older black women, well over half of whom are near-poor.

An additional set of problems are the complexities of state and federal assistance programs, whose regu-lations continually change and whose application pro-cesses are not particularly accessible. A study released by the Census Bureau in late December 1988 showed that without Social Security and other government pay-ments such as Medicare and Medicaid, *nearly half* the nation's elderly would be living below the poverty line (*Los Angeles Times*, December 28, 1988, Part I, page 4).

[4] The situation may be even worse. As Zarit (1980) suggests, the illnesses of older people violate a "law" that the medical profession lives by, for these maladies are often incurable. Some of the impa-tience may therefore stem from the fact that most older patients do not get well.

Many of the homeless (discussed in Box 21.3, page 620) are older adults whose circumstances have deteriorated so severely that they have had to take to the streets. In considering the many statistics that federal and state governments compile on income and poverty, it should be borne in mind that the same degree of material deprivation probably has a more negative impact on an older person than on a younger one, given the reduced physical and in some case mental abilities possessed by many of those over the age of sixty-five.

Where the Elderly Live

One of the more prevalent myths regarding the aged is that the majority live in institutions. In fact, at any given time 95 percent of the aged reside in the community, living either by themselves or with a spouse, adult relatives, or friends. In 1980, 68 percent of the community elderly lived with their families. As summarized in a recent report from the Congressional Budget Office (1988), the trend is clearly for older adults to reside in settings where they live either alone or with their spouse. The percentages of these "independent" noninstitutionalized adults over the age of sixty-five rose from 20 percent in 1960 to 33 percent in 1984. Even though millions of the elderly are at or below the poverty line, most are able to afford their own residences and want very much to do so. Of course, the financial situation of older adults affects the quality of their housing. Up to 30 percent of older persons in the United States are estimated to live in substandard housing, largely because their incomes are marginal (American Association of Retired Persons, 1982).

It is nonetheless predicted that independent living will become more prevalent as incomes (and pensions) increase and as the average decline in number of children per family simply makes it less feasible for increasing numbers of seniors to move in with their adult offspring. Those least likely to live outside of institutions are solitary very old women and, in general, the disabled and frail, whose numbers are expected to increase in coming decades as the elderly population ages.

Although only 4 to 5 percent of the elderly population live in institutions at any one time, this percentage increases dramatically with age. The National Nursing Home Survey conducted in 1977 showed that only one of every hundred persons in the sixty-five to seventy-four age group is in a nursing home on a given day (National Center for Health Statistics, 1979). This number climbs to seven out of every hundred persons in the seventy-four to eighty-four age group and to more than one out of five persons in the eighty-five and over population. The often-cited statistic that only 4 to 5 percent of older adults reside in nursing homes at any given

time has been called the 4 percent fallacy (Kastenbaum and Candy, 1973), for this figure does not tell us the likelihood of spending some time in an institution at some period during late life. In a careful review of several studies of nursing home utilization, Wingard, Jones, and Kaplan (1987) concluded that at the time of death, about 20 percent of older adults lived in such institutions, with percentages ranging from a low of 9 percent to as high as 46 percent. Not surprisingly, the chances of being in a nursing home increase with age and are higher for women, for those without caregivers who could look after them in a home setting, and for those whose poor health prevents them from being able to perform normal daily activities.

Societal Expectations

One final social factor to be considered as we provide a context for our study of the psychological disorders of the elderly concerns society's attitudes toward the aged and in particular the myths held about late life. A survey of Americans of all ages showed a wide gap between their view of the problems of old age and that of the old people actually experiencing them (Harris, 1981). The ten problems listed in Figure 17.1 were perceived as more common or serious for older adults than the aged actually found them to be. For example, only 13 percent of the aged actually reported loneliness to be a problem, whereas 65 percent of those under sixty-five and 45 percent of the aged *expected* it to be a problem. The gloomy expectations, which exceeded the reality of the problems, were held not only by those under sixty-five but by those over sixty-five as well. We are as yet unsure how these myths about late life may affect the mental health of older adults. But if someone believes that senility is an inevitable consequence of aging, which it is not, an older relative may be treated as though he or she were senile when in fact this may not be the case.

Ageism or discrimination against older adults can take several forms. The negative type of ageism casts all elderly people as sexless, senile, and feeble. In another, more subtle form of ageism, which is potentially as dangerous, we smile a special smile or shout a special hooray when a ninety-two-year-old man crosses the finish line at a sporting event. Gatz, Pearson and Fuentes (1984) have called negative ageism myth and positive ageism countermyth. Myths emphasize disadvantage and deterioration, the mistaken beliefs given in Figure 17.1. Countermyths find no problems in aging, such as there being no decline in sexual capacity with age. As the truth probably lies somewhere between these two extremes, either form of ageism can be harmful to older adults.

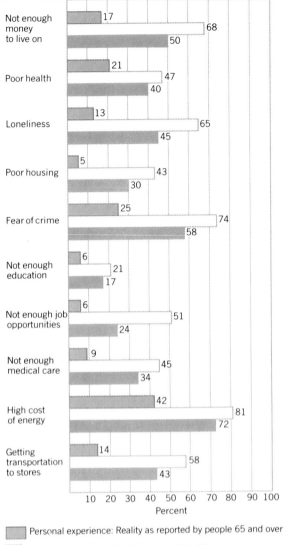

Personal experience: Reality as reported by people 65 and over

Public expectation: Belief of people 16 to 64

Public expectation: Belief of people 65 and over

FIGURE 17.1
Myth versus the reality of aging. Elderly people experiencing problems never report them to be as serious as the general public expects them to be. After Harris (1981).

Brain Disorders of Old Age

Although the vast majority of older people, approximately 85 to 90 percent, do not have organic brain disorders, these problems account for more admissions and hospital inpatient days than any other condition of geriatric adults (Christie, 1982). Two principal types of brain disorders are distinguished, ***dementia*** and ***delirium.*** A complete description and a discussion of causes are found in the Appendix (page 636); our focus here is primarily on the psychological factors surrounding brain disorders in older adults (Box 17.1).

Dementia

Clinical Description

The most prevalent form of dementia in the elderly is Alzheimer's disease. In fact, it accounts for 50 percent of the cases of senile dementia. Dementia is what laypeople call senility; it is a gradual deterioration of intellectual abilities to the point that social and occupational functioning are impaired. Memory abilities decline, as well as at least one other of the following realms of mental activity—abstract thinking, judgment, language, and personality. Generally, difficulty in remembering things is the most prominent symptom of dementia. People may leave tasks unfinished because they forget to return to them after an interruption. A person who had started to fill a teapot at the sink will leave the water running. Parents may become unable to remember the name of a daughter or son and later not even recall that they have children. Hygiene may become poor and appearance slovenly as the person loses awareness of when they last bathed and knowledge of how to dress adequately.

Judgment may become faulty, and there may be difficulty in comprehending personal situations and making plans or decisions. The demented also lose their standards and control of their impulses; they may use coarse language, tell inappropriate jokes, shoplift, and make sexual advances to strangers. The course of dementia may be progressive, static, or remitting, depending on the cause. Eventually, many with progresive dementia become withdrawn and apathetic. In the terminal phase of the illness, the personality has lost its sparkle and integrity. Relatives and friends will say that the person is just not himself any more. Social involvement with others keeps narrowing. In the end, the person is oblivious to his surroundings.

The prevalence of definite cases of dementia in the aged has been estimated at approximately 2 to 5 percent when noninstitutionalized adults are considered, and another 2 to 3 percent are added from the institutionalized aged (Gurland and Cross, 1982). Only a small proportion of persons under sixty suffer from dementia, but approximately 20 percent of individuals over the age of eighty do (see Box 17.2) (Bergmann *et al.*, 1971; Gurland and Cross, 1982; LaRue, Dessonville, and Jarvik, 1985; Jarvik, Ruth, and Matsuyama, 1980).

BOX 17.1

CEREBROVASCULAR DISEASES—STROKE AND ITS AFTERMATH

The blood vessels supplying the brain are subject to several types of malfunction. In atherosclerosis, deposits of fatty material narrow the lumen, or inner passageway, of the arteries of the body. When those in the brain are affected, some areas may not receive enough blood and hence insufficient oxygen and glucose. If the shortage is prolonged, the brain tissue, which is particularly dependent on receiving adequate supplies, softens, degenerates, and is even destroyed. The effects of cerebral atherosclerosis vary widely, depending on what area of the brain has clogged arteries and whether it is also supplied by nonaffected blood vessels. About three million Americans are presently incapacitated in some way by cerebral atherosclerosis.

In *cerebral thrombosis* a blood clot forms at a site narrowed by atherosclerosis and blocks circulation. Carbon dioxide builds up and damages the neural tissues. The loss of consciousness and control is referred to as apoplexy or *stroke.* The patient may die, suffer paralysis or decreased sensation from one side of the body or of an arm or leg, or lose other motor and sensory functions. The impairments of the patients who survive may disappear spontaneously, or they may be lessened through therapy and determined effort. Usually there is some residual damage. When only a small vessel is suddenly blocked, the patient suffers transient confusion and unsteadiness. A succession of these small strokes will bring cumulative damage, however.

In *cerebral hemorrhage* a blood vessel ruptures because of a weakness in its wall, damaging the brain tissue on which the blood spills. Cerebral hemorrhages are frequently associated with hypertension. The psychological disturbance produced depends on the size of the vessel that has ruptured and on the extent and the location of the damage. Often the person suffering a cerebral hemorrhage is overtaken suddenly and rapidly loses consciousness. When a large vessel ruptures, the person suffers a major stroke. All functions of the brain are generally disturbed—speech, memory, reasoning, orientation, and balance. The person usually lapses into a coma, sometimes with convulsions, and may die within two to fourteen days. If the person survives, he or she will probably have some paralysis and difficulties with speech and memory, although in some cases appropriate rehabilitation restores nearly normal functioning. Cerebral thromboses and hemorrhages together kill about 200,000 Americans each year (Terry and Wisniewski, 1974).

A frequent impairment is *aphasia,* a disturbance of the ability to use words. The cause of this damage may be a clot in the middle cerebral artery supplying the parieto-temporal region, usually of the dominant cerebral hemisphere. A right-handed person depends on the parieto-

Physical therapy is almost always needed for stroke victims.

temporal region in the left hemisphere for language skills; a left-handed person may depend on this region in the right hemisphere or in the left.

Aphasia is generally divided into two types, receptive or sensory and executive or motor. In sensory aphasias, individuals have difficulty in understanding the meaning of words. They may have auditory aphasia and not understand the words spoken to them or visual aphasia and not understand the printed word. They will, however, be able to speak properly; and they may, for example, be able to read but not understand spoken speech, or they may understand spoken speech but not be able to read. With motor aphasia a person suffers no deficit in comprehension but has problems in speaking words and sentences. He or she may transpose syllables, utter words of a sentence out of order, or be unable to recall names of common objects.

The following case illustrates the human impact of a stroke and efforts that can be made to restore some semblance of normalcy.

At age sixty-eight, Mr. H., a retired small businessman, was active in community affairs and with his hobby of woodworking. He had high blood pressure that was well controlled on medication and had had diabetes for several years, which was controlled with insulin. Mr. H. was accustomed to being independent and in charge of things, and this was acceptable to his wife of forty-five years. Mr. H. believed that any reduction of his independent status would be a sign of weakness. He was generally even tempered but would become angry when he was hindered from completing a task he had set out to do. . . .

Mrs. H. was active with her church group and had frequent visitors. She was in good health but had only moderate physical strength. She prepared well-balanced meals for both of them, including the special diet required for Mr. H. because of his diabetes and high blood pressure. They had two children, both of whom were married and living out of state, but who visited at holiday times.

One morning Mrs. H. entered her husband's workshop and found him sitting on a chair and unable to speak. The right side of his face drooped and he was unable to move his right arm or leg. He did not seem to see her when she approached him from his right but could see her when she moved to his left side. He made a few attempts to speak but was unsuccessful. Mrs. H. called their physician, who arranged for ambulance transportation to the hospital. Detailed examination and testing revealed that Mr. H. had sustained a stroke due to the occlusion of an artery supplying the left side of his brain. After receiving acute care including that necessary to prevent complications and reaching a stabilized condition, Mr. H. was transferred to a comprehensive medical rehabilitation center.

Mr. H.'s medical records were reviewed by the rehabilitation physician, he was examined, and his wife was informed of the results. She was also interviewed by a social worker who obtained further background information and answered questions about the facility. Mrs. H. found that she would be part of the rehabilitation process, that the staff would work closely with her, and that she would receive training necessary to help in her husband's care when he returned home. She would also receive counseling to aid her in coping skills and help her adapt to this change in their life situation. Mr. H. had a urinary catheter and had become constipated because of his illness and inactivity. These problems were attended to by the rehabilitation nursing staff, which also kept close watch on skin condition, both because of his impaired mobility and his diabetes. They monitored his blood pressure and regularly checked his urine for sugar. As Mr. H. progressed in the program, they taught him how to inject his insulin with his left hand and taught his wife how to draw up the proper amount in the syringe.

Mr. H. began to regain some communication ability, and his function was carefully evaluated by the speech pathologist, who aided him in improving general communication abilities. She informed Mrs. H. and the rehabilitation team members about how best to communicate with Mr. H. Speech therapy was also used to improve the volume and clarity of his speech.

As communication abilities improved, a psychologist evaluated Mr. H.'s mental status and cognitive skills and helped him to adapt to the frustrations of his disability and his feelings of [not] being in control. The psychologist also helped Mr. H. direct his anger in a more productive manner rather than diffusely taking out frustrations on the staff or on his wife. . . .

The physical therapist gradually helped Mr. H. improve his bed mobility and transfers, and eventually he progressed to the point where he was ambulating, first with a broad-based four-pointed cane and maximum assistance, and ultimately with a straight cane with his wife standing by. The occupational therapist worked on teaching Mr. H. to use his nondominant hand while he was also working to improve function in the weak right hand. He was taught to feed himself, to dress himself, and to perform the basic activities of daily living. He was also given exercises and training that would [allow him to pursue] his woodworking hobby, at least to a limited degree.

The recreational therapist helped Mr. H. to reach some self-fulfillment during his leisure time. His leisure activities were geared to those he had previously enjoyed, adapted to his disability. Transportation and financial status were discussed with Mrs. H. and also with her husband, and appropiate community agency referrals were made. An occupational therapist went out to the house to evaluate the existence of architectural barriers and to make recommendations for safety.

During this course of events, the rehabilitation team met weekly to discuss the problems that Mr. H. was experiencing, to compare ideas on solving these problems, and to plan the treatment approach for the forthcoming week. After about a month of this treatment Mr. H. was able to return home with his wife at a semi-independent level, with plans to return for outpatient treatment in order further to increase his strength, mobility, self-care, and communication skills. (Zarit, 1980, pp. 179–180)

Treatment of Dementia

If the dementia is found to have a reversible cause, appropriate medical treatment should begin immediately, for example, correcting a nutritional deficiency. To date, however, no clinically significant treatment has been found for Alzheimer's disease, although investigations are numerous. It is a degenerative disease and suggests continued deterioration of the patient. Certain drugs can bring mild improvements in learning and memory for short periods of time, particularly in mildly impaired people, but long-term treatments have not been found (Bartus *et al.*, 1982). Zarit (1980) has succinctly summarized the interventions that make sense in these situations.

The treatment of persons with [progressive] senile dementia is basically supportive both of affected individuals and of their social networks. At present there are no methods that can effectively restore intellectual function or prevent further deterioration in cases of senile brain disease. Treatment involves minimizing the disruption caused by the disorder. Goals for treatment include: maintaining the person in a community setting; allowing affected persons the opportunity of discussing their illness and its consequences; giving information to family members and other concerned persons about the nature of this disorder; supporting family members so that they can continue to provide assistance to the affected person; and using behavioral and problem-solving methods to deal with specific issues that arise as the result of the brain disorder.
(p. 356)

For every individual with a severely disabling dementia living in an institution, there are two living in the community (Gurland and Cross, 1982), usually supported by a spouse, daughter, or other family member. The burden of caring for the elderly with dementia usually falls on family members. Thus not only does the individual need to be considered in treatment but the family as well. Family caregivers and friends, faced with taxing demands on their time, energies, and emotions, can become depressed. One form of support is accurate information on the nature of the person's problems. For example, people with Alzheimer's have great difficulty placing new information into memory. This means that they can engage in a reasonable conversation but will forget a few minutes later what has been discussed. A caregiver may become impatient unless he or she understands that this impairment is to be expected because of the underlying brain damage. Making increased demands on the patient, perhaps in the belief that he or she is expressing hostility in a passive-aggressive manner, is likely to be aggravating for the

Memory aids, like the label on this patient's shirt, are used to help members of an Alzheimer's group.

person making them, and for other family members, and is not likely to help the elderly person's recollections. Homespun memory drills are also ill-advised, for there are no known techniques for improving the memories of persons with this disease.

Families can be taught, however, how to help their relatives cope with lost functions. Substituting recognition for recall in daily situations may help patients and families better manage their lives. Families can be taught to ask questions embedding the answer. It is much easier to respond to "Was the person you just spoke to on the phone Harry or Tom?" than to "Who just called?" Labels on drawers, appliances, and rooms help orient a person. If the individual has lost the ability to read, pictures can be used instead of verbal labels. Prominent calendars and clocks and strategic notes can also help, as can an automatic dialer on a telephone.

Caregivers should also be informed that patients do not always appreciate their limitations and may attempt to engage in activities beyond their abilities, sometimes in a dangerous manner. Although it is not advisable to coddle patients, it is important to set limits in light of their obliviousness to their own problems and impairments. Sometimes the caregiver's reactions to the patient's problems require attention. The daughter-in-law of a woman was offended by the woman's color combinations in clothing and wished to take over responsibility for coordinating her wardrobe, even though the woman was capable of dressing herself in an adequate, although not spiffy, fashion. The caregiver was urged not to impose her standards and taste on the woman, and to understand that her ability to dress herself and to take responsibility for her clothes was more important than adherence to conventional appearance (Zarit, 1980).

There are several other ways in which counselors and therapists can help those responsible for looking after people with dementia at home. Many caregivers are afraid to leave the infirm person alone, and as a consequence they exhaust themselves by paying constant attention to him or her. They may deny themselves simple diversions and pleasures because they view their leaving the house as neglect of the spouse or parent. In many instances their overattentiveness is inappropriate to the situation. If the infirm person's needs are really critical, outside help from a nurse or other professional should be sought. Sadly though, many families cannot afford such respite services, or such services are not available in their area.

The counselor must bear in mind that some of the tensions between caregiver and patient may well have their roots in aspects of the relationship that predate the onset of the dementia. There is a tendency to consider the most obvious facet of a situation, here the impairments of a sick person, as the cause of all difficulties. Counseling directed to long-standing problems may be called for.

The paranoid delusions sometimes found in dementia can be disruptive. As with paranoia generally, the beliefs should not be challenged directly. It is better to try to work around them, concentrating on aspects of the person's behavior that are more intact. The delusions in dementia diminish with time, as memory worsens with the progressive cerebral deterioration; the prognosis for this aspect of the illness is, in a sad sort of way, good.

Counseling the impaired person is difficult and, with the more severely deteriorated, of apparently little long-term benefit because of their cognitive losses. But some patients seem to enjoy and be reassured by occasional conversations with professionals and with others not directly involved in their lives. It would appear important not to discount entirely their ability to participate in their caregiver's discussions of ways to cope with the problems they face. Their inherent cognitive limitations must be appreciated, however; Zarit (1980) even suggests that no efforts be made to get them to admit to their problems, for their denial may be the most effective coping mechanism available.

The cognitive limitation of senile persons should always be treated with gentleness. Others should not consider them nonbeings, talking about their debilities in their presence, making fun of their occasional antics and forgetfulness, discounting their paranoid suspicions about others. Older people, even those with no organic disorder, are often infantilized or ignored by their juniors, a sign of disrespect that demeans not only the elderly person but the person showing the discourtesy.

Perhaps the most heart-rending decision is whether and when to institutionalize the impaired person. At some point the nursing needs may become so onerous and the mental state of the person so deteriorated that placement in a nursing home is the only realistic option, for the benefit not only of the person but of his or her family. The conflicts encountered in making this decision are not to be underestimated. The counselor can be a source of information about nearby facilities as well as a source of support for making and implementing the decision (Zarit, 1980).

Delirium

Clinical Description

The term delirium is derived from the Latin words *de* meaning from or out of and *lira* meaning furrow or track. The term thus implies being off track or deviating from the individual's usual state (Wells and Duncan, 1980). Although delirium is one of the most frequent organic mental disorders in older adults, it has been neglected in research and is, like dementia, often misdiagnosed. Progress in diagnosis has been impeded largely by terminological chaos. The literature reveals thirty or more synonyms signifying delirium (Liston, 1982), acute confusional state and acute brain syndrome being the two most common.

Delirium is described in DSM-IIIR as a "clouded state of consciousness." The patient, sometimes rather suddenly, has great trouble concentrating and focusing attention, and cannot maintain a coherent and directed stream of thought. In the early stages of delirium, the person is frequently restless, particularly at night. The sleep–waking cycle becomes disturbed so that he or she is drowsy during the day, and awake, restless, and agitated during the night. The individual is generally worse during sleepless nights and in the dark. Vivid dreams and nightmares are common.

People of any age are subject to delirium, but it is more common in children and older adults. Investigators have reported that 10 to 15 percent of older general-surgery patients become delirious after their operations (Miller, 1981). A review of the literature on delirium concluded that between one-third and one-half of all the hospitalized elderly are likely to be delirious at some point during their stay (Lipowski, 1983). Although the rates vary widely, even the lowest figures indicate that delirium is a serious health problem for older adults.

T.H. is a fifty-six-year-old right-handed businessman who had entered the hospital for cervical disk surgery. Because of his busy schedule and his anxiety relating to surgery, he had canceled his admission on two previous occasions. The patient was a fairly heavy social drinker but not to the point of interfering in any way with his business performance. The surgery was uneventful and there were no immediate complications of the procedure. The patient was greatly relieved and seemed to be making a normal recovery until the third postoperative night. During that night he became quite restless and found it difficult to sleep. The next day he was visibly fatigued but otherwise normal. The following night his restlessness became more pronounced, and he became fearful and anxious. As the night progressed, he thought that he saw people hiding in his room, and shortly before dawn he reported to the nurse that he saw some strange little animals running over his bed and up the drapes. At the time of morning rounds, the patient was very anxious and frightened. He was lethargic, distractible, and quite incoherent when he tried to discuss the events of the night before. He knew who he was and where he was but did not know the date or when he had had his surgery. During that day his mental status fluctuated, but by nightfall he had become grossly disoriented and agitated. At this point, psychiatric consultation was obtained.

The consultant's diagnosis was acute postoperative confusional state. The cause was probably due to a combination of factors: withdrawal from alcohol, fear of surgery, use of strong analgesics, stress of the operation, pain, and the sleepless nights in an unfamiliar room. The treatment consisted of a reduction in medications for pain, partial illumination of the room at night, and a family member in attendance at all times. These simple changes in conjunction with 50 mg of chlorpromazine (Thorazine) three times daily and 500 mg of chloral hydrate at bedtime reversed his confusional state within two days, and he was able to return home in a week with no residual evidence of abnormal behavior. To date there has been no recurrence of these problems. (Strub and Black, 1981, pp. 89–90)

Delirious patients may experience extreme difficulty in collecting their thoughts; they may be impossible to engage in conversation because of their wandering attention and fragmented thinking. Words are slurred, or they have difficulty finding them, and handwriting and spelling may become impaired. In severe delirium speech is sparse or pressured and incoherent. Bewildered and confused, delirious individuals may become disoriented for time, place, and sometimes for person. But very often they are so inattentive that they cannot be questioned about orientation. In the course of a twenty-four-hour period, however, they will have lucid intervals and become alert and coherent. These fluctuations help to distinguish delirium from other syndromes.

Perceptual disturbances are common; individuals mistake the unfamiliar for the familiar. For example, they state that they are in a hotel instead of a hospital, and see the attending nurse as a room clerk. Moreover, they may see objects as too small, too big, misshapen, or duplicated. Although illusions and hallucinations are common, particularly visual and mixed visual–auditory ones, they are not always present in delirium. Paranoid delusions have been noted in 40 to 70 percent of the delirious aged. These delusions tend to be poorly worked out, fleeting, changeable, and tied to the surroundings.

Accompanying their disordered thoughts and perceptions are swings in activity and mood. Delirious people can be erratic, ripping their clothes one moment and sitting lethargically the next. They are in great emotional turmoil and may shift rapidly from one emotion to another—depression, anxiety, and fright, anger, euphoria, and irritability. Fever, flushed face, dilated pupils, rapid tremors, rapid heartbeat, elevated blood pressure, and incontinence of urine and feces are also common. If the delirium proceeds, the person will completely lose touch with reality and may become stuperous (Lipowski, 1980, 1983; Strub and Black, 1981).

Although delirium usually develops swiftly, within a matter of hours or days, the exact mode of onset depends on the underlying cause. Delirium resulting from a toxic reaction or concussion will have an abrupt onset; when infection or metabolic disturbance underlies delirium, the onset of symptoms is gradual, over an extended period of time.

Why are the elderly especially vulnerable to delirium? Many explanations have been offered. There are the physical declines of aging, the increased general susceptibility to chronic diseases, the many medications prescribed for older patients, and vulnerability to stress. One other factor, brain damage, increases the risk of delirium. The elderly with dementing disorders appear to be the most susceptible of all. A retrospective review of 100 hospital admissions of people all ages who had a diagnosis of delirium revealed that 44 percent of them had a delirium superimposed on another organic brain condition (Purdie, Honigman, and Rosen, 1981).

Treatment of Delirium

Complete recovery is possible if the syndrome is correctly identified and the underlying cause—for example, drug intoxication, nutritional imbalance, infection, stress—is promptly and effectively treated. Generally, the condition takes one to four weeks to clear, although it takes longer in the elderly than in the young. If the underlying causative condition is not treated, however, the brain can be permanently damaged and the patient may die. The mortality rate for delirium is extremely high; approximately 40 percent of the patients die, either from the underlying condition or from exhaustion (Rabins and Folstein, 1982). In fact, when fatality rates for dementia and delirium are compared over a one-year period of time, the rates are higher for delirium than for dementia, 37.5 compared to 16 percent. Thus delirium in an older adult is a very serious matter.

One often neglected aspect of the management of delirium is educating the family of a senile parent to recognize the symptoms of delirium and its reversible nature. They may interpret the onset of delirium as a new stage of a progressive dementing condition. For example, a father with Alzheimer's disease may run a high fever from an internal infection and begin to hallucinate and otherwise act bizarrely. These new symptoms, superimposed on the intellectual deterioration to which members of the family have become accustomed, may alarm them into concluding that he is losing ground fast and irreversibly. They may be rushed into a premature decision to institutionalize him. Proper diagnosis and treatment, however, can usually return the person to his earlier state, which, although problematic, was being coped with by those in the home.

Psychological Disorders of Old Age

In an earlier discussion the point was made that transsexuals tend to attribute whatever personal unhappiness they experience to the discrepancy between their anatomy and their gender identity. A similar process operates with old people, at least as they are viewed by others. The most obvious characteristic of a seventy-five-year-old man is that he is old. If he is cranky, it is because he is old. If he is depressed, it is because he is old. Even when he is happy, it is assumed to be because of his age. Moreover, the "old-age explanation" is generally a somatic one, even if this is not made explicit. Some ill-defined physical deterioration is assumed to underlie not only the physical problems of old people but all their psychological problems as well.

Although a psychological disorder at any age may have a physical explanation, this explanation can be problematic with older adults because it locates the cause of their problems within them and can blind us to other factors that may have much to do with whatever mental or emotional distress they are suffering. The fact is that most psychopathology to be found in the aged has *not* been directly linked to the physiological processes of aging. Whether the person brings maladaptive personality traits and inadequate coping skills into old age plays a role, as do health, genetic predisposition, and life stressors (Box 17.2).

Depression

Extent of the Problem

According to NIMH data, mood disorders are less common in older adults than in younger adults (Myers *et al.*, 1984; Regier *et al.*, 1988), but they are estimated to account for nearly half the admissions of older adults to acute psychiatric care (Gurland and Cross, 1982; Redick and Taube, 1980). Unipolar depressions are much more common in the elderly than bipolar depressions (Post, 1978; Regier *et al.*, 1988). In fact, the onset of manic-depressive illness after the age of sixty-five is believed to be rare (Jamison, 1979); Regier *et al.* found almost no person aged sixty-five or older who met diagnostic criteria for mania. For this reason the following discussion will be of unipolar depression in older adults.

Mood disorders are less frequent in older adults than among younger adults.

BOX 17.2

PREVALENCE OF MENTAL DISORDERS IN LATE LIFE

Is age itself a contributing factor to emotional and mental malfunction? Do more old people than young people have mental disorders? Whether mental disorders become more prevalent with age is not clear, partly because of the methodological and conceptual difficulties that we have already discussed. Comprehensive and systematic research on the incidence and prevalence of various psychiatric disorders in late adulthood is just beginning (LaRue, Dessonville, and Jarvik, 1985; Stenmark and Dunn, 1982). The already mentioned extensive cross-sectional study conducted by the National Institute of Mental Health, using the DSM-III criteria for disorders, has yielded valuable data on mental disorders in all age groups, including the elderly.

First some background. The Epidemiological Catchment Area program sponsored by the NIMH is a collaborative effort of five major United States cities to give the Diagnostic Interview Schedule (DIS) at six-month intervals to large general-population samples in order to estimate current and lifetime prevalences of psychiatric disorders. Current prevalence is the proportion of persons in the sample who at present have a given disorder; lifetime prevalence is the proportion of persons who have *ever* had the disorder up to the date of assessment, whether or not they have it at present.

Initial results from three of the cities show that current prevalence rates for a sample of 9000 people indicated that persons over sixty-five had the lowest overall rates of all age groups when the disorders were grouped together. Indeed, schizophrenia and substance abuse are extremely rare in people in the upper age ranges. The primary problem of old age was found to be *cognitive impairment.* In the NIMH study, rates for mild cognitive impairment were about 14 percent for elderly males and females, and

for severe cognitive impairment 5.5 percent for men and 4.7 percent for women (Myers *et al.,* 1984). These rates tell us only the overall prevalence of cognitive impairment in the aged, not whether the causes were reversible or irreversible. As we shall see, this is an important issue.

What of lifetime prevalence? We would expect that because older adults have lived through a longer risk period in which disorders could develop, they would have the highest overall lifetime rates. Again, however, the lifetime rates of those sixty-five and older were the lowest.

What can explain these findings? Disordered older people might have been absent from the community samples through mortality or institutionalization. Older adults may also have attributed their symptoms to physical illness or forgotten past episodes (Robins *et al.,* 1984). Moreover, as we have said before, we do not really know whether we can measure disorders the same way in the old as we do in younger people. Some disorders, such as schizophrenia, were said to have a maximum age for onset; DSM-III held that individuals do not become schizophrenic after age forty-five. Finally, perhaps there has been a true historical increase in psychiatric disorders in the last few generations, as compared to our current generation of older adults. Today's younger and middle-aged adults may have significantly higher rates of mental disorders than their parents and grandparents (Robins *et al.,* 1984).

All in all, the majority of persons sixty-five years of age and older are free from serious psychopathology, but 10 to 20 percent do have psychological problems, either cognitive or mental, severe enough to warrant professional attention (Birren and Sloane, 1980; Gurland and Cross, 1982; LaRue, Dessonville, and Jarvik, 1985).

Women have more periods of depression than men for most of their lives, except possibly when they reach old-old age. More than 30 percent of older individuals who have chronic health problems or are confined in hospitals are depressed (Blazer, 1982). Moreover, people with a dementing disorder such as Alzheimer's may simultaneously become depressed; 20 percent of those with dementia are estimated to have a superimposed depression (Reifler, Larson, and Hanley, 1982).

Depression in Older versus Younger Adults
Is depression in older adults the same as or different from that in younger adults? Blazer (1982) states that worry, feelings of uselessness, sadness, pessimism, fatigue, inability to sleep, and volitional difficulties are

common symptoms of depression in the elderly. These symptoms are of course similar to those of depression in other age groups. When Blazer (1982) compared the symptoms of depression in the aged to those of three younger adult populations being treated for depression, however, he noted some interesting differences. Feelings of guilt were found less often in the depressed elderly, whereas somatic complaints were more common. Thoughts of suicide were also less common in older patients, which contrasts with our knowledge that in older men acutal suicide attempts and successes increase (see page 501).

Depression versus Dementia
A number of case histories and research studies doc-

ument that symptoms of elderly individuals, seemingly of dementia, remit spontaneously or improve with treatment for depression (Kiloh, 1961; Post, 1975; Folstein and McHugh, 1978; McAllister and Price, 1982). On the other hand, cases of depression are often misdiagnosed as a dementing disorder. This is an important issue in differential diagnosis because depression is generally reversible whereas dementia is not.

Depressed patients may complain more of forgetfulness than patients with dementia, a distinction which may be clinically useful (Kahn *et al.*, 1975; Raskin and Rae, 1981). Those with dementia may forget that they forget! In testing, depressed patients tend to underestimate their abilities and to be preoccupied with negative feedback (Miller, 1975; Weingartner and Silberman, 1982). Depressed older adults, although they complain more than nondepressed controls about memory problems, do not in fact perform less well than do controls on a laboratory memory test (O'Hara *et al.*, 1986); and their performance on memory tests is above average or superior even if they complain about memory deficits (Williams, Little, Scates, and Blockman, 1987). This discrepancy between memory complaints and actual memory deficits among depressed people is found as well among younger subjects (page 227) and probably reflects self-deprecating evaluations in the clinical syndrome of depression (Coyne and Gotlib, 1983).

The depressed also tend to have more errors of omission: they may not answer a question because it is just too much effort for them, or because they expect to make mistakes. Those with dementia, on the other hand, tend to make random or confabulatory errors (Whitehead, 1973). Finally, as noted earlier, patients can suffer from both dementia and depression: a depressed person may develop Alzheimer's (but the reader should not infer that depression is a cause of Alzheimer's), and an Alzheimer's patient can become depressed over his growing physical and cognitive limitations (Reifler *et al.*, 1982; Teri and Reifler, 1987).

Correlates of Depression in the Aged

As indicated earlier, many aged in poor physical health are depressed., In a survey of 900 elderly people living in the community, Blazer and Williams (1980) found that 44 percent of people with depressive symptoms were medically ill. Moreover, older men who have their first onset of depression in late life are likely to have undergone surgery before psychiatric admission, to have unusually high rates of chronic illness, and to have suffered from more medical conditions than other persons do (Roth and Kay, 1956). Physicians who care for elderly medical patients are insensitive to the likelihood of depression coexisting with physical illnesses and more

often than not fail to diagnose and therefore to treat the psychological condition (Rapp, Parisi, Walsh, and Wallace, 1988; Rapp, Parisi, and Walsh, 1988). This oversight can worsen not only the depression but the medical problem itself.

Physical illness and depression are linked for reasons other than the disheartening aspects of an illness. Medications prescribed to treat a chronic condition can aggravate a depression that already exists, cause a depression to start, or produce symptoms that resemble the disorder but are not in fact a true depression (Klerman, 1983). The drugs that are the most likely to do this are antihypertensive medications, which cause depression in 20 percent of adults who take them. Other possibilities include hormones, corticosteroids, and anti-Parkinsonian medications. Longitudinal and retrospective studies have pointed out that, on the other side of the coin, individuals who are originally depressed may be predisposed to develop physical illness (Vaillant, 1979; Wigdor and Morris, 1977).

As we grow older, we almost inevitably experience a number of life events that could cause depression. The elderly are commonly bereaved of their loved ones. Various studies have documented higher rates of illness and death among the widowed (Parkes and Brown, 1972; Clayton, 1973), and bereavement has been hypothesized to be a common precipitationg factor for depressions that hospitalize elderly patients (Turner and Sternberg, 1978). And yet longitudinal studies have found relatively low rates of depression in the bereaved, and it has been concluded that the symptoms of depression in bereft individuals are generally less severe and fewer than those in individuals institutionalized for depression (Clayton *et al.*, 1972; Bornstein *et al.*, 1973; Gallagher *et al.*, 1982). Few older people, then, appear to develop a disabling depressive illness following an expected loss of a loved one.

Retirement has also been assumed to have negative consequences for the person, but research does not generally support this assumption (Atchley, 1980; George, 1980). The ill effects of retirement found by studies may have had much to do with the poor health and low incomes of the retirees.

Each older person brings to late life a developmental history that makes his or her reactions to common problems unique. Their coping skills and personality determine how effectively they will respond to new life events (Butler and Lewis, 1982). We should not assume that depression rather than adaptation is the common reaction to losses and stress in late life.

Treatment of Depression

Although clinical lore commonly holds that depressions in the elderly last longer and are more resistant to treatment, these claims are not substantiated (Small and Jarvik, 1982). Indeed, there is substantial evidence that depressed older adults can be helped by psychological interventions. Gallagher and Thompson (1982, 1983) compared cognitive, behavioral, and brief psychodynamic psychotherapies for older depressed individuals. All three were found equally effective, and in a recent study (Thompson, Gallagher, and Breckenridge, 1987), 70 percent of the patients were judged either completely "cured" or markedly improved. This compares very favorably with psychotherapy in younger depressed age groups. Another notable finding is that untreated control patients did not improve, suggesting that older adults are less likely than younger to recover unless they are treated.

The use of antidepressant drugs with older adults is complicated by side effects like postural hypotension; some patients treated with tricyclic antidepressants become dizzy and fall. There is also risk to the cardiovascular system, with the danger of a heart attack. Older people are also at high risk for toxic reactions to medications generally. Especially since the efficacy of antidepressants with older adults is in question (Beutler *et al.*, 1987), nonpharmacological approaches to depression in the elderly are particularly important (Bressler, 1987).

Delusional (Paranoid) Disorders

A sixty-six-year-old married woman reluctantly agreed to a clinical evaluation. She [had] a six-week history of bizarre delusions and hallucinations of her husband spraying the house with a fluid that smelled like "burned food." She complained that he sprayed the substance everywhere around the house, including draperies and furniture, although she had never seen him do it. She could smell the substance almost constantly, and it affected her head, chest, and rectum. She also complained that someone in the neighborhood had been throwing bricks and rocks at her house. In addition, she suspected her husband of having affairs with other women, whose footprints she claimed to have seen near home.

She gave a vague history of marital distress for about six years. Yet she had no history of a similar episode earlier in life, no history of previous psychiatric treatment, and no history of

long-term suspiciousness or mistrust. The patient had been a domestic servant for thirty years and was still working. She was described as a loyal, active church member and as socially outgoing. Interviews revealed a sullen woman who was extremely hostile toward her husband. She focused on the delusion that he was spraying an unusual substance in an attempt to upset her; other issues in the relationship seemed secondary. No cognitive dysfunction could be determined in interviews, and her behavior with interviewers was otherwise socially appropriate. She denied vehemently that anything was wrong with her and insisted that her husband was the one with a problem. She looked very sad at times and would occasionally wipe away a tear; but her predominant affect was extreme hostility and consternation about her husband's alleged behavior. . . .

Medical evaluation revealed no abnormalities. The only suggestion of a precipitating event was the death of a son five years earlier. Though denying emotional problems of her own, she reluctantly agreed to come for weekly interviews with the clinic social worker and to take haloperidol, 1 mg three times per day. She began to suppress her delusional concerns after about three weeks, and the therapist was able to draw her into other topics during the interviews. She has been maintained on the same dosage of haloperidol for about seven months and has remained in remission. (Varner and Gaitz, 1982, pp. 108–109)

As we can understand from this case history, paranoia may have a disturbing and immediate impact on others, often bringing angry reactions and contributing to a decision to institutionalize the older adult (Berger and Zarit, 1978). Yet how common is paranoia in late life? As with depression, this depends on the diagnostic criteria used. When DSM-III criteria for paranoid disorders were applied consistently in 800 older patients at the Texas Research Institute of Mental Science for a period of five years, a 2 percent incidence for outpatients and a 4.6 percent incidence for inpatients were found (Varner and Gaitz, 1982). Yet paranoid symptomatology is held to be a general complaint of many elderly psychiatric patients (Pfeiffer, 1977). One study of geriatric inpatients found that 32 percent of them had paranoid symptoms associated with some other form of mental illness (Whanger, 1973). Because the term paranoia is loosely applied, the exact prevalence cannot be known.

Clinicians report an interesting and striking difference between the paranoid delusions of older people and those of younger individuals. The suspicions of older adults are more down to earth, concerned with persons in their immediate surroundings—such as neighbors, sons and daughters, people in stores, and the like. In contrast, the persecutors of younger paranoids are often located far away, in the C.I.A. or the F.B.I. or even outer space. Younger paranoids are given to more grandiosity than older ones (Post, 1987). Moreover, older patients are more likely to be women who are in good health, except for problems with vision and, as we shall see, hearing.

Causes of Paranoia

Paranoia in the aged may be the continuation of a disorder that began earlier in life. It may also accompany organic brain conditions such as delirium and dementia. In fact, paranoia may serve a function for the demented, filling in the gaps caused by memory loss. Instead of admitting "I can't remember where I left my keys," they think "Someone must have come in and taken my keys" (Zarit, 1980). Paranoid ideation has also been linked to sensory losses, in particular hearing. Older people with severe paranoid disorders tend to have longstanding hearing loss in both ears, which makes them socially deaf (Post, 1980). An older woman who is deaf may believe that other people are whispering about her, so that she cannot hear what is being said. Her paranoid reactions may be an attempt to fill in the blanks caused by sensory loss (Pfeiffer, 1977; see Box 17.3). By explaining bewildering events, delusions are in a sense adaptive and understandable. Often the earlier social adjustment of paranoid patients has been poor; the onset of their symptoms may follow a period in which they have become increasingly isolated. And isolation itself limits a person's opportunities to check his or her suspicions about the world, making it easier for delusions to take hold. The individual builds a "pseudocommunity" rather than social relations based on good communication and mutual trust (Cameron, 1959).

Like other kinds of psychopathology, paranoia may be maintained, at least in part, by reinforcement from others. A lonely woman gets action from police and relatives if she complains of intruders. Sadly enough, sometimes such attention is the best the old person can manage, for as just stated, many of those who develop paranoia have been socially isolated throughout their lives. But it should not be supposed that the adoption of a paranoid belief is deliberate, nor does it seem plausible that reinforcement patterns can explain why a person began having delusions in the first place.

Older people are especially vulnerable to all kinds of abuse from others. They may be talked about behind their backs, or even to their faces, as though they were not present, and taken advantage of by others in many small and larger ways. There is thus a danger that a complaint of persecution from an older person will be quickly dismissed as "just" a sign of late-life paranoia. An older client of one of the authors complained bitterly about being followed by a detective hired by her "evil" husband. Inquiry revealed that the husband was worried that she was having an affair and had indeed hired someone to follow her! It should always be determined whether suspicions have any bases in reality before they are attributed to paranoia.

Treatment of Paranoia

The treatment of paranoia in older adults is much the same as for younger adults. Clinical lore suggests that a patient, supportive approach is best; the therapist should provide empathic understanding of the person's concerns. Directly challenging the paranoid delusion or attempting to reason the person out of his or her beliefs is seldom effective. Rather, recognition of the distress caused by the paranoia is more likely to promote a therapeutic relationship with the person. Therapists should be mindful that, by the time the patient sees a health professional, many others—family, friends, the police—have probably tried, to no avail, to reason the person out of his or her delusional beliefs.

If the person has a hearing or visual problem, a hearing aid or corrective lenses may alleviate some of the symptoms. If the individual is socially isolated, efforts can be made to increase his or her activities and contacts. Regular supportive therapy may help the patient in reestablishing relations with family members and friends. Attention should be provided for appropriate behavior. Even if these straightforward measures do not relieve paranoia, they may be beneficial in other areas of the person's life.

Studies of therapy outcomes indicate that delusions in the elderly can be treated successfully with phenothiazines (Post, 1980). Unfortunately, paranoid individuals are generally suspicious of the motives of those who give them drugs. Toxicity from medications must also be considered, given the particular sensitivity of older people to drugs. Institutionalization, best considered as a last resort, may do little good. In practice, the decision depends more on how tolerant the person's social environment is than on how severe and disruptive are the paranoid beliefs.

BOX 17.3

PARTIAL DEAFNESS, GROWING OLD, AND PARANOIA

A relationship between hearing problems in old age and the development of paranoid thinking was noted many years ago by Emil Kraepelin and has been verified since by careful laboratory studies (Cooper *et al.*, 1974). The connection appears to be specific to paranoia, for the relationship between difficulties in hearing and depression in older individuals is not as great. Since hearing losses appear to predate the onset of paranoid delusions, this may be a cause–effect relationship of some importance.

Stanford psychologist Philip Zimbardo and his associates conducted an ingenious experiment to study the relation of poor hearing to paranoia. They reasoned that loss of hearing acuity might set the stage for the development of paranoia if the person does not acknowledge, or is unaware of, the hearing problem (Zimbardo, Andersen, and Kabat, 1981). If I have trouble hearing people around me, which makes them seem to be whispering, I may conclude that they are whispering *about me,* and that what they say is unfavorable. I will think this way, however, only if I am unaware of my hearing problem. If I know that I am partially deaf, I will appreciate that I do not hear them well because of my deafness and will not think that they are whispering. A hard-of-hearing grandfather may eventually challenge the light-voiced, gesturing grandchildren he believes are whispering about him; and they will deny that they are. A tense cycle of allegations, denials, and further accusations will isolate the increasingly hostile and suspicious grandfather from the company of his grandchildren.

The experiment done by Zimbardo and his group examined the initial stage of this hypothesized development of paranoia. College students, previously determined to be easily hypnotized and capable of responding to a posthypnotic suggestion of partial deafness, participated in what they believed to be a study of the effects of various hypnotic procedures on creative problem solving. Each of the subjects sat in a room with two others who were actually confederates of the experimenter. The trio were provided a task to perform either cooperatively or by themselves; they were to make up a story concerning a TAT picture. The picture was shown on the screen, and projected first was the word "FOCUS." The confederates, as planned, began to joke with each other as they made decisions about the story, inviting the subject to join them in the cooperative venture. After the story was completed, the subject was left alone to fill out the questionnaires, among them MMPI measures of paranoia and an adjective checklist to assess mood.

As described so far, there is nothing particularly interesting about the experiment. The actual manipulations took place earlier, *before* the TAT picture was presented. Each subject had been hypnotized and given one of the three following posthypnotic suggestions.

1. *Induced partial deafness without awareness.* Each member of the first group was told that when he saw the word "FOCUS" projected on a screen in the next room, he would have trouble hearing noises and whatever other people might be saying, that they would seem to be whispering, and that he would be concerned about not being able to hear. He was also instructed that he would not be aware of this suggestion until an experimenter removed the amnesia by touching his shoulder.

Schizophrenia

Does schizophrenia ever appear for the first time in old age? Debate on this question has raged for years. According to DSM-III, first-time onset of schizophrenia after the age of sixty-five was very rare. However, explicit allowance for late-onset schizophrenia is made in DSM-IIIR in order to facilitate further study of people who seem to become schizophrenic after the age of forty-five.

When schizophrenia does make an appearance in older adults, it is often called paraphrenia (Roth, 1955). These patients are reported to have a milder form of the disorder than patients with early onset. They also tend to be unmarried, live in isolation, have few surviving relatives, have hearing losses and a family history of schizophrenia, and belong to the lower socioeconomic classes (Post, 1987). In the United States the term paraphrenia, like paranoia, has been inconsistently used and the phenomenon little studied (Berger and Zarit, 1978; Bridge and Wyatt, 1980). Some researchers believe that the older patients diagnosed as having paraphrenia by Roth actually had a mood disorder (Cooper, Garside, and Kay, 1976; Cooper and Porter, 1976; Kay *et al.*, 1976), for in many with prominent symptoms, cognition and overall functioning were preserved.

Large-scale surveys have estimated the overall prevalence of schizophrenia at 1 percent or less in persons over the age of sixty (LaRue, Dessonville, and Jarvik, 1985; Myers *et al.*, 1984; Reiger *et al.*, 1988). Ninety percent of the geriatric patients with schizophrenia acquired the disorder before the age of forty, which means that very few have late onset (Gurland and Cross, 1982;

2. *Induced partial deafness with awareness.* Subjects in the second group, the control group, were given the same partial-deafness suggestion, but they were instructed to remember that their hearing difficulty was by posthypnotic suggestion.

3. *Posthypnotic-suggestion control.* Subjects in the third group, controls for the effectiveness of posthypnotic suggestion, were instructed to react to the word "FO-CUS" by experiencing an itchiness in the left earlobe, with amnesia for this suggestion until touched on the left shoulder by the experimenter.

After being given their posthypnotic suggestions, all subjects were awakened from the hypnotic state and ushered into the next room, where the experiment proceeded with the TAT picture, as already described. It can now be appreciated that participants who had deafness without awareness might perceive the joking of the confederates as directed toward them, for they would have trouble hearing what was being said and would be unlikely to attribute this difficulty to any hearing problem of their own. Subjects who had deafness with awareness would have the same problem hearing the joking, but they would know that they had a temporary decrement in hearing through hypnotic suggestion. The other control subjects would have no hearing problems, just itchy earlobes. At the completion of the study, all subjects were carefully informed about the purposes of the study, and steps were taken to ensure that the posthypnotic suggestions of partial deafness and itchy earlobes had been lifted.

The results are fascinating. The experience of being partially deaf without awareness showed up significantly on cognitive, emotional, and behavioral measures. As compared to members of the two control groups, these subjects scored more paranoid on the MMPI scales and described themselves as more irritated, agitated, and hostile. The two confederates who were in the same room with these subjects rated them as more hostile than the controls. (The confederates were of course not aware of which group a given subject was in.) When the confederates invited each subject to work with them in concocting the TAT story, only one of six experimental subjects accepted the overture, although most of the control subjects agreed. At the end of the study, just before the debriefing, all subjects were asked whether they would like to participate in a future experiment with the same partners; none of the deafness-without-awareness subjects said that he would, but most of the controls did.

The overall reaction of subjects who had trouble hearing and had no ready explanation for it, other than that others were whispering, was suspicion, hostility, agitation, and unwillingness to affiliate with these people. This pattern is similar to what Zimbardo hypothesizes to be the earliest stage of the development of some paranoid delusions. The creation of this "analogue incipient paranoia" in the laboratory by inducing deafness without awareness of the deafness is consistent with the view that when people's hearing becomes poor in old age, they are susceptible to paranoia *if,* for whatever reasons, they do not acknowledge their deafness.

Bollerup, 1975). In these cases paranoid symptoms are almost always present (Fish, 1960; Roth, 1955), and the schizophrenia of these people does not have the classical pattern (Post, 1987).

The next question of interest is what happens to schizophrenic symptomatology as people become older. Now that the advent of neuroleptics, such as Thorazine, and political decisions to reduce the number of patients in mental hospitals have ushered in a veritable revolution in the treatment of schizophrenia, many more schizophrenics live at home or elsewhere in the community than was the case twenty or thirty years ago. They are less likely to have been institutionalized for long periods of time and have not suffered from the secondary problems of institutionalization. Mortality rates for this group are higher than those of age-matched

controls, in part because their rates of suicide and traumatic death are higher (Post, 1980).

Given that many of the schizophrenics who do survive beyond the age of sixty-five are not in hospitals, and given that their symptoms are controlled somewhat by drugs, did the distortions of their thinking become less as they entered old age? Some researchers claim that schizophrenia sometimes "burns out" (Bridge, Cannon, and Wyatt, 1978), that positive symptoms (see Chapter 14, page 386) become somewhat muted; hallucinations and delusions decrease in intensity and frequency, and the capacity for social interactions improves. But, as Lawton (1972) cautions, these findings are based primarily on hospitalized patients who are taking drugs. As yet the course of schizophrenia in old age has really not been adequately studied.

Psychoactive Substance Use Disorders

Alcohol Abuse and Dependence

Alcoholism is generally believed to be less prevalent in the elderly than in younger cohorts. It is estimated that between 2 and 10 percent of the elderly are alcoholic or abuse alcohol. Prevalence estimates vary, however, because studies employ different definitions of the older age group (Whittington, 1984). In a recent study examining NIMH Epidemiological Catchment Area data of one-month prevalence rates (Regier *et al.*, 1988), only 0.9 percent of community-dwelling adults age sixty-five and over were found to be abusing alcohol. This compares with 4.1 percent of those eighteen to twenty-four, 36 percent from twenty-four to forty-four, and 2.1 percent from forty-five to sixty-four. More men were having alcohol problems than women.[5]

Problem drinkers are not likely to survive to old age. The peak years for death from cirrhosis are between fifty-five and sixty-four years of age. Older people may also develop physiological intolerance for alcohol, counteracting its positive effects on mood (Gurland and Cross, 1982).

It is believed that older alcoholics fall into two groups, the two-thirds or more who began drinking in early or middle adulthood and who have continued their pattern into late life, and the small percentage who took to drink after age fifty (Rosin and Glatt, 1971). Alcoholics who started late either had intermittent drinking problems in the past and now abuse alcohol regularly in late life or had no history of alcohol problems until their late years (Zimberg, 1978). The late-starting abuser is more likely to be separated or divorced, more likely to live alone, and more likely to have serious health difficulties (Schuckit and Moore, 1979). Age-related circumstances, such as retirement, may have provoked some of them to drink (Rosin and Glatt, 1971).

However, not all workers support this distinction; Borgatta, Montgomery, and Borgatta (1982), for example, argue that there is no firm evidence for late-onset alcoholism. One conclusion that *can* be drawn from research is that alcoholism is not a self-limiting problem: if a person is a problem drinker in his or her younger years, chances are that he or she will remain so later in life (if the person lives that long).

As people age, their tolerance for alcohol is reduced, for they metabolize it more slowly. Thus the drug may cause greater changes in their brain chemistry than in that of the young and may more readily bring on toxic effects such as delirium. A number of neuropsychological studies have shown that cognitive deficits associated with alcohol abuse are likely to be more pronounced in the aged alcoholic than in younger individuals with comparable drinking histories (Brandt *et al.*, 1983). Although some intellectual functioning is recovered with abstinence, residual effects may remain long after the older person has stopped drinking.

Unfortunately, clinicians may be less likely to look for alcoholism in older people and instead attribute symptoms such as poor motor coordination and impaired memory to an organic problem or to late-life depression. If alcohol abuse goes unrecognized, treatment of the patient will be severely compromised.

Illegal Drug Abuse

The current older population abuses illegal drugs infrequently compared to other age groups. In the previously cited NIMH survey (Regier *et al.*, 1988), none of those aged sixty-five and older, and only 0.1 percent of those between forty-five and sixty-four years of age, had a drug abuse or dependency disorder, compared to much higher rates for younger age groups. Studies of the few older narcotics abusers indicate that they began their habit early in life and reduced their drug intake as they grew older (Ball and Chambers, 1970). It is believed by many experts, however, that the abuse of illegal drugs is higher than these formal estimates and that as younger cohorts age, there will be explosive growth in the prevalence of drug abuse in the elderly (Whittington, 1984). Early beliefs that addicts "mature out" of their drug abuse (Winick, 1962) are unfounded (Schuckit and Moore, 1979).

Medication Misuse

The misuse of prescription and over-the-counter medicines is a much greater problem in the aged population than drug or alcohol abuse (LaRue, Dessonville, and Jarvik, 1985). Since all phases of drug intake are altered in the elderly—absorption, distribution, metabolism, and excretion—they are more likely, as we have noted, to react adversely to medications in even normal doses and to experience more side effects to a wider range of drugs. Community surveys of the aged show that they have a higher overall rate of legal drug intake than any other group (Warheit, Arey, and Swanson, 1976); although they comprised only 11.3 percent of the population, they consumed 25 percent of all prescribed medications at that time.

Abuse of prescription or legal drugs can be deliberate or inadvertent. Some may seek out drugs to abuse, obtaining medications from a number of sources. Others may not take medications as they are prescribed, perhaps through misunderstanding, ignorance, or lim-

---

[5]Although the ECA survey will eventually publish data on both community and institutionalized samples, it has done only community-dwelling groups so far. Since there may be a bias toward institutionalized care for older adults' mental health needs, the statistics cited above may underestimate actual prevalence.

Medication misuse is a serious problem among the aged.

ited financial resources. One study showed that more than half of a group of aged could not afford to take their medications the way they were prescribed (Brand, Smith, and Brand, 1977). A careful interview study of 141 well-functioning middle-class elderly people living in their own homes found that almost half reported having misused prescription or over-the-counter drugs at least once over a period of six months (Folkman, Bernstein, and Lazarus, 1987). The chance for misuse is believed to increase the more medications are taken and the more complex are the instructions. Dependence on medications can develop, particularly in anxious, depressed, and hypochondriacal older adults (LaRue, Dessonville, and Jarvik, 1985). One side effect of medications, confusion, may be misdiagnosed as dementia, and the side effect of lethargy may be mistaken for depression. More serious still is a recent finding from a report of the Department of Health and Human Services that 51 percent of deaths from drugs in the United States involve people over the age of sixty who make up only 17 percent of the population (Eastman, 1989).

Individuals of any age need to understand why they are taking a drug, what it is called, when and how often they should take it, and under what conditions, for example, before meals, on an empty stomach, and so on. Their comprehension of the instructions should be tested. An older woman who had been given an antibiotics prescription that cautioned against taking it before or after meals came to the attention of one of the authors. She believed that this warning meant she could not eat at all while taking the medication! Since visual acuity declines with age and susceptibility to glare in-

creases, printing instructions in small type on a shiny label—a common practice of drug companies—is bad. A chart on which the forgetful person can check off when he or she has taken medication, taped in a prominent place, serves as a useful reminder.

Hypochondriasis

Older adults complain of a multitude of physical problems, among them sore feet and backs, poor digestion, constipation, labored breathing, and cold extremities. All are to be taken seriously by responsible health professionals. But some of the elderly only believe themselves to be ill and complain unendingly about aches and pains for which there are no plausible physical causes. Indeed, it has been widely believed that hypochondriasis is especially common in the elderly. Busse and Blazer (1979) estimated the prevalence in community-residing elderly to be between 10 and 20 percent. New cases of hypochondriasis in the elderly are found to peak between the ages of sixty and sixty-five, with a greater proportion of women affected than men (Busse, 1976).

Some new data, however, suggest that the proportion of hypochondriasis is *not* greater in old age than at any other age (Siegler and Costa, 1985). In fact, the elderly as a whole tend to *under*report somatic symptoms rather than overreport them and often fail to seek help for serious illnesses (Besdine, 1980).

We do not imply that there are no older hypochondriacs, however. Longitudinal survey data indicate that health concerns do not increase with age but rather remain fairly stable over the life span (cf. stability of personality as discussed earlier, page 103); since actual health *problems* do increase with age without accompanying increases in *concerns* about health, such data support the idea that people do not become more hypochondriacal as they get older (Costa et al., 1987). Rather, as Siegler and Costa (1985) state, older persons who have many physical complaints have long-standing personality traits that predict such complaining. Their excessive somatic complaints appear to be associated with neuroticism or poor adjustment, which are *not* associated with age. In addition, the recent NIMH study (Regier et al., 1988) found only 0.1 percent of those aged sixty-five years or older to have Somatization Disorder, which is the same rate as in younger age groups; this confirms an earlier NIMH catchment area study (Myers et al., 1984) that found no increases in hypochondriasis among older adults. The discrepancy between this low rate and the much higher rates reported by others is probably due to stricter definitions used in the Regier et al. survey.

Causes of Hypochondriasis

It has been suggested that for older adults of this and previous generations, emotional concerns and distress are more difficult to talk about than physical ailments. The language they use to express unhappiness, then, is somatic. It is not that my feelings are hurt because my son never visits me. Rather, I can't keep my food down and my arms keep aching. Studies have indicated that somatizing is more frequent among lower-middle-class or semiskilled workers (Pilowsky, 1970) than among better-educated people, who presumably have greater psychological sophistication and are more accepting of nonmedical explanations for their psychological distress. Perhaps, then, hypochondriacal complaints in some older adults represent in part a cohort effect. The next generation of older people have lived in a social climate in which psychological problems are more openly discussed and in which seeing a "shrink" and taking medications for emotional disorders are more acceptable than they were to the previous generation. These future older adults may somatize even less.

Treatment of Hypochondriasis

No controlled studies of the treatment of hypochondriasis have been done. Clinicians generally agree, however, that reassuring the person that he or she is really healthy is generally useless, for these people are not swayed by negative laboratory tests or authoritative pronouncements from "official sources." Some tentative evidence suggests that ignoring the somatic complaints and concentrating instead on more positive aspects of existence can be helpful (Goldstein and Birnbom, 1976). I know that you're feeling bad and that your feet really hurt, but let's take a walk in Palisades Park anyway. Diverting activities may allow these individuals at least to function in the face of their perceived medical ills and perhaps obtain some positive satisfactions from life.

Insomnia

DSM-IIIR has added a new section on several types of sleep disorders. Of special interest for older adults are the Insomnia Disorders: Primary Insomnia, Insomnia Related to Another Mental Disorder (Nonorganic), and Insomnia Related to a Known Organic Factor. Insomnia is a frequent complaint among the elderly. One national survey found serious sleep disturbances in 25 percent of respondents aged sixty-five to seventy-nine as compared to 14 percent in the eighteen to thirty-four age group; another 20 percent have less serious but still problematic insomnia (Mellinger, Balter, and Uhlrnhuth, 1985).

The most common problems are awakening often at night, frequent early-morning awakenings, difficulties in falling asleep, and daytime fatigue (Miles and Dement, 1980). These complaints have been found to parallel the physiological changes that occur normally in the sleep patterns of older adults (Bootzin, Engle-Friedman, and Hazelwood, 1983). For example, the total time that the elderly devote to sleep appears to be somewhat less than or the same as that of younger age groups. But sleep is more often spontaneously interrupted as people grow older. Thus older people generally sleep less in relation to the total time they spend in bed. In addition, the elderly spend less absolute time in a phase known as rapid eye movement (REM) sleep; and stage 4 sleep, the deepest, is virtually absent. In general, elderly men appear to have more disturbances of their sleep than do women, a difference found to a lesser extent in young adults (Dement, Laughton, and Carskadon, 1981).

Causes of Insomnia

Besides the changes in sleep associated with aging, various illnesses, medications, caffeine, stress, anxiety, depression, lack of activity, and poor sleep habits may make insomniacs of older adults. Depressed mood—in the absence of a full-blown mood disorder—has been shown to be related to sleep disturbances in older adults, especially early-morning awakening.(Rodin, McAvay, and Timko, 1988). Pain, particularly that of arthritis, is a principal disrupter of their sleep (Prinz and Raskin, 1978). Sleep apnea, a respiratory disorder in which breathing ceases for a period of ten seconds or more repeatedly through the night, increases with age (Bliwise, Carskadon, Carey, and Dement, 1984). Whatever the cause of insomnia at any age, it is worsened by self-defeating actions like ruminating over it and counting the number of hours slept and those spent waiting to fall asleep.

Treatment of Insomnia

Over-the-counter medications and prescription drugs are taken by many older insomniacs. The little bottle of sleeping pills is a familiar companion to the many medications that sit on the night table. The elderly are major consumers of sleep aids, yet these rapidly lose their effectiveness and may in fact with continuous use make sleep light and fragmented. REM rebound sleep, an increase in REM sleep after prolonged reliance on drugs, is fitful (Bootzin, Engle-Friedman, and Hazelwood, 1983). In fact, medications can bring about what is called a drug-dependent insomnia. These so-called aids can also give people drug hangovers and increase respiratory difficulties, which in the elderly is a great hazard, given the increased prevalence of sleep apnea.

There is now considerable evidence that sleep medication is not the appropriate treatment for the chronic insomniac of any age, but particularly not for the elderly insomniac. Still, a U.S. Public Health Survey found sleep medications being prescribed for over 94 percent of nursing home residents (U.S. Public Health Service, 1976); in many instances such medication was being administered daily without evidence of a sleep disturbance (Cohen *et al.*, 1983).

Nonpharmacological treatment of sleep disorders in the elderly has not been researched very much, perhaps because workers have assumed that the normal age-related changes in sleep patterns noted earlier preclude effective intervention (Bootzin and Engle-Friedman, 1987). Nonetheless, improvement is possible. Explaining the nature of sleep and the changes that take place as a normal part of the aging process can reduce the worry that older persons have about their sleep pattern, concern which in itself can interfere with sleep. The therapist should also reassure them that it is not a calamity to go without sleep. It will not cause irreversible brain damage or insanity, fears that some people have. Some individuals are given relaxation training, to help them fall asleep, and instructions that will help them develop good sleep habits—rising at the same time every day; avoiding activities at bedtime that are inconsistent with falling asleep, such as watching television and reading; lying down only when sleepy; and if unable to go to sleep, getting up and going into another room. All these tactics can loosen the grip of insomnia in adults of all ages (Bootzin *et al.*, 1983, Morin and Azrin, 1988).

Suicide

Several factors put people in general at especially high risk for suicide: serious physical illness, feelings of hopelessness, social isolation, loss of loved ones, dire financial circumstances, and depression (see Chapter 9). Because these problems are widespread among the elderly, we should not be surprised to learn that suicide rates for people over sixty-five are high, perhaps three times greater than the rate for younger individuals (Osgood, 1984; Pfeiffer, 1977).

Although persons over age sixty-five comprise but 12 percent of the population, they commit 23 percent of all reported suicides in the United States (National Center for Health Statistics, 1985). An examination of cross-sectional data indicates that the suicide rate for males rises from youth and increases in a linear fashion with age (Atchley, 1982). White older men are more likely to commit suicide than any other group; their peak ages for taking their lives are from eighty to eighty-four. The rate for women peaks before they reach fifty

and declines steadily thereafter. Thus rates of suicide in white men increase sharply during old age, and rates for women decline somewhat. Throughout the life span men have higher suicide rates than women, but the difference is most notable in the old-old. Marked increases have also been noted recently among nonwhite men (Manton, Blazer, and Woodbury, 1987). What all of this means is that, as more and more people survive longer, the number of suicides in the over sixty-five age group could double over the next forty years (Blazer, Bachar, and Manton, 1986).

Older persons communicate their intentions to commit suicide less often than the young and make fewer attempts. When they do make an attempt, however, they are more successful in killing themselves. Suicide attempts by people younger than thirty-five fail more often than they succeed, but those of people over fifty are more likely to be lethal. Once people are past sixty-five, their attempts rarely fail (Butler and Lewis, 1982). Furthermore, the statistics given are probably underestimates; older adults have many opportunities to "give up" on themselves by neglecting their diet or medications, thus killing themselves in a more passive fashion. Moreover, Butler and Lewis (1982) have argued that suicide of older adults may more often be a rational or philosophical decision than that of younger people. Consider, for example, the elderly man who faces the intractable pain of a terminal illness and knows that with each passing day his medical care is using up more and more of the money he might otherwise leave to his widow and his family.

Intervention to prevent the suicide of an older person is similar to that discussed earlier. In general, the therapist tries to persuade the person to regard his problems in less desperate terms. Mental health professionals, who are usually younger and healthier, may unwittingly try less hard to prevent an older person's suicide attempt. But even the older person, once the crisis has passed, is usually grateful that he or she has another chance at living.

Sexuality and Aging

Frequency of Sexual Activity

Biases against the expression of sexuality in old age and disbelief in older people's capacity for sex have abounded in our culture. Men and women alike have been expected to lose interest in and capacity for sex once they reach their senior years. Some believe that old people are unable to enjoy anything more passionate than an affectionate hug and a kiss on the cheek. An older male who shows sexual interest in much younger women is called a "dirty old man." And, after the strong sexual

"I don't even feel the same way about myself as I did when I was twenty-one. How could I feel the same way about you?"

value placed on them when younger, older women are not considered especially sexual. Furthermore, their capacity for sexual arousal is confused with their postmenopausal inability to procreate.

The facts are that older people have considerable sexual interest and capacity. A recent study found that this held true even for many healthy eighty- to one-hundred-year-old individuals, the preferred activities being caressing and masturbation, with some occasions of sexual intercourse as well (Bretschneider and McCoy, 1988). As we review the data, it will be important to bear in mind that sexual interest and activity vary greatly in younger adults; disinterest or infrequent sex in an older person should not be blithely taken as evidence that older people are inherently asexual. The sixty-eight-year-old man who has no sex life may well have had little if any interest at age twenty-eight. Whether the person is twenty-eight or sixty-eight, one of the best predictors of continued sexual activity is past sexual enjoyment and frequency (Solnick and Corby, 1983).

The frequencies of sexual activity and interest in sex have been determined in several large-scale surveys, among them the famous Kinsey reports (Kinsey, Pomeroy, and Martin, 1948; Kinsey *et al.,* 1953) and the Duke Longitudinal Studies (Pfeiffer, Verwoerdt, and Wang, 1968, 1969; George and Weiler, 1980). The picture that emerges from these surveys varies according to when the study was conducted.

The earlier studies, such as the Kinsey reports and the first Duke longitudinal study, noted a decline in heterosexual intercourse, masturbation, and homosex-

ual intercourse beginning around age thirty and continuing across the life span. The belief that sex necessarily becomes less important to people in their middle years and in old age was not substantiated by later research, however. The second Duke study (George and Weiler, 1980) covered the years 1968 through 1974 and indicated no decline in the sexual activity of people between ages forty-six and seventy-one, and in fact indicated that 15 percent of older persons increased their sexual activity as they aged. Other studies show that about half of those between the ages of sixty and seventy-one still have regular and frequent intercourse (Comfort, 1980; Turner and Adams, 1988).

These facts can be interpreted in several ways. Clearly older people can be sexually active; even the earlier surveys indicated that. But it is noteworthy that the second Duke study did not reveal the decline of the first. The older people surveyed in the second study may have had less negative stereotyping to contend with, and they may have been healthier, both of which would be cohort effects. They may also have been more willing to discuss their sexual interests and activities with researchers because the cultural atmosphere has become more supportive, a time-of-measurement effect. Historical factors and sexual attitudes in society at large may affect sexuality among older adults. In one study seventy- and eighty-year-olds reported rates of intercourse much like those that Kinsey found in forty-year-olds in the 1940s and 1950s (Starr and Weiner, 1981). Perhaps sexual activity in the elderly will continue to rise as today's young grow older.

Older people still have both sexual interest and capacity.

Physiological Changes in Sexual Response with Aging
Among the volunteer subjects studied by Masters and Johnson (1966) were a number of older adults. We know a great deal about sexuality in older adults both from their physiological research and from more recent work by Comfort (1984), O'Donohue (1987), and Weg (1983). What is true of both sexes is that there are wide individual differences in sexual capacity and behavior among older adults, as indeed is the case for other areas in the lives of seniors. The following differences have been found between older and younger adults.

Men Older men take longer to have an erection, even when they are being stimulated in a way they like. They can maintain an erection longer before ejaculating than younger men, however, and the feeling that ejaculation is inevitable may disappear. It is not known whether physiological changes or control learned over the years explains this. During the orgasm phase, contractions are less intense and fewer in number, and the seminal fluid expelled is less in volume and under less pressure. Once orgasm has occurred, erection is lost more rapidly in older men, and the capacity for another erection cannot be regained as quickly as in younger men. In fact, the refractory period begins to lengthen in men in their twenties (Rosen and Hall, 1984).

Older men are capable of the same pattern of sexual activity as younger men, the major difference being that things take longer to happen, and when they do, there is less urgency. The way men and their partners view normal, age-related physiological changes may contrib-

ute to sexual dysfunction, however. If, for example, a man or his partner reacts with alarm to a slow buildup of sexual arousal, the stage is set for performance fears, which have been proclaimed a principal reason for psychosexual dysfunction. Unfortunately, changes that occur with aging are often misinterpreted as evidence that older men are becoming impotent. An important point to remember is that an older man does not lose his capacity for erection and ejaculation unless physical or emotional illness interferes (Kaiser *et al.,* 1988).

Women A number of age-related differences have been found in older women, but again none of them justifies the conclusion that they are incapable of a satisfactory sex life. In fact, like younger women, they are capable of at least as much sexual activity as are men. There are even reports of women becoming orgasmic for the first time in their lives at age eighty. Like men, older women need more time to become sexually aroused. Vaginal lubrication is slower and reduced because estrogen levels are lower, and there may be vaginal itching and burning. Steroid replacement can reduce many of these symptoms and be helpful against osteoporosis, a disease causing brittleness of the bones. There are risks, however, such as developing endometrial (uterine) cancer. Vaginal contractions during orgasm are fewer in number compared to those of younger women. Spastic contractions of the vagina and uterus, rather than the rhythmic ones of orgasm in younger women, can cause discomfort and even pain in the lower abdomen and legs. Direct stimulation of the clitoris may be painful in some older women. Like older men, older women return more quickly to a less-aroused state. There is some evidence that these physical changes are not as extensive in women who have been sexually stimulated on a regular basis once or twice a week throughout their sexual lives.

Age-Related Problems None of these changes, however, need have a significant negative impact on the enjoyment of sexual activity. Sexual relations of older people can be fulfilling, especially if the partners understand these age-related changes in physiological responding and do not view them as abnormal or in decline. Indeed, the ability of the older man to maintain an erection for longer periods of time may make intercourse more enjoyable for both him and his partner (Solnick and Corby, 1983). Nonetheless, physical illness can interfere, as it can in younger people. And because the elderly suffer from many chronic ailments, the potential for interference from illness and medications is greater (Mulligan *et al.,* 1988). This is particularly true for men; any disease that disrupts male hormone balance, the nerve pathways to the pelvic area, or blood supply to the penis can prevent erection. Tranquilizers and antihypertensive drugs can also bring about sexual dysfunctioning, as can fatigue and excessive drinking and eating. Older adults are sometimes challenged as well by having to adjust to disease-related bodily changes, such as alterations in the genitalia from treatment of urological cancer (Anderson and Wolf, 1986).

Fears of resuming sexual activities after a heart attack have inhibited older men and their lovers, but for most of them the fears are exaggerated (Friedman, 1978). Regrettably, physicians often fail to provide accurate information to postcoronary patients; for example, heart rate is frequently higher during activities such as climbing stairs than it is during intercourse. The situation for patients with congestive heart failure, in which the heart is unable to maintain an adequate circulation of blood in the tissues of the body, or to pump out venous blood returned by the venous circulation, does create for some a risk in intercourse, but less strenuous sexual activity is not a problem (Kaiser *et al.*, 1988).

Although women experience fewer physical problems than men, they are subject to all the myths about aging women's sexuality (Gatz, Pearson, and Fuentes, 1984). In addition, a heterosexual woman's sexual activity typically centers on having a partner and on whether or not he is well. Thus sexual activity of older women is less than that of older men, perhaps because they lack a partner or because they tend to be married to men older than they who may have significant health problems.

Treatment of Sexual Dysfunction

Making the facts of sexuality in old age available to the general public and to the professionals who look after their medical and mental health needs is likely to benefit many older people. As with younger adults, a degree of permission-giving is useful, especially in the light of widespread societal stereotypes of the asexuality of seniors. Physicians in particular have been guilty of telling the older patient to forget about sex or of not raising the issue when discussing the patient's adjustment, perhaps because of their own discomfort, lack of knowledge, or ageism. Clinicians need to bear in mind that the current cohort of people over sixty-five was socialized into sexuality at a time when the open discussion of sex was in no way as prevalent as it has been for the past twenty years. Nursing homes are often intolerant of sexuality among their residents; a married couple residing in the same nursing home may not be allowed to share a room (Comfort, 1984). The authors have also witnessed nurses in geriatric wards caution residents against stimulating themselves in public while at the same time not allowing for privacy.

Some older people will prefer not to be sexually ac-

tive, but for older adults who are experiencing and are troubled by sexual dysfunctions, indications are that they are good candidates for the type of sex therapy given by Masters and Johnson (Berman and Lief, 1976). Greater attention must be paid, however, to physical condition than is usual with younger adults, and this includes creative and open discussion of sexual techniques and positions that take into consideration physical limitations from illnesses such as arthritis (Zeiss, Zeiss, and Dornbrand, 1988).

General Issues in Treatment and Care

Access to Services

Older adults apparently do not receive their just share of mental health services (Redick and Taube, 1980). It has been estimated that only 2.7 percent of clinical services provided by psychologists go to older adults (VandenBos, Stapp, and Kilburg, 1981). Nearly 70 percent of psychologists report never seeing an older client (Dye, 1978; VandenBos, Stapp, and Kilburg, 1981). Moreover, of persons diagnosed as having a psychiatric condition, younger adults are more likely to receive treatment than are older adults (Myers and Weissman, 1980). Although they comprise about 12 percent of the U.S. population, older adults represent only 6 percent of those served by community mental health centers and only 2 percent of those seen by private therapists (Flemming, Rickards, Santos, and West, 1986; MacDonald, 1987; Roybal, 1988). This underservice is especially serious for minority and rural elderly.

Why this apparent underservice to the mental health needs of older adults? Some feel that those who are currently elderly are reluctant to define their problems in psychological terms, and that this lack of psychological mindedness keeps them out of therapy (Lawton, 1979). Also at fault is inadequate (though slowly improving) geriatric training for both medical and mental health professionals. The research that has been done, however, suggests that older adults are really not more reluctant to seek treatment (Knight, 1983; Zarit, 1980), nor are they more likely to drop out of treatment than other age groups (Knight, 1983).

The way services are provided may fail the elderly. Older adults often come to mental health centers through referrals. Yet research has shown that older people are less likely than younger adults to be referred (Ginsburg and Goldstein, 1974; Kucharski, White, and Schratz, 1979). The reimbursement system may pose some problems, for it is biased toward inpatient care and pays less for outpatient therapy, especially for mental health services (Gatz and Pearson, 1988). Moreover, Medicare does not cover supportive care for persons with Alzheimer's disease.

Various studies have shown that clinicians do not expect to treat the elderly with as much success as the young (Dye, 1978; Ford and Sbordonne, 1980; Settin, 1982). In one study older patients were rated by therapists as having more severe psychopathology, less motivation for treatment, a poorer prognosis, and less insight than younger patients (Karasu, Stein, and Charles, 1979). Yet, in fact, research does not suggest that psychotherapy of the elderly is less successful (Garfield, 1978). If the aged are viewed as having limited possibilities for improvement, they may not be treated. But a therapist may also lack the knowledge necessary to give good treatment to older people, which will keep them from improving.

Provision of Services

Admissions of older adults to state and county mental hospitals and to psychiatric wards of city hospitals have substantially decreased in the past few years. Older people needing mental health treatment now live in nursing homes or receive community-based care.

Nursing Homes

The evidence indicates that nursing homes are becoming the major locus for institutional care for the aged with severe chronic illnesses and mental disorders (Kramer, 1977). According to forecasts based on current estimates, the number of older people residing in nursing homes is expected to increase from 1.2 million in 1980 to 2.2 million by the turn of the century, and by the year 2050 to triple to 5.4 million (U.S. Bureau of the Census, 1984). Given these projected future increases, it does not appear that enough people are being trained to provide mental health services within these nursing homes. This is a matter of concern, particularly since only 30 percent of the nation's 15,000 nursing homes offer counseling as a routine service, and at least 50 percent of patients have diagnosed emotional disorders (National Center for Health Statistics, 1979).

Fifteen years ago the news media were filled with exposés and lawsuits concerning ineptitude and brutality in some nursing homes. Violations of building codes, neglect, overmedication, intimidation, excessive billing, and other unethical and illegal practices have made people wary about the honesty of nursing home operators and occasioned considerable anxiety among families and old people themselves about the nursing home as the best place to spend final months or years.

These concerns have been raised again by a recent federal government report from the Health Care Financing Administration (Rosenblatt and Spiegel, 1988). Among the negative findings about the nation's nursing homes are the following:

17 percent failed to give residents adequate privacy during treatments, and for the care of personal needs.

43 percent did not ensure that food was properly refrigerated and served under sanitary conditions.

30 percent did not provide consistent daily hygiene care.

18 percent failed to provide adequate care to residents with catheters.

22 percent did not provide rehabilitation services to prevent residents from losing the ability to walk or move about freely.

29 percent failed to administer drugs according to physician's instructions.

15 percent failed to keep electrical and mechanical equipment in safe operating condition.

25 percent failed to follow proper isolation procedures to reduce the spread of infection.

These problems are all the more serious given the frail state of most nursing home residents. Although objections to the report have been raised by various nursing home organizations (especially in California, where the figures were considerably worse than the national averages), the report drives home the point that many major problems are still with us.[6]

There may also be more subtle complications in placing someone in a nursing home, perhaps even when the more flagrant violations just noted are absent. A dramatic study by Blenker (1967) highlights the problem. Elderly people who came to a family service center were *randomly* assigned to one of three treatments, intensive, intermediate, and minimal. Intensive treatment involved the services of a nurse and a social worker, and intermediate somewhat less professional attention. Minimal treatment consisted of information and referral to community-based services. We might expect intensive treatment to be the most effective, but quite the

---

[6]More alarming still are the conditions of so-called board-and-care homes, institutional settings, usually in houses and seldom licensed, which are frequently crawling with cockroaches, totally lacking in professional supervision, and preying on the fears that some seniors have of being entirely without shelter. Oversight of these residential settings seems thus far to have fallen through the cracks of federal and state governments.

The deplorable conditions of some nursing homes have attracted considerable attention.
Some nursing homes, however, are well-run, attractive residences.

opposite was the case. After half a year the death rate of members of the intensive-care group was four times that of people in the minimal-care group! The intermediate-care group was less worse off than the intensive-care group; the death rate of its members was "only" twice that of the minimal-care group. What happened? It turned out that the major factor was being placed in an institution such as a nursing home. A person was much more likely to be institutionalized if a nurse and social worker were intensively involved in planning his or her care, and that is where excessive death rates were found. Since people had been assigned randomly to the three treatments, it is unlikely that the death rates were related to differences existing before treatment began.

What is there about nursing homes that contributes to such decline? First, relocation to a new setting is in itself stressful and is believed to play a role in increased mortality (Aldrich and Mendkoff, 1963; Schulz and Brenner, 1977). Once in the nursing home, the extent and nature of care discourage rehabilitation and even maintenance of whatever self-care skills and autonomous activities the resident may be capable of. For example, a resident able to feed herself, but slowly and with occasional spills, will be assisted at mealtime and even fed like a child to shorten the time devoted to serving meals, as well as to decrease the chances of messes on the floor and stains on the woman's clothing. The resident no longer thinks of herself as someone able to eat without help, which is likely to lead to still more loss of function and lowered morale. Muscles

themselves weaken and deteriorate through disuse (DeVries, 1975). Relatives of the resident, anxious to know that they have made the right decision and that Mom is being well cared for, are pleased by the tidiness and orderliness that are the result of excessive staff involvement in all details of living.

Custodial care may be excessive, but treatments to improve a patient's mental condition do not have priority. We know that depression is found in some older people, especially those in nursing homes. The type of psychoactive drug prescribed, however, is more likely to be a tranquilizer than an antidepressant; a less agitated, relatively inactive patient is easier to handle. Psychological interventions are virtually unheard of, for the staff either is untrained in their implementation or operates under the widely held assumption that such therapy is inappropriate for an old person.

In sum, all the problems of institutionalization are in bold and exaggerated relief in nursing homes. Independence is inadvertently, but with sad consequences, discouraged, and both physical and mental deteriorations, because they are expected, are obtained (see Box 17.4).

The prevalent myth is that families dump their older relatives into institutions at the first sign of frailty. The data indicate, however, that families usually explore all their alternatives and exhaust their own resources before they institutionalize an older relative. Thus the decision to institutionalize comes as a last resort, not as a first choice. Institutionalization is also believed to

BOX 17.4

LOSS OF CONTROL AND MINDLESSNESS IN NURSING HOMES

Ellen Langer has advanced an argument relating lack of control over life circumstances to the deterioration in both physical and mental health often found in some of the elderly. The reasoning behind her research program is this. Since we know that a perceived or actual lack of control leads to deterioration in adaptive behavior, at least some of what we regard as senility—the inactivity of elderly people and their poor adjustment to changing circumstances—may be caused by loss of control rather than progressive brain disease (Langer, 1981).

Langer points out that our society actually *teaches* the elderly—and sometimes the nonelderly as well!—that older adults are incompetent, or at least far less competent than they were before they became old. In our eagerness to help them, we seem to protect old people from having to make decisions that they might, in fact, be able to make. In our concern to protect them from physical harm, we arrange environments that require little effort to control. And, of course, we set ages for compulsory retirement, overlooking the large individual differences of old people. These practices, especially in a society that values competence and activity, do much to destroy an elderly person's belief that he or she is still effective, that indeed life is worthwhile.

Langer and Rodin (1976b) argue that the crucial problem in nursing homes is loss of opportunity to exercise control and personal responsibility. In one study patients were assigned a particular fifteen-minute period during which the nurse would be on call specifically for them, thus increasing each individual's control over his or her own caretaking. The health of these patients improved more than that of the control group, and they were more sociable (Rodin, 1980).

In another study Langer and Rodin (1976a) told one group of residents that they would be given a variety of decisions to make, instead of the staff's making decisions for them; they were also given plants to take care of. A control group was told how eager the staff was to take care of them; the plants they were given would be looked after by the staff. Although initially matched on variables such as health, these two groups of elderly residents differed three weeks later on several measures of alertness, happiness, and general well-being. Members of the group given enhanced responsibility—and presumably a sense of greater control—tested superior on these measures. Even more impressive was the finding eighteen months later that only half as many of the experimental group, seven out of forty-seven, had died as had members of the control group, thirteen out of forty-four. Moreover, the group given responsibilities continued to show better psychological and physical health (Rodin and Langer, 1977). Similar results have been reported for older adults living in independent and assisted sections of retirement villages (Slivinske and Fitch, 1987), and the general issue of personal autonomy has been focused on by a project of a private research and service organization, the Retirement Research Foundation's Personal Autonomy in Long Term Care Initiative (Hofland, 1988).

Not only may our treatment of old people engender in them a sense of lost control, but their repetitious, unchallenging environments—especially the surroundings of those who are hospital patients or live in nursing homes—may encourage a mode of cognitive functioning that Langer terms "mindlessness." Mindlessness is a kind of automatic information processing studied by cognitive psychologists, a mode of thinking that is adaptive when people are in situations that recur frequently, for example, remembering a familiar sequence such as tying one's shoes. In fact, attending to such overlearned activities—making the information processing conscious, not mindless—can actually *interfere* with performance! When a situation is novel and requires our attention, we want to operate *mindfully*.

What are the clinical implications of too much mindlessness, this mode of mental functioning that entails little cognitive effort? The elderly may be afforded too few opportunities to be thoughtful and to maintain an alert state of mind. Because of the restricted mobility of nursing home residents and hospital patients and because little is demanded of them, their experiences tend to be repetitious and boring. The Langer and Rodin nursing home research may well demonstrate that conscious *thinking* per se as well as perceived control is essential in maintaining emotional and physical well-being. Lack of control and mindlessness are probably related, for what is there really to think about when people believe that they have lost control over the events in their lives?

have a negative impact on family relations. One study, however, found that for a large number of families, moving the parent to a nursing home strengthened family ties and brought a renewed closeness between the parent and the child who was the primary caregiver. The care provided by the home alleviated the strain and pressure caused by the multiple physical or mental problems of the parent. In only about 10 percent of the families were relations worsened by the move (Smith and Bengston, 1979).

Community-Based Care

Since 95 percent of the aged at any given time reside in the community, what in general can be said about community-based care for them? Traditional individual,

family, and marital counseling, pet therapy,[7] and peer counseling have all been shown effective to some degree in relieving depression, anxiety, and loneliness; most of these therapies are described elsewhere. The frail elderly have an urgent need for help with their daily living arrangements. We discuss here some general principles that can foster the development of effective and comprehensive-community care (Zarit, 1980).

Comprehensive Community-Based Services Sound community care should provide a continuum of aid, ranging from information to services that allow the frail elderly to remain in their homes. Some communities are organized to provide telephone reassurance, daily phone calls to old persons living alone, to check that they are all right; home services, such as Meals on Wheels, which brings a hot meal a day to the old person's door, visits from homemakers who cook meals and see to the household, shopping help from young people, light repair work by volunteers; a community day center for older people, which may also serve a hot lunch and provide help with state and federal forms; sheltered

housing, apartments in which several old people may live together semi-independently; home visits by health professionals and social workers, who can assess the actual needs of old people and treat them; and regular social visits from community neighbors. A range of available services allows a true match with the needs of the older person. Otherwise he or she will have too much or not enough help. There is some research indicating that community-based outreach projects can enhance the quality of life of elderly people and reduce their dependency on institutional care (e.g., Knight, 1983; Nocks, Learner, Blackman, and Brown, 1986).

Working with the members of families who care for older relatives is especially important. They need information on how to handle problem situations and on how to keep the older relative in poor health as independent as possible. They also need support and encouragement, opportunities to vent their feelings of guilt and resentment. Some may need permission to take time off, or to feel that they will be able to, should the pressure become too great. Especially stressful is caring for a person with Alzheimer's disease (Anthony-Bergstone, Zarit, and Gatz, 1988; Gwynther and George, 1986; Zarit, Todd, and Zarit, 1986).

Coordination of Services Mere availability of services is not enough, however. They must be coordinated, and regrettably they are not in most localities. All too often an older person and his or her family are shuffled from one agency to another, getting lost in Kafkaesque bureaucracies. In fact, even professionals who have experience with the system often have difficulties working

---

[7]Pet therapy builds on age-old observations that people who have pets to take care of benefit from the companionship of their animals. The dependence of a domesticated animal on a human being can help the person physically and emotionally, by keeping him or her active and feeling useful. A pet's acceptance of us is usually more nearly unconditional than that given by people. Sheer physical contact with an animal is also beneficial. We do not argue that older adults, or anyone else, are better off taking care of household pets than having human companions. But the responsibility and pleasure of taking care of a cat, dog, or bird does enhance simple daily living, fosters healthful thoughts and actions (Brickel, 1984), and improves the morale of those living alone (Goldmeier, 1988).

through it to get needed services for their clients! Moreover, frustrating rules can interfere with the very goals for which programs were instituted. In California, for example, Medicare does not always pay for rehabilitation services, such as physical therapy after a broken hip has healed. As a consequence, many older people do not regain the function that they might have and may suffer additional physical and emotional deterioration, exacerbations that require more expensive services.

Issues Specific to Therapy with Older Adults

As mentioned throughout this chapter, discussing a group of people who share only chronological age runs the risk of overlooking important differences in their backgrounds, developmental histories, and personalities. Although adults over sixty-five do have in common physical and psychological characteristics that make them different from younger adults, they are nonetheless *individuals,* each of whom has lived a long time and experienced unique joys and sorrows. In spite of this uniqueness, there are a few general issues important to consider in the conduct of therapy with older people. They can be divided into issues of content and issues of process (Zarit, 1980).

Content

The incidence of organic brain syndromes does increase with age, but other mental health problems of older adults are not that different from those experienced earlier in life. Although the clinician should appreciate how physical incapacities and medications may intensify psychological problems, consistency and continuity from earlier decades of the older person's life should be noted too.

The clinician must also bear in mind that the emotional distress of older adults may be a realistic reaction to problems in living. Medical illnesses can create irreversible difficulties in walking, seeing, and hearing. Finances may be a problem, particularly for the older woman who lives alone. To suggest that all psychological distress is pathological rather than an understandable response to real-life problems is unfair and inaccurate.

The older person's worries about impending death are another realistic source of stress. Much psychological turmoil about dying can be reduced by encouraging the client to attend to such concrete details as ensuring that estate and will are in order and that funeral or cremation plans are explicit and satisfactory. If clients deplore and dread the artificial life-support treatments sometimes applied in terminal illnesses, the therapist should suggest that they consider a Living Will to provide to those they choose to be responsible for them.

Family members are wisely included in discussions, for their own concerns about death often influence their dealings with the old person.

Older clients may also be counseled to examine their lives from a philosophical or a religious perspective. Leo Tolstoy was but one of many people who became increasingly religious as they grew old. Philosophical and religious perspectives can help the client transcend the limitations aging imposes on human existence. When the person is finally dying, discussions of the meaning of the individual's life can facilitate self-disclosure and enhance his or her sense of well-being and personal growth. The loved ones, who will experience the inevitable loss, will also benefit from such discussions.

Process

Many clinicians have asked whether older adults require entirely different treatments from younger adults, or whether they can benefit from the same treatments. We have already indicated that traditional individual, family, and marital therapies are effective with the elderly (Gatz *et al.,* 1985). Some clinicians make adaptations and focus on here-and-now problems. They hold that therapy with the elderly needs to be more active and directive, providing information, taking the initiative in seeking out agencies for necessary services, and helping the client and his or her family through the maze of federal and local laws and offices that are in place to help the aged.

In recent years several books have been published on therapy with older adults (Herr and Weakland, 1979; Hussian, 1981; Knight, 1986; Lewinsohn and Teri, 1983; Sherman, 1981; Storandt, 1983; Zarit, 1980). Establishing a good relationship with the older person; providing constructive contingencies in the surroundings; fostering a sense of control, self-efficacy, and hope; and elucidating a sense of meaning are believed to be the common mechanisms of change (Gatz *et al.,* 1985).

Summary

Until recently the psychological problems of older people have been neglected by mental health professionals. As the proportion of people who live beyond sixty-five continues to grow, it will become ever more important to learn about the disorders suffered by some older people and the most effective means of preventing or ameliorating them. Although physical deterioration is an obvious aspect of growing old, it appears that most of the emotional distress to which old people are prone is psychologically produced.

Serious brain disorders affect a very small minority

of older people, fewer than 10 percent. Two principal ones have been distinguished, dementia and delirium. In dementia the person's intellectual functioning goes downhill; memory, abstract thinking, and judgment deteriorate. If the dementia is progressive, as most are, the individual seems another person altogether and is in the end oblivious to his surroundings. A variety of diseases can cause this deterioration, the most important of which is an Alzheimer-type disease, in which cortical cells waste away. In delirium there is sudden clouding of consciousness and other problems in thinking, feeling, and behaving—fragmented and undirected thought, incoherent speech, inability to sustain attention, hallucinations, illusions, disorientation, lethargy or hyperactivity, and mood swings. The condition is reversible, provided the underlying cause is self-limiting or adequately treated. Brain cells malfunction but are not necessarily destroyed. Causes include overmedication, infection of brain tissue, high fevers, malnutrition, dehydration, endocrine disorders, head trauma, and cerebrovascular problems.

The treatments of these two disorders are quite different from each other. If delirium is suspected, there should be a search for the cause so that the pathogenic situation can be rectified. Dementia, on the other hand, usually cannot be treated, but the person and the family affected by the disease can be counseled on how to make the remaining time reasonable and even rewarding. If adequate support is given to caregivers, many dementia patients can be looked after at home. There usually comes a time, however, when the burden of care impels most families to place the person in a nursing home or hospital.

Older people suffer from the entire spectrum of psychological disorders, in many instances brought with them into their senior years. The newer cognitive behavior therapies are being applied to depression of the elderly, and results so far are encouraging.

Although not as widespread as depression, paranoia is a problem for older people and for those who have a relationship with them. In contrast to the persecutors of young paranoids, distant agencies such as the F.B.I. and aliens from outer space, those of older individuals live closer to home—the neighbor who opens her mail, the ungrateful son who is conniving to steal his mother's money, the physician who prescribes drugs that pollute the mind. Paranoia is sometimes brought on by brain damage in dementia, but more often it is apparently caused by psychological factors. Paranoia may be a reaction to hearing difficulties. If I cannot hear what they are saying—especially if I do not acknowledge my hearing problem—perhaps it is because they are whispering nasty things about me. Isolation as well can be a factor;

when a person has little social intercourse, and indeed many old people have too little, it is difficult to verify impressions and suspicions, setting the stage for delusions to develop. Other psychological disorders discussed are schizophrenia; substance abuse, in particular the misuse of medication; hypochondriasis; and insomnia.

White males, as they enter old age, are at increasing risk of suicide. More of the suicide attempts of old people result in death than do those of younger people. Mental health professionals, most of them younger than sixty-five, may assume that the old and debilitated have nothing to live for. This attitude may reflect their own fear of growing old.

Considerable mythology has surrounded sexuality and aging, the principal assumption being that at the age of sixty-five sex becomes improper, unsatisfying, and even impossible. Evidence indicates otherwise. Barring serious physical disability, older people, even those well into their eighties, are capable of deriving enjoyment from sexual intercourse and other kinds of lovemaking. There are differences as people age; it takes longer to become aroused and the orgasm is less intense. Dissemination of accurate information about sexual capacity in old age would probably prevent much unnecessary sexual dysfunction and disinterest.

Nursing homes and other extended-care facilities often do little to encourage residents to maintain or enhance whatever skills and capacities they still have; both physical and mental deteriorations are the rule. Nowadays care is provided in the community whenever possible. There should be comprehensive services, such as Meals on Wheels, regular home visits by health professionals, and support for caregivers. Such services should be coordinated so that people do not have to confront a bureaucratic maze. And intervention should be minimal so that old people remain as independent as their circumstances permit.

Many older people can benefit from psychotherapy, but several issues specific to treating the older adult should be borne in mind. The emotional distress of the elderly is sometimes realistic in content. They have often suffered irreplaceable losses and face real medical and financial problems; it is unwise always to attribute their complaints to a psychopathological condition. Death is a more immediate issue as well. As for the process of therapy, clinicians should sometimes be active and directive, providing information and seeking out the agencies that give the social services needed by their clients. Therapy should also foster a sense of control, self-efficacy, and hope and should help the older person elucidate a sense of meaning as the end of life is approached.

Adolph Gottlieb. *Hands of Oedipus.* 1943. © 1980 Adolph and Esther Gottlieb Foundation. New York. Photo: O. Nelson.

Intervention

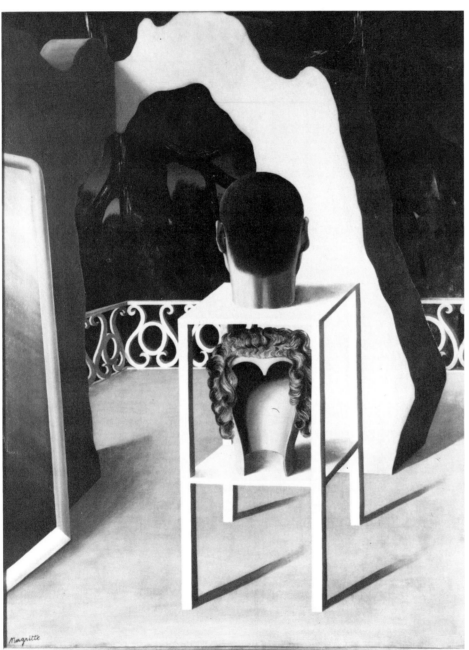

Chapter 18

Insight Therapy

The Placebo Effect
Psychoanalytic Therapy
   Basic Techniques and Concepts on Psychoanalysis
   Ego Analysis
   Evaluation of Analytic Therapy
Humanistic and Existential Therapies
   Carl Rogers's Client-Centered Therapy
   Existential Therapy
   Gestalt Therapy
Summary

Throughout our account of the various psychopathologies, we have considered the ways in which therapists of varying persuasions attempt to prevent, lessen, and even eliminate mental and emotional suffering. The Chapter 2 descriptions of the several paradigms of treatment—physiological, psychoanalytic, learning, cognitive, and humanistic—laid the groundwork. As we have seen in Chapters 6 through 17, some forms of intervention are more appropriate than others for particular problems. Through our understanding of physiological processes, new parents now have means of halting or at least reducing certain forms of genetically transmitted mental retardation. And through better understanding of the process of learning, retarded children are now acquiring more cognitive, social, and self-care skills than was earlier thought possible. Psychoanalytic theory helps therapists in treating dissociative disorders, for it alerts them to the possibility that an amnesic patient, for example, cannot remember because the pain of certain past events forced them to be massively repressed. Humanistic treatment helps clients explore the depth and causes of their psychological pain and encourages them to take action, make choices, and assume responsibility for bettering their lives.

Now it is time to take a closer, more intensive look at therapy, to consider issues of general importance, to explore controversies, and to make comparisons. What we have studied so far of psychopathology and treatment should enable us to do so with some sophistication and perspective.

Shorn of its theoretical complexities, any psychotherapy "is a situation in which one human being (the therapist) tries to act in such a way as to enable another human being to act and feel differently" (Wachtel, 1977, p. 271). The basic assumption, indeed article of faith, is that particular kinds of verbal and nonverbal exchanges in a trusting relationship can achieve goals such as reducing anxiety and eliminating self-defeating or dangerous behavior.

Simple as this definition may seem, there is little general agreement about what *really* constitutes psychotherapy. A person's next-door neighbor might utter the same words of comfort as would a clinical psychologist, but should we regard this as psychotherapy? In what way is psychotherapy different from such nonprofessional reassurance? Is the distinction made on the straightforward basis of whether the dispenser of reassurance has a particular academic degree or license? Does it relate to whether the giver of information has a theory that dictates or at least guides what he or she says? Does it depend on how sound the basic assumptions of the theory are? These are difficult questions, and, as in other areas of abnormal psychology, there is less than perfect agreement among professionals.

It is important to note at the outset that the people who seek or are sent for *professional* help are probably those who have tried the nonproessional avenues to feeling better and have failed to obtain relief. Before an individual goes to a therapist, he or she has confided in friends or in a spouse, perhaps spoken to the family doctor, has often consulted with a member of the clergy, and may have tried several of the vast number of self-help books and programs that are so popular nowadays. For most people in psychological distress, one or more

What is the distinction between the verbal interchange of client and therapist and of two friends?

A traditional psychoanalytic therapy session.

of these options provide enough relief, and they seek no further help (Bergin, 1971). But for others these attempts fall short, and individuals are left feeling helpless, often hopeless. These are the people who go to mental health clinics, university counseling centers, and the private offices of independent practitioners. Whatever the nature and efficacy of any form of psychotherapy, we should keep in mind that professionals generally have as clients the especially troubled people who have not been helped by other means.

Therapeutic activities and theories are very great in number. There are scores, perhaps hundreds, of schools of therapy, each with its band of enthusiastic adherents (both therapists and patients) proposing procedures ranging from screaming and writhing nude on the floor to forced inactivity and sleep for several weeks. One could almost say "You name it, someone thinks it's therapeutic." Because it would be impossible and unenlightening to examine every variation, we have opted for a focused review of the field, presenting sufficient detail about the major approaches to allow a grasp of the basic issues and an overall perspective on the therapeutic enterprise.

London (1964; 1986) categorizes psychotherapies into *insight* and *action* (behavioral) therapies. Behavior therapy is the subject of Chapter 19. **Insight therapy,** which is discussed in depth in this chapter, assumes that behavior, emotions, and thoughts become disordered because people do not adequately understand what motivates them, especially when their needs and drives conflict. Insight therapy tries to help them discover the true reasons they behave, feel, and think as they do.

The assumption is that greater awareness of motivations will yield greater control over and subsequent improvement in thought, emotion, and behavior. The emphasis is less on changing people directly than on uncovering the causes of their distress—both historical and current. To facilitate such insights, therapists of different theoretical persuasions have employed a variety of techniques, ranging from the free association of psychoanalysis to the reflection of feelings practiced in client-centered therapy.

Our principal concern in this chapter and the next is individual therapy, that is, therapy conducted by a clinician with one patient or client. But it should be noted that nearly everything said in these two chapters is relevant also for therapy in groups, a subject dealt with more completely as one of three principal topics in Chapter 20.

The Placebo Effect

For reasons that will become clear, it is appropriate to begin our discussion of intervention with what has become known as the ***placebo effect.*** The term refers to improvement in physical or psychological condition that is attributable to a patient's expectations of help rather than to any specific active ingredient in a treatment. Frank (1973) relates placebo effects to faith healing in prescientific or nonscientific societies. For centuries, suffering human beings have derived benefit from making pilgrimages to sanctified places such as Lourdes and from ingesting sometimes foul-smelling concoctions.

Many people tend to dismiss placebo reactions as "not real" or second-best. After all, if a person has a tension headache, what possible benefit can he or she hope to get from a pill that is totally devoid of chemical action or direct physiological effect? The fact is, however, that such benefits can sometimes be significant and even long lasting. For example, Lasagna and his colleagues (1954) reported impressive relief from pain in surgical patients receiving saline injections. And Frank (1973) furnishes extensive evidence attesting to improvement in a variety of physical and mental problems after ingestion of placebo "sugar pills" and from exposure to other ministrations that, in themselves, could not possibly account for this relief.

The definition of placebo drawn from pharmacological research, however, must be tempered with the observation that in psychotherapy, the expectation of being helped can be an active ingredient! If the theory adopted by the therapist holds positive expectancy of improvement to be an active ingredient, then improvement arising from the expectancy would, by definition, *not* be considered a placebo effect. Indeed, Lambert, Shapiro, and Bergin (1986) argue that "placebo factors" should be replaced with the concept "common factors" in the study of the effects of psychotherapy. They remind us of Rosenthal and Frank's (1956) early caveat that a placebo as something therapeutically inert can be understood only from the standpoint of a particular *theory* of change, and they define common factors as "those dimensions of the treatment setting . . . that are not specific to a particular technique. Those factors that are common to most therapies (such as expectation for improvement, persuasion, warmth and attention, understanding, encouragement, etc.) should not be viewed as theoretically *inert* nor as *trivial;* they are central to psychological treatments and play an active role in patient improvement" (p. 163). Indeed, patients in so-called placebo control groups, as Lambert *et al.* (1986) point out, generally improve more than patients in no treatment groups—though often not as much as patients in treatment groups.

The place of placebo control groups in psychotherapy research is an often-debated and complex topic, the intricacies of which are beyond the scope of this book. Let it be noted, though, that a study that compares a particular therapy to no treatment at all and finds that therapy brings more improvement indeed tells us something important, namely, that being treated is better than receiving no treatment. But a given therapy usually tries to create improvement in a particular way, by removing the person's defenses, by easing the individual's way to self-actualization, by enhancing responsible choices, by counterconditioning fears, and so forth. To determine whether these *processes* are at work and are effective, a study does need a control group of patients who are primarily instilled with expectancies of help, who believe that something worthwhile and beneficial is being done for them. *All* therapies derive at least some of their power from the faith that people have in the healer and from their profound hope to get better.

Psychoanalytic Therapy

Despite the numerous critical attacks made on psychoanalytic theory and the claims that psychoanalytic therapy has limited effectiveness, psychoanalysis and its many offshoots remain an important force in American psychiatry and clinical psychology. In this section we summarize and evaluate the important elements of both

classical—that is, traditional—psychoanalysis and ego analysis.

Basic Techniques and Concepts in Psychoanalysis

The overall purpose of psychoanalysis derives from the Freudian assumption that psychopathology develops when people remain unaware of their true motivations and fears. They can be restored to healthy functioning only by becoming conscious of what has been repressed. When people can understand *what* is motivating their actions, they have a greater number of choices. Where id is, let there ego be, to paraphrase a maxim of psychoanalysis. The ego, being the primarily conscious, deliberating, choosing portion of the personality, can better guide the individual in rational, realistic directions if repressions are at a minimum.

Wachtel's (1977) woolly mammoth (see page 41) is an apt metaphor for the unresolved, buried conflicts from which psychoanalytic theory assumes neurotic problems arise. The proper focus of therapy then is not on the presenting problem, such as fears of being rejected, but on unconscious conflicts existing in the psyche from childhood. Only by lifting the repression can the person confront the underlying problem and reevaluate it in the context of his or her adult life.

Free Association

Psychoanalysts use a number of techniques to help the patient recover conflicts that have been repressed. Perhaps the best known and most important is free association: the patient, reclining on a couch, is encouraged to give free rein to thoughts and feelings, and to verbalize whatever comes to mind. The assumption is that with enough practice free association will facilitate the uncovering of unconscious material.[1] The analysand must follow the fundamental rule of reporting thoughts and feelings as accurately as possible, without screening out the elements he feels are unimportant or shameful. Freud assumed that thoughts and memories occurred in associative chains and that recent ones reported first would ultimately trace back to earlier crucial ones. In order to get to these earlier events, however, the therapist has to be very careful not to guide or direct the patient's thinking, and he or she usually sits behind the patient to minimize such influence. Ford and Urban (1963) have

---

[1]The adjective "free," however, does not mean uncaused, only free from conscious censorship and control. "As an avowed determinist, Freud believed that unconscious mechanisms governed by psychological laws produced the flow of free associations. Free associations are thus not truly free" (Morse, 1982, p. 215). Indeed, it is the assumption that they are *not* free that makes this technique important in psychoanalysis.

paraphrased the analyst's directions for free association.

In ordinary conversation, you usually try to keep a connecting thread running thorugh your remarks, excluding any intrusive ideas or side issues so as not to wander too far from the point, and rightly so. But in this case you must talk differently. As you talk various thoughts will occur to you which you like to ignore because of certain criticisms and objections. You will be tempted to think, "That is irrelevant or unimportant or nonsensical," and to avoid saying it. Do not give in to such criticism. Report such thoughts in spite of your wish not to do so. Later, the reason for this injunction, the only one you have to follow, will become clear. Report whatever goes through your mind. Pretend that you are a traveler, describing to someone beside you the changing views which you see outside the train window. (p. 168)

Resistance

But blocks do arise, virtually thrusting themselves across the thoughts supposedly given free rein. Patients may suddenly change the subject or be unable to remember how a long-ago event ended. They will try any tactic to interrupt the session, remaining silent, getting up from the couch, looking out the window, making jokes and personal remarks to the analyst. Patients may even come late or "forget" sessions altogether. Such obstacles to free association—*resistances*—were noted by Freud and contributed to the development of the concept of repression. He asserted that interference with free association can be traced to unconscious control over sensitive areas; it is precisely these areas that psychoanalytic therapists must thoroughly probe. Indeed, in some respects these resistances, these failures in free association, provide the analyst with the most critical information about the patient.

Analysis of Dreams

Akin to free association is dream analysis. Freud assumed that during sleep the ego defenses are lowered, allowing repressed material to come forth, usually in disguised form. Concerns of the patient are often expressed in symbols (*latent content*) to help protect the conscious ego from the true significance of dream material. The *manifest content* of dreams—what is immediately apparent—may be regarded as a sort of compromise between repression of true meaning and a full expression of unconscious material. The cutting down of a tall tree (manifest content) might symbolize the patient's anger toward his father (latent content). The content of dreams, then, is distorted by unconscious defensive structures, which, never completely abandoned, even in sleep, continue their fight to protect the ego from repressed impulses.

Interpretation and Denial

As presumably unconscious material begins to appear, another technique comes into play, *interpretation.* According to Freud, this stage helps the person face the hitherto repressed and emotionally loaded conflict. At the "right time" the analyst begins to point out to the patient his defenses and the underlying meaning of his dreams. Great skill is required lest an interpretation be offered too early, for the patient may so totally reject it that he leaves treatment. To be effective, interpretations should reflect insights that the patient is on the verge of making himself; they can then be claimed by the patient as his own, rather then coming from the analyst. Presumably an interpretation that a patient attributes to himself will be more readily accepted and thereby have a stronger therapeutic effect.

Interpretation then is the analyst's principal weapon against the continued use of defense mechanisms. She points out how certain verbalizations of the patient relate to repressed unconscious material, and she suggests what the manifest content of dreams *truly* means. If the interpretation is timed correctly, the patient can start to examine the repressed impulse in the light of present-day reality. In other words, he begins to realize that he no longer has to fear the expression of the impulse.

Feeling safe under the undemanding conditions arranged by the analyst, the patient presumably uncovers more and more repressed material. Interpretations are held to be particularly helpful in establishing the meaning of the resistances that disturb the patient's free association. The therapist may, for example, point out how the patient manages to avoid a topic, and it is common for the analysand to deny the interpretation. Interestingly, this denial is sometimes interpreted as a sign that the therapist's interpretation is correct rather than incorrect. In the slow process of "working through" the disturbing conflicts, of confronting them again and again, the patient gradually faces up to the validity of the analyst's interpretations, often with great emotion.

Determining when an analysand's *denial* of an interpretation means that it is correct is, in our opinion, one of the thorniest problems in psychoanalysis. When, in truth, is it appropriate to consider that a No is really a Yes? Great abuse is possible here, and psychoanalysts are often satirized for these decisions. But the analyst, like any clinician, does not judge in a vacuum. She formulates hypotheses over time about the patient, noticing how one problem area relates to others. Like a detective, the therapist searches for clues in a slowly developing picture, and every statement, every gesture of the patient, is viewed within this scheme. A patient's No is considered a Yes only in the *context* of other ideas already formed by the analyst. And in part the analyst bases her judgment on how vigorously the patient

BOX 18.1

EXCERPT FROM A PSYCHOANALYTIC SESSION, AN ILLUSTRATION OF TRANSFERENCE

Patient: (a fifty-year-old male business executive): I really don't feel like talking today.

Analyst: (Remains silent for several minutes, then) Perhaps you'd like to talk about why you don't feel like talking.

Patient: There you go again, making demands on me, insisting I do what I just don't feel up to doing. (Pause) Do I always have to talk here, when I don't feel like it? (Voice becomes angry and petulant) Can't you just get off my back? You don't really give a damn how I feel, do you?

Analyst: I wonder why you feel I don't care.

Patient: Because you're always pressuring me to do what I feel I can't do.

Comments. This excerpt must be viewed in context. The patient had been in therapy for about a year, complaining of depression and anxiety. Although extremely successful in the eyes of his family and associates, he himself felt weak and incompetent. Through many sessions of free association and dream analysis, the analyst had begun to suspect that the patient's feelings of failure stemmed from his childhood experiences with an extremely punitive and critical father, a man even more successful than the client, and a person who seemed never to be satisfied with his son's efforts. The exchange quoted was later interpreted by the analyst as an expression of resentment by the patient of his *father's* pressures on him and had little to do with the analyst himself. The patient's tone of voice (petulant), as well as his overreaction to the analyst's gentle suggestion that he talk about his feelings of not wanting to talk, indicated that the patient was angry not at his analyst but at his father. The expression of such feelings to the analyst, that is, transferring them from the father to the analyst, was regarded as significant by the therapist and was used in subsequent sessions in helping the patient to reevaluate his childhood fears of expressing aggression toward his father.

denies an interpretation, generally regarding as defensive a denial expressed in an excessive manner. As Queen Gertrude in Shakespeare's *Hamlet* commented, "The lady doth protest too much, methinks" (Act III, Scene 2).

Transference

The core of psychoanalytic therapy is the ***transference neurosis.*** Freud noted that his patients sometimes acted toward him in an emotion-charged and unrealistic way. For example, a patient much older than Freud would behave in a childish manner during a therapy session. Although these reactions were often positive and loving, many times they were quite negative and hostile. Since these feelings seemed out of character with the ongoing therapy relationship, Freud assumed that they were relics of attitudes *transferred* to him from those held in the past toward important people in the patient's history, primarily parents. That is, he felt that patients responded to him *as though* he were one of the important people in their past. Freud utilized this transference of attitudes, which he came to consider an inevitable aspect of psychoanalysis, as a means of explaining to patients the childhood origin of many of their concerns and fears. This revelation and explanation tended also to help lift repressions and allow the confrontation of hitherto buried impulses. In psychoanalysis, transfer-

ence is regarded as essential to a complete cure. Indeed, it is precisely when analysts notice transference developing that they take hope that the important neurotic conflict from childhood is being approached.

Analysts encourage the development of transference by intentionally remaining shadowy figures, generally sitting behind the patient while the patient free-associates and serving as relatively blank screens on which the important persons in the neurotic conflicts can be projected. They take pains to reveal as little as possible of their own personal lives. Analysts are also caring persons, which may remind the patient of attributes, real or hoped for, in his or her parents. Because the therapy setting is so different from the childhood situation, analysts can readily point out to patients the irrational nature of their fears and concerns (see Box 18.1).

Countertransference

Related to transference is ***countertransference,*** the feelings of the analyst toward the patient. The analyst must take care lest she lay her own emotional vulnerabilities on the analysand. Her own needs and fears must be recognized for what they are; she should have enough understanding of her own motivations to be able to see the client clearly, without distortion. The problem has been well articulated in a discussion of therapy with depressed people, during which countertransference is a continuing challenge to a therapist.

Depressed patients bring their hopelessness and despair into therapy, and the therapist may be affected. If the depression improves slowly, or not at all, the therapist may feel guilty, angry, and/or helpless. After seeing several severely depressed patients in a day, the therapist may feel quite drained and eventually may become unwilling to work in the future with similar patients. Suicidal patients can evoke particularly difficult countertransferences. . . .

One safeguard against such difficulties is the therapist's continuing awareness of these feelings and their relation to his or her own psychodynamics. A suffering patient may mobilize the therapist's fantasy of being able to heal and earn gratitude, deftly and single-handedly; or may stir up the therapist's anger at the existence of suffering. An abiding awareness of these reactions will help the therapist maintain the patience and satisfaction with small gains that are necessary for conducting psychotherapy with severely depressed patients. At the same time, the therapist must avoid overstepping his/her role and trying to do all the work for an apparently weak patient (Jacobson and McKinney, 1982, p. 215).

For this reason a "training analysis," or *Lehranalyse,* is a formal part of the education of an analyst. Although many therapists of different theoretical persuasions consider it useful to have been in therapy themselves, a personal therapy is *required* in analytic training institutes. It is essential that analysts reduce to a minimum the frequency and intensity of countertransference toward their clients.

The Detachment of the Analyst
The analyst, moreover, must *not* become actively involved in helping the analysand deal with everyday problems. He assiduously avoids any intervention, such as a direct suggestion how to behave in a troublesome situation. Short-term relief might deflect the patient's efforts to uncover the repressed conflicts. Freud was emphatic on this point, writing in 1918 that the analyst must take care not to make the patient's life so comfortable that he or she is no longer motivated to delve into the unconscious. He put it this way in his criticism of nonanalytic helpers.

Their one aim is to make everything as pleasant as possible for the patient, so that he may feel well there and be glad to take refuge there again from the trials of life. In so doing, they make no attempt to give him more strength for facing life and more capacity for

carrying out his actual tasks in it. In analytic treatment, all such spoiling must be avoided. As far as his relations with the physician are concerned, the patient must be left with unfulfilled wishes in abundance. It is expedient to deny him precisely those satisfactions which he desires most intensely and expresses most importunately. (Freud, 1955, p. 164)

The detachment of the analyst has often been ridiculed or misinterpreted, which does an injustice both to analytic theory and to the people who apply it. When a person is in pain and is needy, the initial impulse is, figuratively, to take the sufferer into one's arms and comfort him or her, providing reassurance that all will be well, that the client will be taken care of. But the truth is that others have probably already tried to provide solace; if sympathy and support were going to help, they probably would already have done so. The analyst must work hard to *resist* showing concern through expressions of support and with concrete advice. Moreover, acting in a directive fashion will interfere with transference, for the therapist necessarily becomes less of a blank screen if he expresses opinions, voices objections, and gives advice and direction. The distance kept by the analyst from the analysand is intended for his or her betterment. This stratagem is consistent with analytic theory and is rather rigidly applied by the more orthodox of psychoanalysts (Box 18.2).

Concluding Comment
Psychoanalysis is directly opposite in thrust to behavior therapy, for behavior therapists, unconcerned with factors that are presumed by analysts to be buried in the unconscious, concentrate precisely on what analysts ignore, namely, helping patients change their attitudes, feelings, and overt behavior in concrete, current life situations. What the analyst, and to a large degree the ego analyst, terms "supportive therapy," the behavior therapist regards as the essence of therapy. By the same token, what the behavior therapist sees as unnecessary and even detrimental to the client—digging into the repressed past and withholding advice on how to make specific changes in the here and now—is judged by the analyst to be essential to complete psychotherapeutic treatment.

Ego Analysis

After Freud's death the most important modifications in psychoanalytic theory came from a group generally referred to as ego analysts. Their views are often seen as constituting contemporary Freudian psychoanalysis. The major figures in this loosely formed movement in-

BOX 18.2

WHAT DOES THE THERAPIST SEE OF THE CLIENT IN TRANSFERENCE?

The American psychiatrist Harry Stack Sullivan (1892–1949) contributed a theoretical perspective to the development of normal and abnormal behavior that is considered a variation of ego psychology. According to Sullivan (1953), the basic difficulty of patients is misperceptions of reality (parataxic distortions) stemming from disorganization in the interpersonal relations of childhood, primarily those between child and parents. This is traditionally Freudian.

Sullivan is perhaps best noted for his conception of the analyst as a "participant observer" in the therapy process. In contrast to the classical or even ego-analytical view of the therapist as a blank screen for the transference neurosis, Sullivan argued that the therapist, like the scientist, is inevitably a part of the process he or she is studying. An analyst does not "see" patients without at the same time affecting them.

In a searching critique of transference, Wachtel (1977) goes even further. Opposing the orthodox psychoanalytic view that a shadowy therapist enables transference to develop, Wachtel hypothesizes that such unvarying behavior on the part of the therapist frustrates the client, who may be seeking some indication of how the therapist feels about what he or she is doing and saying. The sometimes childish reactions assumed to be part of the transference neurosis Wachtel regards, in part, as the normal reactions of an adult who is thwarted! The troubled client sees the analyst as a professional person who remains distant and noncommittal in the face of his or her increasing expression of emotion. Thus, rather than being exclusively an unfolding of the client's personality, "transference" may actually be

Harry Stack Sullivan modified the traditional psychoanalytic notions of transference.

in some measure his or her extreme frustration with minimal feedback. Moreover, because the analyst restricts his own behavior so severely in the consulting room, and intentionally limits the setting to which the client is exposed, he can sample only a limited range of the client's behavior, attitudes, and feelings. In contrast, behavior therapists and others who believe more than analysts do that behavior is in large part situationally determined often role-play someone in the person's life to see how the client reacts.

clude Karen Horney (1942), Anna Freud (1946), Erik Erikson (1950), David Rapaport (1951), and Heinz Hartmann (1958).[2] Although Freud by no means ignored the interactions of the organism with the environment, his view was essentially a "push model," one in which people are driven by intrapsychic urges. The ego analysts place greater emphasis on a person'a ability

to control the environment and to select the time and the means for satisfying certain instinctual drives. Their basic contention is that the individual is as much ego as id. They also focus on current living conditions to a greater extent than Freud did, although they still advocate delving deeply into the historical causes of an individual's behavior.

The ego analysts do not view man as an automaton pushed hither and yon by imperative innate energies on the one hand and by situational events on the other, constantly seeking some compromise among these conflicting influences. When behavior develops in a healthy fashion, man controls both it and the influence of situational events, selectively responding to consequences he has thoughtfully selected. . . . Man is not at the mercy of either [innate energies or situa-

---

[2]In analytic circles distinctions are often drawn between ego analysts and neo-Freudians. Horney and Harry Stack Sullivan are often considered neo-Freudians. Neo-Freudians regard Freud's model of humankind as too dependent on instinctual drives. The ego analysts introduced into Freudian circles a greater concern with adaptation to environmental demands; hence the "ego" in their name. A concern for adaptation, however, does seem at least implicitly to downplay the role of instinctual drives, thus blurring the distinction between ego analysis and neo-Freudianism. The intricacies of these similarities and differences have provided grist for the mill of lively debates between theoreticians both loyal to and rebellious against Freud.

tional events]. He can impose delay and thought be-
tween innate energies and action, thus postponing the
reduction of such energies indefinitely. Learned re-
sponses, primarily thought, make this possible, and al-
though originally they may be learned as a conse-
quence of their energy-reducing function, later they
may become relatively independent of such influences
(drives) and control them. (Ford and Urban, 1963,
pp. 187–188)

We have, then, a set of important ego functions that
are primarily conscious, capable of controlling both id
instincts and the external environment, and that more
significantly, do not depend on the id for their energy.
Ego analysts assume that these functions and capabilities are present at birth and then develop through experience. Underemphasized by Freud, ego functions
have energies and gratifications of their own, usually
separate from the reduction of id impulses. And whereas
society was, for Freud, essentially a negative inhibition
against the unfettered gratification of libidinal impulses,
the ego analysts hold that an individual's social interactions can provide their own special kind of gratification.

In spite of these changes, however, we cannot con-
clude that most ego analysts have entirely renounced
Freud's repression theory. Consider this from Karen
Horney (1885–1952).

The . . . task awaiting the patient is to change those
factors within himself which interfere with his best de-
velopment. This does not mean only a gross modifica-
tion in action or behavior, such as gaining or regain-
ing the capacity for public performance, for creative
work . . . or losing phobias or tendencies toward
depression. These changes will automatically take
place in a successful analysis. They are not primary
changes, however, but result from less visible changes
within the personality. . . . (1942, pp. 117–118).

Evaluation of Analytic Therapy

In clinical circles there are few issues more controversial
than the question whether psychoanalysis and related
therapies work. Some clinicians are uneasy with the
psychoanalytic concepts themselves, especially those that
seem wedded to a notion of *an* unconscious.

Paradigmatic differences bear on any evaluation of
the effectiveness of psychoanalysis, in all its various
forms. It is very difficult to evaluate scientifically. What,
for example, are the criteria for improvement? A principal one is the lifting of repressions, making the unconscious conscious. But how is that to be demon-

strated? How do we determine whether a repression
has been lifted? Attempts to assess outcome have sometimes relied on projective tests like the Rorschach, which,
in turn, rely on the concept of the unconscious. Clearly,
if this very concept is rejected a priori, little credence
will be given to the use of projective tests.

The central concept of insight is also questioned.
Rather than accept insight as the recognition by the
client of some important, externally valid historical connection or relationship, several writers (e.g., Bandura,
1969; London, 1964) propose that the development of
insight is better understood as a *social conversion process,* whereby the patient comes to accept the belief
system of his or her therapist. Marmor (1962) has suggested that insight means different things depending on
the school of therapy; a patient treated by a proponent
of any one of the various schools develops insights along
the lines of its particular theoretical predilections.
Freudians tend to elicit insights regarding oedipal dilemmas, Sullivanians insights regarding interpersonal
relationships.

Should we be concerned whether an insight into the
past is a true one? If an insight is in fact part of a social
conversion process, do we need to concern ourselves
with the truth of it? When we examine cognitive behavior therapy in the next chapter, especially Ellis's
rational-emotive therapy, we encounter this question
again. Therapists who encourage clients to look at things
differently—as do all the therapists discussed in this
chapter and the cognitive behavior therapists of the
next—believe that an insight may help the client to
change an outlook, whether or not the insight is true.
Because of the immense complexity of human lives, it
is impossible to know with any degree of certainty whether
an event really happened and, if it did, whether it caused
the current problem.[3]

With all these cautions in mind, let us consider what
efforts researchers have made to evaluate the efficacy
of psychoanalytic and ego-analytic therapy. Like all
therapy research, psychoanalytic research can be divided into studies concentrating on outcome and those
concentrating on process. **Outcome studies** ask whether
therapy works. **Process studies** focus on what happens
during therapy that can be related to the outcome. For
example, does transference have to occur for beneficial
change to take place?

---

[3]The issue has other ramifications. In our discussion of ethics in therapy in Chapter 21, we review suggestions that psychotherapy is inherently, ultimately, a moral enterprise. That is, therapists, sometimes unwittingly, convey to clients messages about how they *ought*
to live their lives. They assume a "secular priest" role (London, 1964,
1986). In this framework the usefulness of a given insight would
depend on whether it helps the client lead a life more consonant with
a particular set of shoulds and oughts.

Outcome Research

The following generalizations about Freudian psychoanalysis were made by Luborsky and Spence (1978), who relied on outcome research conducted with some measure of controlled observation.

1. Patients with severe psychopathology (e.g., schizophrenia) do not do as well as those with anxiety disorders. This is understandable in view of Freud's admitted emphasis on neurosis rather than psychosis and in view of the heavy reliance psychoanalysis places on rationality and verbal abilities.

2. The more education a patient has, the better he or she does in analysis, probably because of the heavy emphasis on verbal interaction.

3. The evidence is conflicting whether the outcome of psychoanalysis is any better than what would be achieved through the mere passage of time or by engaging other professional help, such as a family doctor (Bergin, 1971). This is *not* to say that psychoanalysis does no good, only that clear evidence is as yet lacking. Given the great diversity in the characteristics of both patients and therapists, and in the severity of patients' problems, the question being asked is probably too complex to yield a single, scientifically acceptable answer.

A widely cited study by Sloane and his colleagues (1975) at the Temple University Outpatient Clinic had three behavior therapists and three psychoanalysts—all of them highly experienced and recognized leaders in their respective fields—treat a total of ninety adult patients for a period of four months. Most of the participants in this study can best be described as neurotic; they were the individuals typically seen in outpatient clinics or in private consulting rooms. For the most part they were troubled by anxiety and disturbed relationships. After being matched on age and sex, as well as severity of problems, they were assigned to behavior therapy or to short-term analytic therapy, meaning ego analysis, presumably. In addition to the ninety people treated, some who had gone through the same comprehensive assessment were assigned to a wait-list control group. They were promised therapy later but were asked to wait while others were in treatment. The purpose of this control group was to judge the effects on patients of having taken steps to enter therapy.

Sloane and his colleagues drew up for their therapists a list of defining characteristics of the analytic and behavior therapy that they intended to compare (Table 18.1) and instructed the therapists to adhere to these definitions as closely as possible. Audiotape recordings of the fifth session of each treatment were analyzed to determine whether these rules were being followed. The judgment was made that they were.

Outcome measures, taken immediately after treatment and at an eight-month follow-up, included personality tests such as the MMPI, ratings of how much symptoms had improved, structured interviews to determine how well the clients were doing in their work and social adjustment, and a global rating of improvement. In addition to the psychiatrist or psychologist who had conducted the therapy, the client, a clinician who had not been involved in treatment and did not know which each participant had received, and a close friend or relative joined in the judgments.

Depending on how we look at the data, and there are many ways, given the complexity of the study and the several measures taken, the findings favor behavior therapy, analytic therapy, or no treatment at all! Immediately after termination of therapy it was determined that the problems of the clients in the two treatment groups had been relieved about equally and that their functioning was similarly improved. The independent clinicians rated 80 percent of the clients in each treatment group improved or cured and 48 percent of the wait-list control group improved or recovered. *But* at the eight-month follow-up the superiority of the two treated groups over the wait-list control group had vanished, for the subjects in the control group had improved markedly. The people waiting for treatment had received a fair amount of attention, for in addition to the initial and later assessments they were called regularly and given encouragement and support.[4]

This ambitious study is subject to several criticisms that are of general importance to the study of therapy. First, did the use of multiple judges—the client, the therapist, an independent clinician, and a close friend or relative—make the information gathered about improvement especially valid? Unlikely. The ratings made by independent clinicians were based entirely on interviews with the clients. It is not surprising that their ratings correlated significantly with those of the clients. Yet these two ratings correlated much less strongly with those of the therapist, friends, and relatives. Which sets of ratings are valid?

Much of the information collected was obtained through interviews. Improvement was rated by what the client said and how he or she said it during treatment or evaluation interviews—except for the judgments of friends and relatives, who presumably observed the daily

---

[4]We can view negatively the fact that the wait-list control group "caught up with" the two therapy groups at the eight-month follow-up. But the same finding can be regarded as positive. The therapy, whether insight or behavioral, *speeded up* the rate of improvement, thus lessening overall the suffering of the clients and those close to them. In this way both types of therapy were helpful and could be judged superior to the attention given the wait-list group.

Chapter 18 / Insight Therapy 523

TABLE 18.1
Characteristics of behavior therapy and psychoanalytically oriented psychotherapy in the Temple University study (*from Sloane et al., 1975*)

1. Specific advice
  b) Given frequently.*
  p) Given infrequently.
	p) Only indirectly encouraged in everyday life. Assertive or aggressive speech which would be inappropriate in everyday life permitted in therapeutic session.

2. Transference interpretation
  b) Avoided.
  p) May be given.
	10. Symptoms
	  b) Interest in the report of symptoms, may explain biologically.
	  p) Report of symptoms discouraged, may interpret symbolically.

3. Interpretation of resistance
  b) Not used.
  p) Used.	

4. Dreams
  b) Polite lack of interest; not used in treatment.
  p) Interest in reported dreams which may be used in treatment.
	11. Childhood memories
	  b) Usually history-taking only.
	  p) Usually further memories looked for.

5. Level of anxiety
  b) Diminished when possible except in implosive therapy.
  p) Maintain some anxiety as long as it does not disrupt behavior.
	12. Aversion, e.g., electric shock
	  b) May be used.
	  p) Not used.

	13. Observers of treatment session
	  b) May be permitted.
	  p) Not usually permitted.

6. Training in relaxation
  b) Directly undertaken.
  p) Only an indirect consequence of sitting, and perhaps the example of the therapist.
	14. Deliberate attempts to stop behavior, such as thoughts, which makes the patient anxious
	  b) May be used.
	  p) Rarely directly attempted.

7. Desensitization
  b) Directly undertaken.
  p) Only an indirect consequence of talking in comfortable circumstances with uncritical therapist.
	15. Role training
	  b) May be used.
	  p) Not used.

8. Practical retraining
  b) Directly undertaken.
  p) Not emphasized.
	16. Repetition of motor habits
	  b) May be used.
	  p) Not used.

9. Training in appropriately assertive action b) Directly undertaken and encouraged in everyday life.	*The items preceded by b apply to behavior therapy, by p to psychoanalysis.

living of the client. No other observation of the client in everyday surroundings or in contrived settings, such as the speech anxiety test employed by Paul (1966) (see page 91) was attempted, however. By not arranging for such observations, Sloane and his colleagues made the assumption that we can know how a client is doing by sampling his or her behavior in the consulting room.

The Sloane study exemplifies a recent trend in analytic therapies, namely, time-limited or **brief therapy,** generally defined as psychotherapy lasting no more than 25 sessions. Interestingly, Freud's conception and implementation of psychoanalysis was itself a brief therapy, focusing on specific problems, making it clear to the patient that therapy would not exceed a certain number of sessions, structuring sessions in a directive fashion, and overall being more active than psychoanalysis eventually developed. Although short-term

therapies are not restricted to analytic approaches, the early pioneers were psychoanalysts: Ferenczi (1920) and Alexander and French (1946).

Specifically, the principal differences between brief analytic or psychodynamic therapy and time-unlimited psychoanalysis lie in interpretations being focused more on present life circumstances and the way the patient handles them (brief analytic) than on the historical significance of feelings and behavior (psychoanalysis) ("Perhaps your anger at your wife is linked to some unresolved conflicts with your mother"). Another key difference is that transference is not encouraged to develop in brief analytic treatment.

Koss and Butcher (1986) recently reviewed studies on brief therapy—including but not restricted to analytic therapies—and found it generally to be no less effective than time-unlimited treatment, perhaps because both therapist and patient work harder and focus on more concrete and more manageable goals than a "personality overhaul." On a very practical note, Koss and Butcher (1986) are of the opinion that time-limited, brief psychotherapy is likely to become more widespread because of the reluctance of insurance companies to reimburse patients for significant portions of their expenses in time-unlimited treatment.

Garfield and Bergin (1986) add some useful perspectives on the trends to brief therapies. Research on classical psychoanalysis has been extremely difficult to do, one reason being that, if a therapy can last upward of six years, funding and many other practical matters militate against such projects. One research project that was ultimately completed at the Menninger Clinic in Topeka, Kansas, took eighteen years from the onset to the final publication (Kernberg *et al.*, 1972)! No surprise then that so little even reasonably controlled research has been done on longer forms of treatment like classical psychoanalysis.

In addition, standards for research have shifted over the past twenty years. It used to be adequate to entrust a group of therapists to use therapy X and then to regard X as the independent variable. But as we have seen in the Sloane study, greater efforts are being made to prescribe or at least to monitor what therapists actually *do* in sessions. An even more recent and perhaps revolutionary development is the use of carefully detailed manuals from which therapists have to work. The NIMH Collaborative Depression Project that we discuss in the next chapter (page 553) is a good example of this trend—therapists are trained to adhere as much as they possibly can to what is in the manuals, and sometimes they are monitored, as in the Sloane study, to help maintain the integrity of the independent variable. (The NIMH study also yielded data favorable to short-term psychodynamic therapy.) It can be mentioned that this development arises directly out of behavior therapy, where the earliest studies were characterized by manuals (e.g., Lang and Lazovick, 1963) and sometimes also by tape recordings played by the therapist-experimenter (e.g., Davison, 1968b). Naturally the feasibility of such control measures is limited by the complexity of the therapy—Davison was able to relax his snake-phobic subjects with prepared tapes, but even so the desensitization itself was carried out "live" because the therapist had to respond to each subject's different reactions to noxious imaginal stimuli.

Process Research

It is difficult to draw general conclusions from process studies of analytic therapy, primarily because the variables are so complex and, as already stated, inextricably bound up with concepts referring to the unconscious.

A number of projects, entailing intensive study of tape recordings and of analysts' notes for individual cases, have been under way for years. One of the factors studied is "associative freedom," or the extent to which the analysand can free-associate. If free association helps the analyst get to hitherto repressed material, great facility in free-associating should predict a good outcome. Unfortunately, the relationship is much more complex, for the patient's free association interacts with the analyst's interpretations, and the effectiveness of these, in turn, depends on their timing—not to mention their accuracy. Because of these difficulties, plus the problems of defining outcome criteria and of designing reliable measures, it is not surprising that process research in psychoanalysis and related therapies has thus far shed little light on how they work.

Humanistic and Existential Therapies

Humanistic and existential therapies, like psychoanalytic therapies, are insight-oriented, being based on the assumption that disordered behavior can best be treated by increasing the individual's awareness of motivations and needs. But there is a useful contrast between psychoanalysis and its offshoots on the one hand and humanistic-existential approaches on the other: humanistic-existential therapies place greater emphasis on the person's freedom of choice. Free will is regarded as the human being's most important characteristic. Free will is, however, a double-edged sword, for it not only offers fulfillment and pleasure but also threatens acute pain and suffering. It is an innately provided gift that *must* be used and that requires special courage to use. Not all of us can meet this challenge; those who cannot are regarded as candidates for client-oriented, existential, and Gestalt therapies.

Carl Rogers's Client-Centered Therapy

Carl Rogers was an American psychologist whose theorizing about psychotherapy grew slowly out of years of intensive clinical experience. After teaching at the university level in the 1940s and 1950s, he helped organize the Center for Studies of the Person in La Jolla, California. Rogers makes several basic assumptions about human nature and the means by which we can try to understand it (Ford and Urban, 1963; Rogers, 1951, 1961).

Carl Rogers.

1. We must adopt a phenomenological point of view (see page 53). People can be understood only from the vantage point of their own perceptions and feelings. It is the way people construe events rather than the events themselves that the investigator must attend to, for a person's phenomenological world is the major determinant of behavior and makes him or her unique.

2. Healthy people are aware of their behavior. In this sense Rogers's system is similar to psychoanalysis and ego analysis, for it emphasizes the desirability of being aware of motives.

3. People are innately good and effective; they become ineffective and disturbed only when faulty learning intervenes.

4. Behavior is purposive and goal-directed; people do not respond passively to the influence of their environment or to their inner drives. They are self-directive. In this assumption Rogers is closer to ego analysts than to orthodox Freudian psychoanalysis.

5. Therapists should not attempt to manipulate events for the individual; rather they should create conditions that will facilitate independent decision making by the client.

Therapeutic Intervention

Assuming that a mature and well-adjusted person makes his own judgments based on what is intrinsically satisfying and actualizing, Rogers avoids imposing goals on the client during therapy. The client is to take the lead and direct the course of the conversation and of the session. The therapist's job is to create conditions so that during their hour together the client can return once again to his basic nature and judge for himself which course of life is intrinsically gratifying to him. Because of Rogers's very positive view of people, he assumes that their decisions will not only make them

happy with themselves but also turn them into good, civilized people.

Rogers's thinking evolved from a clear specification of techniques (Rogers, 1942) to an emphasis on the attitude and emotional style of the therapist and a deemphasis of specific procedures (Rogers, 1951). The therapist should have three core qualities. *Genuineness,* sometimes called congruence, encompasses spontaneity, openness, and authenticity. The therapist has no phoniness and no professional facade, self-disclosing himself, his feelings, and his thoughts informally and candidly to the client. In a sense the therapist through honest self-disclosure provides a model for what the client can become. He is in touch with his feelings and is able to express them and to accept responsibility for doing so. He has the courage to present himself to others as he really is. The second attribute of the successful therapist, according to Rogers, is being able to extend *unconditional positive regard.* Other people set what Rogers called "conditions of worth"—I will love you if. . . . The client-centered therapist prizes clients as they are, and conveys unpossessive warmth for them, even if he does not approve of their behavior. People have value merely for being people, and the therapist must care deeply for and respect a client, for the simple reason that he or she is another human being, engaged in the struggle of growing and being alive. The third quality, *accurate empathic understanding,* is the ability to see the world through the eyes of clients from moment to moment, to understand the feelings of clients both from their own phenomenological vantage point, which is known to them, and from perspectives that they may be only dimly aware of.

Empathy

Let us examine empathy more closely. Empathizing—the acceptance, recognition, and clarification of feelings—is one of the few techniques of Rogerian therapy.

BOX 18.3

EXCERPT FROM A CLIENT-CENTERED THERAPY SESSION

Client: (an eighteen-year-old female college student): My parents really bug me. First it was Arthur they didn't like, now it's Peter. I'm just fed up with all their meddling.

Therapist: You really are angry at your folks.

Client: Well, how do you expect me to feel? Here I am with a 3.5 GPA, and providing all sorts of other goodies, and they claim the right to pass on how appropriate my boyfriend is. (Begins to sob.)

Therapist: It strikes me that you're not just angry with them. (Pause) Maybe you're worried about disappointing them.

Client: (Crying even more) I've tried all my life to please them. Sure their approval is important to me. They're really pleased when I get A's, but why do they have to pass judgment on my social life as well?

Comments. Although the emotion expressed initially was one of anger, the therapist believed that the client was really fearful of criticism from her parents. She therefore made an advanced empathic statement in an effort to explore with the client what was only implied but not expressed. Previous sessions had suggested that the client worked hard academically primarily to please her parents and to avoid their censure. She had always been able to win their approval by getting good grades, but more recently the critical eyes of her mother and father were directed at the young men she was dating. The client was beginning to realize that she had to arrange her social life to please her parents. Her fear of disapproval from her parents became the focus in therapy after the therapist had helped her see beyond her anger.

Within the context of a warm therapeutic relationship, the therapist encourages the client to talk about his or her most deeply felt concerns and attempts to restate the emotional aspects, not just the content, of what the client says. This reflection of feelings to the client is meant to remove gradually the emotional conflicts that are blocking self-actualization. Because feelings are mirrored back without judgment or disapproval, the client can look at them, clarify them, and acknowledge and accept them. Feared thoughts and emotions that were previously too threatening to enter awareness can become part of the self-concept. The therapist, it should be noted, is not being truly nondirective, a term often applied to Rogers, for he selectively attends to evaluative statements and feelings expressed by the client. He believes that these are the matters the client should be helped to examine.

If therapeutic conditions allowing self-acceptance are established, clients begin to talk in a more honest and emotional way about themselves. Rogers assumes that such talk in itself is primarily responsible for changing behavior.

Rogers's application of empathy is sometimes mistakenly assumed to be an easy, straightforward matter, but it is not. In fact, it requires much subtlety and constitutes strong "medicine" indeed. The therapist does not always restrict herself to merely finding words for the emotional aspects of what the client says but, in what one writer called *advanced accurate empathy* (Egan, 1975), she goes beyond to what she believes *lies behind* the client's observable behavior (see Box 18.3). The therapist makes an inference about what is troubling the client. She interprets what the client has told her in a way that seems different from the client's actual statements. In a sense, advanced empathy represents theory building on the part of the therapist: after considering over a number of sessions what the client has been saying and how he or she has been saying it, the therapist generates a hypothesis about what may be the true source of distress and yet remains hidden from the client.[5] The following is an example.

Client: I don't know what's going on. I study hard, but I just don't get good marks. I think I study as hard as anyone else, but all of my efforts seem to go down the drain. I don't know what else I can do.

Counselor A: You feel frustrated because even when you try hard you fail [primary empathy].

Counselor B: It's depressing to put in as much effort

---

[5]Whether an advanced empathy statement by the therapist should even be regarded as *accurate* is another interesting question. These interpretations by client-centered therapists can never be known for sure to be true. Rather, like scientific theories and insights into the past, they may be more or less *useful.*

as those who pass and still fail. It gets you down and maybe even makes you feel a little sorry for yourself [advanced empathy]. (Egan, 1975, p. 135)

In *primary empathy* the therapist tries to restate to clients their thoughts, feelings, and experiences *from their own point of view*. The work here is at the phenomenological level; the therapist views the client's world from the client's perspective and then communicates to the client that this frame of reference is understood and appreciated. In advanced empathy the therapist generates a view that takes the client's world into account but conceptualizes things, it is hoped, in a more constructive way. The therapist presents to the client a way of considering himself or herself that may be quite different from the client's accustomed perspective.

To understand this important distinction, we must bear in mind that therapists operating within the client-centered framework assume that the client views things in an unproductive way, as evidenced by the psychological distress that has brought the client into therapy. At the primary empathic level the therapist accepts this view, understands it, and communicates to the client that it is appreciated. But at the advanced or interpretive level the therapist offers something new, a perspective she hopes is better and more productive and implies new modes of action. Advanced empathizing builds on the information made available over a number of sessions in which the therapist has concentrated on making primary-level empathic statements.

The client-centered therapist, operating within a phenomenological philosophy, *must* have as her goal the movement of a client from his or her present phenomenological world to another one; hence the importance of the advanced empathy stage. Since people's emotions and actions are determined by how they construe themselves and their surroundings, by their phenomenology, those who are dysfunctional or otherwise dissatisfied with their present mode of living are in need of a *new* phenomenology. From the very outset, then, client-centered therapy—and all other phenomenological therapies—have perforce been interested in clients' adopting frameworks different from what they had upon beginning treatment. Merely to reflect back to clients their current phenomenology cannot in itself bring therapeutic change. A new phenomenology must be acquired.

Evaluation

Largely because of Rogers's own insistence that the outcome and process of therapy be carefully scrutinized and empirically validated, numerous studies have attempted to evaluate client-centered therapy. Indeed, Rogers can be credited with originating the whole field of psychotherapy research. He and his students deserve the credit for removing the mystique and excessive privacy of the consulting room; for example, they pioneered the tape recording of therapy sessions for subsequent analysis by researchers.

Research on Rogerian therapy has focused principally on relating outcome to the personal qualities of therapists and has yielded inconsistent results, casting doubt on the widely held assumption that positive outsome is strongly related to the therapist's empathy, genuineness, and warmth (Beutler, Crago, and Arizmendi, 1986; Lambert *et al.*, 1986). It is probably useful to continue emphasizing such qualities in the training of young clinicians, however, for they would seem to help create for the client an atmosphere of trust and safety within which to reveal the deep inner workings of the self. But it is not justifiable, from a research perspective, to assert that these qualities, by themselves, are sufficient to help clients change.

In keeping with Rogers's phenomenological approach, self-reports by clients have been the usual measures of the effectiveness of therapy. Research on Rogerian therapy has until recently paid little attention to how patients actually *behave* following therapy. Rogers's basic datum was the individual's own phenomenological evaluation of and reaction to himself and events in his world; the overt behavior, it is held, follows from these perceptions and has not generally been the proper object of study by the client-centered therapy researcher.

Rogers's emphasis on subjective experience raises epistemological problems, for the therapist must be able to make accurate and incisive inferences about what the client is feeling or thinking. Although the method seems to rely entirely on what the client says, Rogers asserts that clients can be unaware of their true feelings; indeed, it is this lack of awareness that brings most of them into therapy in the first place. As with psychoanalysis, we must ask how a therapist is to make an inference about internal processes of which a client is seemingly unaware, and they by what procedures the usefulness or validity of that inference is to be evaluated.

The early use of only self-descriptive measures of outcome from client-centered therapy has, however, given way to more direct and theoretically neutral measures that tap into the patient's daily functioning in life, such as the adequate performance of social roles. An associated trend is the use of multiple methods of assessing therapeutic change (Beutler, 1983; Lambert *et al.*, 1986) as investigators have come increasingly to appreciate the complex nature of behavior and the need to assess along many dimensions. For example, physiological measures can be supplemented with self-report from the patient-subjects as well as with reports from significant others (e.g., spouses). Valuable and differing kinds of information are available from looking at change in a multidimensional fashion. We saw examples of this in the Sloane *et al.* (1975) study and in the earlier classic study of Gordon Paul (1966) (page 91).

Rogers may also be criticized for assuming that self-actualization is the principal human motivation. Rogers infers the self-actualization motive from his observation that people seek out situations offering fulfillment. But then the self-actualization tendency is proposed as an *explanation* of the search for these situations. Circular reasoning again!

Another point to consider is how faulty ideas are learned from the evaluation of others. Why does the master motive not always dominate the individual's learning? If the person is indeed always self-actualizing, under what circumstances does faulty learning take place, and what motives and needs are satisfied by such faulty learning?

Finally, Rogers assumes both that the psychologically healthy person makes choices to satisfy self-actualizing tendencies and that people are by their very natures good. But some social philosophers have taken a less optimistic view of human nature. Thomas Hobbes, for example, stated that life is "nasty, brutish, and short." How do we explain a person who behaves in a brutish fashion and yet asserts that this behavior is intrinsically gratifying and, indeed, self-actualizing?

It may be that the problem of extreme unreasonableness was not adequately addressed by Rogers because he and his colleagues concentrated on people who are only mildly disturbed. As a way to help unhappy but not severely disturbed people understand themselves better (and *perhaps* even to help them behave differently), client-centered therapy may very well be appropriate and effective. This humanistic approach remains popular in the encounter group movement (see page 574). Rogerian therapy may not, however, be appropriate for a severe psychological disorder, as Rogers himself warned.

Existential Therapy

Those most commonly associated with existentialism are the Danish philosopher Sören Kierkegaard and the German philosophers Edmund Husserl and Martin Heidegger, and with existential therapy the Swiss psychiatrists Ludwig Binswanger and Medard Boss and the Austrian psychiatrist Viktor Frankl, whose logotherapy and views on depression were discussed earlier (see page 240). In this country the principal proponents of existential therapy, or existential analysis as it is some-

times called, have been Rollo May and the late Abraham Maslow (1908–1970).

Basic Concepts of Existentialism
The following is a distillation of the existential position.

Man has the capacity for being aware of himself, of what he is doing, and what is happening to him. As a consequence, he is capable of making decisions about these things and of taking responsibility for himself. He can also become aware of a possibility of becoming completely isolated and alone, that is, nothing, symbolized by the ultimate nothingness of death. This is innately feared. He is not a static entity but in a constant state of transition. He does not exist; he is not a being; rather he is coming into being, emerging, becoming, evolving toward something. His ways of behaving toward himself and other events are changing constantly. His significance lies not in what he has been in the past, but in what he is now and the direction of his development, which is toward the fulfillment of his innate potentiality. (Ford and Urban, 1963, p. 448)

The existential point of view, like humanism, emphasizes personal growth. There are, though, some important distinctions. Humanism, as exemplified by Rogers's views, stresses the goodness of human nature. If unfettered by groundless fears and societal restrictions, human beings will develop normally, even exceptionally, much as a flower will sprout from a seed if only given enough light, air, and water. Existentialism is gloomier, having a strain of darkness within it. Although it embraces free will and responsibility, existentialism stresses the anxiety that is inevitable in making important choices, the existential choices on which existence depends, such as staying or not staying with a spouse, with a job, or even with this world. Hamlet's famous soliloquy beginning "To be, or not to be—that is the question" (Act III, Scene 1) is a classic existential statement. To be truly alive is to confront the anxiety that comes with existential choices. Existential anxiety comes from several sources (Tillich, 1952). We are all aware that one day we shall die; when we with honesty confront this inescapable reality, we face up to existential anxiety. We are also aware of our helplessness against chance circumstances that can forever change our lives, such as an automobile accident that cripples us. Third, we are aware that we must ultimately make decisions, act, and live with the consequences. Fourth, we must ourselves create the meaning of our lives; the ultimate responsibility for endowing our world and our lives with

Rollo May, one of the central figures in existential therapy.

Abraham Maslow, the humanistic therapist who made Carl Jung's term self-actualization central to his psychology.

substance and purpose rests with each of us. And finally, we know that we are ultimately alone.

To avoid choices, to pretend that they do not have to be made, may protect the individual from anxiety, but it also deprives him of living a life with meaning and is at the core of psychopathology. Thus whereas the humanistic message is upbeat, almost ecstatic, the existential is tinged with sadness and anxiety, but not despair, unless the exercise of free will and assumption of responsibility that accompanies it are avoided.

The Goals of Therapy

So oftentimes it happens that we live our lives in chains, and we never even know we have the key. ("Already Gone," by Jack Tempchin and Robb Strandlund, 1973 and 1975)

A person is the sum of the choices he makes. Difficulties in making choices can be understood only by exploring experience. The existential therapist, by offering support and empathy through adoption of the individual's phenomenological frame of reference, helps him explore his behavior, feelings, relationships, and what his life means to him. But the therapist also en-

courages the client to confront and clarify past and present choices. Present choices are the most important.

In addition, existential therapy helps people relate *authentically* to others. People are assumed to define their identity and existence in terms of their personal relationships; a person is threatened with nonbeing— or alienation—if isolated from others. Even though he may be effective in dealing with people and his world, he can become anxious if deprived of open and frank relationships. Hence, although the existential view is a highly subjective one, it strongly emphasizes *relating to others* in an open, honest, spontaneous, and loving manner.[6] The encounter group movement (page 574) owed much to this existential tenet.

The therapeutic relationship should be an authentic encounter between two human beings so that the patient has some practice in relating to another individual

---

[6]At the same time each of us is ultimately and basically *alone*. Although existentialism asserts that we must relate authentically to others, the paradox of life is that we are inherently separate from others, that we came into this world alone and must create our own existence in the world alone.

in a straightforward fashion.[7] The therapist, through her own honesty and self-disclosure, helps the client learn authenticity. This can take the form of the therapist's openly expressing her strong disapproval of what the client is doing—but without rejecting the client as a worthwhile human being.

The principal goal of existential therapy is to make the patient more aware of his or her own potential for choice and growth. In the existential view people create their existence anew at each moment. The potential for disorder as well as for growth is ever present. Individuals must be encouraged to accept the responsibility for their own existence and to realize that, within certain limits, they can redefine themselves at any moment and behave and feel differently within their own social environment. But this freedom to choose and the responsibility that comes with it are not easy for humankind to accept and work with. Many people are afraid of this freedom, and as they begin to make choices, they realize that fulfillment is a *process,* that they must constantly choose and accept responsibility if they are to be truly human and fulfill their potential. Their prospects then are not cheery; with greater awareness of their freedom to choose comes more existential anxiety. One of the goals of therapy is to bolster their resolve and ability to cope with this inescapable anxiety and to continue growing.

The existential writers, however, are very vague about what therapeutic techniques will help the client grow. Indeed, a reliance on technique may be seen as an objectifying process, that is, a process in which the therapist acts upon the client as though he or she were a thing to be manipulated (Prochaska, 1984). The existential approach is a general *attitude* taken by certain therapists toward human nature, rather than a set of therapeutic techniques.

Evaluation

Research on existential therapy per se may be inherently impossible, for, as just mentioned, it represents not a set of definable techniques but an epistemological stance, whereby the therapist must do her utmost to view the world as the client perceives it, and a general commitment to certain goals of human conduct—authenticity, spontaneity, choice, growth, assumption of responsibility. Therapeutic change is achieved by help-

ing the client to shift from his or her perceived reality and to develop the human qualities prized by existentialist philosophers. Existential therapy lacks the definable, concrete operations on which scientific research can be conducted. Indeed, no research has been done, although existential therapists have published numerous case reports relating successes with a variety of clinical problems.

Moreover, contemporary science is seen as dehumanizing by existentialists, hence to be *avoided.* They believe that applying science to individuals denies their unique humanness. Several of the criticisms of client-centered therapy apply too to existential treatment. Since by definition a person's subjective experience is unique to himself, how can the therapist know that she is truly understanding a patient's world as it appears to him? Yet attention to subjective impressions is not necessarily unproductive. Paying heed to our freedom to choose and ability to change at any time may be an important means of improving behavior. Indeed, the message implicit in existentialism, that our existence is constantly being reaffirmed and that we are not prisoners of our past mistakes and misfortunes, might well be incorporated into *any* therapy.

Gestalt Therapy

Another humanistic therapy that has developed over the past forty years is Gestalt therapy; its most important proponent was the late Frederich S. Perls (see Box 18.4). After receiving a medical degree in Germany in 1921, Perls became a psychoanalyst. But he was rejected by European analysts because he challenged some of the basic precepts of psychoanalytic theory, particularly the important place accorded to the libido and its various transformations in the development of neurosis (Perls, 1947). He emigrated to Holland in 1933, shortly after Hitler came to power, because he was opposed to totalitarianism, and to South Africa in 1934, as the country's first teaching analyst. There he developed the basics of Gestalt therapy. He took up residence in the United States in 1946 and eventually settled at Esalen, a center for humanistic–existential therapy in Big Sur, California. Here his ideas and techniques of therapy underwent impressive growth, especially as applied in groups (Perls, Hefferline, and Goodman, 1951; Perls, 1970).

Basic Concepts of Gestalt Therapy

Like Rogers, Perls held that people have an innate goodness and that this basic nature should be allowed to express itself. Psychological problems originate in

---

[7]It is interesting to note that this approach, which places so much emphasis on a person's perceptions, understanding, feelings, and other internal processes, is in a way very behavioristic. The person must at some point during therapy begin to behave differently, both toward the therapist and toward the outside world, in order for his or her own existential condition to be changed.

BOX 18.4

A GLIMPSE OF FRITZ PERLS

As Joe got on the elevator, he hardly noticed the short, gray-bearded man standing against the wall. Then recognition hit him. "Uh, Dr. Perls, I'm, uh, honored to meet you. I've read your work, and it's such—such an honor to meet—to be in your presence. . . ." Joe's stammering speech trailed away with no effect. The old man did not move.

The elevator slowed and Joe, realizing that an opportunity was slipping away, heard himself say, hopelessly, "I'm really nervous." Perls turned and smiled at him. As the doors opened, he took Joe's arm and said, "Now let us talk" (Gaines, 1974).

Frederich (Fritz) Perls (1893–1970), colorful founder of Gestalt therapy.

frustrations and denials of this innate goodness. Gestalt therapy, along with other humanistic approaches, tends to emphasize the creative and expressive aspects of people, rather than the negative and distorted features on which psychoanalysis seems to concentrate.

A basic assumption of Gestalt therapy is that all of us bring our needs and wants to any situation. We do not merely perceive situations "as they are"; instead we engage our social environment by projecting our needs, or fears, or desires onto what is "out there." Thus if I am talking to a stranger, I do not merely react to the person as that person exists; I react to the stranger in the context of my needs. Sometimes there is "unfinished business" with an important person from one's past; this can affect how we deal with someone in the present.

Gestalt therapists working with groups sometimes have people pair off, close their eyes, and imagine the face of an individual to whom they have a strong emotional attachment. They are encouraged to concentrate on the feelings they have about that person. Then all open their eyes and look at their partner. After a few moments they are instructed to close their eyes again and think now of something neutral, such as an arithmetic problem. They then open their eyes again and look a second time at their partner. Finally, they are asked whether there was an important difference in the ways they felt about their partner in the two situations. This exercise is designed to exaggerate what is assumed to be inevitable in all our social interactions, namely, the intrusion of our feelings into whatever is happening at any particular moment.

Perls and his followers have concentrated on the here and now and on the individual as an actor, as a being who is responsible for his or her own behavior and who is capable of playing a central role in bringing about beneficial changes.

The patient who comes for help, seeking to relate more adequately with other people and to be able to express his feelings more directly, is instructed to express what he is feeling at that moment to another person. The ways in which he stops, blocks, and frustrates himself quickly become apparent, and he can then be assisted in exploring and experiencing the blockings and encouraged to attempt other ways of expressing himself and of relating.

Thus, the general approach of Gestalt theory and therapy requires the patient to specify the changes in himself that he desires, assists him in increasing his awareness of how he defeats himself, and aids him in experimenting and changing. Blocks in awareness and behavior emerge [during the session] in the same way that they manifest themselves in a person's life; his increased awareness of his avoidances and his relief as he becomes able to expand his experience and behavior are felt immediately in increases in capacity for living. (Fagan and Shepherd, 1970, p. 2)

The foregoing description of the theorizing behind Gestalt therapy does not distinguish it very well from what Rogers prescribes. But Gestalt therapy is supposedly related to Gestalt psychology, a branch of psychology concerned primarily with perception. Their closest similarity may be in their attention to *wholes*. Perls wanted to make individuals *whole* by increasing their awareness of unacknowledged feelings and having them reclaim the parts of the personality that have been denied or disowned.

The Gestalt therapists focuses on what a client is doing in the consulting room here and now, without delving into the past, for the most important event in the client's life is what is happening at this moment. In Gestalt therapy all that exists is the Now. If the past is bothersome, it is brought into the present. "Why" questions are discouraged, for searching after causes in the past is considered an attempt to escape responsibility for making choices in the present, a familiar existential theme. Clients are exhorted, cajoled, sometimes even coerced into awareness of what is happening now. Awareness is an immediate and direct thinking and sensing. Individuals must know what is going on about them, what they think and fantasize, want and feel, what they are doing at the moment, and they must also sense posture, facial expressions, muscular tensions, and gestures, the words they use, the sound of their voice. Perls believed that awareness is curative. People have only to be moved away from their ideas about themselves to an awareness of what they are feeling and doing at this exact moment.

Gestalt Therapy Techniques

Gestalt therapy is noted for its emphasis on techniques, in contrast to their paucity in the humanistic and existential therapies discussed so far.[8] The techniques described here are but a small sample of current Gestalt practices.

The Gestalt therapist insists that the client talk in the present tense. This is one way of directing his attention to current feelings and activities. To help him bear continuing responsibility for what he is and what he is to become, the therapist instructs him to change "it" language into "I" language.

Therapist: What do you hear in your voice?

Patient: My voice sounds like it is crying.

---

[8]Although Gestalt therapy over the years has tended to become identified with a set of techniques, many contemporary workers assert that it is not a set of defined procedures, or for that matter a particular theory of behavior and experience. Rather, Gestalt therapy entails a particular *attitude* toward the nature of humankind and toward treatment. A Gestalt therapist is constantly creative, is open to new experiences, and talks openly to the client on a person-to-person basis, the I–thou which is a tenet of existential philosophy. The core of therapy is to help the client be creative and open too. The Gestalt therapist is trained to "fine-tune" the person so that he or she can encounter the world on an immediate, nonjudgmental, nonreflective basis. We agree that equating Gestalt therapy with techniques does not tell the whole story. Gestalt therapy does indeed encourage both therapists and clients to be spontaneous and open to new experience in a general way. At the same time, though, Gestalt therapists employ a body of procedures on a rather consistent basis. Many of them have even been adopted by therapists of other persuasions.

Therapist: Can you take responsibility for that by saying, I am crying? (Levitsky and Perls, 1970, p. 142)

This simple change in language, besides encouraging the patient to assume responsibility for feelings and behavior, reduces his sense of being alienated from aspects of his very being. It helps the patient see himself as active rather than passive, as an open and searching person rather than as someone whose behavior is determined entirely by external events.

In one procedure of Gestalt therapy, the empty-chair technique, a client projects and then talks to his projection of a feeling, or of a person, object, or situation. Thus, seeing that a patient is crying, the Gestalt therapist might ask him to regard the tears as being in an empty chair opposite him and to speak *to* the tears. This tactic often seems to help people confront their feelings. Indeed, to ask a person to talk *about* his tears is assumed to encourage him to establish still greater distance between himself and his feelings—something Gestalt therapists assert interferes with psychological well-being.

Another technique is to have the person behave opposite to the way he feels. Someone who is excessively timid might be asked during the therapy session to behave like an outgoing person. Perls assumed that the opposite side of the coin actually lies within the being of the person and that acting out feelings not usually expressed allows the person to become aware of a part of himself that has thus far been submerged.

All therapists pay attention to nonverbal and paralinguistic cues given by the client. Nonverbal cues are body movements, facial expressions, gestures, and the like; paralinguistic cues are the tone of voice, the rapidity with which words are spoken, and other audible components of speech beyond its content. People can negate with their hands or their eyes what they are saying with the larynx. Perls placed special emphasis on these nonlinguistic signals, closely observing them to determine what clients might really be feeling. "What we say is mostly lies or bullshit. But the voice is there, the gesture, the posture, the facial expression, the psychosomatic language" (Perls, 1969, p. 54).

During the therapy session Gestalt therapists often create unusual episodes to externalize, to make more vivid and understandable, a problem they believe a client is having. In one session that we observed, a husband and wife sat together on a sofa, bickering about the woman's mother. The husband seemed very angry with his mother-in-law, and the therapist surmised that she was getting in the way of his relationship with his wife. The therapist wanted to demonstrate to the couple how frustrating this must be for both of them, and he also wished to goad both of them to do something about it. Without warning, he rose from his chair and wedged himself between the couple. Not a word was said. The husband looked puzzled, then hurt, and gradually became angry at the therapist. He asked him to move so that he could sit next to his wife again. The therapist shook his head. When the husband repeated his request, the therapist removed his jacket and placed it over the wife's head so that the husband could not even see her. A long silence followed, during which the husband grew more and more agitated. The wife meanwhile was sitting quietly, covered by the therapist's coat. Suddenly the husband stood up, walked past the therapist, and angrily removed the coat; then he pushed the therapist off the sofa. The therapist exploded in good-natured laughter. "I wondered how long it would take you to do something!" he roared.

This staged scene drove several points home in a way that mere words might not have. The husband—having been trained already by the therapist to get in better touch with his feelings and to express them without fear or embarrassment—reported tearfully that he had felt cut off from his wife by the therapist, in much the same way that he felt alienated from her by her mother. The mother was intruding, and he was not doing anything about it. He did not trust himself to assert his needs and to take action to satisfy them. The fact that he was able to remove the coat and the therapist as well made him wonder whether he might not behave similarly toward his mother-in-law. As he spoke, his wife began to sob; she confided to her husband that all along she had been wanting him to take charge of the problem with her mother. So far so good. But then the therapist turned to the woman and asked her why she had not removed the coat herself! The husband grinned as the therapist gently chided the wife for being unduly passive about her marital problems. By the end of the session, the clients, although emotionally drained, felt in better contact with each other and expressed resolve to work together actively to alter their relationship with her mother.

The interpretation of dreams is another important part of Gestalt therapy. Gestalt analysis of them is quite different from the psychoanalytic. The dream is not considered a rich source of symbolism relating to unconscious processes; rather,

Every image in the dream, whether human, animal, vegetable, or mineral, is taken to represent an alienated portion of the self. By reexperiencing and retelling the dream over and over again in the present tense, from the standpoint of each image, the patient can begin to reclaim these alienated fragments, and accept

them, live with them and express them more appropriately. (Enright, 1970, p. 121)

For example, a woman in Gestalt therapy dreamed of walking down a crooked path among tall, straight trees. The therapist asked her to *become* one of the trees, and this made her feel serene and more deeply rooted. She then expressed her desire for such security. When she was asked to become the crooked path, tears welled as she confronted the deviousness of the way in which she lived. Once again the Gestalt therapist helped the client to externalize feelings customarily avoided, so that she could become aware of them, acknowledge them as her own, and then perhaps decide to change them.

Consistent with their phenomenological approach, Gestalt therapists encourage clients to recount, with emotion, the meaning that the dream has for them at that very moment. Even though the therapist may have a hypothesis about what a particular dream means to the client, care is taken not to impose that meaning on the dreamer, for it is the dreamer's dream. The only significance it has for the dreamer is the meaning it holds as it is discussed in the session. In this sense Gestalt therapy does not have a theory of dreams; rather it concerns itself with dream *work*, the analysis of dreams by the client with support from the therapist. Since only the phenomenal world has importance for each client, his or her immediate experience is the one thing worth focusing on.

Evaluation

The clinical literature suggests that Gestalt therapists spend much or most of their time urging clients to be more expressive, spontaneous, and responsive to their own needs. Perls describes this activity as making the person more attentive to emerging gestalts. Therapy also attempts to make the person whole by encouraging a reclamation of parts of the personality hitherto denied. The psychotherapy is therefore aligned with the experimental findings of Gestalt psychology. It is open to question, however, whether Perls's description is the most accurate or parsimonious way of talking about the techniques, and, more importantly, whether such concepts assist in the effective training of good therapists.

Gestalt therapy does forcefully convey the existential message that a person is not a prisoner of his past, that he can at any time make the existential choice to be different, and that the therapist will not tolerate stagnation. No doubt this optimistic view helps many people change. If the person does not know how to behave differently, however, considerable damage can be done to an already miserable individual.

Perls's emphasis on responsibility is not to be confused with commitment or obligation to others. Even as a therapist Perls did not present himself as a person who assumes responsibility for others, and he did not urge this on his patients either. The individual has the responsibility to take care of himself, to meet his *own* needs as they arise. This apparent egocentrism may be troubling for people with a social conscience and for those who have in the past made commitments to others. Indeed, Perls believed that commitments should never be made in the first place (Prochaska, 1984).

The same complaint voiced about Rogers's client-centered therapy applies to Gestalt therapy. Indeed, it may be common to all humanistic therapies. According to humanists, people are, by their very nature, good, purposive, and resourceful. If they are, it would be reasonable to trust this intrinsic good nature and to encourage direct expression of needs. But are people always good? Sometimes clients—especially those who are psychologically troubled—feel they must do something that, in the judgment of the professional, is not in their own best interests. Suppose that a client feels the need to murder someone or to engage in other behavior that, to outside observers, is surely undesirable. What is the therapist's responsibility? At what point does the therapist intervene and impose his or her judgment?[9] We believe that Gestalt therapists do *not* abdicate all decisions to their clients and that they *do* exert considerable influence on them, if only by virtue of the models they themselves provide. We have already indicated that Perls was a very charismatic figure. It is likely that most people adopt the values of their therapist, regardless of theoretical orientation (Rosenthal, 1955; Pentony, 1966), and it seems preferable to us to admit this social influence so that it can be dealt with, rather than to deny that such influence exists and perhaps allow for even greater "tyranny" of therapists over patients. This issue is discussed at length in Chapter 21.

A few studies have attempted to examine aspects of Gestalt therapy, in particular the empty-chair technique. Conoley and his colleagues (1983) found, in an analogue study with college undergraduates, that self-rated anger was reduced after a twenty-minute empty-chair exercise. Greenberg and Rice (1981) report that the technique increases awareness and emotional expression. There is now a growing trend for those interested in Gestalt therapy to attempt to study parts of it in a reasonably controlled fashion.

All therapies are subject to abuse; Gestalt is no exception. Indeed, it may present special problems. It is

not difficult, even for trainees with a minimum of experience, to induce clients to express their feelings. Some Gestalt techniques may in themselves be so powerful in opening people up that clients can be harmed unintentionally. The forcefulness of Perls's personality and his confrontational style have led some therapists to mimic him without the thoughtfulness, skill, and caring he appeared to possess in unusual abundance. The responsible Gestalt therapist is a professional who keeps the client's interests at the forefront, and who understands that the expression of strong emotion for its own sake is seldom enough to ease an individual's suffering. The nature of Gestalt therapy and the fact that a cult has grown up around the memory of Fritz Perls are reasons why practicing Gestalt therapists should strive for an extra measure of caution and humility.

Summary

Insight therapies share the basic assumption that a person's behavior is disorderd because he is not aware of what motivates his actions. Psychoanalysis and ego analysis tend to emphasize factors from the past, whereas most humanistic and existential approaches, such as those of Rogers and Perls, emphasize the currenty determinants of behavior.

Consistent with Freud's second theory of neurosis, psychoanalysis tries to uncover childhood repressions so that infantile fears of libidinal expression can be examined by the adult ego in the light of present-day realities. Ego analysis puts more emphasis on the need and ability of the patient to achieve greater control over the environment and over instinctual gratification.

Rogers trusts the basic goodness of the drive to self-actualize, and he proposes the creation of nonjudgmental conditions in therapy. Through empathy and unconditional positive regard for their clients, therapists help them to view themselves more accurately and to trust their own instincts for self-actualization. Existential therapists, influenced primarily by European existential philosophy, similarly regard people as having the innate ability to realize their potential; they also have the freedom to decide at any given moment to become different. Both Rogers and the existentialists assume that the only reality is the one perceived by the individual; thus the therapist must try to view the world from the client's phenomenological frame of reference, rather than from his own.

The Gestalt therapy of Perls is usually regarded as

---

[9]As we shall see in Chapter 21, when we discuss the Tarasoff ruling, therapists now have no choice but to take action in such circumstances, even against the client's wishes.

humanistic, yet it is different in important ways from the therapies of Rogers and the existentialists. Perls stressed living in the now, and the many techniques he and his followers have introduced are designed to help clients experience their current needs and feel comfortable about satisfying them as they emerge. The emphasis is on changing behavior, and yet considerable attention is directed toward increasing the individual's awareness of what he or she is doing at the present moment and accepting responsibility for it.

In addition to the specific criticisms we have made of each of these insight therapies, all have a common problem which impedes progress and refinement. Carefully controlled studies to support the claims of efficacy and the assertions that changes do occur for the reasons expounded by the various theorists are scarce. Some theorists—expecially the existentialists—dismiss a priori and paradigmatically the need for and even the possibility of the kind of controlled research that most social scientists deem important. The practical question is whether people are helped by therapists. The scientific question is whether improvement is actually due to the reasons proposed by the originators and adherents of the particular therapy.

Henri Matisse, Icarus from *Jazz*. © 1989 Succession H. Matisse/ARS, New York/Art Resource.

Chapter 19

Cognitive and Behavior Therapies

Counterconditioning
   Systematic Desensitization
   Aversion Therapy
Operant Conditioning
   The Token Economy
   Operant Work with Children
Modeling
   Problems Treated by Modeling
   The Role of Cognition
Cognitive Restructuring
   Ellis's Rational-Emotive Therapy
   Beck's Cognitive Therapy
   *The Therapies of Beck and Ellis—
      Some Comparisons*
   Social Problem Solving
   Some Reflections on Cognitive Behavior Therapy
Behavioral Medicine
   Chronic Pain and Activity
   Chronic Diseases and Life-style
   Biofeedback

**Generalization and Maintenance of
   Treatment Effects**
   Intermittent Reinforcement
   Environmental Modification
   Self-Reinforcement
   Eliminating Secondary Gain
   Relapse Prevention
   Attribution to Self
Some Basic Issues in Behavior Therapy
   Internal Behavior and Cognition
   Underlying Causes
   Broad-Spectrum Treatment
   Relationship Factors
   Flesh on the Theoretical Skeleton
   *Psychoanalysis and Behavior Therapy—
      A Rapprochement?*
Summary

Over the past four decades a new way of treating psychopathology has been developed. Called *behavior therapy,* it was initially restricted to procedures based on classical and operant conditioning, but today it is characterized more by its epistemological stance—its search for rigorous standards of proof—than by allegiance to any particular set of concepts (Davison and Goldfried, 1973). In brief, behavior therapy is an attempt to change abnormal behavior, thoughts, and feelings by drawing on the methods used and the discoveries made by experimental psychologists in their study of both normal and abnormal behavior.

That the most effective clinical procedures will be developed through science is an *assumption.* There is nothing inherent in the scientific method that guarantees victories for those studying human behavior by its principles. Because we have reached the moon and beyond by playing the science game does not mean that the same set of rules should be applied to human behavior. The existentialists, who emphasize free will, assume that the nature of humankind cannot be meaningfully probed by following the rules favored by the authors of this textbook. Although we are placing our bets on the scientific work described in this chapter, it nonetheless remains an article of faith that behavior therapy will prove the best means of treating disordered behavior, cognition, and affect.

Sometimes the term "behavior modification" has been used interchangeably with behavior therapy; therapists using operant conditioning as a means of treatment have often preferred this term. But we have argued elsewhere (Davison and Stuart, 1975) that the term behavior therapy should be employed to differentiate this approach from others. After all, every therapy—whether is be psychoanalysis or psychosurgery—has as its ultimate goal the modification of behavior.

Just when behavior therapy first began to be developed is difficult to date. In any event, some social scientist did not wake up one morning and proclaim that from this day forward people with psychological problems should be treated with techniques suggested by experimental findings. Rather, over a number of years people in the clinical field began to formulate a new set of assumptions about the best means of dealing with the problems that they encountered. Although there are areas of overlap, we have found it helpful to distinguish four theoretical approaches applied in behavior therapy—counterconditioning, operant conditioning, modeling, and cognitive restructuring. After reviewing these, we discuss behavioral medicine, a new specialization that blends behavioral and biomedical knowledge to enhance physical health and lessen physical illness.

Counterconditioning

In counterconditioning, illustrated in Figure 2.5 (page 48), a response (R_1) to given stimulus (S) is eliminated by eliciting different behavior (R_2) in the presence of that stimulus. For example, if a man is afraid (R_1) of enclosed spaces (S), the therapist attempts to help him have a calm reaction (R_2) when he is in such situations. Experimental evidence suggests that unrealistic fears can be eliminated in this way. An early and now famous clinical demonstration of counterconditioning was a case reported by Mary Cover Jones (1924). She successfully eliminated a little boy's fear of rabbits by feeding him in the presence of a rabbit. The animal was at first kept several feet away and then gradually moved closer on successive occasions. In this fashion the fear (R_1) produced by the rabbit (S) was "crowded out" by the stronger positive feelings associated with eating (R_2).

Systematic Desensitization

Three decades later Joseph Wolpe (1958) employed similar techniques with fearful adults. He found that many of his clients, like the child treated by Jones, could be encouraged to expose themselves gradually to the situation or object they feared if they were at the same time engaging in behavior that inhibited anxiety. Rather than have his patients eat, however, as Mary Cover Jones did, Wolpe taught these adults deep muscle re-

Joseph Wolpe, one of the pioneers in behavior therapy. He is known particularly for systematic desensitization, a widely applied behavioral technique.

laxation. His training procedures were adapted from earlier work by Edmond Jacobson (1929), who had shown that strong emotional states like anxiety could be markedly inhibited if a person is in a state of deep relaxation.

Many of the fears felt by Wolpe's patients were so abstract—for example, fear of criticism and fear of failure—that it was impractical to confront them with *real-life* situations that would evoke these fears. Following earlier proposals by Salter (1949), Wolpe reasoned that he might have fearful patients *imagine* what they feared. Thus he formulated a new technique that he called *systematic desensitization,* a term originally applied to the medical procedure of administering increasing doses of allergens to hay fever and asthma sufferers to reduce their sensitivity to these allergens. In systematic desensitization a deeply relaxed person is asked to imagine a graded series of anxiety-provoking situations; the relaxation tends to inhibit any anxiety that might otherwise be elicited by the imagined scenes. If relaxation does give way to anxiety, the client signals to the therapist by raising an index finger, stops imagining the situation in mind, rests, reestablishes relaxation, and then reimagines the situation. If anxiety drives out relaxation again, the client goes back to an earlier situation and later tries to handle the more difficult one. Over successive sessions a client is usually able to tolerate increasingly more difficult scenes as he or she climbs the hierarchy in imagination. As has been documented by Wolpe as well as by many other clinicians (e.g., Goldfried and Davison, 1976), the ability to tolerate stressful imagery is generally followed by a reduction of anxiety in related real-life situations. The case study on page 48 illustrates the application of this technique.

Between therapy sessions clients are usually instructed to place themselves in progressively frightening real-life situations. These homework assignments help to move their adjustment from imagination to actuality (e.g., Davison, 1968b; Sherman, 1972). As noted earlier in Chapter 6 (page 146), exposure to feared real-life situations has long been known to be an important means of reducing unwarranted anxieties.

Clinicians have treated a great variety of anxiety-related problems by systematic desensitization. The technique appears deceptively simple. But as with any therapy for people in emotional distress, its proper application is a complicated affair. First, the clinician must determine, by means of a comprehensive behavioral assessment, that the situations the client is reacting anxiously to do not warrant such fearful reactions. If a person is anxious because she lacks the skills to deal with a given set of circumstances, desensitization would not be appropriate; to be anxious, for example, about

piloting an airplane is logical when the individual does not know how to operate the aircraft! Desensitization, then, is an appropriate treatment if a client seems to be inhibited by anxiety from behaving in customary and known ways.

Sometimes the technique can be used when the client does not appear openly anxious. For example, a middle-aged construction worker sought help for his depression (Goldfried and Davison, 1976). He was having trouble getting out of bed in the morning and viewed his job and life in general with dread and foreboding. Careful assessment by the clinician revealed that the man was inordinately concerned whether the men working under him liked and approved of him. His depression had set in after he had been promoted to foreman, a position that required him to issue orders and monitor and criticize the activities of other workers. His men would occasionally object to his instructions and comments, and the client found their resentful stares and sullen silences very upsetting. He agreed with the therapist that a hierarchy of situations in which he was criticized and rejected by others would be appropriate. The reduction in job-related anxiety that followed treatment by desensitization succeeded in lifting his depression.

As with all the techniques described in this chapter, very rarely is only one procedure used exclusively. A person fearful of social interactions might well be given training in conversational and other social skills in addition to desensitization. In the most general sense, the treatments chosen and their applicability depend largely on the therapist's ingenuity in discovering the source of the anxiety underlying a client's problems.

The Outcome Question

Researchers became interested in studying desensitization because clinical reports indicated that the technique is effective. Initial steps in the experimental investigation of the procedure were taken by Lazovik and Lang (1960; Lang and Lazovik, 1963). They were concerned primarily with assessing the procedure under relatively controlled laboratory conditions. In the earlier clinical reports, improvement had been judged by the clinicians who had given the treatment, and other therapeutic procedures were usually employed along with desensitization. Lang and Lazovik decided that to eliminate bias in evaluating desensitization of the simple phobia chosen, fear of snakes, testers who were *not* treating the subjects should measure their pretreatment and posttreatment ability to approach snakes. They also restricted treatment to desensitization. Their experiments showed that, indeed, desensitization alone can measurably and significantly reduce avoidance of a phobic object.

Systematic desensitization being conducted with a group by Arnold Lazarus.

One of the most widely known and highly regarded experiments in systematic desensitization, and in psychotherapy research as a whole, was conducted by Gordon Paul (1966). His purpose was to compare systematic desensitization, a placebo, and insight therapy for their effectiveness in reducing unrealistic fear. He recruited students who were taking a required public-speaking course and were all fearful of speaking in front of groups. Prior to treatment all students had to deliver a speech before an audience, and numerous measures of their anxiety were taken—self-reports, behavior observa-

Snake phobias were often studied in early outcome research on systematic desensitization.

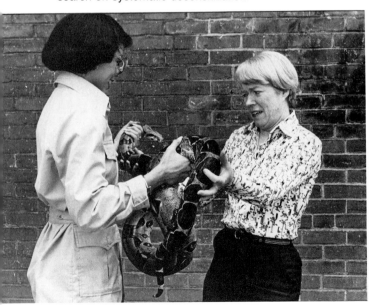

tions, and two physiological measures, of pulse rate and sweat (see page 91).

After delivering one speech, students were assigned to one of three treatments. The first was systematic desensitization. The second was an attention-placebo treatment. Subjects in the second group met with a sympathetic therapist who led them to believe that a pill would reduce their overall sensitivity to stress. To convince them, the therapist had them listen to a tape that he said had been used in training astronauts to function under stress. They listened to this "stress tape" for several sessions after ingesting the "tranquilizer." In reality, the pill was a placebo, and the tape contained various nonverbal sounds that had been shown in other research to be quite boring. In this ingenious way Paul raised subjects' expectations that their social anxieties could be lessened by taking a pill.

The third treatment was insight therapy. Subjects met with skilled insight-oriented therapists to talk over their anxieties; the therapists were free to structure the sessions in any way they saw fit. All treatments were limited to five sessions, a number settled on by the insight therapists when they were asked how many sessions they would need to make a measurable impact on this kind of problem. An important feature of Paul's experimental design was training insight therapists to do systematic desensitization. In fact, insight therapists gave all three treatments. By doing this, Paul attended to the criticism that any superiority of systematic desensitization could be attributed to greater enthusiasm shown by desensitization therapists. A fourth group or students did not receive any treatment; the anxiety of these students was measured as they gave two speeches along with the others, one before and one after the treatment sessions.

The results of this important study revealed that subjects who had received systematic desensitization improved much more than did the no-treatment group and more than did the attention-placebo and insight therapy subjects, who reacted about the same to their forms of therapy. Students receiving the latter two treatments did, however, show significant improvement. The results, then, indicated that systematic desensitization is superior both to insight therapy and to attention plus a placebo in lessening anxiety about making speeches. These results persisted in a two-year follow-up (Paul, 1967). Subsequent research has attested to the effectiveness of desensitization in reducing a wide range of anxieties.

The Process Question

Behavioral researchers are interested not only in whether a given technique works—the outcome question—but also in *why*—the process question. Wolpe suggests that counterconditioning underlies the efficacy of desensitization; a state or response antagonistic to anxiety is substituted for anxiety as the person is exposed gradually to stronger and stronger doses of what he or she is afraid of. Many experiments (e.g., Davison, 1968b) suggest that there may be a specific learning process underlying the technique and that, indeed, it may be counterconditioning. But a number of other explanations are possible. Some workers attach importance to exposure to what the person fears per se; relaxation is then considered merely a useful way to encourage a frightened individual to confront what he or she fears (Wilson and Davison, 1971).

Aversion Therapy

Aversion therapy attempts to attach negative feelings to stimuli that are considered inappropriately attractive.[1] The literature on classical aversive conditioning of animals (i.e., pairing a neutral or positive stimulus with an unpleasant unconditioned stimulus such as shock; see Box 6.3, page 138) led therapists to believe that negative reactions could be conditioned in human beings, and they formulated treatment programs along these lines. The method is similar to desensitization but has the opposite goal, since the new response of anxiety, or an aversion reaction, is to be substituted for a positive response. Among the problems treated with aversion therapy are excessive drinking, smoking, transvestism, exhibitionism, and overeating. For example, an excessive drinker who wishes to be discouraged from drinking is asked to taste, see, or smell alcohol and is then made uncomfortable while doing so. In addition to employing painful but not harmful shock to the hands as the unconditioned stimulus, some therapists have adopted use of emetics, drugs that make the client nauseous when presented with the undesirable stimulus.

Recent research in chemical aversion with alcoholism and nicotine dependence (see page 291 and 307) lends some support to the proposition that nausea paired with the taste of alcohol or with inhaling a cigarette can produce stable conditioned aversions and subsequent abstinence from alcohol or tobacco (e.g., Cannon, Baker,

"DON'T SHOOT. I AM DR. CRANISH, AND THIS IS MY PATIENT. I AM A PIONEER IN EXCITEMENT THERAPY."

Gino, and Nathan, in press; Baker and Brandon, 1988). These and similar findings, however, have been criticized by Wilson (1987) among others. Debate continues to be lively.

Aversion therapy has been controversial also for ethical reasons. A great outcry was raised about inflicting pain and discomfort on people, even when they asked for it. Perhaps the greatest ethical concern and anger were voiced by gay liberation organizations. They held that homosexuals who requested painful treatment to help them shift sexual preference were actually seeking to punish themselves for behavior that a prejudiced society had convinced them was dirty. They accused behavior therapists of impeding the acceptance of homosexuality as a legitimate life-style when they acceded to such requests (Silverstein, 1972). The issue has been a difficult one to resolve and led several behavior therapists to question whether therapists should ever agree to help homosexuals change their sexual orientation (see Box 21.5, page 630).

Behavior therapists who choose aversive procedures seldom use them alone. Instead, more positive techniques are instituted to teach new behavior to replace that eliminated. Even if the effects of aversion therapy are ephemeral, or short-lived, the temporary reduction in undesirable behavior can create some "space," which can be taken up by responses judged by the person or

---

[1]Some commentators (e.g., Sandler, 1986) consider aversion therapy to be a form of punishment and place it under the general rubric of operant conditioning. Our preference is otherwise, though we accept the widely held assumption in learning theory that all classical conditioning procedures have operant elements, and that all operant conditioning procedures have Pavlovian features. The issue appears to be whether, as in classical conditioning, the therapist or experimenter attempts to pair a *stimulus* with an aversive event, regardless of what the person is doing; or whether, as in operant conditioning, the effort is made to pair a *response* with an aversive event. In practice there is more overlap than the conceptual scheme implies.

the culture to be more appropriate. When aversion therapy is employed, it is generally chosen as a last resort.

Operant Conditioning

In the 1950s a number of investigators suggested that therapists should try to shape overt behavior through rewards and punishments (Skinner, 1953). In the belief that they could through operant conditioning exercise some control over the complex, puzzling, often frenetic behavior of hospitalized patients, many experimentally minded psychologists determined to try to bring practical order into the chaos of institutions for the severely disturbed.

In addition to the familiar use of praise, tokens, and food as positive reinforcers, and of verbal or physical punishment as negative reinforcers, operant workers have developed other reinforcers. The "Premack principle" (Premack, 1959) holds that in a given situation a more probable behavior can serve as a reinforcer for a less probable behavior. For example, if you know that John would rather watch a football game than do the laundry, you can make the former contingent on the latter: allowing John to watch football can function as a positive reinforcer for washing the clothes. Most of us have applied this principle to our own behavior many times, as when we resolve not to reward ourselves with going to a movie unless we first complete a task that holds less appeal for us. Another operant tool is "time out," which refers to removing a person from an environment in which he or she can earn positive reinforcers. For example, rather than just ignoring undesirable behavior—the typical extinction method—one banishes the person for a stated period of time to a dreary room where positive reinforcers are unavailable. Finally, "overcorrection" is a punisher that requires the person not only to restore an environment he or she has sullied but also to improve upon its original condition (e.g., Azrin, Sneed, and Foxx, 1973). Thus, if a destructive child tears the sheets off his bed instead of making it, the therapist requires him to make not only his own bed but others as well. Generally speaking, operant treatments work best with clients whose intellectual capacities are limited and in situations in which considerable control can be exercised by the therapist.

The Token Economy

An early example of work within the operant tradition is the token economy of Ayllon and Azrin (1968). On the basis of research that Staats and Staats (1963) had

The token economy was one of the first therapeutic applications of operant conditioning.

done with children, they set aside an entire ward of a mental hospital for a series of experiments in which rewards were provided for activities such as making beds and combing hair and were not given when behavior was withdrawn or bizarre. The forty-five female patients, who averaged sixteen years of hospitalization, were systematically rewarded for their ward work and self-care by giving them plastic tokens that could later be exchanged for special privileges, such as listening to records and going to the movies, renting a private room, and extra visits to the canteen. The entire life of each patient was as far as possible controlled by this regime.

The rules of the token economy—the medium of exchange; the chores and self-care to be rewarded, and by what number of tokens; the items and privileges that can be purchased, and for how many tokens—are carefully established and usually posted. These regimes have demonstrated how even markedly regressed adult hospital patients can be significantly affected by systematically manipulating reinforcement contingencies, that is, rewarding some behavior to increase its frequency, or ignoring other behavior to reduce its frequency. To show that a stimulus following behavior actually reinforces it, an experiment has to demonstrate not only that behavior increases when followed by a positive event, but also that behavior declines when nothing positive happens as a consequence. In Chapter 5 the ABAB design was presented as a method for studying the effect of contingencies. Ayllon and his associates demonstrated in this way the effect of contingencies on the behavior of their ward patients. Figure 19.1 indicates that conduct such as brushing teeth and making beds markedly decreased when rewards were withdrawn, but became more frequent again when rewards were reinstated.

Since the publication of Ayllon's early studies of the token economy, many similar programs have been in-

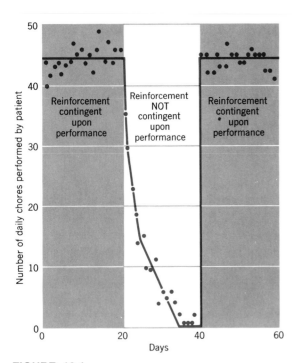

FIGURE 19.1
When receiving tokens was the contingency, patients on a ward spent more time grooming themselves and doing chores than when they were given no reward. Adapted from Ayllon and Azrin (1965).

stituted throughout the country. The most impressive was reported by Gordon Paul and Robert Lentz (1977) and has already been mentioned (page 405). The long-term, regressed, and chronic schizophrenic patients in their program are the most severely debilitated institutionalized adults ever studied systematically. Some of these patients screamed for long periods, some were mute; many were incontinent, a few assaultive. Most of them no longer used silverware, and some buried their faces in their food. The patients were matched for age, sex, socioeconomic background, symptoms, and length of hospitalization and then assigned to one of three wards—social learning (behavioral), milieu therapy, and routine hospital management. Each ward had twenty-eight residents. The two treatment wards shared extensive objectives: to teach self-care, housekeeping, communication, and vocational skills; to reduce symptomatic behavior; and to release patients to the community.

1. **Social-Learning Ward.** Located in a new mental health center, the social-learning ward was operated on a token economy embracing all aspects of the residents' lives. Their appearance had to pass muster each morning, in eleven specific ways, in order to earn a token. Well-made beds, good behavior at

mealtime, classroom participation, and socializing during free periods were other means of earning tokens. Residents learned to do as they should through modeling, shaping, prompting, and instructions. They were also trained to communicate better with one another and participated in problem-solving groups. Tokens were a necessity, for they purchased meals as well as small luxuries. In addition to living by the rules of the token economy, each individual received behavioral treatments tailored to his needs. Residents were kept busy learning to behave better 85 percent of their waking hours.

2. **Milieu Therapy Ward.** Another ward of the center operated on the principles of Jones's (1953) "therapeutic community." These residents too were kept busy 85 percent of their waking hours. Both individually and as a group, they were expected to act responsibly and to participate in decisions about how the ward was to function. In general, they were treated more as normal individuals than as incompetent mental patients. Staff members impressed on the residents their positive expectations of them and praised them for doing well. When they behaved symptomatically, staff members stayed with them, making clear their expectations that they would soon behave more appropriately.

3. **Routine Hospital Management.** These patients continued their accustomed hospital existence in an older state institution, receiving custodial care and heavy antipsychotic medication. Except for the 5 percent of their waking hours occupied by occasional activity, and recreational, occupational, and individual and group therapies, these people were on their own.

Before the program began, the staffs of the two treatment wards were carefully trained to adhere to detailed instructions in therapy manuals; regular observations confirmed that they were implementing the principles of a social-learning or a milieu therapy program. Over the four and a half years of hospitalization and the one and a half years of follow-up, the patients were carefully evaluated at regular six-month intervals by structured interviews and by meticulous, direct, behavioral observations.

The results? Both the social-learning and the milieu therapy reduced symptomatic behavior, with the social-learning ward achieving better results than the milieu ward on a number of measures. The residents acquired self-care, housekeeping, social, and vocational skills. The behavior of members of these two groups within the institution was superior to that of the residents of the hospital ward. By the end of treatment, more of them had been discharged. In fact, over 10 percent of the social-learning patients left the center for indepen-

BOX 19.1

TOKEN ECONOMIES, ASYLUMS, AND THE METRICS OF HUMAN EXISTENCE

Despite the success of Paul and Lentz's landmark study, questions have been raised about token economies in institutional settings. Some of these concern the basic assumptions of these behavior control regimens (Gagnon and Davison, 1976).

David Rothman (1971), a historian, has traced the development of mental hospitals in this country during the nineteenth century. He shows that asylums of the time were instituted as they were because much of the madness of the day was assumed caused by the hurly-burly of a vigorous democratic society, which offered endless opportunities—and therefore possibilities for failure. Asylums were to be havens for those who could not keep up with the rapid economic and social expansion that had followed the industrial revolution.

Consider how this view of the mental hospital as refuge contrasts with the way token economies are organized. The disease, if you will, now becomes the doctor. The token economy is the nineteenth-century asylum on its head, for this innovation introduces into the hospital the very conditions that were assumed in the previous century to have caused mental disorders. Instead of protecting patients from the strains of an achievement-oriented, money-dominated society, the token economy introduces commercial relationships into the asylum.

Can we claim on these historical grounds that token economies are necessarily bad? Can we really say that commercialism is likely to cause or aggravate mental illness? After all, have we not made some progress in understanding mental disorder since the early nineteenth century? Readers may judge for themselves by reflecting on the material presented in the preceding chapters of this book. It would seem that for the more serious disorders—schizophrenia, in particular—genetic factors and the biochemistry and pathology of the brain have provided and will provide the major clues to etiology. Economic failure may be a factor, but probably as a stressor that activates a diathesis.

Other issues can be raised that are not tied to history. Token economies are effective in ward *management*. They do seem to introduce order where there has been only chaos; helping a regressed schizophrenic dress herself and arrive on time to a hospital dining hall is a significant

accomplishment. And if the remarkable success of Paul and Lentz in returning chronic schizophrenics to the community, to live in sheltered residences, can be duplicated by other clinicians, the token economy will have proved of value in helping resocialize mental patients.

But what, in fact, do patients really learn on a token economy? Gagnon and Davison (1976) take an unusual position on this.

One thing that is learned is that producing certain kinds of behavior produces a stable response from the token-emitting behavioral engineer. . . . The value of any act is metrically stable, and its value can be compared to [that of] other acts [in] number of tokens. . . . [Is this a good thing for mental patients to learn if they are to be prepared for life outside the confines of the institution?] The exchanges that characterize most conventional social life [suggest] that things do not come out even. . . . [Sanity] is largely the capacity to tolerate interactions which have low predictability of outcome [and] to survive the fact that life is unjust: sometimes you get what you pay for, sometimes you get more than you pay for, sometimes you get less than you pay for. . . . Indeed, to stay "sane," you commonly have to doctor the books. (pp. 532–534, emphasis added)

Finally, a token regimen may encourage people to view themselves and others in ways that are undesirable. Human relationships and human feelings run the risk of being cheapened when reduced to a monetary metric. If a patient, for example, has to have twenty tokens to see a clergyman, will this adversely affect how he feels about religion? If thirty tokens are required for a weekend pass, how will a patient feel about the people she sees while she is on leave?

We are unaware of attempts by behavior therapists to answer such questions. The failure to address these issues does *not* represent callousness to the human condition; such an allegation would be unfair and incorrect. Rather, apparently because of their professional training, psychologists and psychiatrists are not especially inclined to view their work in historical and sociological contexts.

---

dent living; 7 percent of the milieu patients achieved this goal, and none of the hospital treatment patients did. Many more patients from all three groups were discharged to community placements such as boarding homes and halfway houses, where there was supervision, to be sure, but considerably less restraint than patients had been experiencing for an average of sev-

enteen years. Members of the social-learning group were significantly better in remaining in these community residences than were patients in the other two groups.

Considering how poorly these patients had been functioning before this treatment project, these results are remarkable. And the fact that the social-learning program was superior to the milieu program is also significant, for milieu treatment is instituted in many mental hospitals. As implemented by Paul's team of clinicians, it provided more attention to patients than was given those on the social-learning ward. This greater amount of attention of the other treatment would appear to control well for the placebo effect of the social-learning therapy.

These results, though, should not be accepted as confirming the usefulness of token economies per se, for the social-learning therapy contained elements that went beyond operant conditioning of overt motor behavior. Staff provided information to residents and attempted verbally to clarify misconceptions. Indeed, Paul (personal communication, 1981) relegates the token economy to a secondary, although not trivial, role. He sees it as a useful device for getting the attention of severely regressed patients in the initial stages of treatment. The token economy created the opportunity for his patients to acquire new information, or, in Paul's informal phrase, to "get good things into their heads."

Paul and Lentz have never claimed that any one of these patients was "cured." Although they were able to live outside the hospital, they continued to manifest many signs of mental disorder, and few of them had gainful employment or participated in the social activities most people take for granted. The outcome, though, is not to be underestimated; chronic mental patients, those typically shut away on back wards and forgotten by society, can be resocialized and taught self-care. They can learn to behave normally enough to be discharged from mental institutions (see Box 19.1).[2]

Yet the success of the Paul–Lentz work has had little impact on the care of hospitalized mental patients. In 1983, Boudewyns, Fry, and Nightingale (1986) surveyed all 152 Veterans Administration Medical Centers. A phenomenal 100 percent response rate revealed that only twenty centers reported having any sort of behavior modification or token economy. Of these twenty, only half modeled their efforts on the work of Paul and Lentz. Thus, of 46,360 schizophrenics with an average stay of 98 days, only 1.01 percent were being exposed to the best-validated therapy program available for hospitalized schizophrenic patients. Why is this model for treatment not more widely used? Speculation includes staff resistance (it requires a way of interacting with patients and of keeping records that is new and perhaps objectionable to mental health staff), problems finding effective reinforcers for chronic patients, high cost, and concerns for patient rights. Boudewyns *et al.* reject as spurious all objections but staff resistance and argue

that educational and incentive methods be explored as ways to interest staff more in becoming involved in token programs.

Operant Work with Children

Some of the best operant conditioning behavior therapy has been done with children, perhaps because much of their behavior is subject to the control of others. Children, after all, tend more than adults to be under continual supervision. At school their behavior is scrutinized by teachers, and when they come home parents frequently oversee their play and other social activities. In most instances the behavior therapist works with the parents and teachers in an effort to change the ways they reward and punish the children for whom they have responsibility. It is assumed that altering the reinforcement practices of the adults in a child's life will ultimately change the child's behavior.

The range of childhood problems dealt with through operant conditioning is very broad, including bed-wetting, thumb-sucking, aggression, tantrums, hyperactivity, disruptive classroom behavior, poor school performance, language deficiency, extreme social withdrawal, and asthmatic attacks. Self-mutilation has also been effectively treated with punishment procedures, sometimes involving the response-contingent application of painful electric shock to the hands or feet (see page 631); such extreme measures are of course used only when less drastic interventions are ineffective and when the problem behaviors are health- or life-threat-

Operant techniques are used frequently with a wide range of childhood problems.

ening (Sandler, 1986). Even gender identity appears susceptible to operant procedures (see page 327). In general, rates of improvement for the above kinds of problems are superior to those reported for traditional forms of therapy (Franks, 1984; O'Leary, Turkewitz, and Taffel, 1973; O'Leary and Wilson, 1987; Ollendick, 1986; Ross, 1981). Operant behavior therapists must of course determine that the behavior being shaped or extinguished is in fact controllable through reward. A child who is crying because of physical pain should be attended to.

Encouraging results have also been achieved by applying operant techniques to the training of retarded and autistic children. As indicated in Chapter 16, many operant conditioners have challenged assumptions about the limited trainability of such children, much to their benefit and their families. Such work is arduous and consumes long stretches of time, but among other problems operant conditioners have been able to improve table manners (Plummer, Baer, and LeBlanc, 1977), social skills (Williams *et al.,* 1975), and hyperactive behavior (Doubros, 1966).

Modeling

Modeling is the third theoretical approach employed by behavior therapists. The importance of modeling and imitation in behavior is self-evident, for children as well as adults are able to acquire complex responses and eliminate emotional inhibitions merely by watching how others handle themselves.

Problems Treated by Modeling

The effectiveness of modeling in clinical work was shown in an early study by Bandura, Blanchard, and Ritter (1969). They were attempting to help people overcome their snake phobias. The researchers had fearful adults view both live and filmed confrontations of people and snakes. In these engagements the models gradually moved closer to the animals. The fears of the patients were decidedly reduced. The pioneering work of Ivar Lovaas mentioned in Chapter 16 employs modeling to teach complex skills such as speech to autistic children (Lovaas, Berberich, Perloff, and Schaeffer, 1966). Sex therapy researchers have found that inhibited adults can become more comfortable with their sexuality if shown tastefully designed explicit films of people touching themselves, masturbating, and having intercourse (Nemetz, Craig, and Reith, 1978; McMullen and Rosen, 1979). Other films or slide presentations have signifi-

cantly reduced children's fears of dogs (Hill, Liebert, and Mott, 1968), of hospitalization (Roberts *et al.,* 1981), of surgery (Melamed and Siegel, 1975), and of dental work (Melamed *et al.,* 1975). Films prepared by Melamed show initially fearful children gradually coping with their anxieties about preparing for and undergoing medical and dental procedures. So helpful do such films appear to be that they have become a routine part of medical and dental practices in a number of hospitals and clinics. These modeling films for reducing children's fears of medical treatments are considered one of the new behavioral medicine or health psychology procedures.

Some of the clinical work of Arnold Lazarus, one of the leading behavior therapists, is also regarded as modeling treatment. As indicated in Chapter 2 (page 49), in *behavior rehearsal* Lazarus (1971) demonstrates for a client a better way to handle a difficult interpersonal problem. The client observes the therapist's exemplary performance and then attempts to imitate it during the therapy session. By continual practice and observation, the client can frequently acquire entire repertoires of more effective and more satisfying behavior. Often videotape equipment can be creatively used to facilitate such modeling and imitation.

In an attempt to expand the kinds of problems handled, some therapists and researchers have tried covert modeling (Cautela, 1971). The client imagines that he is watching a model, sometimes the client himself, coping with an object he fears or handling a situation requiring assertion. Research suggests that covert modeling can reduce fears and promote more assertive behavior (Kazdin, 1975). Covert procedures, in which the patient does nothing overt and has no real-life contact with what is feared or upsetting, are of course adopted when direct experience is not possible. Imagined substitutes are not expected to be as effective as actual exposure to threat and actual practice in confronting it (Bandura, 1977).

Behavior therapy programs for hospitalized patients also make use of modeling. Bellack, Hersen, and Turner (1976) contrived social situations for three chronic schizophrenic patients and then observed whether they behaved appropriately to the situation. For instance, a given patient would be told to pretend that he had just returned home from a weekend trip to find his lawn had been mowed. As he gets out of the car, his next-door neighbor approaches him and says that he has cut the patient's grass because he was already cutting his own. The patient must then respond to the situation. As expected, patients were initially not very good at making a socially appropriate response, which in this instance would have been some sort of thank-you. Training followed; the therapist encouraged the patient to respond, commenting helpfully on his efforts. If necessary, the therapist also modeled appropriate behavior so that the patient could observe and then try to imitate it. This combination of role playing, modeling, and positive reinforcement effected significant improvement in all three patients. There was even generalization to social situations that had not been worked on during the training. This study, and others like it (e.g., Wallace *et al.*, 1985), indicate that many severely disturbed patients can be taught new social behavior that may help them function better both inside *and outside* the hospital.

The Role of Cognition

It is still unclear, however, *how* the observation of a model is translated into changes in overt behavior. In their original writings on modeling, Bandura and Walters (1963) asserted that an observer could, somehow, learn new behavior by watching others. Given the emphasis that much of experimental psychology places on learning through doing, this attention to learning without doing was important. But it left out the processes that could be operating. A moment's reflection on the typical modeling experiment suggests the direction theory and research have taken in recent years. The observer, a child, sits in a chair and watches a film of another child making a number of movements, such as hitting a Bobo doll in a highly stereotyped manner, and he hears the child uttering peculiar sounds. An hour later the youngster is given the opportunity to imitate what he saw and heard earlier. He is able to do so, as common sense and folk wisdom would predict. How shall we understand what happened? Since the observer did not *do* anything of interest in any motoric way while watching the film, except perhaps fidget in his chair, it would not be fruitful to look at overt behavior for a clue. Obviously, the child's cognitive processes were engaged, including his ability to remember later on what had happened.

Bandura (1986) has written extensively on the cognitive factors involved in modeling, which he defines as a process by which a person rather efficiently acquires rules for the generation of adaptive behavior. This interest has led Bandura to formulate a "social cognitive" theory of behavior in which the person's symbolic, cognitive processes play a key role. Bandura, Jeffrey, and Bachica (1974), drawing on experimental cognitive research, showed that having a code by which to summarize information helps a person retain it better. In addition, they found that the use of such a code helped observers pattern their actions on what they had seen modeled. Other theories about memory storage and retrieval may shed light on how people acquire new and complex patterns of behavior "simply" by watching others. The word "simply" is placed in quotation marks because, in fact, the process is not simple at all. The literature on modeling, which at first offered straightforward, commonsensical social-learning explanations, now regards modeling interventions as a type of cognitive behavior therapy, to which we now turn.

Cognitive Restructuring

In the therapies discussed thus far, the emphasis has been on the direct manipulation of overt behavior and occasionally of covert behavior. Relatively little attention has been paid to direct alteration of the thinking and reasoning processes of the client. Perhaps it was in reaction to insight therapy that behavior therapists initially discounted the importance of cognition, regarding any appeal to thinking as a return to the "mentalism" that John Watson had vigorously objected to in the early part of the twentieth century (see page 43).

If behavior therapy is to be taken seriously as applied experimental psychology, however, it should incorporate theory and research on cognitive processes. Indeed, for a number of years behavior therapists have paid attention to "private events"—to thoughts, perceptions, judgments, and self-statements—and they have studied and manipulated these processes in their attempts to understand and modify overt and covert disturbed behavior (Mahoney, 1974). The cognitive-restructuring treatment of the man with "pressure points" described in Chapter 2 (page 50) is one early example. Cognitive restructuring is a general term for changing a pattern of thought that is presumed to be causing a disturbed emotion or behavior. It is carried out in several ways by cognitive behavior therapists.

Ellis's Rational-Emotive Therapy

For many years the work of a New York clinical psychologist, Albert Ellis, existed outside the mainstream of behavior therapy, but eventually it engaged the interest of behavior therapists. The principal thesis of Ellis's rational-emotive therapy (RET) is that sustained emotional reactions are caused by internal sentences that people repeat to themselves. The aim of therapy is to eliminate the wrongheaded beliefs of disturbed people through a rational examination of them. As indicated earlier, anxious persons may create their own problems by adopting unrealistic expectations, such as "I must win the love of everyone." Or a depressed person may say several times a day, "What a worthless jerk I am." Ellis proposes that people interpret what is happening around them, that sometimes these interpretations can cause emotional turmoil, and that a therapist's attention should be focused on these internal sentences, rather than on historical causes or, indeed, overt behavior (Ellis, 1957, 1962, 1984).

Ellis lists a number of irrational beliefs that people can harbor; these beliefs underlie their negative self-statements and cause their distress. One very common notion is that people must be thoroughly competent in everything they do. Ellis suggests that many people actually believe this untenable assumption, and that they evaluate every event within this context. Thus, if a person makes an error, it becomes a catastrophe since it violates his deeply held conviction that he must be perfect. It sometimes comes as a shock to clients to realize that they actually believe such strictures and as a consequence run their lives so that it becomes virtually impossible to live comfortably or productively.

Clinical Implementation

After becoming familiar with the client's problems, the therapist presents the basic theory of rational-emotive therapy so that the client can understand and accept it.[3] The following transcript is from a session with a young man who had inordinate fears about speaking in front of groups. The therapist guides the client to view his "inferiority complex" in terms of the unreasonable things he may be telling himself. The therapist's thoughts during the interview are indicated in italics.

Client: My primary difficulty is that I become very uptight when I have to speak in front of a group of people. I guess it's just my own inferiority complex.

Therapist: [*I don't want to get sidetracked at this point by talking about that conceptualization of his problem. I'll just try to finesse it and make a smooth transition to something else.*] I don't know if I would call it an inferiority complex but I do believe that people can, in a sense, bring on their own upset and anxiety in certain kinds of situations. When you're in a particular situation, your anxiety is often not the result of the situation itself, but rather the way in which you *interpret* the situation—what you tell yourself about the situation. For example, look at this pen. Does this pen make you nervous?

Client: No.

Therapist: Why not?

Client: It's just an object. It's just a pen.

Therapist: It can't hurt you?

Client: No. . . .

Therapist: It's really not the object that creates emotional upset in people, but rather what you think about the object. [*Hopefully, this Socratic-like dialogue will eventually bring him to the conclusion that self-statements can mediate emotional arousal.*] Now this holds true for . . . situations where emotional upset is caused by what a person tells himself about the situation. Take, for example, two people who are about to attend the same social gathering. Both of them may know exactly the same number of people at the party, but one person can be optimistic and relaxed about the situation, whereas the other one can be worried about how he will appear, and consequently be very anxious. [*I'll try to get him to verbalize the basic assumption that attitude or perception is most important here.*] So, when these two people walk into the place where the party is given, are their emotional reactions at all associated with the physical arrangements at the party?

Client: No, obviously not.

Therapist: What determines their reactions, then?

Client: They obviously have different attitudes toward the party.

Therapist: Exactly, and their attitudes—the ways in which they approach the situation—greatly influence their emotional reactions. (Goldfried and Davison, 1976, pp. 163–165)

Having persuaded the client that his emotional problems will benefit from rational examination, the therapist proceeds to teach the person to substitute for irrational self-statements an internal dialogue meant to ease his emotional turmoil. At the present time therapists who implement Ellis's ideas differ greatly on how they persuade clients to change their self-talk. Some rational-emotive therapists, like Ellis himself, argue with clients, cajoling and teasing them, sometimes in very blunt language, to change their minds. Others, believing that social influence should be more subtle and that individuals should participate in changing themselves, encourage clients to discuss their own irrational thinking and then gently lead them to discover more rational ways of regarding the world.

One variation of rational-emotive therapy, **systematic rational restructuring** (Goldfried, Decenteceo, and Weinberg, 1974), is modeled after systematic desensi-

---

[3]We said in Chapter 18 that the usefulness of an insight into the past or of an empathy statement does not depend on whether it is true. Nor does the usefulness of rational-emotive therapy. Ellis's views may be only partially correct, or even entirely wrong, and yet it may be helpful for a client to act as though they are true.

tization. The therapist and client draw up a hierarchy of anxiety-provoking situations, but instead of having the client relax while imagining each, the therapist teaches the client to talk to himself differently about the situation. Anxiety, it is hoped, will be reduced during the visualization itself. Reasonably well-controlled studies attest to the effectiveness of systematic rational restructuring (e.g., Goldfried, Linehan, and Smith, 1978).

Once a client verbalizes a different belief or self-statement during a therapy session, it must be made part of everyday thinking. In recent years, Ellis and his followers have paid particular attention to homework assignments designed to provide opportunities for the client to experiment with the new self-talk and to experience the positive consequences of viewing life in less catastrophic ways. Indeed, Ellis emphasizes the importance of getting the patient to *behave* differently, both to test out new beliefs and to learn to cope with life's disappointments.

Research on Efficacy

In a recent review of outcome studies in RET, Haaga and Davison (1989) came to the following conclusions:

1. RET reduces self-reports of general anxiety, speech anxiety, and test anxiety.

2. In social anxiety RET effects improvements in both self-report and behavior though it may be inferior to systematic desensitization.

3. RET is inferior to exposure-based treatments for agoraphobia, but it remains to be studied whether combining the two approaches leads to better maintenance of exposure-produced gains.

4. Preliminary evidence suggests that RET may be useful in treating excessive anger, depression, and antisocial behavior.

5. RET has utility only as part of more comprehensive behavioral programs for sexual dysfunction.

6. As described in Chapter 8, RET shows promise in reducing the type A behavior pattern but, as with other psychological interventions, has not yet shown its utility in preventing coronary heart disease (Haaga, 1987).

7. There is some preliminary evidence that RET may be useful in a preventive fashion for untroubled people, that is, to help currently well people cope better with everyday stress.

8. Systematic rational restructuring is useful with test anxiety, self-reported social anxiety, and nonassertiveness, and may be as effective with social anxiety as is systematic desensitization. However, it is inferior to *in vivo* exposure for treating simple phobias

and may add little to behavior rehearsal in the treatment of nonassertiveness.

9. There is only some tentative evidence (e.g., Smith, 1983) that RET achieves its effects through a reduction in the irrationality of thought. Not to be underestimated in importance is the support RET gives patients to confront what they fear and to take risks with new, more adaptive behavior.

As with most other clinical procedures, the relevance of RET to a given problem is dependent in part on how the clinician *conceptualizes* the patient's predicament. Thus, if one is trying to help an overweight person lose pounds, one might conceptualize the eating as a way of reducing anxiety; in turn, the anxiety is viewed as due to social distress that is itself caused by extreme fear of rejection arising from an irrational need to please everyone and never make a mistake. The RET therapist would direct her efforts to the irrational beliefs about pleasing others and being perfect, the rationale being that this will alleviate the patient's distress and ultimately the overeating. This kind of analysis into underlying causes is discussed at the end of this chapter (see Box 19.2 for RET with children).

The Ethics of RET

It can be argued that Ellis is preaching an ethical system, for he suggests that a great deal of emotional suffering is engendered by goals that *he* asserts are wrong. He proposes that by altering these goals a person can reduce subjective discomfort. Indeed, he proposes that the reduction of stress can often improve performance so that, ironically, it more closely approximates the goal previously viewed as a "must" or a "should."

Ellis's overall views have not gone unchallenged, however. In a thoughtful philosophical essay, Bandura (1986) suggests that RET therapists link certain beliefs and demanding patterns of thought to psychopathology because their clients are mostly people whose emotions and actions are disordered. There are, Bandura argues, many who seem to think "irrationally," according to Ellis, yet in spite of their allegedly troubled thoughts often make important contributions to society—indeed, who distinguish themselves *because of* their "irrational" thoughts. The theme of *utility* that we have mentioned several times runs through Bandura's thinking:

Visionaries and unshakable optimists, whose misbeliefs foster hope and sustain their efforts in endeavors beset with immense obstacles, do not flock to psychotherapists. . . . Similarly, the efforts of social reformers rest on illusions about the amount of social change their collective actions will accomplish. Although their fondest hopes are likely to be unrealized during their

BOX 19.2

RATIONAL-EMOTIVE THERAPY AND EDUCATION FOR CHILDREN

Though he works almost exclusively with adults, Ellis has been interested for some years in extending RET to problems of childhood and especially to education. Recently, several reports have appeared that attempt to apply the principles of rational-emotive therapy to children and adolescents (Ellis and Bernard, 1983). Although there is not yet enough evidence that children can understand and accept the tenets of RET or that the sometimes complex intellectual discussions with an RET therapist can be adapted to a level appropriate for a youngster, a number of preliminary studies suggest that the enterprise holds some promise.

In their review of RET, Haaga and Davison (1989) distinguish between RET applied to normal children and RET employed with clinically disordered children. With normals, workers have experimented with what is called Rational-Emotive Education. REE consists of classroom lectures, typically conducted by specially trained teachers, that explain the general cognitive rationale that people's thoughts influence their feelings and behavior; that certain kinds of thoughts are irrational; and that troublesome interpersonal situations like being teased can be made less so by altering one's way of thinking about them (one is reminded of the old childhood refrain about sticks and stones breaking bones but names not being able to harm one). The teacher conducts classroom discussions and tells stories to bring the concepts to life. Specially designed cartoon materials and coloring books are also sometimes used. The overall rationale for REE is that it might be *preventive* in its effects, that is, that children given such education may later in life be spared some of the emotional distress that burdens many adults. In this respect REE can be considered a form of *primary prevention* within the framework of community psychology (see page 586).

What are the results of studies of Rational-Emotive Education? Cangelosi, Gressard, and Mines (1980) showed that a twenty-four-session "rational thinking group" intervention improved self-concept among high school volunteer subjects more than did loosely structured group discussions or no treatment at all. Unfortunately there was no long-term follow-up to assess the possible preventive benefits of REE. In a study with sixth graders, Knaus and Bokor (1975) found superior reductions in test anxiety and increases in self-esteem from an REE program consisting of 85 ten- to thirty-minute sessions as compared to a non-RET-based self-concept enhancement program and a no-treatment control. It is also encouraging that the REE sessions were conducted by regular classroom teachers after only three hours of training; this suggests excellent disseminability of the REE treatment. Other studies (e.g., Jasnow, 1982) support the belief that REE can have positive effects on nonclinical samples of children and adolescents, but as yet follow-up measures, to assess its preventive impact, are lacking.

REE has been applied as well to some clinical problems in children. Von Pohl (1982) employed REE in a residential and day treatment facility with six disturbed children, focusing mostly on "acting out" problems (extreme misbehavior). The study suggested beneficial effects on behaviors such as talking out of turn, complaining, and being out of seat. A twenty-four-session REE class improved level of aspiration and anxiety in a group of learning disabled children in a study by Omizo, Cubberly and Omizo (1985). Both studies, however, have methodological flaws that warrant considerable caution in viewing the results as strongly supportive for REE.

The promise is there, but REE with children is still very much in its infancy.

---

lifetime, nevertheless their concerted efforts achieve some progress and strengthen the perceived efficacy of others to carry on the struggle. For those leading impoverished, oppressed lives, realism can breed despair. . . . Clearly the relationship between illusion and psychological functioning is a complex one. (Bandura, 1986, p. 516)

Beck's Cognitive Therapy[4]

The reader will recall that Beck (see page 226) holds that numerous disorders, particularly depression, are caused by the negative patterns in which individuals think about themselves, the world, and the future. These negative patterns of thought, or negative schemata, are maintained by one or more errors in logic, such as arbitrary inference or selective abstraction. The overall goal of Beck's therapy is to provide the client with experiences, both within and without the consulting room, that will disconfirm the dark conclusions drawn through errors in logic and ultimately to alter the negative schemata in a favorable way. Thus if a client, through his ineptness schema, bemoans his witlessness because he burned the roast, he is encouraged to view the failure as regrettable but not to overgeneralize (one of the errors in logic) and conclude, through his hopelessness schema, that he can do no good on future occasions. The therapist tries to break into the vicious cycle of a negative schema fueling an illogicality, which in turn fuels the negative schema.

---
[4]Some of this section is based on Haaga and Davison (1986).

Clinical Implementation

Attempts to change negative thinking are made at both the behavioral and cognitive levels. One behavioral technique, useful for clients who are convinced that they are depressed all the time, and who become still more deeply depressed because of this belief, is to have them record their moods at regular intervals during the day. If it turns out that these reports show some variability, as indeed often happens even with very depressed people, this information can serve to challenge their general belief that life is always miserable. This change in thinking can then serve as the basis for a change in behavior, such as getting out of bed in the morning, doing a few chores, or even going to work.

Similarly, depressed clients often do very little because tasks seem insurmountable, and they believe they can accomplish nothing. To test this hypothesis or schema of insurmountableness, the therapist breaks down a particular task into small steps and encourages the client to focus on just one step at a time. If this tactic is skillfully handled, and a good therapeutic relationship is obviously important, the client finds that she can, in fact, accomplish *something*. Her accomplishments are then discussed with the therapist as inconsistent with her notion that tasks are beyond her efforts. As the client begins to change her view of herself, tasks of greater difficulty appear less forbidding, and success can build upon success, with still further beneficial changes in the client's beliefs about herself and her world.

"Collaborative empiricism" is inherent to Beck's therapy. Therapist and client work as co-investigators to uncover and examine any maladaptive interpretations of the world that may be aggravating the client's depression and general life condition. They try to uncover both "automatic thoughts" and "dysfunctional assumptions." Automatic thoughts are the things we tell or picture to ourselves as we go about our daily business, the running dialogue we have with ourselves as we drive to school, listen to a friend, or watch others crossing the street. Clients usually need practice in taking note of such thoughts and images, especially the ones that are associated with their depressed mood. For example, a father hears his daughter tell him that she failed a test at school, and he thinks to himself, "What a lousy parent I am." Thereafter he feels blue. The therapist helps the client monitor such thoughts, and together they examine their validity. Why should your daughter's problems at school mean that you are a bad parent? What else affects your youngster and determines whether she does well at school? In this fashion the therapist teaches the man to check his thoughts against the available information and to entertain hypotheses that might explain his daughter's failure on the test, other than his being a bad parent.

This phase of identifying and modifying automatic thoughts is followed by a more subtle phase, the identification of underlying dysfunctional assumptions. These can be likened to a *leitmotiv* in music, a dominant, recurring theme. The father may come to realize that he believes himself responsible for the happiness and welfare of his entire family, including how good a student his daughter is. The therapist can examine with the man the implications of the worst possible case, that the evidence does indeed indicate that he is a bad father. Is this something to be clinically depressed about? To be sure, his concern and desire to do something about his daughter's problems are understandable, but these reactions can energize a person to new action, not plunge him into despair.

How can the therapist help the individual to alter his or her dysfunctional assumptions? In addition to verbal persuasion, the therapist may encourage the client to behave in a way inconsistent with them. For example, a woman who believes that she must please everyone at her office can decline the next unreasonable request made of her and see whether, as she has been assuming, the sky will fall. If the situation has been properly analyzed ahead of time by client and therapist, clearly a necessary step, the woman can experience what happens when she acts against her absolutist belief.

Beck's therapy, like others that alter thinking, is *difficult!* Clients would probably not be depressed if they were readily convinced by mastery experiences that they are worthwhile individuals. Our brief account is only an outline; the implementation is invariably less systematic, less unidirectional, and certainly more arduous than the description implies.

Research on Efficacy

The effectiveness of Beck's approach is under intensive study. A noteworthy effort was reported by Rush, Beck, and their colleagues (1977). Two groups of severely depressed men and women, outpatients with an average age of thirty-six, were treated, one group with a daily bedtime dose of imipramine or Tofranil, a psychoactive drug widely and effectively used for depression, the other with twenty sessions of Beck's therapy. The depression of these outpatients had been with them for about twelve months. The median number of therapists already seen by the patients, unsuccessfully, was two. Three-quarters of them had thought about suicide. After the twelve-week period of treatment, 79 percent of the cognitive-therapy group were very much improved or completely themselves, compared to 20 percent of those taking imipramine. There were also fewer dropouts from the cognitive-therapy group. Since people who terminate therapy prematurely are usually doing poorly, this was an early indication that these people were receiving more help than those who took the drug. Patients who had received cognitive therapy remained less depressed at six-month follow-up- and for at least a year after termination of treatment (Kovacs *et al.,* 1981).[5]

In light of the demonstrated efficacy of imipramine in treating depression, these findings are praise indeed for Beck's treatment. Other research as well indicates that this cognitive-restructuring therapy is effective in relieving depression (Shaw, 1977; Wilson, Goldin, and Charbonneau-Powis, 1983). Haaga and Davison (1989) also cite some preliminary evidence that Beck's therapy may be better than drug therapy for patients with high pretreatment levels of "learned resourcefulness" as measured by Rosenbaum's (1980) Self-Control Schedule (Simons, Lustman, Wetzel, and Murphy, 1985); and that it may have a preventive effect relative to drug treatment, a consideration of major importance in light of the oft-observed tendency for depressive episodes to recur (Blackburn, Eunson, and Bishop, 1986). Perhaps cognitive therapy patients acquire some useful cognitive behavior skills that they are able to use following termination of therapy. And as seen in Chapter 17, because older patients can be extremely sensitive to medications and can also suffer from medical problems that contraindicate prescribing psychoactive drugs, therapists often treat their depression cognitively. A recent large-scale study on Beck's cognitive therapy is described in Box 19.3.

Yet to be demonstrated is that when cognitive therapy works, it does so because it helps patients change their cognitions to bring them more in line with external reality. As Hollon and Beck (1986) point out, predictable changes in cognitions do occur in cognitive therapy—*but* they are found as well in successful treatment of depression by drugs (e.g., Rush *et al.,* 1982). Cognitive change may be the *consequence* of change produced by other means. Or, at least with depression (the disorder in which cognitive therapy has been researched), cognitive change may be the mediator of therapeutic improvement brought about by *any* therapy, whether it be Beck's cognitive therapy, psychoanalysis, or drugs.

The Therapies of Beck and Ellis— Some Comparisons

The views and techniques of Ellis and Beck are widely used by therapists nowadays. With the inevitable changes that inventive clinicians make as they apply the work of others, and with the evolution in the thinking of the theorists themselves, the differences between the two therapies can sometimes be difficult to discern. They do contrast, however, in interesting ways (Haaga and Davison, 1986).

To the father who became depressed when he learned that his daughter had failed a test at school, Ellis, in essence, would say immediately, "So what if you are a bad father? It is irrational to be depressed about being a bad parent." Beck, in contrast, would first examine the evidence for the conclusion. His is a more empirical approach. "What evidence is there for thinking that you are a bad father?" If proof is lacking, this discovery in itself will be therapeutic. Ellis regards his own type of solution as more thoroughgoing. *Even if* the man is a bad father, the world will not end, for he does not have to be competent in everything he does. Beck may also eventually question with the man whether one has to be competent in everything to feel good about oneself, but not until the evidence that they accumulate suggests that the man is not a good father.

The Beckian therapist certainly has preconceptions, primarily about the forms that maladaptive, illogical thinking takes, such as overgeneralization. But working with a depressed individual is a collaborative, *inductive* procedure by which client and therapist attempt to discover the particular dysfunctional assumptions underlying the client's negative thoughts. Rational-emotive therapists, by contrast, are *deductive*. They are confident that a distressed person subscribes to one or more of a finite list of common irrational beliefs.

Beckian and standard rational-emotive practices differ in style on this inductive–deductive basis. Beck suggests that the therapist avoid being overly didactic, but Ellis often uses mini-lectures and didactic speeches. Beck proposes calling negative thoughts "unproductive ideas" to promote rapport with clients. He does not favor adjectives such as "irrational" or "nutty," which might be heard—with supportive humor, it must be pointed out—from Ellis. Finally, Beck recommends that the therapist begin by acknowledging the client's frame of reference and asking for an elaboration of it. Having had a chance to present his or her case and feel understood, the client may be more willing to go through the collaborative process of undermining beliefs. Ellis, on the other hand, supposes that quite forceful interventions are necessary to disrupt a well-learned maladaptive pattern of thinking; he will therefore directly confront the client's irrational beliefs, sometimes within minutes in the first session.

Social Problem Solving

Some psychological distress can be regarded as a reaction to problems for which people believe they have

---

[5]This 20 percent improvement figure for tricyclic drugs is well below the benefits reported in most other drug studies, including the recently completed NIMH study to be described shortly. It has been suggested that the drug condition in the Rush *et al.* study was not an optimal one (Becker and Schuckit, 1978).

BOX 19.3

NIMH TREATMENT OF DEPRESSION COLLABORATIVE RESEARCH PROGRAM

In 1977 the National Institute of Mental Health undertook a large, complex, and expensive three-site study of Beck's cognitive therapy, comparing it to another brief psychotherapy and to pharmacotherapy (Elkin, Parloff, Hadley, and Autry, 1985). Called the Treatment of Depression Collaborative Research Program (TDCRP), this is the first multisite coordinated study initiated by NIMH in the field of psychotherapy (the NIMH has fruitfully conducted such research in pharmacology).

SELECTION OF THERAPIES

Three criteria were employed in selecting a psychotherapy to be compared with Beck's: it had to have been developed for treating depression; it had to be explicit and standardized enough to allow for instructing other therapists (preferably using a manual); and it had to have empirically shown some efficacy with depressed patients. It was also preferable that there be little overlap with Beck's cognitive therapy. The NIMH team selected Gerald Klerman's Interpersonal Psychotherapy, which is a psychodynamic, Sullivanian, insight-oriented approach that focuses on current problems and interpersonal relationships and which has demonstrated effectiveness for depression (Klerman, Weissman, Rounsaville, and Chevron, 1984; Weissman *et al.*, 1979). It is, however, not as much intrapsychic as it is interpersonal; it emphasizes better understanding of the interpersonal problems assumed to give rise to depression and aims at improving relationships with others. As such, the focus is on better communication with others, reality-testing, developing more effective social skills, and meeting present social role requirements. Actual techniques include somewhat nondirective discussion of interpersonal problems, exploration of and encouragement to express unacknowledged negative feelings, improvement of both verbal and nonverbal communications, and problem solving.*

A pharmacological therapy, imipramine, a well-tested tricyclic drug widely regarded as a standard therapy for depression, was used as a reference against which to evaluate the two psychotherapies. Dosages were adjusted according to predetermined guidelines that were flexible enough to allow for some clinical judgment of the psychiatrist in the context of "clinical management," that is, in a warm, supportive atmosphere (Fawcett *et al.*, 1987). Indeed, Elkin *et al.* (1985) regard this almost as a drug-plus-

supportive therapy condition, "supportive" referring to the nature of the doctor–patient relationship, not to the application of any explicit psychotherapeutic techniques.

A fourth and final condition was a placebo–clinical management group, against which to judge the efficacy of imipramine. It was also conceived of as a partial control for the two psychotherapies because of the presence of strong support and encouragement. In a double-blind design like that used in the imipramine condition, patients in this group received a placebo that they believed might be an effective antidepressant medication; they were also given direct advice when considered necessary. As placebo conditions go, this was a very "strong" one, that is, it included much more psychological support and even intervention than do most placebo control groups in both the psychotherapy and pharmacotherapy literatures. It should be noted that "clinical management"—support and advice—was common to both this and the imipramine groups.

All treatments lasted sixteen weeks, with slight differences in numbers of sessions, depending on the treatment manuals. For example, cognitive therapy patients received twelve sessions during the first eight weeks, followed by weekly sessions during the second half of the study. These twenty sessions exceeded the sixteen for interpersonal therapy, which, however, could number as many as twenty at the therapist's discretion. Throughout all therapies, patients were closely monitored and all professional safeguards were employed to minimize risk, for example, excluding imminently suicidal patients and, in general, maintaining close and regular contact during the study. These considerations were particularly important in the placebo condition.

SELECTION AND TRAINING OF THERAPISTS

An important feature of this study was the care and thoroughness of therapist selection and training at each of the

---

*Though technique differences have been noted between the therapies of Beck and Klerman (DeRubeis, Hollon, Evans, and Bemis, 1982), in our eyes there is considerable overlap, for both emphasize improving accuracy in perception as well as efficacy in social behavior. The reader may want to consider this when the results of this milestone study are described.

no solution. I am late with a term paper and am upset about it. Shall I approach the professor, or is it better to deal at least initially with her teaching assistant? Should I request an Incomplete, or will it look bad on my transcript, which is going to be sent out soon to the graduate programs I am applying to? But isn't an In-

complete better than a C? Students caught in such a predicament can be helped by knowing how to solve a problem in the most effective, efficient manner.

Therapists have devised what is called *social problem solving* (SPS) (D'Zurilla and Goldfried, 1971; Goldfried and D'Zurilla, 1969; Kanfer and Busenmeyer, 1982).

treatment sites. This phase took almost two years, beginning with careful screening of recruits for general clinical competence and some experience in one of the three modalities under study. Altogether twenty-eight therapists were selected—ten each for Interpersonal Therapy and drug therapy and eight for Cognitive Therapy.

Clearly this was not a random selection of therapists, for they had to seek participation, be accepted after rigorous screening, and agree to adhere to an established treatment protocol, as well as have each of their therapy sessions videotaped for concurrent as well as subsequent scrutiny to ensure adherence to the respective therapy protocol. Training itself took months and was very rigorous, involving 119 patients. This selection and training phase itself constituted an achievement in psychotherapy research and has already been reported on by those involved in instruction and supervision (Rounsaville, Chevron, and Weissman, 1984; Shaw, 1984; Waskow, 1984). This lengthy procedure was taken to ensure the integrity of the independent variable (page 120). Only recently have psychotherapy outcome studies devoted suitable attention to the training and monitoring of therapist-experimenters to ensure that the independent variables are, in fact, being manipulated in the study. Subjects began to be treated in May 1982.

The overall design of the study is shown in Table 19a. It should be noted that each site administered each therapy as well as the placebo condition, with two to four therapists per treatment. The plan allowed for 240 patients, in anticipation of some attrition. (Actually, 250 patients began the study.)

SELECTION OF PATIENT–SUBJECTS

Who were these patients and how were they selected? The principal consideration was that they met Research Diagnostic Criteria for Definite Major Depressive Disorder but not be imminently suicidal or have medical contraindications for the use of imipramine (in case they were assigned to the drug condition). All were outpatients, nonbipolar and nonpsychotic. Many other pieces of information were gathered on the patients so that these could later

TABLE 19a
Design of NIMH depression outcome study (*from Elkin et al., 1985, p. 309*)

Research Sites	Treatment Condition, No. of Patients (No. of Therapists)				
	Cognitive Behavior Therapy	Interpersonal Psychotherapy	Imipramine + Clinical Management	Pill-Placebo + Clinical Management	Total
George Washington University, Washington, D.C.	20 (3)	20 (3)	20 (3)	20	80 (9)
University of Pittsburgh	20 (2)	20 (4)	20 (4)	20	80 (10)
University of Oklahoma, Oklahoma City	20 (3)	20 (3)	20 (3)	20	80 (9)
Total	60 (8)	60 (10)	60 (10)	60	240 (28)

Training clients in SPS consists of a number of steps, the first being to regard their distress as a reaction to unsolved problems and even to regard problems as challenges or opportunities rather than as threats (D'Zurilla, 1986). They are then taught to identify what the problems might be; to brainstorm—to generate as many alternative solutions as possible without evaluating their feasibility or possible effectiveness; to assess the likely consequences of each solution; and to implement a decision and evaluate its effectiveness for achieving their particular goals. Clients often have to cycle back to earlier stages, for their initial solution may not work

be related to treatment outcome (e.g., is melancholia a negative factor in cognitive therapy? do minority patients drop out of therapy more often than others?). Seventy percent of the sample was female (which corresponds well to the 2:1 ratio of women to men with this disorder), and patients were on average moderately to severely depressed for an outpatient sample, with 38 percent classified as endogenous. Of those who began treatment, 162, or 68 percent, completed at least fifteen weeks and twelve sessions; although more patients in the placebo condition dropped out of treatment, their number was not statistically greater than those in the other three, active treatment groups.

TYPES OF ASSESSMENTS

A wide range and large number of assessments were made at pre- and posttreatment, as well as three times during treatment and again at six-, twelve-, and eighteen-months follow-up. Measures included some that might shed light on processes of change. For example, do interpersonal therapy patients learn to relate better to others during therapy and, if so, is this improvement correlated with clinical outcome? Do cognitive therapy patients manifest less cognitive distortion during the latter sessions than at the beginning of treatment and, if so, is this shift associated with better clinical outcome? Assessment instruments included those that tap the perspectives of the patient, the therapist, an independent clinical evaluator blind to treatment condition, and, whenever possible, a significant other from the patient's life, for example, a spouse. Three domains of change were assessed: depressive symptomatology, overall symptomatology and life functioning, and functioning related to particular treatment approaches (e.g., the Dysfunctional Attitudes Scale of Weissman and Beck (1978), to assess cognitive change).

RESULTS

Initial analyses of the data suggest variations among research sites, between those who completed treatment and the total sample (including dropouts), and among assessments with different perspectives (e.g., patient versus clinical evaluator judgments). Some of the complex initial findings can be summarized as follows (Elkin *et al.*, 1986; Elkin *et al.*, in press):

1. At termination and without distinguishing subjects according to severity of depression, there were no significant differences in reduction of depression or improvement in overall functioning between cognitive therapy (CT) and interpersonal therapy (IPT) or between either of them and imipramine plus clinical management. In general, then, the three active treatments achieved significant *and equivalent* degrees of success. The placebo plus clinical management subjects also showed significant improvement. Imipramine was faster than the other treatments in reducing depressive symptoms. By the end of sixteen weeks, however, the two psychotherapies had caught up with the drug.

2. On some measures the less severely depressed placebo subjects were doing as well at termination as were the less depressed people in the three active treatment conditions.

3. Severely depressed patients did not fare as well in the placebo condition as did those in the three active treatments.

4. There was little evidence that particular treatments effected change in expected domains. for example, IPT patients showing more improvement in social functioning than imipramine or CT patients.

Other papers are being prepared for publication on different aspects of this complex study, especially on the follow-up data—a very critical issue because imipramine subjects, though improving more rapidly, may relapse more quickly or more severely than patients in the psychotherapy groups (cf. Blackburn *et al.*, 1986). At this juncture it appears that "the general lack of differences between the two psychotherapies, together with the good results for the [Placebo–Clinical Management] condition, suggests once again the importance of common factors in different types of psychologically-mediated treatment" (Elkin *et al.*, in press, p. 26 of prepublication manuscript, quoted by permission). The data from this major study constitute a mine that will be worked by scientists for many years.

out. People with even serious problems often have "second chances" to solve them.

Some clinical research finds SPS training to be useful. For example, depressed older adults in a nursing home shed more of their depression after such training than patients given a more behaviorally based treatment (Hussian and Lawrence, 1981). Similarly good outcomes were achieved by Nezu (1986), who found greater reductions in depression among subjects who received the entire SPS package as compared to a control condition whose group discussions about problems did not contain systematic procedures for solving them and

BOX 19.4

ASSERTION TRAINING

"Children should be seen and not heard." "Keep a stiff upper lip." "He's the strong silent type." Our society does not generally value the open expression of beliefs and feelings, and yet people seem to pay an emotional price for concealing their thoughts and suppressing their feelings. Peoples' wants and needs may not be met if they shy away from stating them clearly. As we have seen, poor communication between sexual partners is one of the major factors contributing to an unsatisfying sexual relationship. Therapists of all persuasions spend a good deal of time encouraging clients to discover what their desires and needs are and then to take responsibility for meeting them. If they have trouble expressing their feelings and wishes to others, assertion training, conducted individually or in groups (see page 577), may be able to help them.

Andrew Salter, in his book *Conditioned Reflex Therapy* (1949), was the first behavior therapist to set assertiveness as a positive goal for clients. Using Pavlovian, classical conditioning terms, Salter said that much human psychological suffering is caused by an excess of cortical inhibition; therefore greater excitation is called for. He encouraged socially inhibited people to express their feelings to others in an open, spontaneous way. They are to do so verbally, telling people when they are happy or sad, angry or resolute; and nonverbally with smiles and frowns, what Salter called facial talk. They are also to contradict people they disagree with, and with appropriate feeling; use the pronoun I as often as possible; express agreement with those who praise them; and improvise, that is, respond intuitively in the moment without ruminating. Although Salter's classical conditioning formulation of assertion has not been verified, assertiveness remains a goal for people in therapy, and his impact on therapeutic practice has been great and enduring.

How are we to define assertion? Is it not inconsiderate to put ourselves forward and express our beliefs and feelings to others? What if we hurt someone else's feelings in doing so? Much effort has gone into articulating the differences between assertive behavior and aggressive behavior. A useful distinction has been drawn by Lange and Jakubowski (1976); they consider assertion as

expressing thoughts, feelings, and beliefs in direct, honest, and appropriate ways which respect the rights of other people. In contrast, aggression involves self-expression which is characterized by violating others' rights and demeaning others in an attempt to achieve one's own objectives. (pp. 38–39)

Arnold Lazarus regards the expression of positive and negative emotions as important for psychological well-being. He argues (1971) that "emotional freedom" in the most general sense of the term is important for many kinds of clients; they need to express affection and approval as well as dislikes and criticisms. In helping clients to assert themselves, behavior therapists, whether they acknowledge it or not, are doing therapeutic work with goals similar to those of humanistic therapists, who also regard expression of positive and negative feelings as a necessary component of effective living.

People may be unassertive for any number of reasons. The specific therapy procedures chosen will depend on the reasons believed to be causing the individual's unassertiveness. Assertion training, then, is actually a set of different techniques, having in common the goal of enhancing assertiveness. Goldfried and Davison (1976) have suggested several factors that can underlie unassertiveness, one or more of which may be found in an unassertive individual.

1. The client may not know what to say. Some unassertive people lack information on what to say in situations

evaluating the effectiveness of the solutions. In another study, school-aged children acquired problem-solving skills that generalized to situations different from those dealt with in the SPS training (Weissberg *et al.*, 1981). In the best of all possible worlds, clients learn a general attitude and set of skills that they can apply to a wide range of future situations, thereby enhancing their general well-being.

"Metacognition," that is, what people know about knowing (Meichenbaum and Asarnow, 1979), is also applied in solving social problems. If I come to a new city, I am likely to get lost without a map. But once I obtain a street map, granted that I have earlier learned the general skill of map reading, I am well able to find my way around. At the metacognitive level I know that to locate streets and areas in a new city, I should get a city map and then read it.

Another example of metacognition is how we react to a problem that we find difficult to solve. We call it an interesting challenge; tell ourselves to go slow; think of as many solutions as possible, without committing ourselves to any particular one; and carefully and without rushing test out each of our alternatives.

SPS training, however, can be criticized for its overall approach to life. Goldfried (1980) points out that such training conveys the message that people *should* strive to take effective action against any frustration or problem, in order to gain or regain control over their situ-

that call for expressiveness. The therapist should supply this information.

2. Clients may not know how to behave assertively. They may not assume the tone and loudness of voice, the fluency of speech, the facial expression and eye contact, and the body posture necessary for assertiveness. Modeling and role playing can help these people acquire the signals of firmness and directness.

3. Clients may fear that something terrible will happen if they assert themselves. Systematic desensitization may reduce this anticipatory anxiety. In others assertiveness seems to be blocked by negative self-statements, such as "If I assert myself and am rejected, that would be a catastrophe" (Schwartz and Gottman, 1976). They will profit from rational-emotive therapy.

4. The client may not feel that it is "proper" or "right" to be assertive. The value systems of some people preclude or discourage assertiveness. For example, some of the problems of a Catholic nun undergoing therapy seemed to relate to her unassertiveness, but through discussion it became clear that she would violate some of her vows were she more expressive and outspoken. By mutual agreement assertion training was not undertaken; instead, therapy focused on helping her work within her chosen profession in ways that were more personally satisfying and yet not more assertive.

Assertion training may begin with conversations in which the therapist tries to get the client to distinguish between assertiveness and aggression. For people who are submissive, even making a reasonable request or refusing a presumptuous one may make them feel that they are being hostile. Then therapists usually give clients sample situations that will leave them feeling put upon if they are unable to handle them. The situations usually require that they stand up for their rights, their time, and their energies.

You have been studying very hard for weeks, taking no time off at all for relaxation. But now a new film, which will play for only a few days, interests you and you have decided to take a few hours and go late this evening to see it. On the way to an afternoon class, your very good friend tells you that she has free tickets to a concert this evening and asks you to go with her. How do you say no?

Behavior rehearsal is a useful technique in assertion training. The therapist discusses and models appropriate assertiveness and then has the client role-play situations. Improvement is rewarded by praise from the therapist or from other members of an assertion training group. Graded homework assignments, such as asking the garageman to explain the latest bill for repairs, then telling an uncle that his constant criticisms are resented, are given as soon as the client has acquired some degree of assertiveness through session work.

Assertion training raises several ethical issues. To encourage assertiveness in people who, like the nun mentioned earlier, believe that self-denial is a greater good than self-expression would violate the client's value system and could generate an unfavorable "ripple effect" in other areas of the person's life. Drawing a distinction between assertion and aggression is also an ethical issue. Behavior considered assertive by one person may be seen by another as aggressive. If we adopt the distinction made by Lange and Jakubowski, that assertion respects the rights of others whereas aggression does not, we still have to make a judgment about what the rights of others are. Thus assertion training touches on moral aspects of social living, namely the definition of other people's rights and the proper means of standing up for one's own.

ation. To view life as full of challenges to be overcome may encourage the development of a type A personality (Price, 1982). Furthermore, SPS training fosters a calculating attitude. Clients are taught, perhaps rather doggedly, to analyze all life's frustrations and difficulties in highly rational terms. Perhaps some problems are best left unexamined by our rational minds.

Some Reflections on Cognitive Behavior Therapy

As we have indicated, behavior therapy initially aligned itself with stimulus–response psychology—with the study of classical and operant conditioning—the assumption being that principles and procedures derived from conditioning experiments could be applied to lessen psychological suffering. The S–R orientation came from behaviorists like Watson and Skinner, who had become dissatisfied with the work done on the contents of the mind and consciousness in Wundt's and Titchener's laboratories and with their use of introspection in these studies. What has now developed and is called cognitive behavior therapy (or sometimes cognitive therapy) may appear to be a radical and novel departure, given the earlier focus of behavior therapists on classical and operant conditioning. But in a historical sense it actually represents a return to the cognitive foci of this earliest period of experimental psychology, and many experimental psychologists have continued through the years to do research into cognition—into the mental processes of perceiving, recognizing, conceiving, judging, and reasoning, of problem solving, imagining, and other symbolizing activities.

Ellis and Beck try directly to change cognitive processes in order to relieve psychological distress. From the beginning, however, behavior therapists have relied heavily on the human being's capacity to symbolize, to process information, to represent the world in words and images. Wolpe's systematic desensitization is a very clear example. This technique, believed by Wolpe to rest on conditioning principles, is inherently a cognitive procedure, for the client *imagines* what is fearful. Indeed, the most exciting overt behavioral event during a regimen of desensitization is the client's occasional signaling of anxiety by raising an index finger! If anything important is happening, it is surely going on "under the skin," and some of this activity is surely cognitive in nature.

As behavior therapy "goes cognitive," however, it is important to bear in mind that contemporary researchers continue to believe that behavioral *procedures* are more powerful than strictly verbal ones in affecting cognitive *processes* (Bandura, 1977). That is, they favor behavioral techniques while maintaining that it is important to alter a person's beliefs in order to effect an enduring change in behavior and emotion. Bandura suggests, in fact, that all therapeutic procedures, to the extent that they are effective, work their improvement by giving the person a sense of mastery, of "self-efficacy." At the same time he finds that the most effective way to gain a sense of self-efficacy, if one is lacking, is by changing behavior. Whether or not we believe self-efficacy to be as important as Bandura does, a distinction can be made between processes that underlie improvement and *procedures* that set these *processes* in motion. Cognitive behavior therapists continue to be behavioral in their use of performance-based procedures and in their commitment to behavioral change, but they are cognitive in the sense that they believe cognitive change to be an important mechanism that accounts for the effectiveness of at least some behavioral procedures. Indeed, cognition and behavior continually and reciprocally influence each other—new behavior can alter thinking, and that new mode of thinking can in turn facilitate the new behavior. In addition, the environment influences both thought and action and is influenced by them. The model, termed **triadic reciprocality** by Bandura (1986), highlights the close interrelatedness of thinking, behaving, and the environment.

All cognitive behavior therapists heed the mental processes of their clients in another way. They pay attention to the world as it is perceived by the client. It is not what impinges on us from the outside that controls our behavior, the assumption that has guided stimulus–response psychology for decades. Rather our feelings and behavior are determined by how we view the world. The Greek philosopher Epictetus stated this in the first century: "Men are disturbed not by things, but by the view they take of them." Thus behavior therapy is being brought closer to the humanistic and existential therapies reviewed in Chapter 18. A central thesis of therapists like Rogers and Perls is that clients must be understood from their own frame of reference, from their phenomenological world, for it is this perception of the world that controls life and behavior.

From the philosophical point of view, such assumptions on the part of those who would understand people and try to help them are profoundly important. Experimentally minded clinicians and researchers are intrigued by how much the new field of cognitive behavior therapy has in common with the humanists and their attention to the phenomenological world of their clients. To be sure, the *techniques* used by cognitive behavior therapists are usually quite different from those of the followers of Rogers and of Perls. But as students of psychotherapy and of human nature, these surface differences should not blind us to the links between the two approaches.

Behavioral Medicine

Behavioral medicine has two roots, the early work in psychosomatic medicine, done primarily by psychiatrists and other physicians, and the later work in behavior therapy, done primarily by psychologists (Brownell, 1982). The contributions of psychiatrists and physicians sensitized mental health workers to the role of psychological factors in both the etiology and the treatment of medical disorders. The contributions of the psychologists were primarily in the techniques of change, the tools by which psychological factors can be analyzed and manipulated to enhance our understanding of illness as well as how to prevent it and treat it.

Behavioral medicine is truly a marriage of two disparate fields, one that seems to be working very well. It is not restricted to a set of techniques or particular principles of changing behavior. Rather, workers in this field employ a wide variety of procedures—from contingency management through operant conditioning to desensitization through counterconditioning—all of which have in common the goal of altering bad living habits, distressed psychological states, and aberrant physiological processes, in order to have a beneficial impact on a person's physical condition. Behavioral medicine has already been mentioned several times in this book. Psychophysiological disorders (Chapter 8) and the problems of seriously ill children (Chapter 15) are treated by behavioral medicine, as are the addictive disorders that threaten health, such as cigarette smoking and alcoholism (Chapter 11). A sampling of other activities will convey an even better sense of the scope of this emerging multidisciplinary field of research and treatment.

Chronic Pain and Activity

Millions of Americans suffer from chronic pain (Bonica, 1981). Defined as pain that persists beyond the healing time of the affected parts of the body, it accounts for millions of dollars of lost work time and disrupts family life, as well as keeping the sufferer in continuous and extreme discomfort. Behavioral medicine assumes that treatment can be psychological as well as medical.

After an attack of severe back muscle spasms, for example, a person may be reluctant to engage in physical activity more vigorous than getting into and out of bed. In the acute phase this is sensible behavior. As the spasms ease, and if no other damage has occurred, such as to the disks between the vertebrae, the patient should begin moving more normally, stretching, and eventually attempting exercises to strengthen the very muscles that had gone into spasm. In a recent comparative study, Fordyce and his colleagues (Fordyce, Brockway, Bergman, and Spengler, 1986) showed the superiority of a behavioral program over a traditional medical one for management of acute back pain. In the traditional program patients exercised and otherwise moved about only until they felt pain, whereas the behavioral management program encouraged them to exercise at a predetermined intensity for a predetermined period of time, even if they experienced pain. Low back pain patients have also been given relaxation training and encouraged to relabel their pain as numbness or tickling (Rybstein-Blinchik, 1979), a cognitive-restructuring procedure. Obviously care must be taken not to push patients beyond activities their bodies are actually ready for. The implicit message seems to be that traditional medical practice has underestimated what chronic pain patients are capable of (Keefe and Gil, 1986).

Other kinds of pain have also been favorably affected by psychological interventions. Wells, Howard, Nowlin, and Vargas (1986) gave twenty-four patients being prepared for a variety of elective surgeries one hour of "stress inoculation training" (Meichenbaum, 1975). The training session consisted of deep breathing, relaxation, pleasant imagery, and the encouragement to use positive coping self-statements. Patients practiced these drills for the week preceding surgery. Compared to a control group, these patients were less anxious both before and after surgery, felt less postsurgical pain, and were discharged on the average of three and one-half days sooner. This last statistic is particularly striking—consider the huge savings in medical costs that could be achieved if these results are replicable and stable.

Chronic Diseases and Life-style

Behavioral medicine is concerned not only with alleviation of illness and pain but with their prevention; when it has this purpose, it is often called health psychology. At the beginning of this century, the leading causes of death were infectious diseases such as influenza and tuberculosis. With these illnesses largely under medical control, the 1980s saw Americans succumbing most often to diseases of the heart, cancer, cerebrovascular diseases such as stroke, and accidents. For each of these the behavior of people over their lifetime—their life-style—is implicated. We have already seen in Chapter 8 that, along with type A personality, a diet high in cholesterol, lack of exercise, and smoking contribute to heart disease.

Physicians have for years been dispensing sound advice about diet, exercise, and smoking, usually with little effect on life-style. Getting people to do what is in the best interest of their health is a challenge! Merely telling a sedentary file clerk that she must exercise for at least fifteen minutes three times a week at 70 percent of her maximum heart rate will probably not rouse her to adhere to such a schedule.

In one study (Epstein *et al.*, 1980) female college students agreed that they would run one to two miles a day for five weeks and made a five-dollar deposit, which was returned to them a dollar at a time as they complied. These young women ran more consistently than those in a control group who had no contingency. A number of similar programs for encouraging regular exercise have also been reported. Of particular interest was the posting of a cartoon at the base of a public stairway and escalator (Brownell, Stunkard, and Albaum, 1980). It portrayed a glum, unhealthy-looking heart taking the escalator, next to a robust, happy heart bounding up a flight of stairs; the caption read, "Your heart needs exercise . . . here's your chance." Simple and inexpensive, the cartoon effected a dramatic change in people passing that way: three times as many used the stairs as had been observed earlier. Stairs are of course far more available than aerobics exercise sessions and climbing them is easier than instituting a jogging regimen. Regular stair use is known to be a very healthful cardiovascular exercise for people throughout their lives.

BOX 19.5

META-ANALYSIS AND THE EFFECTS OF PSYCHOTHERAPY

A development in psychotherapy research that has attracted enormous attention in recent years is **meta-analysis**. Devised by Smith, Glass, and Miller (1980), it can be summarized as

a quantitative method for averaging and integrating the standardized results of a large number of different studies. The unit of analysis is the effect size (ES), a quantitative index of the size of the effect of therapy . . . [arrived at] by subtracting the mean of the control group from the mean of the treatment group and dividing that difference by the standard deviation of the control group. . . . The larger the ES, the greater the effect of therapy. . . . For example, Smith and Glass (1980) claimed that the ES for all psychological therapies . . . was 0.68, which means that the average client receiving therapy would do better than 75% of those who do not receive therapy. Once the ES's from a large number of different studies have been calculated, statistical analyses can be carried out to answer different questions about treatment outcome, such as comparing the effects of different therapies. . . . A consensually validated statistical method, meta-analysis aims to eliminate or at least minimize the subjectivity and reviewer bias to which traditional "literary reviews" of the evidence are susceptible. (O'Leary and Wilson, 1987, p. 178)

The basis of comparison need not be Therapy A versus Therapy B, rather, one can compare on dimensions such as type of subjects and settings in which therapy was administered. The independent variables, in other words, can be any factors considered to be influential in the outcome of an intervention. The great advantage of meta-analysis is that it provides a common metric across studies conducted in diverse settings by different investigators at different times (Kazdin, 1986).

In their original and oft-cited report, Smith *et al.* (1980) meta-analyzed 475 psychotherapy outcome studies involving more than 25,000 subjects and 1700 effect sizes and came to two conclusions that have attracted considerable attention and created controversy. First, they concluded that a wide range of therapies produce larger effect sizes than no treatment. Specifically, treated patients were found to be better off than almost 80 percent of untreated patients. Confirming results have been reported by others as well (e.g., Howard, Kopta, Krause, and Orlinsky, 1986). Second, Smith *et al.* contend that effect sizes across diverse modes of intervention are not different from each other.

The psychotherapy research literature is now replete with references to and use of meta-analysis in efforts to sort through scores of studies and to bring a sense of order

and fairness to the task of making comparative statements on the merits of contrasting kinds of therapy. Indeed, the current edition of a standard handbook of psychotherapy and behavior change (Garfield and Bergin, 1986) relies heavily on literature reviews utilizing this technique. As part of a growing trend toward eclecticism in psychotherapy, reviewers of the literature rely increasingly on meta-analysis as an evaluative and comparative tool. In this spirit, Lambert *et al.* (1986) draw several conclusions about psychotherapy *in general,* that is, without explicit consideration of *differences among* theoretical orientations. Although in our view this tactic runs the risk of comparing the proverbial apples and oranges, their conclusions are nonetheless useful in our broad-gauged study of this field.

1. Lambert *et al.* (1986) go beyond the findings of Smith *et al.* (1980) as well as others to find that many psychotherapeutic interventions surpass in effectiveness a number of so-called attention-placebo control groups. Their conclusion is that psychotherapists are more than "placebologists" (p. 163). By the same token, what Lambert *et al.* call "common factors" (see page 516), rather than placebo factors, namely, warmth, trust, and encouragement, do themselves effect significant and even lasting improvement in a broad range of anxiety and affective disorders.

2. They found that the positive effects of psychotherapy tend to be maintained for many months following termination. Lambert *et al.* (1986) base this sanguine conclusion on a meta-analysis of 67 outcome studies by Nicholson and Berman (1983), mostly behavioral in nature, with patients other than those diagnosed as psychotic, organic-disordered, antisocial personality, or addictive-disordered. Posttreatment status correlated well with follow-up status and, in general, group differences at follow-up were similar to those immediately following termination of therapy. This finding is obviously important to the client and to the individual therapist (who hopes that his or her patients will continue to do well once they stop coming for regular sessions); it is important as well to psychotherapy researchers, who often have to undertake expensive and very arduous follow-up measures to convince their colleagues that the effects of a given treatment are enduring. And yet Lambert *et al.* (1986) remind us that some disorders probably need to be followed up more than others, for example, depression, which is known to be recurrent.

3. There is considerable variability in therapy effects. Although treatment group X may, on average, show sig-

nificant improvement, there are often patients in that group who get worse. This "deterioration effect" is discussed in greater detail in Box 20.1.

4. Recent meta-analytic studies comparing insight therapy to cognitive and behavioral interventions show a slight but consistent advantage to the latter, although there is criticism by proponents of insight therapy that behavioral and cognitive therapies focus on milder disorders.*

However, meta-analysis has been criticized by a number of psychotherapy researchers for the following reasons.

1. The behavioral researchers Wilson and Rachman (Rachman and Wilson, 1980; Wilson and Rachman, 1983) allege that many behavior therapy studies, in particular those employing single-subject designs (see page 124), were omitted in the Smith *et al.* (1980) review. The claim is that the exclusion of these studies weakened the case for behavior therapy.

2. A more general problem is the quality control of studies that are included in a meta-analysis. Therapy studies differ in their internal and external validity *as judged by particular researchers*. Because the meta-analyses of Smith *et al.* give equal weight to all studies, a situation is created where a poorly controlled outcome study receives as much attention as a well-controlled one. When Smith *et al.* attempted to address this problem by comparing effect sizes of good versus poor studies and found no differences, they were further criticized for the criteria they employed in separating the "good" from the "not-so-good" (Rachman and Wilson, 1980)! They were criticized also for using the results of this closer scrutiny to conclude that good and bad studies can be lumped together, the criticism being that "if poor-quality research agrees with good research, include it. . . . If poor research disagrees, disregard it" (Mintz, 1983, p. 74). O'Leary and Wilson (1987) consider other critiques as well and conclude that the ultimate problem is that *someone* has to make a judgment of good versus poor quality in psychotherapy research and that *others* can find fault with that judgment.

This would appear to be an insoluble problem, one that has existed for years in reviews of therapy outcome research. There are times when a scholar has no choice but to make his or her own judgment about the validity of a piece of research and to decide whether or not to ignore it. Perhaps Mintz (1983) is correct in saying that the move toward meta-analysis in this field has at least sensitized us to the subjectivity that is inherent in passing judgment on research, and has also encouraged greater explicitness in the criteria used to accept or to reject the findings of a given outcome study. Moreover, meta-analysis has uncovered deficiencies in some published research, for example, inadequate reporting of means and standard deviations and the collection of outcome data by persons not blinded to the treatment condition to which subjects were assigned (Shapiro and Shapiro, 1983). A long-term beneficial effect of meta-analysis may, then, be an improvement in research practices and a tightening of publication standards (Kazdin, 1986).

3. The overwhelming majority of outcome studies employ more than one measure. In their original work, Smith *et al.* (1980) computed effect sizes separately for each measure in each study; this led to greater weight being given to studies with larger numbers of outcome measures. Efforts to correct this inequity (e.g., Landman and Dawes, 1980; Prioleau, Murdock, and Brody, 1983) included combining separate measures to come up with a single effect size estimate for each study. At first blush this seems a good and fair solution, but as O'Leary and Wilson (1987) point out, it obscures the different information that different measures can provide, and also overlooks the fact that different measures may change at different rates from a given intervention. They point out, for example, that rapid weight reduction programs can lead to quick weight loss *but* to an increase in depression (Stunkard and Rush, 1974). If one statistically combines these two measures into a single one, a finding of no significant effect emerges, thus concealing a clinically important outcome.

4. Insight-oriented therapists claim that there is a bias against them because most of the therapy outcome research has been done by cognitive and behavioral therapists (Lambert *et al.*, 1986). This is troublesome because Smith *et al.* (1980) found larger effect sizes for those techniques to which the investigator had a prior allegiance.

With all its attendant problems, meta-analysis, properly and creatively applied, promises to bring a measure of greater objectivity to the evaluation of psychotherapy. The continuing challenge, in our view, is the seemingly inescapable role of the investigator's own paradigm in judging the merits of another's meta-analysis.

---

*As one might expect, charges of bias go back and forth between proponents of diverse approaches. Dispassionate, paradigm-free interpretations of data are no less difficult to come by in therapy research than in psychopathology.

Many industries and corporations now maintain their own health and fitness programs, screening their employees for such illnesses as hypertension and providing facilities and incentives for taking regular exercise, even during work hours. More than magnanimity is operating here; such programs are known to reduce absenteeism and improve health generally, making them cost-effective for the company.

Biofeedback

A visit to the commercial exhibit area of any psychological or psychiatric convention will reveal a plentiful display of complex biofeedback apparatus, touted as an efficient, even miraculous, means of helping people control one or another bodily-mental state. Basically, by using sensitive instrumentation, biofeedback gives a person prompt and exact information, otherwise unavailable, on muscle activity, brain waves, skin temperature, heart rate, blood pressure, and other bodily functions. It is assumed that a person can achieve greater voluntary control over these phenomena—most of which were once considered to be under involuntary control and completely unresponsive to will—if he or she knows immediately, through an auditory or visual signal, whether a somatic activity is increasing or decreasing. Because anxiety has generally been viewed as a state involving the autonomic ("involuntary") nervous system, and because psychophysiological disorders afflict organs innervated by this system, it is obvious why researchers and clinicians became intrigued with biofeedback. Indeed, biofeedback was for a time virtually synonymous with behavioral medicine.

In a series of studies at Harvard Medical School, Shapiro, Tursky, and Schwartz (1970; Schwartz, 1973) demonstrated that human volunteers could achieve significant short-term changes in blood pressure and in heart rate. They found that some subjects could even be trained to increase their heart rate while decreasing blood pressure. Achievement of this fine-grained control lent impetus to biofeedback work with human beings and awakened hope that certain clinical disorders might be alleviated in this new way.

In the move from analogue to the more challenging world of the clinic, at least three vital questions must be asked. First, can persons whose systems are *malfunctioning* achieve the same biofeedback control over bodily events that normal subjects can acquire? Second, if actual patients can achieve some degree of control, will it be enough to make a significant difference in their problems? And third, can the control achieved by patients hooked up to and receiving immediate feedback from a remarkable apparatus be carried over to real-

life situations in which they will have no special devices to inform them of the state of the bodily functions that they have learned to control?

Research with patients suffering from essential hypertension has been somewhat encouraging, but results have not been certain enough to establish biofeedback as a standard treatment for the problem (Shapiro and Surwit, 1979). Moreover, some (Blanchard *et al.*, 1979) believe that relaxation training, which is often given along with biofeedback, does more to reduce blood pressure than the biofeedback itself, a conclusion recently concurred with in recent reviews by Emmelkamp (1986), O'Leary and Wilson (1987), and Reed, Katkin, and Goldband (1986).

The control of migraine headache by biofeedback was reviewed in Chapter 8 (page 212). Tension headaches, believed to be caused by excessive and persistent tension in the frontalis muscles of the forehead and in the muscles of the neck, have also been approached within this framework, the standard treatment entailing feedback of tension in the frontalis muscles. Although such biofeedback has indeed been shown to be effective (e.g., Birbaumer, 1977), recent studies suggest that cognitive factors may play a role. For example, Holroyd *et al.* (1984) found that *believing* that one was reducing frontalis tension via biofeedback was associated with reductions in tension headaches, whether or not such reductions were actually being achieved. Enhanced feelings of self-efficacy and internal control appear to have inherent stress-reducing properties, a theme we encountered back in Chapter 6 when we discussed control and anxiety. It is possible that biofeedback strengthens the sense of control, thereby reducing general anxiety levels and ultimately tension headaches. Other studies

Biofeedback was the principal therapy used in the early days of behavioral medicine.

(e.g., Blanchard *et al.*, 1982; Cox, Freundlich, and Meyer, 1975) suggest that relaxation per se is the critical variable, similar to the beliefs about treating essential hypertension.

The control of various forms of epilepsy through biofeedback has been attempted with some success. Several patients have reduced the frequency of seizures through intensive biofeedback training to increase brain activity in the sensorimotor cortex, but this improvement did not invariably persist when training sessions were discontinued (Sterman, 1973).

In Raynaud's disease, blood flow to the hands and feet, and sometimes to the face, nose, and ears, is reduced by spasms of small peripheral arteries and can be quite serious if not corrected. Because drug treatment to dilate vessels is often ineffective and can have negative side effects, behavioral medicine researchers have successfully experimented with both relaxation and biofeedback to increase finger temperature (Surwit, 1982; Freedman, Ianni, and Wenig, 1985). It is far from clear, however, whether the biofeedback is an improvement over straightforward relaxation training (Reed, Katkin, and Goldband, 1986). Indeed, it is questionable whether increases in finger temperature effected by biofeedback are correlated at all with improvement in Raynaud symptoms (Keefe, Surwit, and Pilon, 1979).

Reports on the use of biofeedback for neuromuscular disorders—cerebral palsy, paralysis in the aftermath of stroke and of diseases such as poliomyelitis—have been more positive. The initial research was done by Basmajian (1977) in the early 1960s. Paralyzed patients proved able to activate single motor cells if informed of their firing by biofeedback. The Biofeedback Society of America is so enthusiastic about the effectiveness of biofeedback for hemiplegia, a paralysis on one side of the body usually caused by stroke, that it is regarded as the treatment of choice (Fernando and Basmajian, 1978). The fact that patients participating in these studies had not earlier been helped by conventional physical therapy lends credibility to the specific effectiveness of biofeedback in allowing them to make minute muscle movements. A 1980 report by the National Institute of Mental Health reasons that biofeedback should be especially useful for neuromuscular disorders because functions that have gone awry are normally under the voluntary control of the central nervous system. If the dysfunction is caused in part by the faintness of the signs of muscle movement in damaged tissue, amplifying these proprioceptive signals by feedback will make the patient aware of them and possibly allow control (Runck, 1980).

Whether or not biofeedback has specific effects or whether it helps patients relax and achieve an enhanced sense of control over stress, clinicians must remain mindful of the complexities of human problems. A man with high blood pressure, for example, might have to alter a tense, driven life-style before he can significantly reduce blood pressure through biofeedback. It is unwise, and a sign of naive clinical practice, to assume that one technique focused on a specific malfunction or problem will invariably cure the patient.[6]

Generalization and Maintenance of Treatment Effects

As we have indicated, generalizing to real life and maintaining whatever gains have been achieved in therapy is a problem common to all treatments. Insight therapists assume that therapeutic effects are made more general through restructuring of the personality. As environmentalists, behavior therapists wonder how changes brought about by their manipulations can be made to persist once clients return to their everyday situations, which are often assumed to have been a factor in creating their problems in the first place! Behavior therapists have tried to meet this challenge in several ways.

Intermittent Reinforcement

Because laboratory findings indicate that intermittent reinforcement—rewarding a response only a portion of the times it appears—makes new behavior more enduring, many operant programs take care to move away from continuous schedules of reinforcement once desired behavior is occurring with satisfactory regularity. For example, if a teacher has succeeded in helping a disruptive boy spend more time in his seat by praising him generously for each arithmetic problem that he finishes there, he or she will gradually reward him for every other success, and ultimately only infrequently. The hope is that the satisfactions of being a good pupil will make the child less dependent on the teacher's approval.

Another strategy is to move from artificial reinforcers to those that occur naturally in the social environment. A token program might be maintained only long enough to encourage certain desired behavior, after which the person is weaned to natural reinforcers such as praise from peers.

---

[6]Of course, medical consultation is always a part of responsible treatment of psychophysiological disorders such as hypertension.

BOX 19.6

SELF-CONTROL—OUTSIDE A BEHAVIORAL PARADIGM?

One of the most exciting areas in behavior therapy concerns the exercise of self-control (Kanfer, 1979; Mahoney, 1972; Runck, 1982). Much of the research and theory reviewed in this chapter seems to assume that the human being is a relatively passive recipient of stimulation from the environment. Given this apparent dependence on the external world, how can we account for behavior that appears to be autonomous, willed, and often contrary to what might be expected in a particular situation? How, for example, do we account for the fact that a person on a diet refrains from eating a luscious piece of chocolate cake even when hungry?

Psychoanalytic writers, including the ego analysts, handle the issue by positing within the person some kind of internal agent. Thus many ego analysts assert that the ego can operate on its own power, making deliberate decisions for the entire psychic system—including decisions that go against the wishes of the id. Behaviorists, especially Skinner (1953), have objected to this "explanation," regarding it as simply a relabeling of the phenomena.

Perhaps the most widely accepted behavioral view of self-control is Skinner's: an individual engages in self-control when he or she arranges the environment so that only certain controlling stimuli are present. A person wishing to lose weight rids his or her home of fattening foods and avoids passing restaurants when hungry. Behavior remains a function of the surroundings, but they are controlled by the individual.

A related behavioral conception of self-control is reflected in Bandura's (1969) explanation of aversive conditioning. Rather than being passively conditioned to feel distaste for stimuli that have been paired with shock, a peson learns a skill of aversive self-stimulation that he or she deliberately applies in real life. According to this view, a person resists a temptation by *deliberately* recalling the earlier aversive experience of being shocked or nauseated during therapy. Here, then, the individual is said to create symbolic stimuli that, in turn, control behavior.

A familiar means of exercising self-control, also discussed in the behavior therapy literature, is setting standards for oneself and denying oneself reinforcement unless they are met (Bandura and Perloff, 1967). One example is a tactic often employed by the authors of this book: I will not leave this desk for a snack until I have finished writing this page. When a person sets goals, and makes a contract with himself about achieving them before enjoying a reward, and then keeps to the contract without obvious external constraints, he can be said to have exercised self-control.

Self-control can be applied with *any* therapy technique. The only stipulation is that the client implement the procedure on his own, after receiving instructions from the therapist. For example, a client who was being desensitized decided on his own to imagine some of the hierarchy scenes while relaxing in a warm tub. A sophisticated and intelligent man, he felt that he understood the rationale of desensitization well enough and had enough control over the processes of his imagination to meet the procedural requirements of the technique. Consequently, after achieving what he felt to be a state of deep relaxation in his bathtub, he closed his eyes and carried out the scene presentation and scene termination as he had learned to do

Environmental Modification

Another strategy for bringing about generalization takes the therapist into the province of community psychology, which will be discussed in the next chapter. Behavior therapists manipulate surroundings, or attempt to do so, to support changes brought about in treatment. As one small example, Lovaas and his colleagues (1973) found that the gains painstakingly achieved in therapy for autistic children were sustained only when their parents continued to reinforce their good behavior.

Self-Reinforcement

Generalization can also be enhanced by assigning the client a more active role, as done by Drabman, Spitalnik, and O'Leary (1973). In a three-month after-school program for disruptive young boys, the teacher re-warded nondisruptive classroom behavior and appropriate reading behavior. Later the boys were allowed to self-rate their behavior according to the teacher's criteria and reward their own good conduct. That is, the pupils were taught that they could earn special privileges not only by behaving well when the teacher dispensed rewards but through honest evaluation of their own good behavior. The findings for the first part of the study were similar to those of many other studies: disruptive behavior decreased and academic behavior improved when the teacher judged them and dispensed the tokens. This improvement then generalized to periods of each class during which the child *himself judged* how well he was doing and *reinforced himself* accordingly; in other words, improved performance was extended to periods of time when the pupils were not under direct external control (see Box 19.6).

from the behavior therapist. Later, when he was with the therapist, they were able to skip the items to which he had desensitized himself in the tub and proceed more rapidly through the anxiety hierarchy.

Implicit in all conceptions of self-control are three criteria: (1) there are *few external controls* that could explain the behavior; (2) control of self is difficult enough that the person has to *put forth some effort;* and (3) the behavior in question is engaged in with *conscious deliberation and choice.* The individual actively decides to exercise self-control either by performing some action or by keeping himself from doing something, such as overeating. He does not do it automatically, nor is he forced to by someone else.

Let us take the example of a male jogger. If an army sergeant is goading this man along, the first criterion is not met and his running would not be an instance of self-control, even though considerable effort is probably required to maintain the running.

If the jogger finds it pleasurable to run, so enjoyable that he would rather do so than engage in other activities, the running cannot be considered an instance of self-control. Self-control is to be seen in the *earliest* stages of jogging, when the man may indeed be exerting great effort. He groans as he dons his Nikes, looks at his watch after only a few minutes of running to see how long this torture has been going on, and collapses in relief after half a mile, glad that the ordeal is over.

The third criterion, acting with conscious deliberation and choice, distinguishes self-control from actions people perform in a mindless way. It is probably a good thing that much of our everyday behavior is mindless, for imagine how fatiguing (and boring!) it would be to mull over and make specific decisions to do such things as look out a window, tie our shoelaces, eat our breakfast, and so on. But these very acts would be categorized as instances of self-control if, on a given occasion, we have to decide whether to engage in them, Eating would require self-control if we were on a strict diet and had agreed, with our spouse, or doctor, or ourselves, to reduce caloric intake.

In our opinion, the concept of self-control places a strain on the behavioristic paradigm, for people are described as acting independently, putting forth effort, deliberating and choosing. Each of these verbs supposes the person to be an *initiator* of action, as the place where control *begins.* Ardent behaviorists, though, will counter by asserting with Skinner that our view of the person as an initiator only indicates our ignorance of the external forces that ultimately control behavior. Thus the person who denies himself an extra dessert is not really controlling himself; rather his self-denial is controlled by some subtle reward unappreciated by the observer, or by a distinct reinforcer, such as being able later on to wear clothes of a smaller size. The flaw in this line of reasoning is that it is purely *post hoc* and irrefutable. We can *always* assert that, down the road, there will arrive the reinforcer that sustains the behavior. Such an "explanation" should be as unsatisfactory to the behaviorist as the psychoanalyst's invocation of an unconscious defense mechanism to account for an action.

The implications are clear. At least for disruptive children, self-evaluating and self-rewarding their own good behavior may be one effective way in which they can maintain it when the original controlling agent is absent.

Eliminating Secondary Gain

Most behavior therapists assign their clients homework, tasks to do between sessions. For example, clients may be asked to listen to audiotapes containing relaxation-training instructions. They sometimes fail to follow through in a consistent fashion, complaining of not having enough quiet time at home to listen to the tapes, or saying that they forgot about the assignment. Many patients are so resistant to doing on their own what they consciously and rationally agree is in their own best interests that therapists often invoke as an explanation the psychoanalytic concept of secondary gain, that the patient derives benefit from his problem. For complex and poorly understood reasons people sometimes act as though they unconsciously wish to keep their symptoms. Therapists, whatever their persuasion, may have to examine the client's interpersonal relationships for clues to why a person suffering directly from a problem seemingly prefers to hold on to it.

Relapse Prevention

Marlatt (1985) has proposed the "abstinence violation effect" as a focus of concern in relapse prevention. His research on alcoholism sensitized him to the generally negative effects of a "slip," as when the former drinker, after a successful period of abstinence, imbibes to a stupor after taking a single drink. Marlatt suggests that the ways the person reacts both cognitively and behaviorally to the slip will determine whether he overcomes the setback and stays on the wagon or whether he relapses and resumes drinking to excess. The consequences of the slip are hypothesized to be worse if the person attributes it to internal, stable, and global factors believed to be uncontrollable—in much the same way as Abramson, Seligman, and Teasdale (1978) theorize about helplessness and depression (see page 229). An example would be a belief that the slip was caused by an uncontrollable disease process that overwhelms the person once a single drink is taken. In contrast, relapse is assumed to be less likely if the individual attributes the slip to causes that are external, unstable, specific, and controllable, such as an expectedly stressful life event. Cognitive behavior therapists attempt to minimize the abstinence violation effect by encouraging attributions to external, unstable, and specific factors *and* by teaching coping strategies to deal with life stressors.

Attribution to Self

Attribution, a subject usually studied by social psychologists, may offer insight on how to maintain treatment gains once therapy is over. How a person explains to himself why he is behaving or has behaved in a particular way presumably helps to determine his subsequent actions. Might not a person who has been in therapy and attributes improvement in his behavior to an external cause, such as a reinforcer from the environment, lose ground once what he considers the external justification for change is gone? In an analogue study on attribution and maintaining a change in behavior (Davison and Valins, 1969), college undergraduates were shocked on their fingertips to determine how much they could bear. Then they took a "fast-acting vitamin compound" and were told that they would now be able to endure greater amounts of shock. And indeed they were, at least in their own minds. The experimenters had surreptitiously lowered the voltage levels to create this belief. Half of the subjects were then told that the capsule ingested was only a placebo, the others that its effects would soon wear off. Those who believed that they had taken a placebo attributed to themselves the greater ability to withstand discomfort and endured higher levels of shock on the third test. Those who believed that they had been given a real drug that was no longer effective were in the third round able to endure only lesser amounts of shock.

In an experiment with a similar design, conducted with people who were having trouble falling asleep, Davison, Tsujimoto, and Glaros (1973) obtained comparable results, indicating that "real" problems may be treated by helping patients to attribute improvements to themselves. Individuals attempting to reduce their smoking (Chambliss and Murray, 1979; Colletti and Kopel, 1979) and to lose weight (Jeffrey, 1974) have similarly benefited from attributing gains to their own efforts and changes in attitudes rather than to external forces. In a series of nonbehavior therapy outcome studies from the Johns Hopkins Psychotherapy Research Unit, patients who attributed their gains to a drug did not maintain their improvement as much as did those who construed their changes as arising from their own efforts (Frank, 1976).

What are the implications of attribution research? Since in behavior therapy most improvement seems to be controlled by environmental forces, especially therapy relying on operant manipulation, it might be wise for behavior therapists to help their clients to feel more responsible. By encouraging an "I did it" attitude, perhaps by motivating them to practice new skills and to expose themselves to challenging situations, therapists may help their clients be less dependent on therapy and therapist and better maintain their treatment gains. Insight therapies have always emphasized the desirability of patients' assuming primary responsibility for their improvement. Behavior therapists have eventually realized that they must come to grips with the issue (Bandura, 1977; Mischel, 1977). On a more general level, the question of attributing improvement underscores the importance of cognitive processes in behavior therapy.

Some Basic Issues in Behavior Therapy

Behavior therapy is expanding each year; with such a proliferation of activity, everyone concerned should remain aware of problems and issues that transcend particular experimental findings. The following considerations, many of which have been alluded to earlier, need to be kept clearly in mind.

Internal Behavior and Cognition

In Chapter 5, we demonstrated that the inference of intervening processes and other explanatory fictions is useful in interpreting data and generating fruitful hypotheses. Behavior therapists are often thought to hold the radical behavioristic positions of Watson and Skinner, that it is not useful or legitimate to make inferences about internal processes of the organism.

The position we share with others (see Bandura, 1969, 1986; Kanfer and Phillips, 1970; Mahoney, 1974; MacCorquodale and Meehl, 1948; Mischel, 1968; O'Leary and Wilson, 1987) is that behavior therapy, as applied experimental psychology, is legitimately concerned with internal as well as external events. provided the internal mediators are securely anchored to observable stimuli or responses.

Underlying Causes

Behavior therapy is sometimes held to deal with symptoms whereas other therapies, particularly psychoanalytically oriented ones, are concerned with "root" or "underlying" causes. To many people a determinant of behavior that is assumed to lie in the unconscious or in the past is somehow more "underlying" or "basic" than a determinant that is anchored in the current environment. This conception fails to consider the fact that science searches for the most significant causes of behavior. If "underlying" is defined as "not immediately obvious," cognitive and behavior therapists indeed search for underlying causes. If such causes are taken to be the most significant ones, that is, the controlling variables, the task of behavior therapists is the same as for all other therapists—to find the most significant causes (Bandura, 1969).

The issue of underlying causes has become even more salient with the growth of cognitive approaches. For some time Ellis, Beck, and their followers have been concerned with the form and nature of beliefs, ideas, assumptions, and schemata that may account for a patient's disordered behavior and emotion and that are seldom openly and directly expressed. These must usually be *inferred* by the clinician or experimenter based on the person's actions or readily detectable thoughts. That is, cognitive behavior therapists, not unlike their analytic counterparts, believe generally that there is more to the patient than immediately meets the eye (Goldfried and Davison, 1976). Guidano and Liotti (1983), for example, speak of the "protective belt" behind which one must search for core beliefs, which themselves are generally related to one's idea of oneself, such as a negative self-image. Mahoney (1982) believes that core, central cognitions may be extremely difficult to change, even when uncovered, because they stem from one's earlier developmental history. And well before the popularity of cognitive behavior therapy, George Kelly distinguished between "core constructs" and "peripheral constructs," the former relating to the person's basic sense of self or identity (Kelly, 1955).

Safran, Vallis, Segal, and Shaw (1986) consider these and other core cognitive processes to be important for cognitive therapists to assess and attempt to change. Although changing core beliefs is not a simple matter for either patient or therapist, it is believed to be essential to cognitive therapy if its positive effects are to be enduring. The subtlety in assessing these variables that are not immediately apparent is discussed later when we consider rapprochement between behavior therapy and psychoanalysis. But the approach is similar also to the discussion in Chapter 18 of advanced accurate empathy (page 526), as can be seen from the following case example given by Safran *et al.* (1986):

For example, a client who failed an exam . . . accessed the automatic thought: "I can't handle university." At this point the therapist could have challenged this belief or encouraged the client to examine evidence relevant to this belief. Instead she decided to engage in a process of vertical exploration. In response to the therapist's probes a constellation of automatic thoughts emerged that revolved around the client's beliefs that he was not smart enough. The client at this point spontaneously recalled two memories of situations in which he had felt humiliated and worthless because he felt he had "been stupid" at the time. As he recounted these memories he became visibly more emotional. Further exploration revealed that these feelings of intellectual inferiority and associated feelings of worthlessness cut across a number of problem situations for the client. It also emerged that he believed that his value as a person was completely dependent upon his intellectual performance. In this situation had the therapist intervened when the first automatic thought emerged, she may not have accessed the entire chain of self-evaluative cognitions and higher level constructs that underlay the client's distress. (p. 515)

Broad-Spectrum Treatment

Our review of behavior therapy has necessarily been fragmented because we have dealt with separate techniques one at a time. In clinical practice, however, behavior therapists employ several procedures at once or sequentially in an attempt to deal with all the important controlling variables; this approach is generally referred to as *broad-spectrum behavior therapy* (Lazarus, 1971). For example, a woman fearful of leaving her home might well undergo *in vivo* desensitization by walking out of her door and gradually engaging in activities that take her farther and farther from her safe haven. Over the years, however, she may also have built up a dependent relationship with her husband. As she becomes bolder in venturing forth, this change in her behavior may disrupt the equilibrium of the relationship that she and her husband have worked out over the years (see page 145). To attend only to her fear of leaving home would be incomplete behavior therapy (Lazarus, 1965) and might even lead to replacement of the agoraphobia with another difficulty that would serve to keep the woman at home—a problem frequently called "symptom substitution."

In a related vein, therapists do not invariably focus only on the patient's complaint as stated during the first interview. A clinical graduate student was desensitizing an undergraduate for test anxiety. The client made good progress up the hierarchy of imagined situations but was not improving at all in the real world of test taking. The supervisor of the graduate student suggested that the therapist find out whether the client was studying for his tests. It turned out that he was not; worry about the health of his mother was markedly interfering with his attempts to study. Thus the goal of making the client nonchalant about taking tests was inappropriate, for he was approaching the tests themselves without adequate preparation. On the basis of additional assessment, the therapy shifted away from desensitization to a discussion of how the client could deal with his realistic fears about his mother's possible death.

Relationship Factors

A good relationship between client and therapist is important for many reasons. As discussed in Chapter 4 (page 76), it seems doubtful that clients will reveal deeply personal information if they do not trust or respect their therapists. Furthermore, since behavior therapy cannot be imposed on an unwilling client, a therapist must obtain the cooperation of the client if there is to be any possibility that techniques will have their desired effect. In desensitization, for example, a client could readily sabotage the best efforts of the therapist by not imagining a particular scene, by not signaling anxiety appropriately, and by not practicing relaxation. And in virtually all other behavior therapy procedures clients are able to, and sometimes will, work against the therapist if relationship factors are neglected (Davison, 1973).

In the Paul (1966) study of anxious public speakers, for example, considerable and long-lasting improvement was observed in subjects who were given the attention-placebo treatment. Thus, although desensitization subjects improved more than the others, the significant improvement in the attention-placebo group demonstrates the substantial contribution of the warm, trusting relationship with a therapist.

Flesh on the Theoretical Skeleton

Determining the most important controlling variables is related to another overlooked aspect of behavior therapy—indeed, of any therapy—namely, moving from a general principle to a concrete clinical intervention.

To illustrate, let us consider a study in which undergraduates were trained to analyze the behavior of severely disturbed children in operant conditioning terms (Davison, 1964). The students were encouraged to *assume* that the important determinants of these children's behavior were the consequences of that behavior. Armed with M & M candies as reinforcers, these student-therapists attempted to bring the behavior of the severely disturbed children under their control. Eventually, one child appeared to be losing interest in earning the candies. Working within a framework that required an effective reinforcer, the therapist looked around for another incentive. Luckily, he noticed that each time the child passed a window, she would pause for a moment to look at her reflection. The therapist obtained a mirror and was subsequently able to make "peeking into the mirror" the reinforcer for desired behavior; the peeks into the mirror were used in the same *functional* way as the M & M candies. Thus, *although guided by a general principle, the therapist had to rely on improvisation and inventiveness as demanded by the clinical situation.*

An outsider can get the impression that devising therapy along behavioral lines is easy and straightforward, that the application of a general principle to a particular case is a simple matter. Although a given theoretical framework helps to guide the clinician's thinking, it is by no means sufficient.

The clinician in fact approaches his work with a given set, a framework for ordering the complex data that are his domain. But frameworks are insufficient. The clinician, like any other applied scientist, must fill out the theoretical skeleton. Individual cases present problems that always call for knowledge beyond basic psychological principles. (Lazarus and Davison, 1971, p. 203)

The preceding quotation from two behavior therapists is very similar to the following one from an article written by two experimental social psychologists.

In any experiment, the investigator chooses a procedure which he intuitively feels is an empirical realization of his conceptual variable. All experimental procedures are "contrived" in the sense that they are invented. Indeed, it can be said that the art of experimentation rests primarily on the skill of the investigator to judge the procedure which is the most accurate realization of his conceptual variable and has the greatest impact and the most credibility for the subject. (Aronson and Carlsmith, 1968, p. 25)

Thus behavior therapists are faced with the same kinds of decision-making challenges that their experimental colleagues face. There are no easy solutions in dealing with human problems.

Psychoanalysis and Behavior Therapy— A Rapprochement?

Is contemporary psychoanalysis compatible with behavior therapy? This question has been discussed for many years, and few professionals are optimistic about a meaningful rapprochement, arguing that these two points of view are incompatible paradigms. But Paul Wachtel, in his work on just such an integration (1977, 1982), has offered a scheme that, in our view, holds considerable promise at least for establishing a dialogue between psychoanalytically oriented therapists and behavior therapists.

As indicated in Chapter 18, ego analysts place much more emphasis on current ego functioning than did Freud. Sullivan, for example, suggested that patients will feel better about themselves and function more effectively if they focus on problems in their current interpersonal behavior. But even Sullivan appears to have been ambivalent about the wisdom of working directly on how people act and feel in the present if this might mean they would not recover memories of repressed infantile conflicts. Wachtel, however, suggests that the therapist *should* help the client change his current behavior, not only so that he can feel better in the here and now but indeed so that he can *change* his childlike fears from the past.

Wachtel bases his principal position on Horney (1939), Sullivan (1953), and Erikson (1950) and calls it "cyclical psychodynamics" (1982). He believes that people maintain repressed problems by their currrent behavior and the feedback it brings from their social relations. Although their problems were set in motion by past repressed events, people keep acting in ways that maintain them. For example, take a young man who has repressed his extreme rage at his mother for having mistreated his father years ago, when he was still a child. To control this rage, as a youngster he developed defenses that took the form of overpoliteness and deference to women. Today this solicitousness and unassertiveness encourage some women to take advantage of him, but he also misperceives situations in which women are genuinely nice to him. Misinterpreting their friendly overtures as condescending insults, he comes to resent women even more and retreats still further. In this fashion his submissiveness, originating in his "woolly mammoth," his buried problem of long ago, creates personal problems in the present and revives his repressed rage. It is as though his adult ego is saying, unconsciously, "You see, women, like my mother, really are bitchy. They're not to be trusted. They're hurtful and sadistic." This present-day confirmation of his belief from childhood turns back upon the buried conflict and, as it were, keeps it alive. The cycle continues, with the young man's own behavior and misconceptions confirming the nastiness of women.

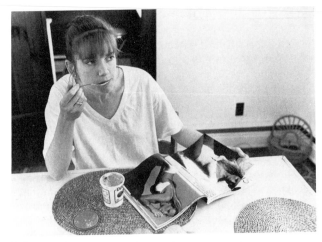

Self-control presents an interesting dilemma for behavior therapists.

The implications for therapy are to alter current behavioral patterns both for their own sake, which is the behavior therapist's credo, and for the purpose of uncovering the underlying psychodynamics. By pointing out that a direct alteration of behavior may help clients attain a more realistic understanding of their past repressed conflicts, traditionally the goal of psychoanalysis, Wachtel hopes to interest his analytic colleagues in the techniques employed by behavior therapists. Wachtel would probably give the deferential young man some assertion training, in hopes of breaking into the vicious cycle by changing his here-and-now relations with women. Once his belief that all women want to take advantage of him is repeatedly disconfirmed, the young man can begin to understand the repressed conflict of love–hate with his mother.

Similarly, Wachtel holds that behavior therapists can learn much from their analytic colleagues, especially concerning the *kinds* of problems people tend to develop. For example, psychoanalytic theory tells us that children have strong and usually ambivalent feelings about their parents, and that, presumably, some of these are so unpleasant that they are repressed, or at least are difficult to focus on and talk about openly.

To a behavior therapist the deferential young man might initially appear fearful of heterosexual relationships. Taking these fears at face value, he or she would work to help him reduce them, perhaps by a combination of desensitization, rational-emotive therapy, and social-skills training. But the behavior therapist will fail to explore the possibility, suggested by the psychoanalytic literature, that the young man is basically *angry* at women. Wachtel advises that the behavior therapist be sensitive to the childhood conflicts that analysts focus on and question the young man about his relationship with his mother. His reply or manner may give a hint of resentment. The therapist will then *see* the defer-

BOX 19.7

RAPPROCHEMENT AND ECLECTICISM—ANOTHER LOOK

Wachtel's efforts at rapprochement are part of a long tradition in the field of psychotherapy. As reviewed by Garfield and Bergin (1986), other efforts preceded his, and still others are developing. An early plea for behavior therapists and psychoanalysts to become conversant with each other's work came from a psychoanalyst, Judd Marmor (1971). And before him was the pioneering conceptual work of Dollard and Miller (1950), whose stimulus–response research and theorizing on anxiety were discussed in Chapter 6. In addition, Jerome Frank (1971, 1973) and Sol Garfield (1974) articulated positions on the nature of effective psychotherapy that cut across doctrinaire lines. Other position statements, for example, Goldfried and Davison (1976), Davison (1977), and Goldfried (1980), were also part of the integrative *Zeitgeist* of the 1970s.

It will be recalled from Chapter 2 (Box 2.3, page 56) that most contemporary therapists identify themselves as eclectic, that is, as using procedures if not also principles from different approaches. Take note, though, of the simple fact that to know that a therapist is eclectic conveys nothing specific or useful about what he or she thinks she is doing during treatment, or about what she actually does during treatment. Eclectic A, then, may be very different from Eclectic B! Perhaps the only informative definition of an eclectic is someone who does not adhere to a single theoretical system. "Therapists can select and use whatever procedures or methods they think works best with particular patients" (Garfield and Bergin, 1986, p. 8).

But now the question arises of what *guides* the therapist's thinking, session planning, and implementation. Without such guideposts, eclecticism runs the risk of being a fancy word for chaos. Are there perhaps some general principles or strategies that are so widely employed and found, at least clinically, to be effective that they might constitute the core of a more general therapy system, one which incorporates the collective wisdom of practicing clinicians as well as the insights of theoreticians and the hard-won findings of researchers?

Marvin Goldfried (1980, 1982) speculates on what these common themes might be, basing part of his thinking on a survey he conducted with a number of well-known therapists (Brady *et al.*, 1980). He suggests, for example, that a common effective ingredient is exposure to what is fearsome (see page 146). However, an analyst might push for exposure to presumed repressed impulses whereas a behavior therapist might concentrate on presumed external environmental stimuli. Another possible commonality in effective therapies might be feedback to the patient on how he or she affects others. Although Goldfried's ideas have not gone unchallenged (e.g., Haaga, 1986), it is fair to say that his approach has appeal among many clinicians, and the organization founded by him and Wachtel—the Society for the Exploration of Psychotherapy Integration—has grown enormously in just a few years and has annual meetings that are known for their liveliness and spirited exchange of ideas among theorists and clinicians who, perhaps only a decade ago, might never even have attended the same convention. What seems to bring them together is dissatisfaction with the limitations imposed by their particular theoretical frameworks and an interest in exploring connections among diverse orientations and in developing new conceptual frameworks for understanding therapeutic processes.

Is a grand, all-encompassing theory or approach necessarily desirable or even possible? We believe not, and our own use of different paradigms in the study of both psychopathology and intervention aligns us more with the views of Garfield and Bergin:

A comprehensive conception of how the body works does not demand that every system or organ of the body operate according to the same principles. Thus, our view of how the circulatory system works is quite different from our view of the nervous system. The forces and actions of the human heart operate according to the principles of fluid mechanics, whereas the principles of electrochemistry apply to the transmission of nerve impulses through the neuron; yet these two quite different processes occur in the same human body and are coordinated harmoniously despite their apparently disparate functions.

Similarly, human personality may operate in accordance with a complex interaction of seemingly disparate processes that act together, though each differently and in its own sphere. Thus, it is conceivable that the same individual may suffer at one time from a repressed conflict, a conditioned response, an incongruent self-image, and irrational cognitions; and that each of these dysfunctions may operate in semi-independent systems of psychic action that are amenable to rather different interventions, each of which is compatible with the "system" to which it is being applied. Diagnosis and therapy might then become concerned with the locus of the disorder or with which portion or portions of the multisystem psyche is involved. (Garfield and Bergin, 1986, p. 10)

ential young man differently and hypothesize that he is not just fearful of women but angry at them as well, because he associates them with a mother who has been the object of both hate and love from early childhood. This additional information will presumably suggest a different behavioral intervention, for the anger must be dealt with.

Wachtel would also have the behavior therapist appreciate that reinforcers can be *subtle* and that, furthermore, a client may deny that he or she really wants something. And the client may well be unaware of this denial. In other words, therapists should attune themselves to unconscious motivation, to the possibility that a person may be motivated or reinforced by a set of events that he or she is not conscious of for psycho-dynamic reasons.

Contemporary psychoanalytic thought may also help the behavior therapist become aware of the *meaning* that a particular intervention has for a client. Consider the case of a young woman with whom a behavior therapist decided to do assertion training. As role-playing procedures were described, the client stiffened in her chair and then began to sob. To proceed with the training without dealing with her reaction to the description of it would of course be insensitive and poor clinical practice. An awareness of psychoanalytic theories had sensitized the therapist to the possibility that assertion *symbolized* something to the client. The therapist gently encouraged the woman to talk freely, to free-associate, to the idea of assertion training. She recalled a series of incidents from childhood in which her parents had criticized the way she acted with her friends, without providing support and constructive suggestions about other ways to behave. Without initially being aware of it herself, the client was reminded of this pain from the past when the therapist suggested that she learn more assertive ways of dealing with others. The psychologist was able to distinguish the current enterprise, assertion training, from the unhelpful and negative criticisms made in the past and thereby persuaded the young woman to try role playing. The incident also pointed up the client's unresolved problems with her parents and with authority figures in general.

In a related vein, Wachtel argues that psychoanalysts are more likely than behavior therapists to consider the nonnormative or unusual concerns, wishes, and fears of their patients. Guided by the view that emotional problems derive from the repression of id conflicts, they consider psychological difficulties to reflect infantile wishes and fears, dark mysteries of primary process thinking. Behavior therapists tend to have a more straightforward, more prosaic, if you will, view of their pateints' problems.

O'Leary and Wilson (1987) have recently replied to Wachtel's criticism that behavior therapists err by taking the patient's complaints at face value. They freely admit that behaviorally oriented therapists eschew inferences to unconscious processes, but at the same time they point out that they have for some time published on the need for therapists to be sensitive to hidden agendas, to distortions in what the client says, and to the possibility that the presenting problem is not invariably the problem that is best for the therapist to work on to relieve the client's distress (cf. Goldfried and Davison, 1976; Lazarus, 1971). "They attend to the same cues as other therapists do. They are alert to patterns of functioning, to inconsistencies between verbal report and action, contradictions in accounts of events, unacknowledged emotional reactions to significant life

events. . . nonverbal cues, and other signs that things don't quite fit together. . . [including] listening with the 'third ear'. . ." (p. 398). In our view, as clinical psychologists who have taught and practiced in a cognitive behavioral framework for many years, O'Leary and Wilson are correct in how they describe the actual *practice* of experienced behavioral clinicians. What is unclear to us, and we believe to Wachtel, is the degree to which this sophisticated practice is derivable from the theories that constitute contemporary behavior therapy. It is the disjunction between theory and practice that lies at the core of Wachtel's critical discussion of behavior therapy and the ways psychoanalysis might enrich both behavioral theory and practice (Box 19.7).

Summary

In this chapter we have reviewed theory and research in cognitive and behavior therapy, a branch of clinical psychology that attempts to apply the methodologies and principles of experimental psychology to the therapeutic modification of human behavior. Several areas of this field were surveyed. Through counterconditioning a substitute desirable response is elicited in the presence of a stimulus that has evoked an undesired response. Systematic desensitization is believed by some to be effective because of counterconditioning. In operant conditioning, desired responses are taught and undesired ones discouraged by applying the contingencies of reward and punishment. The token economy is a prime example of the clinical application of operant conditioning. Modeling—helping the client to acquire new responses and unlearn old ones by observing models—is useful in eliminating fears and efficient in teaching new patterns of behavior. Cognitive-restructuring techniques, such as rational-emotive therapy, alter the thoughts that are believed to underlie emotional disorders. Self-control was examined and found to present some interesting challenges to the behavioral paradigm; an active and conscious human being by autonomous and deliberate choice acts independently of environmental influences. Behavioral medicine was reviewed as a specialty that attempts to alter bad living habits, distressed psychological states, and aberrant physiological processes by psychological procedures, in order to prevent and to treat medical illnesses. Finally, several important issues in cognitive and behavior therapy—such as the role of underlying causes, relationship factors, and the possibilities of integrating some parts of psychoanalytic theorizing into behavior therapy—were discussed in the hope of providing the reader with a better and more sophisticated grasp of a field that is both promising and controversial.

Oskar Schlemmer, *Lounge*, 1925. Staatsgalerie Stuttgart. © 1989 The Oskar Schlemmer Family Estate, Badenweiler, West Germany.

Chapter 20

Group, Couples and Family Therapy, and Community Psychology

Group Therapy
  Insight-Oriented Group Therapy
  Behavior Therapy Groups
  Evaluation of Group Therapy
Couples and Family Therapy
  The Normality of Conflict
  From Individual to Conjoint Therapy
  The Essentials of Conjoint Therapy
  Special Considerations
  Research in Couples and Family Therapy
Community Psychology
  Prevention and Seeking
  Values and the Question of Where to Intervene
  Community Mental Health Centers
  *Suicide Prevention Centers and Telephone
    Crisis Services*
  The Use of Media to Change Harmful Life-styles
  Halfway Houses and Aftercare
  Self-Help Movement
  Competency Enhancement and Family Problems
  *Overall Evaluation of Community
    Psychology Work*
Summary

In this chapter we review three means of therapeutic intervention. Although different from one another in many important ways, they are similar in making far more efficient use of professional time and are more economical than the one-to-one therapies reviewed in the preceding two chapters. As we shall soon see, however, economy is not the primary reason that any of these is chosen. Rather, each treatment has developed from a particular rationale for providing effective help. In group therapy a professional treats a number of patients simultaneously; in couples and family therapy, committed partners and sometimes children are seen together in conjoint sessions; and community psychology is oriented toward prevention and treats the problems of patients without removing them from their customary surroundings.

Group Therapy

Most group therapists regard their form of treatment as uniquely appropriate for accomplishing certain goals. For example, group members can learn vicariously (see page 46) when attention is focused on another participant. Social pressures, too, can be surprisingly strong in groups. If a therapist tells an individual client that his or her behavior seems hostile even when hostility is not intended, the message may be rejected; however, if three or four other people agree with the interpretation, the person may find it much more difficult to dismiss. In addition, many people derive comfort and support solely from the knowledge that others have problems similar to their own.

The encounter groups of the early 1960s relied heavily on touching exercises.

Virtually every technique or theory employed in individual therapy has been, or can be, used for treating people in groups. Thus there are psychoanalytic groups (Slavson, 1950; Wolf, 1949), Gestalt groups (Perls, 1969), client-centered groups (Rogers, 1970), behavior therapy groups (Lazarus, 1968a; Paul and Shannon, 1966; Upper and Ross, 1980), and countless other kinds. Group therapies have also been used with children and their parents, with adolescents, with patients suffering from a host of medical illnesses, with the aged and their caregivers, with abusive parents, with delinquents, with gays, and with hospitalized mental patients (Lubin, 1983). Another major type of group, the so-called self-help group, is discussed under Community Psychology (page 594). We shall examine closely a few group psychotherapies, in hopes of imparting some idea of the range of prevailing theories and procedures, and then review the evidence bearing on their effectiveness.

Insight-Oriented Group Therapy

Sensitivity Training and Encounter Groups
Aronson (1972) differentiates the sensitivity training or T-group from the more radical "encounter group," which grew in popularity primarily on the West Coast at such places as the Esalen Institute, where Perls was in residence in the 1960s. T-groups tend to rely more on verbal procedures and to avoid the physical contact, touching exercises, and unrestrained expressions of emotion employed by many encounter groups. Aronson's distinction is not accepted by all workers, however. Rogers (1970) traces the development of encounter groups to his training of counselors at the University of Chicago in 1946, in which he emphasized personal growth and improved interpersonal communication. We would agree with his judgment that T-groups and encounter groups are usually impossible to distinguish from each other nowadays.

The T-group was originally conceived in 1947, and the National Training Laboratory was established through conferences on small-group dynamics held in Bethel, Maine. The impetus came from colleagues of Kurt Lewin, who was a famous social psychologist at MIT (Lubin, 1983). The original groups were made up of people in industry, and the goal was to increase efficiency in business practices at the highest levels of management by making executives more aware of their impact on other people and of their own feelings about others. Over the past thirty-five years millions of people have participated in such groups, including no doubt some readers of this book. Attention has shifted in these years from group dynamics to individual growth.

The T-group is best viewed as educational; it was not designed for those who are seriously disturbed. The T-group promotes personal growth and better understanding in people who are functioning reasonably well. Generally speaking, members are encouraged to focus on their "here and now" relationships with one another. Individuals are often drawn to T-groups because, even though their lives are not full of problems, they feel that they are missing something, that their days are lived through without intensity and intimacy. Aronson lists some general goals of T-groups.

1. To develop a willingness to examine one's behavior and to experiment with new ways of behaving.
2. To learn more about people in general.
3. To become more authentic and honest in interpersonal relations.
4. To work cooperatively with people rather than assuming an authoritarian or submissive manner.
5. To develop the ability to resolve conflicts through logical and rational thinking rather than through coercion and manipulation of others.

In the most general terms, T-groups and encounter groups provide a setting wherein people are encouraged to behave in an unguarded fashion. They are then helped to receive and give feedback, to see how they come across to and affect others, and to examine how they feel about their behavior and that of others. They are expected to become more aware and accepting of themselves and of other group members. Aronson (1972) provides the following description of a group session getting started.

He [the leader] . . . falls into silence. Minutes pass. They seem like hours. The group members may look at each other or out the window. Typically, participants may look at the trainer for guidance or direction. None is forthcoming. After several minutes, someone might express his discomfort. This may or may not be responded to. Eventually, in a typical group, someone will express annoyance at the leader: "I'm getting sick of this. This is a waste of time. How come you're not doing your job? What the hell are we paying you for? Why don't you tell us what we're supposed to do?" There may be a ripple of applause in the background. But someone else might jump in and ask the first person why he is so bothered by a lack of direction—does he need someone to tell him what to do? And the T-group is off and running. (p. 241)

Levels of Communication Figure 20.1 is Aronson's schematic representation of a dyadic or two-person interaction. In our everyday lives we usually operate at level P_3, namely, behaving in some verbal or nonverbal way toward another person. Usually the recipient of our P_3 behavior responds at level R_4, evaluating us. There are obviously many points at which misjudgments can occur. For example, at level R_3 the recipient may misinterpret P's intention. Even though the person, a man, may feel warmly (P_1) toward his friend the recip-

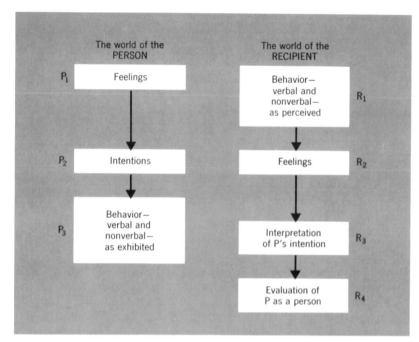

FIGURE 20.1

Schematic representation of a two-person interaction. The diagram illustrates the different levels of communication possible. After Aronson. 1972.

"I wouldn't call two 'Gesundheit's in seven years a sincere effort to communicate."

(Drawing by Geo. Price; copyright © 1971 The New Yorker Magazine, Inc.)

ient, he may have difficulty expressing warmth and therefore show sarcasm at P_3. The recipient will then interpret P's intention as a wish to hurt him (R_3), rather than as a desire to express warm feelings toward him. Without the open discussion that is encouraged in a T-group, the recipient can reject (R_4) the person as a nasty individual and never come to understand that the person really feels warmly (P_1) but has just not learned to express his feelings (P_3) appropriately. A properly run T-group encourages the participants to break down their personal communications and reactions into all the various components so that they can examine their true feelings toward other persons and their perceptions of what they are receiving from them.

Within the T-group people talk frankly and listen to one another. Usually the group works on the ongoing interactions, rather than examining past histories, as would be the case in a psychoanalytically oriented group. The emphasis on openness is not necessarily a violation of a person's right to privacy, although there is little question that in some groups people feel pressured to reveal more about themselves than they might wish. Experienced and competent group leaders watch for undue coercion and direct the stream of conversation away from an individual when they sense excessive probing into the person's private feelings. They will make every effort not to impose their will and ideas on the other participants, but they are of course aware of the very powerful position that they occupy in the group. It seems likely that some of the unfortunate abuses of

encounter and T-groups can be attributed to the all-too-human tendency of some trainers to wield this power unwisely.

Variations   Particular sensitivity and encounter groups may vary in a number of ways. Rogers's (1970) groups tend to operate according to his individual client-centered therapy as outlined in Chapter 18; the leader tries to clarify the feelings of group members, on the assumption that growth can occur as people confront their emotions with honesty. The group leader—or "facilitator"—tends to be less active than in the T-groups Aronson describes. Some groups may meet for hours at a time, perhaps over a weekend, with little if any sleep allowed. Such *marathons* (Bach, 1966; Mintz, 1967; Stoller, 1968) rely on fatigue and extended exposure to a particular set of social conditions to weaken "defenses" and help the participants become more open and presumably more authentic.

Behavior Therapy Groups

Individualized Behavior Therapy in Groups
Arnold Lazarus (1968a), a pioneer in group behavior therapy, pointed out that a behavior therapists may, primarily for reasons of efficiency, choose to treat several people suffering from the same kind of problem by seeing them in a group rather than individually. The emphasis, as in one-to-one therapy, remains on inter-

a

b

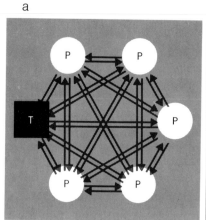
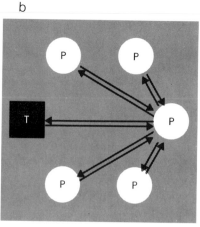

FIGURE 20.2

Distinction between (a) individualized group therapy and (b) group therapy in which interactions among all the members are regarded as important. Arrows indicate lines of communication and influences; T stands for therapist, P for patient.

actions between the therapist and each individual patient or client (Figure 20.2a).[1]

Group desensitization (Lazarus, 1961) is a good example of this individualized approach. A single therapist can teach deep muscle relaxation and present a hierarchy to each member of the group simultaneously, thus saving therapist time. Fears handled in this manner include test anxiety (Nawas, Fishman, and Pucel, 1970), snake phobias (Ritter, 1968), anxiety about public speaking (Paul and Shannon, 1966), and social anxiety (Wright, 1976).

Groups using behavioral techniques to help individual members lose weight (Wollersheim, 1970) and stop smoking (Koenig and Masters, 1965) have also been successful. Whether this should be considered group therapy is open to question. The members of these special-purpose groups do seem to provide valuable encouragement and social support for one another, however.

Social-Skills Training Groups

Social skills are taught to groups of people who have similar deficits in relating to others, for example, job interview skills or conversational and dating skills; efforts are usually made to treat people with comparable levels of deficiency so that an appropriate pace can be maintained for all group members (Kelly, 1985). Participants rehearse together the skills that they are learning and thus provide one another unique and appro-

priate help in changing behavior. Because members interact, the lines of communication are among all participants, not just between therapist and participant (Figure 20.2b). Groups of depressed people, for example, have learned social skills that are likely to bring them more reinforcement from others (Lewinsohn, Weinstein, and Alper, 1970; Teri and Lewinsohn, 1986).

Assertion Training Groups

A particularly important social skill is assertiveness (see page 556). Lazarus conducts assertion training groups composed of about ten people of the same sex. At the first meeting he describes the general goals of the therapy group, commenting particularly on the problems that unassertiveness can create for individuals in our society. He also suggests that the therapy group can provide a good setting for cooperative problem solving. Like Rogers, he calls for honesty and acceptance within the group and prescribes constructive criticism and the diligent practice of new skills. Then members introduce themselves briefly, and the others are encouraged to comment on the manner in which they presented themselves, especially if they were apologetic.

Members of the group are then given a situation that calls for an assertive response. The therapist turns the situation into a skit and demonstrates being assertive. Then group members, in pairs or larger groupings, take turns playing out the skit. The therapist and other members tell the persons practicing assertiveness what they are doing right and doing wrong. Assertiveness is rehearsed again and again in this fashion. Of particular importance are assignments carried out by the members between sessions. People are encouraged to describe both successful and unsuccessful attempts at assertive behavior in their everyday activities, and they often role-play within the group to help them improve on their assertion in past or anticipated situations. The emphasis is at all times on the benefits to be derived

---

[1]Gestalt therapy groups generally operate in this fashion as well. The therapist works with one group member at a time; often this individual will sit in a particular chair, or on a particular pillow, referred to as "the hot seat." Recent developments indicate that some Gestalt groups also use the uniqueness of the group setting to good advantage. One member's emotional discussion of the loss of a loved one evolved into a group discussion of how the group felt about the imminent "loss" of the therapist, who had to go out of town. A kind of group theme or gestalt is said to have emerged from that interaction (Harman, 1984).

from appropriate and effective expression of both positive and negative feelings. If the therapist is sensitive and skillful, he or she is able to create an atmosphere in which group members begin to trust themselves to express criticism without fearing that they are hurting other people's feelings. Assertion groups may even be effective in reducing the compliant, withdrawn behavior of chronic schizophrenics (Bloomfield, 1973).

There are some similarities between Lazarus's assertion training groups and the sensitivity training groups described earlier, but an important difference is the attention Lazarus pays to between-session activities; people are trained within the group to make specific changes later, outside the group therapy setting. Although T-groups are similarly concerned with helping people change their everyday lives, much less systematic attention is paid to what clients do between group sessions.

In general, behavioral and cognitive-behavioral approaches utilize the uniqueness of the group setting. For example, Rose (1986) describes problem-solving groups on college campuses in which members help each other generate possible solutions to each other's life challenges. Some group leaders also do what can be termed "problem-solving the group," whereby group members are challenged to deal with a particular problem—such as a few people doing all the talking. The group process itself thus becomes material for the honing of problem-solving skills. This general approach has been followed for many years in sensitivity training and encounter groups as well.

Evaluation of Group Therapy

Like other therapies, the T-group and encounter movement has its share of glowing testimonials.

I have known individuals for whom the encounter experience has meant almost miraculous change in the depth of their communication with spouse and children. Sometimes for the first time real feelings are shared. . . . I have seen teachers who have transformed their classroom . . . into a personal, caring, trusting, learning group, where students participate fully and openly in forming the curriculum and all the other aspects of their education. Tough business executives who described a particular business relationship as hopeless have gone home and changed it into a constructive one. (Rogers, 1970, p. 71)

Such observations, especially by a highly skilled and respected clinician, contribute to the faith many people have in encounter groups. Comments of this nature do not, however, satisfy most scientists of human behavior.

Some critics have suggested that those who participate in T-groups learn only how to participate in T-groups. They are not able to transfer to real-life situations the insights and skills that have been acquired in a group (Houts and Serber, 1972). Transfer of learning is a difficult problem for, whether we like it or not, the real world is not set up to encourage openness and frankness. Those who are not operating by the rules of a T-group may be offended by the open and honest expression of feelings. Indeed, as Aronson reminds us, it someone insists that others be totally open when they do not want to be, he or she is being insensitive to their feelings and so really has *not* learned some of the essentials from what might have seemed a good T-group experience. This is not to say that T-group experiences can never transfer to the real world. Knowledge of how a person feels about others and comes across to them may be extremely useful in everyday activities, even though the overt behavior encouraged in a T-group or encounter group is not continued.

Because the independent variables are so complex and difficult to control, it is extraordinarily difficult to do good research with groups. As will all psychotherapy research, there is little agreement on what are the best means of measuring success. There is also wide disparity in how often groups meet and for how long, and the people assembled are quite diverse. Few studies have employed credible controls for the placebo effect. Most importantly, little attention is paid to what actually *happens* in the group. Mindful of these methodological shortcomings, Smith (1975) offered the following tentative conclusions about T-groups that met for at least twenty hours and were compared to no-treatment controls.

1. T-group participants tend to view themselves more favorably after a group experience, and this effect often persists for months afterward.

2. Some studies suggest that group members come to view themselves as more in control of their behavior, more responsible for themselves.

3. There is little if any good evidence that T-groups help participants become more open-minded and less prejudiced.

4. Some documentation suggests that participants become more willing to disclose personal information about themselves.

5. Since the purpose of a sensitive training group is to foster understanding of others and their needs, it is surprising how little evidence shows participants becoming more empathic.

6. Some evidence suggests that participants improve more than controls in communication skills.

7. Some data indicate that associates of former group participants see them as functioning better in their everyday activities. For example, they seem more relaxed, more communicative. But in most instances the observers knew that their friends and colleagues had been in a group program, thus weakening the import of this observation.

Additional generalizations about other kinds of groups come from careful reviews of studies that met certain methodological criteria, such as random assignment of subjects to different treatments and the presence of appropriate control groups; but "these constraints . . . excluded the bulk of the potential literature" (Bednar and Kaul, 1978, p. 772), a sad commentary on the state of research in the complicated area of group therapy. Indeed, in their updated review, Kaul and Bednar (1986), after locating 477 articles in more than 900 journals and 1500 books published between 1977 and 1983, regarded only 17 as having sufficient internal validity to warrant discussion! The following conclusions are based on their literature reviews except as noted:

1. In general, group therapies of different kinds appear to have beneficial effects on a wide variety of clients, and in some instances these favorable outcomes endure at several months' follow-up.

2. Dependent people appear to do better in a highly structured group, whereas independent, better-functioning individuals improve to a greater extent in groups that have less structure and offer more opportunity for self-expression.

3. Little research has been directed at the factors generally assumed to be of principal therapeutic value in groups, such as learning by imitation, realizing that others have the same problems, acquiring feelings of belongingness, and inculcation of hope (Yalom, 1985).

4. Marathon groups may have no particular advantage over similarly constituted groups that meet for shorter periods of time; in fact, concentrating group hours in a few marathon sessions may accomplish less than spreading them over more sessions.

5. A variety of group therapies do initiate beneficial and lasting changes in the behavior of individual members, but seldom have there been appropriate attention-placebo controls for nonspecific factors. (This complaint should by now be familiar to the reader.)

6. Casualties of therapy, people who become worse in the course of treatment, are very few, with most studies finding rates of less than 3 percent. Members who do become worse are usually particularly disturbed or lacking in self-esteem. Those responsible for selecting group members try to screen out people who might need more individual attention or for whom the stress of confrontation and open sharing of feelings with others might be too great. Particular *styles* of leadership, such as a challenging, authoritative attitude that pushes group members to deal with more feeling, especially anger, than they are ready for, may be harmful (Lieberman, Yalom, and Miles, 1973; see Box 20.1).

In a recent study of Lifespring, a large group awareness training business, approximately three-hundred undesignated people spent sixty hours together over the course of five days. They were guided by leaders who encouraged them to confront their life problems and experiment with new ways of being. Lieberman (1987) found little evidence for casualties that could reasonably be attributed solely or primarily to the group experience. Although the methodological challenges of such research are daunting, these findings suggest that, when problems like depression or fearfulness were found after the group training, they were in people who had such problems from time to time in their past. Though the findings of this ambitious study are not easy to interpret, it is fair to say that casualties, although not entirely absent, occur infrequently and, when they do, are probably attributable more to preexisting conditions than to anything new and harmful resulting from the group training.

7. No body of evidence supports the superiority of one kind of group therapy over another. Although one theoretical approach may be more suitable than another for treating a particular problem, research has only begun to address such questions.

8. Cohesive groups may produce better results for their members than do less cohesive groups, giving them comfort and courage (Budman *et al.*, 1987).

9. It has long been assumed that progress in group therapy is facilitated by feedback, by candid comments made by one person to another about the feelings he or she arouses, the impressions made, "how you're comin' across." Evidence indicates that feedback is indeed useful, especially when negative feedback, "You sound imperious when you ask things of people," is accompanied by positive feedback, "I like the way you said that" (Jacobs *et al.*, 1973).

10. There is evidence for the effectiveness of behavioral and cognitive behavioral groups (Rose, 1986).

BOX 20.1

THERAPY, FOR BETTER OR FOR WORSE

In 1966 Allen Bergin applied the term *deterioration effect* to the harm that can come to someone from therapy. Several reviews of the literature since his initial report (Bergin, 1971; Bergin and Lambert, 1978; Lambert, Bergin, and Collins, 1977; Strupp, Hadley, and Gomes-Schwartz, 1977) indicate an unpleasant fact of life: although individual psychotherapy benefits many people, some are hurt by the experience. Group therapy (Yalom and Lieberman, 1971) and marital and family treatment (Gurman, Kniskern, and Pinsoff, 1986) also have casualties. Risk of being harmed is of course not peculiar to psychological intervention. Patients have been made worse by a wide range of medical procedures as well, including electroconvulsive therapy (Elmore and Sugerman, 1975) and the prescription of psychoactive drugs (Shader and DiMascio, 1970), both of which aim at psychological change. Some people who do *not* seek treatment also deteriorate. Avoiding contact with a mental health professional is no guarantee against getting worse!*

What are the factors that might be responsible for the deterioration effect? Highly disturbed people and those with great expectations and a need to improve are among those often harmed. Another factor is the therapist's failure to structure sessions properly, inadequately focusing on important issues and instead allowing the patient to ramble. Other therapist factors include failure to deal with the patient's negative attitudes toward therapy or the therapist, dealing inadequately with patient resistance, and timing interpretations poorly (Sachs, 1983). Indeed, there

is evidence that just as there are therapists whose work is associated with a disproportionate number of therapy casualties, there are also therapists who seldom have patients get worse and who generally help their patients (Lambert *et al.*, 1986).

Therapies of all orientations are subject to the deterioration effect. Reports from the Menninger Foundation, a renowned center for research and training in psychoanalysis, suggest that Freudian therapy may be too stressful for people with little "ego strength," poor personal relationships, and little ability to tolerate anxiety and frustration (Kernberg, 1973; Horwitz, 1974).

The therapist will bear ultimate responsibility for harm to the client. Lieberman, Yalom, and Miles (1973) found casualties in encounter groups that were led by an "aggressive stimulator," by a challenging, authoritative person who insisted on self-disclosure and catharsis of group participants even when they were not willing or ready for it. Any therapy can be abused by a practitioner who follows it foolishly, without tailoring it to the needs of the client. Some clients, desperate for support, reassurance, and advice and lacking in interpersonal skills, may become worse if a client-centered therapist unflinchingly declines to provide some guidance. Other clients, already overly dependent on others, may not be able to make choices and grow if the behavior therapist does not recognize this as a need and, instead, takes total charge of their lives. Any therapist or community worker can err when assessing the patient's problem, thereby embarking on treatment that cannot possibly help him or her. In addition, therapists, it must be remembered, are only human beings! Their training and experience do not qualify them as Superpeople in Mental Health. Their own needs and personal problems, even though they know they should not allow them to intrude, can blind them to the needs of the client and can otherwise reduce their ability and willingness to work on the client's behalf. Sadly, some therapists are unethical as well. A few go so far as to claim that clients (always the more attractive ones) can profit from a sexual encounter with the therapist; these workers sometimes initiate or permit sexual intimacies. Licensing laws and codes of ethics do not themselves ensure that therapists will always act wisely and humanely. Most do, and the vast majority of clients are *not* hurt by them. But the deterioration effect has been observed too often to be disregarded or underestimated.

*Several noted behavior therapists have examined the studies on which Bergin and others base their claim of a deterioration effect. They (Mays and Franks, 1980; Rachman and Wilson, 1980) suggest that the evidence is far weaker than assumed earlier. It is proving as difficult to show that therapy can sometimes harm as it has been to show that it can help. One problem is insufficient information on "spontaneous deterioration," that is, on the rate at which people who receive no therapy at all become worse. We know that some disturbed and untreated people do get worse. "If spontaneous deterioration did not take place, mental health workers would join the ranks of the unemployed" (Rachman and Wilson, 1980, p. 99). But therapy outcome studies have thus far failed to assess this deterioration adequately. Thus certain people who deteriorate while in therapy may do so not because of the therapy itself, but because of factors outside the consulting room, beyond the control of the therapist. Even so, some patients clearly worsen during therapy, which raises serious empirical and ethical questions.

Couples and Family Therapy

Many married couples who seek or who are referred for therapy to deal with problems in their relationship have children. Sometimes the problems that parents

have with a child arise from conflicts in the marriage; other times a child's behavior creates distress in an otherwise well-functioning couple. The line between marital therapy and family therapy is often blurred, and professionals who specialize in working with couples often find themselves working with the children as well.

For these reasons we have elected to discuss couples and family therapy together, distinguishing between the two when useful.

In addition, changing mores prompt us sometimes to use the term couples therapy rather than marital therapy because of the growing numbers of couples who live together in a committed relationship and yet are not married. These include both heterosexual and gay couples, and children are sometimes part of the therapeutic picture for both kinds of couples. There may, therefore, be family therapy without the adult partners being either married or of the opposite sex.

The Normality of Conflict

There is almost universal agreement among couples therapists and researchers, regardless of theoretical orientation, that conflict is *inevitable* in a marriage or in any other long-term relationship. The aura of the honeymoon passes when the couple makes unromantic decisions about where to live, where to seek employment, how to budget money, what kind of meals to prepare and the sharing of that responsibility, when to visit in-laws, when to have children if they plan to do so, and whether to experiment with novel sexual techniques. Now, in addition, they have the changed nature of gender roles to negotiate. For example, if both spouses work, shall their place of residence be determined by the husband's employment or by the wife's? These sources of conflict must be handled by any two people living together, whether they are married or not, whether they are of the opposite sex or not. Authorities agree that it is the way couples deal with such inherent conflicts that determines the quality and duration of their cohabitation relationship (e.g., Schwartz and Schwartz, 1980).

A strategy some couples adopt, deliberately or unconsciously, is to avoid acknowledging disagreements and conflicts. Because they believe in the reality of the fairy tale ending, "And they lived happily ever after," any sign that their own relationship is not going smoothly is so threatening that it must be ignored. Unfortunately, dissatisfactions and resentments usually develop and begin to take their toll as time goes by. Because the partners do not quarrel, they may appear "a perfect couple" to outside observers. But without opening the lines of communication, they may drift apart emotionally.

From Individual to Conjoint Therapy

The terms family therapy and marital therapy do not denote a set procedure. Although the focus is on at least two members of a family, how the therapist views the problem, what techniques are chosen to alleviate it, how often family members are seen, and whether children and even grandparents are included are all variables of treatment.

Couples and family therapy share some of the same theoretical frameworks as individual therapy. Psychoanalytic marital therapists, for example, focus on the way a person seeks or avoids a partner who resembles, to his or her unconscious, the opposite-sexed parent. Frustrated and unsatisfied by his love-seeking attempts as a child, the adult man may unconsciously seek maternal nurturance from his wife and make excessive, even infantile, demands of her. Much of the discussion will center around the conflicts he is having with his wife and, presumably, the repressed strivings for maternal love that underlie his immature ways of relating to her. These unconscious forces will be plumbed, with the wife assisting and possible revealing some of her own unresolved yearnings for her father.

Wachtel's interpersonal psychoanalytic views, which we have discussed elsewhere in this book, have recently been applied to marital and family therapy (Wachtel and Wachtel, 1986). The concern with interactions among people has the Wachtels bring families together in the consulting room so that interactions can be directly observed, commented upon to all family members, and hopefully altered by gentle prodding, encouragement, and reinforcement. Although this approach sounds similar to social-learning methods, the difference lies in the assumptions made by the Wachtels of the importance of the client's unconscious wishes and fears, along the lines of the individual therapy that Wachtel (1977) advocates.

Ellis's rational-emotive therapy has also been applied to marital conflict. Again the perspective is individualistic or intrapsychic; the therapist assumes that something going on within one or both of the partners is causing the marital distress. The wife, for example, may harbor the irrational belief that her husband must constantly adore her, that his devotion must never falter. She is likely then to overreact when at a social gathering he enjoys himself away from her side, talking to other men and women.

Early sex therapy treated a psychosexual problem of one or both partners directly, expecting that whatever other difficulties the couple might have—anger, resentment—would dissipate thereafter. This pattern undoubtedly holds for many sexually distressed couples. But, as already mentioned in Chapter 13, the increasing popularity of sex therapy since Masters and Johnson's *Human Sexual Inadequacy* was published in 1970 has brought to the attention of sex therapists many troubled couples for whom the sexual problem is but one aspect of a more complex *system* (Friedman and Hogan, 1985). Marital and family therapy looks for these systems. The

"You wait here. I'll talk to him."

following case history illustrates how a sexual dysfunction can serve a *useful* purpose in maintaining a couple's relationship and how its apparently successful treatment can actually worsen their overall connection and cut short their newfound sexual enjoyment.

A couple with a marriage of twenty years duration sought treatment for the male's problem of total inability to have an erection. This had been a problem for over nineteen of their twenty years of marriage. Successful intercourse had only taken place in the first few months of the marriage. The woman in this couple was also unable to reach an orgasm, and indeed had never had an orgasm from any form of stimulation, in her entire life. However, she reported that she greatly enjoyed sex and was extremely frustrated by her husband's inability to have an erection.

In treating this couple, through techniques [based on those of Masters and Johnson], very rapid progress was made. The husband very quickly began to have erections in response to his wife's manual stimulation of his genitals.

She also learned to have orgasm, first through her own masturbation and then through her husband's manual and oral stimulation of her genitals. By session 10 of weekly therapy, the couple was able to engage in normal intercourse with both of them having orgasm. Thus, the case was essentially "cured" within ten sessions.

However, at this point, something rather peculiar happened. Rather than continuing intercourse after this success, the couple discontinued all sexual activity for the next several weeks. Upon careful exploration by the therapist a rather interesting picture emerged. First, it became clear that the husband had a great need to remain distant and aloof from his wife. He had great fears of being overwhelmed and controlled by her, and found closeness to be very uncomfortable. He himself had had a rather disturbed relationship with his mother, with her being extremely controlling, manipulating, and intrusive in his life, well into his adulthood. For him, the inability to have an erection served to keep his wife distant from him, and to maintain his need for privacy, separateness, and autonomy in the relationship.

In exploring the situation with the wife, [the therapist found] in contrast to her overt statements . . . an extremely ambivalent attitude toward sex. She had been raised in a very anti-sexual family. While she claimed to have rejected these anti-sexual teachings in her own late adolescence and adulthood, in point of fact this rejection had occurred only at a superficial intellectual level. Emotionally, she still had a great deal of difficulty in accepting her sexual feelings. She had fears of being overwhelmed by uncontrollable sexual urges if she allowed herself to enjoy sex. Thus, her husband's erectile problems served to protect her from her own fears about sex. Furthermore, over the nineteen years of her husband being unable to attain an erection, she had come to have a very powerful position in the relationship. She very often reminded her husband that he owed her a lot because of her sexual frustration. Thus, she was essentially able to win all arguments with him, and to get him to do anything that she wanted.

For this couple, the rapid resolution of their sexual dysfunction threatened elements in both their own personalities, and in the way their relationship was structured. In exploring their inability to continue having intercourse, once they had succeeded, they came to realize the [link] between their sexual problems and the structure of their [marriage]. With several additional weeks of therapy focused on resolving these individual and relationship factors, they were able to resume sexual activity successfully. (LoPiccolo and Friedman, 1985, pp. 465–466).

The Essentials of Conjoint Therapy

It has been noticed that many people who improve through individual therapy, usually in an institution, have a relapse when they return home. Theories blaming family relationships for schizophrenia were based on such observations. Sometimes forces work the other way around: improvement of the "identified patient" can be destructive to the family, as in the case description just given. Apparently the family unit and the relationships within it are sometimes distorted and need restructuring. As an overall approach, family and couples therapy seems to have begun with the work of John

Bell (1975), a psychologist working in the 1950s at the Mental Research Institute in Palo Alto, California. In the past forty years an increasing number of mental health professionals have devoted their professional lives to this kind of work. During the 1960s the efforts of Virginia Satir (1967), a psychiatric social worker, and of Donald Jackson (and Weakland, 1961), a psychiatrist, also at MRI, provided the field with fresh impetus.

The MRI people identify faulty communication patterns, uneasy relationships, and inflexibility. Members of the family come to realize how their behavior affects their relations with others. They then devote their energies to making specific changes. Few family therapists are concerned with past history, and none believes that working with only one member of the family can be fruitful. Whatever the clinical problem, the family therapist views it as that of a system, the family, and therefore treated to the best advantage within this group context.[2]

Most marital therapy is conjoint, that is, the partners are *together* in sessions with a therapist. Initially, distressed couples do not react very positively toward each other, which is not surprising! Jacobson and Margolin (1979), two behavioral marital therapists, recommend attending to this problem as an initial step in helping a couple improve their marriage. One strategy is the "caring days" idea of Richard Stuart (1976). The wife agrees to devote herself to doing nice things for her husband on a given day, without expecting anything in return. The husband will do the same for her on another day. If successful, this strategy accomplishes at least two important things: first, it breaks the cycle of distance, suspicion, and aversive control of each other; and second, it shows the giving partner that he or she is able to affect the spouse in a positive way. This enhanced sense of positive control is achieved simply by pleasing the partner. The giving can later be more reciprocal; each partner may agree to please the other in certain specific ways, in anticipation of the partner's reciprocating. For example, a husband may agree to prepare dinner on Tuesdays, and on that day the wife contracts to stop at the supermarket on her way home from work and do the weekly shopping. The improved atmosphere that develops as a consequence of each partner's doing nice things for the other and having nice things done for him or her in return helps each become motivated to please the other person on future occasions.

Behavioral marital therapists generally adopt Thibaut and Kelley's (1959) exchange theory of interaction. According to this view of human relationships, people value others if they receive a high ratio of benefits to

---

[2]An example of Salvador Minuchin's family systems therapy was given earlier in our discussion of anorexia nervosa (see page 43).

costs, that is, if they see themselves getting at least as much from the other person as they have to expend. Furthermore, people are assumed to be more disposed to continue a given relationship if other alternatives are less attractive to them, promising fewer benefits and costing more. Therapists therefore try to encourage a mutual dispensing of rewards by spouse A and spouse B.

Behavioral marital therapy has in common with other approaches a focus on enhancing communication skills between the partners, but the emphasis is more on increasing the ability of each partner to please the other, the core assumption being that "the relative rates of pleasant and unpleasant interactions determine the subjective quality of the relationship" (Wood and Jacobson, 1985). Indeed, this is claimed by such therapists to be more than an assumption, for they can point to data supporting the view that distressed couples differ from nondistressed ones in reporting lower frequencies of positive exchanges and higher frequencies of unsatisfying exchanges. Moreover,

distressed spouses are highly reactive to immediate or recent events in their relationship, while happy couples tend to maintain their satisfaction independently of recent events (Jacobson, Waldron, and Moore, 1980; Margolin, 1981). . . . They are also more likely to reciprocate negative or punishing behaviors initiated by their partners (Billings, 1979; Gottman, 1979; Margolin and Wampold, 1981). In contrast, nondistressed marriages are relatively resilient, even in the face of unpleasant events, and less vulnerable to the impact of negative interchange. While happy couples also respond to variability in the quality of day-to-day interactions, their degree of affective reactivity is much lower than that of distressed couples. (Wood and Jacobson, 1985, p. 345)

For these reasons, behavioral marital therapy concentrates on increasing positive marital exchanges, the hope being not only that short-term satisfaction will increase but also that a foundation will be laid for long-term trust and positive feelings, qualities that the aforementioned research shows to be characteristic of nondistressed marriages. Cognitive change is also seen as important, for couples often need training in problem solving (see page 552) and encouragement to acknowledge when positive changes are occurring (distressed couples often *perceive* inaccurately the ratio of positive to negative exchanges, tending to overlook the former and fixate on the latter).

In all forms of couples therapy, each partner is trained to listen empathically to the other and to state clearly to the partner what he or she understands is being said

Family therapy can include not only the parents but also the children.

and what the feelings behind the remarks are. One way to improve communication is to distinguish between the intent of a remark and its impact.[3] Partner A, for example, may wish to be helpful by asking partner B whether he can get her something from the store, but this question may have a negative impact if she would prefer him to stay home and help her with a project. The husband's intent, then, would be positive, but his question would affect his wife negatively. Research has shown that the communications of distressed and happy couples may not differ so much in intent as in impact. In one study Gottman and his colleagues (1976) found that both types of couples made the same number of positive statements to partners, but distressed spouses reported having *heard* fewer positive statements than satisfied spouses. Gottman proposed a technique for clarifying intent when two partners are in a heated argument going nowhere. The husband calls "Stop action" and asks his wife to tell him what she believes he is trying to say. Or the wife asks the same of her husband. The feedback indicates immediately whether remarks are having the intended impact.

Marital and family therapy has made creative use of the good-quality videotape equipment now available. A couple can be given a problem to solve during part of a therapy session, such as where to go on vacation, and can be videotaped while thay attempt to solve it. The ways in which they push forward their own wishes—or fail to—and the ways in which they accommodate to the other's wishes—or fail to—are but one aspect of their communication that a therapist can glean from later viewing of the tape, oftentimes with the couple themselves watching too. Patterns of communication

_____

[3]The reader will find the following similar to Aronson's analysis of a two-person exchange.

and miscommunication can be more readily discerned. The husband and wife can agree to try out new ways of negotiating and new ways of dealing with conflictual issues (Margolin and Fernandez, 1985). Recently, attempts are being made to combine formally certain kinds of cognitive therapy with the problem-solving, communication training and behavioral contracting that have long characterized behavioral marital therapy (Baucom and Lester, 1986).

Many operant behavior therapists follow Gerald Patterson's (1974a) practice of working with the parents to alter reinforcement of a child whose behavior is a problem. The child is involved little if at all in treatment. An improvement in the child's behavior often reduces much distress between husband and wife. But sometimes a child's aberrant behavior can be traced to the marital distress; although the child may be the "identified patient," his or her "problems" may better be regarded as reflecting marital conflict. In such instances family-marital therapists usually decide to intervene in the marital relationship, hoping that the child's difficulties will diminish if the parents learn to get along better. Unfortunately, there is little decisive information on where it is best to intervene. Some research done by a Stony Brook group suggests that altering the child's problematic behavior can improve the marital relationship (Oltmanns, Broderick, and O'Leary, 1976), but other research done by the same group indicates that successful marital treatment has a favorable impact on children's problems (Turkewitz and O'Leary, 1977).

Special Considerations

The marital dysfunction treated by therapists is not all the same, as Margolin and Fernandez (1985) remind us. One couple may seek professional assistance when there is only dissatisfaction in their relationship, but another may wait until the crisis is so great that one or both partners have already consulted a divorce lawyer. There are, then, different *stages* of marital distress (Weiss and Cerreto, 1980; Duck, 1984), and different therapeutic approaches may be called for, depending on where the therapist judges the couple to be.

Indeed, conjoint therapy may not even be the best tack, if, for example, one of the parties suffers from a psychological problem that disrupts the home but is itself related to issues outside the home. If a husband is depressed because of self-doubts about his job, there is little reason to alter the marital relationship. Such a strategy might lift his depression somewhat, but it will hardly address the source of the problem. Even so, married partners are usually the most significant people in each other's lives and thereby control many of the

most powerful reinforcers that can be brought to bear on their partners. If the depressed man will benefit from being assertive at his job, his wife could encourage this by working with him first on becoming more assertive in the marriage (Jacobson and Margolin, 1979).

Divorce counseling is a new facet of marital therapy. Until recently marital-family therapists have regarded divorce as an evil to be avoided at all costs, but the advocacy of women's rights, the increasing acceptability of single-parent families, and the greater expectations people have of marriage have prompted mental health workers to explore ways of helping people leave a marriage that appears beyond repair (Kaslow, 1981). Therapists of this new specialty help the divorced or separated partner deal with the loss of the spouse, regain self-esteem—a person is likely to blame himself or herself for the "failure" of the marriage—and foster independence (Gurman and Kniskern, 1978). Sometimes divorce counseling or therapy begins while the couple are still living together; the participants might regard as successful a resolution of their ambivalence and fear about separating.

Research in Couples and Family Therapy

Studies have been conducted on *divorce mediation*, consultations occurring before a divorce has been achieved. An alternative to the usual adversarial process, mediation is conducted by a third party (a lawyer, counselor, or even trained layperson) who strives for neutrality and whose goal is to help the distressed couple reach agreement on child custody and financial arrangements before involving their own respective lawyers. Data indicate that mediation is associated with "(1) a higher rate of pretrial agreements; (2) a higher level of satisfaction with the agreements; (3) major reductions in the amount of litigation after final court orders; (4) an increase in joint custody agreements; and (5) . . . decrease in public expenses such as custody studies and court costs (Sprenkle and Storm, 1983)" (Gurman, Kniskern, and Pinsoff, 1986, p. 589).

Considerable research has also been published over the past decade on the effectiveness of family and marital therapies (e.g., Weiss and Wider, 1982; Jacobson and Margolin, 1979; Jacobson, Follette, Revenstorf, Baucom, Hahlweg and Margolin, 1984; Lieberman, Wheeler, and Kuehnel, 1983; O'Leary and Turkewitz, 1978; Stuart, 1980). A recent meta-analysis of twenty carefully selected outcome studies meeting stringent methodological standards concludes that, overall, family therapy has beneficial effects for many family problems (Hazelrigg, Cooper, and Borduin, 1987). Comprehensive reviews of the area by Gurman and Kniskern (1978) and Gurman, Kniskern, and Pinsoff (1986) reach the following conclusions about outcome and process in couples and family therapy:

1. Conjoint therapy for marital problems appears to be more successful than individual therapy with one partner. Indeed, the state of about 10 percent of patients seen individually for marital problems worsens.

2. As summarized in Box 20.2, reducing the level of expressed emotion in the families of schizophrenics discharged from hospital and maintained on neuroleptics lowers relapse rates.

3. Although focused on the fearfulness of one partner, Barlow's exposure treatment, which involves encouragement and collaboration by the spouse, has proven effective in reducing agoraphobia (see Chapter 6, page 144) and has avoided the deterioration in the marital relationship that has sometimes been reported when the agoraphobic partner gets better (Himandi, Cerny, Barlow, Cohen, and O'Brien, 1986).

4. Not surprisingly, marital therapy results are generally better for younger couples and when no steps have yet been taken toward divorce.

5. Process research lags far behind outcome research, though some components are coming under empirical scrutiny, such as session-to-session changes as a function of specific ingredients of therapy sessions, like the degree to which negative affect is focused on by the therapist (Pinsof, 1985).

6. Overall, most nonbehavioral approaches, such as analytic and humanistic, have not been subjected to as much controlled research as have behavioral and systems approaches, a probable reflection of the lesser research emphasis in these paradigms. A noteworthy exception is a report by Johnson and Greenberg (1985), who found superiority of a Gestalt therapy-based marital intervention that focused on uncovering unacknowledged feelings and needs as compared to the problem-solving component of behavioral marital therapy. As Johnson and Greenberg speculate, it may be important for a marital intervention to work directly on increasing trust and sensitivity to one's own unmet needs and hidden fears as well as those fears and needs of one's partner. Indeed, increasing attention is being paid by behavioral marital therapists to the affective dimensions of marital conflict, yet another sign of the move toward rapprochement among contrasting therapeutic orientations (page 569).

Community Psychology

Prevention and Seeking

Community psychology's focus on prevention sets it apart from most of what we have studied so far. Gerald Caplan (1964), whose writings have had considerable impact, distinguishes three levels of prevention. ***Tertiary prevention*** is in many respects equivalent to the treatment of disorders already discussed. It also seeks to reduce the long-term consequences of having a disorder; for example, mental health workers help those who have recovered from mental illness to participate fully in the occupational and social life of the community. ***Secondary prevention*** consists of efforts to detect problems early, before they become serious, and to prevent their development into chronic disabilities. Quick and accurate assessment by community people—physicians, teachers, clergymen, police officers, court officials, social workers—allows remedial procedures to begin early. Crisis-intervention work and twenty-four-hour emergency services are examples of secondary prevention.

Primary prevention tries to reduce the incidence of new cases of social and emotional problems in a population. Altering stressful and depriving conditions in the environment and strengthening individuals so that they can resist stress and cope with adversity are two primary means of prevention. Some examples of primary prevention measures include attention to overcrowding, poor housing, job discrimination, neighborhood recreation, and school curricula and neighborhood

Job training could be viewed as an instance of primary prevention.

group work with children from broken homes. Genetic counseling, prenatal care for ghetto mothers, school lunches, and Meals on Wheels are also primary prevention measures. Community psychologists concentrate their efforts on primary and secondary prevention.

Nearly all the therapies reviewed thus far are administered by professional persons with advanced degrees who make themselves available by appointment in offices, clinics, and hospitals. They provide assistance to individuals who initiate the contact themselves or are referred by the courts. Such delivery of services has been referred to as in the **waiting mode** (Rappaport and Chinsky, 1974). In contrast, community psychology operates in the **seeking mode,** that is, those who are troubled or are likely one day to be so are sought out by community workers, some of whom are paraprofessionals supervised by psychologists, psychiatrists, or social workers. Mental health services are often provided outside of offices and clinics, in the schools, businesses, and factories of the person's own community.

Rappaport and Chinsky (1974) proposed that every type of mental health care has two components, the delivery and the conceptual. The delivery component relates to the difference between seeking and waiting, that is, an *attitude* about making services available. As noted, community psychology has a seeking orientation. The conceptual component, on the other hand, consists of the *theoretical* and *data-based underpinnings* of the services. Two examples are psychoanalytic and

learning approaches. Table 20.1 illustrates how these two conceptual modes combine with either style of the delivery component. For example, a twenty-four-hour-a-day hot line in a suicide prevention center would be in the community psychology seeking mode. But what *specifically* the people answering the phones say and do when a call comes in depends on the conceptual mode. One worker might take a psychoanalytic approach; another might construe suicide threats in learning terms. Clearly, these two workers would treat the calls differently—but both would be delivering community psychology. The conceptual components section of Table 20.1 could, of course, be expanded almost indefinitely. Further, the question whether a particular conceptual orientation is more suited to one of the two delivery modes than to the other is a separate, and crucial, issue, one that creates ongoing controversy among community psychologists and psychiatrists.

Values and the Question of Where to Intervene

In an effort to explain the essence of community psychology, Rappaport (1977) proposes that we view society as composed of four levels: the individual, the small group, the organization, and the institution. Therapists will intervene at a given level, depending on their values and goals for people. For example, if the therapist assumes that society itself is benign, human prob-

TABLE 20.1

Some possible models for mental health service (*adapted from Rappaport and Chinsky, 1974*)

Conceptual Component*	Delivery Component	
	Waiting Mode	**Seeking Mode**
Psychoanalytic approach	Psychodynamic explanations of abnormal behavior. Therapist waits for patient to initiate contact and then uses insight therapy.	Psychodynamic explanations of abnormal behavior. Professional attempts to prevent illness through public education and extends traditional treatments into community settings.
Learning approach	Learning theory interpretation of emotional dysfunction. Therapist waits for client to initiate contact and then uses techniques such as systematic desensitization.	Learning theory interpretation of emotional dysfunction. Professional extends services into the community through public education; trains various nonprofessionals in behavior therapy techniques and social-learning principles.

*Listed here as examples are only two of a large number of possible conceptual components.

BOX 20.2

EMPOWERMENT, SMALL WINS, AND BROAD-SCALE SOCIAL CHANGE

We have repeatedly found that people need to feel in control of their lives, for if they do not, they are subject to anxiety, depression, and psychophysiological disorders. Primary prevention workers are on fairly solid empirical ground in concentrating on what Rappaport (1981) calls empowerment.

Indeed, it has been argued by some distinguished community psychologists (Joffee and Albee, 1981) that powerlessness underlies the entire range of social problems and psychopathology.

It makes little sense to develop separate programs for the prevention of child abuse, spouse abuse, elder abuse, the exploitation of women, minority group members, migrant farmworkers, the handicapped, the mentally ill, and the mentally retarded. If we see all these groups as powerless because of socioeconomic conditions, then a logical approach is to determine whether there might be an equitable redistribution of power. . . . Without meaning to be simplistic, we would like to suggest that we examine the arguments . . . for a redistribution of power through a redistribution of wealth in our society. (p. 332)

These words counsel action on a grand scale—what could be wider-ranging than a redistribution of wealth? Other community psychologists define large social problems as made up of smaller, more manageable chunks (Weick, 1984). An example would be the increasing use of nonsexist language—he or she; plural pronouns like "they" rather than the singular ones; female pronouns where earlier only masculine pronouns would have been used, as in speaking of physicians; and conversely, male

Empowerment is viewed by community psychologists as a critical aspect of the solution to many social problems.

pronouns where earlier only female pronouns would have been heard, as in discussing elementary school teachers. This "small win" has been achieved in a relatively short time.

Weick argues that small, focused shifts are more readily accepted by opponents and attract resources for the next effort at change—since everyone loves a winner. The failure of a too-ambitious attempt can be demoralizing, but small wins make more small wins possible, and in this stepwise fashion more sweeping changes can be achieved over time.

lems will be seen as failures to *adjust* to this benign system. Treatment will therefore attempt to change the *individual* so that he or she will fit into society. This tertiary prevention is pursued in a number of ways—from behavior therapy to psychoanalysis to chemotherapy—but in all these modes of intervention society is considered good and people in need of adjustment to it.[4] In contrast, human problems may be assumed to derive from interpersonal difficulties such as conflicts

within families, at work, and in other *small groups*. The therapist applies family and encounter therapy to help members of the group communicate better. The therapist does *not* try to change just the individual because the problem is assumed to lie in group processes.

If the third level, that of *organizations*, is considered at fault, therapists have another view of human disorders. They "blame" the way units such as schools and prisons operate. To help a child who is failing in her academic work, for example, therapists examine the school curriculum and how it is implemented by principals and teachers; they do *not* provide remedial tutoring for the pupil. Community psychology operates at this level and at the *institutional* level, which is closely related to it but is more abstract and all-inclusive. Institutions refer not to physical entities such as school buildings and prisons but to the basic values and ideologies that characterize a society, its religion, and its

_____

[4]Of course, a therapist can work with individuals and help them change so that they are better able to deal with a society that is *not* benign. In other words, therapists treating individuals may at the same time view society as exerting a negative, even evil, influence on people. They may decide that it is easier to help the client cope with negative societal forces, rather than try to change the negative aspects of society. The community psychologist is concerned, however, that negative societal forces will be overlooked when all the attention is paid to the individual. Indeed, therapists are commonly accused of helping their troubled clients *adjust* to an evil society.

politics. For example, the community psychologist may assert that people are unhappy because of a lopsided distribution of wealth and power. Professional efforts would then be directed at political parties, the courts, legislatures, and the like, *not* to encourage them to function more efficiently but rather to shift their goals and basic assumptions so that they work toward a more equitable social distribution of wealth and power (see Box 20.2).

Rappaport's analysis makes it clear why some community workers tend to be impatient with individual and group therapy. They do not believe that problems lie with the individual or the group, and they even assert that by concentrating on these levels the therapist will "blame the victim" (Ryan, 1971) and overlook the real problems of organizations and institutions. For these reasons community psychologists work in the seeking mode and make no pretense, as some individual and group therapists frequently do, of being politically and ethically neutral.

Why a shift to community activism in the treatment of mental disorders? For many years it had been obvious how few people could avail themselves of psychotherapeutic services, which were usually very expensive, in short supply, and apparently geared to so-called YAVIS clients—individuals who are young, attractive, verbal, intelligent, and successful (Schofield, 1964). Eysenck (1952) had also questioned the effectiveness of most kinds of psychotherapy, finding treated patients' rates of improvement no better than the spontaneous remission rate. Although Eysenck's criticisms were compellingly rebutted by a number of scholars (e.g., Bergin, 1971), the idea had taken hold among mental health professionals that psychotherapy aimed at changing the individual might not be the best way to alleviate the psychological problems of the majority of people. Focus began to shift from repressions, conflicts, and neurotic fears to large-scale social problems such as poverty, overcrowding, poor education, segregation, the alienation felt in large cities, and the impersonalism of many aspects of persent-day living.

The shift from intrapsychic factors to social factors probably reflected the *Zeitgeist* or tenor of the times. The 1960s were a period of tremendous social upheaval and activism. Institutions of all kinds were being challenged. Cities and college campuses were erupting in riots, and a range of minority groups, from blacks in urban ghettoes to gays in the larger cities, charged racism and political repression. This social upheaval, which at times seemed to border on revolution, further encouraged a search for causes of individual suffering in social institutions. At the same time the Kennedy and Johnson administrations (1961–1968) lent the monetary clout of the federal government to a progressive lib-

eralism. John Kennedy's New Frontier and Lyndon Johnson's Great Society programs poured tens of millions of dollars into attempts at bettering the human condition.

Community Mental Health Centers

The greatest single impetus to the community psychology movement was a practical one. In 1955 Congress authorized the Joint Commission on Mental Illness and Health to examine the state mental hospitals. On the basis of its six-year survey, the commission concluded that the care offered was largely custodial and that steps must be taken to provide effective treatment. Its 1961 report recommended that no additional large hospitals be built and that instead community mental health clinics be established. In 1963 President Kennedy sent a message to Congress calling for a "bold new approach," proposing the Community Mental Health Centers Act to provide comprehensive services in the community and to implement programs for the prevention and treatment of mental disturbances. The act was passed. For every 100,000 people a mental health center was to provide outpatient therapy, short-term inpatient care, day hospitalization for those able to go home at night, twenty-four-hour emergency services, and consultation and education to other agencies in the community.

Additional impetus came from the 1965 Swampscott Conference (Bennett *et al.*, 1966), which had been organized around the growing dissatisfaction felt by many clinical psychologists about the inherent limitations of traditional delivery of mental health services and for what they perceived as the need for a new commitment to the promotion of human welfare on a broad scale. Though the political climate in the country in the 1980s has not been particularly supportive of community psychology and related efforts, five NIMH-sponsored Preventive Intervention Research Centers have recently been established (Gesten and Jason, 1987).

The principal objective of a community mental health center is to provide outpatient mental health care in a person's own community and at a cost that is not beyond the means of most people. The increased availability of clinical services presumably means that fewer individuals will require institutionalization and can, instead, remain with their families and friends and continue to work while receiving therapy locally several times a week. The community health center also provides short-term inpatient care, usually on a psychiatric ward of a community general hospital, again where relatives and friends of patients may conveniently visit them. When it is needed, partial hospitalization, during the day or sometimes for the night, is usually available on a psy-

BOX 20.3

COMMUNITY PSYCHOLOGY AND COMMUNITY MENTAL HEALTH—RELATED BUT DIFFERENT

Although related, the community mental health movement and community psychology should be distinguished from each other. Community psychology is concerned primarily with primary prevention, with intervention where no dysfunctions are yet evident. Community psychology shows its concern for individuals by trying to alter social systems on the institutional level and by creating different and, it is hoped, better environments for people to live in, both to reduce the forces that are thought to bring maladaptions and to promote opportunities for individuals to realize their potential. Community psychology requires intervention with the courts, police, schools, and city services and planning agencies. Political more than clinical skills are required for such work; in fact, relatively little time is spent dealing directly with the individuals affected by the larger social forces.

Community mental health, by contrast, provides care for the needy, troubled people who have traditionally been underserved by the mental health professions. Because community mental health delivers mental health services for needy individuals, its orientation is often as individualistic as traditional consulting room therapy of the kind discussed in Chapters 18 and 19. On the staffs of mental health centers are psychiatrists, clinical psychologists, and social workers who conduct individual or group therapy in offices at the center. The two movements are sometimes equated; the inclusion of community mental health in this discussion of community psychology reflects the relationship between these two forces in psychology today. Nonetheless, their differences are as important to appreciate as are their similarities.

chiatric ward. A twenty-four-hour walk-in crisis service offers emergency consultation around the clock and "rap sessions" for members of the community. In Chapter 12 (page 343) we discussed rape crisis work, a service often run by community mental health centers.

Centers are staffed by psychiatrists, psychologists, social workers, and nurses, and sometimes by paraprofessionals who live in the neighborhood and can help bridge the gap between the middle- and upper-middle-class professionals and community members to whom mental health service is sometimes an alien concept. Paraprofessionals and volunteers can provide needed staffing for the centers within their limited budgets.

The first program involving paraprofessionals was probably that at Harvard University (Umbarger *et al.*, 1962), in which students spent several hours per week as companions to patients in mental hospitals. Community acceptance of these workers would seem to be a vital factor in community-based programs. They usually bring a fresh commitment to their work and sincere and warm interest in the patients. Yet a nonprofessional may not have all the qualities and talents necessary to make effective therapeutic interventions. Surely much depends on *what* the paraprofessional is supposed to do.

A wide range of services is included under the rubrics of "consultation" and "education." A principal one is to educate other community workers, the teachers, clergymen, and police, in the principles of preventive mental health and in how to extend help themselves (see Box 20.3). Consider the crisis-intervention effort made

by the Westside Community Health Center in 1971. The staff tried to help children adjust to enforced school busing in San Francisco.

We designed a program in which we placed a professional staff person on a school bus to ride to and from school with grade school children; in addition this staff person had streetcorner meetings with the parents about their busing concerns, and acted also as their advocate to the schools. Knowing the children would be experiencing separation anxiety in this [situation], we had our Hospital Art Department design coloring books with maps of the territory they would cover on the bus route; we attempted to introduce play materials and games that would be helpful to the children, would encourage the children to carry "transitional objects" from home . . . such as dolls, teddy bears, special favorite toys. Our staff member met with the children before they boarded the bus, talked to them on the bus, again in their new schoolyard and on the way back home again. (Heiman, 1973, p. 60)

Other initiatives taken by staff members at a mental health center might be to call a rent strike, should they decide that better housing would alleviate emotional suffering. Or suggestions might be made by a center's staff to change the work environment in a local factory in order to reduce the boredom or tension of performing particular kinds of work. Moreover, organized interventions such as these need not emanate solely from community mental health centers. Workers can operate from university departments, social welfare agencies, and even private offices and still undertake activities that would be best characterized as community psychology.

Suicide Prevention Centers and Telephone Crisis Services

Many suicide prevention centers are modeled after the Los Angeles Suicide Prevention Center, founded in 1958 by Farberow and Shneidman. There are at present more than 200 such centers in the United States. Staffed largely by nonprofessionals under the supervision of psychologists or psychiatrists, these centers attempt to provide twenty-four-hour consultation to people in suicidal crises. Usually the initial contact is made by telephone. The center's phone number is well publicized in the community. The worker tries to assess the likelihood that the caller will actually make a serious suicide attempt, and, most importantly, tries to establish personal contact and dissuade the caller from suicide. The summary sheet on page 592, used by telephone workers at the Los Angeles center, speeds the recording of crucial bits of information.

Specialists hold that phone attendants in these centers should work toward the following goals (Speer, 1972).

1. "Tuning in," communicating empathy to the caller.
2. Conveying understanding of the problem.
3. Providing information regarding sources of help, for example, mental health clinics, psychologists, and psychiatrists.
4. Obtaining an agreement from the caller to take some specific steps away from suicide, for example, making an appointment to come to the center itself.
5. Providing some degree of hope to the caller that the crisis will end and that life will not always appear so hopeless.

The potential value of such community facilities rests in the fact that most suicides give warnings—"cries for help"—before taking their lives (see page 246). Ambivalence about living or dying is the hallmark of the suicidal state (Shneidman, 1976). Usually their pleas are directed first to relatives and friends, but many potential suicides are isolated from these sources of emotional support; a hot-line service may save the lives of such individuals.

It is exceedingly difficult to do controlled research on suicide. Evaluating the effectiveness of suicide prevention centers is similarly problematic, for a large portion of those who call are not heard from again (Stein and Lambert, 1984). For example, Speer (1971) found that more than 95 percent of callers did not use the service repeatedly. Does this mean that the phone contact helped so much that no further consultation was needed? Perhaps so, but it is also possible that many callers killed themselves after the phone call. Some workers (e.g., Jennings, Barraclough, and Moss, 1978; Weiner, 1969) found no difference in the suicide rates of cities with hot-line services and of those without. Although numerous factors might have masked real differences, we cannot conclude from these data that the centers have demonstrated their effectiveness. Indeed, a recent meta-analysis of five studies on the effectiveness of suicide prevention centers fails to demonstrate that rates decline after the implementation of services (Dew, Bromet, Brent, and Greenhouse, 1987).

Once again, we are left with little if any convincing evidence. Human lives are precious, however, and since many people who contact prevention centers weather

Reaching out into the community is one of the key features of community psychology.

LOS ANGELES SUICIDE PREVENTION CENTER - TELEPHONE SERVICE

CALL DATA

Day Of The Week (1)
- ☐ 1. Sun.
- ☐ 2. Mon.
- ☐ 3. Tue.
- ☐ 4. Wed.
- ☐ 5. Thu.
- ☐ 6. Fri.
- ☐ 7. Sat.

Date (2-6)
Month	Date	Year

Time (7-10)
Hours	Minutes

Call Duration (11-12)
Minutes

Called Before (13)
- ☐ 1. Yes ☐ 2. No

NAMES

Client

Name _____
First   Last

Address _____

Phone _____ Work Phone _____

Third Party Caller (14)
- ☐ 1. Yes ☐ 2. No

Name _____

Address _____

Phone _____ Work Phone _____

Relationship To Client _____

CLIENT DATA

Age (15-16) _____

Sex (17)
- ☐ 1. M ☐ 2. F

Marital Status (18)
- ☐ 1. Single ☐ 2. Married ☐ 3. Divorced ☐ 4. Separated
- ☐ 5. Widowed ☐ 6. Living Together

Race (19)
- ☐ 1. White ☐ 2. Black ☐ 3. Spanish ☐ 4. Oriental
- ☐ 5. Other _____

Employment (20)
- ☐ 1. Full Time ☐ 2. Part Time ☐ 3. Unemployed
- ☐ 4. Retired ☐ 5. Disabled ☐ 6. Housewife ☐ 7. Student

CLIENT'S RESOURCES

Living Alone (21)
- ☐ 1. Yes ☐ 2. No

Social Contact (22)
- ☐ 0. None ☐ 1. Minimal ☐ 2. Moderate ☐ 3. Frequent

Friends/Relatives (23)   List on other side
- ☐ 1. Yes ☐ 2. No

Finances (24)
- ☐ 0 None ☐ 1 Cash
- ☐ 2 Medi-cal ☐ 3 Insurance

Insurance Co. _____

SUBSTANCE ABUSE

Alcohol History (25)
- ☐ 0. None ☐ 1. Moderate ☐ 2. Severe

Current Alcohol Problem (26)
- ☐ 0. None ☐ 1. Moderate ☐ 2. Severe

Drinking At Time (27)
- ☐ 1. Yes ☐ 2. No ☐ 3. Can't Decide

Current Drug Problem (28)
- ☐ 0. None ☐ 1. Moderate ☐ 2. Severe

SUICIDAL HISTORY

How Long Since First Attempt (29)
- ☐ 0. None ☐ 1. 3 Mos or Less ☐ 2. 3 Mos - 1 Yr.
- ☐ 3. 1 - 5 Yrs. ☐ 4. Over 5 Yrs.

How Long Since Last Attempt (30)
- ☐ 0. None ☐ 1. 3 Mos or Less ☐ 2. 3 Mos. - 1 Yr.
- ☐ 3. 1 - 5 Yrs. ☐ 4. Over 5 Yrs.

Number Of Attempts (31)
- ☐ 0. None ☐ 1. One ☐ 2. Two
- ☐ 3. Three ☐ 4. Four or More

Current Behavior (32)
- ☐ 0. None ☐ 1. Thoughts ☐ 2. Threats
- ☐ 3. Preparation ☐ 4. Low Risk Attempt
- ☐ 5. High Risk Attempt

Plan (33)
- ☐ 0. None ☐ 1. Gun ☐ 2. Pills
- ☐ 3. Cutting ☐ 4. Jumping ☐ 5. Other _____

TREATMENT

Hospitalization (34)
- ☐ 1. Yes ☐ 2. No

Therapy (35)
- ☐ 0. None ☐ 1. Prior ☐ 2. Current

PRESENTING PROBLEMS

Presenting Problems (36-37)   Check One Only
- ☐ 1 Bizarre/Psychotic
- ☐ 2 Emotional/Psychological Long Term
- ☐ 3 Emotional/Psychological Short Term
- ☐ 4 Interpersonal Loss
- ☐ 5 Relationships
- ☐ 6 Depression
- ☐ 7 Medical
- ☐ 8 Lonely
- ☐ 9 Alcohol
- ☐ 10 Drugs
- ☐ 11 Marital/Family
- ☐ 12 Material Needs
- ☐ 13 Violence/Homicide
- ☐ 14 Multiple
- ☐ 15 Other _____

RESOLUTION

Service Provided (38)
- ☐ 1. Support/Reinforce ☐ 2. Refer to Prof. Help
- ☐ 3. Refer to Emergency Help
- ☐ 4. Spc. Called Emergency Help
- ☐ 5. Service Rejected ☐ 6. No Service

RATES

Suicide Risk (39)
- ☐ 1. Low ☐ 2. Moderate ☐ 3. High

Emergency Risk (40)
- ☐ 1. Low ☐ 2. Moderate ☐ 3. High

a suicidal crisis successfully, there is at present no reason to discontinue these efforts.

The Use of Media To Change Harmful Life-styles

Cardiovascular diseases, such as high blood pressure and coronary heart disease, are responsible for more deaths in the United States than any other single group of illnesses. In many respects the life-style of an affluent, industrialized society increases risk of premature cardiovascular diseases. A group of researchers at Stanford University, led by Nathan Maccoby, a psychologist noted for his work in communications, have for several years been studying ways to educate large numbers of people about the desirability of altering their life-styles in order to reduce their risk of cardiovascular diseases. For the Three Communities Project they chose a media campaign and a direct, intensive instructional program (Maccoby *et al.*, 1977; Maccoby and Alexander, 1980; Meyer *et al.*, 1982).

Three towns in northern California were studied; Watsonville and Gilroy were the two experimental towns, and Tracy was the control town. For two years both experimental towns were bombarded by a mass media campaign to inform citizens about cardiovascular diseases. It consisted of television and radio spots, weekly newspaper columns, and newspaper advertisements and stories, all urging them to stop smoking, to exercise more, and to eat foods low in cholesterol. Posters in buses and in stores conveyed briefly and graphically such vital information as the desirability of eating fewer eggs, since the yolks are rich in cholesterol. In addition, a sample of Watsonville residents at high risk for heart disease received intensive instruction consisting of group sessions and individual home counseling over a ten-week period. The researchers wanted to examine whether information and exhortations to alter life-style delivered face-to-face might add to whatever positive benefits derived from the mass media campaign.

The control town, Tracy, had media services that were quite different from those of the two experimental towns. Tracy is separated from Watsonville and Gilroy by a range of low mountains and therefore has entirely separate local television stations. The inhabitants of Tracy were of course not imprisoned in their hometown for the duration of the two-year study, but for the most part they did not receive through their media the messages conveyed to the citizens of the two experimental towns. Because all three towns had sizable numbers of Mexican and Chicano people, all media messages were in Spanish as well as in English.

The findings reveal that through the mass media campaign citizens of Watsonville and Gilroy did significantly increase their knowledge of cardiovascular risk factors; people in the control town did not gain in such knowledge. Egg consumption was reduced more in Watsonville and Gilroy than in Tracy, and clinically significant blood pressure decreases were observed in the two experimental towns, as contrasted with small increases in the control town. The high-risk people of Watsonville who participated in the special, intensive instruction program reaped even greater benefits in lower egg consumption and blood pressure. Finally, the researchers considered the townspeople's overall measure of risk, a weighted average of the several known physical risk factors—high blood levels of cholesterol, smoking cigarettes, and not exercising enough. Not surprisingly, they found highly significant drops in risk in the experimental townspeople, an important result since we know from previous research, the famous Framingham, Massachusetts, longitudinal study of risk factors in cardiovascular diseases (Truett, Cornfield, and Kannel, 1967), that elevated risk scores predict reasonably well the incidence of heart disease over a twelve-year period.

This work of Maccoby and his colleagues is important as a community psychology effort, for it demonstrates that laypeople can learn from the mass media what is known about cardiovascular diseases, and that they will also act in many ways on this knowledge to reduce their overall risk for such diseases. The two-year span of the study is a considerable length of time as far as experiments in psychology are concerned! But in terms of the serious health problems that develop through long-standing detrimental patterns of behavior, this is not a very long time at all.

There is also evidence that mass media programs can reduce deaths from cardiovascular disease via the life-style health changes they foster (Puska, Nissinen, Salonen, and Tuomilehto, 1983). Moreover, their potential for prevention of serious medical illnesses is likely to contribute more to the promotion of good health than strictly medical practices, for

disease-oriented services may retard the progression of debilities and provide some relief from ailments. But a broader socially oriented approach is needed . . . [because] people's health is largely in their own hands rather than in those of physicians. To prevent the ravages of disease, people must be provided with the knowledge and skills to exercise control over their habits and the environmental conditions that impair their health. (Bandura, 1986, p. 178).

Halfway Houses and Aftercare

Some people function too well to remain in a mental hospital and yet do not function independently enough to live on their own or even within their own families. For such individuals there are halfway houses. These are protected living units, typically located in large, formerly private residences. Here patients discharged from a mental hospital live, take their meals, and gradually return to ordinary community life by holding a part-time job or going to school. Living arrangements may be relatively unstructured; some houses set up money-making enterprises that help to train and support the residents. Depending on how well funded the halfway house is, the staff may include psychiatrists or clinical psychologists. The most important staff members are paraprofessionals, often graduate students in clinical psychology or social work who live in the house and act both as administrators and as friends to the residents. Group meetings, at which residents talk out their frustrations and learn to relate to others in honest and constructive ways, are often part of the routine.

The nation's requirements for effective halfway houses for ex-mental patients cannot be underestimated. Properly run residences are scarce. In several states there has been pressure from governors and from legislators to discharge as many hospital patients as possible. But discharge has all too often been bad for the patients. Some local communities object to the presence of shabbily dressed, often inappropriately behaving ex-patients in their neighborhoods. They have sometimes been exploited by entrepreneurs who, for their federal disability money, house them in unsanitary, poorly administered hotels and motels. Many ex-patients reenter the hospital in what has been termed the "revolving door" syndrome. Clearly, it is not enough merely to discharge mental patients. They must have outpatient services and a protective place to live (page 618).

A model of what aftercare can be is provided by the Paul and Lentz (1977) comparative treatment study discussed in Chapter 19 (page 543). When patients were discharged from any of the three wards of the program, social-learning, milieu therapy, or routine hospital management, they usually went to live in nearby boarding homes. These homes, often converted motels, were staffed by workers who had been trained by the Paul–Lentz project to treat the ex-patients according to social-learning principles. These workers, some of whom had B.A. degrees, attended to the specific problems of the ex-patients, using rewards, including tokens for a time, to encourage more independence and normal functioning. They positively reinforced appropriate behavior of the residents and did not attend much to bizarre behavior, as they had done before their training.

The staff knew at all times how a particular patient was doing, because assessment was careful and ongoing. The mental health center project, and this is of paramount importance, acted as consultant to these com-munity boarding homes in order to help their staff work with the ex-patients in as effective a manner as possible. Some boarding homes for ex-mental patients are supported financially by the state as part of the mental health system, but only rarely have the procedures followed in these homes been carefully planned and monitored by professional mental health staff.

In spite of many practical problems, such as staff layoffs, the results were as positive as had been the impact of the social-learning ward program. The ex-patients seemed to benefit from the aftercare; more than 90 percent of the patients discharged from the social-learning ward were able to remain continuously in the community residences during the year-and-a-half follow-up period. Some had been living in the community residences for over five years. The revolving-door syndrome in this instance was halted. Finally, in a finding rather critical in these days of diminishing public funds, the social-learning program—the mental health center treatment combined with the aftercare—was much less expensive than the institutional care such patients usually receive.

Self-Help Movement

It is estimated that over 15 million Americans participate in some 500,000 self-help groups (Riessman, 1985). Alcoholics Anonymous (page 289) is a classic example. These groups operate with minimal or no guidance from mental health professionals, relying more on the mutual support that people in similar circumstances can often give each other as experiences and coping strategies are shared. Some self-help groups include the parents of severely disturbed children and of children who died from accidents, suicide, or murder; people recently divorced or separated; and terminal or recovering cancer patients (Spiegel, Bloom, and Yalom, 1981; Videka-Sherman and Lieberman, 1985).

Since these groups virtually by definition do not include mental health professionals, research has seldom been conducted on them, but there is some evidence that those who care for Alzheimer's patients, usually a close family member, can be helped to feel less lonely (George and Gwyther, 1985). In addition, discharged mental patients have been supported emotionally and socially so as to reduce the frequency of rehospitalization (Edmunson, Bedell, and Gordon, 1984).

Competency Enhancement and Family Problems

The negative effects that *nonsexual* child abuse has on perpetrators, the victim, and other family members render this problem one of considerable social and psychological importance. A number of preventive approaches are under study by community psychologists (Rosenberg and Reppucci, 1985). One approach emphasizes "competency enhancement," that is, instruction in parenting skills so that the various challenges of child-rearing are more familiar and less daunting. If parents know what to expect in child development—that contrariness and selfishness are normal in two- and three-year-olds, for example—they may react less negatively when their child acts in these ways. Also, learning ways to cope with their children's behavior and to control them in nonaversive ways may help parents to be less emotionally coercive and physically punitive. Some programs utilize live or videotaped skits that model assertive problem solving (Gray, 1983, reported in Rosenberg and Reppucci, 1985). Results from several large-scale programs suggest positive attitudinal changes, but the actual impact on lessening child abuse has yet to be assessed.

Similarly indeterminate are the effects of community-wide media campaigns and hot lines available to parents under stress. Indications are that crisis services like hot lines are utilized less often to prevent child abuse than to report abuse or to seek referrals for handling abuse that has already occurred. Better validation exists for efforts directed at high-risk groups, families that are more likely than others to have child abuse and neglect problems, for example, teenage and single-parent mothers. One such study (Olds, 1984, reported in Rosenberg and Reppucci, 1985) added regular visits by a nurse to other postnatal services during the baby's first two years of life. Special intervention included parent education and enhancement of social support networks. Results indicated that nurse-visited mothers had fewer conflicts with their babies and punished them less. Most importantly, the frequency of child abuse/neglect was less as compared to controls.

Some efforts to reduce child *sexual* abuse focus on children themselves, such as instructing them in their rights to control access to their bodies and in assertive behaviors when adults talk to or touch them in discomfiting ways. Data are lacking on the effectiveness of such efforts, however, and there are anecdotal reports of negative effects of such open discussions, for example, nightmares. Documentation of results is clearly of paramount importance (Reppucci, 1987).

Gersten and Jason (1987) review a number of other primary prevention programs aimed at enhancing competence among high-risk individuals. For example, efforts have been made by several community research teams to prevent the frequently observed adverse effects of separation and divorce on both the couple and the children (cf. Wallerstein, 1983). Bloom, Hodges, Kern,

and McFaddin (1985) conducted a six-month program for recently separated people. It was designed to provide both social support and skills training in areas believed to be important for such individuals, for example, child-rearing, employment, and financial management. Four-year follow-ups revealed lower levels of self-reported anxiety and greater self-satisfaction, but other difficulties, like loneliness and employment problems, remained. Similarly mixed results have been reported by others (e.g., Warren *et al.*, 1984)

Children of divorced couples have also been attended to by community researchers. In their Children of Divorce Intervention Program, Pedro-Carrol and Cowen (1985) and Pedro-Carrol, Cowen, Hightower, and Guare (1986) have school-based groups of fourth- to sixth-graders discuss common concerns in a supportive group atmosphere and learn useful skills such as anger control. A subsequent program also involved some of the youngsters serving on an "expert panel," fielding questions from peers about coping with their parents' divorce. Results generally demonstrate fewer classroom adjustment problems and lower anxiety levels as compared to control groups. Similar programs (e.g., Stolberg and Garrison, 1985) report encouraging findings. What remains unexamined, in these and in most other primary prevention studies, is the degree to which they truly reduce the incidence of psychopathology. This is a tall order indeed, but the aspirations and rhetoric of community psychologists have been ambitious and should perhaps be judged by the criteria they themselves have set.

Overall Evaluation of Community Psychology Work

Primary Prevention

It has been suggested that the results of community psychology have not lived up to the rhetoric (Bernstein and Nietzel, 1980). Nowhere are successes more notably lacking than in primary prevention (Cowen, 1983), in keeping disorders from developing in the first place.

One infrequently discussed reason for the limited effectiveness of primary prevention efforts may be that some of the problems community psychologists are trying to prevent are not readily amenable to environmental or social manipulation, for they have major genetic or biological components that are left untouched by the kinds of community-based interventions described in this chapter. As we saw in Chapter 14, for example, there is very strong evidence that schizophrenia has some kind of biological diathesis. Although an environmental preventive effort may conceivably reduce the amount of stress that a predisposed individual is subject to in normal daily living, it seems unlikely that any realistic social change will be able to keep stress levels low enough to prevent schizophrenic episodes from occurring or recurring in high-risk people. Family therapy for reducing expressed emotion (page 581) is a prototype of what might be necessary on a societal scale to have a positive impact on the recurrence of schizophrenic episodes. How practical is it, however, to apply such an approach on a broad scale?

Paraprofessionals and Ethnicity

Community psychology programs often rely on peers, on people who come from the same backgrounds as those receiving services; these paraprofessionals have some training but not the credentials for mental health work. The prevailing belief is that these individuals will better know the life circumstance of those in need, and, most importantly, will be more acceptable to them. Extensive research on modeling provides some justification for these assumptions. Subjects in studies of learning through observation are found to acquire information more readily from models who are perceived as credible and relevant to them; similarity of age and background are important determinants of credibility and relevance (Rosenthal and Bandura, 1978). We can therefore expect that individuals unaccustomed to the standard middle-class fare of a professional office and formal appointments will find the activities and advice of helpers similar to themselves more acceptable.

Few models seem as plausible or relevant as people who have shared but overcome clients' own problems. This is critical if a client rejects staff members as reference figures because they appear too remote in age, education, status, ethnicity, and so on, for suitable comparisons with self, or are perceived as outsiders, lacking vivid conversance with the client's burdens and viewpoint. (Rosenthal and Bandura, 1978, p. 649).

Several studies have examined the effects of race on the counseling relationship. A review of them suggests that black clients prefer black counselors to white counselors, engage in more self-exploration with counselors of their own race, and in general feel more positively toward black helpers than toward white helpers (Jackson, 1973). At the same time the studies suggest that race differences are *not* insurmountable barriers to understanding between counselor and client. Counselors with considerable empathy are perceived as more helpful by clients, regardless of the racial mix. None of these studies investigated whether the therapy provided to black clients by white and black counselors differed in effectiveness.

What Is New in CMHCs?

Problems of community mental health centers were examined more than a decade ago in a rather controversial critique by Ralph Nader's Center for Study of Responsive Law (Holden, 1972). This report held that the centers are based on a good and commendable set of ideas but that the implementation has been rather poor. Often the problem is one of old wine in new bottles. Nader's group pointed out that centers are usually controlled by psychiatrists whose training and outlook are tied to one-to-one therapy, typically along psychoanalytic lines; the "fit" between treatment and the problems of lower-income people who are the centers' primary constituencies is often poor. Indeed, a study conducted by Hollica and Milic (1986) in a Connecticut community mental center indicated that assignment to psychotherapy was made more often for patients of higher social class, who had more education and better employment status. On the plus side was the finding that lower-class patients had indeed been able to obtain some access to outpatient therapy, so-called "categorical" treatment that focused on specific problems like alcohol and drug abuse. What this study does not address, of course, is who is better off in their respective treatment assignment.

Fewer than 800 of the 2000 community mental health centers envisioned by Congress and needed to provide care have been established. An earlier report from the President's Commission on Mental Health (1978) found that centers were not providing good services to underserved populations such as the aged and the chronically mentally ill. More recent data, however, suggest a positive change. For example, day treatment and partial hospitalization are on the rise, and child-oriented services show greater attention to specific pressing problems such as child abuse prevention (Jerrell and Larsen, 1986).

Social and Ethical Factors in Community Psychology

Enthusiasm for community psychology must unfortunately be tempered with awareness of social reality—the conditions of deprivation that community psychologists assume are important in producing and maintaining disordered behavior. To train a black youngster for a specific vocational slot can have a beneficial long-term outcome for the individual only to the extent that society at large provides the appropriate opportunity to use these skills. Those who work in community psychology are aware that racial and social prejudices play a central role in limiting the access of many minority groups to the rewards of the culture at large. Although efforts to improve the socio-cultural milieu must of course continue if our society has any commitment to fostering social and mental well-being, programs may raise expectations that will only be dashed by the realities of the larger culture. This is the quandary of any mental health professional who ventures forth from the consulting room into the community.

Community psychology has as its goal the change of large systems and groups of people rather than treating individual problems. And it is in the seeking mode; psychologists take the initiative in serving people, rather than waiting for individuals in need to come to them. On the face of it, this is a tall order. What do we know about the principles that operate to produce change in societal values and institutions? When a community psychologist organizes a rent strike, for example, what are the best ways of doing so, that is, of persuading the greatest number of tenants to work together in the joint effort? Will gentle persuasion be most effective, or does the situation call for harangues against the landlord? Further, if the community psychologist hopes to take actions that meet the wishes and needs of the community, how does he or she determine them? Recall from Chapters 3 and 4 the difficulties the psychologist has in assessing the needs of an individual client with whom there is extensive direct contact. How much more difficult, then, to assess the needs of thousands of people!

Community psychologists necessarily become social activists to some degree, which raises the danger that these well-meaning professionals may *impose* values and goals on their clients. John Kennedy's launching of the community mental health movement proclaimed that the federal government is rightfully concerned about improving the mental health of Americans. But what is mental health? Who is to decide? To what extent do the people being served by community psychologists have a say in how they are to be helped?

These are but a few of the nettlesome questions that must continually be posed if community psychology is to act responsibly and effectively. The focus of this field is on large-scale factors. Many people are involved; many lives, then, will be affected by decisions and actions. Questions of values and of effectiveness are inherent in any effort to alter the human condition, but they are of special importance when the clients themselves do not seek the intervention.

Psychologists are generally uneasy about entering the arenas of public policy and social values. Their training as social *scientists* does not encourage their professional involvement in large-scale social issues. Community psychologists are different, and recent reviews and policy statements encourage still greater involvement in what are judged to be serious health issues both now and in the near future. In their *Annual Review of Psy-*

chology article, Gesten and Jason (1987) cite the following statistics and projections for the U.S. population:

At any one time 15 to 35 percent of the population needs mental health services (Kiesler, 1985), and contrary to popular opinion, the rate of mental hospital admissions has been *increasing* linearly over the past fifteen years, despite the deinstitutionalization movement (Shadish, 1984).

Half a million children are under temporary care in the foster parent system. Two thousand others die of neglect and abuse each year (Zigler and Finn, 1982).

More than three million children have serious emotional problems, but over 90 percent of them receive no professional treatment. Half of the 7 million who suffer from learning disabilities do not receive adequate care (Alpert, 1985).

By the year 2005, millions more people will need mental health services if for no other reason than that better medical care prolongs life expectancy. There will also be more single-parent homes, many with working mothers (Kramer, 1982).

Expansion of high technology and increased population density are likely to increase levels of social stress, including loss of privacy and autonomy (Sundberg, 1985).

These and other epidemiological facts prompt Gesten and Jason (1987) to argue that "continuing to view ourselves as disinterested scientist-professionals *outside and apart from* the political and economic system will leave us ill prepared for the tasks of the future . . . . [And yet] we seem nonetheless uncertain about how or whether to prepare for the attendant new roles" (pp. 451–452, italics in original).

Their call is clearly for renewed commitment to the original goals of community psychology. At the very least a major contribution of the community psychology movement is in sensitizing mental health professionals to the social, political, and ethical factors in human behavior. These "macro" variables are assumed to be critical in influencing behaviour, and community psychologists are so bold as to try to manipulate them.

Summary

Group therapy takes advantage of some special properties of the group itself. A group can exert especially strong social pressure for change. Members also benefit from sharing common concerns and aspirations. Sensitivity training and encounter groups enable people to learn how they affect others and are affected by them. Efforts are made to get behind the social facades that people present to the world, so that they may deal honestly and more effectively with one another. Controlled research on outcome and process in group therapy of all kinds is just beginning to be done.

In family therapy the problems of the "identified" patient are considered the manifestation of disturbances within the family unit. Family members learn how their behavior and attitudes affect one another, that flexibility and changing communication patterns can bring greater harmony. Marital or couples therapy helps unhappy couples resolve the conflicts inevitable in any ongoing relationship of two adults living together. One technique consists of caring days; one partner at a time concentrates on giving pleasure to the other, breaking the cycle of bitterness and hostility plaguing them. Couples therapists of all theoretical allegiances try to improve partners' communication of needs and wants to each other. An act may be well intentioned but have a negative impact. Talking openly about this problem appears to ease the tensions of many couples. Continuing research in family and marital therapies promises to elucidate the problems for which they are the most appropriate and the processes by which they bring relief.

Community psychology and the related community mental health movement try to prevent mental disorders from developing, to seek out troubled people, and to find the social conditions that may be causing or exacerbating human problems. Community workers must make their values explicit, for they are often fostering social change rather than helping individuals adjust to what some consider untenable social conditions. Deinstitutionalization, the policy of having former mental patients live, if at all possible, at home or in small residences, is part of this movement. Much work needs to be done, however, in designing and supplying adequate sheltered residences and care that will help them live in the community. Primary prevention is difficult to institute, a reflection of our inadequate knowledge of how disordered behavior develops. More needs to be learned about how to determine the needs of a community or how to mobilize large groups of people for change.

Adolph Gottlieb, *Hands of Oedipus*, 1943. © 1980 Adolph and Esther Gottlieb Foundation, New York. Photo: O. Nelson.

Chapter 21

Legal and Ethical Issues

Criminal Commitment

   The Insanity Defense

   Competency to Stand Trial

Civil Commitment

   Problems in the Prediction of Dangerousness

   Recent Trends for Greater Protection

   *Deinstitutionalization, Civil Liberties, and
     Mental Health*

**Ethical Dilemmas in Therapy
and Research**

   Ethical Restraints on Research

   Informed Consent

   Treatment or Research?

   Confidentiality and Privileged Communication

   Who Is the Client?

   Choice of Goals

   Choice of Techniques

   Concluding Comment

Summary

Amendment 1 Congress shall make no law respecting an establishment of religion, or prohibiting the free exercise thereof; or abridging the freedom of speech, or of the press; or the right of the people peaceably to assemble, and to petition the Government for a redress of grievances.

Amendment 4 The right of the people to be secure in their persons, houses, papers, and effects, against unreasonable searches and seizures, shall not be violated. . . .

Amendment 5 No person . . . shall be compelled in any criminal case to be a witness against himself, nor be deprived of life, liberty, or property, without due process of law. . . .

Amendment 6 In all criminal prosecutions, the accused shall enjoy the right to a speedy and public trial . . . ; to be confronted with the witnesses against him; to have compulsory process for obtaining witnesses in his favor, and to have the Assistance of Counsel for his defense.

Amendment 8 Excessive bail shall not be required, nor excessive fines imposed, nor cruel and unusual punishment inflicted.

Amendment 13 . . . Neither slavery nor involuntary servitude, except as a punishment for crime whereof the party shall have been duly convicted, shall exist within the United States, or any place subject to their jurisdiction. . . .

Amendment 14 . . . No State shall . . . deprive any person of life, liberty, or property, without due process of law; nor deny to any person within its jurisdiction the equal protection of the laws.

Amendment 15 . . . The right of citizens of the United States to vote shall not be denied or abridged by the United States or by any State on account of race, color, or previous condition of servitude.

These elegant statements describe and protect some of the rights of American citizens and others residing in this country. Against what are these rights being protected? Be mindful of the circumstances under which most of these statements were issued. After the Constitutional Convention delegates had delineated the powers of government in 1787, the first Congress saw fit in 1789 to amend what they had framed and to set specific limits on the federal government. Amendments beyond the original ten have been added since that time. In particular, the fourteenth amendment is directed to the states, which, as will be seen, are playing increasingly important roles in the protection of the rights of mental patients. The philosophical ideal of American government has always been to allow citizens the maximum degree of liberty consistent with preserving order in the community at large.

We open our final chapter in this way because the legal and mental health systems collaborate continually, although often subtly, to deny a substantial proportion of our population their basic civil rights. With the best of intentions, judges, governing boards of hospitals, bar associations, and professional mental health groups have worked over the years to protect society at large from the actions of people regarded as mentally ill or mentally defective and considered dangerous to themselves or to others. But in so doing they have abrogated the rights of thousands of people in both criminal and civil commitment proceedings. The mentally ill who have broken the law, or who are alleged to have done so, can be committed to a prison hospital through *criminal commitment* proceedings. *Civil commitment* is a set of procedures by which a person who has not broken a law can be deprived of his or her liberty and incarcerated in a mental hospital. In effect, both commitments remove individuals from the normal processes of the law.

Criminal Commitment

We shall examine first the role of psychiatry and psychology in the criminal justice system. Almost as early as the concept of *mens rea* or guilty mind and the rule "No crime without an evil intent" had begun to be accepted in English common law, insanity had to be taken into consideration, for a disordered mind may be regarded as unable to formulate and carry out a criminal purpose. In other words, a disordered mind could not be a guilty mind, because only a guilty mind is one whose actions can be culpable. At first insanity was not a trial defense, but the English crown sometimes granted pardons to people who had been convicted of homicide if they were judged completely and totally mad (A. A. Morris, 1968). By the reign of Edward I (1272–1307), the concept of insanity had begun to be argued in court and could lessen punishment. Then during the course of the fourteenth century it became the rule of law that a person proved to be wholly and continually mad could be defended against a criminal charge.

In modern times judges and lawyers have called on psychiatrists, and recently clinical psychologists as well, for assistance in dealing with criminal acts thought to result from the accused's disordered mental state, not from his free will. Are such emotionally disturbed perpetrators less criminally responsible than those who are not distraught but commit the same crimes? Should such individuals even be brought to trial for transgressions

"BUT YOU JUST CAN'T PLEAD INSANITY
DUE TO AN EXTRA Y-CHROMOSOME IN
A CASE OF EMBEZZLING."

against society's laws? Although efforts to excuse or protect the accused through the insanity defense or by judging them incompetent to stand trial are undoubtedly well intentioned, invoking these doctrines can often subject the accused to a greater denial of his liberties than he would experience without them.

The Insanity Defense

A staggering amount of material has been written on the insanity defense, even though it is pled in only about 2 percent of all cases that reach trial and is rarely successful (N. Morris, 1968; Morse, 1982b; Steadman, 1979). Alan A. Stone (1975), a professor of law and psychiatry at Harvard, proposed an intriguing reason for this great interest. Criminal law rests on the assumption that people have free will and that, if they do wrong, they have *chosen* to do so and should therefore be punished. "Our jurisprudence . . . while not oblivious to deterministic components, ultimately rests on a premise of freedom of will" (*United States* v. *Brawner*[1]). Stone suggests that the insanity defense strengthens the concept of free will by pointing to the few people who constitute an exception because they do not have it, namely, those judged to be insane. These individuals are assumed to have less responsibility for their actions because of a mental defect, an inability to distinguish between right and wrong, or both. They lack the degree of free will that would justify holding them legally accountable for criminal acts. By exclusion, everyone else *has* free will! "The insanity defense is in every sense the exception that

proves the rule. It allows the courts to treat every other defendant as someone who chose 'between good and evil' " (Stone, 1975, p. 222).

Landmark Cases and Laws

Historically, in modern Anglo-American criminal law, there have been three important court rulings and two sets of principles that bear on the problems of legal responsibility and mental illness. The so-called "irresistible-impulse" concept was formulated in 1834 in a case in Ohio wherein it was decided that an insanity defense was legitimate if a pathological impulse or drive that the person could not control had compelled him to commit the criminal act. The irresistible impulse test was confirmed in two subsequent court cases, *Parsons* v. *State* and *Davis* v. *United States*.[2]

The second well-known concept, the M'Naghten rule, was announced in the aftermath of a murder trial in England in 1843. The defendant, Daniel M'Naghten, had meant to kill the British prime minister but had instead mistaken the secretary of Sir Robert Peel for his employer. M'Naghten claimed that he had been instructed to kill Lord Peel by the "voice of God." The judges ruled that

to establish a defence of insanity, it must be clearly proved that, at the time of the committing of the act, the party accused was labouring under such a defect of reason, from disease of the mind, as not to know the nature and quality of the act he was doing; or if he did know it, that he did not know he was doing what was wrong.

By the beginning of the twentieth century, this "right–wrong" test was being used in all the states except New Hampshire and in all federal courts. By the late 1980s it was the sole test in eighteen states, and in several others is applied in conjunction with irresistible impulse. However, a committee of the American Psychiatric Association expressed the view that understanding the difference between right and wrong was out of step with modern conceptions of insanity (Slicker, 1985). It was in this context that a third important court decision was made.

Judge David Bazelon ruled in 1954, in the case of *Durham* v. *United States*,[3] that the "accused is not criminally responsible if his unlawful act was the product of mental disease or mental defect." Bazelon believed that by referring simply to mental illness he would leave the profession of psychiatry free to apply its full knowledge.

---

[1]*United States* v. *Brawner*, No. 22,714 (D.C. Cir. June 23, 1972).

[2]*Parsons* v. *State*, 2 So. 854, 866–67 (Ala. 1887); *Davis* v. *United States*, 175 U.S. 373, 378 (1897).

[3]*Durham* v. *United States*, 214 F. 2d 862, 876 (D.C. Cir. 1954).

BOX 21.1

THE AFTERMATH OF THE JOHN HINCKLEY CASE

In the foreword to a recent book on the insanity defense (Simon and Aaronson, 1988), Judge Barrington D. Parker of the United States District Court for the District of Columbia describes the aftermath of the unexpected NGRI verdict in the trial of John Hinckley, Jr., the man who almost assassinated President Ronald Reagan on March 30, 1981. Judge Parker, who presided over the trial, received a flood of mail from outraged citizens that a would-be assassin of an American president had not been held criminally responsible and had "only" been committed to an indefinite stay in a mental hospital until deemed mentally healthy enough for release. (As we write this in mid-1989, Hinckley has been incarcerated in St. Elizabeth's Hospital for over eight years but could be released whenever his mental health is deemed adequate.)

Because of the publicity of the trial and the public outrage at the NGRI verdict, the insanity defense became a target of vigorous and sometimes vituperative criticism from many quarters. As Judge Parker put it: "For many, the [Hinckley] defense was a clear manifestation of the failure of our criminal justice system to punish individuals who have clearly violated the law." (Simon and Aaronson, 1988, p. vii).

As a consequence of political pressures to "get tough" on criminals, Congress enacted, in October 1984, the Insanity Defense Reform Act, the first time this body had

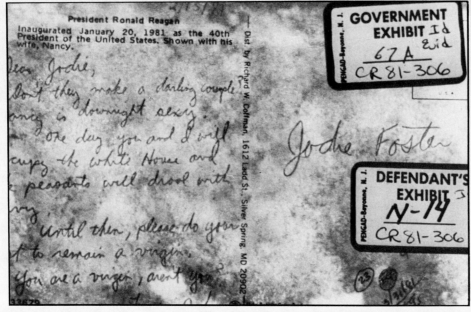

(Top) John Hinckley, President Reagan's assailant, on his way back to St. Elizabeth's following a judicial hearing. (Bottom) Letter by Hinckley to Jodie Foster expressing his dream of marrying her and becoming president.

It would no longer be limited to considering impulses or knowledge of right and wrong. Judge Bazelon purposely did not incorporate in what would be called the Durham test any particular symptoms of mental disorder that might later become obsolete. The psychiatrist was accorded great liberty to convey to the court his or her own evaluation of the accused's mental condition.

Forcing the jury to rely to this extent on expert testimony did not prove workable courtroom practice, however. Since 1972 the Durham test is no longer used in any jurisdiction, and even Judge Bazelon has withdrawn his support for it, feeling that it allowed too much leeway to expert witnesses.

In 1962 the American Law Institute (ALI) proposed

addressed the insanity defense. This new law, which has been adopted in all federal courts, contains several provisions:

1. It eliminates the irresistible-impulse component of the ALI rules, which referred to inability of the person to conform to the requirements of the law as a result of a mental disease or defect. This volitional and behavioral aspect of the ALI guidelines had been subjected to especially strong invective because one could regard *any* criminal act as arising from an inability to stay within the limits of the law. Furthermore, as Richard Bonnie, Professor of Law at the University of Virginia, testified before Congress, "there is . . . no objective basis for distinguishing between offenders who were undeterrable and those who were merely undeterred, between the impulse that was irresistible and the impulse not resisted. . . . To ask [such questions] at all, in my opinion, invites fabricated claims, undermines equal administration of the penal law, and compromises its deterrent effect" (Testimony by Bonnie before 98th Congress, 1984, as cited in Simon and Aaronson, 1988, pp. 49–50).

2. It changes ALI's lack of "substantial capacity . . . to appreciate" to "unable to appreciate." This alteration in the cognitive component of the law is intended to tighten the grounds for an insanity defense.

3. The 1984 act also stipulates that the mental disease or defect be "severe," the intent being to exclude insanity defenses on the bases of nonpsychotic disorders such as antisocial personality disorder.*

4. The Insanity Defense Reform Act of 1984 also shifts the burden of proof from the prosecution to the defense. Instead of the prosecution having to prove that the person was sane beyond a reasonable doubt at the time of the crime (the most stringent criterion, consistent with the constitutional requirement that people are considered innocent until proven guilty), the defense must prove that he was not sane, and must do so with "clear and convincing evidence" (a less stringent but still demanding standard of proof). The importance of this shift can be appreciated by keeping in mind that, if the prosecution bears the burden of proof beyond a reasonable doubt, then the defense need only introduce a reasonable doubt to defeat the prosecution's efforts to prove sanity. The heavier burden that the 1984 Reform Act places on the defense is, like the other provisions, designed to make it more difficult to relieve a defendant of moral and legal responsibility.†

5. Finally, the new act responds to what many felt to be the most annoying possibility allowable under existing laws, namely, release from commitment after a shorter period of time than an ordinary sentence would have provided. If the person is judged to have recovered from his mental illness, then instead of allowing his release from the prison hospital, the period of incarceration can be extended to the maximum allowable for the actual crime.

The full impact of this federal law is yet to be felt in the American judicial system.

---

*Recall that the ALI guidelines had been developed to impose similar restrictions, by the use of the phrase "substantial" incapacity; this apparently was not considered strong enough in the immediate aftermath of the Hinckley acquittal. Also abolished by the Reform Act were defenses relying on "diminished capacity" or "diminished responsibility," based on such mitigating circumstances as extreme passion or "temporary insanity" such that the accused lacked the capacity for a specific type of crime, for example, the premeditation required for first-degree murder, permitting him to be convicted instead on a lesser charge, such as manslaughter.

†According to Simon and Aaronson (1988), this provision arose in large measure from the inability of the prosecution to prove John Hinckley's sanity when he shot Reagan and three others. Several members of the jury testified after the trial to a subcommittee of the Senate Judiciary Committee that the judge's instructions on the burden of proof played a role in their verdict of NGRI. Even before the Act, almost half the states required that the defendant must prove his insanity, but only one, Arizona, had the "clear and convincing" standard. Since *Hinckley,* about two-thirds of the states now place the proof of burden on the defense, albeit with the least exacting of legal standards of proof, "by a preponderance of the evidence."

---

its own guidelines, which were intended to be more specific and informative to lay jurors than other tests.

1. A person is not responsible for criminal conduct if at the time of such conduct as a result of mental disease or defect he lacks substantial capacity either to

appreciate the criminality (wrongfulness) of his conduct or to conform his conduct to the requirements of law.

2. As used in the Article, the terms "mental disease or defect" do not include an abnormality manifested only

by repeated criminal or otherwise antisocial conduct.
(The American Law Institute, 1962, p. 66)

The first of the ALI guidelines in a sense combines the M'Naghten rule and the irresistible-impulse concept. The second ALI guideline concerns those who are repeatedly in trouble with the law; they are not to be deemed mentally ill only because they keep committing crimes. Indeed, the phrase "substantial capacity" in the first guideline is designed to limit an insanity defense to those with the most serious of mental disorders. Until 1984 the ALI test was in use in more than half the states and in all federal courts. Some scholars, however, argued that words like "substantial" and "appreciate" introduce ambiguities that foster disagreements among both expert witnesses and jurors as to whether a defendant's state of mind is sufficiently awry to justify a verdict of not guilty by reason of insanity (Simon and Aaronson, 1988).

In the past several years there has been a fifth major effort in the United States to clarify the legal defense of insanity, strengthened by the controversy created by the not guilty by reason of insanity (NGRI) verdict in the highly publicized trial of John Hinckley, Jr.'s assassination attempt of then President Ronald Reagan. (See Box 21.1.) Eleven states have recently supplemented the NGRI insanity defense with what seems to be a compromise verdict, namely, "guilty but mentally ill" (GBMI). Initially adopted by Michigan in 1975, this principle allows an accused person to be found legally guilty of a crime—thus maximizing the chances of incarceration—but allows for psychiatric judgment of how to deal with the convicted person if he or she is considered to have been mentally ill when the act was committed. Thus, even a seriously ill person can be held morally and legally responsible, but can then be committed to a prison hospital or other suitable facility for psychiatric treatment rather than to a regular prison for punishment.

This trend reflects the uneasiness of the legal and mental health professions in excusing a person who, in Thomas Szasz's terms, is *descriptively* responsible for a crime—that is, there is no disputing that he or she actually committed the act—without being held *ascriptively* responsible for it—that is, without having to suffer some sort of societal negative consequence for having broken the law (Box 21.2). This legal modification avoids the irony of (1) determining that a person committed a crime, (2) that he is not to be held legally responsible because of insanity at the time of the crime—the NGRI defense— and that (3) by the time he is to be criminally committed, he is judged to be no longer mentally ill, and (4) he is *not* incarcerated (or is released after a shorter confinement than he would have been subject

to if he had been found guilty of the crime he committed).[4] A GBMI verdict allows the usual sentence to be imposed for being found guilty of a given crime, but also allows for the person to be treated for his mental illness during incarceration.

So far, however, evidence does not indicate that the GBMI alternative per se results in appropriate psychiatric treatment for those convicted (Fentiman, 1985). The GBMI verdict is opposed by both the American Psychiatric Association and the American Bar Association and also lacks support from professionals outside of the eleven states that currently allow the verdict (Simon and Aaronson, 1988).

In applying the insanity defense, an abstract principle must be fit to specific life situations. As in all aspects of the law, terms can be defined in a number of ways— by defendants, defense lawyers, prosecutors, judges, and, of course, by jurors—and testimony can be presented in diverse fashion, depending on the skill of the interrogators and the intelligence of the witnesses. Furthermore, because only the defendant's mental condition *at the time the crime was committed* is in question, retrospective, often speculative, judgment on the part of attorneys, judges, jurors, and psychiatrists is required. And disagreement between defense and prosecution psychiatrists and psychologists is the rule.

The Case of *Jones* v. *United States*

Case Description To illustrate the predicament that a person can get into if he or she raises insanity as an excusing condition for a criminal act, we consider a Supreme Court case.[5] Michael Jones was arrested unarmed on September 19, 1975, for attempting to steal a jacket from a department store in Washington, D.C. He was charged the following day with attempted petty larceny, a misdemeanor punishable by a maximum prison sentence of one year. The court ordered that he be committed to St. Elizabeth's Hospital, a public mental hospital in Washington, D.C., for a determination of his competency to stand trial. On March 2, 1976, almost six months after the alleged crime, a hospital psychologist reported to the court that Jones was competent to stand trial, although he suffered from "schizophrenia, paranoid type." The psychologist also reported that the alleged crime itself was caused by Jones's condition, his paranoid schizophrenia. This is noteworthy because he

---

[4]Things can go the other way, however, as demonstrated in the case of *Jones* v. *United States* described shortly.

[5]*Jones* v. *United States*, 463 U.S. _____, 103 S. Ct. _____, L.Ed. 2d _____, 51 U.S.L.W. 5041 (1983).

was not asked to offer an opinion on the nature of the crime itself, only on whether Jones was competent to stand trial. Jones then decided to plead not guilty by reason of insanity. Ten days later, on March 12, the court found him not guilty by reason of insanity and formally committed him to St. Elizabeth's Hospital for treatment of his mental disorder.

On May 25, 1976, a customary fifty-day hearing was held to determine whether Jones should remain in the hospital any longer. A psychologist from the hospital testified that, indeed, Jones still suffered from paranoid schizophrenia and was therefore still a danger to himself and to others. A second hearing was held on February 22, 1977, seventeen months after the commission of the crime and Jones's original commitment to St. Elizabeth's for determination of competency. The defendant demanded release since he had already been hospitalized longer than the one-year maximum sentence he would have served had he been found guilty of the theft of the jacket. The court denied the request and returned him to St. Elizabeth's.

The District of Columbia Court of Appeals agreed with the original court. Ultimately, in November 1982, more than seven years after his hospitalization, Jones's appeal to the Supreme Court was heard. On June 29, 1983, by a five-to-four decision, the Court affirmed the earlier decision: Jones was to remain at St. Elizabeth's.

The Decision of the Supreme Court The basic question that Jones took to the Supreme Court was whether someone "who was committed to a mental hospital upon being acquitted of a criminal offense by reason of insanity, must be released because he has been hospitalized for a period longer than he might have served in prison had he been convicted" (*Jones* v. *United States*, p. 700). Having already spent more time in the prison hospital than he would have served in prison had he been convicted, Jones believed that he should be released.

The Supreme Court, however, saw matters differently.

An insanity acquittee is not entitled to his release merely because he has been hospitalized for a period longer than he could have been incarcerated if convicted. The length of a sentence for a particular criminal offense is based on a variety of considerations, including retribution, deterrence, and rehabilitation. However, because an insanity acquittee was not convicted, he may not be punished. The purpose of his commitment is to treat his mental illness and protect him and society from his potential dangerousness. There simply is no necessary correlation between the length of the acquittee's hypothetical criminal sentence

and the length of time necessary for his recovery. (p. 700, emphasis added)[6]

Where [the] accused has pleaded insanity as a defense to a crime, and the jury has found that the defendant was, in fact, insane at the time the crime was committed, it is just and reasonable . . . that the insanity, once established, should be presumed to continue and that the accused should automatically be confined for treatment until it can be shown that he has recovered (S Rep No. 1170, 84th Cong, 1st Sess 13 (1955), as cited in *Jones* v. *United States*, p. 705)

And because it is impossible to predict how long it will take for any given individual to recover—or indeed whether he ever will recover—Congress has chosen, as it has with respect to civil commitment, to leave the length of commitment interdeterminate, subject to periodic review of the patient's suitability for release. (p. 708)

The fact that Jones was acquitted means, said the Court, that he cannot be punished for the crime. For to be punished, the individual must be blameworthy. Jones's insanity left him legally blameless, for he could not possess *mens rea*, a guilty mind. His free will to have committed the theft was deemed to have been superseded by his disturbed mental state. This is the logic of the insanity defense. Furthermore, said the Court, since punishment cannot have any of its intended individual or societal effects on a mentally disturbed person—rehabilitation, deterrence, or retribution—it was irrelevant that Jones was being held longer than a normal prison sentence.

Critique of the Supreme Court Decision The burden of proof was on Jones, the acquittee, to prove that he was no longer mentally ill, or dangerous to society. This contrasts with the normal practice of justice in the United States, that a person's *accusers* have the burden to prove him or her guilty. It is different as well from civil commitment, in which the government, not the person, bears the burden of proof; Jones was denied this civil right.

The Court was concerned about Jones's illness-produced dangerousness. What the Court said about "dangerousness" is therefore interesting. Jones argued in his petition to the Supreme Court that his theft of the jacket was not dangerous because his was not a violent crime. The Court stated, however, that for there to be violence in a criminal act, the act itself need not be dangerous. It cited a previous decision that a nonviolent theft of

---

[6]This absence of correlation between the criminal act and the length of incarceration can also work the other way, namely, "no matter how serious the act committed by the acquittee, he may be released within fifty days of his acquittal if he has recovered" (p. 708).

BOX 21.2

THOMAS S. SZASZ AND THE CASE AGAINST FORENSIC PSYCHIATRY AND PSYCHOLOGY

HIS POLEMIC

By codifying acts of violence as expressions of mental illness, we neatly rid ourselves of the task of dealing with criminal offenses as more or less rational, goal-directed acts, no different in principle from other forms of conduct. (Szasz, 1963, p. 141)

This quotation from one of Thomas Szasz's most widely read books enunciates the basic theme of his argument against the weighty role that his own profession of psychiatry plays in the legal system. We have already mentioned Szasz's distinction between descriptive and ascriptive responsibility. To hold a person criminally responsible is to ascribe legal responsibility for an act for which he is descriptively responsible. A given social group makes the judgment that the person who is descriptively responsible for a criminal act will receive criminal punishment. As Szasz points out, being criminally responsible is not an inherent trait that society uncovers. Rather, society at a given time and for a given criminal act decides that it will hold the perpetrator legally responsible and will punish him.

Szasz goes on to suggest that mental illness began to be used as an explanation for criminal behavior when people acted in a way that was considered particularly irrational and threatening to society. According to Szasz, these exceptional cases all involved violence against people of high social rank. In shooting at Lord Onslow in 1724, a man named Arnold was believed to have as little understanding of his murderous act as "a wild beast." Another man, James Hadfield, was deemed deranged for attempting to assassinate King George III in 1800 as he sat in a box at the Theatre Royal. And a third, Oxford by name, was regarded as insane for trying to kill Queen Victoria in 1840. The best-known case has already been mentioned, that of David M'Naghten (1843), who killed Sir Robert Peel's private secretary after mistaking him for Peel. In all these cases from English law, which forms the basis for all American law, people of low social rank openly attacked their superiors. Szasz believes that "the issue of insanity may have been raised in these trials in order to obscure the social problems which the crimes intended to dramatize" (1963, p. 128).

Other cases here and abroad, such as the assassinations

Thomas S. Szasz, noted psychiatrist who argues strongly against the use of the insanity defense.

of John and Robert Kennedy, the South African prime minister Hendrik Verwoerd, Martin Luther King, and John Lennon, and the attempted assassinations of Ronald Reagan and Pope John Paul II, may to a degree reflect the social ills of the day. Moreover, events in the Soviet Union have reflected the role of politics in criminal and civil commitment. In *A Question of Madness*, the well-known Russian biochemist Zhores Medvedev (1972) told how Soviet psychiatrists collaborated with the state in attempting to muzzle his criticism of the government. They diagnosed him as suffering from paranoid delusions, split personality, and other mental ailments that would make it dangerous for him to be at large in society. In the present age of *Glasnost* and increasing political freedom in the Soviet Union, such abuses may decline. Time will tell.

But pleas of insanity are generally made in far more ordinary cases. Of course Szasz does not claim that all these pleas involve some sort of silent conspiracy of the establishment to cover up social problems. Szasz sets forth a polemic much broader in scope. His basic concern is with individual freedom, which includes the right to deviate from prevailing mores. Far from advocating that people be held *less* accountable for antisocial acts, he argues that legal responsibility be extended to *all,* even to those whose

an article such as a watch may frequently result in violence through the efforts of the criminal to escape, or of the victim to protect his property, or of the police to apprehend the fleeing thief.[7]

The dissenting justices of the Court commented that the longer someone like Jones had to remain in the

hospital, the more difficult it would be for him to demonstrate that he is no longer a dangerous person nor mentally ill. Extended institutionalization would likely make it more difficult for him to afford medical experts other than those associated with the hospital and to behave like someone who is not mentally ill.

The current [use of] psychotropic drugs . . . may render mental patients docile . . ., but it does not "cure"

[7]*Overholser* v. *O'Beorne,* 112 App. D.C. 267, 302 F. 2d 852, 861 (1961).

actions are so far beyond the limits of convention that some people explain their behavior in terms of mental illness. Szasz's overall lament is that

instead of recognizing the deviant as an individual different from those who would judge him, but nonetheless worthy of their respect, he is first discredited as a self-responsible human being and then subjected to humiliating punishment defined and disguised as treatment. (1963, p. 108)

EVALUATION OF SZASZ'S POSITION

The Insanity Defense Reform Act of 1984 (Box 21.1) as well as changes in civil commitment to be described shortly are consistent with the arguments that Szasz has put forward for the past thirty years. Indeed, these shifts in the direction of holding the mentally ill accountable for their actions and thereby more deserving of protection of their civil rights are probably due in large measure to his unrelenting attacks on the liaison between the law and the mental health professions.

However, Szasz has not gone uncriticized by those who sincerely believe that psychiatry and psychology should have an important role in deciding how to deal with people whose criminal acts seem attributable to mental illness. The abuses documented by Szasz should not blind us to the fact that—for whatever combination of physiological and psychological reasons—some people are, at times, a danger to others and to themselves. Although Szasz and others object to mental illness as an explanation, it is difficult to deny that there is, indeed, madness in the world. People *do* occasionally imagine persecutors, whom they sometimes act against with force. Some people *do* hallucinate and on this basis may behave in a dangerous fashion. Our concern for the liberties of one individual has always been tempered with our concern for the rights of others.

But does it help a criminal acquitted by reason of insanity to place him in a prison mental hospital with an indeterminate sentence, pending his rehabilitation? The answer can surely not be an unqualified yes. Should such a person, then, be treated like any other convicted felon and be sent to a penitentiary? Considering the psychic damage that we know may occur in ordinary prisons, a yes to this question cannot be enthusiastic either. But a prison

sentence is more often a finite term of incarceration. If we cannot demonstrate that people are rehabilitated in mental hospitals, perhaps it is just as well to rely on our prisons and on the efforts of penologists to improve these institutions and to find ways of helping inmates alter their behavior so that they will not be antisocial after release.*

Stephen J. Morse, a University of Pennsylvania law professor and a leading theorist in forensics, has also written on the need to treat mentally ill people as responsible individuals and on the associated need to improve the prison system.

If involuntary commitment is abolished, there may well be an increase in the processing of cases of relatively mild deviance through the criminal justice system and increased numbers of crazy persons may spend some time in unpleasant and often terrible jails. But, if crazy persons are almost always responsible for their behavior, and if incarceration in a jail is justified, there is no reason why they should not go to jail. This outcome is in fact more respectful of the dignity and autonomy of crazy persons than assuming that they are nonresponsible and must be "fixed." Jails and locked hospitals are both massive intrusions on liberty. The best response to the argument that jails are bad places, as they surely are for non-crazy and crazy inmates alike, is to clean them up. Using unjustified hospitalization—merely another form of incarceration that offers little if any of the benefits it promises—to avoid jails is not a sensible solution to the problems of criminal justice: it merely allows us to avoid those problems. (Morse, 1982a, p. 98)

---

*The treatment model, however, has been challenged by simple, old-fashioned, retributive justice (Monahan, 1977; Morse, 1979). Today punishment rather than rehabilitation is likely to be the primary purpose of imprisonment. Prisoners given treatment, whether job training or psychotherapy, have no different crime rates after release than inmates who simply sat out their terms in their cells and led a routine prison life. Prisoners themselves have been agitating for finite sentences, rather than the indeterminate sentence that promises early parole depending on "rehabilitation." On the other hand, the guilty but mentally ill trend reviewed may well return a mental health focus to jails and penitentiaries if persons judged to be in need of treatment are sent there with instructions that they receive psychiatric care during their sentence.

---

them or allow them to demonstrate that they would remain non-violent if they were not drugged. . . . At petitioner's May 1976 hearing, the Government relied on testimony [from hospital mental health experts] that petitioner was "not always responsive in a positive way to what goes on" and was "not a very active participant in the informal activities on the Ward" to support its contention that he had not recovered. (p. 716, fn 16)

Competency To Stand Trial

The insanity defense concerns the accused's mental state *at the time of the crime.* A second issue, whether the person is competent to stand trial, concerns the defendant's mental condition *at the time of his or her trial.* It is obviously possible for a person to be judged competent to stand trial yet be acquitted by reason of insanity. By the same token, a person can be deemed incompetent to stand trial when no final courtroom consideration has yet been given to his criminal responsibility for the act in question.

Far greater numbers of people are committed to prison hospitals after being judged incompetent to stand trial than are tried and acquitted by reason of insanity. In fact, it has been estimated that as many as forty-five people are confined in prison hospitals because of incompetency to stand trial for every one ultimately sent there for having been found not guilty by reason of insanity (Steadman, 1979). Our criminal justice system is so organized that the fitness of individuals to stand trial must be decided before it can be determined whether they are responsible for the crime of which they are accused.

With the Supreme Court case *Pate* v. *Robinson*[8] as precedent, the defense attorney, prosecutor, or judge may raise the question of mental illness whenever there is reason to believe that the accused's mental condition might interfere with the upcoming trial. Over the years most jurisdictions in this country have shown concern that the accused may be "presently insane and otherwise so mentally incompetent as to be unable to understand the proceedings against him or properly to assist in his own defense" (Pfeiffer, Eisenstein, and Dabbs, 1967, p. 322). Another way of stating this problem of competency is to say that the courts do not want a person to be brought to trial *in absentia*, which is a basic principle of English common law going back to the eighteenth century. A disturbed person can of course be physically present; what is referred to here is his or her mental state. If after examination the person is deemed too mentally ill to participate meaningfully in a trial, the trial is routinely delayed. The accused is incarcerated in a prison hospital with the hope that means of restoring adequate mental functioning can be found. This happened to Jones, immediately after his arrest.

Being judged incompetent to stand trial can have severe consequences for the individual. Bail is automatically denied, even though it might be routinely granted if the question of incompetency had not been raised. The accused is kept in a facility for the criminally insane for the pretrial examination; these institutions are not the best of hospitals. The accused may well lose employment and undergo the trauma of being separated from family and friends and from familiar surroundings for months or even years, perhaps making his emotional condition even worse and thereby delaying his fitness to stand trial. Some people have languished in a prison hospital for many years, waiting to be found competent to stand trial.

Many psychiatrists, when asked to render a com-

petency judgment, assume that if they judge the person to be mentally disturbed in any way, it follows that he or she cannot stand trial. Robey (1965) pointed out, however, that even a psychotic person may sufficiently understand his position in the legal proceedings to participate in them and to talk with his attorney rationally. Robey proposes that a person be allowed to come to trial *even though* he may behave in a bizarre manner before and during the proceedings. The accused may be at a severe disadvantage if, during the trial, he is confused, deluded, hallucinating, and so on, but a somewhat inequitable trial may be preferable to being incarcerated until behavior is judged normal once again. It should be kept in mind that some of the people we are talking about are proved, once they have been brought to trial, *not* to have committed the crimes of which they were accused.

A 1972 Supreme Court case, *Jackson* v. *Indiana*,[9] forced the states to a shorter-term determination of incompetency. The case concerned a mentally retarded deaf-mute man who was deemed not only incompetent to stand trial but unlikely ever to become competent. The Court ruled that the length of pretrial confinement must be limited to the time it takes to determine whether treatment during this detainment is likely to render the defendant competent to stand trial. If the defendant is unlikely ever to become competent, the state should after this period either institute civil commitment proceedings or release the defendant. It has been suggested that lawyers participate with mental health professionals in making the competency determination, for a knowledgeable lawyer understands exactly what the defendant must be able to do to participate in his own trial (Roesch and Golding, 1980). Legislation has been drafted in most states to define more precisely the minimal requirements for competency to stand trial, ending the latitude that has deprived thousands of people of their rights to due process (Amendment 14) and a speedy trial (Amendment 6).

The era of modern medicine has also had an impact on the competency issue. The concept of "synthetic sanity" (Schwitzgebel and Schwitzgebel, 1980) has been introduced: if a drug like Thorazine temporarily produces a modicum of rationality in an otherwise deranged defendant, the trial may proceed. The likelihood that the defendant will again become incompetent to stand trial if and when the drug is withdrawn will not disqualify him from having his day in court.[10] Furthermore, if the defendant wishes, the effects of the med-

---

[8]*Pate* v. *Robinson*, 384 U.S. 375 (1966).

[9]*Jackson* v. *Indiana*, 406 U.S. 715 (1972).

[10]*State of Louisiana* v. *Hamptom*, 216 So. 2d 311 (1969); *State of Tennessee* v. *Stacy*, No. 446 (Crim. App., Knoxville, TN, August 4, 1977); *United States* v. *Hayes*, 589 F. 2d 811 (1979).

ication must be explained to the jury, lest—if the defendant is pleading NGRI—the jury conclude, from his relatively calm and rational drug-produced demeanor, that he could not have been insane at the time of the crime.[11]

Civil Commitment

Civil commitment affects far greater numbers of people than criminal commitment. It is beyond the scope of this book to examine in detail the variety of state civil commitment laws and regulations. Each state has its own, and they are in almost constant flux. Our aim instead is to provide an overview that will give the reader a basic understanding of the issues and of the current directions of change.

In virtually all states of the union, a person can be committed to a mental hospital against his or her will if a judgment is made that he or she (1) is mentally ill and (2) a danger to self—that is, unable to provide for his or her basic physical needs of food, clothing, and shelter—or a danger to others (Warren, 1982). At present, dangerousness to others is more often the second criterion, and recent court rulings point to *imminent* dangerousness as the principal criterion.[12]

Historically, governments have had the duty to protect their citizens from harm. We take for granted the right and duty of government to set limits on our freedom for the sake of protecting us. Few drivers, for example, question the limits imposed on them by traffic signals. We usually go along with the Food and Drug Administration when it bans uncontrolled use of drugs that cause cancer in laboratory animals, although some people, to be sure, feel they have the right to decide for themselves what risks to take with their own bodies. Government, then, has a long-established right to protect us both from ourselves—the *parens patriae* power of the state; and from others—the police power of the state. Civil commitment is one further exercise of these powers.

Specific commitment procedures are generally of two types, formal and informal. Formal or judicial commitment is by order of a court. It can be requested by any responsible citizen; usually the police, a relative, or a friend seeks the commitment. If the judge believes that there is good reason to pursue the matter, he or she will order a mental health examination. The person has the right to object to these attempts to "certify" him, and a court hearing can be scheduled to allow him to present evidence against commitment.

Informal, emergency commitment can be accomplished without initially involving the courts. For example, a hospital administrative board may decide that a voluntary patient requesting discharge is too disturbed and dangerous to be released. They are able to detain the patient with a temporary, informal commitment order.

Any person acting wildly may be taken immediately to the state hospital by the police. Perhaps the most common informal commitment procedure is the "2PC" or "two physicians' certificate." In most states two physicians, not necessarily psychiatrists, can sign a certificate that will allow a person to be incarcerated for some period of time, ranging from twenty-four hours to as long as twenty days.[13] Detainment beyond this period requires formal judicial commitment.

Problems in the Prediction of Dangerousness

Civil commitment is necessarily a form of preventive detention: the prediction is made that a person judged mentally ill may in the future behave in a dangerous manner and should therefore be detained. Ordinary prisoners, however, are released from penitentiaries, even though statistics show that most will commit additional crimes. Moreover, conviction by a court of law and subsequent imprisonment are carried out only after a person has done some harm to others. Some may say it is like closing the barn door after the horses have thundered out. But our entire legal and constitutional system is organized to protect people from preventive detention. Even if witnesses have seen a person commit a serious crime, he or she is assumed innocent until proven guilty by the courts. The person who openly threatens to inflict harm on others, such as a man who for an hour each day stands in the street and shouts threats to people in a nearby apartment house, is another matter. Does the state have to wait until he acts on his threats? No. Here the civil commitment process can be brought into play, although the person must be

---

[11]*State* v. *Jojola*, 89 N.M. 489, 553 P. 2d 1296 (Ct. App. 1976). This ruling relates to our earlier comment about the difficulty of concluding, from retrospective evidence, what a defendant's mental state was at the time of committing his crime, perhaps years earlier than his trial. This legal principle would seem to acknowledge that juries form their judgment of legal responsibility or insanity at least in part on how the defendant appears during the trial. If he or she seems "too normal," they may be less likely to believe the crime to have been an act of a disturbed mental state than of free will.

[12]*Suzuki* v. *Yuen*, 617 F. 2d 173 (1980).

[13]Special issues are involved in the commitment, institutionalization, and treatment of the mentally retarded, juveniles, drug addicts, and the aged.

deemed not only an imminent danger to others but mentally ill as well (Schwitzgebel and Schwitzgebel, 1980). Most mental health professionals, in agreement with the lay public, will conclude that a person has to be insane to behave in this way.

The likelihood of committing a dangerous act is central to civil commitment, but is "dangerousness" easily predicted? Studies have examined how reliably mental health professionals predict that a person will commit a dangerous act (e.g., Kozol, Boucher, and Garofalo, 1972; Stone, 1975; Monahan, 1973, 1976); they were found to be poor at making this judgment. Some workers have even argued that civil commitment for the purposes of preventive detention should be abolished. Monahan (1978), however, carefully scrutinized these studies and concluded that the professional's ability to predict violence is still an open question. Most of the studies conformed to the following methodological pattern.

1. People were institutionalized for mental illness and for being a danger to the community.

2. While these people were in the hospital, some of them were again predicted to be violent if they were released into the community.

3. After a period of time, these people were released, thus putting together the conditions for "a natural experiment."

4. Checks on the behavior of the released patients over the next several years did not reveal much dangerous behavior.

What is wrong with such research? Monahan points out that little if any consideration was given to changes that institutionalization itself might have effected. In the studies reviewed, the period of incarceration ranged from several months to fifteen years. Prolonged periods of enforced hospitalization might very well make patients more docile, if for no other reason than that they become that much older. Furthermore, the conditions in the open community where the predicted violence would be done can vary widely. We should not expect this kind of prediction to have great validity (Mischel, 1968).

These studies, which have occasioned such pessimism about predicting whether a patient is dangerous, are therefore flawed. Yet they have also been used in arguments against emergency commitment. The fact of the matter is that neither these studies nor any others have examined this specific issue! Monahan, however, has theorized that prediction of dangerousness is probably far easier and surer in true emergency situations than after extended periods of hospitalization. When an emergency commitment is sought, the person may appear out of control and be threatening violence in his or her own living room or, like the man in the street shouting threats. He or she may also have been violent in the past—a good predictor of future violence—and victims and weapons may be on hand. A dangerous outburst seems imminent. Thus, unlike the danger to society predicted in the studies previously examined, the violence requiring an emergency commitment is expected almost immediately and in a known situation. Common sense tells us that such predictions of violence are likely to be very accurate. To test the validity of these expectations, we would have to leave alone half the people predicted to be immediately violent and later compare their behavior to that of persons hospitalized in such emergency circumstances. Such an experiment would be ethically irresponsible. Mental health professionals must apply logic and make the most prudent judgments possible.

There are indications in what Monahan (1984) has called a "second generation of violence" prediction that suggest greater accuracy in predicting dangerousness. A review of these studies led Litwack (1985) to delineate conditions under which the prediction of violence might be good enough to be relied upon to make forensic decisions, whether involving mental patients or others. He suggests that violence prediction has been or will be found to be best under the following conditions (note the role played by situational factors, sometimes in interaction with personality variables):

1. If a person has been repeatedly violent in the recent past, it is reasonable to predict he or she will be violent in the near future unless there have been major changes in his attitudes or in the circumstances where he has been violent. Thus, if a violent person is placed in a restrictive environment like a prison or high-security psychiatric hospital facility, he may well not be violent, given the markedly changed environment.

2. If violence is in the person's distant past, if it was even just a single but a very serious act, and if that person has been incarcerated for a period of time, then violence can be expected upon release if there is reason to believe that his predetention personality and physical abilities have not changed and if he is going to return to the same environment in which he was previously violent.

3. If there is no history of violence, one can still predict it if the person is judged to be on the brink of a violent act, for example, the man already mentioned who is pointing a loaded gun at an occupied building.

Although convincing data on the ability of mental health professionals to predict violence are very difficult to obtain, Litwack argues that at the very least such individuals have the tools to gather the kinds of information that seem useful in predicting violence, for example, interview procedures that can uncover violent intentions, as well as other assessment techniques that can determine whether a person still has personality characteristics that are believed to have contributed to violent behavior in the past.

The basic question is how good a prediction has to be for someone's civil rights to be interfered with. Once again, there is a balancing act between individual liberty and the obligation of government to protect its citizens. Litwack makes the important point that different degrees of certainty are required for different legal and societal purposes. He points out, for example, that the Supreme Court case of *Addington* v. *Texas* (1979)[14] requires "clear and convincing evidence" of violence-proneness and mental illness to justify *extended* civil commitment; presumably a lesser quality of evidence would be enough for short-term, emergency commitment. If confinement is to be relatively brief (e.g., a few days), the downside risk for the individual detained would be only a few days' loss of freedom, whereas the possible benefit to society would be saving another from harm or from murder. This is a legal and moral decision, not a psychological or psychiatric one (see also Box 21.3).

Recent Trends for Greater Protection

The United States Constitution is a remarkable document. It lays down the basic duties of our elected federal officials and guarantees a set of civil rights. But there is often some distance between the abstract delineation of a civil right and its day-to-day implementation. Moreover, judges must *interpret* the Constitution as it bears on specific contemporary problems. Since nowhere in this cornerstone of our democracy is there specific mention of committed mental patients, lawyers and judges interpret various sections of the document to justify what they consider necessary changes in society's treatment of people whose mental health is in question.

In 1972 voluntary admissions to mental hospitals began to outnumber involuntary admissions. But a great number of people admitted to a state or county mental

hospital are still there against their wishes. Moreover, it is impossible to know how many of those who admit themselves voluntarily do so under threat of civil commitment. One survey (Gilboy and Schmidt, 1971) revealed that 40 percent of patients who had "voluntarily" admitted themselves to a mental hospital in Chicago had actually been threatened with commitment by the police officers who had brought them there. The issue of enforced mental hospitalization is still very much with us. Even though psychiatrists, psychologists, the courts, and hospital staff are apparently growing more reluctant to commit, tens of thousands ot mental patients are in hospitals against their will.

In a democratic society the most grievous wrong that can be suffered by a citizen is loss of liberty. The situation of mental patients is improving, however. The rights accorded to ordinary citizens, and even to criminals, are gradually being extended to those threatened with civil commitment and to those who have already been involuntarily hospitalized. No longer is it assumed that deprivation of liberty for purposes of mental health care is reason to deny to the individual all other rights. For example, a 1976 federal court decision in Wisconsin, *Lessard* v. *Schmidt*,[15] gives a person threatened with civil commitment the right to timely, written notice of the proceeding, opportunity for a hearing with counsel, the right to have the hearing decided by jury, Fifth Amendment protection against self-incrimination, and other similar procedural safeguards already accorded defendants in criminal actions. As mentioned earlier, a 1979 Supreme Court decision, *Addington* v. *Texas*, further provides that the state must produce "clear and convincing evidence" that a person is mentally ill and dangerous before he can be involuntarily committed to a mental hospital. And in 1980 the Ninth Circuit Court of Appeals ruled that this danger must be "imminent."[16] Clearly the trend is to restrict the power of the state to curtail individual freedoms because of "mental illness." Although protection of the rights of the mentally ill will add tremendously to the burden of both civil courts and state and county mental hospital staffs, it is a price a free society will have to pay.

Given the record of past [criminal proceedings and] the tragic parody of legal commitment used to warehouse American citizens, it is . . . important that the individual feel sure that the [present] mental health

---

[14]*Addington* v. *Texas*, 99 S. Ct. 1804 (1979). The "clear and convincing" standard of proof, however, still protects the person less than would application of the criminal standard of "beyond a reasonable doubt." The criminal standard—beyond a reasonable doubt—is referred to as the 90 percent standard. The clear and convincing standard is set at 75 percent certainty.

[15]*Lessard* v. *Schmidt*, 349 F. Supp. 1078 (E.D. Wisc. 1972), *vacated and remanded on other grounds*, 94 S. Ct. 712 (1974), *reinstated* 413 F. Supp, 1318 (E.D. Wisc. 1976).

[16]*Suzuki* v. *Yuen*, 617 F. 2d 173 (1980). See Box 21.3 for the tumult created when one big city mayor tried to modify this imminence criterion.

*system [in particular] cannot be so used and
abused . . . for while the average citizen may have
some confidence that if called by the Great Inquisitor
in the middle of the night and charged with a given
robbery, he may have an alibi or be able to prove his
innocence, he may be far less certain of his capacity,
under the press of fear, to instantly prove his sanity.*
(Stone, 1975, p. 57)

Least Restrictive Alternative

Civil commitment rests on presumed dangerousness,
but, as argued earlier by Litwack (1985), dangerousness
is being considered not an unvarying trait of the individual but behavior occurring in a specific social context. Thus a person may be deemed dangerous if allowed to live by himself in an apartment, but not
dangerous if living in a boarding home and taking prescribed psychoactive drugs every day under medical supervision. The "least restrictive alternative" to freedom
is to be provided when treating disturbed people and
protecting them from harming themselves and others.
A number of court rulings, for example, *Lake* v. *Cameron* and *Lessard* v. *Schmidt*, require that only mental
patients who cannot be adequately looked after in less
restrictive homes be confined in hospitals. Thus commitment is no longer necessarily in an institution. Rather
a patient might well be required to reside in a supervised
boarding home or in other sheltered quarters (Schwitzgebel and Schwitzgebel, 1980). Of course, this principle
will have meaning only if society provides suitable residences.

Right to Treatment

Another aspect of civil commitment that has come to
the attention of the courts is the so-called right to treatment, a principle first articulated by Birnbaum (1960).
If a person is deprived of liberty because he or she is
mentally ill and is a danger to self or others, is not the
state required to provide treatment to alleviate these
problems? Is it not unconstitutional (and even indecent)
to incarcerate someone without afterward providing the
help he or she is supposed to need? This important
question has been the subject of several court cases.

The right to treatment has gained in legal status since
the 1960s and was extended to all civilly committed
patients in a landmark case, *Wyatt* v. *Stickney*.[17] In 1971
a class action suit was filed on behalf of Ricky Wyatt,
and all others similarly situated at the Partlow school
in Tuscaloosa, Alabama, against Dr. Stickney, a new

Commissioner of Mental Health. Dr. Stickney was a
willing defendant, for he wanted very much to mod-
ernize the Alabama hospitals and the care they provided. In *Wyatt* v. *Stickney* an Alabama federal court
ruled in 1972 that the only justification for the civil
commitment of patients to a state mental hospital is
treatment. As stated by Judge Frank Johnson, "to deprive any citizen of his or her liberty upon the altruistic
theory that the confinement is for humane and therapeutic reasons and then fail to provide adequate treatment violates the very fundamentals of due process."
Rather, committed mental patients, "have a constitutional right to receive such individual treatment as will
give each of them a realistic opportunity to be cured or
to improve his or her mental condition." This ruling,
upheld on appeal, is frequently cited as ensuring protection of people confined by civil commitment, at least
to this extent: the state cannot simply put them away
without meeting minimal standards of care.

The *Wyatt* ruling, although it applied only in Alabama, was significant, for in the past the courts had
asserted that it was beyond their competence to pass
judgment on the care given to mental patients. The
courts had assumed that mental health professionals
possess special and exclusive knowledge about psychopathology and its treatment. Repeated reports of abuses,
however, gradually prodded the American judicial system to rule on what goes on within the walls of mental
institutions (Schwitzgebel and Schwitzgebel, 1980). The
Wyatt decision set forth very specific requirements, such
as dayrooms of at least forty square feet; curtains or
screens for privacy in multipatient bedrooms, to accommodate no more than five persons; a comfortable bed;
one toilet per eight persons; the right to wear any clothing the patient wishes, provided it is not deemed dangerous; opportunities to interact with members of the
opposite sex; and no physical restraints, except in emergency situations. And to provide care twenty-four hours
a day, seven days a week, there should be, for every
250 patients, at least two psychiatrists, three additional
physicians, twelve registered nurses, ninety attendants,
four psychologists, and seven social workers. When the
Wyatt action was taken, Alabama state mental facilities
averaged one physician per 2000 patients, an extreme
situation indeed.[18]

---

[17]*Wyatt* v. *Stickney*, 325 F. Sup. 781 (M.D. Ala. 1971), *enforced in*
334 F. Supp. 1341 (M.D. Ala. 1971), 344 F. Supp. 373, 379 (M.D.
Ala. 1972), *aff'd sub nom Wyatt* v. *Anderholt*, 503 F. 2d 1305 (5th
Cir. 1974).

[18]Of course, the underlying assumption is that patients civilly committed to public mental hospitals will receive adequate care there.
The evidence is weak, however. Even though the extremely negligent
conditions that the *Wyatt* decision remedied in Alabama seldom hold
today, it is questionable, argues Morse (1982a), whether forced hospitalization benefits patients. But public mental hospitals can provide,
at the very least, shelter, food, protection, and custodial care, which
many deinstitutionalized patients lack.

The trend of the *Wyatt* ruling, however, may have been weakened by a more recent 1982 Supreme Court decision, *Youngberg* v. *Romeo*,[19] regarding the treatment of a mentally retarded boy, Nicholas Romeo, who had been placed in physical restraints on occasion to keep him from hurting himself and others. Holding that the patient had a right to reasonable care and safety, the decision deferred to the professional judgment of the mental health professionals responsible for the boy: "courts must show deference to the judgment exercised by a qualified professional . . . the decision, if made by a professional, is presumptively valid" (pp. 322, 323).

In a more celebrated case,[20] which eventually found its way to the Supreme Court, a civilly committed mental patient sued two state hospital doctors for his release and for money damages, on the grounds that he had been incarcerated against his will for fourteen years without being treated and without being dangerous to himself or to others. In January 1957, at the age of forty-nine, Kenneth Donaldson had been committed to the Florida state hospital at Chattahoochee on petition by his father, who felt that his son was delusional. Donaldson was found at a brief court hearing before a county judge to be a paranoid schizophrenic and was committed for "care, maintenance, and treatment." The Florida statute then in effect allowed for such commitment on the usual grounds of mental illness and dangerousness. At that time, "dangerousness" could be defined as inability to manage property and to protect oneself from being taken advantage of by others.

In 1971, Donaldson sued Dr. O'Connor, the hospital superintendent, and Dr. Gumanis, a hospital psychiatrist, for release. Evidence presented at the trial in a United States district court in Florida indicated that the hospital staff could have released Donaldson at any time following a determination that he was not a dangerous person. Testimony made it clear that at no time during his hospitalization had Donaldson's conduct posed any real danger to others or to himself. In fact, just before his commitment in 1957, he had been earning a living and taking adequate care of himself (and immediately upon discharge he secured a job in hotel administration). Nonetheless, O'Connor had repeatedly refused the patient's requests for release, feeling it was his duty to determine whether a committed patient could adapt successfully outside the institution. His judgment was that Donaldson could not. In deciding the question of dangerousness on the basis of "adjustment outside the institution," O'Connor continued to apply a more re-

Kenneth Donaldson, displaying a copy of the Supreme Court opinion stating that nondangerous mental patients cannot be confined against their will under civil commitment.

strictive standard than that on which most state laws for commitment rested.

Several responsible people had attempted to obtain Donaldson's release by guaranteeing that they would look after him. For example, in 1963 a halfway house formally requested that Donaldson be released to its care, and between 1964 and 1968 a former college classmate made four separate attempts to have the patient released to his care. O'Connor refused, saying that the patient could be released only to his parents, who by this time were quite old and infirm.

The evidence indicated that Donaldson received only custodial care during his hospitalization. No treatment that could conceivably alleviate or cure his assumed mental illness was undertaken.[21] The "milieu therapy" that O'Connor claimed Donaldson was undergoing consisted, in actuality, of being kept in a large room with sixty other patients, many of whom were under criminal commitment. Donaldson had been denied privileges to stroll around the hospital grounds or even to discuss his case with Dr. O'Connor.

[19]*Youngberg* v. *Romeo*, 102 S. Ct. 2462 (1982).

[20]*O'Connor* v. *Donaldson*, 95 S. Ct. 2486 (1975).

[21]Donaldson was prescribed psychotropic drugs, but he refused them because of his Christian Science beliefs, an action Dr. O'Connor considered evidence of Donaldson's mental illness. O'Connor also regarded as delusional Donaldson's expressed desire to write a book about his hospital experiences, which Donaldson did, in fact, do after his release.

The original trial and a subsequent appeal concluded that Donaldson was not dangerous and had been denied his constitutional right to treatment, a right based on the Fifth Amendment to the Constitution. Throughout this litigation Donaldson declared that he was neither dangerous nor mentally ill. *But*, went his claim, *even if* he were mentally ill, he should be released because he was not receiving treatment.

On appeal to the Supreme Court, it was ruled, on June 26, 1975, that "a State cannot constitutionally confine . . . a nondangerous individual who is capable of surviving safely in freedom by himself or with the help of willing and responsible family members or friends." In 1977 Donaldson ultimately settled for $20,000 from Dr. Gumanis and from the estate of Dr. O'Connor, who had died during the appeals process.

The Supreme Court decision on *O'Connor* v. *Donaldson* created a stir when it was issued, and is certain to give mental health professionals pause in detaining patients. Although this decision is often cited as yet another affirmation of "right to treatment," the Supreme Court did not, in fact, rule on the constitutionality of this doctrine. Indeed, Chief Justice Warren E. Burger issued some warnings about the right to treatment.

Given the present state of medical knowledge regarding abnormal human behavior and its treatment, few things would be more fraught with peril than [for] a State's power to protect the mentally ill [to depend on its ability to provide] such treatment as will give them a realistic opportunity to be cured. Nor can I accept the theory that a State may lawfully confine an individual thought to need treatment and justify that deprivation of liberty solely by providing such treatment. Our concepts of due process would not tolerate such a "trade off." (pp. 588–589)

The *Donaldson* decision did say that a committed patient's status must be periodically reviewed, for the grounds on which a patient was initially committed cannot be assumed to continue in effect forever. In other words, people can change while in a mental hospital and may no longer require confinement. This seems straightforward enough! The Court reminded mental hospital officials that they must not forget their patients. It is a sad commentary on the mental hospital system that the Supreme Court of the United States saw the need to caution it about the obvious and routine.

Right to Refuse Treatment

If a committed mental patient has the right to expect appropriate treatment, since he has lost his freedom because he needs help, does he have a right to *refuse* treatment, or a particular kind of treatment? The answer appears to be yes, for a right to obtain treatment does not oblige the patient to *accept* treatment (Schwitzgebel and Schwitzgebel, 1980). But there are qualifications. A state hospital may have adequate staff to provide up-to-date chemotherapy as well as group therapy but lack the professional resources to offer individual therapy. Suppose that patient X refuses the available modalities and insists on individual therapy. Would he later be able to sue the hospital for not offering the specific services requested? If the patient has the right to refuse certain forms of treatment, how far should the courts go in ensuring this right, remaining at the same time realistic about the state's ability to provide alternatives? When should the judgment of a professional staff override the wishes of a patient, especially one who is grossly psychotic? Are the patient's best interests always served if he or she can veto the plans of those responsible for care (Stone, 1975)?

Some recent court decisions illustrate the thorny issues that arise when the right to refuse treatment is debated. In a decision on some cases in which "unjustified polypharmacy" and "force or intimidation" had allegedly been applied, without due consideration for the serious negative side effects of drugs, the judge in a New Jersey federal district court concluded that drugs can actually inhibit recovery, that therefore, except in emergencies, even an involuntarily committed patient could refuse to take them, based on the rights of privacy (First Amendment) and due process (Fourteenth Amendment).[22] He ordered that there be advocates in each state mental hospital to help patients exercise the right to refuse treatment, and that there be posted in each hospital ward a listing of all the side effects of drugs that might be given to patients. A similar court ruling in Massachusetts[23] occasioned widespread medical refusals, with subsequent deterioration in the condition of many patients. In a reconsideration of the 1979 *Rennie* v. *Klein* decision,[24] however, the judge incorporated the *Youngberg* v. *Romeo* decision and stated that the judgment of the health professional must take precedence over the right to refuse treatment when patients are a danger to themselves or to others, in other words, in emergency situations.

Not surprisingly, the rights of committed patients to refuse psychotropic drugs are hotly debated. Although somatic therapies like electroconvulsive therapy and psychosurgery have for some time been subject to ju-

---

[22]*Rennie* v. *Klein*, Civil Action No. 77-2624, Federal District Court of New Jersey, 14 September 1979.

[23]*Rogers* v. *Okin*, 478 F. Supp. 1342 I.D. Mass. 1979; *Rogers* v. *Okin*, 239, F. 2d (1st Cir. 1984).

[24]*Rennie* v. *Klein*, 720 F. 2d 266 (3d Cir. 1983).

dicial review and control, only recently has close attention been paid to drugs used with mental patients. Legal and ethical issues surrounding the use of psychotropic medication are important: the side effects of most neuroleptic drugs are often very aversive to the patient and sometimes harmful and irreversible, and they do not truly address all of the patient's psychosocial problems (see discussion of negative symptoms on page 386). Moreover, neuroleptic drugs are often the only kind of treatment a patient in a state hospital receives with any regularity.

The question of refusing medication continues to be the subject of lawsuits on behalf of both involuntary and voluntary mental hospital patients.[25] Decisions on behalf of patients judged incompetent are frequently made by the hospital professional staff. Although there is inconsistency among different jurisdictions and although the forensic picture is still developing, there appears to be a trend that even involuntarily committed mental patients have certain rights to refuse psychotropic medication.

Opponents of the right to refuse treatment are concerned that mental hospitals will revert to being warehouses of poorly treated patients. Psychiatrists fear that legal experts, unfamiliar with hospitals and with the people in them, will "take at face value the verbal statements of such patients rather than also taking into account other communications which may convey a different message than those uttered" (McGarry and Chodoff, 1981, p. 217). In lay terms, they fear that lawyers and judges will not accept that some people are too mentally deranged to be believed, too mentally disturbed to be able to make sound judgments about their treatment. When a patient is believed to be too psychotic to give informed consent about a treatment, mental health law sometimes invokes the doctrine of *substituted judgment*, the decision that the patient *would have made* if he or she had been able or competent to make a decision. Obviously this principle creates problems as well as solving them.

Does civil commitment imply an incompetency that renders the patient incapable of forming reasonable opinions concerning therapies? The issue is similar to the problem in criminal commitment proceedings, when a judgment that the accused is mentally ill can deny him access to the courts. Stone believes that a civilly committed person may indeed be competent to refuse a given treatment, and recent legal opinion (e.g., *Rivers* v. *Katz*, 1986) supports him. The reasons one can commit (danger to self or others and being mentally ill) are

not the same as those for forcing treatment on a person (e.g., to help the person be able one day to leave the hospital) (Clayton, 1988).

Law, Free Will, and Ethics

Mental health law construes voluntariness somewhat differently from the way many social scientists do. The latter group operates within paradigms that tend to assign less importance to the concept of free will than does the law, which rests utterly on that idea. As psychologists (who, moreover, are familiar with actual practices in mental hospitals), we are aware of the subtle coercion that can operate on hospitalized patients, even those who entered voluntarily. A hospital patient is subject to strong persuasion and pressure to accept the treatment recommendations of professional staff. Although one could argue that this is as it should be, the fact remains, in our view, that even a "voluntary" and informed decision to take psychotropic medication or to participate in any other therapy regimen is often (maybe usually) less than free. The issue then is even more complicated and thorny than most mental health law thus far conceives—and the arguments of the legal profession do not lack for complexity and thorniness! Related questions of freedom of choice are discussed in Box 21.5.

That we are dealing ultimately with an ethical issue is suggested by Clayton (1988):

The most important force behind the notion of a patient's right to reject therapy is the recognition that the weighing of risks and benefits inherent in a decision to undergo or to defer treatment is value-laden. Personal preferences play a role in determining which risks are unacceptable and which benefits are desirable. For instance, the doctor's decision to treat an objecting patient with psychotropic drugs is a value judgment; it reflects the physician's view that freedom from psychosis outweighs the costs of overriding the patient's wishes and of exposing him or her to side effects. This means, at a minimum, that a physician and patient may not always agree on what constitutes the "best" therapy. . . . [Furthermore, the argument that the psychiatrist is acting only in the patient's best interests] assumes a general entitlement to intervene in another's best interest. Society, however, does not generally overrule an individual's decisions merely because they are not objectively self-regarding, to say nothing of not being in his or her best interest. People are permitted to engage in all sorts of dangerous activities, from hang-gliding to cigarette smoking. (pp. 19–20)

---

[25]*Mills* v. *Rogers*, 457 U.S. 291 (1982); *Pennhurst State School and Hospital* v. *Halderman* 465 U.S. 89 (1984); *Rivers* v. *Katz*, 67 N.Y. 2d (1986).

**Rights to Treatment, To Refuse Treatment,
and To Be Treated in the Least Restrictive Setting—
Can They Be Reconciled?**

We have reviewed several legal principles developed over the years that guide the courts and mental health professionals in meeting their constitutional obligations to civilly committed mental patients. Actions taken to implement one principle may conflict with another, however. The basic question is whether the right to be treated in the least restrictive residence can be reconciled with both the right to treatment and the right to refuse treatment. A creative proposal was put forth by Paul and Lentz (1977) in their report on social-learning and milieu therapies on wards at a mental health center. They argue that under certain conditions a committed mental patient can and should be coerced into a particular therapy program, even if the patient states that he or she does not wish to participate. Further, these conditions would not, as *Rennie* v. *Klein* requires, have to be emergencies.

They propose that some hospital treatments have minimal goals and others optimal, and that institutions should have the right and the duty to do whatever is reasonable to move patients toward minimal goals. Achievement of minimal goals—self-care, such as getting up in the morning, bathing, eating meals, and the like; being able to communicate with others on the most basic level; and not being violent or assaultive—will allow patients to move into a less restrictive residence. The elimination of symptomatic behavior would also be regarded as a minimal goal if the local community requires patients to conform, at least to some extent, to community standards.[26] Paul and Lentz go on to argue that if empirical evidence indicates that particular treatments do achieve minimal goals—as the social-learning program did in their study—patients might justifiably be forced to participate in them, even if they or their legal guardians will not give consent voluntarily. Protection of their interests would be the responsibility of an institutional review board, a group of professionals and laypeople who would review all therapy and research activities for a given hospital. The board would decide *for* patients which therapy is likely to achieve minimal goals that would allow them to leave the hospital.

If the patient is determined to be operating above minimal levels, he should have the right to refuse treatments that have optimal goals, such as acquiring vocational skills, obtaining a high school diploma, and

other "luxury" items that can enhance the quality of a patient's life. According to Paul and Lentz, these goals should not be considered so vital that the patient is forced into working toward them.

Deinstitutionalization, Civil Liberties, and Mental Health

The cumulative impact of court rulings such as *Wyatt* v. *Stickney* and *O'Connor* v. *Donaldson* was to put mental health professionals on notice that they must be more careful about keeping people in mental hospitals against their will, and that they must attend more to the specific treatment needs of committed patients. Pressure was placed on state governments in particular to upgrade the quality of care in mental institutions. In view of the abuses that have been documented in hospital care, these are surely encouraging trends.

But the picture is not all that rosy. For judges to declare that patient care must meet certain minimal standards does not automatically translate into that praiseworthy goal. There is not an unlimited supply of money, and care of the mentally ill has never been one of government's high priorities. Nor is support of research in the social and behavioral sciences.

Over the past thirty years, many states have been embarked on a policy of deinstitutionalization, discharging as many patients as possible from mental hospitals and also discouraging admissions. As we have just seen, civil commitment is more difficult to achieve now than it was forty and more years ago, and even if committed, patients are able, with the help of civil rights-minded lawyers, to refuse much of the treatment made available to them in the hospital. At its peak in the 1950s, state mental hospitals housed almost half a million patients; by the late 1980s, the population had dropped to about 130,000. The maxim has become "Treat them in the community," the assumption being that virtually anything is preferable to institutionalization.

But what is this community that former mental patients are supposed to find more helpful to them upon discharge? Facilities outside the hospitals are not prepared to cope with the influx of former mental patients. Some promising programs were described in Chapter 20, but these are very much the exception, not the rule. The state of affairs in many large metropolitan areas is an unrelenting social crisis, for hundreds of thousands of chronically ill mental patients have been released onto the street without sufficient job training and without community services to help them. It is doubtful even that deinstitutionalization has reduced the rate of chronic mental illness, and, as Gralnick (1987) has argued, the acutely ill are largely neglected because it is very difficult

[26]Many therapists are accused of forcing patients to conform to community standards that are themselves open to question. But the basic issue here is not whether mental patients wear clean pants with a belt to hold them up, but whether they wear pants at all.

to commit them unless they are found to be a danger to themselves and to others, a condition that can take years to develop. By that time, Gralnick suggests, the problems may have become chronic and more difficult to deal with. The irony is that deinstitutionalization may be contributing to the very problem it was designed to alleviate, chronic mental illness.

Many discharged mental patients are eligible for benefits from the Veterans Administration and for Social Security Disability Insurance, but a large number are not receiving them. Homeless persons do not have fixed addresses and need assistance in establishing eligibility and residency for the purpose of receiving benefits. A study by the Community Service Society (Baxter and Hopper, 1981), an old and respected social agency in New York City, found them living in the streets, in train and bus terminals, in abandoned buildings, on subways, in cavernous steam tunnels running north from Grand Central Station in Manhattan, and some of them in shelters operated by public agencies, churches, and charitable organizations. The lives of these homeless are desperate.

The homeless suffer from numerous psychological problems, including both alcoholism and schizophrenia.

[In a train station at 11:00 P.M.] . . . the attendant goes off duty and women rise from separate niches and head for the bathroom. There they disrobe, and wash their clothes and bodies. Depending on the length of [the] line at the hand dryers, they wait to dry their clothes, put them in their bags or wear them wet. One woman cleans and wraps her ulcerated legs with paper towels every night. The most assertive claim toilet cubicles, line them with newspapers for privacy and warmth and sleep curled around the basin. Once they are taken, the rest sleep along the walls, one on a box directly beneath the hand dryer which she pushes for warm air. One of the women regularly cleans up the floors, sinks and toilets so that no traces of their uncustomary use remain. (p. 77)

No one knows how many of the homeless are deinstitutionalized mental patients. Those who are not homeless live marginal and unhealthful lives in nursing homes, jails, and rundown hotels. They are a visible part of the population, but their proportions may be diminishing with so many other people being dispossessed from their homes and apartments and losing their industrial jobs. The very state of homelessness undoubtedly exacerbates the emotional suffering of former mental patients. Whatever their numbers, the mentally ill remain an especially defenseless segment of the homeless population.

The relationships between homelessness and mental health have recently been enumerated and analyzed by a committee of the National Academy of Sciences

(Committee on Health Care for Homeless People, 1988, as summarized in Leeper, 1988). It is estimated that 25 to 40 percent of the homeless are alcoholics, with similar proportions suffering from some form of serious mental illness, usually schizophrenia. No doubt such problems are exacerbated further by their nomadic and dangerous existence; homeless people, especially women, are likely victims of violence and rape. Children, too, are among the homeless, a fact that the NAS committee terms "a national disgrace," for these youngsters are forced to live their formative years in chaotic and dangerous situations, with parents under severe stress. One committee member noted in an interview that "many children have developmental delays. I've seen two-year-olds who can't walk, six-month-olds who don't cuddle in your arms, and four-year-olds acting like mothers to one-year-olds because their mother isn't giving them the care they need" (Leeper, 1988, p. 8). That such children often drop out of school and suffer from anxiety, depression, and substance abuse, and are subject as well to physical and sexual abuse, should come as no surprise.

Do such appalling facts justify reversing the policy of deinstitutionalization? The NAS committee thinks not because, in their view, the problem lies with the failure of communities to provide suitable living and rehabilitation conditions, a theme sounded earlier in this book.

[The] vulnerability [of former patients] . . . became clear in January 1982, when a sixty-one-year-old for-

BOX 21.3

THE STRANGE CASE OF "BILLIE BOGGS"

The conflict between individual civil rights and the responsibility of the government to care for its citizens was recently played out in an almost surreal way in the case of "Billie Boggs," a forty-year-old New York City homeless woman (Hornblower and Svoboda, 1987; Kasindorf, 1988). Her real name is Joyce Brown, and she achieved notoriety in 1987 when the sometime flamboyant and always forthright mayor, Edward Koch, concerned about the living conditions of his city's homeless, decided in October to round up those homeless who seemed to be mentally ill and to hospitalize them, even if they did not want it. Mayor Koch had come under intense political pressure to do something about homeless people freezing to death in the shadows of luxurious Manhattan skyscrapers. (The above-mentioned Project HELP had been started by Koch in 1982 but was stymied by difficulties encountered in getting mentally ill street people hospitalized. The incident that follows arose from a reinterpretation of case law that city attorneys told Koch would permit commitment if a person could be judged a danger to himself or others "in the reasonably foreseeable future" rather than at the moment.)

On a tour with other city officials, Koch came upon Ms. Brown lying near a heating grate with her jaw swollen and, when told that she could not be committed, he said to one of the officials, "You're looney yourself." Brown was then taken involuntarily to Bellevue Hospital with the diagnosis of paranoid schizophrenia, based on such behavior as screaming and cursing at black men on the street ("Come suck my d--k, you black motherf----r"), lifting her skirt to expose her bare buttocks and shouting "Kiss my black ass, you motherf-----g nigger," defecating in her clothes or on the pavement, tearing up and burning money, and talking to herself—in addition to living in the streets.

Brown's family background was a conventional middle-class one. She graduated from high school and worked for

Billie Boggs, along with her lawyers, after being released from her confinement in a mental hospital.

ten years as a secretary. Never married, she lived at home with her mother, who died in 1979. Brown had been a heavy user of cocaine and heroin since high school, and she ultimately lost her job in 1983 because of spotty at-

mer psychiatric patient was found dead in a cardboard box on a New York City street. She had been living in the box for eight months after her entitlements were revoked for failure to appear for recertification. She had refused the efforts of various agencies to relocate her, and she died of hypothermia hours before a court order was obtained directing her removal to a hospital.

This case led to the creation of Project HELP, the Homeless Emergency Liaison Project, which is a mobile, psychiatric outreach team that identifies homeless people in need of psychiatric aid, and has authority under State and local laws to involuntarily remove homeless people in danger to themselves to a hospital

for help and evaluation. (Committee on Government Operations, 1985, p. 5) (Box 21.3).

Gralnick (1986) fears that schizophrenics will increasingly be seen as misfits, drug-abusers, and panhandlers rather than as ill people in need of professional care.[27] Jails, shelters, and church basements will be seen

---

[27]Note: One might reply that, in fact, this is precisely what we see—bedraggled social misfits who are drunk or on drugs much of the time, who live in the streets, and who sometimes unabashedly accost passersby for money! If this is the case, it is because deinstitutionalization and the lack of proper outpatient aftercare have produced this sorry outcome.

tendance and bizarre behavior, like swearing at people for no reason. Her life began to come apart, and she began to hear voices and to talk to herself. One day she went into a store with one of her sisters and, seeing a security guard, began for no reason to curse at him loudly. "It was 'Motherf----r this and motherf----r that' " reported a sister (Kasindorf, 1988, p. 38). She also developed the idea that she would marry a handsome, professional white man, and started to harass someone with phone calls about this. From time to time she lived with one or more of her four sisters and in 1985 was removed from a Newark, New Jersey, shelter for disruptive behavior. She was seen by more than one psychiatrist, was prescribed Thorazine (which she refused to take), and had numerous mental health clinic contacts. During this time she became obsessed with Bill Boggs, the host of a local TV talk show program, and tried to engage him in conversation when she visited the television station. Boggs reported that the conversations never made any sense to him. She thereafter adopted his name. Her sisters attempted more than once to commit her after trying valiantly to house her in their own homes or in apartments they found for her and partially paid for.

Five days after being picked up on Mayor Koch's orders, she appeared before a judge who would rule on whether she could be detained longer against her will. Brown was calm and articulate, explaining away much of her unusual behavior; for example, because the nearest public toilet was too far away to reach she would sometimes defecate in her pants. Four city psychiatrists testified that she was mentally ill, but she was declared sane by three psychiatrists hired by American Civil Liberties Union attorneys, who had taken a civil rights interest in her. Indeed, when she testified on her own behalf, she was lucid, calm, and intelligent, a fact that her attorneys claimed showed that she was not mentally ill but that the city psychiatrists claimed

was irrelevant in that mentally ill people are not necessarily retarded nor do they always appear disturbed.

Unable to obtain guidance from the diametrically opposed psychiatric testimony of the city and of the patient, the judge focused on Brown's in-court demeanor and determined that, even if she were mentally ill, she was neither malnourished, suicidal, nor dangerous to others. He declared further that, while living in the streets may be an "offense to aesthetic senses, freedom, constitutionally guaranteed, is the right of all, no less of those who are mentally ill . . . beggars can be choosers" (*Time*, 1988, p. 29).

She was, however, detained in Bellevue while the city contested the judge's ruling to release her. On several appeals, the ACLU and other civil rights minded people claimed that all the mayor was concerned about was cleaning up the streets so that rich constituents would not be confronted with destitute homeless people. Koch and others claimed that the city had a responsibility to help the helpless. The public debate was loud and bitter, Brown's lawyers calling Koch a demagogue and Koch calling them loonies. During her enforced stay at Bellevue, Brown cooperated not at all with any treatment program and refused all psychotropic medication.

In January 1988 Brown was released from Bellevue and became a *cause célèbre* in the ongoing efforts of homeless advocates to force city and state government to provide adequate housing and, to the mentally ill, appropriate outpatient mental health services. She appeared on several local New York talk programs and even on CBS's *Sixty Minutes*. Two weeks after a February 1988 appearance at the Harvard Law School Forum, where she was as big a hit as she had been on the television programs, she was back on the streets again, panhandling and swearing at black people.

as appropriate places for them rather than mental wards. Furthermore, to the extent that treatment will be seen as an (outpatient) option, it will, he predicts, be somatic and drug-based, the reason being that it is cheaper, more straightforward, and does not require the close interpersonal relationship that is intrinsic to any psychotherapy. Gralnick predicts also that biological factors will be focused on *to the exclusion of* psychological factors.[28] This will interfere with achieving full understanding of serious mental illness, which, along with most workers in the field (including the authors of this textbook), he views as a complex interaction between biological diatheses and environmental stressors. Gral-

nick recommends, among other things, that the psychiatric hospital be restored to its previous position as the place of choice to treat and do research in schizophrenia, and that research be more vigorously pursued in aftercare for patients who are discharged.

---

[28] He is not arguing that major advances are not being made in somatic approaches to diagnosis, etiology, and treatment—one would have to be out of contact with reality to believe this. Rather, he is concerned that scientific advances will be *coupled to* a distancing from the personal plight of schizophrenics and lead to a scientifically unjustified and socially questionable neglect of their sad living situation in the era of what he and others regard as misguided deinstitutionalization.

Ethical Dilemmas in Therapy and Research

In this textbook we have examined a variety of theories and a multitude of data focusing on *what is* and *what is thought to be.* Ethics and values, often embodied in our laws, are a different order of discussion. They concern *what ought to be,* having sometimes little to do with what is. It is extremely important to recognize the difference. Within a given scientific paradigm we are able to examine what we believe is reality. As the study of philosophy and ethics reveals, however, the statements that people have made for thousands of years about what *should* be are another matter. The Ten Commandments are such statements. They are prescriptions and proscriptions about human conduct. For example, the eighth commandment, "Thou shalt not steal," in no way describes human conduct, for stealing is not uncommon. It is, instead, a pronouncement of an ideal that people *should* aspire to. The integrity of an ethical code that proscribes stealing does not depend on any evidence concerning the percentage of people who steal. Morals and data are two separate realms of discourse.

The legal trends reviewed thus far in this chapter place limits on the activities of mental health professionals. These legal constraints are important, for laws are one of society's strongest means of forcing all of us to behave in certain ways. Psychologists and psychiatrists also have professional and ethical constraints. All professional groups promulgate "shoulds" and "should nots" and by guidelines and mandates they limit to some degree what therapists and researchers may do with their patients, clients, and subjects. Courts as well have ruled on some of these questions. We examine now the ethics of making psychological inquiries and interventions into the lives of other human beings.

Ethical Restraints on Research

It is basic to science that what can be done is likely to be attempted. The most reprehensible ethical insensitivity is documented in the brutal experiments conducted by certain German physicians on concentration camp prisoners during the Third Reich. One experiment, for example, investigated how long people lived when their heads were bashed repeatedly with a heavy stick. Even if important information might be obtained from this kind of atrocity, which seems extremely doubtful, such actions cannot be allowed. The Nuremberg trials, conducted by the Allies following the war, brought these and other barbarisms to light and meted out severe punishment to soldiers, physicians, and other Nazi officials who had engaged in or contributed to such actions, even when they claimed that they had merely been following orders.

It would be reassuring to be able to say that such gross violations of human decency take place only during incredible and cruel epochs such as the Third Reich, but unfortunately this is not the case. Spurred on by a blind enthusiasm for their work, researchers in this country have sometimes dealt with human subjects in reproachable ways.[29]

Henry K. Beecher, a research professor at Harvard Medical School, surveyed medical research since 1945 and found that "many of the patients [used as subjects in experiments] never had the risk satisfactorily explained to them, and . . . further hundreds have not known that they were the subjects of an experiment although grave consequences have been suffered as the direct result" (1966, p. 1354). One experiment compared penicillin to a placebo as a treatment to prevent rheumatic fever. Even though penicillin had already been acknowledged as the drug of choice to give people with a streptococcal respiratory infection in order to protect them from later contracting rheumatic fever, placebos were administered to 109 servicemen without their knowledge or permission. More men received penicillin than the placebo, but three members of the control group contracted serious illnesses—two had rheumatic fever and one acute nephritis, a kidney disease—as compared to none of those who had received penicillin.

The training of scientists equips them splendidly to pose interesting questions, sometimes even important ones, and to design experiments that are as free as possible of confounds. They have no special qualifications, however, for deciding whether a particular line of inquiry that involves humankind *should* be followed. Society needs knowledge, and a scientist has a right in a democracy to seek that knowledge. The ordinary citizens employed as subjects in experiments must, however, be protected from unnecessary harm, risk, humiliation, and invasion of privacy.[30] There are several international codes of ethics for the conduct of scientific research—the Nuremberg Code formulated in the aftermath of the Nazi war crime trials, the Declaration of Helsinki, and statements from the British Medical Research Council. Closer to home, in the early 1970s the

---

[29]Researchers who use animals in their experiments have also occasionally dealt with their subjects in gratuitously harsh fashion. The American Psychological Association has guidelines for handling laboratory animals that are intended to minimize their discomfort and danger. More recently, strict standards have been promulgated by the National Institutes of Health.

[30]This very statement is an ethical, not an empirical, one.

Department of Health, Education and Welfare began to issue guidelines and regulations governing scientific research that employs human subjects. In addition, a blue-ribbon panel, the National Commission for the Protection of Human Subjects of Biomedical and Behavioral Research, conducted hearings and inquiries into restrictions that the federal government might impose on research performed with mental patients, prisoners, and children. And for several years now the proposals of behavioral researchers, many of whom conduct experiments related to psychopathology and therapy, have been reviewed for safety and general ethical propriety by "human subjects committees" and "institutional review boards" in hospitals, universities, and research institutes. Such committees—and this is very significant—are composed not just of behavioral scientists but of citizens from the community, lawyers, students, and specialists in a variety of disciplines, such as professors of English, history, and comparative religion. They are able to block any research proposal or require questionable aspects to be modified if in their collective judgment the research will put participating subjects at too great risk.

Informed Consent

Participation in research brings up the all-important concept of *informed consent.* Just as committed mental patients are gaining some right to refuse treatment, so may anyone refuse to be a subject in an experiment. The investigator must provide enough information to enable subjects to judge whether they want to take the risks inherent in being a participant. The prospective subjects must be legally capable of giving consent, and there must be no deceit or coercion in obtaining it. For example, an experimental psychologist might wish to determine whether imagery helps college students associate one word with another. One group of subjects will be asked to associate pairs of words in their minds by generating a fanciful image connecting the two, such as "a CAT riding on a BICYCLE." If a prospective subject decides that the experiment is likely to be boring, that subject may decline to participate and, in fact, may withdraw from the experiment at any time, without any fear of penalty.

Paired-associates research like this is relatively innocuous, but what if the experiment poses real risks, such as ingesting a drug? Or what if the prospective subject is a committed mental patient, or a retarded child, unable to understand fully what is being asked? Such a subject may not feel free or even be able to refuse participation. And what of the rights of the researcher, which often are not as carefully considered as

those of subjects, and of the cost to society of important research left undone? Will scientists become reluctant to undertake certain types of work because review committees make the process of obtaining informed consent unduly onerous and time-consuming?

It is in fact not easy to demonstrate that a researcher has obtained informed consent. Epstein and Lasagna (1969) found that only one-third of subjects volunteering for an experiment really understood what the experiment entailed. In a more elaborate study Stuart (1978) discovered that most college students could not accurately describe a simple experiment, even though it had just been explained to them and they had agreed to participate. A signature on a consent form is no assurance that informed consent has really been obtained, which poses a challenge to investigators and members of review panels who are committed to upholding codes of ethics governing participation of human subjects in research. Similar problems have been found in clinical settings, where there is a question of whether psychiatric patients understand the nature of neuroleptic medication. Irwin *et al.* (1985) found that while most patients *said* they understood the benefits and side effects of their drugs, only a quarter of them actually did when queried specifically. The authors' conclusions are that simply reading information to hospitalized patients—especially the more disturbed ones—is no guarantee that they fully comprehend; therefore, *informed* consent cannot be said to have been obtained.

Davison and Stuart (1975) proposed a scheme (Table 21.1) that might protect subjects' rights when they participate in research, without hampering researchers in their quest for knowledge. In determining how careful the researchers must be when obtaining informed consent, Davison and Stuart would ask four questions.

1. What is the level of risk? Little harm is likely in a memory experiment, but a study requiring subjects to withstand electric shock applied to the fingers poses some risk.

2. Is the research of potential benefit to the subject or client? A subject might stand to gain a great deal from being in the study or to gain nothing directly, except the satisfaction of having helped a scientist find out something new.

3. Is the technique an established one, whose risks and benefits are known, or is it new and experimental, so that the researcher is unable to indicate how beneficial, harmful, or discomfiting participation might be?

4. Is the subject realistically free to give consent or to refuse participation? A college student has great freedom to refuse, but a prisoner would probably

feel considerable coercion to participate in an experiment if asked to do so.

These four questions are not the only ones that might be asked, and the numbered consent procedures in Table 21.1 are merely suggestions. Clearly, the judgment of many other people would be needed to establish meaningful values and to work out a set of procedures. The scheme, however, may help human subjects committees organize their thinking about the problem of obtaining informed consent in a variety of circumstances.

Treatment or Research?

What is the difference between treatment and research? This is a question that people attempting to replace old procedures with newer, possibly more effective methods must address. Martin (1975) considered the following example. In school district A a teacher who has read about some of the token economy research in classrooms (e.g., O'Leary and O'Leary, 1977) has adopted token reinforcement as a means of persuading a group of underachieving and often disruptive students to attend to their lessons. The results have been quite encouraging: the classroom is quieter, the students are in

TABLE 21.1

Guidelines for protecting subjects' right to participate only in experiments of own choice
(*after Davison and Stuart, 1975*)

Level of Risk	Freedom to Give Consent	High Potential Benefit to Subject		Low Potential Benefit to Subject, High Potential Benefit to Society	
		Established Procedure	Experimental Procedure	Established Procedure	Experimental Procedure
Low risk	Great freedom	2,3,4*	4	2,3,4	4–5
	Feels some coercion	5	5	5–6	7
High risk	Great freedom	4	5	5–6	7
	Feels some coercion	6	6	7	8

* The numbers indicate the degree of care that should be exercised in obtaining consent, corresponding to the numbered list.

1. *No consent by the subject is necessary.* The nonobtrusive observation of traffic flow in public places or other public behavior might fall into this category. This procedure and the next are permissible only when a review panel has determined that the potential risk of harm to the anonymously observed subjects is nil.

2. *Subject is simply asked to sign a consent form for participation in research as a subject of observations, with no explanation of the nature of the study.* One example would be observing the supermarket shopping habits of individuals; an explanation of the objectives of the study might change relevant behavior.

3. *Subject is asked to sign a consent form for participation in research, with "debriefing" following participation.* Such a study might examine interpersonal behavior in public places; prior disclosure of the hypotheses could change behavior. A panel of experts would have to determine that subjects risked little in participating, including minimal humiliation following debriefing.

4. *Subject is asked to sign a consent form for participation in a project, after full disclosure of the objectives and methods of the research.* This procedure would be applied in efforts to evaluate treatment by randomly assigning subjects to experimental, to placebo control, and to no-treatment control groups. A review panel must judge that risk of harm to control subjects is equal to or less than it would be were there no experiment.

5. *Subject is asked to sign a consent form for participation in a project, after full disclosure of the objectives and methods of the research and in the presence of at least one witness who is not involved in the research.* This procedure would be appropriate any time a review panel senses that subjects may feel obliged to participate. Research with adjudicated offenders could fall into this category.

6. *Subject is asked to sign a consent form for participation in a project, after full disclosure of the objectives and methods of the research and in the presence of witnesses. The consent is reviewed by an independent human subjects committee within the institution.* The procedure might be applied in the experimental evaluation of a program carrying out an institutional objective, for example, vocational training in prisons and mental hospitals.

7. *Subject is asked to sign a consent form for participation in a project, after full disclosure of the objectives and methods of the research and in the presence of witnesses. The consent is reviewed by an independent human subjects committee within the institution and by a similar committee outside the institution.* The procedure could be applied when the research concerns behavior changes that are not strictly related to institutional objectives, for example, a study of the role of repetition when mental patients are taught phrases in a foreign language.

8. *No consent is possible because the rights of the subjects cannot be protected.*

their seats more often, and their academic performance has improved. Moreover, the students themselves like the program. Is this an experiment? Should the teacher have obtained informed consent from the parents? A few miles away in school district B another teacher is also applying a token economy. The project is funded by a federal grant, calls itself experimental, and routinely obtained the informed consent that is commonplace for research. There is no doubt that *this* program is research but does the similarity of district A's program to this one make it research as well?

Because of their relative newness, the application of behavioral procedures is likely to be construed as research, even though not so intended, and to be viewed with some apprehension. And yet we often take for granted—in fact, we applaud—an elementary school teacher who finds a novel way of exciting children about the learning process. "She's really a creative teacher. She doesn't content herself with the curriculum and the materials provided by the school board." To be sure, in many instances the difference between treatment and research is clear. For example, the drug Anectine, a paralytic agent often used to relax patients about to receive electroconvulsive therapy, was imposed on a prisoner for a different purpose, to produce a frightening "unconditioned response"—inability to breathe—in an aversion therapy endeavor. Although the drug is in routine use to protect electroconvulsive therapy patients from physical harm, a judge ruled that employing it in this way without obtaining informed consent appeared to be cruel and unusual punishment.[31]

Confidentiality and Privileged Communication

When an individual consults a physician, a psychiatrist, or a clinical psychologist, he or she expects all that goes on in the session to remain confidential. Nothing will be revealed to a third party, excepting only to other professionals and those intimately involved in the treatment, such as a nurse or medical secretary. The ethical codes of the various helping professions dictate this *confidentiality*.[32]

A *privileged communication* is one between parties in a confidential relation that is protected by statute. The recipient cannot be compelled to disclose it as a witness. The right of privileged communication is a major exception to the access that courts have to evidence in judicial proceedings. Society believes that, in the long

term, the interests of people are best served if communications to a spouse and to certain professionals remain off limits to the prying eyes and ears of the police, judges, and prosecutors. The husband–wife, doctor–patient, pastor–penitent, and attorney–client relationships are the traditional ones, but in recent years states have extended the right of privileged communication to the clients of licensed psychologists.

There are important limits to the client's right of privileged communication, however. For example, according to the current California psychology licensing law (similar elements are present in other state laws), this right is eliminated for any of the following reasons.

1. If the client is accused of a crime and has requested that a determination be made about his sanity.

2. If the client has accused the therapist of malpractice; the therapist, in other words, can divulge information about the therapy in order to defend himself in any legal action initiated by the client.

3. If the client is under sixteen, and the therapist has reason to believe that the child has been a victim of a crime, such as child abuse. In fact, the psychologist is *required* to report to the police within thirty-six hours any suspicion he or she has that the child client has been physically abused, including being sexually molested.

4. If the client initiated therapy in hopes of evading the law for having committed a crime or for planning to do so.

5. If the therapist judges that the client is a danger to himself or to others, and if disclosure of information is necessary to ward off such danger (see Box 21.4).

Who is the Client?

Is it always clear to the clinician who the client is? In private therapy, when an adult pays a clinician a fee for help with a personal problem that has nothing to do with the legal system, the consulting individual is clearly the client. But an individual may be seen by a clinician for an evaluation of his or her competency to stand trial. Or the clinician may be hired by an individual's family to assist in civil commitment proceedings. Perhaps the clinician is employed by a state mental hospital as a regular staff member and sees a particular patient about problems in controlling aggressive impulses. It should be clear, although it is alarming how seldom it *is* clear, that in these instances the clinician is serving more than one client. In addition to the patient, he or she serves the family or the state, and it is incumbent on the mental health professional to inform the patient

[31]*Mackey v. Procunier*, 477 F. 2d 877 (9th Cir. 1973).

[32]Family and marital therapies introduce complexities of their own, discussed in Margolin (1982).

BOX 21.4

THE TARASOFF CASE—THE DUTY TO WARN AND TO PROTECT

The client's right to privileged communication—the legal right of a client to require that what goes on in therapy remain confidential—is an important protection, but as we have seen, it is not absolute. Society has long stipulated certain conditions in which confidentiality in a relationship should not be maintained because of the harm that can befall others. A famous California court ruling in 1974* described circumstances in which a therapist not only may but should breach the sanctity of a client's communication. First, what appear to be the facts of the case.

In the fall of 1968, Prosenjit Poddar, a graduate student from India studying at the University of California at Berkeley, met Tatiana (Tanya) Tarasoff at a folk dancing class. They saw each other weekly during the fall, and on New Year's Eve she kissed him. Poddar interpreted this act as a sign of formal engagement (as it might have been in India, where he was a member of the Harijam or "untouchable" caste). [But] Tanya told him that she was involved with other men, and indicated that she did not wish to have an intimate relationship with him.

Poddar was depressed as a result of the rebuff, but he saw Tanya a few times during the spring (occasionally tape recording their conversations in an effort to understand why she did not love him). Tanya left for Brazil in the summer, and Poddar at the urging of a friend went to the student health facility where a psychiatrist referred him to a psychologist for psychotherapy. When Tanya returned in October 1969, Poddar discontinued therapy. Based in part on Poddar's stated intention to purchase a gun, the psychologist notified the campus police, both orally and in writing, that Poddar was dangerous and should be taken to a community mental health center for psychiatric commitment.

The campus police interviewed Poddar, who seemed rational and promised to stay away from Tanya. They released him and notified the health service. No further efforts at commitment were made because the supervising psychiatrist apparently decided that such was not needed and, as a matter of confidentiality, requested that the letter to the police as well as certain therapy records be destroyed.

On October 27, Poddar went to Tanya's home armed with a pellet gun and a kitchen knife. She refused to speak to him. He shot her with the pellet gun. She ran from the house, was pursued, caught, and repeatedly and fatally stabbed. Poddar was found guilty of voluntary manslaughter rather than first- or second-degree murder. The defense established, with the aid of the expert testimony of three psychiatrists, that Poddar's diminished mental capacity, paranoid schizophrenia, precluded the malice necessary for first- or second-degree murder. After his prison term, he returned to India, where, according to his own report, he is happily married. (Schwitzgebel and Schwitzgebel, 1980, p. 205)

Under the privileged-communication statute of California, the counseling center psychologist properly breached the confidentiality of the professional relationship and took steps to have Poddar civilly committed, for he judged him to be an imminent danger. Poddar had stated that he intended to purchase a gun, and by his other words and actions he had convinced the therapist that he was desperate enough to harm Tanya. What the psychologist did not do, and what the court decided he should have done, was to warn the likely victim, Tanya Tarasoff, that her former friend had bought a gun and might use it against her. Such a warning would have been consistent with previous court decisions that require physicians to warn the public when they are treating people with contagious diseases, and that require mental institutions to warn others when a dangerous patient has escaped (Knapp and Vandecreek, 1982). Or, as stated by the California Supreme Court in *Tarasoff:* "Once a therapist does in fact determine, or under applicable professional standards reasonably should have determined, that a patient poses a serious danger of violence to others, he bears a duty to exercise reasonable care to protect the foreseeable victims of that danger."

A subsequent California court ruling† held by a bare majority that foreseeable victims include those in close relationship to the identifiable victim, in this instance the son of a woman who was shot by a patient. The mother was hurt by a shotgun fired by the dangerous patient, and her seven-year-old son was present when this happened. The boy later sued the psychologists for damages brought on by emotional trauma. Since a young child is likely to

---

Tarasoff v. *Regents of the University of California*, 529 P. 2d 553 (Cal. 1974), *vacated, reheard in bank, and affirmed* 131 Cal. Rptr. 14, 551 P. 2d 334 (1976). The 1976 California Supreme Court ruling was by a four-to-three majority.

†*Hedlund* v. *Superior Court of Orange County*, 194 Cal. Rptr. 805 (Cal. 1983).

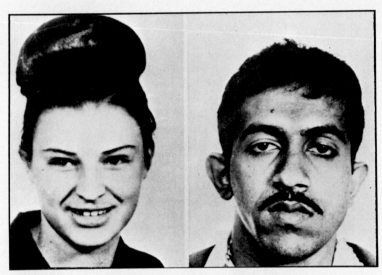

Tatiana Tarasoff and Prosenjit Poddar, who was convicted of manslaughter in her death. The court ruled that his therapist, who had become convinced Prosenjit might harm Tatiana, should have warned her of the impending danger.

be in the company of his mother, the court concluded in *Hedlund* that the *Tarasoff* ruling extended to him.

The duty to warn and to protect principle may be having a profound impact on psychotherapists, some claim a chilling effect, for it imposes on them a new obligation. They argue that if clients are informed of this limitation to the confidentiality of what they say to their therapists—and professional ethics require therapists to provide this information—clients may become reluctant to express feelings of extreme anger to therapists, for fear therapists will notify the people at whom they are angry. Clients may become less open with their therapists, perhaps derive less benefit from therapy, and even become *more* likely to inflict harm on others for not having disclosed their fury as a first step toward controlling it. The welfare of the people whom the *Tarasoff* decision intends to protect may be endangered by the very ruling itself!

The *Tarasoff* ruling, now being applied in other states as well, requires clinicians, in deciding when to violate confidentiality, to use the very imperfect skill of predicting dangerousness. A survey of over 1200 psychologists and psychiatrists in California (Wise, 1978) indicated how the *Tarasoff* decision was affecting their thinking and practices. On the plus side, one-third reported consulting more often with colleagues concerning cases in which violence was an issue. This should have a good outcome, since input from other professionals may improve the solitary clinician's decision making, presumably to the benefit of the client. On the minus side, about 20 percent of the respondents indicated that they now avoid asking their clients questions about violence, an ostrichlike stance that may keep the clinician from obtaining important information and yet, in a legal sense, reduces his or her legal liability should the client harm another person. And a substantial number of therapists keep less detailed records, again in an effort to reduce legal liability.

A 1983 decision of a federal circuit court in California‡ may alter some of these tactics of evasion. The court ruled that Veterans Administration psychiatrists should earlier have warned the murdered lover of an outpatient, Phillip

---

‡*Jablonski by Pahls* v. *United States*, 712 F. 2d 391 (1983).

Jablonski, that she was a foreseeable victim, even though the patient had never made an explicit threat against her to the therapists. The reasoning was that Jablonski, having previously raped and otherwise harmed his wife, would likely direct his continuing "violence . . . against women very close to him" (p. 392).

The court also found the hospital psychiatrists negligent in not obtaining Jablonski's earlier medical records. These records showed a history of harmful violent behavior that, together with the present threats his lover was complaining about, should have moved the hospital to institute emergency civil commitment. The court ruled that the failure to warn was a proximate or immediate cause of the woman's murder. Proper consideration of the medical records, said the judge, would have convinced the psychiatrists that Jablonski was a real danger to others and should be committed.

This broadening of the duty to warn now places mental health professionals in California in an even more difficult predicament, for the potentially violent patient need not even mention whom specifically he may harm. It is up to the therapist to deduce who are possible victims, based on what he or she can learn of the patient's past and present circumstances. Ironically, Jablonski's lover realized that she was in danger, having recently moved out of the apartment she was sharing with him and having complained to her priest and to the Veterans Administration psychiatrists themselves that she feared for her safety. One of the psychiatrists had even advised her to leave Jablonski, at least while he was being evaluated at the medical center. But "when [the lover] responded 'I love him,' [the psychiatrist] did not warn her further because he believed she would not listen to him" (p. 393). The court found this warning "totally unspecific and inadequate under the circumstances" (p. 398).

More recently *Tarasoff* has been extended by a Vermont State Supreme Court ruling, *Peck* v. *Counseling Service of Addison County*,§ which held that a mental health practitioner had a duty to warn a third party if there was a danger of *damage of property*. The case involved a twenty-nine-year-old male patient who, after a heated argument with his father, told his therapist that he wanted to get back at his father and indicated that he might do so by burning down his father's barn. He proceeded to do so. No people or animals were harmed in the arsonous conflagration; the barn housed no animals and was located 130 feet away from his parents' home. The court's conclusion that the therapist had a duty to warn was based on reasoning that arson is a violent act and therefore a lethal

---

§*Peck* v. *Counseling Service of Addison County*, 499 A. 2d 422 (Vt. 1985).

threat to people who may be in the vicinity of the fire. This can be seen as an extension of the *Hedlund* court decision as well; whereas *Hedlund* speaks of humans who may be at risk because of possible physical proximity to the endangered victim, *Peck* speaks of humans who could be harmed via threat to an inanimate object. Furthermore, since some chronic psychiatric patients have a history of fire-setting (Geller and Bertsch, 1985), Stone (1986) predicts that there will be future lawsuits based on this Vermont decision.

As problematic as *Tarasoff* and associated rulings may be for the mental health professions, the situation may not be as bleak as it has appeared to many. When the original 1974 *Tarasoff* ruling was reaffirmed in 1976 by the California Supreme Court, the duty to warn was broadened to a duty to *protect* (see the earlier quotation from the 1976 decision), and it is this seemingly slight change that makes it possible for practitioners to adhere to *Tarasoff* without necessarily breaking confidentiality, that is, without having always to warn a potential victim. As Appelbaum (1985) points out, clinicians can undertake such preventive measures as increased frequency of sessions, initiation of or changes in psychotropic medication, and, in general, closer supervision of the patient. He suggests further that if such measures are judged reasonable, the therapist is unlikely to be held liable if the patient does ultimately harm somebody.

One strategy described by Appelbaum involved an eighteen-year-old patient who threatened during a session that he would beat up his landlady for not permitting her son to associate with him. On the basis of other information about the patient, the therapist determined that *Tarasoff* was relevant. He decided to involve the patient in the discussion, explaining his legal responsibility to protect a potential victim, yet his reluctance to break therapeutic confidentiality. He presented to the patient the choice between hospitalization (the patient was indeed sometimes psychotic) and warning the landlady. The patient preferred to stay out of the hospital and said he would not object to the therapist calling the landlady. When this was done, the landlady told the therapist that the young man had threatened her previously and that she knew how to take care of herself. In other words, she did not take the threats literally. Appelbaum observes that the patient's threats seemed to be manipulative—he succeeded in once again issuing a verbal threat to his landlady, this time through his psychotherapist. But the psychotherapist succeeded as well in involving the patient in the decision making as well as preserving trust in the therapeutic relationship. As anxiety-provoking as *Tarasoff* can be to clinicians, it does not call for therapists to reflexively pick up the phone to call a possible victim whenever a patient expresses a threat.

that this is so. This dual allegiance does not necessarily indicate that the patient's own interests will be sacrificed, but it does mean that discussions will not inevitably remain secret and that the clinician may in the future act in a way that displeases the individual.

Choice of Goals

Ideally the client sets the goals for therapy, but in practice it is naive to assume that some are not imposed by the therapist and even go against the wishes of the client. School systems often want to institute programs that will teach children to "be still, be quiet, be docile" (Winett and Winkler, 1972, p. 499). Many behavior therapists have assumed that young children *should* be compliant, not only because the teacher can then run a more orderly class but because children are assumed to learn better when they are so. But do we really know that the most efficient and most enjoyable learning takes place when children are forced to remain quietly in their seats? Some advocates of "open classrooms" believe that curiosity and initiative, even in the youngest elementary school child, are at least as important as the acquisition of academic skills. As is generally the case in psychology, evidence is less plentiful than are strongly held and vehemently defended opinions. But the issue is clear: any professionals consulted by a school system should be mindful of their own personal biases with respect to goals and should be prepared to work toward different ones if the parents and school personnel so

wish. Any therapist of course retains the option of not working for a client whose goals and proposed means of attaining them are abhorrent in his or her view.

This question of goals is particularly complex in family and marital therapy (Margolin, 1982). If several people are clients simultaneously—inevitable in family treatment!—an intervention that benefits one or more individuals may well work to the disadvantage of one or more of the others. This can happen if one partner in marital therapy really wants to end the relationship, but the other sees the therapy as a way to save it. People often do not openly express their real concerns and wishes at the very beginning of marital therapy; the therapist can already be deeply enmeshed in their lives before learning that the two partners have conflicting goals (Gurman and Kniskern, 1981).

Although the plight of people who voluntarily consult therapists is in no way as expressly confining as that of institutionalized patients, they do operate within constraints on their freedom. The issue has been stated by Seymour Halleck (1971), a psychiatrist, who asserts that the neutrality of the therapist is a myth. In his opinion therapists influence their clients in ways that are subtle yet powerful.

At first glance, a model of psychiatric [or psychological] practice based on the contention that people should just be helped to learn to do the things they want to do seems uncomplicated and desirable. But it is an unobtainable model. Unlike a technician, a psy-

(Left) Typical classroom. (Right) "Open" classroom. An important but not thoroughly answered question is which environment best fosters learning.

BOX 21.5

NOT CAN BUT OUGHT: AN OPINION ON THE TREATMENT OF HOMOSEXUALITY

Several psychologists have argued that the social pressures on homosexuals to become heterosexual make it difficult to believe that the small minority of people who consult therapists for help in changing from same-sex to opposite-sex partners act with free choice (Silverstein, 1972; Davison, 1974, 1976; Begelman, 1975). Although most states have dropped their sodomy laws, which used to be enforced selectively against homosexual acts, there still remains some legal pressure against homosexuality: a 1986 U.S. Supreme Court decision* refused to find constitutional protection in the right to privacy for consensual adult homosexual activity and thereby upheld a Georgia law that prohibits oral–genital and anal–genital acts, even in private and between consenting adults. Silverstein's statement about the pressures homosexuals are under to want to become heterosexual was given in Chapter 12 (page 346). It has further been suggested that the mere availability of change-of-orientation programs serves to condone the prejudice against homosexuality. Clinicians work to develop procedures and study their effects only if they are concerned about the problem to be dealt with by their techniques. The therapy literature contains scant material on helping homosexuals develop as individuals without changing their sexual orientation, in contrast to the many articles and books on how best to discourage homosexual behavior and substitute for it heterosexual patterns. Aversion therapy used to be the most widely used behavioral technique (Davison and Wilson, 1973; Henkel and Lewis-Thomé, 1976). "What are we really saying to our clients when, on the one hand, we assure them that they are not abnormal and on the other hand, present them with an array of techniques, some of them painful, which are aimed at eliminating that set of feelings and behavior that we have just told them is okay?" (Davison, 1976, p. 161).

For these reasons it has been proposed that therapists not help homosexuals become heterosexual even when such treatment is requested. This is obviously a radical proposal, and it has evoked some strong reactions. Gay-activist groups are understandably pleased, considering the suggestion concrete support for the belief that homosexuality per se is not a mental disorder. But many psychologists and psychiatrists are concerned about limiting the choices available to people seeking therapy. Why should a therapist decide for potential clients which options should be available? Do not therapists have a responsibility to satisfy the needs expressed by their clients (Sturgis and Adams, 1978)? A reply to this important criticism would be that therapists always decide what therapy they will offer when they refuse to take as clients people whose goals they disagree with. The request of a patient for a certain kind of treatment has never been sufficient justification for providing it (see

Bowers v. *Hardwick*, 106 S. Ct. 2841 (1986).

Davison, 1978).

It has been asserted that continued research will help develop sex reorientation programs that are even more effective than those already available (Sturgis and Adams, 1978). To discourage such work would deprive today's homosexuals of promising therapies and tomorrow's homosexuals of improved treatments. This objection, however, is not relevant. The fact that we *can* do something does not indicate that we *should*. The proposal to deny sexual reorientation therapy is philosophical-ethical in nature, not empirical. The decision whether we should change sexual orientation will have to be made on moral grounds.

Will numbers of people be hurt by eliminating the sex reorientation option? Some have raised the specter of an upsurge in suicides among homosexuals if therapists refuse to help them switch. These are very serious concerns, but they overlook the possibility, some would say the fact, that far greater numbers of people have been hurt over the years by the availability of sex reorientation programs. As already argued, the existence of these treatments is consistent with societal prejudices and discrimination against homosexuals.

It is noteworthy that since 1975 there has been a dramatic reduction in the use of aversion therapy for changing homosexual orientation to heterosexual (Rosen and Beck, 1988) and a sharp decrease also in reports of other procedures for altering homosexuality. Other signs of increased acceptance of homosexuality as a life-style are the elimination of ego-dystonic homosexuality from the DSM-IIIR and the establishment within the American Psychological Association of the Division of Lesbian and Gay Psychologists and the Committee on Lesbian and Gay Concerns on the Board of Social and Ethical Responsibility.

The proponents who wish to terminate change-of-orientation programs believe that much good can come of their proposal. Homosexuals would be helped to think better of themselves, and greater efforts could be directed toward the problems homosexuals have, rather than to the problem of homosexuality.

It would be nice if an alcoholic homosexual, for example, could be helped to reduce his or her drinking without having his or her sexual orientation questioned. It would be nice if a homosexual fearful of interpersonal relationships, or incompetent in them, could be helped without the therapist assuming that homosexuality lies at the root of the problem. It would be nice if a nonorgasmic or impotent homosexual could be helped as a heterosexual would be rather than [being guided] to change-of-orientation regimens . . . the hope [is] that therapists will concentrate their efforts on such human problems rather than focusing on the most obvious "maladjustment"—loving members of one's own sex. (Davison, 1978, p. 171)

chiatrist [or psychologist] cannot avoid communicating and at times imposing his own values upon his patients. The patient usually has considerable difficulty in finding the way in which he would wish to change his behavior, but as he talks to the psychiatrist his wants and needs become clearer. In the very process of defining his needs in the presence of a figure who is viewed as wise and authoritarian, the patient is profoundly influenced. He ends up wanting some of the things the psychiatrist thinks he should want. (p. 19)

Psychologists agree, and research (e.g., Rosenthal, 1955) supports the contention that patients are indeed influenced by the values of their therapists. A person not only seeks out a therapist who suits his taste and meets what he believes are his needs but also adopts some of the ideals, sometimes even the mannerisms, of the therapist. Most therapists are keenly aware of this modeling after themselves, which surely increases the already heavy responsibilities of their professional role. Perry London (1964, 1985), a leading writer on the ethics of therapeutic intervention, has even suggested that therapists are contemporary society's secular priests, purveyors of values and ethics to help clients live "the good life" (see Box 21.5).

Choice of Techniques

The end does not justify the means. Most of us take in this maxim with our mother's milk. It is said to be intrinsic to a free society. In recent years questions concerning behavioral techniques have been debated among professionals and have even been the subject of court rulings. Perhaps because the various insight therapies emphasize listening, they have seldom been scrutinized as behavior therapy has. The very concreteness, specificity, and directiveness of behavioral techniques have called attention to them, as has their alignment with experimental psychology. It is offensive to some to believe that our understanding of human beings could possibly be advanced by employing rats and pigeons as subject analogues.

Particular concern has been expressed about the ethics of inflicting pain for purposes of therapy. To some people the very term behavior therapy conjures up an image of the violent protagonist in Kubrick's *Clockwork Orange*, eyes popped open with a torturous apparatus, being made nauseous by a drug while scenes of violence flashed on a screen. Aversion therapy programs never really reach this level of coercion and drama, but certainly any such procedure entails making the patient uncomfortable, sometimes extremely so. Making patients vomit or cringe with pain from electric shock applied to the extremities are two aversion techniques worthy of their name. Can there be any circumstances that justify therapists inflicting pain on clients?

Before too glibly exclaiming "No!" consider the following report.

The patient was a nine-month-old baby who had already been hospitalized three times for treatment of vomiting and chronic rumination (regurgitating food and rechewing it in the mouth). A number of diagnostic tests, including an EEG, plus surgery to remove a cyst on the right kidney, had revealed no organic basis for the problems, and several treatments, including a special diet, had been attempted without success. When referred to Lang and Melamed (1969), two behavior therapists, the child was in critical condition and was being fed by tubes leading from the nose directly into the stomach. The attending physician had stated that the infant's life was in imminent danger if the vomiting could not be halted.

Treatment consisted of delivering a series of one-second-long electric shocks to the infant's calf each time he showed signs of beginning to vomit. Sessions followed feeding and lasted under an hour. After just two sessions, shock was rarely required, for the infant learned quickly to stop vomiting in order to avoid the shock. By the sixth session he was able to fall asleep after eating. Nurses reported that the in-session inhibition of vomiting generalized as the infant progressively reduced his vomiting during the rest of the day and night. About two weeks later the mother began to assume some care of the hospitalized child, and shortly thereafter the patient was discharged with virtually complete elimination of the life-threatening pattern of behavior. Throughout the three weeks of treatment and observation, the child gained weight steadily. One month after discharge the child weighed twenty-one pounds and was rated as fully recovered by the attending physician. Five months later he weighed twenty-six pounds and was regarded as completely normal, both physically and psychologically.

The use of aversion therapy has been subject to an understandably high degree of regulation. An additional reason for administrative and judicial concern is that aversion techniques smack more of research than of standard therapy. The more established a therapeutic procedure, whether it be medical or psychological, the less likely it is to attract the attention of the courts or other governmental agencies. Paul and Lentz (1977) had a few very assaultive patients. Their account of administrative problems demonstrates that patients might be subject to more extreme procedures because special attention is paid to new techniques.

Some consideration was given to the contingent use of mild electric shock. . . . However, early in the explorations of the necessary safeguards and review procedures to be followed before evaluating such methods, the department director telephoned to explain that aversion conditioning was a politically sensitive issue. Therefore, more than the usual proposal, preparation, documentation, and committee reviews would be required—to the extent that approval would probably take about eighteen months. Instead, it was suggested that convulsive shock (which can cause tissue damage) be employed since "ECT is an accepted medical treatment." With those alternatives, our choice was to abandon either use of shock. (p. 499)

Mindful that short-term application of electric shock can sometimes keep retarded and autistic children from their self-destructive acts, Martin (1975) proposed that

the test should be that aversive therapy might be used where other therapy has not worked, where it can be administered to save the individual from immediate and continuing self-injury, when it allows freedom from physical restraints which would otherwise be continued, when it can be administered for only a few short instances and when its goal is to make other nonaversive therapy possible. Such an aversive program certainly requires consent from a guardian and immediate review of the results of each separate administration. (p. 77)[33]

Extra precautions such as these are necessary when treatment deliberately inflicts pain on a patient or client; they are especially necessary when the patient cannot realistically be expected to give informed consent. But should we be concerned only with physical pain? The anguish we suffer when a loved one dies is psychologically painful. It is perhaps more painful than an electric shock of 1500 microamperes. Who is to say? Since we allow that pain can be psychological, shall we permit a Gestalt therapist to make a patient cry by confronting him with feelings he has turned away from for years? Shall we forbid a psychoanalyst from guiding a patient to an insight that will likely cause great anguish, all the

more so for the conflict's having been repressed for years?

Concluding Comment

An underlying theme of this book concerns the nature of knowledge. How do we decide that we understand a phenomenon? The branch of philosophy concerned with the methods and grounds for knowledge is called epistemology. The rules of the science game that govern our definition of and search for knowledge require theories that can be tested, experiments that can be replicated, and data that are public. But given the complexity of abnormal behavior and given the vast areas of ignorance, far more extensive than the domains that have already been mapped by science as it is currently practiced, we have great respect for theoreticians and clinicians, those inventive souls who make suppositions, offer hypotheses, follow hunches—all based on rather flimsy data but holding some promise that scientific knowledge will be forthcoming.

This final chapter demonstrates again something emphasized at the very beginning of this book, namely, that the behavioral scientists and mental health professionals who conduct research and give treatment are only human beings. They suffer from the same foibles that sometimes plague nonspecialists. They occasionally act with a certainty their evidence does not justify, and they sometimes fail to anticipate the moral and legal consequences of the ways in which they conduct research and apply the tentative findings of their young discipline. When society acts with great certainty on the basis of expert scientific opinion, particularly when that opinion denies to an individual the rights and respect accorded others, it may be well to let Szasz (1963) remind us that Sir Thomas Browne, a distinguished British physician, testified in a British court of law in 1664 that witches did indeed exist, "as everyone knew."

The authors of this textbook hope that they have communicated in some measure their love for the subject matter and, more importantly, their commitment to the kind of questioning, doubting stance that wrests useful knowledge from nature and will yield more as new generations of scholars build upon the achievements of their predecessors.

---

[33]In addition to being humane, Martin's suggestions are consistent with an established legal principle that holds that therapy should begin with the technique that intrudes least on the patient's freedom and exposes him or her to the least possible risk (Morris, 1966).

Summary

This final chapter dealt with legal and ethical issues in treatment and research. Some of the civil liberties of people are rather routinely set aside when judgments are made by mental health professionals and the courts that mental illness has played a role in determining their behavior. Criminal commitment sends a person to a hospital, either before a trial for an alleged crime, because he is deemed incompetent to stand trial; or after an acquittal by reason of insanity, because a mental defect, the inability to know right from wrong, or both, are believed to have played a role in his committing a criminal act. A person who is considered ill and dangerous to himself and to others, though he has not broken a law, can be civilly committed to an institution. Recent court rulings have provided greater protection to all committed mental patients, particularly those under civil commitment: they have the right to written notification, to counsel, to a jury decision concerning their commitment, and to Fifth Amendment protection against self-incrimination; the right to the least restrictive treatment setting; the right to be treated; and, in most circumstances, the right to refuse treatment, particularly any procedure that entails considerable risk. Finally, a number of moral issues in therapy and research were reviewed: ethical restraints on research, the duty of scientists to obtain informed consent from prospective human subjects, the question whether a program is treatment or research, the right of clients to confidentiality, the setting of therapy goals, and the choice of techniques.

Appendix

Brain Dysfunctions and Abnormal Behavior

Organic Mental Syndromes

Dementia

Delirium

Amnestic Syndrome

Organic Delusional Syndrome

Organic Hallucinosis

Organic Mood Syndrome

Organic Anxiety Syndrome

Organic Personality Syndrome

Organic Mental Disorders

Dementias Arising in the Senium and Presenium

When the brain becomes dysfunctional, a whole host of impairments, of sensory and motor functions as well as emotional and psychological ones, are likely. The disorders to be considered here are psychological and behavioral abnormalities that are caused by transient or permanent brain dysfunctions; they are often similar to the psychopathologies considered in earlier chapters. For this reason it is always important for a clinician to be aware that an apparent psychological problem or symptom may have a clear physiological cause.

DSM-IIIR distinguishes two major categories, *organic mental syndromes* and *organic mental disorders* (Table A.1). The several types of organic mental syndromes, for example, organic mood syndrome and organic hallucinosis, each have specific groups of psycho-

logical and behavioral symptoms that can be produced by several different causes. Each of the organic mental disorders, in contrast, has a specific presumed organic cause. The symptoms for disorders in the two categories may be similar. For example, hallucinations are principal symptoms both of organic hallucinosis, an organic mental syndrome and of alcohol withdrawal delirium and alcohol hallucinosis, two of the alcohol organic mental disorders. The difference is that in organic mental disorders a presumed organic cause of the symptoms is part of the diagnosis itself (e.g., dementia of the Alzheimer type).

Organic Mental Syndromes

Dementia

In Chapter 17 (page 485) we described the memory loss and other cognitive, social, and occupational impairments associated with dementia. In this section we describe the varied causes of the syndrome. Surveys have shown that in 10 to 20 percent of older people who have dementia, the condition is reversible (Cummings and Benson, 1983; Gurland and Cross, 1982; Small, Liston, and Jarvik, 1981; Spar, 1982; Task Force Report, 1980; Wells, 1978). For example, when alcohol and medication toxicities, malnutrition, metabolic disorders, or depression cause dementia, it is reversible.

A number of infectious diseases can also produce dementia. Encephalitis is a generic term that refers to inflammation of brain tissue. A large number of living and nonliving agents can enter the body by various routes and inflame the brain. Most are living, and the most important are several viruses, usually carried by insects such as mosquitoes and ticks. In other cases, though, infection may have spread from another part of the body, for example, the sinuses and ears. Epidemics of one form, encephalitis lethargica, were widespread in the United States and Europe about the time of World War I. It was referred to as sleeping sickness because those infected were extremely lethargic and slept for days and weeks at a time, only to be roused from stupor for brief intervals. The epidemics were suspected of having an influenza virus as their cause, one that apparently and mysteriously vanished from the face of the earth, for the epidemics stopped occurring around 1926.

The major symptoms of encephalitis are vomiting, headache, drowsiness and lethargy, a stiff neck and back, fever, tremors, and sometimes convulsive seizures and coma. In the acute phase of the disease, patients

---

TABLE A.1 The categories of brain disorders in DSM-IIIR

I. *Organic Mental Syndromes* (symptoms presumed to be caused by a brain dysfunction but with many possible etiologies for each)
   A. Delirium.
   B. Dementia.
   C. Amnestic syndrome.
   D. Organic delusional syndrome.
   E. Organic hallucinosis.
   F. Organic mood syndrome.
   G. Organic anxiety syndrome.
   H. Organic personality syndrome.
   I. Intoxication.
   J. Withdrawal.

II. *Organic Mental Disorders* (symptoms linked to specific known or presumed organic causes)
   A. Dementias Arising in the Senium and Presenium
      1. Primary degenerative dementia of the Alzheimer type.
      2. Multi-infarct dementia.
   B. Psychoactive Substance-Induced Organic Mental Disorders (diagnosis usually made in conjunction with Substance Use Disorders)
      1. Alcohol-induced organic mental disorders.
      2. Sedative-, hypnotic-, or anxiolytic-induced organic mental disorders.
      3. Opioid organic mental disorders.
      4. Cocaine organic mental disorder.
      5. Amphetamine or similarly acting sympathomimetic organic mental disorders.
      6. Phencyclidine (PCP) or similarly acting arylcyclohexylamine organic mental disorders.
      7. Hallucinogen-induced organic mental disorders.
      8. Cannabis organic mental disorders.
      9. Nicotine-induced organic mental disorder.
      10. Caffeine organic mental disorder.
      11. Inhalant-induced organic mental disorder.

are delirious and disoriented. Later they may remain depressed and irritable and have dementia. Recovery is usually complete, but some patients may have permanent paralysis of an arm or leg, uncontrollable tremors, seizures, deafness, speech disturbances, and dementia. If the disorder occurs in infants, they will often be mentally retarded; their developing brains are particularly susceptible to damage from infection.

The symptoms of meningitis, an inflammation of the meninges (see Box A.1), are quite similar to those of encephalitis. The causes are varied but usually bacterial. The principal epidemic form, meningococcal meningitis, occurs all over the world; epidemics of major proportions happen every eight to twelve years.

The syphilitic spirochete *Treponema pallidum* invades the body through mucous membranes after being contracted during either intercourse or oral–genital relations. The disorder may also be transmitted from an infected mother to her fetus. The first indication of the disorder is a small sore on the site of the infection—lips, genitals, or anus—which appears after ten to twenty days and then in a few weeks disappears. Before the sore disappears, a diffuse, copper-colored rash may cover the body. Fatigue, headache, and fever may accompany the rash, as well as sore throat, inflammation of the eyes, vague pains in bones and joints, and lesions in the mucous membranes of mouth and genitals.[1] Thereafter no overt difficulties are evident for many years, but during this period spirochetes may be invading the lymph glands, the bone marrow, and the other tissues and organs of the body. Damage usually becomes observable when the individual is in his or her forties or fifties and the spirochetes have either invaded the walls of the heart, causing a heart attack, or penetrated the neural tissue. About 30 percent of those infected will ultimately have neurological impairment.

The clinical picture in dementia caused by the syphilitic spirochete depends on the area of the nervous system affected. In some cases the meninges of the brain are infected, in others the motor nerves of the spinal cord. The most severe damage is done when the cerebral cortex, usually that of the frontal areas, is invaded, producing the syndrome called general paresis. The convolutions of the cerebral cortex flatten through atrophy; on autopsy, the shrinkage is obvious. The first symptoms are irritability, fatigue, depression, loss of motivation at work, irresponsibility in personal affairs, and inattention to personal appearance. The individual becomes progressively more callous and forgetful and

grossly lacking in judgment. Some become euphorically expansive and have absurd and grandiose delusions of position, power, wealth, and physical prowess. Others are depressed and hopeless.

Loss of tone in the facial muscles and failure of the pupils to contract to light are obvious signs. Tremors of the eyelids, lips, facial muscles, and fingers, mispronunciation and slurring of words, deterioration of handwriting, and a wobbly gait indicate loss of control of the voluntary musculature. Massive confusion gradually replaces psychosis. In the final stages the individual is paralyzed, inarticulate, and subject to convulsions, for the mind and body have all but ceased functioning.

With trauma, or injury to the brain, there is often some degree of hemorrhaging and destruction of brain tissue. If the damage is severe, dementia may result. One of the most frequent traumas causing dementia is the **subdural hematoma.** The skull is fractured and bone tears the arachnoid membrane (see Box A.1), causing blood to fill the subdural space between the dura mater and the arachnoid and to destroy much neural tissue. Other causes of dementia include multiple sclerosis and neurological diseases such as Huntington's chorea and Parkinson's disease.

Delirium

The difficulties in concentration and incoherence associated with delirium were described in Chapter 17 (page 489). The causes of delirium in the aged can be grouped into several general classes: drug intoxications, metabolic and nutritional imbalances, infections or fevers, neurological disorders, and the stress of a change in the person's surroundings (Habot and Libow, 1980; Lipowski, 1980). It may also occur following major surgery (hip surgery is especially common; Gustafson *et al.*, 1988), during psychoactive substance withdrawal, and following head trauma or seizures. Common physical illnesses causing delirium in this age group include congestive heart failure, pneumonia, urinary tract infection, cancer, uremia, malnutrition, dehydration, and cerebrovascular accidents or strokes. Probably the single most frequent cause of delirium in the aged is intoxication with prescription drugs (Besdine, 1980; Lipowski, 1983). In most cases, however, the delirium has more than one cause (Sloane, 1980).

Complete recovery is possible if the syndrome is correctly identified and the underlying cause promptly and effectively treated. Generally, the condition takes one to four weeks to clear, although it takes longer in the elderly than in the young. If the underlying causative condition is not treated, however, the brain can be per-

---

[1]Unfortunately, these early signs do not always appear, making detection of the disease difficult. For this reason blood tests are recommended if there is any suspicion of venereal disease after sexual contact with a highly experienced person or with a relative stranger.

BOX A.1

STRUCTURE AND FUNCTION OF THE HUMAN BRAIN

The brain is located within the protective coating of the skull and is enveloped with three layers of nonneural tissue, membranes referred to as *meninges*. The three membranes are the outer, tough, dura mater, the intermediate, weblike arachnoid, and the inner, soft pia mater. Viewed from the top, the brain is divided by a midline fissure into two mirror-image *cerebral hemispheres;* together they constitute most of the cerebrum. The major connection between the two hemispheres is a band of nerve fibers called the *corpus callosum*. Figure A.1 shows the surface of one of the cerebral hemispheres. The upper, side, and some of the lower surfaces of the hemispheres constitute the *cerebral cortex*. The cortex consists of six layers of tightly packed neuron cell bodies with many short, unsheathed interconnecting processes. These neurons, estimated to be 10 to 15 billion in number, make up a thin outer covering, the so-called gray matter of the brain. The cortex is vastly convoluted; the ridges are called *gyri* and the depressions between them *sulci* or fissures. Deep fissures divide the cerebral hemispheres into several distinct areas, called lobes. The *frontal lobe* lies in front of the central sulcus; the *parietal lobe* is behind it and above the lateral sulcus; the *temporal lobe* is located below the lateral sulcus; and the *occipital lobe* lies behind the parietal and temporal lobes. Different functions tend to be localized in particular areas of the lobes—vision in the occipital; discrimination of sounds in the temporal; reasoning and other higher mental processes, plus the regulation of fine voluntary movement, in the frontal; initiation of movements of the skeletal musculature in a band in front of the central sulcus; in a band behind this sulcus, receipt of sensations of touch, pressure, pain, temperature, and body position from skin, muscles, tendons,

and joints.

The two hemispheres of the brain have different functions. The left hemisphere, which generally controls the right half of the body by a crossing over of motor and sensory fibers, is usually dominant; it is responsible for speech and, according to some neuropsychologists, for analytical thinking in right-handed people and in a fair number of left-handed people as well. The right hemisphere controls the left side of the body, discerns spatial relations and patterns, and is involved in emotion and intuition. But analytical thinking cannot be located exclusively in the left hemisphere or intuitive and even creative thinking in the right; the two hemispheres communicate with each other constantly via the corpus callosum. Localization of apparently different modes of thought is probably not as clearcut as some would have us believe.

If the brain is sliced in half, separating the two cerebral hemispheres (Figure A.2), additional important features can be seen. The gray matter of the cerebral cortex does not extend throughout the interior of the brain. Much of the interior is *white matter* and is made up of large tracts or bundles of myelinated (sheathed) fibers that connect cell bodies in the cortex with those in the spinal cord and in other centers lower in the brain. These centers are additional pockets of gray matter, referred to as *nuclei*. The nuclei serve both as way stations, connecting tracts from the cortex with other ascending and descending tracts, and as integrating motor and sensory control centers. Some cortical cells project their long fibers or axons to motor neurons in the spinal cord, but others project them only as far as these clusters of interconnecting neuron cell bodies. Four masses are deep within each hemisphere, called

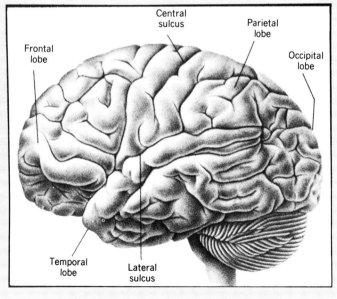

Frontal lobe

Central sulcus

Parietal lobe

Occipital lobe

Temporal lobe

Lateral sulcus

FIGURE A.1 (left)
Surface of the left cerebral hemisphere, indicating the lobes and the two principal fissures of the cortex.

FIGURE A.2 (right)
Slice of brain through the medial plane, showing the internal structures.

collectively the basal ganglia. Deep within the brain too are cavities, called *ventricles,* which are continuous with the central canal of the spinal cord and which are filled with cerebrospinal fluid.

In Figure A.2 are shown four important functional areas or structures.

1. The ***diencephalon,*** connected in front with the hemispheres and behind with the midbrain, contains the *thalamus* and the ***hypothalamus,*** which consist of groups of nuclei. The thalamus is a relay station for all sensory pathways except the olfactory. The nuclei making up the thalamus receive nearly all impulses arriving from the different sensory areas of the body before passing them on to the cerebrum, where they are interpreted as conscious sensations. The hypothalamus is the highest center of integration for many visceral processes. Its nuclei regulate metabolism, temperature, water balance, sweating, blood pressure, sleeping, and appetite.

2. The ***midbrain*** is a mass of nerve fiber tracts connecting the cerebral cortex with the pons, the medulla oblongata, the cerebellum, and the spinal cord.

3. The ***brain stem*** is made up of the ***pons*** and ***medulla oblongata*** and functions primarily as a neural relay station. The pons contains tracts that connect the cerebellum with the spinal cord and the cerebellum with motor areas of the cerebrum. The medulla oblongata serves as the main line of traffic for tracts ascending

from the spinal cord and descending from the higher centers of the brain. At the bottom of the medulla, many of the motor fibers cross to the opposite side. The medulla also contains nuclei that maintain the regular life rhythms of the heartbeat, of the rising and falling diaphragm, and of the constricting and dilating blood vessels. In the core of the brain stem is the *reticular formation,* sometimes called the reticular activating system because of the important role that it plays in arousal and in the maintenance of alertness. The tracts of the pons and medulla send in fibers to connect with the profusely interconnected cells of the reticular formation, which in turn send fibers to the cortex, the basal ganglia, the hypothalamus, the septal area, and the cerebellum.

4. The ***cerebellum,*** like the cerebrum, is made up for the most part of two deeply convoluted hemispheres with an exterior cortex of gray matter and an interior of white tracts. The cerebellum receives sensory nerves from the vestibular apparatus of the ear and from muscles, tendons, and joints. The information received and integrated relates to balance and posture and equilibrium and to the smooth coordination of the body when in motion.

A fifth important part of the brain, not shown in Figure A.2, is the ***limbic system,*** structures that are continuous with one another in the lower cerebrum, and that developed earlier than did the mammalian cerebral cortex. The limbic system controls the visceral and physical expressions of emotion—quickened heartbeat and respiration, trembling, sweating, and alterations in facial expressions—and the expression of appetitive and other primary drives—hunger, thirst, mating, defense, attack, and flight. This system is made up of cortex that is phylogenetically older than the so-called neocortex, which covers most of the hemispheres. The juxallocortex, which consists of four or five layers of neurons, surrounds the corpus callosum and the underlying thalamus. The cingulate gyrus stretching about the corpus callosum is an important structure made up of this juxallocortex. The allocortex, with only three layers of neurons, makes up the cortex of the septal area, which is anterior to the thalamus; the long, tubelike hippocampus, which stretches from the septal area into the temporal lobe; and the part of the lower temporal lobe that surrounds the under portions of the hippocampus and the amygdala (one of the basal ganglia), which is embedded in its tip. The amygdala and the septal area itself, which also consists of nuclei, are sometimes considered part of the limbic system because of their anatomical and functional connections to its other structures.

Corpus callosum

Hypothalamus
Thalamus
} Diencephalon

Brain stem {
Midbran
Pons
Medulla

Cerebellum

manently damaged and the patient may die. The mortality rate for delirium is extremely high; approximately 40 percent of the patients die, either from the underlying condition or from exhaustion (Rabins and Folstein, 1982). In fact, when fatality rates for dementia and delirium are compared over a one-year period of time, the rates are higher for delirium than for dementia, 37.5 compared to 16 percent. Thus delirium in an older adult is a very serious matter.

Diagnosis of Delirium

The accurate diagnosis of delirium and its differentiation from conditions that resemble it are obviously critical to the welfare of older persons. Recognition and differentiation, however, presuppose knowledge of the distinguishing clinical symptoms. An elderly woman, for example, was found in a filthy apartment with no food. Initially believed by a poorly informed physician to be demented, she was simply given routine custodial care in a nursing home. Fortunately, a professional knowledgeable about delirium learned that she had become depressed over the loss of a loved one and had neglected her diet. Once this was recognized, appropriate attention was given to her nutritional deficiencies, and her condition improved to the point that she was discharged back to her own home after one month (Zarit, 1980).

This case is not atypical. Cameron *et al.* (1987) assessed 133 consecutive admissions to an acute medical ward. They found fifteen cases of delirium but only one of these had been detected by the admitting physician. Older adults are often mistaken for "senile" and therefore beyond hope. A decision for long-term institutional care is all too often viewed as the only sound one, in spite of the fact that the person may have a reversible condition. The older adult who has cognitive impairment must be examined thoroughly for all possible reversible causes of the disorder, such as drug intoxications, infections, fever, malnutrition, and head trauma, and then treated accordingly.

Amnestic Syndrome

The principal symptom of **amnestic syndrome** is impairment in both short- and long-term memory when there is no delirium and dementia, no clouding of consciousness, and no intellectual deterioration. The person has difficulties recalling previously acquired information and cannot learn new material. Events from the distant past are usually recalled better than more recent events. The memory problems usually create some disorientation; sometimes the individual resists acknowledging memory difficulties through **confabulation,** filling in gaps with fictions.

Amnestic syndrome is brought on by damage to either side of the brain, in certain diencephalic and temporal lobe structures. Although there are many possible causes—head trauma, infection, infarction of the posterior cerebral arteries—the most common are chronic alcohol use and thiamine deficiency.

One specific amnestic syndrome, **Wernicke's disease,** is frequent among alcoholics, who often do not eat properly. Symptoms include confusion and drowsiness, partial paralysis of the muscles that control eye movements, and an unsteady gait. Autopsy reveals lesions in the pons and cerebellum and in the mammillary bodies, two small, rounded structures of the hypothalamus that contain nuclei. In addition, there is atrophy in the gray matter surrounding several of the ventricles.

A sizable number of patients with Wernicke's disease also develop **Korsakoff's psychosis.** The primary symptoms are the inability to recall information and confabulation. Shortly after dinner a patient with Korsakoff's psychosis may be asked what he had for the evening meal. Unable to recall the details, he quickly provides a description of an imaginary meal. It often happens, however, that such descriptions are patently false and elaborate fabrications. A patient in a mental institution may state that he has just finished a meal of Beef Wellington with a delightful sauce containing truffles, apparently not recognizing the extreme improbability of being served such a dinner.

Patients with Korsakoff's psychosis are usually lucid and friendly, yet they lack judgment, being unaware of the implausibility of the stories they tell and only poorly planning other aspects of their lives. They may become apathetic and sometimes grossly confused and severely disoriented. On autopsy, these patients reveal a pattern of brain damage similar to that of Wernicke's disease, but in addition they also have lesions in the thalamus.

Organic Delusional Syndrome

The delusions in **organic delusional syndrome** are caused by physiological factors that do not cloud consciousness or cause any significant loss of intellectual abilities. Mild impairments may be evident, however, and the person's speech may be somewhat incoherent and rambling. The patient may be either hyperactive, pacing and rocking back and forth, or apathetically immobile. Mood is anxious or depressed. Drugs such as amphetamines, marijuana, and hallucinogens as well as brain lesions, particularly to the nondominant hemisphere, can cause the syndrome. A number of people with temporal lobe epilepsy also have delusions, even between seizures.

There are various forms of epilepsy, in all of which consciousness is altered by sudden disruption of the usual rhythmical electric discharge of brain cells.[2] In *temporal lobe epilepsy* the focus of the abnormal and excessive electric discharge is in the temporal lobes of the brain. The seizures begin with an aura, a signal of the forthcoming attack, which may take the form of dizziness, fear, or unusual sensory experiences such as ringing in the ears or unusual odors. Then the person loses contact with the environment. But during the attack the epileptic appears conscious and engages in some sort of routine or organized activity. The act may be simple and repetitive, such as chewing or moving the limbs in a particular way, or the epileptic may engage in a complex and prolonged series of activities. These seizures may last only a few seconds or minutes but occasionally much longer. After the attack, individuals have no memory of their actions. The behavior of these people is often psychotic, even between seizures (Glaser, Newman, and Schafer, 1963).

Organic Hallucinosis

In *organic hallucinosis* the patient experiences persistent and recurrent hallucinations when alert, well oriented, and in a state of full wakefulness. The use of hallucinogens and prolonged heavy drinking of alcohol are the major causes. Hallucinogens generally bring

---

[2]The other major forms of epilepsy are grand mal, petit mal, and Jacksonian or focal epilepsy. *Grand mal* begins with an aura. In the tonic phase the muscles of the body suddenly become rigid. The patient loses consciousness and falls heavily to the ground if he has not been able to prepare for the attack. The arms and trunk are flexed, the legs outstretched and breathing ceases. After about half a minute, in the clonic phase, which lasts another one or several minutes, the muscles alternately contract and relax, producing violent contortions and jerking movements of the limbs. Breathing resumes. The jaws also open and close, and saliva collects on the lips. Eventually, as the convulsive movements dissipate, the epileptic seizure passes from the clonic phase into coma. The individual remains unconscious and the muscles relax. Upon awakening, perhaps almost immediately or only after several hours, the individual has no memory of what happened after the beginning of the tonic phase. *Petit mal*, more frequent in children and rare after twenty years of age, is only a short (15 to 50 seconds) disturbance or alteration of consciousness. The person stops what he is doing and his eyes roll up. There may be a few twitches of the eye and face muscles, but in most instances such seizures are difficult to recognize. The person may be aware only that his mind has gone blank for a few moments. *Jacksonian* or *focal* epilepsy muscle spasms are limited to particular areas of the body. There are several variants, depending on the area of the brain in which the neurons discharge abnormally. A motor seizure may begin with discharge near the lateral sulcus and be manifested as twitches of the thumb and index finger. A discharge beginning in the visual cortex may produce hallucinations. Sometimes these seizures remain localized and there is no loss of consciousness. But they may also spread, perhaps beginning with the thumb and index finger and then extending to the hand, arm, and shoulder, and sometimes ultimately throughout the entire body.

visual hallucinations, and long-term alcohol abuse brings auditory hallucinations. In the course of the DTs, during withdrawal from alcohol, however, the hallucinations are visual. The sensory deprivations of blindness and deafness may cause hallucinations. Those who are blind have visual ones, and the deaf have auditory hallucinations. Untreated cataracts and otosclerosis may cause chronic hallucinosis. Finally, seizures located in the temporal or occipital lobes may also cause hallucinations.

Organic Mood Syndrome

The affective disturbances of *organic mood syndrome* resemble those of either mania or depression and are usually caused by toxic or metabolic factors. As with the other organic syndromes, these affective disturbances must occur without delirium or dementia to warrant the diagnosis. Depressive symptoms may be brought on by drugs such as reserpine, which is used to treat hypertension, and by methyldopa, used in the treatment of Parkinson's disease. Viral illnesses, strokes, and endocrine disturbances may also bring on an organic mood syndrome.

Endocrine glands secrete their hormones directly into the bloodstream. Thus these powerful substances are delivered to nearly every cell in the body, including the neurons of the brain. Either oversecretions or undersecretions of the thyroid gland may bring on affective problems. In hyperthyroidism or *Graves' disease,* first described by an Irish physician, Robert Graves, early in the nineteenth century, an oversecretion of the hormone thyroxin speeds up metabolic processes, causing weight loss, sweating, and motor agitation and inducing a state of apprehension, restlessness, and either elated mood or irritability. Thinking proceeds at a rapid pace; persons with Graves' disease may be misdiagnosed as suffering an episode of mania. About 20 percent of hyperthyroid patients may have transitory delusions and hallucinations. Hypothyroidism, which brings on a condition called *myxedema* in adults, is a deficiency in thyroid hormone. Metabolic processes are slowed and so too are speech and thinking. The individual has poor emotional control, suffers from fatigue, and gains weight. He or she moves as little as possible and loses interest in activities and surroundings. As the disorder progresses, the skin becomes dry and brittle, and hair is lost from the eyebrows and the genital area. In severe cases depression may be deep enough to be considered psychotic. In children the disorder causes mental retardation. Fortunately, hypothyroidism is a very rare condition today, for the iodine of iodized salt prevents the thyroid deficiency.

The adrenal cortex is centrally invovled in the activation of emergency physiological responses and the energy needs of the human organism. A chronic insufficiency of cortisone secretion by the adrenal cortex produces **Addison's disease,** first described by the English physician Thomas Addison. The patient loses weight, suffers from low blood pressure, and is irritable and easily fatigued; skin and mucuous membranes also darken. The person becomes depressed and less sociable. When abnormal growths on the cortices of the adrenal glands make them secrete too much cortisone, the condition produced is called **Cushing's syndrome.** Harvey Cushing, the American brain surgeon, described this rare disease, which usually affects young women. The afflicted individual has severe mood swings, none of them pleasant. She is most often depressed but may then become anxious, agitated, and irritable. Physical changes, some quite disfiguring ones—obesity, muscle wasting, changes in skin color and texture, and bone porosity that may bring spinal deformity—can also occur.

Organic Anxiety Syndrome

The central features of **organic anxiety syndrome** are either recurrent panic attacks or generalized anxiety. Some cognitive impairments such as the inability to maintain attention are also frequently present.

The disorder is most often due to endocrine disturbances or psychoactive substances. Common endocrine disturbances include hyper- or hypothyroidism, hypoglycemia, and hypercortisolemia. Use of stimulants, such as caffeine, amphetamines, and cocaine, may cause the syndrome as can withdrawal from alcohol and sedatives.

Organic Personality Syndrome

In **organic personality syndrome** the personality undergoes a great change, usually because of damage to the brain. The specific nature of the personality change, although very difficult to predict, depends to some extent on function and location of the brain structures that are altered. Some people become emotionally labile and unable to control themselves. They may have sudden bouts of crying and temper outbursts with little provocation. Or they may be sexually indiscrete, shoplift, and act otherwise inappropriately with little concern for consequences. Others may become apathetic, losing interest in their daily activities, friends, and hobbies. Still others may develop a paranoid suspiciousness.

The syndrome occurs sometimes between episodes of seizures among those with temporal lobe epilepsy.

Multiple sclerosis, cerebrovascular disease, and Huntington's chorea are other causes. The disorder may also be produced by a brain **tumor** or **neoplasm,** an abnormal growth that can produce a wide variety of psychological as well as physical symptoms. Tumors are either malignant or benign. Malignant growths interfere directly with neural functioning by destroying the original brain tissue from which they started to grow. Benign tumors do not destroy tissue but may, as they grow, increase intracranial pressure and thus disrupt the normal functioning of the brain. Brain tumors usually originate either in glial cells—which support and protect neurons, determine their supply of nutrients and enzymes, and remove dead cells—or in the dura, the outermost membrane covering the brain. Metastatic tumors, though, can invade the brain after being carried by the blood from another area of the body such as the lung.

In addition to causing persistent headaches, vomiting, and sensory and motor impairments—double vision, jerky reflexes and coordination, visual, olfactory, and auditory hallucinations, seizures, and paralysis—tumors in the frontal, temporal, and parietal lobes may first disturb the personality. The individual may be preoccupied and confused, depressed and irritable, and careless about dress, appearance, and work. Very occasionally, the person explodes in a sudden and destructive outburst, totally out of character and completely incomprehensible to family, friends, and society at large. After the event it is usually realized, however, that the individual has had earlier warning symptoms and has even communicated them.

If either a benign or a malignant tumor continues to grow, the patient usually dies. Even if the tumor is removed, the functions that have been lost through the destruction of neural tissue do not return because brain cells do not regenerate.

The two lesser brain traumas—the **concussion,** a brief loss of consciousness caused by a jarring blow to the head; and the **contusion,** a bruise of neural tissue and coma when a blow shifts the brain and compresses it against the opposite side of the skull—are serious enough but will not usually change the personality.[3] But a **laceration,** a direct wound to the brain when an object enters the skull and pierces, ruptures, or tears tissue, may affect personality. A famous historical case, reported by Dr. J. M. Harlow (1896), illustrates vividly some personality changes following a severe laceration.

---

[3]A series of severe blows to the head, such as a boxer suffers, can eventually lead to a brain syndrome called "punch-drunkenness." Areas of brain tissue become permanently damaged by the accumulation of injuries; the individual cannot pay attention or concentrate, and memory as well as motor functions are groggy and slow. A person speaks as though slightly drunk. Emotions are unstable and poorly controlled; intellectual impairment is sometimes profound.

The patient, Phineas Gage, was working on evacuation of rocks for the roadway of the Rutland and Burlington Railroad in Cavendish, Vermont, when a premature blast sent a tamping iron, three feet, seven inches in length and over an inch in diameter, through his left cheek, upward, and through the top of his skull. Although Gage recovered with no loss of motor or sensory functions, he was a changed person. Dr. Harlow described how the injury later affected Gage's behavior.

> His physical health is good, and I am inclined to say that he has recovered. Has no pain in head, but says it has a queer feeling which he is not able to describe. Applied for his situation as foreman, but is undecided whether to work or travel. His contractors, who regarded him as the most efficient and capable foreman in their employ previous to his injury considered the change in his mind so marked that they could not give him his place again. The equilibrium or balance, so to speak, between his intellectual faculties and animal propensities, seems to have been destroyed. He is fitful, irreverent, indulging at times in the grossest profanity (which was not previously his custom), manifesting but little deference for his fellows, impatient of restraint or advice when it conflicts with his desires, at times pertinaciously obstinate, yet capricious and vascillating, devising many plans for future operations, which are no sooner arranged than they are abandoned in turn for others . . . his mind is radically changed, so decidedly that his friends and acquaintances said he was "no longer Gage." (pp. 339–340)

Organic Mental Disorders

Two major classes of organic mental disorders are distinguished, **Dementias Arising in the Senium and Presenium** and **Psychoactive Substance-Induced Mental Disorders.** The senium refers to age sixty-five or older and the presenium to age sixty-five and under. The substance-induced disorders are the specific effects, such as intoxication, withdrawal, delirium, hallucinations, and memory dysfunctions, brought on by ingesting alcohol, narcotics, barbiturates, amphetamines, cocaine, and the

other substances covered in Chapter 11. Therefore what remains to be presented are the dementias.

Dementias Arising In the Senium and Presenium

Primary Degenerative Dementia of the Alzheimer Type

In **Alzheimer's disease** the brain tissue deteriorates, with death usually occurring ten or twelve years after the onset of symptoms. The disorder is somewhat more prevalent among women than among men. The disease was first described by the German neurologist Alois Alzheimer in 1860. It commences with difficulties in concentration; the individual appears absent-minded and irritable, shortcomings that soon begin to interfere with the way she leads her life. She blames others for personal failings and has delusions of being persecuted. Memory continues to deteriorate, with the individual becoming increasingly disoriented and agitated.

The primary physiological change in the brain, evident at autopsy, is a general atrophy of the cerebral cortex as neurons are lost, particularly axons and dendrites rather than the cell bodies themselves (Kowall and Beal, 1988). The fissures widen and the ridges become narrower and flatter. The ventricles also become enlarged. Moreover, senile plaques—small round areas consisting of the remnants of the lost neurons and amyloid, a waxy substance deposited when protein synthesis is disturbed—are scattered throughout the cortex; tangled abnormal protein filaments, neurofibrillary tangles, accumulate within the cell bodies of neurons. These plaques and tangles are present throughout the cerebral cortex and the hippocampus.

Although neural pathways using different transmitters deteriorate (Wester *et al.*, 1988), those using acetylcholine are of particular importance. There is evidence that anticholinergic drugs can produce in normals memory impairments similar to those in Alzheimer's patients. Cholinergic agents have been used, with mixed results, in attempts to improve memory in Alzheimer's patients (Summers, 1986). Furthermore, levels of the major metabolite of acetylcholine are low in Alzheimer's patients and are related to the extent of the patient's mental deterioration (Wester *et al.*, 1988).

The risk for Alzheimer's is increased in first-degree relatives of afflicted individuals (Mohs *et al.*, 1987) and among some families the pattern of inheritance suggests the operation of a single dominant gene. Furthermore, the gene controlling the protein responsible for the formation of plaques has been shown to be on the long arm of chromosome 21 and a recent linkage study has demonstrated an association between this gene and the expression of the disease (Tanzi *et al.*, 1987). Although another linkage study did not confirm these results (Schellenberg *et al.*, 1988), it involved patients of a much younger age, raising the possibility that early and late onset of Alzheimer's have different etiologies.

Pick's Disease

Another dementia was first described by Arnold Pick, a Prague physician, in 1892. *Pick's disease* is a degenerative disorder of the central nervous system in which the frontal and temporal lobes atrophy and the ventricles enlarge. As the disease progresses, the deterioration becomes more and more pervasive. The total weight of the brain may be reduced to less than 1000 grams from the usual weight of about 1300 grams. The age of onset is generally in the forties and fifties, and symptoms are similar to those of Alzheimer's disease. Women are affected more often than men. The patient has difficulties with memory and in abstract thinking; he or she is confused and unable to concentrate and has transitory speech impairment. But in Pick's disease affect may be blunted, and the patient is likely to become apathetic and inactive. Life expectancy after onset is usually four to seven years. Microscopic examination of the brain reveals loss of neurons and the presence of Pick's bodies, masses of cytoskeletal elements. Risk among first-degree relatives is heightened, suggesting the importance of genetic mechanisms (Heston, White and Mastri, 1987).

Multi-Infarct Dementias

These dementias are caused by cerebrovascular disease (stroke) most often due to hypertension. In contrast to Alzheimer's disease, the onset is rather sudden and the course is variable with "ups" and "downs." Impairment is less general than in Alzheimer's with specific cognitive deficits determined by the areas of the brain that have been injured. Age of onset is also earlier than in Alzheimer's.

AIDS Dementia Complex

One would not find it too surprising if individuals under the severe emotional, social, and physical duress of being diagnosed with AIDS began to display symptoms such as mild to moderate depression, generalized malaise, and forgetfulness, just to name a few. In fact, the initial response of the medical profession to these problems in AIDS patients was that these symptoms were due to psychological stress. This view has been challenged by those who considered the possibility that an organic mental syndrome may indeed be a facet of HIV virus. Snider (1983) reported on the neurological complica-

tions of AIDS patients. Of his fifty patients, eighteen showed subacute encephalitis, which he thought was due to cytomegalovirus infection. Other types of infections included meningeal invasion. But most importantly, Snider noted diffuse brain damage without focal (specific) lesions in his patients who were suffering from malaise, social withdrawal, and dementia. Two questions arise: What is the source of this diffuse encephalopathy, and is it related to these symptoms?

Nurnberg (1984) was among the first to describe an AIDS patient with an organic mental syndrome that he felt was attributable specifically to the HIV virus rather than to the psychosocial stressors the AIDS patient faces or to opportunistic infections such as cytomegalovirus that HIV allows to gain hold in the individual. "Mr. A", as Nurnberg called him, was a patient who tested positive for the HIV antibodies and was diagnosed as having AIDS. Mr. A, hospitalized for depression, also exhibited anxiety, mild insomnia, anhedonia, anorexia (a 30-lb. weight loss), and lack of libido. As time progressed, he began having hallucinations. Mr. A failed to remember days of the week, reversed digits when trying to repeat them, and failed to recall items on simple memory exercises. In addition to these deficits, apparently in short-term memory, he was also unable to interpret proverbs or abstract similarities between objects. Notably, Nurnberg's patient showed no signs of cytomegalovirus or other opportunistic neurological infections. After Nurnberg's report, the search was on to see if HIV directly affected the brain.

Ho and his colleagues (1985) were the first to isolate HIV from the cerebrospinal fluid and neural tissues of patients demonstrating neurological symptoms similar to Nurnberg's patient, symptoms characteristic of what is now known as AIDS dementia complex (ADC). This was the first evidence conclusively showing that HIV has the ability to cross the brain–blood barrier, a defense mechanism that normally allows only oxygen, nutrients, and waste to flow between the blood vessels and the cerebrospinal fluid. If HIV acts directly on the brain to cause ADC, the virus must come into contact with the brain in some way (either the virus itself or some product it is producing). Isolation of HIV from neural tissue and cerebrospinal fluid shows that it is able to cross the brain–blood barrier, and that it may indeed be responsible for ADC. Subsequent studies have confirmed a role for the HIV virus in producing dementia. White matter in the cerebral cortex and basal ganglia are most affected (Pumarol *et al.*, 1986) and the virus invades macrophages in these areas, where it then replicates (Koenig *et al.*, 1986).

Huntington's Chorea

The degenerative disorder *Huntington's chorea* was first described by the American neurologist George Huntington in 1872, after his father and grandfather, both physicians, had observed the disease in several generations of a family. Symptoms usually begin when the individual is in the thirties, and thereafter deterioration is progressive. The early behavioral signs are slovenliness, disregard for social convention, violent outbursts, depression, irritability, poor memory, euphoria, poor judgment, delusions, suicidal ideas and attempts, and hallucinations. The term chorea was applied to the disorder because of the patient's choreiform movements—involuntary, spasmodic twitching and jerking of the limbs, trunk, and head. These signs of neurological disturbance do not appear until well after behavior has already started to deteriorate. Facial grimaces, a smacking of the lips and tongue, and explosive, often obscene speech are other symptoms. The afflicted individual is likely to have severe problems in speaking, walking, and swallowing. Through the course of the disorder, the suicide rate becomes high, and eventually there is a total loss of bodily control. Death is inevitable, but it may be delayed for ten to twenty years after the onset of illness. The incidence is about 5 cases per 100,000 persons (Boll, Heaton, and Reitan, 1974). The following excerpts from the biography of the American folksinger Woody Guthrie illustrate the development of the disorder, some of the prominent clinical symptoms, and the personal tragedy of the illness.

[Describing the first signs, Woody's wife, Marjorie, commented] "What confused me, and Woody himself, in the early stage of the illness was that by nature he was a rather moody person. As early as 1948, we began to notice that he was more reflective, and often depressed by trivial things. . . . [Shortly thereafter] the symptoms of the disease had become more obvious. Woody developed a peculiar lopsided walk and his speech became explosive. He would take a deep sigh before breathing out the words. The moods and depressions became more exaggerated and more frequent. . . ." [In 1952 the first serious attack occurred. As his wife described it,] "Woody had a violent outburst and foamed at the mouth." [He was hospitalized for three weeks and diagnosed as an alcoholic. After his release he had another violent seizure which, this time, led to a three-month hospitalization. Later] "the disease was making rapid progress. Woody found it increasingly difficult to control his movements, appearing to be drunk even when he wasn't drinking. Friends watched with apprehension as he dived into traffic, oblivious

of danger, Chaplinlike, warding off each car as it sped toward him."

[Finally, in 1956, it was recognized that Guthrie had Huntington's chorea, and he spent his remaining years in hospitals. One incident related by his wife, which occurred shortly after his hospitalization, is especially poignant.] "In the early years of his stay in hospitals, Woody would leave every now and then on his own. One day he took the wrong bus and landed in some town in New Jersey. Noticing his disheveled appearance, his distraught air and halting gait, a policeman picked him up, took him to the local police station, and booked him on a vagrancy charge.

"Woody told the police that he was not a homeless bum but a sick man. He explained that he was staying at a New York hospital and begged them to get him home. 'Well,' they said, 'if you're sick you can stay in our hospital.' Finally they let him call me and I went tearing out to New Jersey.

"When I arrived I was received by a staff doctor, a Viennese psychiatrist. 'Your husband is a very disturbed man,' he said imperiously, 'with many hallucinations. He says that he has written a thousand songs.'[4]

'It is true,' I said.
'He also says he has written a book.'
'That's also true.'
'He says that a record company has put out nine records of his songs!' The doctor's voice dripped disbelief.
'That is also the truth,' I said." (Yurchenco, 1970, pp. 139–148)

The disorder is a genetically determined one, passed on by a single dominant gene. The offspring of an individual with the disorder have a 50 percent chance of being afflicted. A recently developed test that can detect the pathogenic gene now presents the children of Huntington's parents with the difficult choice of whether to learn if he or she is going to contract the disease. A postmortem examination of the brain of an individual with Huntington's chorea reveals widespread atrophy

---

[4]In addition to misdiagnosing Mr. Guthrie, the physician had confused the concepts of delusion and hallucination.

and scarring. The major pathological change is a loss of neurons in the caudate nucleus, one of the basal ganglia. The cerebral cortex also atrophies, especially the frontal areas. High levels of dopamine in the caudate nucleus appear to be primarily responsible for the choreiform movements.

Parkinson's Disease

In 1817 James Parkinson described a slowly progressive degeneration thst begins later in life, between the ages of fifty and seventy. The primary symptoms of ***Parkinson's disease*** are severe and continual muscular tremors, usually occurring at a rate of four to eight movements per second, which rhythmically agitate the limbs, hands, neck, and face. The tremor may begin in one hand or arm, spread to the leg of that side, then to neck, jaw, and face, and finally to the two other limbs. Only muscles that are at rest are subject to tremors, however, not those of the sleeping body or those that are engaged in a coordinated movement. But handwriting becomes small, and this and other manual skills may eventually be lost; speech, swallowing, and chewing are laborious. Other physiological effects include muscular rigidity, akinesia—an inability to initiate movements—and defects in balance. The face later becomes masklike and expressionless, the head shakes, the fingers make pill-rolling movements, and the gait is stiff and distinctive, with the upper part of the body moving forward ahead of the legs. The individual may have difficulty concentrating, become apathetic, and withdraw from social contact. About 90 percent of patients with Parkinson's disease are depressed, and in 30 percent intellectual deterioration is evident (DeJong and Sugar, 1971). About one and a half million Americans are afflicted with the disorder (Stang, 1970).

The etiology of Parkinson's disease varies. It is at times attributable to atherosclerosis; other cases are the aftereffects of encephalitis. The basic brain pathology is a loss of the deeply pigmented nerve cells in the substantia nigra, a nucleus within the midbrain that is an important motor relay station. The neurons in the substantia nigra that are destroyed are those that release dopamine. With reduced amounts of dopamine in the corpus striatum, which consists of the caudate and lenticular nuclei, the action of the neurotransmitter acetylcholine released by the cholinergic motor neurons in the caudate nucleus is insufficiently opposed. And because the neurotransmitter of the cholinergic tracts is not under the inhibitory control of dopamine, too many of the postsynaptic motor neurons fire, producing the uncontrollable muscular tremors and stiffness of Parkinson's disease. Parkinsonism can be treated either by administering anticholinergic drugs to reduce the action of the cholinergic neurons, or by giving the patient a precursor of dopamine, L-dopa. Encouraging as much movement as possible and speech therapy are also helpful.

Glossary

Acetylcholine. A *neurotransmitter*[1] of the central, somatomotor, and *parasympathetic* nervous systems and of the ganglia and the neuron–sweat gland junctions of the *sympathetic*.

Addiction. See *substance dependence*.

Addison's disease. An endocrine disorder produced by *cortisone* insufficiency and marked by weight loss, fatigue, and a darkening of the skin.

Adrenal glands. Two small areas of tissue, located just above the kidneys; the inner core of each gland, the medulla, secretes *epinephrine* and *norepinephrine,* the outer cortex secretes *cortisone* and other steroid hormones.

Adrenaline. A hormone that is secreted by the *adrenal glands*; also called *epinephrine*.

Adrenergic system. All the nerve cells for which *norepinephrine* and *epinephrine* (and more broadly, other *monoamines, dopamine* and *serotonin*) are the transmitter substances, as opposed to the *cholinergic,* which consists of the nerve cells activated by *acetylcholine*.

Advanced accurate empathy. A form of *empathy* in which the therapist infers concerns and feelings that lie behind what the client is saying; it represents an *interpretation*. Compare with *primary empathy*.

Affect. A subjective feeling or emotional tone often accompanied by bodily expressions noticeable to others.

Affirming the consequent. An error in logic by which, if A causes B on one occasion, it is assumed that A is the cause when B is observed on any other occasion.

Age effects. The consequences of being a given chronological age. Compare with *cohort effects*.

Ageism. Prejudicial attitudes toward old people.

Agoraphobia. A cluster of fears centering around being in open spaces and leaving the home.

Alcoholism. A behavioral disorder in which consumption of alcoholic beverages is excessive and impairs health and social and occupational functioning; a physiological dependence on alcohol. See *substance dependence*.

Alkaloid. An organic base found in seed plants, usually in mixture with a number of similar alkaloids. Alkaloids are the active chemicals that give many drugs their medicinal properties and other powerful physiological effects.

Alogia. A *negative symptom* in *schizophrenia,* marked by blocking and poverty of speech content.

Alpha rhythm. A dominant pattern (8 to 13 cps) of the *brain waves* of a resting but awake adult.

Altruistic suicide. As defined by Durkheim, self-annihilation that the person feels will serve a social purpose, such as the self-immolations practiced by Buddhist monks during the Vietnam war.

Alzheimer's disease. A *dementia* involving a progressive atrophy of cortical tissue and marked by memory impairment, involuntary movements of limbs, occasional *convulsions,* intellectual deterioration, and psychotic behavior.

Ambivalence. The simultaneous holding of strong positive and negative emotional attitudes toward the same situation or person.

American Law Institute Guidelines. Rules proposing insanity to be a legitimate defense plea if during criminal conduct an individual could not judge right from wrong or control his or her behavior as required by law. Repetitive criminal acts are disavowed as a sole criterion. Compare *M'Naghten rule* and *irresistible impulse*.

Amino acid. One of a large class of organic compounds, important as the building blocks of proteins.

Amnesia. Total or partial loss of memory that can be associated with a *dissociative disorder,* an *organic brain syndrome,* or *hypnosis*.

Amniocentesis. A prenatal diagnostic technique in which fluid drawn from the uterus is tested for birth defects such as *Down's syndrome* and Tay–Sachs disease.

Amphetamines. A group of stimulating drugs that produce heightened levels of energy and, in large doses, nervousness, sleeplessness, and paranoid *delusions*.

Anal personality. An adult who, when anal retentive, is found by psychoanalytic theory to be stingy and sometimes obsessively clean; when anal expulsive, to be aggressive. Such traits are assumed to be caused by *fixation* through either excessive or inadequate gratification of *id* impulses during the *anal stage* of *psychosexual* development.

Anal stage. In psychoanalytic theory, the second *psychosexual stage,* occurring during the second year of life, during which the anus is considered to be the principal *erogenous zone*.

Analgesia. An insensitivity to pain without loss of consciousness; sometimes found in *conversion disorder*.

Analogue experiment. An experimental study of a phenomenon different from but related to the actual interests of the investigator.

Analysand. A person being psychoanalyzed.

Analysis of defenses. The study by a *psychoanalyst* of the ways a patient avoids troubling topics by the use of *defense mechanisms*.

Analyst. See *psychoanalyst*.

---

[1]Italicized words or variants of these terms are themselves defined elsewhere in the glossary.

Anesthesia. An impairment or loss of sensation, usually of touch but sometimes of the other senses, that is often part of *conversion disorder.*

Angina pectoris. A coronary heart disease.

Anhedonia. A *negative symptom* in *schizophrenia,* in which the individual is unable to feel pleasure

Animal phobias. The fear and avoidance of small animals.

Anomic suicide. As defined by Durkheim, self-annihilation triggered by the person's inability to cope with sudden and unfavorable change in a social situation.

Anorexia nervosa. A disorder in which a person is unable to eat or to retain any food or suffers a prolonged and severe diminution of appetite. The individual has an intense fear of becoming obese, feels fat even when emaciated, and, refusing to maintain a minimal body weight, loses at least 25 percent of original weight.

Anosmia. A *conversion disorder* marked by loss or impairment of the sense of smell.

Anoxia. A deficiency in oxygen reaching the tissues that is severe enough to damage the brain permanently.

Antabuse (*disulfiram*). A drug that makes the drinking of alcohol produce nausea and other unpleasant effects.

Antidepressant. A drug that alleviates *depression,* usually by energizing the patient and thus elevating mood.

Antisocial personality. Also called a psychopath or a sociopath; this person is superficially charming and a habitual lair, has no regard for others, shows no remorse after hurting them, has no shame for behaving in an outrageously objectionable manner, is unable to form relationships and take responsibility, and does not learn from punishment.

Anxiety. An unpleasant feeling of fear and apprehension accompanied by increased physiological arousal. In learning theory it is considered a drive that mediates between a threatening situation and avoidance behavior. Anxiety can be assessed by self-report, by measuring physiological arousal, and by observing overt behavior.

Anxiety disorders. Disorders in which fear or tension is overriding and the primary disturbance: *phobic disorders, panic disorder, generalized anxiety disorder, obsessive-compulsive disorder;* and *posttraumatic stress disorder.* Major category of DSM-IIIR covering most of what used to be referred to as the *neuroses.*

Anxiety neurosis. DSM-II term for what are now diagnosed as *panic disorder* and *generalized anxiety disorder.*

Anxiolytics. Anxiety-reducing drugs, formerly called tranquilizers.

Aphasia. The loss or impairment of the ability to use language because of lesions in the brain. **Executive,** difficulties in speaking or writing the words intended. **Receptive,** difficulties in understanding written or spoken language.

Aphonia. A *conversion disorder* marked by a loss of voice.

Apnea. Cessation of breathing for short periods of time, sometimes occurring during sleep.

Applied behavior analysis. The study of the antecedent conditions and *reinforcement* contingencies that control behavior; see also *operant conditioning.*

Arousal. A state of activation, either behavioral or physiological.

Ascriptive responsibility. The social judgment assigned to someone who has committed an illegal act and who, it is decided, should be punished for it. Contrast with *descriptive responsibility.*

Asociality. A *negative symptom* in *schizophrenia,* marked by inability to form close relationships and feel intimacy.

Assertion training. *Behavior therapy* procedures that attempt to help a person express more easily thoughts, wishes, and beliefs and legitimate feelings of resentment or approval.

Asthma. A *psychophysiological disorder* characterized by narrowing of the airways and increased secretion of mucus, which often cause breathing to be extremely labored and wheezy.

Asylum. A refuge established in western Europe in the fifteenth century as a place to confine and provide for the mentally ill; the forerunner of the mental hospital.

Attention-deficit hyperactivity disorder. A disorder in children marked by difficulties in focusing adaptively on the task at hand and by inappropriate fidgeting and antisocial behavior.

Attribution. The explanation a person has for his or her behavior.

Aura. A signal or warning of an impending epileptic *convulsion,* taking the form of dizziness or an unusual sensory experience.

Autistic disorder. An absorption in self or fantasy as a means of avoiding communication and escaping objective reality. In this *pervasive developmental disorder,* the child's world is one of profound aloneness.

Automatic thoughts. In Beck's theory, the things people picture or tell themselves as they make their way in life.

Autonomic lability. Tendency for the *autonomic nervous system* to be easily aroused.

Autonomic nervous system. The division of the nervous system that regulates involuntary functions; innervates *endocrine glands, smooth muscle,* and heart muscle; and initiates the physiological changes that are part of expression of emotion. See *sympathetic* and *parasympathetic nervous system.*

Aversion therapy. A *behavior therapy* procedure that pairs a noxious stimulus, such as a shock, with situations that are undesirably attractive, the intent being to make the latter less appealing.

Aversive stimulus. A stimulus that elicits pain, fear, or avoidance.

Avoidance learning. An experimental procedure in which a neutral stimulus is paired with a noxious one so that the organism learns to avoid the previously neutral stimulus.

Avoidant disorder of childhood or adolescence. A persistent shrinking from strangers and from peers, despite a clear desire for affection, to the extent that social functioning is impaired; relations with family members are warm.

Avoidant personality. Thinking poorly of themselves, individuals with an avoidant personality are extremely sensitive to potential rejection and remain aloof from others, even though they very much desire affiliation and affection.

Avolition. A *negative symptom* in *schizophrenia*, in which the individual lacks interests and drive.

Barbiturate. A class of synthetic *sedative* drugs that are addictive and in large doses can cause death because the diaphragm relaxes almost completely.

Baseline. The state of a phenomenon before the *independent variable* is introduced, providing a standard against which the effects of the variable can be measured.

Behavior genetics. The study of individual differences in behavior that are attributable in part to differences in genetic makeup.

Behavior modification. A term sometimes used interchangeably with *behavior therapy*.

Behavior rehearsal. A *behavior therapy* technique in which a client practices new behavior in the consulting room, often aided by demonstrations of the therapist.

Behavior therapy. A branch of psychotherapy narrowly conceived as the application of *classical* and *operant conditioning* to the alteration of clinical problems, but more broadly conceived as applied experimental psychology in a clinical context.

Behavioral assessment. A sampling of ongoing cognitions, feelings, and overt behavior in their situational context. To be contrasted with the *projective test* and *personality inventory*.

Behavioral medicine. A new area of behavioral therapy procedures that apply to *psychophysiological disorders*.

Behavioral pediatrics. A branch of *behavioral medicine* concerned with psychological aspects of childhood medical problems.

Behaviorism. The school of psychology associated with John B. Watson, who proposed that observable behavior, not consciousness, is the proper subject matter of psychology. Currently, many who consider themselves behaviorists do use *mediational* concepts, provided they are firmly anchored to observables.

Bell and pad. A *behavior therapy* technique for eliminating nocturnal *enuresis*; if the child wets, an electric circuit is closed and a bell sounds, waking the child.

Beta rhythm. The dominant pattern (14 to 25 cps) of *brain waves* found in an alert adult responding to a stimulus. See also *alpha rhythm*.

Bioenergetics. The therapy based on Wilheim Reich's unorthodox analytic theory that all psychological distress is caused by problems in achieving full sexual satisfaction.

Biofeedback. A term referring to procedures that provide an individual immediate information on even minute changes in muscle activity, skin temperature, heart rate, blood pressure, and other somatic functions. It is assumed that voluntary control over these bodily processes can be achieved through this knowledge, thereby ameliorating to some extent certain *psychophysiological disorders*.

Bipolar disorder. A term applied to the disorder of people who have experienced episodes of both *mania* and *depression* or of mania alone.

Bisexual. One who engages in both *heterosexual* and *homosexual* relations.

Blocking. A disturbance associated with thought disorders in which a train of speech is interrupted by silence before an idea is fully expressed.

Body dysmorphic disorder. Preoccupation with an imagined or exaggerated defect in appearance, for example, facial wrinkles or excess facial or body hair.

Borderline personality. This impulsive and unpredicatable person has an uncertain self-image, intense and unstable social relationships, and extreme swings of mood.

Brain stem. The part of the brain connecting the spinal cord with the *cerebrum*. It contains the *pons* and *medulla oblongata* and functions as a neural relay station.

Brain wave. The rhythmic fluctuations in voltage between parts of the brain produced by the spontaneous firings of its *neurons*; recorded by the *electroencephalograph*.

Brief reactive psychosis. A disorder in which the person has a sudden onset of *psychotic* symptoms—incoherence, *loosening of associations*, *delusions*, *hallucinations*—immediately after a severely disturbing event; the symptoms last more than a few hours but for no more than two weeks. See *schizophreniform disorder*.

Brief therapy. Time-limited psychotherapy, generally lasting no more than twenty-five sessions.

Briquet's syndrome. See *somatization disorder*.

Bulimia. Episodic uncontrollable eating binge, often followed by purging either by vomiting or by laxatives.

Cannabis sativa. See *marijuana*.

Cardiovascular disorders. Medical problems involving the heart and blood circulation system, such as *hypertension* and *coronary heart disease*.

Case study. The collection of historical or biographical information on a single individual, often including experiences in therapy.

Castration. The surgical removal of the *testes*.

Castration anxiety. The fear of having the genitals removed or injured.

CAT scan. Computerized axial tomography, a method of diagnosis employing X-rays taken from different angles and then analyzed by computer to produce a representation of the part of the body in cross section. It can be used on the brain.

Catatonic immobility (catatonia). A fixity of posture, sometimes grotesque, maintained for long periods with accompanying muscular rigidity, trancelike state of consciousness, and *waxy flexibility.*

Catatonic schizophrenic. A *psychotic* patient whose primary symptoms alternate between stuporous immobility and excited agitation.

Catecholamines. *Monoamine* compounds (NH_2), each having a catechol portion (C_6H_6). Catecholamines known to be *neurotransmitters* of the central nervous system are *norepinephrine* and *dopamine;* another, *epinephrine,* is principally a hormone.

Catechol-O-methyltransferase (COMT). An enzyme that deactivates *catecholamines* in the *synapse.*

Cathartic method. A therapeutic procedure introduced by Breuer and developed further by Freud in the late nineteenth century whereby a patient recalls and relives an earlier emotional catastrophe and reexperiences the tension and unhappiness.

Central nervous system. The part of the nervous system that in vertebrates consists of the brain and spinal cord and to which all sensory impulses are transmitted and from which motor impulses pass out; it also supervises and coordinates the activities of the entire nervous system.

Cerebellum. An area of the hindbrain concerned with balance, posture, and motor coordination.

Cerebral atherosclerosis. A chronic disease impairing intellectual and emotional life, caused by a reduction in the brain's blood supply through a buildup of fatty deposits in the arteries.

Cerebral contusion. A bruising of neural tissue marked by swelling and hemorrhage and resulting in coma; it may permanently impair intellectual functioning.

Cerebral cortex. The thin outer covering of each of the *cerebral hemispheres,* highly convoluted, and made up of nerve cell bodies, which constitute the *gray matter* of the brain.

Cerebral hemisphere. Either of the two halves that make up the *cerebrum.*

Cerebral hemmorrhage. Bleeding onto brain tissue from a ruptured blood vessel.

Cerebral thrombosis. The formation of a blood clot in a cerebral artery that blocks circulation in that area of brain tissue and produces paralysis, loss of sensory functions, and possibly death.

Cerebrovascular diseases. Illnesses that disrupt blood supply to the brain, as in *stroke.*

Cerebrum. The two-lobed structure extending from the *brain stem* and constituting the anterior part of the brain. It is the largest and most recently developed portion of the brain, which coordinates sensory and motor activities as well as being the seat of higher cognitive processes.

Character disorder. The old term for *personality disorder.*

Childhood onset pervasive developmental disorder. DSM-III term for a disorder of children older than thirty months but younger than twelve who indicate little empathy or emotional responsiveness to their peers, cling to their parents, take peculiar postures or make stereotyped movements, resist any change, have sudden anxieties and unexplained rages, and may occasionally be self-injurious; it replaced the DSM-II diagnosis of *childhood schizophrenia* and has been replaced in DSM-IIIR by *pervasive developmental disorder.*

Childhood schizophrenia. DSM-II diagnosis replaced by *childhood onset pervasive developmental disorder.*

Chlorpromazine. The generic term for one of the most widely prescribed antipsychotic drugs, sold under the name *Thorazine.*

Cholinergic system. All the nerve cells for which *acetylcholine* is the transmitter substance, in contrast to the *adrenergic,* or more precisely the *monoaminergic.*

Choreiform. Pertaining to the involuntary, spasmodic, jerking movements of the limbs and head found in *Huntington's chorea* and other nervous disorders.

Chromosomes. The threadlike bodies within the nucleus of the cell, DNA being the principal constituent; regarded as carrying the genes.

Chronic. Of lengthy duration or recurring frequently, often with progressing seriousness.

Chronic brain syndrome. See *senile dementia.*

Chronic schizophrenic. A *psychotic* patient who had earlier deteriorated over a long period of time and who has usually been hospitalized for more than two years.

Civil commitment. A procedure whereby a person can be legally certified as mentally ill and hospitalized, even against his will.

Classical conditioning. A basic form of learning, sometimes referred to as Pavlovian conditioning, in which a neutral stimulus is repeatedly paired with another stimulus (called the *unconditioned stimulus,* UCS) that naturally elicits a certain desired response (UCR). After repeated trials the neutral stimulus becomes a *conditioned stimulus* (CS) and evokes the same or similar response, called now the *conditioned response* (CR).

Classificatory variables. The characteristics that subjects bring with them into scientific investigations, such as sex, age, and mental status; studied by *correlational* research and *mixed designs.*

Client-centered therapy. A *humanistic-existential insight therapy,* developed by Carl Rogers, which emphasizes the importance of the therapist's understanding the client's subjective experiences and assisting him or her to gain more awareness of the current motivations for behavior; the goal is not only to reduce anxieties but also to foster actualization of the client's potential.

Clinical psychologist. An individual who has earned a Ph.D. degree in psychology or a Psy.D. and whose training has included an internship in a mental hospital or clinic.

Clinical psychology. The special area of psychology concerned with the study of psychopathology, its causes, prevention, and treatment.

Clitoris. The small, heavily innervated erectile structure located above the vaginal opening; the primary site of female responsiveness to sexual stimulation.

Clonic phase. The stage of violent contortions and jerking of limbs in a *grand mal epileptic* attack.

Cocaine. A pain-reducing, stimulating and addictive *alkaloid,* obtained from coca leaves, which increases mental powers, produces euphoria, heightens sexual desire, and in large doses causes *paranoia* and *hallucinations.*

Cognition. The process of knowing; the thinking, judging, reasoning, and planning activities of the human mind. Behavior is now often explained as depending on the course these processes take.

Cognitive restructuring. Any *behavior therapy* procedure that attempts to alter the manner in which clients think about life so that they change their overt behavior and emotions.

Cohort effects. The consequences of having been born in a given year and having grown up during a particular time period with its own unique pressures, problems, challenges, and opportunities. To be distinguished from *age effects.*

Coitus. Sexual intercourse.

Colic. A condition found in infants in which gas collects in the stomach and produces distress.

Community mental health. The delivery of services to needy, underserved groups through centers that offer outpatient therapy, short-term in-patient care, day hospitalization, twenty-four-hour emergency services, and consultation and education to other community agencies such as the police.

Community psychology. An approach to therapy that emphasizes prevention and the seeking out of potential difficulties rather than waiting for troubled individuals to initiate consultation. The location for professional activities tends to be in the persons' natural surroundings rather than in the therapist's office. See *prevention.*

Competency to stand trial. A legal decision on whether a person can participate meaningfully in his or her own defense.

Compulsion. The irresistible impulse to repeat an irrational act over and over again.

Concordance. As applied in *behavior genetics,* the similarity in psychiatric diagnosis or in other traits in a pair of twins.

Concurrent validity. See *validity.*

Concussion. A jarring injury to the brain produced by a blow to the head that usually involves a momentary loss of consciousness followed by transient disorientation and memory loss.

Conditioned response (CR). The response elicited by a given neutral stimulus (CS), after it has become conditioned by repeated contingent pairings with another stimulus (UCS) that naturally elicits the same or a similar response.

Conditioned stimulus (CS). A neutral stimulus that, after repeated contingent pairings with another stimulus (UCS) that naturally elicits a certain response (UCR), comes to elicit the same or a similar response, called the *conditioned response* (CR).

Conduct disorders. Patterns of extreme disobedience in youngsters, including theft, vandalism, lying, and early drug use; may be precursors of *antisocial personality* disorder.

Confabulation. Filling in gaps in memory caused by brain dysfunction with made-up and often improbable stories that the subject accepts as true.

Confidentiality. A principle observed by lawyers, doctors, pastors, psychologists, and psychiatrists that the goings-on in a professional and private relationship are not divulged to anyone else. See *privileged communication.*

Conflict. A state of being torn between competing forces.

Confounds. Variables whose effects are so intermixed that they cannot be measured separately, making the design of the *experiment* internally invalid and its results impossible to interpret.

Congenital. Existing at or before birth but not acquired through heredity.

Conjoint therapy. Couple or *family therapy* where partners are seen together, and children are seen with their parents and possibly with an extended family.

Construct. An entity inferred by a scientist to explain observed phenomena. See also *mediator.*

Contingency. A close relationship, especially of a causal nature, between two events, one of which regularly follows the other.

Control group. The subjects in an *experiment* for whom the *independent variable* is not manipulated, thus forming a *baseline* against which the effects of the manipulation of the experimental group can be evaluated.

Controlled drinking. A pattern of alcohol consumption that is moderate and avoids the extremes of total abstinence and of inebriation.

Conversion disorder. A *somatoform disorder* in which sensory or muscular functions are impaired, usually suggesting neurological disease, even though the bodily organs themselves are sound; *anesthesias* and paralyses of limbs are examples.

Convulsion. Violent and extensive twitching of the body caused by involuntary pathological muscle contractions.

Convulsive therapy. See *electroconvulsive therapy.*

Coronary heart disease. Angina pectoris, chest pains caused by insufficient supply of blood and thus oxygen to the heart; and myocardial infarction, or heart attack, in which the blood and oxygen supply is reduced so much that heart muscles are damaged.

Corpus callosum. The large band of nerve fibers connecting the two *cerebral hemispheres.*

Correlational method. The research strategy used to establish whether two or more variables are related. Such relationships may be positive—as values for one variable increase, those for the other do also; or negative—as values for one variable increase, those for the other decrease.

Cortisone. A hormone secreted by the adrenal cortices.

Co-twin. In *behavior genetics* research using the *twin method*, the member of the pair who is tested later to determine whether he has the same diagnosis or trait discovered earlier in his birth partner, the *index case* or *proband*.

Counseling psychology. A mental health specialty related to *clinical psychology* but usually concerned with less serious forms of maladjustment.

Counterconditioning. Relearning achieved by eliciting a new response in the presence of a particular stimulus.

Countertransference. Feelings that the *analyst* unconsciously directs to the *analysand* but that come from his or her own emotional vulnerabilities and unresolved *conflicts*.

Covert sensitization. A form of *aversion therapy* in which the subject is told to imagine the undesirably attractive situations and activities at the same time that unpleasant feelings are also induced by imagery.

Cretinism. A condition beginning in prenatal or early life characterized by *mental retardation* and physical deformities, caused by severe deficiency in the output of the *thyroid gland*.

Criminal commitment. A procedure whereby a person is confined in a mental institution either for determination of *competency to stand trial* or after acquittal by reason of insanity.

Critical period. A stage of early development in which an organism is susceptible to certain influences and during which important irreversible patterns of behavior are acquired. See *imprinting*.

Cross-dependent. Acting on the same receptors, as *methadone* does with *heroin;* see *heroin substitute*.

Cross-sectional research. Studies in which different age groups are compared at the same time. Compare with *longitudinal research*.

Crystallized intelligence. Semantic knowledge, such as grammar structure and conceptual knowledge. Tends to increase rather than decrease with age.

Cultural-familial retardation. A mild backwardness in mental development with no indication of brain pathology but evidence of similar limitation in at least one of the parents or siblings.

Cunnilingus. The oral stimulation of female genitalia.

Cushing's syndrome. An endocrine disorder usually affecting young women, produced by oversecretion of *cortisone* and marked by mood swings, irritability, agitation, and physical disfigurement.

Cyclical psychodynamics. The reciprocal relations between current behavior and repressed conflicts, such that they mutually reinforce each other.

Cyclothymic disorder. Swings between elation and depression, but not severe enough to warrant the diagnosis of *bipolar disorder*.

Defect theorist. In the study of *mental retardation*, a person who believes that the cognitive processes of retardates are qualitatively different from those of normal individuals; contrast with *developmental theorist*.

Defense mechanism. In psychoanalytic theory, a reality-distorting strategy unconsciously adopted to protect the ego from anxiety.

Delay of reward gradient. The learning theory term for the finding that rewards and punishments lose their effectiveness the farther in time they are removed from the response in question.

Delirium. A state of great mental confusion in which consciousness is clouded, attention cannot be sustained, and the stream of thought and speech is incoherent. The person is probably disoriented, emotionally erratic, restless or lethargic, and often has *illusions, delusions,* and *hallucinations*.

Delirium tremens (DTs). One of the *withdrawal* symptoms when a period of heavy alcohol consumption is terminated; marked by fever, sweating, trembling, cognitive impairment, and *hallucinations*.

Delta rhythm. See *slow brain waves*.

Delusion. A belief contrary to reality, firmly held in spite of evidence to the contrary; common in *paranoid disorders*. **Of control**, belief that one is being manipulated by some external force such as radar, TV, or a creature from outer space. **Of grandeur**, belief that one is an especially important or powerful person. **Of persecution**, belief that one is being plotted against or oppressed by others.

Delusional disorder. See *paranoid disorder*.

Delusional jealousy. The unfounded conviction that one's mate is unfaithful. The individual may collect small bits of "evidence" to justify the *delusion*.

Dementia. The deterioration of mental faculties—of memory, judgment, abstract thought, control of impulses, intellectual ability—that impairs social and occupational functioning and eventually changes the personality.

Dementia praecox. An older term for *schizophrenia*, chosen to describe what was believed to be an incurable and progressive deterioration of mental functioning beginning in adolescence.

Demographic variable. A varying characteristic that is a vital or social statistic of an individual, sample group, or population, for example, age, sex, *socioeconomic status*, racial origin, education, and the like.

Demonology. The doctrine that a person's abnormal behavior is caused by an autonomous evil spirit.

Denial. *Defense mechanism* in which a thought, feeling, or action is disavowed by the person.

Dependent personality. Lacking in self-confidence, people with a dependent personality passively allow others to run their lives and make no demands on them, lest they endanger these protective relationships.

Dependent variable. In a psychological *experiment*, the behavior that is measured and is expected to change with manipulation of the *independent variable.*

Depersonalization. An alteration in perception of the self in which the individual loses a sense of reality and feels estranged from the self and perhaps separated from the body. It may be a temporary reaction to stress and fatigue or part of *panic disorder, depersonalization disorder,* or *schizophrenia.*

Depersonalization disorder. A *dissociative disorder* in which the individual feels unreal and estranged from the self and surroundings enough to disrupt functioning. The patient may feel that the extremities have changed in size or that he or she watches the self from a distance.

Depression. An emotional state marked by great sadness and apprehension, feelings of worthlessness and guilt, withdrawal from others, loss of sleep, appetite, and sexual desire, or interest and pleasure in usual activities; and either lethargy or agitation. Called *major depression* in DSM-IIIR and *unipolar depression* by others. It can be an associated symptom of other disorders.

Derealization. Loss of the sense that the surroundings are real. It is present in several psychological disorders, such as *panic disorder, depersonalization disorder,* and *schizophrenia.*

Descriptive responsibility. In legal proceedings, the judgment that the accused performed an illegal act. Contrast with *ascriptive responsibility.*

Deterioration effect. In abnormal psychology, a harmful outcome from being in psychotherapy.

Detumescence. The flow of blood out of the genital area.

Developmental arithmetic disorder. Difficulties dealing with arithmetic symbols and operations.

Developmental language disorder. Difficulties understanding spoken language (receptive) or expressing thoughts verbally (expressive).

Developmental reading disorder. See *dyslexia.*

Developmental theorist. In the study of *mental retardation,* a person who believes that the cognitive development of retardates has simply been slower than that of normal individuals, and not qualitatively different. Contrast with *defect theorist.*

Diagnosis. The determination that the set of symptoms or problems of a patient indicates a particular disorder.

Diathesis. *Predisposition* toward a disease or abnormality.

Diathesis–stress paradigm. A view that, as applied in psychopathology, assumes that individuals predisposed toward a particular mental disorder will be particularly affected by stress and will then manifest abnormal behavior.

Dichotic listening. An experimental procedure in which a subject hears two taped messages simultaneously through earphones, one in each ear, usually with the instruction to attend to only one of the messages.

Diencephalon. The lower area of the forebrain, containing the *thalamus* and *hypothalamus.*

Direct analysis. John Rosen's variation of *psychoanalysis* in which the patient's *defense mechanisms* are attacked quickly, forcefully, and often graphically.

Directionality problem. A difficulty in *correlational* research whereby it is known that two variables are related, but it is unclear which is causing the other.

Disease. The medical concept that distinguishes an impairment of the normal state of the organism by its particular group of symptoms and its specific cause.

Disease model. See *medical model.*

Disorganized schizophrenic. A person with *schizophrenia* who has rather diffuse and regressive symptoms; the individual is given to silliness, facial grimaces, and inconsequential rituals and has constantly changeable moods and poor hygiene. There are few significant remissions and eventually considerable deterioration. This form of schizophrenia was formerly called *hebephrenia.*

Disorientation. A state of mental confusion with respect to time, place, identity of self, other persons, and objects.

Displacement. A *defense mechanism* whereby an emotional response is unconsciously redirected from a perhaps dangerous object or concept to a substitute less threatening to the *ego.*

Dissociation. A process whereby a group of mental processes is split off from the mainstream of consciousness, or behavior loses its relationship with the rest of the personality.

Dissociative disorders. Disorders in which the normal integration of consciousness, memory, or identity is suddenly and temporarily altered: *psychogenic amnesia, psychogenic fugue, multiple personality,* and *depersonalization disorder* are examples.

Dizygotic (fraternal) twins. Birth partners who have developed from separate fertilized eggs and who are only 50 percent alike genetically, no more so than siblings born from different pregnancies.

Dominant gene. One of a pair of *genes* that predominates over the other and determines that the *trait* it fosters will prevail in the *phenotype.*

Dopamine. A *catecholamine* that is both a precursor of *norepinephrine* and itself a *neurotransmitter* of the central nervous system. Disturbances in certain of its tracts apparently figure in *schizophrenia* and *Parkinson's disease.*

Double bind. An interpersonal situation in which an individual is confronted, over long periods of time, by mutually inconsistent messages to which she or he must respond, formerly believed by some theorists to cause *schizophrenia.*

Double-blind procedure. A method for reducing the biasing effects of the expectations of subject and experimenter; neither is allowed to know whether the *independent variable* of the *experiment* is being applied to the particular subject.

Down's syndrome (*mongolism*).   A form of *mental retardation* generally caused by an extra *chromosome*. The child's IQ is usually less than 50, and his or her physical characteristics are distinctive, the one most often noted being slanted eyes.

Dream analysis.   A key psychoanalytic technique in which the unconscious meanings of dream material are uncovered.

Drive.   A *construct* explaining the motivation of behavior, or an internal physiological tension impelling an organism to activity.

Drug abuse.   See *substance abuse.*

Drug addiction.   See *substance dependence.*

DSM-IIIR.   The current diagnostic and statistical manual of the American Psychiatric Association.

Dualism.   Philosophical doctrine that a human being is both mental and physical and that these two aspects are separate but interacting. It was advanced in its most definitive statement by Descartes. Contrast with *monism.*

Durham decision.   A 1954 American court ruling that an accused person is not *ascriptively responsible* if his or her crime is judged attributable to mental disease or defect.

Dysfunction.   An impairment or disturbance in the functioning of an organ, organ system, behavior, or cognition.

Dyslexia.   A disturbance in the ability to read; a *learning disability* or *specific developmental disorder.*

Dyspareunia.   Painful or difficult sexual intercourse, the pain or difficulty usually being caused by infection or a physical injury such as torn ligaments in the pelvic region.

Dysthymic disorder.   Long-lasting state of depression but not severe enough for the diagnosis of *major depression.*

Echolalia.   The immediate and sometimes pathological repetition of the words of others; a speech problem often found in autistic children. In **delayed echolalia** this inappropriate echoing takes places hours or weeks later.

Eclecticism.   In psychology, the view that more is to be gained by employing concepts from various theoretical systems than by restricting oneself to a single theory.

Ego.   In psychoanalytic theory, the predominantly conscious part of the personality, responsible for decision making and for dealing with reality.

Ego-alien.   Foreign to the self, such as a *compulsion.*

Ego analysis.   An important set of modifications of classical *psychoanalysis,* based on a conception of the human being as having a stronger, more autonomous ego with gratifications independent of *id* satisfactions. Sometimes called ego psychology.

Ego-dystonic homosexuality.   According to DSM-III, a disorder of people who are persistently dissatisfied with their

homosexuality and wish instead to be attracted to members of the opposite sex.

Egoistic suicide.   As defined by Durkheim, self-annihilation committed because the individual feels extreme alienation from others and from society.

Ejaculate.   To expel semen, typically during male orgasm.

Elective mutism.   A pattern of continuously refusing to speak in almost all social situations, including school, even though the child understands spoken language and is able to speak.

Electra complex.   See *Oedipus complex.*

Electrocardiograph.   A device for recording the electrical activity that occurs during the heartbeat.

Electroconvulsive therapy (ECT).   A treatment that produces a *convulsion* by passing electric current through the brain. It can be useful in alleviating profound *depression,* although sometimes an unpleasant and occasionally dangerous procedure.

Electroencephalogram (EEG).   A graphic recording of electrical activity of the brain, usually that of the *cerebral cortex,* but sometimes the electrical activity of lower areas.

Empathy.   Awareness and understanding of another's feelings and thoughts. See *primary empathy* and *advanced accurate empathy.*

Empty-chair technique.   A *Gestalt therapy* procedure for helping the client become more aware of denied feelings; the client talks to important people or to feelings as though they were present and seated in a nearby vacant chair.

Encephalitis.   Inflammation of brain tissue caused by a number of agents, the most important being several viruses carried by insects.

Encephalitis lethargica.   Known as sleeping sickness, a form of encephalitis that occurred earlier in this century and was characterized by lethargy and prolonged periods of sleeping.

Encopresis.   A disorder in which, through faulty control of the sphincters, the person repeatedly defecates in his or her clothing after an age at which continence is expected.

Encounter group.   See *sensitivity group.*

Endocrine gland.   Any of a number of ductless glands that release *hormones* directly into the blood or lymph. The secretions of some endocrine glands increase during emotional arousal.

Endogenous.   Attributable to internal causes.

Endorphins.   *Opiates* produced within the body; they may have an important role in the processes by which the body builds up *tolerance* to drugs and is distressed by their *withdrawal.*

Enuresis.   A disorder in which, through faulty control of the bladder, the person wets repeatedly during the night (nocturnal enuresis) or during the day after an age at which continence is expected.

Enzyme.   A complex protein produced by the cells to act as a catalyst in regulating metabolic activities.

Epidemiology.   The study of the frequency and distribution of illness in a population.

Epilepsy.   An altered state of consciousness accompanied by sudden changes in the usual rhythmical electrical activity of the brain. See also *grand mal, petit mal, Jacksonian,* and *psychomotor epilepsy.*

Epinephrine.   A hormone (a *catecholamine*) secreted by the medulla of the *adrenal gland;* its effects are similar, but not identical, to those of stimulating the *sympathetic* nerves. It causes an increase in blood pressure, inhibits peristaltic movements, and liberates glucose from the liver. Also called *adrenalin.*

Ergot.   See *LSD.*

Erogenous.   Capable of giving sexual pleasure when stimulated.

Eros (libido).   Freud's term for the life-integrating instinct or force of the *id,* sometimes equated with sexual drive. Compare *Thanatos.*

Essential hypertension.   A *psychophysiological disorder* characterized by high blood pressure that cannot be traced to an organic cause. Over the years it causes enlargement and degeneration of small arteries, enlargement of the heart, and kidney damage.

Estrogen.   A female sex hormone produced especially in the ovaries that stimulates the development and maintains the secondary sex characteristics, such as breast enlargement.

Etiological validity.   See *validity.*

Etiology.   All the factors that contribute to the development of an illness or disorder.

Eugenics.   The field concerned with improving the hereditary qualities of the human race through social control of mating and reproduction.

Ex post facto analysis.   In *correlational research,* an attempt to reduce the *third-variable problem* by picking subjects who are matched on characteristics that may be *confounds.*

Excitement phase.   As applied by Masters and Johnson, the first stage of sexual arousal that is initiated by any appropriate stimulus.

Executive functioning.   The *cognitive* capacity to plan how to do a task, how to devise strategies, and how to monitor one's performance.

Exhibitionism.   Marked preference for obtaining sexual gratification by exposing one's genitals to an unwilling observer.

Existential analysis.   See *humanistic-existential therapy.*

Exogenous.   Attributable to external causes.

Exogenous depression.   A profound sadness assumed to be caused by an environmental event.

Exorcism.   The casting out of evil spirits by ritualistic chanting or torture.

Experiment.   The most powerful research technique for determining causal relationships, requiring the manipulation of an *independent variable,* the measurement of a *depen-*

dent variable, and the *random assignment* of subjects to the several different conditions being investigated.

Experimental hypothesis.   What the investigator assumes will happen in a scientific investigation if certain conditions are met or particular variables are manipulated.

Expressed emotion.   In the literature on *schizophrenia,* the amount of hostility and criticism directed from other people to the patient, usually within a family.

External validity.   See *validity.*

Extinction.   The elimination of a classically *conditioned response* by the omission of the *unconditioned stimulus.* In *operant conditioning,* the elimination of the conditioned response by the omission of *reinforcement.*

Extradural hematoma.   Hemorrhage and swelling between the skull and dura mater when a *meningeal* artery is ruptured by a fractured bone of the skull.

Extroversion.   See *introversion—extroversion.*

Factitious disorder.   A disorder in which the individual's physical or psychological symptoms appear under voluntary control and are adopted merely to assume the role of a sick person. This goal is not voluntary, however, and implies a severe disturbance. Compare with *malingering.*

Falsifiability.   See *testability.*

Familiar.   In witchcraft, a supernatural spirit often embodied in an animal and at the service of a person.

Family interaction method.   A procedure for studying family behavior by observing their interaction in a structured laboratory situation.

Family method.   A research strategy in *behavior genetics* in which the frequency of a *trait* or of abnormal behavior is determined in relatives who have varying percentages of shared genetic background.

Family systems.   A general approach to etiology and treatment that focuses on the complex interrelationships within families.

Family therapy.   A form of *group therapy* in which members of a family are helped to relate better to one another.

Fear-drive.   In the Mowrer–Miller theory, an unpleasant internal state that impels avoidance. The necessity to reduce a fear-drive can form the basis for new learning.

Fear-response.   In the Mowrer–Miller theory, a response to a threatening or noxious situation that is covert and unobservable but that is assumed to function as a stimulus to produce measurable physiological changes in the body and observable overt behavior.

Fellatio.   Oral stimulation of the *penis.*

Female sexual arousal disorder.   Formally called frigidity; the inability of a female to reach or maintain the lubrication swelling stage of sexual excitement, or the inability to enjoy a subjective sense of pleasure or excitement during sexual activity.

Fetal alcohol syndrome.   Retarded growth of the developing fetus and infant; cranial, facial, and limb anomalies, and *mental retardation* caused by heavy consumption of alcohol by the future mother during pregnancy.

Fetishism.   A reliance on an inanimate object for sexual arousal.

First-rank symptoms.   In *schizophrenia,* specific *delusions* and *hallucinations* proposed by Schneider as particularly important for its more exact diagnosis.

Fixation.   In psychoanalytic theory, the arrest of *psychosexual* development at a particular stage through too much or too little gratification at that stage.

Flashback.   An unpredictable recurrence of *psychedelic* experiences from an earlier drug trip.

Flat affect.   A deviation in emotional response wherein virtually no emotion is expressed whatever the stimuli, emotional expressiveness is blunted, or a lack of expression and muscle tone is noted in the face.

Flight of ideas.   A symptom of *mania* that involves a rapid shift from one subject to another in conversation with only superficial associative connections.

Flooding therapy.   A *behavior therapy* procedure in which a fearful person exposes himself or herself to what is frightening, in reality or in the imagination, for extended periods of time and without opportunity for escape.

Fluid intelligence.   Involves short-term memory, abstract thinking, creativity, and reaction time speed. Tends to decline with age.

Follow-up study.   A research procedure whereby individuals observed in an earlier investigation are contacted at a later time.

Forced-choice item.   A format of a *personality inventory* in which the response alternatives for each item are equated for *social desirability.*

Forensic psychiatry or psychology.   The branch of psychiatry or psychology that deals with the legal questions raised by disordered behavior.

Fragile X syndrome.   Associated with *moderate mental retardation;* a malformation of the X chromosome, and in some cases the chromosome may break in two. Symptoms include large, underdeveloped ears, long thin face, broad nasal root, and enlarged testicles in males, and many persons show attention deficits and hyperactivity.

Free association.   A key psychoanalytic procedure, in which the *analysand* is encouraged to give free rein to his or her thoughts and feelings, verbalizing whatever comes into the mind without monitoring its content. The assumption is that, over time, hitherto *repressed* material will come forth for examination by the analysand and *analyst.*

Freebase.   The most potent part of *cocaine,* obtained by heating the drug with ether.

Free-floating anxiety.   Continual anxiety not attributable to any specific situation or reasonable danger. See *generalized anxiety disorder.*

Frontal lobe.   The forward or upper half of each *cerebral hemisphere,* in front of the *central sulcus,* that is active in reasoning and other higher mental processes.

Fugue.   See *psychogenic fugue.*

Functional psychosis.   A condition in which thought, behavior, and emotion are disturbed without known pathological changes in tissues or the conditions of the brain.

Galvanic skin response (GSR).   A change in electric conductivity of the skin caused by an increase in activity of sweat glands when the *sympathetic nervous system* is active, in particular when the organism is anxious.

Gay.   A colloquial term for a homosexual, now often adopted by homosexuals who have openly announced their sexual orientation.

Gay liberation.   The often militant movement seeking to achieve civil rights for homosexuals and recognition of the normality of *homosexuality.*

Gender identity.   The deeply ingrained sense a person has of being either a man or a woman.

Gender identity disorders.   Disorders in which there is a deeply felt incongruence between anatomic sex and the sensed gender; *transsexualism* and *gender identity disorder of childhood* are examples.

Gene.   An ultramicroscopic area of the *chromosome,* the gene is the smallest physical unit of the DNA molecule that carries a piece of heredity information.

General paresis.   See *neurosyphilis.*

Generalized anxiety disorder.   One of the *anxiety disorders,* where anxiety is so chronic, persistent, and pervasive that it seems *free-floating.* The individual is jittery and strained, distractible and apprehensive that something bad is about to happen. A pounding heart, fast pulse and breathing, sweating, flushing, muscle aches, a lump in the throat, and an upset gastrointestinal tract are some of the bodily indications of this extreme anxiety.

Genital stage.   In psychoanalytic theory, the final *psychosexual stage* reached in adulthood, in which heterosexual interests predominate.

Genotype.   An individual's unobservable, physiological genetic constitution; the totality of *genes* possessed by an individual. Compare *phenotype.*

Germ theory.   The general view in medicine that disease is caused by infection of the body by minute organisms and viruses.

Gerontology.   The interdisciplinary study of aging and of the special problems of the aged.

Gestalt therapy.   A *humanistic therapy,* developed by Fritz Perls, that encourages clients to satisfy emerging needs so that their innate goodness can be expressed, to increase their awareness of unacknowledged feelings, and to reclaim parts of the personality that have been denied or disowned.

Gestation period.   The length of time, normally nine months in human beings, during which a fertilized egg develops into an infant ready to be born.

Glans.   The heavily innervated tip of the *penis.*

Glove anesthesia.　A hysterical lack of sensation in the part of the hand that would usually be covered by a glove.

Grand mal epilepsy.　The most severe form of *epilepsy*, involving loss of consciousness and violent *convulsions*.

Grandiosity.　An inflated appraisal of one's worth, power, knowledge, importance, or identity.

Graves' disease.　An endocrine disorder resulting from oversecretion of the hormone *thyroxin,* in which metabolic processes are speeded up, producing apprehension, restlessness, and irritability.

Gray matter.　The neural tissue made up largely of nerve cell bodies that constitutes the cortex covering the *cerebral hemisphere,* the *nuclei* in lower brain areas, columns of the spinal cord, and the ganglia of the *autonomic nervous system.*

Grimace.　A distorted facial expression, often a symptom of *schizophrenia.*

Group therapy.　Method of treating psychological disorders whereby several persons are seen simultaneously by a single therapist.

Gyrus.　A ridge or convolution of the *cerebral cortex.*

Habituation.　In physiology, a process whereby an organism's response to the same stimulus temporarily lessens with repeated presentations.

Halfway house.　A homelike residence for people who are considered too disturbed to remain in their accustomed surroundings but do not require the total care of a mental institution.

Hallucination.　A perception in any sensory modality without relevant and adequate external stimuli.

Hallucinogen.　A drug or chemical whose effects include *hallucinations.* Hallucinogenic drugs such as *LSD, psyilocybin,* and *mescaline* are often called *psychedelic.*

Hashish.　The dried resin of the *Cannabis* plant, stronger in its effects than the dried leaves and stems that constitute *marijuana.*

Health psychology.　A branch of psychology dealing with the role of psychological factors in health and illness.

Hebephrenia.　See *disorganized schizophrenic.*

Helplessness.　A *construct* referring to the sense of having no control over important events; considered by many theorists to play a central role in *anxiety* and *depression.* See *learned helplessness.*

Hermaphrodite.　A person with parts of both male and female genitalia.

Heroin.　An extremely addictive *narcotic* drug derived from *morphine.*

Heroin antagonist.　Drugs, like naxolone, which prevent a heroin user from experiencing any high.

Heroin substitute.　Narcotics, like *methadone,* which are *cross-dependent* with *heroin* and thereby replace it and the body's craving for it.

Heterosexual.　One who desires or engages in sexual relations with members of the opposite sex.

Hidden observer.　In hypnosis, the part of the self that is aware of things outside conscious awareness.

High-risk method.　A research technique involving the intensive examination of people who have a high probability of later becoming abnormal.

Histrionic personality.　This person is overly dramatic and given to emotional excess, impatient with minor annoyances, immature, dependent on others, and often sexually seductive, without taking responsibility for flirtations. Formerly called hysterical personality.

Homophobia.　Fear of *homosexuality.*

Homosexuality.　Sexual desire or activity directed toward a member of one's own sex.

Homovanillic avid.　A major metabolite of *dopamine.*

Hormone.　A chemical substance produced by an *endocrine gland* and released into the blood or lymph for the purpose of controlling the function of a distant organ or organ system. Metabolism, growth, and development of secondary sexual characteristics are among the functions so controlled.

Humanistic-existential therapy.　A generic term for an *insight* psychotherapy that emphasizes the individual's subjective experiences, free will, and ever-present ability to decide on a new life course.

Huntington's chorea.　A fatal *presenile dementia*, passed on by a single *dominant gene.* The symptoms includes spasmodic jerking of the limbs, psychotic behavior, and mental deterioration.

5-Hydroxyindoleacetic acid (5-HIAA).　The major metabolite of *serotonin* that is present in the cerebrospinal fluid.

Hyperactivity.　See *attention-deficit hyperactivity disorder.*

Hyperkinesis.　See *hyperactivity.*

Hypertension.　Abnormally high arterial blood pressure, with or without known organic causes. See *essential hypertension.*

Hyperventilation.　Very rapid and deep breathing associated with high levels of anxiety that causes level of carbon dioxide in blood to be lowered with possible loss of consciousness.

Hypnosis.　A trancelike state or behavior resembling sleep, characterized primarily by increased suggestibility and induced by suggestion.

Hypoactive sexual desire disorder.　The absence of or deficient sexual fantasies and urges.

Hypochondriasis.　A *somatoform disorder* in which the person, misinterpreting rather ordinary physical sensations, is preoccupied with fears of having a serious disease and is not dissuaded by medical opinion. Difficult to distinguish from *somatization disorder.*

Hypomania.　An above-normal elevation of mood, but not as extreme as *mania.*

Hypothalamus.　A collection of *nuclei* and fibers in the lower part of the *diencephalon,* concerned with the regulation of many visceral processes, such as metabolism, temperature, water balance, and so on.

Hysteria (hysterical state). A disorder, known to the ancient Greeks, in which a physical incapacity, a paralysis, an anesthesia, or an analgesia, is not due to a physiological dysfunction, for example, *glove anesthesia;* an older term for *conversion disorder.* In the late nineteenth century *dissociative disorders* were identified as such and considered hysterical states.

Hysterical neurosis. The DSM-II category for *dissociative* and *somatoform disorders.*

Id. In psychoanalytic theory, that part of the personality present at birth, composed of all the energy of the *psyche,* and expressed as biological urges that strive continually for gratification.

Ideas of reference. *Delusional* thinking that reads personal significance into seemingly trivial remarks and activities of others and completely unrelated events.

Identity crisis. A developmental period in adolescence marked by concerns about who one is and what one is going to do with his or her life.

Idiographic. In psychology, relating to investigative procedures that consider the unique characteristics of a single person, studying them in depth, as in the *case study.* Contrast with *nomothetic.*

Idiot savant. An individual with a rare form of *mental retardation,* being extraordinarily talented in one or a few limited areas of intellectual achievement.

Illusion. A misperception of a real external stimulus, such as hearing the slapping of waves as footsteps.

Imipramine. An *antidepressant drug,* one of the *tricyclic* group.

Imprinting. The irreversible acquisition of behavior by a neonate of a social species during a *critical period* of development. The neonate is attracted to and mimics the first moving object seen, thereby acquiring specific patterns of behavior.

In absentia. Literally, "in one's absence." Courts are concerned that a person be able to participate personally and meaningfully in his or her own trial and not be tried *in absentia* because of a distracting mental disorder.

In vivo. As applied in psychology, taking place in a real-life situation.

Inappropriate affect. Emotional responses that are out of context, such as laughter when hearing sad news.

Incest. Sexual relations between close relatives for whom marriage is forbidden, most often between daughter and father or between brother and sister.

Incidence. In community studies of a particular disorder, the rate at which new cases occur in a given place at a given time; compare with *prevalence.*

Incoherence. In *schizophrenia,* an aspect of *thought disorder* wherein verbal expression is marked by disconnect-

edness, fragmented thoughts, jumbled phrases, and *neologisms.*

Independent variable. In a psychological *experiment,* the factor, experience, or treatment that is under the control of the experimenter and that is expected to have an effect on the subjects as assessed by changes in the *dependent variable.*

Index case. The person who in a genetic investigation bears the diagnosis or *trait* that the investigator is interested in: same as *proband.*

Indoleamines. *Monoamine* compounds (NH_2), each containing an indole portion (C_8H_7N); indoleamines believed to act in neurotransmission are *serotonin* and tryptamine.

Infectious disease. An illness caused when a microorganism, such as a bacterium or a virus, invades the body, multiplies, and attacks a specific organ or organ system; pneumonia is an example.

Informed consent. The agreement of a person to serve as a research subject or to enter therapy after being told the possible outcomes, both benefits and risks.

Inhibited female orgasm. A recurrent and persistent delay or absence of orgasm in a woman during sexual activity adequate in focus, intensity, and duration; in many instances the woman may experience considerable sexual excitement nonetheless.

Inhibited male orgasm. A recurrent and persistent delay or absence of ejaculation after an adequate phase of sexual excitement.

Inhibited sexual desire. Sexual interest that is less than the individual, the partner, or both regard as sufficient.

Inhibited sexual excitement. A recurrent and persistent lack of sexual excitement during sexual activity. The new tern for *impotence* in men, frigidity in women. See also *inhibited female orgasm.*

Insanity defense. The legal argument that a defendant should not be held *ascriptively responsible* for an illegal act if the conduct is attributable to mental illness.

Insight therapy. The general term for any *psychotherapy* that attempts to impart greater awareness to a patient of what motivates his or her behavior, the assumption being that disordered behavior is caused by *repression* or other unconscious *conflicts.*

Instrumental learning. See *operant conditioning.*

Intelligence quotient (IQ). A standardized measure indicating how far an individual's raw score on an *intelligence test* falls away from the average raw score of his or her chronological age group.

Intelligence test. A standardized means of assessing a person's current mental ability, for example, the Stanford–Binet test and the Wechsler Adult Intelligence Scale.

Internal validity. See *validity.*

Interpretation. In *psychoanalysis,* a key procedure in which the *analyst* points out to the *analysand* where *resistances* exist and what certain dreams and verbalizations reveal about impulses repressed in the *unconscious;* more generally, any statement by a therapist that construes the client's problem in a new way.

Introjection. In psychoanalytic theory, the unconscious incorporation of the values, attitudes, and qualities of another person into the individual's own ego structure.

Intromission. Insertion of *penis* into *vagina* or anus.

Introspective method. A procedure whereby trained subjects are asked to report on their conscious experiences. This was the principal method of study in early twentieth-century psychology.

Involutional melancholia. A *mood disorder* characterized by profound sadness and occurring at a person's *climacteric* in late middle age; a DSM-II diagnosis that does not appear in DSM-IIIR.

Irrational beliefs. Self-defeating assumptions that are assumed by *rational-emotive* therapists to underlie psychological distress.

Irresistible impulse. The term used in an 1834 Ohio court ruling on criminal responsibility in which it was decided that an *insanity defense* can be established by proving that the accused had an uncontrollable urge to perform the act.

Jacksonian epilepsy. A form of *epilepsy* in which muscle spasms are limited to a particular part of the body.

Korsakoff's psychosis. A chronic brain disorder associated with *Wernicke's disease* and marked by loss of recent memories and associated *confabulation*, and by additional lesions in the *thalamus*.

La belle indifférence. The blasé attitude people with *conversion disorder* have toward their symptoms.

Labelling theory. The general view that serious pyschopathology, like *schizophrenia*, is caused by society's reactions to unusual behavior.

Labile. Easily moved or changed, quickly shifting from one emotion to another or easily aroused.

Laceration. A jagged wound; in the brain, a tearing of tissue by an object entering the skull, often causing paralysis, change in personality, intellectual impairment, and even death.

Latency period. In psychoanalytic theory, the years between ages six and twelve during which *id* impulses play a minor role in motivation.

Latent content. In dreams, the presumed true meaning hidden behind the *manifest content*.

Learned helplessness. An individual's passivity and sense of being unable to act and to control his or her life, acquired through unpleasant experiences and traumas in which efforts made were ineffective; according to Seligman, this brings on *depression*.

Learning disabilities. Problems in mastering reading, arithmetic, or speech that are not caused by *mental retardation*, impairment of visual or auditory functions, other psycho-

logical disorders, or cultural disadvantage. Called *specific developmental disorders* in DSM-IIIR.

Learning paradigm. As applied in abnormal psychology, a set of assumptions that abnormal behavior is learned in the same way as other human behavior.

Least restrictive alternative. The legal principle according to which a committed mental patient must be treated in a setting that imposes as few restrictions as possible on his or her freedom.

Lesbian. Female homosexual.

Lesion. Any localized abnormal structural change in organ or tissue caused by disease or injury.

Libido. See *Eros*.

Lifespan developmental psychology. The study of changes in people as they grow from infancy to old age.

Life Change Unit (LCU) **score.** A score produced by totaling ratings of the stressfulness of recently experienced life events; high scores are found to be related to the contracting of a number of physical illnesses.

Limbic system. The lower parts of the *cerebrum* made up of primitive cortex that controls visceral and bodily changes associated with emotion and regulates drive-motivated behavior.

Linkage analysis. A technique in genetic research where occurrence of a disorder in a family is evaluated alongside a known genetic marker.

Lithium carbonate. A drug useful in treating both *mania* and *depression* in *bipolar disorder*.

Lobotomy. A brain operation in which the nerve pathways between the *frontal lobes* of the brain and the *thalamus* and *hypothalamus* are cut in hopes of effecting beneficial behavioral change.

Logotherapy. Existential *psychotherapy* developed by Viktor Frankl, aimed at helping the demoralized client restore meaning to life by placing his or her suffering in a larger spiritual and philosophical context. The individual assumes responsibility for his or her existence and for pursuing a meaningful life.

Longitudinal research. Investigation that collects information on the same individuals repeatedly over time, perhaps many years, in an effort to determine how phenomena change. Compare with *cross-sectional research*.

Loose association. In *schizophrenia*, an aspect of *thought disorder* wherein the patient has difficulty sticking to one topic and drifts off on a train of associations evoked by an idea from the past.

LSD (*d*-lysergic acid diethylamide). A drug synthesized in 1938 and discovered to be a *hallucinogen* in 1943. It is derived from lysergic acid, the principal constituent of the *alkaloids* of ergot, a grain fungus that in earlier centuries brought on epidemics of spasmodic ergotism, a nervous disorder sometimes marked by *psychotic* symptoms.

Luria–Nebraska test. A battery of *neuropsychological* tests that can detect impairment in different parts of the brain.

Magical thinking. The conviction of the individual that his or her thoughts, words, and actions may in some manner cause or prevent outcomes in a way that defies the normal laws of cause and effect.

Mainstreaming. A policy of placing handicapped children in regular classrooms; special classes are provided for them as needed, but they share as much as possible in the opportunities and ambience afforded normal youngsters.

Major depression. A disorder of individuals who have experienced episodes of *depression* but not of *mania;* DSM-IIIR term. Also called *unipolar depression.*

Male erectile disorder. Formerly known as impotence; the inability of a male to become erect or to sustain erection through sexual activity, or the inability to enjoy a subjective sense of pleasure or excitement during sexual activity.

Malingering. Faking a physical or psychological incapacity in order to avoid a responsibility or gain an end; the goal is readily recognized from the individual's circumstances. To be distinguished from *conversion disorder,* in which the incapacity is assumed to be beyond voluntary control.

Malleus Maleficarum ("the witches' hammer"). A manual written by two Dominican monks in the fifteenth century to provide rules for identifying and trying witches.

Mammillary body. Either of two small rounded structures located in the *hypothalamus* and consisting of *nuclei.*

Mania. An emotional state of intense but unfounded elation evidenced in talkativeness, *flight of ideas* and distractibility, grandiose plans, and spurts of purposeless activity. Called *bipolar disorder* in DSM-IIIR.

Manic-depressive illness, manic-depressive psychosis. Originally described by Kraepelin, a *mood disorder* characterized by alternating euphoria and profound sadness or by one of these moods. Called *bipolar disorder* in DSM-IIIR.

Manifest content. The immediately apparent, conscious content of dreams; compare with *latent content.*

Marathon group. A group session run continuously for a day or even longer, typically for *sensitivity training,* the assumption being that defenses can be worn down by the physical and psychological fatigue generated through intensive and continuous group interaction.

Marijuana. A drug derived from the dried and ground leaves and stems of the female hemp plant, *Cannabis sativa.*

Marital therapy. Any professional intervention that treats relationship problems of a couple.

Masochism. A marked preference for obtaining or increasing sexual gratification through subjection to pain.

Masturbation. Self-stimulation of the genitals, typically to *orgasm.*

M'Naghten rule. A British court decision of 1843 that stated that an *insanity defense* can be established by proving that the defendant did not know what he was doing or did not realize that it was wrong.

Mediation theory. In psychology, the general view that certain stimuli do not directly initiate an overt response but activate an intervening process, which in turn initiates the response. It explains thinking, drives, emotions, and beliefs in terms of stimulus and response.

Mediator. In psychology, an inferred state intervening between the observable stimulus and response, being activated by the stimulus and in turn initiating the response; in more general terms, a thought, drive, emotion, or belief. Also called a *construct.*

Medical model (disease model). As applied in abnormal psychology, a set of assumptions that conceptualizes abnormal behavior as being similar to physical diseases.

Medulla oblongata. An area in the *brain stem* through which nerve fiber tracts ascend to or descend from higher brain centers.

Megalomania. A paranoid *delusion* of *grandeur* in which an individual believes himself to be an important person or to be carrying out great plans.

Melancholia. A vernacular diagnosis of several millenniums' standing for profound sadness and depression. In *major depression* with melancholia the individual is unable to feel better even momentarily when something good happens, regularly feels worse in the morning and awakens early, and suffers a deepening of other symptoms of depression.

Meninges. The three layers of nonneural tissue that envelop the brain and spinal cord. They are the dura mater, the arachnoid, and the pia mater.

Meningitis. An inflammation of the *meninges* through infection, usually by a bacterium, or through irritation. **Meningococcal,** the epidemic form of the disease caused by *Neisseria meningitidis,* takes the life of 10 percent who contract it and causes cerbral palsy, hearing loss, speech defects, and other forms of permanent brain damage in one of four who recover.

Mental age. The numerical index of an individual's cognitive development determined by standardized *intelligence tests.*

Mental retardation. Subnormal intellectual functioning associated with impairment in social adjustment and identified at an early age.

Meprobamate. Generic term for *Miltown,* an *anxiolytic,* the first introduced and for a time one of the most widely used.

Mescaline. A *hallucinogen* and *alkaloid* that is the active ingredient of *peyote.*

Mesmerize. The first term for hypnotize, after Franz Anton Mesmer, an Austrian physician who in the late eighteenth century treated, and cured, hysterical or *conversion disorders* by what he considered the animal magnetism emanating from his body and permeating the universe.

Meta-analysis. A quantitative method of analyzing and comparing various therapies by standardizing their results.

Metabolism. The sum of the intracellular processes by which large molecules are broken down into smaller ones, releasing energy and wastes, and by which small molecules are built up into new living matter by consuming energy.

Metacognition. The knowledge people have about the way they know their world, such as recognizing the usefulness of a map if one has to find one's way in a new city.

Methadone. A synthetic addictive *heroin substitute* for treating *heroin* addicts that acts as a substitute for heroin by eliminating its effects and the craving for it.

Methedrine. A very strong *amphetamine*, sometimes shot directly into the veins.

3-Methoxy-4-hydroxyphenylethylene glycol (MHPG). A major metabolite of *norepinephrine*.

Midbrain. The middle part of the brain that consists of a mass of nerve fiber tracts connecting the spinal cord and *pons*, *medulla*, and *cerebellum* to the *cerebral cortex*.

Migraine headache. Extremely debilitating headache caused by sustained dilation of the extracranial arteries, the temporal artery in particular; the dilated arteries trigger pain-sensitive nerve fibers in the scalp.

Mild mental retardation. A limitation in mental development measured on IQ tests at between 50–55 and 70; children with such a limitation are considered the educable mentally retarded and are placed in special classes.

Milieu therapy. A treatment procedure that attempts to make the total environment and all personnel and patients of the hospital a *therapeutic community,* conducive to psychological improvement; the staff conveys to the patients the expectation that they can and will behave more normally and responsibly.

Miltown. The trade name for *meprobamate,* one of the principal *anxiolytics.*

Minimal brain damage. The term sometimes applied to *hyperactive* children, reflecting the belief that at least some of these youngsters suffer from minor brain defects.

Minnesota Multiphasic Personality Inventory (MMPI). A lengthy *personality inventory* by which an individual is diagnosed through his true–false replies to groups of statements indicating states such as *anxiety, depression,* masculinity–femininity, and paranoia.

Mixed design. A research strategy in which both *classificatory* and *experimental* variables are used; assigning subjects from discrete populations to two experimental conditions is an example.

Model. A set of concepts from one domain applied to another by analogy. For example, in trying to understand the brain we may assume that it functions like a computer.

Modeling. Learning by observing and imitating the behavior of others.

Moderate mental retardation. A limitation in mental development measured on IQ tests between 35–40 and 50–55; children with this degree of retardation are often institutionalized, and their training is focused on self-care rather than development of intellectual skills.

Modified leucotomy. A surgical procedure that severs an area near the *corpus callosum* to relieve *obsessive-compulsive disorders.*

Mongolism. See *Down's syndrome.*

Monism. Philosophical doctrine that ultimate reality is a unitary organic whole and that therefore mental and physical are one and the same. Contrast with *dualism.*

Monoamine. An organic compound containing nitrogen in one amino group (NH_2). Some of the known *neurotransmitters* of the central nervous system, called collectively brain amines, are *catecholamines* and *indoleamines,* which are monoamines.

Monoamine oxidase (MAO). An enzyme that deactivates *catecholamines* and *indoleamines* within the presynaptic *neuron,* indoleamines in the *synapse.*

Monoamine oxidase inhibitors. A group of *antidepressant* drugs that keep the enzyme *monoamine oxidase* from deactivating *neurotransmitters* of the central nervous system.

Monozygotic twins. Genetically identical siblings who have developed from a single fertilized egg.

Mood disorder. A disorder in which there are disabling disturbances in emotion.

Moral anxiety. In psychoanalytic theory, the *ego's* fear of punishment for failure to adhere to the *superego's* standards of proper conduct.

Moral treatment. A therapeutic regimen, introduced by Philippe Pinel during the French Revolution, whereby mental patients were released from their restraints and were treated with compassion and dignity rather than with contempt and denigration. *Milieu therapy* gives patients similar encouraging attention.

Morbidity risk. The probability that an individual will develop a particular disorder.

Morphine. An addictive narcotic *alkaloid* extracted from *opium,* used primarily as an analgesic and as a *sedative.*

Mourning work. In Freud's theory of *depression,* the recall by a depressed person of memories associated with a lost one, serving to separate the individual from the deceased.

Multiaxial. Having several dimensions, each of which is employed in categorizing; the DSM-IIIR is an example.

Multifactorial. Referring to the operation of several variables influencing in complex fashion the development or maintenance of a phenomenon.

Multiple-baseline design. An experimental design in which two behaviors of a single subject are selected for study and a treatment is applied to one of them. The behavior that is not treated serves as a baseline against which the effects of the treatment can be determined. This is a common design in operant research.

Multiple personality. A very rare *dissociative disorder* in which two or more fairly distinct and separate personalities are present within the same individual, each of them with its own memories, relationships, and behavior patterns and only one of them dominant at any given time.

Mutism. The inability or refusal to speak.

Myocardial infarction. See *coronary heart disease.*

Myxedema. An endocrine disorder of adults produced by thyroid deficiency; metabolic processes are slowed, and the patient becomes lethargic, slow-thinking, and depressed.

Narcissistic personality. Extremely selfish and self-centered, people with a narcissistic personality have a grandiose view of their uniqueness, achievements, and talents and an insatiable craving for admiration and approval from others. They are exploitative to achieve their own goals and expect much more from others than they themselves are willing to give.

Narcosynthesis. A psychiatric procedure originating during World War II in which a drug was employed to help stressed soldiers recall the battle trauma underlying their disorder.

Narcotic. One of the addictive *sedative* drugs, for example, *morphine* and *heroin,* that in moderate doses relieve pain and induce sleep.

Negative symptoms. In *schizophrenia,* these are behavioral deficits such as *flat affect* and *apathy.*

Negativism. A tendency to behave in a manner opposite to the desires of others or to what is expected or requested.

Neo-Freudian. A person who has contributed to the modification and extension of Freudian theory.

Neologism. A word made up by the speaker that is usually meaningless to a listener.

Neoplasm. See *tumor.*

Neurodermatitis. A chronic (*psychophysiological*) disorder in which patches of skin become inflamed.

Neuroleptic. A *psychoactive drug,* such as *Thorazine,* that reduces *psychotic* symptoms but has side effects resembling symptoms of neurological diseases.

Neurology. The scientific study of the nervous system, especially its structure, functions, and abnormalities.

Neuron. A single nerve cell.

Neuropsychological tests. Psychological tests, like the *Luria-Nebraska,* which can detect impairment in different parts of the brain.

Neuropsychology. A psychological specialty concerned with the relationships among cognition, affect, and behavior on the one hand, and brain function on the other.

Neurosis. One of a large group of nonpsychotic disorders characterized by unrealistic *anxiety* and other associated problems, for example, phobic avoidances, *obsessions,* and *compulsions.*

Neurosyphilis (general paresis). Infection of the central nervous system by the spirochete *Treponema pallidum* that destroys brain tissue; marked by eye disturbances, tremors, and disordered speech as well as severe intellectual deterioration and *psychotic* symptoms.

Neurotic anxiety. In psychoanalytic theory, a fear of the consequences of expressing previously punished and repressed id impulses; more generally, unrealistic fear.

Neurotransmitter. A chemical substance important in transferring a nerve impulse from one *neuron* to another.

Niacin. One of the complex of B vitamins.

Nicotine. The principal *alkaloid* of tobacco and its addicting agent.

Niemann–Pick disease. An inherited disorder of lipid (fat) metabolism that produces *mental retardation,* paralysis and brings early death.

Nomenclature. A system or set of names or designations used in a particular discipline, such as the DSM-IIIR.

Nomothetic. Relating to the abstract, recurrent, universal, to the formulation of general laws that explain a range of phenomena. Contrast with *idiographic.*

Norepinephrine. A *catecholamine* that is a *neurotransmitter* of the central nervous system. Disturbances in its tracts apparently figure in *depression* and *mania.* It is also a neurotransmitter secreted at the nerve endings of the *sympathetic nervous system,* a hormone liberated with *epinephrine* in the adrenal medulla and similar to it in action, and a strong vasoconstrictor.

Normal curve. As applied in psychology, the bell-shaped distribution of a measurable *trait* depicting most people in the middle and few at the extremes.

Nosology. A systematic classification of diseases.

Nucleus. In anatomy, a mass of nerve cell bodies (*gray matter*) within the brain or spinal cord by which descending nerve fibers connect with ascending nerve fibers.

Object choice. In the psychology of sex, the type of person or thing selected as a focus for sexual activity.

Objective anxiety. In psychoanalytic theory, the *ego's* reaction to danger in the external world; the same as realistic fear.

Observer drift. The tendency of two raters of behavior to begin to agree with each other, achieving unusually high levels of *reliability;* their way of coding behavior differentiates their scores from those of another pair of raters. This is regarded as a threat to reliable and valid *behavioral assessment.*

Obsession. An intrusive and recurring thought that seems irrational and uncontrollable to the person experiencing it.

Obsessive-compulsive disorder. An *anxiety disorder* in which the mind is flooded with persistent and uncontrollable thoughts or the individual is compelled to repeat certain acts again and again, causing significant distress and interference with everyday functioning.

Obsessive compulsive personality. Perfectionistic and work- rather than pleasure-oriented, people with a compulsive personality have inordinate difficulty making decisions, are overconcerned with details and efficiency, and relate poorly to others because they demand that things be done their way. They are unduly conventional, serious, formal, and stingy with their emotions.

Occipital lobe. The posterior area of each *cerebral hemisphere,* situated behind the *parietal* and above the *temporal lobes,* that is responsible for reception and analysis of visual information and for some visual memory.

Oedipus complex. In Freudian theory, the desire and conflict of the four-year-old male child who wants to possess his mother sexually and to eliminate the father rival. The threat of punishment from the father makes the boy *repress* these id impulses. Girls have a similar sexual desire for the father, which is repressed in analogous fashion and is called the **Electra complex**.

Operant behavior. A response that is supposedly voluntary and operates on the environment, modifying it so that a reward or goal is attained.

Operant conditioning. The acquisition or elimination of a response as a function of the environmental contingencies of *reward* and *punishment.*

Operational definition. A definition of a theoretical concept that equates it with a set of observable operations that can be measured.

Operationism. A school of thought in science that holds that a given concept must be defined in terms of a single set of identifiable and repeatable operations that can be measured.

Opium. The dried milky juice obtained from the immature fruit of the opium poppy. This addictive *narcotic* produces euphoria and drowsiness and reduces pain.

Oral stage. In psychoanalytic theory, the first *psychosexual stage* that extends into the second year, during which the mouth is the principal *erogenous zone.*

Organic mental disorder. DSM-IIIR category for organic psychological problems that are linked to a specific known or presumed somatic cause, for example alcohol-induced organic mental disorder.

Organic mental syndrome. DSM-IIIR category for organic psychological problems that are believed caused by more than one specific somatic factor, for example, organic mood syndrome.

Organismic variable. The physiological or psychological factor assumed to be operating "under the skin"; these variables are one of the foci of *behavioral assessment.*

Orgasm (climax). The involuntary, intensely pleasurable, climactic phase in sexual arousal that lasts a number of seconds and usually involves muscular contractions and *ejaculation* in the male and similar contractions in the genitalia of the female.

Orgasmic reorientation. A *behavior therapy* technique for altering classes of stimuli to which people are sexually attracted; individuals are confronted by a conventionally arousing stimulus while experiencing *orgasm* for another, undesirable reason.

Outcome research. Research on the effectiveness of *psychotherapy.* Contrast with *process research.*

Overcontrolled. In reference to childhood disorders, problems that create distress for the child, such as *anxiety* and *social withdrawal.*

Panic disorder. An *anxiety disorder* in which the individual has sudden and inexplicable attacks of jarring symptoms, such as difficulty breathing, heart palpitations, dizziness, trembling, terror, and feelings of impending doom. In DSM-IIIR, said to occur with or without *agoraphobia.*

Paradigm. A set of basic assumptions that outline the universe of scientific inquiry, specifying both the concepts regarded as legitimate and the methods to be used in collecting and interpreting data.

Paranoia. The general term for *delusions* of persecution, *grandiosity,* or both; found in several pathological conditions, *paranoid disorders, paranoid schizophrenia, and paranoid personality* disorder. Can be produced as well by large doses of certain drugs, such as *cocaine* or *alcohol.*

Paranoid disorder. A disorder in which the individual has persistent persecutory *delusions* or *delusional jealousy*—an unfounded conviction that his or her mate is unfaithful—is very often contentious, but has no *thought disorder* and does not *hallucinate.*

Paranoid personality. This person, expecting to be mistreated by others, becomes suspicious, secretive, jealous, and argumentative. He or she will not accept blame and appears cold and unemotional.

Paranoid schizophrenic. A *psychotic* patient who has numerous systematized *delusions* as well as *hallucinations* and *ideas of reference.* He or she may also be agitated, angry, argumentative, and sometimes violent.

Paraphilias. Sexual attraction to unusual objects and sexual activities unusual in nature.

Paraphrenia. Term sometimes used to refer to *schizophrenia* in an older adult.

Paraprofessional. In clinical psychology, an individual lacking a doctoral degree but trained to perform certain functions usually reserved for clinicians, for example, a college student trained and supervised by a behavioral therapist to shape the behavior of *autistic* children through contingent reinforcers.

Parasympathetic nervous system. The division of the *autonomic nervous system* that is involved with maintenance; it controls many of the internal organs and is active primarily when the organism is not aroused.

Paresthesia. *Conversion disorder* marked by a sensation of tingling or creeping on the skin.

Parietal lobe. The middle division of each *cerebral hemisphere,* situated behind the central sulcus; above the lateral sulcus; is the receiving center for sensations of the skin and of bodily positions.

Parkinson's disease. A *presenile dementia* characterized by uncontrollable and severe muscle tremors, a stiff gait, a masklike, expressionless face, and withdrawal.

Passive-aggressive personality. People with a passive-aggressive personality indirectly resist the demands of others by such exasperating behavior as being late, missing appointments, not answering calls, and making foolish mistakes; their dawdling is considered a hostile way to control others without assuming responsibility for their own anger.

Pathology. The anatomical, physiological, and psychological deviations of a disease or disorder, and the study of these abnormalities.

PCP. See *phencyclidine.*

Pearson product moment correlation coefficient (r). A statistic, ranging in value from −1.00 to +1.00; the most common means of denoting a correlational relationship. The sign indicates whether the relationship is positive or negative and the magnitude indicates the strength of the relationship.

Pedophilia. A preference for obtaining sexual gratification through contact with youngsters defined legally as underage; one of the *paraphilias.*

Penile plethysmograph. A device for detecting blood flow and thus for recording changes in size of the *penis.*

Penis. The male organ of copulation.

Perseveration. The persistent repetition of words and ideas, often found in *schizophrenics.*

Personality disorders. A heterogeneous group of disorders, listed separately on axis II, that are regarded as long-standing, inflexible, and maladaptive traits that impair social and occupational functioning but not contact with reality.

Personality inventory. A self-report questionnaire by which an examinee indicates whether statements assessing habitual tendencies apply to him or her.

Personality structure. See *trait.*

Pervasive developmental disorder. Severe childhood problems marked by profound disturbances in social relations and oddities in behavior. *Autistic disorder* is one.

PET scan. Computer-assisted motion pictures of the living brain, created by analysis of radioactive particles from isotopes injected into the bloodstream.

Petit mal epilepsy. A form of *epilepsy* involving a momentary alteration in consciousness, more frequent in children than adults.

Peyote. A *hallucinogen* obtained from the root of the peyote cactus, the active ingredient being the *alkaloid mescaline.*

Phallic stage. In psychoanalytic theory, the third *psychosexual stage,* extending from ages three to six, during which maximal gratification is obtained from genital stimulation.

Phencyclidine. Also known as PCP, angel dust, PeaCE Pill, zombie, and other street names. This very powerful and hazardous drug causes profound disorientation, agitated and often violent behavior, and even seizures, coma, and death.

Phenomenology. As applied in psychology, the philosophical view that the phenomena of subjective experience should be studied because behavior is considered to be determined by how people perceive themselves and the world rather than by objectively described reality.

Phenothiazine. The class name for a group of drugs that relieve psychotic symptoms and are considered *neuroleptics;* their molecular structure, like that of the *tricyclic drugs,* consists of three fused rings.

Phenotype. The totality of observable characteristics of a person. Compare with *genotype.*

Phenylketonuria (PKU). A genetic disorder that, through a deficiency in a liver enzyme, phenylalanine hydroxylase, causes severe *mental retardation* unless phenylalanine can be largely restricted from diet until the age of six.

Phobic disorder. An *anxiety disorder* in which there is intense fear and avoidance of specific objects and situations, recognized as irrational by the individuals.

Physiological paradigm. A broad theoretical point of view holding that mental disorders are caused by aberrant *somatic* processes.

Physiology. The study of the functions and activities of living cells, tissues, and organs and of the physical and chemical phenomena involved.

Pick's disease. A *presenile dementia* involving diffuse atrophy of *frontal* and *temporal lobes,* which impairs memory, concentration, and ability to think abstractly and eventually results in *psychosis* and death.

Placebo. Any inactive therapy or chemical agent, or any attribute or component of such a therapy or chemical, that affects a person's behavior for reasons having to do with his or her expectation of change.

Placebo effect. The action of a drug or psychological treatment that is not attributable to any specific operations of the agent. For example, a tranquilizer can reduce anxiety both because of its special biochemical action and because the recipient expects relief. See *placebo.*

Plateau phase. According to Masters and Johnson, the second stage in sexual arousal, during which excitement and tension have reached a stable high level before *orgasm.*

Play therapy. The use of play as a means of uncovering what is troubling a child and of establishing *rapport.*

Pleasure principle. In psychoanalytic theory, the demanding manner by which the *id* operates, seeking immediate gratification of its needs.

Plethysmograph. An instrument for determining and registering variations in the amount of blood present or passing through an organ.

Polydrug abuse. The misuse of more than one drug at a time, such as drinking heavily and taking cocaine.

Pons. An area in the *brain stem* containing nerve fiber tracts connecting the *cerebellum* with the spinal cord and with motor areas of the *cerebrum.*

Positive spikes. An EEG pattern recorded from the *temporal lobe* of the brain, with frequencies of 6 to 8 cps and 14 to 16 cps, that is often found in impulsive and aggressive people.

Positive symptoms. In *schizophrenia,* behavioral excesses such as *hallucinations* and bizarre behavior. Compare with *negative symptoms.*

Posttraumatic stress disorder. An *anxiety disorder* in which a particularly stressful event, such as military combat, rape, or a natural disaster, brings in its aftermath intrusive reexperiencings of the trauma, a numbing of responsiveness to the outside world, estrangement from others, a tendency to be easily startled, nightmares, recurrent dreams, and otherwise disturbed sleep.

Poverty of content. Reduced meaningfulness in speech, one of the *negative symptoms* of *schizophrenia*.

Poverty of speech. Reduced amount of talking, one of the *negative symptoms of schizophrenia*.

Predictive validity. See *validity*.

Predisposition. An inclination or *diathesis* to respond in a certain way, either inborn or acquired; in abnormal psychology, a factor that lowers the ability to withstand stress and inclines the individual toward *pathology*.

Premature ejaculation. Inability of the male to inhibit his *orgasm* long enought for mutually satisfying sexual relations.

Premorbid adjustment. In research on *schizophrenia*, the social and sexual adjustment of the individual before the onset or diagnosis of his symptoms. Patients with good premorbid adjustment are those found to have been relatively normal earlier, but those with poor premorbid adjustment had inadequate interpersonal and sexual relations.

Preparedness. In *classical conditioning* theory, a biological *predisposition* to associate particular stimuli readily with the *unconditioned stimulus*.

Presenile dementia. An often progressive mental deterioration occurring when the individual is in his or her forties or fifties.

Prevalence. In *epidemiological* studies of a disorder, the percentage of a population that has it at a given time. Compare with *incidence*.

Prevention. **Primary,** efforts in *community psychology* to reduce the incidence of new cases of psychological disorder by such means as altering stressful living conditions and genetic counseling. **Secondary,** efforts to detect disorders early, so that they will not develop into full-blown, perhaps chronic disabilities. **Tertiary,** efforts to reduce the long-term consequences of having a disorder, equivalent in most respects to therapy.

Primary empathy. A form of *empathy* in which the therapist understands the content and feeling of what the client is saying and expressing from the client's *phenomenological* point of view. Compare with *advanced accurate empathy*.

Primary narcissism. In psychoanalytic theory, the part of the *oral stage* of *psychosexual* development during which the ego has not yet differentiated from the *id*.

Primary process. In psychoanalytic theory, one of the *id's* means of reducing tension; by imagining what it desires.

Privileged communication. The communication between parties in a confidential relation that is protected by statute. A spouse, doctor, lawyer, pastor, psychologist, or psychiatrist cannot be forced, except under unusual circumstances, to disclose such information.

Proband. The person who in a genetic investigation bears the diagnosis or *trait* that the investigator is interested in; the same as *index case*.

Process-reactive. A dimension used to distinguish schizophrenics; process schizophrenics suffer long-term and gradual deterioration before the onset of their illness, whereas reactive schizophrenics have a better premorbid history prior to a more rapid onset of symptoms. See *premorbid adjustment*.

Process research. Research on the mechanisms by which a therapy may bring improvement. Compare with *outcome research*.

Profound mental retardation. A limitation in mental development measured on IQ tests at less than 20–25; children with this degree of retardation require total supervision of all their activities.

Progestins. Steroid progestational hormones that are regarded as the biological precursors of androgens, the male sex hormones.

Prognosis. A prediction of the likely course and outcome of an illness.

Projection. A *defense mechanism* whereby characteristics or desires unacceptable to the *ego* are attributed to someone else.

Projective hypothesis. The notion that highly unstructured stimuli, as in the *Rorschach,* are necessary to bypass defenses in order to reveal repressed unconscious motives and conflicts.

Projective test. A psychological assessment device employing a set of standard but vague stimuli on the assumption that unstructured material will allow unconscious motivations and fears to be uncovered. The *Rorschach* series of inkblots is an example.

Pronoun reversal. A speech problem in which the child refers to himself as "he" or "you" and uses "I" or "me" in referring to others; often found in the speech of children with *autistic disorder*.

Pseudocommunity. An illusory world built up by a *paranoid* person, dominated by false beliefs that are not properly verified and shared by others.

Psilocybin. A *psychedelic* drug extracted from the mushroom *Psilocybe mexicana*.

Psyche. The soul, spirit, or mind as distinguished from the body. In psychoanalytic theory, it is the totality of the *id, ego,* and *superego* including both conscious and unconscious components.

Psychedelic. A drug that expands consciousness. See also *hallucinogen*.

Psychiatrist. A physician (M.D. degree) who has taken specialized postdoctoral training, called a residency, in the diagnosis, treatment, and prevention of mental and emotional disorders.

Psychoactive drug. A chemical compound having a psychological effect that alters mood or thought process. Valium is an example.

Psychoactive substance abuse. Less severe form of *psychoactive substance dependence.*

Psychoactive substance dependence. The abuse of a drug accompanied by impairment in social and occupational functioning and by physiological dependence upon it; formerly called *addiction.*

Psychoanalysis. A term applied primarily to the therapy procedures pioneered by Freud, entailing *free association, dream interpretation,* and *working through* the *transference neurosis.* More recently the term has come to encompass the numerous variations on basic Freudian therapy.

Psychoanalyst (analyst). A therapist who has taken specialized post-doctoral training in psychoanalysis after earning either an M.D. or a Ph.D.

Psychodynamic. In psychoanalytic theory, it relates to the mental and emotional forces and processes that develop in early childhood and their effects on behavior and mental states.

Psychogenesis. Development from psychological origins as distinguished from somatic origins. Contrast with *somatogenesis.*

Psychogenic amnesia. A *dissociative disorder* in which the person suddenly becomes unable to recall important personal information, to an extent that cannot be explained by ordinary forgetfulness.

Psychogenic fugue. A *dissociative disorder* in which the person, totally amnesic and unable to recall the past, suddenly moves to a new location and assumes a new identity.

Psychological autopsy. The analysis of an individual's *suicide* through the examination of his letters and through interviews with friends and relatives in the hope of discovering why he or she committed suicide.

Psychological deficit. The term used to indicate that performance of a pertinent psychological process is below that expected of a normal person.

Psychological dependency. The term sometimes applied to the reason for *substance abuse;* the reliance on a drug because its effects make stressful situations more bearable, without physiological addiction to it.

Psychological test. A standardized procedure designed to measure a subject's performance of a particular task or to assess his or her personality.

Psychomotor epilepsy. A form of epileptic seizure in which the individual loses contact with the environment but appears conscious and performs some routine, repetitive act or engages in more complex activity.

Psychopath. See *antisocial personality.*

Psychopathologist. A mental health professional who conducts research into the nature and develoment of mental and emotional disorders; their academic backgrounds can differ, some having been trained as experimental psychologists, others as psychiatrists, and still others as biochemists.

Psychophysiological disorder. A disorder with physical symptoms that may involve actual tissue damage, usually in one organ system, and that are produced in part by continued mobilization of the *autonomic nervous system* under stress. Hives and ulcers are examples. No longer listed in DSM-IIIR in a separate category, such disorders are now diagnosed on axis I as psychological factor influencing a physical condition; on axis III the specific physical condition is given.

Psychophysiology. The discipline concerned with the bodily changes that accompany psychological events.

Psychosexual stages. In psychoanalytic theory, critical developmental phases that the individual passes through, each stage characterized by the body area providing maximal erotic gratification. The adult personality is formed by the pattern and intensity of instinctual gratification at each stage.

Psychosexual trauma. As applied by Masters and Johnson, earlier frightening or degrading sexual experience that is related to a present *sexual dysfunction.*

Psychosis. A severe mental disorder in which thinking and emotion are so impaired that the individual is seriously out of contact with reality.

Psychosomatic disorder. See *psychophysiological disorder.*

Psychosurgery. Any surgical technique in which neural pathways in the brain are cut in order to change behavior. See *lobotomy.*

Psychotherapy. A primarily verbal means of helping troubled individuals change their thoughts, feelings, and behavior to reduce distress and to achieve greater life satisfaction. See *insight therapy* and *behavior therapy.*

Psychotic depression. A profound sadness and unjustified feelings of unworthiness in which there are also *delusions.*

Punishment. In psychological experiments, any noxious stimulus imposed on the animal to reduce the probability that it will behave in the way deemed by the experimenter to be incorrect.

Random assignment. A method of assigning subjects to groups in an *experiment* that gives each subject an equal chance of being in each group. The procedure helps to ensure that groups are comparable before the experimental manipulation begins.

Rape. To force sexual intercourse or other sexual activity on another person. **Forcible rape** is the legal term. **Statutory rape** is sexual intercourse between an adult male and someone who is under the age of consent.

Rapid-smoking treatment. A *behavior therapy* technique for reducing cigarette smoking in which the person is instructed to puff much more quickly than usual in an effort to make the whole experience an aversive one.

Rapport. A close, trusting relationship.

Rational-emotive therapy. A *cognitive-restructuring behavior therapy* introduced by Albert Ellis and based on the assumption that much disordered behavior is rooted in absolutistic demands that people tell themselves. The therapy aims to alter the unrealistic goals individuals set for themselves, such as "I must be universally loved."

Rationalization.   A *defense mechanism* in which a plausible reason is unconsciously invented by the *ego* to protect itself from confronting the real reason for an action, thought, or emotion.

Raynaud's disease.   A *psychophysiological disorder* in which capillaries, especially of the fingers and toes, are subject to spasm. It is characterized by cold, moist hands, commonly accompanied by pain and may progress to local gangrene.

Reaction formation.   A *defense mechanism* whereby an unconscious and unacceptable impulse or feeling that would cause anxiety is converted into its opposite so that it can become conscious and be expressed.

Reaction time test.   A procedure for determining the interval between the application of a stimulus and the beginning of the subject's response.

Reactivity.   The phenomenon whereby the object of observation is changed by the very fact that it is being observed.

Reality principle.   In psychoanalytic theory, the manner in which the *ego* delays gratifications and otherwise deals with the environment in a planful, rational fashion.

Receptive language disorder.   Difficulties understanding spoken language.

Receptor.   Proteins embedded in the membrane covering a neural cell that interact with a *neurotransmitter.*

Recessive gene.   A *gene* that must be paired with one identical to it in order to determine a *trait* in the *phenotype.*

Recovery time.   The period it takes for a physiological process to return to *baseline* after the body has responded to a stimulus.

Refractory phase.   The brief period after stimulation of a nerve, muscle, or other irritable element during which it is unresponsive to a second stimulus; or the period after intercourse during which the male cannot have another orgasm.

Regression.   A *defense mechanism* in which anxiety is avoided by retreating to the behavior patterns of an earlier *psychosexual stage.*

Reinforcement.   In *operant conditioning,* increasing the probability that a response will recur either by presenting a contingent positive event or by removing a negative one.

Reliability.   The extent to which a test, measurement, or classification system produces the same scientific observation each time it is applied.

Repression.   A *defense mechanism* whereby impulses and thoughts unacceptable to the *ego* are pushed into the *unconscious.*

Residual schizophrenia.   Diagnosis given to patients who have had one episode of schizophrenia but who presently show no psychotic symptoms, though signs of the symptoms do exist.

Resistance.   During *psychoanalysis,* the defensive tendency of the unconscious part of the *ego* to ward off from consciousness particularly threatening *repressed* material.

Resistance to extinction.   The tendency of a *conditioned response* to persist in the absence of any *reinforcement.*

Resolution phase.   The last stage in the sexual arousal cycle, during which sexual tensions abate.

Response acquiescence.   A "yea"-saying *response set,* or agreeing with a question regardless of its content.

Response cost.   An *operant conditioning* punishment procedure in which the misbehaving person is fined already earned reinforcers.

Response deviation.   A tendency to answer questionnaire items in an uncommon way, regardless of their content.

Response hierarchy.   The ordering of a series of responses according to the likelihood of their being elicited by a particular stimulus.

Response prevention.   A *behavior therapy* technique in which the person is discouraged from making an accustomed response; used primarily with *compulsive* rituals.

Response set.   The tendency of an individual to respond in a particular way to questions or statements on a test—for example, with a "False"—regardless of the content of each query or statement.

Reticular formation.   Network of *nuclei* and fibers in the central core of the *brain stem* that is important in arousing the cortex and maintaining alertness, in the processing of incoming sensory stimulation, and in adjusting spinal reflexes.

Retrospective report.   A recollection by an individual of a past event.

Reversal design (ABAB design).   An experimental design in which behavior is measured during a baseline period (A), during a period when a treatment is introduced (B), during the reinstatement of the conditions that prevailed in the baseline period (A), and finally during a reintroduction of the treatment (B). It is commonly used in operant research to isolate cause–effect relationships.

Reward.   Any satisfying event or stimulus that, by being contingent upon a response, increases the probability that the subject will so respond again.

Rh factor.   Substances present in the red blood cells of most people. If Rh factors are present in the blood of a fetus but not in that of the mother, her system produces antibodies that may enter the bloodstream of the fetus and indirectly damage the brain.

Right to refuse treatment.   A legal principle according to which a committed mental patient may decline to participate in unconventional or risky treatments.

Right to treatment.   A legal principle according to which a committed mental patient must be provided some minimal amount and quality of professional intervention, enough to provide a realistic opportunity for meaningful improvement.

Risk factor.   A condition or variable that, if present, increases the likelihood of developing a disorder.

Rorschach test.   A *projective test* in which the examinee is instructed to interpret a series of ten inkblots reproduced on cards.

Role playing.   See *behavioral rehearsal.*

Rosenthal effect.   The tendency for results to conform to experimenters' expectations unless stringent safeguards are instituted to minimize human bias; named after Robert Rosenthal, who performed many of the original experiments revealing the problem.

Rubella (German measles).   An infectious disease that if contracted by the mother during the first three months of pregnancy has a high risk of causing *mental retardation* and physical deformity in the child.

Sadism.   A marked preference for obtaining or increasing sexual gratification by inflicting pain on another person.

Schema.   A mental structure for organizing information about the world. Pl. schemata.

Schizoaffective disorder.   Diagnosis to be applied when it is difficult to determine whether a patient has an *affective disorder* or either *schizophreniform disorder* or *schizophrenia.*

Schizoid personality.   This person, emotionally aloof and indifferent to the praise, criticism, and feelings of others, is usually a "loner" with few, if any, close friends and with solitary interests.

Schizophrenia.   A group of *psychotic* disorders characterized by major disturbances in thought, emotion, and behavior—disordered thinking in which ideas are not logically related; faulty perception and attention; bizarre distrubances in motor activity; flat or inappropriate emotion; reduced tolerance for stress of interpersonal relations. It causes a patient to withdraw from people and reality, often into a fantasy life of *delusions* and *hallucinations.* The problems must last at least six months at some time during the person's life. See *schizoaffective disorder, schizophreniform disorder,* and *brief reactive psychosis.*

Schizophreniform disorder.   Diagnosis for people who have all the symptoms of *schizophrenia,* except that the disorder lasts more than two weeks and less than six months. See *brief reactive psychosis.*

Schizophrenogenic.   Causing or contributing to the development of *schizophrenia;* often applied to the cold, conflict-inducing mother who is alleged to make her children schizophrenic.

Schizotypal personality.   This eccentric individual has oddities of thought and perception—*magical thinking, illusions, depersonalization, derealization*—speaks digressively and with overelaborations, and is usually socially isolated. Under stress he or she may appear *psychotic.*

School phobia.   An acute, irrational dread of attending school, usually accompanied by somatic complaints. It is the most common *phobia* of childhood.

Secondary gain.   Benefits that a person unconsciously obtains from a disability.

Secondary process.   The reality-based decision-making and problem-solving activities of the *ego.* Compare with *primary process.*

Sedative.   A drug that slows bodily activities, especially those of the central nervous system; it is used to reduce pain and tension and to induce relaxation and sleep.

Selective mortality.   A possible confound in *longitudinal research,* whereby the less healthy people in a sample are more likely to drop out.

Self-actualization.   Fulfilling one's potential as an always growing human being; believed by *client-centered therapists* to be the master motive.

Self-monitoring.   In *behavioral assessment,* a procedure whereby the individual observes and reports certain aspects of his or her own behavior, thoughts, or emotions.

Self psychology.   Kohut's variant of psychoanalysis, in which the focus is on the development of the person's self-worth from acceptance and nurturance by key figures in childhood.

Semantic Differential.   A self-report inventory requiring the respondent to rate each concept, such as mother, in one of seven positions between a number of polar adjectives, such as clean–dirty, strong–weak.

Senile dementia.   A disorder that can be brought on by progressive deterioration of the brain caused in part by aging; marked by memory impairment, inability to think abstractly, loss of standards and control of impulses, poor personal hygiene, great *disorientation,* and eventually obliviousness.

Senile plaques.   Small areas of tissue degeneration in the brain, made up of granular material and filaments.

Sensate focus.   A term applied to exercises prescribed at the beginning of the Masters and Johnson sex therapy program; partners are instructed to fondle each other to give pleasure but to refrain from intercourse, thus reducing anxiety about sexual performance.

Sensitivity (encounter) group.   A small group of people who spend a period of time together both for therapy and for educational purposes; participants are encouraged or forced to examine their interpersonal functioning and their often-overlooked feelings about themselves and others.

Sensory-awareness procedures.   Techniques that help clients tune into their feelings and sensations, as in *sensate-focus* exercises, and to be open to new ways of experiencing and feeling.

Separation anxiety disorder.   A disorder in which the child feels intense fear and distress when away from someone on whom he or she is very dependent; it is said to be an important cause of *school phobia.*

Serotonin.   An *indoleamine* that is a *neurotransmitter* of the central nervous system. Distrubances in its tracts apparently figure in *depression* and *mania.*

Severe mental retardation.   A limitation in mental development measured in IQ tests at between 20–25 and 35–

40. Individuals so afflicted often cannot care for themselves, communicate only briefly, and are listless and inactive.

Sex-change surgery. An operation removing existing genitalia of a *transsexual* and constructing a substitute for the genitals of the opposite sex.

Sexual aversion disorder. Avoidance of nearly all genital contact with another person.

Sexual disorders. Disorders of sexual functioning including *gender identity disorders, paraphilias,* and *sexual dysfunctions.*

Sexual dysfunctions. Dysfunctions in which the appetitive or psychophysiological changes of the normal sexual response cycle are inhibited.

Sexual orientation disturbance. An earlier term for DSM-III's *ego-dystonic homosexuality.*

Sexual response cycle. The general pattern of sexual physical processes and feelings, building to an orgasm by stimulation and made up of five phases: *interest, excitement, plateau, orgasm,* and *resolution.*

Sexual script. Rules people have for guilding their actions in sexual situations.

Sexual value system. As applied by Masters and Johnson, the activities that an individual holds to be acceptable and necessary in a sexual relationship.

Shaping. In *operant conditioning,* reinforcing responses that are successively closer approximations of the desired behavior.

Shell shock. A term from World War I for what is now referred to as *posttraumatic stress disorder;* it was believed to be due to sudden atmospheric changes from nearby explosions.

Sibling. One of two or more persons having the same parents.

Sidestream smoke. The smoke from the burning end of a cigarette, which contains higher concentrations of ammonia, carbon monoxide, nicotine, and tar than that inhaled by the smoker.

Significant difference. See *statistical significance.*

Single-subject experimental designs. Designs for experiments conducted with a single subject; these procedures include the *reversal* and *multiple-baseline* designs in operant research.

Situational determinants. The environmental conditions that precede and follow a particular piece of behavior, being a primary focus of *behavioral assessment.*

Situational orgasmic dysfunction. Inability of a woman to have an *orgasm* in particular situations.

Skeletal (voluntary) muscle. One of the muscles that clothe the skeleton of the vertebrate, that is attached to bone, and is under voluntary control.

Skinner box. A laboratory apparatus in which an animal is placed for an *operant conditioning* experiment. It contains a lever or other device that the animal must manipulate to obtain a reward or avoid punishment.

Sleeping sickness. See *encephalitis lethargica.*

Slow brain waves. The theta rhythm (4 to 7 cps) usually recorded by an EEG from subcortical parts of the brain and the delta rhythm (less than 4 cps) normally recorded during deep sleep; sometimes recorded in awake sociopaths.

Smooth (involuntary) muscle. Thin sheets of muscle cells associated with *viscera* and walls of blood vessels that perform functions not usually under direct voluntary control.

Social desirability. In completion of *personality inventories,* the tendency of the responder to give what he or she considers the socially acceptable answer, whether or not it is accurate.

Social drift theory. Attempt to explain the correlation between social class and *schizophrenia* by proposing that schizophrenics move downward in social positions.

Social phobia. A collection of fears linked to the presence of other people.

Social-skills training. *Behavior therapy* procedures for teaching socially unknowledgeable individuals how to meet others, to talk to them and maintain eye contact, to give and receive criticism, offer and accept compliments, to make requests and express feelings, and how otherwise to improve their relations with other people. *Modeling* and *behavior rehearsal* are two such procedures.

Social-withdrawal disorder. A disorder of extremely shy children who never "warm up" to new people both young and old, even after prolonged exposure to them. They have loving relations within the family; but they do not join in group play, and in crowded rooms they cling to their parents or hide.

Socioeconomic status. A relative position in the community as determined by occupation, income, and amount of education.

Sociopath. See *antisocial personality.*

Sodomy. Originally, penetration of the male organ into the anus of another male, it was later broadened in English law to include heterosexual anal intercourse and by some state statutes to cover unconventional sex generally.

Soma. The totality of an organism's physical makeup.

Somatic weakness. The vulnerability of a particular organ or organ system to psychological stress and thereby to a particular *psychophysiological disorder.*

Somatization disorder. A *somatoform disorder* in which the person continually seeks medical help for recurrent and multiple physical symptoms that have no discoverable physical cause. The medical history is complicated and dramatically presented. It is also called Briquet's syndrome. Compare with *hypochondriasis.*

Somatoform disorders. Disorders in which physical symptoms suggest a physical problem but have no known physiological cause; they are therefore believed to be linked to psychological conflicts and needs but not voluntarily assumed; *somatization disorder* (Briquet's syndrome), *conversion disorder, somatoform pain disorder, hypochondriasis.*

Somatoform pain disorder. A *somatoform disorder* in which the person complains of severe and prolonged pain that is not explainable by organic pathology; it tends to be stress-related or permits the patient to avoid an aversive activity and/or to gain attention and sympathy.

Somatogenesis. Development from bodily origins as distinguished from psychological origins. Compare with *psychogenesis.*

SORC. An acronym for the four sets of variables that are the focus of *behavioral assessment: situational determinants, organismic variables,* overt respones, and *reinforcement* contingencies.

Specific developmental disorders. Delays in the development of language and articulation, in being able to read and do arithmetic, skills that are related to maturation. Some signs of the disturbances are often evident in adulthood. Also called *learning disabilities;* listed on axis II.

Specific-reaction theory. The hypothesis that an individual develops a given *psychophysiological disorder* because of the innate tendency of the autonomic system to respond in a particular way to stress, for example, by increasing heart rate or developing tension in the forehead.

Spectator role. As applied by Masters and Johnson, a pattern of behavior in which the individual's focus on and concern for sexual performance impedes his or her natural sexual responses.

Stability-lability. A dimension of classifying the responsiveness of the *autonomic nervous system.* Labile individuals are those in whom a wide range of stimuli can elicit autonomic *arousal.* Stable individuals are not so easily aroused.

State-dependent learning. The phenomenon whereby an organism shows the effects of learning that took place in a special condition, such as intoxication, better than in another condition.

State-dependent memory. The phenomenon whereby people are more able to remember an event if they are in the same state as when it happened. If they are in a greatly different state when they try to remember—happy now, and sad then, for example—memory is poorer.

Statistical significance. A magnitude of difference that has a low probability of having occurred by chance alone and is by convention regarded as important.

Statutory rape. Sexual intercourse, whether forced or not, with someone who is below an age fixed by local statute as that of consent.

Steppingstone theory. The belief that the use of one kind of drug, such as *marijuana,* leads to the use of a more dangerous one, such as *cocaine.*

Stimulant. A drug that increases alertness and motor activity and at the same time reduces fatigue, allowing an individual to remain awake for an extended period of time.

Strategic processing. The use of *cognitive* strategies to solve problems; it is said to be defective in the *mentally retarded.*

Stress. A stimulus that strains the physiological or psychological capacities of an organism.

Stroke. A sudden loss of consciousness and control followed by paralysis; caused when a blood clot obstructs an artery or by hemorrhage into the brain when an artery ruptures.

Subdural hematoma. Hemorrhage and swelling of the arachnoid torn by a fractured bone of the skull.

Subintentioned death. A death that is believed to have been caused in some measure by the person's unconscious intentions.

Substance abuse. The use of a drug for at least a month to such an extent that the person is often intoxicated throughout the day and fails in important obligations and in attempts to abstain, but where there is no physiological dependence. See *psychological dependency.*

Substance dependence. The abuse of a drug accompanied by a physiological dependence on it, made evident by *tolerance* and *withdrawal symptoms;* also called *addiction.*

Substance use disorders. Disorders in which drugs like *alcohol* and *cocaine* are abused to such an extent that behavior becomes maladaptive; social and occupational functioning is impaired, and control or abstinence becomes impossible. Reliance on the drug may be either psychological, as in *substance abuse,* or physiological, as in *substance dependence* or *addiction.*

Successive approximations. Responses that closer and closer resemble the desired response in *operant conditioning.* See *shaping.*

Suicide. The taking of one's own life intentionally.

Sulcus (fissure). A shallow furrow in the *cerebral cortex* separating adjacent convolutions or *gyri.*

Superego. In psychoanalytic theory, the part of the personality that acts as the conscience and reflects society's moral standards as they have been learned from parents and teachers.

Symbolic loss. In psychoanalytic theory, the unconscious interpretation by the *ego* of an event like rejection as a total loss such as suffered in the death of a loved one.

Sympathetic nervous system. The division of the *autonomic nervous system* that acts on bodily systems—for example, speeding up the contractions of the blood vessels, slowing those of the intestines, and increasing the heartbeat—to prepare the organism for exertion, emotional stress, and extreme cold.

Symptom. An observable physiological or psychological manifestation of a disease, often occurring in a patterned group of symptoms to constitute a *syndrome.*

Synapse. A small gap between two *neurons* where the nerve impulse passes from the axon of the first to the dendrites or cell body of the second.

Syndrome. A group or pattern of *symptoms* that tend to occur together in a particular *disease.*

Systematic desensitization. A major *behavior therapy* procedure that has a fearful person, while deeply relaxed, imagine a series of progressively more fearsome situations. The two responses of relaxation and fear are incompatible and fear is dispelled. It is useful for treating psychological problems in which *anxiety* is the principal difficulty.

Systematic rational restructuring. A variant of *rational-emotive therapy* in which the client imagines a series of increasingly anxiety-provoking situations while attempting to reduce distress by talking about them to the self in a more realistic, defusing fashion.

Tachycardia. A racing of the heart, often associated with high levels of anxiety.

Tarantism. Wild dancing *mania*, prevalent in the thirteenth century in western Europe, supposedly incited by the bite of a tarantula.

Tardive dyskinesia. A muscular disturbance of older patients who have taken *phenothiazines* for a very long time, which is marked by involuntary lip-smacking and chin-wagging.

Taylor-Manifest Anxiety Scale. Fifty items drawn from the MMPI as a self-report questionnaire to assess anxiety.

Temporal lobe. A large area of each *cerebral hemisphere* situated below the *lateral sulcus* and in front of the *occipital lobe* that contains primary auditory projection and association areas and general association areas.

Testability. The extent to which a scientific assertion is amenable to systematic probes, any one of which could negate the scientist's expectations.

Testes. Male reproductive glands or gonads; the site where sperm develop and are stored.

Testosterone. Male sex hormone secreted by the *testes* that is responsible for the development of sex characteristics such as enlargement of the testes and growth of facial hair.

Tetrahydrocannabinol (THC). The major active chemical in *marijuana* and *hashish*.

Thalamus. A major brain relay station consisting of two egg-shaped lobes located in the *diencephalon* that receives impulses from all sensory areas except for the olfactory and transmits them to the *cerebrum*.

Thanatos. In psychoanalytic theory, the death instinct that is the second of the two basic instincts within the *id*, the other being *Eros*.

Thematic Apperception Test (TAT) A *projective test* consisting of a set of black and white pictures reproduced on cards, each depicting a potentially emotion-laden situation. The examinee, presented with the cards one at a time, is instructed to make up a story about each situation.

Theory. A formally stated and coherent set of propositions that purport to explain a range of phenomena, order them in a logical way, and suggest what additional information might be gleaned under certain conditions.

Therapeutic community. A concept in mental health care that views the total environment as contributing to prevention or treatment.

Thiamine. One of the complex of B vitamins.

Third-variable problem. The difficulty in *correlational research* on two variables whereby their relationship may be attributable to a third factor.

Thorazine. Trade name for *chlorpromazine*, one of the *neuroleptics* and a member of the *phenothiazine* group of drugs.

Thought disorder. A symptom of *schizophrenia*, evidenced by problems such as *incoherence, loose associations,* and *concrete reasoning* and speech marked by *neologisms* and *clang associations*.

Thyroid gland. An endocrine structure whose two lobes are located on either side of the windpipe; it secretes *thyroxin*.

Time-of-measurement effects. A possible confound in *longitudinal research*, whereby events at a particular point in time can have a specific effect on a variable one is studying over time.

Time-out. An *operant conditioning* punishment procedure in which for bad behavior the person is temporarily removed from a setting where reinforcers can be obtained and placed, for example, in a boring room.

Token economy. A *behavior therapy* procedure, based on *operant conditioning* principles, in which institutionalized patients are given script rewards such as poker chips for socially constructive behavior. The tokens themselves can be exchanged for desirable items and activities such as cigarettes and extra time away from the ward.

Tolerance. A physiological process in which greater and greater amounts of an addictive drug are required to produce the same effect. See *psychoactive substance dependence*.

Tonic phase. The state of rigid muscular tension and suspended breathing in a *grand mal epileptic* attack.

Trait. A somatic characteristic or an enduring *predisposition* to respond in a particular way, distinguishing one individual from another.

Trance logic. A way of thinking during *hyponosis* that allows a person to entertain as real phenomena notions and images that are inherently contradictory, such as seeing two people in place of one.

Tranquilizer. A drug that reduces anxiety and agitation, such as *Valium*; see *anxiolytic*.

Transference. The venting of the *analysand's* emotions, either positive or negative, by treating the *analyst* as the symbolic representative of someone important in the past. An example is the analysand's becoming angry with the analyst to release emotions actually felt toward his or her father.

Transference neurosis. A crucial phase of *psychoanalysis* during which *analysand* reacts emotionally toward the *analyst*, treating him as a parent and reliving childhood experiences in his presence. It enables both analyst and analysand to examine hitherto *repressed* conflicts in the light of present-day reality.

Transsexual. A person who believes he is opposite in sex to his biological endowment and often desires *sex-change surgery.*

Transvestic fetishism. The practice of dressing in the clothing of the opposite sex, usually for the purpose of sexual arousal.

Trauma. A severe physical injury or wound to the body caused by an external force, or a psychological shock having a lasting effect on mental life.

Traumatic disease. An illness produced by external assault such as poison, a blow, or stress, for example, a broken leg.

Tremor. An involuntary quivering of voluntary muscle, usually limited to small musculature of particular areas.

Triadic reciprocality. The influence of cognition and behavior on each other through the relationship between thinking, behaving, and the environment.

Tricyclic drug. One of a group of *antidepressants* so-called because the molecular structure of each is characterized by three fused rings. Tricyclics are assumed to interfere with the reuptake of *norepinephrine* and *serotonin* by a *neuron* after it has fired.

Trisomy. A condition wherein there are three rather than the usual pair of *chromosomes* within the cell nucleus.

Tumescence. The flow of blood into the genitals.

Tumor (neoplasm). Abnormal growth that when located in the brain can be either malignant and directly destroy brain tissue, or benign and disrupt functioning by increasing intracranial pressure.

Twin method. Research strategy in *behavior genetics* in which *concordance* rates of *monozygotic* and *dizygotic* twins are compared.

Two-factor theory. Mowrer's theory of avoidance learning according to which (1) fear is attached to a neutral stimulus by pairing it with a noxious *unconditioned stimulus,* and (2) a person learns to escape the fear elicited by the *conditioned stimulus,* thereby avoiding the UCS. See *fear-drive.*

Type A and type B. Two contrasting psychological patterns revealed through studies seeking the cause of *coronary heart disease.* Type A people are competitive, rushed, hostile, and overcommitted to their work, type Bs more relaxed and relatively free of pressure. Type As are believed to be at heightened risk for heart disease.

Ultrasound. The use of controlled sound waves to visualize internal organs without having to use X-rays.

Unconditional positive regard. According to Rogers, a crucial attitude for the *client-centered* therapist to adopt toward the client, who needs to feel accepted totally as a person in order to evaluate the extent to which his current behavior contributes to his self-actualization.

Unconditioned response (UCR). A behavior elicited by a stimulus (UCS) on an instinctual basis.

Unconditioned stimulus (UCS). A stimulus that elicits an instinctual, *unconditioned response;* meat powder producing salivation is an example.

Unconscious. A state of unawareness without sensation or thought. In psychoanalytic theory, it is the part of the personality, in particular the *id* impulses, or *id* energy, of which the *ego* is unaware.

Undercontrolled. In reference to childhood disorders, problem behavior of the child that creates trouble for others, such as his or her disobedience and aggressiveness.

Undifferentiated schizophrenia. Dignosis given for patients whose psychotic symptoms do not fit a listed category, or that meet the criteria for more than one category.

Unipolar depression. A term applied to the disorder of individuals who have experienced episodes of *depression* but not of *mania;* referred to as major depression in DSM-IIIR.

Vagina. The sheathlike female genital organ that leads from the uterus to the external opening.

Vaginal barrel. The passageway of the vaginal canal leading from the external opening to the uterus.

Vaginal orgasm. The sexual climax experienced through stimulation of the *vagina.*

Vaginal plethysmograph. A device for recording the amount of blood in the walls of the *vagina* and thus for measuring arousal.

Vaginismus. Painful, spasmodic contractions of the outer third of the *vaginal barrel* that make insertion of the *penis* impossible or extremely difficult.

Validity—internal. The extent to which experimental results can be confidently attributed to the manipulation of the *independent variable.* **External,** the extent to which research results may be generalized to other populations and settings. As applied to psychiatric diagnoses, **concurrent,** the extent to which previous undiscovered features are found among patients with the same diagnosis; **predictive,** the extent to which predictions can be made about the future behavior of patients with the same diagnosis; **etiological,** the extent to which a disorder in a number of patients is found to have the same cause or causes.

Valium. An anxiety-reducing drug or *anxiolytic,* believed to be the most widely prescribed of those available to physicians.

Variable. A characteristic or aspect in which people, objects, events, or conditions vary.

Vasoconstriction. A narrowing of the space within the walls (lumen) of a blood vessel, implicated in diseases such as *hypertension.*

Vicarious conditioning. Learning by observing the reactions of others to stimuli or through listening to what they say.

Vineland Adaptive Behavior Scale. An instrument for assessing how many age-appropriate, socially adaptive behaviors a child engages in.

Viscera. The internal organs of the body located in the great cavity of the trunk proper.

Vitamin. Any of various organic substances that are, as far as is known, essential to the nutrition of many animals, acting usually in minute quantities to regulate various metabolic processes.

Voodoo death. The demise of a member of a primitive culture after breaking a tribal law or being cursed by the witch doctor.

Voyeurism (peeping). Marked preference for obtaining sexual gratification by watching others in a state of undress or having sexual relations.

Vulnerability schema. People who are socially anxious and who generally think about danger, harm, and unpleasant events that may come to them.

Waxy flexibility. An aspect of *catatonia* in which the patient's limbs can be moved into a variety of positions and thereafter maintained for unusually long periods of time.

Wernicke's disease. A chronic brain disorder produced by a deficiency of B-complex vitamins that is marked by confusion, drowsiness, partial paralysis of eye muscles, and unsteady gait and by lesions in the *pons, cerebellum,* and *mammillary bodies.* Chronic alcoholics are especially susceptible.

White matter. The neural tissue, particularly of the brain and spinal cord, consisting of tracts or bundles of myelinated (sheathed) nerve fibers.

Withdrawal symptoms. Negative physiological and psychological reactions evidenced when a person suddenly stops taking an addictive drug; cramps, restlessness, and even death are examples. See *psychoactive substance abuse.*

Wooly mammoth. A metaphor for the way the repressed conflicts of psychoanalytic theory are encapsulated in the *unconscious,* making them inaccessible to examination and alteration; thus maintained they cause disorders in adulthood.

Working through. In *psychoanalysis,* the arduous, time-consuming process through which the *analysand* confronts repressed conflicts again and again and faces up to the validity of the analyst's *interpretations* until problems are satisfactorily solved.

Zeitgeist. The German word for the trends of thought and feeling of culture and taste of a particular time period.

Zygote. The fertilized egg cell formed when the male sperm and female ovum unite.

References

Abel, G.G., Barlow, D.H., Blanchard, E. B., & Guild, D. (1977). The components of rapists' sexual arousal. *Archives of General Psychiatry,* **34,** 895–903.

Abel, G.G., Becker, J.V., Murphy, W.D., & Flanagan, B. (1981). Identifying dangerous child molesters. In R. Stuart (Ed.), *Violent behavior: social learning approaches to prediction, management, and treatment.* New York: Brunner.

Abel, G.G., Blanchard, E.B., & Barlow, D.H. (1981). Measurement of sexual arousal in several paraphilias: The effects of stimulus modality, instructional set, and stimulus content. *Behaviour Research and Therapy,* **19,** 25–33.

Abel, G.G., Cunningham-Rathner, J., Becker, J.V., & McHugh, J. (1983). *Motivating sex offenders for treatment with feedback of their psychophysiologic assessment.* Paper presented at the World Congress of Behavior Therapy, Washington, D.C. As cited in Rosen and Beck (1988).

Abel, G.G., Mittelman, M.S., & Becker, J.V. (1985). Sexual offenders: Results of assessment and recommendations for treatment. In M.H. Ben-Aron, S.J. Hucker, & C.D. Webster (Eds.), *Clinical criminology: The assessment and treatment of criminal behavior.* Toronto: M & M Graphics.

Abraham, K. (1911). Notes on the psychoanalytical investigation and treatment of manic-depressive insanity and allied conditions. In E. Jones (Ed.), *Selected papers of Karl Abraham, M.D.* London: Hogarth Press, 1927.

Abramovitz, S.I. (1986). Psychosocial outcomes of sex reassignment surgery. *Journal of Consulting and Clinical Psychology,* **54,** 183–189.

Abrams, R. (1975). What's new in convulsive therapy? In S. Arieti & G. Chrzanowski (Eds.), *New dimensions in psychiatry.* New York: Wiley.

Abramson, L.Y., Garber, J., Edwards, N. B., & Seligman, M.E.P. (1978). Expectancy changes in depression and schizophrenia. *Journal of Abnormal Psychology,* **87,** 102–109.

Abramson, L.Y., Metalsky, G.I., & Alloy, L.B. (in press). Hopelessness depression: A theory-based subtype of depression. *Psychological Review.*

Abramson, L.Y., Seligman, M.E.P., & Teasdale, J.D. (1978). Learned helplessness in humans. Critique and reformulation. *Journal of Abnormal Psychology,* **87,** 49–74.

Achenbach, T.M. (1982). *Developmental psychopathology* (2nd ed.). New York: Wiley.

Achenbach, T.M., & Edelbrock, C.S. (1978). The classification of child psychopathology: A review of empirical efforts. *Psychological Bulletin,* **85,** 1275–1301.

Achenbach, T.M., & Edelbrock, C.S. (1981). Behavioral problems and competencies reported by parents of normal and disturbed children aged 4 through 16. *Monographs of the Society for Research in Child Development,* **46,** Serial No. 188.

Achenbach, T.M., & Edelbrook, C. (1983). *Manual for the child behavior checklist.* Burlington, Vt: Author.

Adams, E.H., & Durell, J. (1984). Cocaine: A growing public health problem. In J. Grabowski (Ed.), *Cocaine: Pharmacology, effects, and treatment of abuse.* Rockville, Md.: NIDA.

Adams, J. (1978). *Psychoanalysis of drug dependence.* New York: Grune & Stratton.

Adams, K.M. (1980). In search of Luria's battery: A false start. *Journal of Consulting and Clinical Psychology,* **48,** 511–516.

Adler, A. (1929). *Problems of neurosis.* New York: Harper & Row.

Adler, A. (1964). Compulsion neurosis, 1931. In H.L. Ansbacher & R.R. Ansbacher (Eds.), *Superiority and social interest.* Evanston, Ill.: Northwestern University Press.

Agras, W.S., Schneider, J.A., Arnow, B., Raeburm, S.D., & Telch, C.F. (1989). Cognitive-behavioral and response-prevention treatments for bulimia nervosa. *Journal of Consulting and Clinical Psychology,* **57,** 215–221.

Agras, S., Sylvester, D., & Oliveau, D. (1969). The epidemiology of common fears and phobias. Unpublished manuscript, 1969.

Aigner, T.G., & Balster, R.L. (1978). Choice behavior in rhesus monkeys: Cocaine versus food. *Science,* **201,** 534–535.

Akhter, S., Wig, N.N., Varma, V.K., Pershad, D., & Verma, S.K. (1975). A phenomenological analysis of symptoms in obsessive-compulsive neurosis. *British Journal of Psychiatry,* **127,** 342–348.

Albee, G.W., Lane, E.A., & Reuter, J.M. (1964). Childhood intelligence of future schizophrenics and neighborhood peers. *Journal of Psychology,* **58,** 141–144.

Aldrich, C.K., & Mendkoff, E. (1963). Relocation of the aged and disabled: A mortality study. *Journal of the American Geriatrics Society,* **11,** 185–194.

Alexander, F. (1950). *Psychosomatic medicine.* New York: Norton.

Alexander, F., & French, T.M. (1946). *Psychoanalytic therapy.* New York: Ronald Press.

Alexander, P.C., & Lupfer, S.L. (1987) Family characteristics and long-term consequences associated with sexual abuse. *Archives of Sexual Behavior,* **16,** 235–245.

Allderidge, P. (1979). Hospitals, mad houses, and asylums: Cycles in the care of the insane. *British Journal of Psychiatry,* **134,** 321–324.

Allen, G.J., Chinsky, J.M., Larsen, S.W., Lockman, J.E., & Selinger, H.V. (1976). *Community psychology and the schools: A behaviorally oriented multilevel preventive approach.* Hillsdale, N.J.: Erlbaum.

Allen, M.G. (1976). Twin studies of affective illness. *Archives of General Psychiatry,* **33,** 1476–1478.

Alloy, L.B., & Abramson, L.Y. (1979). Judgment of contingency in depressed and nondepressed students: Sadder but wiser? *Journal of Experimental Psychology: General,* **108,** 441–485.

Alloy, L.B., Kelly, K.A., Mineka, S., & Clements, C.M. (in press). Comorbidity in anxiety and depressive disorders: A helplessness/hopelessness perspective. In J.D. Maser and C.R. Cloninger (Eds.), *Comorbidity in anxiety and mood disorders.* Washington, D.C.: American Psychiatric Press.

Allport, G.W. (1937). *Personality: A psychological interpretation.* New York: Holt, Rinehart & Winston.

Allport, G.W. (1961). *Pattern and growth in personality.* New York: Holt, Rinehart & Winston.

Allport, G.W. (1954). *The nature of prejudice.* Cambridge, Mass:, Addison–Wesley.

American Cancer Society. (1976). *Task force on tobacco and cancer—Target 5.* Report to the Board of Directors, American Cancer Society.

American Heart Association Heart Facts 1982. (1981). Dallas: American Heart Association.

American Law Institute (1962). *Model penal code: Proposed official draft.* Philadelphia: The American Law Institute.

American Psychiatric Association. *Diagnostic and statistical manual of mental disorders.* First edition, 1952; second edition, 1968; third edition, 1980; revised, 1987. Washington, D.C.: American Psychiatric Association.

Anderson, B.J., & Wolf, F.M. (1986). Chronic physical illness and sexual behavior: Psychological issues. *Journal of Consulting and Clinical Psychology,* **54,** 168–175.

Anderson, B.L. (1983). Primary orgasmic dysfunction: Diagnostic considerations and review of treatment. *Psychological Bulletin,* **93,** 105–136.

Andreasen, N.C. (1979). Thought, language, and communication disorders: II. Diagnostic significance. *Archives of General Psychiatry,* **36,** 1325–1330.

Andreasen, N.C. (1982). Negative symptoms in schizophrenia. Definition and reliability. *Archives of General Psychiatry,* **39,** 784–787.

Andreasen, N.C. (1984). *The broken brain.* New York: Harper & Row.

Andreasen, N.C., Nasrallah, H.A., Dunn, V., Olson, S.C., Ehrhardt, J.C., Coffman, J. A., & Crosset, J.H.W. (1986). Structural abnormalities in the frontal system of schizophrenia. *Archives of General Psychiatry,* **40,** 258–263.

Andreasen, N.C., & Olsen, S.A. (1982). Negative versus positive schizophrenia. Definition and validation. *Archives of General Psychiatry,* **39,** 789–794.

Andreasen, N.C., Olsen, S.A., Dennert, J. W., & Smith, M.R. (1982). Ventricular enlargement in schizophrenia: Relationship to positive and negative symptoms. *American Journal of Psychiatry,* **139,** 297–302.

Andreasen, N.C., Rice, J., Endicott, J., Coryell, W., Grove, W.W., & Reich, T. (1987). Familial rates of affective disorder. *Archives of General Psychiatry,* **44,** 461–472.

Angrist, B., Lee, H.K., & Gershon, S. (1974). The antagonism of amphetamine-induced symptomatology by a neuroleptic. *American Journal of Psychiatry,* **131,** 817–819.

Aniline, O., & Pitts, F.N., Jr. (1982). Phencyclidine (PCP): A review and perspectives. *CRC Critical Review of Toxicology,* **10,** 145–177.

Anthony-Bergstone, C., Zarit, S.H., & Gatz, M. (1988). Symptoms of psychological distress among caregivers of dementia patients. *Psychology and Aging,* **3,** 245–248.

Appelbaum, P.S. (1985). *Tarasoff* and the clinician: Problems in fulfilling the duty to protect. *American Journal of Psychiatry,* **142,** 425–429.

Appley, M., & Trumball, R. (1967). *Psychological Stress.* NY: Appleton-Century-Crofts.

Aragone, J., Cassady, J., & Drabman, R.S. (1975). Treating overweight children through parental training and contingency contracting. *Journal of Applied Behavior Analysis,* **8,** 269–278.

Arieti, S. (1955). *Interpretation of schizophrenia.* New York: Basic Books.

Arieti, S. (1979). New views on the psychodynamics of phobias. *American Journal of Psychotherapy,* **33,** 82–95.

Arkonac, O., & Guze, S.B. (1963). A family study of hysteria. *New England Journal of Medicine,* **268,** 239–242.

Armor, D.J., Polich, J.M., & Stambul, H. B. (1978). *Alcoholism and treatment.* New York: Wiley.

Aronson, E. (1972). *The social animal.* San Francisco: Freeman.

Aronson, E., & Carlsmith, J.R. (1968). Experimentation in social psychology. In G. Lindzey & E. Aronson (Eds.). *The handbook of social psychology: Vol 2. Research methods.* Menlo Park, Calif.: Addison–Wesley.

Ashcroft, G., Crawford, T., & Eccleston, E. S. (1966). 5-Hydroxyindole compounds in the cerebrospinal fluid of patients with psychiatric or neurological disease. *Lancet,* **2,** 1049–1052.

Atchley, R. (1980). Aging and suicide: Reflection of the quality of life. In S. Haynes & M. Feinleib (Eds.), *Proceedings of the Second Conference on the Epidemiology of Aging.* National Institute of Health, Washington, D.C.: U.S. Government Printing Office.

Atkinson, R.C., & Shiffrin, R.M. (1969). Human memory: A proposed system and its control processes. In K.W. Spence & J.T. Spence (Eds.), *The psychology of learning and motivation: Advances in research and theory* (Vol. 2). New York: Academic Press.

Atthowe, J.M. (1976). Treating the hospitalized person. In W.E. Craighead, A.E. Kazdin, & M.J. Mahoney (Eds.), *Behavior modification: Principles, issues, and applications.* Boston: Houghton Mifflin.

August, G.J., Stewart, M.A., & Tsai, L. (1981). The incidence of cognitive disabilities in siblings of autistic children. *British Journal of Psychiatry,* **138,** 416–422.

Ausubel, D.P. (1961). Causes and types of narcotic addictions: A psychosocial view. *Psychiatric Quarterly,* **35,** 523–531. (a)

Ausubel, D.P. (1961). Personality disorder is disease. *American Psychologist,* **16,** 69–74. (b)

Ax, A.F. (1953). The physiological differentiation between fear and anger in humans. *Psychosomatic Medicine,* **15,** 433–442.

Axline, V.M. (1964). *Dibs: In search of self.* New York: Ballantine.

Ayllon, T., & Azrin, N.H. (1968). *The token economy: A motivational system for therapy and rehabilitation.* New York: Appleton–Century–Crofts.

Azrin, N.H., Sneed, T.J., & Foxx, R.M. (1973). Dry bed: A rapid method of eliminating bedwetting (enuresis) of the retarded. *Behaviour Research and Therapy,* **11,** 427–434.

Bach, G.R. (1966). The marathon group: Intensive practice of intimate interactions. *Psychological Reports,* **181,** 995–1002.

Bagby, E. (1922). The etiology of phobias. *Journal of Abnormal Psychology,* **17,** 16–18.

Bahm, A.K., Chandler, C., & Eisenberg, L. (1961). *Diagnostic characteristics related to service on psychiatric clinics for children.* Paper presented at the 38th Annual Convention of Orthopsychiatry, Munich.

Baker, T., and Brandon, T.H. (1988). Behavioral treatment strategies. In *A report of the Surgeon General: The health consequences of smoking: Nicotine addiction.* Rockville, Md.: U.S. Department of Health and Human Services.

Bakwin, H. (1973). The genetics of enuresis. In J. Kolvin, R.C. MacKeith, & S.R. Meadow (Eds.), *Enuresis and encopresis.* Philadelphia: Lippincott.

Ball, J.C., & Chambers, C.D. (Eds.) (1970). *The epidemiology of opiate addiction in the United States.* Springfield, Ill.: Charles C. Thomas.

Ball-Rokeach, S.J., Rokeach, M., & Grube, J.W. (1984). *The great American values test.* New York: Free Press.

Ballenger, J.C., Burrows, G.O., DuPont, R.L., Lesser, M., Noyes, R.C. et al. (1988). Aprazolam in panic disorder and agoraphobia, results from multicenter trial. *Archives of General Psychiatry,* **45,** 413–421.

Baller, W.R. (1975). *Bed-wetting: Origin and treatment.* Elmsford, N.Y.: Pergamon.

Bancroft, J.H., Jones, G.H., & Pullan, B. R. (1966). A simple transducer for measuring penile erections, with comments on its use in the treatment of sexual disorders. *Behaviour Research and Therapy,* **4,** 239–241.

Bancroft, J.L., & Bell, C. (1985). Simultaneous recording of penile diameter and penile arterial pulse during laboratory-based erotic stimulation in normal subjects. *Journal of Psychosomatic Research,* **29,** 303–313.

Bandura, A. (1969). *Principles of behavior modification.* New York: Holt, Rinehart & Winston.

Bandura, A. (1973). *Aggression: A social learning analysis.* Englewood Cliffs, N.J.: Prentice–Hall.

Bandura, A. (1977). Self-efficacy: Toward a unifying theory of behavioral change. *Psychological Review,* **84,** 191–215.

Bandura, A. (1982). The psychology of chance encounters. *American Psychologist,* **37,** 747–755.

Bandura, A. (1986). *Social foundations of thought and action: A social cognitive theory.* Englewood Cliffs, N.J.: Prentice–Hall.

Bandura, A., Blanchard, E.B., & Ritter, B. (1969). Relative efficacy of desensitization and modelling approaches for inducing behavioral, affective, and attitudinal changes.

Journal of Personality and Social Psychology, **13**, 173–199.

Bandura, A., Grusec, J.E., & Menlove, F. L. (1967). Vicarious extinction of avoidance behavior. *Journal of Personality and Social Psychology*, **5**, 16–23.

Bandura, A., Jeffrey, R.W., & Bachicha, D. L. (1974). Analysis of memory codes and cumulative rehearsal in observational learning. *Journal of Research in Personality*, **7**, 295–305.

Bandura, A., & Menlove, F.L. (1968). Factors determining vicarious extinction of avoidance behavior through symbolic modeling. *Journal of Personality and Social Psychology*, **8**, 99–108.

Bandura, A., & Perloff, B. (1967). Relative efficacy of self-monitored and externally imposed reinforcement systems. *Journal of Personality and Social Psychology*, **7**, 111–116.

Bandura, A., & Rosenthal, T.L. (1966). Vicarious classical conditioning as a function of arousal level. *Journal of Personality and Social Psychology*, **3**, 54–62.

Bandura, A., & Walters, R.H. (1959). *Adolescent aggression*. New York: Ronald Press.

Bandura, A., & Walters, R.H. (1963). *Social learning and personality development*. New York: Holt, Rinehart & Winston.

Banis, H.T., Varni, J.W., Wallander, J.L., Korsch, B.M., Jay, S.M., Adler, R., Garcia-Temple, E., & Negrete, V. (1988). Psychological and social adjustment of obese children and their families. *Child: Care, Health, and Development*, **14**, 157–173.

Barabee, H.E., Marshall, W.L., & Lanthier, R. (1979). Deviant sexual arousal in rapists. *Behaviour Research and Therapy*, **17**, 215–222.

Barahal, H.S. (1958). 1000 prefrontal lobotomies: Five-to-ten-year follow-up study. *Psychiatric Quarterly*, **32**, 653–678.

Barbach, L.G. (1975). *For yourself*. New York: Doubleday.

Barber, T.X. (1969). *Hypnosis: A scientific approach*. New York: Van Nostrand–Reinhold.

Barber, T.X., & Silver, M.J. (1968). Fact, fiction, and the experimenter bias effect. *Psychological Bulletin, Monograph Supplement*, **70**, 1–29.

Barefoot, J.C., Dahlstrom, G., & Williams, R.B. (1983). Hostility, CHD incidence, and total mortality: A 25-year follow-up study of 255 physicians. *Psychosomatic Medicine*, **45**, 59–63.

Barkley, R.A. (1981). *Hyperactive children: A handbook for diagnosis and treatment*. New York: Guilford.

Barkley, R.A., & Cunningham, C.E. (1979). The effects of methylphenidate on the mother–child interactions of hyperactive children. *Archives of General Psychiatry*, **36**, 201–208.

Barkley, R.A., Hasting, J.E., Tousel, R. E., & Tousel, S.E. (1976). Evaluation of a token system for juvenile delinquents in a residential setting. *Journal of Behavior Therapy and Experimental Psychiatry*, **7**, 227–230.

Barlow, D.H., Abel, G.G., & Blanchard, E.B. (1979). Gender identity change in transsexuals. *Archives of General Psychiatry*, **36**, 1001–1007.

Barlow, D.H., Becker, R., Leitenberg, H., & Agras, W.S. (1970). A mechanical strain gauge for recording penile circumference. *Journal of Applied Behavior Analysis*, **3**, 73–76.

Barlow, D.H., Cohen, A.B., Waddell, M. T., Vermilyea, B.B., Klosko, J.S., Blanchard, E.B., & DiNardo, P.A. (1984). Panic and generalized anxiety disorders: Nature and treatment. *Behavior Therapy*, **15**, 431–449.

Barlow, D.H., Reynolds, E.J., & Agras, W.S. (1973). Gender identity change in a transsexual. *Archives of General Psychiatry*, **29**, 569–576.

Barlow, D.H., Sakheim, D.K., & Beck, J. G. (1983). Anxiety increases sexual arousal. *Journal of Abnormal Psychology*, **92**, 49–54.

Barlow, D.H., & Waddell, M.T. (1985). Agoraphobia. In D.H. Barlow (Ed.), *Clinical handbook of psychological disorders*. New York: Guilford.

Baron, R.A., & Byrne, D. (1977). *Social psychology: Understanding human interaction* (2nd ed.). Boston: Allyn & Bacon.

Barrett, C.L. (1969) Systematic desensitization versus implosive therapy. *Journal of Abnormal Psychology*, **74**, 587–592.

Barrett, C.L., Hampe, E., & Miller, L. (1978). Research on psychotherapy with children. In S.L. Garfield & A.E. Bergin (Eds.), *Handbook of psychotherapy and behavior change: An empirical analysis* (2nd ed.). New York: Wiley.

Bartlett, F. (1932). *Remembering*. Cambridge, England: Cambridge University Press.

Bartus, R.T., Dean, R.L., Beer, B., & Lippa, A.S. (1982). The cholinergic hypothesis of geriatric memory dysfunction. *Science*, **217**, 408–417.

Basedow, H. (1925). *The Australian aboriginal*. London: Adelaide.

Basmajian, J.V. (1977). Learned control of single motor units. In G.E. Schwartz & J. Beatty (Eds.), *Biofeedback: Theory and Research*. New York: Academic Press.

Bates, G.W., Campbell, I.M., & Burgess, P.M. (in press). Assessment of articulated thoughts in social anxiety: Modification of the ATSS procedure. *British Journal of Clinical Psychology*.

Bateson, G., Jackson, D.D., Haley, J., & Weakland, J. (1956). Toward a theory of schizophrenia. *Behavioral Science*, **1**, 251–264.

Battle, E.S., & Lacey, B.A. (1972). Context for hyperactivity in children, over time. *Child Development*, **43**, 757–773.

Baucom, D.H., & Lester, G.W. (1986). The usefulness of cognitive restructuring as an adjunct to behavioral marital therapy. *Behavior Therapy*, **17**, 385–403.

Bauer, D.H. (1976). An exploratory study of developmental changes in children's fears. *Journal of Child Psychology and Psychiatry*, **17**, 69–74.

Baum, M. (1970). Extinction of avoidance responding through response prevention (flooding). *Psychological Bulletin*, **74**, 276–284.

Baumeister, A.A. (1984). Some methodological and conceptual issues in the study of cognitive processes with retarded people. In P.H. Brooks, R. Sperber, & C. McCauley (Eds.), *Learning and cognition in the mentally retarded*. Hillsdale, N.J.: Erlbaum.

Baumeister, A.A., & Berkson, G. (1980). FY 1981 Appropriations Statement on Appropriations to the National Institute of Child Health and Human Development.

Baumeister, A.A., & Maclean, W.E., Jr. (1979). Brain damage and mental retardation. In N.R. Ellis (Ed.), *Handbook of mental deficiency, psychological theory and research* (2nd ed.). Hillsdale, N.J.: Erlbaum.

Baxter, E., & Hopper, K. (1981). *Private lives/public places: Homeless adults on the streets of New York City*. New York: Community Service Society.

Beck, A.T. (1967). *Depression: Clinical, experimental and theoretical aspects*. New York: Harper & Row.

Beck, A.T. (1976). *Cognitive therapy and the emotional disorders*. New York: International Universities Press.

Beck, A.T. (1986). Hopelessness as a predictor of eventual suicide. In J.J. Mann & M. Stanley (Eds.), *Psychobiology of suicidal behavior*. New York: New York Academy of Sciences. (a)

Beck, A.T. (1986). Cognitive therapy: A sign of retrogression or progress. *The Behavior Therapist*, **9**, 2–3. (b)

Beck, A.T., Brown, G., Steer, R.A., Eidelson, J.I., & Riskind, J.H. (1987). Differentiating anxiety and depression: A test of the cognitive-content-specificity hypothesis. *Journal of Abnormal Psychology*, **96**, 179–183.

Beck, A.T., & Emery, G. (1985). *Anxiety disorders and phobias: A cognitive perspective*. New York: Basic Books.

Beck, A.T., Kovacs, M., & Weissman, A. (1975). Hopelessness and suicidal behavior: An overview. *Journal of the American Medical Associations*, **234**, 1146–1149.

Beck, A.T., Kovacs, M., & Weissman, A. (1979). Assessment of suicidal ideation: The

Scale for Suicide Ideation. *Journal of Consulting and Clinical Psychology, 47,* 343–352.

Beck, A.T., Rush, A.J., Shaw, B.F., & Emery, G. (1979). *Cognitive therapy of depression.* New York: Guilford.

Beck, A.T. Schuyler, D., & Herman, I. (1974). Development of suicidal intent scales. In A.T. Beck, H.L.P. Resnik, & D.J. Lettieri (Eds.), *The prediction of suicide.* Bowie, Md.: Charles Press.

Beck, A.T., Steer, R.A., Kovacs, M., & Garrison, B. (1985). Hopelessness and eventual suicide: A 10-year prospective study of patients hospitalized with suicidal ideation. *American Journal of Psychiatry, 142,* 559–563.

Beck, A.T., & Ward, C.H. (1961). Dreams of depressed patients: Characteristic themes in manifest content. *Archives of General Psychiatry, 5,* 462–467.

Beck, A.T., Ward, C.H. Mendelson, M., Mock, J.E., & Erbaugh, J.K. (1962). Reliability of psychiatric diagnosis: II. A study of consistency of clinical judgments and ratings. *American Journal of Psychiatry, 119,* 351–357.

Beck, J.G., Barlow.D.H., Sakheim, D.K., & Abrahamson, D.J. (1984). *Sexual responding during anxiety: Clinical versus nonclinical patterns.* Paper presented at the 18th annual convention of the Association for Advancement of Behavior Therapy, Philadelphia. As cited in Barlow, D.H. (1986). Causes of sexual dysfunction: The role of anxiety and cognitive interference. *Journal of Consulting and Clinical Psychology, 54,* 140–148.

Beck, J.G., Sakheim, D.K., & Barlow, D. H. (1983). Operating characterisitcs of the vaginal photoplethysmograph: Some implications for its use. *Archives of Sexual Behavior, 12,* 43–58.

Beck, M. (1979, November 12). Viet vets fight back. *Newsweek,* 44–49.

Becker, C., & Kronus, S. (1977). Sex and drinking patterns: An old relationship revisited in a new way. *Social Problems, 24,* 482–497.

Becker, J.V. (1988). Adolescent sex offenders. *The Behavior Therapist, 11,* 185–187.

Becker, J., & Schuckit, M.A. (1978). The comparative efficacy of cognitive therapy and pharmacotherapy in the treatment of depression. *Cognitive Therapy and Research, 2,* 193–197.

Bednar, R.L., & Kaul, T.J. (1978). Experiential group research: Current perspectives. In S.L. Garfield & A.E. Bergin (Eds.), *Handbook of psychotherapy and behavior change: An empirical analysis* (2nd ed.). New York: Wiley.

Beecher, H.K. (1966). Ethics and clinical research. *New England Journal of Medicine,* **274,** 1354–1360.

Begab, M.J. (1974). The major dilemma of mental retardation: Shall we prevent it? (Some implications of research in mental retardation). *American Journal of Mental Deficiency, 78,* 519–529.

Begelman, D.A. (1975). Ethical and legal issues of behavior modification. In M. Hersen, R. Eisler, & P.M. Miller (Eds.). *Progress in behavior modification.* New York: Academic Press.

Bell, A.P., & Wineberg, M.A. (1978). *Homosexualities: A study of diversity among men and women.* New York: Simon & Schuster.

Bell, J.E. (1975). *Family therapy.* New York: Jason Aronson.

Bellack, A.S., Hersen, M., & Turner, S.M. (1976). Generalization effects of social skills training in chronic schizophrenics: An experimental analysis. *Behavior Research and Therapy, 14,* 391–398.

Bellack, A.S., Turner, S.M., Hersen, M., & Luber, R.F. (1984). An examination of the efficacy of social skills training for chronic schizophrenic patients. *Hospital and Community Psychiatry, 35,* 1023–1028.

Belliveau, E., & Richter, L. (1970). *Understanding "Human Sexual Inadequacy."* New York: Bantam.

Belmont, J.M., & Butterfield, E.C. (1969). The relations of short-term memory to development and intelligence. In L.P. Lipsitt & H.W. Reese (Eds.), *Advances in Child Development and Behavior* (Vol. 4). New York: Academic Press.

Belmont, J.M., & Butterfield, E.C. (1971). Learning strategies as determinants of memory deficiencies. *Cognitive Psychology, 2,* 411–420.

Bem, D.J., & Allen, A. (1974). On predicting some of the people some of the time: The search for cross-situational consistencies in behavior. *Psychological Review, 81,* 506–520.

Bem, S.L. (1974). The measurement of psychological androgyny. *Journal of Consulting and Clinical Psychology, 42,* 155–162.

Bem, S.L. (1984). Gender schema theory and its implications for child development: Raising gender-aschematic children in a gender-schematic society. *Signs: Journal of Women in Culture and Society, 8,* 598–616.

Bemis, K.M. (1978). Current approaches to the etiology and treatment of anorexia nervosa. *Psychological Bulletin, 85,* 593–617.

Bender, L., & Blau, A. (1937). The reactions of children to sexual relations with adults. *American Journal of Orthopsychiatry, 7,* 500–518.

Bennett, C.C., Anderson, L.S., Cooper, S., Hassol, L., Klein, D.C., & Rosenblum, G. (Eds.). (1966). *Community psychology: A report of the Boston Conference on the education of psychologists for community mental health.* Boston: Boston University Press.

Bennett, I. (1960). *Delinquent and neurotic children.* London: Tavistock Publications.

Bennett, W. (1980). The nicotine fix. *Harvard Magazine, 82,* 10–14.

Benowitz, N.L., & Jacob, P., III. (1984). Daily intake of nicotine during cigarette smoking. *Clinical Pharmacology Therapeutics, 35,* 499–504.

Benson, H. (1975). *The relaxation response.* New York: Morrow.

Ben-Tovim, M.V., & Crisp, A.H. (1979). Personality and mental state within anorexia nervosa. *Journal of Psychosomatic Research, 23,* 321–325.

Benton, A. (1978). Some conclusions about dyslexia. In A.L. Benton & D. Pearl (Eds.), *Dyslexia.* New York: Oxford University Press.

Berger, K.S., & Zarit, S.H. (1978). Late life paranoid states: Assessment and treatment. *American Journal of Orthopsychiatry, 48,* 528–537.

Berger, P.A., & Dunn, M.J. (1982). Substance induced and substance use disorders (opioids, cocaine, amphetamines and similarly acting sympathomimetics, phencyclidine (PCP), inhalants, hallucinogens, and cannabis, tobacco, caffeine). In J.H. Greist, J.W. Jefferson, & R.L. Spitzer (Eds.), *Treatment of mental disorders.* New York: Oxford University Press.

Bergin, A.E. (1966). Some implications of psychotherapy research for therapeutic practice. *Journal of Abnormal Psychology, 71,* 235–246.

Bergin, A.E. (1971). The evaluation of therapeutic outcomes. In A.E. Bergin & S.L. Garfield (Eds.), *Handbook of psychotherapy and behavior change: An empirical analysis.* New York: Wiley.

Bergin, A.E., & Lambert, M.J. (1978). The evaluation of therapeutic outcomes. In S. L. Garfield & A.E. Bergin (Eds.), *Handbook of psychotherapy and behavior change: An empirical analysis* (2nd ed.). New York: Wiley.

Bergler, E. (1946). Personality traits of alcohol addicts. *Quarterly Journal of Studies on Alcohol, 7,* 356–361.

Bergman, J.D., Dykens, E., Watson, M., Ort, S.I., & Leckman, J.F. (1987). Fragile-X syndrome: Variability of phenotypic expression. *Journal of the American Academy of Child and Adolescent Psychiatry, 26,* 463–467.

Bergmann, K., Kay, D.W.K., Foster, E. M., McKechnie, A.A., & Roth, M. (1971). A follow-up study of randomly selected community residents to assess the effects of chronic organic brain syndrome and cerebrovascular disease. *Psychiatry,* Part II,

Proceedings of the Fifth World Congress of Psychiatry, Mexico.

Berlin, F.S., & Meinecke, C.F. (1981). Treatment of sex offenders with antiandrogenic medication: Conceptualization, review of treatment modalities, and preliminary findings. *American Journal of Psychiatry, 138,* 601–607.

Berman, E.M., & Lief, H.I. (1976). Sex and the aging process. In W.W. Oaks, G. A. Melchiode, & I. Ficher (Eds.), *Sex and the life cycle.* New York: Grune & Stratton.

Bernard, J. (1973). *The future of marriage.* New York: Bantam.

Bernstein, D.A., & Nietzel, M.T. (1980). *Introduction to clinical psychology.* New York: McGraw–Hill.

Berry, J.C. (1967). *Antecedents of schizophrenia, impulsive character and alcoholism in males.* Paper presented at the 75th Annual convention of the American Psychological Association, Washington, D.C.

Besdine, R.W. (1980). Geriatric medicine: An overview. In C. Eisodorfer (Ed.), *Annual review of gerontology and geriatrics.* New York: Springer.

Bettelheim, B. (1967). *The empty fortress.* New York: Free Press.

Bettelheim, B. (1969). *Children of the dream.* London: Collier–Macmillan.

Bettelheim, B. (1973). Bringing up children. *Ladies Homes Journal, 90,* 28.

Bettelheim, B. (1974). *A home for the heart.* New York: Knopf.

Beutler, L.E. (1983). *Eclectic psychotherapy: A systematic approach.* New York: Pergamon.

Beutler, L.E., Cargo, M., & Arizmendi, T. G. (1986). Therapist variables in psychotherapy process and outcome. In S.L. Garfield & A.E. Bergin (Eds.), *Handbook of psychotherapy and behavior change* (3rd ed.). New York: Wiley.

Beutler, L.E., Scogin, F., Kirkish, P., Schretlen, D., Corbishley, A., Hamblin, D., Meredith, K., Potter, R., Bamford, C.R., & Levenson, A.I. (1987). Group cognitive therapy and alprazolam in the treatment of depression in older adults. *Journal of Consulting and Clinical Psychology, 55,* 550–556.

Bibring, E. (1953). The mechanism of depression. In P. Greenacre (Ed.), *Affective disorders.* New York: International Universities Press.

Bieber, I., Dain, H.J., Dince, P.R., Drellich, M.G., Grand, H.C., Gundlach, R. H., Kremer, M.W., Rifkin, A.H., Wilbur, C.B., & Bieber, T.B. (1962). *Homosexuality: A psychoanalytical study.* New York: Random House.

Biederman, J., Rivinus, T.M., Herzog, D. B., Ferber, R.A., Harper, G.P., Orsulak, P.J., Harmatz, J.S., & Schildkraut, J.J. (1984). Platelet MAO activity in anorexia nervosa patients with and without a major depressive disorder. *American Journal of Psychiatry, 141,* 1244–1247.

Billings, A. (1979). Conflict resolution in distressed and nondistressed married couples. *Journal of Consulting and Clinical Psychology, 47,* 368–376.

Billings, A.G., Cronkite, R.C., & Moos, R.H. (1983). Social-environmental factors in unipolar depression: Comparisons of depressed patients and nondepressed controls. *Journal of Abnormal Psychology, 92,* 119–133.

Bindrim, P. (1968). A report on a nude marathon: The effect of physical nudity upon the practice interaction in the marathon group. *Psychotherapy: Theory, Research and Practice, 5,* 180–188.

Birbaumer, H. (1977). Biofeedback training: A critical review of its clinical applications and some possible future directions. *European Journal of Behavioural Analysis and Modification, 4,* 235–251.

Birnbaum, M. (1960). The right to treatment. *American Bar Association Journal, 46,* 499–505.

Biron, M., Risch, N., Hamburger, R., Mandel, B., Kushner, S., Newman, M., Drumer, D., & Belmaker, R.H. (1987). Genetic linkage between X-chromosome markers and bipolar affective illness. *Nature, 326,* 289–292.

Birren, J.E., & Sloane, R.B. (Eds.). (1980). *Handbook of mental health and aging.* Englewood Cliffs, N.J.: Prentice–Hall.

Bitterman, M.E. (1975). Issues in the comparative psychology of learning. In R.B. Masterson, M.E. Bitterman, C.B.G. Campbell, & N. Hotten (Eds.), *The evolution of brain and behavior in vertebrates.* Hillsdale, N.J.: Erlbaum.

Bjorkqvist, S.E. (1975). Clonidine in alcohol withdrawal. *Acta Psychiatrica Scandinavica, 52,* 256–263.

Blackburn, I.M., Eunson, K.M., & Bishop, S. (1986). A two-year naturalistic follow-up of depressed patients treated with cognitive therapy, pharmacotherapy, and a combination of both. *Journal of Affective Disorders, 10,* 67–75.

Blanchard, E.B., Andrasik, F., Neff, D.F., Arena, J.G., Ahles, T.A., Jurish, S.E., Pallmeyer, T.P., Saunders, N.L., & Teders, S.J. (1982). Biofeedback and relaxation training with three kinds of headache: Treatment effects and their prediction. *Journal of Consulting and Clinical Psychology, 50,* 562–575.

Blanchard, E.B., & Miller, S.T. (1977). Psychological treatment of cardiovascular disease. *Archives of General Psychiatry, 34,* 1402–1413.

Blanchard, E.B., Miller, S.T., Abel, G.G., Haynes, M.R., & Wicker, R. (1979). Evaluation of biofeedback in the treatment of borderline essential hypertension. *Journal of Applied Behavior Analysis, 12,* 99–109.

Blanchard, E.B., Theobald, E.E., Williamson, D.A., Silver, B.V., & Brown, D.A. (1978). Temperature biofeedback in the treatment of migraine headaches: A controlled evaluation. *Archives of General Psychiatry, 35,* 581–588.

Bland, K., & Hallam, R. (1981). Relationship between response to graded exposure and marital satisfaction in agoraphobics. *Behaviour Research and Therapy, 19,* 335–338.

Blatt, B. (1966). The preparation of special educational personnel. *Review of Educational Research, 36,* 151–161.

Blazer, D.G. (1982). *Depression in late life.* St. Louis: Mosby. (a)

Blazer, D.G. (1982). Social support and mortality in an elderly community population. *American Journal of Epidemiology, 115,* 684–694. (b)

Blazer, D.G., Bachar, J.R., & Manton, K. G. (1986). Suicide in late life: Review and commentary. *Journal of the American Geriatrics Society, 34,* 519–525.

Blazer, D.G., & Siegler, I.C. (1984). *A family approach to health care of the elderly.* Menlo Park, Calif.: Addison–Wesley.

Blazer, D.G., & Williams, C.D. (1980). Epidemiology of dysphoria and depression in the elderly population. *American Journal of Psychiatry, 137,* 439–444.

Blenker, M. (1967). Environmental change and the aging individual. *Gerontologist, 7,* 101–105.

Bleuler, E. (1923). *Lehrbuch der psychiatrie* (4th ed.). Berlin: Springer.

Bliss, E.L. (1980). Multiple personalities: A report of 14 cases with implications for schizophrenia and hysteria. *Archives of General Psychiatry, 37,* 1388–1397.

Bliss, E.L. (1983). Multiple personalities, related disorders, and hypnosis. *American Journal of Clinical Hypnosis, 26,* 114–123.

Bliwise, D., Carskadon, M., Carey, E., & Dement, W. (1984). Longitudinal development of sleep-related respiratory disturbance in adult humans. *Journal of Gerontology, 39,* 290–293.

Bloch, S., and Reddaway, P. (1977). *Psychiatric terror: How Soviet psychiatry is used to suppress dissent.* New York: Basic Books.

Block, J. (1971). *Lives through time.* Berkeley, Calif.: Bancroft Books.

Bloom, B.L., Hodges, W.F., Kern, M.B., & McFaddin, S.C. (1985). A preventive intervention program for the newly separated:

Final evaluations. *American Journal of Orthopsychiatry, 55,* 9–26.

Bloomfield, H.H. (1973). Assertive training in an outpatient group of chronic schizophrenics: A preliminary report. *Behavior Therapy, 4,* 277–281.

Blumenthal, J.A., Williams, R.B., Kong, Y., Schanberg, S.M., & Thompson, I.W. (1978). Type A behavior and angiographically documented coronary disease. *Circulation, 58,* 634–639.

Bobruff, A., Gardos, G., Tarsy, D., Rapkin, R.M., Cole, J.O., & Moore, P. (1981). Clonazepan and phenobarbital in tardive dyskinesia. *American Journal of Psychiatry, 138,* 189–193.

Bockhoven, J. (1963). *Moral treatment in Amerian psychiatry.* New York: Springer.

Bohman, M., Cloninger R.C., Sigvardsson, S., & Knorring, A. von. (1982). Predisposition to criminality in Swedish adoptees: I. Genetic and environmental heterogeneity. *Archives of General Psychology, 39,* 1233–1241.

Bohman, M., Sigvardsson, S., & Cloninger, C.R. (1981). Maternal inheritance of alcohol abuse. *Archives of General Psychiatry, 38,* 965–969.

Boll, T.J. (1985). Developing issues in clinical neuropsychology. *Journal of Clinical and Experimental Neuropsychology, 7,* 473–485.

Boll, T.J., Heaton, R., & Reitan, R.M. (1974). Neuropsychological and emotional correlates of Huntington's chorea. *Journal of Nervous and Mental Disease, 158,* 61–69.

Bollerup, T. (1975). Prevalence of mental illness among 70 year olds domiciled in nine Copenhagen suburbs. *Acta Psychiatrica Scandinavica, 51,* 327–339.

Bond, I.K., & Hutchinson, H.C. (1960). Application of reciprocal inhibition therapy to exhibitionism. *Canadian Medical Association Journal, 83,* 23–25.

Bonica, J.J. (1981). Pain research and therapy: Past and current status and future needs. In L. Ng & J.J. Bonica (Eds.), *Pain, discomfort, and humanitarian care.* New York: Elsevier.

Bootzin, R.R., & Engle-Friedman, M. (1987). Sleep disturbances. In L.L. Carstensen & B.A. Edelstein (Eds.), *Handbook of clinical gerontology.* New York: Pergamon.

Bootzin, R.R., Engle-Friedman, M., & Hazelwood, L. (1983). Sleep disorders and the elderly. In P.M. Lewinsohn & L. Teri (Eds.), *Clinical geropsychology: New directions in assessment and treatment.* New York: Pergamon.

Borgatta, E.F., Montgomery, R.J.Y., & Borgatta, M.L. (1982). Alcohol use and abuse, life crisis events, and the elderly. *Research on Aging, 4,* 378–408.

Borkovec, T.D., & O'Brien, G.T. (1976). Methodological and target behavior issues in analogue outcome research. In M. Hersen, R.M. Eisler, & P.M. Miller (Eds.), *Progress in behavior modification* (Vol. 3). New York: Academic Press.

Bornstein, P.E., Clayton, P.J., Halikas, J. A., & Robins, E. (1973). The depression of widowhood after thirteen months. *British Journal of Psychiatry, 122,* 561–566.

Bornstein, P.H., Hamilton, P., Miller, D., Quevillon, C., & Spitzform, R. (1977). Reliability and validity enhancement: A treatment package for increasing fidelity of self-report. *Journal of Clinical Psychology, 33,* 861–866.

Bornstein, R.F., Leone, D.R., & Galley, D.J. (1987). The generalizability of subliminal mere exposure effects: Influence of stimuli perceived without awareness on social behavior. *Journal of Personality and Social Psychology, 53,* 1070–1079.

Bosch, G. (1970). *Infantile autism.* New York: Springer-Verlag.

Boskind-Lodahl, M., & White, W.C. (1978). The definition and treatment of bulimarexia in college women—A pilot study. *Journal of American College Health Association, 27,* 84–97.

Botwinick, J. (1977). Intellectual abilities. In J.E. Birren & K.W. Schaie (Eds.), *Handbook of the psychology of aging.* New York: Van Nostrand–Reinhold.

Botwinick, J. (1984). *Aging and Behavior* (3rd ed.). New York: Springer.

Boudewyns, P.A., Fry, T.J., & Nightingale, E.J. (1986). Token economy programs in VA medical centers: Where are they today? *The Behavior Therapist, 9,* 126–127.

Bourne, P.G. (1970). *Men, stress, and Vietnam.* Boston: Little, Brown.

Bourne, P.G., Alford, J.A., & Bowcock, J. Z. (1966). Treatment of skid row alcoholics with disulfiram. *Quarterly Journal of Studies on Alcohol, 27,* 42–48.

Bower, G.H. (1981). Mood and memory. *American Psychologist, 36,* 129–148.

Bower, G.H. (in press). Temporary emotional states act like multiple personalities. In R. Klein & B. Doane, (Eds.), *Psychological concepts and dissociative disorders: Reverberating implications.* Hillside, N.J.: Erlbaum.

Bower, G.H., Black, J.B., & Turner, T.J. (1979). Scripts in memory for text. *Cognitive Psychology, 11,* 177–220.

Bowers, M.B., Jr. (1974). Central dopamine turnover in schizophrenic syndromes. *Archives of General Psychiatry, 31,* 50–54.

Bowlby, J. (1973). *Attachment and loss: Vol. 2. Separation.* New York: Basic Books.

Bowlby, J. (1980). *Attachment and loss; Sadness and depression.* New York: Basic Books.

Brady, J.P., Davison, G.C., Dewald, P.A., Egan, G., Fadiman, J., Frank, J.D., Gill, M.M., Hoffman, I., Kempler, W., Lazarus, A.A., Raimy, V., Rotter, J.B., & Strupp, H.H. (1980). Some views on effective principles of psychotherapy. *Cognitive Therapy and Research, 4,* 271–306.

Brand, F.N., Smith, R.T., & Brand, P.A. (1977). Effect of economic barriers to medical care on patients' noncompliance. *Public Health Reports, 92,* 72–78.

Brand, R.J., Rosenman, R.H., Jenkins, C. D., Sholtz, R.L., & Zyzanski, S.J. (in press). Comparison of coronary heart disease prediction in the Western Collaborative Group Study using the structured interview and the Jenkins Activity Survey assessments of coronary-prone Type A behavior pattern. *Journal of Chronic Diseases.*

Brandt, J., Butters, N., Ryan, C., & Bayog, R. (1983). Cognitive loss and recovery in chronic alcohol abusers. *Archives of General Psychiatry, 40,* 435–442.

Bransford, J.D., & Johnson, M.K. (1973). Considerations of some problems of comprehension. In W.G. Chase (Ed.), *Visual information processing.* New York: Academic Press.

Brecher, E.M., & the Editors of *Consumer Reports* (1972). *Licit and illicit drugs,* Mount Vernon, N.Y.: Consumers Union.

Brehony, K.A., & Geller, E.S. (1981). Agoraphobia: Appraisal of research and a proposal for an integrative model. In M. Hersen, R.M. Eisler, & P.M. Miller (Eds.), *Progress in behavior modification* (Vol. 12). New York: Academic Press.

Breier, A., Charney, D.S., & Heninger, G.R. (1986). Agoraphobia with panic attacks. *Archives of General Psychiatry, 43,* 1029–1036.

Bressler, R. (1987). Drug use in the geriatric patient. In L.L. Carstensen & B.A. Edelstein (Eds.), *Handbook of clinical gerontology.* New York: Pergamon.

Bretschneider, J.G., & McCoy, N.L. (1988). Sexual interest and behavior in healthy 80- to 102-year-olds. *Archives of Sexual Behavior, 17,* 109–129.

Breuer, J., & Freud, S. (1895). *Studies in hysteria.* Translated and edited by J. Strachey, with the collaboration of A. Freud. New York: Basic Books, 1982.

Brewer, W.F., & Treyens, J.C. (1981). Role of schemata in memory for places. *Cognitive Psychology, 13,* 207–230.

Brickel, C.M. (1984). The clinical use of pets with the aged. *Clinical Gerontologist, 2,* 72–75.

Brickman, A.S., McManus, M., Grapentine, W.L., & Alessi, N. (1984). Neuropsychological assessment of seriously delinquent adolescents. *Journal of the American Academy of Child Psychiatry, 23,* 453–457.

Bridge, T.B., & Wyatt, R.J. (1980). Paraphrenia: Paranoid states of late life. II. American research. *Journal of the American Geriatrics Society, 28,* 205–210.

Bridge, T.P., Cannon, H.E., & Wyatt, R. J. (1978). Burned-out schizophrenia: Evidence for age effects on schizophrenic symptomatology. *Journal of Gerontology, 33,* 835–839.

Bridger, W.H., & Mandel, I.J. (1965). Abolition of the PRE by instructions in GSR conditioning. *Journal of Experimental Psychology, 69,* 476–482.

Brodie, H.K.H., & Leff, M.J. (1971). Bipolar depression: A comparative study of patient characteristics. *American Journal of Psychiatry, 127,* 1086–1090.

Brooks, J., & Weinraub, M. (1976). A history of infant intelligence testing. In M. Lewis (Ed.), *Origins of intelligence: Infancy and early childhood.* New York: Plenum.

Broverman, J.K., Broverman, D.M., & Clarkson, F.E. (1970). Sexual stereotypes and clinical judgments of mental health. *Journal of Consulting and Clinical Psychology, 34,* 1–7.

Brown, A.L. (1974). The role of strategic behavior in retardate memory. In N.R. Ellis (Ed.), *International review of research in mental retardation* (Vol. 7). New York: Academic Press.

Brown, G.W., & Birley, J.L.T. (1968). Crises and life changes and the onset of schizophrenia. *Journal of Health and Social Behavior, 9,* 203–214.

Brown, G.W., Bone, M., Dalison, B., & Wing, J.K. (1966). *Schizophrenia and social care.* London: Oxford University Press.

Brown, G.W., & Harris, T.O. (1978). *Social origins of depression.* London: Tavistock.

Browne, A., & Finkelhor, D. (1986). Impact of child sexual abuse: A review of the research. *Psychological Bulletin, 99,* 66–77.

Brownell, K.D. (1982). Behavioral medicine. In C.M. Franks, G.T. Wilson, P.C. Kendall, & K.D. Brownell (Eds.), *Annual review of behavior therapy: Theory and practice* (Vol. 8). New York: Guilford.

Brownell, K.D., Hayes, S.C., & Barlow, D.H. (1977). Patterns of appropriate and deviant sexual arousal: The behavioral treatment of multiple sexual deviations. *Journal of Consulting and Clinical Psychology, 45,* 1144–1155.

Brownell, K.D., Stunkard, A.J., & Albaum, J.M. (1980). Evaluation and modification of exercise patterns in the natural environment. *American Journal of Psychiatry, 137,* 1540–1545.

Brownmiller, S. (1975). *Against our will: Men, women and rape.* New York: Simon & Schuster.

Bruch, H. (1980). Preconditions for the development of anorexia nervosa. *American Journal of Psychoanalysis, 40,* 169–172.

Bruch, H. (1981). Developmental considerations of anorexia nervosa and obesity. *Canadian Journal of Psychiatry, 26,* 212–217.

Buchsbaum, M.S., Kessler, R., King, A., Johnson, J., & Cappelletti, J. (1984). Simultaneous cerebral glucography with positron emission tomography and topographic electroencephalography. In G. Pfurtscheller, E.J. Jonkman, & F.H. Lopes da Silva (Eds.), *Brain ischemia: Quantitative EEG and imaging techniques.* Amsterdam: Elsevier.

Budman, S.H., Demby, A., Feldstein, M., Redondo, J., Scherz, B., Bennett, M.J., Koppenaal, G., Daley, B.S., Hunter, M., & Ellis, J. (1987). Preliminary findings on a new instrument to measure cohesion in a group psychotherapy. *International Journal of Group Psychotherapy, 37,* 75–94.

Buell, T., Stoddard, P., Harris, F.R., & Baer, D.M. (1968). Collateral social development accompanying reinforcement of outdoor play in a preschool child. *Journal of Applied Behavior Analysis, 1,* 167–173.

Buglass, D., Clarke, J., Henderson, A.S., Kreitman, N., & Presley, A.S. (1977). A study of agoraphobic housewives. *Psychological Medicine, 7,* 73–86.

Bukovsky, V. (1977, May 3). General Svetlichny: "We will let him rot in the insane asylum!" *The New York Times.*

Bunney, W.E., Goodwin, F.K., & Murphy, D.L. (1972). The "Switch Process" in manic-depressive illness. *Archives of General Psychiatry, 27,* 312–317.

Bunney, W.E., Murphy, D.L., Goodwin, F.K., & Borge, G.F. (1970). The switch process from depression to mania: Relationship to drugs which alter brain amines. *Lancet, 1,* 1022.

Burgess, A.W., & Holmstrom, L.L. (1974). *Rape: Victims of crisis.* Bowie, Md.: Robert J. Brady Company.

Burnam, M.A., Stein, J.A., Golding, J. M., Siegel, J.M., Sorenson, S.B., Forsythe, A.B., & Telles, C.A. (1988). Sexual assault and mental disorders in a community population. *Journal of Consulting and Clinical Psychology, 56,* 843–850.

Burwen, L.S., & Campbell, D.T. (1957). The generality of attitudes toward authority and nonauthority figures. *Journal of Abnormal and Social Psychology, 54,* 24–31.

Buss, A.H. (1966). *Psychopathology,* New York: Wiley.

Busse, E.W. (1976). Hypochondriasis in the elderly: A reaction to social stress. *Journal of the American Geriatrics Society, 24,* 145–149.

Busse, E.W., & Blazer, D.G. (1979). Disorders related to biological functioning. In E.W. Busse & D. Blazer (Eds.), *Handbook of geriatric psychiatry.* New York: Van Nostrand-Reinhold.

Butler, R.N., & Lewis, M.I. (1982). *Aging and mental health: Positive psychosocial approaches* (3rd ed.). St. Louis: Mosby.

Butterfield, E.C., & Belmont, J.M. (1975). Assessing and improving the executive cognitive functions of mentally retarded people. In I. Bialer & M. Sternlicht (Eds.), *Psychological issues in mental retardation.* New York: Psychological Dimensions.

Butterfield, E.C., & Belmont, J.M. (1977). Assessing and improving the cognitive functions of mentally retarded people. In I. Bialer and M. Sternlicht (Eds.), *The psychology of mental retardation: Issues and approaches.* New York: Psychological Dimensions.

Caccioppo, J.T., Glass, C.R., & Merluzzi, T.V. (1979). Self-statements and self-evaluations: A cognitive-response analysis of heterosexual social anxiety. *Cognitive Therapy and Research, 3,* 249–262.

Caddy, G.R. (1983). Alcohol use and abuse. In B. Tabakoff, P.B. Sutker, C.L. Randell (Eds.), *Medical and social aspects of alcohol use.* New York: Plenum.

Caddy, G.R. (1985). Cognitive behavior therapy in the treatment of multiple personality. *Behavior Modification, 9,* 267–292.

Cadoret, R.J. (1978). Evidence for genetic inheritance of primary affective disorder in adoptees. *American Journal of Psychiatry, 135,* 463–466. (a)

Cadoret, R.J. (1978). Psychopathology in adopted-away offspring of biologic parents with antisocial behavior. *Archives of General Psychiatry, 35,* 176–184. (b)

Cadoret, R.J., Cain, C.A., & Grove, W. M. (1980). Development of alcoholism in adoptees raised apart from alcoholic biologic relatives. *Archives of General Psychiary, 37,* 561–563.

Calhoun, J.B. (1970). Space and the strategy of life. *Ekistics, 29,* 425–437.

Calhoun, K.S., Atkeson, B.M., & Resick, P.A. (1982). A longitudinal examination of fear reactions in victims of rape. *Journal of Counseling Psychology, 29,* 655–661.

Cameron, D.J., Thomas, R.I., Mulvihill, M., & Bronheim, H. (1987). Delirium: A test of the Diagnostic and Statistical Manual III criteria on medical inpatients. *Journal of the American Geriatrics Society, 35,* 1007–1010.

Cameron, N. (1959). The paranoid pseudo-community revisited. *American Journal of Sociology, 65,* 52–58.

Cameron, N. (1963). *Personality development and psychopathology: A dynamic approach.* Boston: Houghton Mifflin.

Cameron, N., & Magaret, A. (1951). *Behavior pathology.* Boston: Houghton Mifflin.

Campbell, M. (1987). Drug treatment of infantile autism: The past decade. In R. Shader (Ed.), *Psychopharmacology: A generation of progress.* New York: Raven Press.

Campbell, M. (1988). Fenfluramine treatment of autism. *Journal of Child Psychology and Psychiatry, 29,* 1–10.

Campbell, M., Adams, P., Small, A.M., Perry, R., Curren, E., Tesch, L. McV., Lynch, N., & Pidhorodeckyj, C. (in press). The effects of fenfluramine on behavioral symptoms and learning: A double-blind and placebo controlled study. (Submitted for publication.) Cited in Campbell (1988).

Campbell, S.B. (1985). Hyperactivity in preschoolers: Correlates and prognostic implications. *Clinical Psychology Review, 5,* 405–428.

Campbell, S.B., & Werry, J.S. (1986). Attention deficit disorder (hyperactivity). In H.C. Quay & J.S. Werry (Eds.), *Psychopathological disorders of childhood* (3rd ed.). New York: Wiley.

Cangelosi, A., Gressard, C.F., & Mines, R. A. (1980). The effects of a rational thinking group on self-concepts in adolescents. *The School Counselor, 27,* 357–361.

Cannon, D.S., & Baker, T.B. (1981). Emetic and electric shock alcohol aversion therapy: Assessment of conditioning. *Journal of Consulting and Clinical Psychology. 49,* 20–23.

Cannon, D.S., Baker, T.B., Gino, A., & Nathan, P.E. (in press). Alcohol aversion therapy: Relationship between strength of aversion and abstinence. In T.B. Baker & D.S. Cannon (Eds.), *Addictive disorders: Psychological research on assessment and treatment.* New York: Praeger.

Cannon, D.S., Baker, T.B., & Wehl, C.K. (1981). Emetic and electric shock alcohol aversion therapy: Six- and twelve-month follow-up. *Journal of Consulting and Clinical Psychology, 49,* 360–368.

Cannon, W.E. (1942). "Voodoo" death. *American Anthropologist, 44,* 169–182.

Cantwell, D.P. (1975) Genetic studies of hyperactive childen. In R. Fieve, D. Rosenthal, & H. Brill (Eds.), *Genetic research in psychiatry.* Baltimore: Johns Hopkins University Press.

Cantwell, D.P. (1983). Childhood depression: What do we know, where do we go? In S.B. Cruze, I.J. Baris, and J.E. Barrett (Eds.), *Childhood psychopathology and development.* New York: Raven Press.

Cantwell, D.P., Baker, L., & Rutter, M. (1978). Family factors. In M. Rutter & E. Schopler (Eds.), *Autism: A reappraisal of concepts and treatment.* New York: Plenum.

Cantwell, D.P., & Carlson, G.A. (1978). Stimulants. In J.S. Werry (Ed.), *Pediatric psychopharmacology: The use of behavior modifying drugs on children.* New York: Brunner/Mazel.

Cantwell, D.P., Russell, A.T., Mattison, R., & Will, L. (1979). A comparison of DSM-II and DSM-III in the diagnosis of childhood psychiatric disorders. *Archives of General Psychiatry, 36,* 1208–1228.

Caplan, G. (1964). *Principles of preventive psychiatry.* New York: Basic Books.

Caporael, L. (1976). Ergotism: The satan loosed in Salem? *Science, 192,* 21–26.

Carey, G., & Gottesman, I.I. (1981). Twin and famiy studies of anxiety, phobic, and compulsive disorders. In D.F. Klein & J.G. Rabkin (Eds.), *Anxiety: New research and changing concepts.* New York: Raven Press.

Carpenter, W.T. (1986). Thoughts on the treatment of schizophrenia. *Schizophrenia Bulletin, 12,* 527–539.

Carpenter, W.T., Murphy, D.L., & Wyatt, R.J. (1975). Platelet monoamine oxidase activity in acute schizophrenia. *American Journal of Psychiatry, 132,* 438–441.

Carr, A.T. (1971). Compulsive neurosis: Two psychophysiological studies. *Bulletin of the British Psychological Society, 24,* 256–257.

Carr, A.T. (1974). Compulsive neurosis: A review of the literature. *Psychological Bulletin, 81,* 311–319.

Carr, E.G., Schreibman, L., & Lovaas, O. I. (1975). Control of echolalic speech in psychotic children. *Journal of Abnormal Child Psychology, 3,* 331–351.

Carroll, B.J. (1982). The dexamethasone suppression test for melancholia. *British Journal of Psychiatry, 140,* 292–304.

Carskadon, M.A., Brown, E., & Dement, W.C. (1980). Respiration during sleep in the elderly. *Sleep Research, 9,* 99.

Cashman, J.A. (1966). *The LSD story.* Greenwich, Conn.: Fawcett.

Casper, R.C., Eckert, E.O., Halmi, K.A., Goldberg, S.C., & Davis, J.M. (1980). Bulimia: Its incidence and clinical importance in patients with anorexia nervosa. *Archives of General Psychiatry, 37,* 1030–1035.

Cassell, S. (1965). Effect of brief puppet therapy upon the emotional responses of children undergoing cardiac catheterization. *Journal of Consulting Psychology, 29,* 1–8.

Casson, I.R., Siegel, O., Sham, R., Campbell, E.A., Tarlau, M., & DiDomenico, J. (1984). Brain damage in modern boxers. *Journal of the American Medical Association, 251,* 2263–2267.

Cautela, J.R. (1966). Treatment of compulsive behavior by covert sensitization. *Psychological Record, 16,* 33–41.

Cautela, J.R. (1971). Covert extinction. *Behavior Therapy, 2,* 192–200.

Chambers, K.C. (1985). Sexual dimorphism as an index of hormonal influence on conditioned food aversions. *Annals of the New York Academy of Sciences, 443,* 110–125.

Chambers, K.C., Resko, J.A., & Phoenix, C. (1982). Correlations of diurnal changes in hormones with sexual behavior and age in male rhesus macques. *Neurobiology of Aging, 3,* 37–42.

Chambliss, C.A., & Murray, E.J. (1979). Efficacy attribution, locus of control, and weight loss. *Cognitive Therapy and Research, 3,* 349–353.

Chao, R.C., Green, D.E., Forrest, J.S., Kaplan, J.N., Winship-Ball, A., & Braude, M. (1976). The passage of ^{14}C-delta^9-tetrahydrocannabinol into the milk of lactating squirrel monkeys. *Research Communications in Chemical Pathology and Pharmacology, 15,* 303–317.

Chapman, L.J., & Chapman, J.P. (1969). Illusory correlation as an obstacle to the use of valid psychodiagnostic signs. *Journal of Abnormal Psychology, 74,* 271–287.

Charlesworth, W.B. (1976). Human intelligence as adaptation. An ethological approach. In L.E. Resnick (Ed.), *The nature of intelligence.* Hillsdale, N.J.: Erlbaum.

Charney, D.S., Heniger, C.R., & Breier, A. (1984). Noradrenergic function in pain attacks. *Archives of General Psychiatry, 41,* 751–763.

Charney, D.S., Heninger, G.R., & Sternberg, D.E. (1984). Serotonin function and the mechanism of action of antidepressant treatment. *Archives of General Psychiatry, 41,* 359–365.

Chein, I., Gerard, D.L., Lee, R.S., & Rosenfield, E. (1964). *The road to H: Narcotics, delinquency, and social policy.* New York: Basic Books.

Chester, P. (1972). *Women and madness.* Garden City, N.Y.: Doubleday.

Chesney, M.A., Eagleston, J.R., & Rosenman, R.H. (1980). The Type A Structured Interview: A behavioral assessment in the rough. *Journal of Behavioral Assessment, 2,* 255–272.

Chesno, F.A., & Kilmann, P.R. (1975). Effects of stimulation intensity on sociopathic avoidance learning. *Journal of Abnormal Psychology, 84,* 144–151.

Christensen, A. (1983). Intervention. In H. H. Kelley, E. Berscheid, A. Christensen, J. H. Harvey, T.L. Huston, G. Levinger, E. McClintock, L.A. Peplau, & D.R. Peterson (Eds.), *Close relationships.* San Francisco: Freeman.

Christensen, A., & Nies, D.C. (1980). The Spouse Observation Checklist: Empirical analysis and critique. *American Journal of Family Therapy, 8,* 69–79.

Christensen, A., Sullaway, M., & King, C. (1982). *Dysfunctional interaction patterns and marital happiness.* Paper presented at the annual meeting of the Association for Advancement of Behavior Therapy, Los Angeles, (As cited in Margolin, Michelli, & Jacobson, 1988.)

Christie, A.B. (1982). Changing patterns in

mental illness in the elderly. *British Journal of Psychiatry,* **140,** 154–159.

Churchill, D.W. (1969). Psychotic children and behavior modification. *American Journal of Psychiatry,* **125,** 1585–1590.

Churchill, W. (1967). *Homosexual behavior among males: A cross-cultural and cross-species investigation.* Englewood Cliffs, N.J.: Prentice–Hall.

Clark, D.F. (1988). The validity of measures of cognition: A review of the literature. *Cognitive Therapy and Research,* **12,** 1–20.

Clark, D.M. (1986). A cognitive approach to panic. *Behavior Research and Therapy,* **24,** 461–470.

Clark, D.M., Salkovskis, P.M., & Chalkley, A.J. (1985). Respiratory control as a treatment for panic attacks. *Journal of Behavior Therapy and Experimental Psychiatry,* **16,** 23–30.

Clark, J.V., & Arkowitz, H. (1975). Social anxiety and the self-evaluation of interpersonal performance. *Psychological Reports,* **36,** 211–221.

Clark, R. (1970). *Crime in America.* New York: Simon & Schuster.

Clark, W.B., & Cahalan, D. (1976). Changes in drinking behavior over a four-year span. *Addictive Behaviors,* **1,** 251–259.

Clausen, J.A., & Kohn, M.L. (1959). Relation of schizophrenia to the social structure of a small city. In B. Pasamanick (Ed.), *Epidemiology of mental disorder.* Washington, D.C.: American Association for the Advancement of Science.

Clayton, E.W. (1988). From Rogers to Rivers: The rights of the mentally ill to refuse medications. *American Journal of Law and Medicine,* **13,** 7–52.

Clayton, P.J. (1973). The clinical morbidity of the first year of bereavement: A review. *Comparative Psychiatry,* **14,** 151–157.

Clayton, P.J., Halikas, J.A., & Maurice, W.L. (1972). The depression of widowhood. *British Journal of Psychiatry,* **129,** 532–538.

Clayton, V.P., & Birren, J.E. (1980). The development of wisdom across the life span: A reexamination of an ancient topic. In P. B. Baltes & O.G. Brim (Eds.), *Life-span development and behavior* (Vol. 3). New York: Academic Press.

Cleckley, J. (1976). *The mask of sanity* (5th ed.). St. Louis: Mosby.

Climko, R.P., Roehrich, H., Sweeney, D. R., & Al-Razi, J. (1987). Ecstasy: A review of MDMA and MDA. *International Journal of Psychiatry in Medicine,* **16,** 359–372.

Cloninger, C.R., Bohman, M., & Sigvardsson, S. (1981). Inheritance of alcohol abuse: Cross fostering analysis of adopted men. *Archives of General Psychiatry,* **38,** 861–868.

Cloninger, C.R., Reich, T., & Guze, S.B. (1975). The multifactorial model of disease transmission: II. Sex differences in the fa-

milial transmission of sociopathy (antisocial personality). *British Journal of Psychiatry,* **127,** 11–22.

Cloninger, R.C., Sigvardsson, S., Bohman, M., & Knorring, A. von (1982). Predisposition to petty criminality in Swedish adoptees: II. Cross-fostering analysis of gene-environment interaction. *Archives of General Psychiatry,* **39,** 1242–1247.

Clunies-Ross, G.G. (1979). Accelerating the development of Down's syndrome infants and young children. *The Journal of Special Education,* **13,** 169–177.

Coates, S., & Person, E.S. (1985). Extreme boyhood femininity: Isolated behavior or pervasive disorder? *Journal of the American Academy of Child Psychiatry,* **24,** 702–709.

Cohen, D., Eisdorfer, C., Prinz, P., Breen, A., Davis, M., & Gadsby, A. (1983). Sleep disturbances in the institutionalized aged. *Journal of the American Geriatrics Society,* **31,** 79–82.

Cohen, D.J., Solnit, A.J., & Wohlford, P. (1979). Mental health services in Head Start. In E. Zigler & J. Valentine (Eds.), *Project Head Start.* New York: Free Press.

Cohen, H.L., & Filipczak, J. (1971). *A New learning environment.* San Francisco: Jossey–Bass.

Cohen, S. (1980). Therapeutic aspects. In *Marijuana research findings: 1980.* Washington, D.C.: U.S. Government Printing Office.

Cohen, S. (1981). Adverse effects of marijuana: Selected issues. *Annals of the New York Academy of Science,* **362,** 119–124.

Cohen, S. (1988). Psychosocial models of the role of social support in the etiology of physical disease. *Health Psychology,* **7,** 269–297.

Cohen, S., and Wills, T.A. (1985). Stress, social support, and the buffering process. *Psychological Bulletin,* **98,** 310–357.

Cole, J.D. (1988). Where are those new antidepressants we were promised? *Archives of General Psychiatry,* **45,** 193–194.

Collaborative study of children treated for phenylketonuria, preliminary report 8 (February 1975). Principal investigator: R. Koch. Presented at the Eleventh General Medicine Conference, Stateline, Nevada.

Colletti, G., & Kopel, S.A. (1979). Maintaining behavior change: An investigation of three maintenance strategies and the relationship of self-attribution to the long-term reduction of cigarette smoking. *Journal of Consulting and Clinical Psychology,* **47,** 614–617.

Combs, G., Jr., & Ludwig, A.M. (1982). Dissociative disorders. In J.H. Greist, J. W. Jefferson, & R.L. Spitzer (Eds.), *Treatment of mental disorders.* New York: Oxford University Press.

Comfort, A. (1980). Sexuality in later life. In J.E. Birren & R.B. Sloane (Eds.), *Hand-*

book of mental health and aging. Englewood Cliffs, N.J.: Prentice–Hall.

Comfort, A. (1984). Sexuality and the elderly. In J.P. Abrahams & V. Crooks (Eds.), *Geriatric mental health.* Orlando, Fla.: Grune & Stratton.

Committee on Health Care for Homeless People (1988). *Homelessness, health, and human needs.* Washington, D.C.: National Academic Press.

Committee on Government Operations (1985). *The federal response to the homeless crisis.* Washington, D.C.: U.S. Government Printing Office.

Conger, J.J. (1951). The effects of alcohol on conflict behavior in the albino rat. *Quarterly Journal of Studies on Alcohol,* **12,** 1–29.

Congress of the U.S., Congressional Budget Office (1988). *Changes in the living arrangements of the elderly: 1960–2030.* Washington, D.C.: U.S. Government Printing Office.

Conners, C.K. (1969). A teacher rating scale for use in drug studies with children. *American Journal of Psychiatry,* **126,** 884–888.

Conners, C.K., Taylor, E., Meo, G., Kurtz, M., & Fournier, M. (1972). Magnesium pemoline and dextroamphetamine: A controlled study in children with minimal brain dysfunction. *Psychopharmacologia,* **26,** 321–336.

Conners, F.A., Caruso, D.R., & Detterman, D.K. (1986). Computer-assisted instruction for the mentally retarded. In N. R. Ellis & N.W. Bray (Eds.), *International review of research in mental retardation* (Vol. 14). New York: Academic Press.

Conoley, C.W., Conoley, J.C., McConnell, J.A., & Kimzey, C.E. (1983). The effect of the ABCs of rational emotive therapy and the empty-chair technique of Gestalt therapy on anger reduction. *Psychotherapy: Theory, Research, and Practice,* **20,** 112–117.

Cooper, A.F., Garside, R.F., & Kay, D.W. K. (1976). A comparison of deaf and non-deaf patients with paranoid and affective psychoses. *British Journal of Psychiatry,* **129,** 532–538.

Cooper, A.F., Kay, D.W.K., Curry, A.R., Garside, R.F., & Roth, M. (1974). Hearing loss in paranoid and affective psychoses of the elderly. *Lancet,* **2,** 851–854.

Cooper, A.F., & Porter, R. (1976). Visual acuity and ocular pathology in the paranoid and affective psychoses of later life. *Journal of Psychosomatic Research,* **20,** 107–114.

Cooper, J.E., Kendell, R.E., Guland, B. J., Sharpe, L., Copeland, J.R.M., & Simon, R. (1972). *Psychiatric diagnosis in New York and London.* London: Oxford University Press.

Coppen, A., Prange, A.J., Whybrow, P.C., & Noguera, R. (1972). Abnormalities in indoleamines in affective disorders. *Archives of General Psychiatry*, **26**, 474–478.

Corey, G. (1977). *Theory and practice of counseling and psychotherapy.* Belmont, Calif.: Wadsworth.

Cornblatt, B., & Erlenmeyer-Kimling, L.E. (1985). Global attentional deviance in children at risk for schizophrenia: Specificity and predictive validity. *Journal of Abnormal Psychology*, **94**, 470–486.

Costa, P.T., Jr., & McCrae, R.R. (1978). Objective personality assessment. In M. Storandt, I.E. Siegler, & M.R. Elias, (Eds.), *The clinical psychology of aging.* New York: Plenum.

Costa, P.T., Jr., McCrae, R.R., Zonderman, A.B., Barbano, H.E., Lebowitz, B., & Larson, D.M. (1986). Cross-sectional studies of personality in a national sample: 2. Stability in neuroticism, extraversion, and openness. *Psychology and Aging*, **1**, 144–149.

Costa, P.T., Jr., Zonderman, A.B., McCrae, R.R., Cornoni-Huntley, J., Locke, B.Z., & Barbano, H.E. (1987). Longitudinal analyses of psychological well-being in a national sample: Stability of mean levels. *Journal of Gerontology*, **42**, 50–55.

Costello, C.G. (1980). Childhood depression: Three basic but questionable assumptions in the Lefkowitz and Burton critique. *Psychological Bulletin*, **87**, 185–190.

Courchesne, E., Yeung-Courchesne, R., Press, G.A., Hesselink, J.R., & Jernigan, T.L. (1988). Hypoplasia of cerebellar vermal lobules VI and VII in autism. *New England Journal of Medicine*, **318**, 1349–1354.

Covi, L., Lipman, R.S., Derogatis, L.R., Smith, J.E., & Pattison, J.H. (1974). Drugs and group psychotherapy in neurotic depression. *American Journal of Psychiatry*, **131**, 191–197.

Cowan, P.A., Hoddinott, B.A., & Wright, B.A. (1965). Compliance and resistance in the conditioning of autistic children: An exploratory study. *Child Development*, **36**, 913–923.

Cowdry, R.W., & Gardner, D.L. (1988) Pharmacotherapy of borderline personality disorders: Aprazolam, carbamazepine, trifluoperazine, and tranykoypromine. *Archives of General Psychiatry*, **45**, 111–119.

Cowen, E.L. (1983). Primary prevention in mental health: Past, present, and future. In R.D. Felner, L.A. Jason, J.N. Moritsugu, & S.S. Farber (Eds.), *Preventive psychology: Theory, research and practice.* New York: Pergamon.

Cox, A., Rutter, M., Newman, S., & Bartak, L. (1975). A comparative study of infantile autism and specific developmental language disorders: II. Parental characteristics. *British Journal of Psychiatry*, **126**, 146–159.

Cox, D.J., Freundlich, A., & Meyer, R.G. (1975). Differential effectiveness of electromyographic feedback, verbal relaxation instructions, and medication placebo with tension headaches. *Journal of Consulting and Clinical Psychology*, **43**, 892–898.

Cox, V.C., Paulus, P.B., & McCain, G. (1984). Prison crowding research: The relevance for prison housing standards and a general approach regarding crowding phenomena. *American Psychologist*, **39**, 1148–1160.

Coyle, J.T., Price, D.L., & Delong, M.R. (1983). Alzheimer's disease: A disorder of cortical cholinergic innervation. *Science*, **219**, 1184–1190.

Coyne, J.C. (1976). Depression and the response of others. *Journal of Abnormal Psychology*, **85**, 186–193.

Coyne, J.C., & Gotlib, I.H. (1983). The role of cognition in depression: A critical appraisal. *Psychological Bulletin*, **94**, 472–505.

Craft, M.J. (1969). The natural history of psychopathic disorder. *British Journal of Psychiatry*, **115**, 39–44.

Craig, M.M., & Glick, S.J. (1963). Ten years' experience with the Glueck social prediction table. *Crime and Delinquency*, **9**, 249–261.

Craik, F.I.M. (1977). Age differences in human memory. In J.E. Birren & K.W. Schaie (Eds.), *Handbook of the psychology of aging.* New York: Van Nostrand–Reinhold.

Creer, T.L. (1982). Asthma. *Journal of Consulting and Clinical Psychology*, **50**, 912–921.

Creer, T.L., Renna, C.M., & Chai, H. (1982). The application of behavioral techniques to childhood asthma. In D.C. Russo & J.W. Varni (Eds.), *Behavioral pediatrics: Research and practice.* New York: Plenum.

Creer, T.L., Weinberg, E., & Molk, L. (1974). Managing a hospital behavior problem: Malingering. *Journal of Behavior Therapy and Experimental Psychiatry*, **5**, 259–262.

Crisp, A.H. (1967). The possible significance of some behavioral correlates of weight and carbohydrate intake. *Journal of Psychosomatic Research*, **11**, 117–131.

Crisp, A.H., Palmer, R.L., & Klucy, R.S. (1976). How common is anorexia nervosa? A prevalence study. *British Journal of Psychiatry*, **128**, 529–554.

Crissey, M.S. (1975). Mental retardation. Past, present, and future. *American Psychologist*, **30**, 800–808.

Crofton, J., Campbell, I.E., Cole, P.V., Friend, J.A.R., Oldham, P.D., Springett, V.H., Berry G., & Raw, M. (1983). Comparison of four methods of smoking withdrawal in patients with smoking related diseases: Report by a Subcommittee of the Research Committee of the British Thoracic Society. *British Medical Journal*, **286**, 595–597.

Cross, D.G., & Sharpley, C.F. (1981). The Locke–Wallace Marital Adjustment Test reconsidered: Some psychometric findings as regards its reliability and factorial validity. *Educational and Psychological Measurement*, **41**, 1303–1306.

Crowe, R.R. (1974). An adoption study of antisocial personality. *Archives of General Psychiatry*, **31**, 785–791.

Crowe, R.R., Noyes, R., Pauls, D.L., & Slymen, D.J. (1983). A family study of panic disorder. *Archives of General Psychiatry*, **40**, 1065–1069.

Crowe, R.R., Pauls, D.L., Slymen, D.J., & Noyes, R. (1980). A family study of anxiety neurosis: Morbidity risk in families of patients with and without mitral valve prolapse. *Archives of General Psychiatry*, **37**, 77–79.

Crown, S., & D'Ardenne, P. (1982). Symposium on sexual dysfunction: Controversies, methods, results. *British Journal of Psychiatry*, **140**, 70–77.

Crtryn, L., & McKnew, D.H. (1979). Affective disorders. In J. Noshpitz (Ed.), *Basic handbook of child psychiatry* (Vol. 2). New York: Basic Books.

Cruickshank, W.M. (1977). Myths and realities in learning disabilities. *Journal of Learning Disabilities*, **10**, 51–63.

Cummings, J.L., & Benson, D.F. (1983). *Dementia: A clinical approach.* Woburn, Mass.: Butterworth.

Cunningham, C.E., & Barkley, R.A. (1979). The interactions of normal and hyperactive children with their mothers in free play and structured tasks. *Child Development*, **50**, 217–224.

Curran, J.P. (1977). Skills training as an approach to the treatment of heterosexual social anxiety. *Psychological Bulletin*, **89**, 140–157.

Curran, J.W. (1985). The epidemiology and prevention of acquired immunodeficiency syndrome. *Annals of Internal Medicine*, **103**, 657–662.

Cutler, S.J., & Grams. A.E. (1988). Correlates of self-reported everyday memory complaints. *Journal of Gerontology*, **43**, 582–590.

Danaher, B.G., Jeffery, R.W., Zimmerman, R., & Nelson, E. (1980). Aversive smoking using printed instructions and audiotape adjuncts. *Addictive Behaviors*, **5**, 353–358.

Daneman, E.A. (1961). Imipramine in office management of depressive reactions (a double-blind study). *Diseases of the Nervous System*, **22**, 213–217.

Davidson, J.T.R., Giller, E.L., Zisook, S., & Overall, J.E. (1988). An efficacy study of isocarboxazid in depression and its relationship to depressive nosology. *Archives of General Psychiatry*, **45**, 120–128.

Davidson, P.R., Malcolm, P.B., Lanthier, R.D., Barbaree, H.E., & Ho, T.P. (1981). Penile response measurement: Operating characteristics of the Parks plethysmograph. *Behavioral Assessment*, **3**, 137–143.

Davidson, W.S., Redner, R., Blakely, C. H., Mitchell, C.M., & Emshoff, J.G. (1987). Diversion of juvenile offenders: An experimental comparison. *Journal of Consulting and Clinical Psychology,* **55,** 68–75.

Davis, J.M. (1976). Overview: Maintenance therapy in psychiatry: II. Affective disorders. *American Journal of Psychiatry,* **133,** 1–13.

Davis, J.M. (1978). Dopamine theory of schizophrenia: A two-factor theory. In L. C. Wynne, R.L. Cromwell, & S. Matthysse (Eds.), *The nature of schizophrenia.* New York: Wiley.

Davis, J.M., Klerman, G., & Schildkraut, J. (1967). Drugs used in the treatment of depression. In L. Efron, J.O. Cole, D. Levine, & J.R. Wittenborn (Eds.), *Psychopharmacology, A review of progress.* Washington, D.C.: U.S. Clearinghouse of Mental Health Information.

Davison, G.C. (1964). A social learning therapy programme with an autistic child. *Behaviour Research and Therapy,* **2,** 146–159.

Davison, G.C. (1966). Differential relaxation and cognitive restructuring in therapy with a "paranoid schizophrenic" or "paranoid state." *Proceedings of the 74th Annual Convention of the American Psychological Association.* Washington, D.C.: American Psychological Association.

Davison, G.C. (1968). Elimination of a sadistic fantasy by a client-controlled counterconditioning technique. *Journal of Abnormal Psychology,* **73,** 84–90. (a)

Davison, G.C. (1968). Systematic desensitization as a counterconditioning process. *Journal of Abnormal Psychology,* **73,** 91–99. (b)

Davison, G.C. (1973). Counter countrol in behavior modification. In L.A. Hamerlynck, L.C. Handy, & E.J. Mash (Eds.), *Behavior change: Methodology, concepts and practice.* Champaign, Ill.: Research Press.

Davison, G.C. (1974). *Homosexuality: The ethical challenge.* Presidential address to the Eighth Annual Convention of the Association for Advancement of Behavior Therapy, Chicago.

Davison, G.C. (1976). Homosexuality: The ethical challenge. *Journal of Consulting and Clinical Psychology,* **44,** 157–162.

Davison, G.C. (1977) *Theory and practice in behavior therapy: An unconsummated marriage.* Paper presented at annual meeting of the Association for Advancement of Behavior Therapy, Atlanta, 1977. Audiotape distributed by Biomonitoring Associates, Guilford Press, New York.

Davison, G.C. (1978). Not can but ought: The treatment of homosexuality. *Journal of Consulting and Clinical Psychology,* **46,** 170–172.

Davison, G.C. (1980). And now for something completely different: Cognition and little r. In M.J. Mahoney (Ed.), *Psychotherapy process: Current issues and future directions.* New York: Plenum.

Davison, G.C., Feldman, P.M., & Osborn, C.E. (1984). Articulated thoughts, irrational beliefs, and fear of negative evaluation. *Cognitive Therapy and Research,* **8,** 349–362.

Davison, G.C., & Goldfried, M.R. (1973). Postdoctoral training in clinical behavior therapy. *Menninger Clinic Bulletin 17.*

Davison, G.C., Haaga, D.A.F., Rosenbaum, J., Dolezal, S.L., & Weinstein, K.A. (1989). *Association of articulated thoughts with overt behavioral and subjective indices of speech anxiety.* Paper presented at Annual Convention of The Association for Advancement of Behavior Therapy, Washington, D.C.

Davison, G.C., Robins, C., & Johnson, M. K. (1983). Articulated thoughts during simulated situations: A paradigm for studying cognition in emotion and behavior. *Cognitive Therapy and Research,* **7,** 17–40.

Davison, G.C., & Stuart, R.B. (1975). Behavior therapy and civil liberties. *American Psychologist,* **30,** 755–763.

Davison, G.C., & Thompson, R.F. (1988). Stress management. In D. Druckman & J. A. Swets (Eds.), *Enhancing human performance: Issues, theories, and techniques.* Washington, D.C.: National Academic Press.

Davison, G.C. Tsujimoto, R.N., & Glaros, A.G. (1973). Attribution and the maintenance of behavior change in falling asleep. *Journal of Abnormal Psychology,* **82,** 124–133.

Davison, G.C., & Valins, S. (1969). Maintenance of self-attributed and drug-attributed behavior change. *Journal of Personality and Social Psychology,* **11,** 25–33.

Davison, G.C., & Wilson, G.T. (1973). Attitudes of behavior therapists toward homosexuality. *Behavior Therapy,* **4,** 686–696.

Davison, G.C., & Zighelbom, V. (1987). Irrational beliefs in the articulated thoughts of college students with social anxiety. *Journal of Rational-Emotive Therapy,* **5,** 238–254.

Dawson, M.E., Schell, A.M., & Banis, H. T. (1986). Greater resistance to extinction of electrodermal responses conditioned to potentially phobic CSs: A noncognitive process? *Psychophysiology,* **23,** 552–561.

deCharms, R. (1968). *Personal causation: The internal affective determinants of behavior.* New York: Academic Press.

DeJong, R.N., & Sugar, O. (1971). *The yearbook of neurology and neurosurgery.* Chicago: Year Book Medical Publishers.

DeJonge, G.A. (1973). Epidemiology of enuresis: A survey of literature. In I. Kolvin, R.C. Mackeith, & S.R. Meadow (Eds.), *Enuresis and encopresis.* Philadelphia: Lippincott.

Dekker, E., & Groen, J. (1956) Reproducible psychogenic attacks of asthma. *Journal of Psychosomatic Research,* **1,** 58–67.

Dekker, E., Pelser, H.E., & Groen, J. (1957). Conditioning as a cause of asthmatic attacks. *Journal of Psychosomatic Research,* **2,** 97–108.

deLint, J. (1978). Alcohol consumption and alcohol problems from an epidemiological perspective. *British Journal of Alcohol and Alcoholism,* **17,** 109–116.

Dement, W.C., Laughton, E., & Carskadon, M.A. (1981). "White paper" on sleep and aging. *Journal of the American Geriatrics Society,* **30,** 25–50.

DeMyer, M. (1975). The nature of the neuropsychological disability of autistic children. *Journal of Autism and Childhood Schizophrenia.,* **5,** 109–127.

DeMyer, M., Barton, S., DeMyer, W.E., Norton, J.A., Allen, J., & Steele, R. (1973). Prognosis in autism: A follow-up study. *Journal of Autism and Childhood Schizophrenia,* **3,** 199–246.

DeMyer, M., Pontius, W., Norton, J.A., Barton, S., Allen, J., & Steele, R. (1972). Parental practices and innate activity in autistic and brain-damaged infants. *Journal of Autism and Childhood Schizophrenia,* **2,** 49–66.

Denhoff, E. (1973). The natural history of children with minimal brain dysfunction. *Annals of the New York Academy of Sciences,* **205,** 188–205.

Depue, R.A., & Monroe, S.M. (1978). Learned helplessness in the perspective of the depressive disorders: Conceptual and definitional issues. *Journal of Abnormal Psychology,* **87,** 3–20.

DeRubeis, R.J., Hollon, S.D., Evans, M. D., & Bemis, K.M. (1982). Can psychotherapies for depression be discriminated? A systematic investigation of cognitive therapy and interpersonal therapy. *Journal of Consulting and Clinical Psychology,* **50,** 744–760.

Detterman, D.K. (1979). Memory in the mentally retarded. In N.R. Ellis (Ed.), *Handbook of mental deficiency, psychological theory and research* (2nd ed.). Hillsdale, N.J.: Erlbaum.

Deutsch, A. (1949). *The mentally ill in America.* New York: Columbia University Press.

DeVries, H.A. (1975). Physiology of exercise and aging. In D.S. Woodruff & J.E. Birren (Eds.), *Aging: Scientific perspectives and social issues.* New York: Van Nostrand–Reinhold.

Dew, M.A., Bromet, E.J., Brent, D., & Greenouse, J.B. (1987). A quantitative literature review of the effectiveness of suicide prevention centers. *Journal of Consulting and Clinical Psychology, 55,* 239–244.

Dewys, W.D., Begg, C., & Lavin, P.T. (1980). Prognostic effect of weight loss prior to chemotherapy in cancer patients. *American Journal of Medicine, 69,* 491–497.

Deykin, E.Y., Alpert, J.J., & McNamarra, J.J. (1985). A pilot study of the effect of exposure to child abuse or neglect on adolescent suicidal behavior. *American Journal of Psychiatry, 142,* 1299–1303.

Diament, C., & Wilson, G.T. (1975). An experimental investigation of the effects of covert sensitization in an analogue eating situation. *Behavior Therapy, 6,* 499–509.

Diamond, M. (1982). Sexual identity, monozygotic twins reared in discordant sex roles and a BBC follow-up. *Archives of Sexual Behavior, 11,* 181–186.

Diamond, S., Baldwin, R., & Diamond, R. (1963). *Inhibition and choice.* New York: Harper & Row.

Didion, J. (1979). *The white album.* New York: Simon & Schuster.

DiMascio, A., Weissman, M.M., Prusoff, B. A., Neu, C., & Zwilling, M. (1979). Differential symptom reduction by drugs and psychotherapy in acute depression. *Archives of General Psychiatry, 36,* 1450–1456.

Dimsdale, J.E. (1988). A perspective on Type A behavior and coronary disease. *The New England Journal of Medicine, 318,* 110–112.

Dimsdale, J.E., Pierce, C., Schoenfeld, D., Brown, A., Zusman, R., & Graham, R. (1986). Suppressed anger and blood pressure: The effects of race, sex, social class, and age. *Psychosomatic Medicine, 48,* 430–436.

Dodge, K.A., & Frame, C.L. (1982). Social cognitive biases and deficits in aggressive boys. *Child Development, 53,* 620–635.

Dodson, B. (1974). *Liberating masturbation.* New York: Bodysex Designs.

Dogoloff, L.I. (1980). Prospect of the 1980s: Challenge and response. *Drug Enforcement, 7,* 2–3.

Dole, V., & Nyswander, M. (1966). Methadone maintenance: A report of two years' experience. In *Problems of drug dependence.* Washington, D.C.: National Academy of Science.

Doleys, D.M. (1977). Behavioral treatments for nocturnal enuresis in childen: A review of the recent literature. *Psychological Bulletin, 8,* 30–54.

Dollard, J., & Miller, N.E. (1950). *Personality and psychotherapy.* New York: McGraw–Hill.

Domino, E.F., Krause, R.R., & Bowers, J. (1973). Various enzymes involved with putative transmitters. *Archives of General Psychiatry, 29,* 195–201.

Donnellan, A.M., Mirenda, P.L., Mesaros, R.A., & Fassbender, L.L. (1984). Analyzing the communicative functions of aberrant behavior. *The Journal of the Association for Persons with Severe Handicaps, 9,* 201–212.

Doran, A.R., Pickar, D., Boronow, J. et al. (1985). CT scans in schizophrenics, medical and normal controls. Annual meeting of the American College of Neuropsychopharmamacology, Maui, HI.

Doris, J., & Sarason, S.B. (1955). Test anxiety and blame assignment in a failure situation. *Journal of Abnormal Psychology, 50,* 335–338.

Doubros, S.G. (1966). Behavior therapy with high level, institutionalized, retarded adolescents. *Exceptional Children, 33,* 229–233.

Douglas, J.D. (1967). *The social meanings of suicide.* Princeton, N.J.: Princeton University Press.

Dovenmuehle, R.H., Recklass, J.B., & Newman, G. (1970). Depressive reactions in the elderly. In Palmore, E.B. *Normal aging.* Durham, N.C.: Duke University Press.

Drabman, R.S., Cordue, G.D., Hammer, D., Jarvie, G.I., & Horton, W. (1979). Developmental trends in eating rates of normal and overweight preschool children. *Child Development, 50,* 211–216.

Drabman, R.S., Spitalnik, R., & O'Leary, K.D. (1973). Teaching self-control to disruptive children. *Journal of Abnormal Psychology, 82,* 10–16.

Drake, R.D., & Sederer, L.I. (1986). The adverse effects of intensive treatment of chronic schizophrenia. *Comprehensive Psychiatry, 27,* 313–326.

Duck, S. (1984). A perspective on the repair of personal relationships. In S. Duck (Ed.), *Personal relationships 5: Repairing personal relationships.* New York: Academic Press.

Dunham, H.W. (1965). *Community and schizophrenia: An epidemiological analysis.* Detroit: Wayne State University Press.

DuPont, R.W. (1976). Testimony before the subcommittee on aging and subcommittee on alcoholism and narcotics of the U.S. Senate Committee on Labor and Public Welfare, Washington, D.C. Cited in D.M. Peterson, F.I. Whittington, & E.T. Beer (1979). Drug use and misuse among the elderly. *Journal of Drug Issues, 9,* 5–26.

Durkheim, E. (1897). *Suicide* (2nd ed., 1930, in French). English translation by J.A. Spaulding & G. Simpson (1951). New York: Free Press.

Dweck, C.S. (1975). The role of expectation and attributions in the alleviation of learned helplessness. *Journal of Personality and Social Psychology, 31,* 674–685.

Dworkin, B.R., Filewich, R.J., Miller, N. E., & Craigmyle, N. (1979). Baroreceptor activation reduces reactivity to noxious stimulation: Implications for hypertension. *Science, 205,* 1299–1301.

Dworkin, R.H. & Lenzenwenger, M.F. (1984). Symptoms and the genetics of schizophrenia: Implications for diagnosis. *American Journal of Psychiatry, 141,* 1541–1546.

Dworkin, R.H., Lenzenwenger, M.F., & Moldin, S.O. (1987). Genetics and the phenomenology of schizophrenia. In P.D. Harvey and E.F. Walker (Eds.), *Positive and negative symptoms of psychosis.* Hillsdale, N.J.: Erlbaum.

Dye, C.J. (1978). Psychologist's role in the provision of mental health care for the elderly. *Professional Psychology, 9,* 38–49.

Dykens, E., Leckman, J.F., Paul, R., & Watson, M. (1988). Cognitive, behavioral, and adaptive functioning in fragile X and non-fragile X retarded men. *Journal of Autism and Developmental Disorders, 18,* 41–52.

Dysken, M.W. (1979). Clinical usefulness of sodium amobarbital interviewing. *Archives of General Psychiatry, 36,* 789–794.

D'Zurilla, T.J., & Goldfried, M.R. (1971). Problem-solving and behavior modification. *Journal of Abnormal Psychology, 78,* 107–126.

D'Zurilla, T.J. (1986). *Problem-solving therapy: A social competence approach to clinical intervention.* New York: Springer.

Eastman, C. (1976). Behavioral formulations of depression. *Psychological Review, 83,* 277–291.

Eastman, P. (1989). America's "other drug problem" overwhelms thousands, experts say, *AARP Newsletter, 30,* 1–3.

Eckert, E.D., Goldberg, S.C., Halmi, K. A., Casper, R.C., & Davis, J.M. (1982). Depression in anorexia nervosa. *Psychological Medicine, 12,* 115–122.

Edmundson, E., Bedell, J. R., & Gordon, R. (1984). In A. Gartner & F. Riessman (Eds.), *The self-help revolution.* New York: Human Sciences Press.

Edwards, A.L. (1957). *The social desirability variable in personality research.* New York: Dryden.

Edwards, G., Gross, M.M., Keller, J., Moser, J., & Room, R. (1977). *Alcohol related disabilities.* Geneva, Switzerland: World Health Organization.

Edwards, G., Hensman, C., Hawker, A., & Williamson, V. (1967). Alcoholics Anonymous: The anatomy of a self-help group. *Social Psychiatry, 1,* 195–204.

Egan, G. (1975). *The skilled helper.* Monterey, Calif.: Brooks/Cole.

Egeland, J.A., Gerhard, D.S., Pauls, D. L., Sussex, J.N., Kidd, K.K., Allen, C. R., Hostetter, A.M., & Housman, D.E. (1987). Bipolar affective disorders linked to DNA markers on chromosome 11. *Nature, 325,* 783–787.

Ehrhardt, A., & Money, J. (1967). Progestin-induced hermaphroditism: IQ and psychosexual identity in a study of ten girls. *Journal of Sex Research,* **3,** 83–100.

Eidelson, R.J., & Epstein, N. (1982). Cognition and relationship maladjustment: Development of a measure of dysfunctional relationship belief. *Journal of Consulting and Clinical Psychology,* **50,** 715–720.

Elkin, I., Parloff, M.B., Hadley, S.W., & Autry, J.H. (1985). NIMH Treatment of Depression Collaborative Research Program. *Archives of General Psychiatry,* **42,** 305–316.

Elkin, I., Shea, T., Imber, S., Pilkonis, P., Sotsky, S., Glass, D., Watkins, J., Leber, W., & Collins, J. (1986). *NIMH Treatment of Depression Collaborative Research Program: Initial outcome findings.* Paper presented to the American Association for the Advancement of Science.

Elkin, I., Shea, M.T., Watkins, J.T., Imber, S.D., Sotsky, S.M., Collins, J.F., Glass, D.R., Pilkonis, P.A., Leber, W.R., Docherty, J.P., Fiester, S.J., & Parloff, M.B. (in press). NIMH Treatment of Depression Collaborative Research Program: I. General effectiveness of treatments. *Archives of General Psychiatry.*

Ellenberger, H.F. (1972). The story of "Anna O": A critical review with new data. *Journal of the History of the Behavior Sciences,* **8,** 267–279.

Ellingson, R.J. (1954). Incidence of EEG abnormality among patients with mental disorders of apparently nonorganic origin: A criminal review. *American Journal of Psychiatry,* **111,** 263–275.

Ellis, A. (1961). *The folklore of sex.* New York: Grove.

Ellis, A. (1962). *Reason and emotion in psychotherapy.* New York: Lyle Stuart.

Ellis, A. (1971). Rational-emotive treatment of impotence, frigidity, and other sexual problems. *Professional Psychology,* **2,** 346–349.

Ellis, A. (1984). Rational-emotive therapy. In R.J. Corsini (Ed.), *Current psychotherapies* (3rd. ed.). Itasca, Ill: Peacock Press.

Ellis, A., & Bernard, M.E. (1983). An overview of rational-emotive approaches to the problems of childhood. In A. Ellis & M.E. Bernard (Eds.), *Rational-emotive approaches to the problems of childhood.* New York: Plenum.

Ellis, H. (1906). *Studies in the psychology of sex.* New York: Random House.

Ellis, N.R. (1963). The stimulus trace and behavioral inadequacy. In N.R. Ellis (Ed.), *Handbook of mental deficiency.* New York: McGraw-Hill.

Ellis, N.R. (1970). Memory processes in retardates and normals. In N.R. Ellis (Ed.), *International review of research in mental retardation* (Vol. 4). New York: Academic Press.

Ellis, N.R., Deacon, J.R., & Wooldridge, P.W. (1985). Structural memory deficits of mentally retarded persons. *American Journal of Mental Deficiency,* **89,** 393–402.

Elmore, A.M. (1979). A comparison of the psychophysiological and clinical response to biofeedback for temporal pulse amplitude reduction and biofeedback for increases in hand temperature in the treatment of migraine. Unpublished doctoral dissertation. State University of New York at Stony Brook.

Elmore, A.M., & Tursky, B. (1978). The biofeedback hypothesis: An idea in search of a theory and method. In A.A. Sugerman & R.E. Tarter (Eds.), *Expanding dimensions of consciousness.* New York: Springer.

Elmore, A.M., & Tursky, B. (1981). A comparison of two psychophysiological approaches to the treatment of migraine. *Headache,* **21,** 93–101.

Elmore, J.L., & Sugerman, A.A. (1975). Precipitation of psychosis during electroshock therapy. *Diseases of the Nervous System,* **3,** 115–117.

Emery, R.E. (1982). Interparental conflict and the children of discord and divorce. *Psychological Bulletin,* **92,** 310–330.

Emery, R.E., & O'Leary, K.D. (1979). *Children's perceptions of marital discord and behavior problems of boys and girls.* Paper presented at the annual meeting of the Association for Advancement of Behavior Therapy, San Francisco.

Emmelkamp, P.M.G. (1986). Behavior therapy with adults. In S.L. Garfield & A.E. Bergin (Eds.), *Handbook of psychotherapy and behavior change* (3rd ed.). New York: Wiley.

Emmons, R.A., & Diener, E. (1986). Situation selection as a moderator of response consistency and stability. *Journal of Personality and Social Psychology,* **51,** 1013–1019.

Endicott, J., Nea, J., Fleiss, J., Cohen, J., Williams, J.B., & Simon, R. (1982). Diagnostic criteria for schizophrenia. Reliability and agreement between systems. *Archives of General Psychiatry,* **39,** 884–889.

Endicott, J., & Spitzer, R.L. (1978). A diagnostic interview: The Schedule for Affective Disorders and Schizophrenia. *Archives of General Psychiatry,* **35,** 837–844.

Engel, B.T., & Bickford, A.F. (1961). Response specificity: Stimulus response and individual response specificity in essential hypertension. *Archives of General Psychiatry,* **5,** 478–489.

Englemann, S. (1969). *Conceptual learning.* San Rafael, Calif.: Dimensions Publishing.

English, H.B. (1929). Three cases of the "conditioned fear response." *Journal of Abnormal and Social Psychology,* **34,** 221–225.

Ennis, B., & Emery, R. (1978). *The rights of mental patients—An American Civil Liberties Union Handbook.* New York: Avon.

Ennis, B., & Siegel, L. (1973). *The rights of mental patients.* American Civil Liberties Union Handbook Series. New York: Avon.

Enright, J.B. (1970). An introduction to Gestalt techniques. In J. Fagan & I.L. Shepherd (Eds.), *Gestalt therapy now: Theory, techniques, applications.* Palo Alto, Calif.: Science and Behavior Books.

Epstein, L.C., & Lasagna, L. (1969). Obtaining informed consent. *Archives of Internal Medicine,* **123,** 682–688.

Epstein, L.H., Beck, S., Figueroa, J., Farkas, G., Kazdin, A.E., Danema, D., & Becker, D. (1981). The effects of point economy and parent management on urine glucose and metabolic control in children with insulin dependent diabetes. *Journal of Applied Behavior Analysis,* **14,** 365–375.

Epstein, L.H., Masek, B.J., & Marshall, W.R. (1978). A nutritionally based school program for control of eating in obese children. *Behavior Therapy,* **9,** 766–788.

Epstein, L.H., Wing, R.R., Thompson, J.K., & Griffen, W. (1980). Attendance and fitness in aerobics exercise: The effects of contract and lottery procedures. *Behavior Modification,* **4,** 465–479.

Epstein, S. (1979). The stability of behavior: On predicting most of the people much of the time. *Journal of Personality and Social Psychology,* **37,** 1097–1126.

Erdberg, P., & Exner, J.E., Jr. (1984). Rorschach assessment. In G. Goldstein & M. Hersen (Eds.), *Handbook of psychological assessment.* New York: Pergamon.

Erikson, E.H. (1950). *Childhood and society.* New York: Norton.

Erikson, E.H. (1959). *Identity and the life cycle. Selected papers.* New York: International Universities Press.

Erlenmeyer-Kimling, L.E., & Cornblatt, B. (1987). The New York high-risk project: A follow-up report. *Schizophrenia Bulletin,* **13,** 451–461.

Esler, J., Julius, S., Sweifler, A., Randall, O., Harburg, E., Gardiner, H., & DeQuattro, V. (1977). Mild high-renin essential hypertension: A neurogenic human hypertension. *New England Journal of Medicine,* **296,** 405–411.

Evans, I.M. (1976). Classical conditioning. In M.P. Feldman & A. Broadhurst (Eds.), *Theoretical and experimental bases of the behaviour therapies.* New York: Wiley.

Evans, R.B. (1969). Childhood parental relationships of homosexual men. *Journal of Consulting and Clinical Psychology,* **33,** 129–135.

Evans, R.I., Rozelle, R.M., Maxwell, S.E., Raines, B.E., Dill, C.A., Guthrie, T.J., Henderson, A.H., & Hill, P.C. (1981). Social modelling films to deter smoking in adolescents: Results of a three-year field investigation. *Journal of Applied Psychology*, **66**, 399–414.

Exner, J.E. (1978). *The Rorschach: A comprehensive system. Vol.2. Current research and advanced interpretation.* New York: Wiley.

Eysenck, H.J. (1952). The effects of psychotherapy: An evaluation. *Journal of Consulting Psychology*, **16**, 319–324.

Eysenck, H.J. (1957). *Dynamics of anxiety and hysteria.* London: Routledge and Kegan Paul.

Eysenck, H.J. (1975). Crime as destiny. *New Behaviour*, **9**, 46–49.

Fagan, J., & Shepherd, I.L. (Eds.). (1970). *Gestalt therapy now: Theory, techniques, applications.* Palo Alto, Calif.: Science and Behavior Books.

Fagan, J.F., & Singer, L.T. (1983). Infant recognition memory as a measure of intelligence. In L.P. Lipsitt (Ed.), *Advances in infancy research* (Vol. 2). Norwood, N.J.: Ablex.

Fagerstrom, K-O. (1978). Measuring degree of physical dependence to tobacco smoking with reference to individualization of treatment. *Addictive Behaviors*, **3**, 235–241.

Fagerstrom, K-O. (1982). A comparison of psychological and pharmacological treatment in smoking cessation. *Journal of Behavioral Medicine*, **5**, 343–351.

Fairburn, C.G. (1980). Self-induced vomiting. *Journal of Psychosomatic Research*, **24**, 193–197.

Fairweather, G.W. (Ed.). (1964). *Social psychology in treating mental illness: An experimental approach.* New York: Wiley.

Falloon, I.R.H., Boyd, J.L., McGill, C.W., Razani, J., Moss, H.B., & Gilderman, A.N. (1982). Family management in the prevention of exacerbation of schizophrenia: A controlled study. *New England Journal of Medicine*, **306**, 1437–1440.

Falloon, I.R.H., Boyd, J.L., McGill, C.W., Williamson, M., Razani, J., Moss, H.B., Gilderman, A.M., & Simpson, G.M. (1985). Family management in the prevention of morbidity of schizophrenia. *Archives of General Psychiatry*, **42**, 887–896.

Farina, A. (1976). *Abnormal psychology.* Englewood Cliffs, N.J.: Prentice–Hall.

Farkas, G., & Rosen, R.C. (1976). The effects of alcohol on elicited male sexual response. *Studies in Alcohol*, **37**, 265–272.

Farris, E.J., Yeakel, E.H., & Medoff, H. (1945). Development of hypertension in emotional gray Norway rats after air blasting. *American Journal of Physiology*, **144**, 331–333.

Favell, J.E., Azrin, N.H., Baumeister, A.A., Carr, E.G., Dorsey, M.F., Forehand, R., Foxx, R.M., Lovaas, O.I., Rincover, A., Risley, T.R., Romanczyk, R.G., Russo, D.C., Schroeder, S.R., & Solnick, J.V. (1982). The treatment of self-injurious behavior. *Behavior Therapy*, **13**, 529–554.

Fawcett, J., Epstein, P., Fiester, S.J., Elkin, I., & Autry, J.H. (1987). Clinical Management—Imipramine/placebo administration manual: NIMH Treatment of Depression Collaborative Research Program. *Psychopharmacology Bulletin*, **23**, 309–324.

Fedora, O., Reddon, J.R., & Yeudall, L.T. (1986). Stimuli eliciting sexual arousal in genital exhibitionists: A possible clinical application. *Archives of Sexual Behavior*, **15**, 417–427.

Fein, D., Pennington, B., Markowitz, P., Braverman, M., & Waterhouse, L. (1986). Toward a neuropsychological model of infantile autism: Are the social deficits primary? *Journal of the American Academy of Child Psychiatry*, **25**, 198–212.

Feingold, B.F. (1973). *Introduction to clinical allergy.* Springfield, Ill.: Charles C. Thomas.

Feingold, B.F. (1975). *Why your child is hyperactive.* New York: Random House.

Feinsilver, D.B., & Gunderson, J.G. (1972). Psychotherapy for schizophrenics—Is it indicated? *Schizophrenia Bulletin*, **1**, 11–23.

Felner, R.D., Stolberg, A., & Cowen, E.L. (1975). Crisis events and school mental health referral patterns of young children. *Journal of Consulting and Clinical Psychology*, **43**, 305–310.

Fenichel, O. (1945). *The psychoanalytic theory of neurosis.* New York: Norton.

Fentiman, L.C. (1985). Guilty but mentally ill: The real verdict is guilty. *Boston College Law Review*, **26**, 601–653.

Ferenczi, S. (1920). The further development of an active therapy in psychoanalysis. In J. Richman (Ed.) (1960). *Further contributions to the theory and technique of psychoanalysis.* London: Hogarth.

Fernando, C.K., & Basmajian, J.V. (1978). Biofeedback in physical medicine and rehabilitation. *Biofeedback and Self-regulation*, **3**, 435–455.

Ferster, C.B. (1961). Positive reinforcement and behavioral deficits of autistic children. *Child Development*, **32**, 437–456.

Ferster, C.B. (1965). Classification of behavioral pathology. In L. Krasner & L.P. Ullmann (Eds.), *Research in behavior modification.* New York: Holt, Rinehart & Winston.

Feuerstein, R. (1980). *Instrumental enrichment: An intervention program for cognitive modifiability.* Baltimore: University Park Press.

Field, T., Goldberg, S., Stern, D., & Sostek, A. (Eds.). (1980). *High-risk infants and children: Adult and peer interactions.* New York: Academic Press.

Field, T., Sostek, A., Goldberg, J., & Shuman, M. (Eds.). (1979). *Infants born at risk.* New York: Spectrum.

Figley, C.R. (1978). Introduction. In C.R. Figley (Ed.), *Stress disorders among Vietnam veterans.* New York: Brunner/Mazel. (a)

Figley, C.R. (1978). Psychosocial adjustment among Vietnam veterans: An overview of the research. In C.R. Figley (Ed.), *Stress disorders among Vietnam veterans.* New York: Brunner/Mazel. (b)

Figley, C.R., & Leventman, S. (1980). Introduction: Estrangement and victimization. In C.R. Figley & S. Leventman (Eds.), *Strangers at home: Vietnam veterans since the war.* New York: Praeger.

Fillmore, K.M., & Caetano, R. (1980). *Epidemiology of occupational alcoholism.* Paper presented at the National Institute on Alcohol Abuse and Alcoholism's Workshop on Alcoholism in the Workplace, Reston, Va., May 22, 1980.

Finkelhor, D. (1979). *Sexually victimized children.* New York: Free Press.

Finn, S.E. (1982). Base rates, utilities, and DSM-III: Shortcomings of fixed-rule systems of psychodiagnosis. *Journal of Abnormal Psychology*, **91**, 294–302.

Firth-Cozens, J., & Brewin, C.R. (1988). Attributional change during psychotherapy. *British Journal of Clinical Psychology*, **27**, 47–54.

Fisch, G.S., Cohen, I.L., Wolf, E.D., Brown, W.T., Jenkins, E.C., & Gross, A. (1986). Autism and the fragile X syndrome. *American Journal of Psychiatry*, **143**, 71–73.

Fischer, M. (1971). Psychoses in the offspring of schizophrenic monozygotic twins and their normal co-twins. *British Journal of Psychiatry*, **118**, 43–52.

Fischetti, M., Curran, J.P., & Wessberg, H.W. (1977). Sense of timing. *Behavior Modification*, **1**, 179–194.

Fish, F. (1960). Senile schizophrenia. *Journal of Mental Science*, **106**, 938–946.

Fisher, C., Cohen, H.D., Schiavi, R.C., Davis, D., Furman, B., Ward, K., Edwards, A., & Cunningham, J. (1983). Patterns of female sexual arousal during sleep and waking: Vaginal thermoconductance studies. *Archives of Sexual Behavior*, **12**, 97–122.

Fleming, M., Steinman, C., & Bocknek, G. (1980). Methodological problems in assessing sex-reassignment surgery. A reply to Meyer and Reter. *Archives of Sexual Behavior*, **9**, 451–456.

Flemming, A.S., Rickards, L.D., Santos, J.F., & West, P.R. (1986). *Report on a survey of community mental health centers* (Vol.

3). Washington, D.C.: Action Committee to Implement the Mental Health Recommendations of the 1981 White House Conference on Aging. As cited in Roybal (1988).

Fletcher, C., & Doll, R. (1969). A survey of doctors' attitudes to smoking. *British Journal of Prevention and Social Medicine, 23,* 145–153.

Fodor, I. (1978). Phobias in women: Therapeutic approaches. In *Helping women change: A guide for professional counseling.* New York: BMA Audio Cassette Program.

Folkman, S., Bernstein, L., & Lazarus, R.S. (1987). Stress processes and the misuse of drugs in older adults. *Psychology and Aging, 2,* 366–374.

Folks, D.G., Ford, C.V., & Regan, W.M. (1984). Conversion symptoms in a general hospital. *Psychosomatics, 25,* 285–295.

Folstein, M.F., & McHugh, P.R. (1978). Dementia syndrome of depression. In R. Katzman, R.D. Terry, & K.L. Bick (Eds.), *Alzheimer's disease: Senile dementia and related disorders. Vol.7. Aging.* New York: Raven Press.

Folstein, S., & Rutter, M. (1978). A twin study of individuals with infantile autism. In M. Rutter & E. Schopler (Eds.), *Autism: A reappraisal of concepts and treatment.* New York: Plenum.

Fontana, A. (1966). Familial etiology of schizophrenia: Is a scientific methodology possible? *Psychological Bulletin, 66,* 214–228.

Ford, C., & Neale, J.M. (1985). Effects of a helplessness induction on judgments of control. *Journal of Personality and Social Psychology, 49,* 1330–1336

Ford, C.S., & Beach, F.A. (1951). *Patterns of sexual behavior.* New York: Harper.

Ford, C.V., & Folks, D.G. (1985). Conversion disorders: An overview. *Psychosomatics, 26,* 371–383.

Ford, C.V., & Sbordone, R.J. (1980). Attitudes of psychiatrists towards elderly patients. *American Journal of Psychiatry, 137,* 571–575.

Ford, D.H., & Urban, H.B. (1963). *Systems of psychotherapy: A comparative study.* New York: Wiley.

Fordney-Settlage, D.S. (1975). Heterosexual dysfunction: Evaluation of treatment procedures. *Archives of Sexual Behavior, 4,* 367–388.

Fordyce, W.E. (1973). An operant conditioning method for managing chronic pain. *Postgraduate Medicine, 53,* 123–128.

Fordyce, W.E. (1976). *Behavioral methods for chronic pain and illness.* St. Louis: Mosby.

Fordyce, W.E., Brockway, J.A., Bergman, J.A., & Spengler, D. (1986). Acute back pain: A control-group comparison of behavioral vs. traditional methods. *Journal of Behavioral Medicine, 9,* 127–140.

Forstein, M. (1988). Homophobia: An overview. *Psychiatric Annals, 18,* 33–36.

Foucault, M. (1965). *Madness and civilization.* New York: Random House.

Foy, D.W., Carroll, E.M., & Donahoe, C.P., Jr. (in press). Etiological factors in the development of PTSD in clinical samples of combat veterans. *Journal of Consulting and Clinical Psychology.*

Foy, D.W., Resnick, H.S., Sipprelle, R.C., & Carroll, E.M. (1987). Premilitary, military, and postmilitary factors in the development of combat-related posttraumatic stress disorder. *The Behavior Therapist, 10,* 3–9.

Frances, A. (1980). The DSM-III personality disorders section: A commentary. *American Journal of Psychiatry, 137,* 1050–1054.

Frank, J.D. (1971). Therapeutic factors in psychotherapy. *American Journal of Psychotherapy, 25,* 350–361.

Frank, J.D. (1973). *Persuasion and healing* (2nd ed.). Baltimore: Johns Hopkins University Press.

Frank, J.D. (1976). Psychotherapy and the sense of mastery. In R.L. Spitzer & D.F. Klein (Eds.), *Evaluation of psychotherapies: Behavioral therapies, drug therapies and their interactions.* Baltimore: Johns Hopkins University Press.

Frankel, B.G., & Whitehead, P.C. (1981). *Drinking and damage: Theoretical advantages and implications for prevention.* Monograph 14. New Brunswick, N.J.: Rutgers Center of Alcohol Studies.

Frankl, V. (1959). *From death camp to existentialism.* Boston: Beacon.

Frankl, V. (1963). *Man's search for meaning.* New York: Washington Square.

Franks, C.M. (1984). Behavior therapy with children and adolescents. In G.T. Wilson, C.M. Franks, K.D. Brownell, & P.C. Kendall (Eds.), *Annual review of behavior therapy: Theory and practice* (Vol. 9). New York: Guilford.

Freed, E.X. (1971). Anxiety and conflict: Role of drug-dependent learning in the rat. *Quarterly Journal of Studies on Alcohol, 32,* 13–29.

Freedman, R.R., Ianni, P., & Wenig, P. (1985). Behavioral treatment of Raynaud's disease: Long-term follow-up. *Journal of Consulting and Clinical Psychology, 53,* 136.

Freeman, B.J., & Ritvo, E.R. (1976). Cognitive assessment. In E.R. Ritvo, B.J. Freeman, E.M. Ornitz, & P.E. Tanguay (Eds.), *Autism: Diagnosis, current research and management.* New York: Spectrum.

Freud, A. (1946). *The ego and mechanisms of defense.* New York: International Universities Press. (a)

Freud, A. (1946). *The psychoanalytic treatment of children: Lectures and essays.* London: Imago. (b)

Freud, S. (1905). Three contributions to the theory of sex. In A.A. Brill (Ed.), *The basic writings of Sigmund Freud.* New York: Modern Library, 1938.

Freud, S. (1909). Analysis of a phobia in a five-year-old boy. In *Collected works of Sigmund Freud* (Vol. 10). London: Hogarth, 1956.

Freud, S. (1915). A case of paranoia running counter to the psychoanalytical theory of the disease. In *Collected papers* (Vol. 2). London: Hogarth, 1956.

Freud, S. (1917). Mourning and melancholia. In *Collected papers* (Vol. 4). London: Hogarth and the Institute of Psychoanalysis, 1950.

Freud, S. (1918). Lines of advance in psychoanalytic therapy. In *The complete psychological works of Sigmund Freud.* Translated by J. Strachey. London: Hogarth and the Institute of Psychoanalysis, 1955.

Freud, S. (1936). *The problem of anxiety.* New York: Norton, 1926.

Freud, S. (1937). Analysis terminable and interminable. *International Journal of Psychoanalysis, 18,* 373–391.

Freud, S. (1949). *A general introduction to psychoanalysis.* New York: Garden City Publishing.

Freund, K. (1963). A laboratory method for diagnosing predominance of homo- and hetero-erotic interest in the male. *Behaviour Research and Therapy, 1,* 85–93.

Friar, L.R., & Beatty, J. (1976). Migraine: Management by trained control of vasoconstriction. *Journal of Consulting and Clinical Psychology, 44,* 46–53.

Friedberg, C.K. (1966). *Diseases of the heart* (3rd ed.). Philadelphia: Saunders.

Friedman, E., Shopsin, B., Sathananthan, G., & Gershon, S. (1974). Blood platelet monoamine oxidase activity in psychiatric patients. *American Journal of Psychiatry, 131,* 1392–1394.

Friedman, J.M. (1978). Sexual adjustment of the postcoronary male. In J.LoPiccolo & L. LoPiccolo (Eds.), *Handbook of sex therapy.* New York: Plenum.

Friedman, J.M., & Hogan, D.R. (1985). Sexual dysfunction: Low sexual desire. In D.H. Barlow (Ed.), *Clinical handbook of psychological disorders.* New York: Guilford.

Friedman, M. (1969). *Pathogenesis of coronary artery disease.* New York: McGraw-Hill.

Friedman, M., Thoresen, C.E., Gill, J.J., Powell, L.H., Ulmer, D., Thompson, L. Price, V.A., Rabin, D.D., Breall, W.S., Dixon, T., Levy, R., & Bourg, E. (1984). Alteration of type A behavior and reduction in cardiac recurrences in postmyocardial infarction patients. *American Heart Journal,* **108,** 237–248.

Friedman, M., Thoresen, C.E., Gill, J.J., Ulmer, D., Thompson, L., Powell, L., Price, A., Elek, S.R., Rabin, D.D., Breall, W.S., Piaget, G., Dixon, T., Bourg, E., Levy, R., & Tasto, D.I. (1982). Feasibility of altering type A behavior pattern after myocardial infarction. *Circulation,* **66,** 83–92.

Friedman, M., & Ulmer, D. (1984). *Treating type A behavior and your heart.* New York: Fawcett Crest.

Friedman, R., & Dahl, L.K. (1975). The effect of chronic conflict on the blood pressure of rats with a genetic susceptibility to experimental hypertension. *Psychosomatic Medicine,* **37,** 402–416.

Frisch, M.B., & Higgins, R.L. (1986). Instructional demand effects and the correspondence among role-play, self-report, and naturalistic measures of social skill. *Behavioral Assessment,* **8,** 221–236.

Fristoe, M., & Lloyd, L.L. (1979). Nonspeech communication. In N.R. Ellis (Ed.), *Handbook of mental deficiency, psychological theory and research* (2nd ed.). Hillsdale, N.J.: Erlbaum.

Fromm-Reichmann, F. (1948). Notes on the development of treatment of schizophrenics by psychoanalytic psychotherapy. *Psychiatry,* **11,** 263–273.

Fromm-Reichmann, F. (1952). Some aspects of psychoanalytic therapy with schizophrenics. In E. Brady & F.C. Redlich (Eds.), *Psychotherapy with schizophrenics.* New York: International Universities Press.

Frude, N. (1982). The sexual nature of sexual abuse: A review of the literature. *Child Abuse and Neglect,* **6,** 211–223.

Furby, L., Weinrott, M.R., & Blacksbaw, L. (1989). Sex offender recidivism. A review. *Psychological Bulletin,* **105,** 3–30.

Furman, W., Rahe, D., & Hartup, W. (1979). Rehabilitation of socially withdrawn preschool children through mixed-age and same-age socialization. *Child Development,* **50,** 915–922.

Gagnon, J.H. (1977). *Human sexualities.* Chicago: Scott, Foresman.

Gagnon, J.H., & Davison, G.C. (1974). *Enhancement of sexual responsiveness in behavior therapy.* Paper presented at the 82nd Annual Convention of the American Psychological Association, New Orleans.

Gagnon, J.H., & Davison, G.C. (1976). Asylums, the token economy, and the metrics of mental life. *Behavior Therapy,* **7,** 528–534.

Gagnon, J.H., & Simon, W. (1973). *Sexual conduct: The social origins of human sexuality.* Chicago: Aldine.

Gaines, J. (1974). The founder of Gestalt

therapy: A sketch of Fritz Perls. *Psychology Today,* **8,** 117–118.

Galin, D., Diamond, R., & Braff, D. (1977). Lateralization of conversion symptoms: More frequent on the left. *American Journal of Psychiatry,* **134,** 578—580.

Gallagher, D., Breckenridge, J.N., Thompson, L.W., Dessonville, C., & Amaral, P. (1982). Similarities and differences between normal grief and depression in older adults. *Essence,* **5,** 127–140.

Gallagher, D., & Thompson, L.W. (1982). *Elders' maintenance of treatment benefits following individual psychotherapy for depression: Results of a pilot study and preliminary data from an ongoing replication study.* Paper presented at the annual meeting of the American Psychological Association, Washington, D.C.

Gallagher, D., & Thompson, L.W. (1983). Cognitive therapy for depression in the elderly. A promising model for treatment and research. In L.D. Breslau & M.R. Haug (Eds.), *Depression and aging: Causes, care and consequences.* New York: Springer.

Garcia, J., McGowan, B.K., & Green, K.F. (1972). Biological constraints on conditioning. In A.H. Black & W.F. Prokasy (Eds.), *Classical conditioning II: Current research and theory.* New York: Appleton–Century–Crofts.

Garfield, S.L. (1974). *Clinical psychology: The study of personality and behavior.* Chicago: Aldine.

Garfield, S.L., & Bergin, A.E. (Eds.). (1986). *Handbook of psychotherapy and behavior change.* (3rd ed.). New York: Wiley. (a)

Garfield, S.L., & Bergin, A.E. (1986). Introduction and historical overview. In S.L. Garfield & A.E. Bergin (Eds.), *Handbook of psychotherapy and behavior change.* (3rd ed.). New York: Wiley (b)

Garfield, S., & Kurtz, R. (1974). A survey of clinical psychologists: Characteristics, activities, and orientations. *The Clinical Psychologist,* **28,** 7–10.

Garfinkel, P.E., & Garner, D.M. (1982). *Anorexia nervosa: A multidimensional perspective.* New York: Brunner/Mazel.

Garfinkel, P.E., Moldofsky, H., & Garner, D.M. (1980). The heterogeneity of anorexia nervosa. *Archives of General Psychiatry,* **37,** 1036–1040.

Garmezy, N. (1977). DSM-III: Never mind the psychologists—Is it good for the children? *The Clinical Psychologist,* **31,** 3–4.

Garner, D.M., Garfinkel, P.E., Schwartz, D., & Thompson, M. (1980). Cultural expectations of thinness in women. *Psychological Reports,* **47,** 483–491.

Garner, D.M., & Rosen, L.W. (in press). Cognitive behavioral treatment for anorexia nervosa and bulimia nervosa. In A.S. Bel-

lack, M. Hersen, & A.E. Kazdin (Eds.), *International handbook of behavior modification and therapy* (2nd ed.). New York: Plenum.

Gatz, M., & Pearson, C.G. (1988). Ageism revised and the provision of psychological services. *American Psychologist,* **43,** 184–188.

Gatz, M., Pearson, C., & Fuentes, M. (1984). Older women and mental health. In A.U. Rickel, M. Gerrard, & I. Iscoe (Eds.), *Social and psychological problems of women: Prevention and crisis intervention.* Washington, D.C.: Hemisphere Publishing.

Gauthier, J., Bois, R., Allaire, D., & Drollet, M. (1981). Evaluation of skin temperature biofeedback training at two different sites for migraine. *Journal of Behavioral Medicine,* **4,** 407–419.

Gauthier, Y., Fortin, C., Drapeau, P., Breton, J., Gosselin, J., Quintal, L., Weisnagel, J., & Lamarre, A. (1978). Follow-up study of 35 asthmatic preschool children. *Journal of the American Academy of Child Psychiatry,* **17,** 679–694.

Gauthier, Y., Fortin, C., Drapeau, P., Breton, J., Gosselin, J., Quintal, L., Weisnagel, J., Tetreault, L., & Pinard, G. (1977). The mother–child relationship and the development of autonomy and self-assertion in young (14–30 months) asthmatic children. *Journal of the American Academy of Child Psychiatry,* **16,** 109–131.

Gawin, F.H., & Kleber, H.D. (1986). Abstinence symptomatology and psychiatric diagnosis in cocaine abusers. *Archives of General Psychiatry,* **43,** 107–113.

Gebhard, P.H., Gagnon, J.H., Pomeroy, W.B., & Christenson, C.V. (1965). *Sex offenders.* New York: Harper & Row.

Geer, J.H., Davison, G.C., & Gatchel, R.I. (1970). Reduction of stress in humans through nonveridical perceived control of aversive stimulation. *Journal of Personality and Social Psychology,* **16,** 731–738.

Geer, J.H., Heiman, J., & Leitenberg, H. (1984). *Human sexuality.* Englewood Cliffs, N.J.: Prentice–Hall.

Geer, J.H., Morokoff, P., & Greenwood, P. (1974). Sexual arousal in women. The development of a measuring device for vaginal blood volume. *Archives of Sexual Behavior,* **3,** 559–566.

Geis, G. (1977). Forcible rape: An introduction. In D. Chappell, R. Geis, & G. Geis (Eds.), *Forcible rape: The crime, the victim, and the offender.* New York: Columbia University Press.

Geis, G., & Monahan, J. (1976). The social ecology of violence. In T. Lickona (Ed.), *Moral development and behavior.* New York: Holt, Rinehart & Winston.

Geller, E., Ritvo, E.R., Freeman, B.J., & Yuwiler, A. (1982). Preliminary observations on the effect of fenfluramine on blood serotonin and symptoms in three autistic boys. *New England Journal of Medicine,* **307,** 165–169.

Geller, E., Yokota, A., Schroth, P., & Novak, P. (1984). Study of fenfluramine in outpatients with the syndrome of autism. *Journal of Pediatrics,* **105,** 823–828.

Geller, J.L., & Bertsch, G. (1985). Fire-setting behavior in the histories of a state hospital population. *American Journal of Psychiatry,* **142,** 464–468.

General Register Office (1968). *A glossary of mental disorders.* Studies on Medical and Population Subjects 22. London: General Register Office.

Gentry, W.D., Chesney, A.P., Gary, H.G., Hall, R.P., & Harburg, E. (1982). Habitual anger-coping styles: I. Effect of mean blood pressure and risk for essential hypertension. *Psychosomatic Medicine,* **44,** 195–202.

Gentry, W.D., Chesney, A.P., Hall, R.P., & Harburg, E. (1981). Effect of habitual anger-coping pattern on blood pressure in black/white, high/low stress area respondents. *Psychosomatic Medicine,* **43,** 88.

George, L.K. (1980). *Role transitions in later life.* Monterey, Calif.: Brooks/Cole.

George, L.K., & Gwynther, L.P. (1985). *Support groups for caregivers of memory impaired elderly: Easing caregiver burden.* Paper presented at the NMHA Commission on the Prevention of Mental and Emotional Disability, Alexandria, Va. (As cited in Gesten & Jason, 1987.)

George, L.K., & Gwynther, L.P. (1986). Caregiver well-being: A multidimensional examination of family caregivers of demented adults. *The Gerontologist,* **26,** 253–259.

George, L.K., & Weiler, S.J. (1981). Sexuality in middle and late life: The effects of age, cohort, and gender. *Archives of General Psychiatry,* **38,** 919–923.

Gerald, P.S. (1980). X-linked mental retardation and an X-chromosome marker. *New England Journal of Medicine,* **303,** 696–697.

Gerbino, L., Oleshansky, M., & Gershon, S. (1978). Clinical use and mode of action of lithium. In M.A. Lipton, A. DiMascio, & F.K. Killam (Eds.), *Psychopharmacology: A generation of progress.* New York: Raven Press.

Gesten, E.L., & Jason, L.A. (1987). Social and community interventions. *Annual Review of Psychology,* **38,** 427–460.

Giarretto, H. (1982). A comprehensive child sexual abuse treatment program. *Child Abuse and Neglect,* **6,** 263–278.

Gibbons, D.C. (1975). *Delinquent behavior.* Englewood Cliffs, N.J.: Prentice–Hall.

Gibbs, J. (Ed.). (1968). *Suicide.* New York: Harper & Row.

Gibson, D., & Harris, A. (1988). Aggregated early intervention effects for Down's syndrome persons: Patterning and longevity of benefits. *Journal of Mental Deficiency Research,* **32,** 1–17.

Gilboy, J.A., & Schmidt, J.R. (1971). "Voluntary" hospitalization of the mentally ill. *Northwestern University Law Review,* **66,** 429–439.

Gilewski, M.J., & Zelinski, E.M. (1986). Questionnaire assessment of memory complaints. In L.W. Poon (Ed.), *Handbook for clinical memory assessment of older adults.* Washington, D.C.: American Psychological Association.

Ginsburg, A.B., & Goldstein, S.G. (1974). Age bias in referral to psychological consultation. *Journal of Gerontology,* **29,** 410–415.

Gittelman-Klein, R., & Klein, D.F. (1976). Methylphenidate effects in learning disabilities. *Archives of General Psychiatry,* **33,** 655–664.

Gittelman-Klein, R., Klein, D.F., Abikoff, H., Katz, S., Gloisten, A.C., & Kates, W. (1976). Relative efficacy of methylphenidate and behavior modification in hyperkinetic children: An interim report. *Journal of Abnormal Child Psychology,* **4,** 361–379.

Gittelman-Klein, R., Klein, D.F., Katz, S., Saraf, K., & Pollack, E. (1976). Comparative effects of methylphenidate and thioridazine in hyperkinetic children. *Archives of General Psychiatry,* **33,** 1217–1231.

Glaser, G.H., Newman, R.J., & Schafer, R. (1963). Interictal psychosis in psychomotor-temporal lobe epilepsy: An EEG psychological study. In G.H. Glaser (Ed.), *EEG and behavior.* New York: Basic Books.

Glass, C.R., & Merluzzi, T.V. (1981). Cognitive assessment of social-evaluative anxiety. In T.V. Merluzzi, C.R. Glass, & M. Genest (Eds.), *Cognitive assessment.* New York: Guilford.

Glassman, A.H., Jackson, W.K., Walsh, B.T., & Roose, S.P. (1984). Cigarette craving, smoking withdrawal, and clonidine. *Science,* **226,** 864–866.

Glassman, A.H., & Roose, S.P. (1981). Delusional depression. *Archives of General Psychiatry,* **38,** 424–427.

Glassman, A.H., Steiner, F., Walsh, T., Raizman, P.S., Fleiss, J.L., Cooper, T.B., & Covey, L.S. (1988). Heavy smokers, smoking cessation, and clonidine. *Journal of the American Medical Association,* **259,** 2853–2866.

Glover, E. (1956). *On the early development of mind.* New York: International Universities Press.

Glueck, S., & Glueck, E. (1959). *Predicting delinquency and crime.* Cambridge, Mass.: Harvard University Press.

Goetzl, U., Green, R., Whybrow, P., & Jackson, R. (1974). X-linkage revisited. *Archives of General Psychiatry,* **31,** 665–671.

Goffman, E. (1961). *Asylums: Essays on the social situation of mental patients and other inmates.* Chicago: Aldine.

Gold, M.S., Pottash, A.C., Sweeney, D.R., & Kleber, H.D. (1980). Opiate withdrawal using clonidine. *Journal of the American Medical Association,* **243,** 343–346.

Gold, M.S., Redmond, D.E., Jr., & Kleber, H.D. (1978). Clonidine in opiate withdrawal. *Lancet,* **1,** 929–930.

Goldberg, E.M., & Morrison, S.L. (1963). Schizophrenia and social class. *British Journal of Psychiatry,* **109,** 785–802.

Goldberg, S.R., Spealman, R.D., & Goldberg, D.M. (1981). Persistent behavior at high rates maintained by intravenous self-administration of nicotine. *Science,* **214,** 573–575.

Goldberg, T.E., Weinberger, D.R., Berman, K.F., Pllskin, N.H., & Podd, M.H. (1987). Further evidence for dementia of prefrontal type in schizophrenia? *Archives of General Psychiatry,* **44,** 1008–1013.

Golden, C.J. (1981). The Luria–Nebraska Children's Battery: Theory and formulation. In G.W. Hynd & J.E. Obrzut (Eds.), *Neuropsychological assessment and the school-age child: Issues and procedures.* New York: Grune & Stratton. (a)

Golden, C.J. (1981). A standardized version of Luria's neuropsychological tests: A quantitative and qualitative approach to neuropsychological evaluation. In S.B. Filskov & T.J. Boll (Eds.), *Handbook of clinical neuropsychology.* New York: Wiley (b)

Golden, C.J., Hammeke, T., & Purisch, A. (1978). Diagnostic validity of a standardized neuropsychological battery derived from Luria's neuropsychological test. *Journal of Consulting and Clinical Psychology,* **46,** 1258–1265.

Goldfried, M.R. (1980). Psychotherapy as coping skills training. In M.J. Mahoney (Ed.), *Psychotherapy process: Current issues and future directions.* New York: Plenum. (a)

Goldfried, M.R. (1980). Toward the delineation of therapeutic change principles. *American Psychologist,* **35,** 991–999. (b)

Goldfried, M.R. (Ed.). (1982). *Converging themes in the practice of psychotherapy.* New York: Springer.

Goldfried, M.R., & Davison, G.C. (1976). *Clinical behavior therapy.* New York: Holt, Rinehart & Winston.

Goldfried, M.R., Decenteceo, E.T., & Weinberg, L. (1974). Systematic rational restructuring as a self-control technique. *Behavior Therapy,* **5,** 247–254.

Goldfried, M.R., & D'Zurilla, T.J. (1969). A behavioral-analytic model for assessing competence. In C.D. Speilberger (Ed.),

Current topics in clinical and community psychology (Vol. 1). New York: Academic Press.

Goldfried, M.R., Linehan, M., & Smith, J.L. (1978). Reduction of text anxiety through cognitive restructuring. *Journal of Consulting and Clinical Psychology, 46,* 32–39.

Goldfried, M.R., Stricker, G., & Weiner, I.B. (1971). *Rorschach handbook of clinical and research applications.* Englewood Cliffs, N.J.: Prentice–Hall.

Goldmeier, J. (1988). Pets or people: Another research note. *The Gerontologist, 26,* 203–206.

Goldstein, A. (1976). Opioid peptides (endorphins) in pituitary and brain. *Science, 193,* 1081–1086.

Goldstein, H.S., Edelberg, R., & Meier, C.F. (1988). Relationship of resting heart rate and blood pressure to experienced anger and expressed anger. *Psychosomatic Medicine, 50,* 321–329.

Goldstein, M., & Rodnick, E. (1975). The family's contribution to the etiology of schizophrenia: Current status. *Schizophrenia Bulletin, 14,* 48–63.

Goldstein, S.E., & Birnbom, F. (1976). Hypochondriasis and the elderly. *Journal of the American Geriatrics Society, 24,* 150–154.

Goodwin, D.W. (1979). Alcoholism and heredity: A review and hypothesis. *Archives of General Psychiatry, 36,* 57–61.

Goodwin, D.W. (1982). Substance induced and substance use disorders: Alcohol. In J.H. Griest, J.W. Jefferson, & R.L. Spitzer (Eds.), *Treatment of mental disorders.* New York: Oxford University Press.

Goodwin, D.W., Crane, J.B., & Guze, S.B. (1969). Alcoholic "blackouts": A review and clinical study of 100 alcoholics. *American Journal of Psychiatry, 26,* 191–198.

Goodwin, D.W., & Guze, S.B. (1984). *Psychiatric diagnosis* (3rd ed.). New York: Oxford University Press.

Goodwin, D.W., Schulsinger, F., Hermansen, L., Guze, S.B., & Winokur, G.A. (1973). Alcohol problems in adoptees raised apart from alcoholic biological parents. *Archives of General Psychiatry, 128,* 239–243.

Goodwin, D.W., Schulsinger, F., Knop, J., Mednick, S.A., & Guze, S.B. (1977). Psychopathology in adopted and nonadopted daughters of alcoholics. *Archives of General Psychiatry, 34,* 1005–1009.

Gorenstein, E.E. (1982). Frontal lobe functions in psychopaths. *Journal of Abnormal Psychology, 91,* 368–379.

Gorman, J.M., Fyer, M.R., Goetz, R., Askanazi, J., Leibowitz, M.R., Fyer, A.J., Kinney, J., & Klein, D.F. (1988). Ventilatory physiology of patients with panic disorder. *Archives of General Psychiatry, 45,* 53–60.

Gorman, J.M., Levy, G.F., Liebowitz, M.R., McGrath, P., Appleby, I.L., Dillon, D.J., Davies, S.O., & Klein, D.F. (1983). Effect of acute beta-adrenergic blockade on lactate-induced panic. *Archives of General Psychiatry, 40,* 1079–1082.

Gorman-Smith, D., & Matson, J.L. (1985). A review of the treatment research for self-injurious and stereotyped responding. *Journal of Mental Deficiency Research, 29,* 295–308.

Gotlib, I.H. (1982). Self-reinforcement and depression in interpersonal interaction: The role of performance level. *Journal of Abnormal Psychology, 93,* 19–30.

Gotlib, I.H., & Asarnow, R.F. (1979). Interpersonal and impersonal problem-solving skills in mildly and clinically depressed students. *Journal of Consulting and Clinical Psychology, 47,* 86–95.

Gotlib, I.H., & Robinson, L.A. (1982). Responses to depressed individuals: Discrepancies between self-report and observer-rated behavior. *Journal of Abnormal Psychology, 91,* 231–240.

Gotlib, I.H., & Whiffen, V.E. (in press). The interpersonal context of depression: Implications for theory and research. In D. Perlman & W. Jones (Eds.), *Advances in personal relationships.* Greenwich: JAI Press.

Gottesman, I. (1962). Differential inheritance of the psychoneuroses. *Eugenics Quarterly, 9,* 223–227.

Gottesman, I.I., McGuffin, P., Farmer, A.E. (1987). Clinical genetics as clues to the "real" genetics of Schizophrenia. *Schizophrenia Bulletin, 13,* 23–47.

Gottesman, I., & Shields, J. (1972). *Schizophrenia and genetics: A twin study vantage point.* New York: Academic Press.

Gottlieb, J., Gottlieb, B.W., Schmelkin, L.P., & Curci, R. (1983). Low- and high-IQ learning disabled children in the mainstream. *Analysis and Intervention in Developmental Disabilities, 3,* 59–69.

Gottman, J.M. (1979). *Marital interaction: Experimental investigations.* New York: Academic Press.

Gottman, J.M., & Levenson, R.W. (1986). Assessing the role of emotion in marriage. *Behavioral Assessment, 8,* 31–48.

Gottman, J.M., Markman, H., & Notarius, C. (1977). The topography of marital conflict: A sequential analysis of verbal and nonverbal behavior. *Journal of Marriage and the Family, 39,* 461–477.

Gottman, J., Notarius, C., Gonso, J., & Markman, H. (1976). *A couple's guide to communication.* Champaign, Ill.: Research Press.

Gove, W.R. (1970). Societal reaction as an explanation of mental illness: An evaluation. *American Sociological Review, 35,* 873–884.

Gove, W.R., & Fain, T. (1973). The stigma of mental hospitalization. *Archives of General Psychiatry, 28,* 494–500.

Gove, W.R., & Tudor, J. (1973). Adult sex roles and mental illness. *American Journal of Sociology, 78,* 812–835.

Goyette, C.H., & Conners, C.K. (1977). *Food additives and hyperkinesis.* Paper presented at the 85th Annual Convention of the American Psychological Association.

Grabowski, J. (Ed.). (1984). *Cocaine: Pharmacology, effects, and treatment of abuse.* Rockville, Md.: National Institute on Drug Abuse.

Graham, D.T. (1967). Health, disease and the mind–body problem: Linguistic parallelism. *Psychosomatic Medicine, 29,* 52–71.

Graham, J.R., & Wolff, H.G. (1938). Mechanisms of migraine headache and action of ergotamine tartrate. *Archives of Neurology and Psychiatry, 18,* 23–45.

Graham, P.J., Rutter, M.L., Yule, W., & Pless, I.B. (1967). Childhood asthma: A psychosomatic disorder? Some epidemiological considerations. *British Journal of Preventive Medicine, 21,* 78–85.

Gralnick, A. (1986). Future of the chronic schizophrenic patient: Prediction and recommendation. *American Journal of Psychotherapy, 40,* 419–429.

Gray, E.B. (1983). *Final report: Collaborative research of community and minority group action to prevent child abuse and neglect. Vol. III: Public awareness and education using the creative arts.* Chicago: National Committee for Prevention of Child Abuse.

Gray, J.A. (1971). *The psychology of fear and stress.* New York: McGraw–Hill.

Gray, J.A. (1982). *The neuropsychology of anxiety.* New York: Oxford University Press.

Green, R. (1974). *Sexual identity conflict in children and adults.* New York: Basic Books.

Green, R. (1976). One hundred ten feminine and masculine boys: Behavioral contrasts and demographic similarities. *Archives of Sexual Behavior, 5,* 425–446.

Green, R. (1985). Gender identity in childhood and later sexual orientation: Follow-up of 78 males. *American Journal of Psychiatry, 142,* 339–341.

Green, R., & Money, J. (1969). *Transsexualism and sex reassignment.* Baltimore: Johns Hopkins University Press.

Greenberg, L., Fine, S.B., Cohen, C., Larson, K., Michaelson-Baily, A., Rubinton, P., & Glick, I.D. (1988). An interdisciplinary psychoeducation program for schizophrenic patients and their families in an acute care setting. *Hospital and Community Psychiatry, 39,* 277–281.

Greenberg, L.S., & Rice, L.N. (1981). The specific effects of a gestalt intervention. *Psy-*

chotherapy: Theory, Research, and Practice, **18,** 31–37.

Greenblatt, D.J., & Shader, R.I. (1978). Pharmacotherapy of anxiety with benzodiazepines and β-adrenergic blockers. In M.A. Lipton, A. DiMascio, & K.F. Killiam (Eds.), *Psychopharmacology: A generation of progress.* New York: Raven Press.

Greenblatt, M., Solomon, M.H., Evans, A.S., & Brooks, G.W. (Eds.). (1965). *Drugs and social therapy in chronic schizophrenia.* Springfield, Ill.: Charles C. Thomas.

Grings, W.W., & Dawson, M.E. (1978). *Emotions and bodily responses: A psychophysiological approach.* New York: Academic Press.

Grinker, R.R., & Spiegel, J.P. (1945). *War neuroses.* New York: Arno Press, 1979.

Gross, M.B., & Wilson, W.C. (1974). *Minimal brain dysfunction.* New York: Brunner/Mazel.

Grossman, H.J. (Ed.). (1983). *Classification in mental retardation.* Washington, D.C.: American Association of Mental Deficiency.

Grosz, H.J., & Zimmerman, J. (1970). A second detailed case study of functional blindness: Further demonstration of the contribution of objective psychological laboratory data. *Behavior Therapy,* **1,** 115–123.

Groth, N.A., & Burgess, A.W. (1977). Sexual dysfunction during rape. *New England Journal of Medicine,* **297,** 764–766.

Groth, N.A., Hobson, W.F., & Gary, T.S. (1982). The child molester: Clinical observations. In J. Conte & D.A. Shore (Eds.), *Social work and child sexual abuse.* New York: Haworth.

Group for Advancement of Psychiatry. (1966). *Psychopathological disorders in childhood: Theoretical considerations and a proposed classification.* Report 62. New York: Mental Health Memorials Center.

Gubbay, S., Lobascher, M., & Kingerlee, P. (1970). A neurological appraisal of autistic children: Results of a Western Australia survey. *Developmental Medicine and Child Neurology,* **12,** 422–429.

Guerney, B.G. (Ed.). (1969). *Psychotherapeutic agents: New roles for nonprofessionals, parents and teachers.* New York: Holt, Rinehart & Winston.

Guidano, V., & Liotti, G. (1983). *Cognitive processes and emotional disorder.* New York: Guilford.

Gunderson, J.G., Kolb, J.E., & Austin, V. (1981). The diagnostic interview for borderline patients. *American Journal of Psychiatry,* **138,** 896–903.

Guralnik, J.M., Yanagashita, M., & Schneider, E.L. (1988). Projecting the older population of the United States: Lessons from the past and prospects for the future. *The Milbank Quarterly,* **66,** 283–308.

Gurland, B.J., & Cross, P.S. (1982). Epidemiology of psychopathology in old age. In L.F. Jarvik & G.W. Small (Eds.), *Psychiatric Clinics of North America.* Philadelphia: Saunders.

Gurman, A.S., & Kniskern, D.P. (1978). Research on marital and family therapy: Progress, perspective, and prospect. In S.L. Garfield & A.E. Bergin (Eds.), *Handbook of psychotherapy and behavior change: An empirical analysis* (2nd ed.). New York: Wiley.

Gurman, A.S., & Kniskern, D.P. (1981). Family therapy outcome research: Knowns and unknowns. In A.S. Gurman & D.P. Kniskern (Eds.), *Handbook of family therapy.* New York: Brunner/Mazel.

Gurman, A.S., Kniskern, D.P., & Pinsoff, W.M. (1986). Research on the process and outcome of marital and family therapy. In S.L. Garfield & A.E. Bergin (Eds.), *Handbook of psychotherapy and behavior change* (3rd ed.). New York: Wiley.

Gustafson, Y., Berggren, D., Bucht, B., Norberf, A., Hansson, L.I., & Winblad, B. (1988). Acute confusional states in elderly patients treated for femoral neck fracture. *Journal of the American Geriatrics Society,* **36,** 525–530.

Guze, S.B. (1967). The diagnosis of hysteria: What are we trying to do? *American Journal of Psychiatry,* **124,** 491–498.

Guze, S.B. (1976). *Criminality and psychiatric disorders.* New York: Oxford University Press.

Gwynther, L.P., & George, L.K. (1986). Caregivers for dementia patients: Complex determinants of well-being and burden. *The Gerontologist,* **26,** 245–247.

Haaga, D.A. (1986). A review of the common principles approach to integration of psychotherapies. *Cognitive Therapy and Research,* **10,** 527–538.

Haaga, D.A. (1987). Treatment of the type A behavior pattern. *Clinical Psychology Review,* **7,** 557–574. (a)

Haaga, D.A. (1987). *Smoking schemata revealed in articulated thoughts predict early relapse from smoking cessation.* Paper presented at the 21st annual convention of the Association for Advancement of Behavior Therapy, Boston. (b)

Haaga, D.A. (1988). Cognitive assessment in the prediction of smoking relapse. Unpublished doctoral dissertation, University of Southern California. (a)

Haaga, D.A. (1988). *Cognitive aspects of the relapse prevention model in the prediction of smoking relapse.* Paper presented at the 22nd annual convention of the Association for Advancement of Behavior Therapy, New York. (b)

Haaga, D.A., & Davison, G.C. (1986). Cognitive change methods. In A.P. Goldstein & F.H. Kanfer (Eds.), *Helping people change* (3rd ed.). Elmsford, N.Y.: Pergamon.

Haaga, D.A., & Davison, G.C. (1989). Outcome studies of rational-emotive therapy. In M.E. Bernard & R. DiGiuseppe (Eds.), *Inside rational-emotive therapy.* New York: Academic Press.

Habot, B., & Libow, L.S. (1980). The interrelationship of mental and physical status and its assessment in the older adult: Mind–body interaction. In J.E. Birren & R.B. Sloane (Eds.), *Handbook of mental health and aging.* Englewood Cliffs, N.J.: Prentice–Hall.

Hafner, R.J. (1982). Marital interaction in persisting obsessive-compulsive disorders. *Australian and New Zealand Journal of Psychiatry,* **16,** 171–178.

Hafner, R.J., Gilchrist, P., Bowling, J., & Kalucy, R. (1981). The treatment of obsessional neurosis in a family setting. *Australian and New Zealand Journal of Psychiatry,* **15,** 145–151.

Haggard, E. (1943). Some conditions determining adjustment during and readjustment following experimentally induced stress. In S. Tomkins (Ed.), *Contemporary psychopathology.* Cambridge, Mass.: Harvard University Press.

Haley, S.A. (1978). Treatment implications of post-combat stress response syndromes for mental health professionals. In C.R. Figley (Ed.), *Stress disorders among Vietnam veterans.* New York: Brunner/Mazel.

Hall, C.S. (1954). *A primer of Freudian psychology.* New York: New American Library.

Hall, C.S., Lindzey, G., Loehlin, J.C., & Manosevitz, M. (1985). *Introduction to theories of personality.* New York: Wiley.

Hall, S.M., Tunstall, C., Rugg, D., Jones, R.T., & Benowitz, N. (1985). Nicotine gum and behavioral treatment in smoking. *Journal of Consulting and Clinical Psychology,* **53,** 256–258.

Halleck, S.L. (1971). *The politics of therapy.* New York: Science House.

Hamilton, E.W., & Abramson, L.Y. (1983). Cognitive patterns and major depressive disorder: A longitudinal study in a hospital setting. *Journal of Abnormal Psychology,* **92,** 173–184.

Hammen, C.L. (1980). Depression in college students: Beyond the Beck Depression Inventory. *Journal of Consulting and Clinical Psychology,* **48,** 126–128.

Hammen, C.L., & Cochran, S.D. (1981). Cognitive correlates of life stress and depression in college students. *Journal of Abnormal Psychology,* **90,** 23–27.

Hammen, C., Marks, T., Mayol, A., & deMayo, R. (1985). Depressive self-schemas, life stress, and vulnerability to depression. *Journal of Abnormal Psychology, 94,* 308–319.

Hampe, E., Noble, H., Miller, L.C., & Barrett, C.L. (1973). Phobic children one and two years posttreatment. *Journal of Abnormal Psychology, 82,* 446–453.

Hansen, W.B., Johnson, C.A., Flay, B.R., Graham, J.W., & Sobel, J. (1988). Affective and social influences approaches to the prevention of multiple substance abuse among seventh grade students. *Preventive Medicine, 17,* 135–154.

Hanusa, B.H., & Schulz, R. (1977). Attributional mediators of learned helplessness. *Journal of Personality and Social Psychology, 35,* 602–611.

Haracz, J.L. (1982). The dopamine hypothesis: An overview of studies with schizophrenic patients. *Schizophrenia Bulletin, 8,* 438–469.

Harburg, E., Erfurt, J.C., Hauenstein, L.S., Chape, C., Schull, W.J., & Schork, M.A. (1973). Socioecological stress, suppressed hostility, skin color, and black–white male blood pressure: Detroit. *Psychosomatic Medicine, 35,* 276–296.

Hare, E. (1969). *Triennial statistical report of the Royal Maudsley and Bethlem Hospitals.* London: Bethlem and Maudsley Hospitals.

Hare, R.D. (1970). *Psychopathy: Theory and research.* New York: Wiley.

Hare, R.D. (1978). Electrodermal and cardiovascular correlates of sociopathy. In R.D. Hare & D. Schalling (Eds.), *Psychopathic behaviour: Approaches to research.* New York: Wiley.

Hare, R.D. (1980). A research scale for the assessment of psychopathy in criminal populations. *Personality and Individual Differences, 1,* 111–119.

Hare, R.D. (1982). Psychopathy and physiological activity during anticipation of an aversive stimulus in a distraction paradigm. *Psychophysiology, 19,* 266–271.

Hare, R.D., & Jutai, J.W. (1983). Psychopathy and electrocortical indices of perceptual processing during selective attention. *Psychophysiology, 20,* 146–151.

Harlow, J.M. (1868). Recovery from the passage of an iron bar through the head. *Publication of the Massachusetts Medical Society, 2,* 327ff.

Harman, R.L. (1984). Recent developments in gestalt group therapy. *International Journal of Group Psychotherapy, 34,* 473–483.

Harrington, A., & Sutton-Simon, K. (1977). Rape. In A.P. Goldstein, P.J. Monti, T.J. Sardino, & D.J. Green (Eds)., *Police crisis intervention.* Kalamazoo, Mich.: Behaviordelia.

Harris, E.L., Noyes, R., Crowe, R.R., & Chaudhry, D.R. (1983). Family study of agoraphobia: Report of a pilot study. *Archives of General Psychiatry, 40,* 1061–1064.

Hart, B.M., Reynolds, N.J., Baer, D.M., Brawley, E.R., & Harris, F.R. (1968). Effect of contingent and noncontingent social reinforcement on the cooperative play of a preschool child. *Journal of Applied Behavior Analysis, 1,* 73–76.

Hartmann, H. (1958). *Ego psychology and the problem of adaptation.* New York: International Universities Press.

Hartsough, C.S., & Lamber, N.M. (1985). Medical factors in hyperactive and normal children: Prenatal, developmental, and health history findings. *American Journal of Orthopsychiatry, 55,* 190–201.

Harvey, J., Judge, C., & Wiener, S. (1977). Familial X-linked mental retardation with an X chromosome abnormality. *Journal of Medical Genetics, 14,* 45–50.

Harvey, P.D. (1987). Laboratory research: Its relevance to positive and negative symptoms. In P.D. Harvey and E.F. Walker (Eds.), *Positive and negative symptoms of psychosis.* Hillsdale, N.J.: Erlbaum.

Hastrup, J.L., Light, K.C., & Obrist, P.A. (1982). Parental hypertension and cardiovascular response to stress in healthy young adults. *Psychophysiology, 19,* 615–622.

Hawley, C., & Buckley, R. (1974). Food dyes and hyperkinetic children. *Academic Therapy, 10,* 27–32.

Haynes, S.N., & Horn, W.F. (1982). Reactivity in behavioral observation: A review. *Behavioral Assessment, 4,* 369–385.

Hays, P. (1976). Etiological factors in manic-depressive psychoses. *Archives of General Psychiatry, 33,* 1187–1188.

Haywood, H.C., Filler, J.W., Jr., Shiffman, M.A., & Chatelanat, G. (1975). Behavioral assessment in mental retardation. In P. McReynolds (Ed.), *Advances in psychological assessment* (Vol. 3). Palo Alto, Calif.: Science and Behavior Books.

Hazelrigg, M.D., Cooper, H.M., & Borduin, C.M. (1987). Evaluating the effectiveness of family therapies: An integrative review and analysis. *Psychological Bulletin 1987, 101,* 428–442.

Heaton, R.K. (1975). Subject expectancy and environmental factors as determinants of psychedelic flashbacks. *Journal of Nervous and Mental Disease, 161,* 157–165.

Heaton, R.K., & Victor, R.G. (1976). Personality characteristics associated with psychedelic flashbacks in natural and experimental settings. *Journal of Abnormal Psychology, 85,* 83–90.

Hechtman, L., Weiss, G., & Perlman, T. (1984). Hyperactives as young adults: Past and current substance abuse and antisocial behavior. *American Journal of Orthopsychiatry, 54,* 415–425.

Hecker, M.H.L., Chesney, M., Black, G.W., and Frautsch, N. (1988). Coronary-prone behavior in the Western Collaborative Group Study. *Psychosomatic Medicine, 50,* 153–164.

Heiman, J.R., & LoPiccolo, J. (1983). Effectiveness of daily versus weekly therapy in the treatment of sexual dysfunction. Unpublished manuscript, State University of New York at Stony Brook.

Heiman, J., LoPiccolo, J., & LoPiccolo, L. (1976). *Becoming orgasmic: A sexual growth program for women.* Englewood Cliffs, N.J.: Prentice–Hall.

Heiman, N.M. (1973). Postdoctoral training in community mental health. *Menninger Clinical Bulletin 17.*

Heller, J. (1974). *Something happened.* New York: Knopf.

Hembree, W.C., Nahas, G.G., & Huang, H.F.S. (1979). Changes in human spermatozoa associated with high dose marihuana-smoking. In G.G. Nahas & W.D.M. Paton (Eds.), *Marihuana: Biological effects.* Elmsford, N.Y.: Pergamon.

Hempel, C. (1958). The theoretician's dilemma. In H. Feigl, M. Scriven, & G. Maxwell (Eds.), *Minnesota studies in the philosophy of science* (Vol. 2). Minneapolis: University of Minnesota Press.

Heninger, G.R., Charney, D.S., & Menkes, D.B. (1983). Receptor sensitivity and the mechanism of action of antidepressant treatment. In P.J. Clayton & J.E. Barrett (Eds.), *Treatment of depression: Old controversies and new approaches.* New York: Raven Press.

Henkel, H., & Lewis-Thomé, J. (1976). *Verhaltenstherapie bei männlichen Homosexuellen.* Diplomarbeit der Studierenden der Psychologie. University of Marburg.

Henker, B., & Whalen, C.K. (1980). The changing face of hyperactivity. In C.K. Whalen & B. Henker (Eds.), *Hyperactive children.* New York: Academic Press.

Henningfield, J.E., Miyasato, K., and Jasinski, D.R. (1983). Cigarette smokers self-administer intravenous nicotine. *Pharmacology and Biochemistry of Behavior, 19,* 887–890.

Henry, J.P., Ely, D.L., & Stephens, P.M. (1972). Changes in catecholamine-controlling enzymes in response to psychosocial activation of defense and alarm reactions. In *Physiology, emotion, and psychosomatic illness.* Ciba Symposium 8. Amsterdam, Netherlands: Associated Scientific Publishers.

Henson, D.E., Rubin, H.B., Henson, C., & Williams, J. (1977). Temperature changes of the labia minora as an objective measure of human female eroticism. *Journal of Behavior Therapy and Experimental Psychiatry, 8,* 401–410.

Hepler, R.S., & Frank, I.M. (1971). Marijuana smoking and intraocular pressure. *Journal of the American Medical Association, 217,* 1392.

Herbert, J. (1965). Personality factors and bronchial asthma. A study of South African Indian children. *Journal of Psychosomatic Research, 8,* 353–364.

Herbert, M. (1978). *Conduct disorders of childhood and adolescence.* New York: Wiley.

Herbert, M. (1982). Conduct disorders. In B.B. Lahey & A.E. Kazdin (Eds.), *Advances in clinical child psychology* (Vol. 5). New York: Plenum.

Herd, J.A. (1986). Neuroendocrine mechanisms in coronary heart disease. Cited in K.A. Matthews, S.M. Weiss, T. Detre, T.M. Dembroski, B.F. Faulkner, S.B. Marruck, & R.B. Williams (Eds.), *Handbook of stress, reactivity, and cardiovascular disease.* New York: Wiley.

Herman, C.P., & Mack, D. (1975). Restrained and unrestrained eating. *Journal of Personality, 43,* 647–660.

Herman, C.P., & Polivy, J. (1980). Restrained eating. In A. Stunkard (Ed.), *Obesity.* Philadelphia: Saunders.

Hermann, D.J. (1982). Know thy memory: The use of questionnaires to assess and study memory. *Psychological Bulletin, 92,* 434–452.

Hernández-Peon, R., Chavez-Ibarra, G., & Aguilar-Figueroa, E. (1963). Somatic evoked potentials in one case of hysterical anesthesia. *EEG and Clinical Neurophysiology, 15,* 889–892.

Herr, J.J., & Weakland, J.H. (1979). *Counseling elders and their families: Practical techniques to applied gerontology.* New York: Springer.

Hersen, M., & Bellack, A.S. (1976). Social skills training for chronic psychiatric patients. *Comprehensive Psychiatry, 17,* 559–580.

Hersen, M., & Bellack, A.S. (Eds.). (1981). *Behavioral assessment: A practical handbook* (2nd ed.). New York: Pergamon.

Hersen, M., & Bellack, A.S. (Eds.). (1988). *Behavioral assessment: A practical handbook* (3rd ed.). New York: Pergamon.

Hertzog, C., & Schaie, K.W. (1988). Stability and change in adult intelligence: 2. Simultaneous analysis of longitudinal means and covariance structures. *Psychology and Aging, 3,* 122–130.

Heston, L.L. (1966). Psychiatric disorders in foster home reared children of schizophrenic mothers. *British Journal of Psychiatry, 112,* 819–825.

Heston, L.L., White, J.A., & Mastri, A.R. (1987). Pick's disease: Clinical genetics and natural history. *Archives of General Psychiatry, 44,* 409–411.

Hetherington, E.M., & Martin, B. (1979). Family interaction. In H.C. Quay & J.S. Werry (Eds.), *Psychopathological disorders of childhood* (2nd ed.). New York: Wiley.

Hewett, F.M. (1965). Teaching speech to an autistic child through operant conditioning. *American Journal of Orthopsychiatry, 33,* 927–936.

Heyd, D., & Bloch, S. (1981). The ethics of suicide. In S. Bloch & P. Chodoff (Eds.), *Psychiatric ethics.* New York: Oxford University Press.

Hibbert, G.A. (1984). Hyperventilation as a cause of panic attacks. *British Medical Journal, 288,* 263–264.

Hickey, T. (1980). *Health and aging.* Belmont, Calif.: Wadsworth.

Higgins, G.F. (1978). Sexuality and the spinal cord injured patient. In J. LoPiccolo & L. LoPiccolo (Eds.), *Handbook of sex therapy.* New York: Plenum.

Hilgard, E.R. (1979). The Stanford hypnotic susceptibility scales as related to other measures of hypnotic responsiveness. *American Journal of Clinical Hypnosis, 21,* 68–83.

Hilgard, E.R., Morgan, A.H., & MacDonald, H. (1975). Pain and dissociation in the cold pressor test: A study of hypnotic analgesia with "hidden reports" through automatic keypressing and automatic talking. *Journal of Abnormal Psychology, 84,* 280–289.

Hill, D. (1952). EEG in episodic psychotic and psychopathic behavior: A classification of data. *EEG and Clinical Neurophysiology, 4,* 419–442.

Hill, J.H., Liebert, R.M., & Mott, D.E.W. (1968). Vicarious extinction of avoidance behavior through films: An initial test. *Psychological Reports, 12,* 192.

Hill, S.Y. (1980). Introduction: The biological consequences. In *Alcoholism and alcohol abuse among women: Research issues.* Rockville, Md.: National Institute on Alcohol Abuse and Alcoholism.

Hilterbrand, K. (1983). Depression in anorexia nervosa. Unpublished manuscript, University of Southern California.

Himadi, W.G., Cerny, J.A., Barlow, D.H., Cohen, S., & O'Brien, G.T. (1986). The relationship of marital adjustment to agoraphobia treatment outcome. *Behaviour Research and Therapy, 24,* 107–115.

Hinshaw, S.P. (1987). On the distinction between attentional deficits/hyperactivity and conduct problems/aggression in child psychopathology. *Psychological Bulletin, 101,* 443–463.

Hinshaw, S.P., Henker, B., & Whalen, C.K. (1984). Self-control in hyperactive boys in anger-inducing situations: Effects of cognitive-behavioral training and of methylphenidate. *Journal of Abnormal Child Psychology, 12,* 55–77.

Hiroto, D.S., & Seligman, M.E.P. (1975). Generality of learned helplessness in man. *Journal of Personality and Social Psychology, 31,* 311–327.

Hirschfeld, R.A., & Cross, C.K. (1982). Epidemiology of affective disorders. *Archives of General Psychiatry, 39,* 35–46.

Hite, S. (1976). *The Hite report.* New York: Macmillan Co.

Ho, D., Rota, T., Schooley, R., Kaplan, J., Allen, J., Groopman, J., Resnick, L., Felsenstein, L., Andrews, C., & Hirsch, M. (1985). Isolation of HTLV-III from cerebrospinal fluid and neural tissues of patients with neurologic symptoms related to the acquired immune deficiency syndrome. *New England Journal of Medicine, 313,* 1493–1497.

Hobbs, S.A., Beck, S.J., & Wansley, R.A. (1984). Pediatric behavioral medicine: Directions in treatment and prevention. In M. Hersen, R.M. Eisler, & P.M. Miller (Eds.), *Progress in behavior modification* (Vol. 16). New York: Academic Press.

Hoch, P.H., & Dunaif, S.L. (1955). Pseudopsychopathic schizophrenia. In P.H. Hoch & J. Zubin (Eds.), *Psychiatry and the law.* New York: Grune & Stratton.

Hoch, P.H., & Polatin, P. (1949). Pseudoneurotic forms of schizophrenia. *Psychiatric Quarterly, 23,* 248–276.

Hodapp, V., Weyer, G., & Becker, J. (1975). Situational stereotypy in essential hypertension patients. *Journal of Psychosomatic Research, 19,* 113–121.

Hodgson, R.J., & Rachman, S.J. (1972). The effects of contamination and washing on obsessional patients. *Behaviour Research and Therapy, 10,* 111–117. (a)

Hodgson, R.J., & Rachman, S.J. (1972). The treatment of chronic obsessive-compulsive neurosis. *Behaviour Research and Therapy, 10,* 181–189. (b)

Hoffman, M.L. (1970). Moral development. In P.H. Mussen (Ed.), *Carmichael's manual of child psychology.* London: Wiley.

Hofland, B.F. (1988). Autonomy in long term care: Background issues and a programmatic response. *The Gerontologist, 28* (Suppl.), 3–9.

Hogan, D. (1978). The effectiveness of sex therapy: A review of the literature. In J. LoPiccolo & L. LoPiccolo (Eds.), *Handbook of sex therapy.* New York: Plenum.

Hogarty, G.E., Anderson, C.M., Reiss, D.J., Kornblith, S.J., Greenwald, D.P., Javna, C.D., & Madonia, M.J. (1986). Family psychoeducation, social skills training, and maintenance chemotherapy in the aftercare treatment of schizophrenia. I: One year effects of a controlled study on relapse and expressed emotion. *Archives of General Psychiatry, 43,* 633–642.

Hogarty, G.E., Goldberg, S.C., Schooler, N.R., Ulrich, R.F., & The Collaborative Study Group (1974). Drug and socio-therapy in the aftercare of schizophrenic patients: II. Two-year relapse rates. *Archives of General Psychiatry, 31,* 603–608.

Hokanson, J.E., & Burgess, M. (1962). The effects of three types of aggression on vascular processes. *Journal of Abnormal and Social Psychology, 65,* 446–449.

Hokanson, J.E., Burgess, M., & Cohen, M.F. (1963). Effects of displaced aggression on systolic blood pressure. *Journal of Abnormal and Social Psychology, 67,* 214–218.

Hokanson, J.E., Willers, K.R., & Koropsak, E. (1968). Modification of autonomic responses during aggressive interchange. *Journal of Personality, 36,* 386–404.

Holden, C. (1972). Nader on mental health centers: A movement that got bogged down. *Science, 177,* 413–415.

Holinger, P.C. (1979). Violent deaths among the young: Recent trends in suicide, homicides, and accidents. *American Journal of Psychiatry, 136,* 1144–1147.

Hollingshead, A.B., & Redlich, F.C. (1958). *Social class and mental illness: A community study.* New York: Wiley.

Hollon, S.D., & Beck, A.T. (1979). Cognitive therapy of depression. In P.C. Kendall & S.D. Hollon (Eds.), *Cognitive-behavioral interventions: Theory, research, and procedures.* New York: Academic Press.

Hollon, S.D., & Beck, A.T. (1986). Cognitive and cognitive-behavioral therapies. In S.L. Garfield & A.E. Bergin (Eds.), *Handbook of psychotherapy and behavior change* (3rd ed.). New York: Wiley.

Hollon, S.D., DeRubeis, R.J., Tuason, V.B., Weimer, M.J., Evans, M.D., & Garvey, M.J. (1989). Cognitive therapy, pharmacotherapy, and combined cognitive-pharmacotherapy in the treatment of depression: I. Differential outcome. Unpublished manuscript, Vanderbilt University.

Hollon, S.D., & Kendall, P.C. (1980). Cognitive self-statements in depression: Development of an automatic thoughts questionnaire. *Cognitive Therapy and Research, 4,* 383–395.

Holmes, T.S., & Holmes, T.H. (1970). Short-term intrusions into the life style routine. *Journal of Psychosomatic Research, 14,* 121–132.

Holmes, T.H., & Rahe, R.H. (1967). The social readjustment rating scale. *Journal of Psychosomatic Research, 11,* 213–218.

Holroyd, K., Penzien, D., Hursey, K., Tobin, D., Rogers, L., Holm, J., Marcille, P., Hall, J., & Chila, A. (1984). Change mechanisms in EMG biofeedback training: Cognitive changes underlying improvements in tension headache. *Journal of Consulting and Clinical Psychology, 52,* 1039–1053.

Holmstrom, L.L., & Burgess, A.W. (1980). Sexual behavior during reported rapes. *Archives of Sexual Behavior, 9,* 427–439.

Honigfeld, G., & Howard, A. (1978). *Psy-chiatric drugs: A desk reference* (2nd ed.). New York: Academic Press.

Hooley, J.M. (1986). Expressed emotion and depression: Interactions between patients and high-versus-low-expressed emotion spouses *Journal of Abnormal Psychology, 95,* 237–246.

Hoon, E.F., & Hoon, P.W. (1978). Styles of sexual expression in women: Clinical implications of multivariate analyses. *Archives of Sexual Behavior, 7,* 105–116.

Hoon, P., Wincze, J., & Hoon, E. (1977). A test of reciprocal inhibition: Are anxiety and sexual arousal in women mutually inhibitory? *Journal of Abnormal Psychology, 86,* 65–74.

Horan, J.J., Linberg, S.E., & Hackett, G. (1977). Nicotine poisoning and rapid smoking. *Journal of Consulting and Clinical Psychology, 45,* 344–347.

Horn, A.S., & Snyder, S.H. (1971). Chlorpromazine and dopamine: Conformational similarities that correlate with the anti-schizophrenic activity of phenothiazine drugs. *Proceedings of the National Academy of Sciences, 68,* 2325–2328.

Horn, J.L. (1985). Remodeling old models of intelligence. In B.B. Wolman (Ed.), *Handbook of intelligence: Theory, measurements, and applications.* New York: Wiley.

Horn, J.L., & Donaldson, G. (1976). On the myth of intellectual decline in adulthood. *American Psychologist, 31,* 701–719.

Hornblower, M., & Svoboda, W. (1987). Down and out—But determined: Does a mentally disturbed woman have the right to be homeless? *Time,* November 23, 1987, p. 29.

Horney, K. (1939). *New ways in psychoanalysis.* New York: International Universities Press.

Horney, K. (1942). *Self-analysis.* New York: Norton.

Horowitz, M.J. (1975). Intrusive and repetitive thoughts after experimental stress. *Archives of General Psychiatry, 32,* 223–228.

Horowitz, M.J., Marmar, C.R., Weiss, D.S., Kaltreider, N.B., & Wilner, N.R. (1986). Comprehensive analysis of change after brief dynamic psychotherapy. *American Journal of Psychiatry, 143,* 582–589.

Horwitz, L. (1974). *Clinical prediction in psychotherapy.* New York: Jason Aronson.

Houts, P.S., & Serber, M. (Eds.). (1972). *After the turn-on, what? Learning perspectives on humanistic groups.* Champaign, Ill.: Research Press.

Howard, K.I., Kopta, S.M., Krause, M.S., & Orlinsky, D.E. (1986). The dose–effect relationship in psychotherapy. *American Psychologist, 41,* 159–164.

Hsu, L.K.G. (1980). Outcome of anorexia nervosa: A review of the literature (1954 to 1978). *Archives of General Psychiatry, 37,* 1041–1046.

Hugdahl, K., Fredrikson, M., & Ohman, A. (1977). Preparedness and arousability as determinants of electrodermal conditioning. *Behaviour Research and Therapy, 15,* 345–353.

Hughes, J.R. (1985). As cited in "Many factors account for failures with nicotine gum." In *Pharmacologic treatment of tobacco dependence.* Report from an International Congress, November 3–5, 1985, New York City.

Hughes, P.L., Wells, L.A., Cunningham, C.J., & Ilstrup, D.M. (1986). Treating bulimia with desipramine. *Archives of General Psychiatry, 43,* 182–186.

Hulicka, I.M. (1967). Short-term learning and memory efficiency as a function of age and health. *Journal of the American Geriatrics Society, 15,* 285–294.

Hull, J.G. (1981). A self-awareness model of the causes and effects of alcohol consumption. *Journal of Abnormal Psychology, 90,* 586–600.

Hunt, D.D., Carr, J.E., & Hampson, J.L. (1981). Cognitive correlates of biologic sex and gender identity in transsexualism. *Archives of Sexual Behavior, 10,* 65–77.

Hunt, W.A., & Bespalec, D.A. (1974). An evaluation of current methods of modifying smoking behavior. *Journal of Clinical Psychology, 30,* 431–438.

Hussian, R.A. (1981). *Geriatric psychology: A behavioral perspective.* New York: Van Nostrand–Reinhold.

Hussian, R.A., & Lawrence, P.S. (1980). Social reinforcement of activity and problem-solving training in the treatment of depressed institutionalized elderly patients. *Cognitive Therapy and Research, 5,* 57–69.

Husted, J.R. (1975). Desensitization procedures in dealing with female sexual dysfunction. *The Counseling Psychologist, 5,* 30–37.

Hutchings, B., & Mednick, S.A. (1974). Registered criminality in the adoptive and biological parents of registered male adoptees. In S.A. Mednick, F. Schulsinger, J. Higgins, & B. Bell (Eds.), *Genetics, environment and psychopathology.* New York: Elsevier.

Hutt, C., Hutt, S.J., Lee, D., & Ounsted, C. (1964). Arousal and childhood autism. *Nature, 204,* 908–909.

Huttenlocher, P.R. (1974). Dendritic development in neocortex of children with mental defect and infantile spasms. *Neurology, 24,* 203–210.

Hyman, B.T., Van Hoesen, G.W., Damasio, A.R., & Barnes, C.L. (1984). Alzheimer's disease: Cell-specific pathology isolates the hippocampal formation. *Science,* **225,** 1168-1170.

Inglis, J. (1969). Electrode placement and the effect of ECT on mood and memory in depression. *Canadian Psychiatric Association Journal,* **14,** 463–471.

Innes, G., Millar, W.M., & Valentine, M. (1959). Emotion and blood pressure. *Journal of Mental Sciences,* **105,** 840–851.

Insell, T.R. (1986). The neurobiology of anxiety. In B.F. Shaw, Z.V. Segal, T.M. Wallis, & F.E. Cashman (Eds.), *Anxiety disorders.* New York: Plenum.

Insell, T.R., Murphy, D.L., Cohen, R.M., Alterman, I., Itts, C., & Linnoila, M. (1983). Obsessive-compulsive disorders. A double-blind trial of clomipramine and clorgyline. *Archives of General Psychiatry,* **40,** 605–612.

Insull, W. (Ed.). (1973). *Coronary risk handbook.* New York: American Heart Association.

Irwin, M., Lovitz, A., Marder, S.R., Mintz, J., Winslade, W.J., Van Putten, T., & Mills, M.J. (1985). Psychotic patients' understanding of informed consent. *American Journal of Psychiatry,* **142,** 1351–1354.

Isen, A.M., Shaiken, T.F., Clark, M., & Karp, L. (1978). Affect, accessibility of material in memory, and behavior: A cognitive loop? *Journal of Personality and Social Psychology,* **36,** 1–12.

Issidorides, M.R. (1979). Observations in chronic hashish users: Nuclear aberrations in blood and sperm and abnormal acrosomes in spermatozoa. In G.G. Nahas & W.D.M. Paton (Eds.), *Marihuana: Biological effects.* Elmsford, N.Y.: Pergamon.

Jackson, A.M. (1973). Psychotherapy: Factors associated with the race of the therapist. *Psychotherapy: Theory, Research, and Practice,* **10,** 273–277.

Jackson, D.D., & Weakland, J. (1961). Conjoint family therapy: Some considerations on theory, technique and results. *Psychiatry,* **24,** 30–45.

Jacob, R.G., & Chesney, M.A. (1986). Psychological and behavioral methods to reduce cardiovascular reactivity. In K.A. Mathews, S.M. Weiss, T. Detre, T.M. Dembroski, B.F. Faulkner, S.B. Manuck, & R.B. Williams (Eds.), *Handbook of stress, reactivity, and cardiovascular disease.* New York: Wiley.

Jacobs, M., Jacobs, A., Gatz, M., & Schaible, T. (1973). Credibility and desirability of positive and negative structured feedback in groups. *Journal of Consulting and Clinical Psychology,* **40,** 244–252.

Jacobson, A., & McKinney, W.T. (1982). Affective disorders. In J.H. Griest, J.W. Jefferson, & R.L. Spitzer (Eds.), *Treatment of mental disorders.* New York: Oxford University Press.

Jacobson, E. (1929). *Progressive relaxation.* Chicago: University of Chicago Press.

Jacobson, N.S., Follette, W.C., & McDonald, D.W. (1982). Reactivity to positive and negative behavior in distressed and nondistressed married couples. *Journal of Consulting and Clinical Psychology,* **50,** 706–714.

Jacobson, N.S., Follette, W.C., Revenstorf, D., Baucom, D.H., Hahlweg, K., & Margolin, G. (1984). Variability of outcome and clinical significance of behavioral marital therapy: A reanalysis of outcome data. *Journal of Consulting and Clinical Psychology,* **52,** 497–504.

Jacobson, N.S., & Margolin, G. (1979). *Marital therapy: Strategies based on social learning.* New York: Brunner/Mazel.

Jacobson, N.S., McDonald, D.W., Follette, W.C., & Berley, R.A. (1985). Attributional process in distressed and nondistressed married couples. *Cognitive Therapy and Research,* **9,** 35–50.

Jacobson, N.S., Waldron, H., & Moore, D. (1980). Toward a behavioral profile of marital distress. *Journal of Consulting and Clinical Psychology,* **48,** 696–703.

Jaffe, J.H. (1985). Drug addiction and drug abuse. In *Goodman and Gilman's the pharmacological basis of therapeutic behavior.* New York: Macmillan Co.

James, N., & Chapman, J. (1975). A genetic study of bipolar affective disorder. *British Journal of Psychiatry,* **126,** 449–456.

Jamison, K.R. (1979). Manic-depressive illness in the elderly. In O.J. Kaplan (Ed.), *Psychopathology of aging.* New York: Academic Press.

Jandorf, L., Deblinger, E., Neale, J.M., & Stone, A.A. (1986). Daily vs. major life events as predictors of symptom frequency. *Journal of General Psychology,* **113,** 205–218.

Jarvik, L.F., Mintz, J., Steuer, J., & Gerner, R. (1982). Treating geriatric depression: A 26-week interim analysis. *Journal of the American Geriatrics Society,* **30,** 713–717.

Jarvik, L.F., & Perl, M. (1981). Overview of physiologic dysfunction related to psychiatric problems in the elderly. *Aging: Neuropsychiatric Manifestations of Physical Disease in the Elderly,* **14,** 1–15.

Jarvik, L.F., Ruth, V., & Matsuyama, S. (1980). Organic brain syndrome and aging: A six-year follow-up of surviving twins. *Archives of General Psychiatry,* **37,** 280–286.

Jarvik, M.E. (1979). Biological influences on cigarette smoking. In N.A. Krasnegor (Ed.), *The behavioral aspects of smoking.* Washington, D.C.: National Institute on Drug Abuse.

Jarvik, M.E., Cullen, J.W., Gritz, E.R., Vogt, T.M., & West, L.J. (Eds.), (1977). *Research on smoking behavior.* Washington, DC: National Institute on Drug Abuse.

Jarvik, M.E., & Schneider, N.G. (1984). Degree of addiction and effectiveness of nicotine gum therapy for smoking. *American Journal of Psychiatry,* **141,** 790–791.

Jarvis, M.J., Raw, M., Russell, M.A.H., & Feyerabend, C. (1982). Randomised controlled trial of nicotine chewing-gum. *British Medical Journal,* **285,** 537–540.

Jasinski, D.R., Johnson, R.E., & Kocher, T.R. (1985). Clonidine in morphine withdrawal. *Archives of General Psychiatry,* **42,** 1063–1066.

Jasnow, N. (1982). *Effects of relaxation training and rational emotive therapy on anxiety reduction in sixth grade children.* Unpublished doctoral dissertation, Hofstra University.

Jay, S.M., Elliott, C.H., Ozolins, M., & Olson, R.A. (1982). *Behavioral management of children's distress during painful medical procedures.* Paper presented at the annual meeting of the American Psychological Association, Washington, D.C.

Jeans, R.F.I. (1976). An independently validated case of multiple personality. *Journal of Abnormal Psychology,* **85,** 249–255.

Jeffrey, D.B. (1974). A comparison of the effects of external control and self-control on the modification and maintenance of weight. *Journal of Abnormal Psychology,* **83,** 404–410.

Jellinek, E.M. (1952). Phases of alcohol addiction. *Quarterly Journal of Studies on Alcohol,* **13,** 673–684.

Jenike, M.A. (1986). Theories of etiology. In M.A. Jenike, L. Baer, & W.E. Minichiello (Eds.), *Obsessive-compulsive disorders.* Littleton, Mass.: PSG Publishing.

Jenkins, C.D. (1971). Psychologic and social precursors of coronary disease. *New England Journal of Medicine,* **284,** 244–255, 307–317.

Jenkins, C.D. (1976). Recent evidence supporting psychologic and social risk factors for coronary disease. *New England Journal of Medicine,* **294,** 987–994, 1033–1038.

Jenkins, C.D., Rosenman, R.H., & Zyzanski, S.J. (1974). Prediction of clinical coronary heart disease by a test for the coronary-prone behavior pattern. *New England Journal of Medicine,* **290,** 1271–1275.

Jenkins, C.D., Zyzanski, S.J., & Rosenman, R.H. (1978). Coronary-prone behavior: One pattern or several? *Psychosomatic Medicine,* **40,** 25–43.

Jenkins, R.L., & Glickman, S. (1947). Patterns of personality organization among delinquents. *Nervous Child,* **6,** 329–339.

Jennings, C., Barraclough, B.M., & Moss, J.R. (1978). Have the Samaritans lowered the suicide rate? A controlled study. *Psychological Medicine, 8*, 413–422.

Jerrell, J.M., & Larsen, J.K. (1986). Community mental health centers in transition: Who is benefitting? *American Journal of Orthopsychiatry, 56*, 78–88.

Jersild, A.T., & Holmes, F.B. (1935). *Children's fears*. New York: Teachers College Press, Columbia University.

Jersild, A.T., Markey, F.V., & Jersild, C.L. (1933). Children's fears, dreams, wishes, daydreams, likes, dislikes, pleasant and unpleasant memories. In A.T. Jersild (Ed.), *Child psychology*. Englewood Cliffs, N.J.: Prentice–Hall, 1960.

Joffee, J.M., & Albee, G.W. (1981). Powerlessness and psychopathology. In J.M. Joffee & G.W. Albee (Eds.), *Prevention through political action and social change: Primary prevention of psychopathology* (Vol. 5). Hanover, N.H.: University Press of New England.

Johnson, A.M., Falstein, E.I., Szurek, S.A., & Svendson, M. (1941). School phobia. *American Journal of Orthopsychiatry, 11*, 701–702.

Johnson, E.H. (1984). Anger and anxiety as determinants of elevated blood pressure in adolescents. Unpublished doctoral dissertation, University of South Florida.

Johnson, S.M., & Greenberg, L.S. (1985). Differential effects of experiential and problem-solving interventions in resolving marital conflict. *Journal of Consulting and Clinical Psychology, 53*, 175–184.

Johnston, D.G., Troyer, I.E., & Whitsett, S.F. (1988). Clomipramine treatment of agoraphobic women. *Archives of General Psychiatry, 45*, 453–459.

Johnston, D.W. (1985). Psychological interventions in cardiovascular disease. *Journal of Psychosomatic Research, 29*, 447–456.

Johnston, M.B., Whitman, T.L., & Johnson, M. (1980). Teaching addition and subtraction to mentally retarded children: A self-instructional program. *Applied Research in Mental Retardation, 1*, 141–160.

Jones, B.M. (1973). Memory impairment on the ascending and descending limbs of the blood alcohol curve. *Journal of Abnormal Psychology, 82*, 24–32.

Jones, B.M., & Parsons, O.A. (1971). Impaired abstracting ability in chronic alcoholics. *Archives of General Psychiatry, 24*, 71–75.

Jones, B.M., & Parsons, O.A. (1975). Alcohol and consciousness: Getting high, coming down. *Psychology Today, 8*, 53–58.

Jones, E. (1955). *The life and work of Sigmund Freud* (Vol. 2). New York: Basic Books.

Jones, M. (1953). *The therapeutic community*. New York: Basic Books.

Jones, M.C. (1924). A laboratory study of fear: The case of Peter. *Pedagogical Seminary, 31*, 308–315.

Jones, M.C. (1964). Personality antecedents and correlates of drinking patterns in young males. *Journal of Consulting and Clinical Psychology, 32*, 2–12.

Jones, M.C. (1968). Personality correlates and antecedants of drinking patterns in males. *Journal of Consulting and Clinical Psychology, 32*, 2–12.

Jones, R.T. (1977). Human effects. In R.C. Peterson (Ed.), *Marijuana research findings: 1976*. NIDA Research Monograph 14. Washington, D.C.: U.S. Government Printing Office.

Jones, R.T. (1980). Human effects: An overview. In *Marijuana research findings: 1980*. Washington, D.C.: U.S. Government Printing Office.

Jones, R.T. (1983). Cannabis and health. *Annual Review of Medicine, 34*, 247–258.

Jones, R.T. (1984). The pharmacology of cocaine. In J. Grabowski (Ed.), *Cocaine: Pharmacology, effects, and treatment of abuse*. Rockville, Md.: National Institute on Drug Abuse.

Jones, R.T., & Benowitz, N. (1976). The 30-day trip—Clinical studies of cannabis tolerance and dependence. In M.C. Braude & S. Szara (Eds.), *Pharmacology of marijuana*. New York: Raven Press.

Jung, C.G. (1982). *Contributions to analytical psychology*. New York: Harcourt Brace Jovanovich.

Justice, B., & Justice, R. (1979). *The broken taboo: Sex in the family*. New York: Human Sciences Press.

Jutai, J.W., & Hare, R.D. (1983). Psychopathy and selective attention during performance of a complex perceptual-motor task. *Psychophysiology, 20*, 140–151.

Kagan, J. (1965). Reflection-impulsivity and reading ability in primary grade children. *Child Development, 36*, 609–628.

Kahn, E. (1985). Heinz Kohut and Carl Rogers: A timely comparison. *American Psychologist, 40*, 893–904.

Kahn, R.L. (1975). The mental health system and the future aged. *The Gerontologist, 15*, Part II, 24–31.

Kahn, R.L., Zarit, S.H., Hilbert, N.M., & Niederehe, G. (1975). Memory complaint and impairment in the aged. *Archives of General Psychiatry, 32*, 1569–1573.

Kaiser, F.E., Viosca, S.P., Morley, J.E., Mooradian, A.D., Davis, S.S., & Korenman, S.G. (1988). Impotence and aging: Clinical and hormonal factors. *Journal of the American Geriatrics Society, 36*, 511–519.

Kammen, D.P. van, Bunney, W.E., Docherty, J.P., Jimerson, D.C., Post, R.M., Sivis, S., Ebart, M., & Gillin, J.C. (1977).

Amphetamine-induced catecholamine activation in schizophrenia and depression. *Advances in Biochemical Psychopharmacology, 16*, 655–659.

Kanas, N. (1986). Group therapy with schizophrenics: A review of controlled studies. *International Journal of Group Therapy, 36*, 339–351.

Kandel, D.B. (1984). Marijuana users in young adulthood. *Archives of General Psychiatry, 41*, 200–209.

Kandel, D.B., Davies, M., Karus, D., & Yamaguchi, K. (1986). The consequences in young adulthood of adolescent drug involvement. *Archives of General Psychiatry, 43*, 746–754.

Kandel, D.B., Murphy, D., & Karus, D. (1985). *National Institute on Drug Abuse Research Monograph Series 61*. Washington, D.C.: NIDA.

Kane, J., Honigfeld, G., Singer, J., Meltzer, H., et al. (1988). Clozapine for treatment resistant schizophrenics. *Archives of General Psychiatry, 45*, 789–796.

Kane, J.M., Woerner, M., Weinhold, P., Wegner, J., Kinon, B., & Bornstein, M. (1986). Incidence of tardive dyskinesia: Five-year data from a prospective study. *Psychopharmacology Bulletin, 20*, 387–389.

Kane, R.L., Parsons, D.A., & Goldstein, G. (1983). Statistical relationships and discriminative accuracy of the Halstead–Reitan, Luria–Nebraska, and Wechsler IQ scores in the identification of brain damage. *Journal of Clinical and Experimental Neuropsychology, 7*, 211–223.

Kanfer, F.H. (1979). Self-management: Strategies and tactics. In A.P. Goldstein & F.H. Kanfer (Eds.), *Maximizing treatment gains: Transfer enhancement in psychotherapy*. New York: Academic Press.

Kanfer, F.H., & Busemeyer, J.R. (1982). The use of problem-solving and decision making in behavior therapy. *Clinical Psychology Review, 2*, 239–266.

Kanfer, F.H., & Nay, W.R. (1982). Behavioral assessment. In G.T. Wilson & C.R. Franks (Eds.), *Contemporary behavior therapy: Conceptual and empirical foundations*. New York: Guilford.

Kanfer, F.H., & Phillips, J.S. (1970). *Learning foundations of behavior therapy*. New York: Wiley.

Kanner, L. (1943). Autistic disturbances of affective contact. *Nervous Child, 2*, 217–250.

Kanner, L. (1973). Follow-up of eleven autistic children originally reported in 1943. In L. Kanner (Ed.), *Childhood psychosis: Initial studies and new insights*. Washington, D.C.: Winston–Wiley.

Kanner, L., & Eisenberg, L. (1955). Notes on the follow-up studies of autistic children. In P. Hoch & J. Zubin (Eds.), *Psychopath-*

ology of childhood. New York: Grune & Stratton.

Kanter, J., Lamb, R., & Loeper, G. (1987). Expressed emotions in families: A critical review. *Hospital and Community Psychiatry,* **38,** 374–380.

Kantor, J.S., Zitrin, C.M., & Zeldis, S.M. (1980). Mitral valve prolapse syndrome in agoraphobic patients. *American Journal of Psychiatry,* **137,** 467–469.

Kantorovich, N.V. (1930). An attempt at associative-reflex therapy in alcoholism. *Psychological Abstracts,* **4,** 493.

Kaplan, H.S. (1974). *The new sex therapy.* New York: Brunner/Mazel.

Karacan, I., Thornby, J., Holzer, C.E., Warheit, G.J., Schwab, J.J., & Williams, R.L. (1976). Prevalence of sleep disturbance in a primarily urban Florida county. *Social Science Medicine,* **10,** 239–244.

Karasu, T.B., Stein, S.P., & Charles, E.S. (1979). Age factors in patient–therapist relationship. *Journal of Nervous and Mental Disease,* **167,** 100–104.

Karrer, R., Nelson, M., & Galbraith, G.C. (1979). Psychophysiological research with the mentally retarded. In N.R. Ellis (Ed.), *Handbook of mental deficiency, psychological theory and research* (2nd ed.). Hillsdale, N.J.: Erlbaum.

Kasindorf, J. (1988). The real story of Billie Boggs: Was Koch right—Or the civil libertarians? *New York,* May 2, 1988, pages 36–44.

Kasl, S.V., & Cobb, S. (1970). Blood pressure changes in men undergoing job loss: A preliminary report. *Psychosomatic Medicine,* **32,** 19–38.

Kaslow, F.W. (1981). Divorce and divorce therapy. In A.S. Gurman & D.P. Kniskern (Eds.), *Handbook of family therapy.* New York: Brunner/Mazel.

Kastenbaum, R., & Candy, S.E. (1973). The 4% fallacy: A methodological and empirical critique of extended care facility population statistics. *International Journal of Aging and Human Development,* **4,** 15–21.

Kaszniak, A.W., Nussbaum, P.D., Berren, M.R., & Santiago, J. (1988). Amnesia as a consequence of male rape: A case report. *Journal of Abnormal Psychology,* **97,** 100–104.

Katchadourian, H.A., & Lunde, D.T. (1972). *Fundamentals of human sexuality.* New York: Holt Rinehart & Winston.

Katz, E.R. (1980). Illness impact and social reintegration. In J. Kellerman (Ed.), *Psychological aspects of childhood cancer.* Springfield, Ill.: Charles C. Thomas.

Katz, E.R., Kellerman, J., & Siegel, S.E. (1980). Behavioral distress in children with leukemia undergoing bone marrow aspirations. *Journal of Consulting and Clinical Psychology,* **48,** 356–365.

Katzman, R. (1976). The prevalence and malignancy of Alzheimer's disease. *Archives of Neurology,* **33,** 217–218.

Kaul, T.J., & Bednar, R.L. (1986). Experiential group research: Results, questions, and suggestions. In S.L. Garfield & A.E. Bergin (Eds.), *Handbook of psychotherapy and behavior change* (3rd ed.). New York: Wiley.

Kawi, A.A., & Pasamanick, B. (1958). Association of factors of pregnancy with reading disorders in childhood. *Journal of the American Medical Association,* **166,** 1420–1432.

Kay, D.W.K., Cooper, A.F., Garside, R.F., & Roth, M. (1976). The differentiation of paranoid from affective psychoses by patient's premorbid characteristics. *British Journal of Psychiatry,* **129,** 207–215.

Kazdin, A.E. (1975). Covert modelling, imagery assessment, and assertive behavior. *Journal of Consulting and Clinical Psychology,* **43,** 716–724.

Kazdin, A.E. (1985). *Treatment of antisocial behavior in children and adolescents.* Homewood, Ill.: Dorsey Press.

Kazdin, A.E. (1986). Research designs and methodology. In S.L. Garfield & A.E. Bergin (Eds.), *Handbook of psychotherapy and behavior change* (3rd ed.). New York: Wiley.

Kazdin, A.E., & Wilson, G.T. (1978). *Evaluation of behavior therapy: Issues, evidence, and research strategies.* Cambridge, Mass.: Ballinger.

Keefe, F.J., & Gil, K.M. (1986). Behavioral concepts in the analysis of chronic pain syndromes. *Journal of Consulting and Clinical Psychology,* **54,** 776–783.

Keefe, F.J., Surwit, R.S., & Pilon, R. (1979). A 1-year follow-up of Raynaud's patients treated with behavioral therapy techniques. *Journal of Behavioral Medicine,* **2,** 385–391.

Keen, S. (1979). Some ludicrous theses about sexuality. *Journal of Humanistic Psychology,* **19,** 15–22.

Kegel, A.H. (1957). Sexual function of the pubococcygeus muscle. *Western Journal of Surgery,* **60,** 521–524.

Keith, S.J., Gunderson, J.G., Reifman, A., Buchsbaum, S., & Mosher, L.R. (1976). Special report: Schizophrenia 1976. *Schizophrenia Bulletin,* **2,** 509–565.

Keller, M.B., Shapiro, R.W., Lavori, P.W., & Wolfe, N. (1982). Relapse in major depressive disorder. *Archives of General Psychiatry,* **39,** 911–915.

Kellerman, J., & Varni, J.W. (1982). Pediatric hematology/oncology. In D.C. Russo & J.W. Varni (Eds.), *Behavioral pediatrics: Research and practice.* New York: Plenum.

Kellner, R. (1982). Disorders of impulse control (not elsewhere classified). In J.H.

Griest, J.W. Jefferson, & R.L. Spitzer (Eds.), *Treatment of mental disorders.* New York: Oxford University Press.

Kelly, E., & Zeller, B. (1969). Asthma and the psychiatrist. *Journal of Psychosomatic Research,* **13,** 377–395.

Kelly, G.A. (1955). *The psychology of personal constructs.* New York: Norton.

Kelly, J.A. (1985). Group social skills training. *The Behavior Therapist,* **8,** 93–95.

Kelly, J.A., & St. Lawrence, J.S. (1988). AIDS prevention and treatment: Psychology's role in the health crisis. *Clinical Psychology Review,* **8,** 255–284. (a)

Kelly, J.A., & St. Lawrence, J.S. (1988). *The AIDS health crisis: Psychological and social interventions.* New York: Plenum. (b)

Kelly, J.A., St. Lawrence, J.S., Hood, H.V., & Brasfield, T. (1988). Behavioral intervention to reduce AIDS risk activities. To be published. As cited in Kelly & St. Lawrence (1988a).

Kelly, J.A., St. Lawrence, J.S., Hood, H.V., Smith, S., Jr., & Cook, D. (1988). Nurses' attitudes towards AIDS. *The Journal of Continuing Education in Nursing,* **19,** 78–83.

Kendall, P.C., & Hollon, S.D. (Eds.). (1981). *Assessment strategies for cognitive-behavioral interventions.* New York: Academic Press.

Kendell, R.E. (1975). *The role of diagnosis in psychiatry.* London: Blackwell.

Kendler, K.S., & Gruenberg, A.M. (1984). Independent analysis of Danish adoption study of schizophrenia. *Archives of General Psychiatry,* **41,** 555–562.

Kennedy, W.A. (1965). School phobia: Rapid treatment of 50 cases. *Journal of Abnormal Psychology,* **70,** 285–289.

Kenney, R.A. (1982). *Physiology of aging.* Chicago: Year Book Medical Publishers.

Kent, R.N., O'Leary, K.D., Diament, C., & Dietz, A. (1974). Expectation biases in observational evaluation of therapeutic change. *Journal of Consulting and Clinical Psychology,* **42,** 774–780.

Kernberg, O.F. (1970). A psychoanalytic classification of character pathology. *Journal of the American Psychoanalytic Association,* **18,** 800–822.

Kernberg, O.F. (1973). Summary and conclusion of "Psychotherapy and psychoanalysis: Final report of the Menninger Foundation's Psychotherapy Research Project." *International Journal of Psychiatry,* **11,** 62–77.

Kernberg, O. (1985). *Borderline conditions and pathological narcissism.* Northvale, N.J.: Jason Aronson.

Kernberg, O.P., Burstein, E.D., Coyne, L., Applebaum, A., Horwitz, L., & Voth, H. (1972). Psychotherapy and psychoanalysis: Final report of the Menninger Foundation's

Psychotherapy Research Project. *Bulletin of the Menninger Clinic*, **36**, 1–276.

Kessel, N., & Grossman, G. (1961). Suicide in alcoholics. *British Medical Journal*, **2**, 1671–1672.

Kessler, J. (1966). *Psychopathology of childhood*. Englewood Cliffs, N.J.: Prentice–Hall.

Kessler, R.C., & McLeod, J.D. (1985). Social support and mental health in community samples. In S. Cohen & S.L. Syme (Eds.), *Social support and health*. New York: Academic Press.

Kety, S.S. (1774). From rationalization to reason. *American Journal of Psychiatry*, **131**, 957–963.

Kety, S.S., Rosenthal, D., Wender, P.H., & Schulsinger, F. (1968). The types and prevalence of mental illness in the biological and adoptive families of adopted schizophrenics. In D. Rosenthal & S.S. Kety (Eds.), *The transmission of schizophrenia*. Elmsford, N.Y.: Pergamon.

Kety, S.S., Rosenthal, D., Wender, P.H., Schulsinger, F., & Jacobson, B. (1975). Mental illness in the biological and adoptive families of adopted individuals who have become schizophrenic: A preliminary report based on psychiatric interviews. In R.R. Fieve, D. Rosenthal, & H. Brill (Eds.), *Genetic research in psychiatry*. Baltimore: Johns Hopkins University Press.

Keuthen, N. (1980). Subjective probability estimation and somatic structures in phobic individuals. Unpublished manuscript, State University of New York at Stony Brook.

Keys, A., Taylor, H.L., et al. (1971). Mortality and coronary heart disease in men studied for 23 years. *Archives of Internal Medicine*, **128**, 201–214.

Kidder, T. (1978). Soldiers of misfortune. *The Atlantic Monthly*, **241**, 41–52.

Kielcolt-Glaser, J.K., Garner, W., Speicher, C.E., Penn, G.M., Holliday, J., & Glaser, R. (1984). Psychosocial modifiers of immunocompetence in medical students. *Psychosomatic Medicine*, **46**, 7–14.

Kiesler, C.A. (1985). Prevention and public policy. In J.C. Rosen & L.J. Solomon (Eds.), *Prevention in health psychology*. Hanover, N.H.: University Press of New England.

Killen, J.D., Maccoby, N., & Taylor, C.B. (1984). Nicotine gum and self-regulation training in smoking relapse prevention. *Behavior Therapy*, **15**, 234–248.

Kiloh, L.G. (1961). Pseudo-dementia. *Acta Psychiatrica Scandinavia*, **37**, 336–351.

Kimble, G.A., Garmezy, N., & Zigler, E. (1980), *Principles of general psychology*. New York: Wiley.

Kimmel, D.C., (1979). Adjustments to aging among gay men. In B. Berzon & R. Leighton (Eds.), *Positively gay*. Millbrae, Calif.: Celestial Arts.

Kimmel, D.C. (1988). Ageism, psychology, and public policy. *American Psychologist*, **43**, 175–178.

Kimura, D. (1983). Sex differences in cerebral organization for speech and praxic functions. *Canadian Journal of Psychology*, **37**, 19–35.

Kinsey, A.C., Pomeroy, W.B., & Martin, C.E. (1948). *Sexual behavior in the human male*. Philadelphia: Saunders.

Kinsey, A.C., Pomeroy, W.B., Martin, C.E., & Gebhard, P.H. (1953). *Sexual behavior in the human female*. Philadelphia: Saunders.

Kinsman, R.A., Spector, S.L., Shucard, D.W., & Luparello, T.J. (1974). Observations on patterns of subjective symptomatology of acute asthma. *Psychosomatic Medicine*, **36**, 129–143.

Klee, G.D., Bertino, J., Weintraub, W., & Calaway, E. (1961). The influence of varying dosage on the effects of lysergic acid diethylamide (LSD-25). *Journal of Nervous and Mental Disease*, **132**, 404–409.

Klee, G.D., & Weintraub, W. (1959). Paranoid reactions following lysergic acid diethylamide (LSD-25). In P.B. Bradley, P. Demicker, & C. Radonco-Thomas (Eds.), *Neuropsychopharmacology*. Amsterdam, Netherlands: Elsvier.

Kleeman, S.T. (1967). Psychiatric contributions in the treatment of asthma. *Annals of Allergy*, **25**, 611–619.

Klein, D.C., & Seligman, M.E.P. (1976). Reversal of performance deficits and perceptual deficits in learned helplessness and depression. *Journal of Abnormal Psychology*, **85**, 11–26.

Klein, D.F., & Davis, J.M. (1969) *Diagnosis and durg treatment of psychiatric disorders*. Baltimore: Williams & Wilkins.

Klein, D.N., Taylor, E.B., Dickstein, S., & Harding, K. (1988). Primary early-onset dysthymia: Comparison with primary nonbipolar nonchronic major depression on demographic, clinical, familial, personality, and socioenvironmental characteristics and short-term outcome. *Journal of Abnormal Psychology*, **97**, 387–398.

Klein, M. (1932). *The psychoanalysis of children*. London: Hogarth.

Kleinke, C.L., Staneski, R.A., & Mason, J.K. (1982). Sex differences in coping with depression. *Sex Roles*, **8**, 877–889.

Kleinmuntz, B. (1967). *Personality measurement: An introduction*. Homewood, Ill.: Dorsey Press.

Klerman, G.L. (1972). Drug therapy of clinical depressions. *Journal of Psychiatric Research*, **9**, 253–270.

Klerman, G.L. (1975). Drug therapy of clinical depressions—Current status and implications for research on neuropharmacology of the affective disorders. In D.F. Klein & R. Gittelman-Klein (Eds.), *Progress in psy-*

chiatric drug treatment. New York: Brunner/Mazel.

Klerman, G.L. (1983). Problems in the definition and diagnosis of depression in the elderly. In M. Hauge & L. Breslau (Eds.), *Depression in the elderly: Causes, care, consequences*. New York: Springer.

Klerman, G.L. (1988). Depression and related disorders of mood (affective disorders). In A.M. Nicholi, Jr. (Ed.), *The new Harvard guide to psychiatry*. Cambridge, Mass.: Harvard University Press.

Klerman, G.L., Weissman, M.M., Rounsaville, B.J., & Chevron, E.S. (1984). *Interpersonal psychotherapy of depression*. New York: Basic Books.

Kluft, R.P. (1984). An introduction to multiple personality disorder. *Psychiatric Annals*, **7**, 19–24. (a)

Kluft, R.P. (1984). Treatment of multiple personality disorder: A study of 33 cases. *Psychiatric Clinics of North America*. **7**, 9–29. (b)

Kluft, R.P. (1985). Using hypnotic inquiry protocols to monitor treatment progress and stability in multiple personality disorder. *American Journal of Clinical Hypnosis*, **28**, 63–75.

Kluger, J.M. (1969). Childhood asthma and the social milieu. *American Academy of Child Psychiatry*, **8**, 353–366.

Knapp, P.H. (1969). The asthmatic and his environment. *Journal of Nervous and Mental Disease*, **149**, 133–151.

Knapp, S., & Vandecreek, L. (1982). Tarasoff: Five years later. *Professional Psychology*, **13**, 511–516.

Knaus, W., & Bokor, S. (1975). The effect of rational-emotive education lessons on anxiety and self-concept in sixth grade students. *Rational living*, **10**, 7–10.

Knight, B. (1983). An evaluation of a mobile geriatric team. In M.A. Smyer & M. Gatz (Eds.), *Mental health and aging: Programs and evaluations*. Beverly Hills, Calif.: Sage.

Knight, B. (1986). *Psychotherapy with older adults*. Beverly Hills, Calif.: Sage.

Knight, R.A., & Prentkey, R.A. (in press). Classifying sexual offenders: The development and corroboration of taxonomic models. In W.R. Marshall, R. Laws, & H. Barbaree (Eds.), *The handbook of sexual assault*. New York: Plenum.

Knight, R.P. (1937). The dynamics of chronic alcoholism. *Journal of Nervous and Mental Disease*, **86**, 538–548.

Koegel, R.L., Schreibman, L., Britten, K.R., Burkey, J.C., & O'Neill, R.E. (1982). A comparison of parent training to direct child treatment. In R.L. Koegel, A. Rincover, & A.L. Egel (Eds.), *Educating and understanding autistic children*. San Diego, Calif.: College-Hill.

Koenig, K., & Masters, J. (1965). Experimental treatment of habitual smoking. *Be-*

haviour Research and Therapy, **3**, 235–243.

Koenig, S., Gendelman, H., Orenstein, J., DelCanto, J.C., Pezeshkpour, G.H., Yungbluth, G., Janotta, F., Aksamit, A., Martin, M., & Feaci, A. (1986). Detection of AIDS virus in macrophages in brain tissue from AIDS patients with encephalopathy. *Science,* **233**, 1089–1093.

Kog, E., & Vandereycken, W. (1985). Family characteristics of anorexia nervosa and bulimia: A review of the research literature. *Clinical Psychology Review,* **5**, 159–180.

Kohn, M.L. (1968). Social class and schizophrenia: A critical review. In D. Rosenthal & S.S. Kety (Eds.), *The transmission of schizophrenia.* Elmsford, N.Y.: Pergamon.

Kohut, H. (1966). Forms and transformations of narcissism. *Journal of the American Psychoanalytic Association,* **14**, 243–272.

Kohut, H. (1971). *The analysis of the self.* New York: International Universities Press.

Kohut, H. (1977). *The restoration of the self.* New York: International Universities Press.

Kohut, H., & Wolf, E.S. (1978). The disorders of the self and their treatment: An outline. *International Journal of Psychoanalysis,* **59**, 413–425.

Kolb, L.C. (1968). *Noyes' modern clinical psychiatry* (7th ed.). Philadelphia: Saunders.

Kolvin, I., MacKeith, R.C., & Meadows, S.R. (1973). *Bladder control and enuresis.* Philadelphia: Lippincott.

Konig, P., & Godfrey, S. (1973). Prevalence of exercise-induced bronchial libility in families of children with asthma. *Archives of Diseases of Childhood,* **48**, 518.

Kopfstein, J.M., & Neale, J.M. (1972). A multivariate study of attention dysfunction in schizophrenia. *Journal of Abnormal Psychology,* **80**, 294–299.

Korchin, S.J. (1976). *Modern clinical psychology.* New York: Basic Books.

Kornetsky, C. (1976). Hyporesponsivity of chronic schizophrenic patients to dextroamphetamine. *Archives of General Psychiatry,* **33**, 1425–1428.

Koss, M.P., & Butcher, J.N. (1986). Research on brief psychotherapy. S.L. Garfield & A.E. Bergin (Eds.). *Handbook of psychotherapy and behavior change* (3rd ed.). New York: Wiley.

Kovacs, M., & Beck, A.T. (1977). The wish to live and the wish to die in attempted suicides. *Journal of Clinical Psychology,* **33**, 361–365.

Kovacs, M., Rush, A.J., Beck, A.T., & Hollon, S.D. (1981). Depressed outpatients treated with cognitive therapy or pharmacotherapy: A one-year follow-up. *Archives of General Psychiatry,* **38**, 33–39.

Kowalik, D.L., & Gotlib, I.H. (1987). Depression and marital interaction: Concordance between intent and perception of communication. *Journal of Abnormal Psychology,* **96**, 127–134.

Kowall, N.K., & Beal, M. F. (1988). Cortical somatostatin, neuropeptide Y, and NADPH diphorase neurons: Normal anatomy and alterations in Alzheimer's disease. *Annals of Neurology,* **23**, 105–113.

Kozel, N.J., & Adams, E.H. (1986). Epidemiology of drug abuse: An overview. *Science,* **234**, 970–974.

Kozel, N.J., Grider, R.A., & Adams, E.H. (1982). National surveilance of cocaine use and related health consequences. *Morbidity and Mortality Weekly Report 31,* **20**, 265–273.

Kozol, H., Boucher, R., & Garofalo, R. (1972). The diagnosis and treatment of dangerousness. *Crime and Delinquency,* **18**, 371–392.

Kraepelin, E. (1883). *Lehrbuch der Psychiatrie* (1st ed., 1883; 8th ed., 1915). *Clinical psychiatry.* Translated from the 7th German edition by A.R. Diefendorf. Delmar, N.Y.: Scholars' Facsimiles and Reprints, 1981.

Kramer, M. (1977). *Psychiatric services and the changing institutional scene 1950–1985.* Washington, D.C.: National Institute of Mental Health.

Krantz, S., & Hammen, C.L. (1979). Assessment of cognitive bias in depression. *Journal of Abnormal Psychology,* **88**, 611–619.

Kranz, H. (1936). *Lebenschicksale krimineller Zwillinge.* Berlin: Springer-Verlag.

Krech, D., Rosenzweig, M., & Bennett, E. (1966). Environmental impoverishment, social isolation, and changes in brain chemistry and anatomy. *Physiology and Behavior,* **1**, 99–104.

Kringlen, E. (1970). Natural history of obsessional neurosis. *Seminars in Psychiatry,* **2**, 403–419.

Kroll, P., Chamberlain, P., & Halpern, D. (1979). The diagnosis of Briquet's syndrome in a male population. *Journal of Nervous and Mental Disease,* **169**, 171–174.

Kucharski, L.T., White, R.M., & Schratz, M. (1979). Age bias, referral for psychological assistance and the private physician. *Journal of Gerontology,* **34**, 423–428.

Kuhn, T.S. (1962). *The structure of scientific revolutions.* Chicago: University of Chicago Press.

Kunst-Wilson, W.R., & Zajonc, R.B. (1980). Affective discrimination of stimuli that cannot be recognized. *Science,* **207**, 557–558.

Kuriansky, J.B., Deming, W.E., & Gurland, B.J. (1974). On trends in the diagnosis of schizophrenia. *American Journal of Psychiatry,* **131**, 402–407.

Kutchinsky, B. (1970). *Studies on pornography and sex crimes in Denmark.* Copenhagen: New Social Science Monographs.

Lacey, J.I. (1967). Somatic response patterning and stress: Some revisions of activation theory. In M.H. Appley & R. Trumball (Eds.), *Psychological stress.* New York: McGraw–Hill.

Ladd, G.W. (1981). Effectiveness of a social learning method for enhancing children's social interaction and peer acceptance. *Child Development,* **52**, 171–178.

La Greca, A.J., Akers, R.L., & Dwyer, J.W. (1988). Life events and alcohol behavior among older adults. *The Gerontologist,* **28**, 552–558.

Laing, R.D. (1964). Is schizophrenia a disease? *International Journal of Social Psychiatry,* **10**, 184–193.

Lamb, H.R., & Zusman, J. (1979). Primary prevention in perspective. *American Journal of Psychiatry,* **36**, 12–17.

Lambert, M.J., Bergin, A.E., & Collins, J.L. (1977). Therapist-induced deterioration in psychotherapy. In A.S. Gurman & A.M. Razin (Eds.), *Effective psychotherapy: A handbook of research.* Elmsford, N.Y.: Pergamon.

Lambert, M.J., Shapiro, D.A., & Bergin, A.E. (1986). The effectiveness of psychotherapy. In S.L. Garfield & A.E. Bergin (Eds.), *Handbook of psychotherapy and behavior change* (3rd ed.). New York: Wiley.

Landman, J. T., & Dawes, R. (1982). Psychotherapy outcome: Smith and Glass's conclusions stand up under scrutiny. *American Psychologist,* **37**, 504–516.

Lando, H.A. (1977). Successful treatment of smokers with a broad-spectrum behavioral approach. *Journal of Consulting and Clinical Psychology,* **45**, 361–366.

Lane, E.A., & Albee, G.W. (1965). Childhood intellectual differences between schizophrenic adults and their siblings. *American Journal of Orthopsychiatry,* **35**, 747–753.

Lang, A.R., Goeckner, D.J., Adessor, V.J., & Marlatt, G.A. (1975). Effects of alcohol on aggression in male social drinkers. *Journal of Abnormal Psychology,* **84**, 508–518.

Lang, A.R., & Marlatt, G.A. (1982). Problem drinking: A social learning perspective. In R.J. Gatchel, A. Baum, & J.E. Singer (Eds.), *Handbook of psychology and health.* Hillsdale, N.J.: Erlbaum.

Lang, P.J. (1969). The mechanics of desensitization and the laboratory study of fear. In C.M. Franks (Ed.), *Behavior therapy: Appraisal and status.* New York: McGraw–Hill.

Lang, P.J., & Lazovik, A.D. (1963). Experimental desensitization of a phobia. *Journal of Abnormal and Social Psychology,* **66**, 519–525.

Lang, P.J., & Melamed, B.G. (1969). Case report: Avoidance conditioning therapy of an infant with chronic ruminative vomiting. *Journal of Abnormal Psychology,* **74**, 1–8.

Lange, A.J., & Jakubowski, P. *Responsible assertive behavior.* Champaign, Ill.: Research Press.

Lange, J. (1929). *Verbrechen als Schicksal.* Leipzig: Georg Thieme Verlag.

Langer, E.J. (1981). Old age: An artifact? In J. McGaugh & S. Kiesler (Eds.), *Aging: Biology and behavior.* New York: Academic Press.

Langer, E.J., & Albelson, R.P. (1974). A patient by any other name . . . : Clinician group difference in labelling bias. *Journal of Consulting and Clinical Psychology, 42,* 4–9.

Langer, E.J., & Rodin, J. (1976). The effects of choice and enhanced personal responsibility for the aged. *Journal of Personality and Social Psychology, 34,* 191–198.

Langevin, R., Paitich, D., Ramsay, G., Anderson, C., Kamrad, J., Pope, S., Geller, G., Pearl, L., & Newman, S. (1979). Experimental studies of the etiology of genital exhibitionism. *Archives of Sexual Behavior, 8,* 307–331.

Langevin, R., Paitich, D., & Steiner, B. (1977). The clinical profile of male transsexuals living as females versus those living as males. *Archives of Sexual Behavior, 6,* 143–154.

Lanyon, R.I. (1986). Theory and treatment of child molestation. *Journal of Consulting and Clinical Psychology, 54,* 176–182.

LaRue, A., Dessonville, C., & Jarvik, L.F. (1985). Aging and mental disorders. In J.E. Birren & K.W. Schaie (Eds.), *Handbook of psychology of aging* (2nd ed.). New York: Van Nostrand–Reinhold.

Lasagna, L., Mosteller, F., Von Felsinger, J.M., & Beecher, H.K. (1954). A study of the placebo response. *American Journal of Medicine, 16,* 770–779.

Lavelle, T.L., Metalsky, G.I., & Coyne, J.C. (1979). Learned helplessness, test anxiety, and acknowledgment of contingencies. *Journal of Abnormal Psychology, 88,* 381–387.

Laws, D.R., & Holmen, M.L. (1978). Sexual response faking by pedophiles. *Criminal Justice and Behavior. 5,* 343–356.

Lawton, M.P. (1972). Schizophrenia forty-five years later. *Journal of Genetic Psychology, 121,* 133–143.

Lawton, M.P. (1979). Clinical geropsychology: Problems and prospects. In *Master lecture series on the psychology of aging.* Washington, D.C.: American Psychological Association.

Layne, C. (1983). Painful truths about depressives' cognitions. *Journal of Clinical Psychology, 39,* 848–853.

Lazar, I. (1979). Social services in Head Start. In E. Zigler & J. Valentine (Eds.), *Project Head Start.* New York: Free Press.

Lazarus, A.A. (1961). Group therapy of phobic disorders by systematic desensitization. *Journal of Abnormal and Social Psychology, 63,* 504–510.

Lazarus, A.A. (1965). Behavior therapy, incomplete treatment, and symptom substitution. *Journal of Nervous and Mental Disease, 140,* 80–86.

Lazarus, A.A. (1968). Behavior therapy in groups. In G.M. Gazda (Ed.), *Basic approaches to group psychotherapy and counseling.* Springfield, Ill.: Charles C. Thomas. (a)

Lazarus, A.A. (1968). Learning theory and the treatment of depression. *Behavior Research and Therapy, 6,* 83–89. (b)

Lazarus, A.A. (1971). *Behavior therapy and beyond.* New York: McGraw–Hill.

Lazarus, A.A., & Davison, G.C. (1971). Clinical innovation in research and practice. In A.E. Bergin & S.L. Garfield (Eds.), *Handbook of psychotherapy and behavior change: An empirical analysis.* New York: Wiley.

Lazarus, A.A., Davison, G.C., & Polefka, D. (1965). Classical and operant factors in the treatment of school phobia. *Journal of Abnormal Psychology, 70,* 225–229.

Lazarus, R.S. (1966). *Psychological stress and the coping process.* New York: McGraw–Hill.

Lazarus, R.S., & Cohen, J.P. (1977). Environmental stress. In I. Altman & J.F. Wohlwill (Eds.), *Human behavior and the environment: Current theory and research.* New York: Plenum.

Lazarus, R.S., & Folkman, S. (1984). *Stress, coping, and adaptation.* New York: Springer.

Lazovik, A.D., & Lang, P.J. (1960). A laboratory demonstration of systematic desensitization psychotherapy. *Journal of Psychological Studies, 11,* 238–247.

Lederman, S. (1956). *Alcohol, alcoholism, alcoholisation: Scientifiques de Caractere Physiologique Economique et Social.* Paris: Presses Universitaires de France.

Lee, D., DeQuattro, V., Cox, T., Pyter, L., Foti, A., Allen, J., Barndt, R., Azen, S., & Davison, G.C. (1987). Neurohormonal mechanisms and left ventricular hypertrophy: Effects of hygienic therapy. *Journal of Human Hypertension, 1,* 147–151.

Lee, T., & Seeman, P. (1977). Dopamine receptors in normal and schizophrenic human brains. *Proceedings of the Society of Neurosciences, 3,* 443.

Lee, V.E., Brooks-Gunn, J., & Schnur, E. (1988). Does Head Start work? A 1-year follow-up comparison of disadvantaged children attending Head Start, no preschool, and other preschool programs. *Developmental Psychology, 24,* 210–222.

Leeper, P. (1988). Having a place to live is vital to good health. *NewsReport, 38,* 5–8.

Leff, J.P. (1976). Schizophrenia and sensitivity to the family environment. *Schizophrenia Bulletin, 2,* 566–574.

Lefkowitz, M.M., & Burton, N. (1978). Childhood depression: A critique of the concept. *Psychological Bulletin, 85,* 716–726.

Lehrer, P.M., & Woolfolk, R.L. (1982). Self-report assessment of anxiety: Somatic, cognitive, and behavioral modalities. *Behavioral Assessment, 4,* 167–177.

Leiblum, S.R., & Rosen, R.C. (Eds.). (1988). *Sexual desire disorders.* New York: Guilford.

Leibtag, D. (1980, July 11). Potent new heroin smoked and snorted. *ADAMHA News.*

Leland, H., & Smith, D. (1965). *Play therapy with mentally subnormal children.* New York: Grune & Stratton.

Lemere, F., & Voegtlin, W.L. (1950). An evaluation of the aversion treatment of alcoholism. *Quarterly Journal of Studies on Alcohol, 11,* 199–204.

Lemieux, G., Davignon, A., & Genest, J. (1956). Depressive states during rauwolfia therapy for arterial hypertension. *Canadian Medical Association Journal, 74,* 522–526.

Leon, G.R., Gillum, B., Gillum, R., & Gouze, M. (1979). Personality stability and change over a 30-year period—Middle age to old age. *Journal of Consulting and Clinical Psychology, 47,* 517–524.

Lerer, B., Bleich, A., Kotler, M., Garb, R., Hertzberg, M., & Levin, B. (1987). Post-traumatic stress disorder in Israeli combat veterans. *Archives of General Psychiatry, 44,* 976–981.

Lesage, A., & Lamontagne, Y. (1985). Paradoxical intention and exposure *in vivo* in the treatment of psychogenic nausea: Report of two cases. *Behavioral Psychotherapy, 13,* 69–75.

Levendusky, P., & Pankratz, L. (1975). Self-control technique as an alternative pain medication. *Journal of Abnormal Psychology, 84,* 165–168.

Levenson, M. (1972). Cognitive and perceptual factors in suicidal individuals. Unpublished doctoral dissertation, University of Kansas.

Levitsky, A., & Perls, F.S. (1970). The rules and games of Gestalt therapy. In J. Fagan & I.L. Shepherd (Eds.), *Gestalt therapy now: Theory, techniques, applications.* Palo Alto, Calif.: Science and Behavior Books.

Levitt, E.E. (1971). Research on psychotherapy with children. In A.E. Bergin & S.L. Garfield (Eds.), *Handbook of psychotherapy and behavior change: An empirical analysis.* New York: Wiley.

Levy, L.H. (1963). *Psychological interpretation.* New York: Holt, Rinehart & Winston.

Levy, R., & Muskin, J. (1973). Somatosensory evoked response in patients with hysterical anesthesia. *Journal of Psychosomatic Research, 17,* 81–84.

Lewinsohn, P.H. (1974). A behavioral approach to depression. In R.J. Friedman & M.M. Katz (Eds.), *The psychology of depression: Contemporary theory and research.* Washington, D.C.: Winston–Wiley.

Lewinsohn, P.H., & Libet, J.M. (1972). Pleasant events, activity schedules and depression. *Journal of Abnormal Psychology,* **79,** 291–295.

Lewinsohn, P.M., Steinmetz, J.L., Larsen, D.W., & Franklin, J. (1981). Depression-related cognitions: Antecedent or consequences? *Journal of Abnormal Psychology,* **90,** 213–219.

Lewinsohn, P.M., & Teri, L. (1983). *Clinical geropsychology: New directions in assessment and treatment.* New York: Pergamon.

Lewinsohn, P.H., Weinstein, M., & Alper, T. (1970). A behavioral approach to the group treatment of depressed persons: A methodological contribution. *Journal of Clinical Psychology,* **26,** 525–532.

Lewinsohn, P.M. (1974). A behavioral approach to depression. In R.J. Friedman and M.M. Katz (Eds.), *The psychology of depression: Contemporary theory and research.* Washington, D.C.: Winston.

Lewinsohn, P.M., Mischel, W., Chaplon, W., & Barton, R. (1980). Social competence and depression: The role of illusory self-perceptions. *Journal of Abnormal Psychology,* **89,** 203–212.

Ley, R. (1987). Panic disorder: A hyperventilation interpretation. In L. Michelson & L.M. Asher (Eds.), *Anxiety and stress disorders.* New York: Guilford.

Liberman, M.A. (1983). Social contexts of depression. In L.D. Breslau & M.R. Haug (Eds.), *Depression and aging: Causes, care and consequences,* New York: Springer.

Liberman, R.P., King, L.W., DeRisi, W.J., & McCann, M. (1975). *Personal effectiveness.* Champaign, Ill.: Research Press.

Liberman, R.P., Wheeler, E.G., & Kuehnel, J.M. (1983). Failures in behavioral marital therapy. In E.B. Foa & P.M.G. Emmelkamp (Eds.), *Failures in behavior therapy.* New York: Wiley.

Lichtenstein, E., & Danaher, B.G. (1977). Modification of smoking behavior: A critical analysis of theory, research, and practice. In M. Hersen, R.M. Eisler, & P.M. Miller (Eds.), *Progress in behavior modification* (Vol. 4). New York: Academic Press.

Lichtenstein, E., Harris, D.E., Birchler, G.R., Wahl, J.M., & Schmahl, D.P. (1973). Comparison of rapid smoking, warm, smoky air, and attention placebo in the modification of smoking behavior. *Journal of Consulting and Clinical Psychology,* **40,** 92–98.

Lieberman, M.A. (1987). Effects of large group awareness training on participants' psychiatric status. *American Journal of Psychiatry,* **144,** 460–464.

Lieberman, M.A., Yalom, J.D., & Miles, M.B. (1973). *Encounter groups: First facts.* New York: Basic Books.

Liebert, R.M., Neale, J.M., & Davidson, E.S. (1973). *The Early Window.* Elmsford, NY: Pergamon.

Liebowitz, M.R., Fyer, A.J., Gorman, J.M., Dillon, D.J., Appleby, I.L., Levy, G.F., Anderson, S., Levitt, M., Palij, M., Davies, S.O., & Klein, D.F. (1984). Lactate provocation of panic attacks. *Archives of General Psychiatry,* **41,** 764–770.

Liebson, I. (1967). Conversion reaction: A learning theory approach. *Behaviour Research and Therapy,* **7,** 217–218.

Lief, H.I. (1988). Foreword. In S.R. Leiblum & R.C. Rosen (Eds.), *Sexual desire disorders.* New York: Guilford.

Liem, J.H. (1974). Effects of verbal communications of parents and children: A comparison of normal and schizophrenic families. *Journal of Consulting and Clinical Psychology,* **42,** 438–450.

Lifton, R.J. (1976). Advocacy and corruption in the healing profession. In N.L. Goldman & D.R. Segal (Eds.), *The social psychology of military service.* Beverly Hills, Calif.: Sage.

Lindsay, W.R. (1986). Cognitive changes after social skills training with young mildly mentally handicapped adults. *Journal of Mental Deficiency Research,* **30,** 81–88.

Linehan, M.M. (1985). Dialectical behavior therapy for borderline personality disorder. *Bulletin of the Menninger Clinic,* **51,** 261–276.

Linehan, M.M., Camper, P., Chiles, J.A., Strosahl, K., & Shearin, E.N. (1987). Interpersonal problem-solving and parasuicide. *Cognitive Therapy and Research,* **11,** 1–12.

Linehan, M.M., & Shearin, E.N. (1988). Lethal stress: A social-behavioral model of suicidal behavior. In S. Fisher & J. Reason (Eds.), *Handbook of life stress, cognition, and health.* New York: Wiley.

Linton, H.B., & Langs, R.J. (1964). Empirical dimensions of LSD-25 reactions. *Archives of General Psychiatry,* **10,** 469–485.

Linz, D.G., Donnerstein, E., & Penrod, S. (1988). Effects of long-term exposure to violent and sexually degrading depictions of women. *Journal of Personality and Social Psychology,* **55,** 758–768.

Lion, J.R. (1978). Outpatient treatment of psychopaths. In W.H. Reid (Ed.), *The psychopath: A comprehensive study of antisocial disorders and behaviors.* New York: Brunner/Mazel.

Lipinski, D.P., Black, J.L., Nelson, R.O., & Ciminero, A.R. (1975). The influence of motivational variables on the reactivity and reliability of self-recording. *Journal of Consulting and Clinical Psychology,* **43,** 637–646.

Lipman, A. (1984). Homosexuals. In E.B. Palmore (Ed.), *Handbook on the aged in the United States,* Westport, CT: Greenwood Press.

Lipowski, Z.J. (1980). *Delirium: Acute brain failure in man.* Springfield, Ill.: Charles C. Thomas.

Lipowski, Z.J. (1983). Transient cognitive disorders (delirium and acute confusional states) in the elderly. *American Journal of Psychiatry,* **140,** 1426–1436.

Lipton, M.A., & Nemeroff, C.B. (1978). The biology of aging and its role in depression. In G. Usdin & C.K. Hofling (Eds.), *Aging: The process and the people.* New York: Brunner/Mazel.

Liskow, B. (1982). Substance induced and substance use disorders: Barbiturates and similarly acting sedative hypnotics. In J.H. Greist, J.W. Jefferson, & R.L. Spitzer (Eds.), *Treatment of mental disorders.* New York: Oxford University Press.

Liston, E.H. (1982). Delirium in the aged. In L.F. Jarvik & G.W. Small (Eds.), *Psychiatric clinics of North America.* Philadelphia: Saunders.

Litwack, T.R. (1985). The prediction of violence. *The Clinical Psychologist,* **38,** 87–90.

Lloyd, L.L., & Karlan, G.R. (1984). Nonspeech communication symbols and systems: Where have we been and where are we going? *Journal of Mental Deficiency Research,* **28,** 3–20.

Lobitz, W.C., & Post, R.D. (1979). Parameters of self-reinforcement and depression. *Journal of Abnormal Psychology,* **88,** 33–41.

Lockyer, L., & Rutter, M. (1969). A five-to-fifteen-year follow-up of infantile psychosis: III. Psychological characteristics. *British Journal of Psychiatry,* **115,** 865–882.

London, P. (1964). *The modes and morals of psychotherapy.* New York: Holt, Rinehart & Winston.

London, P. (1986). *The modes and morals of psychotherapy* (2nd ed.). New York: Hemisphere Publishing.

Loney, J., Langborne, J.E., Jr., & Paternite, C.E. (1978). An empirical basis for subgrouping the hyperkinetic-minimal brain dysfunction syndrome. *Journal of Abnormal Psychology,* **87,** 431–441.

Lopez, S., & Hernandez, P. (1986). How culture is considered in evaluations of psychopathology. *Journal of Nervous and Mental Disease,* **176,** 598–606.

Lopez, S., & Nunez, J.A. (1987). Cultural factors considered in selected diagnostic criteria and interview schedules. *Journal of Abnormal Psychology,* **96,** 270–272.

LoPiccolo, J. (1977). Direct treatment of sexual dysfunction in the couple. In J. Money & H. Musaph (Eds.), *Handbook of sexology,* New York: Elsevier/North-Holland.

LoPiccolo, J., & Friedman, J.M. (1985). Sex

therapy: An integrated model. In S.J. Lynn & J.P. Garskee (Eds.), *Contemporary psychotherapies: Models and methods.* New York: Merrill.

LoPiccolo, J., & Hogan, D.R. (1979). Multidimensional treatment of sexual dysfunction. In O.F. Pomerleau & J.P. Brady (Eds.), *Behavioral medicine: Theory and practice.* Baltimore: Williams & Wilkins.

LoPiccolo, J., & Lobitz, W.C. (1972). The role of masturbation in the treatment of orgasmic dysfunction. *Archives of Sexual Behavior, 2,* 163–171.

LoPiccolo, J. & Lopiccolo, L. (1978) (Eds.), *Handbook of sex therapy.* New York: Plenum.

LoPiccolo, J., & Stock, W. (1986). Treatment of sexual dysfunction. *Journal of Consulting and Clinical Psychology, 54,* 158–167.

LoPiccolo, J., & Stock, W. (in press). Sexual counseling in gynecological practice. In Z. Rosenwaks, F. Benjamin, & M. Stone (Eds.), *Basic gynecology,* New York: Macmillan Co.

Loranger, A., Oldham, J., Russakoff, L.M., & Susman, V. (1987). Structured interviews and borderline personality disorder. *Archives of General Psychiatry, 41,* 565–568.

Loranger, A.W., Oldham, J.M., & Tulis, E.H. (1983). Familial transmission of DSM-III borderline personality disorder. *Archives of General Psychiatry, 40,* 795–799.

Lothstein, L.M. (1980). The postsurgical transsexual: Empirical and theoretical considerations. *Archives of Sexual Behavior, 9,* 547–564.

Lothstein, L.M. (1983). *Female-to-male transsexualism: Historical, clinical, and theoretical issues.* Boston: Routledge and Kegan Paul.

Lotter, V. (1966). Epidemiology of autistic conditions in young children: I. Prevalence. *Social Psychiatry, 1,* 124–137.

Lotter, V. (1974). Factors related to outcome in autistic children. *Journal of Autism and Childhood Schizophrenia., 4,* 263–277.

Lotter, V. (1978). Follow-up studies. In M. Rutter & E. Schopler (Eds.), *Autism: A reappraisal of concepts and treatment.* New York: Plenum.

Lovaas, O.I. (1977). *The autistic child: Language development through behavior modification.* New York: Irvington.

Lovaas, O.I. (1987). Behavioral treatment and normal educational and intellectual functioning in young autistic children. *Journal of Consulting and Clinical Psychology, 55,* 3–9.

Lovaas, O.I., Berberich, J.P., Perloff, B.F., & Schaeffer, B. (1966). Acquisition of imitative speech by schizophrenic children. *Science, 151,* 705–707.

Lovaas, O.I., Freitag, G., Gold, V.J., & Kassorla, I.C. (1965). Experimental studies in childhood schizophrenia: Analysis of self-destructive behavior. *Journal of Experimental Child Psychology, 2,* 67–84.

Lovaas, O.I., Koegel, R., Simmons, J.Q., & Long, J.S. (1973). Some generalization and follow-up measures on autistic children in behavior therapy. *Journal of Applied Behavior Analysis, 6,* 131–166.

Lovaas, O.I., Litrownik, A., & Mann, R. (1971). Response latencies to auditory stimuli in autistic children engaged in self-stimulatory behavior. *Behaviour Research and Therapy, 9,* 39–49.

Lovaas, O.I., Newsom, C., & Hickman, C. (1987). Self-stimulatory behavior and perceptual reinforcement. *Journal of Applied Behavior Analysis, 20,* 45–68.

Lovaas, O.I., Schreibman, L., Koegel, R., & Rehm, R. (1971). Selective responding by autistic children to multiple sensory input. *Journal of Abnormal Psychology, 77,* 221–222.

Lovibond, S.H. (1964). *Conditioning and enuresis.* Oxford, England: Pergamon.

Lovibond, S.H., & Caddy, G. (1970). Discriminated aversive control in the moderation of alcoholics' drinking. *Behavior Therapy, 1,* 437–444.

Lowen, A. (1958). *The physical dynamics of character structure.* New York: Grune & Stratton.

Lowenthal, M.F., Berkman, P., & Associates (1967). *Aging and mental disorder in San Francisco.* San Francisco: Jossey–Bass.

Lubin, B. (1983). Group therapy, In I.B. Weiner (Ed.), *Clinical methods in psychology* (2nd ed.). New York: Wiley.

Lubin, R.A. (1977). Influences of alcohol upon performance and performance awareness. *Perceptual and Motor Skills, 45,* 303–310.

Luborsky, L., & Spence, D.P. (1978). Quantitative research on psychoanalytic therapy. In S.L. Garfield & A.E. Bergin (Eds.), *Handbook of psychotherapy and behavior change: An empirical analysis* (2nd ed.). New York: Wiley.

Luparello, T.J., McFadden, E.R., Lyons, H.A., & Bleecker, E.R. (1971). Psychologic factors and bronchial asthma, *New York State Journal of Medicine, 71,* 2161–2165.

Luria, A.R. (1961). *The role of speech in the regulation of normal and abnormal behavior.* New York: Pergamon.

Luria, D.B. (1970). *Overcoming drugs: program of action.* New York: McGraw–Hill.

Luthe, W., & Schultz, J.H. (1969). *Autogenic therapy.* Vol. 1. *Autogenic methods.* New York: Grune & Stratton.

Lyght, C.E. (Ed.). (1966). *The Merck manual of diagnosis and therapy* (11th ed.). Rahway, N.J.: Merck Sharp and Dohme Research Laboratories.

Lykken, D.T. (1957). A study of anxiety in the sociopathic personality. *Journal of Abnormal and Social Psychology, 55,* 6–10.

Lyon, G.R., & Moats, L.C. (1988). Critical issues in the instruction of the learning disabled. *Journal of Consulting and Clinical Psychology, 56,* 830–835.

Lystad, M.M. (1957). Social mobility among selected groups of schizophrenics. *American Sociological Review, 22,* 288–292.

Maccoby, N., & Alexander, J. (1980). Use of media in lifestyle programs. In P.O. Davidson & S.M. Davidson (Eds.), *Behavioral medicine: Changing health lifestyles.* New York: Brunner/Mazel.

Maccoby, N., Farquhar, J.W., Wood, P.D., & Alexander J. (1977). Reducing the risk of cardiovascular disease: Effects of a community-based campaign on knowledge and behavior. *Journal of Community Health, 3,* 100–114.

Maccoby, E.E., & Jacklin, C.N. (1974). *The psychology of sex differences.* Stanford, Calif.: Stanford University Press.

MacCorquodale, K., & Meehl, P. (1948). On the distinction between hypothetical constructs and intervening variables. *Psychological Review, 5,* 95–107.

MacDonald, D.I. (1987, March). Testimony before the U.S. Senate of Representatives Committee on Appropriations, Subcommittee on the Departments of Labor, Health and Human Services, and Education, 100th Congress, 1st Session. Washington, D.C.: U.S. Government Printing Office. As cited in Roybal (1988).

MacFarlane, J.W., Allen, L., & Honzik, M.R. (1954). *A developmental study of the behavior problems of normal children between 21 months and 14 years.* Berkeley, Calif.: University of California Press.

Mackay, A.V.P., Iversen, L.L., Rossor, M., Spokes, E., Arregio, A., Crease, I., & Snyder, S.H. (1982). Increased brain dopamine and dopamine receptors in schizophrenia. *Archives of General Psychiatry, 39,* 991–997.

Macleod, C., & Hemsley, D.R. (1985). Visual feedback of vocal intensity in the treatment of hysterical aphonia. *Journal of Behaviour Therapy and Experimental Psychiatry, 4,* 347–353.

MacMillan, J.F., Gold, A., Crow, T.J., Johnson, A.L., & Johnstone, E.C. (1986). Expressed emotion and relapse. *British Journal of Psychiatry, 148,* 133–143.

MacPhillamy, D.J., & Lewinsohn, P.M. (1973). A scale for the measurement of positive reinforcement. Unpublished manuscript, University of Oregon.

MacPhillamy, D.J., & Lewinsohn, P.M. (1974). Depression as a function of levels of desired and obtained pleasure. *Journal of Abnormal Psychology, 83,* 651–657.

Magenis, R.E., Overton, K.M., Chamberlin, J., Brady, T., & Lovrien, E. (1977). Paternal origin of the extra chromosome in Down's syndrome. *Human Genetics, 37,* 7–16.

Maher, B.A. (1966). *Principles of psychopathology: An experimental approach.* New York: McGraw–Hill.

Maher, B.A. (1974). *Journal of Consulting and Clinical Psychology, 42,* 1–3 (editorial).

Mahoney, M.J. (1972). Research issues in self-management. *Behavior Therapy, 3,* 45–63.

Mahoney, M.J. (1974). *Cognition and behavior modification.* Cambridge, Mass.: Ballinger.

Mahoney, M.J. (1982). Psychotherapy and human change processes. In *Psychotherapy research and behavior change* (Vol. 1). Washington, D.C.: American Psychological Association.

Main, T.F. (1958). Perception and ego-function. *British Journal of Medical Psychology, 31,* 1–7.

Malamuth, N.M. (1981). Rape proclivity among males. *Journal of Social Issues, 37,* 138–157.

Malamuth, N.M., & Check, J.V.P. (1981). The effects of mass media exposure on acceptance of violence against women: A field experiment. *Journal of Research in Personality, 15,* 436–446.

Malamuth, N.M., & Check, J.V.P. (1983). Sexual arousal to rape depictions: Individual differences. *Journal of Abnormal Psychology, 92,* 55–67.

Malamuth, N.M., Feshbach, S., & Jaffe, Y. (1977). Sexual arousal and aggression: Recent experiments and theoretical issues. *Journal of Social Issues, 33,* 110–133.

Malin, H., Coakley, J., Kaelber, C., Munch, N., & Holland, W. (1982). An epidemiologic perspective on alcohol abuse in the United States. In *Alcohol consumption and related problems.* National Institute of Alcohol Abuse and Alcoholism. Washington, D.C.: U.S. Government Printing Office.

Malloy, T.R., Wein, A.J., & Carpiniello, V.L. (1980). Comparison of the inflatable penile and the small carrion prostheses in the surgical treatment of erectile impotence. *Journal of Urology, 123,* 678–679.

Mandler, G. (1966). Anxiety. In D.L. Sills (Ed.), *International encyclopedia of the social sciences.* New York: Macmillan Co.

Mandler, G. (1972). Helplessness: Theory and research in anxiety. In C.D. Spielberger (Ed.), *Anxiety: Current trends in theory and research.* New York: Academic Press.

Mann, V.A., & Brady, S. (1988). Reading disability: The role of language deficiencies. *Journal of Consulting and Clinical Psychology, 56,* 811–816.

Mannello, T.A., & Seaman, F.J. (1979). *Prevalence, costs, and handling of drinking problems on seven railroads.* Washington, D.C.: University Research Corporation.

Manton, K.G., Blazer, D.G., & Woodbury, M.A. (1987). Suicide in middle age and later life: Sex and race specific life table and co-

hort analyses. *Journal of Gerontology, 42,* 219–227.

Manuck, S.B., Kaplan, J.R., & Clarkson, T.B. (1983). Behaviorally induced heart rate reactivity and atherosclerosis in cynomolgus monkeys. *Psychosomatic Medicine, 49,* 95–108.

Manuck, S.B., and Krantz, D.S. (1986). Psychophysiologic reactivity in coronary heart disease and essential hypertension. In K.A. Matthews, S.M. Weiss, T. Detre, T.M. Dembroski, B.F. Faulkner, S.B. Manuck, & R.B. Williams (Eds.), *Handbook of stress, reactivity, and cardiovascular disease.* New York: Wiley.

Marcus, J., Hans, S.L., Nagler, S., Auerbach, J.G., Mirsky, A.F., & Aubrey, A. (1987). Review of the NIMH Israeli Kibbutz-City and the Jerusalem infant development study. *Schizophrenia bulletin, 13,* 425–438.

Margolin, G. (1978). The relationship among marital assessment procedures: A correlational study. *Journal of Consulting and Clinical Psychology, 46,* 1556–1558.

Margolin, G. (1981). Behavior exchange in happy and unhappy marriages: A family cycle perspective. *Behavior Therapy, 12,* 329–343.

Margolin, G. (1982). Ethical and legal considerations in marital and family therapy. *American Psychologist, 37,* 788–801.

Margolin, G., & Fernandez, V. (1985). Marital dysfunction. In M. Hersen & A.S. Bellack (Eds.), *Handbook of clinical behavior therapy with adults.* New York: Plenum.

Margolin, G., Michelli, J., & Jacobson, N.S. (1988). Assessment of marital dysfunction. In M. Hersen & A.S. Bellack (Eds.), *Behavioral assessment: A practical handbook.* (3rd ed.). New York: Pergamon.

Margolin, G., & Wampold, B.F. (1981). Sequential analysis of conflict and accord in distressed and non-distressed marital partners. *Journal of Consulting and Clinical Psychology, 49,* 554–567.

Margolin, G., & Weiss, R.L. (1978). Comparative evaluation of therapeutic components associated with behavioral marital treatment. *Journal of Consulting and Clinical Psychology, 46,* 1476–1486.

Marijuana research findings. (1980). Washington, D.C.: U.S. Government Printing Office.

Marks, I.M. (1969). *Fears and phobias.* New York: Academic Press.

Marks, I.M. (1981). *Care and cure of neuroses: Theory and practice of behavioral psychotherapy.* New York: Wiley. (a)

Marks, I.M. (1981). Review of behavioral psychotherapy: I. Obsessive-compulsive disorders. *American Journal of Psychiatry, 138,* 584–592. (b)

Marks, I. (1983). Behavioral psychotherapy

for anxiety disorders. *Psychiatric Clinics of North America, 8,* 25–34. (a)

Marks, I. (1983). Are there anticompulsive or antiphobic drugs? Review of the evidence. *British Journal of Psychiatry, 143,* 338–347. (b)

Marks, I.M., & Gelder, M.G. (1967). Transvestism and fetishism: Clinical and psychological changes during faradic aversion. *British Journal of Psychiatry, 113,* 711–729.

Marks, I.M., Gelder, M.G., & Bancroft, J. (1970). Sexual deviants two years after electrical aversion. *British Journal of Psychiatry, 117,* 73–85.

Marlatt, G.A. (1983). The controlled drinking controversy: A commentary. *American Psychologist, 38,* 1097–1110.

Marlatt, G.A. (1985). Relapse prevention: Theoretical rationale and overview of the model. In G.A. Marlatt & J. Gordon (Eds.), *Relapse prevention: Maintenance strategies in addictive behavior change.* New York: Guilford.

Marlatt, G.A., Demming, B., & Reid, J.B. (1973). Loss of control drinking in alcoholics: An experimental analogue. *Journal of Abnormal Psychology, 81,* 233–241.

Marmor, J. (1962). Psychoanalytic therapy as an educational process: Common denominators in the therapeutic approaches of different psychoanalytic schools. In J.H. Masserman (Ed.), *Science and psychoanalysis.* Vol. 5. *Psychoanalytic education.* New York: Grune & Stratton.

Marmor, J. (1971). Dynamic psychotherapy and behavior therapy: Are they irreconcilable? *Archives of General Psychiatry, 24,* 22–28.

Marshall, W.L., Gauthier, J., & Gordon, A. (1979). The current status of flooding therapy. In M. Hersen, R.M. Eisler, & P.M. Miller (Eds.), *Progress in behavior modification* (Vol. 7). New York: Academic Press.

Marshall, W.L., Parker, L., & Hayes, B.M. (1982). Treating public speaking problems. *Behavior Modification. 6,* 147–170.

Marston, A., & Marston, M. (1980). *Comprehensive weight control.* New York: BMA Cassettes.

Martin, B. (1961). The assessment of anxiety by physiological behavioral measures. *Psychological Bulletin, 58,* 234–255.

Martin, D., & Lyon, P. (1972). *Lesbian/woman.* New York: Bantam.

Martin, R. (1975). *Legal challenges to behavior modification: Trends in schools, corrections, and mental health.* Champaign, Ill.: Research Press.

Maruish, M.E., Sawicki, R.F., Franzen, M.D., & Golden, C.J. (1984). Alpha coefficient reliabilities for the Luria–Nebraska Neuropsychological Battery summary and localization scales by diagnostic category.

The International Journal of Clinical Neuropsychology, 7, 10–12.

Maslow, A.H. (1968). *Toward a psychology of being.* New York: Van Nostrand–Reinhold.

Massie, H.N., & Beels, C.C. (1972). The outcome of family treatment of schizophrenia. *Schizophrenia Bulletin, 1,* 24–36.

Masters, W.H., & Johnson, V.E. (1966). *Human sexual response.* Boston: Little, Brown.

Masters, W.H., & Johnson, V.E. (1970). *Human sexual inadequacy.* Boston: Little, Brown.

Mateer, C.A., Polen, S.B., & Ojemann, G.A. (1982). Sexual variation in cortical localization of naming as determined by stimulation mapping. *The Behavioral and Brain Sciences, 5,* 310–311.

Mathe, A., & Knapp, P. (1971). Emotional and adrenal reactions of stress in bronchial asthma. *Psychosomatic medicine, 33,* 323–329.

Matheny, A.P., Jr., Dolan, A.B., & Wilson, R.S. (1976). Twins with academic problems: Antecedent characteristics. *American Journal of Orthopsychiatry, 46,* 464–469.

Mathews, A.M., Bancroft, J., Whitehead, A., Hackmann, A., Julier, D., Bancroft, J., Gath, D., & Shaw, P. (1976). The behavioural treatment of sexual inadequacy: A comparative study. *Behaviour Research and Therapy, 14,* 427–436.

Mattes, J.A., & Gittelman, R. (1983). Growth of hyperactive children on maintenance regimen of methylphenidate. *Archives of General Psychiatry, 40,* 317–321.

Matthews, K.A. (1978). Assessment and developmental antecedents of pattern A behavior in children. In T.M. Dembroski, S.M. Weiss, J.L. Shields, S.G. Haynes, & M. Feinleib (Eds.), *Coronary-prone behavior,* New York: Springer-Verlag.

Matthews, K.A. (1982). Psychological perspectives on the type A behavior pattern. *Psychological Bulletin, 91,* 293–323.

Matthews, K.A., Glass, D.C., Rosenman, R.H., & Bortner, R.W. (1977). Competitive drive, pattern A, and coronary heart disease: A further analysis of some data from the Western Collaborative Group Study. *Journal of Chronic Diseases, 30,* 489–498.

Matthews, K.A., Krantz, D.S., Dembroski, T.M., & McDongal, J.M. (1982). Unique and common variance in Structured Interview and Jenkins Activity Survey measures of the type A behavior pattern. *Journal of Personality and Social Psychology, 42,* 303–313.

Matthews, K.A., & Rakaczky, C.J. (1987). Familial aspects of type A behavior and physiologic reactivity to stress. In T. Dembroski and T. Schmidt (Eds.), *Behavioral factors in coronary heart disease.* Heidelberg: Springer-Verlag.

Mausner, B. (1973). An ecological view of cigarette smoking. *Journal of Abnormal Psychology, 81,* 115–126.

May, P.R.A. (1986). *Treatment of schizophrenia: A comparative study of five treatment methods.* New York: Science House.

May, P.R.A. (1974). Psychotherapy research in schizophrenia—Another view of present reality. *Schizophrenia Bulletin, 1,* 126–132.

May, P.R.A., Tuma, A.H., Yale, C., Potepan, P., & Dixon, W.J. (1976). Schizophrenia—A follow-up study of results of treatment: II. Hospital stay over two to five years. *Psychiatry, 33,* 481–486.

Maynard, R. (1970, June 29). Omaha pupils given "behavior" drugs. *Washington Post.*

Mays, D.T., & Franks, C.M. (1980). Getting worse: Psychotherapy or no treatment—The jury should still be out. *Professional Psychology, 11,* 78–92.

McAdoo, W.G., & DeMyer, M.K. (1978). Personality characteristics of parents. In M. Rutter & E. Schopler (Eds.), *Autism: A reappraisal of concepts and treatment.* New York: Plenum.

McAllister, T.W., & Price, T.R.P. (1982). Severe depressive pseudodementia with and without dementia. *American Journal of Psychiatry, 139,* 626–629.

McCary, J.L. (1973). *Human sexuality* (2nd ed.). New York: Van Nostrand–Reinhold.

McConaghy, N. (1967). Penile volume change to moving pictures of male and female nudes in heterosexual and homosexual males. *Behavior Therapy, 5,* 43–48.

McCord, J., McCord, W., & Thurber, S. (1962). Some effects of paternal absence on male children. *Journal of Abnormal and Social Psychology, 64,* 361–369.

McCord, W., & McCord, J. (1964). *The psychopath: An essay on the criminal mind.* New York: Van Nostrand–Reinhold.

McCord, W., McCord, J., & Gudeman, J. (1959). Some current theories of alcoholism. *Quarterly Journal of Studies on Alcohol, 20,* 727–749.

McCord, W., McCord, J., & Gudeman, J. (1960). *Origins of alcoholism.* Stanford. Calif.: Stanford University Press.

McCrady, B.S. (1985). Alcoholism. In D.H. Barlow (Ed.), *Clinical handbook of psychological disorders.* New York: Guilford.

McCrae, R.R. (1982). Age differences in the use of coping mechanisms. *Journal of Gerontology, 37,* 454–460.

McCrae, R.R., & Costa, P.T., Jr. (1984). *Emerging lives, enduring dispositions: Personality in adulthood.* Boston: Little, Brown.

McCrae, R.R., Costa, P.T., Jr., & Arenberg, D. (1980). Constancy of adult personality structure in males: Longitudinal, cross-sectional and times-of-measurement analysis. *Journal of Gerontology, 35,* 877–883.

McFall, R.M., & Hammen, C.L. (1971). Motivation, structure, and self-monitoring: Role of nonspecific factors in smoking reduction. *Journal of Consulting and Clinical Psychology, 37,* 80–86.

McFall, R.M., & Lillesand, D.B. (1971). Behavior rehearsal with modeling and coaching in assertion training. *Journal of Abnormal Psychology, 77,* 313–323.

McGarry, L., & Chodoff, P. (1981). The ethics of involuntary hospitalization. In S. Bloch & P. Chodoff (Eds.), *Psychiatric ethics,* New York: Oxford University Press.

McGeer, E., & McGeer, P.L. (1976). Neurotransmitter metabolism in the aging brain. In R.D. Terry & S. Gershon (Eds.), *Aging* (Vol. 3). New York: Raven Press.

McGhie, A., & Chapman, J.S. (1961). Disorders of attention and perception in early schizophrenia. *British Journal of Medical Psychology, 34,* 103–116.

McGlashan, T.M. (1983). The borderline syndrome: I. Testing three diagnostic systems. *Archives of General Psychiatry, 40,* 1311–1318.

McGuiness, D. (1981). Auditory and motor aspects of language development in males and females. In A. Ansara (Ed.), *Sex differences in dyslexia.* Towson, Md.: The Orton Dyslexia Society.

McGuiness, D. (1985). *When children don't learn.* New York: Basic Books.

McGuire, R.J., Carlisle, J.M., & Young, B.G. (1965). Sexual deviations as conditioned behaviour: A hypothesis. *Behaviour Research and Therapy, 2,* 185–190.

McKnight, D.L., Nelson, R.O., Hayes, S.C., & Jarrett, R.B. (1984). Importance of treating individually assessed response classes in the amelioration of depression. *Behavior Therapy, 15,* 315–335.

McLeod, C., Mathews, A., & Tata, P. (1986). Attentional bias in emotional disorders. *Journal of Abnormal Psychology, 95,* 15–20.

McMahon, R.C. (1980). Genetic etiology in the hyperactive child syndrome: A critical review. *American Journal of Orthopsychiatry, 50,* 145–150.

McMullen, S., & Rosen, R.C. (1979). Self-administered masturbation training in the treatment of primary orgasmic dysfunction. *Journal of Consulting and Clinical Psychology, 47,* 912–918.

McNally, R.J., & Reiss, S. (1982). The preparedness theory of phobias and human safety-signal conditioning. *Behaviour Research and Therapy, 20,* 153–159.

McNeal, E.T., & Cimbolic, P. (1986). Antidepressants and biochemical theories of depression. *Psychological Bulletin, 99,* 361–374.

McNeill, E. (1967). *The quiet furies.* Englewood Cliffs, N.J.: Prentice–Hall.

Medical Research Council Working Party on Mild to Moderate Hypertension. Adverse reactions to bendroflumethiazide and propanalol for the treatment of mild hypertension. *Lancet, 11,* 539.

Mednick, S.A., Gabrielli, W.F., & Hutchings, B. (1984). Genetic influences in criminal convictions: Evidence from an adoption cohort. *Science* **224,** 891–894.

Mednick, S.A., & Hutchings, B. (1978). Genetic and psychophysiological factors in psychopathic behaviour. In R.D. Hare & D. Schalling (Eds.), *Psychopathic behavior: Approaches to research.* New York: Wiley.

Mednick, S.A., Machon, R., Huttunen, M.O., & Bonett, D. (1988). Fetal viral infection and adult schizophrenia. *Archives of General Psychiatry, 45,* 189–192.

Mednick, S.A., & Schulsinger, F. (1968). Some premorbid characteristics related to breakdown in children with schizophrenic mothers. In D. Rosenthal & S.S. Kety (Eds.), *The transmission of schizophrenia.* Elmsford, N.Y.: Pergamon.

Mednick, S.A., Schulsinger, F., & Griffith, J. (1981). Children of schizophrenic mothers: The Danish high-risk study. In F. Schulsinger, S.A. Mednick, & J. Knop (Eds.), *Longitudinal research: Methods and uses in behavioral science.* Hingham, Mass.: Martinus Nijhoff.

Medvedev, Z. (1972). *A question of madness.* New York: Knopf.

Meehl, P.E. (1962). Schizotaxia, schizotypy, schizophrenia. *American Psychologist, 17,* 827–838.

Meichenbaum, D. (1975). A self-instructional approach to stress management: A proposal for stress inoculation training. In I. Sarason & C.D. Spielberger (Eds.), *Stress and anxiety* (Vol. 2). New York: Wiley.

Meichenbaum, D.H., & Asarnow, J. (1979). Cognitive-behavioral modification and metacognitive development: Implications for the classroom. In P.C. Kendall & S.D. Hollon (Eds.), *Cognitive-behavioral interventions: Theory, research, and procedures.* New York: Academic Press.

Meichenbaum, D.H., & Goodman, J. (1969). Reflection-impulsivity and verbal control of motor behavior. *Child Development, 40,* 785–797.

Meichenbaum, D.H., & Goodman, J. (1971). Training impulsive children to talk to themselves. A means of developing self-control. *Journal of Abnormal Psychology, 77,* 115–126.

Meiselman, K.C. (1978). *Incest: A psychological study of causes and effects with treatment considerations.* San Francisco, Calif.: Jossey-Bass.

Melamed, B.G., Hawes, R.R., Heiby, E., & Glick, J. (1975). Use of filmed modeling to reduce uncooperative behavior of children during dental treatment. *Journal of Dental Research, 54,* 797–801.

Melamed, B.G., & Siegel, L.J. (1975). Reduction of anxiety in children facing hospitalization and surgery by use of filmed modeling. *Journal of Consulting and Clinical Psychology, 43,* 511–521.

Mellinger, G.D., Balter, M.B., & Uhlenhuth, E.H. (1985). Insomnia and its treatment. *Archives of General Psychiatry, 42,* 225–232.

Mello, N.K., & Mendelson, J.H. (1970). Experimentally induced intoxication in alcoholics: A comparison between programmed and spontaneous drinking. *Journal of Pharmacology and Experimental Therapy, 173,* 101.

Mellor, C.S. (1970). First rank symptoms of schizophrenia. *British Journal of Psychiatry, 117,* 15–23.

Meltzer, H.Y., Sachar, E.J., & Frantz, A.G. (1974). Serum prolactin levels in acutely psychotic patients: An indirect measurement of central dopaminergic activity. In E. Usdin (Ed.), *Neuropsychopharmacology of monoamines and their regulatory enzymes.* New York: Raven Press.

Mendels, J. (1970). *Concepts of depression.* New York: Wiley.

Mendels, J., & Cochrane, C. (1968). The nosology of depression, The endogenous-receptive concept. *American Journal of Psychiatry, 124,* 1–11.

Mendels, J., Fieve, A., Fitzgerand, R.G., Ramsey, T.A., & Stokes, J.W.. (1972). Biogenic amine metabolites in cerebrospinal fluid of depressed and manic patients. *Science, 175,* 1380–1382.

Mendels, J., Stinnett, J.L., Burns, D., & Frazer, A. (1975). Amine precursors and depression. *Archives of General Psychiatry, 32,* 22–30.

Mendelson, J.H. (1964). Experimentally induced chronic intoxication and withdrawal in alcoholics. *Quarterly Journal of Studies on Alcohol,* Supplement 2.

Mendelson, J. H., Rossi, A.M., & Meyer, R.E. (Eds.). (1974). *The use of marijuana: A psychological and physiological inquiry.* New York: Plenum.

Mendlewicz, J., & Rainer, J.D. (1977). Adoption study supporting genetic transmission in manic-depressive illness. *Nature, 268,* 327–329.

Merskey, H. (1979). *The analysis of hysteria.* London: Bailliere Tindall.

Metalsky, G.I., Abramson, L.V., Seligman, M.E.P., Semmel, A., & Peterson, C. (1982). Attributional styles and life events in the classroom: Vulnerability and invulnerability to depressive mood reactions. *Journal of Personality and Social Psychology, 43,* 612–617.

Metalsky, G.I., Haberstadt, L.J., & Abramson, L.Y. (1987). Vulnerability and invulnerability to depressive mood reactions: Toward a more powerful test of the diathesis–stress and causal mediation components of the reformulated theory of depression. *Journal of Personality and Social Psychology, 52,* 386–393.

Metzner, R., Litwin, G., & Weil, G.M. (1965). The relation of expectation and mood to psilocybin reactions. *Psychedelic Review, 5,* 3–39.

Mey, B.J.V., & Neff, R.L. (1982). Adult–child incest: A review of research and treatment. *Adolescence, 17,* 717–735.

Meyer, A. (1917). The aims and meaning of psychiatric diagnosis. *American Journal of Insanity, 74,* 163–168.

Meyer, A., Nash, J., McAlister, A., Maccoby, N., & Farquhar, J. (1980). Skills training in a cardiovascular health education campaign. *Journal of Consulting and Clinical Psychology, 48,* 129–142.

Meyer, J., & Reter, D.J. (1979). Sex reassignment follow-up. *Archives of General Psychiatry, 36,* 1010–1015.

Meyer, V. (1966). Modification of expectations in cases with obsessional rituals. *Behaviour Research and Therapy, 4,* 273–280.

Meyer, V., & Chesser, E.S. (1970). *Behavior therapy in clinical psychiatry.* Baltimore: Penguin.

Meyer, V., Robertson, J., & Tatlow, A. (1975). Home treatment of an obsessive-compulsive disorder by response prevention. *Journal of Behavior Therapy and Experimental Psychiatry, 6,* 37–38.

Meyer-Bahlburg, H. (1979). Sex hormones and female homosexuality: A critical examination. *Archives of Sexual Behavior, 8,* 101–119.

Michelson, L., Sugai, D.P., Wood, R.P., & Kazdin, A.E. (1983). *Social skills assessment and training with children: An empirically based handbook.* New York: Plenum.

Miklich, D.R., Rewey, H.H., Weiss, J.H., & Kolton, S. (1973). A preliminary investigation of psychophysiological responses to stress among different subgroups of asthmatic children. *Journal of Psychosomatic Research, 17,* 1–8.

Miklowitz, D.J. (1985). Family interaction and illness outcome in bipolar and schizophrenic patients. Unpublished Ph.D. thesis, UCLA.

Miklulineen, M., & Solomon, Z. (1988). Attributional style and posttraumatic stress disorder. *Journal of Abnormal Psychology, 97,* 308–313.

Miles, L.E., & Dement, W.C. (1980). Sleep and aging. *Sleep, 3,* 119–220.

Milgram, N.A. (1973). Cognition and language in mental retardation: Directions and implications. In D.K. Routh (Ed.), *The experimental psychology of mental retardation*. Chicago: Aldine.

Miller, E. (1975). Impaired recall and the memory disturbance in presenile dementia. *British Journal of Social and Clinical Psychology, 14*, 73–79.

Miller, H.R. (1981). Psychiatric morbidity in elderly surgical patients. *British Journal of Psychiatry, 138*, 17–20.

Miller, I.W., & Norman, W.H. (1979). Learned helplessness in humans: A review and attribution theory model. *Psychological Bulletin, 86*, 93–118.

Miller, N.E. (1948). Studies of fear as an acquirable drive. I. Fear as motivation and fear-reduction as reinforcement in the learning of new responses. *Journal of Experimental Psychology, 38*, 89–101.

Miller, N.E. (1959). Liberalization of basic S–R concepts: Extensions to conflict behavior, motivation, and social learning. In S. Koch (Ed.), *Psychology: A study of a science* (Vol. 2). New York: McGraw-Hill.

Miller, R.G., Palkes, H.S., & Stewart, M.A. (1973). Hyperactive children in suburban elementary schools. *Child Psychiatry and Human Development, 4*, 121–127.

Miller, W.R., Seligman, M.E.P., & Kurlander, H.M. (1975). Learned helplessness, depression, and anxiety. *Journal of Nervous and Mental Disease, 161*, 347–357.

Millon, T. (1981). *Disorders of personality: DSM III. Axis II*. New York: Wiley.

Milton, F., & Hafner, J. (1979). The outcome of behavior therapy for agoraphobia in relation to marital adjustment. *Archives of General Psychiatry, 36*, 807–811.

Milton, O., & Wahler, R.G. (Eds.). (1969). *Behavior disorders: Perspectives and trends* (2nd ed.). Philadelphia: Lippincott.

Mineka, S. (1985). Animal models of anxiety-based disorders: Their usefulness and limitations. In A.H. Tuma & J.D. Maser (Eds.), *Anxiety and the anxiety disorders*. New York: Erlbaum.

Mineka, S., Davidson, M., Cook, M., & Keir, R. (1984). Observational conditioning of snake fear in rhesus monkeys. *Journal of Abnormal Psychology, 93*, 355–372.

Mintz, E. (1967). Time-extended marathon groups. *Psychotherapy, 4*, 65–70.

Mintz, J. (1983). Integrating research evidence. *Journal of Consulting and Clinical Psychology, 51*, 71–75.

Mintz, R.S. (1968). Psychotherapy of the suicidal patient. In H.L.P. Resnik (Ed.), *Suicidal behaviors*. Boston: Little, Brown.

Minuchin, S. (1974). *Families and family therapy*. Cambridge, Mass.: Harvard University Press.

Minuchin, S., Baker, L., Rosman, B.L., Liebman, R., Milman, L., & Todd, T.C.

(1975). A conceptual model of psychosomatic illness in children: Family organization and family therapy. *Archives of General Psychiatry, 32*, 1031–1038.

Mirenda, P.L., Donnellan, A.M., & Yoder, D.E. (1983). Gaze behavior: A new look at an old problem. *Journal of Autism and Developmental Disorders, 13*, 397–409.

Mischel, W. (1968). *Personality and assessment*. New York: Wiley.

Mischel, W. (1973). Toward a cognitive social learning reconceptualization of personality. *Psychological Review, 80*, 252–283.

Mischel, W., (1977). On the future of personality assessment. *American Psychologist, 32*, 246–254.

Mischel, W., & Peake, P.K. (1982). Beyond déjà vu in the search for cross-situational consistency. *Psychological Review, 89*, 730–755.

Mitchell, J.E., Hatsukami, D., Eckert, E.D., & Pyle, R.L. (1985). Characteristics of 275 patients with bulimia. *American Journal of Psychiatry, 142*, 482–485.

Mohr, J.W., Turner, R.E., & Jerry, M.B. (1964). *Pedophilia and exhibitionism*. Toronto: University of Toronto Press.

Mohs, R.C., Breitner, J.C.S., Silverman, J.M., & Davis, K.L. (1987). Alzheimer's disease: Morbid risk among first-degree relatives approximates 50% by 90 years of age. *Archives of General Psychiatry, 44*, 405–408.

Mollica, R.F., & Milic, M. (1986). Social class and psychiatric practice: A revision of the Hollingshead and Redlich model. *American Journal of Psychiatry, 143*, 12–17.

Monahan, J. (1973). The psychiatrization of criminal behavior. *Hospital and Community Psychiatry, 24*, 105–107.

Monahan, J. (1976). The prevention of violence. In J. Monahan (Ed.), *Community mental health and the criminal justice system*. Elmsford, N.Y.: Pergamon.

Monahan, J. (1977, April 30). Prisons: A wary verdict on rehabilitation. *Washington Post*, page A13.

Monahan, J. (1978). Prediction research and the emergency commitment of dangerous mentally ill persons: A reconsideration. *American Journal of Psychiatry, 135*, 198–201.

Monahan, J. (1981). *The clinical prediction of violent behavior*. Rockville, Md.: National Institute of Mental Health.

Monahan, J. (1984). The prediction of violent behavior: Toward a second generation of theory and policy. *American Journal of Psychiatry, 141*, 10–15.

Monahan, J., Caldeira, C. & Friedlander, H. (1979). The police and the mentally ill: A comparison of arrested and committed persons. *International Journal of Law and Psychiatry, 2*, 509–518.

Money, J., & Ehrhardt, A. (1972). *Man and woman, boy and girl*. Baltimore: Johns Hopkins University Press.

Money, J., Hampson, J.G., & Hampson, J.L. (1955). An examination of some basic sexual concepts: The evidence of human hermaphroditism. *Johns Hopkins Hospital Bulletin, 97*, 301–319.

Moniz, E. (1936). *Tentatives opératoires dans le traitement de certaines psychoses*. Paris: Masson.

Moos, R.H. (1974). *Evaluating treatment environments*. New York: Wiley.

Morganstern, K.P. (1973). Implosive therapy and flooding procedures: A critical review. *Psychological Bulletin, 79*, 318–334.

Morin, C.M., & Azrin, N.H. (1988). Behavioral and cognitive treatments of geriatric insomnia. *Journal of Consulting and Clinical Psychology, 56*, 748–753.

Morokoff, P. (1985). Effects of sex guilt, repression, sexual "arousability," and sexual experience on female sexual arousal during erotica and fantasy. *Journal of Personality and Social Psychology, 49*, 177–187.

Morris, A.A. (1968). Criminal insanity. *Washington Review, 43*, 583–622.

Morris, J. (1974). *Conundrum*. New York: Harcourt Brace Jovanovich.

Morris, J.B., & Beck, A.T. (1974). The efficacy of antidepressant drugs. *Archives of General Psychiatry, 30*, 667–674.

Morris, N. (1966). Impediments to legal reform. *University of Chicago Law Review, 33*, 627–656.

Morris, N. (1968). Psychiatry and the dangerous criminal. *Southern California Law Review, 41*, 514–547.

Morrison, J.R., & Stewart, M.A. (1971). A family study of the hyperactive child syndrome. *Biological Psychiatry, 3*, 189–195.

Morrison, J.R., & Stewart, M.A. (1973). The psychiatric status of the legal families of adopted hyperactive children. *Archives of General Psychiatry, 28*, 888–891.

Morse, S.J. (1978). Crazy behavior, morals, and science: An analysis of mental health law. *Southern California Law Review, 51*, 527–654.

Morse, S.J. (1979). Diminished capacity: A moral and legal conundrum. *International Journal of Law and Psychiatry, 2*, 271–298.

Morse, S.J. (1982). A preference for liberty: The case against involuntary commitment of the mentally disordered. *California Law Review, 70*, 54–106. (a)

Morse, S.J. (1982). Failed explanation and criminal responsibility: Experts and the unconscious. *Virginia Law Review, 678*, 971–1084. (b)

Morse, S.J. (1982, June 23). In defense of the insanity defense. *Los Angeles Times*. (c)

Moser, C., & Levitt, E.E. (1987). An exploratory-descriptive study of a sadomasochistically oriented sample. *The Journal of Sex Research, 23,* 322–337.

Moses, J.A. (1983). Luria–Nebraska Neuropsychological Battery performance of brain dysfunctional patients with positive or negative findings on current neurological examination. *International Journal of Neuroscience, 22,* 135–146.

Moses, J.A., & Schefft, B.K. (1984). Interrater reliability analyses of the Luria–Nebraska Neuropsychological Battery. *The International Journal of Clinical Neuropsychology, 7,* 31–38.

Mowrer, O.H. (1939). A stimulus–response analysis of anxiety and its role as a reinforcing agent. *Psychological Review, 46,* 553–565.

Mowrer, O.H. (1947). On the dual nature of learning—A reinterpretation of "conditioning" and "problem-solving." *Harvard Educational Review, 17,* 102–148.

Mowrer, O.H. (1950). *Learning theory and personality dynamics.* New York: Ronald Press.

Mowrer, O.H., & Mowrer, W.M. (1938). Enuresis: A method for its study and treatment. *American Journal of Orthopsychiatry, 8,* 436–459.

Mowrer, O.H., & Viek, P. (1948). An experimental analogue of fear from a sense of helplessness. *Journal of Abnormal and Social Psychology, 43,* 193–200.

Mrazek, F.J. (1984). Sexual abuse of children. **In** B. Lahey & A.E. Kazdin (Eds.), *Advances in child clinical psychology* (Vol. 6). New York: Plenum.

Mulligan, T., Retchin, S. M., Chinchilli, V.M., & Bettinger, C.B. .(1988). *Journal of the American Geriatrics Society, 36,* 520–524.

Munby, M., & Johnston, D.W. (1980). Agoraphobia: The long-term follow-up of behavioural treatment. *British Journal of Psychiatry, 137,* 418–427.

Munjack, D.J., & Kanno, P.H. (1979). Retarded ejaculation: A review. *Archives of Sexual Behavior, 8,* 139–150.

Murphy, D.L., & Wyatt, R.J. (1972). Reduced MAO activity in blood platelets from schizophrenic patients. *Nature, 238,* 225–226.

Murphy, G.E., Simons, A.D., Wetzel, R.D., & Lustman, P.J. (1984). Cognitive therapy and pharmacotherapy: Singling out together in the treatment of depression. *Archives of General Psychiatry, 41,* 33–41.

Murphy, J. (1976). Psychiatric labeling in cross-cultural perspective. *Science, 191,* 1019–1028.

Muscettola, G., Potter, W.Z., Pickar, D., & Goodwin, F.K. (1984). Urinary 3-methoxy-4-hydroxyphenylglycol and major affective disorders. *Archives of General Psychiatry, 41,* 337–342.

Myers, J.K., & Weissman, M.M. (1980).

Psychiatric disorders and their treatment. *Medical Care, 18,* 117–123.

Myers, J. K., Weissman, M. M., Tischler, G.L., Holzer, C.E., Leaf, P.J., Orvaschel, H.A., Anthony, J.C., Boyd, J.H., Burke, J.E., Kramer, M., & Stoltzman, R. (1984). Six-month prevalence of psychiatric disorders in three communities: 1980–1982. *Archives of General Psychiatry, 41,* 959–967.

Naranjo, C., Shulgin, A.T., & Sargent, T. (1976). Evaluation of 3,4-methylenedioxyamphetamine (MDA) as an adjunct to psychotherapy. *Medical Pharmacological Experiments, 17,* 359–364.

Nathan, P.E., & Goldman, M.S. (1979). Problem drinking and alcoholism. In O.F. Pomerleau & J.P. Brady (Eds.), *Behavioral medicine: Therapy and practice.* Baltimore: Williams & Wilkins.

Nathan, P.E., Samaraweera, A., Andberg, M.M., & Patch, V.D. (1968). Syndromes of psychosis and psychoneurosis. *Archives of General Psychiatry, 19,* 704–716.

Nathan, P.E., Titler, N.A., Lowenstein, L.W., Solomon, P., & Rossi, A.M. (1970). Behavioral analysis of chronic alcoholism. *Archives of General Psychiatry, 22,* 419–430.

National Cancer Institute (1977). *The smoking digest: Progress report on a nation kicking the habit.* Washington, D.C.: U.S. Department of Health, Education and Welfare.

National Center for Health Statistics (1979). *The National Nursing Home Survey: 1977 Summary for the United States.* Department of Health, Education and Welfare Publication (PHS) 79–1794. Hyattsville, Md.: U.S. Department of Health and Human Services.

National Center for Health Statistics (1985). *Vital statistics of the United States, 1980.* Vol. II—*Mortality, Part B.* Hyattsville, Md.: U.S. Department of Health and Human Services.

National Center for Health Statistics (1988). Advance report of final mortality statistics, 1986. *NCHS Monthly Vital Statistics Report, 37,* (Suppl. 6).

National Council on Alcoholism (1986). *Facts on alcoholism.* New York: Author.

National Institute on Alcohol Abuse and Alcoholism. (1983). *Special Report to the U.S. Congress on Alcohol and Health.* Washington, D.C.: U.S. Government Printing Office.

National Institute on Drug Abuse (1988). *National household survey on drug abuse: Main findings 1985.* Washington, D.C.: Department of Health and Human Services.

National Institute on Drug Abuse. (1983). *Population projections, based on the Na-*

tional Survey on Drug Abuse, 1982. Rockville, Md.: Author.

National Survey on Drug Abuse. (1979). Washington, D.C.: National Institute on Drug Abuse.

National Survey on Drug Abuse. (1982). Washington, D.C.: Department of Health and Human Services, National Institute on Drug Abuse.

National Survey on Drug Abuse: Main Findings 1982. (1983). NIDA, Department of Health and Human Services Publication No. (ADM) 83-1263. Washington, D.C.: U.S. Government Printing Office.

Navia, B.A., Cho, E., Petito, C.K., & Price, R.W. (1986). The AIDS dementia complex: II. Neuropathology. *Annals of Neurology, 19,* 525–535.

Nawas, M.M., Fishman, S.T., & Pucel, J.C. (1970). The standardized densensitization program applicable to group and individual treatment. *Behaviour Research and Therapy, 6,* 63–68.

Neale, J.M. (1971). Perceptual span in schizophrenia. *Journal of Abnormal Psychology, 77,* 196–204.

Neale, J.M., & Katahn, M. (1968). Anxiety, choice and stimulus uncertainty. *Journal of Personality, 36,* 238–245.

Neale, J.M., & Liebert, R.M. (1980). *Science and behavior: An introduction to methods of research* (2nd ed.). Englewood Cliffs, N.J.: Prentice–Hall.

Neisser, U. (1976). *Cognition and reality.* San Francisco: Freeman.

Nelson, J.C., & Bowers, M.B. (1978). Delusional unipolar depression. *Archives of General Psychiatry, 35,* 1321–1328.

Nelson, R.E., & Craighead, W.E. (1977). Selective recall of positive and negative feedback, self-control behaviors, and depression. *Journal of Abnormal Psychology, 86,* 379–388.

Nelson, R.O. (1977). Assessment and therapeutic functions of self-monitoring. In M. Hersen, R. M. Eisler, & P. M. Miller (Eds.), *Progress in behavior modification.* New York: Academic Press.

Nelson, R.O., Lipinski, D. P., & Black, J.L. (1975). The effects of expectancy on the reactivity of self-recording. *Behavior Therapy, 6,* 337–349.

Nelson, R.O., Lipinski, D.P., & Black, J.L. (1976). The reactivity of adult retardates' self-monitoring: A comparison among behaviors of different valences, and a comparison with token reinforcement. *Psychological Record, 26,* 189–201.

Nelson, R.O., Lipinski, D.P., & Boykin, R.A. (1978). The effects of self-recorders' training and the obtrusiveness of the self-recording device on the accuracy and reactivity of self-monitoring. *Behavior Therapy, 9,* 200–208.

Nemetz, G.H., Craig, K.D., & Reith, G. (1978). Treatment of female sexual dysfunction through symbolic modeling. *Journal of Consulting and Clinical Psychology, 46,* 62–73.

Nettelbeck, T. (1985). Inspection time and mild mental retardation. In N.R. Ellis & N.W. Bray (Eds.), *International review of research in mental retardation* (Vol. 13). New York: Academic Press.

Neugarten, B.L. (1977). Personality and aging. In J.E. Birren & K.W. Schaie (Eds.), *Handbook of the psychology of aging.* New York: Van Nostrand–Reinhold.

Neugebauer, R. (1979). Mediaeval and early modern theories of mental illness. *Archives of General Psychiatry, 36,* 477–484.

Neugebauer, R. (1987). Exploitation of the insane in the new world: Benoni Buck, the first reported case of mental retardation in the American colonies. *Archives of General Psychiatry, 44,* 481–483.

Neuhaus, E.C. (1958). A personality study of asthmatic and cardiac children. *Psychosomatic Medicine, 20,* 181–186.

Neuringer, C. (1964). Rigid thinking in suicidal individuals. *Journal of Consulting Psychology, 28,* 54–58.

Newman, J.P., & Kosson, D.S. (1986). Passive avoidance learning in psychopathic and nonpsychopathic offenders. *Journal of Abnormal Psychology, 95,* 257–263.

Newman, J.P., Patterson, C.M., & Kosson, D.S. (1987). Response perseveration in psychopaths. *Journal of Abnormal Psychology, 96,* 145–149.

Nezu, A.M. (1986). Efficacy of a social problem-solving therapy approach for unipolar depression. *Journal of Consulting and Clinical Psychology, 54,* 196–202.

Nicholson, R.A., & Berman, J.S. (1983). Is follow-up necessary in evaluating psychotherapy? *Psychological Bulletin, 93,* 261–278.

Nihira, K., Foster, R., Shellhaas, M., & Leland, H. (1975). *AAMD-Adaptive Behavior Scale.* Washington, D.C.: American Association on Mental Deficiency.

Nisbett, R.E., & Wilson, T.D. (1977). Telling more than we can know: Verbal reports on mental processes. *Psychological Review, 84,* 231–259.

Nocks, B.C., Learner, R.M., Blackman, D., & Brown, T.E. (1986). The effects of a community-based long term care project on nursing home utilization. *The Gerontologist, 26,* 150–157.

Nogrady, H., McConkey, K.M., Laurence, J.R., & Perry, C. (1983). Dissociation, duality, and demand characteristics in hypnosis. *Journal of Abnormal Psychology, 92,* 223–235.

Nolen-Hoeksema, S. (1987). Sex differences in unipolar depression: Evidence and theory. *Psychological Bulletin, 101,* 259–282.

North, A.F. (1979). Health services in Head Start. In E. Zigler & J. Valentine (Eds.), *Project Head Start.* New York: Free Press.

Norton, G.R., Harrison, B., Hauch, J., & Rhodes, L. (1985). Characteristics of people with infrequent panic attacks. *Journal of Abnormal Psychology, 94,* 216–221.

Norton, J.P. (1982). Expressed emotion, affective style, voice tone and communication deviance as predictors of offspring schizophrenia spectrum disorders. Unpublished doctoral dissertation, University of California at Los Angeles.

Notarius, C.I., & Markman, H.J. (1989). Coding marital interaction: A sampling and discussion of current issues. *Behavioral Assessment, 11,* 1–11.

Notarius, C.I., Markman, H.J., & Gottman, J.M. (1983). Couples Interaction Scoring System: Clinical implications. In E.E. Filsinger (Ed.), *Marriage and family assessment.* Beverly Hills: Sage.

Nowlan, R., & Cohen, S. (1977). Tolerance to marijuana: Heart rate and subjective "high." *Clinical Pharmacology Therapeutics, 22,* 550–556.

Noyes, R., Anderson, D.J., Clancy, J., Crowe, R.R., Slyman, D.J., Ghoneim, M.M., & Hinrichs, J.V. (1984). Diazepam and propanolol in panic disorder and agoraphobia. *Archives of General Psychiatry, 41,* 287–292.

Noyes, R., Crowe, R.R., Harris, E.L., Hamra, B.J., McChesney, C.M., & Chandry, D.R. (1986). Relationship between panic disorder and agoraphobia: A family study. *Archives of General Psychiatry, 43,* 227–232.

Nunnally, J.C. (1967). *Psychometric theory.* New York: McGraw–Hill.

Nurnberg, H.G., Prudic, J., Fiori, M., & Freedman, E. (1984). Psychopathology complicating acquired immune deficiency syndrome (AIDS). *American Journal of Psychiatry, 141,* 95–96.

Obler, M. (1973). Systematic desensitization in sexual disorders. *Journal of Behavior Therapy and Experimental Psychiatry, 4,* 93–101.

Obrist, P.A., Gaebelein, C.J., Teller, E.S., Langer, A.W., Grignolo, A., Light, K.C., & McCubbin, J.A. (1978). The relationship among heart rate, carotid *dP/dt,* and blood pressure in humans as a function of the type of stress. *Psychophysiology, 15,* 102–115.

Ochitil, H. (1982). Conversion disorder. In J.H. Greist, J.W. Jefferson, & R.L. Spitzer (Eds.), *Treatment of mental disorders.* New York: Oxford University Press.

Ockene, J.K. (1984). Toward a smoke-free society. *American Journal of Public Health, 74,* 1198–1200.

O'Connor, R.D. (1969). Modification of social withdrawal through symbolic modeling. *Journal of Applied Behavior Analysis, 2,* 15–22.

O'Donohue, W.T. (1987). The sexual behavior and problems of the elderly. In L.L. Carstensen & B.A. Edelstein (Eds.), *Handbook of clinical gerontology.* New York: Pergamon.

O'Hara, M.W., Hinrichs, J.V., Kohout, F.J., Wallace, R.B., & Lemke, J.H. (1986). Memory complaint and memory performance in the depressed elderly. *Psychology and Aging, 1,* 208–214.

Ohman, A., Erixon, G., & Lofberg, I. (1975). Phobias and preparedness: Phobic versus neutral pictures as conditional stimuli for human autonomic responses. *Journal of Abnormal Psychology, 34,* 41–45.

Olds, D.L. (1984). *Final report: Prenatal/early infancy project.* Washington, D.C.: Maternal and Child Health Research, National Institute of Health.

O'Leary, K.D. (1980). Pills or skills for hyperactive children. *Journal of Applied Behavior Analysis, 13,* 191–204.

O'Leary, K.D., & O'Leary, S.G. (Eds.). (1977). *Classroom management* (2nd ed.). Elmsford, N.Y.: Pergamon.

O'Leary, K.D., Pelham, W.E., Rosenbaum, A., & Price, G.H. (1976). Behavioral treatment of hyperkinetic children: An experimental evaluation of its usefulness. *Clinical Pediatrics, 15,* 510–515.

O'Leary, K.D., & Turkewitz, H. (1978). Marital therapy from a behavioral perspective. In T.J. Paolino, Jr., & B.S. McCrady (Eds.), *Marriage and marital therapy.* New York: Brunner/Mazel.

O'Leary, K.D., Turkewitz, H., & Taffel, S.J. (1973). Parent and therapist evaluation of behavior therapy in a child psychological clinic. *Journal of Consulting and Clinical Psychology, 41,* 289–293.

O'Leary, K.D., & Wilson, G.T. (1975). *Behavior therapy: Application and outcome.* Englewood Cliffs, N.J.: Prentice–Hall.

O'Leary, K.D., & Wilson, G.T. (1987). *Behavior therapy: Application and outcome.* (2nd ed.). Englewood Cliffs, N.J.: Prentice–Hall.

Ollendick, T.H. (1986). Child and adolescent behavior therapy. In S.L. Garfield, & A.E. Bergin (Eds.), *Handbook of psychotherapy and behavior change.* (Third edition). New York: Wiley.

Oltmanns, T. F., Broderick, J.E., & O'Leary, K.D. (1976). *Marital adjustment and the efficacy of behavior therapy with children.* Paper presented at the Association for the Advancement of Behavior Therapy, New York City.

Omizo, M.M., Cubberly, W.E., & Omizo, S.A. (1985). The effects of rational-emotive education groups on self-concept and locus of control among learning disabled children. *The Exceptional Child, 32,* 13–19.

O'Neal, J.M. (1984). First person account: Finding myself and loving it. *Schizophrenia Bulletin, 10,* 109–110.

Orne, M.T. (1959). The nature of hypnosis: Artifact and essence. *Journal of Abnormal and Social Psychology, 58,* 277–299.

Orne, M.T., Dinges, D.F., & Orne, E.C. (1984). The differential diagnosis of multiple personality in the forensic court. *International Journal of Clinical and Experimental Hypnosis, 32,* 118–169.

Ornitz, E. (1973). Childhood autism: A review of the clinical and experimental literature. *California Medicine, 118,* 21–47.

Orris, J.B. (1967). Visual monitoring performance in three subgroups of male delinquents. Unpublished M.A. thesis, University of Illinois.

Osgood, N.J. (1984). Suicides. In E.B. Palmore (Ed.), *Handbook on the aged in the United States.* Westport, Conn.: Greenwood Press.

Pahnke, W.N. (1963). Drugs and mysticism. Unpublished doctoral dissertation, Harvard University.

Palmore, E.B. (1986). Trends in the health of the aged. *The Gerontologist, 26,* 298–302.

Parfitt, D.N., & Gall, C. (1944). Psychogenic amnesia: The refusal to remember. *Journal of Mental Science, 90,* 511–531.

Parkes, C.M., & Brown, R.J. (1972). Health after bereavement: A controlled study of young Boston widowers. *Psychosomatic Medicine, 34,* 49–461.

Parks, C.V., Jr., and Hollon, S.D. (1988). Cognitive assessment. In A.S. Bellack, & M. Hersen (Eds.), *Behavioral assessment,* (Third edition). Elmsford, NY: Pergamon Press.

Parloff, M.B., Waskow, I.E., & Wolfe, B.E. (1978). Research on therapist variables in relation to process and outcome. In S.L. Garfield & A.E. Bergin (Eds.), *Handbook of psychotherapy and behavior change: An empirical analysis* (2nd ed.). New York: Wiley.

Parsons, O.A. (1975). Brain damage in alcoholics: Altered states of consciousness. In M.M. Gross (Ed.), *Alcohol intoxication and withdrawal.* New York: Plenum.

Pasamanick, B., Rogers, M., & Lilienfeld, M.A. (1956). Pregnancy experience and the development of behavior disorder in children. *American Journal of Psychiatry, 112,* 613–617.

Patel, C., Marmot, M.G., Terry, D.J., Carruthers, M., Hunt, B., & Patel, M. (1985). Trial of relaxation in reducing coronary risk: Four year follow-up. *British Medical Journal, 290,* 1103–1106.

Paternite, C.E., & Loney, J. (1980). Childhood hyperkinesis: Relationships between symptomatology and home environment. In C.K. Whalen & B. Henker (Eds.), *Hyperactive children.* New York: Academic Press.

Patsiokas, A.T., Clum, G.A., & Luscomb, R.L. (979). Cognitive characteristics of suicide attempters. *Journal of Consulting and Clinical Psychology, 47,* 478–484.

Patterson, G.R. (1974). A basis for identifying stimuli which control behaviors in natural settings. *Child Development, 45,* 900–911. (a)

Patterson, G.R. (1974). Interventions for boys with conduct problems: Multiple settings, treatments, and criteria. *Journal of Consulting and Clinical Psychology, 42,* 471–481. (b)

Patterson, G.R. (1982). *Coercive family process.* Eugene, Oreg.: Castalia.

Patterson, G.R. (1986). Performance models for antisocial boys. *American Psychologist, 41,* 432–444.

Patterson, G.R., Cobb, J.A., & Ray, R.S. (1973). A social engineering technology for retraining families of aggressive boys. In H.E. Adams & I.P. Unikel (Eds.), *Issues and trends in behavior therapy.* Springfield, Ill.: Charles C. Thomas.

Patterson, G.R., Ray, R.S., Shaw, D.A., & Cobb, J.A. (1969). *Manual for coding of family interactions.* New York: ASIS/NAPS, Microfiche Publications.

Patterson, G.R., & Reid, J.B. (1970). Reciprocity and coercion: Two facets of social systems. In C. Neuringer & J. Michael (Eds.), *Behavior modification in clinical psychology.* New York: Appleton–Century–Crofts.

Paul, G.L. (1966). *Insight vs. desensitization in psychotherapy.* Stanford, Calif.: Stanford University Press.

Paul, G.L. (1967). Insight versus desensitization in psychotherapy two years after termination. *Journal of Consulting Psychology, 31,* 333–348.

Paul, G.L. (1969). Chronic mental patient: Current status–future directions. *Psychological Bulletin, 71,* 81–94.

Paul, G.L., & Lentz, R.J. (1977). *Psychosocial treatment of chronic mental patients: Milieu versus social learning programs.* Cambridge, Mass.: Harvard University Press.

Paul, G.L., & Shannon, D.T. (1966). Treatment of anxiety through systematic desensitization in therapy groups. *Journal of Abnormal Psychology, 71,* 124–135.

Paulauskas, S.L., & Campbell, S.B.G. (1979). Social perspective-taking and teacher ratings of peer interaction in hyperactive boys. *Journal of Abnormal Child Psychology, 7,* 483–493.

Pavlov, I.P. (1928). *Lectures on conditioned reflexes.* New York: International Publishers.

Paykel, E.S. (1979). Recent life events in the development of the depressive disorders. In R.A. Depue (Ed.), *The psychobiology of the depressive disorders.* New York: Academic Press.

Pearlin, L.I. (1983). Role strains and personal stress. In H.B. Kaplan (Ed.), *Psychosocial stress: Trends, theory and research.* New York: Academic Press.

Pearson, C., & Gatz, M. (1982). Health and mental health in older adults: First steps in the study of a pedestrian complaint. *Rehabilitation Psychology, 27,* 37–50.

Pechacek, T.F. (1979). Modification of smoking behavior. In N.A. Krasnegor (Ed.), *The behavioral aspects of smoking.* Washington, D.C.: National Institute on Drug Abuse.

Pecknold, J.C., Rifkin, A., & Swenson, R.P. Alprazolam in panic disorder and agoraphobia: Results from a multicenter trial. *Archives of General Psychiatry, 45,* 413–421.

Pedro-Carroll, J.L., & Cowen, E.L. (1985). The children of divorce intervention program: an investigation of the efficacy of a school-based prevention program. *Journal of Consulting and Clinical Psychology, 53,* 603–611.

Pedro-Carroll, J.L., Cowen, E.L., Hightower, A.D., & Guare, J.C. (1986). Preventive intervention with latency-aged children of divorce: A replication study. *American Journal of Community Psychology, 14,* 277–290.

Pendery, M.L., Maltzman, I.M., & West, L.J. (1982). Controlled drinking by alcoholics? New findings and a reevaluation of a major affirmative study. *Science, 217,* 169–175.

Penk, W.E., Robinowitz, R., Roberts, W.R., Patterson, E.T., Dolan, M.P., & Atkins, H.G. (1981). Adjustment differences among male substance abusers varying in degree of combat experience in Vietnam. *Journal of Consulting and Clinical Psychology, 49,* 426–437.

Pennebaker, J., Kielcolt-Glaser, J.K., & Glaser, R. (1988). Disclosure of traumas and immune function: Health implications for psychotherapy. *Journal of Consulting and Clinical Psychology, 56,* 239–245.

Pennington, B.F., & Smith, S.D. (1988). Genetic influences on learning disabilities: An update. *Journal of Consulting and Clinical Psychology, 56,* 817–823.

Pentoney, P. (1966). Value change in psychotherapy. *Human Relations, 19,* 39–46.

Perley, M.J., & Guze, S.B. (1962). Hysteria—The stability and usefulness of clinical criteria. *New England Journal of Medicine, 266,* 421–426.

Perlmutter, M. (1978). What is memory aging the aging of? *Developmental Psychology, 14,* 330–345.

Perlmutter, M., & Hall, E. (1985). *Adult development and aging.* New York: Wiley.

Perls, F.S. (1947). *Ego, hunger, and aggression.* New York: Vintage.

Perls, F.S. (1969). *Gestalt therapy verbatim.* Moab, Utah: Real People Press.

Perls, F.S. (1970). Four lectures. In J. Fagan & I.L. Shepherd (Eds.), *Gestalt therapy now: Therapy, techniques, applications.* Palo Alto, Calif.: Science and Behavior Books.

Perls, F.S., Hefferline, R.F., & Goodman, P. (1951). *Gestalt therapy: Excitement and growth in the human personality.* New York: Julian Press.

Perris, L. (1969). The separation of bipolar (manic-depressive) from unipolar recurrent depressive psychoses. *Behavioral Neuropsychiatry, 1*, 17–25.

Perry, J.D., & Whipple, B. (1981). Pelvic muscle strength of female ejaculators: Evidence in support of a new theory of orgasm. *Journal of Sex Research, 17*, 22–39.

Pervin, L.A. (1963). The need to predict and control under conditions of threat. *Journal of Personality, 31*, 570–585.

Peters, J.J. (1977). The Philadelphia rape victim project. In D. Chappell, R. Geis, & G. Geis. (Eds.), *Forcible rape: The crime, the victim, and the offender.* New York: Columbia University Press.

Peterson, C., & Seligman, M.E.P. (1984). Causal explanations as a risk factor for depression: Theory and evidence. *Psychological Review, 91*, 347–374.

Pfeiffer, E. (1977). Psychopathology and social pathology. In J.E. Birren & K.W. Schaie (Eds.), *Handbook of psychology and aging.* New York: Van Nostrand–Reinhold.

Pfeiffer, E., & Busse, E.W. (1973). Mental disorders in later life—Affective disorders: Paranoid, neurotic and situational reactions. In E.W. Busse & E. Pfeiffer (Eds.), *Mental illness in later life.* Washington, D.C.: American Psychiatric Association.

Pfeiffer, E., Eisenstein, R.B., & Dabbs, G.E. (1967). Mental competency evaluation for the federal courts: I. Methods and results. *Journal of Nervous and Mental Disease, 144*, 320–328.

Pfeiffer, E., Verwoerdt, A., & Wang, H.S. (1968). Sexual behavior in aged men and women: I. Observations on 254 community volunteers. *Archives of General Psychiatry, 19*, 753–758.

Pfeiffer, E., Verwoerdt, A., & Wang, H.S. (1969). The natural history of sexual behavior in a biologically advantaged group of aged individuals. *Journal of Gerontology, 24*, 193–198.

Phares, J. (1979). *Clinical psychology: Concepts, methods, and professions.* Homewood, Ill.: Dorsey Press.

Phillips, D.P. (1974). The influence of suggestion on suicide: Substantive and theoretical implications of the Werther effect.

American Sociological Review, 39, 340–354.

Phillips, D.P. (1977). Motor vehicle fatalities increase just after publicized suicide stories. *Science, 196*, 1464–1465.

Phillips, D.P. (1985). The found experiment: A new technique for assessing impact of mass media violence on real-world aggressive behavior. In G. Comstock (Ed)., *Public communication and behavior* (Vol. 1). New York: Academic Press.

Phillips, E.I. (1968). Achievement Place: Token reinforcement procedures in a home style rehabilitation setting for predelinquent boys. *Journal of Applied Behavior Analysis, 1*, 213–223.

Phillips, L. (1953). Case history data and prognosis in schizophrenia. *Journal of Nervous and Mental Disease, 117*, 515–525.

Phillips, R.D. (1985). Whistling in the dark? A review of play therapy research. *Psychotherapy, 22*, 752–760.

Pierce, C.M. (1980). Enuresis. In H.I. Kaplan, A.H. Friedman, & B.J. Sadock (Eds.), *Comprehensive textbook of psychiatry* (3rd ed). Baltimore: Williams & Wilkins.

Pierce, C.M. (1985). Enuresis. In H.I. Kaplan & B.J. Sadock (Eds.), *Comprehensive textbook of psychiatry* (4th ed.). Baltimore: Williams & Wilkins.

Pilowsky, I. (1970). Primary and secondary hypochondriasis. *Acta Psychiatrica Scandinavica, 46*, 273–285.

Pinel, P. (1962). *A treatise on insanity, 1801.* English translation by D.D. Davis. New York: Hafner.

Pinsoff, W.M. (1985). The process of family therapy: The development of the Family Therapist Coding System. In L. Greenberg & W.M. Pinsoff (Eds.), *The psychotherapeutic process: A research handbook.* New York: Guilford.

Piran, N., Kennedy, S., Garfinkel, P.E., & Owens, M. (1985). Affective disturbance and eating disorders. *The Journal of Nervous and Mental Disease. 173*, 395–400.

Pirsig R.M. (1974). *Zen and the art of motorcycle maintenance: An inquiry into values.* New York: Morrow.

Plummer, S., Baer, D.M., & LeBlanc, J.M. (1977). Functional consideration in the use of time out and an effective alternative. *Journal of Applied Behavior Analysis, 10*, 689–706.

Pokorny, A.D. (1968). Myths about suicide. In H.L.P. Resnik (Ed.), *Suicidal behaviors.* Boston: Little, Brown.

Poland, R.E., Rubin, R.T., Lesser, I.M., Lane, L.A., & Hart, P. J. (1987). Neuroendocrine aspects of primary endogenous depression. *Archives of General Psychiatry, 44*, 790–796.

Polivy, J. (1976). Perception of calories and regulation of intake in restrained and un-

restrained eaters. *Addictive Behavior, 1*, 237–243.

Poon, L.W. (1985). Differences in human memory with aging: Nature, causes, and clinical implications. In J.E. Birren & K.W. Schaie (Eds.), *Handbook of the psychology of aging.* New York: Van Nostrand– Reinhold.

Pope, H.G., & Hudson, J.I. (1984). *New hope for binge eaters: Advances in the understanding and treatment of bulimia.* New York: Harper & Row.

Pope, H.G., Jonas, J.M., Hudson, J.I., Cohen, B.M., & Gunderson, J.G. (1983). The validity of DSM-III borderline personality disorder. *Archives of General Psychiatry, 40*, 23–30.

Post, F. (1975). Dementia, depression, and pseudodementia. In D.F. Benson & D. Blumer (Eds.), *Psychiatric aspects of neurologic disease.* New York: Grune & Stratton.

Post, F. (1978). The functional psychosis. In A.D. Isaacs & F. Post (Eds.), *Studies in geriatric psychiatry.* Chichester, England: Wiley.

Post, F. (1980). Paranoid, schizophrenia-like and schizophrenic states in the aged. In J.E. Birren & R.B. Sloane (Eds.), *Handbook of mental health and aging.* Englewood Cliffs, N.J.: Prentice–Hall.

Post, F. (1987). Paranoid and schizophrenic disorders among the aging. In L.L. Carstensen & B.A. Edelstein (Eds.), *Handbook of clinical gerontology.* New York: Pergamon.

Post, R.M., Fink E., Carpenter, W.T., & Goodwin, F.K. (1975). Cerebrospinal fluid amine metabolites in acute schizophrenia. *Archives of General Psychiatry, 32*, 1063–1069.

Poster, D.S., Penta, J.S., Bruno, S., & Macdonald, J.S. (1981). Delta 9-tetrahydrocannabinol in clinical oncology. *Journal of the American Medical Association, 245*, 2047–2051.

Powell, L.H., Friedman, M., Thoresen, C.E., Gill, J.J., & Ulmer, D.K. (1984). Can the type A behavior pattern be altered after myocardial infarction? A second year report from the Recurrent Coronary Prevention Project. *Psychosomatic Medicine, 46*, 293–313.

Premack, D. (1959). Toward empirical behavior laws: I. Positive reinforcement. *Psychological Review, 66*, 219–233.

President's Commission on Mental Health (1978). Report to the President. Washington, D.C.: Superintendent of Documents, U.S. Government Printing Office.

Price, L.H., Charney, D.S., Rubin, A.L., & Heninger, G.R. (1986). Alpha-2 adrenergic receptor function in depression. *Archives of General Psychiatry, 43*, 849–860.

Price, V.A. (1982). *Type A behavior pattern:*

A model for research and practice. New York: Academic Press.

Prien, R.F., Kupfer, D.J., Mansky, P.A., Small, J.G., Tuason, V.B., Voss, C.B., & Johnson, W.E. (1984). Drug therapy in the prevention of recurrences in unipolar and bipolar affective disorders. *Archives of General Psychiatry, 41, 1096–1104.*

Prinz, P., & Raskind, M. (1978). Aging and sleep disorders. In R. Williams & R. Karacan (Eds.), *Sleep disorders: Diagnosis and treatment.* New York: Wiley.

Prioleau, L., Murdock, M., & Brody, N. (1983). An analysis of psychotherapy versus placebo studies. *The Behavioral and Brain Sciences, 6, 275–310.*

Prizant, E.M. (1983). Echolalia in autism: Assessment and intervention. *Seminars in Speech and Language, 4, 63–77.*

Prochaska, J.O. (1984). *Systems of psychotherapy* (2nd ed.). Homewood, Ill.: Dorsey Press.

Proctor, J.T. (1958). Hysteria in childhood. *American Journal of Orthopsychiatry, 28, 394–407.*

Pu, T., Mohamed, E., Imam, K., & El-Roey, A.M. (1986). One hundred cases of hysteria in eastern Libya. *British Journal of Psychiatry, 148, 606–609.*

Puig-Antich, J., Lukens, E., Davies, M., Goetz, D., Brennan-Quattrock, J., & Todak, G. (1985). Psychosocial functioning in prepubertal major depressive disorders. I. Interpersonal relationships during the depressive episode. *Archives of General Psychiatry, 42, 500–507.*

Pumarola, S.T., Navis, B.A., Cordon-Cardo, C., Cho, E.S., & Price, R.W. (1987). HIV antigen in the brains of patients with the AIDS dementia complex. *Annals of Neurology, 21, 490–496.*

Purcell, K., Brady, K., Chai, H., Muser, J., Molk, L., Gordon, N., & Means, J. (1969). The effect on asthma in children of experimental separation from the family. *Psychosomatic Medicine, 31, 144–164.*

Purcell, K., & Weiss, J.H. (1970). Asthma. In C.G. Costello (Ed.), *Symptoms of psychopathology: A handbook.* New York: Wiley.

Purdie, F.R., Honigman, T.B., & Rosen, P. (1981). Acute organic brain syndrome: A view of 100 cases. *Annals of Emergency Medicine, 10, 455–461.*

Purpura, D.P. (1976). Discussants' comments. In T.D. Tjossem (Ed.), *Intervention strategies for high risk infants and young children.* Baltimore: University Park Press.

Puska, P., Nissinen, A., Salonen, J.T., & Toumilehto, J. (1983). Ten years of the North Karelia project: Results with community-based prevention of coronary heart disease. *Scandinavian Journal of Social Medicine, 11, 65–68.*

Putnam, F.W., Post, R.M., & Guroff, J.J. (1983). *100 cases of multiple personality disorder.* Paper presented at the Annual Meeting of the American Psychiatric Association, New York.

Quay, H.C. (1964). Personality dimensions in delinquent males as inferred from the factor analysis of behavior ratings. *Journal of Research in Crime and Delinquency, 1, 33–37.*

Quay, H.C. (1965). Psychopathic personality as pathological stimulus seeking. *American Journal of Psychiatry, 122, 180–183.*

Quay, H.C. (1979). Classification. In H.C. Quay & J.S. Werry (Eds.), *Psychopathological disorders of childhood* (2nd ed.), New York: Wiley.

Quay, H.C. (1986). Conduct disorders. In H.C. Quay & J.S. Werry (Eds.), *Psychopathological disorders of childhood* (3rd ed.). New York: Wiley.

Quinsey, V.L., & Chaplin, T.C. (1982). Penile responses to nonsexual violence among rapists. *Criminal Justice and Behavior. 9, 372–384.*

Rabavilas, A., & Boulougouris, J. (1974). Physiological accompaniments of ruminations, flooding and thought-stopping in obsessional patients. *Behaviour Research and Therapy, 12, 239–244.*

Rabins, P.V., & Folstein, M.F. (1982). Delirium and dementia: Diagnostic criteria and fatality rates. *British Journal of Psychiatry, 140, 149–153.*

Rachman, S.J. (1966). Sexual fetishism: An experimental analogue. *Psychological Record, 16, 293–296.*

Rachman, S., & deSilva, P. (1978). Abnormal and normal obsessions. *Behavior Research and Therapy, 16, 233–248.*

Rachman, S.J., & Hodgson, R.J. (1980). *Obsessions and compulsions.* Englewood Cliffs, N.J.: Prentice–Hall.

Rachman, S.J., & Wilson, G.T. (1980). *The effects of psychological therapy* (2nd ed.). Elmsford, N.Y.: Pergamon.

Radloff, L. (1975). Sex differences in depression: The effects of occupation and marital status. *Sex Roles, 1, 249–265.*

Ragland, D.R., & Brand, R.J. (1988). Type A behavior and mortality from coronary heart disease. *The New England Journal of Medicine, 318, 65–69.*

Rahe, R.H., & Holmes, T.H. Life crises and disease onset: A prospective study of life crises and health changes. Unpublished manuscript.

Rahe, R.H., & Lind, E. (1971). Psychosocial factors and sudden cardiac death: A pilot study. *Journal of Psychomatic Research, 15, 19–24.*

Ramey, C.T., MacPhee, D., & Yeates, K.O. (1982). Preventing developmental retardation. A general systems model. In L. Bond & J. Joffee (Eds.), *Facilitating infant and early childhood development.* Hanover, N.H.: University Press of New England.

Rank, O. (1936). *Will therapy.* New York: Knopf.

Rapaport, D. (1951). *The organization and pathology of thought.* New York: Columbia University Press.

Rapaport, K., & Burkhart, B.R. (1984). Personality and attitudinal characteristics of sexually coercive college males. *Journal of Abnormal Psychology, 93, 216–221.*

Rapoport, J.L., Buchsbaum, M.S., Zahn, T.P., Weingartner, H., Ludlow, D., & Mikkelson, E.J. (1978). Dextroamphetamine: Cognitive and behavioral effects in normal prepubertal boys. *Science, 199, 560–563.*

Rapp, S.R., Parisi, S.A., & Walsh, D.A. (1988). Psychological dysfunction and physical health among elderly medical inpatients. *Journal of Consulting and Clinical Psychology, 56, 851–855.*

Rapp, S.R., Parisi, S.A., Walsh, D.A., & Wallace, C.E. (1988). Detecting depression in elderly medical inpatients. *Journal of Consulting and Clinical Psychology, 56, 509–513.*

Rappaport, J. (1977). *Community psychology: Values, research, and action.* New York: Holt, Rinehart & Winston.

Rappaport, J. (1981). In praise of paradox: A social policy of empowerment over prevention. *American Journal of Community Psychology, 9, 1–25.*

Rappaport, J., & Chinsky, J.M. (1974). Models for delivery of service from a historical and conceptual perspective. *Professional Psychology, 5, 42–50.*

Raskin, F., & Rae, D.S. (1981). Psychiatric symptoms in the elderly. *Psychopharmacology Bulletin, 17, 96–99.*

Raymond, E.F., Michaels, T.J., & Steer, R.A. (1980). Prevalence and correlates of depression in elderly persons. *Psychological Reports, 47, 1055–1061.*

Raymond, J.G. (1979). *The transsexual empire: The making of the she-male.* Boston: Beacon.

Redfield, J., & Stone, A.A. (1979). Individual viewpoints of stressful life events. *Journal of Consulting and Clinical Psychology, 47, 147–154.*

Redick, R.W., & Taube, C.A. (1980). Demography and mental health care of the aged. In J.E. Birren & R.B. Sloane (Eds.), *Handbook of mental health and aging.* Englewood Cliffs, N.J.: Prentice–Hall.

Redmond, D.E. (1977). Alterations in the function of the nucleus locus coeruleus. In I. Hanin & E. Usdin (Eds.), *Animal models in psychiatry and neurology.* New York: Pergamon.

Reed, D., McGhee, D., Yano, K., & Feinleib, M. (1983). Social networks and coronary heart disease among Japanese men in Hawaii. *American Journal of Epidemiology,* **119,** 356–370.

Reed, S.D., Katkin, E.S., & Goldband, S. (1986). Biofeedback and behavioral medicine. In F.H. Kanfer & A.P. Goldstein (Eds.), *Helping people change: A textbook of methods* (3rd ed.). Elmsford, NY: Pergamon.

Rees, L. (1963). The significance of parental attitudes in childhood asthma. *Journal of Psychosomatic Research,* **7,** 181–190.

Rees, L. (1964). The importance of psychological, allergic and infective factors in childhood asthma. *Journal of Psychosomatic Research,* **7,** 253–262.

Reeve, V.C. (1979). Incidence of marijuana in a California impaired driver population. Sacramento: State of California, Department of Justice, Division of Law Enforcement Investigative Service.

Regier, D.A., Boyd, J.H., Burke, J.D., Jr., Rae, D.S., Myers, J.K., Kramer, M., Robins, L.N., George, L.K., Karno, M., & Locke, B.Z. (1988). One-month prevalence of mental disorders in the United States. *Archives of General Psychiatry,* **45,** 977–1986.

Reich, J. (1987). Sex distribution of DSM-III personality disorders in psychiatric outpatients. *American Journal of Psychiatry,* **144,** 485–488.

Reich, W. (1942). *The function of the orgasm.* New York: Noonday Press.

Reid, E.C. (1910). Autopsychology of the manic-depressive. *Journal of Nervous and Mental Disease,* **37,** 606–620.

Reifler, B.V., Larson, E., & Hanley, R. (1982). Co-existence of cognitive impairment and depression in geriatric outpatients. *American Journal of Psychiatry,* **139,** 623–626.

Rekers, G.A., & Lovaas, O.I. (1974). Behavioral treatment of deviant sex role behaviors in a male child. *Journal of Applied Behavioral Analysis,* **7,** 173–190.

Reppucci, N.D. (1987). Prevention and ecology: Teen-age pregnancy, child sexual abuse, and organized youth sports. *American Journal of Community Psychology,* **15,** 1–22.

Rescoria, R.A., & Solomon, R.L. (1967). Two-process learning theory: Relationships between Pavlovian conditioning and instrumental learning. *Psychological Review,* **74,** 151–182.

Research on the treatment of narcotic addiction: State of the art. (1983). National Institute on Drug Abuse Treatment Monograph Series. Department of Health and Human Services Publication No. (ADM) 83–1281. Washington, D.C.: U.S. Government Printing Office.

Resick, P.A., Veronen, L.J., Calhoun, K.S., Kilpatrick, D.G., & Atkeson, B.M. (1986). Assessment of fear reactions in sexual assault victims: A factor-analytic study of the Veronen–Kilpatrick Modified Fear Survey. *Behavioral Assessment,* **8,** 271–283.

Resnik, H.L.P. (Ed.). (1968). *Suicidal behaviors.* Boston: Little, Brown.

Rice, J., Reich, T., Andreasen, N.N., Endicott, J., Eerdewegh, M. Van, Fishman, R., Hirschfeld, R.M.A., & Klerkman, G.L. (1987). The familial transmission of bipolar illness. *Archives of General Psychiatry,* **44,** 451–460.

Richards, P., Berk, R.A., & Forster, B. (1979). *Crime as play: Delinquency in a middle class suburb.* Cambridge, Mass.: Ballinger.

Richardson, S.A., Katz, M., & Koller, H. (1986). Sex differences in number of children administratively classified as mildly mentally retarded: An epidemiological review. *American Journal of Mental Deficiency,* **91,** 250–256.

Richter, C.P. (1957). On the phenomenon of sudden death in animals and man. *Psychosomatic Medicine,* **19,** 191–198.

Ricks, D.M. (1972). The beginning of vocal communication in infants and autistic children. Unpublished dissertation. University of London.

Rie, H.E., Rie, E.D., Stewart, S., Ambuel, F.P. (1976). The effects of methylphenidate on underachieving children. *Journal of Consulting and Clinical Psychology,* **44,** 250–260.

Rieder, R.O., Mann, L.S., Weinerger, D.R., Kammen, D.P. van, & Post, R.M. (1983). Computer tomographic scans in patients with schizophrenia, schizoaffective, and bipolar affective disorder. *Archives of General Psychiatry,* **40,** 735–739.

Riessman, F. (1985). New dimensions in self-help. *Social Policy,* **15,** 2–5.

Rimland, B. (1964). *Infantile autism.* New York: Appleton–Century–Crofts.

Rimland, B. (1969). Psychogenesis versus biogenesis: The issues and the evidence. In S.C. Plog & R.B. Edgerton (Eds.), *Changing perspectives in mental illness.* New York: Holt, Rinehart & Winston.

Rimm, D.C., & Masters, J.C. (1979). *Behavior therapy: Techniques and empirical findings* (2nd ed.). New York: Academic Press.

Ritter, B. (1968). The group treatment of children's snake phobias, using vicarious and contact desensitization procedures. *Behaviour Research and Therapy,* **6,** 1–6.

Ritvo, E.R., Freeman, B.J., Geller, E., & Yuwiler, A. (1983). Effects of fenfluramine on 14 outpatients with the syndrome of autism. *Journal of the American Academy of Child Psychiatry,* **22,** 549–558.

Ritvo, E.R., Yuwileer, A., Geller, E., Ornitz, E.M., Saeger, K., & Plotkin, S. (1970). Increased blood serotonin and platelets in early infantile autism. *Archives of General Psychiatry,* **23,** 556–572.

Robbin, A.A. (1958). A controlled study of the effects of leucotomy. *Journal of Neurology, Neurosurgery, and Psychiatry,* **21,** 262–269.

Robbin, A.A. (1959). The value of leucotomy in relation to diagnosis. *Journal of Neurology, Neurosurgery, and Psychiatry,* **22,** 132–136.

Roberto, L.G. (1983). Issues in diagnosis and treatment of transsexualism. *Archives of Sexual Behavior,* **12,** 445–473.

Roberts, M.C., Wurtele, S.K., Boone, R.R., Ginther, L.J., & Elkins, P.D. (1981). Reduction of medical fears by use of modeling: A preventive application in a general population of children. *Journal of Pediatric Psychology,* **6,** 293–300.

Robey, A. (1965). Criteria for competency to stand trial: A checklist for psychiatrists. *American Journal of Psychiatry,* **122,** 616–622.

Robins, E., & Guze, S.B. (1970). Establishment of diagnostic validity in psychiatric illness: Its application to schizophrenia. *American Journal of Psychiatry,* **126,** 983–987.

Robins, L.N. (1966). *Deviant children grown up.* Baltimore: Williams & Wilkins.

Robins, L.N. (1972). Follow-up studies of behavior disorders in children. In H.C. Quay & J.S. Werry (Eds.), *Psychopathological disorders of childhood.* New York: Wiley.

Robins, L.N., Helzer, J.E., Croughan, J., & Ratliff, K.S. (1981). National Institute of Mental Health: Diagnostic Interview Schedule. *Archives of General Psychiatry,* **38,** 381–389.

Robins, L.N., Helzer, J.E., Weissman, M.M., Orvaschel, H., Gruenberg, E., Burke, J.D., & Reiger, D.A. (1984). Lifetime prevalence of specific psychiatric disorders in three sites. *Archives of General Psychiatry,* **41,** 942–949.

Robinson, N.M., & Robinson, H.B. (1976). *The mentally retarded child* (2nd ed.). New York: McGraw–Hill.

Rodin, J. (1980). Managing the stress of aging: The control of control and coping. In H. Ursin & S. Levine (Eds.), *Coping and Health.* New York: Academic Press.

Rodin, J., & Langer, E.J. (1977). Long-term effects of a control-relevant intervention with the institutionalized aged. *Journal of Personality and Social Psychology,* **35,** 897–902.

Rodin, J., Mcavay, G., & Timko, C. (1988). A longitudinal study of depressed mood and sleep disturbances in elderly adults. *Journal of Gerontology: Psychological Sciences,* **43,** P45–P53.

Roesch, R., & Golding, S.L. (1980). *Competency to stand trial.* Urbana, Ill.: University of Illinois Press.

Rofman, E.S., Askinazi, C., & Fant, E. (1980). The prediction of dangerous behavior in emergency commitment. *American Journal of Psychiatry,* **137,** 1061–1064.

Rogers, C.R. (1942). *Counseling and psychotherapy: New concepts in practice.* Boston: Houghton Mifflin.

Rogers, C.R. (1951). *Client-centered therapy.* Boston: Houghton Mifflin.

Rogers, C.R. (1961). *On becoming a person: A therapist's view of psychotherapy.* Boston: Houghton Mifflin.

Rogers, C.R. (1970). *Carl Rogers on encounter groups.* New York: Harper & Row.

Rogers, C.R., Gendlin, G.T., Kiesler, D.V., & Truax, C.B. (1967). *The therapeutic relationship and its impact: A study of psychotherapy with schizophrenics.* Madison: University of Wisconsin Press.

Rokeach, M. (1973). *The nature of human values.* New York: Free Press.

Romanczyk, R.G., Diament, C., Goren, E.R., Trundell, G., & Harris, S.L. (1975). Increasing isolate and social play in severely disturbed children: Intervention and postintervention effectiveness. *Journal of Autism and Childhood Schizophrenia,* **43,** 730–739.

Romanczyk, R.G., Kent, R.N., Diament, C., & O'Leary, K.D. (1973). Measuring the reliability of observational data: A reactive process. *Journal of Applied Behavior Analysis,* **6,** 175–184.

Rooth, F.G. (1973). Exhibitionism, sexual violence, and pedophilia. *British Journal of Psychiatry,* **122,** 705–710.

Rorschach, H. (1921). *Psychodiagnostics: A diagnostic test based on perception.* Translation and English edition by P. Lemkau & B. Kronenberg (9th ed.). New York: Grune & Stratton, 1981.

Rose, S.D. (1986). Group methods. In F.H. Kanfer & A.P. Goldstein (Eds.), *Helping people change: A textbook of methods* (3rd ed.). Elmsford, N.Y.: Pergamon.

Rosen, E., Fox, R., & Gregory, I. (1972). *Abnormal psychology* (2nd ed.). Philadelphia: Saunders.

Rosen, J.C., & Leitenberg, H.C. (1985). Exposure plus response prevention treatment of bulimia. In D.M. Garner & P.E. Garfinkel (Eds.), *Handbook of psychotherapy for anorexia nervosa and bulimia.* New York: Guilford.

Rosen, J.C., & Leitenberg, H. (1982). Bulimia nervosa: Treatment with exposure and response prevention. *Behavior Therapy,* **13,** 117–124.

Rosen, J.N. (1964). A method of resolving acute catatonic excitement. *Psychiatric quarterly,* **20,** 183–198.

Rosen, R.C., & Beck, J.G. (1988). *Patterns of sexual arousal: Psychophysiological processes and clinical applications.* New York: Guilford.

Rosen, R.C., & Hall, E. (1984). *Sexuality.* New York: Random House.

Rosen, R.C., & Rosen, L. (1981). *Human sexuality.* New York: Knopf.

Rosenbaum, M. (1980). The role of the term schizophrenia in the decline of diagnoses of multiple personality. *Archives of General Psychiatry,* **37,** 1383–1385.

Rosenbaum, M. (1980). A schedule for assessing self-control behaviors: Preliminary findings. *Behavior Therapy,* **11,** 109–121.

Rosenberg, M.S., & Reppucci, N.D. (1985). Primary prevention of child abuse. *Journal of Consulting and Clinical Psychology,* **53,** 576–585.

Rosenblatt, R.A. (1988, December 4). Some seniors protest higher medicare tax. *Los Angeles Times.*

Rosenblatt, R.A., & Spiegel, C. (1988, December 2). Half of state's nursing homes fall short in federal study. *Los Angeles Times,* Part I, pages 3, 34.

Rosenhan, D.L. (1973). On being sane in insane places. *Science,* **179,** 250–258.

Rosenhan, R.H., Brand, R.J., Jenkins, C.D., Friedman, M., Straus, R., & Wurm, M. (1975). Coronary heart disease in the Western Collaborative Group Study: Final follow-up experience of 8½ years. *Journal of the Amerian Medical Association,* **233,** 872–877.

Rosenman, R.H., Friedman, M., Straus, R., Wurm, M., Kositichek, R., Hahn, W., & Werthessen, N.T. (1964). A predictive study of coronary heart disease. *Journal of the American Medical Association,* **189,** 103–110.

Rosenthal, D. (1955). Changes in some moral values following psychotherapy. *Journal of Consulting Psychology,* **19,** 431–436.

Rosenthal, D. (1970). *Genetic Theory and Abnormal Behavior.* NY: McGraw-Hill.

Rosenthal, N.E., Carpenter, C.J., James, S.P., Parry, B.L., Rogers, S.L.B., & Wehr, T.A. (1986). Seasonal affective disorder in children and adolescents. *American Journal of Psychiatry,* **143,** 356–358.

Rosenthal, N.E., Sack, D.A., Carpenter, C.J., Parry, B.L., Mendelson, W.B., & Wehr, T.A. (1985). Antidepressant effects of light in seasonal affective disorder. *American Journal of Psychiatry,* **142,** 163–170.

Rosenthal, R. (1966). *Experimenter bias in behavioral research.* New York: Appleton–Century–Crofts.

Rosenthal, T.L., & Bandura, A. (1978). Psychological modeling: Theory and practice. In S.L. Garfield & A.E. Bergin (Eds.), *Handbook of psychotherapy and behavior change: An empirical analysis* (2nd ed.). New York: Wiley.

Rosin, A.J., & Glatt, M.M. (1971). Alcohol excess in the elderly. *Quarterly Journal of Studies on Alcoholism,* **32,** 53–59.

Rosman, B.L., Minuchin, S., & Liebman, R. (1975). Family lunch session: An introduction to family therapy in anorexia nervosa. *American Journal of Orthopsychiatry,* **45,** 846–852.

Rosman, B.L., Minuchin, S., & Liebman, R. (1976). Input and outcome of family therapy of anorexia nervosa. In J.L. Claghorn (Ed.), *Successful psychotherapy.* New York: Brunner/Mazel.

Ross, A.O. (1981). *Psychological disorders of childhood: A behavioral approach to theory, research, and practice* (2nd ed.). New York: McGraw–Hill.

Ross, D.M., & Ross, S.A. (1973). Storage and utilization of previously formulated mediators in educable mentally retarded children. *Journal of Educational Psychology,* **65,** 205–210.

Ross, D.M., & Ross, S.A. (1976). *Hyperactivity: Research, theory, and action.* New York: Wiley.

Ross, J.L. (1977). Anorexia nervosa: An overview. *Bulletin of the Menninger Clinic,* **41,** 418–436.

Rossiter, E.M., & Wilson, G.T. (1985). Cognitive restructuring and response prevention in the treatment of bulimia nervosa. *Behaviour Research and Therapy,* **23,** 349–359.

Roth, D., & Rehm, L.P. (1980). Relationships among self-monitoring processes, memory, and depression. *Cognitive Therapy and Research,* **4,** 149–157.

Roth, M. (1955). The natural history of mental disorder in old age. *Journal of Mental Science,* **99,** 439–450.

Roth, M., & Kay, D.W.K. (1956). Affective disorder arising in the senium: II. Physical disability as an etiological factor. *Journal of Mental Science,* **102,** 141–150.

Roth, S., & Kubal, L. (1975). The effects of noncontingent reinforcement on tasks of differing importance: Facilitation and learned helplessness effects. *Journal of Personality and Social Psychology,* **32,** 680–691.

Rothman, D. (1971). *The discovery of the asylum.* New York: Harper & Row.

Rounsaville, B.J., Chevron, E.S., & Weissman, M.M. (1984). Specification of techniques in Interpersonal Psychotherapy. In J.B.W. Williams & R.L. Spitzer (Eds.), *Psychotherapy research: Where are we and where should we go?* New York: Guilford.

Roy, A. (1982). Suicide in chronic schizophrenics. *British Journal of Psychiatry,* **141,** 171–177.

Roy, A., Everett, D., Pickar, D., & Paul, S.M. (1987). Platelet tritiated imipramine binding and serotonin uptake in depressed patients. *Archives of General Psychiatry,* **44,** 320–327.

Roybal, E.R. (1988). Mental health and aging: The need for an expanded federal response. *American Psychologist,* **43,** 189–194.

Ruberman, W., Weinblatt, E., Goldberg, J.D., and Chaudhary, B.S. (1984). Psychosocial influences on mortality after myocardial infarction. *New England Journal of Medicine, 311,* 552–559.

Runck, B. (1980). *Biofeedback—Issues in treatment assessment.* Rockville, Md.: National Institute of Mental Health.

Runck, B. (1982). *Behavioral self-control: Issues in treatment assessment.* Rockville, Md.: National Institute of Mental Health.

Rush, A.J., Beck, A.T., Kovacs, M., & Hollon, S.D. (1977). Comparative efficacy of cognitive therapy and pharmacotherapy in the treatment of depressed outpatients. *Cognitive Therapy and Research, 1,* 17–39.

Rush, A.J., Beck, A.T., Kovacs, M., Weissenberger, J., & Hollon, S. D. (1982). Comparison of the effects of cognitive therapy on hopelessness and self-concept. *American Journal of Psychiatry, 139,* 862–866.

Rusin, M., & Siegler, I.C. (1975). *Personality differences between participants and dropouts in a longitudinal study.* Paper presented at the Gerontological Society, Louisville, Ky.

Ruskin, A., Board, O.W., & Schaffer, R.L. (1948). Blast hypertension: Elevated arterial pressure in victims of the Texas City disaster. *American Journal of Medicine, 4,* 228–236.

Russell, D.E.H. (1982). *Rape in marriage.* New York: Macmillan Co.

Russell, M.A.H., Feyerabend, C., & Cole, P.V. (1976). Plasma nicotine levels after cigarette smoking and chewing nicotine gum. *British Medical Journal. 1,* 1043–1046.

Russell, M.A.H. Merriman, R., Stapleton, J., & Taylor, W. (1983). Effect of nicotine chewing gum as an adjunct to general practitioners' advice against smoking. *British Medical Journal, 287,* 1782–1785.

Russo, D.C., & Varni, J.W. (1982). Behavioral pediatrics. In D.C. Russo & J.W. Varni (Eds.), *Behavioral pediatrics: Research and practice.* New York: Plenum.

Rutter, M. (1966). Prognosis: Psychotic children in adolescence and early adult life. In J.K. Wing (Ed.), *Childhood autism: Clinical, educational, and social aspects.* Elmsford, N.Y.: Pergamon.

Rutter, M. (1967). Psychotic disorders in early childhood. In A.J. Cooper (Ed.), *Recent developments in schizophrenia. British Journal of Psychiatry,* Special Publication.

Rutter, M. (1971). Parent–child separation: Psychological effects on the children. *Journal of Child Psychology and Psychiatry, 12,* 233–260.

Rutter, M. (1978). Diagnosis and definition. In M. Rutter & E. Schopler (Eds.), *Autism: A reappraisal of concepts and treatment.* New York: Plenum.

Rutter M. (1979). Maternal deprivation. 1972–1978: New findings, new concepts, new approaches. *Child Development, 50,* 283–305.

Rutter, M., & Lockyer, L. (1967). A five to fifteen year follow-up of infantile psychosis: I. Description of sample. *British Journal of Psychiatry, 113,* 1169–1182.

Rutter, M., Tizard, J., & Whitmore, K. (1970). *Education, health, and behavior.* London: Longmans.

Ryall, R. (1974). Delinquency: The problem for treatment. *Social Work Today, 15,* 98–104.

Ryan, W. (1971). *Blaming the victim.* New York: Random House.

Rybstein-Blinchik, E. (1979). Effects of different cognitive strategies on chronic pain experience. *Journal of Behavioral Medicine, 2,* 93–101.

Sachs, J.S. (1983). Negative factors in brief psychotherapy: An empirical assessment. *Journal of Consulting and Clinical Psychology, 51,* 557–564.

Sackeim, H.A., Nordlie, J.W., & Gur, R.C. (1979). A model of hysterical and hypnotic blindness: Cognition, motivation and awareness. *Journal of Abnormal Psychology, 88,* 474–489.

Safer, D.J., & Allen, R.P. (1976). *Hyperactive children: Diagnosis and management.* Baltimore: University Park Press.

Safran, J.D., Vallis, T.M., Segal, Z.V., & Shaw, B.F. (1986). Assessment of core cognitive processes in cognitive therapy. *Cognitive Therapy and Research, 10,* 509–526.

Sajdel-Sulkowska, E.M., & Marotta, C.A. (1984). Alzheimer's disease brain: Alterations in RNA levels and in ribonuclease-inhibitor complex. *Science, 225,* 947–949.

Sakel, M. (1938). The pharmacological shock treatment of schizophrenia. *Nervous and Mental Disease Monograph 62.*

Sallan, S.E., Zinberg, N.E., & Frei, E. (1975). Antiemetic effect of delta-9-THC in patients receiving cancer chemotherapy. *New England Journal of Medicine, 293,* 795–797.

Salter, A. (1949). *Conditioned reflex therapy.* New York: Farrar, Straus.

Salzman, L. (1980). *Psychotherapy of the obsessive personality.* New York: Jason Aronson.

Salzman, L. (1985). Psychotherapeutic management of obsessive-compulsive patients. *American Journal of Psychotherapy, 39,* 323–330.

Salzman, L., & Thaler, F.H. (1981). Obsessive-compulsive disorders: A review of the literature. *American Journal of Psychiatry, 138,* 286–296.

Sandler, J. (1986). Aversion methods. In F.H. Kanfer & A.P. Goldstein (Eds.), *Helping people change: A textbook of methods* (3rd ed.). Elmsford, N.Y.: Pergamon.

Sarent, J.D., Green, E.E., & Walters, E.D. (1972). Preliminary report on the use of autogenic feedback techniques in the treatment of migraine headaches. *Headache, 12,* 120–124.

Sargent, J.D., Green, E.E., & Walters, E.D. (1973). The use of autogenic feedback training in a pilot study of migraine and tension headaches. *Psychosomatic Medicine, 35,* 129–135.

Sartorius, N., Shapiro, R., & Jalonsky, A. (1974). The international pilot study of schizophrenia. *Schizophrenia Bulletin, 2,* 21–35.

Sassenrath, E.N., Chapman, L.F., & Goo, G.P. (1979). Reproduction in rhesus monkeys chronically exposed to moderate amounts of delta-9-tetrahydrocannabinol. In G.G. Nahas & W.D.M. Paton (Eds.), *Marihuana: Biological effects.* Elmsford, N.Y.: Pergamon.

Satterfield, J.H., Cantwell, D.P., Lesser, L.I., & Podosin, R.L. (1972). Physiological studies of the hyperactive child. *American Journal of Psychiatry, 128,* 1418–1424.

Satterfield, J.H., Hoppe, C.M., & Schell, A.M. (1982). A prospective study of delinquency in 110 adolescent boys with attention deficit disorder and 88 normal adolescent boys. *American Journal of Psychiatry, 139,* 795–798.

Scarlett, W. (1980). Social isolation from agemates among nursery school children. *Journal of Child Psychology and Psychiatry, 21,* 231–240.

Schachter, S. (1977). Nicotine regulation in heavy and light smokers. *Journal of Experimental Psychology: General, 106,* 5–12.

Schachter, S. (1978). Pharmacological and psychological determinants of smoking. *Annals of Internal Medicine, 88,* 104–114.

Schachter, S., Kozlowski, L.T., & Silverstein, B. (1977). Effects of urinary pH on cigarette smoking. *Journal of Experimental Psychology: General, 106,* 13–19.

Schachter, S., & Latané, B. (1964). Crime, cognition, and the autonomic nervous system. In D. Levine (Ed.), *Nebraska symposium on motivation* (Vol. 12). Lincoln: University of Nebraska Press.

Schachter, S., Silverstein, B., Kozlowski, L.T., Herman, C.P., & Liebling, B. (1977). Effects of stress on cigarette smoking and urinary pH. *Journal of Experimental Psychology: General, 106,* 24–30.

Schachter, S., Silverstein, B., & Perlik, O. (1977). Psychological and pharmacological explanations of smoking under stress. *Journal of Experimental Psychology: General, 106,* 31–40.

Schaie, K.W. (1980). Intelligence and problem solving. In J.E. Birren & R.B. Sloane (Eds.), *Handbook of mental health and aging.* Englewood Cliffs, N.J.: Prentice–Hall.

Schaie, K.W., & Hertzog, C. (1982). Longitudinal methods. In B.B. Wolman (Ed.), *Handbook of developmental psychology.* Englewood Cliffs, N.J.: Prentice–Hall.

Schain, R.J., & Reynard, C.J. (1975). Effects of a central stimulant drug (methylphenidate) in children with hyperactive behavior. *Pediatrics, 55,* 709–716.

Schank, R., & Abelson, R. (1977). *Scripts, plans, goals, and understanding.* Hillsdale, N.J.: Erlbaum.

Schatzberg, A.F., Orsulak, P.J., Rosenbaum, A.H., Cole, J.O., & Scheerenberger, R.C. (1983). *A history of mental retardation.* Baltimore: P.H. Brookes.

Scheerenberger, R.C. (1984). *A history of mental retardation.* Baltimore, MD: P.H. Brookes.

Scheerer, M., Rothman, E., & Goldstein, K. (1945). A cse of "idiot savant": An experimental study of personality organization. *Psychological Monographs, 58* (whole No. 269).

Scheff, T.J. (1966). *Being mentally ill: A sociological theory.* Chicago: Aldine.

Schellenberg, G.D., Bird, T.D., Wijsman, E.M., Moore, D.K., Boehkne, E.M., Bryant, E.M., Lampe, T.H., Nochlin, D., Sumi, S.M., Deeb, S.S., Beyreuther, K., & Martin, G.M. (1988). Absence of linkage of chromosome 21q21 markers to familial Alzheimer's disease. *Science, 241,* 1507–1510.

Schildkraut, J.J. (1965). The catecholamine hypothesis of affective disorders. *American Journal of Psychiatry, 122,* 509–522.

Schildkraut, J.J. (1983). Biochemical subtypes of unipolar depressions. In P.J. Clayton & J.E. Barrett (Eds.), *Treatment of depression: Old controversies and new approaches.* New York: Raven Press.

Schinke, S.P., & Gilchrist, L.D. (1985). Preventing substance abuse with children and adolescents. *Journal of Consulting and Clinical Psychology, 53,* 596–602.

Schlesier-Stropp, B. (1984). Bulimia: A review of the literature. *Psychological Bulletin, 95,* 247–257.

Schmauk, F.J. (1970). Punishment, arousal, and avoidance learning in sociopaths. *Journal of Abnormal Psychology, 76,* 443–453.

Schneider, K. (1959). *Clinical psychopathology.* New York: Grune & Stratton.

Schneider, N.G. (1987). Nicotine gum in smoking cessation: Rationale, efficacy, and proper use. *Comprehensive Therapy, 13,* 32–37.

Schneider, N.G., & Jarvik, M.E. (1984). Time course of smoking withdrawal symptoms as a function of nicotine replacement. *Psychopharmacology, 82,* 143–144.

Schneider, N.G., Jarvik, M.E., & Forsythe, A.B. (1984). Nicotine vs. placebo gum in the alleviation of withdrawal during smoking cessation. *Addictive Behaviors, 9,* 149–156.

Schneider, N.G., Jarvik, M.E., Forsythe, A.B., Read, L.L., Elliott, M.L., & Schweiger, A. (1983). Nicotine gum in smoking cessation: A placebo-controlled, double-blind trial. *Addictive Behaviors, 8,* 253–261.

Schoenbach, V., Kaplan, B.H., Fredman, L., & Kleinaum, D.G. (1986) Social ties and mortality in Evans County, Georgia. *American Journal of Epidemiology, 123,* 577–591.

Schoeneman, T.J. (1977). The role of mental illness in the European witchhunts of the sixteenth and seventeenth centuries: An assessment. *Journal of the History of the Behavioral Sciences, 13,* 337–351.

Schofield, W. (1964). *Psychotherapy: The purchase of friendship.* Englewood Cliffs, N.J.: Prentice–Hall.

Schuckit, M.A. (1983). The genetics of alcoholism. In B. Tabakoff, P.B. Sutker, & C.L. Randall (Eds.), *Medical and social aspects of alcohol use.* New York: Plenum.

Schuckit, M.A., & Gold, E.O. (1988). A simultaneous evaluation of multiple ethanol challenges to sons of alcoholics and controls. *Archives of General Psychiatry, 45,* 211–216.

Schuckit, M.A., & Moore, M.A. (1979). Drug problems in the elderly. In O.J. Kaplan (Ed.), *Psychopathology of aging.* New York: Academic Press.

Schuckit, M.A., & Rayses, V. (1979). Ethanol ingestion: Differences in blood acetaldehyde concentrations in relatives of alcoholics and controls. *Science, 203,* 54–55.

Schulsinger, F. (1972). Psychopathy: Heredity and environment. *International Journal of Mental Health, 1,* 190–206.

Schultz, R., & Brenner, G. (1977). Relocation of the aged: A review and theoretical analysis. *Journal of Gerontology, 32,* 323–333.

Schutz, W.C. (1967). *Joy.* New York: Grove.

Schwab, J.J., Fennell, E.B., & Warheit, G.J. (1974). The epidemiology of psychosomatic disorders. *Psychosomatics, 15,* 88–93.

Schwarz, J.R. (1981). *The Hillside strangler: A murderer's mind.* New York: New American Library.

Schwartz, G.E. (1973). Biofeedback as therapy: Some theoretical and practical issues. *American Psychologist, 28,* 666–673.

Schwartz, G.E., & Weiss, S. (1977). What is behavioral medicine? *Psychosomatic Medicine, 36,* 377–381.

Schwartz, G.E., & Weiss, S.M. (1978). Behavioral medicine revisited: An amended definition. *Journal of Behavioral Medicine, 1,* 249–252.

Schwartz, G.J. (1977). College students as contingency managers for adolescents in a program to develop reading skills. *Journal of Applied Behavior Analysis, 10,* 645–655.

Schwartz, J.L. (1987). *Review and evaluation of smoking cessation methods: The United States and Canada 1978–1985.* U.S. Department of Health and Human Services, National Institutes of Health, NIH Publication No. 87–2940.

Schwartz, M.A., Wyatt, R.J., Yang, H., & Neff, N. (1974). Multiple forms of monamine oxidase in brain: A comparison of enzymatic activity in mentally normal and chronic schizophrenic individuals. *Archives of General Psychiatry, 31,* 557–560.

Schwartz, M.S. (1946). The economic and spatial mobility of paranoid schizophrenics. Unpublished M.A. thesis, University of Chicago.

Schwartz, R., & Schwartz, L.J. (1980). *Becoming a couple.* Englewood Cliffs, N.J.: Prentice–Hall.

Schwartz, R.M., & Gottman, J.M. (1976). Toward a task analysis of assertive behavior. *Journal of Consulting and Clinical Psychology, 44,* 910–920.

Schwartz, S.H., & Inbar-Saban, N. (1988). Value self-confrontation as a method to aid in weight loss. *Journal of Personality and Social Psychology, 54,* 396–404.

Schwitzgebel, R.L., & Schwitzgebel, R.K. (1980). *Law and psychological practice.* New York: Wiley.

Scientific perspectives on cocaine abuse. (1987). *Pharmacologist, 29,* 20–27.

Seeman, T.E. & Syme, S.L. (1987). Social networks and coronary artery disease: A comparison of the structure and function of social relations as predictors of disease. *Psychosomatic Medicine, 49,* 381–406.

Segovia-Riquelman, N., Varela, A., & Mardones, J. (1971). Appetite for alcohol. In Y. Israel & J. Mardones (Eds.), *Biological basis of alcoholism.* New York: Wiley.

Seidman, L. J. (1983). Schizophrenia and brain dysfunction: An integration of recent neurodiagnostic findings. *Psychological Bulletin, 94,* 195–238.

Seiden, R.H. (1974). Suicide: Preventable death. *Public Affairs Report, 15,* 1–5.

Seigel, R.K. (1982). Cocaine smoking. *Journal of Psychoactive Drugs, 14,* 277–359.

Seligman, M.E.P. (1971). Phobias and preparedness. *Behavior Therapy, 2,* 307–320.

Seligman, M.E.P. (1973). Fall into helplessness. *Psychology Today, 7,* 43–48.

Seligman, M.E.P. (1974). Depression and learned helplessness. In R.J. Friedman & M.M. Katz (Eds.), *The psychology of depression: Contemporary theory and research.* Washington, D.C.: Winston–Wiley.

Seligman, M.E.P. (1975). *Helplessness: On depression, development, and death.* San Francisco: Freeman.

Seligman, M.E.P. (1978). Comment and integration. *Journal of Abnormal Psychology,* **87,** 165–179.

Seligman, M.E.P., Abramson, L.V., Semmel, A., & Von Beyer, C. (1979). Depressive attributional style. *Journal of Abnormal psychology,* **88,** 242–247.

Seligman, M.E.P., Castellon, C., Cacciola, J., Schulman, P., Luborsky, L., Ollove, M., & Downing, R. (1988). Explanatory style change during cognitive therapy for unipolar depression. *Journal of Abnormal Psychology,* **97,** 13–18.

Seligman, M.E.P., & Hager, M. (Eds.). (1972). *Biological boundaries of learning.* New York: Appleton–Century–Crofts.

Selling, L.S. (1940). *Men against madness.* New York: Greenberg.

Selye, H. (1950). *The physiology and pathology of exposure to stress.* Montreal: Acta.

Serban, G., Conte, H.R., & Plutchik, R. (1987). Borderline and schizotypal personality disorders: Mutually exclusive or overlapping? *Journal of Personality Assessment,* **5,** 15–22.

Settin, J.M. (1982). Clinical judgment in geropsychology practice. *Psychotherapy: Theory, Research and Practice,* **19,** 397–404.

Shader, R.I., Caine, E.D., & Meyer, R.E. (1975). Treatment of dependence on barbiturates and sedative hypnotics. In R.I. Shader (Ed.), *Manual of psychiatric therapeutics: Practical psychopharmacology and psychiatry.* Boston, Mass.: Little, Brown.

Shader, R.I., & DiMascio, A. (1970). *Psychotropic drug side-effects: Clinical and theoretical perspectives.* Baltimore: Williams & Wilkins.

Shadish, W.R. (1984). Policy research: Lessons from the implementation of deinstitutionalization. *American Psychologist,* **39,** 725–738.

Shapiro, A.P. (1961). An experimental study of comparative responses of blood pressure to different noxious stimuli. *Journal of Chronic Diseases,* **13,** 293–311.

Shapiro, D.A., & Shapiro, D. (1983). Comparative therapy outcome research: Methodological implications of meta-analysis. *Journal of Consulting and Clinical Psychology,* **51,** 42–53.

Shapiro, D., & Surwit, R.S. (1979). Biofeedback. In O.F. Pomerleau & J.P. Brady (Eds.), *Behavioral medicine: Theory and practice.* Baltimore: Williams & Wilkins.

Shapiro, D., Tursky, B., & Schwartz, G.E. (1970). Control of blood pressure in man by operant conditioning. *Circulation Research,* **26,** 127–132.

Shatan, C.F. (1978). Stress disorders among Vietnam veterans: The emotional content of combat continues. In C.R. Figley (Ed.), *Stress disorders among Vietnam veterans.* New York: Brunner/Mazel.

Shaw, B.F. (1977). Comparison of cognitive therapy and behavior therapy in the treatment of depression. *Journal of Consulting and Clinical Psychology,* **45,** 543–551.

Shaw, B.F. (1984). Specification of the training and evaluation of cognitive therapists for outcome studies. In J.B.W. Williams & R.L. Spitzer (Eds.), *Psychotherapy research: Where are we and where should we go?* New York: Guilford.

Shaywitz, S.E., Cohen, D.J., & Shaywitz, B.A. (1978). The biochemical basis of minimal brain dysfunction. *The Journal of Pediatrics,* **92,** 179–187.

Shekelle, R.B., Hulley, S.B., Neaton, J., Billings, J., Borlani, N., Gerace, T., Jacobs, D., Lasser, N., & Stamler, J. (1983). Type A behavior pattern and coronary death in MRFIT. *American Heart Association Cardiovascular Disease Newsletter,* **33,** 34.

Sher, K.J., Frost, R.O., & Otto, R. (1983). Cognitive deficits in compulsive checkers: An exploratory study. *Behaviour Research and Therapy,* **21,** 357–363.

Sher, K.J., & Levenson, R.W. (1982). Risk for alcoholism and individual differences in the stress-response-dampening effects of alcohol. *Journal of Abnormal Psychology,* **91,** 350–367.

Sherman, A.R. (1972). Real-life exposures as a primary therapeutic factor in the desensitization treatment of fear. *Journal of Abnormal Psychology,* **79,** 19–28.

Sherman, E. (1981). *Counseling the aging: An integrative approach.* New York: Free Press.

Shevitz, S.A. (1976). Psychosurgery: Some current observations. *American Journal of Psychiatry,* **133,** 266–270.

Shilling, L.E. (1984). *Perspectives on counseling therapies.* Englewood Cliffs: N.J.: Prentice–Hall.

Shneidman, E.S. (1973). Suicide. In *Encyclopedia Britannica.* Chicago: Encyclopedia Britannica.

Shneidman, E.S. (1976). A psychological theory of suicide. *Psychiatric Annals,* **6,** 51–66.

Shneidman, E.S. (1985). *Definition of suicide.* New York: Wiley.

Shneidman, E.S. (1987). A psychological approach to suicide. In G.R. VandenBos & B.K. Bryant (Eds.), *Cataclysms, crises, and catastrophes: Psychology in Action.* Washington, D.C.: American Psychological Association.

Shneidman, E.S., & Farberow, N.L. (1970). A psychological approach to the study of suicide notes. In E.S. Shneidman, N.L. Farberow, & R.E. Litman (Eds.), *The psychology of suicide.* New York: Jason Aronson.

Shneidman, E.S., Farberow, N.L., & Litman, R.E. (Eds.). (1970). *The psychology of suicide.* New York: Jason Aronson.

Shopsin, B., Friedman, E., & Gershon, S. (1976). Parachlorophenylalanine reversal of tranylcypromine effects in depressed patients. *Archives of General Psychiatry,* **33,** 811–819.

Shopsin, B., Gershon, S., Thompson, H., & Collins, P. (1975). Psychoactive drugs in mania. *Archives of General Psychiatry,* **32,** 34–42.

Short, J.F., & Nye, F.I. (1958). Extent of unrecorded juvenile delinquency: Tentative conclusions. *Journal of Criminal Law, Criminology, and Police Science,* **29,** 296–302.

Siegel, J.M., Sorenson, S.B., Golding, J.M., Burnam, M.A., & Stein, J.A. (1987). The prevalence of childhood sexual assault: The Los Angeles Epidemiological Catchment Area Project. *American Journal of Epidemiology,* **126,** 1141–1153.

Siegel, R.A. (1978). Probability of punishment and suppression of behavior in psychopathic and nonpsychopathic offenders. *Journal of Abnormal Psychology,* **87,** 514–522.

Siegler, I.C., & Costa, P.T., Jr. (1985). Health behavior relationships. In J.E. Birren & K.W. Schaie (Eds.), *Handbook of the psychology of aging* (2nd ed.). New York: Van Nostrand–Reinhold.

Seigler, I.C., George, L.K., & Okun, M.A. (1979). A cross sequential analysis of adult personality. *Developmental Psychology,* **15,** 350–351.

Siemens, A.J. (1980). Effects of cannabis in combination with ethanol and other drugs. In *Marijuana research findings: 1980.* Washington, D.C.: U.S. Government Printing Office.

Siever, L.J., & Uhde, T.W. (1984). New studies and perspectives on the noradrenergic receptor system in depression. *Biological Psychiatry,* **19,** 131.

Silverstein, C. (1972). *Behavior modification and the gay community.* Paper presented at the annual convention of the Association for Advancement of Behavior Therapy, New York City.

Simeons, A.T.W. (1961). *Man's presumptuous brain: An evolutionary interpretation of psychosomatic disease.* New York: Dutton.

Simon, R.J., & Aaronson, D.E. (1988). *The insanity defense: A critical assessment of law and policy in the post-Hinckley era.* New York: Praeger.

Simons, A.D., Lustman, P.J., Wetzel, R.D., & Murphy, G.E. (1985). Predicting response to cognitive therapy of depression: The role of learned resourcefulness. *Cognitive Therapy and Research,* **9,** 79–89.

Simons, A.D., Murphy, G.E., Levine, J.L., & Wetzel, R.D. (1985). Sustained improvement one year after cognitive and/or pharmacotherapy of depression. *Archives of General Psychiatry, 43,* 43–48.

Simpson, G.M., & May, P.R.A. (1982). Schizophrenic disorders. In J.H. Greist, J.W. Jefferson, & R.L. Spitzer (Eds.), *Treatment of mental disorders.* New York: Oxford University Press.

Simpson, M.T., Olewine, D.A., Jenkins, F.H., Ramsey, S.J., Zyzanski, S.J., Thomas, G., & Hames, C.G. (1974). Exercise-induced catecholamines and platelet aggregation in the coronary-prone behavior pattern. *Psychosomatic Medicine, 36,* 476–487.

Singer, M., & Wynne, L.C. (1963). Differentiating characteristics of the parents of childhood schizophrenics. *American Journal of Psychiatry, 120,* 234–243.

Sintchak, G.H., & Geer, J.H. (1975). A vaginal plethysmograph system. *Psychophysiology, 12,* 113–115.

Sisson, L.A., Van Hasselt, V.B., Hersen, M., & Aurland, J.C. (in press). Tripartite behavioral intervention to reduce stereotypic and disruptive behaviors in young multihandicapped children. *Behavior Therapy.*

Sizemore, C.C., & Pittillo, E.S. (1977). *I'm Eve.* Garden City, N.Y.: Doubleday.

Skinner, B.F. (1984). "Superstition" in the pigeon. *Journal of Experimental Psychology, 38,* 168–172.

Skinner, B.F. (1953). *Science and human behavior.* New York: Macmillan Co.

Skinner, H.A., & Allen, B.A. (1982). Alcohol dependence syndrome: Measurement and validation. *Journal of Abnormal Psychology, 91,* 199–209.

Skinner, H.A., Jackson, D.N., & Hoffman, H. (1974). Alcoholic personality types: Identification and correlates. *Journal of Abnormal Psychology, 83,* 658–666.

Sklar, L.A., & Anisman, H. (1979). Stress and coping factors influence tumor growth. *Science, 205,* 513–515.

Skrzypek, G.J. (1969). The effects of perception isolation and arousal on anxiety, complexity preference and novelty preference in psychopathic and neurotic delinquents. *Journal of Abnormal Psychology, 74,* 321–329.

Slater, E. (1938). Erbpathologie des manisch-depression Irreseins. Die Eltern und Kinder von Manisch-Depressiven. *Zeitschrift für die gesamte Neurologie und Psychiatrie, 163,* 1–17.

Slater, E. (1961). The thirty-fifth Maudsley lecture: Hysteria 311. *Journal of Mental Science, 107,* 358–381.

Slater, E., & Glithero, E. (1965). A follow-up of patients diagnosed as suffering from hysteria. *Journal of Psychosomatic Research, 9,* 9–13.

Slater, E., & Shields, J. (1969). Genetic aspects of anxiety. In M.H. Lader (Ed.), *Studies of anxiety.* Ashford, England: Headley Brothers.

Slavson, S.R. (1950). *Analytic group psychotherapy with children, adolescents and adults.* New York: Columbia University Press.

Slicker, W.D. (1985). Current perspectives on the insanity defense. *Case and Comment, 90,* 22–28.

Slivinske, L.R., & Fitch, V.L. (1987). The effect of control enhancing interventions on the well-being of elderly individuals living in retirement communities. *The Gerontologist, 27,* 176–181.

Sloane, R.B. (1980). Organic brain syndrome. In J.E. Birren & R.B. Sloane (Eds.), *Handbook of mental health and aging.* Englewood Cliffs, N.J.: Prentice–Hall.

Sloane, R.B., Staples, F.R., Cristol, A.H., Yorkston, N.J., & Whipple, K. (1975). *Psychoanalysis versus behavior therapy.* Cambridge, Mass.: Harvard University Press.

Small, G.W., & Jarvik, L.F. (1982). The dementia syndrome. *Lancet,* 1443–1446.

Small, G.W., Liston, E.H., & Jarvik, L.F. (1981). Diagnosis and treatment of dementia in the aged. *The Western Journal of Medicine, 135,* 469–481.

Smith, D.W., Bierman, E.L., & Robinson, N.M. (1978). *The biologic ages of man: From conception through old age.* Philadelphia: Saunders.

Smith, K.F., & Bengston, V.L. (1979). Positive consequences of institutionalization: Solidarity between elderly parents and their middle aged children. *The Gerontologist, 5,* 438–447.

Smith, M.L., Glass, G., & Miller, T. (1980). *The benefits of psychotherapy.* Baltimore: Johns Hopkins University Press.

Smith, P.B. (1975). Controlled studies of the outcome of sensitivity training. *Psychological Bulletin, 82,* 597–622.

Smith, T., Snyder, C.R., & Perkins, S.C. (1983). Self-serving funciton of hypochondriacal complaints: Physical symptoms as self-handicapping strategies. *Journal of Personality and Social Psychology, 44,* 787–797.

Smith, T.W. (1983). Change in irrational beliefs and the outcome of rational-emotive psychotherapy. *Journal of Consulting and Clinical Psychology, 51,* 156–157.

Smith, T.W., & Frohm, K.D. (1985). What's so unhealthy about hostility? Construct validity and psychosocial correlates of the Cook and Medley Ho scale. *Health Psychology, 4,* 503–520.

Snider, V.D., Simpson, D.M., Nielsen, S., Gold, J.W.M., Metroka, C.E., & Posner, J.B. (1983). Neurological complications of acquired immune deficiency syndrome: Analysis of 50 patients. *Annals of Neurology, 14,* 403–418.

Snyder, D.K. (1979). Multidimensional assessment of marital satisfaction. *Journal of Marriage and the Family, 41,* 121–131.

Snyder, M. (1983). The influence of individuals on situations: Implications for understanding the links between personality and social behavior. *Journal of Personality, 51,* 497–516.

Snyder, S.H. (1974). *Madness and the brain.* New York: McGraw–Hill.

Snyder, S.H., Banerjee, S.P., Yamamura, H.I., & Greenberg, D. (1974). Drugs, neurotransmitters, and schizophrenia. *Science, 184,* 1243–1253.

Sobell, M.B., & Sobell, L.C. (1976). Second-year treatment outcome of alcoholics treated by individualized behavior therapy: Results. *Behaviour Research and Therapy, 14,* 195–215.

Sobell, M.B., & Sobell, L.C. (1978). *Behavioral treatment of alcohol problems: Individualized therapy and controlled drinking.* New York: Plenum.

Solan, H.A. (1982). Understanding learning disabilities. In J.R. Lachenmeyer & M.S. Gibbs (Eds.), *Psychopathology in childhood.* New York: Gardner.

Solnick, R.L., & Corby, N. (1983). Human sexuality and aging. In D.S. Woodruff & J.E. Birren (Eds.), *Aging: Scientific perspectives and social issues* (2nd ed.). Monterey, Calif.: Brooks/Cole.

Soloff, P.H. et al. (1986). Paradoxical affects of amitriptyline on borderline patients. *American Journal of Psychiatry, 143,* 1603–1605.

Solomon, Z., Mikulincev, M., & Flum, H. (1988). Negative life events, coping response, and combat-related psychopathology: A prospective study. *Journal of Abnormal Psychology, 97,* 302–307.

Sommer, R. (1969). *Personal space: The behavioral basis of design.* Englewood Cliffs, N.J.: Prentice–Hall.

Sorotzin, B. (1984). Nocturnal enuresis: Current perspectives. *Clinical Psychology Review, 4,* 293–316.

Soueif, M.I. (1976). Some determinants of psychological deficits associated with chronic cannabis consumption. *Bulletin of Narcotics, 28,* 25–42.

Spadoni, A.J., & Smith, J.A. (1969). Milieu therapy in schizophrenia. *Archives of General Psychiatry, 20,* 547–557.

Spanier, G.B. (1976). Measuring dyadic adjustment: New scales for assessing the quality of marriage and similar dyads. *Journal of Marriage and the Family, 38,* 15–28.

Spanos, N.P. (1978). Witchcraft in histories of psychiatry: A critical appraisal and an alternative conceptualization. *Psychological bulletin, 35,* 417–439.

Spanos, N.P. (1982). Hypnotic behavior: A cognitive, social psychological perspective. *Research Communications in Psychology, Psychiatry, and Behavior, 7,* 199–213.

Spanos, N.P., Gwynn, M.I., & Stam, H.J. (1983). Instructional demands and ratings of overt and hidden pain during hypnotic analgesia. *Journal of Abnormal Psychology, 92*, 479–488.

Spanos, N.P., Weekes, J.R., & Bertrand, L.D. (1985). Multiple personality: A social psychological perspective. *Journal of Abnormal Psychology, 94*, 362–376.

Spar, J.E. (1982). Dementia in the aged. In L.F. Jarvik & G.W. Small (Eds.), *Psychiatric clinics of North America*. Philadelphia: Saunders.

Sparrow, S.S., Ballo, D.A., & Cicchetti, D.V. (1984). *Vineland Adaptive Behavior Scales*. Circle Pines, Minn.: American Guidance Service.

Special Report to the U.S. Congress on Alcohol and Health (1983). Washington, D.C.: NIAA.

Speer, D.C. (1971). Rate of caller re-use of a telephone crisis service. *Crisis Intervention, 3*, 83–86.

Spengler, A. (1977). Manifest sadomasochism of males: Results of an empirical study. *Archives of Sexual Behavior, 6*, 441–456 .

Sperling, M. (1973). Conversion hysteria and conversion symptoms: A revision of classification and concepts. *Journal of the American Psychoanalytic Association, 21*, 745–771.

Spiegel, D., Bloom, J.R., & Yalom, I. (1981). Group support for patients with metastatic cancer: A randomized prospective outcome study. *Archives of General Psychiatry, 38*, 527–534.

Spielberger, C.D. (1988). *State-trait anger expression inventory: Professional manual*. Odessa, Fla.: Psychological Assessment Resources.

Spielberger, C.D., Johnson, E.H., Russell, S. F., Crane, R.J. & Worden. T.J. (1985). The experience and expression of anger. In M.A. Chesney & R.H. Rosenman (Eds.), *Anger and hostility in cardiovascular and behavioral disorders*. New York: Hemisphere Publishers.

Spiers, P.A. (1982). The Luria–Nebraska Neuropsychological Battery revisited: A theory in practice or just practicing? *Journal of Consulting and Clinical Psychology, 50*, 301–306.

Spinetta, J.J. (1980). Disease-related communication: How to tell. In J. Kellerman (Ed.), *Psychological aspects of childhood cancer*. Springfield, Ill.: Charles C. Thomas.

Spitz, H.H., Carroll, J.G., & Johnson, S.J. (1975). Hypothesis-testing from a limited set: An example of mentally retarded subjects outperforming college subjects. *American Journal of Mental Deficiency, 79*, 736–741.

Spitzer, R.L., & Endicott, J. (1978). *Schedule for affective disorders and schizophrenia*. New York: New York State Psychiatric Institute, Biometrics Research Division.

Spitzer, R.L., Endicott, J., & Gibbon, M. (1979). Crossing the border into borderline personality and borderline schizophrenia. *Archives of General Psychiatry, 36*, 17–24.

Spitzer, R.L., Endicott, J., & Robins, E. (1977). *Research diagnostic criteria* (3rd ed.). New York: New York State Psychiatric Institute, Biometrics Research Division.

Spitzer, R., & Williams, J.D.W. (1986). *Structured clinical interview for DSM-IIR*. New York: New York State Psychiatric Institute, Biometrics Research Division.

Spitzer, R.L., & Williams, J.D.W. (1985). *Structured clinical interview for DSM-IIIR. Patient version*. New York: New York State Psychiatric Institute, Biometrics Research Division.

Sprague, R.L., & Gadow, K.D. (1976). The role of the teacher in drug treatment. *School Review, 85*, 109–140.

Sprague, R.L., & Sleator, E.K. (1977). Methylphenidate in hyperkinetic children: Differences in dose effects on learning and social behavior. *Science, 198*, 1274–1276.

Sprenkle, D.H., & Storm, C.L. (1983). Divorce therapy outcome research: A substantive and methodological review. *Journal of Marital and Family Therapy, 9*, 239–258.

Srole, L., Langner, T.S., Michael, S.T., Opler, M.K., & Rennie, T.A.C. (1962). *Mental health in the metropolis: The midtown Manhattan study*. New York: McGraw–Hill.

Sroufe, L.A. (1975). Drug treatment of children with behavior problems. In F. Horowitz (Ed.), *Review of child development research*. Chicago: University of Chicago Press.

Staats, A.W., & Butterfield, W.H. (1965). Treatment of nonreading in a culturally deprived juvenile delinquent: An application of learning principles. *Child Development, 36*, 925–942.

Staats, A.W., & Staats, C.K. (1963). *Complex human behavior*. New York: Holt, Rinehart & Winston.

Stang, R.R. (1970). The etiology of Parkinson's disease. *Diseases of the Nervous System, 31*, 381–390.

Stanton, A.H., & Schwartz, M.S. (1954). *The mental hospital*. New York: Basic Books.

Stanton, M.D., & Bardoni, A. (1972). Drug flashbacks: Reported frequency in a military population. *American Journal of Psychiatry, 129*, 751–755.

Stanton, M.D., & Figley, C.R. (1978). Treating the Vietnam veteran within the family system. In C.R. Figley (Ed.), *Stress disorders among Vietnam veterans*. New York: Brunner/Mazel.

Starfield, B. (1972). Enuresis: Its pathogenesis and management. *Clinical Pediatrics, 11*, 343–350.

Starr, B.D., & Weiner, M.B. (1981). *The Starr–Weiner report on sex and sexuality in the mature years*. New York: Stein & Day.

Staub, E., Tursky, B., & Schwartz, G.E. (1971). Self-control and predictability: Their effects on reactions to aversive stimulation. *Journal of Personality and Social Psychology, 18*, 157–162.

Steadman, H.J. (1979). *Beating a rap: Defendants found incompetent to stand trial*. Chicago: University of Chicago Press.

Steele, C.M., & Josephs, R.A. (1988). Drinking your troubles away II: An attention-allocation model of alcohol's effects on psychological stress. *Journal of Abnormal Psychology, 97*, 196–205.

Stein, D.M., & Lambert, M.I. (1984). Telephone counseling and crisis interventions: A review. *American Journal of Community Psychology, 12*, 101–126.

Stein, Z., & Susser, M.A. (1971). Changes over time in the incidence and prevalence of mental retardation. In J. Hellmuth (Ed.), *Exceptional infant*. New York: Brunner/Mazel.

Stenmark, D.E., & Dunn, V.K. (1982). Issues related to the training of geropsychologists. In J.F. Santos & G.R. VandenBos (Eds.), *Psychology and the older adult*. Washington, D.C.: American Psychological Association.

Sterman, H.B. (1973). Neurophysiologic and clinical studies of sensorimotor EEG biofeedback training: Some effects on epilepsy. *Seminars in Psychiatry, 5*, 507–525.

Stern, D.B. (1977). Handedness and the lateral distribution of conversion reactions. *Journal of Nervous and Mental Disease, 164*, 122–128.

Stern, R.S., & Cobb, J.P. (1978). Phenomenology of obsessive-compulsive neurosis. *British Journal of Psychiatry, 132*, 233–234.

Stern, S.L., Rush, J., & Mendels, J. (1980). Toward a rational pharmacotherapy of depression. *American Journal of Psychiatry, 137*, 545–552.

Sternbach, R.A. (1966). *Principles of psychophysiology:* New York: Academic Press.

Steuer, J.L., & Hammen, C.L. (1983). Cognitive-behavioral group therapy for the depressed elderly: Issues and adaptations. *Cognitive Theory and Research, 7*, 285–296.

Stevenson, J., & Jones, I.H. (1972). Behavior therapy technique for exhibitionism: A preliminary report. *Archives of General Psychiatry, 27*, 839–841.

Stewart, M.A., Plitts, F.N., Craig, A.G., & Dieruf, W. (1966). The hyperactive child syndrome. *American Journal of Orthopsychiatry, 36*, 861–867.

Stolberg, A.L., & Garrison, K.M. (1985). Evaluating a primary prevention program for children of divorce. *American Journal of Community Psychology, 13*, 111–124.

Stoller, F.H. (1968). Accelerated interaction: A time-limited approach based on the brief intensive group. *International Journal of Group Psychotherapy, 18*, 220–235.

Stone, A.A. (1975). *Mental health and law: A system in transition.* Rockville, Md.: National Institute of Mental Health.

Stone, A.A. (1986). Vermont adopts *Tarasoff:* A real barn-burner. *American Journal of Psychiatry,* **143,** 352–355.

Stone, A.A., Cox, D.S., Valdimarsdottir, H., Jandorf, L., & Neale, J.M. (1987). Evidence that secretory IgA antibody is associated with daily mood. *Journal of Personality and Social Psychology,* **52,** 988–993.

Stone, A.A., and Neale, J.M. (1982). Development of a methodology for assessing daily experiences. In A. Baum and J. Singer (Eds.), *Environment and health.* Hillsdale, N.J.: Erlbaum.

Stone, A.A., & Neale, J.M. (1984). The effects of "severe" daily events on mood. *Journal of Personality and Social Psychology,* **46,** 137–144.

Stone, A.A., Reed, B.R., and Neale, J.M. (1987). Changes in daily event frequency precede episodes of physical symptoms. *Journal of Human Stress,* **13,** 70–74.

Stone, G. (1982). *Health psychology,* a new journal for a new field. *Health Psychology,* **1,** 1–6.

Stone, L.J., & Hokanson, J.E. (1967). Arousal reduction via self-punitive behavior. *Journal of Personality and Social Psychology,* **12,** 72–79.

Stone, M.H. (1986). Exploratory psychotherapy in schizophrenia-spectrum patients: A reevaluation in the light of long-term follow-up of schizophrenic and borderline patients. *Bulletin of the Menninger Clinic,* **50,** 287–306.

Stone, M.H. (1987) Psychotherapy of borderline patients in light of long-term follow-up. *Bulletin of the Menninger Clinic,* **51,** 231–247.

Stringer, A.Y., & Josef, N.C. (1983). Methylphenidate in the treatment of aggression in two patients with antisocial personality disorder. *American Journal of Psychiatry,* **140,** 1365–1366.

Storandt, M. (1977). Age, ability level and methods of administering and scoring the WAIS. *Journal of Gerontology,* **32,** 175–178.

Storandt, M. (1983). *Counseling and therapy with older adults.* Boston: Little, Brown.

Strub, R.L., & Black, F.W. (1981). *Organic brain syndromes: An introduction to neurobehavioral disorders.* Philadelphia: F.A. Davis.

Strupp, H.H., Hadley, S.W., & Gomes-Schwartz, B. (1977). *Psychotherapy for better or worse: An analysis of the problem of negative effects.* New York: Jason Aronson.

Stuart, F.M., Hammond, D.C., & Pett, M.A. (1987). Inhibited sexual desire in women. *Archives of Sexual Behavior,* **16,** 91–106.

Stuart, R.B. (1976). An operant interpersonal program for couples. In D.H.L. Olson (Ed.), *Treating relationships.* Lake Mills, Iowa: Graphic Publishing Company.

Stuart, R.B. (1978). Protection of the right to informed consent to participate in research. *Behavior Therapy,* **9,** 73–82.

Stuart, R.B. (1980). *Helping couples change: A social learning approach to marital therapy.* New York: Guilford.

Stunkard, A.J., & Rush, J. (1974). Dieting and depression reexamined: A critical review of reports of untoward responses during weight reduction for obesity. *Annals of Internal Medicine,* **81,** 526–533.

Sturgis, E.T., & Adams, H.E. (1978). The right to treatment: Issues in the treatment of homosexuality. *Journal of Consulting and Clinical Psychology,* **46,** 165–169.

Sullivan, H.S. (1929). Research in schizophrenia. *American Journal of Psychiatry,* **9,** 553–567.

Sullivan, H.S. (1953). *The interpersonal theory of psychiatry.* New York: Norton.

Summit, R.C. (1983). The child sexual abuse accommodation syndrome. *Child Abuse and Neglect,* **7,** 177–193.

Sundberg, N.D. (1985). The use of future studies in training for prevention and promotion in mental health. *Journal of Primary Prevention,* **6,** 98–114.

Sunderland, A., Watts, K., Baddeley, A.D., & Harris, J.E. (1986). Subjective memory assessment and test performance in elderly adults. *Journal of Gerontology,* **41,** 376–384.

Surwit, R.S. (1982). Behavioral treatment of Raynaud's syndrome in peripheral vascular disease. *Journal of Consulting and Clinical Psychology,* **50,** 922–932.

Sutherland, S., & Scheri, D.J. (1977). Crisis intervention with victims in rape. In D. Chappell, R. Geis, & G. Geis (Eds.), *Forcible rape: The crime, the victim and the offender.* New York: Columbia University Press.

Swartz, M., Blazer, D., George, L., & Landerman, R. (1986). Somatization disorder in a community population. *American Journal of Psychiatry,* **143,** 1403–1408.

Sweer, L., Martin, D.C., Ladd, R.A., Miller, J.K., & Karpf, M. (1988). The medical evaluation of elderly patients with major depression. *Journal of Gerontology: Medical Sciences,* **43,** M53–M58.

Sweet, J.J., Carr, M.A., Rossini, E., & Kasper, C. (1986). Relationship between the Luria–Nebraska Neuropsychological Battery and the WISC-R: Further examination using Kaufman's factors. *International Journal of Clinical Neuropsychology,* **8,** 177–180.

Swift, W.J., Andrews, D., & Barklage, N.E. (1986). The relationship between affective disorder and eating disorders: A review of the literature. *American Journal of Psychiatry,* **143,** 290–299.

Syndulko, K. (1978). Electrocortical investigations of sociopathy. In R.D. Hare & D. Schalling (Eds.), *Psychopathic behaviour: Approaches to research.* New York: Wiley.

Szasz, T.S. (1960). The myth of mental illness. *American Psychologist,* **15,** 113–118.

Szasz, T.S. (1963). *Law, liberty, and psychiatry.* New York: Macmillan Co.

Szasz, T.S. (Ed.). (1974). *The age of madness: The history of involuntary hospitalization.* New York: Jason Aronson.

Tanzi, R.E., Gusella, F., Watkins, P.C., Bruns, G.A.P., St. George-Hyslop, P., Van Keunen, M.L., *et al.* (1987). Amyloid B protein gene: cDNA, mRNA distribution, and genetic linkage near the Alzheimer locus. *Science,* **235,** 880–884.

Tashkin, D.P., Calvarese, B., & Simmons, M. (1978). Respiratory status of 75 chronic marijuana smokers: Comparison with matched controls. University of California at Los Angeles School of Medicine. Abstract in *American Review of Respiratory Diseases,* **117,** 261.

Tate, B.G., & Baroff, G.S. (1966). Aversive control of self-injurious behavior in a psychotic boy. *Behaviour Research and Therapy,* **4,** 281–287.

Taylor, C.B. (1983). DSM-III and behavioral assessment. *Behavioral Assessment,* **5,** 5–14.

Taylor, J.A. (1953). A personality scale of manifest anxiety. *Journal of Abnormal and Social Psychology,* **48,** 285–290.

Teasdale, J.D., Fennell, M.J.V., Hibbert, G.A., & Amies, P.L. (1984). Cognitive therapy for major depressive disorder in primary care. *British Journal of Psychiatry,* **44,** 400–406.

Teri, L., & Lewinsohn, P.M. (1986). Individual and group treatment of unipolar depression: Comparison of treatment outcome and identification of predictors of successful treatment outcome. *Behavior Therapy,* **17,** 215–228.

Teri, L., & Reifler, B.V. (1987). Depression and dementia. In L.L. Carstensen & B.A. Edelsein (Eds.), *Handbook of clinical gerontology.* New York: Pergamon.

Terry, R.D., & Wisniewski, H.M. (1974). Sans teeth, sans eyes, sans taste, sans everything. *Behavior Today,* **5,** 84.

Terry, R.D., & Wisiniewski, H.M. (1977). Structural aspects of aging of the brain. In C. Eisdorfer & R.O. Friedel (Eds.), *Cognitive and emotional disturbances in the elderly.* Chicago: Year Book Medical Publishers.

Thaker, G.K., Tamminga, C.A., Alphs, L.D., Lafferman, J., Ferraro, T.N., & Hare, T.A. (1987). Brain γ-aminobutyric acid abnormality in tardive dyskinesia. *Archives of General Psychiatry,* **44,** 522–531.

The Harvard Medical School Mental Health Letter, 1987, **4,** 1–3.

The sourcebook of criminal justice statistics. (1983) Washington, D.C.: Bureau of Justice and Statistics.

Theodor, L.H., & Mandelcorn, M.S. (1973). Hysterical blindness: A case report and study using a modern psychophysical technique. *Journal of Abnormal Psychology, 82,* 552–553.

Thibaut, J.W., & Kelley, H.H. (1959). *The social psychology of groups.* New York: Wiley.

Thigpen, C.H., & Cleckley, H. (1954). *The three faces of Eve,* Kingsport, Tenn.: Kingsport Press.

Thompson, L.W., Gallagher, D., & Breckenridge, J.S. (1987). Comparative effectiveness of psychotherapies for depressed elders. *Journal of Consulting and Clinical Psychology, 55,* 385–390.

Thoresen, C.E., Friedman, M., Powell, L.H., Gill, J.J., & Ulmer, D.K. (1985). Altering the type A behavior pattern in postinfarction patients. *Journal of Cardiopulmonary Rehabilitation, 5,* 258–266.

Thorndike, E.L. (1935). *The psychology of wants, interests and attitudes.* New York: Appleton–Century.

Thyer, B.A. & Curtis, G.C. (1984). The effects of ethanol on phobic anxiety. *Behaviour Research and Therapy, 22,* 599–610.

Tienari, P., Sorri, A., Lahti, I., Naarala, M.N., Wahlberg, E., Moring, J., Pohjola, J., & Wynne, L.C. (1987). Genetic and psychosocial factors in schizophrenia: The Finnish adoptive family study. *Schizophrenia Bulletin, 13,* 477–484.

Tillich, P. (1952). *The courage to be.* New Haven, Conn.: Yale University Press.

Tippin, J., & Henn, F.A. (1972). Modified leucotomy in the treatment of intractable obsessional neurosis. *American Journal of Psychiatry, 139,* 1601–1603.

Tolber, N. (1986). Meta-analysis of 143 adolescent drug prevention programs: Quantitative outcome results of program participants compared to a control or comparison group. *Journal of Drug Issues, 16,* 537–568.

Tollefson, D.J. (1972). The relationship between the occurrence of fractures and life crisis events. Unpublished master of nursing thesis, University of Washington, Seattle.

Tomlinson, B.E., & Henderson, G. (1976). Some quantitative findings in normal and demented old people. In R.D. Terry & S. Gershon (Eds.), *Neurobiology of aging.* New York: Raven Press.

Torgersen, S. (1983). Genetic factors in anxiety disorders. *Archives of General Psychiatry, 40,* 1085–1089.

Torgerson, S. (1986). Genetics of somatoform disorder. *Archives of General Psychiatry, 43,* 502–505.

Tramontana, J., & Stimbert, V. (1970). Some techniques of behavior modification with an autistic child. *Psychological Reports, 27,* 498.

Treffert, D.A., McAndrew, J.B., & Dreifuerst, P. (1973). An inpatient treatment program and outcome for 57 autistic and schizophrenic children. *Journal of Autism and Childhood Schizophrenia, 3,* 138–153.

Truett, J., Cornfield, J., & Kannel, W. (1967). Multivariate analysis of the risk of coronary heart disease in Framingham. *Journal of Chronic Disease, 20,* 511–524.

Trull, T.J., Widiger, T.A., & Frances, A. (1987). Covariation of criteria for avoidant, schizoid, and dependent personality disorders. *American Journal of Psychiatry, 144,* 767–771.

Tuckman, J., Kleiner, R.J., & Lavell, M. (1959). Emotional content of suicide notes. *American Journal of Psychiatry, 116,* 59–63.

Turkat, I.D., and Maisto, S.A. (1985). Personality disorders: Application of the experimental method to the formulation and modification of personality disorders. In D.H. Barlow (Ed.), *Clinical handbook of psychological disorders.* New York: Guilford.

Turkewitz, H., & OLeary, K.D. (1977). *A comparison of communication and behavioral marital therapy.* Paper presented at the Eleventh Annual Convention of the Association for Advancement of Behavior Therapy, Atlanta.

Turner, B.F., & Adams, C.G. (1988). Reported change in preferred sexual activity. *The Journal of Sex Research, 25,* 289–303.

Turner, R.J., & Sternerg, M.P. (1978). Psychosocial factors in elderly patients admitted to a psychiatric hosital. *Age and aging, 7,* 171–177.

Turner, R.J., & Wagonfeld, M.O. (1967). Occupational mobility and schizophrenia. *American Sociological Review, 32,* 104–113.

Twentyman, C.T., & McFall R.M. (1975). Behavioral training of social skills in shy males. *Journal of Consulting and Clinical Psychology, 43,* 384–395.

Ullmann, L., & Krasner, L. (1975). *A psychological approach to abnormal behavior* (2nd ed.). Englewood Cliffs, N.J.: Prentice–Hall.

Ultmann, M., Belman, A., Ruff, H., Novick, B., Cone-Wesson, B., Cohen, H., & Rubinstein, A. (1985). Developmental abnormalities in children with acquired immune deficiency syndrome (AIDS) and AIDS-related complex. *Developmental Medicine and Child Neurology, 27,* 563–571.

Umbarger, C.C., Dalsimer, J.S., Morrison, A.P., & Breggin, P.R. (1962). *College students in a mental hospital.* New York: Grune & Stratton.

Upper, D. & Ross, S.M. (Eds.), (1980). *Behavioral group therapy 1980: An annual review.* Champaign, Ill.: Research Press.

U.S. Bureau of the Census (1986). *Statistical brief.* Washington, D.C.: U.S. Government Printing Office.

U.S. Bureau of the Census (1987). *America's centenarians (data from the 1980 census).* Washington, D.C.: U.S. Government Printing Office.

U.S. Bureau of the Census (1988). *United States population estimates, by age, sex, and race: 1980–1987.* Washington, D.C.: U.S. Government Printing Office.

U.S. Department of Commerce, U.S. Bureau of the Census (1988). *Poverty in the United States: 1986.* Washington, D.C.: U.S. Government Printing Office.

U.S. Department of Health and Human Services (1982). *Prevention in adulthood: Self-motivated quitting.* In *Cancer: The health consequences of smoking, a report of the Surgeon General.* Washington, D.C.: U.S. Government Printing Office.

U.S. Public Health Service (1976). *Physicians' drug prescribing patterns in skilled nursing facilities.* Washington, D.C.: U.S. Department of Health, Education, and Welfare.

Vaillant, G.E. (1979). Natural history of male psychologic health: Effects of mental health on physical health. *New England Journal of Medicine, 301,* 1249–1254.

Vaillant, G.E. (1983). *The natural history of alcoholism: Causes, patterns, and paths to recovery.* Cambridge, Mass.: Harvard University Press.

Valenstein, E.S. (1973). *Brain control.* New York: Wiley.

van Egeren, L.F., & Mararasmi, S. (1987). A computerized diary for ambulatory blood pressure monitoring. In N. Schneiderman (Ed.), *Handbook on methods and measurements in cardiovascular behavioral medicine.* New York: Plenum.

Van Praag, H., Korf, J., & Schut, D. (1973). Cerebral monamines and depression: An investigation with the probenecid technique. *Archives of General Psychiatry, 28,* 827–831.

Van Putten, T., May, P.R.A., Marder, S.R., & Wittman, L.A. (1981). Subjective response to antipsychotic drugs. *Archives of General Psychiatry, 38,* 187–190.

VandenBos, G.R., Stapp, J., & Kilburg, R.R. (1981). Health service providers in psychology: Results of the 1978 APA Human Resources Survey. *American Psychologist, 36,* 1395–1418.

Vardaris, R.M., Weisz, D.J., Fazel, A., & Rawitch, A.B. (1976). Chronic administration of delta-9-tetrahydrocannabinol to pregnant rats: Studies of pup behavior and placental transfer. *Pharmacology and Biochemistry of Behavior, 4,* 249–254.

Varner, R.V., & Gaitz, C.M. (1982). Schizophrenic and paranoid disorders in the aged.

In L.F. Jarvik & G.W. Small (Eds.), *Psychiatric clinics of North America*. Philadelphia: Saunders.

Varni, J.W. (1981). Self-regulation techniques in the management of chronic arthritic pain in hemophilia. *Behavior Therapy, 12,* 185–194.

Varni, J.W., & Dietrich, S.L. (1981). Behavioral pediatrics: Towards a reconceptualization. *Behavioral Medicine Update, 3,* 5–7.

Varni, J.W., & Wallander, J.L. (1984). Adherence to health-related regimens in pediatric chronic disorders. *Clinical Psychology Review, 4,* 585–596.

Vaughn, C.E., & Leff, J.P. (1976). The influence of family and social factors on the course of psychiatric illness. A comparison of schizophrenic and depressed neurotic patients. *British Journal of Psychiatry, 129,* 125–137.

Verbrugge, L.M. (1979). Female illness rates and illness behavior. *Women's Health, 4,* 61–79.

Videka-Sherman, L., & Lieberman, M. (1985). The effects of self-help and psychotherapy interventions on child loss: The limits of recovery. *American Journal of Orthopsychiatry, 55,* 70–82.

Vincente, K., Wiley, J.A., & Carrington, R.A. (1979). The risk of institutionalization before death. *Gerontologist, 19,* 361–367.

Voeltz, L.M. (1977). Syntactic rule mediation and echolalia in autistic children. Unpublished manuscript, University of Hawaii.

Voeltz, L.M. (1980). Children's attitudes toward handicapped peers. *American Journal of Mental Deficiency, 84,* 455–464.

Voeltz, L.M. (1982). Effects of structured interactions with severely handicapped peers on children's attitudes. *American Journal of Mental Deficiency, 86,* 380–390.

Volkmar, F., & Cohen, D.J. (1985). The experience of infantile autism: A first-person account by Tony W. *Journal of Autism and Developmental Disorders, 15,* 47–54.

Von Felsinger, J.M., Lasagna, L., & Beecher, H.K. (1956). The response of normal men to lysergic acid derivatives. *Journal of Clinical and Experimental Psychopathology, 17,* 414–428.

Von Pohl, R. (1982). A study to assess the effects of rational- emotive therapy with a selected group of emotionally disturbed children in day and residential treatment. Unpublished doctoral dissertation, University of Alabama.

Von Wright, J.M., Pekanmaki, L., & Malin, S. (1971). Effects of conflict and stress on alcohol intake in rats. *Quarterly Journal of Studies on Alcohol, 32,* 420–441.

Vygotsky, I .S. (1978). *Mind in society: The development of higher psyhological processes*. Edited and translated by M. Cole, V. John-Steiner, S. Scribner, & E. Souberman. Cambridge, Mass.: Harvard University Press.

Wachtel, E.F., & Wachtel, P.L. (1986). *Family dynamics in individual psychotherapy: A guide to clinical strategies*. New York: Guilford.

Wachtel, P.L. (1973). Psychodynamics, behavior therapy, and the implacable experimenter: An inquiry into the consistency of personality. *Journal of Abnormal Psychology, 82,* 324–334.

Wachtel, P. (1977). *Psychoanalysis and behavior therapy: Toward an integration*. New York: Basic Books.

Wachtel, P.L. (1982). Vicious circles: The self and the rhetoric of emerging and unfolding. *Contemporary Psychoanalysis, 18,* 259–273.

Wadden, T.A. (1984). Relaxation therapy for essential hypertension: Specific or nonspecific effects. *Journal of Psychosomatic Research, 28,* 53–61.

Waldfogel, S. (1959). Emotional crisis in a child. In A. Burton (Ed.), *Case studies in counseling and psychotherapy*. Englewood Cliffs, NJ: Prentice-Hall.

Waldron, I. (1978). The coronary-prone behavior pattern, blood pressure, employment and socio-economic status in women. *Journal of Psychosomatic Research, 22,* 79–87.

Walen, S., Hauserman, N.M., & Lavin, P. J. (1977). *Clinical guide to behavior therapy*. Baltimore: William & Wilkins.

Wallace, C.J., Boone, S.E., Donahoe, C.P., & Foy, D.W. (1985). The chronically mentally disabled: Independent living skills training. In D.H. Barlow (Ed.), *Clinical handbook of psychological disorders*. New York: Guilford.

Wallace, C.J., & Liberman, R.P. (1985). Social skills training for patients with schizophrenia: A controlled clinical trial. *Psychiatry Research, 15,* 239–247.

Wallace, C.J., Nelson, C.J., Liberman, R.P., Aitchison, R.A., Lukoff, D., Elder, J.P., & Ferris, C. (1980). A review and critique of social skills training with schizophrenic patients. *Schizophrenia Bulletin, 6,* 42–63.

Walker, E., Bettes, B.A., Kain, E., & Harvey, P. (1985). Relationship of gender and marital status with symptomatology in psychotic patients. *Journal of Abnormal Psychology, 94,* 42–50.

Wallander, J.L., & Hubert, N.C. (1985). Long-term prognosis for children with attention deficit disorder with hyperactivity (ADD/H). In B.B. Lahey & A.E. Kazdin (Eds.), *Advances in child clinical psychology* (Vol. 8). New York: Plenum.

Wallerstein, J.S. (1983). Children of divorce: Stress and developmental tasks. In N. Gar-

mezy & M. Rutter (Eds.), *Stress, coping and development in children*. New York: McGraw-Hill.

Walsh, B.T., Stewart, J.W., Roose, S.P., Gladis, M., & Glassman A.H. (1984). Treatment of bulimia with phenelzine. *Archives of General Psychiatry, 41,* 1105–1109.

Walton, D. (1961). The application of learning theory to the treatment of a case of somnambulism. *Journal of Clinical Psychology, 37,* 96–99.

Ward, C.H., Beck, A.T., Mendelson, M., Mock, E., & Erbaugh, J.K. (1962). The psychiatric nomenclature: Reasons for diagnostic disagreement. *Archives of General Psychiatry, 7,* 198–205.

Warheit, G.J., Arey, S.A., & Swanson, E. (1976). Patterns of drug use: An epidemiologic overview. *Journal of Drug Issues, 6,* 223–237.

Warner, K.E. (1977). The effects of the antismoking campaign on cigarette consumption. *American Journal of Public Health, 67,* 645–650.

Warren, C.A.B. (1982). *The court as last resort: Mental illness and the law*. Chicago: University of Chicago Press.

Warren, N.J., Grew, R.S., Ilgen, E.R., Konanc, J.T., Washton, A.M., & Resnick, R.B. (1980). Clonidine for opiate detoxification: Outpatient clinical trials. *American Journal of Psychiatry, 137,* 1121–1122.

Warren, R., Smith, G., & Velten, E. (1984). Rational-emotive therapy and the reduction of interpersonal anxiety in junior high school students. *Adolescence, 19,* 643–648

Waskow, I.E. (1984). Specification of the technique variable in the NIMH Treatment of Depression Collaborative Research Program. In J.B.W. Williams & R.L. Spitzer (Eds.), *Psychotherapy research: Where are we and where should we go?* New York: Guilford.

Watson, G.C., & Buranen, C. (1979). The frequency and identification of false positive conversion reactions. *Journal of Nervous and Mental Disease, 167,* 243–247.

Watson, J.B. (1913). Psychology as the behaviorist views it. *Psychological Review, 20,* 158–177.

Watson, J.B., & Rayner, R. (1920). Conditioned emotional reactions. *Journal of Experimental Psychology, 3,* 1–14.

Watt, N.F. (1974). Childhood and adolescent roots of schizophrenia. In D. Ricks, A. Thomas, & M. Roff (Eds.), *Life history research in psychopathology* (Vol. 3). Minneapolis: University of Minnesota Press.

Watt, N.F., Stolorow, R.D., Lubensky, A.W., & McClelland, D.C. (1970). School adjustment and behavior of children hospitalized for schizophrenia as adults. *American Journal of Orthopsychiatry, 40,* 637–657.

Webster, J.S., & Hammer, D. (1983). Thermistor measurement of male sexual arousal. *Psychophysiology, 20,* 111–115.

Weg, R.B. (Ed.). (1983). *Sexuality in the later years: Roles and behavior.* New York: Academic Press.

Wegner, D.M., Schneider, D.J., Carter, S.R., & White, T.L. (1987). Paradoxical effects of thought suppression. *Journal of Personality and Social Psychology, 53,* 5–13.

Weick, K.E. (1984). Small wins: Redefining the scale of social problems. *American Psychologist, 39,* 40–49.

Weinberg, G. (1972). *Society and the healthy homosexual.* New York: St. Martin's Press.

Weinberger, D.R., Cannon-Spoor, H.E., Potkin, S.G., & Wyatt, R.J. (1980). Poor premorbid adjustment and CT scan abnormalities in chronic schizophrenia. *American Journal of Psychiatry, 137,* 1410–1413.

Weinberger, D.R., Wagner, R.L., & Wyatt, R.J. (1983). Neuropathological studies of schizophrenia: A selective review. *Schizophrenia Bulletin, 9,* 193–212.

Weiner, B. (1986). An attributional theory of motivation and emotion. Unpulished manuscript, UCLA.

Weiner, B., Frieze, L., Kukla, A., Reed, L., Rest, S., & Rosenbaum, R.M. (1971). *Perceiving the causes of success and failure.* New York: General Learning Press.

Weiner, H. (1977). *Psychobiology and human disease.* New York: Elsevier.

Weiner, J.W. (1969). The effectiveness of a suicide prevention program. *Mental Hygiene, 53,* 357–363.

Weingartner, H., & Silverman, E. (1982). Models of cognitive impairment: Cognitive changes in depression. *Psychopharmacology Bulletin, 18,* 27–42.

Weinstein, K.A., Davison, G.C., DeQuattro, V., & Allen, J.W. (1986). *Type A behavior and cognitions: Is hostility the bad actor?* Paper presented at the 94th annual convention of the American Psychological Association, Washington, D.C.

Weintraub, M., & Standish, R. (1983). Nabilone: An antiemetic for patients undergoing cancer chemotherapy. *Hospital Formulary. 18,* 1033–1035.

Weintraub, S., Liebert, D.E., & Neale, J.M. (1975). Teacher ratings of children vulnerable to psychopathology. *American Journal of Orthopsychiatry, 45,* 838–845.

Weintraub, S. Prinz, R., & Neale, J.M. (1978). Peer evaluations of the competence of children vulnerable to psychopathology. *Journal of Abnormal Child Psychology, 6,* 461–473.

Weiss, B., Weisz, J.R., & Bromfield, R. (1986). Performance of retarded and nonretarded persons on information-processing tasks: Further tests of the similar structure hypothesis. *Psychological Bulletin, 100,* 157–175.

Weiss, G. (1983). Long-term outcome: Findings, concepts, and practical implications. In M. Rutter (Ed.), *Developmental neuropsychiatry.* New York: Guilford.

Weiss, R.L., & Cerreto, M.C. (1980). The Marital Status Inventory: Development of a measure of dissolution potential. *American Journal of Family Therapy, 8,* 80–85.

Weiss, R.L., Hops, H., & Patterson, G.R. (1973). A framework for conceptualizing marital conflict, a technology for altering it, some data for evaluating it. In L.A. Hamerlynck, L.C. Handy, & E.J. Mash (Eds.), *Behavior change: Methodology, concepts, and practice.* Champaign, Ill.: Research Press.

Weiss, R.L., & Perry, B.A. (1983). The Spouse Observation Checklist: Development and clinical applications. In E.E. Filsinger (Ed.), *Marriage and family assessment.* Beverly Hills, Calif.: Sage.

Weiss, R.L., & Wieder, G.B. (1982). Marital and family distress. In A.S. Bellack, M. Hersen, & A.E. Kazdin (Eds.), *International handbook of behavior modification.* New York: Plenum.

Weiss, S. (1986). Introduction and overview. In K.A. Matthews, S.J. Weiss, T. Detre, T.M. Dembroski, B. Falkner, S.B. Manuck, & R.B. Williams (Eds.), *Handbook of stress, reactivity, and cardiovascular disease.* New York: Wiley.

Weisserg, R.P., Gesten, E.L., Rapkin, B.D., Cowen, E.L., Davidson, E., deApodaca, R.F., & McKim, B.J. (1981). Evaluation of a social-problem-solving training program for suburban and inner-city third-grade children. *Journal of Consulting and Clinical Psychology, 49,* 251–261.

Weissman, A.N., & Beck, A.T. (1978). *Development and validation of the Dysfunctional Attitude Sale.* Paper presented at the 12th annual convention of the Association for Advancement of Behavior Therapy, Chicago.

Weissman, M.M., Kidd, K.K., & Prusoff, B.A. (1982). Variability in rates of affective disorders in relatives of depressed and normal probands. *Archives of General Psychiatry, 39,* 1397–1403.

Weissman, M.M., Klerman, G.L., & Paykel, E.S. (1971). Clinical evaluation of hostility in depression. *American Journal of Psychiatry, 128,* 261–266.

Weissman, M.M., Klerman, G.L., Prusoff, B.A., Sholomskas, D., & Padian, N. (1981). Depressed outpatients. Results one year after treatment with drugs and/or interpersonal psychotherapy. *Archives of General Psychiatry, 38,* 51–56.

Weissman, M.M., & Myers, J.K. (1978). Affective disorders in a U.S. urban community. *Archives of General Psychiatry, 35,* 1304–1310.

Weissman, M.M., Prusoff, B.A., DiMascio, A., New, C., Goklaney, M., & Klerman, G.L. (1979). The efficacy of drugs and psychotherapy in the treatment of acute depressive episodes. *American Journal of Psychiatry, 36,* 555–558.

Weisz, J.R., & Yeates, K.D. (1981). Cognitive development in retarded and nonretarded persons: Piagetian tests of the similar structure hypothesis. *Psychological Bulletin, 90,* 153–178.

Weitzenhoffer, A.M., & Hilgard, E.R. (1959). *Stanford hypnotic susceptibility scale, Forms A and B.* Palo Alto, Calif: Consulting Psychologists Press.

Wells, C.C. (1978). Chronic brain disease: An overview. *American Journal of Psychiatry, 135,* 1–12.

Wells, C.E., & Duncan, G.W. (1980). *Neurology for psychiatrists.* Philadelphia: F.A. Davis Co.

Wells, J.K., Howard, G.S., Nowlin, W.F., & Vargas, M.J. (1986). Presurgical anxiety and postsurgical pain and adjustment: Effects of a stress inoculation procedure. *Journal of Consulting and Clinical Psychology, 54,* 831–835.

Wender, P.H., Kety, S.S., Rosenthal, D., Schulsinger, F., Ortmann, J., & Lunde, I. (1986). Psychiatric disorders in the biological and adoptive families of adopted individuals with affective disorders. *Archives of General Psychiatry, 43,* 923–929.

Werry, J.S., Methven, R.J., Fitzpatrick, J., & Dixon, H. (1983). The interrater reliability of DSM-III in children. *Journal of Abnormal Child Psychology, 11,* 341–354.

Wertsch, J. (1979). From social interactions to higher psychological processes: A clarification and application of Vygotsky's theory. *Human Development, 22,* 1–22.

Wester, P., Eriksson, S., Forsell, A., Puu, G., & Adolfsson, R. (1988). Monoamine metabolite concentrations and cholinesterase activities in cerebrospinal fluid of progressive dementia paients: Relation to clinical parameters. *Acta Neurologica Scandinavica, 77,* 12–21.

Whalen, C.K. (1983). Hyperactivity, learning problems, and the attention deficit disorders. In T.H. Ollendick & M. Hersen (Eds.), *Handbook of child psychopathology.* New York: Plenum.

Whalen, C.K., & Henker, B. (1985). The social worlds of hyperactive (ADDH) children. *Clinical Psychology Review, 5,* 447–478.

Whanger, A.D. (1973). Paranoid syndrome of the senium. In E. Eisdorfer & W.E. Fann (Eds.), *Psychopharmacology—Aging.* New York: Plenum.

White, J., Davison, G.C., & White, K. Articulated thoughts and cognitive distortion in depressed and non-depressed psychiatric patients. Unpublished manuscript, University of Southern California, 1989.

White, W.A. (1932). *Outlines of psychiatry* (13th ed.). New York: Nervous and Mental Disease Publishing Company.

White, W.C. & Boskind-White, M. (1981). An experiential-behavioral approach to the treatment of bulimarexia. *Psychotherapy: Theory, Research, and Practice*, **18**, 501–507.

Whitehead, A. (1973). Verbal learning and memory in elderly depression. *British Journal of Psychiatry*, **123**, 203–208.

Whitlock, F.A. (1967). The aetiology of hysteria. *Acta Psychiatrica Scandinavica*, **43**, 144–162.

Whittington, F.J. (1984). Addicts and alcoholics. In E.B. Palmore (Ed.), *Handbook on the aged in the United States*. Westport, Conn.: Greenwood Press.

Wickens, D.D. Allen, C.K., & Hill, F.A. (1963). Effects of instruction on extinction of the conditioned GSR. *Journal of Experimental Psychologoy*, **66**, 235–240.

Wicks-Nelson, R., & Israel, A.C. (1984). *Behavior disorders of childhood*. Englewood Cliffs, N.J.: Prentice–Hall.

Widiger, T.A., Frances, A. Spitzer, R.L., & Williams, J.B.W. (1988). The DSM-III personality disorders: An overview. *American Journal of Psychiatry*, **145**, 786–795.

Widiger, T.A., Frances, A., & Trull, T.J. (1987). A psychometric analysis of the social-interpersonal and cognitive-perceptual items for the schizotypal personality disorder. *Archives of General Psychiatry*, **44**, 741–745.

Widiger, T.A., Trull, T.J., Hurt, S., Clarkin, J., & Frances, A. (1987). A multidimensional scaling of the DSM-III personality disorders. *Archives of General Psychiatry*, **44**, 557–566.

Wiener G. (1970). Varying psychological sequelae of lead ingestion in children. *Public Health Reports*, **85.** 19–24.

Wiens, A.N., & Menustik, C.E. (1983). Treatment outcome and patient characteristics in an aversion therapy program for alcoholism. *American Psychologist*, **38**, 1089–1096.

Wig, N.N., & Varma, V.K. (1977). Patterns of long-term heavy cannabis use in North India and its effects on cognitive functions. A preliminary report. *Drug and Alcohol Dependence*, **2**, 211–219.

Wigdor, B., & Morris, G. (1977). A comparison of twenty-year medical histories of individuals with depressive and paranoid states. *Journal of Gerontology*, **32**, 160–163.

Wiggins, J. (1968). Inconsistent socialization. *Psychological Reports*, **23**, 303–336.

Wikler, A. (1980). *Opiod dependence: Mechanisms and treatment*. New York: Plenum.

Wilkins, L.T. (1969). *Evaluation of penal measures*. New York: Random House.

Williams, H., & McNicol, K.N. (1969). Prevalence, natural history and relationship of wheezy bronchitis and asthma in children: An epidemiological study. *British Medical Journal*, **4**, 321–325.

Williams, J.M., Little, M.M., Scates, S., & Blockman, N. (1987). Memory complaints and abilities among depressed older adults. *Journal of Consulting and Clinical Psychology*, **55**, 595–598.

Williams, K., Goodman, M., & Green, R. (1985). Parent–child factors in gender role socialization in girls. *Journal of the American Academy of Child Psychiatry*, **26**, 720–731.

Williams, L., Martin, G.L., McDonald, S., Hardy, L., & Lambert, L., Sr. (1975). Effects of a backscratch contingency of reinforcement for table serving on social interaction with severely retarded girls. *Behavior Therapy*, **6**, 220–229.

Williams, M.E., Davison, G.C., & DeQuattro, V. Cognitions of type A and type B individuals in response to social criticism. Unpublished manuscript, University of Southern California, Los Angeles, 1989.

Williams, R.B. (1987). Psychological factors in coronary artery disease: Epidemiological evidence. *Circulation*, **76**, 117–123.

Williams, R.B., Barefoot, J.C., Haney, T.H., Harrell, F.E., Blumenthal, J., Pryor, D.B., & Peterson, B. (1986). *Type A behavior and angiographically documented coronary atherosclerosis in a sample of 2,289 patients*. Paper presented at the annual meeting of the Psychosomatic Society.

Williams, R.B., Haney, T.L., Lee, K.L., Kong, Y., Blumenthal, J.A., & Whalen, R.E. (1980). Type A behavior, hostility, and coronary atherosclerosis. *Psychosomatic Medicine*, **42**, 539–549.

Williams, S.L., & Rappoport, A. (1983). Cognitive treatment in the natural environment for agoraphobics. *Behavior Therapy*, **14**, 299–313.

Wilson, G.T. (1987). Chemical aversion conditioning as a treatment for alcoholism: A re-analysis. *Behaviour Research and Therapy*, **25**, 503–516.

Wilson, G.T., & Abrams, D. (1977). Effects of alcohol on social anxiety and physiological arousal: Cognitive versus pharmacological processes. *Cognitive Therapy and Research*, **1**, 195–210.

Wilson, G.T. & Davison, G.C. (1969). Aversion techniques in behavior therapy: Some theoretical and metatheoretical considerations. *Journal of Consulting and Clinical Psychology*, **33**, 327–329.

Wilson, G.T., & Davison, G.C. (1971). Processes of fear reduction in systematic desensitization. Animal studies. *Psychological Bulletin*, **76**, 1–14.

Wilson, G.T., & Lawson, D.M. (1976). The effects of alcohol on sexual arousal in wo-

men. *Journal of Abnormal Psychology*, **85**, 489–497.

Wilson, G.T., & O'Leary, K.D. (1980). *Principles of behavior therapy*. Englewood Cliffs, N.J.: Prentice–Hall.

Wilson, G.T., & Rachman, S. (1983). Meta-analysis and the evaluations of psychotherapy outcome: Limitations and liabilities. *Journal of Consulting and Clinical Psychology*, **51**, 54–64.

Wilson, R.C., Christensen, P.R., Merrifield, P.R., & Guilford, J.P. (1975). *Alternative uses test*. Beverly Hills, Calif.: Sheridan Psychological Co.

Wilson, T.D., Goldin, J.C., & Charbonneau-Powis, M. (1983). Comparative efficacy of behavioral and cognitive treatments of depression. *Cognitive Therapy and Research*, **7**, 111–124.

Wilson, W.R. (1975). Unobtrusive induction of positive attitudes. Unpublished doctoral dissertation, University of Michigan.

Wiltz, N.A., & Patterson, G.R. (1974). An evaluation of parent training procedures designed to alter inappropriate aggressive behavior of boys. *Behavior Therapy*, **5**, 215–224.

Wincze, J.P., Bansal, S., & Malamud, M. (1986). The effects of medroxyprogesterone acetate on subjective arousal, arousal to erotic stimulation, and nocturnal penile tumescence in male sex offenders. *Archives of Sexual Behavior*, **15**, 293–305.

Winett, R.A., & Winkler, R.C. (1972). Current behavior modification in the classroom: Be still, be quiet, be docile. *Journal of Applied Behavior Analysis*, **5**, 499–504.

Wing, L. (1976). Diagnosis, clinical description, and prognosis. In L. Wing (Ed.), *Early childhood autism: Clinical, educational, and social aspects*. New York: Pergamon.

Wingard, D.L., Jones, D.W., & Kaplan, R.M. (1987). Institutional care utilization by the elderly: A critical review. *The Gerontologist*, **27**, 156–163.

Winick, C. (1962). Maturing out of narcotic addiction. *Bulletin on Narcotics*, **14**, 1–7.

Winkler, R. (1977). What types of sex-role behavior should behavior modifiers promote? *Journal of Applied Behavior Analysis*, **10**, 549–552.

Winokur, G. (1963). Sexual behavior: Its relationship to certain effects and psychiatric diseases. In G. Winokur (Ed.), *Determinants of human sexual behavior*. Springfield, Ill.: Charles C. Thomas.

Winokur, G. (1979). Unipolar depression. *Archives of General Psychiatry*, **36**, 47–52.

Winokur, G., & Clayton, P.J. (1967). Family history studies: I. Two types of affective disorders separated according to genetic and clinical factors. In J. Wortis (Ed.), *Recent advances in biological psychiatry* (Vol. 9). New York: Plenum.

Winokur, G., Clayton, P.J., & Reich, T. (1969). *Manic-depressive illness*. St. Louis: Mosby.

Winokur, A., March, V., & Mendels, J. (1980). Primary affective disorder in relatives of patients with anorexia nervosa. *American Journal of Psychiatry, 137,* 695–698.

Winters, K.C., & Neale, J.M. (1985). Mania and low self-esteem. *Journal of Abnormal Psychology, 94,* 282–290.

Winters, K.C., Weintraub, S., & Neale, J.M. (1981). Validity of MMPI codetypes in identifying DSM-III schizophrenics, unipolars and bipolars. *Journal of Consulting and Clinical Psychology, 49,* 486–487.

Wise, R.A., (1987). The neurobiology of craving: Implications for the understanding and treatment of addiction. *Journal of Abnormal Psychology, 97,* 118–132.

Wise, T. (1978). Where the public peril begins: A survey of psychotherapists to determine the effects of Tarasoff. *Stanford Law Review, 31,* 165–190.

Wolberg, L.R. (1954). *The technique of psychotherapy*. New York: Grune & Stratton.

Wolchik, S.A., Spencer, S.L., & List, I.S. (1983). Volunteer bias in research employing vaginal measures of sexual arousal. *Archives of Sexual Behavior, 12,* 399–408.

Wold, D.A. (1968). *The adjustment of siblings to childhood leukemia*. Unpublished medical thesis, University of Washington, Seattle.

Wolf, A. (1949). The psychoanalysis of group. *American Journal of Psychotherapy, 3,* 16–50.

Wolf, M., Risley, T., & Mees, H. (1964). Application of operant conditioning procedures to the behavior problems of an autistic child. *Behaviour Research and Therapy, 1,* 305–312.

Wolf, M.M. (1978). Social validity: The case for subjective measurement or how applied behavior analysis is finding its heart. *Journal of Applied Behavior Analysis, 11,* 203–214.

Wolin, S.J. (1980). Introduction: Psychosocial consequences. In *Alcoholism and alcohol abuse among women: Research issues*. Rockville, Md.: National Institute on Alcohol Abuse and Alcoholism.

Wolpe, J. (1958). *Psychotherapy be reciprocal inhibition*. Stanford, Calif.: Stanford University Press.

Wolpe, J. (1980). Cognitive behavior and its role in psychotherapy: An integrative account. In M.J. Mahoney (Ed.), *Psychotherapy process: Current issues and future directions*. New York: Plenum.

Wolpe, J., & Rachman, S.J. (1960). Psychoanalytic "evidence," A critique based on Freud's case of Little Hans. *Journal of Nervous and Mental Disease, 131,* 135–147.

Wong, D.F., Wagner, H.N. Tune, L.E., Dannals, R.F., Pearlson, G.D., Links, J.M., *et al.* (1986). Positron emission tomography reveals elevated D2 dopamine receptors in drug-naive schizophrenics. *Science, 234,* 1558–1562.

Wood, D.L., Sheps, S.G., *et al.* (1984). Cold pressor test as a predictor of hypertension. *Hypertension, 6,* 301–306.

Wood, L.F., & Jacobson, N.S. (1985). Marital distress. In D.H. Barlow (Ed.), *Clinical handbook of psychological disorders*. New York: Guilford.

Woodruff, R.A., Goodwin, D.W., & Guze, S.B. (1974). *Psychiatric diagnosis*. New York: Oxford University Press.

Woods, S.W., Charney, D.S., Goodman, W.K., and Heninger, G.R. (1987). Carbon dioxide induced anxiety. *Archives of General Psychiatry, 44,* 365–375.

World Health Organization (1948). *Manual of the international statistical classification of diseases, injuries and causes of death*. Geneva: WHO.

Wortman, C.B., & Brehm, J.W. (1975). Responses to uncontrollable outcomes: An integration of the reactance theory and the learned helplessness model. In L. Berkowitz (Ed.), *Advances in social psychology*. New York. Academic Press.

Wright, D.S. (1971). *The psychology of moral behavior*. Harmondsworth, England: Penguin.

Wright, J.C. (1976). A comparison of systematic desensitization and social skill acquisition in the modification of social fear. *Behavior Therapy, 7,* 205–210.

Wurmser, L. (1981). Psychodynamics of substance abuse. In J. Lowinson & P. Ruiz (Eds.), *Substance abuse: Clinical problems and perspectives*. Baltimore: Williams & Wilkins.

Yalom, I.D. (1980). *Existential psychotherapy*. New York: Basic Books.

Yalom, I.D. (1985). *The theory and practice of group psychotherapy* (3rd ed.). New York: Basic Books.

Yalom, I.D., Green, R., & Fisk, N. (1973). Prenatal exposure to female hormones: Effect on psychosexual development in boys. *Archives of General Psychiatry, 28,* 554–561.

Yurchenco, H. (1970). *A mighty hard road: The Woody Guthrie Story*. New York: McGraw–Hill.

Zane, M.D. (1984). Psychoanalysis and contextual analysis of phobias. *Journal of the American Academy of Psychoanalysis, 12,* 553–568.

Zarit, S.H. (1980). *Aging and mental disorders: Psychological approaches to assessment and treatment*. New York: Free Press.

Zarit, S.H., Eiler, J., & Hassinger M. (1985). Clinical assessment. In J.E. Birren & K.W. Schaie (Eds.), *Handbook of psychology of aging* (2nd ed.). New York: Van Nostrand–Reinhold.

Zarit, S.H., Todd, P.A., & Zarit, J.M. (1986). Subjective burden of husbands and wives as caregivers: A longitudinal study. *The Gerontologist, 26,* 260–266.

Zeaman, D., & Hanley, P. (1983). Stimulus preferences as structural features. In T.J. Tighe & B.E. Shepp (Eds.), *Perception, cognition, and development*. Hillsdale, N.J.: Erlbaum.

Zeaman, D., & House, B.J. (1979). A review of attention theory. In N.R. Ellis (Ed.), *Handbook of mental deficiency, psychological theory and research* (2nd ed.). Hillsdale, N.J.: Erlbaum.

Zeigob, L.E., Arnold, S., & Forehand, R. (1975). An examination of observer effects in patient–child interactions. *Child Development, 46,* 509–512.

Zeiss, A.M., Zeiss, R.A. & Dornbrand L. (1988). *Assessing and treating sexual problems in older couples*. Paper presented at the meeting of the Gerontological Society of America, San Francisco, November, 1988.

Zerbin-Rüdin, E. (1972). Genetic research and the theory of schizophrenia. *International Journal of Mental Health, 1,* 42–62.

Ziegler, F.J., Imboden, J.B., & Meyer, E. (1960). Contemporary conversion reactions: A clinical study. *American Journal of Psychiatry, 116,* 901–910.

Zigler, E. (1967). Familial mental retardation: A continuing dilemma. *Science, 155,* 292–298.

Zigler, E. (1969). Development versus difference theories of mental retardation and the problem of motivation. *American Journal of Mental Deficiency, 73,* 536–556.

Zigler, E., & Finn, M. (1982). A vision of child care in the 1980s. In L.A. Bond & J.M. Joffe (Eds.), *Facilitating infant and early child development*. Hanover, N.H.: University Press of New England.

Zilbergeld, B., & Evans, M. (1980). The inadequacy of Masters and Johnson, *Psychology Today, 14,* 28–43.

Zilboorg, G., & Henry, G.W. (1941). *A history of medical psychology*. New York: Norton.

Zillman, D., & Bryant, J. (1984). Effects of massive exposure to pornography. In N.M. Malamuth & E. Donnerstein (Eds.), *Pornography and sexual aggression*. New York: Academic Press.

Zimbardo, P.G., Andersen, S.M., & Kabat, L.G. (1981). Paranoia and deafness: An experimental investigation, *Science, 212,* 1529–1531.

Zimberg, S. (1978). Diagnosis and treatment of elderly alcoholics. *Alcoholism: Clinical and Experimental Research, 2,* 27–29.

Zimmerman, M. (1988). Why are we rushing to publish DSM-IV? *Archives of General Psychiatry, 45,* 1135–1138.

Zimmerman, M. Coryell, W., Pfohl, B., & Stangl, D. (1986). The validity of four types of endogenous depression. *Archives of General Psychiatry, 43,* 234–245.

Zitrin, C.M., Klein, D.F., & Woerner, M.G. (1980). Treatment of agoraphobia with group exposure *in vivo* and imipramine. *Archives of General Psychiatry, 37,* 63–72.

Zitrin, C.M., Klein, D.F., Woerner, M.G., & Ross, D.C. (1983). Treatment of phobias 1. Comparison of imipramine hydrochloride and placebo. *Archives of General Psychiatry, 40,* 125–138.

Zohar, J., Insel, T.R., Zohar-Kadouch, R.C. Hill, J.Z., & Murphy, D. L. (1988). Serotenergic responsivity in obsessive-compulsive disorder. *Archives of General Psychiatry, 45,* 167–175.

Zucker, K.J., Finegan, J.K., Deering, R.W., & Bradley, S.J. (1984). Two subgroups of gender-problem children. *Archives of Sexual Behavior, 13,* 27–39.

Zung, W.W.K. (1967). Depression in the normal aged. *Psychosomatics, 8,* 287–292.

Zuroff, D.C. (1986). Was Gordon Allport a trait theorist? *Journal of Personality and Social Psychology, 51,* 993–1000.

Quotation Credits

Photo Credits

Page vi: Hazel Hankin.

Chapter 1
Page 8: National Library of Medicine / Page 9: The New York Public Library / Page 10: Historical Pictures Service, Inc. / Page 11 (Top Right): The Bettmann Archive / Page 11 (Top Left): Radio Times Hulton Picture Library / Page 11 (Bottom): From Sandel L. Gilman, *Seeing the Insane* / Page 12: Courtesy of The Commonwealth of Massachusetts / Page 13 (Top): From P. Boyer and S. Nissenbaum *Ergotism: The Satan Loosed in Salem* / Page 13 (Bottom): Courtesy of The Historical Society of Pennsylvania / Page 15: © Mary Evans Picture Library/ Photo Researchers, Inc. / Page 18 (Top): National Library of Medicine / Page 18 (Bottom): National Library of Medicine / Page 20: H. Roger-Viollet / Page 21: The Bettmann Archive / Page 23: Courtesy Stanford University

Chapter 2
Page 34 (Top): The Bettmann Archive / Page 34 (Bottom): Edmund Engelman / Page 35 (Top): Edmund Engelman / Page 35 (Bottom): Courtesy of Weidenfied and Nicolson / Page 38: Sidney Harris / Page 39 (Top): Courtesy Adler Consultation Center, New York / Page 39 (Bottom): Courtesy Jon Erikson, 1976 / Page 41 (Top Right): Ellis Herwing/Stock, Boston / Page 41 (Top Left): Harvey Stein / Page 43 (Top): Culver Pictures / Page 43 (Bottom): Culver Pictures / Page 45: Ken Heyman/ Black Star / Page 46: Cary Wolinsky/ Stock, Boston / Page 53: © Ulrike Welsch, 1988 / Page 54 (Top): Michael Rougier/*Life Magazine*, © Time, Inc. / Page 54 (Bottom): Mark Antman/The Image Works, Inc.

Page 65 (Top Left): J.P. Laffont/Sygma / Page 65 (Top Right): Bill Strode/Black Star / Page 65 (Bottom): John Griffin/ The Image Works, Inc. / Page 66 (Top): Michael Weisbrot/Stock, Boston / Page 66 (Bottom Left): Bob Combs/Rapho/Photo Researchers, Inc. / Page 66 (Bottom Right): Mark Antman/The Image Works, Inc. / Page 71: Peter Southwick/Stock, Boston

Chapter 4
Page 77: Michal Heron/Woodfin Camp & Associates / Page 78: Nancy Bates/The Picture Cube / Page 80: © 1942 by the President and the fellows of Harvard College. © 1971, Henry A. Murray / Page 81: Courtesy Dr. Henri F. Ellenberger / Page 83: Arthur Grace/Stock, Boston / Page 85: Arthur Glauberman/Photo Researchers, Inc. / Page 86: Spencer Grant/Photo Researchers, Inc. / Page 87: Van Bucher/Photo Researchers, Inc. / Page 88: Ulrike Welsch / Page 98: Michal Heron/Woodfin Camp & Associates / Page 99: Courtesy of Daniel O'Leary/ photo by S. Kupferberg / Page 101: Paul Fortin/Stock, Boston / Page 102: Hazel Hankin/Stock, Boston / Page 107: Charlyce Jones

Chapter 5
Page 111: Joel Gordon / Page 114: Springer/Bettmann Film Archive / Page 119: George Malave/Stock, Boston / Page 123: Courtesy Harry F. Harlow; Regional Primate Research Center / Page 128: Dave Schaefer/The Picture Cube

Chapter 6
Page 133: Harvey Stein / Page 136: Jeff Albertson/Stock, Boston / Page 140: Courtesy Dr. Susan Mineka / Page 141: Patsy Davidson/The Image Works / Page 142: Nancy Durrell McKenna/Photo Researchers, Inc. / Page 143: Enrico Ferorelli/Dot / Page 145: Courtesy of Dr. David H. Barlow/Center for Stress & Anxiety Disorders / Page 147: Sidney Harris / Page 152: Sidney Harris / Page 154: Syndicated International/Photo Trends / Page 157: David Turnley/Detroit Free Press/Black Star / Page 159: The Bettmann Archive / Page 160: Owen Franken/Sygma / Page 161: Bettye Lane/ Photo Researchers, Inc. / Page 163: Eric Knoll/Taurus

Page 172: © Joan Menschenfreund / Page 176: Culver Pictures, Inc. / Page 180: Geral Martineau, *The Washington Post* / Page 181: Sidney Harris / Page 182: Topham/The Image Works, Inc. / Page 184: Ken Robert Buck/The Picture Cube

Chapter 8
Page 190: Courtesy of Central Museum der Gemeente Utrecht / Page 192 (Left): Rose Skytta/Jeroboam / Page 192 (Top Right): David S. Strickler/The Picture Cube / Page 192 (Bottom Right): Joan Liftin / Page 200: Michael Austin/Photo Researchers, Inc. / Page 201 (Top): Joe Rodriguez/Black Star / Page 201 (Bottom): Spencer Grant/Photo Researchers, Inc. / Page 203: Louis Fernandez/Black Star / Page 214: Alexander Lowry/Photo Researchers, Inc. / Page 216 (Top): Phil Huber/Black Star / Page 216 (Bottom): Spencer Grant/ Photo Researchers, Inc.

Chapter 9
Page 221: Bruce Davidson/Magnum / Page 223 (Top): Jean-Claude Lejeune/ Stock, Boston / Page 223 (Bottom): Courtesy of Dr. Norman E. Rosenthal, NIMH / Page 224 (Left): Library of Congress / Page 224 (Middle): The Bettmann Archive / Page 224 (Right): The Bettmann Archive / Page 225: Ulrike Welsch / Page 234: Mark Antman/The Image Works, Inc. / Page 240: Courtesy Jean Weyrich, Luxembourg / Page 241: Paul Fusco/Magnum / Page 246: UPI/ Bettmann Newsphotos / Page 247: © 1980 Hazel Hankin / Page 248: Mary Kate Denny/PhotoEdit

Chapter 10
Page 257: Jerry Ohlinger's Movie Material Store / Page 258: AP/World Wide Photos / Page 263: Gale Zucker/Stock, Boston / Page 264: Ellis Herwig/The Picture Cube / Page 266: Daily Telegraph Magazine/Woodfin Camp & Associates / Page 268: © 1978 by William L. Apple / Page 271: Abram G. Shoenfeld/Photo Researchers, Inc. / Page 273: Stephen L. Feldman/Photo Researchers, Inc.

Page 278: Ed Lettean/Photo Researchers, Inc. / Page 280: W. Marc Bernsau/The Image Works, Inc. / Page 282: Peter Menzel/Stock, Boston / Page 283: Chris Gray/The Image Works, Inc. / Page 284: Culver Pictures, Inc. / Page 286: Catherine Ursillo/Photo Researchers, Inc. / Page 289: Marty Heitner/The Picture Cube / Page 293: Culver Pictures,

Name Index

Aaronson, D.E., 604–606
Abel, G.G., 329, 330, 339, 342
Abelson, R.P., 26, 27
Abraham, K., 225
Abramovitz, S.I., 326, 327
Abramson, L.Y., 229, 230, 232, 234, 566
Abramson, D.J., 367
Achenbach, T.M., 90, 412, 413, 430, 431
Adams, C.G., 502
Adams, E.H., 294, 297, 298, 310, 311
Adams, H.E., 630
Adams, J., 284
Adams, K.M., 87
Adler, A., 38, 39, 52, 155
Agras, W.S., 328, 435
Agras, S., 133
Akhter, S., 154
Al-Razi, J., 314
Albaum, J.M., 559
Albee, G.W., 398, 588
Aldrich, C.K., 506
Alessi, N., 88
Alexander, F., 42, 144, 198, 211, 523
Alexander, J., 593
Alexander, P.C., 332, 333
Alford, J.A., 289
Allaire, D., 213
Allderidge, P., 12
Allen, C.K., 137
Allen, J.W., 94, 204, 206, 214
Allen, L., 430
Allen, M.G., 236
Allen, R.P., 416
Allen, G.J., 430
Alloy, L.B., 232, 234
Allport, G.W., 105, 116, 476
Alper, T., 577
Alpert, J.J., 431
Alpert, R., 315, 597
Alzheimer, A., 643, 644
Amies, P.L., 239
Andersen, B.L., 368, 370
Andersen, S.M., 496
Anderson, B.J., 504
Andreasen, N.C., 236, 380, 386, 387, 394
Andrews, D., 436
Angrist, B., 393
Aniline, O.I., 316
Anisman, H., 192
Anna, O., 21, 22, 173
Anthony-Bergstone, C., 508
Appelbaum, P.S., 628
Appley, M., 191
Aquilar-Figueroa, E., 177
Aragone, J., 435
Aretaeus, 220
Arey, S.A., 498
Arieti, S., 136

Aristotle, 8
Arizmendi, M.J., 527
Arkonac, O., 172
Arkowitz, H., 140
Armor, D.J., 292
Arnold, S., 99
Arnold, 608
Aronson, E., 568, 574, 575, 576, 578, 584
Asarnow, R.F., 234
Asarnow, J., 556
Asclepius, 7
Atchley, R., 493, 501
Atkeson, B.M., 336
Atkinson, R.C., 448
August, G.J., 469
Austin, V., 257
Ausubel, D.P., 31, 299
Autry, J.H., 553
Ax, A.F., 200
Axline, V., 428
Ayllon, T., 406, 542, 543
Azen, S., 214
Azrin, N.H., 406, 501, 542, 543

Bach, G.R., 576
Bachar, J.R., 501
Bachica, D., 547
Baddeley, A.D., 482
Baer, D.M., 546
Bagby, E., 137
Bahm, A.K., 421
Baker, T.B., 291, 541
Baker, T., 307, 308, 541
Baker, L., 468
Bakwin, H., 414
Baldwin, R., 466
Ball, J.C., 498
Ball-Rokeach, S.J., 365
Balla, D.A., 444
Ballenger, J.C., 147
Baller, W.R., 414, 415
Balster, R.L., 298
Balter, M.B., 500
Bancroft, J., 342, 368
Bancroft, J.H., 328
Bancroft, J.L., 328
Bandura, A., 46, 49, 51, 106, 138, 152, 198, 245, 338, 422, 521, 546, 547, 549, 550, 558, 564, 566, 567, 593, 596
Banis, H.T., 137, 435
Bansal, S., 343
Barabee, H.E., 339
Barbach, L.G., 369
Barbano, H.E., 482
Barber, T.X., 24, 122
Bardoni, A., 317
Barefoot, J.C., 206
Barklage, N.E., 436
Barkley, R.A., 90, 418

Barlow, D.H., 144–146, 152, 328–330, 339, 342, 367, 586
Barnt, R., 214
Baroff, G.S., 124, 125
Baron, R.A., 331
Barraclough, B.M., 591
Barrett, C.L., 428, 429
Bartlett, F., 95
Bartus, R.T., 488
Basedow, H., 148
Basmajian, J.V., 563
Bates, G.W., 94
Bateson, G., 396
Battle, E.S., 418
Baucom, D.H., 585
Bauer, D.H., 425
Baumeister, A.A., 448, 450
Baxter, E., 619
Bazelon, D., 603
Beach, F.A., 332
Beal, M.F., 643
Beatty, J., 213
Beck, A.T., 51, 52, 70, 94, 95, 141, 149, 163, 216, 225–228, 232, 239, 240, 242, 243, 247, 249, 250, 254, 550–553, 555, 558, 567
Beck, J.G., 329, 344, 342, 344, 367, 630
Beck, S.J., 435
Becker, J., 202, 552
Becker, J.V., 329, 339, 342, 344
Bedell, J.R., 594
Bednar, R.L., 579
Beecher, H., 622
Beecher, H.K., 317
Begab, M.J., 456
Begelman, D.A., 630
Bell, A.P., 479
Bell, C., 328
Bell, J., 583
Bellack, A.S., 103, 405, 546
Belmont, J.M., 448, 449
Bem, S.L., 135, 325
Bemis, K.M., 432, 433, 553
Bender, L., 332
Bengston, V.L., 507
Benjamin, H., 327
Bennet, E., 450
Bennet, I., 263
Bennett, W., 303
Benowitz, N., 307
Benowitz, N.L., 304, 313
Benson, D.F., 636
Benson, H., 212
Berberich, J.P., 546
Berger, K.S., 494
Berger, P.A., 296
Bergin, A.E., 515, 516, 522, 524, 560, 570, 580, 589
Bergler, E., 284
Bergman, J.A., 559
Bergman, J.D., 451

Bergman, K., 485
Berk, R.A., 423
Berley, R.A., 101
Berlin, F.S., 343
Berman, E.M., 504
Berman, J.S., 560
Bernard J., 230, 550
Bernstein, D.A., 99, 595
Bernstein, L., 499
Berry, J.C., 398
Bertrand, L.D., 183
Bertsch, G., 628
Besdine, R.W., 499, 637
Bespalec, D.A., 306
Bettelheim, B., 414, 418, 468, 472
Bettinger, C.B., 503
Beutler, L.E., 494, 527
Bianchi, E., 183
Bibring, E., 228
Bickford, A.F., 202
Bieber, I., 346, 347
Biederman, J., 436
Bierman, E.L., 450
Billings, A., 584
Billings, A.G., 233
Binet, A., 84
Bini, L., 241
Binswanger, L., 528
Bintz, J., 261
Birbaumer, H., 562
Birchler, G.R., 306
Birley, J.L.T., 392
Birnbaum, M., 614
Birnbom, F., 500
Biron, M., 236
Birren, J.E., 481, 492
Bishop, S., 239, 552
Bitterman, M.E., 139
Bjorkqvist, S.E., 305
Black, F.W., 490
Black, J.L., 92
Blackburn, I.M., 239, 552, 555
Blackman, D., 508
Blackshaw, L., 344
Blanchard, E.B., 49, 213, 214, 330, 339, 546, 562, 563
Bland, K., 145
Blatt, B., 456
Blau, A., 332
Blazer, D.G., 196, 492, 493, 499, 501
Blazer, D., 479
Blenker, M., 505
Bleuler, E., 376–378, 386, 407
Bliss, E.L., 180, 182
Bliwise, D., 500
Block, J., 106
Block, S., 242
Blockman, N., 493
Bloom, B.L., 595
Bloom, J.R., 594
Bloomfield, H.H., 578

Blumenthal, J.A., 204
Board, O.W., 200
Bockhoven, J., 18
Bocknek, G., 326
Bohman, M., 265, 288
Bois, R., 213
Bokor, S., 550
Boll, T.J., 86, 88, 645
Bollerup, T., 497
Bond, I.K., 335
Bonica, J.J., 559
Bonnie, R., 605
Bootzin, R.R., 500, 501
Borduin, C.M., 585
Borgatta, E.F., 498
Borgatta, M.L., 498
Bornstein, P.E., 493
Bornstein, P.H., 92
Bornstein, R.F., 175
Bosch, G., 469
Boskind-Lodahl, M., 435
Boskind-White, M., 435
Boss, M., 528
Botwinick, J., 481
Boucher, R., 612
Boudewyns, P.A., 545
Boulougouris, J., 155
Bourne, P.G., 158, 159, 289
Bowcock, J.Z., 289
Bower, G.H., 184, 185
Bowers, M.B., 223, 393
Bowlby, J., 232, 422
Boykin, R.A., 92
Brady, J.P., 570
Brady, S., 441
Braff, D., 177
Braid, J., 22, 23
Brand, F.N., 499
Brand, P.A., 499
Brand, R.J., 206
Brandon, T.H., 307, 308, 541
Brandt, J., 498
Bransford, J., 50
Brasfield, T., 365
Braverman, M., 465
Brecher, E.M., 279, 293, 296, 302
Breckenridge, J.S., 494
Brehm, J.W., 229
Brehony, K.A., 135, 145
Breier, A., 146, 147
Brennan-Quatrock, J., 431
Brenner, G., 506
Brent, D., 591
Bressler, R., 494
Breuer, J., 21, 22, 33, 56, 162, 173, 186
Brewer, W.F., 95
Brewin, C.R., 240
Brickel, C.M., 508
Brickman, A.S., 88
Bridge, T.B., 496
Bridge, T.P., 497
Bridger, W.H., 137
Briquet, P., 170
Brockway, J.A., 559
Broderick, J.E., 585
Brodie, H.K.H., 235
Brody, N., 561
Bromet, E.J., 591
Bromfield, R., 450
Brooks, J., 443

Brooks-Gunn, J., 457
Broverman, D.M., 230
Broverman, J.K., 135, 230
Brown, A., 201
Brown, J., 620
Brown, G.W., 233, 234, 392, 398
Brown, R.J., 493
Brown, T.E., 508
Brown, W.T., 451
Browne, A., 333
Browne, T., 632
Brownell, K.D., 342, 558, 559
Brownmiller, S., 337, 338, 339
Bruch, H., 436
Bruno, S., 313
Bryant, J., 338
Buchsbaum, M.S., 394
Buck, B., 17
Buckley, R., 418
Budman, S.H., 579
Buglass, D., 136
Bunney, W.E., 237
Buranen, C., 170
Burger, W.E., 616
Burgess, A.W., 336, 337
Burgess, M., 200
Burgess, P.M., 94
Burkhart, B.R., 336
Burnam, M.A., 332
Burton, N., 430
Burwen, L.S., 106
Busenmeyer, J.R., 553
Buss, A.H., 182
Busse, E.W., 499
Butcher, J.N., 523, 524
Butterfield, E.C., 448, 449
Buttler, R.N., 482, 493, 501
Byrne, D., 331

Caccioppo, J.T., 95
Caddy, G.R., 185, 290
Cadoret, R.J., 236, 265, 285, 288
Caetano, R., 285
Cain, C.A., 288
Caine, E.D., 295
Calhoun, K.S., 336
Cameron, D.J., 640
Cameron, N., 152, 163, 495
Campbell, D.T., 106
Campbell, I.M., 94
Campbell, M., 472
Campbell, S.B., 416, 418
Camus, A., 244
Candy, S.E., 484
Cangelosi, A., 550
Cannon, D.S., 291, 541
Cannon, H.E., 497
Cannon, W., 148, 190
Cantwell, D.P., 417, 430, 468
Caplan, G., 586
Caporael, L., 15
Carey, E., 500
Carey, G., 156
Carlisle, J.M., 335
Carlsmith, J.R., 568
Caroll, E.M., 158, 160
Carpenter, W.T., 407
Carpiniello, V.L., 371
Carr, A.T., 155
Carr, E.G., 470

Carr, J.E., 323
Carr, M.A., 88
Carroll, B.J., 238
Carruthers, M., 214
Carskadon, E., 500
Caruso, D.R., 463
Cashman, J.A., 314
Casper, R.C., 432
Cassady, J., 435
Cassell, S., 428
Casson, I.R., 88
Cautela, J.R., 290, 342, 546
Cerletti, U., 241
Cerny, J.A., 145, 586
Cerreto, M.C., 585
Chai, H., 211
Chalkley, A.J., 147
Chamberlain, P., 171
Chambers, C.D., 498
Chambers, K.C., 291, 343
Chambliss, C.A., 566
Chandler, C., 421
Chapman, J.P., 80, 236
Chapman, J.S., 380, 382
Chapman, L.F., 312
Chapman, L.J., 80
Chapman, T.C., 339
Charbonneau-Powis, M., 532
Charcot, J.M., 21, 22, 174, 185
Charles, I (King), 17
Charles, E.S., 505
Charlesworth, W.B., 444
Charney, D.S., 149, 237
Charpentier, P., 400
Chavez-Ibara, G., 177
Check, J.V.P., 338
Chein, I., 299
Chesler, P., 230
Chesney, M.A., 203, 204, 214
Chesser, E.S., 155
Chevron, M.M., 554
Chevron, E.S., 553
Chichilli, V.M., 503
Chinsky, J.M., 430, 587
Cho, E., 364
Chodoff, P., 617
Christ, 7
Christensen, A., 101, 102
Christie, A.B., 485
Christina (Queen of Sweden), 10
Churchill, D.W., 466
Churchill, W., 346
Cicchetti, D.V., 444
Cimbolic, P., 237, 238
Clark, D.F., 95
Clark, D.M., 147
Clark, J.V., 140
Clark, R., 273
Clark, W.B., 282
Clarkson, F.E., 230
Clarkson, T.B., 205
Clausen, J.A., 396
Clavarese, B., 313
Clayton, E.W., 617
Clayton, P.J., 493
Clayton, V.P., 481
Cleckley, H., 114, 115, 262, 263, 270, 273
Clements, C.M., 232
Climko, R.P., 314
Cloninger, C.R., 171, 288, 421

Cloninger, R.C., 265
Clum, G.A., 247
Clunies-Ross, G.G., 459
Coates, S., 325
Cobb, J.A., 424
Cobb, J.P., 153
Cobb, S., 200
Cochran, S.D., 233
Cohen, D., 500
Cohen, D.J., 418, 457, 467
Cohen, I.L., 451
Cohen, M.F., 200
Cohen, S., 145, 195, 196, 313, 586
Cole, J.D., 237
Cole, P.V., 307
Colleti, G., 566
Collins, J.L., 580
Combs, G. Jr., 185
Comfort, A., 502–504
Conger, J.J., 286
Conners, C.K., 90, 418
Conners, F.A., 463
Conoley, C.W., 534
Conte, H.R., 257
Cook, D., 366
Cooper, A.F., 496
Cooper, H.M., 585
Cooper, J.E., 379
Coppen, A., 237
Corby, N., 502, 503
Corey, G., 403
Cornblatt, B., 399
Cornfield, J., 593
Cornoni-Huntley, J., 482
Costa, P.T., Jr., 481, 482, 499
Costelo, C.G., 430
Courchesne, E., 469
Covi, L., 239
Cowdry, R.W., 272
Cowen, E.L., 422, 594, 595
Cox, A., 468
Cox, D.J., 563
Cox, T., 214
Coyne, J.C., 232, 234, 439
Craft, M.J., 273
Crago, M., 527
Craig, K.D., 546
Craig, M., 421
Craighead, W.E., 95, 227
Craik, F.I.M., 481
Crane, J.B., 282
Creer, T.L., 207, 211, 435
Crider, R.A., 297
Crisp, A.H., 431, 432
Crissey, M.S., 457
Crofton, J., 307
Cronkite, R.C., 233
Cross, C.K., 222
Cross, D.G., 100
Cross, P.S., 485, 488, 491, 492, 496, 498, 636
Croughan, J., 77
Crowe, R.R., 146
Crown, S., 368
Cubberly, W.E., 550
Cummings, J.L., 636
Cunningham, C.J., 435
Cunningham, C.E., 90, 418
Cunningham-Rather, J., 329
Curran, J.W., 364
Curran, J.P., 140

Curtis, G.C., 286
Cushing, H., 642
Cutler, S.J., 482
Cytryn, L., 431

D'Ardenne, P., 368
D'Zurilla, T., 553, 554
Dabbs, G.E., 610
Dahl, L.K., 202
Dahlstrom, G., 206
Danaher, B.G., 307
Daneman, E.A., 239
Davies, M., 431
Davignon, A., 237
Davis, J.M., 242, 394
Davis, P., 316
Davison, G.C., 50, 52, 92, 94,
    114, 116, 134, 137, 141,
    145, 149, 152, 204, 206,
    214, 216, 227, 241, 242,
    329, 340, 342, 347, 348,
    369, 425, 429, 470, 524,
    538, 539, 541, 544, 548–550,
    552, 566–568, 570, 571, 623,
    624, 630
Dawes, R., 561
Dawson, M.E., 95, 137
Deacon, J.R., 448
Decenteceeo, E.T., 548
Dederich, C., 301
DeHaan, R., 355
DeJong, R.N., 646
Dement, W.C., 500
Deming, B., 282
Deming, W.E., 378
DeMyer, M.K., 468
DeMyer, M., 464, 468, 469
Depue, R.A., 223, 232
DeQuatro, V., 94, 204, 206, 214
DeRisi, W.J., 405
DeRubeis, R.J., 239, 553
Descartes, R., 190, 244
deSilva, P., 155
Dessonville, C., 478, 485, 492,
    496, 498, 499
Detterman, D.K., 448, 463
Deutsch, A., 15
DeVries, H.A., 506
Dew, M.A., 591
Dewys, W.D., 435
Deykin, E.Y., 431
Diamond, R., 177, 466
Diamond, S., 466
Didion, J., 212
Diener, E., 106
Dietrich, S.L., 434
Dimasio, A., 580
Dimsdale, J.E., 201, 206
Dinges, D.F., 183
Dodge, K.A., 424
Dodson, B., 369
Dolan, A.B., 441
Dole, V., 300
Doleys, D.M., 415
Dolezal, S.L., 94
Doll, R., 304
Dollard, J., 286, 570
Donahoe, C.P. Jr., 158
Donaldson, G., 481
Donaldson, K., 615, 616
Donerstein, E., 338
Donnellan, A.M., 465, 470

Doran, A.R., 394
Doris, J., 233
Dornbrand, L., 504
Doubros, S.G., 546
Douglass, J.D., 244
Down, L., 450
Drabman, R.S., 435, 564
Drake, R.D., 402
Dreifurst, P., 468
Drollet, M., 213
Duck, S., 585
Dunaif, S.L., 378
Duncan, G.W., 498
Dunham, H.W., 396
Dunn, M.J., 296
Dunn, V.K., 492
Durkheim, E., 161, 245
Durrell, J., 298
Dweck, C.S., 230
Dworkin, B.R., 198
Dworkin, R.H., 390
Dye, C.J., 504, 505
Dykens, E., 451
Dysken, M.W., 186

Eagleston, J.R., 203, 204
Eastman, P., 499
Eckert, E.D., 434, 436
Edelbrook, C.S., 413, 430
Edelbrook, C., 90
Edmunson, E., 594
Edwards, A.L., 83
Edwards, G., 290
Edward, I., 602
Egan, G., 526, 527
Egeland, J.A., 236
Ehrhardt, A., 324
Eidelson, R.J., 101
Eiler, J., 478
Eisenberg, L., 421, 468
Eisenstein, R.B., 610
Elkin, I., 553–555
Ellenberger, H.F., 22
Ellingson, R.J., 265
Ellis, A., 51, 52, 94, 100, 145,
    216, 226, 239, 354, 363,
    521, 547–550, 552, 558, 567,
    581
Ellis, H., 352, 353
Ellis, N.R., 448, 449
Elmore, A.M., 211, 212, 213
Elmore, J.L., 580
Ely, D.L., 202, 434, 435
Emery, G., 140, 149
Emery, R.E., 421, 422
Emmelkamp, P.M.G., 144, 562
Emmons, R.A., 106
Endicott, J., 77, 78, 255, 257,
    379
Engel, B.T., 202
Engle-Friedman, M., 500, 501
English, H.B., 137
Enright, J.B., 533
Epictetus, 558
Epstein, L.C., 623
Epstein, L.H., 435, 559
Epstein, N., 101
Epstein, S, 106
Erdberg, P., 80
Erikson, E., 39, 40, 41, 42, 52,
    520, 569
Erixon, G., 139

Erlenmeyer-Kimling, L.E., 399
Esler, J., 214
Eunson, K.M., 239, 552
Evans, I.M., 139
Evans, M., 368
Evans, M.D., 239, 553
Evans, R.B., 346
Evans, R.I., 308
Exner, J.E., 80
Eysenck, H.J., 141, 421, 589

Fagan, J., 531
Fagan, J.F., 443
Fain, T., 69
Fairburn, C.G., 435
Fairweather, G.W., 19
Falloon, I.R.H., 404, 405
Farberow, N.L., 248, 591
Farina, A., 14
Faris, E.J., 202
Farkas, G., 281
Farmer, A.E., 387
Favell, J.E., 461
Fawcett, J., 553
Fedora, O., 335
Fein, D., 465
Feingold, B.F., 417–419
Feinsilver, D.B., 403
Feldman, P.M., 94
Felner, R.D., 422
Fenell, E.B., 191
Fenichel, O., 284
Fennell, M.J.V., 239
Fentiman, L.C., 606
Ferenczi, S., 523
Fernandez, V., 584
Fernando, C.K., 563
Ferster, C.B., 468
Feshbach, S., 338
Feyerabend, C., 306
Field, T., 455
Figley, C.R., 159, 160, 161, 163
Fillmore, K.M., 285
Finkelhor, D., 332, 333
Finn, M., 597
Finn, S.E., 72
Fiori, M., 364
Firth-Cozens, J., 240
Fisch, G.S., 451
Fischetti, M., 140
Fish, F., 497
Fisher, M., 328, 390
Fishman, S.T., 577
Fisk, N., 324, 441
Fitch, V.L., 507
Flanagan, B., 339
Flay, B.R., 308
Fleming, A.S., 504
Fleming, M., 326
Fletcher, C., 304
Fodor, I., 135
Folkman, S., 192, 499
Folks, D.G., 169, 171, 176, 177
Follette, W.C., 100, 101, 585
Folstein, M.F., 491, 493, 640
Folstein, S., 469
Ford, C., 234
Ford, C.S., 332
Ford, C.V., 177, 505
Ford, D.H., 516, 521, 524, 528
Ford, D.V., 169, 171
Fordney-Settlage, D.S., 369

Fordyce, W.E., 559
Forehand, R., 99
Forstein, M., 348
Foster, B., 423
Foti, A., 214
Foucault, M., 12
Fox, R., 282
Foxx, R.M., 542
Foy, D.W., 158, 160, 162
Frame, C.I., 424
Frances, A., 254, 259
Frank, J.D., 515, 566
Frank, J., 570
Frankl, V., 240, 528
Franks, C.M., 546, 580
Franzen, M.D., 88
Fredrikson, M., 139
Freed, E.X., 286
Freedman, E., 364
Freedman, R.R., 563
Freeman, B.J., 464
Frei, E., 313
Freitag, G., 461
French, T.M., 42, 144, 523
Freud, A., 41, 428, 520
Freud, S., 22, 32, 33, 36, 37, 38,
    41, 42, 52, 56, 59, 116, 132,
    134, 135, 136, 139, 144, 146,
    155, 169, 173, 174, 175,
    178, 186, 225, 226, 245,
    297, 303, 346, 354, 360,
    377, 385, 388, 389, 401,
    432, 516–521, 523, 534, 569
Freund, K., 328
Freundlich, A., 563
Friar, L.R., 213
Frias, A.S., 10
Friedberg, C.K., 202
Friedman, E., 237
Friedman, J.M., 504, 581, 583
Friedman, M., 203, 215
Friedman, R., 202
Frisch, M.B., 93
Fristoe, M., 447, 462
Fromm-Reichman, F., 396, 402,
    403
Frost, R.O., 156
Frude, N., 332
Fry, T.J., 545
Fuentes, M., 484, 504
Furby, L., 344

Gabrielli, W.F., 265
Gadow, K.D., 418
Gage, P., 643
Gagnon, J.H., 338, 341, 347,
    353, 354, 368, 369, 544
Gahalan, D., 282
Gaines, J., 531
Gaitz, C.M., 494
Galbraith, G.C., 450
Galen, 8, 19
Galin, D., 177
Gall, C., 185
Gallagher, D., 493, 494
Galley, D.J., 175
Garcia, J., 138
Gardner, D.L., 272
Garfield, S., 56
Garfield, S.L., 505, 524, 560,
    570
Garfinkel, P.E., 432, 436

Garmezy, N., 389, 416
Garner, D.M., 432, 435
Garofalo, R., 612
Garrison, K.M., 595
Garside, R.F., 496
Garvey, M.J., 239
Gatchel, R.I., 149
Gath, D., 368
Gatz, M., 476, 483, 484, 504, 505, 508, 509
Gauthier, J., 213
Gawin, F.H., 298
Gebhart, P.H., 332, 333, 338
Geer, J.H., 149, 328, 329, 332, 343, 357
Gelder, M.G., 135, 342
Geller, E., 472
Geller, E.S., 135, 145
Geller, G.L., 628
Genest, J., 237
Gentry, W.D., 201
George, L.K., 482, 493, 502, 508, 594
George III (King), 608
Gerson, S., 237, 393
Gesten, E.L., 309, 589, 595, 597
Giarretto, H., 343
Gibbon, M., 255, 257
Gibbons, D.C., 423
Gibbs, J., 244
Gibson, D., 459
Gil, K.M., 556
Gilboy, J.A., 613
Gilchrist, L.D., 308
Gilewski, M.J., 482
Gino, A., 291, 541
Ginsburg, A.B., 504
Glaros, A.G., 566
Glaser, G.H., 641
Glaser, R., 120
Glass, C.R., 95, 140
Glass, G., 560
Glassman, A.H., 223, 305
Glatt, M.M., 498
Glick, S.J., 421
Glithero, E., 170
Glueck, F., 422
Glueck, S., 422
Godfrey, S., 210
Goetz, D., 431
Goffman, E., 18
Gold, E.O., 288
Gold, M.S., 305
Gold, V.J., 461
Goldband, S., 213, 562, 563
Goldberg, E.M., 396
Goldberg, S.R., 304
Goldberg, T.E., 394
Golden, C.J., 87, 88
Goldfried, M.R., 52, 80, 92, 152, 538, 539, 548, 549, 553, 556, 567, 570, 571
Goldin, J.C., 552
Golding, S.L., 610
Goldman, M.S., 290
Goldmeier, J., 508
Goldstein, A., 294
Goldstein, G., 87
Goldstein, H.S., 201
Goldstein, K., 458
Goldstein, M., 397
Goldstein, S.E., 500, 504

Gomes-Schwartz, B., 580
Goo, G.P., 312
Goodman, J., 462
Goodman, M., 325
Goodman, P., 530
Goodwin, D.W., 222, 282, 287, 288, 289, 292, 296, 297, 310
Goodwin, F.K., 237
Gordon, R., 594
Gorman, J.M., 147
Gorman-Smith, D., 461
Gotlib, I.H., 234, 493
Gottesman, I.I., 156, 177, 387, 390
Gottman, J., 557
Gottman, J.M., 100, 101, 584
Gove, W.R., 69, 388
Goyette, C.E., 418
Grabowski, J., 298
Graham, D.T., 190
Graham, J.R., 213
Graham, J.W., 308
Graham, P.J., 207
Graham, R., 201
Gralnick, A., 618, 620, 621
Grams, A.E., 482
Grapentine, W.L., 88
Graves, R., 641
Gray, E.B., 595
Gray, J.A., 149
Green, E.E., 212
Green, K.F., 138
Green, R., 324, 325
Greenberg, L.S., 406, 534, 586
Greenblatt, D.J., 146
Greenblatt, M., 19
Greenhouse, J.B., 591
Greenwood, P., 328
Gregory, I., 282
Gressard, C.F., 550
Griesinger, W., 19, 20
Griffith, J., 399
Grings, W.W., 95
Grinker, R.R., 162
Gross, A., 451
Gross, M.B., 417, 418
Grossman, G., 243
Grossman, H.J., 442
Grosz, H.J., 174, 176
Groth, N.A., 333, 337
Grove, W.M., 288
Gruenberg, A.M., 387
Grusec, J.E., 427
Guare, J.C., 594
Gubbay, S., 469
Gudeman, J., 285
Guidano, V., 567
Gunderson, J.G., 257, 272, 403
Gur, R.C., 173
Guralnik, J.M., 479
Gurland, B.J., 378, 485, 488, 491, 492, 496, 498, 636
Gurman, A.S., 580, 585, 629
Gustafson, Y., 637
Guthrie, W., 645
Guze, S.B., 171, 172, 220, 222, 282, 296, 297, 310, 421
Gwynn, M.I., 24
Gwynther, L.P., 508, 594

Haaga, D.A., 94, 95, 215, 241, 549, 550, 552, 570

Habot, B., 637
Hacket, G., 307
Hackman, A., 368
Hadfield, J., 608
Hadley, S.W., 553, 580
Hafner, J., 145
Hafner, R.J., 154
Hager, M., 139
Haggard, E., 149
Hahlweg, K., 585
Halam, R., 145
Halberstadt, L.J., 230
Haley, S.A., 158, 162
Hall, C.S., 41
Hall, E., 481, 503
Hall, S.M., 307
Halleck, S., 629
Halpern, D., 171
Halstead, W.C., 86
Hamilton, E.W., 234
Hammeke, T., 87
Hammen, C.L., 92, 227, 232, 233
Hammer D., 328
Hammond, D.C., 356
Hammond, W., 158
Hampe, E., 428, 429
Hampson, J.L., 323, 325
Hampson, J.G., 325
Hanley, P., 448
Hanley, R., 492
Hansen, W.B., 308, 309
Hanusa, B.H., 233
Haracz, J.L., 394
Harburg, E., 200
Hare, R.D., 176, 263, 267, 270
Haris, J.E., 482
Harlow, J.M., 642, 643
Harman, A., 17
Harman, R.L., 577
Harrington, A., 336
Harris, A., 459
Harris, D.E., 306
Harris, E.L., 144, 484, 485
Harris, T.O., 233, 234
Hartman, H., 42, 520
Hartsough, C.S., 416, 418
Harvey, J., 17, 451
Harvey, P.D., 387
Hassinger, M., 478
Hastrup, J.L., 202
Hathaway, S.R., 84
Hatsukami, D., 434
Hauserman, N.M., 178
Hawley, C., 418
Haves, S.C., 240, 342
Haynes, S.N., 92, 103
Hays, P., 236
Hazelrigg, M.D., 585
Hazelwood, L., 500
Heaton, R.K., 317, 318
Heaton, R., 645
Hechtman, H., 285
Hecker, M.H.L., 206
Hefferline, R.F., 530
Heidegger, M., 52, 244, 528
Heiman, J., 332, 343, 357, 367
Heiman, N.M., 370, 590
Heinman, J.R., 369
Heller, J., 132
Helzer, J.E., 77
Hembel, C., 111

Hembree, W.C., 312
Hemsley, D.R., 178
Heninger, G.R., 237
Henkel, H., 630
Henker, B., 417, 418, 424
Henn, F.A., 157
Henningfield, J.E., 304
Henry, G.W., 378
Henry, J.P., 202
Henry, VIII, 13
Henson, C., 328
Henson, D.E., 328
Herbert, J., 210
Herbert, M., 421
Herd, J.A., 206
Herman, I., 247
Hernandez, P., 77
Hernandez-Peon, R., 177
Herr, J.J., 509
Herrman, D.J., 482
Hersen, M., 103, 405, 546
Hertzog, C., 477, 481
Hesselink, J.R., 469
Heston, L.L., 390, 391, 397, 644
Hetherington, E.M., 423
Hewett, F.M., 466, 470
Heyd, D., 242
Hibbert, G.A., 147, 239
Hickey, T., 479
Hickman, C., 466
Higgins, G.F., 362
Higgins, R.L., 93
Hightower, A.D., 594
Hilgard, E.R., 22, 23, 24, 25
Hill, F.A., 137
Hill, J.H., 546
Hill, S.Y., 282
Hilterbrand, K., 436
Himadi, W.G., 145, 586
Hinkley, J., Jr., 604, 605, 606
Hinrichs, J.V., 493
Hinshaw, S.P., 416, 424
Hippocrates, 8, 19, 32, 169, 220
Hiroto, D.S., 229
Hirschfeld, R.A., 222
Hite, S., 358
Hitler, A., 530
Ho, D., 644
Hobbs, S.A., 435
Hobbs, T., 528
Hoch, P.H., 378
Hodapp, V., 202
Hodges, W.F., 595
Hodgson, R.J., 152, 155, 156
Hoffman, H., 285
Hoffman, M.L., 421
Hofland, B.F., 507
Hofman, A., 314
Hogan, D., 370
Hogan, D.R., 369, 581
Hogarty, G.E., 401, 404
Hokanson, J.E., 200
Holden, C., 596
Holinger, P.C., 244
Hollingshead, A.B., 395, 396
Hollon, S.D., 94, 227, 239, 552, 553
Holmen, M.L., 329
Holmes, F.B., 426
Holmes, O.W., 22
Holmes, T.H., 193
Holmstrom, L.L., 336

Holroyd, K., 562
Honigman, T.B., 490
Honingfeld, G., 242, 299
Honzik, M.R., 430
Hood, H.V., 365, 366
Hooley, J.M., 234
Hoon, E.F., 358, 367
Hoon, P.W., 358, 367
Hope, C.M., 419
Hopper, K., 619
Horan, J.J., 307
Horn, A.S., 393
Horn, J.L., 481
Horn, W.F., 92, 103
Hornblower, M., 620
Horney, K., 42, 520, 569
Horowitz, M., 155
Horwitz, L., 580
Houts, P.S., 578
Howard, A., 242, 299
Howard, G.S., 559
Howard, K.I., 560
Hsu, L.K.G., 431
Huang, H.F.S., 312
Hubert, N.C., 417
Hudson, J.I., 435, 436
Hugdahl, K., 139
Hughes, J.R., 307
Hughes, P.L., 435
Hulicka, I.M., 482
Hunt, B., 214
Hunt, D.D., 323
Hunt, W.A., 306
Huntington, G., 645
Husserl, E., 528
Hussian, R.A., 509, 555
Husted, J.R., 369
Hutchings, B., 265
Hutchison, H.C., 335, 342
Hutt, C., 469
Huttenlocher, P.R., 450

Ianni, P., 563
Ilstrup, D.M., 435
Imboden, J.B., 169
Inbar-Saban, N., 365
Innes, G., 200
Innocent, VIII, 9
Insell, T.R., 150
Institoris, H., 9
Insull, W., 202
Irwin, M., 623
Isen, A.M., 227
Israel, A.C., 425
Issidorides, R.M., 312

Jablonski, P., 628
Jablonsky, A., 379
Jacklin, C.N., 230
Jackson, A.M., 596
Jackson, D., 583
Jackson, D.N., 285
Jackson, W.K., 305
Jacob, P., 304
Jacob, R.G., 214
Jacobs, M., 579
Jacobson, A., 519
Jacobson, E., 212, 539
Jacobson, N.S., 100, 101, 583–585
Jaffe, J.H., 280, 294, 299, 300, 301, 302, 303, 313, 315

Jaffe, Y., 338
Jakubowski, P., 556
James, N., 236
James, W., 278
Jamison, K.R., 491
Jandorf, L., 194
Janet, P., 21, 22, 156
Jarrett, R.B., 240
Jarvik, L.F., 478, 479, 485, 492, 494, 496, 498, 499, 636
Jarvik, M.E., 304, 306, 307, 308
Jarvis, M.J., 306
Jasinski, D.R., 305
Jasnow, N., 550
Jason, L.A., 309, 589, 595, 597
Jay, S.M., 434
Jeans, B.F., 180, 182
Jeffrey, D.B., 566
Jeffrey, R.W., 307, 547
Jellinek, E.M., 282
Jenike, M.A., 156, 157
Jenkins, C.D., 202, 203, 204
Jenkins, E.C., 451
Jennings, C., 591
Jernigan, T.L., 469
Jerrell, J.M., 596
Jerry, M.B., 335
Jersild, A.T., 425, 426
Jersild, C.L., 425
Joffee, J.M., 588
Johnson, A.M., 427
Johnson, C.A., 308
Johnson, F., 614
Johnson, L., 481, 483, 589
Johnson, M.K., 50, 94
Johnson, R.E., 305
Johnson, S.M., 586
Johnson, V.E., 328, 336, 352–356, 358, 359, 361–363, 367–370, 372, 503, 504, 581, 582
Johnston, D.W., 144, 214
Johnston, E.H., 146, 201
Johnston, M.B., 462
Jones, B.M., 280, 283
Jones, D.W., 484
Jones, E., 134
Jones, I.H., 335
Jones, M., 19, 543, 606, 607
Jones, M.C., 285, 427, 538
Jones, R.T., 307, 311, 312, 313
Jorgesen, C., 326
Josef, N.C., 273
Josephs, R.A., 286, 287
Judge, C., 451
Julier, D., 368
Jung, C.G.,22, 38, 52, 392
Jutai, J.W., 267, 270

Kabat, L.G., 496
Kagan, J., 247
Kagen, S., 314
Kahn, R.L., 482, 493
Kaiser, F.E., 503, 504
Kammen, D.P., 394
Kamp, M., 170
Kanas, N., 402
Kandel, D.B., 311, 312
Kane, J.M., 401
Kane, R.L., 87
Kanfer, F.H., 89, 98, 553, 564, 567

Kannel, W., 593
Kanner, L., 463, 465, 468
Kanno, P.H., 358
Kant, I., 244
Kanter, J., 398
Kantor, J.S., 146
Kantorovich, N.V., 290
Kaplan, H.S., 352, 353, 354, 356, 357, 358, 367, 368, 370
Kaplan, J.R., 205
Kaplan, R.M., 484
Karasu, T.B., 505
Karlan, G.R., 462
Karrer, R., 450
Karus, D., 311
Kasanin, J., 378
Kasindorf, J., 620, 621
Kasl, S.V., 200
Kaslow, F.W., 585
Kasper, C., 88
Kastenbaum, R., 484
Kaszniak, A.W., 168
Katahn, M., 149
Katchadourian, H.A., 334
Katkin, E.S., 213, 562, 563
Katz, E.R., 434
Katz, M., 449
Kaul, T.J., 579
Kawi, A.A., 441
Kay, D.W.K., 493, 496
Kazdin, A.E., 424, 430, 546, 560, 561
Keefe, F.J., 559, 563
Keen, S., 360
Kegel, A.H., 371
Keith, S.J., 406
Keller, M.B., 224
Kellerman, J., 434
Kelley, H.H., 583
Kellner, R., 273
Kelly, E., 210
Kelly, G., 567
Kelly, J., 364, 365, 366, 577
Kelly, K.A., 232
Kemp, R., 17
Kendall, P.C., 94, 227
Kendell, R.E., 62
Kendler, K.S., 387
Kennedy, J., 481, 589, 597 608
Kennedy, R., 608
Kennedy, S., 436
Kennedy, W.A., 427
Kenney, R.A., 479
Kent, R.N., 103, 122
Kern, M.B., 595
Kernberg, O.F., 258, 272, 580
Kernberg, O.P., 524
Kessel, N., 243
Kessler, J., 492
Kessler, R.C., 196
Kety, S., 391, 392
Keuthen, N., 137
Keys, A., 206
Kidder, T., 163
Kiclcolt-Glaser, J.K., 120, 196
Kierkegaard, S., 52, 528
Kiesler, C.A., 597
Kilburg, R.R., 504
Killen, J.D., 307
Kiloh, L.G., 493
Kilpatrick, D.G., 336
Kimble, G.A., 389

Kimmel, D.C., 476, 479
Kimura, D., 441
King, C., 102
King, L.W., 405
King, M.L., 608
Kingerlee, P., 469
Kinsey, A., 353, 358, 359, 346, 502
Kinsman, R.A., 207
Kleber, H.D., 298, 305
Klee, G.D., 317
Kleeman, S.T., 209
Klein, D.C., 227
Klein, D.F., 146
Klein, D.N., 224
Klein, M., 428
Kleiner, R.J., 245
Kleinke, C.L., 230
Kleinmuntz, B., 82
Klerman, G.L., 226, 239, 242, 493, 553
Klucy, R.S., 431
Kluft, R.P., 182, 185
Kluger, J.M., 210
Knap, S., 626
Knapp, P., 207, 210
Knaus, W., 550
Knight, B., 504, 508, 509
Knight, R.A., 337
Kniskern, D.P., 580, 585, 629
Koch, E., 620
Kocher, T.R., 305
Koegel, R.L., 471
Koenig, K., 577
Koenig, S., 644
Kog, E., 433
Kohn, M.L., 395, 396
Kohut, F.J., 493
Kohut, H., 258
Kolb, J.E., 257
Koller, H., 449
Kolvin, I., 414
Konig, P., 210
Kopel, S.A., 566
Kopfstein, J.M., 118
Kopta, S.M., 560
Korchin, S.J., 42
Kornetsky, C., 394
Koropsak, E., 200
Koss, M.P., 523, 524
Kosson, D.S., 268, 269
Kossorla, I.C., 461
Kovaks, M., 239, 243, 247, 552
Kowalik, D.L., 234
Kowall, N.K., 643
Kozel, N.J., 294, 297, 298, 310, 311
Kozol, H., 612
Kraeplin, E., 20, 62, 220, 376–378, 385, 392, 407, 496
Kraft-Ebbing, R. von, 20
Kramer, M., 505, 597
Krantz, D.S., 205
Krantz, S., 227
Kranz, H., 264
Krasner, L., 176
Krause, M.S., 560
Krech, D., 450
Kringlen, E., 152
Kroll, P., 171
Kubal, L., 229
Kucharski, L.T., 504

Kuehnel, J.M., 585
Kuhn, T.S., 23, 26, 353
Kunst-Wilson, W.R., 175
Kuriansky, J.B., 378
Kurlander, H.M., 229
Kurtz, R., 56
Kutchinsky, B., 334

Laboit, 399, 400
Lacey, B.A., 418
Lacey, J.I., 141, 197, 270
Ladd, G.W., 430
Laing, R., 389
Lamber, N.M., 416, 418
Lambert, M.J., 516, 527, 560, 561, 580, 591
Lamontagne, Y., 178
Lamp, R., 398
Landman, J.T., 561
Lando, H.A., 306
Lane, E.A., 398
Lang, A.R., 281, 292
Lang, P.J., 104, 105, 524, 539, 631
Lange, A.J., 556, 557
Lange, J., 264
Langer, E., 507
Langer, E.J., 26, 27
Langevin, R., 323
Langhorne, J.E., 416
Langs, R.J., 317
Lanthier, R., 339
Lanyon, R.I., 333, 341, 343
Larsen, J.K., 596
Larsen, S.W., 430
Larson, D.M., 482
Larson, E., 492
LaRue, A., 478, 485, 492, 496, 498, 499
Lasagna, L., 317, 515, 623
Latané, B., 268, 269, 270
Laughton, E., 500
Laurence, J.R., 25
Lavell, M., 245
Lavelle, T.L., 232
Lavin, P.J., 178
Lawrence, P.S., 555
Laws, D.R., 329
Lawson, D.M., 281
Lawton, M.P., 497, 504
Layne, C., 227
Lazar, I., 457
Lazarus, A.A., 114, 116, 145, 292, 340, 429, 546, 556, 567, 568, 571, 574, 576–578
Lazarus, R., 49, 191, 192
Lazarus, R.S., 499
Lazovick, A.D., 524, 539
Learner, R.M., 508
Leary, T., 315
LeBlanc, J.M., 546
Lebowitz, B., 482
Leckman, J.F., 451
Lederman, S., 285
Lee, D., 214
Lee, H.K., 393
Lee, T., 393
Lee, V.E., 457
Leeper, P., 619
Leff, J.P., 398, 401
Leff, M.J., 236
Lefkowitz, M.M., 430

Lehrer, P.M., 105
Leiblum, S.R., 356
Leitenberg,H., 332, 343, 357, 433, 435
Lejeune, J., 450
Leland, H., 460
Lemieux, G., 237
Lemke, J.H., 493
Lennon, J., 608
Lentz, R.J., 19, 402, 406, 594, 618, 632
Lentz, R., 543–545
Lenzenweger, M.F., 390
Leone, D.R., 175
Lerer, B., 163
Lesage, A., 178
Lester, G.W., 585
Levenson, M., 247
Levenson, R.W., 101, 286
Leventman, S., 159, 160, 161
Levine, J.L., 239
Levitsky, A., 532
Levitt, E.E., 340
Levy, R., 177
Lewin, K., 574
Lewinsohn, P.H., 577
Lewinsohn, P.M., 227, 234, 509, 577
Lewis, M.I., 493, 501
Lewis, N., 482
Lewis-Thomé, J., 630
Ley, R., 147
Liberman, R.P., 405
Libow, L.S., 637
Lichtenstein, E., 306
Lieberman, M.A., 579, 580
Lieberman, M., 594
Lieberman, R.P., 585
Liebert, D.E., 234
Liebert, R.M., 120, 422, 546
Liebman, R., 433
Liebson, I., 178
Lief, H.I., 356, 504
Liem, J.H., 397
Lifton, R.J., 162, 163
Light, K.C., 202
Lillesand, D.B., 93
Linberg, S.E., 307
Lind, E., 193, 203
Lindsay, W.R., 462
Linehan, M.M., 243, 245, 247, 272, 549
Linton, H.B., 317
Linz, D.G., 338
Linzey, G., 41
Lion, J.R., 273
Liotti, G., 567
Lipinski, D.P., 92
Lipman, A., 479
Lipowski, Z.J., 489, 490, 637
Lisi, I.S., 329
Liskow, B., 295, 301
Liston, E.H., 489, 636
Litman, R.E., 248
Litrownik, A., 466
Little, M.M., 493
Litwack, T.R., 612–614
Litwin, G., 317
Lloyd, L.L., 447, 462
Lobascher, M., 469
Lobitz, W.C., 227, 370
Lock, B.Z., 482

Lockman, J.E., 430
Lockyer, L., 464
Loehlin, J.C., 41
Loeper, G., 398
Löfberg, I., 139
London, P., 93, 515, 521, 631
Loney, J., 416
Lopez, S., 77
LoPiccolo, J., 359, 367–370, 583
LoPiccolo, L., 368, 370
Loranger, A., 254, 257
Lord Onslow, 608
Lothstein, L.M., 326, 327
Lotter, V., 464, 468
Louis XIV, 10
Lovaas, O.I., 327, 461, 466, 470, 471, 546, 564
Lovibond, S.H., 290
Lowen, A., 360
Lowenthal, M.F., 482
Luborsky, L., 522
Ludwig, A.M., 185
Lukens, E., 431
Lunde, D.T., 334
Luparelo, T.J., 209
Lupfer, S.L., 332, 333
Luria, A., 87
Luscomb, R.L., 247
Lustman, P.J., 552
Luthe, W., 212
Lyght, C.E., 199
Lykken, D.T., 267, 268, 269
Lyon, G.R., 442
Lyon, P., 346
Lystad, M.M., 396

M'Naghten, D., 603, 606, 608
Mac Farlane, J.W., 430
Maccoby, E.E., 230
Maccoby, N., 307, 593
MacCorquodale, K., 567
MacDonald, D.I., 504
MacDonald, H., 24
MacDonald, J.S., 313
MacKay, A.V.P., 393
MacKeith, R.C., 414
MacLean, W.E., Jr., 450
MacLeod, C., 149, 178
MacMillan, J.F., 398
Madarasmi, S., 96
Magaret, A., 163
Magenis, R.E., 451
Maher, B.A., 30, 105, 127
Mahoney, M.J., 547, 564, 567
Main, T.F., 37
Maisto, S.A., 272
Malamud, M., 343
Malamuth, N.M., 338
Malin, H., 283
Malin, S., 286
Malloy, T.R., 371
Maltzman, I.M., 292
MaNally, R.J., 139
Mandel, I.J., 137
Mandelcorn, M.S., 173
Mandler, G., 148, 232
Mann, V.A., 441, 466
Mannello, T.A., 285
Manosevitz, M., 41
Manton, K., 501
Manton, K.G., 501
Manuck, S.B., 205

March, V., 436
Marcus, J., 399
Mardones, J., 287
Margolin, G., 100, 583–585, 625, 629
Mark, 7
Markey, F.V., 425
Markman, H.J., 100
Markowitz, P., 465
Marks, I.M., 135, 136, 139, 146, 156, 342
Marlatt, G.A., 282, 292, 565, 566
Marmor, J., 521, 570
Marmot, M.G., 214
Marshall, W.L., 339
Marshall, W.R., 435
Marston, A., 211
Marston, M., 211
Martin, B., 104, 423
Martin, C.E., 346, 502
Martin, D., 346
Martin, R., 624, 632
Maruish, M.E., 88
Masek, B.J., 435
Maslow, A., 52, 528
Masters, J., 577
Masters, W.H., 328, 336, 352–356, 358, 359, 361–363, 367–370, 372, 502, 504, 581, 582
Mastri, A.R., 644
Mateer, C.A., 441
Mathaney, A.P., Jr., 441
Mathe, A., 210
Mathews, A.M., 368
Mathews, K.A., 204, 206, 215
Matson, J.L., 461
Matsuyama, S., 485
Mausner, B., 304
May, P.R.A., 404
May, R., 528
Mays, D.T., 580
McAdoo, W.G., 468
McAllister, T.W., 493
McAndrew, J.B., 468
McAvay, G., 500
McCann, M., 405
McCary, J.L., 334
McConkey, K.M., 25
McCord, J., 263, 273, 285, 422
McCord, W., 263, 273, 285, 422
McCrady, B.S., 292, 293
McCrae, R.R., 482
McDonald, D.W., 100, 101
McFaddin, S.C., 595
McFall, R.M., 92, 93, 140
McGarry, L., 617
McGhie, A., 380, 382
McGlashan, T.M., 257
McGowan, B.K., 138
McGuffin, P., 387
McGuiness, D., 441
McGuire, R.J., 335
McHugh, J., 329
McHugh, P.R., 493
McKinley, J.C., 84
McKinney, W.T., 519
McKnew, D.H., 431
McKnight, D.L., 240
McLeod, J.D., 196
McManus, M., 88

McMullen, S., 370, 546
McNamara, J.J., 431
McNeal, E.T., 237, 238
McNeil, E., 260, 261
McNicol, K.N., 208
Meadow, S.R., 414
Mednick, S.A., 265, 395, 398, 399, 408
Medoff, H., 202
Medvedev, Z., 608
Meehl, P., 387, 389, 567
Mees, H., 470
Meichenbaum, D.H., 462, 556, 559
Meinecke, C.F., 343
Meiselman, K.C., 332
Melamed, B.G., 546, 631
Mellinger, G.D., 500
Mello, N.K., 283
Mellor, C.S., 381, 382
Melville, H., 244, 245
Mendels, J., 69, 237, 436
Mendelson, J.H., 283, 286, 313
Mendkoff, E., 506
Mendlewicz, J., 236
Menkes, D.B., 237
Menlove, F.L., 46, 427
Merluzzi, T.V., 95, 140
Merriman, R., 308
Merskey, H., 183
Mesmer, F.A., 21, 22, 23, 185
Metalsky, G.I., 230, 232
Metzner, R., 317
Mey, B.J.V., 332
Meyer, A., 378
Meyer, E., 169
Meyer, J., 326, 327
Meyer, R.E., 295, 313
Meyer, R.G., 563
Meyer, V., 152, 155, 157, 593
Meyer-Bahlburg, H., 324
Michelli, J., 100
Michelson, L., 430
Miklich, D.R., 210
Miklowitz, D.J., 397
Miles, L.E., 500
Miles, M.B., 579, 580
Milgram, N.A., 462
Millar, W.M., 200
Miller, E., 493
Miller, H.R., 489
Miller, I.W., 229
Miller, L., 428
Miller, L.C., 429
Miller, N.E., 46, 47, 50, 112, 286, 570
Miller, R.G., 417
Miller, S.T., 214
Miller, T., 560
Miller, W.R., 229
Milton, F., 145
Milton, O., 31, 261
Mineka, S., 137, 139, 232
Mines, R.A., 550
Mintz, E., 576
Mintz, J., 561
Mintz, R.S., 245
Minuchin, S., 422, 433, 583
Mirenda, P.L., 465
Mischell, W., 88, 103, 104, 106, 566, 567
Mitchell, J.E., 434

Mittelman, M.S., 342
Moats, L.C., 442
Mohr, J.W., 335
Mohs, R.C., 643
Moldofsky, H., 432
Molk, L., 435
Monahan, J., 609, 612
Money, J., 324, 325
Moniz, E., 399
Monroe, S.M., 223, 232
Montgomery, R.J.Y., 498
Moore, D., 584
Moore, M.A., 498
Moos, R.H., 18, 233
Morgan, A.H., 24
Morin, C.M., 501
Moris, N., 603
Morokoff, P., 328, 329
Morris, A.A., 602
Morris, G., 493
Morris, J., 326
Morris, J.B., 242
Morrison, J.R., 417
Morrison, S.L., 396
Morse, J., 603, 609, 614
Morse, S.J., 516
Moser, C., 340
Moses, A., 88
Moss, J.R., 591
Mott, D.E.W., 546
Mowrer, O.H., 46, 47, 50, 137, 148, 415
Mowrer, W.M., 415
Mrazek, F.J., 333
Mulligan, T., 503
Munby, M., 144
Munjack, D.J., 358
Murad, Sultan, IV, 302
Murdock, M., 561
Murphy, D., 311
Murphy, D.L., 237
Murphy, G.E., 239, 552
Murphy, J., 388
Murphy, W.D., 339
Murray, E.J., 566
Muscettola, G., 237
Muskin, J., 177
Myers, J.K., 113, 133, 146, 222, 223, 279, 491, 492, 496, 499, 504

Nader, R., 596
Nahas, G.G., 312
Naranjo, C., 314
Nason, A., 355
Nathan, P.E., 259, 286, 290, 291, 541
Navia, B.A., 364
Nawas, M.M., 577
Nay, F.H., 98
Neale, J.M., 83, 118, 120, 126, 149, 194–197, 234, 235, 348
Neff, R.L., 332
Neisser, U., 50
Nelson, E., 307
Nelson, J.C., 223
Nelson, M., 450
Nelson, R.E., 95, 227
Nelson, R.O., 92, 240
Nemetz, G.H., 546
Netter, F.H., 169
Nettlebeck, T., 449

Neugebauer, R., 12, 17
Neuhaus, E.C., 210
Neuringer, C., 247
Newman, J.B., 268, 269
Newman, R.J., 641
Newsom, C., 466
Nezu, A.M., 555
Nicholson, R.A., 560
Nies, D.C., 101
Nietzel, M.T., 99, 595
Nightingale, E.J., 545
Nihira, K., 444
Nisbett, R.E., 175, 233
Nissinen, A., 593
Noble, H., 429
Nocks, B.C., 508
Nogrady, H., 25
Nolen-Hoeksema, S., 230
Nordlie, J.W., 173
Norman, W.H., 229
North, A.F., 457
Norton, J.P., 397
Notarious, C.I., 100
Nowlan, R., 313
Nowlin, W.F., 559
Noyes, R., 144, 147
Nunez, J.A., 77
Nunnally, J.C., 80
Nurnberg, H.G., 364, 644
Nye, F.I., 420
Nyswander, M., 300

O'Brien, G.T., 145, 586
O'Connor, R.D., 430, 615
O'Donohue, W.T., 503
O'Hara, M.W., 493
O'Leary, K.D., 103, 144, 412, 416, 421, 546, 560, 562, 564, 567, 571, 585, 624
O'Leary, S.G., 624
O'Neal, J.M., 376
Obler, M., 367
Obrist, P.A., 201, 202
Ochitil, H., 178
Ockene, J.K., 306
Ohman, A., 139
Ojemann, G.A., 441
Okun, M.A., 482
Oldham, J.M., 257
Olds, D.L., 595
Oliveau, D., 133
Ollendick, T.H., 546
Olsen, S.A., 387
Oltmanns, T.F., 585
Omizo, M.M., 550
Omizo, S.A., 550
Orlinsky, D.E., 560
Orne, E.C., 183
Orne, M.T., 22, 183
Ornitz, E., 469
Orris, J.B., 270
Ort, S.I., 451
Osborn, C.E., 94
Osgood, N.J., 501
Osler, W., 203
Otto, R., 156
Owens, M., 436

Pahnke, W.N., 317
Paitich, D., 323
Palkes, H.S., 417
Palmer, R.L., 431

Palmore, E.B., 479
Pappenheim, B., 22
Parfitt, D.N., 185
Paris, S., 14
Parisi, S.A., 493
Parker, B.D., 604
Parkes, C.M., 493
Parkinson, J., 646
Parks. C.W., Jr., 94
Parloff, M.B., 553
Parsons, D.A., 87
Parsons, O.A., 280, 283
Pasamanick, B., 441
Pasteur, L., 30
Patel, C., 214
Patel, M., 214
Paternite, C.E., 416
Paterson, C.M., 268
Paterson, G., 89, 585
Patsiokas, A.T., 247
Patterson, G.R., 421, 423, 424
Paul, G.L., 19, 91, 98, 104, 402, 406, 523, 528, 540, 543–545, 568, 574, 577, 594, 618, 632
Paul, R., 451
Pauster, L., 20
Pavlov, I., 43, 45, 138
Paykel, E.S., 226, 233
Peake, P.K., 106
Pearson, C., 483, 484, 504
Pearson, C.G., 476, 505
Pearson, K., 117
Pedro-Carrol, J.L., 595
Peel, R., 603, 608
Pekanmaki, L., 286
Pendery, M.L., 292
Penk, W.E., 159
Pennebaker, J., 120, 121, 122
Pennington, B., 465
Pennington, B.F., 441
Penrod, S., 338
Penta, J.S., 313
Pentoney, P., 534
Perkins, S.C., 177
Perl, M., 479
Perley, M.J., 171
Perlman, T., 285
Perlmutter, M., 481
Perloff, B.F., 546, 564
Perls, F.S., 530, 531–535, 558, 574
Perris, L., 235
Perry, B.A., 100
Perry, C., 25
Perry, J.D., 354
Person, E.S., 325
Pervin, L.A., 149
Pet, M.A., 356
Peters, J.J., 201, 343
Peterson, C., 230
Petito, C.K., 364
Pfeiffer, E., 494, 495, 501, 502, 610
Phares, J., 104
Phillips, D.P., 245, 428
Phillips, J.S., 89, 567
Phillips, L., 378
Phoenix, C., 343
Pick, A., 644
Pierce, C., 201
Pierce, C.M., 414
Pilon, R., 563

Pilowsky, I., 500
Pinel, P., 15, 16, 17, 18, 260, 261
Pinsoff, W.M., 580, 585, 586
Piran, N., 436
Pirsig, R., 23
Pittillo, E.S., 115
Pitts, F.N. Jr., 316
Plath, S., 244
Plato, 8, 346
Plummer, S., 546
Plutchik, R., 257
Poddar, P., 626
Pokorny, A.D., 243
Polatin, P., 378
Polefka, D., 145, 429
Polen, S.B., 441
Polich, J.M., 292
Polland, R.E., 238
Pomeroy, W.B., 346, 502
Poon, L.W., 481, 482
Pope, H.G., 257, 435, 436
Porter, R., 496
Post, F., 393, 491, 493, 495–497
Post, R.M., 393
Poster, D.S., 313
Pottash, A.C., 305
Powell, L.H., 215
Premack, D., 542
Prentky, R.A., 337
Press, G.A., 469
Price, L.H., 238
Price, R.W., 364
Price, T.R.P., 493
Price, V.A., 199, 215, 557
Prichard, J., 260, 261
Prien, R.F., 242
Prinz, P., 500
Prinz, R., 234
Prioleau, L., 561
Prizant, E.M., 466
Prochaska, J.O., 530, 534
Proctor, J.T., 176
Prudic, J., 364
Pryor, R., 297
Pu, T., 176
Pucel, J.C., 577
Puig-Antich, J., 431
Pullan, B.R., 328
Pumarola, S.T., 644
Purcell, K., 207, 209
Purdie, F.R., 490
Purisch, A., 87
Purpura, D.P., 450
Puska, P., 593
Putnam, F.W., 182
Pyle, R.L., 435
Pyter, L., 214

Quay, H.C., 270, 416, 419, 421, 425
Queen Victoria, 608
Quinsey, V.L., 339

Rabavilas, A., 155
Rabins, P.V., 491, 640
Rachman, S.J., 134, 152, 155, 156, 331, 561, 580
Radloff, L., 230
Rae, D.S., 493
Ragland, D.R., 206

Rahe, R.H., 193, 203
Rainer, J.D., 236
Rank, O., 52
Rapaport, D., 520
Rapaport, K., 336
Rapoport, A., 145
Rapoport, J.L., 418
Rapp, S.R., 493
Rappaport, J., 587–589
Raskin, F., 493
Raskin, M., 500
Ratliff, K.S., 77
Ray, R.S., 424
Raymond, J.G., 325
Rayner, R., 45, 136, 137
Reagan, R., 604–606, 608
Reddon, J.R., 335
Redfield, J., 194
Redick, R.W., 491, 504
Redlich, F.S., 395, 396
Redmond, D.E., 149
Redmond, D.E., Jr., 305
Reed, B.R., 195, 196, 197
Reed, S.D., 213, 562, 563
Reeve, V.C., 312
Regan, W.M., 169, 171
Regier, D.A., 491, 496, 498, 499
Rehm, L.P., 227
Reich, J., 258
Reich, T., 421
Reich, W., 360
Reid, E.C., 220
Reid, J.B., 282
Reifler, B.V., 492, 493
Reiss, L., 209, 210
Reiss, S., 139
Reitan, R.M., 86, 645
Reith, G., 546
Rekers, G.A., 327
Renna, C.M., 211
Reppuci, N.D., 595
Rescorla, R.A., 105
Resick, P.A., 336
Resko, J.A., 343
Resnick, H.S., 160
Resnik, H.L.P., 244
Reter, D.G., 326, 327
Reuter, J.M., 398
Revenstorf, D., 585
Reynard, C.J., 416
Reynolds, E.J., 328
Rice, J., 236
Rice, L.N., 534
Richards, P., 423
Richardson, S.A., 449
Richter, C.P., 148
Rickards, L.D., 505
Ricks, D.M., 465
Rieder, R.O., 394
Riesman, F., 594
Rimland, B., 48, 70, 463, 465, 468, 469
Risley, T., 470
Ritter, B., 49, 546, 577
Ritvo, E.R., 464, 472
Roberto, L.G., 327
Roberts, M.C., 546
Robey, A., 610
Robins, C., 94
Robins, E., 220

Robins, L.N., 77, 171, 263, 264, 267, 421, 492
Robinson, H.B., 445, 460
Robinson, L.A., 234
Robinson, N.M., 445, 450, 460
Rodin, J., 500, 507
Rodnick, E., 397
Roehrich, H., 314
Roesch, R., 610
Rogers, C., 38, 52, 53, 54, 152, 403, 524–528, 530, 534, 535, 558, 574, 576–578
Rokeach, M., 365
Romanczyk, R.G., 99, 470
Romeo, N., 615
Roose, S.P., 223, 305
Roosevelt, T., 293
Rooth, F.G., 335
Rorschach, H., 81, 88
Rose, S.D., 578, 579
Rosen, E., 282, 322, 332, 358, 359, 368
Rosen, J., 402, 403
Rosen, J.C., 433, 435
Rosen, L.W., 435
Rosen, P., 490
Rosen, R.C., 281, 322, 329, 332, 342, 344, 354, 356, 358, 359, 368, 370, 503, 546, 630
Rosenbaum, J., 94
Rosenbaum, M., 180, 552
Rosenberg, M.S., 595
Rosenblatt, R.A., 483, 505
Rosenhan, D.L., 18
Rosenman, R.H., 203, 204, 205
Rosenthal, D., 390, 516, 534, 631
Rosenthal, N.E., 224
Rosenthal, R., 103, 120
Rosenthal, T.L., 139, 596
Rosenzweig, M., 450
Rosin, A.J., 498
Rositer, E.M., 435
Rosman, B.L., 433
Ross, A.O., 413, 546
Ross, D.M., 418, 462
Ross, J.L., 432
Ross, S.A., 418, 462
Ross, S.M., 574
Rossi, A.M., 313
Rossini, E., 88
Roth, D., 227
Roth, M., 493, 496, 497
Roth, S., 229
Rothman, D., 544
Rothman, E., 458
Rounsaville, B.J., 553, 554
Roy, A., 238, 243
Roybal, E.R., 504
Ruberman, W., 196
Rubin, H.B., 328
Rugg, D., 307
Runck, B., 563, 564
Rush, A.J., 239, 551, 552
Rush, B., 13
Rush, J., 561
Ruskin, A., 200
Russell, D.E.H., 338
Russell, M.A.H., 306, 308
Russo, D.C., 434
Ruth, V., 485

Rutter, M., 421, 422, 430, 464, 465, 468, 469
Ryall, R., 422
Ryan, W., 332, 589
Rybstein-Blinchik, E., 559

Sachs, J.S., 580
Sackeim, H.A., 173, 174
Safer, D.J., 416
Safran, J.D., 567
Sagan, C., 23
Sakel, M., 399
Sakheim, D.K., 329, 367
Sallan, S.E., 313
Salonen, J.T., 593
Salter, A., 539, 556
Salzman, L., 153, 156
Sandler, J., 541, 546
Santos, J.F., 504
Sarason, S.B., 233
Sargent, J.D., 212
Sargent, T., 314
Sartorius, N., 379
Sartre, J.P., 52
Sassenrath, E.N., 312
Satir, V., 583
Satterfield, J.H., 419
Sawicki, R.F., 88
Scates, S., 493
Schachter, S., 268, 269, 270, 304
Schaeffer, B., 546
Schafer, R., 641
Schaffer, R.L., 200
Schaie, K.W., 477, 478
Schain, R.J., 416
Scheerenberger, R.C., 459
Scheerer, M., 458
Scheff, T.J., 388
Schefft, B.K., 88
Schell, A.M., 137, 419
Scheri, D.J., 343
Schildkraut, J.J., 236
Schinke, S.P., 308
Schlesier-Stropp, B., 433, 435
Schmal, D.P., 306
Schmauk, F.J., 269
Schmidt, J.R., 613
Schneider, E.L., 479
Schneider, K., 381, 382
Schneider, N.G., 306, 307
Schnur, E., 457
Schoeneman, T.J., 10
Schoenfeld, D., 201
Schofield, W., 589
Schratz, M., 504
Schreibman, L., 470
Schuckit, M.A., 288, 498, 552
Schulsinger, F., 265, 398, 399, 408
Schultz, J.H., 212
Schulz, R., 233, 506
Schuyler, D., 247
Schwab, J.J., 191
Schwartz, D., 432
Schwartz, G.E., 149, 192, 211, 214, 562
Schwartz, J.L., 306, 581
Schwartz, J.R., 183
Schwartz, M.S., 18, 396

Schwartz, R., 581
Schwartz, R.M., 557
Schwartz, S.H., 365
Schwitzgebel, R.K., 610, 612, 614, 616, 626
Schwitzgebel, R.L., 610, 612, 614, 616, 626
Seaman, F.J., 285
Sederer, L.I., 402
Seeman, P., 393
Segal, Z.V., 567
Segovia-Riquelman, N., 287
Seguin, E., 457
Seiden, R.H., 244
Seidman, L.J., 394
Seligman, M.E.P., 138, 139, 220, 228, 229–232, 239, 240, 566
Selinger, H.V., 430
Selling, L.S., 16
Selye, H., 191
Seneca, 242
Serban, G., 257
Serber, M., 578
Settin, J.M., 505
Shader, R.I., 146, 295, 580
Shadish, W.R., 597
Shakespeare, W., 281, 518
Shannon, D.T., 574, 577
Shapiro, A.P., 202
Shapiro, D., 211, 214, 561, 562
Shapiro, D.A., 561
Shapiro, R., 379
Sharpley, C.F., 100
Shaw, B.F., 552, 554, 567
Shaw, P., 368
Shaywitz, B.A., 418
Shaywitz, S.E., 418
Shearin, E.N., 243, 245
Shekelle, R.B., 205
Shepherd, I.L., 531
Sher, K.J., 156, 286
Sherman, A.R., 539
Sherman, E., 509
Shields, J., 149, 390
Shiffrin, R.M., 448
Shilling, L.E., 404
Shneidman, E.S., 243–249, 591
Shoenbach, V., 196
Shopsin, B., 237
Short, J.F., 420
Shulgin, A.T., 314
Siegel, J.M., 332
Siegel, L.J., 546
Siegel, R.K., 298
Siegel, S.E., 434
Siegler, I.C., 479, 481, 482, 499
Siemens, A.J., 313
Siever, L.J., 149
Sigvardsson, S., 288
Silberman, E., 493
Silver, M.J., 122
Silverstein, C., 346, 347, 541, 630
Simeons, A.T.W., 198
Simmons, M., 313
Simon, R.J., 604–606
Simon, W., 341
Simons, A.D., 239, 552
Singer, L.T., 443
Singer, M., 468

Sintchak, G.H., 328
Sipprelle, R.C., 160
Sizemore, C.C., 115
Skinner, B.F., 45, 50, 90, 105, 542, 557, 564, 566
Skinner, H.A., 285
Sklar, L.A., 192
Skrzypek, G.J., 270
Slater, E., 149, 170, 177, 235
Sleator, E.K., 419
Slicker, W.D., 603
Slivinske, L.R., 507
Sloane, R.B., 492, 522–524, 528, 637
Small, G.W., 494, 636
Smith, D., 460
Smith, D.W., 450
Smith, J.L., 549
Smith, K.F., 507
Smith, M.L., 560, 561
Smith, P.B., 578
Smith, R.T., 499
Smith, S., Jr., 366
Smith, S.D., 441
Smith, T., 177
Smith, T.W., 549
Sneed, T.J., 542
Snider, V.D., 644
Snow, J., 113
Snyder, C.R., 177
Snyder, M., 106
Snyder, S.H., 295, 393
Sobel, J., 308
Sobell, L.C., 290
Sobell, M.B., 290
Solan, H.A., 442
Solnick, R.L., 502, 503
Solnit, A.J., 457
Soloff, P.H., 272
Solomon, R.L., 105
Solomon, Z., 158
Sorotzin, B., 414
Soueif, M.I., 312
Spanier, G.B., 100
Spanos, N.P., 10, 24, 25, 183
Spar, J.E., 636
Sparrow, S.S., 444
Speer, D.C., 591
Spence, D.P., 522
Spencer, S.L., 329
Spengler, A., 340
Spengler, D., 559
Sperling, M., 173
Spiegel, C., 505
Spiegel, D., 594
Spiegel, J.P., 162
Spielberger, C.D., 201
Spiers, P.A., 87
Spinetta, J.J., 434
Spinoza, B., 110
Spitalnik, R., 564
Spitzer, R.L., 77, 78, 255, 257
Sprague, R.L., 418, 419
Sprenger, J., 9
Sprenkle, D.H., 585
Srole, L., 395
Sroufe, L.A., 418
St Augustine, 242
St Tomas Aquinas, 242
St. Lawrence, J.S., 365, 366
St. George-Hyslop, 644

Staats, A.W., 542
Staats, C.K., 542
Stam, H.J., 24
Stambul, H.B., 292
Standish, R., 313
Stang, R.R., 646
Stanton, A.H., 18
Stanton, M.D., 163, 317
Stapleton, J., 308
Stapp, J., 504
Starfield, B., 414, 415
Starr, B.D., 502
Staub, E., 149
Steadman, H.J., 603, 610
Steele, C.M., 286, 287
Stein, D.M., 591
Stein, S.P., 505
Steiner, B., 323
Steinman, C., 326
Stenmark, D.E., 492
Stephens, J.H., 170
Stephens, P.M., 202
Sterback, R.A., 190
Sterman, H.B., 563
Stern, D.B., 177
Stern, R.S., 153
Sternberg, M.P., 493
Stevenson, J., 335
Stewart, M.A., 416, 417, 469
Stimbert, V., 466
Stock, W., 359, 369
Stolberg, A., 422
Stolberg, A.L., 595
Stoller, F.H., 576
Stone, A.A., 603, 612, 614, 616, 617, 628
Stone, A., 194, 195, 196, 197
Stone, G., 192
Stone, L.J., 200
Stone, M.H., 272, 403
Storandt, M., 509
Storm, C.L., 585
Strandlund, R., 529
Stricker, G., 80
Stringer, A.Y., 273
Strub, R.L., 490
Strupp, H.H., 580
Stuart, F.M., 356
Stuart, R.B., 100, 538, 583, 585, 623, 624
Stunkard, A.J., 559, 561
Sturgis, E.T., 630
Sugai, D.P., 430
Sugar, O., 646
Sugerman, A.A., 580
Sullaway, M., 102
Sullivan, H.S., 42, 378, 379, 402, 403, 520, 569
Summit, R.C., 333
Sundberg, N.D., 597
Sunderland, A., 482
Surwit, R.S., 562, 563
Sutherland, S., 343
Sutton-Simon, K., 336
Svoboda, W., 620
Swanson, E., 498
Swartz, M., 171
Sweeney, D.R., 305, 314
Sweet, J.J., 88
Swift, W.J., 436
Sylvester, D., 133

Symonds, 193
Syndenham, T., 19
Syndulko, K., 267
Szasz, T., 17, 31, 606, 608, 609, 632

Taffel, S.J., 546
Tarasoff, T., 626
Tashkin, D.P., 313
Tate, B.G., 124, 125
Taube, C.A., 491, 504
Taylor, C.B., 72, 307
Taylor, J.A., 104
Taylor, W., 308
Teasdale, J.D., 229, 239, 566
Tempchin, J., 529
Teri, L., 493, 509, 577
Terry, D.J., 214
Terry, R.D., 486
Thaker, G.K., 401
Thaler, F.H., 153
Theodor, L.H., 173
Thibaut, J.W., 583
Thigpen, C.H., 114, 115
Thompson, L.W., 494
Thompson, M., 432
Thompson, R.F., 215
Thoresen, C.E., 215
Thorndike, E., 45, 137
Thurber, S., 422
Thyer, B.A., 286
Tienari, P., 397
Tillich, P., 529
Timko, C., 500
Tippin, J., 157
Titchener, E., 43, 557
Tituba, 14
Tizard, J., 430
Tobler, N., 308
Todack, G., 431
Todd, P.A., 508
Tollefson, D.J., 193
Tolstoy, L., 244, 509
Torgersen, S., 144, 146, 149, 177
Tramontana, J., 466
Treffert, D.A., 468
Treyens, J.C., 95
Truet, J., 593
Trull, T.J., 254, 259
Trumball, R., 191
Tsai, L., 469
Tsujimoto, R.N., 566
Tuason, V.B., 239
Tuckman, J., 245
Tuke, W., 18
Tulis, E.H., 257
Tunstall, C., 307
Tuomilehto, J., 593
Turkat, I.D., 272
Turkewitz, H., 546, 585
Turner, B.F., 502
Turner, R.E., 335
Turner, R.J., 396, 493
Turner, S.M., 405, 546
Tursky, B., 149, 211, 213, 214, 562
Twain, M., 420
Twentyman, C.T., 140

Uhde, T.W., 149

Uhlrnhuth, E.H., 500
Ullmann, L., 176
Ulmer, D., 215
Ultman, M., 364
Umbarger, C.C., 590
Upper, D., 574
Urban, H.B., 516, 521, 524, 528

Vaillant, G., 293, 493
Valentine, M., 200
Valins, S., 566
Vallis, T.M., 567
Van Putten, T., 401
Vandecreek, L., 626
VandenBos, G.R., 504
Vandereycken, W., 433
vanEgeren, L.F., 96
Vardaris, R.M., 312
Varela, A., 287
Vargas, M.J., 559
Varma, V.K., 312
Varner, R.V., 494
Varni, J.W., 434, 435
Vaughn, C.E., 398, 401
Verbrugge, L.M., 195
Veronen, L.J., 336
Verowerd, H., 608
Verwoerdt, A., 502
Vesalius, 19
Victor, R.G., 317, 318
Videka-Sherman, L., 594
Viek, P., 148
Volkmar, F., 467
Voltaire, 244
Von Felsinger, J.M., 317
Von Wright, J.M., 286
VonPohl, R., 550
Vygotsky, L.S., 449

Wachtel, E.F., 581
Wachtel, P.L., 32, 36, 41, 42,
    56, 102, 104, 105, 106, 144,
    514, 516, 569, 570, 571, 581
Waddell, M.T., 144
Wadden, T.A., 214
Wagner, R.L., 394
Wagonfeld, M.O., 396
Wahl, J.M., 306
Wahler, R.G., 31, 261
Waldfogel, S., 426
Waldron, H., 584
Waldron, I., 204
Walen, S., 178
Walker, E., 399
Wallace, C.E., 493
Wallace, C.J., 547
Wallace, R.B., 493
Wallander, J.L., 435
Walsh, B.T., 305
Walsh, D.A., 493
Walters, E.D., 212
Walters, R.H., 422, 547
Walton, D., 186
Wampold, B.F., 584, 585
Wang, H.S., 502
Wansley, R.A., 435
Ward, C.H., 225

Ward, W.S., 22
Waren, C.A.B., 611
Warheit, G.J., 191, 498
Warner, K.E., 302
Warren, R., 595
Waskow, I.E., 554
Waterhouse, L., 465
Watson, G.C., 170
Watson, J., 547, 557, 560
Watson, J.B., 43, 44, 136, 137
Watson, M., 451
Watt, N.F., 398
Watts, K., 482
Weakland, J.H., 509
Webster, J.S., 328
Weekes, J.R., 183
Weg, R.B., 503
Wegner, D.M., 155
Wehl, C.K., 291
Weick, K.E., 588
Weil, G.M., 317
Weiler, S.J., 502
Weimer, M.J., 239
Wein, A.J., 371
Weinber, G., 346
Weinberg, E., 435
Weinberg, L., 548
Weinberg, M.A., 479
Weinberger, D.R., 394
Weiner, B., 229, 232
Weiner, H., 199
Weiner, J.W., 591
Weiner, I.B., 80
Weiner, M.B., 502
Weiner, S., 451
Weinraub, M., 443
Weinrott, M.R., 344
Weinstein, K.A., 94, 204, 206
Weinstein, M., 577
Weintraub, M., 313
Weintraub, S., 83, 234
Weintraub, W., 317
Weisman, A.N., 555
Weiss, B., 450
Weiss, G., 285, 419
Weiss, J.H., 208
Weiss, R.L., 100, 585
Weiss, S., 199
Weiss, S.M., 192
Weissberg, R.P., 556
Weissman, A., 247
Weissman, M.M., 222, 223, 226,
    236, 504, 553, 554
Weisz, J.R., 450
Weitzenhoffer, A.M., 23
Wells, C.C., 636
Wells, C.E., 489
Wells, J.K., 559
Wells, L.A., 435
Wender, P.H., 236
Wenig, P., 563
Werry, J.S., 418
Wessberg, H., 140
West, L.J., 292
West, P.R., 504
Wester, P., 643
Wetzel, R.D., 239, 552

Weyer, G., 202
Whalen, C.K., 413, 416–418,
    424
Whanger, A.D., 495
Wheeler, E.G., 585
Whiffin, V.E., 234
Whipple, B., 354
White, J., 94, 227
White, J.A., 644
White, K., 94, 227
White, R.M., 504
White, W.A., 380
White, W.C., 435
Whitehead, A., 368, 493
Whitlock, F.A., 170
Whitmore, K., 430
Whittington, 498
Wickens, D.D., 137
Wicks-Nelson, 425
Widiger, T.A., 254, 255, 259
Wieder, G.B., 585
Wiener, G., 418
Wig, N.N., 312
Wigdor, B., 493
Wiggins, J., 264
Wikler, A., 284, 301
Wilkins, L.T., 273
Willers, K.R., 200
Williams, C.D., 493
Williams H., 208
Williams, J., 172, 328
Williams, J.D.W., 78
Williams, J.M., 493
Williams, K., 324, 325
Williams, L., 546
Williams, R.B., 205, 206
Williams, S.L., 145
Wills, T.A., 195
Wilson, G.T., 134, 144, 281,
    291, 412, 435, 541, 546,
    560, 561, 562, 567, 571,
    580
Wilson, R., 261
Wilson, R.C., 247
Wilson, R.S., 441
Wilson, T.D., 175, 233, 552
Wilson, W.C., 417, 418
Wilson, W.R., 175
Wiltz, N.A., 421
Wincze, J.P., 343, 367
Winett, R.A., 629
Wing, L., 469
Wingard, D.J., 484
Winick, C., 498
Winkler, R., 328
Winkler, R.C., 629
Winokur, A., 436
Winokur, G., 236, 371
Winters, K.C., 83, 235
Wise, T., 305, 627
Wisniewski, H.M., 484
Woerner, M.G., 146
Wohlford, P., 457
Wolchik, S.A., 329
Wold, D.A., 193
Wolf, E.D., 451
Wolf, E.S., 258

Wolf, F.M., 504
Wolf, H.G., 213
Wolf, M., 90, 470
Wolin, S.J., 282
Wolpe, J., 48, 50, 134, 144, 148,
    538, 539, 540, 558
Wong, D.F., 393
Wood, D.L., 202
Wood, L.F., 584
Wood, R.P., 430
Woodbury, M.A., 501
Woodruff, R.A., 222
Woods, S.W., 149
Wooldridge, P.W., 448
Woolf, V., 244
Woolfolk, R.L., 105
Wortman, C.B., 229
Wright, D.S., 421
Wundt, W., 43, 557
Wyatt, R.J., 394, 496, 497
Wynne, L.C., 468

Yalom, I., 594
Yalom, I.D., 30, 52, 56, 324
Yalom, J.D., 579, 580
Yanagashita, M., 479
Yeakel, E.H., 202
Yeates, K.D., 450
Yeudall, L.T., 335
Yeung-Courchesne, R., 469
Yoder, D.E., 465
Young, B.G., 335
Yurchenco, H., 645

Zajonc, R.B., 175
Zane, M.D., 146
Zarit, S.H., 478, 483, 487–489,
    495, 496, 504, 508, 509,
    640
Zeaman, D., 448
Zeigler, E., 389
Zeigob, L.E., 99
Zeiss, A.M., 504
Zeldis, S.M., 146
Zelinski, E.M., 482
Zeller, B., 210
Zess, R.A., 504
Ziegler, F.J., 169
Zighelboim, V., 94, 141
Zigler, E., 449, 597
Zilbergeld, B., 368
Zilboorg, G., 378
Zilboorg, G.W., 10
Zillman, D., 338
Zimbardo, P.G., 496
Zimberg, S., 498
Zimmerman, J., 174, 176
Zimmerman, M., 73, 223
Zimmerman, R., 307
Zinberg, N.E., 313
Zitrin, C.M., 146
Zohar, J., 156
Zonderman, A.B., 482
Zucker, K.J., 325
Zuroff, D.C., 105
Zusman, R., 201
Zyzanski, S.J., 204, 205

Subject Index

ABAB (reversal) design, 124, 542
Abortion, 454
Academic skills:
  attention-deficit hyperactivity disorder,
    416
  learning disabilities, 440
  mental retardation, 447
Academic skills disorder, 440–441
Accident(s), see Brain damage; Head injury
Achenbach Child Behavior Checklist, 90
Acquired fear, 111
Acquired immune deficiency syndrome
    (AIDS):
  dementia complex, 644
  described, 364–366, 367
Acrophobia, 133
Addiction, see also Psychoactive substance
    use disorder(s)
  barbiturate abuse, 295
  caffeine, 296
  cigarette smoking, 303, 304
  cocaine, 298
  defined, 279n1
  marijuana, 313
  nicotine, 302
  opiates abuse, 293, 294
  theories, 299
Addison's disease, 642
Adolescence, see also Childhood disorder(s)
  anorexia nervosa, 431–433
  attention-deficit hyperactivity disorder,
    417
  autistic disorder, 469
  conduct disorder, 419
  diagnostic categories, 65
Advertising, 309
Affective disorder(s), see Mood disorder(s)
After care, 621. See also Halfway house(s)
Age effect, 477
Ageism, 484–485
Age level, see also Adolescence; Aging;
    Childhood disorder(s)
  attention-deficit hyperactivity disorder,
    416
  barbiturate abuse, 295
  childhood fears, 425
  cigarette smoking, 302–303
  delirium, 489
  depression, 492
  marijuana use, 310
  mental retardation, 444, 447–448
  opiates abuse, 294
  paranoid delusions, 495
  schizophrenia, 376, 378
  toilet training, 414
Aggression:
  alcohol and, 281
  behavioral variability and, 107
  conduct disorders, 419, 420–421, 422
  essential hypertension, 200
  rape and, 338, 339
Aging, 475–510
  brain disorders, 485–491

cerebrovascular diseases, 486–487
concepts relative to, 476–478
delirium, 489–491, 637
delusional (paranoid) disorder, 494–497
dementia, 485, 488–489
depression, 491–494
facts about, 478–485
hypochondriasis, 499–500
insomnia, 500–501
problems of, 476
psychoactive substance abuse disorders,
  498–499
psychological disorders, 491–504
schizophrenia, 496–497
sexuality and, 501–504
suicide, 501
treatment and care issues, 504–509
Agoraphobia:
  defined, 133
  described, 135–136
  diagnostic category, 67
  family therapy, 145n5
  panic disorder, 147
  sex role, 135
  treatment of, 144, 145
AIDS, see Acquired immune deficiency
    syndrome (AIDS)
Akasthesia, 401
Al-Anon Family Groups, 289
Alateen, 289
Alcohol abuse, 280
Alcohol dependence, 280
Alcoholics Anonymous (AA), 289–290, 594
Alcoholism, 279–293. See also Psychoactive
    substance user disorder(s)
  aging and, 498
  amnestic syndrome and, 640
  antisocial personality disorder and, 265
  anxiety and, 146
  aversion therapy for, 541
  barbiturate abuse and, 295
  clonidine treatment for withdrawal, 305
  effects of (long-term), 281–284
  effects of (short-term), 280–281
  fetal alcohol syndrome and, 283, 455
  homelessness and, 619
  organic hallucinosis and, 641
  overview of, 279–280
  relapse prevention and, 565–566
  sexual dysfunction and, 362
  suicide and, 243n5
  theories, 284–288
  therapy for, 289–293
Allergy:
  asthma and, 210
  cigarette smoking and, 303
  psychophysiological disorders and, 198
Altruistic suicide, 245
Alzheimer's disease, 451. See also Dementia
  aging and, 485, 488–489
  described, 643–644
Amenorrhea, 431
American Law Institute, 604–606

American Psychiatric Association, see entries
    under DSM
Amnesia, see also Memory
  alcoholism, 283
  psychogenic amnesia, 179
  psychogenic fugue, 179
Amnestic syndrome, 640
Amniocentesis, 444
Amobarbital, 295
Amphetamine abuse, 278, 295–296. See also
    Psychoactive substance user disorder(s)
Analogue experiment, 123–124
Anal stage, 33
Anger, see Hostility
Anger-control training, 424
Animal experimentation, 122–124, 622n30
Animal magnetism, 21
Anomic suicide, 245
Anorexia nervosa, 431–433, 436. See also
    Bulimia nervosa
Antabuse (disulfiram), 289
Antidepressants, 146, 147
Antisocial behavior, 285
Antisocial personality disorder, 259, 260–271
  alcoholism and, 292
  avoidance learning and, 267–270
  barbiturate abuse, 295
  case histories of, 260–262
  central nervous system and, 265–267
  conduct disorders compared, 422, 423
  criteria in, 262–263
  diagnostic category of, 67
  family and, 263–264
  genetics and, 264–265
  historical perspective on, 260
  therapy for, 273–274
  underarousal and, 270–271
Anxiety:
  alcoholism and, 287
  antisocial personality disorder and, 268
  assessment of, 91, 98, 104–105
  autonomic nervous system measurement,
    96
  behavior therapy and, 48
  biofeedback and, 562
  bulimia nervosa and, 434
  cognitive behavior therapy and, 51
  death and, 509
  depression and, 232
  DSM-III definition of, 132
  learning paradigms and, 47
  obsessive-compulsive disorder and, 155
  organic anxiety syndrome, 642
  phobias and, 134
  psychoanalytic paradigm, 36
  psychophysiological disorders and, 211
  sexual dysfunctions and, 359, 360, 367
  social withdrawal (childhood), 429
  systematic desensitization and, 538–539
  theoretical concept of, 111–112
Anxiety disorder(s), 132–165
  diagnostic categories, 67, 132–133
  generalized anxiety disorder, 147–152

Anxiety disorder(s) (*Continued*)
  obsessive-compulsive disorder, 152–157
  panic disorder, 146–147
  phobias, 133–146
  physiological approaches to, 32
  posttraumatic stress disorder, 157–164
Anxiety hierarchy, 49
Anxiety reduction technique(s), 370
Anxiolytics (sedatives):
  abuse of, 293–295
  therapy with, 146, 147
Aphasia, 87, 486–487
Applied behavior analysis, 460–462
Aptitude, 84
Arousal:
  antisocial personality disorder and, 270–271
  attention-deficit hyperactivity disorder, 418
  sexual arousal, 281, 328–329, 356–357
Arousal reduction, 216
Articulated Thoughts During Simulated Situations (ATSS), 94, 95
Assasination, 604–605, 608–609
Assertion training:
  behavior therapy, 49
  described, 556–557
  group therapy, 577–578
Assessment of Daily Experience (ADE), 194–195
Assessment procedure(s), 76–107
  anxiety and, 104–105
  behavioral assessment, 88–103
  behavioral consistency and variability and, 103–107
  brain abnormality and, 85–88
  clinical interview, 76, 78–79
  psychological testing, 78, 80–85
Asthma, 207–211
  amphetamine treatment for, 295
  described, 207–208
  etiology of, 208–211
  psychophysiological disorders, 198
  therapy for, 211
Astrology, 106n7
Asylums, 12–18, 544. *See also* Mental hospital(s)
Atherosclerosis, 202, 286–287
Attention, 382–383, 448
Attention-deficit hyperactivity disorder, 413, 416–419
  classification of, 413, 416–417
  psychological theories of, 418
  physiological theories of, 417–418
  treatment of, 418–419
Attribution, 229–230, 233, 482
Attributional-Style Questionnaire, 231, 232, 234
Attribution to self, 566
Autistic disorder, 463–472
  descriptive characteristics of, 463–468
  Education for All Handicapped Children Act and, 459
  ethics and, 632
  etiology of, 468–470
  first-person account of, 467
  mental retardation compared, 443n1
  operant conditioning and, 546
  self-injurious behavior and, 461
  treatment of, 470–472
Autonomic (involuntary) nervous system, 96, 141

Aversion therapy:
  alcoholism, 290, 291
  behavior therapy and, 49
  described, 541–542
  ethics and, 631–632
  homosexuality and, 630
  paraphilias and, 342
  self-injurious behavior and, 461
  smoking cessation programs and, 309
Avoidance conditioning, 47, 136–139
Avoidance learning, 267–270
Avoidance personality disorder, 259
Awareness, 175

Bail, 610
Barbiturate abuse, 278, 294–295. *See also* Psychoactive substance use disorder(s)
Baseline, 122
Beck Depression Inventory, 228, 232
Bedlam, 13
Beggars, 12
Behavioral assessment, 88–103
  behavioral consistency/variability, 103–107
  behavior therapy and, 98
  cognitive assessment, 94–95
  direct observation, 89–92
  interview/self-report measures, 92–93
  marital assessment, 100–102
  overview of, 88–89
  physiological measurement, 95–98
  reliability of, 98–99
  validity of, 99, 103
Behavioral marital therapy, 100–102, 583–584. *See also* Couples and family therapy
Behavioral medicine, 558–563
  biofeedback, 562–563
  chronic pain, 559
  origins of, 558–559
  prevention and, 559, 562
  psychophysiological disorders, 211
Behavioral pediatrics, 343–345
Behavioral skills training, 217, 370
Behavior genetics, 142–143
Behavior rehearsal, 546, 557
Behavior therapy, 538–571
  behavioral assessment and, 98
  behavioral pediatrics, 434–435
  broad-spectrum treatment, 567–568
  causation and, 567
  client-therapist relationship, 568
  cognitive behavior therapy, 50–51
  cognitive restructuring, 547–554, 557–558
  conduct disorders, 424
  counterconditioning, 538–642
  described, 48–49
  development of, 42–46
  dissociative disorders and, 186
  ethics and, 631–632
  family therapy, 100–102, 583–584
  gender identity disorder, 327–330
  generalization/maintenance issues in, 563–566
  generalized anxiety disorder and, 150–152
  group therapy, 576–578
  homosexuality and, 630
  internal events and cognitions, 566–567
  inventiveness and, 568
  modeling, 546–547
  obsessive-compulsive disorders and, 155, 156–157
  operant conditioning and, 542–546

overview of, 538
paradigm and, 26–27
paraphilias, 341–342, 343
personality disorders and, 272–273
phobias and, 134–135, 136–141, 144–146
psychoanalysis and, 522–524, 569–571
psychophysiological disorders and, 211
schizophrenia and, 406
self-injurious behavior and, 461
smoking cessation programs and, 307
somatoform disorders and, 176–177, 178
Bell and pad apparatus, 415
Bereavement, 493
Bias, 103, 347, 561
Bible, 7
Bile(s), 8
Biochemistry:
  attention-deficit hyperactivity disorder, 417–418
  depression in the elderly, 493
  mood disorders and, 236–238
  schizophrenia and, 392–394
Bioenergetics, 360
Biofeedback:
  described, 562–563
  hypertension and, 214
  migraine headache and, 212–213
  psychophysiological disorders and, 211
  stress management techniques and, 216
Biological factors, *see also* Physical health; *entries under* Organic
  alcoholism, 280, 282–284
  brain, 638–639
  obsessive-compulsive disorders, 156
  psychophysiological disorders, 190–191
  sexual physiology, 354–355
  somatoform disorders, 177
  stress and, 196–197
Bipolar disorder:
  aging and, 491–492
  borderline personality disorder and, 257
  childhood disorders, 430–431
  diagnostic category, 66, 222
  genetics and, 235–236
  heterogeneity within, 223–224
  learned helplessness and, 232
  major depression contrasted, 223
  pharmacotherapy for, 242
  theories, 235
Birth anxiety, 36
Bisexuality, 346
Blackout (alcoholic), 282
Blaming the victim, 589
Blindness, 173–174
Blood pressure, 96, 199–202
Body dysmorphic disorder, 168
Body image, 432
Borderline personality disorder, 272
Brain, *see also* Organic mental disorder(s); Organic mental syndrome(s)
  aging and, 485–491
  anatomy of, 638–639
  antisocial personality disorder, 265–267
  assessment of abnormality of, 85–88
  Down's syndrome and, 451
  drug abuse and, 294, 295, 297
  electroconvulsive therapy and, 242
  learning disabilities and, 441
  mood disorders and, 236–237
  obsessive-compulsive disorders and, 156, 157
  schizophrenia and, 394–395

somatoform disorders, 177
somatogenesis, 8, 20
Brain damage, *see also* Head injury
  attention-deficit hyperactivity disorder, 418
  dementia, 637
  mental retardation, 449, 450
  neuropsychological assessment, 86–88
Brief (time-limited) therapy, 523–524
Briquet's syndrome, *see* Somatization disorder (Briquet's syndrome)
Broad-spectrum behavior therapy, 567–568
Bulimia nervosa, 432, 433–435, 436

Caffeine, 296
Cancer, 302, 313, 314*n*20
Cannabis sativa, 309. *See also* Marijuana
Cardiovascular disease, 199–207, 593
Case study method, 113–116, 186*n*10, 260–262
Castration anxiety, 331, 335
Catatonic immobility, 383, 386
Cathartic method, 21
Causation, 110, 113, 119, 123, 567
Central nervous system, *see also* Brain
  alcohol effects on, 280
  antisocial personality disorder and, 265–267
  attention-deficit hyperactivity disorder, 418
  autistic disorder, 470
  narcotics abuse, 293
Cerebral palsy, 447*n*3, 563
Cerebrovascular disease, 486–487
Character disorder, 254. *See also* Personality disorder(s)
Chemical imbalance, 20, 32. *See also* Biochemistry
Chemotherapy, 313
Child molestation, 333, 594–595
Childhood disorder(s), 412–437
  adult disorders contrasted, 412–413
  affective disorders, 430–431
  anorexia nervosa, 431–433
  attention-deficit hyperactivity disorder, 413, 416–419
  autistic disorder, 463–472
  bulimia nervosa, 433–435
  classification of, 65, 412–413
  conduct disorders, 419–425
  dissociative disorders, 182
  fears, 425–429
  gender identity disorder, 322–325
  learning disabilities, 440–442
  mental retardation, 442–463
  overcontrolled behavior, 425–431
  social withdrawal, 429–430
  undercontrolled behavior, 413–425
Childhood onset pervasive developmental disorder, 464. *See also* Autistic disorder
Child psychology, 39
Child rearing, *see* Family
Children:
  asthma, 207–210
  ethical issues, 629
  homelessness and, 619
  operant conditioning and, 545–546
  posttraumatic stress disorder, 157–158
  rational-emotive therapy and, 550
Chlorpromazine, 400
Cholesterol, 202
Chronic affective disorder, 224

Cigarette smoking, *see* Nicotine and cigarette smoking
Cirrhosis of the liver, 283
Civil commitment, 611–621, 625
Civil liberties, 618–621
Civil rights, 602, 613
Classical conditioning:
  described, 43–45
  enuresis, 415
  phobias, 136, 137, 138
  psychophysiological disorders, 198–199
Classification, *see* Diagnostic classification
Classificatory variable, 118–120
Claustrophobia, 133
Client-centered therapy, 53–54, 211, 524–528, 568
Clinical assessment, *see* Assessment procedure(s)
Clinical interview, 76, 78–79, 92–93, 94–95
Clinical psychology, 6
Clitoris, 354, 355
Clonidine, 305
Clozapine, 401*n*13
Cocaine abuse, 296–298, 300
Code V, 68
Coercion hypothesis, 423
Coffee, 296
Cognition:
  aging and, 489
  alcohol and, 280, 286
  behavior therapy and, 88, 566–567
  generalized anxiety disorder and, 149
  learning disabilities and, 442
  mental retardation and, 448
  modeling and, 547
  neuropsychological assessment and, 88
  post-Freudian perspective and, 39
  senile dementia and, 489
  suicide and, 246, 247
Cognitive assessment, 94–95, 101
Cognitive-behavior therapy:
  AIDS prevention and, 365
  causation and, 567
  described, 50–51
  generalized anxiety disorder and, 148–149
  mental retardation and, 460, 462
  paradigm of, 49–52, 57
  perspectives on, 557–558
  learned helplessness concept and, 228–234
Cognitive restructuring, 547–554
  behavior therapy and, 557–558
  cognitive therapy and, 550–552
  example of, 50–51
  rational-emotive therapy, 547–550
  social problem solving, 552–557
  stress management, 216–217
Cognitive set (schema), 50, 95, 226
Cognitive therapy:
  conduct disorders, 424
  depression, 226–234, 239–240
  described, 550–552
  hypertension and, 214
  mood disorders and, 239
  obsessive-compulsive disorder and, 155–156
  phobias and, 145
  rational-emotive therapy compared, 552
Cohort effect, 477
Collective unconscious, 38
Combat stress, 158–162, 169
Commitment, *see* Civil commitment; Criminal commitment

Communication:
  autistic disorder, 465–466
  behavioral marital assessment, 100
  delirium, 489
  family therapy, 584–585
  group therapy, 575–576
  medical model and, 31
  mental retardation, 446–447, 462
  sexual dysfunction, 367
  stroke, 486–487
Communication training, 370
Community psychology:
  aging and, 507–509
  conduct disorders and, 423
  described, 586–597
  generalized anxiety disorder, 152
  stress management techniques, 217
Competency to stand trial, 606–607, 609–611, 625
Compulsion(s), *see also* Obsessive-compulsive disorder
  autistic disorder, 466
  content of, 154
  described, 153–154
  pedophilia, 333
Computer-assigned instruction, 462–463
Computerized axial tomography (CAT scan), 85, 394–395
Concordant twin, 142
Concurrent validity, 71
Concussion, 642
Conditioned stimulus/response, 44, 45, 47, 137
Conditioning, *see* Classical conditioning; Operant conditioning
Condom, 365
Conduct disorder(s), 419–425
  attention-deficit hyperactivity disorder contrasted, 416
  classification of, 419–421
  etiology of, 421–423
  treatment of, 423–425
Confabulation, 640
Confidentiality, 625, 626–628
Confound(s), 121
Conscience, 33
Consciousness, 33
Constitution (U.S.), 602, 613, 616
Content analysis, 99
Continuum, 70
Control, 148, 234
Control group, 121, 122
Controlled drinking, 290–292
Contusion, 642
Conversion disorder(s), *see also* Somatoform disorder(s)
  behavioral theory, 176
  described, 168–170
  diagnostic category, 67
  psychoanalysis and, 173, 178
  psychophysiological disorder contrasted, 191
  somatization disorder and, 171
Coping, 192, 215–217
Coprophilia, 341
Coronary heart disease, 199, 202–207, 211
Correlational method(s), 116–120, 126–127
Correlation coefficient, 117
Counseling psychology, 7
Counterconditioning, 48, 518–519, 538–542

Couples and family therapy, 580–586
  agoraphobia and, 145n5
  anorexia nervosa, 433
  confidentiality issue, 625n33
  conjoint therapy essentials, 583–585
  described, 428
  individual to conjoint therapy, 581–583
  normality of conflict, 581
  obsessive-compulsive disorder, 154
  overview of, 580–581
  research in, 585–586
  schizophrenia, 404–405
  sexual dysfunction, 370
  special considerations in, 585
Couples Interaction Scoring System, 100, 101
Covert modeling, 546
Covert sensitization, 342
Crack cocaine, 297
Creativity, 110–111
Crime, *see also* Law
  alcoholism and, 279, 281–282
  antisocial personality disorder and, 261, 264–265, 273–274
  juvenile delinquency, 419–420
  rape, 336
Criminal commitment, *see also* Civil commitment
  competency to stand trial, 609–611
  historical perspective on, 602
  insanity defense, 603–609
Cross-dependence (drug abuse), 300
Cross-dressing, 323, 324, 331
Cross-sectional research design, 477
Crystallized intelligence, 481
Culture:
  alcoholism and, 285
  diagnosis and, 77
  gender identity disorder and, 325
  homosexuality and, 346
  incest and, 332
  MMPI and, 83n1
  rape and, 337–338
  schizophrenia and, 388–389
  sexual dysfunction and, 362
  trait orientation and, 106n7
Cushing's syndrome, 642
Cyclazocine, 300

Dangerousness:
  civil commitment and, 611–613, 614
  criminal commitment and, 602, 607–608
  duty to warn and to protect, 626–628
Dark Ages, 8–13, 30
Daytop Village, 301
Deafness, 496–497
Death, *see* Mortality
Defense mechanism, 33, 36–37, 42
Degenerative disease, 20
Deinstitutionalization, 19, 457, 459, 618–621
Delay of reward gradient, 286
Delirium, 489–491, 637, 640
Delirium tremens (DTs), 279, 283
Delusion(s):
  amphetamines and, 295
  cognitive behavior therapy and, 51
  homosexuality and, 384–385
  mood disorders and, 223
  schizophrenia and, 66, 380–383, 386, 406–407
  senile dementia and, 489

transsexualism and, 323
witchcraft and, 10
Delusional (paranoid) disorder, 66, 384, 494–497
Dementia:
  aging and, 485, 488–489
  Alzheimer's disease, 485, 488–489, 643–644
  depression compared, 492–493
  multi-infarct dementias, 644
  organic mental disorders, 643–646
  organic mental syndromes, 636–637
Dementia praecox, 20, 376. *See also* Schizophrenia
Demonology, 7–12
Denial, 517–518
Dependency:
  depression and, 225
  psychoactive substances, 279
  school phobia and, 427
Dependent personality disorder, 259, 271
Dependent variable, 121
Depersonalization, 146
Depersonalization disorder, 67, 179
Depression, *see also* Bipolar disorder; Major depression
  aging and, 491–494
  bulimia nervosa and, 434
  childhood disorders and, 430–431
  cognitive therapy and, 50, 51, 550–551
  countertransference and, 518–519
  described, 220–221
  diathesis-stress approach, 55
  eating disorders and, 436
  electroconvulsive shock treatment, 32
  existentialism and, 240
  learning paradigms and, 48
  medical model and, 30
  mood disorder classification and, 66
  National Institute of Mental Health research program on, 553–555
  stress and, 233
  systematic desensitization and, 539
Depressive attributional style, 158
Derealization, 146
Desensitization, *see* Systematic desensitization
Detachment, 519
Deterioration effect, 580
Determinism, 33
Detoxification, 299
Detumescence, 353
Development, *see also* Childhood disorder(s)
  diagnostic category, 68
  post-Freudian perspective, 39–41
  psychoanalytic paradigm, 33
Developmental arithmetic disorder, 440
Developmental articulation disorder, 441
Developmental coordination disorder, 441
Developmental expressive writing disorder, 440
Developmental reading disorder, 440
Deviant behavior, 30, 47–48
Devil, *see* Demonology
Dexamethasone suppression test, 238
Diagnostic classification, *see also entries under* DSM
  clinical psychology and, 6
  criticism of practices in, 70–71
  cultural differences and, 77
  DSM-III and DSM-IIIR, 62–68, 71–73

epidemiology and, 113
historical perspective on, 20, 62
medical model and, 30, 31
relevance issues in, 69
Diathesis–stress model, 55–57, 107, 418
Diet:
  alcoholism and, 282, 283
  attention-deficit hyperactivity disorder, 417–418
  coronary heart disease, 202–203
  phenylketonuria (PKU), 32, 454
Differential deficit, 127
Diptheria-pertussis-tetanus (DPT) vaccine, 456
Directionality problem, 119
Direct observation:
  behavioral assessment, 89–92, 100
  case study method, 113–116
  psychoanalytic paradigm, 37
  scientific method, 23
  somatogenesis, 8
Disease model, 30, 31
Disorganized schizophrenia, 385–386. *See also* Schizophrenia
Displacement, 36
Dissociative disorder(s), 168, 179–186
  depersonalization disorder, 179
  diagnostic category, 67
  multiple personality, 179–182
  psychogenic amnesia and fugue, 179
  theories, 182–185
  therapy for, 185–186
Distortion, 226–227
Disulfiram (Antabuse), 289
Divorce, 422, 585, 595
Dizygotic twin, 142. *See also* Twin studies
Dopaminergic system, 392–394, 418
Double-blind procedure, 122
Down's syndrome (trisomy 21), 450–451
Dream analysis:
  depression and, 225
  described, 517
  gestalt therapy and, 533
  phobias and, 144
  psychoanalytic therapy and, 42
Drive theory, 38
Drug abuse, *see* Psychoactive substance use disorder(s)
DSM-I, 62, 378, 412
DSM-II, 62
  borderline personality disorder, 256n3
  childhood disorders, 412, 464
  criticism of, 70, 71
  dissociative disorders, 186
  DSM-III compared, 68n2, 72
  homosexuality and, 345
  hysteria and, 185n9
  neuroses and, 132
  schizophrenia and, 378, 379
DSM-III, 62–68
  alcoholism, 279
  antisocial personality disorder, 262–263
  anxiety, 132
  autistic disorder, 463
  borderline personality disorder, 257
  childhood disorders, 412, 464
  cultural differences, 77
  diagnostic categories in, 62–68, 71–73
  dissociative disorders, 179
  homosexuality, 323, 345–347
  MMPI and, 83n1

personality disorders, 254, 271
posttraumatic stress disorder, 158
schizophrenia, 496
transsexualism, 323n1
DSM-IIIR:
  agoraphobia, 135n3
  alcoholism, 280
  antisocial personality disorder, 263
  anxiety disorders, 132–133
  autistic disorder, 464
  brain abnormality, 85
  bulimia nervosa, 433
  childhood disorders, 412–413, 414, 416,
    425, 430, 440
  classification issues, 64, 71–73
  clinical interview, 78
  cultural differences, 77
  delirium, 489
  histrionic personality disorder, 258
  homosexuality, 345, 347–348
  malingering, 170n1
  mental retardation, 442, 445, 446
  mood disorders, 222–224
  multiple personality, 179–180
  neurosis, 132
  organic mental disorders/syndromes, 636
  orgasm disorders, 357
  panic disorder, 146
  paranoid delusions, 384
  personality disorders, 254, 255, 272
  phobias, 145
  posttraumatic stress disorder, 157–158
  psychophysiological disorders, 191
  psychosis, 132n1
  rape, 336, 337
  sadomasochism, 340
  schizophrenia, 379, 384–385, 403, 496
  school phobia, 427
  sexual disorders, 322–323, 330, 331, 341
  sexual dysfunctions, 352, 353, 356, 361
  somatization disorder, 171
  somatoform disorder, 168
  transsexualism, 323, 326
Due process, 460
Durham test, 603–604
Duty to warn and to protect, 626–628
Dyadic Adjustment Scale, 100
Dyslexia, 440
Dyspareunia, 359
Dyssomnias, 67
Dysthymic disorder, 224

Early infantile autism, *see* Autistic disorder
Eating disorder, *see* Anorexia nervosa;
  Bulimia nervosa
Echolalia, 465–466
Eclecticism, 56, 570
Ecological validity, *see* External validity;
  Validity
Ecstasy (drug), 314n20
Education for All Handicapped Children
  Act, 459–460
EEG, *see* Electroencephalography
Egalitarianism, 17
Ego, 32–33, 37, 38, 41, 42
Ego analysis:
  behavior therapy and, 569
  described, 519–521
  phobias and, 144
  post-Freudian perspective, 39, 42
  psychophysiological disorders, 211

psychotherapy and, 42
  schizophrenia, 402–403
Ego-dystonic homosexuality, 323, 345–347.
  See also Homosexuality
Egoistic suicide, 245
Ejaculation (premature), 358–359
Elderly, *see* Aging
Elective autism, 429
Electra complex, 33
Electrocardiography, 96
Electroconvulsive shock treatment (ECT),
  32, 241–242, 400, 616–617, 632
Electrodermal responding, 96, 97
Electroencephalography, 85, 265–267, 469
Empathy, 54, 76, 292n4, 525–527, 567
Empowerment, 588
Empty-chair technique, 152, 532
Encephalitis, 156, 636–637
Encounter group, 574–576, 580
Endocrine system, 238, 641–642
Endorphins, 294
English common law, 602, 610
Enuresis, 414–415
Environment, *see also* Situation
  behavioral consistency/variability, 103
  diathesis-stress approach, 55–56
  generalization, 564
  generalized anxiety disorder, 148
Environmental hazard (toxins), 455–456
Enzyme deficiency, 32
Epidemiology:
  alcoholism, 279–280, 285–286
  antisocial personality disorder, 260
  asthma, 207–208
  attention-deficit hyperactivity disorder, 417
  autistic disorder, 463
  cigarette smoking, 302–303
  cirrhosis of the liver, 283
  conduct disorders, 421
  marijuana use, 310
  obsessive-compulsive disorder, 152
  panic disorder, 146
  paraphilias, 330
  phobias, 133
  research described, 113, 116
  schizophrenia, 295–296, 298–299
  schizophrenia in the aging, 496–497
  senile dementia, 485
  suicide in the aging, 501
  transsexuals, 323
Epilepsy, 469, 563, 640–641
Ergot poisoning, 14–15
Eros, 32
Essential hypertension, 199–202, 211, 214,
  562
Ethics, 622–632. *See also* Law
  antisocial personality disorder, 260, 273n8
  assertion training, 557
  aversion therapy, 541
  behavioral techniques, 631–632
  civil commitment, 617–618
  classical conditioning, 44–45
  client allegiance, 625, 629
  community psychology, 596–597
  confidentiality/privileged communication,
    625
  electroconvulsive therapy, 242
  goal selection, 629–631
  homosexuality, 630
  informed consent, 623–624
  psychoanalysis, 521n3

rational-emotive therapy, 549–550
  research restraints, 622–623
  sexual encounters with patient, 580
  suicide, 249
  treatment/research dichotomy, 624–625
Ethnicity, 285. *See also* Culture; Race
  differences
Etiological validity, 70–71
Etiology, 31
Eugenics movement, 456–457
Evolution theory, 197–198
Excess dopamine activity, 392–394
Exhibitionism, 334–335, 342
Existentialism:
  concepts of, 528–529
  depression, 240
  described, 528–530
  humanistic paradigm and, 52, 53
  posttraumatic stress disorder, 161
  schizophrenia, 389, 403
Exorcism, 7
Experimental cognitive psychology, 95
Experimental effect, 121, 122
Experimental hypothesis, *see* Hypothesis
Experimental psychology:
  alcoholism, 280–281, 286
  cocaine, 298
  dissociative disorders, 183
  ethics, 622–623
  generalized anxiety disorder, 148–149
  informed consent, 623–624
  learned helplessness concept, 228–229
  unconscious and, 175
Experimental research, 120–127
  analogue experiments, 123–124
  design features, 120–121
  external validity, 122–123
  internal validity, 121–122
  mixed designs, 126–127
  overview of, 120
  single-subject, 124–125
Expressed emotion (EE), 398, 405
External validity, 103, 122–123. *See also*
  Validity
Extinction, 298
Extinction curve, 44
Extraversion/introversion, 38
Extreme autistic aloneness, 463, 464–465.
  See also Autistic disorder

Falsifiability, 110
Family:
  aging and, 488, 491, 506
  antisocial personality disorder, 263–264
  asthma, 209–210
  attention-deficit hyperactivity disorder, 418
  autistic disorder, 465, 468–469, 471
  child abuse prevention, 594–595
  childhood depression, 431
  cigarette smoking, 303n11
  conduct disorders, 421, 422, 424
  schizophrenia, 396–398
Family therapy, *see* Couples and family
  therapy
Fantasy, 32–33, 183, 330, 340
Fear(s):
  acquired fear, 111
  childhood disorders, 425–429
  learning paradigms, 47
Female sexual arousal disorder, 356–357
Femininity, 324–325

Feminism, 239
Fenfluramine, 472
Fetal alcohol syndrome, 283, 455
Fetishism, 49, 330–331
Fetus, *see* Pregnancy
Fixation, 33
Flashback(s), 317–318
Flight of ideas, 222
Flooding, 145
Fluid intelligence, 481. *See also* Intelligence
Forcible rape, 336. *See also* Rape
Forensic psychiatry/psychology, 608–609.
    See also Law
Fragile X syndrome, 451
Free association:
    described, 42, 516–517
    dissociative disorders and, 185
    outcome studies and, 524
    phobias and, 144
Free-floating anxiety, *see* Generalized anxiety
    disorder
Free will, 53, 524, 603, 617–618
Frigidity, *see* Female sexual arousal disorder
Frottage, 465
Frotteurism, 341
Fugue, *see* Psychogenic fugue

GABA, 149–150
Galvanic skin response, *see* Electrodermal
    responding
Gender identity disorder, 323–330
    childhood, 322–325
    homosexuality, 346–347
    therapies for, 325–330, 546
    transsexualism, 323–324
General adaptation syndrome (GAS), 191
Generalization:
    behavior therapy, 563–566
    environmental modification, 564
    intermittent reinforcement, 563
    scientific method, 111
    secondary gain elimination, 565
    self-reinforcement, 564–565
Generalized anxiety disorder, 67, 147–152
General paresis, 20
Genetic counseling, 456n5
Genetics, *see also* Twin studies
    alcoholism, 287–288
    antisocial personality disorder, 264–265
    attention-deficit hyperactivity disorder,
        417, 418
    autistic disorder, 469
    behavior genetics, 142–143
    childhood depression, 431
    conduct disorders, 421
    diathesis-stress approach, 55
    eugenics movement, 456–457
    generalized anxiety disorder, 149
    Huntington's chorea, 644–646
    learning disabilities, 441
    medical model, 30
    mental retardation, 450–451, 454
    mood disorders, 235–236
    panic disorder, 146
    phenylketonuria (PKU), 32, 454
    phobias, 144
    schizophrenia, 387, 390–392
    schizotypal personality disorder, 255
    somatoform disorders, 177
Genital stage, 33
Genotype, 142
Geriatrics, *see* Aging

Germ theory of disease, 20, 30
Gestalt therapy, 152, 530–534, 577n1
Glove anesthesia, 169–170
Grandiose delusions, 384, 386
Graves' disease, 641
Group for Advancement of Psychiatry, 412
Group therapy, 574–579
    behavior therapy, 576–578
    insight-oriented, 574–576
    outcomes, 578–579
    overview of, 574
    posttraumatic stress disorder, 164
Guilt and shame, 36, 263
Guilty but mentally ill verdict, 606

Halfway house(s), 593–594, 615
Hallucination:
    schizophrenia and, 66, 382–383, 406–407
    substance abuse and, 283, 297
    witchcraft, 10
Hallucinogen(s), 314–318, 641
Halstead–Reitan battery, 86–87
Harms, 580, 611, 626–627
Harrison Narcotics Act of 1914, 293
Hashish, 309
Headache, *see* Migraine headache
Head injury, *see also* Brain; Brain damage
    delirium, 637
    dementia, 637
    mental retardation, 454
    neuropsychological assessment, 88
    obsessive-compulsive disorder, 156
    organic personality syndrome, 642–643
Head Start program, 457, 459
Hearing problems, 496–497
Heart, *see also* Cardiovascular disease,
        Coronary heart disease
    cocaine and, 297
    panic disorder and, 146
Heart rate, 97–98, 101, 148, 196
Helplessness, 148, 152, 426, 468. *See also*
        Learned helplessness
Heredity, *see* Genetics
Heretics, 9
Hermaphroditism, 323
Heroin abuse, 293–294
Heroin antagonists, 300
Heuristics, 69n5, 116
High-risk method, 119
Histrionic personality disorder, 257–258, 271
Homelessness, 619–621
Homophobia, 346, 348
Homosexuality, 345–348
    aging and, 479
    DSM-IIIR and, 347–348
    ego-dystonic homosexuality, 345–347
    ethical issues, 630
    future research in, 348
    gender identity and, 346–347
    historical perspective on, 345–346
    homophobia and, 346
    paranoia and, 37, 384–385
    sexual dysfunction, 362
    transvestistic fetishism contrasted, 331
Homovanillic acid, 393, 418
Hopelessness, 232
Hospitalization, 289. *See also*
        Institutionalization; Mental hospital(s)
Hostility, 198, 201, 225–226, 238
Humanistic-existential therapy, 524–534. *See*
        also Existentialism
    client-centered therapy, 524–528

existential therapy, 528–530
    gestalt therapy, 530–534
Humanistic therapy, 53–54
    clinical interview, 76
    described, 52–53
    generalized anxiety disorder, 149, 152
    paradigm consequences, 57
    post-Freudian perspective, 38
    schizophrenia, 403
    sexual dysfunction, 359
Humanitarian treatment, 15–18
Humors, 8
Huntington's chorea, 644–646
Hyperactivity, 285. *See also* Attention-deficit
        hyperactivity disorder
Hypertension, *see* Essential hypertension
Hyperventilation, 147
Hypnosis:
    dissociative disorders, 184–185, 186
    historical perspective on, 21, 22–23
    hysteria, 185–186
    paradigm clash, 24–25
Hypoactive sexual desire disorder, 356
Hypochondria, 171
Hypochondriasis, 67, 168, 499–500
Hypomania, 223
Hypothesis, 110, 116, 120, 127, 517
Hysteria, *see also* Conversion disorder(s)
    described, 169
    DSM-II and, 185n9
    historical perspective on, 21
    witchcraft and, 10

Iatrogenic disease, 456. *See also* Harms
Id, 32, 37, 38, 41, 52, 53, 136
Ideas of reference, 386
Identity crisis, 40–41
Idiographic context, 116
Idiot savant, 458
Illusion, 255
Immune system, 197, 364
Impotence, *see* Male erectile disorder
Imprisonment, *see* Incarceration;
        Institutionalization
Inappropriate affect, 383
Incarceration, *see also* Institutionalization
    antisocial personality disorder, 273–274
    civil commitment compared, 611
    conduct disorders, 423–424
    criminal commitment compared, 606–607
    punishment/rehabilitation goals in, 609
    sex offenders, 344
Incest, 332–333, 342–343
Incidence, 113. *See also* Epidemiology
Income, *see* Socioeconomic class
Independent variable, 120–121
Index case (proband), 142
Individual, 53, 54, 588
Individual differences, 407, 417, 476–477
Individualized group therapy, 576–577
Individual psychology, 38–39
Infancy, 65, 443
Infantile autism, *see* Pervasive developmental
        disorder (infantile autism)
Infantile sexuality, 37
Infection, 454, 470, 478, 636–637
Inferiority, 38
Informed consent, 623–624
Inhibited female orgasm, 357–358
Inhibited male orgasm, 358–359
Inquisition, 9–10
Insanity, 602

Insanity defense, 183, 603–609
Insanity Defense Reform Act, 604–605, 609
Insight, 111, 521, 524
Insight therapy, 515, 540, 574–576
Insomnia, *see* Sleep disorder(s)
Institutionalization, *see also* Incarceration;
    Mental hospital(s)
  autistic disorder, 472*n*8
  deinstitutionalization, 618–621
  mental retardation, 456, 457, 459
  nursing homes, 505–507
  schizophrenia, 497
  senile dementia, 489
Insulin coma therapy, 399
Intelligence, 58, 142, 399, 481
Intelligence testing, 84–85, 443, 463, 464
Intermittent reinforcement, 563
Internal behavior, 566–567
Internal validity, 121–122. *See also* Validity
Interpersonal relations:
  attention-deficit hyperactivity disorder, 417
  autistic disorder, 463
  bulimia nervosa, 435
  cocaine, 297
  depression, 234
  opiates abuse, 294
  sexual dysfunctions, 352
  stress, 195–196
  voyeurism, 334
Interpretation, 517–518
Intervention, 587–589
Interview, *see* Clinical interview
Introjection, 225
Introspection, 43
Involuntary commitment, *see* Criminal
    commitment
Involuntary nervous system, *see* Autonomic
    (involuntary) nervous system
Irrationality and irrational beliefs, 51, 227,
    548
Irresistable-impulse concept, 603

Jealousy, 386
Juvenile delinquency, 419–420. *See also*
    Conduct disorder(s)
Juvenile justice system, 425. *See also*
    Incarceration

Kidney failure, 199
Klismaphilia, 341
Korean War, 158
Korsakoff's psychosis, 283, 540

Labeling, 31, 388–389
La belle indifférence, 170
Laceration (brain), 642–643
Lactate, 147
Language:
  autistic disorder, 463, 465–466
  learning disabilities, 440–441
  mental retardation, 449, 462
  stroke, 486–487
Latency period, 33
Law, *see also* Ethics
  antisocial personality disorder, 260
  cigarette smoking, 304
  civil commitment, 611–621
  criminal commitment, 18, 602–611
  cross-dressing, 323
  duty to warn and to protect, 626–628
  historical perspective, 17
  homosexuality, 630

  mental retardation, 460
  pedophilia, 333
  privileged communication, 625
  rape, 336
  sex offenders, 344
  suicide, 242–243
Law of effect, 45
Lead poisoning, 455–456
Learned helplessness, 228–234, 239–240. *See*
    also Helplessness
Learning curve, 44
Learning disability, 416, 440–442
Learning theory, 26–27, 42–49
  alcoholism, 286–287
  attention-deficit hyperactivity disorder,
    418, 419
  behavior therapy, 42–46, 48–49
  classical conditioning, 43–45
  cognitive paradigms, 49–52
  conduct disorders, 422
  deviant behavior, 47–48
  dissociative disorders, 182–183
  enuresis, 415
  fetishism, 331
  generalized anxiety disorder, 148
  learned helplessness, 228–234
  mediational, 46–47
  modeling, 46
  operant conditioning, 45
  phobias, 136–137
Least restrictive alternative principle, 614,
    618
Legitimacy, 112
Libido, 32, 38
Life-span developmental psychology, 39. *See*
    also Childhood disorder(s);
    Development; *entries under*
    Developmental
Life style changes, 593
Limbic system, 639
Linkage analysis, 236
Lithium, 223, 242
Little Hans case, 134
Liver, 280, 283
Lobotomy, 399
Logotherapy, 240
Longitudinal research design, 477–478
Loose association, 380
LSD, 278, 314–318. *See also* Psychoactive
    substance abuse
Luria-Nebraska battery, 87–88
d-Lysergic acid diethylamide (LSD), 278,
    314–318

Madness, *see* Insanity
Magical thinking, 255
Magnetism, 21
Maintenance, 563–566
Major depression, *see also* Bipolar disorder;
    Depression
  aging, 491–492
  bipolar disorder contrasted, 223
  borderline personality disorder, 257
  childhood disorders, 430–431
  cognitive theories of, 226–234
  diagnostic category, 66, 222
  genetics, 235–236
  heterogeneity within, 223–224
  interpersonal aspects of, 234
  psychoanalytic theories of, 225–226
  therapy for, 238–242
Male erectile disorder, 356–357

Malingering, 170
Malnutrition, 282, 283. *See also* Diet
Mania, 220, 221–222, 235. *See also* Bipolar
    disorder
Manic-depressive psychosis, 20
MAO inhibitor(s), *see* Monoamine oxidase
    (MAO) inhibitor(s)
Marijuana, 309–314
Marital assessment, *see* Behavioral marital
    therapy; Couples and family therapy
Marriage:
  aging and, 479
  conduct disorders, 422
  sexual dysfunctions, 352
  stress measurement, 193
Masculinity, 324–325
Masochism, 336–337, 339–341
Masturbation, 322, 342, 354, 365, 370
Media, 593
Mediational learning, 46–47, 50
Mediator, 45
Medical model, 30, 31
Medical student syndrome, 254*n*1
Medicare and Medicaid, 482–483
Medroxyprogesterone acetate (MPA), 343
Megalomania, 483
Melancholia, 220, 223
Memory:
  aging, 481–482, 493
  alcoholism, 283
  cognitive assessment, 95
  defense mechanism, 36
  dissociative disorders, 184–185
  electroconvulsive therapy, 242
  marijuana, 310, 311
  mental retardation, 448–449
  obsessive-compulsive disorder, 156
  organic amnestic syndrome, 640
  psychogenic amnesia, 179
Meningitis, 637
Mens rea concept, 602, 607
Menstruation, 355, 431
Mental health professions, 6–7
Mental hospital(s), *see also* Asylums; Civil
    commitment; Criminal commitment;
    Institutionalization
  aging, 505
  alcoholism, 279
  civil commitment, 611
  community mental health, 589–590
  ethical issues, 625
  halfway houses, 593–594
  historical perspective, 12–18, 544
  medical model, 30
  modeling techniques in, 546–547
  modern, 18–19
  token economy procedures in, 542–545
Mental retardation, 442–463
  autistic disorder and, 463–464
  competency to stand trial, 610
  concept of, 442–444
  diagnostic classification of, 58, 68, 445–446
  etiology of, 449–456
  intelligence testing and, 84
  nature of, 446–449
  operant conditioning, 546
  phenylketonuria, 32, 69
  prevention of, 456–457
  somatogenesis, 20
  treatment for, 457, 459–463
Mescaline, 314–315
Meta-analysis, 560–561

Metabolism, 280
Metacognition, 556
Methadone, 300
Methadyl acetate, 300
Methaqualone abuse, 295n6
Methedrine, 296
Methodology, *see* Research methods
Middle Ages, 8–13, 62
Migraine headache, 212–213, 562
Milieu therapy, 19, 543–545
Mind-body problem, 190. *See also*
    Psychophysiological disorder(s)
Minnesota Multiphasic Personality Inventory
    (MMPI), 82–84
Minorities, *see* Ethnicity; Race differences
Mitral valve prolapse, 146
M'Naghten rule, 603
Modeling:
    behavior therapy, 49
    childhood fears, 427
    conduct disorders, 422
    described, 46, 546–547
    phobias, 138–139, 145
Modified leucotomy, 157
Monasteries, 9
Monoamine oxidase (MAO) inhibitor(s),
    236, 237–238, 242, 493
Monozygotic twin, 142. *See also* Twin studies
Mood, 197
Mood disorder(s), 220–250. *See also* Bipolar
    disorder; Depression; Major depression
    aging, 491–494
    alcoholism, 292
    cyclothymic disorder, 224
    depression and, 220–221
    diagnostic categories, 66, 222–224
    dysthymic disorder, 224
    mania, 221–222
    organic mood syndrome, 641–642
    physiological theories of, 235–238
    psychological theories of, 224–235
    suicide and, 242–249
    therapy for, 238–242
Moral anxiety, 36
Moral awareness, 421, 422
Morality, 33
Moral treatment, 15–18
Mores, *see* Norms
Morphine abuse, 293–294
Mortality:
    aging, 478
    anxiety, 509
    caffeine abuse, 296
    cigarette smoking, 302
    Down's syndrome, 451
    essential hypertension, 199
    life style changes, 593
    PCP abuse, 316
    schizophrenia, 497
    senile delirium, 491
    stroke, 486
    structural support, 196
    suicide, 243–244
Motor effect, 383, 401, 464
Mourning work, 225
Multiaxial system, 62–64
Multi-infarct dementia, 644
Multiple-baseline procedure, 124–125
Multiple personality, 67, 114–115, 179–182,
    183
Myocardial infarction, 202, 297
Myxedema, 641

Naloxone, 300
Narcissistic personality disorder, 67, 258–259
Nacotics abuse, 293–294. *See also*
    Psychoactive substance use disorder(s)
National Institute of Mental Health, 553–555
Nazi Germany, 456n5, 622
Necrophilia, 341
Neo-Freudianism, 42, 520n2
Neologism, 380, 466
Nervous system, *see also* Autonomic
    (involuntary) nervous system; Brain;
    Central nervous system; Somatic
    nervous system
    generalized anxiety disorder, 149–151
    medical model, 30
    mental disorders, 20
Neurobiology, 149–151
Neuroendocrine system, *see* Endocrine
    system
Neuroleptic drugs, 400–401, 407
Neurology:
    autistic disorder, 469–470
    brain abnormality assessment, 85
    conversion disorders, 170
    neuropsychologist contrasted, 86n2
    schizophrenia, 394–395
Neuromuscular disease, 563
Neuropsychology, 86–88, 177
Neurosis, 132, 223
Neurotic anxiety, 36, 41. *See also* Anxiety
Neurotransmitter, 150–151, 236–238, 418
Nicotine and cigarette smoking, 302–309
    abuse, 278
    addiction, 304
    alcoholism and, 280
    clonidine treatment, 305
    consequences of, 302–304
    coronary heart disease, 202
    history of, 302
    treatment/prevention, 304, 306–309
Nicotine gum, 306–307, 308
Nomothetic context, 116
Norepinephrine, 236
Normal curve, 57–58
Norms:
    abnormal definition and, 58
    antisocial personality disorder, 67, 263
    conduct disorders, 420
    cultural differences, 77
    smoking cessation programs, 308
Not guilty by reason of insanity verdict, 604–
    605, 606, 607, 610, 611
Noxious chemicals, *see* Toxins
Nuclear magnetic response imaging, 85
Nursing homes, 505–507

Objective anxiety, 36. *See also* Anxiety
Objectivity, 5–6, 26, 31
Obscene telephone call, 341
Observation, *see* Direct observation
Obsession(s), *see also* Compulsion(s)
    autistic disorder, 466
    content of, 154
    described, 152–153
Obsessive-compulsive disorder, 67, 152–157
Obsessive-compulsive personality disorder,
    259
Occupation, 285–286. *See also*
    Socioeconomic class
Odyssey House, 301
Oedipus complex, 33, 134
Operant behavior therapy, 585

Operant conditioning:
    aversion therapy contrasted, 541n1
    children and, 545–546
    conduct disorders, 422
    described, 45, 542–546
    phobias, 139–140, 145
    psychophysiological disorders, 198–199
    self-report measure and, 90
    token economy, 542–545
Operationist concept, 112
Opium abuse, 293
Oral phase, 33, 225
Organic anxiety syndrome, 642
Organic brain syndrome, *see* Organic mental
    syndrome(s)
Organic delusional syndrome, 640–641
Organic hallucinosis, 641
Organic mental disorder(s), 643–646
    AIDS dementia complex, 644
    Alzheimer's disease, 643–644
    amnesia, 179
    diagnostic categories, 65, 636
    Huntington's chorea, 644–646
    muli-infarct dementias, 644
    Parkinson's disease, 646
    Pick's disease, 644
Organic mental syndrome(s), 636–643
    aging, 509
    amnestic syndrome, 179, 640
    delirium, 637, 640
    dementia, 636–637
    DSM-IIIR, 636
    medical model, 30
    organic anxiety syndrome, 642
    organic delusional syndrome, 640–641
    organic hallucinosis, 641
    organic mood syndrome, 641–642
    organic personality syndrome, 642–643
Organic mood syndrome, 641–642
Organic origin, *see* Somatogenesis
Organic personality syndrome, 642–643
Organizations, 588–589
Orgasm, 354–355
Orgasm disorder, 357–359
Orgasmic reorientation, 342
Outcomes:
    community psychology, 595–597
    group therapy, 578–579
    harmful, 580
    meta-analysis, 560–561
    psychoanalytic therapy, 521–524
Overcontrolled behavior, 425–431
Overcorrection technique, 542

Pain:
    aversion therapy ethics, 631–632
    behavioral medicine, 599
    cocaine and, 296–297
    hypnosis, 24–25
    medical model, 31
    narcotics abuse, 293
    sexual pain disorder, 359
    somatoform pain disorder, 168
Panic, 149–151
Panic attack, 315, 642
Panic disorder, 67, 146–147
Paradigm(s):
    abnormal psychology and, 26–27
    choice of terms in, 30
    clinical interview, 76
    cognitive paradigm, 49–52
    consequences of adopting, 55–57

diathesis-stress approach, 55–57
eclecticism, 56
humanistic paradigm, 52–54
hypnosis and, 24–25
learning paradigm, 42–49
physiological treatment, 32
psychoanalytic paradigm, 32–42
subjectivity, 26
validity, 103
Paralysis, 168, 169–170
Paranoid delusion, *see also* Delusional (paranoid) disorder
aging, 489, 494–497
homosexuality, 37, 384–385
Paranoid personality disorder, 254–255
Paranoid schizophrenia, 386. *See also* Schizophrenia
Paraphilia(s), 330–345
atypical, 341
defined, 330
diagnostic category, 67
exhibitionism, 334–335
fetishism, 330–331
incest, 332–333
pedophilia, 333
rape, 336–339
sadomasochism, 339–341
therapy for, 341–343
transvestistic fetishism, 331
voyeurism, 334
Paraprofessional, 590, 596
Parasomnias, 67
Parasympathetic nervous system, 96. *See also* Autonomic (involuntary) nervous system
Parens patriae power, 611
Parent-management training, 424
Paresis, 20, 31
Parkinson's disease, 401, 646
Passive-aggressive personality disorder, 259, 271–272
Pathology, 30
PCP (phencyclidine), 278, 316
Pediatrics, *see* Behavioral pediatrics; Childhood disorder(s)
Pedophilia, 333
Peer relations, 308, 309, 417, 430, 431, 465. *See also* Interpersonal relations
Pellagra, 20
Penile implant, 371
Penile plethysmograph, 328–329, 335, 339
Penis, 355
Pentobarbital, 295
Perception:
alcohol, 286
learning disabilities, 441
schizophrenia, 382–383
Persecution delusion, 381, 384. *See also* Delusional (paranoid) disorder
Personal growth movement, *see* Humanistic therapy
Personality:
aging and, 482
alcoholism and, 285
asthma and, 210
organic personality syndrome, 642–643
post-Freudian perspective, 38
psychoanalytic paradigm, 33
type A behavior, 203–207, 214–215
Personality disorder(s), 254–275
antisocial personality disorder, 259, 260–271

avoidant personality disorder, 259
borderline personality disorder, 256–257
dependent personality disorder, 259
diagnostic classification, 67, 254, 255, 259
histrionic personality disorder, 257–258
narcissistic personality disorder, 258–259
obsessive-compulsive personality disorder, 259
paranoid personality disorder, 254–255
passive-aggressive personality disorder, 259
schizoid personality disorder, 255
schizotypal personality disorder, 255
therapy for, 271–273
Personality inventory, 81–84, 98*n*5
Personality structure, 88
Personality trait, *see* Traits
Pervasive developmental disorder (infantile autism), 68
Phallic stage, 33
Pharmacology and pharmacotherapy:
aging, 482, 494, 498–499
AIDS, 364
alcoholism, 289
amphetamines, 295
antisocial personality disorder, 273–274
anxiety disorders, 32
attention-deficit hyperactivity disorder, 418, 419
autistic disorder, 472
cocaine, 296–297
competency to stand trial, 610–611
criminal commitment, 608–609
dissociative disorders, 186
ethics and, 622
generalized anxiety disorder, 149, 150, 152
hypertension, 214
informed consent, 623
mood disorders, 223, 236–238, 239, 242
obsessive-compulsive disorder, 156, 157
opium abuse, 293
organic mood syndrome, 641
panic disorder, 147
paraphilias, 343
phobias, 146
placebo effect, 515–516
psychiatry and, 6
psychoactive substance use disorders, 299–300
psychophysiological disorders, 211
right to refuse treatment, 616–617
schizophrenia, 392, 400–401, 406–407
sexual dysfunctions, 371
Phencyclidine (PCP), 278, 316
Phenomenology, 6, 38, 53, 525, 527
Phenotiazines, 392–394, 400–401, 407
Phenotype, 142
Phenylketonuria (PKU), 32, 69, 454
Phlegm, 8
Phobia(s), 133–146
behavioral theories of, 136–141, 144–146
defined, 133
diagnostic classification, 67, 133–136
genetics and, 144
incidence of, 133
modeling and, 546
predisposing factors in, 141–144
psychoanalytic theory of, 136, 144
school phobia, 426–427
therapy for, 144–146
Phoenix House, 301

Physical health, *see also Biological factors; entries under* Organic
aging and, 478, 479–481, 483
alcoholism, 280
cigarette smoking, 302–304, 308
depression in the elderly, 493
hypochondriasis, 499
marijuana, 312–313
stress, 192
Physiological measurement, 95–98
Physiological treatment, 32
Physiology, *see* Psychophysiology
Pick's disease, 644
PKU, *see* Phenylketonuria (PKU)
Placebo effect, 122*n*8, 515–516
Play therapy, 428
Pleasure principle, 32
Politics, 102
Polydrug abuse, 278, 280
Pornography, 334, 338, 546
Positron emission tomography, 85, 393–394
Post-Freudian perspective, 38–41
Posttraumatic stress disorder, 67, 157–164, 336
Predictive validity, 71
Predisposition, 55
Prefrontal lobotomy, 399
Pregnancy:
attention-deficit hyperactivity disorder, 418
cigarette smoking, 303
Down's syndrome, 450–451
fetal alcohol syndrome, 283, 455
marijuana use, 312
mental retardation, 444, 454
sexual activity during, 355
syphilis, 637
Premack principle, 542
Premature birth, 454–455
Premature ejaculation, 358–359
Preparedness, 138–139
Presenile psychosis, 20
Prevalence, 113. *See also* Epidemiology
Prevention:
AIDS, 365
behavioral medicine, 559, 562
child abuse, 594–595
cigarette smoking, 304, 306–309
community psychology, 586–587
conduct disorders, 424–425
drug abuse, 301–302
empowerment, 588
mental retardation, 456–457
Primary prevention, 586–587, 588, 595–596
Primary process, 32
Prison, *see* Criminal commitment; Incarceration
Privileged communication, 625, 626–628
Probability, 117–118
Proband (index case), 142
Problem drinker, 292*n*3
Process-reactive dimension, 378
Projection, 36
Projective personality test, 80–81, 98*n*5
Pronoun reversal, 466
Proposition, 110
Psilocybin, 314–315, 317
Psychedelics, *see* LSD
Psychiatric social work, 7
Psychiatry, 6
Psychoactive drugs, *see* Pharmacology and pharmacotherapy
Psychoactive substance abuse, 279

Psychoactive substance dependence, 279
Psychoactive substance use disorder(s), 278–319
  addiction theories, 299
  aging and, 498–499
  alcoholism, 279–293
  clonidine treatment, 305
  diagnostic categories, 58, 65–66, 279
  historical perspective on, 278
  LSD/psychedelics, 314–318
  marijuana, 309–314
  nicotine, 302–309
  polydrug abuse, 278
  prevention, 301–302
  sedatives, 293–295
  stimulants, 295–298
  therapy for, 299–301
Psychoanalysis, 516–524
  alcoholism, 284
  autistic disorder, 472
  behavior therapy and, 522–524, 569–571
  conduct disorders, 422
  conversion disorders, 178
  defense mechanism, 36–37
  described, 6, 42
  dissociative disorders, 182, 185–186
  ego analysis, 519–521
  enuresis, 415
  evaluation of, 521–524
  family therapy, 581
  fetishism, 330–331
  generalized anxiety disorder, 148, 150
  humanistic paradigm contrast, 52–53
  major depression, 225–226
  mood disorders, 238–239
  obsessive-compulsive disorders, 155, 156
  paradigm of, 26–27, 32–42, 52–53, 57, 88, 132
  paranoid delusions, 384–385
  paraphilias, 341
  phobias, 134, 135, 136, 144
  post-Freudian psychodynamic perspectives, 38–41
  psychological testing, 80
  psychophysiological disorders, 198, 211
  schizophrenia and, 377, 388
  self psychology, 258
  sexual dysfunctions, 359
  somatoform disorders, 173–174
  suicide, 245
  techniques and concepts in, 516–519
Psychodynamics, 33, 370–371. *See also* Psychoanalysis
Psychogenesis, 20–22, 469
Psychogenic amnesia, 67, 179
Psychogenic fugue, 67, 179, 183
Psychological autopsy, 248
Psychological paradigm, *see* Paradigm(s)
Psychological tests and testing, 78, 80–85, 235, 246–247. *See also entries under names of tests*
Psychopath, 260. *See also* Antisocial personality disorder
Psychopathologist and psychopathology, 5, 7–22
Psychophysiological disorder(s), 190–217
Psychophysiology, 95–98, 101, 104–105, 339
Psychosexual development, 33
Psychosis, 132*n*1, 223
Psychosomatic disorders, 67, 190. *See also* Psychophysiological disorder(s)
Psychosurgery, 157, 616–617

Psychotherapy, 6, 56, 401–404, 560–561. *See also* Psychoanalysis
Psychotomimetic drugs, 314, 608–609
Pulse, *see* Heart rate
Punishment procedures, 545. *See also* Operant conditioning
Pure Food and Drugs Act, 297

Questionnaires, *see* Psychological tests and testing; Self-report measures; *entries under names of specific tests*

Race differences, *see also* Ethnicity
  aging and, 483
  community psychology and, 596
  diagnosis and, 77
  essential hypertension and, 200–201
  MMPI and, 83*n*1
Random assignment, 122
Rape, 336–339
  criminality and, 336
  exhibitionism and, 335
  homelessness and, 619
  posttraumatic stress disorder and, 162
  psychophysiological analysis of, 339
  rapist profile, 336–339
  sexual dysfunction and, 363
  therapy for, 343–344
  victims of, 336
Rapid-smoking treatment, 306–307
Rapport, 76. *See also* Empathy
Rational-emotive therapy:
  behavioral marital assessment, 100*n**
  children and, 550
  cognitive therapy compared, 552
  described, 51, 547–550
  family therapy, 581
  mood disorders, 240–241
  personality disorders, 272
  sexual dysfunction, 370
Rationalization, 37
Raynaud's disease, 563
Reaction formation, 36–37
Reactivity, 92
Readiness, 442
Reading-disabled children, 442
Reality principle, 33
Recidivism, 423–424
Reflex activity, 32
Regression, 37
Reinforcement, 45, 48, 178
Relapse, 565–566, 583
Relativity, 47
Relaxation training, 51, 152, 214, 539
Relevance, 69
Reliability, 70, 98–99, 110
Religion:
  aging and, 509
  demonology and, 8–10
  incest and, 332
  pedophilia and, 333
  post-Freudian perspective, 38
  sexual dysfunction and, 361
Repression, 36, 41, 80, 136, 144
Reproductive system, 312. *See also* Sexual disorder(s); Sexual dysfunction(s)
Research methods, 110–128
  aging and, 476–478
  case study method, 113–116
  correlational method, 116–120
  epidemiological research, 113
  ethical constraints on, 622–623

  experimentation, 120–127
  homosexual studies, 347
  mixed designs, 126–127
  overview of, 112–113
  scientific method and, 110–112
  therapy compared, 624–625
Resistance, 517
Respiration, 147, 148, 208–210
Retirement, 493
Retrospective report, 137*n*4, 263
Reversal (ABAB) design, 124, 542
Rewards, *see* Operant conditioning
Right to refuse treatment principle, 616–618
Right to treatment principle, 614–616, 618
Risk factor, 113, 398–399, 622, 623–624
Role playing, 49
Rorschach inkblot test, 80–81
Rosenthal effect, 103, 122

Sadism, 336–337, 339–341
Sadness, 220, 225. *See also* Depression
Salt, 202
Scale for Suicide Ideation, 247
Schedule for Affective Disorders and Schizophrenia, 78
Schema concept, 50, 95, 226
Schizoaffective psychosis, 378. *See also* Schizophrenia
Schizoid personality disorder, 67, 255, 272
Schizophrenia, 376–408
  aging and, 496–497
  amphetamines, 295
  biochemical factors in, 392–394
  childhood onset of, 464
  clinical symptoms of, 379–384
  cognitive behavior therapy, 50–51
  correlational method, 118, 119, 120
  depersonalization disorder and, 179*n*6
  diagnostic categories, 66, 379
  diathesis-stress approach, 56–57
  electroconvulsive therapy for, 241
  existentialism and, 389
  experimental research, 123
  family and, 396–398
  genetics and, 30, 387, 390–392
  high-risk studies of, 398–399
  historical perspective, 20, 376–379
  homelessness and, 619–621
  labeling theory and, 388–389
  medical model of, 31
  mixed experimental designs, 126–127
  multiple personality contrasted, 180*n*7
  neurological findings in, 394–395
  paradigm selection and, 55
  psychoanalysis and, 388
  psychophysiology, 96–97
  schizotypal personality disorder and, 255
  socioeconoimc class and, 395–396
  subcategories of, 384–387
  suicide and, 243*n*5
  therapy for, 399–407
  token economies and, 543
  transsexualism and, 323
Schizotypal personality disorder, 255
School phobia, 426–427
Scientific method, 22–27, 37, 110–112. *See also* Research methods
Secobarbital abuse, 295
Secondary gain elimination, 565
Secondary prevention, 586
Secondary process, 33
Sedatives, *see* Anxiolytics

Seeking mode, 587
Seizures, 241–242, 469, 640–641
Selective abstraction, 51
Self-actualization, 38, 52, 53, 528
Self-efficacy, 51
Self-help movement, 594
Self-help skills, 447, 461
Self-injurious behavior, 124, 461
Self-monitoring, 91–92
Self-mutilation, 545
Self psychology, 258
Self-reinforcement, 564–565
Self-report measures, 81–84, 90, 92–93, 94–95, 137, 193–194
Senile psychosis, 20
Senility, *see* Aging; Dementia
Sensitivity training, 574–576, 578–579
Sensorimotor skills, 441, 447
Sensory-awareness procedures, 370
Separation, *see* Divorce
Separation anxiety disorder, 427
Serotonin, 236, 472
Sex change surgery, 323, 325–327. *See also* Transsexualism
Sex differences, *see also* Sex role
  aging, 479
  alcohol, 281, 282
  anorexia nervosa, 431
  antisocial personality disorder, 260
  autistic disorder, 464
  barbiturate abuse, 295
  borderline personality disorder, 257
  cigarette smoking, 302–303
  cirrhosis of the liver, 283
  conduct disorder, 421
  conversion disorder, 169
  coronary heart disease, 202
  depression, 230, 492
  essential hypertension, 200
  fragile X syndrome, 451
  gender identity disorder, 325n3
  histrionic personality disorder, 258
  learning disabilities, 441
  mental retardation, 449
  mood disorders, 236
  obsessive-compulsive personality disorder, 259
  paraphilias, 330
  Pick's disease, 644
  sadomasochism, 340
  sexual activity among the aging, 503
  somatization disorder, 171
Sex education, 370
Sexism, 337, 396n11
Sex role, *see also* Sex differences
  agoraphobia, 135
  behavioral marital assessment, 102
  rape, 336
  sexual dysfunction, 362
Sex therapy, 581–583
Sexual arousal, 281, 328–329
Sexual arousal disorder, 356–357
Sexual assault, 116. *See also* Rape
Sexual aversion disorder, 356
Sexual desire disorder, 356
Sexual disorder(s), 322–349. *See also* Paraphilia(s)
  diagnostic category, 67
  gender identity disorders, 323–330
  homosexuality, 345–348
  overview of, 322–323
  paraphilias, 330–345

Sexual dysfunction(s), 351–372
  aging, 501–504
  bioenergetic approach to, 360
  diagnostic categories, 67, 356
  orgasm disorders, 357–359
  relationships and, 352
  sex therapy, 581–583
  sexual arousal disorders, 356–357
  sexual desire disorders, 356
  sexual pain disorder, 359
  sexual response cycle and, 352–353
  theories, 359–367
  therapy for, 367–371
Sexual orientation imbalance, 345
Sexual response cycle, 352–353
Shame and guilt, 36, 263
Shaping procedure, 45
Shell shock, 158. *See also* Posttraumatic stress disorder
Short-term memory, *see* Memory
Siblings, 431
Significance, 122
Simple phobia, 135. *See also* Phobia(s)
Single-subject experimental research design, 124–125
Situation, *see also* Environment
  behavioral assessment, 88, 93, 105–107, 151
  clinical interview, 76
  cognitive assessment, 94
  direct observation, 90
Skills training, 217, 370
Sleep disorder(s), 67, 157–158, 500–501
Sleeping sickness, 636. *See also* Encephalitis
Smoking cessation programs, 91–92, 95n4, 211, 541. *See also* Nicotine and cigarette smoking
Social anxiety, 140–141
Social class, *see* Socioeconomic class
Social drift theory, 396
Social factors, *see* Socioeconomic class
Social-learning theory, 19, 468, 470–472
Social-learning ward, 543–545
Social networks, *see* Interpersonal relations
Social phobias, 136. *See also* Phobia(s)
Social problem solving, 552–557
Social Readjustment Rating Scale, 192–194
Social relations, *see* Interpersonal relations
Social skills, 447
Social-skills training, 178, 240–241, 577
Social support, 195–196. *See also* Interpersonal relations
Social withdrawal, 429–430, 464–465
Sociocultural factors, 38, 174, 176. *See also* Culture
Socioeconomic class:
  aging and, 482–485
  community psychology, 589, 596–597
  conduct disorders, 423
  heroin abuse, 294n5
  mental retardation, 450
  paradigm selection, 55
  psychoanalysis, 37
  schizophrenia, 395–396, 496
  somatoform disorder, 176
Sociogenic hypothesis, 396
Sociology, 245
Sociopathy, *see* Antisocial personality disorder
Somatic approach, 146
Somatic nervous system, 96
Somatic passivity, 381

Somatic-weakness theory, 197
Somatization disorder (Briquet's syndrome), 67, 170–172, 177
Somatoform disorder(s), 67, 168–178
Somatoform pain disorder, 67, 168
Somatogenesis, 8, 19–20
Somnambulism, 186
SORC factors, 89, 93
Specific developmental disorders, 440. *See also* Learning disabilities
Specific-reaction theory, 197
Spectator role, 357, 361, 363
Speech, 440–441, 462. *See also* Language
Spouse Observation Checklist, 100–101
Standardization, 80, 81
Stanford-Binet test, 84
State-dependent memory, 184–185
Statistical significance, 117–118
Statistics, 57–58, 78, 80, 116–120. *See also* Correlational method(s)
Statutory rape, 336. *See also* Rape
Stereotyped behavior, 461, 466
Sterilization laws, 456–457
Stigma, 69, 416, 479
Stimulant abuse, 293, 295–298
Stimulants therapy, 418–419
Stress, *see also* Posttraumatic stress disorder
  alcoholism and, 286–287
  Assessment of Daily Experience, 194–195
  asthma and, 210
  attention-deficit hyperactivity disorder, 418
  concept of, 191–192
  depression and, 233
  diathesis-stress approach, 55–57
  essential hypertension, 200, 202
  illness, 192
  management techniques for, 215–217
  mediators of, 195–197
  schizophrenia and, 392
  Social Readjustment Rating Scale, 192–194
  theories, 197–199
Stroke, 199, 486–487, 563
Structuralism, 42
Structured Clinical Interview (SCID), 78, 79
Subdural hematoma, 637
Subjectivity, 5–6, 26, 31, 110, 527
Submission-domination, 340–341
Substance use disorders, *see* Psychoactive substance use disorder(s)
Successive approximation, 45
Suffering, 58
Suicidal Intent Scale, 247
Suicide, 242–249
  aging and, 501
  alcoholism, 279
  barbiturates and, 295
  childhood depression, 431
  ethics and, 249
  facts about, 243–244
  historical perspective on, 242–243
  myths about, 243
  perspectives on, 245–246
  predictive tests for, 246–247
  prevention of, 247–249
  substance abuse and, 278
Suicide prevention center, 248, 591–593
Superego, 32, 33, 37
Supernatural, 7, 8, 148, 190
Supreme Court (U.S.), 607–609, 610, 615–616

Symbolic loss, 225
Symbolism, 38, 517
Sympathetic nervous system, 96, 295. *See also* Autonomic (involuntary) nervous system; Nervous system
Symptom, 20, 30, 31
Synanon, 301
Syndrome, 20
Synesthesias, 315
Synthetic sanity concept, 610–611
Syphilis, 20, 637
Systematic desensitization:
    behavior therapy and, 48
    described, 538–541
    generalized anxiety disorder, 151
    personality disorders, 272
    phobias, 144, 145

Tardive dyskinesia, 401, 407
Taylor Manifest Anxiety Scale, 104
Teleology, 38
Telephone crisis service, 591–593
Telephone scatologia, 341
Television, 422
Tertiary prevention, 586
Testability, 110
Testing, *see* Psychological tests and testing
T-group, *see* Group therapy; Sensitivity training
Thalidomide, 455
Thanatos, 32, 245
Thematic Apperception Test (TAT), 80, 98n5
Therapy, *see entries under names of specific therapeutic techniques; entries under names of specific disorders*
Third-variable problem, 119–120
Thorazine, 610–611
Thyroid gland, 641, 642
Time-of-measurement effect(s), 477, 478
Time out procedure, 542
Tobacco, *see* Nicotine and cigarette smoking
Toilet training, 33, 155, 414, 415, 461
Token economy, 49, 542–545

Tolerance, 279, 295–296, 304
Tomboy, 324–325
Toxins, 455–456, 636, 641
Traits, 88, 103–107, 254
Tranquilizers, *see* Anxiolytics
Transference, 518, 520
Transsexualism, 323–324, 325
Transvestistic fetishism, 331. *See also* Cross-dressing
Trauma, 361–362
Treponema pallidum, 637
Triadic reciprocality, 558
Tricyclic antidepressants, 236, 494
Trisomy 21, *see* Down's syndrome (trisomy 21)
Tumescence, 353
Tumor, 642
Twin studies, *see also* Genetics
    alcoholism, 288
    antisocial personality disorder, 264–265
    autistic disorder, 469
    conduct disorders, 421
    genetics and, 142–143
    learning disabilities, 441
    mood disorders, 236
    schizophrenia, 387, 390
    somatoform disorders, 177
Two physicians' certificate, 611
Type A behavior, 203–207, 214–215

Ulcer, 198
Unconditional positive regard, 53, 54
Unconditioned stimulus/response, 44, 45, 46–47
Unconscious, 33, 36, 38, 41, 175
Underarousal, *see* Arousal
Unipolar depression, *see* Major depression

Vaginismus, 359, 362
Validity, *see also* External validity; Internal validity
    behavioral assessment, 99, 103
    case study method, 115–116
    classification issues, 70–71

Valium, 32
Values, 587–589
Variables, 120–121
Venereal disease, 367. *See also* Acquired immune deficiency syndrome (AIDS); Syphilis
Vicarious conditioning, 138–139. *See also* Modeling
Vicarious learning, 574
Vietnam War, 158–162
Violence, *see* Dangerousness
Vitamin deficiency, 20, 283
Vocational skills, 447
Voluntary commitment, 613
Voluntary nervous system, *see* Somatic nervous system
Voodoo death, 148, 190
Voyeurism, 334
Vulnerability schema, 140

Waiting mode, 587
Waxy flexibility, 383
Wechsler Adult Intelligence Scale, 84
Wernicke's disease, 640
Witchcraft, 9–12, 14–15
Withdrawal, *see* Social withdrawal
Withdrawal reaction:
    alcoholism, 282, 283
    barbiturates, 295
    clonidine treatment for, 305
    cocaine, 298
    detoxification and, 299
    nicotine, 304
    psychoactive substance use disorder, 279
Women's movement, *see also* Feminism; Sex differences; Sexism; Sex role
    agoraphobia and, 135
    divorce counseling and, 585
    rape and, 337–338
World Health Organization (WHO), 62, 379
World War I, 158, 636
World War II, 158, 162, 295, 468

X-ray, 85